LEARNING CANADIAN CRIMINAL LAW

Fourteenth Edition

CARSWELL

LEARNING CANADIAN CRIMINAL LAW

Fourteenth Edition

by

DON STUART
B.A., LL.B., Dip. Crim., D. Phil.
Faculty of Law
Queen's University

and

STEVE COUGHLAN
B.A., M.A., LL.B., Ph.D.
Faculty of Law
Dalhousie University

 THOMSON REUTERS®

[43] My colleague, Arbour J., by contrast, takes the view that s. 43 is unconstitutionally vague, a point of view also expressed by Deschamps J. Arbour J. argues first that the foregoing analysis amounts to an impermissible reading down of s. 43. This contention is answered by the evidence in this case, which established a solid core of meaning for s. 43; to construe terms like "reasonable under the circumstances" by reference to evidence and argument is a common and accepted function of courts interpreting the criminal law. To interpret "reasonable" in light of the evidence is not judicial amendment, but judicial interpretation. It is a common practice, given the number of criminal offences conditioned by the term "reasonable". If "it is the function of the appellate courts to rein in overly elastic interpretations" (Binnie J., at para. 122), it is equally their function to define the scope of criminal defences.

[44] Arbour J. also argues that unconstitutional vagueness is established by the fact that courts in the past have applied s. 43 inconsistently. Again, the inference does not follow. Vagueness is not argued on the basis of whether a provision has been interpreted consistently in the past, but whether it is capable of providing guidance for the future. Inconsistent and erroneous applications are not uncommon in criminal law, where many provisions admit of difficulty; we do not say that this makes them unconstitutional. Rather, we rely on appellate courts to clarify the meaning so that future application may be more consistent. I agree with Arbour J. that Canadians would find the decisions in many of the past cases on s. 43 to be seriously objectionable. However, the discomfort of Canadians in the face of such unwarranted acts of violence toward children merely demonstrates that it is possible to define what corrective force is reasonable in the circumstances. Finally, Arbour J. argues that parents who face criminal charges as a result of corrective force will be able to rely on the defences of necessity and "*de minimis*". The defence of necessity, I agree, is available, but only in situations where corrective force is not in issue, like saving a child from imminent danger. As for the defence of *de minimis*, it is equally or more vague and difficult in application than the reasonableness defence offered by s. 43.

ARBOUR J. (dissenting):

[Justice Arbour would have held that s. 43 was vague. She engaged in a comprehensive discussion of the case law under the section, pointing to acquittals under it where corporal punishment had been applied: by teachers; for blows to the face or head; to teenagers; to children under two; and through the use of implements. She argued that the majority was not "interpreting" s. 43 but simply engaging in judicial rewriting of the section.]

[181] In my view, the case law speaks for itself with respect to whether s. 43 delineates the appropriate boundaries of legal debate. It is wholly unpersuasive for this Court to declare today what the law is de novo and to assert that this

now frames the legal debate: i.e., anything outside the framework was simply wrongly decided! This approach robs the test in Nova Scotia Pharmaceutical, supra, of any usefulness. There is no need to speculate about whether s. 43 is capable, in theory, of circumscribing an acceptable level of debate about the scope of its application. It demonstrably has not succeeded in doing so. Canadian courts have been unable to articulate a legal framework for s. 43 despite attempts to establish guidelines.

[183] "Reasonableness" with respect to s. 43 is linked to public policy issues and one's own sense of parental authority. "Reasonableness" will always entail an element of subjectivity. As McCombs J. recognized in the case at bar, "[b]ecause the notion of reasonableness varies with the beholder, it is perhaps not surprising that some of the judicial decisions applying s. 43 to excuse otherwise criminal assault appear to some to be inconsistent and unreasonable" ((2000), 49 O.R. (3d) 662, at para. 4). It is clear, however, that the concept of reasonableness, so widely used in the law generally, and in the criminal law in particular, is not in and of itself unconstitutionally vague. "Reasonableness" functions as an intelligible standard in many other criminal law contexts. This Court has been clear that constitutional analysis must always be contextual (*Law v. Canada (Minister of Employment and Immigration)*, [1999] 1 S.C.R. 497, at para. 6). Accordingly, whether a given phrase is unconstitutionally vague must also vary with context.

[184] Other instances of the words "reasonable under the circumstances" may not be overly vague because they occur in contexts in which the factors for assessing reasonableness are clear and commensurable. Some general agreement as to the standard against which to measure the "reasonableness" of conduct will assist in providing sufficient clarity to a standard of "reasonableness". For example, reasonable force in self-defence can be measured for proportionality against the assault for which one is defending oneself. Similarly, it is possible to frame a legal debate about the proper boundaries of the use of reasonable force in performing an arrest (see *Asante-Mensah*, *supra*, per Binnie J., at paras. 51-59). This is not so in the case of corporal punishment of children, where there is no built-in commensurability between physical punishment and bad behaviour that can be used to assess proportionality. Indeed the Chief Justice concludes, at para. 35, that the gravity of the child's conduct is not a "relevant contextual consideration" as it invites a punitive, rather than a corrective focus.

[185] Corporal punishment is a controversial social issue. Conceptions of what is "reasonable" in terms of the discipline of children, whether physical or otherwise, vary widely, and often engage cultural and religious beliefs as well as political and ethical ones. Such conceptions are intertwined with how other controversial issues are understood, including the relationship between the state and the family and the relationship between the rights of the parent and the rights

of the child. Whether a person considers an instance of child corporal punishment "reasonable" may depend in large part on his or her own parenting style and experiences. While it may work well in other contexts, in this one the term "reasonable force" has proven not to be a workable standard. Lack of clarity is particularly problematic here because the rights of children are engaged. This Court has confirmed that children are a particularly vulnerable group in society (*Sharpe, supra*, at para. 169, and *Winnipeg Child and Family Services v. K.L.W.*, [2000] 2 S.C.R. 519, 2000 SCC 48 at para. 73). Vagueness in defining the terms of a defence which affects the physical integrity of children may be even more invidious than is vagueness in defining an offence or a defence in another context, and may therefore call for a stricter standard.

[186] Canada's international obligations with respect to the rights of the child must also inform the degree of protection that children are entitled to under s. 7 of the *Charter*. As the Chief Justice notes (at para. 32), Canada is a party to both the United Nations Convention on the Rights of the Child, Can. T.S. 1992 No. 3, and the International Covenant on Civil and Political Rights, Can. T.S. 1976 No. 47. . . . .

[187] It is notable that the Committee has not recommended clarifying these laws so much as abolishing them entirely. The Chief Justice notes, at para. 33, that neither the Convention on the Rights of the Child nor the International Covenant on Civil and Political Rights "require state parties to ban all corporal punishment of children". However, the Committee's Concluding Observations on Canada's First Report are illustrative:

> [P]enal legislation allowing corporal punishment of children by parents, in schools and in institutions where children may be placed [should be considered for review]. In this regard ... physical punishment of children in families [should] be prohibited. In connection with the child's right to physical integrity ... and in the light of the best interests of the child, ... the possibility of introducing new legislation and follow-up mechanisms to prevent violence within the family [should be considered], and ... educational campaigns [should] be launched with a view to changing attitudes in society on the use of physical punishment in the family and fostering the acceptance of its legal prohibition. [Emphasis added.]

(Committee on the Rights of the Child, Report adopted by the Committee at its 233rd meeting on 9 June 1995, Ninth Session, CRC/C/43, at para. 93)

[188] In its most recent Concluding Observations, the Committee expressed "deep concern" that Canada had taken "no action to remove section 43 of the *Criminal Code*" and recommended the adoption of

> legislation to remove the existing authorization of the use of "reasonable force" in disciplining children and explicitly prohibit all forms of violence against children, however light, within the family, in schools and in other institutions where children may be placed.

(Committee on the Rights of the Child, Consideration of Reports Submitted by State Parties Under Article 44 of the Convention, Thirty-fourth Session, CRC/ C/15/Add. 215 (2003), at paras. 32-33)

[190] In the Chief Justice's reasons, it is useful to note how much work must go into making the provision constitutionally sound and sufficiently precise: (1) the word "child" must be construed as including children only over age 2 and younger than teenage years; (2) parts of the body must be excluded; (3) implements must be prohibited; (4) the nature of the offence calling for correction is deemed not a relevant contextual consideration; (5) teachers are prohibited from utilizing corporal punishment; and (6) the use of force that causes injury that is neither transient nor trifling (assault causing bodily harm) is prohibited (it seems even if the force is used by way of restraint). At some point, in an effort to give sufficient precision to provide notice and constrain discretion in enforcement, mere interpretation ends and an entirely new provision is drafted. As this Court concluded in *R. v. Heywood*, [1994] 3 S.C.R. 761, at p. 803:

> The changes which would be required to make s. 179(1)(b) [here, s. 43] constitutional would not constitute reading down or reading in; rather, they would amount to judicial rewriting of the legislation. [Emphasis added.]

The restrictions put forth by the Chief Justice with respect to the scope of the defence have not emerged from the existing case law. These restrictions are far from self-evident and would not have been anticipated by many parents, teachers or enforcement officials.

[191] In my view, we cannot cure vagueness from the top down by declaring that a proper legal debate has taken place and that anything outside its boundaries is simply wrong and must be discarded. Too many people have been engaged in attempting to define the boundaries of that very debate for years in Canadian courtrooms to simply dismiss their conclusions because they do not conform with a norm that was never apparent to anyone until now. As demonstrated earlier, s. 43 has been subject to considerable disparity in application, some courts justifying conduct that other courts have found wholly unreasonable, despite valiant efforts by the lower courts to give intelligible content to the provision. Attempts at judicial interpretation which would structure the discretion in s. 43 have, in my opinion, failed to provide coherent or cogent guidelines that would meet the standard of notice and specificity generally required in the criminal law. Thus, despite the efforts of judges, some of whom have openly expressed their frustration with what has been described as "no clear test" and a "legal lottery" in the criminal law (McGillivray, "'He'll learn it on his body': Disciplining childhood in Canadian law", supra, at p. 228; *James*, *supra*, per Weagant Prov. J., at paras. 11-12), the ambit of the justification

remains about as unclear as when it was first codified in 1892. As Lamer C.J. stated in *R. v. Morales*, [1992] 3 S.C.R. 711, at p. 729:

> A standardless sweep does not become acceptable simply because it results from the whims of judges and justices of the peace rather than the whims of law enforcement officials. Cloaking whims in judicial robes is not sufficient to satisfy the principles of fundamental justice.

This would not only raise the already high bar set in *Nova Scotia Pharmaceutical, supra*; it would essentially make it unreachable.

[192] As a result, I find that the phrase "reasonable under the circumstances" in s. 43 of the *Code* violates children's security of the person interest and that the deprivation is not in accordance with the relevant principle of fundamental justice, in that it is unconstitutionally vague.

The other dissenters, Justices Binnie and Deschamps, found that s. 43 violated equality protections under s. 15. Binnie J. was of the view that the violation could be saved under s. 1 for parents and those standing in the place of parents but not for teachers. Deschamps J. found that the violation could not be demonstrably justified.

Which judgment is more activist? That of Chief Justice McLachlin or that of Justice Arbour?

Are there problems with the regime for s. 43 declared by the majority? See critical comments by Tim Quigley, "Correction of Children: The Supreme Court Divided" (2004) 16 C.R. (6th) 286 and Sanjeev Anand, "Reasonable Chastisement: A Critique of the Supreme Court's Decision in the Spanking Case" (2004) 41 Alberta. L. Rev. 871.

The tougher criteria read in by the majority have since not always been faithfully applied, so judicial subjectivity and acquittals are still a major problem. See for example *R. v. Kaur* (2004), 27 C.R. (6th) 224 (Ont. C.J.) (mother lightly tapped cheek of 12 year old daughter because of her silent treatment), criticized by Drew Mitchell, "Child Assault and Children's Rights after Foundation for Children" (2005), 27 C.R. (6th) 230; *R. v. Plummer*, Ont. C.J., June 6, 2006 (use of belt to correct causing no pain); and *R. v. Swan*, Ont. S.C. March 13, 2008 (throwing teenage daughter into truck to rescue her from party and her boyfriend).

In *Swan* the trial judge convicted on the basis of s. 43 based on the synopsis in Martin's *Criminal Code* that s. 43 "does not apply to force to children under two or teenagers". On appeal Justice Robertson acquitted, deciding this was a misreading as the SCC was referring at that point only to corporal punishment. This is certainly true and it seems clear that the Supreme Court envisaged s. 43 as capable of authorizing physical restraint by parents as well as teachers. However, Robertson J. overlooks other general limits required by the Supreme Court, in particular against the use of force where there is a risk of bodily harm and the quite clear pronouncement that the gravity of the precipitating event is not to be considered.

It is fundamentally problematic as pointed out by Arbour J. that, unlike normal defences to assault such as self-defence, the Supreme Court allows no consideration of proportionality given that the gravity of the precipitating event is stated to be irrelevant. It doesn't matter whether the child spat or burnt down the barn. The assaulter also cannot be acting out of frustration or anger. So we are left with justifying coolly premeditated minor physical correction without reference to context. Trial judges will surely have difficulty, as did Robertson J., in not considering the precipitating event.

Would the better approach be to repeal s. 43 and catch Canada up to the worldwide trend to abolish the right to physically discipline children? The European Global Initiative to End All Corporal Punishment of Children in Europe and article 19 of the UN Convention on the Rights of Children have led to the abolition of any right to hit children in over 50 countries. Well over 500 professional child care and health organizations in Canada have endorsed a call presently before the Senate for repeal of s. 43. There is now overwhelming evidence that physical discipline of children likely causes mental and physical harm and will later likely cause victims to discipline their children in the same way. The Truth and Reconciliation Commission called for s. 43's repeal. Senator Sinclair's speech to the Senate on March 7, 2017 documents how the culture of violent discipline in residential schools has had a lasting effect.

If Canada followed this trend defences available to parents, caregivers and teachers would be those available to anyone charged with assault, including the defences of self-defence, duress and necessity, and possibly the emerging doctrine of *de minimis non curat lex* (see later). The power of physical restraint would be limited to that presently authorized in s. 27, which allows physical force where reasonably necessary to prevent crime or harm to others and which involves an assessment of what the child actually did. Section 27 would indeed have been the better basis for the acquittal in *Swan*.

In three major decisions in 2011, 2012 and 2013, Chief Justice McLachlin, writing for the full Court, reconsidered, developed and finally sought to separate the s. 7 challenges of arbitrariness, overbreadth and gross disproportionality.

In *PHS Community Services Society v. Canada (Attorney General)*, 86 C.R. (6th) 223, [2011] 3 S.C.R. 134, the prohibition of drug possession under the *Controlled Drugs and Substances Act* was held to engage the rights to life and security of the person of the clients and staff of Insite, Vancouver's supervised injection site. The Court held that the prohibition itself did not violate principles of fundamental justice as overbroad because the Minister's power under s. 56 to grant an exemption meant that it could be limited to appropriate circumstances.

However, the Supreme Court unanimously held that the Minister's refusal to grant such an exemption to the Vancouver safe injection site was not in accordance with principles of fundamental justice as it was arbitrary and also grossly disproportionate in its effects. The remedy was to order the Minister to grant an exemption. The denial to Insite had been arbitrary given evidence that traditional criminal law prohibitions had done little to reduce drug use in that area of Vancouver; the risk to injection drug users of death and disease had been reduced when they injected under the supervision of a health professional; and the presence of Insite had reduced crime rates, incidents of public injection and relapse rates, and no overdose deaths had occurred at the facility.

The evidentiary record will rarely be as clear and uncontested as it was in *PHS*. It showed the effectiveness of Insite in reducing severe health and public safety risks in a particularly vulnerable population. Furthermore, Vancouver Health, police authorities, and the municipal and B.C. provincial governments all read the evidence as favouring the maintenance of the Insite Clinic. It was only federal government law and order ideology that did not.

Chief Justice McLachlin added enigmatically:

> [132]. . .The jurisprudence on arbitrariness is not entirely settled. In *Chaoulli*, three justices (per McLachlin C.J. and Major J.) preferred an approach that asked whether a limit was "necessary" to further the state objective: paras. 131-32. Conversely, three other justices (per Binnie and LeBel JJ.), preferred to avoid the language of necessity and instead approved of the prior articulation of arbitrariness as where "[a] deprivation of a right . . . bears no relation to, or is inconsistent with, the state interest that lies behind the legislation": para. 232. It is unnecessary to determine which approach should prevail, because the government action at issue in this case qualifies as arbitrary under both definitions. (ed. Note: In *Chaoulli* the Court divided 3-3 on whether Quebec legislation prohibiting private insurance to cover delays in medical insurance was arbitrary and therefore contrary to s.7.)

In *R. v. Khawaja*, 97 C.R. (6th) 223, [2012] 3 S.C.R. 555, the Court decided that terrorism provisions in the *Criminal Code* were not overbroad or grossly disproportional. Based on a purposive interpretation of the *actus reus* and *mens rea* requirements of s. 83.18, the Court concluded that it did not allow convictions for: (i) innocent or socially useful conduct undertaken absent any specific intent to enhance the abilities of a terrorist group to facilitate or carry out a terrorist activity; or (ii) conduct that a reasonable person would not view as capable of materially enhancing the abilities of a terrorist group to facilitate or carry out a terrorist activity. She added that it was not necessary to decide whether overbreadth and gross disproportionality were distinct constitutional doctrines.

Finally, in its ruling in *Bedford* (2013), the Court struck down the existing prostitution laws:

BEDFORD v. CANADA (ATTORNEY GENERAL)

2013 SCC 72, 7 C.R. (7th) 1, [2013] 3 S.C.R. 1101, 303 C.C.C. (3d) 146

The applicants, B, L and S, challenged the constitutionality of the *Criminal Code* provisions prohibiting common bawdy-houses (s. 210), living on the avails of prostitution (s. 212(1)(j)) and communicating for the purpose of prostitution (s. 213(1)(c)). The applicants were current or former prostitutes who sought to operate common bawdy-houses in which they would earn income from their own prostitution or the prostitution of other women. The applicants argued that the provisions violated their s. 7 rights to liberty and security of the person by putting the safety and lives of prostitutes at risk, and by preventing them from implementing safety measures — such as hiring security guards or "screening" potential clients — that could protect them from violence. The evidentiary record amounted to over 25,000 pages of affidavits, and experts and documentary evidence in the form of studies, reports of expert panels and Parliamentary records. Some of the affiants were cross-examined. The application judge accepted the applicants' arguments and invalidated the challenged provisions. The Crown appealed.

Five justices of the Ontario Court of Appeal allowed the appeal in part. The offences of keeping a common bawdy-house and living off the avails of prostitution were unanimously held to be unconstitutional. The living off the avails offence was read down to only apply to exploitative relationships. A 3-2 majority upheld the constitutionality of the offence of communicating for the purpose of prostitution.

The Attorney General appealed and B, L and S cross-appealed on the constitutionality of s. 213(1)(c) and in respect of the s. 210 remedy.

The Supreme Court dismissed the appeal and allowed the cross-appeal.

Chief Justice McLachlin for a unanimous Court declared that ss. 210, 212(1)(j) and 213(1)(c) of the *Criminal Code* were inconsistent with s. 7 of the *Charter*. The declaration of invalidity was suspended for one year. The Court ruled that the impugned laws negatively impact security of the person rights of prostitutes and thus engage s. 7. The prohibitions all heighten the risks the applicants face in prostitution — itself a legal activity. They do not merely impose conditions on how prostitutes operate. They go a critical step further by imposing *dangerous* conditions on prostitution. They prevent people engaged in a risky — but legal — activity from taking steps to protect themselves from the risks. Prostitutes are prevented from working in a fixed indoor location. The Court ruled that while some prostitutes may fit the description of persons who freely choose (or at one time chose) to engage in the risky economic activity of prostitution, many prostitutes have no meaningful choice but to do so. It makes no difference that the conduct of pimps and johns is the immediate source of the harm suffered by prostitutes. The violence of a john does not diminish the role of the state in making a prostitute more vulnerable to that violence.

The Court then discussed the relevant principles of fundamental justice of arbitrariness, overbreadth and gross disproportionality:

[105] The overarching lesson that emerges from the case law is that laws run afoul of our basic values when the means by which the state seeks to attain its objective is fundamentally flawed, in the sense of being arbitrary, overbroad, or having effects that are grossly disproportionate to the legislative goal. To deprive citizens of life, liberty, or security of the person by laws that violate these norms is not in accordance with the principles of fundamental justice.

[106] As these principles have developed in the jurisprudence, they have not always been applied consistently. The Court of Appeal below pointed to the confusion that has been caused by the "commingling" of arbitrariness, overbreadth, and gross disproportionality (at paras. 143-51). This Court itself recently noted the conflation of the principles of overbreadth and gross disproportionality (*R. v. Khawaja*, 2012 SCC 69, [2012] 3 S.C.R. 555, at paras. 38-40; see also *R. v. S.S.C.*, 2008 BCCA 262, 257 B.C.A.C. 57, at para. 72). In short, courts have explored different ways in which laws run afoul of our basic

values, using the same words — arbitrariness, overbreadth, and gross disproportionality — in slightly different ways.

[107] Although there is significant overlap between these three principles, and one law may properly be characterized by more than one of them, arbitrariness, overbreadth, and gross disproportionality remain three distinct principles that stem from what Hamish Stewart calls "failures of instrumental rationality" — the situation where the law is "inadequately connected to its objective or in some sense goes too far in seeking to attain it" (*Fundamental Justice: Section 7 of the Canadian Charter of Rights and Freedoms* (2012), at p. 151). As Peter Hogg has explained:

> The doctrines of overbreadth, disproportionality and arbitrariness are all at bottom intended to address what Hamish Stewart calls "failures of instrumental rationality", by which he means that the Court accepts the legislative objective, but scrutinizes the policy instrument enacted as the means to achieve the objective. If the policy instrument is not a rational means to achieve the objective, then the law is dysfunctional in terms of its own objective.
> ("The Brilliant Career of Section 7 of the Charter" (2012), 58 *S.C.L.R.* (2d) 195, at p. 209 (citation omitted))

[108] The case law on arbitrariness, overbreadth and gross disproportionality is directed against two different evils. The first evil is the absence of a connection between the infringement of rights and what the law seeks to achieve — the situation where the law's deprivation of an individual's life, liberty, or security of the person is not connected to the purpose of the law. The first evil is addressed by the norms against arbitrariness and overbreadth, which target the absence of connection between the law's purpose and the s. 7 deprivation.

[109] The second evil lies in depriving a person of life, liberty or security of the person in a manner that is grossly disproportionate to the law's objective. The law's impact on the s. 7 interest is connected to the purpose, but the impact is so severe that it violates our fundamental norms.

[110] Against this background, it may be useful to elaborate on arbitrariness, overbreadth and gross disproportionality.

[111] Arbitrariness asks whether there is a direct connection between the purpose of the law and the impugned effect on the individual, in the sense that the effect on the individual bears some relation to the law's purpose. There must be a rational connection between the object of the measure that causes the s. 7 deprivation, and the limits it imposes on life, liberty, or security of the person (Stewart, at p. 136). A law that imposes limits on these interests in a way that bears *no connection* to its objective arbitrarily impinges on those interests. Thus, in *Chaoulli*, the law was arbitrary because the prohibition of private health insurance was held to be unrelated to the objective of protecting the public health system.

[112] Overbreadth deals with a law that is so broad in scope that it includes *some* conduct that bears no relation to its purpose. In this sense, the law is arbitrary *in part*. At its core, overbreadth addresses the situation where there is no rational connection between the purposes of the law and *some*, but not all, of its impacts. For instance, the law at issue in *Demers* required unfit accused to attend repeated review board hearings. The law was only disconnected from its purpose insofar as it applied to permanently unfit accused; for temporarily unfit accused, the effects were related to the purpose.

[113] Overbreadth allows courts to recognize that the law is rational in some cases, but that it overreaches in its effect in others. Despite this recognition of the scope of the law as a whole, the focus remains on the individual and whether the effect on the individual is rationally connected to the law's purpose. For example, where a law is drawn broadly and targets some conduct that bears no relation to its purpose in order to make enforcement more practical, there is still no connection between the purpose of the law and its effect on the *specific individual*. Enforcement practicality may be a justification for an overbroad law, to be analyzed under s. 1 of the *Charter*.

[114] It has been suggested that overbreadth is not truly a distinct principle of fundamental justice. The case law has sometimes said that overbreadth straddles both arbitrariness and gross disproportionality. Thus, in *Heywood*, Cory J. stated: "The effect of overbreadth is that in some applications the law is arbitrary or disproportionate" (p. 793).

[115] And in *R. v. Clay*, 2003 SCC 75, [2003] 3 S.C.R. 735, the companion case to *Malmo-Levine*, Gonthier and Binnie JJ. explained:

> Overbreadth in that respect addresses the potential infringement of fundamental justice where the adverse effect of a legislative measure on the individuals subject to its strictures is grossly disproportionate to the state interest the legislation seeks to protect. Overbreadth in this aspect is, as Cory J. pointed out [in *Heywood*], related to arbitrariness. [Emphasis deleted; para. 38.]

[116] In part this debate is semantic. The law has not developed by strict labels, but on a case-by-case basis, as courts identified laws that were inherently bad because they violated our basic values.

[117] Moving forward, however, it may be helpful to think of overbreadth as a distinct principle of fundamental justice related to arbitrariness, in that the question for both is whether there is *no connection* between the effects of a law and its objective. Overbreadth simply allows the court to recognize that the lack of connection arises in a law that goes too far by sweeping conduct into its ambit that bears no relation to its objective.

[118] An ancillary question, which applies to both arbitrariness and overbreadth, concerns how significant the lack of correspondence between the objective of

the infringing provision and its effects must be. Questions have arisen as to whether a law is arbitrary or overbroad when its effects are *inconsistent* with its objective, or whether, more broadly, a law is arbitrary or overbroad whenever its effects are *unnecessary* for its objective (see, e.g., *Chaoulli*, at paras. 233-34).

[119] As noted above, the root question is whether the law is inherently bad because there is *no connection*, in whole or in part, between its effects and its purpose. This standard is not easily met. The evidence may, as in *Morgentaler*, show that the effect actually undermines the objective and is therefore "inconsistent" with the objective. Or the evidence may, as in *Chaoulli*, show that there is simply no connection on the facts between the effect and the objective, and the effect is therefore "unnecessary". Regardless of how the judge describes this lack of connection, the ultimate question remains whether the evidence establishes that the law violates basic norms because there is *no connection* between its effect and its purpose. This is a matter to be determined on a case-by-case basis, in light of the evidence.

[120] Gross disproportionality asks a different question from arbitrariness and overbreadth. It targets the second fundamental evil: the law's effects on life, liberty or security of the person are so grossly disproportionate to its purposes that they cannot rationally be supported. The rule against gross disproportionality only applies in extreme cases where the seriousness of the deprivation is totally out of sync with the objective of the measure. This idea is captured by the hypothetical of a law with the purpose of keeping the streets clean that imposes a sentence of life imprisonment for spitting on the sidewalk. The connection between the draconian impact of the law and its object must be entirely outside the norms accepted in our free and democratic society.

[121] Gross disproportionality under s. 7 of the *Charter* does *not* consider the beneficial effects of the law for society. It balances the negative effect on the individual against the purpose of the law, *not* against societal benefit that might flow from the law. As this Court said in *Malmo-Levine*:

> In effect, the exercise undertaken by Braidwood J.A. was to balance the law's salutary and deleterious effects. In our view, with respect, that is a function that is more properly reserved for s. 1. These are the types of social and economic harms that generally have no place in s. 7. [para. 181]

[122] Thus, gross disproportionality is not concerned with the number of people who experience grossly disproportionate effects; a grossly disproportionate effect on one person is sufficient to violate the norm.

[123] All three principles — arbitrariness, overbreadth, and gross disproportionality — compare the rights infringement caused by the law with the objective of the law, not with the law's effectiveness. That is, they do not

look to how well the law achieves its object, or to how much of the population the law benefits. They do not consider ancillary benefits to the general population. Furthermore, none of the principles measure the percentage of the population that is negatively impacted. The analysis is qualitative, not quantitative. The question under s. 7 is whether *anyone's* life, liberty or security of the person has been denied by a law that is inherently bad; a grossly disproportionate, overbroad, or arbitrary effect on one person is sufficient to establish a breach of s. 7.

[Having explained the relevant principles of fundamental justice, the Court found that the three provisions being challenged all violated s. 7 of the *Charter.*]

(4) Do the Impugned Laws Respect the Principles of Fundamental Justice?

(a) Section 210: The Bawdy-House Prohibition

(i) The Object of the Provision

[131] The appellant Attorneys General argue that the object of this provision, considered alone and in conjunction with the other prohibitions, is to deter prostitution. The record does not support this contention; on the contrary, it is clear from the legislative record that the purpose of the prohibition is to prevent community harms in the nature of nuisance.

[132] There is no evidence to support a reappraisal of this purpose by Parliament. The doctrine against shifting objectives does not permit a new object to be introduced at this point (*R. v. Zundel*, [1992] 2 S.C.R. 731). On its face, the provision is only directed at in-call prostitution, and so cannot be said to aim at deterring prostitution generally. To find that it operates with the other Criminal Code provisions to deter prostitution generally is also unwarranted, given their piecemeal evolution and patchwork construction, which leaves out-calls and prostitution itself untouched. I therefore agree with the lower courts that the objectives of the bawdy-house provision are to combat neighbourhood disruption or disorder and to safeguard public health and safety.

(ii) Compliance With the Principles of Fundamental Justice

[The Court concluded that the bawdy-house provisions were grossly disproportionate to their objective. They noted that allowing a prostitute to work from a bawdy-house would provide the "safety benefits of proximity to others, familiarity with surroundings, security staff, closed-circuit television and other such monitoring that a permanent indoor location can facilitate", which had to be balanced against the fact that "complaints about nuisance arising from indoor prostitution establishments are rare" (para. 134).]

[135] The Court of Appeal acknowledged that empirical evidence on the subject is difficult to gather, since almost all the studies focus on street prostitution.

However, it concluded that the evidence supported the application judge's findings on gross disproportionality — in particular, the evidence of the high homicide rate among prostitutes, with the overwhelming number of victims being street prostitutes. The Court of Appeal agreed that moving indoors amounts to a "basic safety precaution" for prostitutes, one which the bawdy-house provision makes illegal (paras. 206-7).

[136] In my view, this conclusion was not in error. The harms identified by the courts below are grossly disproportionate to the deterrence of community disruption that is the object of the law. Parliament has the power to regulate against nuisances, but not at the cost of the health, safety and lives of prostitutes. A law that prevents street prostitutes from resorting to a safe haven such as Grandma's House while a suspected serial killer prowls the streets, is a law that has lost sight of its purpose. [Editors' note: "Grandma's House" was a safe house in the downtown east side of Vancouver established as a place for street prostitutes to bring clients. It was shut down after bawdy-house charges were laid.]

(b) Section 212(1)(j): Living on the Avails of Prostitution

(i) The Object of the Provision

[137] This Court has held, per Cory J. for the majority in *Downey*, that the purpose of this provision is to target pimps and the parasitic, exploitative conduct in which they engage. . .

(ii) Compliance With the Principles of Fundamental Justice

[139] The courts below concluded that the living on the avails provision is overbroad insofar as it captures a number of non-exploitative relationships which are not connected to the law's purpose. The courts below also concluded that the provision's negative effect on the security and safety of prostitutes is grossly disproportionate to its objective of protecting prostitutes from harm.

[140] I agree with the courts below that the living on the avails provision is overbroad.

[141] The provision has been judicially restricted to those who provide a service or good to a prostitute because she is a prostitute, thus excluding grocers and doctors, for instance (*Shaw v. Director of Public Prosecutions*, [1962] A.C. 220 (H.L.)). It also has been held to require that exploitation be proven in the case of a person who lives with the prostitute, in order to exclude people in legitimate domestic relationships with a prostitute (*Grilo*). These refinements render the prohibition narrower than its words might suggest.

[142] The question here is whether the law nevertheless goes too far and thus deprives the applicants of their security of the person in a manner unconnected to the law's objective. The law punishes everyone who lives on the avails of prostitution without distinguishing between those who exploit prostitutes (for example, controlling and abusive pimps) and those who could increase the safety and security of prostitutes (for example, legitimate drivers, managers, or bodyguards). It also includes anyone involved in business with a prostitute, such as accountants or receptionists. In these ways, the law includes some conduct that bears no relation to its purpose of preventing the exploitation of prostitutes. The living on the avails provision is therefore overbroad.

[143] The appellant Attorneys General argue that the line between an exploitative pimp and a prostitute's legitimate driver, manager or bodyguard, blurs in the real world. A relationship that begins on a non-exploitative footing may become exploitative over time. If the provision were tailored more narrowly — for example, by reading in "in circumstances of exploitation" as the Court of Appeal did — evidentiary difficulties may lead to exploiters escaping liability. Relationships of exploitation often involve intimidation and manipulation of the kind that make it very difficult for a prostitute to testify. For these reasons, the Attorneys General argue, the provision must be drawn broadly in order to effectively capture those it targets.

[144] This argument is more appropriately addressed under the s. 1 analysis. As stated above, if a law captures conduct that bears no relation to its purpose, the law is overbroad under s. 7; enforcement practicality is one way the government may justify an overbroad law under s. 1 of the Charter.

[145] Having found that the prohibition on living on the avails of prostitution is overbroad, I find it unnecessary to consider whether it is also grossly disproportionate to its object of protecting prostitutes from exploitative relationships.

(c) Section 213(1)(c): Communicating in Public for the Purposes of Prostitution

(i) The Object of the Provision

. . . .

[147] It is clear from these reasons [those in the *Prostitution Reference*, the previous challenge to the constitutionality of this law] that the purpose of the communicating provision is not to eliminate street prostitution for its own sake, but to take prostitution "off the streets and out of public view" in order to prevent the nuisances that street prostitution can cause. The *Prostitution Reference* belies the argument of the Attorneys General that Parliament's overall objective in these provisions is to deter prostitution.

(ii) Compliance With the Principles of Fundamental Justice

[148] The application judge concluded that the harm imposed by the prohibition on communicating in public was grossly disproportionate to the provision's object of removing the nuisance of prostitution from the streets. This was based on evidence that she found established that the ability to screen clients was an "essential tool" to avoiding violent or drunken clients (application decision, at para. 432).

[149] The majority of the Court of Appeal found that the application judge erred in her analysis of gross disproportionality by attaching too little importance to the objective of s. 213(1)(c), and by incorrectly finding on the evidence that face-to-face communication with a prospective customer is essential to enhancing prostitutes' safety (paras. 306 and 310).

[150] In my view, the Court of Appeal majority's reasoning on this question is problematic, largely for the reasons set out by MacPherson J.A., dissenting in part. Four aspects of the majority's analysis are particularly troubling.

[151] First, in concluding that the application judge accorded too little weight to the legislative objective of s. 213(1)(c), the majority of the Court of Appeal criticized her characterization of the object of the provision as targeting "noise, street congestion, and the possibility that the practice of prostitution will interfere with those nearby" (C.A., at para. 306). But the application judge's conclusion was in concert with the object of s. 213(1)(c) established by Dickson C.J. in the *Prostitution Reference*, which the majority of the Court of Appeal endorsed earlier in their reasons (para. 286).

[152] Compounding this error, the majority of the Court of Appeal inflated the objective of the prohibition on public communication by referring to "drug possession, drug trafficking, public intoxication, and organized crime" (para. 307), even though Dickson C.J. explicitly excluded the exposure of "related violence, drugs and crime" to vulnerable young people from the objectives of s. 213(1)(c). At most, the provision's effect on these other issues is an ancillary benefit — and, as such, it should not play into the gross disproportionality analysis, which weighs the actual objective of the provision against its negative impact on the individual's life, liberty and security of the person.

[153] The three remaining concerns with the majority's reasoning relate to the other side of the balance: the assessment of the impact of the provision.

[154] First, the majority of the Court of Appeal erroneously substituted its assessment of the evidence for that of the application judge. It found that the application judge's conclusion that face-to-face communication is essential to enhancing prostitutes' safety was based only on "anecdotal evidence . . .

informed by her own common sense" (para. 311). This was linked to its error, discussed above, in according too little deference to the application judge on findings of social and legislative facts. MacPherson J.A. for the minority, correctly countered that the evidence on this point came from both prostitutes' own accounts and from expert assessments, and provided a firm basis for the application judge's conclusion (paras. 348-50).

[155] Second, the majority ignored the law's effect of displacing prostitutes to more secluded, less secure locations. The application judge highlighted this displacement (at para. 331), citing the evidence found in the report of the House of Commons Standing Committee on Justice and Human Rights Subcommittee on Solicitation Laws (*The Challenge of Change: A Study of Canada's Criminal Prostitution Laws* (2006)) on the effects of s. 213(1)(c). The majority's conclusion that the application judge did not have a proper basis to conclude that face-to-face communication enhances safety may be explained in part by their failure to consider the impact of the provision on displacement.

[156] Related to this is the uncontested fact that the communication ban prevents street workers from bargaining for conditions that would materially reduce their risk, such as condom use and the use of safe houses.

[157] Finally, the majority of the Court of Appeal majority, in rejecting the application judge's conclusions, relied on its own speculative assessment of the impact of s. 213(1)(c):

> While it is fair to say that a street prostitute might be able to avoid a "bad date" by negotiating details such as payment, services to be performed and condom use up front, it is equally likely that the customer could pass muster at an early stage, only to turn violent once the transaction is underway. It is also possible that the prostitute may proceed even in the face of perceived danger, either because her judgment is impaired by drugs or alcohol, or because she is so desperate for money that she feels compelled to take the risk. [para. 312]

[158] It is certainly conceivable, as this passage suggests, that some street prostitutes would not refuse a client even if communication revealed potential danger. It is also conceivable that the danger may not be perfectly predicted in advance. However, that does not negate the application judge's finding that communication is an essential tool that can decrease risk. The assessment is qualitative, not quantitative. If screening could have prevented one woman from jumping into Robert Pickton's car, the severity of the harmful effects is established.

[159] In sum, the Court of Appeal wrongly attributed errors in reasoning to the application judge and made a number of errors in considering gross disproportionality. I would restore the application judge's conclusion that s. 213(1)(c) is grossly disproportionate. The provision's negative impact on the

safety and lives of street prostitutes is a grossly disproportionate response to the possibility of nuisance caused by street prostitution.

[The Court found that the s. 7 violations were not saved under s. 1. A portion of their reasoning on that subject is included later.]

Each of arbitrariness, overbreadth and gross disproportionality concern in some way comparing the effect of a law to its purpose. This means that in the case of those particular principles of fundamental justice, it is essential to first identify exactly what the purpose of the law in question *is*: a law might be overbroad with respect to one purpose but not another, for example. The Court has offered some guidance about the proper approach to this step.

R. v. SAFARZADEH-MARKHALI

[2016] 1 S.C.R. 180, 334 C.C.C. (3d) 1, 27 C.R. (7th) 265

McLachlin C.J.:

[24] Whether a law is overbroad within the meaning of s. 7 turns on the relationship between the law's purpose and its effect: *R. v. Moriarity*, 2015 SCC 55, [2015] 3 S.C.R. 485, at para. 24. It is critically important, therefore, to identify the purpose of the challenged law at the outset of the s. 7 inquiry.

[25] *Moriarity* summarizes the considerations that guide the task of properly characterizing Parliament's purpose in a s. 7 analysis into overbreadth.

[26] First, the law's purpose is distinct from the means used to achieve that purpose: *Moriarity*, at para. 27. A law's means may be helpful in determining its objective, but the two must be treated separately.

[27] Second, the law's purpose should be characterized at the appropriate level of generality, which "resides between the statement of an 'animating social value' — which is too general — and a narrow articulation" that amounts to a virtual repetition of the challenged provision, divorced from its context: *Moriarity*, at para. 28.

[28] Third, the statement of purpose should be both precise and succinct: *Moriarity*, at para. 29. Precision requires that courts focus on the purpose of the particular statutory provision subject to constitutional challenge: *ibid.*; see also *RJR-MacDonald Inc. v. Canada (Attorney General)*, [1995] 3 S.C.R. 199, at para. 144.

[29] Fourth, the analysis is not concerned with the appropriateness of the legislative purpose. The court must take the legislative objective "at face value" and assume that it is appropriate and lawful: *Moriarity*, at para. 30. The

appropriateness of a legislative objective may be relevant to its constitutionality under other *Charter* provisions. But it has no place in the s. 7 analysis of overbreadth

. . . .

[31] To determine a law's purpose for a s. 7 overbreadth analysis, courts look to (1) statements of purpose in the legislation, if any; (2) the text, context, and scheme of the legislation; and (3) extrinsic evidence such as legislative history and evolution: *Moriarity*, at para. 31.

Bedford is important for deciding that *Charter* challenges for arbitrariness, overbreadth and gross disproportionality are distinct. In setting out these general principles the Court strives to achieve greater clarity. At face value it appears that the Court has emphasized that laws can be struck down as *arbitrary* if there is no rational connection with the objective, as *overbroad* only where the law is only partially arbitrary, and as *grossly disproportionate* in extreme cases of arbitrariness. Greater clarity might have been achieved by folding the three doctrines under the one heading of arbitrariness. At one point the Chief Justice refers to her broader view in *Chaoulli v. Quebec (Attorney General)* (as cited above in *PHS*) that overbreadth concerns a consideration of whether the law was necessary to achieve its objective but she now opts for the Court for the narrower test of rationality:

[119]. . .The root question is whether the law is inherently bad because there is no connection, in whole or in part, between its effects and its purpose.

The Chief Justice adds that:

This standard is not easily met.

Notwithstanding this caveat, the Court's applications of these principles to strike down all the prostitution-related offences appears to reinvigorate power for courts to strike down legislation judges found to be irrational when measured against the legislative objective. Clearly, arbitrariness and overbreadth are lower standards than gross disproportionality. In *R. v. Malmo-Levine*, 2003 SCC 74, [2003] 3 S.C.R. 571, 16 C.R. (6th) 1 and *R. v. Clay*, 16 C.R. (6th) 117, [2003] 3 S.C.R. 735, Justice Binnie for the majority, in rejecting such challenges to marijuana laws, had called for considerable deference to legislative choices and had asserted a test of gross disproportionality for challenges based on vagueness or overbreadth. There is now no such limit.

Some media commentary predicted that the *PHS* ruling would lead to a more activist role for the courts in striking down legislation. One senior judge, who wished to remain anonymous, was quoted in the *Globe and Mail* (October 11, 2011) as saying that the Court had "opened a can of worms" and that many judges were "uncomfortable" in the role of assessing the effectiveness of governmental policy. However, assessing trends in the approach of the Court is a challenging task. *Bedford* itself was a significant decision that seemed to signal a strong approach to judicial independence. On the other hand, it was one of the only 2 out of 11 *Charter* cases in 2013 in which the applicant succeeded (see Sonia Lawrence, "2013: Constitutional Cases in Review" (2014) 67 S.C.L.R. (2d) 4). In 2015 there were 28 *Charter* cases with the challenge succeeding in 13, but only 4 of these resulted in legislation being struck down (see Lorne Sossin, "Constitutional Cases 2015: An Overview" (2016) 76 S.C.L.R. (2d) 1). In the 6 years after *PHS* s. 7 challenges to legislation were heard by the Court in 11 cases and succeeded 6 times (and in one case the challenge succeeded under s. 12 instead).

Simply looking at whether a s. 7 challenge succeeds or fails does not tell the whole story, however, because of another option sometimes adopted by courts: to impose a particular interpretation on the relevant statute and then conclude that there is no violation because of that interpretation. This was what happened in *Canadian Foundation for Children, Youth & the Law*.

On December 6, 2014, new legislation concerning prostitution came into force. It criminalizes the purchase but not the sale of sexual services. Minister of Justice MacKay said it was based on the Nordic model but "made in Canada". He indicated that the government was seeking to protect prostitutes who are "victims" and to go after johns who are "perverts" (*CBC News*, June 4, 2014). Prime Minister Harper later indicated that:

> We understand the fundamental truth that the activities around prostitution are illegal because they are bad for women and society more broadly (Toronto Sun, June 9, 2014).

Section 286.1 criminalizes:

> Everyone who, in any place obtains for consideration, or communicates with anyone for the purpose of obtaining for consideration, the sexual services of a person.

Section 286.2 criminalizes:

> Everyone who receives a financial or other material benefit, knowing that it is obtained by or directly or indirectly from the commission of an offence under s. 286.1.

There are complicated provisions purporting to exempt relationships that are not exploitative (the solution adopted by the Ontario Court of Appeal).
Section 286.4 criminalizes:

> Everyone who knowingly advertises an offer to provide sexual services for consideration.

There is an immunity from ss. 286.2 and 286.4 for a sex-trade worker who advertises his or her own services. However, it is an offence for anyone to communicate in a public place that "is or is next to a school ground, playground or daycare centre".

Whether these new laws will survive another *Charter* challenge remains to be seen. Immediately after the laws came into force, some provinces expressed concern that they were not constitutional and expressed hesitation about them, but ultimately no province has concluded that it will not enforce them. The bill has been applauded by those who see all prostitution as immoral and those who, like the government, see sex work as not ever a free choice but always exploitative, degrading and dangerous to women. It has been decried by others, often speaking for street-trade workers, who see the laws as driving prostitution underground and making their choice of work more dangerous: see, especially, Pivot Legal Society, *My Work Should Not Cost Me My Life. The Case Against Criminalizing the Purchase of Sex in Canada* (2014). Clearly making prostitution in part criminal will make *Charter* s. 7 overbreadth challenges more difficult: see Lisa Dufraimont in Supreme Court Law Review. On the other hand, the broad criminalization of advertising may raise freedom of expression issues and there may be an argument under s. 15 for a discriminatory impact of the laws against men.

(iii) *Oakes test for section 1*

R. v. OAKES

[1986] 1 S.C.R. 103, 50 C.R. (3d) 1, 24 C.C.C.(3d) 321,
1986 CarswellOnt 95, 1986 CarswellOnt 1001

DICKSON C.J.C. (CHOUINARD, LAMER, WILSON and LE DAIN JJ. concurring):

It is important to observe at the outset that s. 1 has two functions: first, it constitutionally guarantees the rights and freedoms set out in the provisions which follow; and, second, it states explicitly the exclusive justificatory criteria (outside of s. 33 of the *Constitution Act, 1982*) against which limitations on those rights and freedoms must be measured. Accordingly, any s. 1 inquiry must be premised on an understanding that the impugned limit violates constitutional rights and freedoms — rights and freedoms which are part of the supreme law of Canada. As Madam Justice Wilson stated in *Singh et al. v. Ministry of Employment and Immigration, supra*, at pp. 218-19: ". . . it is important to remember that the courts are conducting this inquiry in light of a commitment to uphold the rights and freedoms set out in the other sections of the *Charter*."

A second contextual element of interpretation of s. 1 is provided by the words "free and democratic society". Inclusion of these words as the final standard of justification for limits on rights and freedoms refers the court to the very purpose for which the *Charter* was originally entrenched in the Constitution: Canadian society is to be free and democratic. The court must be guided by the values and principles essential to a free and democratic society which I believe embody, to name but a few, respect for the inherent dignity of the human person, commitment to social justice and equality, accommodation of a wide variety of beliefs, respect for cultural and group identity, and faith in social and political institutions which enhance the participation of individuals and groups in society. The underlying values and principles of a free and democratic society are the genesis of the rights and freedoms guaranteed by the *Charter* and the ultimate standard against which a limit on a right or freedom must be shown, despite its effect, to be reasonable and demonstrably justified.

The rights and freedoms guaranteed by the *Charter* are not, however, absolute. It may become necessary to limit rights and freedoms in circumstances where their exercise would be inimical to the realization of collective goals of fundamental importance. For this reason, s. 1 provides criteria of justification for limits on the rights and freedoms guaranteed by the *Charter*. These criteria impose a stringent standard of justification, especially when understood in terms of the two contextual considerations discussed above, namely, the violation of a constitutionally guaranteed right or freedom and the fundamental principles of a free and democratic society.

The onus of proving that a limit on a right or freedom guaranteed by the *Charter* is reasonable and demonstrably justified in a free and democratic society rests upon the party seeking to uphold the limitation. It is clear from the text of s. 1 that limits on the rights and freedoms enumerated in the *Charter* are exceptions to their general guarantee. The presumption is that the rights and freedoms are guaranteed unless the party invoking s. 1 can bring itself within the exceptional criteria which justify their being limited. This is further substantiated by the use of the word "demonstrably" which clearly indicates that the onus of justification is on the party seeking to limit: *Hunter v. Southam Inc.*, *supra*.

The standard of proof under s. 1 is the civil standard, namely, proof by a preponderance of probability. The alternative criminal standard, proof beyond a reasonable doubt, would, in my view, be unduly onerous on the party seeking to limit. Concepts such as "reasonableness", "justifiability" and "free and democratic society" are simply not amenable to such a standard.

. . . .

To establish that a limit is reasonable and demonstrably justified in a free and democratic society, two central criteria must be satisfied. First, the objective, which the measures responsible for a limit on a *Charter* right or freedom are designed to serve, must be "of sufficient importance to warrant overriding a constitutionally protected right or freedom": *R. v. Big M Drug Mart Ltd.*, *supra*, at p. 352. The standard must be high in order to ensure that objectives which are trivial or discordant with the principles integral to a free and democratic society do not gain s. 1 protection. It is necessary, at a minimum, that an objective relate to concerns which are pressing and substantial in a free and democratic society before it can be characterized as sufficiently important.

Second, once a sufficiently significant objective is recognized, then the party invoking s. 1 must show that the means chosen are reasonable and demonstrably justified. This involves "a form of proportionality test": *R. v. Big M Drug Mart Ltd.*, *supra*, at p. 352. Although the nature of the proportionality test will vary depending on the circumstances, in each case courts will be required to balance the interests of society with those of individuals and groups. There are, in my view, three important components of a proportionality test. First, the measures adopted must be carefully designed to achieve the objective in question. They must not be arbitrary, unfair or based on irrational considerations. In short, they must be rationally connected to the objective. Second, the means, even if rationally connected to the objective in this first sense, should impair "as little as possible" the right or freedom in question: *R. v. Big M Drug Mart Ltd.*, *supra*, at p. 352. Third, there must be a proportionality between the *effects* of the measures which are responsible for limiting the *Charter* right or freedom, and the objective which has been identified as of "sufficient importance".

With respect to the third component, it is clear that the general effect of any measure impugned under s. 1 will be the infringement of a right or freedom guaranteed by the *Charter*; this is the reason why resort to s. 1 is necessary. The inquiry into effects must, however, go further. A wide range of rights and freedoms are guaranteed by the *Charter*, and an almost infinite number of factual situations may arise in respect of these. Some limits on rights and freedoms protected by the *Charter* will be more serious than others in terms of the nature of the right or freedom violated, the extent of the violation, and the degree to which the measures which impose the limit trench upon the integral principles of a free and democratic society. Even if an objective is of sufficient importance, and the first two elements of the proportionality test are satisfied, it is still possible that, because of the severity of the deleterious effects of a measure on individuals or groups, the measure will not be justified by the purposes it is intended to serve. The more severe the deleterious effects of a measure, the more important the objective must be if the measure is to be reasonable and demonstrably justified in a free and democratic society.

Although the form of the *Oakes* test has stayed consistent since it was first created, the way in which each individual step is understood has undergone some evolution. The current approach is illustrated by a recent description of the test.

R. v. J. (K.R.)

[2016] 1 S.C.R. 906, 337 C.C.C. (3d) 285, 30 C.R. (7th) 1

Karakatsanis J.:

[58] ... To establish that the limitation on the appellant's s. 11(i) right is reasonable and demonstrably justified, the government must show that the 2012 amendments have a sufficiently important objective "and that the means chosen are proportional to that object[ive]" (*Carter v. Canada (Attorney General)*, 2015

SCC 5, [2015] 1 S.C.R. 331, at para. 94). A law is proportionate if (1) there is a rational connection between the means adopted and the objective; (2) it is minimally impairing in that there are no alternative means that may achieve the same objective with a lesser degree of rights limitation; and (3) there is proportionality between the deleterious and salutary effects of the law (*R. v. Oakes*, [1986] 1 S.C.R. 103; *Carter*, at para. 94). The proportionality inquiry is a normative and contextual one, which requires courts to examine the broader picture by "balanc[ing] the interests of society with those of individuals and groups" (*Oakes*, at p. 139).

. . . .

[61] A law that limits a constitutional right must do so in pursuit of a sufficiently important objective that is consistent with the values of a free and democratic society. This examination is a threshold requirement that is undertaken without considering the scope of the right infringement, the means employed, or the relationship between the positive and negative effects of the law.

. . . .

[67] In assessing the proportionality of a law, a degree of deference is required. As this Court recently wrote in *Carter*:

> At this stage of the analysis, the courts must accord the legislature a measure of deference. Proportionality does not require perfection: *Saskatchewan (Human Rights Commission) v. Whatcott*, 2013 SCC 11, [2013] 1 S.C.R. 467, at para. 78. Section 1 only requires that the limits be "reasonable". [para. 97]

(a) Rational Connection

[68] At this first step of the proportionality inquiry, the government must demonstrate that the means used by the limiting law are rationally connected to the purpose the law was designed to achieve. "To establish a rational connection, the government need only show that there is a causal connection between the infringement and the benefit sought 'on the basis of reason or logic'" (*Carter*, at para. 99, citing *RJR-MacDonald Inc. v. Canada (Attorney General)*, [1995] 3 S.C.R. 199, at para. 153).

. . . .

(b) Minimal Impairment

[70] The question at this second stage is whether the 2012 amendments are minimally impairing, in the sense that "the limit on the right is reasonably tailored to the objective" (*Carter*, at para. 102). It is only when there are alternative, less harmful means of achieving the government's objective "in a real and substantial manner" that a law should fail the minimal impairment test

(*Alberta v. Hutterian Brethren of Wilson Colony*, 2009 SCC 37, [2009] 2 S.C.R. 567, at para. 55).

. . . .

(c) Proportionality of Effects

[77] At this final stage of the proportionality analysis, the Court must "weig[h] the impact of the law on protected rights against the beneficial effect of the law in terms of the greater public good" (*Carter*, at para. 122). This final stage is an important one because it performs a fundamentally distinct role. As a majority of this Court observed in *Thomson Newspapers Co. v. Canada (Attorney General)*, [1998] 1 S.C.R. 877:

> The focus of the first and second steps of the proportionality analysis is not the relationship between the measures and the Charter right in question, but rather the relationship between the ends of the legislation and the means employed. . . . The third stage of the proportionality analysis provides an opportunity to assess, in light of the practical and contextual details which are elucidated in the first and second stages, whether the benefits which accrue from the limitation are proportional to its deleterious effects as measured by the values underlying the *Charter*. [para. 125]

[78] It is for this reason that Aharon Barak, former President of the Supreme Court of Israel, has described this final step as "the very heart of proportionality" ("Proportional Effect: The Israeli Experience" (2007), 57 *U.T.L.J.* 369, at p. 380). And in *Hutterian Brethren*, Abella J. wrote: "... most of the heavy conceptual lifting and balancing ought to be done at the final step — proportionality. Proportionality is, after all, what s. 1 is about" (para. 149).

[79] I agree. While the minimal impairment test has come to dominate much of the s. 1 discourse in Canada, this final step permits courts to address the essence of the proportionality enquiry at the heart of s. 1. It is only at this final stage that courts can transcend the law's purpose and engage in a robust examination of the law's impact on Canada's free and democratic society "in direct and explicit terms" (J. Cameron, "The Past, Present, and Future of Expressive Freedom Under the *Charter*" (1997), 35 *Osgoode Hall L.J.* 1, at p. 66). In other words, this final step allows courts to stand back to determine on a normative basis whether a rights infringement is justified in a free and democratic society. Although this examination entails difficult value judgments, it is preferable to make these judgments explicit, as doing so enhances the transparency and intelligibility of the ultimate decision. Further, as mentioned, proceeding to this final stage permits appropriate deference to Parliament's choice of means, as well as its full legislative objective.

A review of many decisions in the Supreme Court applying the *Oakes* blueprint to s. 1 shows that the *Oakes* test is formalistic. Whether a limit can be demonstrably justified under s. 1 almost always turns on what has become known as the "minimal impairment" test of whether the limitation restricts the *Charter* right as little as possible. Even in the context of criminal law, there seems to be a trend towards judicial deference to legislative choices.

In *R. v. Chaulk*, [1990] 3 S.C.R. 1303, it was argued that the presumption of sanity then contained in s. 16(4) of the *Criminal Code*, placing the onus of proving the defence of insanity on the accused, was an unconstitutional violation of the presumption of innocence in s. 11(d). Chief Justice Lamer, writing for himself and four other judges, held that there had been a violation but it could be justified under s. 1. The objective of the presumption was to "avoid placing an impossible burden of proof on the Crown". Citing recent judgments of the court, indicating that Parliament was not required to adopt the absolutely least intrusive means, Chief Justice Lamer saw the issue as "whether a less intrusive means would achieve the same objective or would achieve the same objective as effectively". The Chief Justice concluded that the alternative of an evidentiary burden requiring that the accused merely raise a reasonable doubt would not be as effective, accepting arguments by Attorneys General that it would be very easy for accused persons to "fake" such a defence.

The sole dissent on this point in *Chaulk* was Madam Justice Wilson, who held that this was not a case for relaxing the minimal impairment test. This might be done where a legislature, mediating between competing groups of citizens or allocating scarce resources, had to compromise on the basis of conflicting evidence. But in *Chaulk* the state was acting as "singular antagonists" of a very basic legal right of an accused and the strict standard of review in *Oakes* should be applied. The government's objective could be quite readily met by a mere burden on the accused to adduce evidence that made insanity "a live issue fit and proper to be left to the jury".

In the decades of jurisprudence since *Oakes*, s. 1 consideration has invariably started with a recitation of the *Oakes* approach, almost as if it were a legislative replacement of the words of s. 1. In *RJR-MacDonald Inc. v. Canada (Attorney General)*, [1995] 3 S.C.R. 199, a major decision on s. 1, McLachlin J. reasserts for the majority that:

> The factors generally relevant to determining whether a violative law is reasonably and demonstrably justified in a free and democratic society remain those set out in *Oakes*. The first requirement is that the objective of the law limiting the *Charter* right or freedom must be of sufficient importance to warrant overriding it. The second is that the means chosen to achieve the objective must be proportional to the objective and the effect of the law — proportionate, in short, to the good which it may produce. Three matters are considered in determining proportionality: the measures chosen must be rationally connected to the objective; they must impair the guaranteed right or freedom as little as reasonably possible (minimal impairment); and there must be overall proportionality between the deleterious effects of the measures and the salutary effects of the law.

In *R. v. Laba* (1994), 34 C.R. (4th) 360 (S.C.C.) the issue was the constitutionality of a provision under s. 394(1)(b) of the *Criminal Code* requiring a person charged with possessing or selling minerals to establish the defence of ownership or lawful authority. Sopinka J., for a court unanimous on this point, held that the Crown could not demonstrably justify this persuasive burden on an accused given a reasonable legislative alternative of an evidentiary burden. In the course of the judgment a reference to *Chaulk* is followed by the remark that:

> it is also important to remember that this is not a case in which the legislature has attempted to strike a balance between the interests of competing individuals or groups. Rather it is a case in which the government (as opposed to other individuals or groups) can be characterised as the singular antagonist of an individual attempting to assert a legal right which is fundamental to our system of criminal justice (at 392).

This appears to endorse the minority Wilson position in *Chaulk*. Since the Court has changed its basic premise, previous s. 1 rulings justifying various *Charter* violations in criminal cases, especially but not only those concerning reverse onus clauses, may well have to be revisited and/or properly distinguished on fresh challenges.

The noteworthy exception to the *Oakes* rule, however, is when the law which has been found to violate the *Charter* is not a statute but a common law rule. In such cases, the Court held in *R. v. Swain*, [1991] 1 S.C.R. 933, C.R. (4th) 253 at 978 [S.C.R.] that:

> Before turning to s. 1, however, I wish to point out that because this appeal involves a *Charter* challenge to a common law, judge-made rule, the *Charter* analysis involves somewhat different considerations than would apply to a challenge to a legislative provision. For example, having found that the existing common law rule limits an accused's rights under s. 7 of the *Charter*, it may not be strictly necessary to go on to consider the application of s. 1. Having come to the conclusion that the common law rule enunciated by the Ontario Court of Appeal limits an accused's right to liberty in a manner which does not accord with the principles of fundamental justice, it could, in my view, be appropriate to consider at this stage whether an alternative common law rule could be fashioned which would not be contrary to the principles of fundamental justice.

> If a new common law rule could be enunciated which would not interfere with an accused person's right to have control over the conduct of his or her defence, I can see no conceptual problem with the Court's simply enunciating such a rule to take the place of the old rule, without considering whether the old rule could nonetheless be upheld under s. 1 of the *Charter*. Given that the common law rule was fashioned by judges and not by Parliament or a legislature, judicial deference to elected bodies is not an issue. If it is possible to reformulate a common law rule so that it will not conflict with the principles of fundamental justice, such a reformulation should be undertaken.

A longstanding view first articulated in *Reference re s. 94(2) of Motor Vehicle Act (British Columbia)*, [1985] 2 S.C.R. 486, 48 C.R. (3d) 289, has been that "[t]his court has expressed doubt about whether a violation of the right to life, liberty or security of the person which is not in accordance with the principles of fundamental justice can ever be justified, except perhaps in times of war or national emergencies". In fact, the Supreme Court has never, to date, saved a s. 7 violation under s. 1, but more recent case law might be read as softening the hard stance against such a possibility.

BEDFORD v. CANADA (ATTORNEY GENERAL)

2013 SCC 72, 7 C.R. (7th) 1, [2013] 3 S.C.R. 1101, 303 C.C.C. (3d) 146

MCLACHLIN C.J.C.:

(b) The Relationship Between Section 7 and Section 1

[124] This Court has previously identified parallels between the rules against arbitrariness, overbreadth, and gross disproportionality under s. 7 and elements of the s. 1 analysis for justification of laws that violate *Charter* rights. These parallels should not be allowed to obscure the crucial differences between the two sections.

[125] Section 7 and s. 1 ask different questions. The question under s. 7 is whether the law's negative effect on life, liberty, or security of the person is in accordance with the principles of fundamental justice. With respect to the principles of arbitrariness, overbreadth, and gross disproportionality, the specific questions are whether the law's purpose, taken at face value, is connected to its effects and whether the negative effect is grossly disproportionate to the law's purpose. Under s. 1, the question is different — whether the negative impact of a law on the rights of individuals is proportionate to the pressing and substantial goal of the law in furthering the public interest. The question of justification on the basis of an overarching public goal is at the heart of s. 1, but it plays no part in the s. 7 analysis, which is concerned with the narrower question of whether the impugned law infringes individual rights.

[126] As a consequence of the different questions they address, s. 7 and s. 1 work in different ways. Under s. 1, the government bears the burden of showing that a law that breaches an individual's rights can be justified having regard to the government's goal. Because the question is whether the broader public interest justifies the infringement of individual rights, the law's goal must be pressing and substantial. The "rational connection" branch of the s. 1 analysis asks whether the law was a rational means for the legislature to pursue its objective. "Minimal impairment" asks whether the legislature could have designed a law that infringes rights to a lesser extent; it considers the legislature's reasonable alternatives. At the final stage of the s. 1 analysis, the court is required to weigh the negative impact of the law on people's rights against the beneficial impact of the law in terms of achieving its goal for the greater public good. The impacts are judged both qualitatively and quantitatively. Unlike individual claimants, the Crown is well placed to call the social science and expert evidence required to justify the law's impact in terms of society as a whole.

[127] By contrast, under s. 7, the claimant bears the burden of establishing that the law deprives her of life, liberty or security of the person, in a manner that is not connected to the law's object or in a manner that is grossly disproportionate

to the law's object. The inquiry into the purpose of the law focuses on the nature of the object, not on its efficacy. The inquiry into the impact on life, liberty or security of the person is not quantitative — for example, how many people are negatively impacted — but qualitative. An arbitrary, overbroad, or grossly disproportionate impact on one person suffices to establish a breach of s. 7. To require s. 7 claimants to establish the efficacy of the law versus its deleterious consequences on members of society as a whole, would impose the government's s. 1 burden on claimants under s. 7. That cannot be right.

[128] In brief, although the concepts under s. 7 and s. 1 are rooted in similar concerns, they are analytically distinct.

[129] It has been said that a law that violates s. 7 is unlikely to be justified under s. 1 of the *Charter* (*Motor Vehicle Reference*, at p. 518). The significance of the fundamental rights protected by s. 7 supports this observation. Nevertheless, the jurisprudence has also recognized that there may be some cases where s. 1 has a role to play (see, e.g., *Malmo-Levine*, at paras. 96-98). Depending on the importance of the legislative goal and the nature of the s. 7 infringement in a particular case, the possibility that the government could establish that a s. 7 violation is justified under s. 1 of the *Charter* cannot be discounted.

The Ontario Court of Appeal adopted the Supreme Court's implicit invitation to save a s. 7 violation under s. 1 in *R. v. Michaud*, 2015 ONCA 585. The accused was a truck driver who was subject to a provincial law requiring him to have a speed limiter device on his truck which prevented it from going more than 105 kph (that is, 5 kph over the speed limit). This law had several goals, including reducing the number and severity of traffic accidents. The evidence showed that in 98% of cases the best way for a truck to avoid an accident was through braking or steering, but that in 2% of cases accelerating would be the better choice, and it was possible that in some portion of those 2% the truck would already be going the maximum speed of 105 kph. The Ontario Court of Appeal concluded "most reluctantly" that this made the legislation overbroad:

> [79] According to *Bedford*, the focus of s. 7 is relentlessly on the individual claimant. If, as the result of legislation, a single individual is left in danger in even a single situation, then the legislation breaches the claimant's s. 7 *Charter* rights. Mr. Michaud meets that test in this case with respect to the speed limiter requirement for his truck.

The Court of Appeal then concluded, however, that this s. 7 violation was saved under s. 1. They noted that there should particularly be judicial deference to legislative choice in the context of regulatory legislation, which did not have the same level of moral blameworthiness as criminal offences. On the particular issue of minimal impairment, they concluded that the challenged law here was part of a complex regulatory response, not an absolute ban on behaviour, and that even the accused's position was only that the device should allow speeds of 110 kph. Further, there was undisputed evidence that the speed limiter devices reduced the severity and frequency of accidents and therefore benefited the public through increased highway safety: this outweighed removing from truck drivers the ability to accelerate in the less than 2% of occasions where that would potentially be helpful.

2.   PROCEDURAL OVERVIEW

(a)   Procedural Classification of Offences

At common law a distinction was drawn between indictable offences (treasons, felonies and misdemeanours) triable only by judge and jury, and offences triable only summarily by justices of the peace sitting without a jury. The distinction between felonies and misdemeanours was important in that the former (e.g., murder, burglary and rape) were punishable by death and resulted in forfeiture of the felon's property, while the latter never involved the death penalty and only rarely forfeiture. It is still maintained in the United States, but was abolished in England in 1967 and in Canada by the *Criminal Code* as early as the nineteenth century.

In the Canadian *Criminal Code* there are, broadly speaking, three types of offences: summary conviction, indictable, and dual (or hybrid) offences. (There is also a fourth type of offence, contraventions offences under the *Contraventions Act*, S.C. 1992, c. 47. These latter offences are regulatory offences and will not be discussed here.) The type of offence is always expressly stipulated in the offence definition; however, this categorization is somewhat misleading. The *Code* never describes an offence as a "hybrid offence". However, some offences indicate that they can be tried by indictment or can be tried summarily. When this is the case, the offence is referred to as a hybrid offence, and the Crown has an election as to which procedure to use. Further, for purposes of mode of trial at least, there are three types of indictable offences. Adding to the confusion, the trial court is determined by the classification of the offence but the *Code* does not set out the classification in an orderly way. Instead, the provisions are haphazardly strewn across the *Code* and are less than explicit in some instances. The best way to explain them, therefore, is by a process of elimination. But, first, a definition of each of the types of offences.

(i)   Offences triable only on indictment

These are more serious offences. Usually the offence section or its penalty section sets out the punishment applicable to the offence. If it does not, s. 743 of the *Code* provides a maximum of five years' imprisonment. Indictable offences are of three types and the type involved has a large bearing on the forum for trial. Where an accused is charged with an indictable offence, generally speaking, he or she must be personally present at all stages of the proceedings, although ss. 650, 650.01, and 650.02 of the *Criminal Code* now permit appearing in other ways in some circumstances.

The most serious offences are given into the exclusive jurisdiction of the superior court of criminal jurisdiction, in Ontario, the Superior Court of Justice.

See ss. 468 and 469. The least serious indictable offences are absolutely within the jurisdiction of a provincial court judge, in Ontario, a judge of the Ontario Court of Justice. See s. 553. For the great bulk of the indictable offences remaining, the accused is entitled to choose the mode of trial. By s. 536(2) the accused will be put to an election and will be asked to choose to be tried by a provincial court judge without a jury, a judge without a jury, or a court composed of a judge and jury. If the accused does not elect a mode of trial, he or she will be deemed to have elected trial by judge and jury, s. 565(1)(c). It is important to note the difference between the exclusive jurisdiction of the superior court at one end of the scale and the absolute jurisdiction of the provincial court judge at the other. The superior court has exclusive jurisdiction: no other court can try these offences. The provincial court judge has absolute jurisdiction: the provincial court judge is absolutely entitled to try these offences in the sense that he or she is not dependent on the accused's electing to be so tried. Other courts of criminal jurisdiction nevertheless have jurisdiction to try the accused for such offences if by happenstance the matter ends up before them: see *R. v. Holliday*, 12 C.C.C. (2d) 56, 26 C.R.N.S. 279 (Alta. C.A.).

Notwithstanding that the accused has elected trial by provincial court judge, the provincial court judge may decide that the matter should be proceeded with by a judge or jury, s. 555, and the Attorney General may also override an accused's decision and compel a jury trial where the offence is punishable by more than five years' imprisonment, s. 568.

There are detailed provisions in the *Criminal Code* which allow an accused person to change his or her mind and to re-elect his or her mode of trial: see ss. 561 to 563.1 and 565. The heart of the re-election provisions is s. 561 which conditions the right to re-elect on the basis of a combination of: (a) the original election; (b) the point in time in the process when the accused wishes to re-elect; and (c) whether the Crown consents to the re-election. The labyrinthine nature of elections is described by Professor Tim Quigley in *Procedure in Canadian Criminal Law*, 2nd ed. (Toronto: Carswell, 2005).

(ii)   Summary conviction offences

Part XXVII of the *Criminal Code* sets out the procedure for the trial of summary conviction offences (i.e., trial before a provincial judge without a jury and without a preliminary inquiry). The maximum penalty for any summary conviction offence, unless otherwise provided, is $5,000 or six months' imprisonment or both: s. 787(1).

Summary conviction offences are always tried in Provincial Court (or its equivalent) or by a justice of the peace (although superior court judges also have the jurisdiction to do so, they rarely exercise it in practice). In theory, Parliament could establish a maximum penalty of up to five years less one day imprisonment without violating the right to a jury trial under s. 11(f) of the *Charter*.

An accused charged with a summary conviction offence normally need not appear personally in court but may instead choose to have a lawyer or some other agent appear for him or her unless the judge orders that he or she must appear personally: s. 800(2) of the *Code*.

(iii) Crown election offences (dual, hybrid)

These are offences for which the prosecution may choose whether to proceed by way of summary conviction or by indictment. If the Crown elects summary conviction, such offences are in all respects summary conviction offences. If the Crown proceeds by indictment, the forum for the trial will depend upon the type of indictable offence involved. As with straight indictable offences, the penalty is usually specified in the enactment but, if not, is governed by s. 743.

Various tactical considerations enter into the Crown election. The higher available penalty for indictable offences, a prior criminal record by the accused, or a desire to require the accused's personal presence throughout may be among the reasons. Sometimes it is a matter of judge-shopping or wishing to get the matter over more quickly.

In 1994 Parliament increased the maximum penalty for several hybrid offences when proceeded against by way of summary conviction to 18 months: see, e.g., assault causing bodily harm (s. 267) and sexual assault (s. 271). Only when the prosecutor elects to proceed by indictment does the accused have the choice under s. 536. If the Crown chooses summary conviction proceedings, the accused no longer has a choice of a preliminary inquiry, trial in superior court or a jury trial. The prosecutor should indicate the nature of the proceeding prior to trial.

The *Interpretation Act*, R.S.C. 1985, c. 1-21, provides:

> 34. (1) Where an enactment creates an offence,
>
>> (a) the offence is deemed to be an indictable offence if the enactment provides that the offender may be prosecuted for the offence by Indictment;

Section 34(1) has been applied to equate Crown election offences with indictable offences in various contexts such as arrest and for the purposes of fingerprinting under the *Identification of Criminals Act*, R.S.C. 1985, c. 11.

PROBLEM 1

How are the following *Criminal Code* offences classified? What options for trial will an accused have in each case?

1. frightening the Queen (s. 49)
2. murder (s. 235(1))
3. robbery (ss. 343, 344)
4. assault (s. 266)
5. assault causing bodily harm (s. 267(b))
6. sexual assault (s. 271)
7. theft (s. 334)
8. causing a disturbance in a public place (s. 175)
9. conspiracy to commit murder (s. 465(1)(a))
10. attempted murder (s. 239)

PROBLEM 2

You are Crown counsel prosecuting a charge of assault causing bodily harm. The accused is charged with striking his wife with his fist. His blow cut her cheek. This required three sutures at the hospital. A senior Crown asks you to try hard to avoid the matter being bumped up to a court in which the accused could choose trial by jury. In the higher court, there is a huge backlog of cases. She advises you to elect to proceed by way of summary conviction. Consider carefully whether you should follow this advice.

PROBLEM 3

A person has been charged with the following three offences: (i) Possession of cocaine for the purposes of trafficking, contrary to s. 5(2) and (3) of the *Controlled Drugs and Substances Act*; (ii) Possession of marijuana, contrary to s. 4(1), (4) and (5) of the *Controlled Drugs and Substances Act*; and (iii) Driving while "over 80", contrary to ss. 253(b) and 255(1) of the *Criminal Code*. How will he be tried on each charge? What considerations should be taken into account by the Crown or defence counsel in making any election which may be available?

It has been well-documented that the criminal jurisdiction of superior courts is shrinking and that the vast percentage of criminal trials now occur in provincial courts (see Webster and Doob, "The Superior/Provincial Criminal Court Distinction: Historical Anachronism or Empirical Reality?" (2004) 48 Crim. L.Q. 77). The major difference is that murder trials and all jury trials are confined to the superior courts.

The general and serious problems of systemic delays, complexity and judge-shopping could be better addressed by returning to the vision of those such as former Attorney General of Ontario Ian Scott and others (see Martin Friedland, "The Provincial Court and the Criminal Law" (2004) 98 Crim. L.Q. 14) who called for just one federal trial court to handle all criminal trials with or without juries. He was pilloried for that view by many members of the superior courts, some members of the profession, and politicians wishing to retain provincial powers to appoint. The *status quo* is currently propped up by claims of special expertise by judges of higher status which increasingly ring hollow given the calibre and workload of current provincial court judges. The single court is already the reality in Nunavut.

(b) Presumption of Innocence

The cornerstone precepts of the presumption of innocence and that the Crown must normally prove to a standard of proof beyond a reasonable doubt were asserted by the House of Lords relatively recently.

(i) **Common law**

WOOLMINGTON v. D.P.P.

[1935] A.C. 462 (H.L.)

May 23. VISCOUNT SANKEY L.C.: — My Lords, the appellant, Reginald Woolmington, after a trial at the Somerset Assizes at Taunton on January 23, at which, after an absence of one hour and twenty-five minutes, the jury disagreed, was convicted at the Bristol Assizes on February 14 of the wilful murder of his wife on December 10, 1934, and was sentenced to death.

. . . .

The facts are as follows. Reginald Woolmington is 21-1/2 years old. His wife, who was killed, was 17-1/2 years old last December. They had known each other for some time and upon August 25 they were married. Upon October 14 she gave birth to a child. Shortly after that there appears to have been some quarrelling between them and she left him upon November 22 and went to live with her mother. Woolmington apparently was anxious to get her to come back, but she did not come. The prosecution proved that at about 9:15 in the morning of the 10th Mrs. Daisy Brine was hanging out her washing at the back of her house at 25 Newtown, Milborne Port. While she was engaged in that occupation, she heard voices from the next door house, No. 24. She knew that in that house her niece, Reginald Woolmington's wife, was living. She heard and could recognize the voice of Reginald Woolmington saying something to the effect "are you going to come back home?" She could not hear the answer. Then the back door in No. 24 was slammed. She heard a voice in the kitchen but could not tell what it said. Then she heard the sound of a gun. Upon that she looked out of the front window and she saw Reginald Woolmington, whose voice she had heard just before speaking in the kitchen, go out and get upon his bicycle, which had been left or was standing against the wall of her house, No. 25. She called out to him but he gave no reply. He looked at her hard and then he rode away.

According to Reginald Woolmington's own story, having brooded over and deliberated upon the position all through the night of December 9, he went on the morning of the 10th in the usual way to the milking at his employer's farm, and while milking conceived this idea that he would take the old gun which was in the barn and he would take it up that morning to his wife's mother's house where she was living, and that he would show her that gun and tell her that he was going to commit suicide if she did not come back. He would take the gun up for the purpose of frightening her into coming back to him by causing her to think that he was going to commit suicide. He finished his milking, went back to his father's house, had breakfast and then left, taking with him a hack saw.

He returned to the farm, went into the barn, got the gun, which had been used for rook shooting, sawed off the barrels of it, then took the only two cartridges which were there and put them into the gun. He took the two pieces of the barrel which he had sawn off and the hack saw, crossed a field about 60 yards wide and dropped them into the brook. Having done that, he returned on his bicycle, with the gun in his overcoat pocket, to his father's house and changed his clothes. Then he got a piece of wire flex which he attached to the gun so that he could suspend it from his shoulder underneath his coat, and so went off to the house where his wife was living. He knocked at the door, went into the kitchen and asked her: "Are you coming back?" She made no answer. She came into the parlour, and on his asking her whether she would come back she replied she was going into service. He then, so he says, threatened he would shoot himself, and went on to show her the gun and brought it across his waist, when it somehow went off and his wife fell down and he went out of the house. He told the jury that it was an accident, that it was a pure accident; that whilst he was getting the gun from under his shoulder and was drawing it across his breast it accidentally went off and he was doing nothing unlawful, nothing wrong, and this was a pure accident. There was considerable controversy as to whether a letter in which he set out his grievances was written before or after the above events. But when he was arrested at 7.30 on the evening of the 10th and charged with having committed murder he said: "I want to say nothing, except I done it, and they can do what they like with me. It was jealousy I suppose. Her mother enticed her away from me. I done all I could to get her back. That's all."

The learned judge in summing-up the case to the jury said:—

> If you accept his evidence, you will have little doubt that she died in consequence of a gunshot wound which was inflicted by a gun which he had taken to this house, and which was in his hands, or in his possession, at the time that it exploded. If you come to the conclusion that she died in consequence of injuries from the gun which he was carrying, you are put by the law of this country into this position: The killing of a human being is homicide, however he may be killed, and all homicide is presumed to be malicious and murder, unless the contrary appears from circumstances of alleviation, excuse, or justification. "In every charge of murder, the fact of killing being first proved, all the circumstances of accident, necessity, or infirmity are to be satisfactorily proved by the prisoner, unless they arise out of the evidence produced against him: for the law will presume the fact to have been founded in malice until the contrary appeareth." That has been the law of this country for all time since we had law. Once it is shown to a jury that somebody has died through the act of another, that is presumed to be murder, unless the person who has been guilty of the act which causes the death can satisfy a jury that what happened was something less, something which might be alleviated, something which might be reduced to a charge of manslaughter, or was something which was accidental, or was something which could be justified.

At the end of his summing-up he added:

> The Crown has got to satisfy you that this woman, Violet Woolmington, died at the prisoner's hands. They must satisfy you of that beyond any reasonable doubt. If they satisfy you of that, then he has to show that there are circumstances to be found in the evidence which has been given from the witness-box in this case which alleviate the crime so that it is

only manslaughter or which excuse the homicide altogether by showing that it was a pure accident.

In the argument before the Court of Criminal Appeal cases were cited by the learned counsel on either side and textbooks of authority were referred to, but the learned judges contented themselves with saying "there can be no question to start with that the learned judge laid down the law applicable to a case of murder in the way in which it is to be found in the old authorities." They repeated the learned judge's words and said: "No doubt there is ample authority for that statement of the law." They then relied, as I have already mentioned, upon the proviso to s. 4 of the *Criminal Appeal Act, 1907*, and dismissed the appeal.

It is true as stated by the Court of Appeal that there is apparent authority for the law as laid down by the learned judge. But your Lordships' House has had the advantage of a prolonged and exhaustive inquiry dealing with the matter in debate from the earliest times, an advantage which was not shared by either of the courts below. Indeed your Lordships were referred to legal propositions dating as far back as the reign of King Canute (994-1035). But I do not think it is necessary for the purpose of this opinion to go as far back as that. Rather would I invite your Lordships to begin by considering the proposition of law which is contained in Foster's Crown Law, written in 1762, and which appears to be the foundation for the law as laid down by the learned judge in this case. It must be remembered that Sir Michael Foster, although a distinguished judge, is for this purpose to be regarded as a textbook writer, for he did not lay down the doctrine in any case before him, but in an article which is described as the "Introduction to the Discourse of Homicide." In the folio edition, published at Oxford at the Clarendon Press in 1762, at p. 255, he states:

> In every charge of murder, the fact of killing being first proved, all the circumstances of accident, necessity, or infirmity, are to be satisfactorily proved by the prisoner, unless they arise out of the evidence produced against him; for the law presumeth the fact to have been founded in malice, until the contrary appeareth. And very right it is, that the law should so presume. The defendant in this instance standeth upon just the same foot that every other defendant doth: the matters tending to justify, excuse, or alleviate, must appear in evidence before he can avail himself of them.

Now the first part of this passage appears in nearly every textbook or abridgment which has been since written. To come down to modern times, the passage appears in Stephen's Digest of the Criminal Law; also in the well-known treatise of Archbold, Criminal Pleading, Evidence and Practice, which is the companion of lawyers who practise in the criminal courts. It also appears most textually in Russell on Crimes and in the second edition of Halsbury's Laws of England, which purports to state the law as on May 1, 1933, where it is said:

> When it has been proved that one person's death has been caused by another, there is a *prima facie* presumption of law that the act of the person causing the death is murder, unless the

contrary appears from the evidence either for the prosecution or for the defence. The onus is upon such person when accused to show that his act did not amount to murder.

The authority for that proposition is given as Foster, pp. 255, 290, and also the case of *Rex v. Greenacre*.

The question arises, Is that statement correct law? Is it correct to say, and does Sir Michael Foster mean to lay down, that there may arise in the course of a criminal trial a situation at which it is incumbent upon the accused to prove his innocence? To begin with, if that is what Sir Michael Foster meant, there is no previous authority for his proposition, and I am confirmed in this opinion by the fact that in all the textbooks no earlier authority is cited for it. Before, however, one considers the earlier criminal law several facts have to be remembered.

First, it was not till 1907 that the Court of Criminal Appeal was set up. It is perfectly true that from time to time there have been famous occasions on which the Judges and Barons were called together to give their opinion upon the law bearing on murder. Examples of this will be found; in the year 1611, in the case of *Mackalley*, all the Judges and Barons were moved to give their opinion; in 1706, in the case of *Reg. v. Mawgridge*, which case was argued before all the judges and all of them except Lord Chief Justice Trevor were of opinion that Mawgridge was guilty of murder; and in 1843 in the case of *Reg. v. M'Naghten*, where all the Judges gave answers to your Lordships' House upon the test of insanity.

M'Naghten's case stands by itself. It is the famous pronouncement on the law bearing on the question of insanity in cases of murder. It is quite exceptional and has nothing to do with the present circumstances. In *M'Naghten's* case the onus is definitely and exceptionally placed upon the accused to establish such a defence. See *Rex v. Oliver Smith*, where it is stated that the only general rule that can be laid down as to the evidence in such a case is that insanity, if relied upon as a defence, must be established by the defendant. But it was added that all the judges had met and resolved that it was not proper for the Crown to call evidence of insanity, but that any evidence in the possession of the Crown should be placed at the disposal of the prisoner's counsel to be used by him if he thought fit. See also Archbold, 29th Edition. It is not necessary to refer to *M'Naghten's* case again in this judgment, for it has nothing to do with it.

It is true that at a later period certain cases were reserved by the judges for the consideration of the Court of Crown Cases Reserved, but many of the propositions with regard to criminal law are contained either in the summing-up of the judges or in text-books of authority as distinguished from a court sitting in banc.

The learned author of Stephen's Digest of the Criminal Law has an interesting note on the definition of murder and manslaughter. But his remarks are rather directed to the ingredients of the crime than to the proof of it. None the less, the author does not hesitate to tread a path of very robust criticism of the previous authorities. He speaks of the "intricacy, confusion and uncertainty of this branch of the law." He refers to the definition of Coke (1552-1623) and says "these passages, overloaded as Coke's manner is, with a quantity of loose, rambling gossip, form the essence of his account of murder." He describes Coke's chapter on manslaughter as "bewildering" and adds that Hale (1609-1676) treats manslaughter in a manner so meagre and yet so confused that no opinion of it can be obtained except by reading through chapters 38 to 40 and trying to make sense of them, and concludes by saying (p. 466) that Sir Michael Foster "to some extent mitigates the barbarous rule laid down by Coke as to unintentional personal violence."

Next it must be remembered that prisoners were not entitled to be represented by counsel, except in cases of felony, where counsel might argue the law on their behalf.

Thirdly, it must not be forgotten that the prisoner himself was not allowed to give evidence before the Act passed in 1898.

Bearing these considerations in mind, I now turn to some of the cases cited to us.

. . . .

The case of *Rex v. Greenacre* was certainly heard by a very distinguished Judge, Tindal, C.J. But it is to be observed that the dictum relied upon by the prosecution in this case — namely:

> that where it appears that one person's death has been occasioned by the hand of another, it behoves that other to show from evidence, or by inference from the circumstances of the case, that the offence is of a mitigated character, and does not amount to the crime of murder,

was contained in the summing-up of the learned judge to the jury. It is the passage in Sir Michael Foster and this summing-up which are usually relied on as the authority for the proposition that at some particular time of a criminal case the burden of proof lies on the prisoner to prove his innocence. The presumption of innocence in a criminal case is strong: see Taylor On Evidence, and it is doubtful whether either of these passages means any such thing. Rather do I think they simply refer to stages in the trial of a case. All that is meant is that if it is proved that the conscious act of the prisoner killed a man and nothing else appears in the case, there is evidence upon which the jury may, not must, find him guilty of murder. It is difficult to conceive so bare and meagre a case, but that does not mean that the onus is not still on the prosecution.

If at any period of a trial it was permissible for the judge to rule that the prosecution had established its case and that the onus was shifted on the prisoner to prove that he was not guilty, and that unless he discharged that onus the prosecution was entitled to succeed, it would be enabling the judge in such a case to say that the jury must in law find the prisoner guilty and so make the judge decide the case and not the jury, which is not the common law. It would be an entirely different case from those exceptional instances of special verdicts where a judge asks the jury to find certain facts and directs them that on such facts the prosecution is entitled to succeed. Indeed, a consideration of such special verdicts shows that it is not till the end of the evidence that a verdict can properly be found and that at the end of the evidence it is not for the prisoner to establish his innocence, but for the prosecution to establish his guilt. Just as there is evidence on behalf of the prosecution so there may be evidence on behalf of the prisoner which may cause a doubt as to his guilt. In either case, he is entitled to the benefit of the doubt. But while the prosecution must prove the guilt of the prisoner, there is no such burden laid on the prisoner to prove his innocence and it is sufficient for him to raise a doubt as to his guilt; he is not bound to satisfy the jury of his innocence.

This is the real result of the perplexing case of *Rex v. Abramovitch*, which lays down the same proposition, although perhaps in somewhat involved language. Juries are always told that, if conviction there is to be, the prosecution must prove the case beyond reasonable doubt. This statement cannot mean that in order to be acquitted the prisoner must "satisfy" the jury. This is the law as laid down in the Court of Criminal Appeal in *Rex v. Davies*, the headnote of which correctly states that where intent is an ingredient of a crime there is no onus on the defendant to prove that the act alleged was accidental. Throughout the web of the English Criminal Law one golden thread is always to be seen, that it is the duty of the prosecution to prove the prisoner's guilt subject to what I have already said as to the defence of insanity and subject also to any statutory exception. If, at the end of and on the whole of the case, there is a reasonable doubt, created by the evidence given by either the prosecution or the prisoner, as to whether the prisoner killed the deceased with a malicious intention, the prosecution has not made out the case and the prisoner is entitled to an acquittal. No matter what the charge or where the trial, the principle that the prosecution must prove the guilt of the prisoner is part of the common law of England and no attempt to whittle it down can be entertained. When dealing with a murder case the Crown must prove (*a*) death as the result of a voluntary act of the accused and (*b*) malice of the accused. It may prove malice either expressly or by implication. For malice may be implied where death occurs as the result of a voluntary act of the accused which is (i.) intentional and (ii.) unprovoked. When evidence of death and malice has been given (this is a question for the jury) the accused is entitled to show, by evidence or by examination of the circumstances adduced by the Crown that the act on his part which caused death was either unintentional or provoked. If the jury are either satisfied with his explanation or, upon a review of all the evidence, are left in reasonable doubt whether, even if his explanation be not accepted, the act was unintentional or provoked, the prisoner is entitled to be acquitted. It is not the law of England to say, as was said in the summing-up in the present case:

> if the Crown satisfy you that this woman died at the prisoner's hands then he has to show that there are circumstances to be found in the evidence which has been given from the witness-box in this case which alleviate the crime so that it is only manslaughter or which excuse the homicide altogether by showing it was a pure accident.

If the proposition laid down by Sir Michael Foster or in the summing-up in *Rex v. Greenacre* means this, those authorities are wrong.

We were then asked to follow the Court of Criminal Appeal and to apply the proviso of s. 4 of the *Criminal Appeal Act, 1907*, which says:

> the court may, notwithstanding that they are of opinion that the point raised in the appeal might be decided in favour of the appellant, dismiss the appeal if they consider that no substantial miscarriage of justice has actually occurred.

There is no doubt that there is ample jurisdiction to apply that proviso in a case of murder. The Act makes no distinction between a capital case and any other case, but we think it impossible to apply it in the present case. We cannot say that if the jury had been properly directed they would have inevitably come to the same conclusion.

In the result we decline to apply the proviso and, as already stated, we order that the appeal should be allowed and the conviction quashed.

Why do we presume innocence in criminal law?

C.K. ALLEN, LEGAL DUTIES AND OTHER ESSAYS IN JURISPRUDENCE

(1931), 286-288

Again, "it is better that ten guilty persons should be acquitted than that one innocent person should be convicted". As Stephen dryly observes, it all depends on what the guilty persons have been doing. It also depends on the general social conditions in which they have been doing it. I have already called attention to the vague fluctuations in the proverbial ratio between the guilty and the innocent; and I have done so in no spirit of levity, for the ratio which it assumes is not without significance. I dare say some sentimentalists would assent to the proposition that it is better that a thousand, or even a million, guilty persons should escape than that one innocent person should suffer; but no sensible and practical person would accept such a view. For it is obvious that if our ratio is extended indefinitely, there comes a point when the whole system of justice has broken down and society is in a state of chaos. In short, it is only when there is a reasonable and uniform probability of guilty persons being detected and convicted that we can allow humane doubt to prevail over security. But we must never forget that ideally the acquittal of ten guilty persons is exactly ten times as great a failure of *justice* as the conviction of one innocent person.

What is a reasonable doubt? Can we define it? Is this standard of proof different from that of proof on a balance of probabilities in civil cases?

(ii) *Reasonable doubt*

R. v. LIFCHUS

[1997] 3 S.C.R. 320, 9 C.R. (5th) 1, 118 C.C.C. (3d) 1,
1997 CarswellMan 392, 1997 CarswellMan 393

The accused was charged with fraud. The trial judge told the jury in her charge on the burden of proof that she used the words "'proof beyond a reasonable doubt' . . . in their ordinary, natural every day sense", and that the words "doubt" and "reasonable" are "ordinary, every day words that . . . you understand". The accused was convicted of fraud. On appeal, he contended that the trial judge had erred in instructing the jury on the meaning of the expression "proof beyond a reasonable doubt". The Court of Appeal allowed the appeal and ordered a new trial. The Supreme Court dismissed the Crown's appeal.

CORY J. (LAMER C.J., SOPINKA, MCLACHLIN, IACOBUCCI and MAJOR JJ. concurring): —

. . . .

The phrase "beyond a reasonable doubt", is composed of words which are commonly used in everyday speech. Yet, these words have a specific meaning in the legal context. This special meaning of the words "reasonable doubt" may not correspond precisely to the meaning ordinarily attributed to them. In criminal proceedings, where the liberty of the subject is at stake, it is of fundamental importance that jurors fully understand the nature of the burden of proof that the law requires them to apply. An explanation of the meaning of proof beyond a reasonable doubt is an essential element of the instructions that must be given to a jury. That a definition is necessary can be readily deduced from the frequency with which juries ask for guidance with regard to its meaning. It is therefore essential that the trial judge provide the jury with an explanation of the expression.

. . . .

Perhaps a brief summary of what the definition should and should not contain may be helpful. It should be explained that:

• the standard of proof beyond a reasonable doubt is inextricably intertwined with that principle fundamental to all criminal trials, the presumption of innocence;

- the burden of proof rests on the prosecution throughout the trial and never shifts to the accused;
- a reasonable doubt is not a doubt based upon sympathy or prejudice;
- rather, it is based upon reason and common sense;
- it is logically connected to the evidence or absence of evidence;[23]
- it does not involve proof to an absolute certainty; it is not proof beyond *any* doubt nor is it an imaginary or frivolous doubt; and
- more is required than proof that the accused is probably guilty — a jury which concludes only that the accused is probably guilty must acquit.

On the other hand, certain references to the required standard of proof should be avoided. For example:

- describing the term "reasonable doubt" as an ordinary expression which has no special meaning in the criminal law context;
- inviting jurors to apply to the task before them the same standard of proof that they apply to important, or even the most important, decisions in their own lives;
- equating proof "beyond a reasonable doubt" to proof "to a moral certainty";
- qualifying the word "doubt" with adjectives other than "reasonable", such as "serious", "substantial" or "haunting", which may mislead the jury; and
- instructing jurors that they may convict if they are "sure" that the accused is guilty, before providing them with a proper definition as to the meaning of the words "beyond a reasonable doubt".

A charge which is consistent with the principles set out in these reasons will suffice regardless of the particular words used by the trial judge. Nevertheless, it may . . . be useful to set out a "model charge" which could provide the necessary instructions as to the meaning of the phrase beyond a reasonable doubt.

Suggested Charge

Instructions pertaining to the requisite standard of proof in a criminal trial of proof beyond a reasonable doubt might be given along these lines:

> The accused enters these proceedings presumed to be innocent. That presumption of innocence remains throughout the case until such time as the Crown has on the evidence put before you satisfied you beyond a reasonable doubt that the accused is guilty.

---

23 The court observed elsewhere in the decision that "certain doubts, although reasonable, are simply incapable of articulation. For instance, there may be something about a person's demeanor in the witness box which will lead a juror to conclude that the witness is not credible. It may be that the juror is unable to point to the precise aspect of the witness's demeanor which was found to be suspicious, and as a result cannot articulate either to himself or others exactly why the witness should not be believed. A juror should not be made to feel that the overall, perhaps intangible, effect of a witness's demeanor cannot be taken into consideration is the assessment of credibility." (para. 29)

What does the expression "beyond a reasonable doubt" mean?

The term "beyond a reasonable doubt" has been used for a very long time and is a part of our history and traditions of justice. It is so engrained in our criminal law that some think it needs no explanation, yet something must be said regarding its meaning.

A reasonable doubt is not an imaginary or frivolous doubt. It must not be based upon sympathy or prejudice. Rather, it is based on reason and common sense. It is logically derived from the evidence or absence of evidence.

Even if you believe the accused is probably guilty or likely guilty, that is not sufficient. In those circumstances you must give the benefit of the doubt to the accused and acquit because the Crown has failed to satisfy you of the guilt of the accused beyond a reasonable doubt.

On the other hand you must remember that it is virtually impossible to prove anything to an absolute certainty and the Crown is not required to do so. Such a standard of proof is impossibly high.

In short if, based upon the evidence before the court, you are sure that the accused committed the offence you should convict since this demonstrates that you are satisfied of his guilt beyond a reasonable doubt.

This is not a magic incantation that needs to be repeated word for word. It is nothing more than a suggested form that would not be faulted if it were used

. . . .

Further, it is possible that an error in the instructions as to the standard of proof may not constitute a reversible error. It was observed in *R. v. W. (D.)*, [1991] 1 S.C.R. 742, at p. 758, that the verdict ought not be disturbed "if the charge, when read as a whole, makes it clear that the jury could not have been under any misapprehension as to the correct burden and standard of proof to apply". On the other hand, if the charge as a whole gives rise to the reasonable likelihood that the jury misapprehended the standard of proof, then as a general rule the verdict will have to be set aside and a new trial directed.

R. v. STARR

[2000] 2 S.C.R. 144, 36 C.R. (5th) 1, 147 C.C.C. (3d) 449,
2000 CarswellMan 449, 2000 CarswellMan 450

The accused had been convicted of two counts of first degree murder. The majority of the Court decided that the reasonable doubt instruction given in the case fell prey to many of the same difficulties outlined in *Lifchus*, and likely misled the jury as to the content of the criminal standard of proof. In allowing the accused's appeal they gave further advice.

IACOBUCCI J. (MAJOR, BINNIE, ARBOUR and LEBEL JJ. concurring): —

. . . .

In the present case, the trial judge did refer to the Crown's onus and to the presumption of innocence, and he stated that the appellant should receive the benefit of any reasonable doubt. The error in the charge is that the jury was not told *how a reasonable doubt is to be defined.* As was emphasized repeatedly in *Lifchus* and again in *Bisson,* a jury *must* be instructed that the standard of proof in a criminal trial is higher than the probability standard used in making everyday decisions and in civil trials. Indeed, it is this very requirement to go beyond probability that meshes the standard of proof in criminal cases with the presumption of innocence and the Crown's onus. However, as Cory J. explained in these earlier decisions, it is generally inappropriate to define the meaning of the term "reasonable doubt" through examples from daily life, through the use of synonyms, or through analogy to moral choices. The criminal standard of proof has a special significance unique to the legal process. It is an exacting standard of proof rarely encountered in everyday life, and there is no universally intelligible illustration of the concept, such as the scales of justice with respect to the balance of probabilities standard. Unlike absolute certainty or the balance of probabilities, reasonable doubt is not an easily quantifiable standard. It cannot be measured or described by analogy. It must be explained. However, precisely because it is not quantifiable, it is difficult to explain.

In my view, an effective way to define the reasonable doubt standard for a jury is to explain that it falls much closer to absolute certainty than to proof on a balance of probabilities. As stated in *Lifchus,* a trial judge is required to explain that something less than absolute certainty is required, and that something more than probable guilt is required, in order for the jury to convict. Both of these alternative standards are fairly and easily comprehensible. It will be of great assistance for a jury if the trial judge situates the reasonable doubt standard appropriately between these two standards. The additional instructions to the jury set out in *Lifchus* as to the meaning and appropriate manner of determining the existence of a reasonable doubt serve to define the space between absolute certainty and proof beyond a reasonable doubt. In this regard, I am in agreement with Twaddle J.A. in the court below, when he said, at p. 177:

> If standards of proof were marked on a measure, proof "beyond reasonable doubt" would lie much closer to "absolute certainty" than to "a balance of probabilities". Just as a judge has a duty to instruct the jury that absolute certainty is not required, he or she has a duty, in my view, to instruct the jury that the criminal standard is more than a probability. The words he or she uses to convey this idea are of no significance, but the idea itself must be conveyed.

See further Patrick Healy, "Direction and Guidance on Reasonable Doubt in the Charge to the Jury" (2001) 6 Can. Crim. L.R. 161.

In 1991 the Supreme Court handed down a decision, *R. v. W. (D.)*, [1991] 1 S.C.R. 742, 63 C.C.C. (3d) 397, 3 C.R. (4th) 302 that was intended to give guidance to judges on how to explain to a jury the process of considering whether they were left with a reasonable doubt or not. Subsequently that court has recognized various criticisms of the *W. (D.)* approach and held that it should not be applied as a "magical incantation".

R. v. S. (J.H.)

2008 SCC 30, 2008 CarswellNS 270, 2008 CarswellNS 271, 57 C.R. (6th) 79, [2008] 2 S.C.R. 152, 231 C.C.C. (3d) 302

A stepfather was charged with sexual assault after the complainant alleged that he had sexually abused her over a number of years, starting when she was approximately four years old. She twice complained to her mother who did not believe her. When the complainant was 15 she went to the police. The accused denied all the allegations and suggested that they were falsely made after he threatened to send her to a Catholic school because of her uncontrollable behaviour. The issue at trial before judge and jury was whether the alleged events had ever happened. The complainant and the accused were the principal witnesses. The trial judge charged the jury on the credibility of the witnesses, instructing them that they had to consider all the evidence and that the trial was not a choice between two competing versions of events. The defence raised no objection to the charge. The jury returned a verdict of guilty.

A majority of the Nova Scotia Court of Appeal set aside the conviction and ordered a new trial. The trial judge had insufficiently explained the principles of reasonable doubt as they applied to credibility. While the *W. (D.)* phrasing was not a magical incantation the charge had failed to express the second *W. (D.)* principle that disbelief in the accused's testimony does not amount to proof of his or her guilt beyond a reasonable doubt. The dissenting judge found that the charge was sufficient.

BINNIE J. (for seven justices): —

8   A series of decisions over at least the past 20 years has affirmed and reaffirmed the proposition that where credibility is a central issue in a jury trial, the judge must explain the relationship between the assessment of credibility and the Crown's ultimate burden to prove the guilt of the accused to the criminal standard. A general instruction on reasonable doubt without adverting to its relationship to the credibility (or lack of credibility) of the witnesses leaves open too great a possibility of confusion or misunderstanding. The so-called *W. (D.)* instruction has long roots: *R. v. Challice* (1979), 45 C.C.C. (2d) 546 (Ont. C.A.), at p. 556; *R. v. Chan* (1989), 52 C.C.C. (3d) 184, (Alta. C.A.), at p. 186; *R. v.*

Morin, [1988] 2 S.C.R. 345, at p. 362; *R. v. H. (C.W.)* (1991), 68 C.C.C. (3d) 146 (B.C.C.A.), at p. 155; *R. v. MacKenzie*, [1993] 1 S.C.R. 212, at pp. 219 and 239; *R. v. Levasseur*, [1994] 3 S.C.R. 518 (upholding Fish J.A.'s dissent reported at (1994), 89 C.C.C. (3d) 508 (Que. C.A.), at p. 534). *W. (D.)* has been cited by Canadian courts at all levels in no fewer than 3,743 subsequent reported cases. It has proven to be a fertile source of appellate review. For a recent application, see *R. v. C.L.Y.*, [2008] 1 S.C.R. 5, 2008 SCC 2.

9 The passage from *W. (D.)* at issue in this case, as in so many others, is found at pp. 757-58, where Cory J. explained:

> Ideally, appropriate instructions on the issue of credibility should be given, not only during the main charge, but on any recharge. A trial judge might well instruct the jury on the question of credibility along these lines:
>
>> First, if you believe the evidence of the accused, obviously you must acquit.
>> Second, if you do not believe the testimony of the accused but you are left in reasonable doubt by it, you must acquit.
>> Third, even if you are not left in doubt by the evidence of the accused, you must ask yourself whether, on the basis of the evidence which you do accept, you are convinced beyond a reasonable doubt by that evidence of the guilt of the accused.
>
> If that formula were followed, the oft repeated error which appears in the recharge in this case would be avoided. The requirement that the Crown prove the guilt of the accused beyond a reasonable doubt is fundamental in our system of criminal law. Every effort should be made to avoid mistakes in charging the jury on this basic principle.
> Nonetheless, the failure to use such language is not fatal if the charge, when read as a whole, makes it clear that the jury could not have been under any misapprehension as to the correct burden and standard of proof to apply...

Essentially, *W. (D.)* simply unpacks for the benefit of the lay jury what reasonable doubt means in the context of evaluating conflicting testimonial accounts. It alerts the jury to the "credibility contest" error. It teaches that trial judges are required to impress on the jury that the burden never shifts from the Crown to prove every element of the offence beyond a reasonable doubt.

10 The precise formulation of the *W. (D.)* questions has been criticized. As to the first question, the jury may believe inculpatory elements of the statements of an accused but reject the exculpatory explanation. In *R. v. Latimer*, [2001] 1 S.C.R. 3, 2001 SCC 1, the accused did not testify, but his description of the killing of his daughter was put into evidence by way of statements to the police. His description of the event itself was obviously believed. The exculpatory explanation did not amount to a defence at law. He was convicted. The principle that a jury may believe some, none, or all of the testimony of any witness, including that of an accused, suggests to some critics that the first *W. (D.)* question is something of an oversimplification.

11 As to the second question, some jurors may wonder how, if they believe none of the evidence of the accused, such rejected evidence may nevertheless of itself raise a reasonable doubt. Of course, some elements of the evidence of an accused may raise a reasonable doubt, even though the bulk of it is rejected. Equally, the jury may simply conclude that they do not know whether to believe the accused's testimony or not. In either circumstance the accused is entitled to an acquittal.

12 The third question, again, is taken by some critics as failing to contemplate a jury's acceptance of inculpatory bits of the evidence of an accused but not the exculpatory elements. In light of these possible sources of difficulty, Wood J.A. in *H. (C.W.)* suggested an additional instruction:

> I would add one more instruction in such cases, which logically ought to be second in the order, namely: "If, after a careful consideration of all the evidence, you are unable to decide whom to believe, you must acquit". [p. 155]

13 In short the *W. (D.)* questions should not have attributed to them a level of sanctity or immutable perfection that their author never claimed for them. *W.(D.)*'s message that it must be made crystal clear to the jury that the burden never shifts from the Crown to prove every element of the offence beyond a reasonable doubt is of fundamental importance but its application should not result in a triumph of form over substance. In *R. v. S. (W.D.)*, [1994] 3 S.C.R. 521, Cory J. reiterated that the *W. (D.)* instructions need not be given "word for word as some magic incantation" (p. 533). In *R. v. Avetysan*, [2000] 2 S.C.R. 745, 2000 SCC 56, Major J. for the majority pointed out that in any case where credibility is important "[t]he question is really whether, in substance, the trial judge's instructions left the jury with the impression that it had to choose between the two versions of events" (para. 19). The main point is that lack of credibility on the part of the accused does not equate to proof of his or her guilt beyond a reasonable doubt.

14 In the present case Oland J.A. agreed that the trial judge did not "call upon the jury to simply decide which of the complainant or [the accused] it believed" (para. 19). Nevertheless, in her view:

> The charge only instructed that probable guilt was not enough to meet the standard of proof beyond a reasonable doubt, that the appellant was to be given the benefit of the doubt, and they did not have to accept or reject all of the testimony of any witness including his, and that they were to consider all of the evidence. Nowhere did it provide any guidance as to how, in the event they were uncertain or unable to resolve the issue of credibility, they were to proceed with their deliberations. *The charge failed to direct that if the jury did not believe the testimony of the accused but were left in a reasonable doubt by that evidence, they must acquit.* [Emphasis added; para. 20.]

In my view, with respect, the reasoning of the majority brushes uncomfortably close to the "magic incantation" error. At the end of the day, reading the charge as a whole, I believe the instruction to this jury satisfied the ultimate test formulated by Cory J. in *W. (D.)* as being whether "the jury could not have been under any misapprehension as to the correct burden and standard of proof to apply" (p. 758).

15 Here the trial judge explained that any reasonable doubt must be resolved in favour of the accused. She also explained that even if they did not accept all of the accused's testimony, they could still accept some of it. She also explained to the jury that they should not see their task as that of deciding between two versions of events. She told them that they could not decide the case simply by choosing between the evidence of the complainant and that of the accused. She reminded them, in that context, that they must consider all of the evidence when determining reasonable doubt. She stated:

> You do not decide whether something happened simply by comparing one version of events with another, or choosing one of them. You have to consider all the evidence and decide whether you have been satisfied beyond a reasonable doubt that the events that form the basis of the crime charged, in fact, took place. [A.R., at p. 54.]
> ...
> Again, you do not decide whether something happened simply by comparing one version of events with the other, or by choosing one of them. You have to consider all of the evidence and decide whether you have been satisfied beyond a reasonable doubt that the events that form the basis of the crimes charges, in fact, took place. [A.R., at p. 55.]

16 In my view, the trial judge got across the point of the second *W. (D.)* question without leaving any realistic possibility of misunderstanding. As stated, she told the jury:

> It is for the Crown counsel to prove beyond a reasonable doubt that the events alleged in fact occurred. It is not for [the accused] to prove that these events never happened. If you have a reasonable doubt whether the events alleged ever took place, you *must* find him not guilty. [Emphasis added; A.R., at p. 54.]

17 There was much discussion at the hearing about defence counsel's failure to object. In my view, he correctly ascertained that the jury had been adequately instructed on the relationship between the assessment of credibility and the ultimate determination of guilt beyond a reasonable doubt. Before the recharge was given he told the trial judge he would "feel more comfortable if simply the wording that was read previously was re-read to the jury again" (A.R., at p. 77). He discharged his duty to the respondent.

Appeal allowed; conviction restored.

Should the Supreme Court have expressly and clearly abandoned the ***W. (D.)*** **approach?** It has been responsible for many, many prolix appeals and orders of new trials. The main problem is that the second question is potentially confusing and/or too generous to accused. See especially the late Jack Gibson, "*R. v. W.D.* Revisited: Is Step Two a Misdirection?" (2003) 11 C.R. (6th) 323.

Justice Binnie might have mentioned the remark of McLachlin J. dissenting in *R. v. S. (W.D.)*, [1994] 3 S.C.R. 521, 93 C.C.C. (3d) 1, 34 C.R. (4th) 1:

> Certainly if the jury rejected (as opposed to being merely undecided about) all of the evidence of the accused, it is difficult to see how that very evidence, having been rejected, could raise a reasonable doubt.

Trial judges are at least now free to reject the complexity of *W. (D.)* as long as they make sure that the jury is warned of the Crown's burden of proof, that it is not just a choice between competing versions and that they may believe some, none or all of the testimony of any witness, including the accused. These principles, of course, apply equally to judge-alone trials.

R. v. MULLINS-JOHNSON

(2007), 50 C.R. (6th) 265, 228 C.C.C. (3d) 505, 2007 CarswellOnt 6660
(C.A.)

In 1993 parents found their four-year-old daughter lying dead on her bed. Her uncle, the accused, who had babysat her the night before, was arrested and charged with first degree murder. He was convicted. He had protested his innocence from the very outset but his appeals to the Ontario Court of Appeal and Supreme Court were rejected. He spent 12 years in jail from the time of his arrest until he was released in 2005 on bail. The Minister of Justice referred the matter to the Court of Appeal under s. 696.3(3)(a)(ii) of the *Criminal Code*, R.S.C. 1985, c. C-46, to determine the case as if it were an appeal on the issue of fresh evidence. The Court heard a number of experts who re-examined the earlier evidence that had led to conviction.

The Ontario Court of Appeal allowed the appeal, quashed the murder conviction and acquitted.

PER O'CONNOR A.C.J.O. (Rosenberg and Sharpe JJ.A concurring):—

...There is no doubt that the new expert opinions in this case are credible and highly cogent. They go to the very core of whether there was an offence committed in this case. The opinions have been provided by some of the leading Canadian and international experts in forensic pathology and pathology. The opinions not only have a profound impact on the reliability of the jury verdict reached at trial, it is submitted that they are dispositive of the result.

Finally, in their excellent factums the parties have fully reviewed for us the entire body of evidence aside from the expert evidence. In short, without the expert evidence there is no case against the appellant and no evidence of a crime. The non-expert evidence, if anything, is inconsistent with guilt and, again, is not indicative of a crime. Now that the trial expert evidence has been completely discredited, there is no case against the appellant and he is clearly entitled to an acquittal.

THE DECLARATION OF INNOCENCE

The fresh evidence shows that the appellant's conviction was the result of a rush to judgment based on flawed scientific opinion. With the entering of an acquittal, the appellant's legal innocence has been re-established. The fresh evidence is compelling in demonstrating that no crime was committed against Valin Johnson and that the appellant did not commit any crime. For that reason an acquittal is the proper result.

There are not in Canadian law two kinds of acquittals: those based on the Crown having failed to prove its case beyond a reasonable doubt and those where the accused has been shown to be factually innocent. We adopt the comments of the former Chief Justice of Canada in The Lamer Commission of Inquiry Pertaining to the Cases of: Ronald Dalton, Gregory Parsons, Randy Druken, Annex 3, pp. 342:

> [A] criminal trial does not address "factual innocence". The criminal trial is to determine whether the Crown has proven its case beyond a reasonable doubt. If so, the accused is guilty. If not, the accused is found not guilty. There is no finding of factual innocence since it would not fall within the ambit or purpose of criminal law.

Just as the criminal trial is not a vehicle for declarations of factual innocence, so an appeal court, which obtains its jurisdiction from statute, has no jurisdiction to make a formal legal declaration of factual innocence. The fact that we are hearing this case as a Reference under s. 696.3(3)(a)(ii) of the *Criminal Code* does not expand that jurisdiction. The terms of the Reference to this court are clear: we are hearing this case "as if it were an appeal". While we are entitled to express our reasons for the result in clear and strong terms, as we have done, we cannot make a formal legal declaration of the appellant's factual innocence.

In addition to the jurisdictional issue, there are important policy reasons for not, in effect, recognizing a third verdict, other than "guilty" or "not guilty", of "factually innocent". The most compelling, and, in our view, conclusive reason is the impact it would have on other persons found not guilty by criminal courts. As Professor Kent Roach observed in a report he prepared for the Commission of Inquiry into Certain Aspects of the Trial and Conviction of James Driskell, "there is a genuine concern that determinations and declarations of wrongful convictions could degrade the meaning of the not guilty verdict" (p. 39). To recognize a third verdict in the criminal trial process would, in effect, create two classes of people: those found to be factually innocent and those who benefited from the presumption of innocence and the high standard of proof beyond a reasonable doubt.

Nothing we have said in these reasons should be taken as somehow qualifying the impact of the fresh evidence. That evidence, together with the other evidence, shows beyond question that the appellant's conviction was wrong and that he was the subject of a terrible miscarriage of justice. We conclude these reasons by paraphrasing what the president of the panel said to

Mr. Mullins-Johnson at the conclusion of the oral argument after entering the verdict of acquittal: it is profoundly regrettable that as a result of what has been shown to be flawed pathological evidence Mr. Mullins-Johnson was wrongly convicted and has spent such a very long time in jail.

(iii) Section 11(d) of the Charter

With the advent of the *Canadian Charter of Rights and Freedoms*, the presumption of innocence has taken on a constitutional dimension. The *Charter* provides in s. 11:

> 11. Any person charged with an offence has the right
>
>   . . . .
>
>   (d) to be presumed innocent until proven guilty according to law in a fair and public hearing by an independent and impartial tribunal.

There is an important distinction between persuasive burdens of proof and evidentiary burdens:

Persuasive burdens of proof (sometimes called legal or ultimate burdens) have three main features. They apply at the end of a case, they never shift in the sense that it is known from the start who bears the burden, and the trier of fact must find against the burdenholder in a borderline case. Normally the burden is on the Crown to prove to a standard of beyond a reasonable doubt. Sometimes the persuasive burden of an issue is placed by Parliament or the courts on the accused to prove on a balance of probabilities. This is called a reverse onus.

There is considerable confusion amongst writers and judges as to the meaning of "evidentiary burdens". This term usually refers to the burden of pointing to evidence to put a legal issue into play (*R. v. Schwartz*, [1988] 2 S.C.R. 443, 45 C.C.C. (3d) 97, 66 C.R. (3d) 251 at 466 [S.C.R.] per Dickson C.J.). Sometimes this is referred to as giving a matter an "air of reality" (an issue we will return to when we discuss defences), providing an evidentiary foundation or a tactical burden. It can be discharged through cross-examination of opposing witnesses or by calling witnesses. It can shift during the ebb and flow of a trial. Used in this sense it has nothing to do with the burden of proof. However, the term "evidentiary burden" is also sometimes used to describe a reverse onus which merely calls upon the accused to provide some evidence to doubt the fact or conclusion in question (see the discussion in "Doubt Mountain and the Presumption of Innocence", p. 108).

On June 15, 2017, Bill C-51 was introduced in Parliament. If passed, it will remove from the *Criminal Code* a number of evidentiary presumptions, particularly those relating to gambling offences, theft and possession of property obtained by crime. In addition it will remove a number of reverse onus provisions in other offences. The government's Backgrounder introducing the bill explains that these provisions could lead to a conviction despite the presence of reasonable doubt, and that they are being removed "to spare the justice system time-consuming and costly *Charter* challenges".

Oakes concerned the constitutionality of a persuasive burden on the accused:

R. v. OAKES

[1986] 1 S.C.R. 103, 50 C.R. (3d) 1, 24 C.C.C.(3d) 321,
1986 CarswellOnt 95, 1986 CarswellOnt 1001

DICKSON C.J.C. (CHOUINARD, LAMER, WILSON and LE DAIN JJ. concurring): —

This appeal concerns the constitutionality of s. 8 of the *Narcotic Control Act*, R.S.C. 1970, c. N-1. The section provides, in brief, that if the court finds the accused in possession of a narcotic, he is presumed to be in possession for the purpose of trafficking. Unless the accused can establish the contrary, he must be convicted of trafficking. The Ontario Court of Appeal held that this provision constitutes a "reverse onus" clause and is unconstitutional because it violates one of the core values of our criminal justice system, the presumption of innocence, now entrenched in s. 11 (d) of the *Canadian Charter of Rights and Freedoms*. The Crown has appealed.

. . . .

The respondent, David Edwin Oakes, was charged with unlawful possession of a narcotic for the purpose of trafficking, contrary to s. 4(2) of the *Narcotic Control Act*. He elected trial by magistrate without a jury. At trial, the Crown adduced evidence to establish that Mr. Oakes was found in possession of eight one gram vials of *cannabis* resin in the form of hashish oil. Upon a further search conducted at the police station, $619.45 was located. Mr. Oakes told the police that he had bought ten vials of hashish oil for $150 for his own use, and that the $619.45 was from a workers' compensation cheque. He elected not to call evidence as to possession of the narcotic. Pursuant to the procedural provisions of s. 8 of the *Narcotic Control Act*, the trial judge proceeded to make a finding that it was beyond a reasonable doubt that Mr. Oakes was in possession of the narcotic.

Following this finding, Mr. Oakes brought a motion to challenge the constitutional validity of s. 8 of the *Narcotic Control Act*, which he maintained imposes a burden on an accused to prove that he or she was not in possession for the purpose of trafficking. He argued that s. 8 violates the presumption of innocence contained in s. 11(*d*) of the *Charter*.

[The trial judge found s. 8 to be inoperative as in conflict with s. 11(d). He afforded the Crown an opportunity to adduce further evidence and the Crown declined. The trial judge acquitted on the offence charged and found the accused guilty of possession only.]

. . . .

To interpret the meaning of s. 11(*d*), it is important to adopt a purposive approach. As this court stated in *R. v. Big M Drug Mart Ltd.*, [1985] 1 S.C.R. 295 at p. 344:

> The meaning of a right or freedom guaranteed by the *Charter* was to be ascertained by an analysis of the *purpose* of such a guarantee; it was to be understood, in other words, in the light of the interests it was meant to protect.
>
> In my view this analysis is to be undertaken, and the purpose of the right or freedom in question is to be sought by reference to the character and the larger objects of the *Charter* itself, to the language chosen to articulate the specific right or freedom, to the historical origins of the concepts enshrined, and where applicable to the meaning and purpose of the other specific rights and freedoms.

To identify the underlying purpose of the *Charter* right in question, therefore, it is important to begin by understanding the cardinal values it embodies.

The presumption of innocence is a hallowed principle lying at the very heart of criminal law. Although protected expressly in s. 11(*d*) of the *Charter*, the presumption of innocence is referable and integral to the general protection of life, liberty and security of the person contained in s. 7 of the *Charter* (see *Reference re s. 94(2) of the Motor Vehicle Act*, December 17, 1985, unreported, per Lamer J.). The presumption of innocence protects the fundamental liberty and human dignity of any and every person accused by the State of criminal conduct. An individual charged with a criminal offence faces grave social and personal consequences, including potential loss of physical liberty, subjection to social stigma and ostracism from the community, as well as other social, psychological and economic harms. In light of the gravity of these consequences, the presumption of innocence is crucial. It ensures that until the State proves an accused's guilt beyond all reasonable doubt, he or she is innocent. This is essential in a society committed to fairness and social justice. The presumption of innocence confirms our faith in humankind; it reflects our belief that individuals are decent and law-abiding members of the community until proven otherwise.

The presumption of innocence has enjoyed longstanding recognition at common law. In the leading case, *Woolmington v. Director of Public Prosecutions*, [1935] A.C. 462 (H.L.), Viscount Sankey wrote at pp. 481-482:

> Throughout the web of the English Criminal Law one golden thread is always to be seen, that it is the duty of the prosecution to prove the prisoner's guilt subject to what I have already said as to the defence of insanity and subject also to any statutory exception. If, at the end of and on the whole of the case, there is a reasonable doubt, created by the evidence given by either the prosecution or the prisoner, as to whether the prisoner killed the deceased with a malicious intention, the prosecution has not made out the case and the prisoner is entitled to an acquittal. No matter what the charge or where thc trial, the principle that the prosecution must prove the guilt of the prisoner is part of the common law of England and no attempt to whittle it down can be entertained.

Subsequent Canadian cases have cited the *Woolmington* principle with approval (see, for example, *Manchuk v. The King*, [1938] S.C.R. 341, at p. 349; *R. v. City of Sault Ste. Marie*, [1978] 2 S.C.R. 1299, at p. 1316).

Further evidence of the widespread acceptance of the principle of the presumption of innocence is its inclusion in the major international human rights documents. Article 11(1) of the *Universal Declaration of Human Rights*, adopted December 10, 1948 by the General Assembly of the United Nations, provides:

> Art. 11(1) Everyone charged with a penal offence has the right to be presumed innocent until proved guilty according to law in a public trial at which he has had all the guarantees necessary for his defence.

In the *International Covenant on Civil and Political Rights*, 1966, art. 14(2) states:

> Art. 14(2) Everyone charged with a criminal offence shall have the right to be presumed innocent until proved guilty according to law.

Canada acceded to this Covenant, and the Optional Protocol which sets up machinery for implementing the Covenant, on May 19, 1976. Both came into effect on August 19, 1976.

In light of the above, the right to be presumed innocent until proven guilty requires that s. 11(*d*) have, at a minimum, the following content. First, an individual must be proven guilty beyond a reasonable doubt. Second, it is the State which must bear the burden of proof. As Mr. Justice Lamer stated in *Dubois v. The Queen* (November 21, 1985, unreported) at p. 6:

> Section 11 (*d*) imposes upon the Crown the burden of proving the accused's guilt beyond reasonable doubt as well as that of making out the case against the accused before he or she need respond, either by testifying or calling other evidence.

Third, criminal prosecutions must be carried out in accordance with lawful procedures and fairness. The latter part of s. 11(*d*), which requires the proof of guilt "according to law in a fair and public hearing by an independent and impartial tribunal", underlines the importance of this procedural requirement.

. . . .

The *Woolmington* case was decided in the context of a legal system with no constitutionally entrenched human rights document. In Canada, we have tempered parliamentary supremacy by entrenching important rights and freedoms in the Constitution. Viscount Sankey's statutory exception proviso is clearly not applicable in this context and would subvert the very purpose of the entrenchment of the presumption of innocence in the *Charter*. . . . Section 8 of the *Narcotic Control Act* is not rendered constitutionally valid simply by virtue of the fact that it is a statutory provision.

. . . .

In general one must, I think, conclude that a provision which requires an accused to disprove on a balance of probabilities the existence of a presumed fact, which is an important element of the offence in question, violates the presumption of innocence in s. 11(*d*). If an accused bears the burden of disproving on a balance of probabilities an essential element of an offence, it would be possible for a conviction to occur despite the existence of a reasonable doubt. This would arise if the accused adduced sufficient evidence to raise a reasonable doubt as to his or her innocence but did not convince the jury on a balance of probabilities that the presumed fact was untrue.

The fact that the standard is only the civil one does not render a reverse onus clause constitutional. As Sir Rupert Cross commented in the *Rede Lectures*, "The Golden Thread of the English Criminal Law: The Burden of Proof", delivered in 1976 at the University of Toronto, at pp. 11-13:

> It is sometimes said that exceptions to the Woolmington rule are acceptable because, whenever the burden of proof on any issue in a criminal case is borne by the accused, he only has to satisfy the jury on the balance of probabilities, whereas on issues on which the Crown bears the burden of proof the jury must be satisfied beyond a reasonable doubt. . . . The fact that the standard is lower when the accused bears the burden of proof than it is when the burden of proof is borne by the prosecution is no answer to my objection to the existence of exceptions to the Woolmington rule as it does not alter the fact that a jury or bench of Magistrates may have to convict the accused although they are far from sure of his guilt.

As we have seen, the potential for a rational connection between the basic fact and the presumed fact to justify a reverse onus provision has been elaborated in some of the cases discussed above and is now known as the "rational connection test". In the context of s. 11(*d*), however, the following question arises: if we apply the rational connection test to the consideration of whether s. 11(*d*) has been violated, are we adequately protecting the constitutional principle of the presumption of innocence? As Professors MacKay and Cromwell point out in their article "Oakes: A Bold Initiative" (1983), 32 C.R. (3d) 221, at p. 233:

> The rational connection test approves a provision that *forces* the trier to infer a fact that may be simply rationally, connected to the proved fact. Why does it follow that such a provision does not offend the constitutional right to be proved guilty beyond a reasonable doubt?

A basic fact may rationally tend to prove a presumed fact, but not prove its existence beyond a reasonable doubt. An accused person could thereby be convicted despite the presence of a reasonable doubt. This would violate the presumption of innocence.

I should add that this questioning of the constitutionality of the "rational connection test" as a guide to interpreting s. 11(*d*) does not minimize its importance. The appropriate stage for invoking the rational connection test, however, is under s. 1 of the *Charter*. This consideration did not arise under the

Canadian Bill of Rights because of the absence of an equivalent to s. 1. At the Court of Appeal level in the present case, Martin J.A. sought to combine the analysis of s. 11(*d*) and s. 1 to overcome the limitations of the *Canadian Bill of Rights* jurisprudence. To my mind, it is highly desirable to keep s. 1 and s. 11(*d*) analytically distinct. Separating the analysis into two components is consistent with the approach this court has taken to the *Charter* to date (see *R. v. Big M Drug Mart Ltd.*, *supra*; *Hunter v. Southam Inc.*, [1984] 2 S.C.R. 145; *Law Society of Upper Canada v. Skapinker*, [1984] 1 S.C.R. 357).

To return to s. 8 of the *Narcotic Control Act*, I am in no doubt whatsoever that it violates s. 11(*d*) of the *Charter* by requiring the accused to prove on a balance of probabilities that he was not in possession of the narcotic for the purpose of trafficking. Mr. Oakes is compelled by s. 8 to prove he is *not* guilty of the offence of trafficking. He is thus denied his right to be presumed innocent and subjected to the potential penalty of life imprisonment unless he can rebut the presumption. This is radically and fundamentally inconsistent with the societal values of human dignity and liberty which we espouse, and is directly contrary to the presumption of innocence enshrined in s. 11(*d*). Let us turn now to s. 1 of the *Charter*.

Subsequently, the Supreme Court has determined that any persuasive burden placed on the accused, whether this relates to an element of the offence or a defence, violates s. 11(d) and the only issue is whether it is saved under s. 1.

Sometimes Parliament resorts to the evidentiary device of a rebuttable presumption to assist the burdenholder. This is usually achieved by a provision that "in the absence of evidence to the contrary" something is presumed. In such cases where the accused points to credible evidence to the contrary the presumption no longer exists. This type of burden is sometimes also confusingly referred to as an evidentiary burden. It has a greater significance than the usual meaning of pointing to evidence in the case. With rebuttable presumptions if the accused does nothing to displace the presumption the presumed fact must be considered proved.

The task of the Crown in proving that a particular element is proven is sometimes made easier by the presence of a "deeming" provision in the *Criminal Code*. Consider an accused who finds a partly-completed building on which no door has yet been installed in the doorway, and who steps halfway in before leaving. Has that accused broken and entered for the purposes of the offence of "break and enter" in s. 348? See s. 350(b)(ii) of the *Criminal Code*. For similar provisions, see s. 139(3), s. 198(2), s. 366(3) and (4), or s. 461. Provisions can also establish that certain matters are *not* proven: see, for example, ss. 304-315 or s. 333.

In *Downey,* the Court decided that rebuttable presumptions also offend s. 11(d) (and would have to be justified under s.1):

R. v. DOWNEY

[1992] 2 S.C.R. 10, 13 C.R. (4th) 129, 72 C.C.C. (3d) 1,
1992 CarswellAlta 56, 1992 CarswellAlta 467

The accused was charged under s. 195 of the *Criminal Code* (later renumbered as s. 212 then struck down in *Canada (Attorney General) v. Bedford,* 2013 SCC 72, (*sub nom.* Canada (Attorney General) v. Bedford) [2013] 3 S.C.R. 1101, 303 C.C.C. (3d) 146, 7 C.R. (7th) 1) with living off the avails of prostitution. Section 195(2) of the *Code* stated that "[e]vidence that a person lives with or is habitually in the company of prostitutes. . . is, in the absence of evidence to the contrary, proof that the person lives on the avails of prostitution". The accused challenged the constitutionality of that mandatory presumption. The Court took the opportunity to articulate the principles governing reverse onus clauses and the presumption of innocence.

. . . .

Cory J.: —

. . . .

Perhaps it may be helpful to summarize the principles to be derived from the authorities.

I — The presumption of innocence is infringed whenever the accused is liable to be convicted despite the existence of a reasonable doubt.

II — If by the provisions of a statutory presumption, an accused is required to establish, that is to say to prove or disprove, on a balance of probabilities either an element of an offence or an excuse, then it contravenes s. 11(d). Such a provision would permit a conviction in spite of a reasonable doubt.

III — Even if a rational connection exists between the established fact and the fact to be presumed, this would be insufficient to make valid a presumption requiring the accused to disprove an element of the offence.

IV — Legislation which substitutes proof of one element for proof of an essential element will not infringe the presumption of innocence if as a result of the proof of the substituted element, it would be unreasonable for the trier of fact not to be satisfied beyond a reasonable doubt of the existence of the other element. To put it another way, the statutory presumption will be valid if the proof of the substituted fact leads inexorably to the proof of the other. However, the statutory presumption will infringe s. 11(d) if it requires the trier of fact to convict in spite of a reasonable doubt.

V — A permissive assumption from which a trier of fact may but not must draw an inference of guilt will not infringe s. 11(d).

VI — A provision that might have been intended to play a minor role in providing relief from conviction will nonetheless contravene the *Charter* if the provision (such as the truth of a statement) must be established by the accused (see *Keegstra, supra*).

VII — It must of course be remembered that statutory presumptions which infringe s. 11(d) may still be justified pursuant to s. 1 of the *Charter*. (As for example in *Keegstra, supra*.)

The Court decided that the rebuttable presumption in s. 195(2) violated s. 11(d) but, by a 4-3 majority, it was saved under s. 1.

STEVE COUGHLAN, DOUBT MOUNTAIN AND THE PRESUMPTION OF INNOCENCE

It can be difficult to conceptualize the various burdens on the Crown and the defence. This is particularly true of the interplay between the onus on the Crown to prove the elements of an offence beyond a reasonable doubt, and the occasional reverse onus provisions in the *Code* which sometimes require an accused to disprove or raise doubt about a particular element. The thought experiment below can be helpful in understanding these issues.

Imagine a hill — Doubt Mountain — on which a two-person game is played (see figure below). The player at the top of the hill is called the "accused"; the player at the bottom is the "Crown". A number of boxes are placed at the bottom of the hill, next to the Crown. Halfway up the hill the "balance of probabilities" (BOP) line is marked on the ground. Somewhere quite close to the top of the hill, but not actually marked on the ground, is the "beyond a reasonable doubt" (BARD) line.

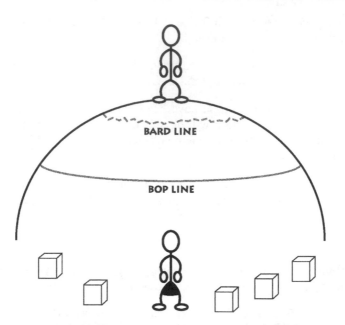

The rules of the game are very simple. The Crown is required to push every box up the hill past the BARD line: if the Crown succeeds in doing this, she wins. If not, the accused wins. Making the game more challenging is the fact that the BARD line does not appear on the hill: until the game is over both players are required to guess, based on their experience with the game, whether a box has been pushed past it or not.

Note that the simplest strategy for the accused is simply to lie down and have a nap. This is not likely to be the *best* strategy, but the rules do not actually require the accused to do anything at all in order to win. At a certain point in the game, though, a lot of the boxes are likely to be a long way up the hill. The accused is likely to think "unless I push some of those boxes below the BARD line, I'm going to lose". A neutral observer (perhaps the neutral observer who will eventually decide the winner) is likely to agree. At that stage it would be true to say that the accused had better do some work or he will lose the game. Note that this does not change the *rule* that the accused is not required to do anything. Tactically, however, it is obvious to everyone that if the accused does nothing he will lose, and so as a practical reality he had better push some boxes down the hill.

Over time it will become obvious to players and observers that some particular routes up the hill are quite easy. In those circumstances an observer will recognize that some boxes are going to be pretty easy to get to the top of the hill, and practically speaking they will almost always end up past the BARD line unless the accused does something about them. Again, though, no change in the rules is implied by this fact.

Now, though, let us consider a possible change in the rules: the addition of a conveyor belt in front of one or more boxes. In those circumstances, we know for certain that the moment the game begins, those boxes shoot up the hill and are past the BARD line. Here we have actually changed the rules: the rules now require the accused to push some boxes down the hill, rather than requiring the Crown to push them up. We could leave the change in the rules at that, and say that the accused is required to push the box below the BARD line. However, we could also make the game even harder than that for the accused. We could say that unless the accused pushes the conveyor belt box down the hill below the BOP line, he loses.

The rules of Doubt Mountain correspond fairly readily to the burdens imposed on the Crown and accused in the criminal justice system. The Crown bears the onus of proof beyond a reasonable doubt, and it is an error to instruct a jury that an accused is required to establish doubt. As a practical matter, however, it is as true in a courtroom as it would be on Doubt Mountain (that is to say, not absolutely clear but reasonably predictable to an informed observer) that sometimes the Crown has done a pretty good job of fulfilling the obligations imposed on it. In those cases, as a tactical decision, the accused ought to choose do some work. It is in one sense accurate in those circumstances to say that unless the accused shows doubt, he will be convicted: the challenge is to distinguish clearly that this is not making it a *rule* that the accused must show doubt. It is simply recognizing that within the rules, which don't insist on the accused doing anything, it has nonetheless become a tactical necessity for the accused to act.

This situation is particularly likely to occur when there is an obvious and reasonable inference to be drawn from facts: or on Doubt Mountain, when the box is on an easy route up the hill. It has often been said, for example, that a person is presumed to intend the natural consequences of his or her actions: if we see an adult pick up a rock, cock her arm, and throw the rock through a pane of glass, we are likely to conclude without any further evidence that she intended to break the window. Unless we hear a reason to think otherwise, we will take the facts to be sufficient to prove the intent. The accused isn't by the rules of the criminal justice system *required* to prove an absence of intent to break the window, just as an easy route up Doubt Mountain isn't a conveyor belt. Still, tactically the accused had better do something or the element will almost certainly be proven. This situation is sometimes described as a "tactical burden".

Sometimes, however, the *Criminal Code* actually imposes a reverse onus on the accused, just as there are sometimes conveyor belts on Doubt Mountain. In those cases it is true *as a matter of law* that an accused who does not show the existence of some doubt will be convicted. If the *Code* provision says that an accused must show "evidence to the contrary",[24] or similar words, that corresponds to pushing the box below the BARD line: the accused is required to show that there is doubt. This type of provision is referred to by the court as an "evidentiary burden". (It is important to note that the phrase "evidentiary burden" is also, and more frequently, used by the court to describe the obligation to present enough evidence to put some legal issue into play, such as, for example, whether an accused acted in self-defence or not). On the other hand if the *Code* provision

---

24 See for example, s. 348(2): "For the purposes of proceedings under this section, evidence that an accused (a) broke and entered a place or attempted to break and enter a place is, in the absence of any evidence to the contrary, proof that he broke and entered the place or attempted to do so, as the case may be, with intent to commit an indictable offence therein."

actually requires the accused to "establish" or "prove" some point,[25] that corresponds to a requirement that the accused push a box far enough down Doubt Mountain that it is below the BOP line. This type of provision is referred to as a "legal burden" on the accused.

Note that a tactical burden and an evidentiary burden (as used in this context) do not differ in the amount of work they call on the accused to do: in each case the accused must show the existence of doubt about whether a particular element has been proven. Those two differ because of the *reason* the accused must do this: because the Crown has done its job well, or because the rules require it. A legal burden, like an evidentiary burden, arises from statute. It differs, though, in that it requires a greater amount of work from the accused: not merely to show that there is doubt whether a point is true, but actually to prove that it is false (that is, push the box halfway down, not just a little way down).

It can be difficult to understand these distinctions in the cases, because judges and the *Code* tend to talk about whether an accused has "proved" a point, but also about whether the Crown has proved its points. As Doubt Mountain attempts to illustrate, it is important to recognize that the Crown and the accused are pushing in different directions. Really it is better to conceptualize the accused as trying to *dis*prove elements, rather than proving anything. The language tends also to talk about an accused "raising" a doubt, which again suggests some positive proof of a point. It is easier to keep the different roles distinct if one thinks of the accused's job as "showing" doubt rather than raising it. This helps keep clear that the accused's task in relation to the "beyond a reasonable doubt" standard is actually easier, not harder, than in relation to the "balance of probabilities" standard.

3. ROLE OF THE CRIMINAL JUSTICE SYSTEM IN CANADIAN SOCIETY

(a) Victims' Rights

It is clear that victims have in the past been ignored and sometimes denigrated by the criminal justice system. Abuses have included unwarranted humiliation on cross-examination, especially in sexual assault trials, the trauma of endless court appearances and delays often without proper explanation, and no consideration in sentencing of the impact of the offence on the victim. Clearly victims have a right to be treated with respect. Legislative changes to better protect interests of victims have included rape shield laws, greater restitution provisions, fine surcharge programs to support victim services, and provisions for bans on publicity of the identity of victims, written victim impact statements on sentencing and victim input into parole decisions.

---

25 See for example, s. 57(3): "Everyone who without lawful excuse, the proof of which lies on him, has in his possession a forged passport or a passport in respect of which an offence under subsection (2) has been committed is guilty of an indictable offence and liable to imprisonment for a term not exceeding five years."

The *Canadian Victims Bill of Rights*, S.C. 2015, c. 13 came into force on April 23, 2015. It specifies that victims of crime have the following rights:

(*a*) the right to information about the criminal justice system, the programs and services that are available to victims of crime and the complaint procedures that are available to them when their rights have been infringed or denied;

(*b*) the right to information about the status of the investigation and the criminal proceedings, as well as information about reviews while the offender is subject to the corrections process, or about hearings after the accused is found not criminally responsible on account of mental disorder or unfit to stand trial, and information about the decisions made at those reviews and hearings;

(*c*) the right to have their security and privacy considered by the appropriate authorities in the criminal justice system;

(*d*) the right to protection from intimidation and retaliation;

(*e*) the right to request testimonial aids;

(*f*) the right to convey their views about decisions to be made by authorities in the criminal justice system that affect the victim's rights under this Act and to have those views considered;

(*g*) the right to present a victim impact statement and to have it considered;

(*h*) the right to have the courts consider making, in all cases, a restitution order against the offender; and

(*i*) the right to have a restitution order entered as a civil court judgment that is enforceable against the offender if the amount owing under the restitution order is not paid.

That Act also expanded who is included in the definition of "victim" in the *Code*, which used to say only

victim includes the victim of an alleged offence

but now reads

victim means a person against whom an offence has been committed, or is alleged to have been committed, who has suffered, or is alleged to have suffered, physical or emotional harm, property damage or economic loss as the result of the commission or alleged commission of the offence and includes, for the purposes of sections 672.5, 722 and 745.63, a person who has suffered physical or emotional harm, property damage or economic loss as the result of the commission of an offence against any other person.

The Truth and Reconciliation Commission, in its 2015 Final Report, observed that

The justice system continues to fail Aboriginal victims of crime. There are few services available for Aboriginal victims of crime. Victim compensation schemes are often lacking and often fail to recognize the distinct needs of Aboriginal victims of crime.

The statistics are startling. Aboriginal people are 58% more likely to be victimized by crime. Aboriginal women report being victimized by violent crime at a rate almost three times higher than non-Aboriginal women—13% of Aboriginal women reported being victimized by violent crime in 2009. In the same year, one in ten Aboriginal people reported being a victim of a non-spousal violent crime, more than double the rate reported by non-Aboriginal people.

It is difficult to obtain accurate information about the rate of victimization in Aboriginal communities. According to some studies, less than one-third of victims of crime report their victimization to police, and police forces across the country do not have a consistent method for recording the Aboriginal identity of victims. Statistics Canada does not provide the kinds of supports necessary to permit some Aboriginal victims to comfortably disclose their experience to researchers. The most recent Statistics Canada data on homicide and family violence fail to report how many victims were Aboriginal, although older data suggest the homicide victimization rate of Aboriginal people between 1997 and 2000 was seven times that of non-Aboriginal people. (footnotes omitted) (p. 179)

The Commission called for the collection of data on the criminal victimization of Aboriginal people, and for the creation of Aboriginal-specific victim programs and services.

Although there are often now calls to recognize new legal and constitutional rights for victims and complaints that accused have too many rights, it is important to think carefully about what sort of rights victims should have. A criminal trial is about determining guilt and just punishment of an accused, not about personal redress for victims. What, for example, if the input of victims were to be determinative on the issue of sentence? Would it be just to have the length of a prison sentence determined by whether the victim wants revenge or compassion? Wouldn't a general right of representation of victims at trial, even on the determination of guilt, hopelessly burden and confuse an already overtaxed and under-resourced criminal justice system?

Constitutional rights for those alleging crimes were directly recognized by the Supreme Court for the first time in its controversial decision in *R. v. O'Connor* (1995) 44 C.R. (4th) 1 (S.C.C.). The Court adopted a special balancing procedure respecting discovery of medical records in the possession of third parties. L'Heureux-Dubé, J., with La Forest, Gonthier and McLachlin JJ. concurring, saw the need to balance the accused's right to a fair trial and full answer and defence with the complainant's rights to privacy and to equality without discrimination. The majority, through a joint judgment by Lamer C.J. and Sopinka J., with Cory, Iacobucci and Major JJ. concurring, determined that the accused's right to full answer and defence should be balanced against the complainant's rights to privacy under ss. 7 and 8. However, the majority, in not referring to a s. 15 equality right for complainants although it was fully argued, implicitly rejected it.

Section 15 equality rights for complainants in sexual assault cases were later asserted by the Supreme Court in *R. v. Mills* (1999), 28 C.R.(5th) 207 (S.C.C.). In *R. v. Shearing* (2002), 2 C.R.(6th) 213 (S.C.C.), the majority of the Court, however, refers to them as "equality interests". See further below in Chapter 4 on Sexual Assault.

Bill C-51, *An Act to amend the Criminal Code and the Department of Justice Act and to make consequential amendments to another Act* will, if it passes, give the complainant in a sexual assault trial the right to counsel in rape shield proceedings, which involve an application to admit evidence about a complainant's prior sexual history in a sexual assault trial.

For full discussion of issues of criminal trials and victims' rights, see David Paciocco, *Getting Away With Murder* (1999) at 351-382. See also Christine Boyle and Marilyn MacCrimmon, "The Constitutionality of Bill C-49: Analyzing Sexual Assault as if Equality Really Mattered" (1998) 41 Crim. L.Q. 198-237.

For strong arguments opposing and supporting *Charter* rights for victims see respectively David Paciocco, "Why the Constitutionalization of Victims' Rights Should Not Occur" (2005) 49 Crim. L.Q. 393 and Alan Young, "Crime Victims and Constitutional Rights" (2005) 49 Crim. L.Q. 432. See too Kent Roach, "Victims' Rights and the *Charter*" (2005) 49 Crim. L.Q. 474, who concludes that "a workable victims' rights amendment to the *Charter* would not benefit crime victims to a significant extent" (at 514).

(b) Scope

"There are acts of wickedness so gross and outrageous that self-protection apart they must be prevented as far as possible at any cost to the offender and punished if they occur with exemplary severity." (J.F. Stephen, *Liberty, Fraternity and Equality*, 2nd ed. (1874) at 178.)

"The only purpose for which power can rightfully be exercised over any member of a civilized community against his will is to prevent harm to others." (John Stuart Mill, *On Liberty* (1859), Chapter 1.)

CANADIAN COMMITTEE ON CORRECTIONS, TOWARDS UNITY: CRIMINAL JUSTICE AND CORRECTIONS (OUIMET REPORT)

(1969), 12-13

1. No act should be criminally proscribed unless its incidence, actual or potential, is *substantially damaging to society*.
2. No act should be criminally prohibited where its incidence may adequately be controlled by social forces other than the criminal process. Public opinion may be enough to curtail certain kinds of behaviour. Other kinds of behaviour may be more appropriately dealt with by non-criminal legal processes, *e.g.* by legislation relating to mental health or social and economic condition.
3. No law should give rise to social or personal damage greater than that it was designed to prevent.

To designate certain conduct as criminal in an attempt to control anti-social behaviour should be a last step. Criminal law traditionally, and perhaps inherently, has involved the imposition of a sanction. This sanction, whether in the form of arrest, summons, trial, conviction, punishment or publicity is, in the view of the Committee, to be employed only as an unavoidable necessity. Men and women may have their lives, public and private, destroyed; families may be broken up; the state may be put to considerable expense: all these consequences are to be taken into account when determining whether a particular kind of conduct is so obnoxious to social values that it is to be included in the catalogue of crimes. If there is any other course open to society when threatened, then that course is to be preferred. The deliberate infliction of punishment or any other state interference with human freedom is to be justified only where manifest evil would result from failure to interfere.

LAW REFORM COMMISSION OF CANADA, REPORT: OUR CRIMINAL LAW

(1976), 27-28

But criminal law is not the only means of bolstering values. Nor is it necessarily always the best means. The fact is, criminal law is a blunt and costly instrument — blunt because it cannot have the human sensitivity of institutions like the family, the school, the church or the community, and costly since it imposes suffering, loss of liberty and great expense.

So criminal law must be an instrument of last resort. It must be used as little as possible. The message must not be diluted by overkill — too many laws and offences and charges and trials and prison sentences. Society's ultimate weapon must stay sheathed as long as possible. The watchword is restraint — restraint applying to the scope of criminal law, to the meaning of criminal guilt, to the use of the criminal trial and to the criminal sentence.

1. Scope of Criminal Law

In re-affirming values criminal law denounces acts considered wrong. Accordingly it has to stick to really wrongful acts. It must not overextend itself and make crimes out of things most people reckon not really wrong or, if wrong, merely trivial. Only those acts thought seriously wrong by our society should count as crimes.

Not all such acts, however, should be crimes. Wrongfulness is a necessary, not a sufficient condition of criminality. Before an act should count as a crime, three further conditions must be fulfilled. First, it must cause harm to other people, to society or, in special cases to those needing protection from themselves. Second, it must cause harm that is serious both in nature and degree. And third, it must cause harm that is best dealt with through the mechanism of the criminal law. These conditions would confine the criminal law to crimes of violence, dishonesty and other offences traditionally in the centre of the stage. Any other offences, not really wrong but penally prohibited because this is the most convenient way of dealing with them, must stay outside the *Criminal Code* and qualify merely as quasi-crimes or violations.

1. **Are there dangers in the Commission's last recommendation?**
2. **Are the proposed criteria of crime helpful?**

ADULT CRIMINAL COURT STATISTICS, 2014/2015

Statistics Canada, February 2017

In 2014/2015, five *Criminal Code* offence types made up close to half (48%) of all completed adult criminal court cases. These included theft (10%), impaired driving (10%), failure to comply with a court order (10%), common assault (9%)

and breach of probation (9%). This was the first time in 10 years that impaired driving was not the most common offence.

Continuing a trend seen over the past decade, more than 6 in 10 (63%) cases completed in adult criminal court in 2014/2015 resulted in a guilty finding. Another 32% of cases were stayed, withdrawn, dismissed or discharged, 4% of cases were acquitted, and the remaining 1% of cases received another type of decision, such as the accused was found not criminally responsible on account of mental disorder.

Probation, either on its own or in combination with another type of sentence, was the most common type of sentence in 2014/2015, at 43% of all guilty cases. The median length of probation was 365 days (one year).

Custodial sentences were imposed in just over one-third (37%) of guilty adult criminal court cases in 2014/2015, the majority (88%) of which received a sentence of six months or less. About 3% of individuals received a custody sentence of two years or more. The median length of custody was 30 days (one month).

INDIGENOUS OVERREPRESENTATION IN THE CRIMINAL JUSTICE SYSTEM
Statistics Canada, January 2017

Indigenous people are overrepresented in Canada's criminal justice system as both victims and offenders. National data on Indigenous people in the criminal justice system includes data on self-reported victimization, police-reported homicide, and provincial/territorial and federal custody.

Indigenous people overrepresented as crime victims, especially females

In 2014, 28% of Indigenous people (aged 15+) reported being victimized in the previous 12 months, compared to 18% of non-Indigenous people. The rate of violent victimization among Indigenous people was more than double that of non-Indigenous people (163 incidents per 1,000 people vs. 74).

Indigenous females had an overall rate of violent victimization that was double that of Indigenous males and close to triple that of non-Indigenous females.

When controlling for various risk factors, Indigenous males were no more at risk of violent victimization than their non-Indigenous counterparts. In contrast, high victimization rates among Indigenous females could not be fully explained by other risk factors. Even when controlling for various risk factors, Indigenous identity remained a risk factor for violent victimization of Indigenous females.

Indigenous adults and youth overrepresented in custody

In 2014/2015, Indigenous adults accounted for 26% of provincial/territorial custody admissions and 25% of the in-custody federal offender population. The proportion of Indigenous adults in custody was about nine times higher than their representation in the adult population (3%). Indigenous adults were overrepresented in provincial/territorial custody in most jurisdictions, especially British Columbia, Saskatchewan, Manitoba and Ontario.

In 2014/2015, Indigenous youth (aged 12-17) accounted for 37% of provincial/territorial custody admissions. The proportion of Indigenous youth in provincial/territorial custody was about five times higher than their representation in the youth population (7%). Indigenous youth were overrepresented in provincial/territorial custody in most jurisdictions, especially British Columbia, Manitoba and Ontario.

Overrepresentation in custody more pronounced for Indigenous females

In 2014/2015, Indigenous men accounted for 24% of adult male provincial/territorial custody admissions and 24% of male offenders in federal custody. By comparison, Indigenous women accounted for 38% of adult female provincial/territorial custody admissions and 36% of female offenders in federal custody. The proportion of Indigenous adults in custody relative to their proportion in the population was eight times higher for Indigenous men and twelve times higher for Indigenous women.

In 2014/2015, male Indigenous youth accounted for 34% of male youth provincial/territorial custody admissions, while female Indigenous youth accounted for 49% of female youth provincial/territorial custody admissions. The proportion of Indigenous youth in provincial/territorial custody relative to their proportion in the population was about five times higher for Indigenous male youth and seven times higher for Indigenous female youth.

R. v. MALMO-LEVINE

16 C.R. (6th) 1, 179 C.C.C. (3d) 417,
2003 CarswellBC 3133, 2003 CarswellBC 3134 (S.C.C.)

In the course of upholding the constitutionality of Canada's marijuana laws the Supreme Court, over the sole dissent of Justice Arbour, firmly rejected the notion that there is a principle of fundamental justice under s. 7 that a criminal prohibition will offend the *Charter* if it can be established that the conduct involved no risk of harm.

GONTHIER and BINNIE JJ.:—

(i) History and Definition of the Harm Principle

What is "the harm principle"? The appellants rely, in particular, on the writings of the liberal theorist, J. S. Mill, who attempted to establish clear boundaries for the permissible intrusion of the state into private life:

> The object of this Essay is to assert one very simple principle, as entitled to govern absolutely the dealings of society with the individual in the way of compulsion and control, whether the means used be physical force in the form of legal penalties, or the moral coercion of public opinion. That principle is, that the sole end for which mankind are warranted, individually or collectively, in interfering with the liberty of action of any of their number, is self-protection. That *the only purpose for which power can be rightfully exercised over any member of a civilised community, against his will, is to prevent harm to others.* His own good, either physical or moral, is not a sufficient warrant. . . . The only part of the conduct of any one, for which he is amenable to society, is that which concerns others. In the part which merely concerns himself, his independence is, of right, absolute. Over himself, over his own body and mind, the individual is sovereign. [Emphasis added.]

> (J. S. Mill, *On Liberty and Considerations on Representative Government*, R. B. McCallum, ed. (1946), at pp. 8-9.)

Thus Mill's principle has two essential features. First, it rejects paternalism — that is, the prohibition of conduct that harms only the actor. Second, it excludes what could be called "moral harm". Mill was of the view that such moral claims are insufficient to justify use of the criminal law. Rather, he required clear and tangible harm to the rights and interests of others.

At the same time, Mill acknowledged an exception to his requirement of harm "to others" for vulnerable groups. He wrote that "this doctrine is meant to apply to human beings in the maturity of their faculties. . . . Those who are still in a state to require being taken care of by others, must be protected against their own actions as well as against external injury" (p. 9).

Mill's statement has the virtues of insight and clarity but he was advocating certain general philosophic principles, not interpreting a constitutional document. Moreover, even his philosophical supporters have tended to agree that justification for state intervention cannot be reduced to a single factor — harm — but is a much more complex matter. One of Mill's most distinguished supporters, Professor H.L.A. Hart, wrote:

> Mill's formulation of the liberal point of view may well be too simple. The grounds for interfering with human liberty are more various than the single criterion of "harm to others" suggests: cruelty to animals or organizing prostitution for gain do not, as Mill himself saw, fall easily under the description of harm to others. Conversely, even where there is harm to others in the most literal sense, there may well be other principles limiting the extent to which harmful activities should be repressed by law. So *there are multiple criteria, not a single criterion, determining when human liberty may be restricted.*

(H. L. A. Hart, "Immorality and Treason", originally appearing in *The Listener* (July 30, 1959), at pp. 162-63, reprinted in *Morality and the Law* (1971), 49, at p. 51 (emphasis added).)

To the same effect, see Professor J. Feinberg, *The Moral Limits of the Criminal Law*, (1984), vol. 1: Harm to Others, at p. 12; also vol. 4: Harmless Wrongdoing, at p. 323.

(ii)   *Is the Harm Principle a Principle of Fundamental Justice?*

The appellants submit that the harm principle is a principle of fundamental justice for the purposes of s. 7 that operates to place limits on the type of conduct the state may criminalize. This limitation exists independently of the division of powers under ss. 91 and 92 of the *Constitution Act, 1867*. In other words, the appellants contend that there is a double threshold. Even if the Crown is able to establish that the creation of a particular criminal offence is a valid exercise of the criminal law power, there is a second level of constraint on the type of conduct that can be made criminal by virtue of s. 7 of the *Charter*.

We agree that there is a form of "double threshold", in that the *Charter* imposes requirements that are separate from those imposed by ss. 91 and 92 of the *Constitution Act, 1867*. However, we do not agree with the attempted elevation of the harm principle to a principle of fundamental justice. That is, in our view the harm principle is not the constitutional standard for what conduct may or may not be the subject of the criminal law for the purposes of s. 7.

In *Re B.C. Motor Vehicle Act, supra*, Lamer J. (as he then was) explained that the principles of fundamental justice lie in "the basic tenets of our legal system. They do not lie in the realm of general public policy but in the inherent domain of the judiciary as guardian of the justice system" (p. 503). This court provided further guidance as to what constitutes a principle of fundamental justice for the purposes of s. 7, in *Rodriguez, supra, per* Sopinka J. (at pp. 590-91 and 607):

> A mere common law rule does not suffice to constitute a principle of fundamental justice, rather, as the term implies, principles upon which there is *some consensus* that they are vital or fundamental to our societal notion of justice are required. Principles of fundamental justice must not, however, be so broad as to be no more than vague generalizations about what our society considers to be ethical or moral. They must be capable of being *identified with some precision* and *applied* to situations in a manner which yields an understandable result. They must also, in my view, be *legal principles*.

> . . . .

> While the principles of fundamental justice are concerned with more than process, reference must be made to principles which are "fundamental" in the sense that they would have *general acceptance among reasonable people*. [Emphasis added.]

The requirement of "general acceptance among reasonable people" enhances the legitimacy of judicial review of state action, and ensures that the values against which state action is measured are not just fundamental "in the eye of the beholder *only*": *Rodriguez*, at pp. 607, and 590 (emphasis in original). In short, for a rule or principle to constitute a principle of fundamental justice for the purposes of s. 7, it must be a legal principle about which there is significant societal consensus that it is fundamental to the way in which the legal system ought fairly to operate, and it must be identified with sufficient precision to yield a manageable standard against which to measure deprivations of life, liberty or security of the person.

a.   Is the Harm Principle a Legal Principle?

In our view, the "harm principle" is better characterized as a description of an important state interest rather than a normative "legal" principle. Be that as it may, even if the harm principle could be characterized as a legal principle, we do not think that it meets the other requirements, as explained below.

b.   There is No Sufficient Consensus that the Harm Principle is Vital or
     Fundamental to Our Societal Notion of Criminal Justice

Contrary to the appellants' assertion, we do not think there is a consensus that the harm principle is the sole justification for criminal prohibition. There is no doubt that our case law and academic commentary are full of statements about the criminal law being aimed at conduct that "affects the public", or that constitutes "a wrong against the public welfare", or is "injurious to the public", or that "affects the community". No doubt, as stated, the presence of harm to others may justify legislative action under the criminal law power. However, we do not think that the absence of proven harm creates the unqualified barrier to legislative action that the appellants suggest. On the contrary, the state may sometimes be justified in criminalizing conduct that is either not harmful (in the sense contemplated by the harm principle), or that causes harm only to the accused.

The appellants cite in aid of their position the observation of Sopinka J., writing for the majority in *Butler*, *supra*, that "[t]he objective of maintaining conventional standards of propriety, independently of any harm to society, is no longer justified in light of the values of individual liberty which underlie the *Charter*" (p. 498). However, Sopinka J. went on to clarify that it is open to Parliament to legislate "on the basis of some fundamental conception of *morality* for the purposes of safeguarding the values which are integral to a free and democratic society" (p. 493 (emphasis added)).

Several instances of crimes that do not cause harm to others are found in the *Criminal Code*. Cannibalism is an offence (s. 182 of the *Code*) that does not harm another sentient being, but that is nevertheless prohibited on the basis of fundamental social and ethical considerations. Bestiality (s. 160 of the *Code*) and cruelty to animals (s. 446 of the *Code*) are examples of crimes that rest on their offensiveness to deeply held social values rather than on Mill's "harm principle".

A duel fought by consenting adults is an example of a crime where the victim is no less culpable than the perpetrator, and there is no harm that is not consented to, but the prohibition (s. 71 of the *Code*) is nevertheless integral to our ideas of civilized society. See also *R. v. Jobidon*, [1991] 2 S.C.R. 714. Similarly, in *R. v. F. (R.P.)* (1996), 105 C.C.C. (3d) 435, the Nova Scotia Court of Appeal upheld the prohibition of incest under s. 155 of the *Criminal Code* despite a *Charter* challenge by five consenting adults. In none of these instances of consenting adults does the criminal law conform to Mill's expression of the harm principle that "[o]ver himself, over his own body and mind, the individual is sovereign", as referenced earlier at para. 106.

Various jurists and commentators are said by the appellants to have endorsed the idea that harm is required, but we think that these sources, read in context, do not support the "harm principle" as defined by the appellants.

One source relied on by the appellants — the writings of Sir James Fitzjames Stephen — illustrates this point. Reference was made to Stephen's statement that the criminal law

> ... must be confined within narrow limits, and can be applied only to definite overt acts or omissions capable of being proved, which acts or omissions inflict definite evils, either on specific persons or on the community at large.

(J. F. Stephen, A History of the Criminal Law of England (1883), vol. II, at pp. 78-79.)

However, Stephen himself was a prominent critic of Mill's harm principle. He believed that "immoral" behaviour can be a proper subject for the criminal law. Clearly, his reference to "evils" inflicted on the community includes the idea of moral harm, which Mill specifically excluded from the scope of his "harm principle". Stephen thus supported a much larger view of the legitimate purposes of the criminal law than is permitted by the appellants' argument.

The appellants also rely on a 1982 report by the Law Reform Commission of Canada entitled *The Criminal Law in Canadian Society* which concludes, at p. 45, that the criminal law "ought to be reserved for reacting to conduct that is seriously harmful". This seems, on its face, to support the harm principle. However, the report goes on to state, at p. 45, that such harm

> ... may be caused or threatened to the collective safety or integrity of society through the infliction of direct damage or the *undermining of what the Law Reform Commission terms fundamental or essential values — those values or interests necessary for social life to be carried on, or for the maintenance of the kind of society cherished by Canadians*. [Emphasis added.]

Such a definition of "harm" is clearly contrary to Mill's harm principle as endorsed by the appellants.

c.   Nor Is There Any Consensus that the Distinction Between Harm to
     Others and Harm to Self Is of Controlling Importance

Our colleague Arbour J. takes the view that when the state wishes to make
imprisonment available as a sanction for criminal conduct, it must be able to
show the potential of such conduct to cause harm to others (para. 56). With
respect, we do not think there is any such principle anchored in our law. As this
court noted in *Rodriguez, supra,* attempted suicide was an offence under
Canadian criminal law (found in the original *Code* at s. 238) until its repeal by
S.C. 1972, c. 13, s. 16. Sopinka J. emphasized, at p. 597, that

> ... the decriminalization of attempted suicide cannot be said to represent a consensus by
> Parliament or by Canadians in general that the autonomy interest of those wishing to kill
> themselves is paramount to the state interest in protecting the life of its citizens.

The offence of attempted suicide was removed from the *Criminal Code* because
Parliament came to prefer other ways of addressing the problem of suicide. In
that case, as here, there was an important distinction between constitutional
competence, which is for the courts to decide, and the wisdom of a particular
measure, which, within its constitutional sphere, is up to Parliament.

Putting aside, for the moment, the proper approach to the appropriateness
of imprisonment (which, as stated, we think should be addressed under s. 12
rather than s. 7), we do not accept the proposition that there is a general
prohibition against the criminalization of harm to self. Canada continues to have
paternalistic laws. Requirements that people wear seatbelts and motorcycle
helmets are designed to "save people from themselves". There is no consensus
that this sort of legislation offends our societal notions of justice. Whether a jail
sentence is an appropriate penalty for such an offence is another question.
However, the objection in that aspect goes to the validity of an assigned
punishment — it does not go to the validity of prohibiting the underlying
conduct.

A recent discussion policy paper from the Law Commission of Canada
entitled *What is a Crime? Challenges and Alternatives* (2003) highlights the
difficulties in distinguishing between harm to others and harm to self. It notes
that "in a society that recognizes the interdependency of its citizens, such as
universally contributing to health care or educational needs, harm to oneself is
often borne collectively" (p. 17).

In short, there is no consensus that tangible harm to others is a necessary
precondition to the creation of a criminal law offence.

d.   The Harm Principle Is Not a Manageable Standard Against Which to
     Measure Deprivation of Life, Liberty or Security of the Person

Even those who agree with the "harm principle" as a regulator of the
criminal law frequently disagree about what it means and what offences will

meet or offend the harm principle. In the absence of any agreed definition of "harm" for this purpose, allegations and counter-allegations of non-trivial harm can be marshalled on every side of virtually every criminal law issue, as one author explains:

> The harm principle is effectively collapsing under the weight of its own success. Claims of harm have become so pervasive that the harm principle has become meaningless: the harm principle no longer serves the function of a critical principle because non-trivial harm arguments permeate the debate. Today, the issue is no longer whether a moral offence causes harm, but rather what type and what amount of harms the challenged conduct causes, and how the harms compare. On those issues, the harm principle is silent.

> (B. E. Harcourt, "The Collapse of the Harm Principle" (1999), 90 J. Crim. L. & Criminology 109, at p. 113)

Professor Harcourt goes on to point out that "[i]t is the hidden normative dimensions . . . [that] do the work in the harm principle, not the abstract, simple notion of harm" (p. 185). In other words, the existence of harm (however defined) does no more than open a gateway to the debate; it does not give any precise guidance about its resolution.

Harm, as interpreted in the jurisprudence, can take a multitude of forms, including economic, physical and social (e.g., injury and/or offence to fundamental societal values). In the present appeal, for example, the respondents put forward a list of "harms" which they attribute to marihuana use. The appellants put forward a list of "harms" which they attribute to marihuana prohibition. Neither side gives much credence to the "harms" listed by the other. Each claims the "net" result to be in its favour.

In the result, we do not believe that the content of the "harm" principle as described by Mill and advocated by the appellants provides a manageable standard under which to review criminal or other laws under s. 7 of the *Charter*. Parliament, we think, is entitled to act under the criminal law power in the protection of legitimate state interests other than the avoidance of harm to others, subject to *Charter* limits such as the rules against arbitrariness, irrationality and gross disproportionality. . . .

R. v. LABAYE

203 C.C.C. (3d) 170, 34 C.R. (6th) 1,
2005 CarswellQue 11495, 2005 CarswellQue 11496, 2005 SCC 80

R. v. KOURI

203 C.C.C. (3d) 217, 34 C.R. (6th) 86,
2005 CarswellQue 11497, 2005 CarswellQue 11498, 2005 SCC 81

The operators of a Montreal "swingers" establishment were charged with keeping a common bawdy-house for the practice of acts of indecency under s. 210(1) of the *Criminal Code*. A 7-2 majority of the Supreme Court abandons the community standard of tolerance test for indecency in favour of an objectively determined harms approach. On that new approach the majority finds that both accused should be acquitted.

In *Labaye* the purpose of the club was to permit couples and single people to meet each other for group sex. Only members and their guests were admitted to the club. Prospective members were interviewed to ensure that they were aware of the nature of the activities of the club and to exclude applicants who did not share the same views on group sex. Members paid an annual membership fee. A doorman manned the main door of the club to ensure that only members and their guests entered. Group sex only took place in an apartment on the third floor. Two doors separated the third floor apartment from the rest of the club. One was marked "Privé" and the other was locked with a numeric key pad. Members of the club were supplied with the appropriate code and permitted to gain access to the third floor apartment. Entry to the club and participation in the activities were voluntary.

At trial, the accused was convicted. The trial judge found that the accused's apartment fell within the meaning of "public place", as defined in s. 197(1) of the *Criminal Code* and that the sexual practices fell below the Canadian community standard of tolerance. She found social harm in the fact that sexual exchanges took place in the presence of other members of the club. This conduct was indecent under the *Criminal Code* because it was degrading and dehumanizing, calculated to induce anti-social behaviour in its disregard for moral values, and raised the risk of sexually transmitted diseases.

A majority of the Quebec Court of Appeal upheld the accused's conviction.

In *Kouri* the accused operated a licensed bar in Montréal. Access to the bar was restricted to couples. A doorman asked prospective clients if they were a "liberated couple", and only couples answering yes were permitted to enter after paying a $6 fee. Every half hour, a translucent curtain closed around the dance floor where people would engage in group sex activities. The trial judge convicted the accused. However, the majority of the Quebec Court of Appeal set aside the conviction, concluding that the acts at issue did not constitute criminal indecency.

In the Supreme Court both appeals were heard together.

McLACHLIN C.J. (MAJOR, BINNIE, DESCHAMPS, FISH, ABELLA and CHARRON JJ. concurring): —

. . . .

2 Defining indecency under the *Criminal Code* is a notoriously difficult enterprise. The *Criminal Code* offers no assistance, leaving the task to judges. The test developed by the cases has evolved from one based largely on subjective considerations, to one emphasizing the need for objective criteria, based on harm. This heightened emphasis on objective criteria rests on the principle that crimes should be defined in a way that affords citizens, police and the courts a clear idea of what acts are prohibited. (See *Reference re ss. 193 and 195.1 (1)(c) of the Criminal Code* (Man.), [1990] 1 S.C.R. 1123, per Lamer J.) We generally convict and imprison people only where it is established beyond a reasonable doubt that they have violated objectively defined norms. Crimes relating to public indecency are no exception.

3 This appeal requires us to apply the norms developed in recent cases to the operation of clubs established to facilitate group sex, a practice colloquially referred to as "swinging". This in turn invites further refinement of the objective criteria for indecency under the *Criminal Code*.

. . . .

4. Analysis

4.1 The Legal Test for Criminal Indecency

4.1.1 The History of Criminal Indecency

13 Section 210(1) of the *Criminal Code* makes it an offence, punishable by two years in prison, to keep a common bawdy-house. A bawdy-house is defined in s. 197(1) of the *Code* as a place kept, occupied, or resorted to "by one or more persons for the purpose of prostitution or the practice of acts of indecency". The only question in this case is whether what went on at l'Orage constituted "acts of indecency".

14 Indecency has two meanings, one moral and one legal. Our concern is not with the moral aspect of indecency, but with the legal. The moral and legal aspects of the concept are, of course, related. Historically, the legal concepts of indecency and obscenity, as applied to conduct and publications, respectively, have been inspired and informed by the moral views of the community. But over time, courts increasingly came to recognize that morals and taste were subjective, arbitrary and unworkable in the criminal context, and that a diverse society could function only with a generous measure of tolerance for minority

mores and practices. This led to a legal norm of objectively ascertainable harm instead of subjective disapproval.

. . . .

4.1.2 Toward a Theory of Harm

26 Developing a workable theory of harm is not a task for a single case. In the tradition of the common law, its full articulation will come only as judges consider diverse situations and render decisions on them. Moreover, the difficulty of the task should not be underestimated. We must proceed incrementally, step by cautious step.

27 The facts of this case require the further exploration of what types of harm, viewed objectively, suffice to found a conviction for keeping a bawdy-house for the purposes of act of indecency. This exploration must be based on the purposes that the offence serves. More precisely, what harms are sought to be curtailed by targeting indecent conduct?

28 The first step is to generically describe the type of harm targeted by the concept of indecent conduct under the *Criminal Code*. In *Butler* at p. 485 and *Little Sisters* at para. 59 , this was described as "conduct which society formally recognizes as incompatible with its proper functioning".

29 Two general requirements emerge from this description of the harm required for criminal indecency. First, the words "formally recognize" suggest that the harm must be grounded in norms which our society has recognized in its Constitution or similar fundamental laws. This means that the inquiry is not based on individual notions of harm, nor on the teachings of a particular ideology, but on what society, through its laws and institutions, has recognized as essential to its proper functioning. Second, the harm must be serious in degree. It must not only detract from proper societal functioning, but must be incompatible with it.

30 It follows that the analysis to be performed in a particular case involves two steps. The first step is concerned with the nature of the harm. It asks whether the Crown has established a harm or significant risk of harm to others that is grounded in norms which our society has formally recognized in its Constitution or similar fundamental laws. The second step is concerned with the degree of the harm. It asks whether the harm in its degree is incompatible with the proper functioning of society. Both elements must be proved beyond a reasonable doubt before acts can be considered indecent under the *Criminal Code*.

. . . .

4.1.5 Summary of the Test

62 Indecent criminal conduct will be established where the Crown proves beyond a reasonable doubt the following two requirements:

1. That, by its nature, the conduct at issue causes harm or presents a significant risk of harm to individuals or society in a way that undermines or threatens to undermine a value reflected in and thus formally endorsed through the Constitution or similar fundamental laws by, for example:

    (a) confronting members of the public with conduct that significantly interferes with their autonomy and liberty; or

    (b) predisposing others to anti-social behaviour; or

    (c) physically or psychologically harming persons involved in the conduct, and

2. That the harm or risk of harm is of a degree that is incompatible with the proper functioning of society.

As the above makes clear, the categories of harm capable of satisfying the first branch of the inquiry are not closed, nor is any one of the listed categories in itself an integral part of the definition of harm. For example, predisposition to anti-social behaviour, while central to this court's analysis in *Butler*, is but one illustration of the type of harm that undermines or threatens to undermine one of society's formally recognized values.

63 This test, applied objectively and on the basis of evidence in successive cases as they arise, is directed to articulating legal standards that enhance the ability of persons engaged in or facilitating sexual activities to ascertain the boundary between non-criminal conduct and criminal conduct. In this way, the basic requirements of the criminal law of fair notice to potential offenders and clear enforcement standards to police will, it is hoped, be satisfied.

4.2 Application of the Test

64 The first question is whether the conduct at issue harmed, or presented a significant risk of harm to individuals or society.

65 The sexual acts at issue were conducted on the third floor of a private club, behind doors marked "Privé" and accessed only by persons in possession of the proper numerical code. The evidence establishes that a number of steps were taken to ensure that members of the public who might find the conduct inappropriate did not see the activities. Pre-membership interviews were

conducted to advise of the nature of the activities and screen out persons not sharing the same interests. Only members and guests were admitted to the premisses. A doorman controlled access to the principal door.

66 On these facts, none of the kinds of harm discussed above was established. The autonomy and liberty of members of the public was not affected by unwanted confrontation with the sexual conduct in question. On the evidence, only those already disposed to this sort of sexual activity were allowed to participate and watch.

67 Nor was there evidence of the second type of harm, the harm of predisposing people to anti-social acts or attitudes. Unlike the material at issue in *Butler*, which perpetuated abusive and humiliating stereotypes of women as objects of sexual gratification, there is no evidence of anti-social attitudes toward women, or for that matter men. No one was pressured to have sex, paid for sex, or treated as a mere sexual object for the gratification of others. The fact that l'Orage is a commercial establishment does not in itself render the sexual activities taking place there commercial in nature. Members do not pay a fee and check consent at the door; the membership fee buys access to a club where members can meet and engage in consensual activities with other individuals who have similar sexual interests. The case proceeded on the uncontested premise that all participation was on a voluntary and equal basis.

68 Finally, there is no evidence of the third type of harm—physical or psychological harm to persons participating. The only possible danger to participants on the evidence was the risk of catching a sexually transmitted disease. However, this must be discounted as a factor because, as discussed above, it is conceptually and causally unrelated to indecency.

69 As stated above, the categories of harm are not closed; in a future case other different harms may be alleged as a basis for criminal indecency. However, no other harms are raised by the evidence in this case. All that is raised, in the final analysis, is the assessment that the conduct amounted to "an orgy" and that Canadian society does not tolerate orgies. (Rochon J.A., at para. 133) This reasoning erroneously harks back to the community standard of tolerance test, which has been replaced, as discussed, by the harm-based test developed in *Butler*.

70 I conclude that the evidence provides no basis for concluding that the sexual conduct at issue harmed individuals or society. *Butler* is clear that criminal indecency or obscenity must rest on actual harm or a significant risk of harm to individuals or society. The Crown failed to establish this essential element of the offence. The Crown's case must therefore fail. The majority of the court of Appeal erred, with respect, in applying an essentially subjective community standard of tolerance test and failing to apply the harm-based test of *Butler*.

71 It is unnecessary to proceed to the second branch of the test. However, if one did, there appears to be no evidence that the degree of alleged harm rose to the level of incompatibility with the proper functioning of society. Consensual conduct behind code-locked doors can hardly be supposed to jeopardize a society as vigorous and tolerant as Canadian society.

72 I would allow the appeal and set aside the conviction.

LeBel J. (Bastarache J. concurring) (dissenting): —

. . . .

75 The majority is in this way departing from the case law of this court and proposing a new approach to indecency that is, in our view, neither desirable nor workable. It constitutes an unwarranted break with the most important principles of our past decisions regarding indecency. Our colleagues' approach replaces the community standard of tolerance with a test that treats harm as the basis of indecency rather than as a criterion for determining the community's level of tolerance. Whether or not serious social harm is sustained has never been the determinative test for indecency, and it cannot take the place of a contextual analysis of the Canadian community standard of tolerance without completely transforming the concept of indecency and rendering it meaningless.

76 In contrast to our colleagues, we propose to continue applying the original test for indecency, which focusses on a contextual analysis of the impugned acts and incorporates the concept of harm as a significant, but not determinative, factor to consider in establishing the applicable level of tolerance. Whether or not harm is sustained is merely one of several indicators or contextual factors that make it possible to gauge the degree of tolerance of the Canadian community. In our view, all the contextual factors must be considered in every case. The application of this test to the facts of the case at bar leads to the conclusion that the impugned acts were indecent and that the appellant's establishment was a common bawdy-house within the meaning of s. 210(1) Cr. C.

. . . .

98 In principle, we consider the change to the legal order proposed by the majority to be inappropriate, particularly because no valid justification is given for departing from the existing test. We are convinced that this new approach strips of all relevance the social values that the Canadian community as a whole believes should be protected.

99 First, our colleagues' approach changes the role of the judge in establishing the standard of tolerance. It is clear from the case law that the judge's role is, through contextual analysis, to interpret the community's view of sexual

practices as expressed in various places at various times. Whether the impugned acts met the Canadian community standard of tolerance is thus a question of law: see *Mara*, at para. 26; *Tremblay*, at p. 946 (per Gonthier J., dissenting, but not on this issue). However, by adopting certain categories of harm that emphasize the mere exposure of the general public to sexual acts or the risk of serious psychological or physical harm, the majority's approach tends to reduce the judge's analysis to a purely fact-based one. The inquiry into the standard of tolerance thus becomes more a question of fact, which is contrary to this court's case law.

100 Second, when the standard of tolerance is established on the basis of the three categories of harm adopted by the majority, it becomes impossible to take into account the multitude of situations that could exceed the threshold for indecency. Granted, the harm-based test for indecency will in most cases yield the same result as a contextual approach. However, it is easy to conceive of situations in which the categories will not reflect the Canadian community standard of tolerance. For example, it is possible that, even in the absence of degrading acts or of harm to the participants, the Canadian community will not tolerate certain acts committed in a given context and place, regardless of whether spectators are present or whether they consent. In other words, sexual acts of any nature performed without an audience would de facto fall outside the ambit of the provisions aimed at prohibiting indecency. In our view, indecency cannot be based solely on the exposure of the general public to sexual acts. This outcome is unacceptable.

101 The Canadian community's tolerance for sexual practices must be assessed independently of the presence of spectators. The nature of the principle that is to be applied must not be forgotten. It consists in establishing not what Canadians think is right for themselves, or what the spectators or participants in question think is right for themselves, but what Canadians would not abide other Canadians seeing: *Towne Cinema*, at pp. 508-9. In a situation in which the Canadian community's tolerance for sexual acts must be established, as opposed to the situation in *Mara*, which concerned indecent performances, the principle will necessarily concern what Canadians would not abide other Canadians doing, taking into account the place and general context, of course. Another thing to bear in mind is that it is the standards of the community as a whole that must be considered and not the standards of a small segment of the community: *Towne Cinema*, at p. 508. Consequently, indecency cannot be based solely on the presence of participants or on their views. The contextual approach allows us to take into account the private nature of the place where the acts are carried out. But for sexual practices in places to which the public has access not to be subject to the standard of tolerance because of their allegedly private nature — we are referring here to the ambiguous concept of relatively private places — would be incompatible with a proper interpretation of the standard of tolerance. An

approach that in many situations, like the situation in the instant case, systematically prevents the standard of tolerance from being established and applied must be rejected.

102 Furthermore, the majority's approach poses serious problems in light of the practical consequences that would result from adopting it. To successfully defend against a charge under s. 210(1) Cr. C. in a context in which there are no degrading acts or in which the participants do not suffer serious harm, it would be enough to ensure that the general public is not a spectator, regardless of the number of participants. It would then be difficult to characterize the acts as indecent, as there would be no evidence of harm.

103 In our opinion, the test adopted by the majority introduces a concept of tolerance that does not seem to be justifiable according to any principle whatsoever. This concept cannot be accepted on the pretext that harm is easier to prove or that it is desirable for this type of offence to have the same rationale as the vast majority of other criminal offences, namely the need to protect the community from harm. Social morality, which is inherent in indecency offences and is expressed through the application of the standard of tolerance, must still be allowed to play a role in all situations where it is relevant. Otherwise, the social values that the Canadian community as a whole considers worth protecting would be stripped of any relevance.

104 Furthermore, the existence of harm is not a prerequisite for exercising the state's power to criminalize certain conduct. The existence of fundamental social and ethical considerations is sufficient: see *R. v. Malmo-Levine*, [2003] 3 S.C.R. 571, 2003 SCC 74, at p. 635. There is no principle that supports the harmonization of offences.

105 The philosophical underpinnings of the majority's harm-based approach are found in the liberal theories of J. S. Mill. This philosopher argued that the only purpose for which state power can be rightfully exercised over a member the community is to prevent harm to others: see J. S. Mill, *On Liberty and Considerations on Representative Government*, at p. 8. This court had occasion to address the principle of harm in *Malmo-Levine*. Although that case concerned the constitutional limits on the state's power to legislate in criminal matters, the majority's reasons stressed that the justification for state intervention cannot be reduced to a single factor. There are multiple criteria for justifying state intervention in criminal matters, even if it restricts human liberty: see *Malmo-Levine*, at p. 632. Offences under the *Criminal Code* are thus based on principles and values other than harm. In the case at bar, the offence relates to social morality. To place excessive emphasis on the criterion of harm will therefore make it impossible to give effect to the moral principles in respect of which there is a consensus in the community.

4.3 Conclusion Regarding Indecency

153 In the case at bar, the impugned sexual acts were very explicit acts, and they took place in a commercial establishment that was easily accessible to the general public. This situation caused a certain form of social harm resulting from the failure to meet the minimum standards of public morality. In light of these contextual factors, we are of the opinion that the sexual acts performed in the appellant's establishment clearly offended the Canadian community standard of tolerance and were therefore indecent. Our analysis does not permit us to conclude that the Canadian community would tolerate the performance, in a commercial establishment to which the public has easy access, of group sexual activities on the scale of those that took place in this case. The appellant's establishment is therefore a common bawdy-house within the meaning of s. 210(1) Cr. C.

5. Disposition

154 We would have dismissed the appeal and upheld the appellant's conviction.

Clarity is a noble and commendable goal when our courts review the exercise of massive state power against the individual. Whether this shift away from the community standard test of tolerance applied in *R. v. Butler*, [1992] 1 S.C.R. 452, *R. v. Tremblay*, [1993] 2 S.C.R. 932 and *R. v. Mara*, [1997] 2 S.C.R. 630 to objectively defined harm has achieved or will achieve greater clarity is, however, debatable. The dissenters are clearly not convinced. **Are you?**

Under the community standard of tolerance test, the Supreme Court has previously decided that strippers dancing for men while the men masturbate is not indecent (*Tremblay*), whereas lap dancing in strip clubs is indecent (*Mara*). Presumably these decisions should now be re-litigated under the objective harm criteria. One wonders, too, whether, given the new approach, there is not now an argument that a keeping a common bawdy-house charge can no longer be sustained based on acts of prostitution in private. See Elaine Craig, "Re-interpreting the Criminal Regulation of Sex Work in Light of *Labaye*" (2008) 1 C.C.L.R. 327. The majority in *Labaye* stress that no one paid for the group sex. **But what about the membership fee?**

The emphasis on evidence of objective harm appears, as Lebel J. points out, to be at odds with the court's earlier decision in *R. v. Malmo-Levine*. **Should Parliament intervene?**

4. ROLES AND RESPONSIBILITIES OF JUDGES AND LAWYERS

(a) The Adversary System

The method of inquiry in our courts is quite distinct from the scientific method; the method of ascertaining the facts at common law is known as adversarial while the scientific method might be labelled inquisitorial. The principal distinguishing characteristic between the two methods resides in the relative passivity of the judge in the adversarial method. The judge's function is to make the ultimate finding of facts but not to personally investigate; rather, to judge the merits of two positions. The tradition in the English-speaking world is to regard the "over-speaking 'judge as no well-tuned cymbal'" (Bacon L.C. as quoted by Lord Denning in *Jones v. National Coal Board*, [1957] 2 Q.B. 55 (C.A.) at 64) and should a trial judge intervene too frequently during the trial he or she runs the risk of being reversed on appeal and a new trial ordered. A frank description of our method of inquiry by the Ontario Court of Appeal appears in *Phillips v. Ford Motor Co.* (1971), 18 D.L.R. (3d) 641 (Ont. C.A.) at 657 where Evans J.A. wrote:

> Our mode of trial procedure is based upon the adversarial system in which the contestants seek to establish through relevant supporting evidence, before an impartial trier of facts, those events or happenings which form the bases of their allegations. This procedure assumes that the litigants, assisted by their counsel, will fully and diligently present all the material facts which have evidentiary value in support of their respective positions and that these disputed facts will receive from a trial judge a dispassionate and impartial consideration in order to arrive at the truth of the matters in controversy. A trial is not intended to be a scientific exploration with the presiding judge assuming the role of a research director; it is a forum established for the purpose of providing justice for the litigants. Undoubtedly a court must be concerned with truth, in the sense that it accepts as true certain sworn evidence and rejects other testimony as unworthy of belief, but it cannot embark upon a quest for the "scientific" or "technological" truth when such an adventure does violence to the primary function of the court, which has always been to do justice, according to law.

The adversary method, however, has been justified over the years by many lawyers as capable of promoting the finest approximation to the truth. As Jerome Frank said:

> They think that the best way for the court to discover the facts in a suit is to have each side strive as hard as it can, in a keenly partisan spirit, to bring to the court's attention the evidence favourable to that side. Macauley said that we obtain the fairest decision "when two men argue, as unfairly as possible, on opposite sides" for then "it is certain that no important consideration will altogether escape notice". (*Courts on Trial* (1949) at 80.)

The diligence of the parties in ferreting out evidence favourable to their side and the vigour with which they attack their opponent's case are seen as finer guarantees of approximating the historical truth than giving the problem for resolution to some government official whose motivation can rarely be of the magnitude of the parties. Also, it is believed that the bias of the decision-maker can be minimized if played to a much less active role than is demanded in the inquisitorial method. The judge who conducts the examination of witnesses is seen as "descend[ing] into the arena and is liable to have his vision clouded by the dust of the conflict. Unconsciously he deprives himself of the advantage of calm and dispassionate observation". (Lord Green M.R. in *Yuill v. Yuill*, [1945] 1 All E.R. 183 (C.A.) at 189.)

Whether the adversary method will more closely approximate truth is certainly open to question. The lawyer is trained to seek success for the client, to win the game. The goal is to present the best picture of the client's position and not the most complete picture. Also, the adversary system presupposes for success some equality between the parties and when this is lacking the "truth" becomes too often simply the view of the more powerful. Most judges will confess to the frequent temptation to reach out and "even the match" but the system cautions against such practice. Perhaps most importantly, while it may be true that in deciding between the validity of two competing theories the decision-maker may be considerably aided by advocates on each side presenting their respective position in the strongest arguments possible, it is certainly questionable whether such a technique is valuable in ensuring that all of the available evidence has been presented by the parties for examination. As Professor Peter Brett has noted:

> observe the practice of scientists and historians in carrying out their investigations. . . . [A] lengthy search will fail to reveal one competent practitioner in either discipline who will willingly and in advance confine himself, in deciding any question involving factual data, to a choice between two sets of existing data proffered to him by rival claimants. In short, the inquisitorial method is the one used by every genuine seeker of the truth in every walk of life (not merely scientific and historical investigations) with only one exception . . . the trial system in the common-law world. (Brett, "Legal Decision-Making Bias: A Critique" (1973) 45 U. Col. L. Rev. 1.)

One large impediment to our search for truth is that the facts to be discovered by our courts are almost always past facts. Our method of discovering them is normally through the oral testimony of witnesses who have personal knowledge about what happened. This personal "knowledge" might perhaps better be described as personal beliefs about what they now remember of facts which they believe they observed. The trier of fact then has regard to what the witness says and, based on observations of what the witness said and of the manner of saying it, comes to an opinion as to whether that is an honest belief. One can do no more. One cannot, as the scientist might, duplicate in the laboratory the actual facts and test the hypothesis proposed. Facts as found by the court are really then only guesses about the actual facts. "Subjectivity piled on subjectivity . . . a trial court's finding of fact is, then, at best, its belief or opinion about someone else's belief or opinion." (Jerome Frank, *Courts on Trial* (1949) at 22.) Recently Mr. Justice Haines of the Ontario Supreme Court described it this way:

> A trial is not a faithful reconstruction of the events as if recorded on some giant television screen. It is an historical recall of that part of the events to which witnesses may be found and presented in an intensely adversary system where the object is quantum of proof. Truth may be only incidental. (*R. v. Lalonde* (1972), 15 C.R.N.S. 1, 5 C.C.C (2d) 168 (H.C.) at 4 (C.R.N.S.)

Besides searching for a different truth than the scientist, our methods are circumscribed by other considerations which require our fact-finding to be done in a way which is acceptable to the parties and to society. Our courts provide a forum for the purpose of resolving disputes between parties which they themselves have been unable to resolve in any other way. Our modern form of trial began simply as a substitute for private duels and feuds which had later been dignified by the process of trial by battle. The resolution of the conflict must be done in a way which ensures social tranquillity generally and is also acceptable to the individual parties. The parties should be able to leave the court feeling that they have had their say, that their case has been presented in the best possible light and that they have been judged by an impartial trier. In judging the efficacy of the legal system's method of fact-finding we must remember that:

> A contested law suit is society's last line of defense in the indispensable effort to secure the peaceful settlement of social conflicts — it is a last-ditch process in which something more is at stake than the truth only of the specific matter in contest. There is at stake also that confidence of the public generally in the impartiality and fairness of public settlement and disputes which is essential if the ditch is to be held and the settlements accepted peaceably. . . . While it is important that the court be right . . . a decision must be made now, one way or the other; . . . to require certainty . . . would be impracticable and undesirable. The law thus compromises. (H. Hart & J. McNaughton, *Evidence and Inference in the Law*, D. Lerner, ed. (1958) at 57.)

With these thoughts in mind we might better understand, and even accept, some of the rules and procedures at work in a criminal trial. For additional thoughts along this line see N. Brooks, "The Judge and the Adversary System" in *The Canadian Judiciary*, A. Linden, ed. (1976).

It would be quite misleading to view the criminal justice system as always leading to an adversarial contest at trial. A large percentage of accused plead guilty. Estimates as to the number of accused charged with criminal offences who plead guilty range between 70 and 90 percent. A large number of guilty pleas are reached as a result of a plea bargain where there is an agreement by the accused to plead guilty with a view to some consideration, usually relating to charge or sentence. The agreement may be reached quite formally after protracted discussion or it may involve a hurried hallway discussion. Usually the plea bargain is entered into following a discussion between the Crown Attorney and the defence counsel but sometimes, although less frequently in Canada, the judge is involved. Sometimes the reality is that the plea bargain can be traced to a discussion between the accused and the police without any lawyer being involved. See generally John F. Klein, *Let's Make A Deal* (1976); R.V. Ericson and P.M. Baranek, *The Ordering of Justice: A Study of Persons as Dependants in the Criminal Process* (1982); and A.H. Warner and K.E. Renner, "The Bureaucratic and Adversary Models of the Criminal Courts: The Criminal Sentencing Process", (1981) 1 *Windsor Yearbook of Access to Justice* 81.

STEVE COUGHLAN, "THE 'ADVERSARY SYSTEM': RHETORIC OR REALITY"

(1993) 8 C.J.L.S. 139 at 154-158

In virtually every criminal case, one of the parties will be the Crown prosecutor. What is the role of the prosecutor? The Supreme Court of Canada has said:

It cannot be over-emphasized that the purpose of a criminal prosecution is not to obtain a conviction, it is to lay before a jury what the Crown considers to be credible evidence relevant to what is alleged to be a crime. Counsel have a duty to see that all available legal proof of the facts is presented; it should be done firmly and pressed to its legitimate strength but it must also be done fairly. *The role of prosecutor excludes any notion of winning or losing*: his function is a matter of public duty than which in civil life there can be none charged with greater personal responsibility. It is to be efficiently performed with an ingrained sense of the dignity, the seriousness and the justness of judicial proceedings.[26] [emphasis added]

The court has also referred to the "fundamental difference in the respective roles of the prosecution and the defence," stating that "the tradition of Crown counsel in this country carrying out their role as 'ministers of justice' and not as adversaries has generally been very high."[27]

Similarly, the Canadian Bar Association Code of Professional Conduct says:

When engaged as a prosecutor, the lawyer's prime duty is not to seek a conviction, but to present before the trial court all available credible evidence relevant to the alleged crime in order that justice may be done through a fair trial upon the merits. The prosecutor exercises a public function involving much discretion and power, and must act fairly and dispassionately.[28]

These authorities do not attach restrictions to the adversarial ways in which a prosecutor may behave: they say that the prosecutor's role is not adversarial. The Crown and defence attorneys in a criminal trial do not occupy equal and opposite positions, as the adversary system would require — Crown counsel is not there as an adversary. How, one must ask, can one have an adversary system with only one adversary?

Most lawyers know prosecutors who clearly do not regard their role in this way: some prosecutors seem to regard themselves as advocates for the police, and are for example unwilling to exercise their own discretion to drop charges.[29] Problems have also been noted owing to Crown prosecutors failing to provide adequate disclosure to the defence.[30] But to the extent that this is true, these Crown prosecutors are failing to perform their jobs properly. Further, this failure illustrates precisely the difficulty in adopting the rhetoric of adversarialism: if prosecutors believe they are adversaries in a competitive activity, we cannot be surprised if they try to win.

---

26 G.R. Williams, *Legal Negotiation and Settlement* (St. Paul, Mn: West Publishing, 1983) also notes that it is difficult for even the most competent negotiator to reach a reasonable settlement if she is not also a competent trial lawyer: in judging the strength of her case, she is required to take into account her own weakness in court.

27 *R. v. Stinchcombe* (1991), 8 C.R. (4th) 277 (S.C.C.) at 283-289.

28 Canadian Bar Association, *Code of Professional Conduct*, (Ottawa: Canadian Bar Association, 1987) commentary 9 to rule IX.

29 See, for example, H. Lilles, "Some Problems in the Administration of Justice in Remote and Isolated Communities" (1990) 15 Queens' L.J. 327 at 340, suggesting that Crown attorneys in the Yukon and Northwest Territories "appear to be reluctant to exercise any significant prosecutorial discretion".

30 See, in particular, *Report of the Commission of Inquiry into the Prosecution of Donald Marshall, Jr.* (Halifax: 1989), finding 1, 4; and *R. v. Stinchcombe, supra* note [27].

One might suggest that the adversary system functions differently in civil and criminal matters, and so the non-adversarial role of Crown counsel is not sufficient to prove that criminal cases are not adversarial. But consider also the role of defence counsel.

One study found, for example, that in 80% of cases where bail was in issue, no hearing took place: 65% of accused were released without formality, and 15% remained in custody.[31] In the remaining 20% of cases, where a bail hearing was held, the accused was released half the time. This means that in two-thirds of all cases, the accused was released on bail because of an agreement between Crown and defence, while only 10% of the time did the defence get the accused released by adversarial means. That is, defence counsel negotiated the release of six clients for every one released through adversarial means.

Similarly, other studies have found that for every charge that results in an acquittal, approximately four charges are stayed or withdrawn without trial.[32] One cannot simply infer from these figures that defence counsel were four times as successful in having clients released through negotiation;[33] it seems, however, a reasonable inference that this strategy must be at least as successful as going to trial.[34]

Of course, one cannot simply say that these results depended solely on the strategy of defence counsel. In most cases it will be obvious to trained counsel whether a particular accused is likely to be released on bail, for example, and if so on what types of conditions. In those cases, defense counsel and prosecutors who reach an agreement are only making use of their expertise. In fact, it is the metasystem, not the system, that is operating. It is not necessary to invoke the rules of the adversary system, or adversary behavior in the broad sense, to explain how these decisions, the majority, are reached. In a system that expects these types of agreements to be reached, excessive adversarial behavior is out of place.[35]

---

31 E. MacKaay, *The Paths of Justice: A Study of the Operation of Criminal Courts in Montreal* (Montreal: Groupe de recherché en jurimétrie, 1976) at 36.

32 See Canada, Policy, Programs and Research Branch, Research and Statistics Section, Department of Justice, *Some Statistics on the Preliminary Inquiry in Canada* (Ottawa: Department of Justice, 1984) at 33, which found that 25% of the charges in the study were stayed or withdrawn, compared to a 6% acquittal rate. See also Canadian Centre for Justice Statistics, "Processing Time in Youth Courts, 1986-87 to 1989-90" 11:4 Juristat 1 at 11, which shows the number of charges stayed or withdrawn in the four years studied ranging from 20.9% to 24.0%, while the number of dismissals or finding of not guilty range from 5.3% to 5.7%.

33 Charges may have been stayed with the intention of relaying them at a later time, for example.

34 A similar example, though one where the benefit to the accused is less obvious, concerns preliminary inquiries. In principle, one would expect lawyers who are trying "to save that client by all means and expedients" (see note 5) [of the original article] routinely to try to use preliminary inquiries as a way of having their client not face trial. In fact, 52% of the time an accused is committed for trial at the preliminary by consent, and a further 40% of the time the defence consents to the admission of some of the Crown's evidence. Only 6% of the time is a preliminary inquiry fully contested. See *Some Statistics on the Preliminary Inquiry in Canada, supra* note [32] at 24-27.

35 But see the discussion below, under "Some Defences of Adversarialism Rejected," for the ethical implications of this observation.

Consider other things a partisan defence counsel will do for a client. If the client is a young offender, alternative measures may be available, provided that the prosecutor believes it is appropriate to use them. Producing that opinion in a prosecutor requires consensus-building and co-operation: a prosecutor must be persuaded, not forced, to recommend alternative measures. The same is true of plea bargaining: the prosecutor cannot be forced to agree. Only a bargain that both parties can accept will be successful — in effect, the win/win model of commercial negotiations, though the "winning" on the part of the accused is a limitation of loss.[36] Indeed, one empirical study of the plea-bargaining process has argued that the prosecutor and defence lawyer generally reach "an agreement that merely reflects the going rate":[37] once again, the meta-system.

Further, a great percentage of criminal charges concern minor offences — shoplifting and similar small-scale property offences.[38] The great majority of these criminal charges result in a finding of guilty, generally by way of guilty plea.[39] Accordingly, one of the most common tasks for many defence counsel is to speak to sentence on a minor matter.[40] Particularly if Crown counsel's role is limited to noting that the facts are unexceptional and that a penalty in the normal range is called for, it is difficult for any defence counsel, try as she might, to be very adversarial.

That is not to say that defence counsel will not zealously act in the interests of her client. Competent defence counsel will call witnesses on sentencing where appropriate, take steps in advance to have the accused enter a treatment program or pay restitution, and argue strongly for the most lenient sentence appropriate. But doing these things is not what we would describe in any other circumstances as adversarial. Counsel is being partisan, and is taking steps to assist the accused; but seeing to it that the accused receives counseling and a psychiatric evaluation is not acting as an adversary.

On the whole, the role of criminal lawyers involves more non-adversarial than adversarial functions. Certainly there are times when counsel will behave adversarially, but non-adversarial roles dominate the criminal lawyer's time.

---

36 But see the Canadian Bar Association *Code of Professional Conduct*, *supra* note [28], commentary 12 to rule IX, allows plea bargaining only where the client is prepared to admit guilt, and so some sentence is inevitable.

37 R.V. Ericson & P.M. Baranek, *The Ordering of Justice: A Study of Accused Persons as Dependants in the Criminal Process* (Toronto: Toronto University Press, 1982) at 117. This study is discussed at greater length below, under "Some Defences of Adversarialism Rejected".

38 Canadian Centre for Justice Statistics, "Preliminary Crime Statistics – 1989" 10:9 Juristat at 2 indicates that, in 1989, approximately 90% of *Criminal Code* offences reported by the police were property crime (59.5%, the majority of which was theft under $1,000) or other crime – "i.e., mischief, disturbing the peace, bail violations" (30.3%).

39 *Some Statistics on the Preliminary Inquiry in Canada*, *supra* note [32] at 66-67 indicates that, in provincial court, a "not guilty" plea is entered only 18% of the time.

40 One cannot make direct inferences about the tasks counsel perform from the statistics on crime. Some counsel restrict themselves to more serious cases. More importantly, the less serious the offence, the less likely it is that an accused person will have counsel: many guilty pleas to minor offences will be entered by the accused personally. Nonetheless, particularly given the existence of legal aid schemes, it seems reasonable to expect a general correlation between the crime statistics and the role of counsel.

See further David Paciocco, "Understanding the Accusatorial System" (2010) 14 Can. Crim. L. Rev. 307.

Is the adversary system and the criminal-law precept that the State must prove guilt beyond reasonable doubt compatible with values of women and Aboriginal people? In arriving at your opinion consider the following views:

CARRIE MENKEL-MEADOW, PORTIA IN A DIFFERENT VOICE: SPECULATION ON A WOMEN'S LAWYERING PROCESS

(1985) 1 Berkeley Women's L.J. 39 at 44-55

In her book, *In a Different Voice: Psychological Theory and Women's Development*, Gilligan observes that much of what has been written about human psychological development has been based on studies of male subjects exclusively. As a consequence, girls and women have either not been described, or they are said to have "failed" to develop on measurement scales based on male norms. Just as Gilligan has observed that studies of human psychological development have been centred on males, feminists have observed the law to be based on male values and behaviours. As Frances Olsen notes:

> Law is supposed to be rational, objective, abstract and principled, like men; it is not supposed to be irrational, subjective, contextualized or personalized like women. The social, political and intellectual practices that constitute "law" were for many years carried out almost exclusively by men. Given that women were long excluded from the practice of law, it should not be surprising that the traits associated with women are not greatly valued by law. Moreover, in a kind of vicious cycle, the "maleness" of law was used as a justification for excluding women from practicing law. While the number of women in law has been rapidly increasing, the field continues to be heavily male dominated.

The male-derived model of moral reasoning and psychological development described by Gilligan values hierarchical thinking based on the logic of reasoning from abstract, universal principles. Gilligan measures her findings against the work of her colleague, Lawrence Kohlberg. His theory of moral development comprised of six "universal" stages is based on a study of 84 *boys* from childhood through adulthood. Gilligan explains that when Kohlberg's model is applied to women, they tend to score at a stage three, a stage characterized by seeing morality as a question of interpersonal relations and caring for and pleasing others. In looking at moral judgments and hearing the "women's voice," Gilligan discovered that:

> When one begins with the study of women and derives developmental constructs from their lives, the outline of a moral conception different from that described by Freud, Piaget, or Kohlberg begins to emerge and informs a different description of development. In this conception, the moral problem arises from conflicting responsibilities rather than from competing rights and requires for its resolution a mode of thinking that is contextual and narrative rather than formal and abstract.

An example drawn from Gilligan's work best illustrates the duality of girls' and boys' moral development. In one of the three studies on which her book is based, a group of children are asked to solve Heinz's dilemma, a hypothetical moral reasoning problem used by Kohlberg to rate moral development on his six-stage scale. The dilemma is that Heinz's wife is dying of cancer and requires a drug which the local pharmacist has priced beyond's Heinz's means. The question is posed: should Heinz steal the drug?

To illustrate and explain the differences between the ways boys and girls approached this problem, Gilligan quotes from two members of her sample, Jake and Amy. Jake, an 11-year-old boy, sees the problem as one of "balancing rights," like a judge who must make a decision or a mathematician who must solve an algebraic equation. Life is worth more than property, therefore Heinz should steal the drug. For Amy, an 11-year-old girl, the problem is different. Like a "bad" law student she "fights the hypo"; she wants to know more facts: Have Heinz and the druggist explored other possibilities, like a loan or credit transaction? Why couldn't Heinz and the druggist simply sit down and talk it out so that the druggist would come to see the importance of Heinz's wife's life? In Gilligan's terms, Jake explores the Heinz dilemma with "the logic of justice" while Amy uses the "ethic of care." Amy scores lower on the Kohlberg scale because she sees the problem rooted in the persons involved rather than in the larger universal issues posed by the dilemma.

In conventional terms Jake would make a good lawyer because he spots the legal issues of excuse and justification, balances the rights, and reaches a decision, while considering implicitly, if not explicitly, the precedential effect of his decision. But as Gilligan argues, and as I develop more fully below, Amy's approach is also plausible and legitimate, both as a style of moral reasoning and as a style of lawyering. Amy seeks to keep the people engaged; she holds the needs of the parties and their relationships constant and hopes to satisfy them all (as in a negotiation), rather than selecting a winner (as in a lawsuit). If one must be hurt, she attempts to find a resolution that will hurt least the one who can least bear the hurt. (Is she engaged in a "deep pocket" policy analysis?) She looks beyond the "immediate lawsuit" to see how the "judgment" will affect the parties. If Heinz steals the drug and goes to jail, who will take care of his wife? Furthermore, Amy is concerned with *how* the dilemma is resolved; the process by which the parties communicate may be crucial to the outcome. (Amy cares as much about procedure as about substance.) And she is being a good lawyer when she inquires whether all the facts have been discovered and considered.

The point here is not that Amy's method of moral reasoning is better than Jake's, nor that she is a better lawyer than Jake. (Some have read Gilligan to argue that the women's voice is better. I don't read her that way.) The point is that Amy does some things differently from Jake when she resolves this dilemma, and these things have useful analogies to lawyering and may not have been sufficiently credited as useful lawyering skills. Jake and Amy have something to learn from one another.

Thus, although a "choice of rights" conception (life v. property) of solving human problems may be important, it is not the only or the best way. Responsibilities to self and to others may be equally important in measuring moral, as well as legal decision making, but have thus far been largely ignored. For example, a lawyer who feels responsible for the decisions she makes with her client may be more inclined to think about how those decisions will hurt other people and how the lawyer and client feel about making such decisions. (Amy thinks about Heinz, the druggist, and Heinz's wife at all times in reaching her decision; Jake makes a choice in abstract terms without worrying as much about the people it affects.)

. . . .

III. THE ADVOCACY-ADVERSARIAL MODEL

The basic structure of our legal system is premised on the adversarial model, which involves two advocates who present their cases to a disinterested third party who listens to evidence and argument and declares one party a winner. In this simplified description of the Anglo-American model of litigation, we can identify some of the basic concepts and values which underlie this choice of arrangements: advocacy, persuasion, hierarchy, competition, and binary results (win/lose). The conduct of litigation is relatively similar (not coincidentally, I suspect) to a sporting event — there are rules, a referee, an object to the game, and a winner is declared after the play is over. As I have argued elsewhere, this conception of the dispute resolution process is applied more broadly than just in the conventional courtroom. The adversarial model affects the way in which lawyers advise their clients ("get as much as you can"), negotiate disputes ("we can really get them on that") and plan transactions ("let's be sure to draft this to your advantage"). All of these activities in lawyering assume competition over the same limited and equally valued items (usually money) and assume that success is measured by maximizing individual gain. Would Gilligan's Amy create a different model?

By returning to Heinz's dilemma we see some hints about what Amy might do. Instead of concluding that a choice must be made between life and property, in resolving the conflict between parties as Jake does, Amy sees no need to hierarchically order the claims. Instead, she tries to account for all the parties' needs, and searches for a way to find a solution that satisfies the needs of both. In her view, Heinz should be able to obtain the drug for his wife and the pharmacist should still receive payment. So Amy suggests a loan, credit arrangement, or a discussion of other ways to structure the transaction. In short, she won't play by the adversarial rules. She searches outside the system for a way to solve the problem, trying to keep both parties in mind. Her methods substantiate Gilligan's observations that women will try to change the rules to preserve the relationships.

Furthermore, in addition to looking for more substantive solutions to the problem (i.e., not accepting the binary win/lose conception of the problem), Amy also wants to change the process. Amy sees no reason why she must act as a neutral arbiter of a dispute and make a decision based only on the information she has. She "belie[ves] in communication as the mode of conflict resolution and [is convinced] that the solution to the dilemma will follow from its compelling representation...." If the parties talk directly to each other, they will be more likely to appreciate the importance of each other's needs. Thus, she believes direct communication, rather than third party mediated debate, might solve the problem, recognizing that two apparently conflicting positions can both be simultaneously legitimate, and there need not be a single victor.

The notion that women might have more difficulty with full-commitment-to-one-side model of the adversary system is graphically illustrated by Hilary, one of the women lawyers in Gilligan's study. This lawyer finds herself in one of the classic moral dilemmas of the adversary system: she sees that her opponent has failed to make use of a document that is helpful to his case and harmful to hers. In deciding not to tell him about the document because of what she sees as her "professional vunerability" in the male adversary system, she concludes that "the adversary system of justice impedes not only the supposed search for truth (the conventional criticism), but also *the expression of concern for the person on the other side.*" Gilligan describes Hilary's tension between her concept of rights (learned through legal training) and her female ethic of care as a sign of her socialization in the male world of lawyering. Thus, the advocacy model, with its commitment to one-side advocacy, seems somehow contrary to "apprehending the reality of the other" which lawyers like Hilary experience. Even the continental inquisitorial model, frequently offered as an alternative to the adversarial model, includes most of these elements of the male system — hierarchy, advocacy, competition and binary results.

So what kind of legal system would Amy and Hilary create if left to their own devices? They might look for ways to alter the harshness of win/lose results; they might alter the rules of the game (or make it less like a game); and they might alter the very structures and forms themselves. Thus, in a sense Amy and Hilary's approach can already be found in some of the current alternatives to the adversary model such as mediation. Much of the current interest in alternative dispute resolution is an attempt to modify the harshness of the adversarial process and expand the kinds of solutions available, in order to respond the better to the varied needs of the parties. Amy's desire to engage the parties in direct communication with each other is reflected in mediation models where the parties talk directly to each other and forge their own solutions. The work of Gilligan and Noddings, demonstrating an ethic of care and a heightened sense of empathy in women, suggests that women lawyers may be particularly interested in mediation as an alternative to litigation as a method of resolving disputes.

Even within the present adversarial model, Amy and Hilary might, in their concern for others, want to provide for a broader conception of interested parties, permitting participation by those who might be affected by the dispute (an ethic of inclusion). In addition, like judges who increasingly are managing more of the details of their cases, Amy and Hilary might seek a more active role in settlement processes and rely less on court-ordered relief. Amy and Hilary might look for other ways to construct their lawsuits and remedies in much the same ways as courts of equity mitigated the harshness of the law court's very limited array of remedies by expanding the conception of what was possible.

The process and rules of the adversary system itself might look different if there were more female voices in the legal profession. If Amy is less likely than Jake to make assertive, rights-based statements, is she less likely to adapt to the male-created advocacy mode? In my experience as a trial lawyer, I observed that some women had difficulty with the "macho" ethic of the courtroom battle. Even those who did successfully adapt to the male model often confronted a dilemma because women were less likely to be perceived as behaving properly when engaged in strong adversarial conduct. It is important to be "strong" in the courtroom, according to the stereotypic conception of appropriate trial behavior. The woman who conforms to the female stereotype by being "soft" or "weak" is a bad trial lawyer, but if a woman is "tough" or "strong" in the courtroom, she is seen as acting inappropriately for a woman. Note, however, that this stereotyping is contextual: the same woman acting as a "strong" or "tough" mother with difficult children would be praised for that conduct. Women's strength is approved of with the proviso that it be exerted in appropriately female spheres.

Amy and Hilary might create a different form of advocacy, one resembling a "conversation" with the fact finder, relying on the creation of a relationship with the jury for its effectiveness, rather than on persuasive intimidation. There is some anecdotal evidence that this is happening already. Recently, several women prosecutors described their styles of trial advocacy as the creation of a personal relationship with the jury in which they urge jurors to examine their own perceptions and values and encourage them to think for themselves, rather than "buying" the arguments of one of the advocates. This is a conception of the relationship between the lawyer and the fact-finder which is based on trust and mutual respect rather than on dramatics, intimidation and power, the male mode in which these women had been trained and which they found unsatisfactory.

In sum, the growing strength of women's voice in the legal profession may change the adversarial system into a more cooperative, less war-like system of communication between disputants in which solutions are mutually agreed upon rather than dictated by an outsider, won by the victor, and imposed upon the loser. Some seeds of change may already be found in existing alternatives to the litigation model, such as mediation. It remains to be seen what further changes Portia's voice may make.

Compare D.L. Rhode, "The Woman's Point of View" (1988) 38 J. Leg. Ed. 39.

MADAM JUSTICE BERTHA WILSON, WILL WOMEN JUDGES REALLY MAKE A DIFFERENCE?

(1990) 28 Osgoode Hall L.J. 507

. . . .

In the literature which is required reading for every newly appointed judge, it is repeatedly stated that judges must be both independent and impartial, that these qualities are basic to the proper administration of justice and fundamental to the legitimacy of the judicial role. The judge must not approach his or her task with preconceived notions about law or policy, with personal prejudice against parties or issues, or with bias toward a particular outcome of a case. Socrates defined the essential qualities of a judge in the following manner: "Four things belong to a judge: to hear courteously, to answer wisely, to consider soberly, and to decide impartially."

. . . .

Many have criticized as totally unreal the concept that judges are somehow superhuman, neutral, above politics and unbiased, and are able to completely separate themselves from their personal opinions and predispositions when exercising their judicial function.

. . . .

Judge Rosalie Abella (Chair of the Ontario Law Reform Commission) also doubts that judicial impartiality is a realistic requirement. In her article "The Dynamic Nature of Equality," she emphasizes that "[e]very decisionmaker who walks into a courtroom to hear a case is armed not only with the relevant legal texts, but with a set of values, experiences and assumptions that are thoroughly embedded."

. . . .

But what has all this got to do with the subject: "Will women judges really make a difference?" It has a great deal to do with it, and whether you agree or not will probably depend on your perception of the degree to which the existing law reflects the judicial neutrality or impartiality we have been discussing. If the existing law can be viewed as the product of judicial neutrality or impartiality, even although the judiciary has been very substantially male, then you may conclude that the advent of increased numbers of women judges should make no difference, assuming, that is, that these women judges will bring to bear the same neutrality and impartiality. However, if you conclude that the existing law, in some areas at least, cannot be viewed as the product of judicial neutrality, then your answer may be very different.

. . . .

Taking from my own experience as a judge of 14 years' standing, working closely with my male colleagues on the bench, there are probably whole areas of the law on which there is no uniquely feminine perspective. This is not to say that the development of the law in these areas has not been influenced by the fact that lawyers and judges have all been men. Rather, the principles and the underlying premises are so firmly entrenched and so fundamentally sound that no good would be achieved by attempting to re-invent the wheel, even if the revised version did have a few more spokes in it. I have in mind areas such as the law of contract, the law of real property, and the law applicable to corporations. In some other areas of the law, however, a distinctly male perspective is clearly discernible. It has resulted in legal principles that are not fundamentally sound and that should be revisited when the opportunity presents itself. Canadian feminist scholarship has done an excellent job of identifying those areas and making suggestions for reform. Some aspects of the criminal law in particular cry out for change; they are based on presuppositions about the nature of women and women's sexuality that, in this day and age, are little short of ludicrous.

But how do we handle the problem that women judges, just as much as their male counterparts, are subject to the duty of impartiality? As was said at the outset, judges must not approach their task with preconceived notions about law and policy. They must approach it with detachment and, as Lord MacMillan said, purge their minds "not only of partiality to persons, but of partiality to arguments." Does this then foreclose any kind of "judicial affirmative action" to counteract the influence of the dominant male perspective of the past and establish judicial neutrality through a countervailing female perspective? Is Karen Selick, writing recently in the *Lawyers Weekly*, correct when she argues that offsetting male bias with female bias would only be compounding the injustice? Does the nature of the judicial process itself present an insuperable hurdle so that the legislatures rather than the courts must be looked to for any significant legal change?

In part this may be so. Certainly, the Legislature is the more effective instrument for rapid or radical change. But there is no reason why the judiciary cannot exercise some modest degree of creativity in areas where modern insights and life's experience have indicated that the law has gone awry. However, and this is extremely important, it will be a Pyrrhic victory for women and for the justice system as a whole if changes in the law come only through the efforts of women lawyers and women judges. The Americans were smart to realize that courses and workshops on gender bias for judges, male and female, are an essential follow-up to scholarly research and learned writing. In Canada, we are just beginning to touch the fringes.

. . . .

I return, then, to the question of whether the appointment of more women judges will make a difference. Because the entry of women into the judiciary is so recent, few studies have been done on the subject. Current statistics show that just over 9 percent of federally appointed judges are women; it is reasonable to assume that more women will be appointed to the Bench as more women become licensed to practise law. Will this growing number of women judges by itself make a difference?

The expectation is that it will, that the mere presence of women on the bench will make a difference. In her article "The Gender of Judges," Suzanna Sherry (an Associate Law Professor at the University of Minnesota) suggests that the mere fact that women are judges serves an educative function; it helps to shatter stereotypes about the role of women in society that are held by male judges and lawyers, as well as by litigants, jurors, and witnesses.

Judge Gladys Kessler (former President of the National Association of Women Judges in the United States) defends the search for competent women appointees to the bench. She says: "But the ultimate justification for deliberately seeking judges of both sexes and all colors and backgrounds is to keep the public's trust. The public must perceive its judges as fair, impartial and representative of the diversity of those who are being judged." Justice Wald has expressed similar sentiments. She believes that women judges are indispensable to the public's confidence in the ability of the courts to respond to the legal problems of all classes of citizens.

. . . .

Some feminist writers are persuaded that the appointment of more women judges will have an impact on the process of judicial decision-making itself and on the development of the substantive law. As was mentioned earlier, this flows from the belief that women view the world and what goes on in it from a different perspective from men. Some define the difference in perspective solely in terms that women do not accept male perceptions and interpretations of events as the norm or as objective reality. Carol Gilligan (a Professor of Education at Harvard University) sees the difference as going much deeper than that. In her view, women think differently from men, particularly in responding to moral dilemmas. They have, she says, different ways of thinking about themselves and their relationships to others.

. . . .

Gilligan's work on conceptions of morality among adults suggests that women's ethical sense is significantly different from men's. Men see moral problems as arising from competing rights; the adversarial process comes easily to them. Women see moral problems as arising from competing obligations, the one to the other; the important thing is to preserve relationships, to develop an ethic of caring. The goal, according to women's ethical sense, is not seen in terms of winning or losing but, rather, in terms of achieving an optimum outcome for all individuals involved in the moral dilemma. It is not difficult to see how this contrast in thinking might form the basis of different perceptions of justice.

There is merit in Gilligan's analysis. In part, it may explain the traditional reluctance of courts to get too deeply into the circumstances of a case, their anxiety to reduce the context of the dispute to its bare bones through a complex system of exclusionary evidentiary rules. This is one of the characteristic features of the adversarial process. We are all familiar with the witness on cross-examination who wants to explain his or her answer, who feels that a simple yes or no is not an adequate response, and who is frustrated and angry at being cut off with a half-truth. It is so much easier to come up with a black and white answer if you are unencumbered by a broader context which might prompt you, in Lord MacMillan's words, to temper the cold light of reason with the warmer tints of imagination and sympathy.

. . . .

Professor Patricia Cain, in her article "Good and Bad Bias: A Comment on Feminist Theory and Judging," says:

> What we want, it seems to me, are lawyers who can tell their clients' story, lawyers who can help judges to see the parties as human beings, and who can help remove the separation between judge and litigant. And, then, what we want from our judges is a special ability to listen with connection before engaging in the separation that accompanies judgment.

Obviously, this is not an easy role for the judge — to enter into the skin of the litigant and make his or her experience part of your experience and only when you have done that, to judge. But we have to do it; or at least make an earnest attempt to do it. Whether the criticism of the justice system comes to us through Royal Commissions, through the media, or just through our own personal friends, we cannot escape the conclusion that, in some respects, our existing system of justice has been found wanting. And as Mr. Justice Rothman says, the time to do something about it is *now*.

One of the important conclusions emerging from the Council of Europe's Seminar on Equality between Men and Women held in Strasbourg last November is that the universalist doctrine of human rights must include a realistic concept of masculine and feminine humanity regarded as a whole, that humankind *is* dual and must be represented in its dual form if the trap of an asexual abstraction in which *human being* is always declined in the masculine is to be avoided. If women lawyers and women judges through their differing perspectives on life can bring a new humanity to bear on the decision-making process, perhaps they *will* make a difference. Perhaps they will succeed in infusing the law with an understanding of what it means to be fully human.

ABORIGINAL PEOPLES AND CRIMINAL JUSTICE

Law Reform Commission of Canada, Report No. 34: (1991), 5-7

The Aboriginal Perspective on Criminal Justice

Aboriginal communities number in the several hundreds and each has had a distinctive experience of the Canadian criminal justice system. Given this diversity, there is necessarily some oversimplification in the following general description of Aboriginal perceptions and aspirations. Nevertheless, we have been struck by the remarkably uniform picture of the system that has been drawn by Aboriginal speakers and writers.

I.   Aboriginal Perceptions

From the Aboriginal perspective, the criminal justice system is an alien one, imposed by the dominant white society. Wherever they turn or are shuttled throughout the system, Aboriginal offenders, victims or witnesses encounter a sea of white faces. Not surprisingly, they regard the system as deeply insensitive to their traditions and values: many view it as unremittingly racist.

Abuse of power and the distorted exercise of discretion are identified time and again as principal defects of the system. The police are often seen by Aboriginal people as a foreign, military presence descending on communities to wreak havoc and take people away. Far from being a source of stability and security, the force is feared by them even when its services are necessary to restore a modicum of social peace to the community.

For those living in remote and reserve communities, the entire court apparatus, quite literally, appears to descend from the sky — an impression that serves to magnify their feelings of isolation and erects barriers to their attaining an understanding of the system.

The process is in reality incomprehensible to those who speak only Aboriginal languages, especially where little or no effort is made to provide adequate interpretation services. Even the English- or French-speaking inhabitants of these communities find the language of the courts and lawyers difficult to understand. Understanding is more than a problem of mere language. Aboriginal persons contend that virtually all of the primary actors in the process (police, lawyers, judges, correctional personnel) patronize them and consistently fail to explain adequately what the process requires of them or what is going to happen to them. Even those who are prepared to acknowledge certain well-intentioned aspects of the present system nevertheless conclude that the system has utterly failed.

Such efforts as have been made to involve the community in the administration of justice are seen as puny and insignificant, and there is little optimism about the future. Elders see the community's young people as the primary victims of the system — cut adrift by it and removed from the community's support as well as from its spiritual and cultural traditions. They recount experiences of children taken from their communities at an early age who later emerge, hardened from the court and correctional processes and ultimately beyond the reach of even imaginative initiatives designed to promote rehabilitation.

Evident and understandable weariness and frustration attend any discussion of approaches to fixing the system or setting it right. For Aboriginal persons, the system presents an unending course of barriers and obstacles, with no avenues of effective complaint or redress. Their sense of injustice is bottomless. They have little or no confidence in the legal profession or in the judiciary to bring about justice or to effect a just resolution of any particular dispute in which they are involved. If the truth be told, most have given up on the criminal justice system.

II. Aboriginal Aspirations

Aboriginal people have a vision of a justice system that is sensitive to their customs, traditions and beliefs. This vision is a natural outgrowth of their aspirations to self-government and sovereignty. They desire a criminal justice system that is Aboriginal-designed, -run and -populated, from top to bottom.

Undoubtedly there are many contrasting visions as to what constitutes an Aboriginal justice system, but fundamental is the belief that the system must be faithful to Aboriginal traditions and cultural values, while adapting them to modern society. Hence, a formal Aboriginal justice system would evince appropriate respect for community Elders and leaders, give heed to the requirements of Aboriginal spirituality and pay homage to the relation of humankind to the land and to nature.

The Aboriginal vision of justice gives pre-eminence to the interests of the collectivity, its overall orientation being holistic and integrative. Thus, it is community-based, stressing mediation and conciliation while seeking an acknowledgment of responsibility from those who transgress the norms of their society. While working toward a reconciliation between the offender and the victim, an Aboriginal justice system would pursue the larger objective of reintegrating the offender into the community as a whole.

The Aboriginal vision challenges both common and civil law concepts. Statute law becomes less important. Within an Aboriginal justice system, laws would not be uniform or homogeneous; they would vary from community to community, depending on customary practices. Customary law would be the binding force promoting harmony within the community.

While possessing common general characteristics, an Aboriginal justice system would of necessity be pluralistic. What such a system would actually look like is unclear. This haziness is a source of frustration. Much essential detail is missing, and Aboriginal people are hesitant to provide that detail, not because they are incapable of providing it — some communities have well-developed and well-articulated models — but because, in their view, they should not have to do so. They aspire to local control. Their contention is essentially: "Give us the keys. Let us control the system. We can hardly do worse than you have."

For accounts of one judge's struggle to deal with cultural diversity in the Yukon Territory, see H. Lilles, "Some Problems in the Administration of Justice in Remote and Isolated Communities" (1990) 15 Queen's L.J. 327 and "A Plea for More Human Values in Our Justice System" (1992) 17 Queen's L.J. 328.

RUPERT ROSS, DANCING WITH A GHOST

Exploring Indian Reality
(Octopus Publishing, 1992), 41-46

[Rupert Ross was an assistant Crown Attorney for the District of Kenora, Ontario, where he worked closely with the Ojibway and Cree peoples to make the court system more responsive to the needs of their communities.]

. . . .

Gradually, though, I began to see and hear things which made me suspect that there might exist a whole range of different explanations where Native people are concerned. One young victim of a rape refused to testify because, as she put it, "It's not right to do this after so much time. He should be finished with it now and getting on with his life." She was 16 years old.

Another woman, the victim of a violent assault by her dangerous nephew, went over her evidence with me in great detail just before court. She insisted (uncharacteristically, I should add) that I do whatever I could to send this uncontrollably violent young man out of the community for as long as possible so that she and her children could live in peace. When she took the witness stand minutes later, however, her refusal to say anything at all about the attack led to his acquittal.

In another case, after a lengthy review of her evidence, the victim, a 15-year-old who had been sexually assaulted by her former boyfriend, told me she thought she could repeat her story in court. As we walked into the courtroom, though, she tugged at my sleeve and asked, "Should I say these things in court? Is it right?"

"Is it right?" That was a dumbfounding question for me. I knew of many significant reasons which made it difficult for people to testify, but it had never occurred to me that in their eyes it might not be the *right* thing to do. I had always assumed that even the most frightened and reluctant witness shared my conviction that testifying was what they should do, even if competing concerns made it impossible for them to go through with it.

What, I asked myself, if we are wrong in that assumption when we deal with Native people? Could they actually believe that coming forward in this fashion was an improper thing to do? If that was the case, then factors such as fear or embarrassment only reinforced the basic disinclination.

It was not until 1986, at a conference in Whitehorse dealing with Native justice issues, that I began to see a little further into the dynamics of such reluctance. It was commonly agreed by the conference participants that Native people, with their belief in consensus decision-making, might find our adversarial system foreign and inappropriate. To explore alternate forms of dealing with social disruption we play-acted a more informal mediation process. In this exercise we devised a scenario in which a youth had broken into the community store and vandalized it. We selected some volunteers from the audience to act as the boy, the store manager and the mediation panel. That panel then asked them both about the break-in, the value of the damage, about how they felt towards each other, and about what could be done to set matters straight between them. It seemed a sensible alternative approach.

One of the mediators, however, was Charlie Fisher, whom I mentioned in Chapter 1. He was asked if such a technique bore any resemblance to what might have been done at Whitedog in more traditional times. His response was a very vehement "no". He then volunteered to make the appropriate changes.

He began by getting rid of the chairs and tables, everyone sat on the floor in a circle, as equals. He then asked for two other people to act as "Representing Elders", one each for the boy and the store manager. As he continued, it became clear that our little experiment in non-adversarial mediation was flawed in virtually every respect. In Charlie's version, the boy and the store manager never spoke in the presence of the panel of Elders. There was no discussion whatever about the break-in, the damage, the feelings of the disputants, or what might be done to set matters straight. There was no *talk* of compensation or restitution, much less the actual imposition of such measures.

Once we understood what was *not* going to take place, we had only one question left: "Why, then, is there a panel at all?"

Charlie Fisher tried to answer us in this way. The duty of each Representing Elder, he explained, was not to speak for the young man or the store manager, but to counsel them in private. That counselling was intended to help each person "rid himself of his bad feelings". Such counselling would continue until the Elder was satisfied that "the person's spirit had been cleansed and made whole again". When the panel convened, an Elder could signify that such cleansing had taken place by touching the ceremonial pipe. The panel would continue to meet until both Elders so signified. At that point, the pipe would be lit and passed to all. As far as the community was concerned, that would be the end of the matter. Whether the two disputants later arranged recompense of some sort was entirely up to them. Passing the pipe signified, as Charlie phrased it, that each had been "restored to the community and to himself".

What was going on here? No fact finding? No allocation of responsibility? No imposition of consequences? Weren't these the very things our courts were created to do? Why didn't the Whitedog people do them in traditional times?

. . . .

I suggest that we must react differently than we have in the past when we find ourselves puzzled by something a Native person has done or, more importantly, when we are about to come to a negative conclusion about it. Rather than assuming that their behaviour stems from principles similar to ours, and then judging that behaviour badly because it does not conform to our own typical behaviour, we must realize that their behaviour is different because it flows from different basic principles. We are not seeing, despite what we *seem* to be seeing, a people who don't care if their friends make dangerous mistakes or if their loved ones fall into self-destructive habits, who don't care about the peace, health and security of their communities. We are instead seeing people whose traditional commandments require that they demonstrate their care in two ways which are fundamentally different from our ways: by conferring virtually absolute freedom on everyone and, when damaging events do occur, by doing whatever is possible to put those events behind them, to let bygones be bygones and to restore essential harmony.

Until we realize that Native people have a highly developed, formal, but radically different set of cultural imperatives, we are likely to continue misinterpreting their acts, misperceiving the real problems they face and imposing, through government policies, potentially harmful "remedies".

We also need to realize that these ethics and attitudes are not necessarily seen as "rules" by Native people themselves, just as we are often unaware that vigorous introspection is an acquired cultural trait with us. These sorts of habits represent, to each group respectively, the way they assume all people are naturally. We are seldom conscious of the fact that at some time we *learned* them, and that we could just as easily have learned different approaches instead.

. . . .

It is also clear that at this stage in history Native people are declaring that they have had enough. After putting up politely with our all-encompassing interference for so long, they are asking us to leave them alone, for in many spheres they have seen only negative results.

The court system is one clear example. The function of traditional Native dispute-resolution systems was the real resolution of disputes. They hoped that at the end of their process the parties would be returned to cooperative co-existence, to real interpersonal harmony. Naturally, they expected that our courts would have the same goal. Little did they know that we do not even pretend to that goal. Our society is a society of strangers. Our judicial processes do not aim at restoring friendship or harmony, if only because between strangers these qualities do not exist in the first place. Instead, we aim at deterring harmful *activity* so that each stranger can continue to follow his private path without interference.

It is little wonder that one Chief recently complained that the court doesn't do what it should do. As he put it, "your court only comes in here to take money in fines and to take our people out to jail, leaving us with the problem." That problem, needless to say, was the unresolved original dispute between people, or the uncorrected dysfunction within an individual accused. Until recently, Native people have been willing to endure many of the traditionally unethical requirements of our legal system in the belief that we too aimed at restoring interpersonal harmony and individual mental health. That belief was mistaken, for our courts focus primarily on the preservation of public peace. They are concerned not with what people are, but with what they do. The Native approach essentially ignores what was done and concentrates instead upon the personal or interpersonal dysfunctions which caused the problem in the first place. Their first priority lies in trying to correct those dysfunctions rather than in trying to keep those continuing dysfunctions from erupting into further harmful or illegal acts.

It is now the judgment of many bands that our system is inappropriate both in its processes and in its goals. If we are not even going to attempt to do what they believe should be done, they don't want us, for our processes themselves are harmful, involving as they do confrontation and the perpetuation of disruptive issues.

HONOURING THE TRUTH, RECONCILING FOR THE FUTURE
Summary of the Final Report of the Truth and Reconciliation Commission of Canada (2015)

Educating lawyers
The criminal prosecution of abusers in residential schools and the subsequent civil law-suits were a difficult experience for Survivors. The courtroom experience was made worse by the fact that many lawyers did not have adequate cultural, historical, or psychological knowledge to deal with the painful memories that the Survivors were forced to reveal. The lack of sensitivity that lawyers often demonstrated in dealing with residential school Survivors resulted, in some cases, in the Survivors' not receiving appropriate legal service. These experiences prove the need for lawyers to develop a greater understanding of Aboriginal history and culture as well as the multi-faceted legacy of residential schools.

Calls to Action

27) We call upon the Federation of Law Societies of Canada to ensure that lawyers receive appropriate cultural competency training, which includes the history and legacy of residential schools, the United Nations Declaration on the Rights of Indigenous Peoples, Treaties and Aboriginal rights, Indigenous law, and Aboriginal — Crown relations. This will require skills-based training in intercultural competency, conflict resolution, human rights, and anti-racism.

28) We call upon law schools in Canada to require all law students to take a course in Aboriginal people and the law, which includes the history and legacy of residential schools, the United Nations Declaration on the Rights of Indigenous Peoples, Treaties and Aboriginal rights, Indigenous law, and Aboriginal — Crown relations. This will require skills-based training in intercultural competency, conflict resolution, human rights, and anti-racism.

R. v. R.D.S.

[1997] 3 S.C.R. 484, 118 C.C.C. (3d) 353, 10 C.R. (5th) 1,
1997 CarswellNS 301, 1997 CarswellNS 302

The accused, a black 15-year-old, was charged with a series of offences arising out of an incident wherein a white police officer had arrested the accused for interfering with the arrest of another youth. The police officer and the accused were the only witnesses at trial. Their accounts of the relevant events differed widely. The trial judge weighed the evidence and determined that the accused should be acquitted. While delivering her oral reasons, the trial judge remarked:

> The Crown says, well, why would the officer say that events occurred the way in which he has relayed them to the court this morning. I am not saying that the Constable has misled the court, although police officers have been known to do that in the past. I am not saying that the officer overreacted, but certainly police officers do overreact, particularly when they are dealing with non-white groups. That to me indicates a state of mind right there that is questionable. I believe that probably the situation in this particular case is the case of a young police officer who overreacted. I do accept the evidence of [R.D.S.] that he was told to shut up or he would be under arrest. It seems to be in keeping with the prevalent attitude of the day. At any rate, based upon my comments and based upon all the evidence before the court I have no other choice but to acquit.

Judge Sparks, the trial judge, was the first black judge appointed in Nova Scotia. **In her decision, was Judge Sparks simply bringing her "different perspective on life" to the bench as Justice Wilson urges in her articles on women judges, or was she acting improperly?** The Crown challenged these comments as raising a reasonable apprehension of bias. The Crown's appeal was allowed and a new trial ordered. This judgment was upheld by a majority of the Nova Scotia Court of Appeal. The accused appealed further.

The Supreme Court allowed the appeal and restored the acquittals. There was a complex division of opinion. **What are the majority rulings on how judges should approach questions of social context at trial and on whether the trial judge's approach in this case created a reasonable apprehension of bias?**

CORY J. (IACOBUCCI J. concurring): —

. . . .

In some circumstances it may be acceptable for a judge to acknowledge that racism in society might be, for example, the motive for the overreaction of a police officer. This may be necessary in order to refute a submission that invites the judge as trier of fact to presume truthfulness or untruthfulness of a category of witnesses, or to adopt some other form of stereotypical thinking. Yet it would not be acceptable for a judge to go further and suggest that all police officers should therefore not be believed or should be viewed with suspicion where they are dealing with accused persons who are members of a different race. Similarly, it is dangerous for a judge to suggest that a particular person overreacted because of racism unless there is evidence adduced to sustain this finding. It would be equally inappropriate to suggest that female complainants, in sexual assault cases, ought to be believed more readily than male accused persons solely because of the history of sexual violence by men against women.

If there is no evidence linking the generalization to the particular witness, these situations might leave the judge open to allegations of bias on the basis that the credibility of the individual witness was prejudged according to stereotypical generalizations. This does not mean that the particular generalization — that police officers have historically discriminated against visible minorities or that women have historically been abused by men — is not true, or is without foundation. The difficulty is that reasonable and informed people may perceive that the judge has used this information as a basis for assessing credibility instead of making a genuine evaluation of the evidence of the particular witness' credibility. As a general rule, judges should avoid placing themselves in this position.

. . . .

The Crown contended that the real problem arising from Judge Sparks' remarks was the inability of the Crown and Constable Stienburg to respond to the remarks. In other words, the Crown attempted to put forward an argument that the trial was rendered unfair for failure to comply with "natural justice". This cannot be accepted. Neither Constable Stienburg nor the Crown was on trial. Rather, it is essential to consider whether the remarks of Judge Sparks gave rise to a reasonable apprehension of bias. This is the only basis on which this trial could be considered unfair.

. . . .

However, there was *no* evidence before Judge Sparks that would suggest that anti-black bias influenced this particular police officer's reactions. Thus, although it may be incontrovertible that there is a history of racial tension between police officers and visible minorities, there was no evidence to link that generalization to the actions of Constable Stienburg. The reference to the fact that police officers may overreact in dealing with non-white groups may therefore be perfectly supportable, but it is nonetheless unfortunate in the circumstances of this case because of its potential to associate Judge Sparks' findings with the generalization, rather than the specific evidence. This effect is reinforced by the statement "[t]hat to me indicates a state of mind right there that is questionable" which immediately follows her observation.

There is a further troubling comment. After accepting R.D.S.'s evidence that he was told to shut up, Judge Sparks added that "[i]t seems to be in keeping with the prevalent attitude of the day". Again, this comment may create a perception that the findings of credibility have been made on the basis of generalizations, rather than the conduct of the particular police officer. Indeed these comments standing alone come very close to indicating that Judge Sparks predetermined the issue of credibility of Constable Stienburg on the basis of her general perception of racist police attitudes, rather than on the basis of his demeanour and the substance of his testimony.

The remarks are worrisome and come very close to the line. Yet, however troubling these comments are when read individually, it is vital to note that the comments were not made in isolation. It is necessary to read all of the comments in the context of the whole proceeding, with an awareness of all the circumstances that a reasonable observer would be deemed to know.

The reasonable and informed observer at the trial would be aware that the Crown had made the submission to Judge Sparks that "there's absolutely no reason to attack the credibility of the officer". She had already made a finding that she preferred the evidence of R.D.S. to that of Constable Stienburg. She gave reasons for these findings that could appropriately be made based on the evidence adduced. A reasonable and informed person hearing her subsequent remarks would conclude that she was exploring the possible reasons why Constable Stienburg had a different perception of events than R.D.S. Specifically, she was rebutting the unfounded suggestion of the Crown that a police officer by virtue of his occupation should be more readily believed than the accused. Although her remarks were inappropriate they did not give rise to a reasonable apprehension of bias.

· · · ·

A high standard must be met before a finding of reasonable apprehension of bias can be made. Troubling as Judge Sparks' remarks may be, the Crown has not satisfied its onus to provide the cogent evidence needed to impugn the impartiality of Judge Sparks. Although her comments, viewed in isolation, were unfortunate and unnecessary, a reasonable, informed person, aware of all the circumstances, would not conclude that they gave rise to a reasonable apprehension of bias. Her remarks, viewed in their context, do not give rise to a perception that she prejudged the issue of credibility on the basis of generalizations, and they do not taint her earlier findings of credibility.

. . . .

I must add that since writing these reasons I have had the opportunity of reading those of Major J. It is readily apparent that we are in agreement as to the nature of bias and the test to be applied in order to determine whether the words or actions of a trial judge raise a reasonable apprehension of bias. The differences in our reasons lies in the application of the principles and test we both rely upon to the words of the trial judge in this case. The principles and the test we have both put forward and relied upon are different from and incompatible with those set out by Justices L'Heureux-Dubé and McLachlin.

MAJOR J. (LAMER C.J. and SOPINKA J. concurring) (dissenting): — The trial judge stated that "police officers have been known to [mislead the court] in the past" and that "police officers do overreact, particularly when they are dealing with non-white groups" and went on to say "[t]hat to me indicates a state of mind right there that is questionable." She in effect was saying, "sometimes police lie and overreact in dealing with non-whites, therefore I have a suspicion that this police officer may have lied and overreacted in dealing with this non-white accused." This was stereotyping all police officers as liars and racists, and applied this stereotype to the police officer in the present case. The trial judge might be perceived as assigning less weight to the police officer's evidence because he is testifying in the prosecution of an accused who is of a different race. Whether racism exists in our society is not the issue. The issue is whether there was evidence before the court upon which to base a finding that *this* particular police officer's actions were motivated by racism. There was no evidence of this presented at the trial.

. . . .

Trial judges have to base their findings on the evidence before them. It was open to the appellant to introduce evidence that this police officer was racist and that racism motivated his actions or that he lied. This was not done. For the trial judge to infer that based on her general view of the police or society is an error of law. For this reason there should be a new trial.

. . . .

The life experience of this trial judge, as with all trial judges, is an important ingredient in the ability to understand human behaviour, to weigh the evidence, and to determine credibility. It helps in making a myriad of decisions arising during the course of most trials. It is of no value, however, in reaching conclusions for which there is no evidence. The fact that on some other occasions police officers have lied or overreacted is irrelevant. Life experience is not a substitute for evidence. There was no evidence before the trial judge to support the conclusions she reached.

. . . .

Canadian Courts have, in recent years, criticized the stereotyping of people into what is said to be predictable behaviour patterns. If a judge in a sexual assault case instructed the jury or him- or herself that because the complainant was a prostitute he or she probably consented, or that prostitutes are likely to lie about such things as sexual assault, that decision would be reversed. Such presumptions have no place in a system of justice that treats all witnesses equally. Our jurisprudence prohibits tying credibility to something as irrelevant as gender, occupation or perceived group predisposition.

. . . .

It can hardly be seen as progress to stereotype police officer witnesses as likely to lie when dealing with non-whites. This would return us to a time in the history of the Canadian justice system that many thought had past. This reasoning, with respect to police officers, is no more legitimate than the stereotyping of women, children or minorities.

. . . .

I agree with the approach taken by Cory J. with respect to the nature of bias and the test to be used to determine if the words or actions of a judge give rise to apprehension of bias. However, I come to a different conclusion in the application of the test to the words of the trial judge in this case. It follows that I disagree with the approach to reasonable apprehension of bias put forward by Justices L'Heureux Dubé and McLachlin.

L'HEUREUX-DUBÉ J. (McLACHLIN J. concurring): —

. . . .

In our view, the test for reasonable apprehension of bias established in the jurisprudence is reflective of the reality that while judges can never be neutral, in the sense of purely objective, they can and must strive for impartiality. It therefore recognizes as inevitable and appropriate that the differing experiences of judges assist them in their decision-making process and will be reflected in their judgments, so long as those experiences are relevant to the cases, are not based on inappropriate stereotypes, and do not prevent a fair and just determination of the cases based on the facts in evidence.

We find that on the basis of these principles, there is no reasonable apprehension of bias in the case at bar. Like Cory J. we would, therefore, overturn the findings by the Nova Scotia Supreme Court (Trial Division) and the majority of the Nova Scotia Court of Appeal that a reasonable apprehension of bias arises in this case, and restore the acquittal of R.D.S. This said, we disagree with Cory J.'s position that the comments of Judge Sparks were unfortunate, unnecessary, or close to the line. Rather, we find them to reflect an entirely appropriate recognition of the facts in evidence in this case and of the context within which this case arose — a context known to Judge Sparks and to any well-informed member of the community.

. . . .

Cardozo recognized that objectivity was an impossibility because judges, like all other humans, operate from their own perspectives. As the Canadian Judicial Council noted in *Commentaries on Judicial Conduct* (1991), at p. 12, "[t]here is no human being who is not the product of every social experience, every process of education, and every human contact". What is possible and desirable, they note, is impartiality:

> . . . [T]he wisdom required of a judge is to recognize, consciously allow for, and perhaps to question, all the baggage of past attitudes and sympathies that fellow citizens are free to carry, untested, to the grave.

> True impartiality does not require that the judge have no sympathies or opinions; it requires that the judge nevertheless be free to entertain and act upon different points of view with an open mind.

. . . .

As discussed above, judges in a bilingual, multiracial and multicultural society will undoubtedly approach the task of judging from their varied perspectives. They will certainly have been shaped by, and have gained insight from, their different experiences, and cannot be expected to divorce themselves from these experiences on the occasion of their appointment to the bench. In fact, such a transformation would deny society the benefit of the valuable knowledge gained by the judiciary while they were members of the Bar. As well, it would preclude the achievement of a diversity of backgrounds in the judiciary. The reasonable person does not expect that judges will function as neutral ciphers; however, the reasonable person does demand that judges achieve impartiality in their judging.

. . . .

An understanding of the context or background essential to judging may be gained from testimony from expert witnesses in order to put the case in context: *R. v. Lavallee*, . . . *R. v. Parks*, . . . and *Moge v. Moge*, . . . from academic studies properly placed before the court; and from the judge's personal understanding and experience of the society in which the judge lives and works. This process of enlargement is not only consistent with impartiality; it may also be seen as its essential precondition.

A reasonable person far from being troubled by this process, would see it as an important aid to judicial impartiality.

. . . .

It is important to note that having already found R.D.S. to be credible, and having accepted a sufficient portion of his evidence to leave her with a reasonable doubt as to his guilt, Judge Sparks necessarily disbelieved at least a portion of the conflicting evidence of Constable Stienburg. At that point, Judge Sparks made reference to the submissions of the Crown that "there's absolutely no reason to attack the credibility of the officer", and then addressed herself to why there might, in fact, be a reason to attack the credibility of the officer in this case. It is in this context that Judge Sparks made the statements which have prompted this appeal.

[The trial judge's] remarks do not support the conclusion that Judge Sparks found Constable Stienburg to have lied. In fact, Judge Sparks did quite the opposite. She noted firstly, that she was *not* saying Constable Stienburg had misled the court, although that could be an explanation for his evidence. She then went on to remark that she was *not* saying that Constable Stienburg had overreacted, though she was alive to that possibility given that it had happened with police officers in the past, and in particular, it had happened when police officers were dealing with non-white groups. Finally, Judge Sparks concluded that, though she was not willing to say that Constable Stienburg did overreact, it was her belief that he *probably* overreacted. And, in support of that finding, she noted that she accepted the evidence of R.D.S. that "he was told to shut up or he would be under arrest".

At no time did Judge Sparks rule that the probable overreaction by Constable Stienburg was motivated by racism. Rather, she tied her finding of probable overreaction to the evidence that Constable Stienburg had threatened to arrest the appellant R.D.S. for speaking to his cousin. At the same time, there was evidence capable of supporting a finding of racially motivated overreaction. At an earlier point in the proceedings, she had accepted the evidence that the other youth arrested that day, was handcuffed and thus secured when R.D.S. approached. This constitutes evidence which could lead one to question why it was necessary for both boys to be placed in choke holds by Constable Stienburg, purportedly to secure them. In the face of such evidence, we respectfully disagree with the views of our colleagues Cory and Major JJ. that there was no evidence on which Judge Sparks could have found "racially motivated" overreaction by the police officer.

While it seems clear that Judge Sparks *did not in fact* relate the officer's probable overreaction to the race of the appellant R.D.S., it should be noted that if Judge Sparks *had* chosen to attribute the behaviour of Constable Stienburg to the racial dynamics of the situation, she would not necessarily have erred. As a member of the community, it was open to her to take into account the well-known presence of racism in that community and to evaluate the evidence as to what occurred against that background.

That Judge Sparks recognized that police officers *sometimes* overreact when dealing with non-white groups simply demonstrates that in making her determination in this case, she was alive to the well-known racial dynamics that may exist in interactions between police officers and visible minorities.

. . . .

Judge Sparks' oral reasons show that she approached the case with an open mind, used her experience and knowledge of the community to achieve an understanding of the reality of the case, and applied the fundamental principle of proof beyond a reasonable doubt. Her comments were based entirely on the case before her, were made after a consideration of the conflicting testimony of the two witnesses and in response to the Crown's submissions, and were entirely supported by the evidence. In alerting herself to the racial dynamic in the case, she was simply engaging in the process of contextualized judging which, in our view, was entirely proper and conducive to a fair and just resolution of the case before her.

GONTHIER J. (LA FOREST J. CONCURRING): — . . . I agree with Cory J. and L'Heureux-Dubé and McLachlin JJ. as to the disposition of the appeal and with their exposition of the law on bias and impartiality and the relevance of context. However, I am in agreement with and adopt the joint reasons of L'Heureux-Dubé and McLachlin JJ. in their treatment of social context and the manner in which it may appropriately enter the decision-making process as well as their assessment of the trial judge's reasons and comments in the present case.

For competing views on *R.D.S.*, see B.P. Archibald, "The Lessons of the Sphinx: Avoiding Apprehensions of Judicial Bias in a Multi-racial, Multi-cultural Society" (1998), 10 C.R. (5th) 54; R.J. Delisle, "An Annotation to R.D.S." (1998), 10 C.R. (5th) 7; and D.M. Paciocco, "The Promise of R.D.S.: Integrating the Law of Judicial Notice and Apprehension of Bias"(1998) 3 Can. Crim. L.R. 319.

(b) Ethical Obligations of Crown and Defence Counsel

See generally, Michel Proulx and David Layton, *Ethics and Canadian Criminal Law* (Irwin Law, 2001).

CANADIAN BAR ASSOCIATION'S
CODE OF PROFESSIONAL CONDUCT (2004)

CONFIDENTIAL INFORMATION

RULE

Maintaining Information in Confidence

1. The lawyer has a duty to hold in strict confidence all information concerning the business and affairs of the client acquired in the course of the professional relationship, and shall not divulge any such information except as expressly or impliedly authorized by the client, required by law or otherwise required by this Code.

Public Safety Exception

2. Where a lawyer believes upon reasonable grounds that there is an imminent risk to an identifiable person or group of death or serious bodily harm, including serious psychological harm that would substantially interfere with health or well-being, the lawyer shall disclose confidential information where it is necessary to do so in order to prevent the death or harm, but shall not disclose more information than is required

THE LAWYER AS ADVOCATE

RULE

When acting as an advocate, the lawyer must treat the tribunal with courtesy and respect and must represent the client resolutely, honourably and within the limits of the law.

Commentary

Guiding Principles

1. The advocate's duty to the client "fearlessly to raise every issue, advance every argument, and ask every question, however distasteful, which he thinks will help his client's case" and to endeavour "to obtain for his client the benefit of any and every remedy and defence which is authorized by law" must always be discharged by fair and honourable means, without illegality and in a manner consistent with the lawyer's duty to treat the court with candour, fairness, courtesy and respect.

Prohibited Conduct

2. The lawyer must not, for example:

    . . . .

    (b) knowingly assist or permit the client to do anything that the lawyer considers to be dishonest or dishonourable;

    . . . .

    (e) knowingly attempt to deceive or participate in the deception of a tribunal or influence the course of justice by offering false evidence, misstating facts or law, presenting or relying upon a false or deceptive affidavit, suppressing what ought to be disclosed or otherwise assisting in any fraud, crime or illegal conduct.

    . . . .

Duties of Prosecutor

9. When engaged as a prosecutor, the lawyer's prime duty is not to seek a conviction, but to present before the trial court all available credible evidence relevant to the alleged crime in order that justice may be done through a fair trial upon the merits. The prosecutor exercises a public function involving much discretion and power and must act fairly and dispassionately. The prosecutor should not do anything that might prevent the accused from being represented by counsel or communicating with counsel and, to the extent required by law and accepted practice, should make timely disclosure to the accused or defence counsel (or to the court if the accused is not represented) of all relevant facts and known witnesses, whether tending to show guilt or innocence, or that would affect the punishment of the accused. There is a clear distinction between prosecutorial discretion and professional conduct. Only the latter can be regulated by a law society. A law society has jurisdiction to investigate any alleged breach of its ethical standards, even those committed by Crown prosecutors in connection with their prosecutorial discretion.

Duties of Defence Counsel

10. When defending an accused person, the lawyer's duty is to protect the client as far as possible from being convicted except by a court of competent jurisdiction and upon legal evidence sufficient to support a conviction for the offence charged. Accordingly, and notwithstanding the lawyer's private opinion as to credibility or merits, the lawyer may properly rely upon all available evidence or defences including so-called technicalities not known to be false or fraudulent.

11. Admissions made by the accused to the lawyer may impose strict limitations on the conduct of the defence and the accused should be made aware of this. For example, if the accused clearly admits to the lawyer the factual and mental elements necessary to constitute the offence, the lawyer, if convinced that the admissions are true and voluntary, may properly take objection to the jurisdiction of the court, or to the form of the indictment, or to the admissibility or sufficiency of the evidence, but must not suggest that some other person committed the offence, or call any evidence that, by reason of the admissions, the lawyer believes to be false. Nor may the lawyer set up an affirmative case inconsistent with such admissions, for example, by calling evidence in support of an alibi intended to show that the accused could not have done, or in fact had not done, the act. Such admissions will also impose a limit upon the extent to which the lawyer may attack the evidence for the prosecution. The lawyer is entitled to test the evidence given by each individual witness for the prosecution and argue that the evidence taken as a whole is insufficient to amount to proof that the accused is guilty of the offence charged, but the lawyer should go no further than that. A lawyer representing an accused or potential accused must not take unfair or improper advantage of an unrepresented complainant by attempting to influence the complainant or potential complainant with respect to the laying, prosecution or withdrawal of a criminal charge.

JUSTICE PETER CORY,
THE INQUIRY REGARDING THOMAS SOPHONOW

2000, Government of Manitoba

The Role of Crown Counsel in the Administration of Justice

Just as it was necessary to express criticism of police officers, I must be critical of some of the actions and omissions of Crown Counsel. The criticism is limited to this case and must not be taken as a general criticism of their work or the work of any particular Crown Attorney.

The role of Crown Counsel is of great importance to the administration of justice and to the welfare of the community. The Crown prosecutor must proceed with the case against the accused fairly and courageously. Prosecutions must proceed even in the face of threats and attempts at intimidation. These insidious threats can on occasion extend to family members. Despite these threats and the danger in which the Crown and at times the family of the Crown are placed, charges must still be vigorously prosecuted. They must be brought to trial and prosecuted with diligence, dispatch and fairness. Crown Counsel are often overworked and paid less than their contemporaries who are in private practice. Nonetheless, they must be industrious to ensure that all the arduous preparation required for each trial or appeal has been completed before the matter comes to court. Crown Counsel must be of absolute integrity and above all suspicion of favouritism or unfair compromise.

Crown Counsel must be a symbol of fairness, prompt to make all reasonable disclosure. As well, they must be scrupulous in the attention given to the welfare and safety of witnesses. They enjoy the respect of all the members of the judiciary. Much is expected of Crown Counsel by society, their community and by the judiciary. The community looks upon the Crown prosecutor as a symbol of fairness, of authority and as a spokesman for the community.

As a rule, Crown Counsel attain and maintain a very high level of professional excellence and fairness. They fulfil all of society's high expectations. It is truly a high office, honoured by the bench, the bar and the community. They should always have, not only the respect of the public and the legal community, but the resources to handle their ever increasing caseloads and the financial compensation that their important office deserves.

The Role of Defence Counsel

There may be some explicit and some implicit criticism of the actions of Defence Counsel, particularly with regard to the disclosure of the alibi evidence. Once again, that criticism arises from the circumstances of this case and it is certainly not a general comment on their work.

The role of Defence Counsel is of great importance to the administration of justice and to our democratic society. Crown Counsel are often regarded by the community as its protector and champion. Frequently, Defence Counsel are associated with their clients. All too often, they are unfairly thought of as those who take advantage of every "loophole" in the law to gain an acquittal. Yet Defence Counsel too must be courageous. They must defend those charged with offences no matter how heinous they may be. It is Defence Counsel who must ensure that no one is found guilty unless the charge is proven beyond a reasonable doubt. They must prepare their case carefully and present it clearly and fearlessly. They are duty bound to ensure that the case proceeds with due attention to the law which binds us all.

It cannot be forgotten that it is often only the Defence Counsel who stands between the lynch mob and the accused. Defence Counsel must be courageous, not only in the face of an outraged and inflamed community, but also, on occasion, the apparent disapproval of the court. Defence Counsel must always act fairly, can never subvert the law and must remember, no matter how trying the circumstances may be, to uphold the dignity of the court.

Our system of justice works best when able and well prepared counsel on both sides make their presentations to an impartial arbiter.

Defence Counsel must ensure that they put forward every reasonable defence on the part of their clients and strive to ensure that only the guilty are convicted.

It cannot be forgotten that there are innocent people who are charged with murder; that there are innocent people charged with sexual assault; that there are innocent people charged with fraud; and, indeed, that innocent people may be charged with any offence set out in the *Criminal Code*. It is the vitally important role of Defence Counsel to ensure that no person is found guilty unless guilt is proven beyond a reasonable doubt. The penalty of imprisonment takes away the most basic liberty of the subject. Indeed, for serious crimes, the deprivation of that liberty may result in a lifetime of imprisonment. The fundamental importance of the role of Defence Counsel in our democratic society is self-evident.

LUBAN, THE ADVERSARY SYSTEM EXCUSE

The Good Lawyer: Lawyers' Rules and Lawyers' Ethics
(Rowman and Allenheld, 1984), 84-88

On February 7, 1973, Richard Helms, the former director of the Central Intelligence Agency, lied to a Senate committee about American involvement in the overthrow of the Allende government in Chile. Santiago proved to be Helms's Waterloo: he was caught out in his perjury and prosecuted. Helms claimed that requirements of national security led him to lie to Congress. We can only speculate, however, on how the court would have viewed this excuse, for in fact the case never came to trial; Helm's lawyer, the redoubtable Edward Bennett Williams, found an ingenious way to back the government down. He argued that national security information was relevant to Helms's defense and must be turned over to Helms, thereby confronting the government with the unpleasant choice of dropping the action or making public classified and presumably vital information. The government chose the first option and allowed Helms to plead guilty to a misdemeanor charge.

I don't know if anyone ever asked Williams to justify his actions; had anyone attempted to do so, they would presumably have been told that Williams was simply doing his job as a criminal defense attorney. The parallel with Helms's own excuse is clear — he was doing his job, Williams was doing his — but it is hard to miss the irony. Helms tried to conceal national security information; therefore he lied. Williams, acting on Helms's behalf, threatened to reveal national security information as part of a tactic that has come to be called "graymailing." One man's ends are another man's means. Neither lying nor graymailing (to say nothing of destabilizing elected regimes) are morally pretty, but a job is a job and that was the job that was. So, at any rate, runs the excuse.

We may want to reject these "good soldier" excuses or we may find them valid and persuasive. That is the issue I shall address here. A second graymailing example will warm us to our topic:

> In instances [of merger cases involving firms in competition with each other] in which the [Federal Trade] commission's legal case looked particularly good and none of the usual defenses appeared likely to work, the staff was confronted several times with the argument that if they did not refrain from prosecution and allow the merger, one of the proposed merger partners would close down its operations and dismiss its employees.

> ... Of course, the mere announcement of the threat to close the plant generates enormous political pressure on the prosecutor not to go forward. Ought lawyers to be engaged in such strategies for the purpose of consummating an otherwise anticompetitive and illegal transaction involving the joinder of two substantial competitors?

On the lawyers' advice, the firms played a nice game of chicken: closing down by stages, they laid off a few workers each day until the FTC cried uncle.

What could justify the conduct of these lawyers? A famous answer is the following statement of Lord Henry Brougham:

> An advocate, in the discharge of his duty, knows but one person in all the world, and that person is his client. To save that client by all means and expedients, and at all hazards and costs to other persons, and, amongst them to himself, is his first and only duty; and in performing this duty he must not regard the alarm, the torments, the destruction which he may bring upon others. Separating the duty of a patriot from that of an advocate, he must go on reckless of consequences, though it should be his unhappy fate to involve his country in confusion.

This speech, made in his 1820 defense of Queen Caroline against King George IV's charge of adultery, was itself an act of graymail. Reminiscing years later, Brougham said that the king would recognize in it a tacit threat to reveal his secret marriage to a Catholic, a marriage that, were it to become public knowledge, would cost him his crown. Knowing this background of Brougham's oft-quoted statement might make us take a dim view of it; it has, nevertheless, frequently been admired as the most eloquent encapsulation of the advocate's job.

Brougham's statement invites philosophical reflection for at first blush it is equally baffling to utilitarianism, and moral rights theory, and Kantianism. The client's utility matters more than that of the rest of the world put together. No one else's moral rights matter. Other people are merely means to the client's ends. Moral theory seems simply to reject Brougham's imperatives.

They are, however, universalizable over lawyers, or so it is claimed. The idea seems to be that the role of lawyer, hence the social institutions that set up this role, reparse the Moral Law, relaxing some moral obligations and imposing new ones. In the words of an Australian appellate court, "Our system of administering justice necessarily imposes upon those who practice advocacy duties which have no analogies, and the system cannot dispense with their strict observance."

The system of which the court speaks is the so-called "adversary system of justice." My main question is this: does the adversary system really justify Brougham's position? I hope that the example of Helms and his lawyers has convinced you that a more general issue is lurking here, the issue of what I shall call *institutional excuses*. We can state the main question in full generality in this way: can a person appeal to a social institution in which he or she occupies a role in order to excuse conduct that would be morally culpable were anyone else to do it? Plausibly, examples exist in which the answer is yes: we do not call it murder when a soldier kills a sleeping enemy, although it is surely immoral for you or me to do it. There are also cases where the answer is no, as in the job "concentration camp commandant" or "professional strikebreaker." Here, we feel, the immorality of the job is so great that it accuses, not excuses, the person who holds it.

This suggests that an important feature of a successful institutional excuse is that the institution is itself justified. I think that is partly right, but I do not think it is the whole story: I shall argue that the *kind* of justification that can be offered of the institution is germane to the success of the excuses it provides.

GEOFFREY HAZARD, ETHICS IN THE PRACTICE OF LAW

(1978), 128

There are several escapes [from moral responsibility]. It is said that no client is guilty until so found by a court; therefore one cannot know what the truth is until then; therefore, one cannot conclude that a client's testimony will constitute perjury. This is pure casuistry. Of course there are doubtful situations, but there are also ones that are not doubtful. A thing is not made true or not by a court's pronouncing on it, and a lawyer can reach conclusions about an issue without having a judge tell him what to think.

See further, Michel Proulx and David Layton, *Ethics and Canadian Criminal Law* (Irwin Law, 2001); and David Tanovich, "Law's Ambition: The Reconstruction of Role Morality in Canada" (2005) 28 Dal. L.J. 267.

GREENSPAN AND JONAS,
GREENSPAN: THE CASE FOR THE DEFENCE

(1987), 260-265

Whenever a crime is committed (or whenever some people in the community suspect that an act may amount to a crime), a large, impersonal machinery goes into motion. Its initial purpose is to determine if some act or event was, in fact, a crime — and if it concludes that it was, to find the individual (or group of individuals) responsible for it.

Once this appears to be accomplished, the machinery shifts into second gear. It tries to establish the accused individual's *degree* of responsibility. Then, in third gear, his or her appropriate punishment. Sometimes there is a fourth gear: the machinery may turn its attention to some social or legal condition in the hope of making it easier to define, prevent, or detect such crimes in the future.

This process can involve dozens and dozens of people in its various stages. Ideally — and often in actual fact — they are highly trained, intelligent, dedicated, and hard-working human beings: people of great personal integrity. They are police officers, forensic experts, medical doctors, prosecuting attorneys, court officials, judges, jurors, parole officials, prison administrators, and lawmakers. Except for the jurors, they are all professionals. Many of them have the authority to knock on anybody's door and ask for information and assistance. Even when they cannot compel people's co-operation by law, they can expect people to co-operate with them as a civic or moral duty. They also have at their disposal support personnel and sophisticated, expensive equipment, the best society can provide, to help them in their work.

There is nothing wrong with any of this, of course. Crime cannot go undetected, undefined, or unpunished. No community could function without protecting itself from crime.

However, this great, impersonal, awesome machinery has one built-in bias. It is an unconscious, functional bias, somewhat like an aircraft's bias for leaving the ground as soon as it has attained a certain speed. The bias of the justice system is to find guilt. That is, first, to define any human act that comes to its attention as a crime; then, to define any suspect as a person who has probably committed such an act; and finally, to define any human being who has committed such an act as a criminal. That's the way the justice system flies.

Everyone knows that in a given individual case none of this may be true — yet the great machine of the criminal justice system may thunder down the runway and take off regardless.

. . . .

Our justice system has tried to counteract this potential by two remedies.

First, on an abstract level, the remedy is the law's presumption that every person is innocent until proven guilty on relevant evidence beyond a reasonable doubt.

By saying "on an abstract level" I don't mean to imply that this presumption is unimportant. On the contrary, it is vital and fundamental. Everything else flows from the presumption of innocence. However, without a second remedy on a concrete level, it could remain as ineffectual as a sheathed sword. Or, to use a more up-to-date metaphor, as an engine without a driver.

This second, concrete remedy is the lawyer for the defence. He drives the abstract engine of the presumption of innocence. He is the one person in the entire world, apart from the accused person's mother, who *starts* with the assumption that the authorities must be mistaken.

To balance the awe-inspiring machinery of the criminal-justice system, the law permits one individual to be the accused person's friend. He is, as the legal expression goes, to be "of counsel" to him. Simply put, his job is to "believe" the accused — or at least not to disbelieve him. His job is to look at every circumstance surrounding the allegations against a defendant with the assumption that they prove, or are consistent with, his innocence.

The defence lawyer is to balance the dozens of powerful professionals whose task is to investigate and prosecute an accused person. We give the defence lawyer this task in the knowledge that a defendant may *be* innocent. Innocent, not just as an abstract legal idea (because in that sense he is innocent anyway until found guilty), but as a matter of plain, actual fact. What he is accused of may not amount to a crime, or he may not have committed it. If it is a crime and he did commit it, it may not be as serious a crime as his adversary, the prosecutor, suggests. And even if it is as serious, there may be something about the circumstances, or about the defendant as a human being, that makes him something else than a criminal deserving the worst punishment.

Since this may be so, our system has decided that there must be one person in the defendant's community who acts as if it were so. One man or woman who is not the defendant's inquisitor, accuser, or judge. One who doesn't merely keep an open mind about him. One person who is the defendant's advocate.

Society assigns this role to the defence lawyer. He is the one person whose duty is to assume the best about a defendant at every step of the way. The defence lawyer alone, among all the defendant's fellow citizens and neighbours, must act on the assumption that whatever the defendant says is true. He must act on the assumption that the defendant's accusers are mistaken. Mistaken — or possibly malicious. They may have their own axe to grind. The defence lawyer must put everything they say about the defendant to the strictest test of proof. In so far as the law permits, he must put the accusers on trial.

This is the defence lawyer's duty. It's a duty not just to his client, but to his society. It is not something the defence lawyer decides in his own mind: it is an obligation the community places on him. The defence lawyer chooses his occupation voluntarily, but he does not choose his role: his society defines his role for him. The moral essence of this role has been distilled by the common experience of our legal tradition over the centuries. It is that a community can retain justice and freedom only as long as it gives standing to one person to take, within the limits of the law, the defendant's side in court.

. . . .

The defence lawyer, as many people have pointed out, only defends a client (or a client's act) and not a crime. Central to any defence, other than a submission in mitigation of sentence, is the position that the client didn't do something. Or that whatever he did was not wrong in law, or at least not as wrong as the prosecution contends. If a lawyer suggested that yes, my client did shoot this man deliberately and in cold blood, but the victim was a nasty fellow who deserved to be shot, *then* he would be defending a crime — but no lawyer does that. (The only exceptions in our times have been some "activist" lawyers who attempted to gain the acquittal of murderers on the basis of some "higher" political or social motive.)

But these are only aberrations — albeit dangerous ones — and we need not concern ourselves with them here. Like most criminal lawyers, I defend clients, not crimes. Which is why I find questions like: "How can you defend those people?" or "Is there any kind of crime at which you'd draw a line?" meaningless.

I haven't the slightest moral conflict defending people accused of homicide, sexual assault, business fraud, environmental offences, or even crimes against humanity. I don't "draw the line" at anything. If I defended *crimes*, maybe I would — but I don't defend crimes. I only defend innocent people. Until they are found guilty there are no other kinds of people for me to defend, and what difference does it make what an innocent person is accused of?

Would you represent any and all accused?

Helen Conway, a sole practitioner and defence counsel in Windsor, Ontario, writing in the *Law Times* of September 10, 2001 under the title "The Spirit of the Law", pointed to statistics of disproportionate rates of depression, addiction and suicide for lawyers, financial strain from low legal aid rates, high overheads and collection difficulties, and a bureaucratic and inefficient criminal justice system. She concludes that the practice of criminal law

> is not for the faint of heart. Lawyers take the heat from all directions and most have even grown accustomed to the overall disrespect and disapproval towards them which exists in the community. Ultimately, however, moral affirmation and professional certainty have to come not from society but from within the knowledge and belief that perhaps lawyers have in some small measure protected the rights of an individual or defended a client who has been wronged or treated unfairly.

> The practice of [criminal] law is, first and finally, a vocation, a call to represent and to advance the ideal of justice. While public in practice, it is also and always personal in spirit (p. 8).

It has been said that there are broadly two models of the practice of criminal law as a defence counsel. Some defence counsel start by advising potential clients that everything told to them will be kept in strictest confidence but that, having heard the full story, the defence counsel may be limited in the ability to present a defence. The client is told that the lawyer cannot participate in perjured testimony. Subject to these limits, the accused is encouraged to tell the defence counsel everything about the case. On the other model, sometimes called "blind person's bluff" the lawyer remains purposefully ignorant about potentially embarrassing facts and discourages the client from telling everything. The accused is never directly asked for his or her version of the facts. Instead, the questions are entirely limited to such questions as whether the accused gave a statement to the police, which witnesses could be of assistance to the defence and what else is known by the police or the Crown Attorney.

What advantages do you see in these models of practice? Which would you follow?

---

1. John Smith has been charged with assault. He asks you to represent him and you agree. He tells you that he beat on the victim during a drunken rage. He imagines that it was because he has never cared for his manner. He knows that he started this particular fracas but also advises you that the victim himself has two previous convictions of common assault, which, he suggests, could be fertile ground for cross-examination. The victim describes the beating in some detail. When the Crown finishes the examination-in-chief you turn to your client who advises: "That's exactly what happened. Now go get him. Destroy his credibility." What do you do?
Your client is convicted. Would you inform the Crown about two other assault convictions registered against your client under another name?

2. Your client is prosecuted for robbery. He committed the crime at 10:45 and has admitted the same to you. The sole prosecution witness identified your client as the robber but mistakenly placed the time at 10:15. Your client has an airtight alibi for 10:00 to 10:30. Will you present the alibi?

3. You have been assigned to prosecute a case of domestic assault. The police laid the charge after they had been called to investigate a disturbance. The wife told the police that her husband had beaten her and that this was not the first time. The trial is to take place tomorrow, three months after the alleged incident. The woman approaches you and wants to withdraw the charge. She tells you that her husband has returned to Alcoholics Anonymous and is participating with her in a marriage-counselling program. The incidence of domestic violence in your community is very high. Will you withdraw?

4. Mr. Murray is a member of the Ontario Bar and certified as a specialist in criminal litigation by the Law Society of Upper Canada. He was retained by Paul Bernardo initially in February 1993 in regard to the

"Scarborough Rapes" and on May 18, 1993, in connection with the murders of L.M. and K.F. and additional related offences.

On May 6, 1993, he went to the Bernardo home after the search warrant for those premises had expired to retrieve personal possessions and evidence that might be helpful to the defence. He had a letter from his client with written instructions that he was only to open it once inside the house. Once inside he opened the sealed envelope, which contained a map and directions to assist in locating six eight-millimetre videotapes from above a pot light. He did so and removed them to his office. Bernardo's written instructions were for his counsel not to view them. The videotapes depicted gross sexual abuse of K.F., L.M., Jane Doe and T.H. by Bernardo and his co-accused Karla Homolka. Without disclosing their existence to the Crown, he retained the tapes for 17 months. He only viewed them at the instruction of Bernardo after he and Bernardo learned of a deal under which Karla Homolka agreed to plead guilty to two counts of manslaughter, with a joint submission to be made for a sentence of 12 years in exchange for her testifying for the Crown in the first degree murder trial of Bernardo. The tapes would be used to aid the defence that Bernardo was guilty of sexual assault but not murder. The Crown was going to portray Homolka as an abused, manipulated victim, while the tapes showed the reverse: that she was not afraid and was an enthusiastic participant in the sexual crimes. He felt obliged to keep the existence of the tapes secret so that the Crown could not prepare Homolka for defence cross-examination.

Trial motions were to begin on September 12, 1994. On September 2, 1994, the accused, through his counsel, applied to the Law Society of Upper Canada for advice. He was advised the tapes should be turned over to the judge and that he should withdraw from the case. Accepting that advice he appeared before the trial judge, who directed that the tapes, their integrity protected by suitable undertakings, go to John Rosen, new counsel for Bernardo, at which time the accused was given leave to withdraw as counsel. Rosen, on September 22, 1994, turned the tapes over to the police and they were used by Crown counsel at the trial. A jury found Bernardo guilty on all charges.

Did Mr. Murray act unethically? If so, what precisely did he do wrong?

See generally A.L. Macdonald and J.E. Pink, "Murder, Silence and Physical Evidence: The Dilemma of Client Confidentiality" (1997) 2 Can. Crim. L.R. 111; Kent Roach, "Smoking Guns: Beyond the Murray Case" (2000) 43 Crim. L.Q. 409; and Wayne Renke, "Real Evidence, Disclosure and the Plight of Counsel" (2003) 47 Crim. L.Q. 175.

Murray was later charged with obstruction of justice but was acquitted on the basis of a lack of proof of intent to mislead and because the rules of professional responsibility in such a situation were quite unclear.

5. Your client says that he is innocent, but that he wants to plead guilty "to get it over with". He is tired of the court delay and does not want to lose any more time off work. The offence is a minor one. Would you assist him in entering his guilty plea? Would you advise him to indicate remorse to secure a minimal penalty?

6. John is observed slipping a box of mints, value $1.75, into his jacket. He is arrested by store security and, following store policy, a charge is laid. John is in his second year of university and hopes to go to law school. He has no prior record. Your brief indicates that he was co-operative during the investigation. He had told the security officer, "I'm dumbfounded. I don't know why I took them". You are approached by a senior defence counsel, acting for John. He's also a friend of John's family. He tells you that John has been going through some rough times of late. John's older brother was recently killed in a car accident and John has just broken up with his girlfriend. He tells you that John is basically a "good kid" but he's under a lot of pressure because exams are just around the corner. Counsel asks if you'll withdraw the charges. Will you?

Suppose that you decide not to withdraw the charge but just as the case is being called by the court clerk you are advised that the store security officer is not present. You can't prove the charge and the trial judge is known not to grant adjournments in such cases. You know that John is about to plead guilty. What do you do?

Chapter 2

THE ACT REQUIREMENT
(ACTUS REUS)

1. INTRODUCTION

C. HOWARD, CRIMINAL LAW

3rd ed. (1977), 9-10

The traditional analysis of a crime at common law is into *actus reus*, or guilty act, and *mens rea*, or guilty mind, but the codes use neither these expressions nor any exact synonyms for them. A writer on the criminal law in Australia therefore has to decide between using different terms according as he is talking about common law or code rules and abandoning the traditional common law terminology altogether. The opinion acted on in this book is that the expressions *actus reus* and *mens rea* are too obscure to be of practical utility in an exposition of the modern law in any context. They therefore do not justify adopting the otherwise disadvantageous course of discussing the principles of the criminal law at common law and under the codes in different language, especially since the principles themselves are the same in all significant respects in both contexts.

The words *actus reus* and *mens rea* are taken from the maxim, *actus non facit reum nisi mens sit rea*, there is no guilty act without a guilty mind. An alternative statement of this principle in English which stresses the implication that the guilty act must be coincidental in time with the guilty mind is, "The intent and the Act must both concur to constitute the crime". The argument in favour of keeping the terms *actus reus* and *mens rea* in common use is that they are the customary language of the courts and that since in themselves they have no special significance, their content being "only one of legal arrangement", there is no point in replacing them with unfamiliar terminology which can be no less arbitrary. Nevertheless there are reasons for thinking that at the present day these particular expressions are responsible for much confusion of thought and should be abandoned in favour of any language which accurately conveys the effect of the law without in itself imposing an unnecessary burden of translation and explanation.

J.F. STEPHEN, A HISTORY OF THE CRIMINAL LAW OF ENGLAND

Vol. 2, (1883), 78-9

No temper of mind, no habit of life, however pernicious, has ever been treated as a crime, unless it displayed itself in some definite overt act. It never entered into the head of any English legislator to enact, or of any English Court, to hold, that a man could be indicted and punished for ingratitude, for hardheartedness, for the absence of natural affection, for habitual idleness, for avarice, sensuality, pride, or, in a word, for any vice whatever as such. Even for purposes of ecclesiastical censure some definite act of immorality was required. Sinful thoughts and dispositions of mind might be the subject of confession and of penance, but they were never punished in this country by ecclesiastical criminal proceedings.

The reasons for imposing this great leading restriction upon the sphere of criminal law are obvious. If it were not so restricted it would be utterly intolerable; all mankind would be criminals, and most of their lives would be passed in trying and punishing each other for offences which could never be proved.

Criminal law, then, must be confined within narrow limits, and can be applied only to definite overt acts or omissions capable of being distinctly proved, which acts or omissions inflict definite evils, either on specific persons or on the community at large.

There are a few provisions in the *Criminal Code* which contemplate potential future behaviour by an accused, rather than responding to a past act. The "peace bond" provisions in s. 810 have long existed, allowing a person who reasonably fears personal injury or property damage at the hands of another person to obtain a "recognizance" in which that other person promises to "keep the peace and be of good behaviour". A person refusing to sign such a recognizance can be jailed for up to 12 months. In recent years, similar provisions dealing with fear of intimidation offences, criminal organization offences, terrorism offences, sexual offences and serious personal injury offences have been brought in: see ss. 810.01, 810.1 and 810.2. These provisions differ from the "personal remedy" offered by a peace bond in that they do not require that the person seeking the order fear that he or she personally will be the victim.

It was noted in Chapter 1 that, as a general rule, the Crown bears the burden of proving all the elements of an offence. In general terms, a distinction is drawn between the external elements of an offence and the fault elements. Chapter 3 will pursue the fault requirement at length, while the focus of this chapter will be on the act requirement. It is important to recognize, however, that the external elements of an offence include more than just the conduct of the accused: other circumstances or consequences will usually also be relevant. It is not an offence to pull a fire alarm if there is actually a fire, for example, and dangerous driving which causes death is a more serious offence than dangerous driving which does not.

Determine what elements need to be established to prove that an accused is guilty of the following *Criminal Code* offences:

- **Defacing current coins - s. 456(b)**
- **Escape from lawful custody - s. 145(1)(a)**
- **Endangering safety of ship - s. 78.1(2)(a)**
- **Carrying weapon while attending public meeting - s. 89**
- **Public mischief - s. 140(1)(c)**
- **Breach of trust by public officer - s. 122**
- **Assault - s. 265(1)(a)**
- **Assaulting a peace officer - s. 270(1)(a)**
- **Assault causing bodily harm - s. 267(b)**
- **Arson - s. 433(a)**
- **Fraud in relation to fares - s. 393(1)(a)**
- **Carrying concealed weapon - s. 90(1)**
- **Robbery - s. 343(c)**
- **Theft - s. 322(1)(a)**

The rest of this chapter will focus on issues surrounding proof that the accused has engaged in the conduct which is forbidden by the offence. It is important to remember, though, that unless *all* elements of the offence are proven by the Crown beyond a reasonable doubt, whether conduct, circumstance or consequence, the accused cannot be found guilty.

We next turn to consider each of the five legal aspects of the act requirement:

1. Commission of an unlawful act;

2. Omission where there was a legal duty to act;

3. Voluntariness;

4. Acting through an innocent agent; and

5. If consequences are part of the offence charged, that the act or omission caused the consequence.

2. COMMISSION OF AN UNLAWFUL ACT

In many, if not most, crimes, the act requirement is self-evident. Stealing requires taking something belonging to someone else, assault is a positive act of applying force, etc. In some instances, however, the law's description of the necessary external circumstance of the offence requires careful judicial analysis because it is vague or involves what appears to be a most minimal form of an act. What follows in this section is a selection of a number of different offences where the definition of the act requirement is difficult and often controversial.

(a) Causing Disturbance in Public Place

R. v. LOHNES

[1992] 1 S.C.R. 167, 10 C.R. (4th) 125, 69 C.C.C. (3d) 289,
1992 CarswellNS 11, 1992 CarswellNS 350

McLachlin J.: — This case requires this court for the first time to consider what constitutes a public disturbance under s. 175(1)(*a*) of the *Criminal Code*, R.S.C. 1985, c. C-46, which makes it an offence to cause a disturbance in or near a public place by, inter alia, fighting, screaming, shouting, swearing, singing or using insulting or obscene language. Shouting or swearing or singing are not in themselves criminal offences. They become criminal only when they cause a disturbance in or near a public place. What constitutes such a disturbance? For example, does mere annoyance or emotional disturbance of the complainant suffice? Or is something more required?

The Facts

The case began as a disagreement between two neighbours in the town of Milton, Nova Scotia. The appellant, Donald Lohnes, lived across the street from a certain Mr. Porter. Mr. Porter, it seems, was given to collecting equipment on his premises and running motors which made loud noises. This disturbed Mr. Lohnes. It disturbed him so much that on two occasions a year apart he went onto the veranda of his house and shouted obscenities at Mr. Porter. The essence of Mr. Lohnes's remarks was that he did not want Mr. Porter "to run that chain saw or that lawn mower or to leave that or have that God-damned junk heap". This was embellished by a string of epithets revealing an impressive command of the obscene vernacular. On the second occasion Mr. Lohnes concluded his oration with the assertion that he would shoot Mr. Porter if he had a gun.

Mr. Porter filed a complaint. He was the only Crown witness. There was no evidence that anyone else heard Mr. Lohnes's statements or that Mr. Porter's conduct was affected by them.

Mr. Lohnes was convicted on the ground that his conduct in itself constituted a disturbance within s. 175(1)(a) of the *Criminal Code*; the trial judge found, as well, that Mr. Porter was "disturbed" by the impugned conduct. The convictions were upheld by the Summary Convictions Appeal Court. The Nova Scotia Supreme Court, Appeal Division refused leave from that decision: (1990), 100 N.S.R. (2d) 268. He now appeals to this court.

Legislation

Section 175 of the *Criminal Code* states:

175. (1) Every one who

(a) not being in a dwelling house, causes a disturbance in or near a public place,

(i) by fighting, screaming, shouting, swearing, singing or using insulting or obscene language,

. . . .

is guilty of an offence punishable on summary conviction.

(2) In the absence of other evidence, or by way of corroboration of other evidence, a summary conviction court may infer from the evidence of a peace officer relating to the conduct of a person or persons, whether ascertained or not, that a disturbance described in paragraph (1)(a) or (d) was caused or occurred.

Analysis

Section 175(1)(a) creates a two-element offence consisting of: (1) commission of one of the enumerated acts; which, (2) causes a disturbance in or near a public place. There is no doubt on the facts of this case that one of the enumerated acts was committed. The only question is whether the evidence establishes that it caused a disturbance in or near a public place.

The word "disturbance" encompasses a broad range of meanings. At one extreme, it may be something as innocuous as a false note or a jarring colour; something which disturbs in the sense of annoyance or disruption. At the other end of the spectrum are incidents of violence, inducing disquiet, fear and apprehension for physical safety. Between these extremes lies a vast variety of disruptive conduct. The question before us is whether all conduct within this broad spectrum elicits criminal liability under s. 175(1), and if not, where the line should be drawn.

The Nova Scotia Supreme Court, Appeal Division, in dismissing Mr. Lohnes's application for leave to appeal, agreed with the finding implicit to the judgments below: all that is required to establish an offence under s. 175(1)(*a*) is one of the forms of prohibited conduct (fighting, screaming, shouting, swearing, singing or using insulting or obscene language) which one ought to know would disturb others. The appellant contends that this interpretation is too broad; there must be some overtly manifested disturbance of the public's use and enjoyment of the public place where the act takes place. The main issue thus turns on how "disturbance" in s. 175(1)(*a*) is defined; does foreseeable emotional upset suffice, or must there be an externally manifested disturbance of a public nature? The appeal, like the judgments below, focuses upon the requisite *actus reus* of the offence, although the issue of *mens rea*, as recognized by the respondent, flows necessarily from a discussion of "disturbance". A subsidiary issue concerns whether the act itself may constitute the disturbance, or whether a secondary disturbance is required.

The values at stake on this appeal are readily discerned. On the one hand lies the freedom of the individual to shout, sing or otherwise express himself or herself. On the other lies the collective right of every subject to peace and tranquillity. Neither right is absolute. The individual right of expression must at some point give way to the collective interest in peace and tranquillity, and the collective right in peace and tranquillity must be based on recognition that in a society where people live together some degree of disruption must be tolerated. The question is where the line is to be drawn.

I propose to consider these issues from the perspectives of the authorities, the principles of statutory construction, and the underlying policy issues. On my reading, these considerations point to the conclusion that s. 175(1)(*a*) of the *Criminal Code* requires an externally manifested disturbance in or near a public place, consisting either in the act itself or in a secondary disturbance.

The Authorities

The offence created by s. 175(1)(*a*) finds its origins in the common law of vagrancy, an "offence against public convenience", which proscribed certain behaviour in order to preserve peace and order in the community: see, for example, *An Act Respecting Vagrants*, S.C. 1869, c. 28. In 1947, the *Criminal Code* created a new and distinct offence of causing a disturbance; the offence was moved from the section of the *Code* entitled "Vagrancy" to the nuisance offences falling under Part V labelled "Offences Against Religion, Morals and Public Convenience", S.C. 1947, c. 55, s. 3. Upon the *Code's* revision in 1955, S.C. 1953-54, c. 51, the offence was included in Part IV, renamed "Sexual Offenses, Public Morals and Disorderly Conduct", as s. 160 under the section entitled "Disorderly Conduct".

Our jurisprudence has exhibited two different doctrinal approaches to the offence dating to the first federal vagrancy enactments. The first line of authority adopts an expansive approach to "disturbance"; the second a narrower approach which would limit "disturbance" by requiring external manifestations of disturbance.

. . . .

Whatever their theoretical pronouncements, Canadian courts have entered few if any convictions under (what is now) s. 175(1)(*a*) absent an overtly manifested disturbance which affected people's conduct, be it found in the act itself or in its effect. In *Swinimer* the accused's fighting, shouting and obscene language in front of his residence interfered with the usual activities of a neighbour as well as her children, to judge from her testimony that she had to return to the bedroom during the episode to calm the children down. The conviction in *R. v. Allick* (February 20, 1976), Munroe J. (B.C. S.C.) [unreported] (cited in *R. v. Peters*, *supra*, at p. 90 [C.C.C., p. 256 C.R.]), arose from a spirited barroom brawl. In *R. v. Chikoski* (1973), 14 C.C.C. (2d) 38 (Ont. Prov. Ct.), the police officer testified that the obscenities which the accused had shouted at him not only offended and disturbed him, but caused a group of men working in a field some 200 feet away to stop their work and look up towards the place where the police officer and the accused were standing. In *R. v. D. (C.)*, the trial judge found that the accused caused an affray in the street by shouting and ramming his car into the back of another car, reducing the wife of the owner to tears. Yet, the Court of Appeal overturned even this conviction, finding that the interruption of "tranquillity" of mind or the "emotional upset" caused the owner and his wife was insufficient to constitute a "disturbance". Shouting abusive language without more was held not to trigger the section in *R. v. Eyre* (1972), 10 C.C.C. (2d) 236 (B.C. S.C.) and *R. v. Peters*. In *R. v. Wolgram*, *supra*, shouting obscenities at police in a barroom was similarly held not to offend the section because "[i]t was not made to appear that any person or persons were so disturbed by what occurred as to cause some disorder or agitation to ensue or that there was any interference with the ordinary and customary use by the public of a public place" (p. 537 [C.C.C.]).

I conclude that the weight of the authority, whether viewed from the point of view of theory or result, suggests that before an offence can arise under s. 175(1) of the *Criminal Code*, the enumerated conduct must cause an overtly manifested disturbance which constitutes an interference with the ordinary and customary use by the public of the place in question. This may be proved by direct evidence or inferred under s. 175(2). It is not necessary that there be a separate disturbance secondary to the disturbing act; the act itself may in some cases amount to a disturbance and "cause" it in this sense. Finally, the principle of legality, alluded to in the judgment of Wilson J. in *Skoke-Graham* suggests that only conduct which may reasonably be expected to cause such a disturbance in the particular circumstances of the case falls within s. 175(1)(*a*) (see p. 14, below).

Principles of Statutory Construction

The word "disturbance" is capable of many meanings. The task is to choose the meaning which best accords with the intention of Parliament.

The following arguments support the conclusion that "disturbance" in s. 175(1)(*a*) involves more than mere mental or emotional annoyance or disruption.

First, the noun "disturbance" may have a different connotation than the verb "to disturb". Not everything that disturbs people results in a disturbance (*e.g.*, smoking). A definition which posits identity between "disturb" and "disturbance" is contrary to ordinary usage, the most fundamental principle of statutory construction. This is not to say that one cannot speak of a purely emotional disturbance, but rather that "disturbance" has a secondary meaning which "disturb" does not possess; a meaning which suggests interference with an ordinary and customary conduct or use.

Second, the context of "disturbance" in s. 175(1)(*a*) suggests that Parliament did not intend to protect society from mere emotional disturbance. Had Parliament sought to protect society from annoyance and anxiety, the section would not be confined to acts occurring in or near a public place, nor would it single out particular forms of objectionable conduct — many other types of conduct disturb us. Parliament could have expressly protected against emotional disturbance, as was done in the *Public Order Act 1986* (U.K.), 1986, c. 64. But, to borrow the language of MacKeigan C.J.N.S. in *Swinimer, supra*, Parliament chose to speak of a disturbance in or near a public place, not in someone's mind. By addressing "disturbance" in the public context, Parliament signalled that its objective was not the protection of individuals from emotional upset, but the protection of the public from disorder calculated to interfere with the public's normal activities.

Third, interpretative aids suggest that s. 175(1)(*a*) is directed at publicly exhibited disorder. As noted in *Skoke-Graham, supra*, headings and preambles may be used as intrinsic aids in interpreting ambiguous statutes. Section 175(1)(*a*) appears under the section "Disorderly Conduct". Without elevating headings to determinative status, the heading under which s. 175(1)(*a*) appears supports the view that Parliament had in mind, not the emotional upset or annoyance of individuals, but disorder and agitation which interferes with the ordinary use of a place.

Fourth, the word used for disturbance in the French version of s. 175(1), "tapage", connotes an externally manifested disturbance involving violent noise or confusion disrupting the tranquillity of those using the area in question. For example, Le Petit Robert 1 (Paris: Le Robert, 1990) defines the term as: "10 Bruit violent, confus, désordonné produit par un groupe de personnes; ... *Tapage injurieux ou nocturne*: consistant à troubler la tranquillité des habitants en faisant du bruit, sans motif légitime". [Emphasis in original.]

Finally, it can be argued that the reference in s. 175(2) to an inference of disturbance from evidence "relating to the *conduct* of a person *or persons*" is consistent with the finding that Parliament had in mind the effect of the shouting, swearing or singing, for example, on the conduct of persons other than the accused. In short, Parliament was concerned with how members of the public other than the accused may have been affected by the impugned act.

Policy

Considerations pertaining to the practical application of the criminal law suggest that the narrower "public disturbance" interpretation of s. 175(1)(a) is preferable to the broader "emotional disturbance" standard.

The first consideration pertains to fundamental justice, and in particular, the principle of legality, which affirms the entitlement of every person to know in advance whether their conduct is illegal. As Wilson J. points out in *Skoke-Graham, supra*, application of the internal test would mean that "anyone in any given situation would act at the risk of causing some unmanifested emotional upset or 'disturbance' to another person" (p. 131 S.C.R.). Read thus, s. 175(1)(a) imposes a duty to ascertain whether one's conduct disturbs or can reasonably be expected to disturb the "mental" or "emotional" tranquillity of others. Such a burden, dependent as it is on time, place, circumstance and the sensitivities of others, verges on the capricious. It may well be questioned whether it could ever be discharged with certainty.

The second consideration is that the narrower "public disturbance" test permits a more sensitive balancing between the countervailing interests at stake. As MacKeigan C.J.N.S. points out in *Swinimer*, the test for a disturbance in or near a public place under s. 175(1)(a) should permit the court to weigh the degree and intensity of the conduct complained of against the degree and nature of the peace which can be expected to prevail in a given place at a given time. A test which accepts mental or emotional disturbance as sufficient to establish the offence does not permit such balancing; all that is required is that the accused should have known that someone might be internally disturbed. A test, on the other hand, which turns on whether the effect of the conduct was such as to interfere with the ordinary and customary use of the premises at the time and place in question, permits the countervailing factors to be weighed and balanced. As such, it arguably strikes a more sensitive balance between the individual interest in liberty and the public interest in going about its affairs in peace and tranquillity.

The final policy consideration takes us into the more precarious terrain of pondering the proper goals and limits of the criminal law. The *Swinimer* standard, adopted by the courts below, would make it a criminal offence to sing or shout in circumstances where a person has reason to believe that his or her conduct might annoy or upset someone else, even though no one may have heard the sound, much less have been affected by it. In support of this interpretation, it was argued that such a stringent standard is necessary in order to nip disturbances in the bud before they become truly disruptive to the public. But it is far from self-evident that the goal of peace and order in our public places requires the criminal law to step in at the stage of foreseeability of mental annoyance. Indeed, our society has traditionally tolerated a great deal of activity in our streets and byways which can and does disturb and annoy others sharing the public space. Given the intrusion on public liberty and the uncertainty in the criminal law which such a rule would introduce, it is arguable that some external manifestation of disorder in the sense of interference with the normal use of the affected place should be required to transform lawful conduct into an unlawful criminal offence.

Conclusion on the Ambit of s. 175(1)(a)

The weight of the authorities, the principles of statutory construction and policy considerations, taken together, lead me to the conclusion that the disturbance contemplated by s. 175(1)(*a*) is something more than mere emotional upset. There must be an externally manifested disturbance of the public peace, in the sense of interference with the ordinary and customary use of the premises by the public. There may be direct evidence of such an effect or interference, or it may be inferred from the evidence of a police officer as to the conduct of a person or persons under s. 175(2). The disturbance may consist of the impugned act itself, as in the case of a fight interfering with the peaceful use of a barroom, or it may flow as a consequence of the impugned act, as where shouting and swearing produce a scuffle. As the cases illustrate, the interference with the ordinary and customary conduct in or near the public place may consist in something as small as being distracted from one's work. But it must be present and it must be externally manifested. In accordance with the principle of legality, the disturbance must be one which may reasonably have been foreseen in the particular circumstances of time and place.

Disposition of the Appeal

There was no evidence of a disturbance of the use of the premises in question by anyone in the case at bar. The trial judge applied a mental disturbance test, convicting on the basis that an "ordinary reasonable individual would be disturbed by language of that nature being shouted in a public area". The convictions were upheld. In denying leave to appeal, the Court of Appeal agreed that language such as that used by the accused was "inherently disturbing and was of itself a disturbance" (p. 270 [N.S.R.]). There was no finding that the conduct of the complainant or anyone else was affected or disturbed by the language. In the absence of such findings, the convictions cannot stand.

I would allow the appeal, quash the convictions, and substitute acquittals in their place.

(b) Vicarious Liability

Under a doctrine of vicarious responsibility, one person is automatically responsible for the wrongdoing of another solely on the basis of a relationship between the parties, irrespective of whether that person was at fault or even acted. In the law of torts it has long been clear common law doctrine that a "master" may be vicariously liable for a tort committed by a "servant" acting in the course and scope of his or her employment. Given that the purpose of torts is compensation, the doctrine has a pragmatic rationale: a master is likely to be in a better position to compensate the victim and an employer profits through his or her employee's work. In this way the employer also bears the risk of employing a bad worker.

In the criminal law where the purpose is just punishment, the emphasis is usually on an individual's own act and fault. Our courts have accordingly been reluctant to impose vicarious responsibility. They have generally done so in the past only where there is an express statutory provision. One such statutory provision has now been held to be unconstitutional.

R. v. BURT

(1985), 47 C.R. (3d) 49, 21 C.C.C. (3d) 138,
1985 CarswellSask 201 (Sask. Q.B.)

GEREIN J.: — The accused was charged that he did contrary to "s. 141 via s. 253 [of the Vehicles Act] as registered owner allow someone to operate vehicle and cause excessive noise in its operation". After a trial which proceeded on the basis of an agreed statement of facts, the learned trial Judge concluded that s. 253 contravened the *Canadian Charter of Rights and Freedoms* and entered an acquittal. From said decision the Crown has appealed.

The agreed facts giving rise to the charge were as follows:

1. THAT on the 4th day of September, 1983 at approximately 2:15 a.m. a Ford pick-up truck, being a motor vehicle registered in the name of the defendant, was operated within the Town of Kindersley, in the Province of Saskatchewan on a public highway.

2. THAT the vehicle was operated in a manner which created excessive or unusual noise, contrary to Section 141 of *The Vehicle* [sic] *Act* for the Province of Saskatchewan. The vehicle left approximately 25 feet of tire marks while crossing Main Street.

3. THAT the Royal Canadian Mounted Police constable on patrol pursued the vehicle, which was approximately two blocks ahead of the police car when it pulled to the right and stopped. As the police vehicle approached the registered owner was observed standing next to the vehicle. The police car stopped and the officer called to the owner who ignored the officer and continued walking into his residence.

4. THAT the driver of the motor vehicle was not identified and the accused is charged as the registered owner of the motor vehicle under the provisions of Section 253 of *The Vehicles Act* for the Province of Saskatchewan.

Section 253 (now s. 169(1)) of the *Vehicles Act*, R.S.S. 1978, c. V-3 (since replaced by the *Vehicles Act, 1983* (Sask.), c. V-3.1), provided:

> 253. The owner of a motor vehicle, tractor or trailer, other than a public service vehicle, is liable for violation of any Provision of this Act in connection with the operation of the motor vehicle, tractor or trailer, unless he proves to the satisfaction of the provincial magistrate or justice of the peace trying the case that at the time of the offence the vehicle, tractor or trailer was not being operated by him, nor by any other person with his consent, express or implied.

The trial Judge held that s. 253 contravened s. 7 of the *Canadian Charter of Rights and Freedoms*, which provides:

> 7. Everyone has the right to life, liberty and security of the person and the right not to be deprived thereof except in accordance with the principles of fundamental justice.

By reason of s. 253 of the *Vehicles Act* an owner of a motor vehicle became vicariously liable for any violation of the Act in which the motor vehicle was involved: see *R. v. Grant* (1957), 29 C.R. 229, 122 C.C.C. 261 (Sask. Police Ct.); *R. v. Davlyn Corp.*, 8 C.R.N.S. 219, [1970] 3 C.C.C. 115 (Alta. C.A.); and *R. v. Budget Car Rentals (Toronto) Ltd.* (1981), 20 C.R. (3d) 66 (C.A.). Thus an owner became liable to be convicted of the substantive violation and not simply of lending or permitting the use of his motor vehicle. On conviction he was subject to punishment, which could be a fine of up to $1,000, imprisonment, suspension of licence or a combination thereof. A person could be asleep at home when events transpire which ultimately result in that person's imprisonment. This could occur even though the person took no part in the violation, even in the sense of aiding or abetting. Thus an owner could be convicted in the absence of *both mens rea* and *actus reus*.

Does this absence of *actus reus* render the legislation invalid? In my opinion it does.

. . . .

Throughout the history of the common law the conduct of the wrongdoer had to compromise the prohibited act. The *actus reus* had to be present. Thus, in *Fowler v. Padget* (1798), 101 E.R. 1103 at 1106, Lord Kenyon C.J. stated:

> . . . it is a principle of natural justice, and of our law, that *actus non facit reum nisi mens sit rea*. The intent and the act must both concur to constitute the crime . . .

In Russell on Crime, 12th ed. (1964), vol. 1, at p. 22, the learned author states:

> The new conception that merely to bring about a prohibited harm should not involve a man in liability to punishment unless in addition he could be regarded as morally blameworthy came to be enshrined in the well-known maxim *actus non facit reum nisi mens sit rea*. This ancient maxim has remained unchallenged as a declaration of principle at common law throughout the centuries up to the present day. So long therefore as it remains unchallenged

no man should be convicted of a crime at common law unless the two requirements which it envisages are satisfied, namely, that there must be both a physical element and a mental element in every crime.

Then, at p. 26:

We may repeat, then, that to constitute a crime at common law there must always be a result brought about by human conduct, a physical event, which the law prohibits, for example the death of a man who is under the Queen's peace; and that it has for some time past been the custom to employ the term *actus reus* to denote a deed so prohibited.

In the text *Criminal Law*, 4th ed. (1978), by Smith and Hogan, the learned authors state at p. 31:

Before a man can be convicted of a crime it is usually necessary for the prosecution to prove (a) that a certain event or a certain state of affairs, which is forbidden by the criminal law, has been caused by his conduct and (b) that this conduct was accompanied by a prescribed state of mind. The event, or state of affairs, is usually called the *actus reus* and the state of mind the *mens rea* of the crime. Both these elements must be proved beyond reasonable doubt by the prosecution.

From my reading, I conclude that traditionally a person was not to be convicted of an offence unless he committed the prohibited act.

The legislative tradition has been more mixed. That a person should not be convicted of an offence committed by someone else unless he has assisted, encouraged, counselled or participated in the offence was enunciated as long ago as *R. v. Huggins* (1730), 92 E.R. 518. However, three exceptions were early recognized, namely: (1) public nuisance committed by an employee; (2) criminal libel; and (3) criminal contempt of court: see *Upholsterers Int. Union of N. Amer., Loc. I v. Hankin & Struck Furniture Ltd.*, [1965] 1 C.C.C. 110 (B.C. C.A.), particularly at p. 40. Then, over the years, other instances of vicarious liability have been created by statute and approved by the courts. By way of example see *Barker v. Levinson*, [1950] 2 All E.R. 825 (Div. Ct.); *R. v. Piggly Wiggly Can. Ltd.* (1933), 60 C.C.C. 104 (C.A.); and *R. v. Kiewel Brewing Co.* (1930), 53 C.C.C. 56 (C.A.). Thus for some considerable time our society has lived with vicarious liability in the field of criminal or quasi-criminal law. Put otherwise, there is a certain legislative tradition of vicarious liability in this country.

Yet instances of vicarious liability have remained the exception rather than the rule. Usually such an approach appears to have been adopted to regulate situations where substantial control over the conduct being regulated and an effective means of enforcing same has reposed in one of the parties, *e.g.*, employment situations: again see *Barker v. Levinson* and *R. v. Kiewel Brewing Co.*

In any event the legislative tradition must be looked at in the light of the then prevailing jurisprudence. More particularly, one must remember that prior to the *Charter* the law was that Parliament and Legislatures were supreme and could enact legislation as they saw fit, subject only to the division of powers as set out in the *British North America Act* [now the *Constitution Act, 1867*]. Thus, it was futile to resist legislation even if it did offend principles of fundamental justice. This situation undoubtedly caused the courts to try to temper certain legislation by resorting to the concept of *mens rea* and implying the requirement of same as often as possible. However, this has now changed. Legislation must now conform to the requirements of the *Charter*.

To ascertain community standards as to *actus reus* is exceedingly difficult. Not only have lay members of society failed to discuss the matter, but the same can be said of the legal community. To my mind this dearth of comment is significant. It suggests that it is generally assumed or taken for granted that *actus reus* will be present when a charge is preferred.

In my opinion, fundamental justice encompasses the concept that a person should not be punished in the absence of a wrongful act. I am satisfied that this is the prevailing view in our society. In speaking about *mens rea* in *R. v. Sault Ste. Marie*, *supra*, Dickson J. (now C.J.C.) said at pp. 362-63:

> Public welfare offences obviously lie in a field of conflicting values. It is essential for society to maintain, through effective enforcement, high standards of public health and safety. Potential victims of those who carry on latently pernicious activities have a strong claim to consideration. On the other hand, there is a generally held revulsion against punishment of the morally innocent.

Surely no less revulsion is held when the person has not even committed the act.

I return now to a consideration of s. 253 itself and in doing so I bear in mind the statement of Dickson J., at p. 51 of *R. v. Big M Drug Mart Ltd.*, *supra*:

> In short, I agree with the respondent that the legislation's purpose is the initial test of constitutional validity and its effects are to be considered when the law under review has passed or, at least, has purportedly passed the purpose test. If the legislation fails the purpose test, there is no need to consider further its effects, since it has already been demonstrated to be invalid. Thus, if a law with a valid purpose interferes by its impact with rights or freedoms, a litigant could still argue the effects of the legislation as a means to defeat its applicability and possibly its validity. In short, the effects test will only be necessary to defeat legislation with a valid purpose; effects can never be relied upon to save legislation with an invalid purpose.

The purpose of the *Vehicles Act* as it existed in 1983, and indeed as it presently exists, was to achieve safe and orderly operation of motor vehicles on public highways. To this end various types of conduct are prohibited and sanctions are provided for any breach thereof. No criticism can be made of the Act as a whole.

The purpose of s. 253 is not so clear. It could not have been enacted to ensure that the owner operates his vehicle in a safe manner. The section itself anticipates that he will not be operating the vehicle and in any event the sections which explicitly govern the operation of a vehicle would cover the situation. I do not think the section was intended to regulate the lending of a motor vehicle.

The very wording of the section does not suggest this. Were it otherwise the Legislature could have so stated. It seems to me that the real purpose of the section is to provide a means whereby a form of coercion can be brought to bear upon the owner of a vehicle to disclose who was driving his vehicle or had possession of it at the time when a violation occurred but the actual malefactor was not apprehended or ascertained. In short, it is a device to facilitate enforcement of the provisions of the Act.

It is of interest to note that s. 231 (now s. 172) required an owner, upon request, to furnish a police officer "with such information as he requires in the fulfilment of his duties". However, I am unable to say that the purpose of the section contravenes the *Charter*.

The result is different when one looks at the effect of the legislation. The owner would not be convicted of having improperly permitted the use of his vehicle by another or refusing to provide information. Rather, he would be convicted of the substantive offence or actual violation; in this case, causing excessive noise. As stated earlier, the owner plays no part in the violation of the Act which gives rise to the charge which is preferred. The result is that the owner becomes subject to punishment for the misconduct of another. As I have earlier concluded that this is contrary to principles of fundamental justice, it follows that s. 253 of the *Vehicles Act* has contravened s. 7 of the *Charter*. I use the past tense as I am concerned only with the former section.

Further, it is my opinion that s. 1 of the *Charter* cannot be utilized to maintain the impugned section. I accept that the *Vehicles Act* has the public welfare as its object and to that end seeks to achieve safe and orderly operation of motor vehicles. I also recognize that motor vehicles are numerous and, by their very nature, highly mobile. Difficulties in enforcement of the provisions of the *Vehicles Act* may result therefrom. While the object is laudable and the difficulties unfortunate, the provisions of s. 253 go beyond the reasonable limits envisaged by s. 1 of the *Charter*.

Appeal dismissed.

The decision in *Burt* was confirmed on appeal by the Saskatchewan Court of Appeal, the majority on the basis that there was no requirement of fault. For discussion of this ruling and other decisions see Lee Stuesser, "Convicting the Innocent Owner: Vicarious Liability Under Highway Traffic Legislation" (1989), 67 C.R. (3d) 316.

A car rental company disputes its responsibility for a municipal by-law parking offence arising from a parking meter violation by a lessee of one of its cars. The by-law declares that a driver of a vehicle who was not the owner is liable to any penalty exacted for a parking by-law offence, but that the owner of the vehicle is also liable "to such a penalty unless at the time the offence was committed the vehicle was in the possession of a person other than the owner or his chauffeur without the owner's consent". Do you think that a constitutional defence along the lines of Burt should succeed?

Compare *R. v. Budget Car Rentals (Toronto) Ltd.* (1981), 20 C.R. (3d) 66, 57 C.C.C. (2d) 201 (C.A.).

Should such a constitutional defence bar enforcement of speeding laws through means of photo radar equipment? Would it be material that the scheme of automatically charging the owner of the vehicle involved fines but no demerit points?

(c)   Possession Offences

Given the definition of "possession" in s. 4(3) of the *Criminal Code* [the older numbering was s. 3(4)] as interpreted in the following decisions, mount defences to charges of possession of marijuana against each of A, B, C and D. The evidence is that at a party in an apartment, A, a guest, passed on a joint to others in a group, without herself smoking, but knowing full well what it was. B did not touch the joint but joined the group in which the joint was being smoked, knowing full well what it was. C joined the group, grabbed the joint and called the police. D, the tenant of the apartment where the party was being held, was not in the group at the time but knew that some of her guests were smoking marijuana. Are there any possible *Charter* arguments? If so, what are they?

MARSHALL v. R.

[1969] 3 C.C.C. 149, 5 C.R.N.S. 348,
1968 CarswellAlta 69 (Alta. C.A.)

McDERMID J.A.: — The appellant was charged jointly with three other persons that:

> Reginald James Smith, Roy Clare Jones, Daniel Joseph Marshall and Frank Nelson Brander stand charged that you on the 5th day of February, A.D. 1968 in the Province of Alberta, near the City of Calgary, in the said Province, were unlawfully in possession of a narcotic, to wit: Cannabis (Marihuana) for the purpose of trafficking, contrary to the provisions of Section 4, sub-section 2 of the *Narcotic Control Act*.

All of the accused were found guilty and the appellant Marshall has appealed against his conviction and sentence.

At the date of the offence the appellant was 16 years of age and was attending school in the city of Calgary. He decided to accompany his friend, one of the accused, Roy Clare Jones, who owned a car, to Vancouver for a short weekend holiday. Also accompanying them were the accused Brander and one, Wes. Cameron. The appellant Marshall did not know Wes. Cameron before the trip to Vancouver. The appellant Marshall only had $15 when he commenced the trip and upon arrival in Vancouver on Friday, February 2, he slept the first night in the car, but subsequently he slept in a suite of a friend of Cameron. Very early Monday morning, February 5, the four who were jointly charged and Wes. Cameron started driving back to Calgary. Shortly after leaving Vancouver the appellant discovered that there was *cannabis* (marijuana) in the car. On the trip marijuana was smoked in the car but not by Marshall.

At Golden, B.C., which is better than halfway on the Trans-Canada Highway to Calgary from Vancouver, while doing 95 m.p.h., the car was stopped by the R.C.M.P. The driver at the time was Cameron. As the highway does not go directly through Golden the police required the car to follow them into Golden. The marijuana was thrown out of the car, but not by the appellant. At Golden as Cameron did not have an identification or a driver's licence he was detained by the police but the other boys were allowed to proceed. Jones, the owner of the car, then drove it. They returned to where they had thrown out the marijuana and it was picked up by one of the boys but not the appellant. They then proceeded on to Calgary, picking up a hitchhiker east of Banff. On the outskirts of Calgary the boys were again stopped by the R.C.M.P. as they only had one light burning. This was in the evening of Monday, February 5. The appellant was sitting in the left rear seat of the car. The R.C.M.P. searched the car and found the marijuana, which was a kilogram or 2.2 lbs. It was on the floor of the rear seat on the right-hand side partially covered by a sweater which belonged to Wes. Cameron. Also in the sleeve of the sweater was found a bag containing additional marijuana.

The police also found a hookah pipe, which is a pipe used for smoking marijuana, the bowl of which was found in the glove compartment and the stem in the pocket of the sweater. With the exception of the hitchhiker all of the boys in the car were arrested and charged as aforesaid. The appellant, Marshall, gave evidence in his defence, and stated that he did not know the marijuana was in the car until they were about 30 miles out of Vancouver on their way home. When asked why he did not leave the car when he found out about the marijuana he said he had no money and he was just getting a ride back to Calgary as he had to get back to classes. He further testified that it was Cameron's marijuana, that he said he did not want to pick up the marijuana after it had been thrown out of the car at Golden, and that when asked by the police about the marijuana he said that whosoever it was would take him off the hook at the trial. When asked why he said that he answered, "Oh I didn't want to, I didn't actually want to tell, say whose it was at the time, what you say squeal on him."

Nowhere does the trial judge throw any doubt on the credibility of the testimony given by Marshall and he did say that he believed that he (Marshall) "did not do anything to exercise control or take control of the marihuana." Such being the case I have accepted the evidence of Marshall even where there is conflict between it and the evidence of others.

Marshall was convicted along with the others by the learned trial judge who stated:

> In the case of Marshall his role at this time was perhaps less of a participant in the sense that he did not drive the car, but certainly at that point he had an opportunity of leaving the car. He may or may not have had an opportunity before reaching Golden. I make no finding on that question but at Golden it is very clear that he had the opportunity of leaving the car, requesting the assistance of the police to get back to Calgary or simply leaving the car and hitch hiking himself if there were no other means.

> . . . .

> Although I believe the evidence of Marshall that he did not do anything to exercise control or take control of the marihuana, yet having ridden in the car as long as he did ride in the car, not having indicated in his evidence any protest or any act on his part separating himself from the actions of the others or from their company, and considering the length of time that transpired, which I think is quite a material consideration, I find that he acquiesced in what the others did, and I also find that in the meaning of the *Narcotic Control Act* and the *Criminal Code*, he was in possession.

The Crown relies upon s. 3(4)(*b*) of the *Criminal Code*, 1953-54, ch. 51, to support the conviction of the appellant, Marshall, The *Narcotic Control Act*, 1960-61, ch. 35, provides that possession means possession as defined in the *Criminal Code*. Section 3(4)(*b*) of the *Criminal Code* provides:

> (4) For the purposes of this Act,

> . . . .

> (b) where one of two or more persons, with the knowledge and consent of the rest, has anything in his custody, it shall be deemed to be in the custody and possession of each and all of them.

There is no doubt that Marshall had knowledge of the marijuana being in the car so the question is did he consent to it being there.

The *Shorter Oxford Dictionary* defines "consent" as: "1. Voluntary agreement to or acquiescence in what another proposes or desires; compliance, concurrence, permission."

The meaning of s. 5(2) in the previous *Code*, which is in substantially the same terms as s. 3(4)(*b*) in the present *Code*, has been dealt with by the British Columbia and the Ontario Courts of Appeal in several cases.

. . . .

It was much pressed on us by counsel for the defence that there must be an element of control in order for there to be possession, and the statement of Cartwright J. (now C.J.) was quoted in *Beaver v. Reg.*, [1957] S.C.R. 531, at

541, 26 C.R. 193, 118 C.C.C. 129, reversing (1956), 25 C.R. 53, 116 C.C.C. 231:

> In my view the law is correctly stated in the following passage in the judgment of O'Halloran J.A., with whom Robertson J.A. concurred, in *Rex. v. Hess* (1949), 8 C.R. 42, 94 C.C.C. 48, at 50-1 (B.C.):
>
> "To constitute 'possession' within the meaning of the criminal law it is my judgment that where, as here, there is manual handling of a thing, it must be co-existent with knowledge of what the thing is, and both these elements must be co-existent with some act of control (outside public duty). When those three elements exist together, I think it must be conceded that under s. 4(1)(*d*) it does not then matter if the thing is retained for an innocent purpose."

However, in that case s. 5(2) was not being considered. The reference was to manual possession.

I find it unnecessary to decide in this case whether there must be some measure of control in order to find the "knowledge and consent" required by s. 3(4)(*b*) of the *Code*. In my opinion, although Marshall certainly had knowledge of the presence of the marijuana he had no control, right to control, nor did he consent to its presence.

The choice facing Marshall was to leave the car at Golden and run the risk of obtaining a ride to Calgary in time to attend his classes, or to stay with the car containing the marijuana. There can be no doubt that he would have been much wiser to have left the car and hitch-hiked to Calgary no matter how long it took him. But to say that a 16-year-old boy faced with this alternative, by choosing to continue his trip to Calgary has consented or agreed or acquiesced to the presence of marijuana in the car is not maintainable. It was certainly an error of judgment on his part to run the risk of being charged with possession of marijuana by being found as an occupant of the car. The trial judge might not have believed his story but once it was believed his decision to continue the journey was consent to riding in the car, but such consent does not mean he consented to the marijuana being in the car. He said he objected to it being picked up again after it was thrown out at Golden. He did nothing to impede the police, although he did not volunteer any assistance to them.

Crown counsel argued that at the time it was stated to the police that Boltwood the hitchhiker had nothing to do with the marijuana that Marshall at that time should also have said he had nothing to do with it. This is, of course, a matter the trial judge could take into consideration in deciding whether to believe Marshall or not. Marshall had no obligation to make a statement. His conduct in the whole matter was not only childish but silly but this does not make him guilty of the offence.

. . . .

In the circumstances of this case the appellant, Marshall, had no power to control the persons possessing the marijuana. He was not the owner of the car. In my opinion, he could not be found guilty of aiding and abetting.

I have been concerned as to the fact that although Marshall stated he did not smoke the marijuana when the pipe was passed to him, he did pass it on. This I think comes very close to a consent, but it could be due almost as a reflex action just as a lighted squib was passed on in the squib case, and in all of the circumstances I do not think constituted consent.

In my opinion, the learned trial judge was in error in drawing the inferences from the facts which he found and he should not have inferred the appellant, Marshall, consented to the others having possession of the drug. Accordingly I would allow the appeal and quash the conviction.

R. v. TERRENCE

33 C.R. (3d) 193, [1983] 1 S.C.R. 357, 4 C.C.C. (3d) 193, 1983 CarswellOnt 67, 1983 CarswellOnt 807

RITCHIE J.: — This is an appeal brought with leave of this court at the instance of the Attorney-General of Ontario, pursuant to s. 621(1)(*b*) of the *Criminal Code*, from a judgment of the Court of Appeal for Ontario whereby that court allowed the appeal and quashed the conviction of the accused entered at trial before Judge P.H. Megginson in the Ontario Provincial Court (Criminal Division) for the County of Frontenac, Ontario, on a charge that he:

> . . . on or about the 30th day of January, 1980 at the Township of Kingston and elsewhere in the County of Frontenac, unlawfully did have in his possession one 1980 Chevrolet automobile, of a value exceeding $200.00, the property of Trudeau Motors, Belleville, Ontario which had been theretofore obtained by a person unknown by an offence committed in Canada punishable on indictment, to wit: theft, the said Kelly Brett Terrence, then knowing the said automobile to have been obtained and did thereby commit an indictable offence, contrary to s. 313(*a*) of the *Criminal Code* of Canada.

The important question raised by this appeal relates to the true meaning to be attached to the word "possession" as the same occurs in the context of s. 3(4)(*b*) of the *Criminal Code* and more particularly whether "possession" as there employed imports control as an essential element. Section 3(4)(*b*) reads as follows:

> 3(4) For the purposes of this Act
>
> . . . .
>
> (*b*) where one of two or more persons, with the knowledge and consent of the rest, has anything in his custody or possession, it shall be deemed to be in the custody and possession of each and all of them.

The only evidence in the record of this appeal which is in any way descriptive of the manner in which the respondent first became aware of the existence of the automobile in question is the evidence of the respondent himself which is, in my view, accurately summarized in the judgment of Mr. Justice MacKinnon at p. 64 of the case on appeal herein as follows [55 C.C.C. (2d) 183 at pp. 184-5, 17 C.R. (3d) 390]:

> The 17-year-old appellant testified at his trial. His evidence was that Bill Rorback, Rorback's brother and one Rick Hayes lives across the street from him in Belleville. He often went across to visit after dinner and he had done so on the evening of January 29, 1980. When he arrived Rick Hayes was not present and the appellant and the two Rorbacks watched television. At about midnight Hayes drove up to the front of the house in a new Camaro automobile and asked if anybody wanted to go for a ride in his "brother-in-law's new car". The appellant said "sure" and went with Hayes.
>
> According to the appellant's evidence, Hayes and the appellant drove around town for three quarters of an hour or so and then started east along Highway 401 towards Kingston. It was established that the Camaro had in fact been recently stolen and the licence plates it carried had recently been stolen from another Camaro in Belleville. The appellant knew that Hayes did not own his own motor vehicle but Hayes had, on previous occasions, borrowed his brother-in-law's car which the appellant described as an old junker". He thought that it was probably time for Hayes' brother-in-law to acquire a new car and as Hayes had the keys to the car, he had no suspicion at the time that the car was stolen.
>
> Hayes turned onto Highway 2 around Napanee and shortly thereafter an O.P.P. cruiser gave chase. Constable Mallock testified that the stolen vehicle, on being pursued, increased its speed to 150 km/h, although the appellant's evidence was that the vehicle did not speed up but rather continued at a constant pace. The car was finally stopped by an O.P.P. roadblock some time shortly after 2:30 a.m. The Camaro pulled over to the shoulder and was apparently slowing down to a stop when the appellant jumped from the moving vehicle, rolled onto the shoulder and ran into the adjoining field. The Camaro collided with a cruiser and then came to a stop . . .

As I have indicated, this was the account given by the respondent and it remains uncontradicted by any direct evidence; it accordingly appears to me that the only basis for doubting the accuracy of this account was the repeated assertion by the trial judge that he "utterly" disbelieved it.

There is no doubt about the fact that the vehicle had been stolen from a garage in Belleville and, indeed, there was evidence to the effect that the theft occurred on the very night when the respondent accepted the invitation from Hayes to go for a ride "in his brother-in-law's car". It was this latter circumstance which permitted the trial judge to say, ". . . this car was as hot as a car could be, having been taken by someone during the same night . . .".

There was, as I have said, no direct evidence to contradict the respondent's version of what occurred, but it is evident from his somewhat acid comments that the judge's finding of "possession" is in great measure based on his disbelief of the respondent and it is apparent that the Judge proceeded on the assumption that the respondent's knowledge of the stolen character of the vehicle was a proven fact.

Based on the assumption that the respondent knew the car to be stolen property, the trial judge went on to find that:

> Even if the accused was not the operator of the vehicle and in that sense had the control of it, if the person who had control of the vehicle had it with his knowledge and consent and he

is in the vehicle as well, in my view, that is sufficient to found the necessary conditions to constitute constructive possession under s. 3(4)(*b*) of the *Criminal Code* as defined.

In the course of his reasons for judgment rendered on behalf of the court of Appeal, Mr. Justice MacKinnon reviewed the relevant cases concerning the ingredients of possession under s. 3(4)(*b*) of the *Criminal Code* and concluded that in order to establish "possession" under that section it was necessary that there should be evidence of control on the part of the accused. In the course of these reasons he said [p. 399]:

> In my view, on the proven facts the necessary measure of control was not established beyond a reasonable doubt by the Crown, nor do those facts allow for the invocation of s. 21. If, by way of example only, it were established that the appellant had directed Hayes to drive to Kingston, that, in light of all the other proven facts, would, in my view, satisfy the requirement of some measure of control over the car. If, by way of further example, he had been seen handing the stolen licence plates to Hayes for them to be placed on the motor vehicle, that, once again in my view, would be sufficient to warrant the application of s. 21 and to establish constructive possession of the car by the appellant.

Section 21 of the *Criminal Code* defines the meaning of "parties" to an offence and involves the question of common intention. It will be remembered that in the present case there is no suggestion that the respondent participated in any way in the actual theft of the car by an unknown person, which took place some time before he was invited to drive in it, and there is nothing to support a finding of common intention in relation to the offence of "possession" with which the respondent is here charged.

The Court of Appeal had reference to the case of *R. v. Lou Hay Hung* (1946), 85 C.C.C. 308, which was a decision of its own court concerned with a charge under the *Opium and Narcotic Drug Act*, 1929 (Can.), c. 49, and in which Mr. Justice Roach in the course of his reasons for judgment, referred to and quoted s. 5(2) of the *Criminal Code*, the predecessor of s. 3(4)(*b*), in the following terms at p. 321 C.C.C.:

> Under s. 5(2), both "knowledge" and "consent" are necessary. I have already stated that, in my opinion, there is no doubt that the appellant knew that the accused Watson had opium in the premises. I have been more than a little concerned with the question whether or not, on the evidence, it should be held that he also consented.

In the same set of reasons, Mr. Justice Roach referred to the judgment of O'Halloran J.A. in *R. v. Colvin and Gladue* (1942), 78 C.C.C. 282 at p. 287, where he said: [at p. 322 C.C.C.]:

> 'Knowledge and consent' which is an integral element of joint possession in s. 5(2) must be related to and read with the definition of 'possession' in the previous s. 5(1)(*b*). It follows that 'knowledge and consent' cannot exist without the co-existence of some measure of control over the subject-matter. If there is the power to consent there is equally the power to refuse and vice versa. They each signify the existence of some power or authority which is here called control, without which the need for their exercise could not arise or be invoked.

In the course of the reasons for judgment rendered by Mr. Justice MacKinnon on behalf of the Court of Appeal in the present case, he had occasion to say of the above passage from Mr. Justice O'Halloran's judgment [at pp. 188-9]:

> The judgment of O'Halloran J.A. in *R. v. Colvin and Gladue* (1942), 78 C.C.C. 282, the relevant passage of which for our purposes being the one quoted by Roach J.A., *supra*, to the effect that "knowledge and consent cannot exist without the co-existence of some measure of control over the subject-matter", has been followed by British Columbia Courts in subsequent decisions: *R. v. Sherman* (1929), 1 C.R. 153; *R. v. Bunyon* (1954), 110 C.C.C. 119; *R. v. Dick and Malley* (1969), 7 C.R.N.S. 75; *R. v. Baker* — May 21, 1976 (B.C. C.A.) (unreported as yet) [reported [1976] W.W.D. 132].

The courts in Quebec have adopted the same reasoning as will be seen by reference to *R. v. Sigouin et al.* (1964) 43 C.R. 211, and *R. v. Fournier* (1979), 43 C.C.C. (2d) 468.

As I have indicated, I agree with the Court of Appeal that a constituent and essential element of possession under s. 3(4)(*b*) of the *Criminal Code* is a measure of control on the part of the person deemed to be in possession by that provision of the *Criminal Code* and, accordingly, I do not consider that the Court of Appeal for the Province of Ontario erred in this regard.

. . . .

Appeal dismissed.

In the next case, the Supreme Court addressed the issue of what constitutes possession in the context of digital information. The accused was charged with possession of child pornography after a warrant was issued to search his home computer. The real issue in the case was whether the warrant had been properly issued, but to answer that question the Court had to decide what it meant to possess an image in a computer.

R. v. MORELLI

[2010] 1 S.C.R. 253, 2010 CarswellSask 151, 252 C.C.C. (3d) 273, 72 C.R. (6th) 208

PER FISH J. (MCLACHLIN C.J.C., BINNIE, and ABELLA JJ. concurring): —

14 In my view, merely viewing in a Web browser an image stored in a remote location on the Internet does not establish the level of control necessary to find possession. Possession of illegal images requires possession of the underlying data files in some way. Simply viewing images online constitutes the separate crime of accessing child pornography, created by Parliament in s. 163.1(4.1) of the *Criminal Code*.

15 For the purposes of the *Criminal Code*, "possession" is defined in s. 4(3) to include personal possession, constructive possession, and joint possession. Of these three forms of culpable possession, only the first two are relevant here. It is undisputed that knowledge and control are essential elements common to both.

16 On an allegation of personal possession, the requirement of knowledge comprises two elements: the accused must be aware that he or she has physical custody of the thing in question, and must be aware as well of what that thing is. Both elements must co-exist with an act of control (outside of public duty): *Beaver v. The Queen*, [1957] S.C.R. 531, at pp. 541-42.

17 Constructive possession is established where the accused did not have physical custody of the object in question, but did have it "in the actual possession or custody of another person" or "in any place, whether or not that place belongs to or is occupied by him, for the use or benefit of himself or of another person" (*Criminal Code*, s. 4(3)(a)). Constructive possession is thus complete where the accused: (1) has knowledge of the character of the object, (2) knowingly puts or keeps the object in a particular place, whether or not that place belongs to him, and (3) intends to have the object in the particular place for his "use or benefit" or that of another person.

18 Here, the appellant is alleged to have had possession of digital images in a computer, rather than tangible objects. The law of possession, however, developed in relation to physical, concrete objects. Its extension to virtual objects — in this case, images stored as digital files and displayed on computer monitors — presents conceptual problems. Unlike traditional photographs, the digital information encoding the image — the image file — can be possessed even if no representation of the image is visible. Likewise, even if displayed on a person's computer monitor, the underlying information might remain firmly outside that person's possession, located on a server thousands of kilometres away, over which that person has no control.

19 Essentially, there are thus two potential "objects" of possession of an image in a computer — the image file and its decoded visual representation on-screen. The question is whether one can ever be said to be in culpable possession of the visual depiction alone, or whether one can only culpably possess the underlying file. Canadian cases appear implicitly to accept only the latter proposition: That possession of an image in a computer means possession of the underlying data file, not its mere visual depiction.

. . . .

25 This is a sensible interpretation for a number of reasons. First, and most important, because Parliament, in s. 163.1(4.1) of the *Criminal Code*, has made accessing illegal child pornography a separate crime, different from possession.

In virtue of s. 163.1(4.2), a person accesses child pornography by "knowingly caus[ing the] child pornography to be viewed by, or transmitted to, himself or herself".

26 Parliament's purpose in creating the offence of accessing child pornography, as explained by the then Minister of Justice, was to "capture those who intentionally view child pornography on the [Inter]net but where the legal notion of possession may be problematic" (Hon. Anne McLellan, House of Commons Debates, vol. 137, 1st Sess., 37th Parl., May 3, 2001, at p. 3581).

27 What made a charge of possession "problematic", of course, is that possessing a digital file and viewing it are discrete operations — one could be criminalized without also criminalizing the other. In the case of child pornography, Parliament has now criminalized both. But viewing and possession should nevertheless be kept conceptually separate, lest the criminal law be left without the analytical tools necessary to distinguish between storing the underlying data file and merely viewing the representation that is produced when that data, residing elsewhere, is decoded. The ITO here is specifically limited to allegations of possession pursuant to s. 163.1(4) of the *Criminal Code* (ITO, preamble and paras. 2, 4 and 16).

28 Interpreting possession to apply only to the underlying data file is also more faithful to a traditional understanding of what it means to "possess" something. The traditional objects of criminal possession — for example, contraband, drugs, and illegal weapons — are all things that could, potentially at least, be transferred to another person.

29 Without storing the underlying data, however, an image on a screen cannot be transferred. The mere possibility of sharing a link to a Web site or enlarging the visual depiction of a Web site, as one could "zoom in" on a TV screen image, is insufficient to constitute control over the content of that site. It is indeed the underlying data file that is the stable "object" that can be transferred, stored, and, indeed, possessed. More broadly, the object possessed must itself have some sort of permanence.

30 Thus, while it does not matter for the purposes of criminal possession how briefly one is in possession of the object, the thing said to be culpably possessed cannot — like a broadcast image flickering across a TV screen or a digital image displayed transiently on-screen — be essentially evanescent.

31 Plainly, the mere fact that an image has been accessed by or displayed in a Web browser does not, without more, constitute possession of that image. An ITO seeking a warrant to search for evidence of possession (rather than accessing) must therefore provide reasonable and probable grounds to believe that the alleged offender possesses (or has possessed) digital files of an illegal

image, and that evidence of that possession will be found in the place to be searched. It is not enough to provide reasonable and probable grounds to believe that the alleged offender viewed or accessed illegal images using a computer, without knowingly taking possession — which includes control — of the underlying files in some way.

32 In applying these principles to the facts of this case, I take care not to be understood to have circumscribed or defined constructive possession of virtual objects. I leave open the possibility, for example, that one could constructively possess a digital file without downloading it to his or her hard drive, using for example a Web-based e-mail account to store illegal material.

33 In short, my purpose here is not to say what constructive possession of virtual objects necessarily is, but rather what it manifestly is not. Plainly, in my view, previous access and the possibility of again accessing a Web site that contains digital images, located on a distant server over which the viewer has no control, do not constitute — either alone or together — constructive possession. However elastic the notion of constructive possession may be, to stretch it that far is to defy the limits of its elasticity.

34 For the sake of greater clarity, I turn now to consider how this understanding of possession applies to files in an Internet cache (that is, copies of files automatically stored on the hard drive by a Web browser).

35 When accessing Web pages, most Internet browsers will store on the computer's own hard drive a temporary copy of all or most of the files that comprise the Web page. This is typically known as a "caching function" and the location of the temporary, automatic copies is known as the "cache". While the configuration of the caching function varies and can be modified by the user, cached files typically include images and are generally discarded automatically after a certain number of days, or after the cache grows to a certain size.

36 On my view of possession, the automatic caching of a file to the hard drive does not, without more, constitute possession. While the cached file might be in a "place" over which the computer user has control, in order to establish possession, it is necessary to satisfy mens rea or fault requirements as well. Thus, it must be shown that the file was knowingly stored and retained through the cache.

37 In the present case, the charge is not based on the appellant using his cache to possess child pornography. It is hardly surprising as most computer users are unaware of the contents of their cache, how it operates, or even its existence. Absent that awareness, they lack the mental or fault element essential to a finding that they culpably possess the images in their cache. Having said that, there may

be rare cases where the cache is knowingly used as a location to store copies of image files with the intent to retain possession of them through the cache.

The dissenting judges (Deschamps J. (Charron and Rothstein JJ. concurring)) felt that the majority understanding of "possession" was too narrow. They argued that there was little difference between exercising control over the hard drive of a computer while on the premises where the computer is located and exercising control over the online space of a web-based hosted service. In their view, the key feature was whether the accused had control over the data, and requiring proof of downloading was a formalistic approach which was tied to the particular state of technology at the time of the decision.

R. v. PHAM

[2005] O.J. No. 5127, 2005 CarswellOnt 6940 (Ont. C.A.)

KOZAK J. (AD HOC) (BLAIR J.A. concurring): —

1 As a result of a police search that took place on March 5, 2003 at unit #4, 28 Overlea Crescent in Kitchener Ontario, the appellant Kim Thi Pham and Lieng Van Nguyen were jointly charged with possession of cocaine for the purpose of trafficking contrary to Section 5(2) of the *Controlled Drugs and Substances Act*. On May 28, 2003, prior to the trial, the charge against Nguyen was withdrawn without explanation. Following a judge alone trial in which the appellant did not testify, she was convicted. There was no evidence of actual possession in that the appellant was not present in the apartment when the search was conducted, so that the Crown's case rested on constructive or joint possession.

2 Ms. Pham appeals her conviction on two grounds:

   (i) the verdict was unreasonable and not supported by the evidence; and

   (ii) the trial judge misapprehended the evidence.

3 The sentence appeal was abandoned since the appellant has served her sentence. For reasons that follow, I would dismiss the conviction appeal.

Position of the Parties

4 The drugs were found in premises primarily occupied by the appellant and then later shared with Nguyen. The appellant contends that Nguyen was trafficking in crack cocaine during her absence and therefore the drugs and money, all of which were found in a common area of the apartment (i.e. the bathroom) could reasonably belong to Nguyen alone. The appellant also argues

that the trial judge misapprehended the evidence in concluding that the drugs found in the residence at the time of the search had been in the apartment prior to the appellant's departure on March 3, 2003, and that Nguyen had not left the apartment between the time of the appellant's departure on March 3, 2003 and the time of the search on March 5, 2003.

5 The Crown takes the position that on the facts of the case, it has proven constructive or joint possession. In this regard the Crown submits that this was a simple trial in which the requisite elements of possession, i.e. knowledge, consent and control were considered by the trial judge in light of all the direct and circumstantial evidence. The Crown contends that in convicting the appellant the trial judge made no palpable and overriding error in his factual findings, nor did he draw any inferences that were clearly wrong, unreasonable, or unsupported by the evidence.

The Facts

6 The appellant moved into the apartment at unit #4 during the month of October 2002, at which time she was the sole occupant. Some two months later Lieng Nguyen moved into the apartment. Ms. Lee Ann Poulton occupied unit #3 which was located directly across from unit #4, and from the peek hole in her door she had a clear view of the entranceway of unit #4.

7 After the appellant moved into the building, numerous visitors came to her door on a consistent basis. As a result of watching through the peek hole, Ms. Poulton saw:

(i) people approach the door to unit #4;

(ii) money being slipped under the door; and

(iii) a clear plastic bag would come out containing white stuff.

The visitors would not usually go inside the appellant's apartment but, instead would participate in short exchanges with someone behind the door. On occasion Ms. Poulton heard voices and was able to identify the appellant as one of the people speaking. On two occasions she saw the appellant open the door. The first was when a man asked if fifty dollars was enough and she let him in. The second was on March 1, 2003 when she saw the exchange of money for a small plastic bag with white stuff in it.

8 Some time during the latter part of December 2002, Lieng Nguyen became an occupant of unit #4.

9 The police were contacted and a surveillance of the building, which was a sixplex, was set up on January 3, 2003. The surveillance continued on the

following days: January 6, 7 and 8; February 25, 27 and 28; and March 3, 4 and 5, 2003. The comings and goings of persons into and out of the building were noted by the surveillance officers. Many of those people were known to the police to have problems with drug addiction.

10 On March 3, 2003 at 4:40 p.m. the appellant was seen (by surveillance) to leave her apartment and did not return prior to the seizure of the drugs on March 5, 2003.

11 On March 4, 2003, during Ms. Pham's absence a person attended at unit #4 briefly and then departed. The police arrested this person and seized from him two pieces of crack cocaine. The police then obtained a search warrant to enter unit #4, and during the early morning hours of March 5, 2003, a search of the apartment was conducted. Lieng Nguyen was the only person in the apartment. During the course of the search two pouches were discovered in the bathroom adjacent to the sink. One pouch was described as a small black cloth purse sitting in full view. Upon opening the purse the police found individually wrapped crack cocaine. On the other side of the sink and sitting in full view was an open pink make-up bag which contained $165.00 of Canadian currency, mostly in 20-dollar bills. It was conceded that the 9.8 grams of crack cocaine was seized from the appellant's apartment which she shared with Nguyen.

Legal Considerations

12 The issue at trial was whether the appellant had knowledge and control of the cocaine found in the bathroom and therefore had it in her possession.

13 Section 2 of the *Controlled Drugs and Substances Act*, S.C. 1996 C.19 adopts the definition of "possession" in subsection 4(3) of the *Criminal Code*. That section reads:

> 4(3) For the purposes of this Act,
>
> > (a) a person has anything in possession when he has it in his personal possession or knowingly:
> >
> > > (i) has it in the actual possession or custody of another person or
> > >
> > > (ii) has it in any place, whether or not that place belongs to or is occupied by him for the use or benefit of himself or another person; and
> >
> > (b) where one of two or more persons with the knowledge and consent of the rest has anything in his custody or possession, it shall be deemed to be in the custody and possession of each and all of them.

14 Section 4(3) of the *Code* creates three types of possession:

> (i) personal possession as outlined in section 4(3)(a);

(ii) constructive possession as set out in section 4(3)(a)(i) and section 4(3)(a)(ii); and

(iii) joint possession as defined in section 4(3)(b).

15 In order to constitute constructive possession, which is sometimes referred to as attributed possession, there must be knowledge which extends beyond mere quiescent knowledge and discloses some measure of control over the item to be possessed. See *R. v. Caldwell* (1972), 7 C.C.C. (2d) 285 (Alberta Supreme Court, Appellate Division); *R. v. Grey* (1996), 28 O.R. (3d) 417 (C.A.).

16 In order to constitute joint possession pursuant to section 4(3)(b) of the Code there must be knowledge, consent, and a measure of control on the part of the person deemed to be in possession. See *R. v. Terrence*, [1983] 1 S.C.R. 357 (S.C.C.); *R. v. Williams* (1998), 40 O.R. (3d) 301 (C.A.); *R. v. Barreau*, 9 B.C.A.C. 290, 19 W.A.C. 290 (B.C.C.A.) and *Re: Chambers and the Queen* (1985), 20 C.C.C. (3d) 440 (Ont. C.A.).

17 The element of knowledge is dealt with by Watt J. in the case of *R. v. Sparling*, [1988] O.J. No. 107 (Ont. H.C.) at p. 6:

> There is no direct evidence of the applicant's knowledge of the presence of narcotics in the residence. It is not essential that there be such evidence for as with any other issue of fact in a criminal proceeding, it may be established by circumstantial evidence. In combination, the finding of narcotics in plain view in the common areas of the residence, the presence of a scale in a bedroom apparently occupied by the applicant, and; the applicants' apparent occupation of the premises may serve to found an inference of the requisite knowledge.

The court of appeal decision in *R. v. Sparling*, [1988] O.J. No. 1877 upheld the above passage as being sufficient evidence to infer knowledge.

18 The onus is on the Crown to prove beyond a reasonable doubt, all of the essential elements of the offence of possession. This can be accomplished by direct evidence or may be inferred from circumstantial evidence. In *Re: Chambers and the Queen, supra* at 448, Martin J.A. noted that the court may draw "appropriate inferences from evidence that a prohibited drug is found in a room under the control of an accused and where there is also evidence from which an inference may properly be drawn that the accused was aware of the presence of the drug."

ANALYSIS

19 The central issue at trial was whether the appellant had knowledge and control of the cocaine found in the black cloth purse in the bathroom, sufficient to constitute constructive or joint possession as defined in paragraphs 4(3)(a) and (b) of the *Code*. In my view the trial judge was entitled to find on the evidence as he did, that she had constructive possession of the cocaine either alone or jointly with Mr. Nguyen.

20 In dealing with the issue of possession the trial judge made it clear that the evidence of Ms. Poulton and the surveillance officers was used only to support a trafficking scheme and not for the purpose of showing propensity. He considered this evidence in the context of the evidence as a whole, as playing a significant role in his assessment of the elements of constructive possession.

21 The trial judge found that the 9.8 grams of cocaine were in the apartment before the appellant left the unit on March 3, 2003. He relied on the evidence of the surveillance officers that Nguyen was in the unit on March 3rd and 4th as the various persons were seen coming and going, and that he was still there at the time of the police entry. In his words:

> I would have to speculate given the evidence before me to find that he left the unit at a point after the accused did, and later returned. I find he did not personally bring the cocaine in after the accused left.

22 That Mr. Nguyen left the unit and returned with the drugs in question (or that someone else brought them in), and therefore that the cocaine was not in Ms. Pham's possession on March 5th, is an argument raised by defence counsel, not on the basis of any evidence but merely as a speculative consideration. In *R. v. Jenner* (2005), 195 C.C.C. (3d) 364 (Man. C.A.) at paragraph 16, this type of approach was dealt with as follows:

> The accused's argument is found not on attempting to rebut the evidence tendered by the crown, but on raising questions and issues that although valid in a rhetorical sort of way add nothing to the issues that the trial judge had to address, and the manner in which he did so. Such a manner of attack was dealt with by this court in *R. v. Drury (L.W.) et al.* (2000), 150 Man. R. (2d) 64, 2000 MBCA 100. Huband J.A. addressed the issue as follows (at paragraph 92):
>
>> This is a question that only the accused Drury could answer, but he elected not to testify. Raising the question and inviting the court to speculate as to the answer does nothing to overcome the body of evidence which overwhelmingly points to guilt.

23 I am inclined to the view that the Manitoba Court of Appeal's reasoning applies in the circumstances of this case. However in the end it does not matter for the purpose of the disposition of this appeal.

24 In his companion reasons which I have had the opportunity of considering, Chief Justice R.R. McMurtry concludes that there was no evidentiary basis upon which the trial judge could conclude beyond a reasonable doubt that the particular drugs in question were in the apartment prior to Ms. Pham's departure. He would therefore allow the appeal. Respectfully I would dismiss the appeal even assuming that Mr. Nguyen or someone else brought the drugs into the apartment during Ms. Pham's absence. The evidence and the trial judge's findings support the conclusion that she was in constructive and/or joint possession of the cocaine even if that were so.

25   The following findings and evidence regarding both knowledge and control of the 9.8 grams of crack cocaine by the accused support that conclusion:

(a)   the accused elected to use her home as a drug trafficking center, and was a key figure in the trafficking scheme carried on out of that center; she continued to be the occupant of unit #4 and retained control of the apartment while she was away;

(b)   both the black cloth purse containing the drugs and the pink make-up bag containing the money were found in full view in the bathroom, a common area of the apartment;

(c)   the cloth purse and the make-up bag are consistent with the personal toiletries of the appellant and were found amidst her personal toiletries and make-up;

(d)   there was no evidence of any men's toiletries in the bathroom;

(e)   the main bedroom was littered with woman's clothing, contained documents (including a passport) in Ms. Pham's name, and was the source of drug-related "dime bags" and cut up newspapers and grocery bags of the type used to wrap a 40 piece of crack cocaine;

(f)   the circumstantial evidence supported as the only logical inference a consistent awareness of, and participation in, all that occurred in her home on the part of Ms. Pham, and demonstrated much more than a quiescent or passive knowledge of the drugs, as well as an element of control over them;

(g)   the role of the accused in the trafficking scheme strongly suggested power and authority over the disposal of the cocaine found, and an ability to withhold consent to the keeping of any drugs in her home; and

(h)   Mr. Nguyen either filled Ms. Pham's shoes as the primary distributor during her absence or she and Mr. Nguyen jointly operated the trafficking scheme.

26   In my view the foregoing provided ample basis to found an inference of the requisite knowledge and supported the trial judge's finding that the appellant had sufficient knowledge and control to constitute constructive possession of the cocaine either personally or jointly with Nguyen. It was agreed that if possession was established, that the possession was for the purpose of trafficking.

27   Whether someone is in possession of something pursuant to section 4(3) of the Code is a question of fact to be determined on the evidence based on the inferences to be drawn in each case. The difficulty in determining the sufficiency

of the evidence required to support an inference of possession is aptly demonstrated in the contrasting decisions of *R. v. Sparling* and *R. v. Grey* mentioned earlier.

28 In *Grey*, the accused was convicted of possession of crack cocaine for the purpose of trafficking. The police found the cocaine hidden in the bedroom of his girlfriend's apartment. The case against the accused rested principally on his regular occupancy of his girlfriend's apartment (i.e. 3 or 4 nights a week) and on the presence of his clothing and other belongings in the bedroom where the crack cocaine was found. The above evidence was found to be insufficient to infer knowledge in that:

(1) there was no direct evidence of the appellant's knowledge. The Crown did not have a witness who could state affirmatively that the appellant knew about the cocaine;

(2) the drugs seized by the police were not in plain view, they were hidden;

(3) the apartment was rented by the co-accused;

(4) other persons frequented the apartment; and

(5) the appellant was not a permanent occupant.

29 In *Sparling* the accused entered into a joint lease and was a full time tenant. The drugs were in full view on the coffee table. This court agreed with Watt J. that direct evidence of knowledge was not essential and that knowledge could be established by circumstantial evidence. *Sparling* is closer to the facts of this case than *Grey*.

CONCLUSION

30 The trial judge instructed himself on reaching a conviction based on inferences from proven facts. At page 4 of the judgment he states as follows:

> If I am to convict on inferences of fact, I must be satisfied beyond a reasonable doubt that guilt is the only reasonable inference to be drawn from all of the proven facts. In assessing inferences for each piece of evidence the reasonable doubt standard is not to be applied each time. I am to consider the inference suggested against any other reasonable inference that can be drawn and attribute weight accordingly. All of the evidence that I determine merits weight is then assessed on the reasonable doubt standard.

This is in keeping with what Lord Wright emphasized in *Caswell v. Powell Duffy Associated Collieries Ltd.*, [1940] A.C. 152, where at p. 169 he stated:

> ... that inference must be carefully distinguished from conjecture or speculation and there can be no inferences unless there are objective facts from which to infer other facts which it is sought to establish.

In *R. v. Lukianchuk*, [2001] B.C.J. No. 3000, 2001 B.C.S.C 119, Romilly J. had this to say at page 7 paragraph 19:

> In *R. v. To*, [1992] B.C.J. No. 1700, supra the accused was arrested after placing a plastic bag in a vehicle. The bag contained several videotapes and 4.4 lbs of heroin. The trial judge disbelieved the accused's evidence that he did not know what was in the bag. McEachern C.J.B.C. stated at page 230:
>
>> It must be remembered that we are not expected to treat real life cases as a completely intellectual exercise where no conclusion can be reached if there is the slightest competing possibility. The criminal law requires a very high degree of proof especially for inferences consistent with guilt, but it does not demand certainty. I do not think it can properly be said that the inferences of knowledge in this case would be unreasonable or unsupported by the evidence.

31 It has not been shown that the trial judge committed any palpable and overriding error or made findings of fact including inferences of fact that are clearly wrong, unreasonable or unsupported by the evidence. The trial judge did not misapprehend the evidence. I would accordingly dismiss the appeal.

32 Like Chief Justice R.R. McMurtry, I agree that the appellant might well have been convicted as a party to the offence, under s. 21(2) of the *Criminal Code*. However, the case was not put on that basis, either at trial or on appeal.

McMURTRY C.J.O. (dissenting): —

44 The only evidence available to the trial judge on which such an inference of knowledge might be drawn is that the appellant was the principal occupant of the premises and that she was actively engaged in the trafficking of drugs. However, the evidence established that the appellant had been absent from the apartment for at least 32 hours before the drugs were discovered by the police. The evidence advanced at trial was not capable of excluding the reasonable inference that someone else left the 9.8 grams of crack cocaine in the bathroom during Ms. Pham's extended absence.

The Supreme Court dismissed the further appeal as of right for the reasons expressed by the majority in the Court below: *R. v. Pham*, 209 C.C.C. (3d) 351, [2006] 1 S.C.R. 940.

R. v. CHALK

(2007), 52 C.R. (6th) 371, 2007 CarswellOnt 7625, 227 C.C.C. (3d) 141
(C.A.)

The accused was convicted by a judge sitting without a jury on a charge of possessing child pornography contrary to s. 163.1(4) of the *Criminal Code*. The pornography consisted of several videos found on the hard drive of a computer kept in the home he occupied with his girlfriend and her two children. The defence acknowledged that several videos found on the computer fell within the definition of child pornography set out in s. 163.1 of the *Criminal Code*. The accused admitted in a statement to the police that he had been aware for several months that there was child pornography on the computer but denied he had intentionally downloaded it to the hard drive. He acknowledged downloading and watching adult pornography sometimes alone and sometimes with his girlfriend. He admitted telling his girlfriend to delete his files after his arrest because he knew the computer would be investigated by the authorities. He did not testify. The trial judge convicted. The accused appealed.

DOHERTY J.A: —

[17] Section 4(3) of the *Criminal Code* contains a definition of possession. Section 4(3)(a)(ii) contains the relevant part of that definition for present purposes:

> a person has anything in possession when he ... knowingly
> (ii) has it in any place ... for the use or benefit of himself or another person;

[18] Possession requires knowledge of the criminal character of the item in issue. In this case, the Crown had to prove that the appellant had knowledge of the contents of the videos in issue. It was, of course, irrelevant whether the appellant knew the contents constituted child pornography: see *Beaver v. The Queen* (1957), 118 C.C.C. 129 at 140 (S.C.C.); *Rex v. Hess (No. 1)* (1948), 94 C.C.C. 48 at 51-52 (B.C.C.A.). The appellant's knowledge of the nature of the videos was established by his statements to the police.

[19] Knowledge alone will not establish possession. The Crown must also prove that an accused with the requisite knowledge had a measure of control over the item in issue. Control refers to power or authority over the item whether exercised or not: *R. v. Mohamad* (2004), 182 C.C.C. (3d) 97 at paras. 60-61 (Ont. C.A.).

[20] In *R. v. Daniels* (2004), 191 C.C.C. (3d) 393 at para. 12 (Nfld. C.A.), a case which also involved a charge of possession of child pornography in the form of material located on a computer hard drive, Welch J.A. explained the concept of control in these terms:

> To be in possession of child pornography, it is not necessary for the individual to have viewed the material. For example, a person may obtain pornographic material in an envelope, but without viewing it, either place it in a drawer or dispose of it in the garbage. *It is the element of control, including deciding what will be done with the material, that is essential to possession.* [Emphasis added.]

[21] In her submissions, Ms. LeRoy argued first that the evidence did not support a finding that the appellant knew that the files contained child

pornography. This submission cannot succeed in the face of the appellant's own admission in his statement to the police.

[22] Ms. LeRoy also submitted that the appellant's direction to Ms. Lewis to delete the files containing the child pornography could not constitute an act of control for the purposes of fixing the appellant with possession of the pornography. She submitted that the appellant's instructions demonstrated an intention to destroy rather than possess the material. She analogized the appellant's position to that of a person who possesses drugs strictly for the purpose of destroying them by flushing them down the toilet. Ms. LeRoy stressed that the trial judge did not find that the appellant played any role in downloading the pornography on to the computer or that he used the computer to view the pornography. She contended that the finding of control was based solely on the instruction to delete and that this instruction was inconsistent with an intention to possess.

[23] There is a line of authority supporting the proposition that exercising control over contraband with the requisite knowledge, but solely with the intent of destroying the contraband or otherwise permanently removing it from one's control does not constitute criminal possession: see *R. v. Glushek* (1978), 41 C.C.C. (2d) 380 (Alta. S.C. App. Div.); *R. v. Christie* (1978), 41 C.C.C. (2d) 282 (N.B. S.C. App. Div.); *R. v. York* (2005), 193 C.C.C. (3d) 331 (B.C.C.A.). In *Christie, supra*, Chief Justice Hughes, in referring to what I would call "innocent possession", said at p. 287:

> In my opinion, there can be circumstances which do not constitute possession even where there is a right of control with knowledge of the presence and character of the thing alleged to be possessed, where guilt should not be inferred, as where it appears there is no intent to exercise control over it. An example of this situation is where a person finds a package on his doorstep and upon opening it discovers it contains narcotics. Assuming he does nothing further to indicate an intention to exercise control over it, he had not, in my opinion, the possession contemplated by the *Criminal Code*. Nor do I think that a person who manually handles it for the sole purpose of destroying or reporting it to the police has committed the offence of possession. ...

[24] The "innocent possession" line of authorities was helpfully examined by Green J. in *R. v. Loukas*, [2006] O.J. No. 2405 (Ont. C.J.). Green J. points out that some of the "innocent possession" cases recognize a public duty defence as for example where an accused takes possession of contraband to deliver it to the authorities. In other cases, "innocent possession" is said to arise from the absence of an intention to exercise control beyond that needed to destroy the contraband or otherwise put it permanently beyond one's control. Green J. observes that in all of these cases there is, despite the existence of possession in the strict sense, an absence of a blameworthy state of mind or blameworthy conduct. Convictions for criminal possession by a technical application of the concepts of knowledge

and control in these circumstances would overreach the purpose underlying the criminal prohibition against possession.

[25] I agree with the analysis described above. There are cases where an individual has the requisite control and knowledge, but cannot be said to be in possession for the purpose of imposing criminal liability. These cases will include cases in which a person takes control of contraband exclusively for the purpose of immediately destroying the contraband or otherwise placing it permanently beyond that person's ability to exercise any control over the contraband. In such cases, the intention is solely to divest oneself of control rather than to possess. Like the other appellate courts whose discussions are referred to above, I do not think that criminal liability should attach to that kind of brief, "innocent possession": see e.g. *R. v. Glushek, supra; R. v. York, supra.*

[26] I am also satisfied, however, that this line of authority has no application to the findings of the trial judge. His findings negate any suggestion of "innocent possession". On the trial judge's findings, the appellant did not have possession of the child pornography strictly for the purposes of destroying that pornography. He knew that the pornography was on the computer's hard drive for several months. During that time, he regularly used the computer and had control over the pornography in the sense that he could have deleted it from the computer at any time had he chosen to do so. On his own admission, he ultimately decided to delete the pornography because he feared that the police would discover it when they examined his computer. In those circumstances, the appellant's instruction to delete the material was a manifestation of his longstanding power or authority over the material. That control had existed for several months and was not merely incidental to an innocent purpose.

[27] I would dismiss the appeal.

(d)   Consent Making Act Lawful

Consent is often referred to as a defence. Where consent of the complainant operates in law to acquit it is better seen as a denial that the Crown has proved an unlawful act. Consent is often the crucial issue in the crime of sexual assault and will be fully considered in Chapter 4.

Here we deal more generally with a series of controversial court rulings where apparent consent is vitiated (considered to be of no legal effect) because of policy limits or because consent was induced by fraud.

R. v. JOBIDON

[1991] 2 S.C.R. 714, 7 C.R. (4th) 233, 66 C.C.C. (3d) 454,
1991 CarswellOnt 110, 1991 CarswellOnt 1023

The accused was tried by judge alone on a charge of manslaughter. A fight had begun in a bar. It was stopped by the bar's owner and the two men agreed it was not over. Outside, the accused struck the victim with his fist. The victim was knocked backwards onto the hood of a car. The trial judge found that the victim had been rendered unconscious by this punch. In a brief flurry lasting no more than a few seconds, the accused struck the unconscious victim a further four to six times on the head. There was one single continuing exchange until the victim rolled off the hood and lay limp. He later died of contusions to the head. The trial judge found as a fact that the accused and the victim had consented to a fair fist fight, and that physical injury was intended. He also found that there was no intent to kill or cause serious bodily harm. He further found that the accused did not intentionally exceed the consent that was given and that he struck the last blows under a reasonable but mistaken apprehension that the victim was still capable of returning the fight and was trying to do so. The cause of death was one or more of the punches thrown by the accused in the parking lot. The trial judge acquitted. He decided that there was no unlawful act which could form the basis for a manslaughter conviction. The connection between the two offences of assault and manslaughter is found in s. 222 of the *Code*. The section provides that culpable homicide is either murder or manslaughter and that a person commits culpable homicide when he or she causes the death of a human being by means of an unlawful act. Since there was a consent to a fair fist fight there was no assault within the meaning of s. 265 of the *Criminal Code* and therefore no unlawful act. The Crown's appeal to the Ontario Court of Appeal was allowed and a conviction of manslaughter substituted. That Court decided that the word "consent" in s. 265 of the *Criminal Code*, defining the crime of assault, should be construed subject to common law limits under which consent to a fight in private or public is not a defence to a charge of assault if actual bodily harm is intended and/or caused. The accused appealed. The Supreme Court dismissed the appeal.

GONTHIER J. (LA FOREST, L'HEUREUX-DUBÉ, CORY and IACOBUCCI JJ. concurring): —

. . . .

There is one principal issue raised in this appeal. The principal issue is whether absence of consent is a material element which must be proved by the Crown in all cases of assault or whether there are common law limitations which restrict or negate the legal effectiveness of consent in certain types of cases.

. . . .

Section 265(1)(*a*) states that an assault occurs when, "without the consent of another person, he applies force intentionally to that other person, directly or indirectly". ... In the appellant's opinion, the trial Judge's finding of consent meant that all the elements of the offence of assault had not been proved. The appellant should therefore have been acquitted on that basis, since the Legislature intended that consent should serve as a bar to conviction.

According to the appellant, the Legislature could have specified that in certain situations, or in respect of certain forms of conduct, absence of consent would not be an operative element of the offence. It has done so with other offences. Parliament has provided that no person is entitled to consent to have death inflicted on him (s. 14). It restricted the concept in ss. 150.1 and 159 of the *Code* by denying defences to sexual offences based on a child's consent. It also did this in s. 286 by negating the validity of a young person's consent to abduction. But with the assault provisions in s. 265, it chose not to insert policy-based limitations on the role of consent.

. . . .

The appellant further observed that, in England, the crime of assault is not defined in a *Criminal Code* but in the common law, to which common law limitations and exceptions more naturally apply. In Canada, we have a code of general principles by which, it is presumed, ambiguity is to be construed in favour of the liberty of the subject.

. . . .

There is no indication in s. 265 that the jurisprudence of the criminal common law was to be undermined by its enactment. There was no hint that traditional policy limits on consent, described below in greater detail, were to be ousted by s. 258 of the first *Criminal Code* of 1892, nor by enactment of its successor provision in s. 244 (now s. 265). This should not be surprising. As the foregoing sketch of the history of the offence demonstrates, far from intending to curtail the authority of that law, the *Code* was a partial expression of it.

All criminal offences in Canada are now defined in the *Code* (s. 9). But that does not mean the common law no longer illuminates these definitions nor gives content to the various principles of criminal responsibility those definitions draw from. As the Law Reform Commission of Canada has noted in its 31st report on recodification, the basic premises of our criminal law — the necessary conditions for criminal liability — are at present left to the common law (*Recodifying Criminal Law*, op. cit., at pp. 17, 28 and 34. Reference may also be made to Eric Colvin, *Principles of Criminal Law* (Toronto: Carswell, 1986), at pp. 16-17). The *Code* itself, in s. 8, explicitly acknowledges the ongoing common law influence.

. . . .

Section 8 expressly indicates that the common law rules and principles continue to apply, but only to the extent that they are not inconsistent with the *Code* or other Act of Parliament and have not been altered by them. While little judicial analysis of this section of the *Code* has been undertaken, the references made to it have predominantly concerned exceptional circumstances which provide defences or which deny certain features of an offence. (See Colvin, op. cit., at pp. 16-17.) This court's leading interpretation of s. 8(3) is found in *R. v. Kirzner*, [1978] 2 S.C.R. 487, 1 C.R. (3d) 138, 38 C.C.C. (2d) 131. Chief Justice Laskin expressly rejected a static view of the common law under s. 8(3) (formerly s. 7(3)). Though speaking in the context of alleged prosecutorial impropriety, and a claimed defence of entrapment, Laskin C.J.C. offered an expansive, developmental view, at p. 496 [S.C.R.]:

> There are good reasons for leaving the question open [re: application of an entrapment defence]. Indeed, if that position is based on a static view of s. 7(3) of the *Criminal Code* I find it unacceptable. I do not think that s. 7(3) should be regarded as having frozen the power of the courts to enlarge the content of the common law by way of recognizing new defences.

The approach of the Chief Justice in *Kirzner* was later reinforced in *R. v. Amato*, [1982] 2 S.C.R. 418, 29 C.R. (3d) 1, 69 C.C.C. (2d) 31. Writing in dissent, on behalf of Laskin C.J.C., McIntyre and Lamer JJ., Estey J. applied what he termed the "ordinary rule of construction where statutes and common law meet" to conclude that "s. 7(3) is the authority for the courts of criminal jurisdiction to adopt, if appropriate in the view of the court, defences including the defence of entrapment" (p. 445 [S.C.R.]). The court's majority did not disagree with this determination.

· · · ·

In light of this communicated understanding of the antecedents and purpose of s. 8(3), it can hardly be said that the common law's developed approach to the role and scope of consent as a defence to assault has no place in our criminal law. If s. 8(3) and its interaction with the common law can be used to develop entirely new defences not inconsistent with the *Code*, it surely authorizes the courts to look to preexisting common law rules and principles to give meaning to, and explain the outlines and boundaries of, an existing defence or justification, indicating where they will not be recognized as legally effective —provided of course that there is no *clear* language in the *Code* which indicates that the *Code* has displaced the common law. That sort of language cannot be found in the *Code*. As such, the common law legitimately serves in this appeal as an archive in which one may locate situations or forms of conduct to which the law will not allow a person to consent.

· · · ·

We have observed from the general analysis of the *Code* and common law that, in the history of our criminal law, codification did not replace common law principles of criminal responsibility, but in fact reflected them. That history also reveals that policy-based limitations of the sort at issue here boast a lineage in the common law equally as long as the factors which vitiate involuntary consent. Since these policy-based limitations also existed before the codification of Canada's criminal law, there is no reason to think they have been ousted by statutory revisions and amendments made to the *Code* along the way.

. . . .

Furthermore, since s. 8(3) of the *Code* expressly confirms the common law's continued authority and provides that exculpatory defences not expressly struck down by the *Code* continue to operate to exclude criminal liability, in this appeal, where the *Code* has not erased the common law limit in fist fights, it must continue to define the scope of legally effective consent. Some may object that s. 8(3) cannot be used to support this interpretation because consent is not really a defence, but instead forms part of the offence; indeed it is the absence of consent that is relevant as an element of the offence of assault. For example, Mewett and Manning, op. cit., at p. 567, write that "Real consent is therefore an essential element of assault going to the *actus reus* in the sense that if consent is present no offence can have been committed." Yet while that objection may have some relevance from a strictly formalistic perspective, it is of little consequence from a substantive point of view. Moreover it conflicts with the spirit of this court's previously expressed understanding of s. 8(3).

Whether consent is formally categorized as part of the *actus reus* of the offence, or as a defence, its essential function remains unaltered — if consent is proved, or if absence of consent is not proved, an individual accused of assault will *generally* be able to rely on the consent of the complainant to bar a conviction. He will be able to lean on the consent as a defence to liability. This basic reality has been widely recognized. English and Canadian courts widely refer to consent as being in the nature of a defence. Leading treatises on criminal law conceive it this way. See Watt, op. cit., at p. 216; Clarkson and Keating, op. cit., at pp. 283-292; Glanville Williams, *Textbook of Criminal Law*, 2nd ed. (London: Steven & Sons, 1983), at pp. 549 and 576-578; and Law Reform Commission of Canada, *Assault*, op. cit., at p. 24. We have also observed, in the general interpretive section above, that the law confers on s. 8(3) an open and developmental view of the common law's role. Section 8(3) strongly suggests preservation of the common law approach to consent in assault.

Assault has been given a very encompassing definition in s. 265. It arises whenever a person intentionally applies force to a person "directly or indirectly", without the other's consent. The definition says nothing about the degree of harm which must be sustained. Nor does it refer to the motives for the touching. If taken at face value, this formulation would mean that the most trivial intended touching would constitute assault. As just one of many possible examples, a father would assault his daughter if he attempted to place a scarf around her neck to protect her from the cold but she did not consent to that touching, thinking the scarf ugly or undesirable. (Even an argument for implied consent would not seem to apply in a case like this.) That absurd consequence could not have been intended by Parliament. Rather its intention must have been for the courts to explain the content of the offence, incrementally and over the course of time.

Furthermore, whereas the factors specified in s. 265(3) are readily identifiable, and are generally applicable to all sorts of situations, that is inherently not true of limitations based on policy considerations, which are fact-specific by nature. It would have been quite impractical, if not impossible, for Parliament to establish an adequate list of exceptions to apply to all situations, old and new. Policy-based limits are almost always the product of a balancing of individual autonomy (the freedom to choose to have force intentionally applied to oneself) and some larger societal interest. That balancing may be better performed in the light of actual situations, rather than in the abstract, as Parliament would be compelled to do.

With the offence of assault, that kind of balancing is a function the courts are well-suited to perform. They will continue to be faced with real situations in which complicated actions and motivations interact, as they have in the past. I do not accept the argument that by failing to enact a list of *objects or forms of conduct* to which one could not validly consent, Parliament intended to eliminate their role in the offence of assault and to rely only on the four factors specified in s. 265(3). Such a major departure from well-established policy calls for more than mere silence, particularly as such a list would have been unduly difficult and impractical to prescribe, and was unnecessary given their existing entrenchment in the common law. The common law is the register of the balancing function of the courts — a register Parliament has authorized the courts to administer in respect of policy-based limits on the role and scope of consent in s. 265 of the *Code*.

. . . .

Limits on consent to assault have long been recognized by English and Canadian courts. ... In present times as well, the English courts have on the whole been very consistent when confronted by assaults arising from fist fights and brawls. Since the English cases have set the overall direction for the Canadian common law in the assault context, and apparently continues to do so, it is of particular relevance in the circumstances of this case. The Canadian authorities also favour limits on consent. However, in recent years there has evolved a mixed record across provincial courts of appeal. This appeal therefore presents a timely opportunity for clarification.

[The Court then reviewed a number of English decisions.]

Finally, in 1980, the English Court of Appeal was asked to state the law in *Attorney General's Reference* (No. 6 of 1980), [1981] 2 All E.R. 1057. It was a reference prompted by a street fight between two young men who, in a relatively calm fashion, had decided to settle differences between them by resorting to their fists. One suffered a bleeding nose and some bruises. The other was charged with assault, but acquitted. The question put to the appellate court was, at p. 1058:

> Where two persons fight (otherwise than in the course of sport) in a public place can it be a defence for one of those persons to a charge of assault arising out of the fight that the other consented to fight?

The court held that because it is not in the public interest that people should cause each other bodily harm for no good reason, consent is no answer to a charge of assault when "actual bodily harm is intended and/or caused" (p. 1059). This meant that most fights would be unlawful regardless of consent. Only minor struggles, or rough but properly conducted sporting events, which may have some positive social value, were combative activities where consent would be an effective bar to a charge of assault. Of course lawful chastisement and reasonable surgical interference were also activities in which the public interest does not require nullification of consent. In such cases the general rule applies: the Crown must prove absence of consent to get a conviction for assault. The English Court of Appeal added that the public nature of the forum in which the fight occurs is not determinative of the effectiveness of consent. Private fights deserved no more protection than public ones.

If determinative of this appeal, the English authorities would undoubtedly support the decision of the court below. Here the assault occurred in circumstances which appear very nearly to have amounted to a disturbance of the peace. And there is no question that the punches thrown by Jobidon were intentional applications of force intended to cause the deceased bodily harm. Rodney Haggart's apparent consent would provide no defence to Jobidon in England.

. . . .

(d) *Summary of the Common Law*

(i) The English Position

Attorney General's Reference makes it clear that a conviction of assault will not be barred if "bodily harm is intended *and/or* caused". Since this test is framed in the alternative, consent could be nullified even in situations where the assailant did not intend to cause the injured person bodily harm but did so inadvertently. In Canada, however, this very broad formulation cannot strictly apply, since the definition of assault in s. 265 is explicitly restricted to *intentional* application of force. Any test in our law which incorporated the English perspective would of necessity have to confine itself to bodily harm intended *and* caused.

(ii)   The Canadian Position

The preceding analysis reveals division in the Canadian jurisprudence. Decisions by courts of appeal in Manitoba, Ontario, Nova Scotia and (lately) Saskatchewan would nullify consent to intentionally inflicted bodily harm arising from a fist fight. Their approach is contained, respectively, in *Buchanan* (1898), *Cullen* (1948), *Squire* (1975), *Jobidon* (1988), *Gur* (1986), *McIntosh* (1991), and *Cey* (1989). (There is of course general support for the idea of policy-based nullification in the Alberta Court of Appeal; witness the language of Laycraft C.J.A. in *R. v. Carriere, supra.*) On the other side are decisions of appellate courts in New Brunswick (*MacTavish* (1972)), Quebec (*Abraham* (1974)), Saskatchewan (*Setrum* (1976)), and Alberta (*Bergner* (1987) and *Loonskin* (1990)).

Although there is certainly no crystal-clear position in the modern Canadian common law, still, when one takes into account the combined English and Canadian jurisprudence, when one keeps sight of the common law's centuries-old persistence to limit the legal effectiveness of consent to a fist fight, and when one understands that s. 265 has always incorporated that persistence, the scale tips rather heavily against the validity of a person's consent to the infliction of bodily injury in a fight.

The thrust of the English common law is particularly important in this regard because it has been consistent for many decades, indeed, centuries. It became an integral component of the Canadian common law and has remained so to this day. Many of the seemingly pivotal pro-consent decisions made by courts in the 1970s were either obiter or were pronounced upon insufficient consideration of the important role of the traditional common law. Moreover they were decided prior to the decision in *Attorney General's Reference* (1980), which offered a very authoritative pronouncement of the common law position. The significance of that decision is perhaps best indicated in the instant appeal, for it provided the basis used by the Ontario Court of Appeal to overrule its decision in *R. v. Dix, supra*. The *Attorney General's Reference* case was again observed to be pivotal in the recent decision of the Appeal Court in Saskatchewan, in *R. v. Cey*. In light of these many considerations, I am of the view that the Canadian position is not as opaque or bifurcated as one might initially think.

Notwithstanding this conclusion, given the residual indeterminacy which admittedly lingers in the recent Canadian cases, it is useful to canvass policy considerations which exert a strong influence in this appeal, for they rather decisively support the respondent, bringing down the scales even more surely in support of the decision in the court below.

(e)   *Policy considerations*

Foremost among the policy considerations supporting the Crown is the social uselessness of fist fights. As the English Court of Appeal noted in the *Attorney General's Reference*, it is not in the public interest that adults should willingly cause harm to one another without a good reason. There is precious little utility in fist fights or street brawls. These events are motivated by unchecked passion. They so often result in serious injury to the participants. Here it resulted in a tragic death to a young man on his wedding day.

There was a time when pugilism was sheltered by the notion of "chivalry". Duelling was an activity not only condoned, but required by honour. Those days are fortunately long past. Our social norms no longer correlate strength of character with prowess at fisticuffs. Indeed, when we pride ourselves for making positive ethical and social strides, it tends to be on the basis of our developing reason. This is particularly true of the law, where reason is cast in a privileged light. Erasing longstanding limits on consent to assault would be a regressive step, one which would retard the advance of civilized norms of conduct.

Quite apart from the valueless nature of fist fights from the combatants' perspective, it should also be recognized that consensual fights may sometimes lead to larger brawls and to serious breaches of the public peace. In the instant case, this tendency was openly observable. At the prospect of a fight between Jobidon and the deceased, in a truly macabre fashion many patrons of the hotel deliberately moved to the parking lot to witness the gruesome event. That scene easily could have erupted in more widespread aggression between allies of the respective combatants. Indeed it happened that the brothers of Jobidon and Haggart also took to each other with their fists.

Given the spontaneous, often drunken nature of many fist fights, I would not wish to push a deterrence rationale too far. Nonetheless, it seems reasonable to think that, in some cases, common law limitations on consent might serve some degree of deterrence to these sorts of activities.

. . . .

Wholly apart from deterrence, it is most unseemly from a moral point of view that the law would countenance, much less provide a backhanded sanction to the sort of interaction displayed by the facts of this appeal. The sanctity of the human body should militate against the validity of consent to bodily harm inflicted in a fight.

. . . .

Some may see limiting the freedom of an adult to consent to applications of force in a fist fight as unduly paternalistic; a violation of individual self-rule. Yet while that view may commend itself to some, those persons cannot reasonably claim that the law does not know such limitations. All criminal law is "paternalistic" to some degree — top-down guidance is inherent in any prohibitive rule. That the common law has developed a strong resistance to recognizing the validity of consent to intentional applications of force in fist fights and brawls is merely one instance of the criminal law's concern that Canadian citizens treat each other humanely and with respect.

Finally, it must not be thought that by giving the green light to the common law, and a red light to consent to fights, this court is thereby negating the role of consent in all situations or activities in which people willingly expose themselves to intentionally applied force. No such sweeping conclusion is entailed. The determination being made is much narrower in scope.

(f) *Conclusion*

How, and to what extent is consent limited?

The law's willingness to vitiate consent on policy grounds is significantly limited. Common law cases restrict the extent to which consent may be nullified; as do the relevant policy considerations. The unique situation under examination in this case, a weaponless fist fight between two adults, provides another important boundary.

The limitation demanded by s. 265 as it applies to the circumstances of this appeal is one which *vitiates consent between adults intentionally to apply force causing serious hurt or non-trivial bodily harm to each other in the course of a fist fight or brawl.* (This test entails that a minor's apparent consent to an adult's intentional application of force in a fight would also be negated.) This is the extent of the limit which the common law requires in the factual circumstances of this appeal. It may be that further limitations will be found to apply in other circumstances. But such limits, if any, are better developed on a case-by-case basis, so that the unique features of the situation may exert a rational influence on the extent of the limit and on the justification for it.

Stated in this way, the policy of the common law will not affect the validity or effectiveness of freely given consent to participate in rough sporting activities, so long as the intentional applications of force to which one consents are within the customary norms and rules of the game. Unlike fist fights, sporting activities and games usually have a significant social value; they are worthwhile. In this regard the holding of the Saskatchewan Court of Appeal in *R. v. Cey, supra*, is apposite.

The court's majority determined that some forms of intentionally applied force will clearly fall within the scope of the rules of the game, and will therefore readily ground a finding of implied consent, to which effect should be given. On the other hand, very violent forms of force which clearly extend beyond the ordinary norms of conduct will not be recognized as legitimate conduct to which one can validly consent.

There is also nothing in the preceding formulation which would prevent a person from consenting to medical treatment or appropriate surgical interventions. Nor, for example, would it necessarily nullify consent between stuntmen who agree in advance to perform risky sparring or daredevil activities in the creation of a socially valuable cultural product. A charge of assault would be barred if the Crown failed to prove absence of consent in these situations, insofar as the activities have a positive social value and the intent of the actors is to produce a social benefit for the good of the people involved, and often for a wider group of people as well. This is a far cry from the situation presented in this appeal, where Jobidon's sole objective was to strike the deceased as hard as he physically could, until his opponent either gave up or retreated. Fist fights are worlds apart from these other forms of conduct.

Finally, the preceding formulation avoids nullification of consent to intentional applications of force which cause only minor hurt or trivial bodily harm. The bodily harm contemplated by the test is essentially equivalent to that contemplated by the definition found in s. 267(2) of the *Code*, dealing with the offence of assault causing bodily harm. The section defines bodily harm as "any hurt or injury to the complainant that interferes with the health or comfort of the complainant and that is more than merely transient or trifling in nature".

On this definition, combined with the fact that the test is restricted to cases involving adults, the phenomenon of the "ordinary" schoolyard scuffle, where boys or girls immaturely seek to resolve differences with their hands, will not come within the scope of the limitation. That has never been the policy of the law and I do not intend to disrupt the status quo. However, I would leave open the question as to whether boys or girls under the age of 18 who truly intend to harm one another, and ultimately cause more than trivial bodily harm, would be afforded the protection of a defence of consent. (As was the accused in *R. v. Barron* (1985), 48 C.R. (3d) 334, 23 C.C.C. (3d) 544 (Ont. C.A.), in which a boy was charged with manslaughter, via assault, for pushing another boy down a flight of stairs thereby causing the boy's death. The trial judge held that the deceased boy had impliedly consented to rough-housing on the stairs as they descended.) The appropriate result will undoubtedly depend on the peculiar circumstances of each case.

· · · ·

I would uphold the decision of the Court of Appeal. The appeal is dismissed.

SOPINKA J. (STEVENSON J. concurring): —

I have had the advantage of reading the reasons of Gonthier J., and while I agree with his disposition of the matter I am unable to agree with his reasons. This appeal involves the role that consent plays in the offence of criminal assault. Unlike my colleague I am of the view that consent cannot be read out of the offence.

. . . .

While the consent of the victim cannot transform a crime into lawful conduct, it is a vital element in determining what conduct constitutes a crime. It is a well-accepted principle of the criminal law that the absence of consent is an essential ingredient of the *actus reus*. Thus it is not theft to steal if the owner consents and consensual intercourse is not sexual assault. In Don Stuart, *Canadian Criminal Law: A Treatise* 2d ed. (Toronto: Carswell, 1987), the author states [at p. 469]:

> The general principle, to which there are exceptions, that the true consent of the victim is always a defence to criminal responsibility is a fundamental principle of the criminal law.

. . . .

In *R. v. Lemieux*, [1967] S.C.R. 492, 2 C.R.N.S. 1, [1968] 1 C.C.C. 187, this court held that the offence of breaking and entering was not made out when it was carried out by pre-arrangement with the agent of the owner. The consent of the owner deprived the activity of an essential feature of the *actus reus*.

. . . .

There is, moreover, no generally accepted exception to this principle with respect to the intentional infliction of physical harm. There are many activities in society which involve the intentional application of force which may result in serious bodily harm but which are not criminal. Surgical operations and sporting events are examples. It was no doubt the absence of an exception to this principle that led Parliament to enact s. 14 of the *Criminal Code*, R.S.C., 1985, c. C-46, which creates an exception for the most serious of assaults, the intentional infliction of death.

In my view, Parliament has chosen to extend this principle to all assaults save murder in the interests of making this aspect of the criminal law certain. I see no evidence in the clear and simple language of s. 265 that it intended to outlaw consensual fighting in the interests of avoiding breaches of the peace or to allow it if a judge thought that it occurred in circumstances that were socially useful. Rather, the policy reflected in s. 265 is to make the absence of consent a requirement in the definition of the offence, but to restrict consent to those intentional applications of force in respect of which there is a clear and effective consent by a victim who is free of coercion or misrepresentation. Instead of reading the words "without the consent of another person" out of s. 265, I am of the opinion that the intention of Parliament is respected by close scrutiny of the scope of consent to an assault. Instead of attempting to evaluate the utility of the activity, the trial judge will scrutinize the consent to determine whether it applied to the very activity which is the subject of the charge. The more serious the assault, the more difficult it should be to establish consent.

2. Interpretation of Section 265

Section 265 states that "[a] person commits an assault when *without the consent of another person*, he applies force intentionally to that other person...." (emphasis added). My colleague Gonthier J. concludes that on the basis of cases which applied the common law, that section should be interpreted as excluding the absence of consent as an element of the *actus reus* in respect of an assault with intent to commit intentional bodily harm. In coming to his conclusion my colleague relies on a number of English authorities. The issue was not finally resolved in England until the decision of the English Court of Appeal on a reference to it by the Attorney General in 1980. See *Attorney General's Reference (No. 6 of 1980)*, [1981] 2 All E.R. 1057. Unconstrained by the expression of legislative policy, the court moulded the common law to accord with the court's view of what was in the public interest. On this basis the court discarded the absence of consent as an element in assaults in which actual bodily harm was either caused or intended. Exceptions were created for assaults that have some positive social value such as sporting events. In Canada, the criminal law has been codified and the judiciary is constrained by the wording of sections defining criminal offences. The courts' application of public policy is governed by the expression of public policy in the *Criminal Code*. If Parliament intended to adopt the public policy which the English Court of Appeal developed it used singularly inappropriate language. It made the absence of consent a specific requirement and provided that this applied to *all* assaults without exception. The conflict in the Canadian cases which my colleague's review discloses is largely due to the application of these two disparate strains of public policy.

In my opinion the above observations as to the appropriate use of public policy are sufficient to conclude that the absence of consent cannot be swept away by a robust application of judge-made policy. This proposition is strengthened and confirmed by the specific dictates of the *Code* with reference to the essential elements of a criminal offence. Section 9(*a*) of the *Code* provides that "[n]otwithstanding anything in this Act or any other Act, no person shall be convicted ... (a) of an offence at common law." The effect of my colleague's approach is to create an offence where one does not exist under the terms of the *Code* by application of the common law. The offence created is the intentional application of force with the consent of the victim. I appreciate that my colleague's approach is to interpret the section in light of the common law but, in my view, use of the common law to eliminate an element of the offence that is required by statute is more than interpretation and is contrary to not only the spirit but also the letter of s. 9(*a*). One of the basic reasons for s. 9(*a*) is the importance of certainty in determining what conduct constitutes a criminal offence. That is the reason we have codified the offences in the *Criminal Code*. An accused should not have to search the books to discover the common law in order to determine if the offence charged is indeed an offence at law. Where does one search to determine the social utility of a fight during a hockey game to take one example? There are those that would argue that it is an important part of the attraction. Judges may not agree. Is this a matter for judicial notice or does it require evidence? The problem of uncertainty which the social utility test creates is greater than searching out the common law, a problem which lead to the prohibition in s. 9(*a*).

. . . .

It appears clear from the findings of the trial judge that the accused had an honest belief in consent, but that consent extended only until Haggart "gave up or retreated". The extent of the consent given by Haggart did not, therefore, extend to being struck once he had been knocked unconscious. The accused knew that Haggart's consent did not extend beyond consciousness.

In my opinion, based on his own findings, the trial judge misconstrued the evidence with respect to the accused's belief that all the blows were struck prior to Haggart losing consciousness.

. . . .

Having found that the accused committed an assault, and given that Mr. Haggart died as a result of that unlawful act, the accused is therefore guilty of manslaughter via *Criminal Code* ss. 222(5)(*a*) and 234. I would therefore dispose of the appeal as proposed by Gonthier J.

For a criticism of the majority's position see Upsrich (1992), 7 C.R. (4th) 235. *Jobidon* was re-asserted by the Supreme Court in *R. v. Paice*, [2005] 1 S.C.R. 339, 29 C.R. (6th) 1, 195 C.C.C. (3d) 97. See editorial by Kent Roach in (2005) 50 Crim. L.Q. 357. *Paice* was applied in *R. v. McDonald* (2012), 284 C.C.C. (3d) 470 (Ont. C.A.), leave to appeal refused (2012), 446 N.R. 389 (note) (S.C.C.), where the Court held that the *Jobidon* policy limit does not apply where non-trivial bodily harm was accidentally rather than intentionally caused.

In *Jobidon*, the Court identifies the limits of consent at "bodily harm" while at other times "serious hurt" or "non-trivial bodily harm". Justice Gonthier later states that the "bodily harm contemplated by [his] test" is "essentially equivalent" to what is now defined in s. 2 of the *Criminal Code* as "any hurt or injury to a person that interferes with the health or comfort of the person and is more than merely transient or trifling in nature".

How have the courts applied this definition of bodily harm?

R. v. MOQUIN

73 C.R. (6th) 310, 253 C.C.C. (3d) 96, 2010 CarswellMan 51 (C.A.)

BEARD J.A.: —

23 What constitutes bodily harm within the meaning of . . . s. 2 was considered by Esson J.A. in *Dixon*, as follows (at pp. 331-32):

> .... The judge clearly found a number of facts. The victim suffered bruises on her arm and head and a laceration two to three inches in length on the back of her head. That wound took "some 10 days to heal". She was "all better within a matter of a month". Having found those facts, the judge had to apply the *Code's* definition of bodily harm. That required him to decide whether the hurt or injury interfered with the victim's health or comfort and whether it was more than merely transient or trifling in nature. I leave aside the question whether there was interference with health because, if there was interference with comfort, that is enough. Transient, trifling and comfort are all words in common usage. The Shorter Oxford English Dictionary, 3rd ed., vol. II, defines "transient" at p. 2346 as: "*Transient* 1. Passing by or away with time; not durable or permanent; temporary, transitory; *esp.* passing away quickly or soon, brief, momentary, fleeting". At p. 2362, it defines "trifling" as: "*Trifling* ... 3. Of little moment or value; trumpery; insignificant, petty". At pp. 373-4, vol. I, it defines "comfort" as: "*Comfort* ... The condition or quality of being comfortable".
>
> . . . .
>
> The findings that "there is no evidence of any interference with the victim's health or comfort" and that "an injury that lasts no longer than a month would fall within the definition of being transient and trifling" demonstrate, in my view, an absence of any reasonable regard for the ordinary meaning of the words. From the time of the assault at least until the medical treatment was completed, it is clear that the victim must have been deprived of any sense of comfort which she might have had before being assaulted. The element of interference with comfort, which is all that the definition requires, must have continued for some time after that. The interference with comfort resulted from a significant injury — one which cannot be described as trifling. There is no necessary connection at all between the duration of the injury and the question whether it is trifling — a life-threatening injury is often resolved in a short time. Transient does relate to time but, in this context, it is simply insupportable to describe as transient an injury that "lasts no longer than a month". .... [emphasis added]

24 This finding in *Dixon* has been applied in a number of appeal cases, including: *R. v. K.(C.)*, 2001 BCCA 379; *R. v. T.G.*, 1999 BCCA 512, 129 B.C.A.C. 148; and *R. v. Van De Wiel (K.W.)* (1997), 158 N.S.R. (2d) 368 (S.C.)

25 Examples of injuries that have been found by courts of appeal to constitute bodily harm within s. 2 of the *Code* are as follows:

— scrapes, lacerations and bruises, especially around the eye and a large amount of hair which had been pulled out by the roots — the court observed that significant bruising will obviously cause discomfort and inconvenience for more than a brief and transitory period — *R. v. Dorscheid*, [1994] A.J. No. 56 (C.A.) (QL);

— superficial injuries, consisting primarily of bruising and abrasions, were found at trial to have interfered with the complainant's health and comfort, which decision was upheld on appeal — *R. v. Rabieifar*, [2003] O.J. No. 3833 (C.A.) (QL);

— a number of bruises to the neck and arms, a number of lacerations to the face, chest, shoulder and wrist which cleared up within a week, difficulty speaking for three or four days as a result of choking and a scar on her forearm from a laceration — the court noted (1) that it was incorrect to find that an injury that would heal within a week could not constitute bodily harm, as life-threatening injuries can be of short duration, and, (2) one must look at the overall effect of a number of injuries, each of which may be trifling, but taken together may be more than trifling and transient — *Garrett*; and

— a sore neck that lasted for approximately one month - the court also noted that medical evidence is not required before making a finding of bodily harm — *R. v. Giroux*, [1995] A.J. No. 900 (C.A.) (QL).

. . . .

27   There is a range of harm occasioned by an assault, and the maximum penalty for the related offences increases as the harm increases. The degrees of harm include bodily harm, serious bodily harm and the harm that is required for an aggravated assault. The Supreme Court of Canada dealt with the interpretation of "serious bodily harm" in *McCraw* as follows (at pp. 80-81):

> .... Giving the word "serious" its appropriate dictionary meaning, I would interpret "serious bodily harm" as being any hurt or injury that interferes in a grave or substantial way with the physical integrity or well-being of the complainant. Thus "serious bodily harm" does not require proof of the same degree of harm required for aggravated assault described in s. 268 of the *Code*; that is to say the wounding, disfiguring or endangering of the life of the complainant. Yet it requires greater harm than the mere "bodily harm" described in s. 267; that is hurt or injury that interferes with the health or comfort of the complainant and that is more than merely transient or trifling in nature.

28   It follows from the decision in *McCraw* that, to constitute bodily harm, an injury does not have to meet the standard of "interferes in a grave or substantial way with the physical integrity or well-being of the complainant," that being the standard for serious bodily harm, which is a higher standard than bodily harm. It should be noted that, for the most part, the offences that incorporated serious bodily harm have been amended to require only bodily harm. Within each offence there is a range of harm, and one of the issues on sentencing is the degree or seriousness of the harm within that range.

PROBLEM

John Jones came into your law office yesterday. He's a man aged 52 who has a son Bill, who is 16. Mr. Jones advised you that his son was involved yesterday in an incident at his school. He says that his son was not the instigator but did respond to taunts from a schoolmate, Spike O'Toole. All of Bill's friends were present in the schoolyard when Spike challenged him to a fight. Bill is a karate expert who is schooled that retreat Is always to be preferred but the pressure of the situation got to him and he took up the challenge. In the result Spike went to the hospital with a broken jaw. Mr. Jones has asked you for advice as to Bill's position.

Compare *R. v. W. (G.)* (1994), 30 C.R. (4th) 393, 90 C.C.C. (3d) 139 (Ont. C.A.) and *R. v. B. (T.B.)* (1994), 34 C.R. (4th) 241 (P.E.I. C.A.).

Jobidon has been applied to decide that for policy reasons there cannot be consent to sexual practices that cause harm: *R. v. Welch* (1995) 43 C.R. (4th) 225 (Ont. C.A.) and *R. v. McIlwane* (1996) 3 C.R. (5th) 76 (Que. C.A.). **Any concerns about this determination?**

In *Jobidon* the issue was consent and the victim in fact died, but it is important to recognize that the case did not concern consenting to death. Two provisions of the *Criminal Code* deal specifically with that issue.

14. No person is entitled to consent to have death inflicted on them, and such consent does not affect the criminal responsibility of any person by who inflicts death on the person who gave consent.

. . . .

241. (1) Everyone is guilty of an indictable offence and liable to imprisonment for a term of not more than 14 years who, whether suicide ensues or not,
(a) counsels a person to die by suicide or abets a person in dying by suicide; or
(b) aids a person to die by suicide.

In *Rodriguez v. B.C. (A. G.)*, [1993] 3 S.C.R. 519, 85 C.C.C. (3d) 15, 24 C.R. (4th) 281 a 5-4 majority held that what was then the prohibition against any form of assisting suicide did not violate *Charter* guarantees of principles of fundamental justice under s. 7, protection against cruel or unusual punishment or treatment under s. 12 nor equality before the law under s. 15.

However in *Carter v. Canada (Attorney General)*, [2015] 1 S.C.R. 331, 320 C.C.C. (3d) 1, 17 C.R. (7th) 1 the Court in a unanimous *per curiam* judgment struck down *Criminal Code* provisions prohibiting assisted suicide as overbroad under the *Bedford* principle, to the extent that they prohibit physician-assisted death for a competent adult person who (i) clearly consents to the termination of life and (ii) has a grievous and irremediable medical condition (including an illness, disease or disability) that causes enduring suffering intolerable to the individual in the circumstances of his or her condition.

The declaration of invalidity was extended for 12 and then for an additional 4 months. After extensive consultations and debate Parliament finally responded by enacting a complex *Criminal Code* regime including a new s. 241.2(2), which authorizes doctor-assisted suicide for persons but only if

(a) they have a serious and incurable illness, disease or disability;
(b) they are in an advanced state of irreversible decline in capability;
(c) that illness, disease or disability or that state of decline causes them enduring physical or psychological suffering that is intolerable to them and that cannot be relieved under conditions that they consider acceptable; and
(d) their natural death has become reasonably foreseeable, taking into account all their medical circumstances, without a prognosis necessarily having been made as to the specific length of time they have remaining.

Clearly Parliament's authorization of doctor-assisted suicide is narrower than that of the Court and a new *Charter* challenge has been launched. Should it succeed? If so on what basis?

The *Criminal Code* used to require that consent is vitiated by "fraud as to the nature and quality of the act".

PROBLEM

A doctor conducted a full vaginal examination of a patient. She consented to the presence of a young medical intern watching the procedure. Unbeknownst to her he was in fact not an intern and the doctor had lied about his status so that his friend could watch. Was her consent vitiated by fraud as to the nature and quality of the act such that the doctor should be convicted of the then-existing crime of indecent assault? Compare *R. v. Bolduc and Bird*, [1967] S.C.R. 677.

In 1983, the law relating to coerced consent was changed. Now, under s. 265(3), applying to all forms of assault and sexual assault,

No consent is obtained where the complainant submits or does not resist by reason of

(a) the application of force to the complainant or to a person other than the complainant;
(b) threats or fear of the application of force to the complainant or to a person other than the complainant;
(c) fraud; or
(d) the exercise of authority.

One particularly difficult issue arises when a person has consented to sexual intercourse with another person while unaware that that other person is HIV-positive. The issue first reached the Supreme Court in *R. v. Cuerrier*, [1998] 2 S.C.R. 371, then came to them again in *R. v. Mabior*, 2012 SCC 47. The issue hinges on s. 265(3), which says that "no consent is obtained where the complainant submits . . . by reason of . . . fraud". When should the failure to disclose HIV-positive status be regarded as fraud within the meaning of that section?

R. v. CUERRIER

[1998] 2 S.C.R. 371, 18 C.R. (5th) 1, 127 C.C.C. (3d) 1,
1998 CarswellBC 1772, 1998 CarswellBC 1773

The accused was charged with two counts of aggravated assault pursuant to s. 268 of the *Criminal Code*. The accused had tested positive for HIV in August 1992. At that time a public health nurse explicitly instructed him to use condoms every time he engaged in sexual intercourse and to inform all prospective sexual partners that he was HIV-positive. The accused angrily rejected this advice. He complained that he would never be able to have a sex life if he told anyone that he was HIV-positive. The accused had unprotected sexual relations with the two complainants without informing them he was HIV-positive. The complainants had consented to unprotected sexual intercourse with the accused, but they testified at trial that if they had known that he was HIV-positive they would never have engaged in unprotected intercourse with him. Fortunately, the complainants did not become HIV-positive.

The trial judge entered a directed verdict acquitting the accused. The Court of Appeal upheld the acquittals. The Supreme Court was unanimous in allowing the appeal and ordering a new trial. The Court was divided in its reasons.

CORY J. (MAJOR, BASTARACHE and BINNIE JJ. concurring): —

. . . .

Section 265(3)(c) simply states that no consent is obtained where the complainant submits or does not resist by reason of "fraud". There are no limitations or qualifications on the term "fraud". It is no longer necessary when examining whether consent in assault or sexual assault cases was vitiated by fraud to consider whether the fraud related to the "nature and quality of the act".

. . . .

. . . A principled approach consistent with the plain language of the section and an appropriate approach to consent in sexual assault matters is preferable. To that end, there is no reason why, with appropriate modifications, the principles which have historically been applied in relation to fraud in criminal law cannot be used.

In criminal law cases dealing with commercial transactions, it has been held that mere negligent misrepresentation would not amount to a fraudulent act. However, deliberately practised fraudulent acts which, in the knowledge of the accused, actually put the property of others at risk is subject to criminal sanction. Non-disclosure can constitute fraud where it would be viewed by the reasonable person as dishonest. The essential elements of fraud then are dishonesty, which can include non-disclosure of important facts, and deprivation or risk of deprivation.

It is now necessary to consider the nature of fraud and how it should be applied in the context of the wording of the present s. 265.

. . . .

At the outset it can be accepted that fraud pertaining to the nature and quality of the act or the identity of the partner will still constitute fraud which can be found to vitiate consent. What other acts of dishonesty which give rise to the risk of deprivation can have the same effect?

. . . .

The deadly consequences that non-disclosure of the risk of HIV infection can have on an unknowing victim, make it imperative that as a policy a broad view of fraud vitiating consent . . . should be adopted. . . . [I]t should now be taken that for the accused to conceal or fail to disclose that he is HIV-positive can constitute fraud which may vitiate consent to sexual intercourse.

Persons knowing that they are HIV-positive who engage in sexual intercourse without advising their partner of the disease may be found to fulfil the traditional requirements for fraud namely dishonesty and deprivation. That fraud may vitiate a partner's consent to engage in sexual intercourse.

. . . .

Without disclosure of HIV status there cannot be a true consent. The consent cannot simply be to have sexual intercourse. Rather it must be consent to have intercourse with a partner who is HIV-positive. True consent cannot be given if there has not been a disclosure by the accused of his HIV-positive status. A consent that is not based upon knowledge of the significant relevant factors is not a valid consent. The extent of the duty to disclose will increase with the risks attendant upon the act of intercourse. To put it in the context of fraud the greater the risk of deprivation the higher the duty of disclosure. The failure to disclose HIV-positive status can lead to a devastating illness with fatal consequences. In those circumstances, there exists a positive duty to disclose. The nature and extent of the duty to disclose, if any, will always have to be considered in the context of the particular facts presented. . . . [T]he Crown will have to establish that the dishonest act . . . had the effect of exposing the person consenting to a significant risk of serious bodily harm. The risk of contracting AIDS as a result of engaging in unprotected intercourse would clearly meet that test.

A position that any fraud that is designed to induce the complainant to submit to the act will vitiate consent and constitute an assault would trivialize the criminal process by leading to a proliferation of petty prosecutions instituted without judicial guidelines or directions. To say that any fraud which induces consent will vitiate consent would bring within the sexual assault provisions of the *Code* behaviour which lacks the reprehensible character of criminal acts.

. . . [S]ome limitations on the concept of fraud as it applies to s. 265(3)(c) are clearly necessary or the courts would be overwhelmed and convictions under the sections would defy common sense. The existence of fraud should not vitiate consent unless there is a significant risk of serious harm.

. . . .

It was contended that criminalization would further stigmatize all persons with HIV/AIDS. However it cannot be forgotten that the further stigmatization arises as a result of a sexual assault and not because of the disease. Just as an HIV-positive individual convicted of armed robbery will be further stigmatized but it will not be related to the status of his health. To proceed by way of a criminal charge for assault is not to "criminalize" the accused's activities. Rather, it is simply to apply the provisions of the *Code* to conduct which could constitute the crime of assault and thereby infringe s. 265.

L'HEUREUX-DUBÉ J.: — . . . [T]he 1983 amendment to the *Criminal Code*, in which the rape and indecent assault provisions were reconstituted as the offence of sexual assault, and the words "false and fraudulent representations as to the nature and quality of the act" were removed, evidences Parliament's intention to move away from the unreasonably strict common law approach to the vitiation of consent by fraud.

. . . Parliament has recognized with s. 265(3), that in order to maximize the protection of physical integrity and personal autonomy, only consent obtained without negating the voluntary agency of the person being touched, is legally valid. . . . [F]raud is simply about whether the dishonest act in question induced another to consent to the ensuing physical act, whether or not that act was particularly risky and dangerous. The focus of the inquiry into whether fraud vitiated consent so as to make certain physical contact non-consensual should be on whether the nature and execution of the deceit deprived the complainant of the ability to exercise his or her will in relation to his or her physical integrity with respect to the activity in question.

. . .

An interpretation of fraud that focuses only on the sexual assault context, and which limits it only to those situations where a "significant risk of serious bodily harm" is evident, is unjustifiably restrictive. Such a particularization and limitation is nowhere present in the assault scheme, because Parliament removed any qualifications to the fraud provision as it relates to sexual assault.

. . . .

Finally, my colleagues' examples of the types of trivial conduct that will be caught by this approach are grossly overstated. Cory J. downplays the limiting effect of the fact that a causal connection must be proven, to the imposing criminal standard, between the accused's dishonest act and his intention to induce the submission of the complainant. For instance, a mere misrepresentation as to a man's professional status, without proof that the man was aware that the complainant was submitting to sexual intercourse with him by reason of his lie, would not constitute sexual assault. See Mewett and Manning, *supra*, at pp. 789-90. Whether a complainant actually submitted to sexual intercourse by reason of an accused's fraud will necessarily depend on an examination of all of the factors, and can only be decided on a case-by-case basis.

McLachlin J.'s predictions are even more cataclysmic. Contrary to her assertion in para. 52 of her reasons, it is not "any deception or dishonesty" that will be criminalized by this approach. McLachlin J. argues that based on the approach to fraud that I have explained, henceforward "the implied consent inherent in the social occasion — the handshake or social buss — are transformed by fiat of judicial pen into crimes". But my approach to fraud will in no way catch such innocent conduct. The very notion of implied consent to touching that is inherent in the social occasion, and indeed, inherent in so many aspects of day to day life, is based on an understanding of social realities and a need for tolerance of a reasonable degree of incidental and trivial contact. Whether or not a man is wearing a false moustache or a woman, alluring make-up, it is inconceivable that the Crown, were it foolish enough to prosecute a case of assault by handshake or social buss, would be capable of establishing beyond a reasonable doubt both that a complainant only consented to the physical contact by reason of the deception, and that the deception was employed with the knowledge and intention of inducing the submission of the complainant. In addition, the principle of *de minimis non curat lex*, that "the law does not concern itself with trifles" might apply in such a case: see *R. v. Hinchey*, [1996] 3 S.C.R. 1128 at para. 69, 111 C.C.C. (3d) 353, 142 D.L.R. (4th) 50, per L'Heureux-Dubé J. Furthermore, I cannot accept McLachlin J.'s criticism that the test suffers from imprecision and uncertainty due to the fact that the dishonesty of the act is to be assessed based on an objective standard. A majority of this court has already accepted such an approach to the assessment of the dishonesty of the act in the criminal fraud context: see *Théroux, supra*, at p. 16, per McLachlin J.

Since Parliament has, through the assault provisions, granted broad protection to individual autonomy and physical integrity in order to guard everyone's right to decide under what conditions another may touch them, it is not for this court to narrow this protection because it is afraid that it may reach too far into the private lives of individuals. One of those private lives presumably belongs to a complainant, whose feeling of having been physically violated, and fraudulently deprived of the right to withhold consent, warrants the protection and condemnation provided by the *Criminal Code*.

Subject to these reasons, I agree with my colleagues' disposition to allow the appeal and order a new trial.

McLACHLIN J. (GONTHIER J. concurring): — For more than a century, the law has been settled; fraud does not vitiate consent to assault unless the mistake goes to the nature of the act or the identity of the partner. Fraud as to collateral aspects of a consensual encounter, like the possibility of contracting serious venereal disease, does not vitiate consent. Parliament did not intend to remove the common law limitations on fraud for assault by amending s. 265(3) of the *Criminal Code* in 1983.

. . . [T]he criminalization of conduct is a serious matter. Clear language is required to create crimes . . . When courts approach the definition of elements of old crimes, they must be cautious not to broaden them in a way that in effect creates a new crime. Only Parliament can create new crimes and turn lawful conduct into criminal conduct . . . [T]he *Interpretation Act*, . . . s. 45(2), . . . provides that an amending enactment shall not be deemed to involve a declaration of a change in the existing law . . . As such, the 1983 amendment of the assault provisions, which removed the qualifier "nature and quality of the act" from the type of fraud sufficient to vitiate consent, should not, in the absence of evidence to the contrary, be taken as a change in the law of assault.

This conclusion is also supported by the rule that where a criminal statute is ambiguous, the interpretation that favours the accused is preferred . . .

. . . [T]he 1983 amendments to the *Criminal Code* did not oust the common law governing fraud in relation to assault. The common law continues to inform the concept of fraud in s. 265(3)(c) of the *Criminal Code*.

. . . .

However, it does not follow that all change to the law of assault is barred. It is open to courts to make incremental changes by extending the common law concepts of nature of the act and identity, provided the ramifications of the changes are not overly complex.

. . . .

It is the proper role of the courts to update the common law from time to time to bring it into harmony with the changing needs and mores of society . . . This applies to the common law concept of fraud in relation to assault.

. . . .

The basic precondition of such change is that it is required to bring the law into step with the changing needs of society.

. . . .

In the case at bar . . . the current state of the law does not reflect the values of Canadian society. It is unrealistic, indeed shocking, to think that consent given to sex on the basis that one's partner is HIV-free stands unaffected by blatant deception on that matter . . . [The] common law [earlier] recognized that deception as to sexually transmitted disease carrying a high risk of infection, constituted fraud vitiating consent to sexual intercourse. Returning the law to this position would represent an incremental change to the law.

. . . .

The question is whether a narrower increment is feasible that catches only harm of the sort at issue in this appeal and draws the required bright line . . . [A] return to the [earlier] common law would draw a clear line between criminal conduct and non-criminal conduct . . . [T]he [earlier] law permitted fraud to vitiate consent to contact where there was (a) a deception as to the sexual character of the act; (b) deception as to the identity of the perpetrator; or (c) deception as to the presence of a sexually transmitted disease giving rise to serious risk or probability of infecting the complainant. This rule is clear and contained. It would catch the conduct here at issue, without permitting people to be convicted of assault for inducements like false promises of marriage or fur coats. The test for deception would be objective, focussing on whether the accused falsely represented to the complainant that he or she was disease-free when he knew or ought to have known that there was a high risk of infecting his partner. The test for inducement would be subjective, in the sense that the judge or jury must be satisfied beyond a reasonable doubt that the fraud actually induced the consent.

. . . .

. . . [A]n explanation may be suggested for why deceit as to venereal disease may vitiate consent while deceit as to other inducements, like promises of marriage or fur coats, does not. Consent to unprotected sexual intercourse is consent to sexual congress with a certain person and to the transmission of bodily fluids from that person. Where the person represents that he or she is disease-free, and consent is given on that basis, deception on that matter goes to the very act of assault. The complainant does not consent to the transmission of diseased fluid into his or her body. This deception in a very real sense goes to the nature of the sexual act, changing it from an act that has certain natural consequences (whether pleasure, pain or pregnancy), to a potential sentence of disease or death. It differs fundamentally from deception as to the consideration that will be given for consent, like marriage, money or a fur coat, in that it relates to the physical act itself. It differs, moreover, in a profoundly serious way that merits the criminal sanction.

The question of when fraud based on non-disclosure of HIV-positive status should vitiate consent to sexual activity where the viral count was low returned to the Supreme Court in 2012.

R. v. MABIOR

2012 SCC 47, 290 C.C.C. (3d) 32, [2012] 2 S.C.R. 584

The accused was charged with aggravated sexual assault in relation to nine complainants. He had tested positive for HIV and received treatment that had reduced his viral load to a low level. The accused told none of the complainants that he was HIV-positive and engaged in a variety of sexual acts with each of them. The complainants testified that they would not have consented to sexual activity had they known of the accused's condition. The trial judge convicted the accused of six counts relating to unprotected sexual intercourse but acquitted the accused with respect to those counts in which the accused used a condom during sexual activity.

The accused appealed his convictions. The Manitoba Court of Appeal allowed the accused's appeal in part, holding that either a low viral load or condom use would negate significant risk, thereby leaving convictions on only two of the counts where the accused's viral load was not yet reduced and he did not use a condom. The Crown appealed the four acquittals to the Supreme Court of Canada.

McLachlin C.J.C. (for the Court)

I. Overview

[4] I conclude that a person may be found guilty of aggravated sexual assault under s. 273 of the *Criminal Code* if he fails to disclose HIV-positive status before intercourse and there is a realistic possibility that HIV will be transmitted. If the HIV-positive person has a low viral count as a result of treatment and there is condom protection, the threshold of a realistic possibility of transmission is not met, on the evidence before us.

(1) Problems With the Existing Interpretation of "Fraud" Vitiating Consent

[12] This Court considered "fraud" under s. 265(3)(c) 14 years ago in *Cuerrier*. The majority test in *Cuerrier* may be stated in different ways, but boils down to two elements: (1) *a dishonest act* (either falsehoods or failure to disclose HIV status); and (2) *deprivation* (denying the complainant knowledge which would have caused her to refuse sexual relations that exposed her to a significant risk of serious bodily harm).

[13] We are invited to revisit the *Cuerrier* test by the parties and by the Manitoba Court of Appeal in this case and the Quebec Court of Appeal in the companion case of *R. v. D.C.*, 2012 SCC 48. Two main criticisms of the *Cuerrier* test are advanced: first, that it is uncertain, failing to draw a clear line between criminal and non-criminal conduct (uncertainty), and second, that it either overextends the criminal law or confines it too closely — the problem of breadth.

[14] I turn first to the criticism that the *Cuerrier* test is uncertain. It is a fundamental requirement of the rule of law that a person should be able to predict whether a particular act constitutes a crime at the time he commits the act. The rule of law requires that laws provide in advance what can and cannot be done: Lord Bingham, *The Rule of Law* (2010). Condemning people for conduct that they could not have reasonably known was criminal is Kafkaesque and anathema to our notions of justice. After-the-fact condemnation violates the concept of liberty in s. 7 of the *Canadian Charter of Rights and Freedoms* and has no place in the Canadian legal system.

[15] The *Cuerrier* test gives rise to two uncertainties — what constitutes "significant risk" and what constitutes "serious bodily harm"? These terms are broad and different people can and do read them in different ways.

[16] About "significant risk", some people say that virtually any risk of serious bodily harm is significant. Others argue that to be significant, the risk must rise to a higher level. These debates centre on statistical percentages. Is a 1% risk "significant"? Or should it be 10% or 51% or, indeed, .01%? How is a prosecutor to know or a judge decide? And if prosecutors, defence counsel and judges debate the point, how — one may ask — is the ordinary Canadian citizen to know? This uncertainty is compounded by the fact that a host of variables may affect the actual risk of infection.

[17] Debate has also surrounded the requirement that the risk be one of "serious bodily harm". Some sexually transmitted diseases involve little beyond treatable temporary discomfort. Yet even that discomfort, while it persists, may be serious from the perspective of the victim. Other STDs, like HIV, are extremely serious, involving permanent and life-altering symptoms, and in some cases death. Between these two extremes lie many other STDs, some more debilitating than others. Which are sufficiently serious to attract the sanction of the criminal law? *Cuerrier* offers no clear answer.

[18] The uncertainty inherent in the concepts of significant risk and serious bodily harm is compounded by the fact that they are interrelated. The more serious the nature of the harm, the lower the probability of transmission need be to amount to a significant risk of serious bodily harm, it is argued. So it is not simply a matter of percentage of risk and seriousness of the potential disease. It is a matter of the two as they relate to each other.

[19] What emerges is a complex calculus that makes it impossible, in many cases, to predict in advance whether a particular act is criminal under s. 265(3)(c) or not. The second major criticism of *Cuerrier* relates to the scope of the conduct it catches. The danger of an overbroad interpretation is the criminalization of conduct that does not present the level of moral culpability and potential harm to others appropriate to the ultimate sanction of the criminal law. A criminal

conviction and imprisonment, with the attendant stigma that attaches, is the most serious sanction the law can impose on a person, and is generally reserved for conduct that is highly culpable — conduct that is viewed as harmful to society, reprehensible and unacceptable. It requires both a culpable act — *actus reus* — and a guilty mind — *mens rea* — the parameters of which should be clearly delineated by the law.

[22] The interpretation of "fraud" vitiating consent to sexual relations is informed by four considerations: (a) the purposes of the criminal law; (b) the common law and statutory history of the concept; (c) *Charter* values, particularly equality, autonomy, liberty, privacy and human dignity; and (d) the experience of other common law jurisdictions. I will consider each in turn.

(a) *The Purposes of the Criminal Law*

[23] The interpretation of fraud vitiating consent to sexual relations should further the purposes of the criminal law, notably identifying, deterring and punishing criminal conduct, defined by a wrongful act and guilty mind. Morality infuses the criminal law. But the law does not seek to criminalize all immorality. The principal objective of the criminal law is the public identification of wrongdoing *qua* wrongdoing which violates public order and is so blameworthy that it deserves penal sanction. . .

[24] The law draws a sharp distinction between civil wrongdoing and criminal wrongdoing. Criminal conduct requires both a wrongful act and a guilty mind. It requires "a significant fault element": *R. v Roy*, 2012 SCC 26, [2012] 2 S.C.R. 60, at para. 32. As Charron J. stated for the majority of this Court in *R. v. Beatty*, 2008 SCC 5, [2008] 1 S.C.R. 49, at para. 34:

> If every departure from the civil norm is to be criminalized, regardless of the degree, we risk casting the net too widely and branding as criminals persons who are in reality not morally blameworthy. Such an approach risks violating the principle of fundamental justice that the morally innocent not be deprived of liberty.

The potential consequences of a conviction for aggravated sexual assault — up to life imprisonment — underline the importance of insisting on moral blameworthiness in the interpretation of s. 265(3)(c) of the *Criminal Code*.

(b) *The Common Law and Statutory History of Fraud Vitiating Consent to Sexual Relations*

[25] The common law history of fraud vitiating consent to sexual relations reveals three periods. The early cases support the view that failure to disclose to a partner the fact that one has a serious sexually transmitted disease could constitute fraud vitiating consent to sexual relations, resulting in convictions for rape or assault. This was reversed in *The Queen v. Clarence* (1888), 22 Q.B.D.

23, which held that fraud was confined to deception as to the sexual nature of the act or as to the identity of the male sexual partner. In the post-*Charter* era, a return to a broader view of fraud vitiating consent is appropriate.

[The Court reviewed cases prior to 1888, noting that until then, if the accused failed to disclose that he had a venereal disease, the complainant was held not to have given a valid consent. With *Clarence* that changed, and the view was adopted that a complainant was not the victim of fraud if she knew that she was consenting to engaging in sexual activity. Consent would only be vitiated by fraud if the complainant had consented to activity but did not know that it was sexual or if she was deceived as to the identity of the person with whom she had sex.]

[42] There are not many cases on the books, to be sure. One understands why when one considers the practical implications of the *Clarence* test. The cases where a woman consents to sex but thinks it is *not* sex or that it is sex with a different man are necessarily rare. Submitting to a medical examination only to discover it is a sexual encounter might be such a case; the complainant does not consent to the sexual act but to a medical procedure. Under *Clarence* and its progeny, if the woman consented to the sexual act with the given man, no matter what the deceit, the man could not be convicted for his act. It is not surprising that the legal lexicon contains few cases dealing with fraud vitiating consent. The stark fact was that in all but rare cases fraud could not vitiate consent.

[43] Canadian common law on fraud vitiating consent to sexual relations has now entered a third, post-*Clarence* era. *Charter* values of equality, autonomy, liberty, privacy and human dignity require full recognition of the right to consent or to withhold consent to sexual relations. Fraud under s. 265(3)(*c*) must be interpreted with these values in mind. The *Clarence* line of jurisprudence, which confined fraud to the question of whether the complainant knew the act was sexual or not, is no longer appropriate in the Canadian context. To hold that a complainant consents to the risk of an undisclosed serious disease because he or she knew the act was sexual affronts contemporary sensibilities and contemporary constitutional values.

(c) *Charter Values*

[44] Courts must interpret legislation harmoniously with the constitutional norms enshrined in the *Charter*: *R. v. Sharpe*, 2001 SCC 2, [2001] 1 S.C.R. 45, at para. 33; *Application under s. 83.28 of the Criminal Code (Re)*, 2004 SCC 42, [2004] 2 S.C.R. 248, at para. 35. *Charter* values are always relevant to the interpretation of a disputed provision of the *Criminal Code*.

[45] The *Charter* values of equality, autonomy, liberty, privacy and human dignity are particularly relevant to the interpretation of fraud vitiating consent to sexual relations. The formerly narrow view of consent has been replaced by a view that respects each sexual partner as an autonomous, equal and free person.

Our modern understanding of sexual assault is based on the preservation of the right to refuse sexual intercourse: sexual assault is wrong because it denies the victim's dignity as a human being. Fraud in s. 265(3)(c) of the *Criminal Code* must be interpreted in light of these values.

[48] In keeping with the *Charter* values of equality and autonomy, we now see sexual assault not only as a crime associated with emotional and physical harm to the victim, but as the wrongful exploitation of another human being. To engage in sexual acts without the consent of another person is to treat him or her as an object and negate his or her human dignity. Although the *Charter* is not directly engaged, the values that animate it must be taken into account in interpreting s. 265(3)(c) of the *Criminal Code*.

(d) *The Experience of Other Common Law Jurisdictions*

[49] The parties and a number of interveners have relied on the approach of foreign legal systems to support their positions.

[50] A survey of comparative law shows that common law jurisdictions criminalize the *actual sexual transmission* of HIV, when the HIV-positive person is aware of his or her serologic status and when the partner does not give informed consent to the risk of infection. Several jurisdictions treat transmission of HIV following non-disclosure as offences involving bodily harm, rather than as sexual offences. Such transmission has been prosecuted on the following legal grounds: in England, for reckless infliction of bodily injury, under s. 20 of *The Offences against the Person Act, 1861*, 24 & 25 Vict., c. 100; in the Australian state of Victoria, for "[c]onduct endangering life" (s. 22 of the *Crimes Act 1958* (Vic.)); and in New Zealand, for, *inter alia*, "reckless disregard for the safety of others" that "causes grievous bodily harm" (s. 188(2) of the *Crimes Act 1961*). See I. Grant, "The Prosecution of Non-disclosure of HIV in Canada: Time to Rethink *Cuerrier*" (2011), 5 *M.J.L.H.* 7, at pp. 31-41.

[51] However, deception that exposes a partner to a *risk of transmission* — but that does not ultimately result in transmission — is not criminalized in many jurisdictions. In England, exposing one's partner to HIV without advising of HIV status does not vitiate consent. Fraud vitiates consent only if it goes to "the nature or purpose of the relevant act", which excludes deception as to HIV status: *R. v. B.*, [2006] EWCA Crim 2945, [2007] 1 W.L.R. 1567, at para. 12. Theoretically, s. 18 of *The Offences against the Person Act, 1861*, which criminalizes intentional infliction of harm, could be used in England to punish non-disclosure of HIV-positive status as a form of *attempted* intentional infliction of harm. However, the high evidentiary burden "of proving that someone actually intended to transmit HIV through sex (as opposed to intending to have unprotected sex)" places a prohibitive onus on the Crown (Grant, at p. 32).

[52] In Australia, six of the nine jurisdictions do not criminalize exposure absent transmission. Of the three jurisdictions that criminalize exposure to a risk of transmission (*Crimes Act 1958* (Vic.), ss. 22 and 23; *Criminal Law Consolidation Act 1935* (S.A.), s. 29; *Criminal Code Act* (N.T.), ss. 174C and 174D), two (Victoria and the Northern Territory) apply lesser criminal offences for cases where no actual transmission resulted from exposure.

[53] In New Zealand, liability hinges, *inter alia*, on whether transmission occurs. Absent transmission, the failure to disclose HIV-positive status prior to sexual relations attracts the lesser offence of criminal nuisance (s. 145 of the *Crimes Act, 1961; R. v. Mwai*, [1995] 3 N.Z.L.R. 149 (C.A.)).

[54] Professor Grant summarizes the contrast between the Canadian approach and the approach taken by England, Australia and New Zealand as follows:

> In Canada, the same charge of aggravated (sexual) assault is typically used regardless of the nature of the deception, whether the virus is transmitted, or whether there is an isolated incident of non-disclosure or an ongoing course of non-disclosure. . . . In all other jurisdictions [canvassed in this study], the offence is characterized as the infliction of bodily harm, and not as non-consensual sexual contact. [p. 42]

[55] In sum, while the experience of other jurisdictions is not conclusive, it sounds a note of caution against extending the criminal law beyond its appropriate reach in this complex and emerging area of the law.

(3) Finding a Solution

[57] The four interpretational considerations suggest that the *Cuerrier* test is valid from the perspective of principle and impact. The *Cuerrier* test, to recap, requires proof of two elements: (1) a dishonest act; and (2) deprivation. It defines the first element broadly in terms of either misrepresentation or non-disclosure of HIV, and the second element equally broadly in terms of whether the act poses a "significant risk of serious bodily harm".

[58] While it may be difficult to apply, the *Cuerrier* approach is in principle valid. It carves out an appropriate area for the criminal law — one restricted to "significant risk of serious bodily harm". It reflects the *Charter* values of autonomy, liberty and equality, and the evolution of the common law, appropriately excluding the *Clarence* line of authority. The test's approach to consent accepts the wisdom of the common law that not every deception that leads to sexual intercourse should be criminalized, while still according consent meaningful scope. While *Cuerrier* takes the criminal law further than courts in other common law jurisdictions have, it can be argued other courts have not gone far enough...

[60] It follows that *Cuerrier* should not be jettisoned. The problems of uncertainty and appropriate reach that have emerged in its application should be

addressed, but to the extent possible within the general framework of *Cuerrier*. This brings us to the suggestions for dealing with the problems of uncertainty and overbreadth that have arisen in applying *Cuerrier*.

[The Court considers and rejects two possible solutions: the "Active Misrepresentation Approach" (which would narrow the concept of dishonest act to active deception such as a clear misrepresentation or a lie in response to a clear question) and the "Absolute Disclosure Approach" (which would require all HIV-positive people to disclose the fact to all sexual partners in all cases). They held that both approaches would solve the uncertainty problem but that the former would be under-inclusive (passive deception could be as blameworthy as active deception) and the latter would be over-inclusive ("People who act responsibly and whose conduct causes no harm and indeed may pose no risk of harm, could find themselves criminalized and imprisoned for lengthy periods"). They also rejected the "Case-by-Case Fact-based Approach" (which is more or less what the Manitoba Court of Appeal had proposed) on the basis that it did not solve the uncertainty problem. After considering and rejecting other options, such as a relationship-based approach or the "Reasonable Partner" approach, they put forward their solution.]

(g) *An Evolving Common Law Approach*

[81] This leaves the option of building greater certainty into the *Cuerrier* test by indicating when the significant risk test is met in terms of principle and concrete situations. Such an approach is consistent with the incremental role of common law courts in adapting the contours of an offence to the requirements of justice and practical application.

[82] The question, building on *Cuerrier*, is: when do sexual relations with an HIV-positive person pose a "significant risk of serious bodily harm"? . . . The terms "serious bodily harm" mean "any hurt or injury, whether physical or psychological, that interferes in a substantial way with the integrity, health or well-being of a victim": *R. v. McCraw*, [1991] 3 S.C.R. 72, at p. 88. Of course, actual transmission of HIV constitutes serious bodily harm.

[83] The courts below answered this question of law differently. The trial judge took the approach that any risk of transmission of HIV, however small, constitutes "significant risk of serious bodily harm" (see reference to the trial judge's reasons, at C.A. para. 66). The Court of Appeal, by contrast, held that "significant risk" connoted a high risk of transmission of HIV. In its view "significant risk of serious bodily harm" under *Cuerrier* requires a "significant or high risk" (para. 80) — the "opposite of evidence of a 'high probability' of no infectiousness" (para. 127).

[84] In my view, a "significant risk of serious bodily harm" connotes a position between the extremes of no risk (the trial judge's test) and "high risk" (the Court

of Appeal's test). Where there is a *realistic possibility of transmission of HIV*, a significant risk of serious bodily harm is established, and the deprivation element of the *Cuerrier* test is met.

· · · ·

[91] These considerations lead me to conclude that the *Cuerrier* requirement of "significant risk of serious bodily harm" should be read as requiring disclosure of HIV status if there is a realistic possibility of transmission of HIV. If there is no realistic possibility of transmission of HIV, failure to disclose that one has HIV will not constitute fraud vitiating consent to sexual relations under s. 265(3)(*c*).

[92] The test of realistic possibility of transmission proposed in these reasons is specific to HIV. As discussed above, "significant risk" depends both on the degree of the harm and risk of transmission. These two factors vary inversely. A treatable sexually transmitted disease that does not seriously alter a person's life or life-expectancy might well not rise to the level of constituting "serious bodily harm", and would also fail to meet the requirement of endangerment of life for aggravated sexual assault under s. 273(1). Where the line should be drawn with respect to diseases other than HIV is not before us. It is enough to note that HIV is indisputably serious and life-endangering. Although it can be controlled by medication, HIV remains an incurable chronic infection that, if untreated, can result in death. As such, the failure to advise a sexual partner of one's HIV status may lead to a conviction for aggravated sexual assault under s. 273(1) of the *Criminal Code*. (This said, it may be that with further medical advances, the death rate may decline to the point where the risk of death is virtually eliminated, reducing the offence to sexual assault *simpliciter* under s. 271(1) of the *Criminal Code*. Similarly, the day may come when researchers will find a cure for HIV, with the possible effect that HIV will cease to cause "serious bodily harm" and the failure to disclose will no longer fall under the category of fraud vitiating consent for the purposes of sexual assault.)

(4) Realistic Possibility of HIV Transmission

[94] This leaves the question of when there is a realistic possibility of transmission of HIV. The evidence adduced here satisfies me that, as a general matter, a realistic possibility of transmission of HIV is negated if (i) the accused's viral load at the time of sexual relations was low, *and* (ii) condom protection was used.

[95] The conclusion that low viral count coupled with condom use precludes a realistic possibility of transmission of HIV, and hence does not constitute a "significant risk of serious bodily harm" on the *Cuerrier* test, flows from the evidence in this case. This general proposition does not preclude the common

law from adapting to future advances in treatment and to circumstances where risk factors other than those considered in this case are at play.

[The Court noted that three factors were relevant to assessing risk: the baseline risk of infection from unprotected vaginal intercourse (somewhere between 0.05% and 0.1%), the percentage by which condom use reduced that risk (something in the range of 80%), and antiretroviral therapy.]

[99] The Court of Appeal, in applying a "high risk" approach, held that condom use reduces the risk of HIV transmission "below the level of significance" (para. 87). However, in my view, the evidence does not establish that condom protection alone precludes a *realistic possibility* of transmission, the standard proposed here. According to the expert evidence, the risk might still fall above the "negligible" threshold: Dr. Smith's report, at p. 6.

[100] This brings us to the final factor, antiretroviral therapy. As noted by the Court of Appeal, the transmissibility of HIV is proportional to the viral load, i.e. the quantity of HIV copies in the blood. The viral load of an untreated HIV patient ranges from 10,000 copies to a few million copies per millilitre. When a patient undergoes antiretroviral treatment, the viral load shrinks rapidly to less than 1,500 copies per millilitre (low viral load), and can even be brought down to less than 50 copies per millilitre (undetectable viral load) over a longer period of time. This appears to be scientifically accepted at this point, on the evidence in this case.

[101] Dr. Smith explained in his report that antiretroviral therapy is not a safe-sex strategy, and that "it is highly advisable that persons even with an undetectable viral load who are having sex with more than one partner unfailingly and correctly use a condom" (pp. 5 and 7). The most recent wide-scale study on this issue, relied on by a number of intervenors, concludes that the risk of HIV transmission is reduced by 89 to 96 percent when the HIV-positive partner is treated with antiretrovirals, irrespective of whether the viral load is low or undetectable: M. S. Cohen et al., "Prevention of HIV-1 Infection with Early Antiretroviral Therapy" (2011), 365 *New Eng. J. Med.* 493. This evidence indicates that antiretroviral therapy, alone, still exposes a sexual partner to a realistic possibility of transmission. However, on the evidence before us, the ultimate percentage risk of transmission resulting from the combined effect of condom use *and* low viral load is clearly extremely low — so low that the risk is reduced to a speculative possibility rather than a realistic possibility.

[102] In reaching this conclusion, I use *low* viral load, rather than *undetectable* viral load, as one of the factors for determining risk. This avoids the evidentiary difficulties associated with establishing an *undetectable* viral load. Dr. Smith presented evidence that various factors such as common infections and treatment issues may lead to fluctuations in a person's viral load. So-called "spikes" or

"blips" bring the viral load of a person treated with antiretrovirals above the detectable level. Furthermore, detectability depends on the accuracy of ever-developing technology: a viral load that assays do not detect today, might very well be detectable by future assays. Finally, it must be observed that Dr. Smith did not accept, and presented as controversial, the 2008 announcement by the Swiss Federal Commission for HIV/AIDS that an HIV-positive person with an undetectable viral load is not sexually infectious (p.5). As he noted, this statement is subject to important qualifications, based only on a review of scientific literature, and requires corroborating research.

[Editors' note: In a later case, *R. v. Thompson*, 2016 NSSC 134, 29 C.R. (7th) 393, Dr. Smith again testified:

[119] Dr. Smith testified that either an undetectable viral load or condom usage would provide protection. He said at the time (2008) when he testified at the *Mabior* trial, doctors were very cautious about what he referred to as the "Swiss Statement" that if the viral load was undetectable, the risk of transmission was negligible. He said it is now accepted.]

[103] This leads to the conclusion that on the evidence before us, the combined effect of condom use *and* low viral load precludes a realistic possibility of transmission of HIV. In these circumstances, the *Cuerrier* requirement of significant risk of serious bodily harm is not met. There is no deprivation within the meaning of *Cuerrier* and failure to disclose HIV status will not constitute fraud vitiating consent under s. 265(3)(*c*) of the *Criminal Code*.

(5) Summary

[104] To summarize, to obtain a conviction under ss. 265(3)(*c*) and 273, the Crown must show that the complainant's consent to sexual intercourse was vitiated by the accused's fraud as to his HIV status. Failure to disclose (*the dishonest act*) amounts to fraud where the complainant would not have consented had he or she known the accused was HIV-positive, and where sexual contact poses a significant risk of or causes actual serious bodily harm (*deprivation*). A significant risk of serious bodily harm is established by a realistic possibility of transmission of HIV. On the evidence before us, a realistic possibility of transmission is negated by evidence that the accused's viral load was low at the time of intercourse and that condom protection was used. However, the general proposition that a low viral load combined with condom use negates a realistic possibility of transmission of HIV does not preclude the common law from adapting to future advances in treatment and to circumstances where risk factors other than those considered in the present case are at play.

[105] The usual rules of evidence and proof apply. The Crown bears the burden of establishing the elements of the offence — a dishonest act and deprivation — beyond a reasonable doubt. Where the Crown has made a *prima facie* case

of deception and deprivation as described in these reasons, a tactical burden may fall on the accused to raise a reasonable doubt, by calling evidence that he had a low viral load at the time and that condom protection was used.

[The Court concluded that here the convictions relating to three complainants in which the accused had a low viral load but did not use a condom should be restored. The accused should not be convicted, however, in relation to the one complainant where the accused had a low viral load and a condom was used.]

The *Mabior* ruling has led to strident criticism from two very different interest groups. Those who see HIV-positive persons as a vulnerable and marginalized group (see, for example, Cecile Kazatchkine et al., "HIV Non-disclosure and the Criminal Law" (2014) 60 Crim. L.Q. 30) cannot see why non-disclosure of HIV-positive status should result in serious criminality given that antiretroviral treatment results in an 89% to 96% reduction in the general low risk of HIV transmission for one sexual act of 0.05% and 0.1%. These advocates argue that forced disclosure of HIV-positive status will discourage HIV testing and inhibit sexual autonomy inherent in truthful but inhibiting disclosures such as "I am HIV positive but my viral count is low so the risk is very small". It is also not clear to these critics that the use of condoms should be mandatory if serious criminality is to be avoided. The Manitoba Court of Appeal's approach in the Court below to the antiretroviral advances was to not require disclosure where the viral count was low OR where a condom was used. So the Supreme Court is much tougher in its approach.

A different criticism is advanced by advocates for sexual assault complainants. Since the approach to consent has long been established as subjective, surely, it is argued, the serious life-threatening risk of HIV transmission, however low, should always be disclosed to allow for informed consent. The retention of the *Cuerrier* approach is decried. See Janine Benedet, "Fraud Vitiating Consent to Sexual Activity after *Mabior* and *C.D.*" (2012), 90 C.R. (6th) 33; Lucinda Vandervort, "HIV, Fraud, Non-Disclosure, Consent and Stark Choice: *Mabior* or Sexual Autonomy" (2014) 60 Crim. L.Q. 301; and prior to *Mabior* in the Supreme Court, Carissima Mathen and Michael Plaxton, "HIV, Consent and Criminal Wrongs" (2011) 57 Crim. L.Q. 464. It is clear that in most of the HIV cases before the courts, the complainants have testified they would never have consented had they known about the HIV positive status. An 80% risk reduction is promised by the Supreme Court's requirement that condoms always be used.

The vehemence and strength of the arguments from these opposed camps suggest that the Supreme Court had to arrive at a compromise on the present state of medical knowledge and that it could not satisfy all competing concerns. Yet the language the Court uses is glaringly inconsistent with its conclusions. Chief Justice McLachlin is eloquent in justifying the Court's approach. She relies on the rule of law requirement of clear notice of criminality ("Condemning people for conduct that they could not have reasonably known was criminal is Kafkaesque and anathema to our notions of justice" (para. 14)); the need to avoid criminal laws being too broad; and *Charter* values of "equality, autonomy, liberty, privacy and human dignity" (para. 45). However, it is hard to see how any of these notions pointed to the broad criminalizing solution the Court actually adopted. Further, it is ironic that the Court's judgment – making the *Cuerrier* test stricter – was penned by the only Justice who had also taken part in deciding *Cuerrier* and who had dissented at the time on the basis that the test created was too strict.

Has Canada adopted the right approach in not following other jurisdictions who only criminalize the actual transmission of HIV? Are we right in calling the crime aggravated sexual assault in *Mabior* rather than aggravated assault as in *Cuerrier*? The Court does not address situations where the HIV-positive accused did disclose his or her HIV status and viral count, whether low or high, and the complainant agreed to sexual conduct with or without a condom. Given the lack of dishonesty, the *Mabior* approach could not be used to say that the consent was vitiated by fraud under s. 265(3)(c). It would, however, be open for a Court on *Jobidon* to come with a new policy-based limit to negate that consent and to convict. That would further broaden Canada's wide criminalization of sexual conduct by HIV-positive persons.

R. v. HUTCHINSON

2014 SCC 19, [2014] 1 S.C.R. 346, 308 C.C.C. (3d) 413, 8 C.R. (7th) 255

The complainant agreed to sexual activity with her partner, the accused, insisting that he use a condom in order to prevent conception. Unknown to her, the accused had poked holes in the condoms they used and the complainant became pregnant. He was charged with aggravated sexual assault. The central dispute among the judges in the case was not whether the accused could claim that the complainant had consented; rather, the issue was the proper basis for rejecting that claim. Broadly, one might say that the complainant had never, in the first place, consented to the sexual activity in question, namely "sex without an effective condom". Alternatively, one might say that she had consented to sex, but that her consent was vitiated by fraud under s. 265(3). By a 4-3 margin, the Court adopted the latter approach.

McLACHLIN C.J.C and CROMWELL J. (for the majority):

[23] The choice between these approaches is a matter of statutory construction. Which approach is correct depends on (1) the wording, scheme and object of the provisions of the *Criminal Code*; (2) the jurisprudence on the provisions and their common law predecessors; and (3) the underlying objectives of the criminal law. We will consider each of these in turn.

(1) The Wording, Scheme and Object of the Legislation and the Scheme of the Provisions

[24] The plain words of the provisions, read in their ordinary and natural sense, support a narrow interpretation of the basic definition of "consent" in s. 273.1(1).

The ordinary meaning of the "sexual activity in question" is the physical act agreed to; there is nothing in the wording to suggest that it includes the conditions or qualifications of the sexual act. . .

(2) The Jurisprudence

. . . .

[39] Both the Court of Appeal majority's approach and the approach proposed by Abella and Moldaver JJ. are also fundamentally at odds with the holdings in *Cuerrier* and *Mabior* that apparent consent is vitiated by fraud only where there is both deception and deprivation. Under the Court of Appeal's approach and that of our colleagues, mistakes — they need not be deceptions — about conditions and qualities of the physical act will result in a finding of no consent under s. 273.1(1) even in the absence of harm or risk of harm. This is contrary to the fundamental point made in *Cuerrier* and affirmed in *Mabior*: "The fraud required to vitiate consent for that offence must carry with it the risk of serious harm": *Cuerrier*, at para. 135.

[40] These inconsistencies are not merely semantic — they may affect outcomes under the "essential features"/"how the act was carried out" approach. HIV status may well be an "essential feature" of the sexual activity under the Court of Appeal majority's approach. It could also be characterized as part of the "how" under Abella and Moldaver JJ.'s approach. If the use of an intact condom goes to the manner in which the sexual activity occurred, why not the exchange of diseased fluids? Thus, under these approaches, deceptions about HIV status could result in a finding of no consent under s. 273.1(1), even where the accused had a low viral load at the relevant time and condom protection was used. That conclusion, however, would be in direct conflict with *Cuerrier* and *Mabior*.

(3) Underlying Objectives of the Criminal Law: Restraint and Certainty

[44] The majority of the Court of Appeal held that the "essential features" of the sexual activity are determined by the complainant's subjective conditions for consent to that activity. There need be no deception or dishonesty on the part of the partner. It follows that the "essential features" of the sexual activity vary from person to person. It would therefore be impossible to predict what a particular person considers "essential". . .

[46] These approaches would also result in the criminalization of acts that should not attract the heavy hand of the criminal law. We have already noted the difficulty of seeing why the presence of a sexually transmitted infection would not be a "component" of the sexual activity or part of "how" the sexual touching occurs. Under the Court of Appeal majority's "essential features" test, a man who pierces a condom may be found guilty of sexual assault; why would a

woman who lies about birth control measures not be equally guilty? Under Abella and Moldaver JJ.'s test, the quality or effectiveness of a condom changes the sexual activity that takes place; why would it not follow that an individual might be prosecuted for using an expired condom or a particular brand of condom? Anomalies abound. The "how the physical act was carried out" test appears not to capture a woman who lies about taking birth control pills, but it might well capture a woman who lies about using a diaphragm.

[47] Conversely, the "how the act was carried out" approach would not capture conduct that is as equally reprehensible as Mr. Hutchinson's actions, like substituting a partner's birth control pills with sugar pills. We do not see any principled basis for criminalizing the act of sabotaging condoms, but not the act of sabotaging birth control pills.

[48] This difficulty is apparent on the facts of this case. The trial judge found that the complainant did not voluntarily agree to sexual intercourse without contraception and that Mr. Hutchinson knew this: paras. 44 and 47. What was critical to her consent was contraception and what she sought to mitigate was the risk of pregnancy. Yet on the approach adopted by our colleagues, her lack of voluntary agreement would result from the use of sabotaged condoms, but not from a lie by Mr. Hutchinson to the effect that he was sterile. These different results on the issue of voluntary agreement respectfully lack rational justification in a case such as this one in which the whole concern of the complainant was pregnancy — a risked consequence of the sexual activity. Her consent did not turn on the "how" of the sexual act, but on whether the risk of pregnancy was mitigated to a degree which she thought sufficient.

The Correct Approach

[54] We conclude that Farrar J.A. was correct to interpret the "sexual activity in question" in s. 273.1(1) to refer simply to the physical sex act itself (for example, kissing, petting, oral sex, intercourse, or the use of sex toys). The complainant must agree to the specific physical sex act. For example, as our colleagues correctly note, agreement to one form of penetration is not agreement to any or all forms of penetration and agreement to sexual touching on one part of the body is not agreement to all sexual touching.

[55] The "sexual activity in question" does not include conditions or qualities of the physical act, such as birth control measures or the presence of sexually transmitted diseases. Thus, at the first stage of the consent analysis, the Crown must prove a lack of subjective voluntary agreement to the specific physical sex act. Deceptions about conditions or qualities of the physical act may vitiate consent under s. 265(3)(c) of the *Criminal Code*, if the elements for fraud are met.

[57] In our view, "voluntary agreement . . . to . . . the sexual activity in question" also encompasses both the sexual nature of the activity (i.e., that the act was sexual in nature as opposed to being for a different purpose, such as a medical examination) and the identity of the partner (defined in the narrow sense of the specific identity of a partner who is personally known to the complainant). While identity and the sexual nature of the act were troublesome issues for the early cases, and while *Cuerrier*, in obiter, suggests that they might be considered at the second stage of the consent analysis under s. 265(3)(c), the better view is that "voluntary agreement . . . to . . . the sexual activity in question" will not exist under s. 273.1(1) if the complainant did not subjectively agree to the sexual nature of the act or the specific identity of the partner. As a result, a complainant's mistaken belief about the identity of the partner or the sexual nature of the act — whether or not that mistake is the result of a deception — will result in no consent under s. 273.1(1) of the *Criminal Code*.

Application

[The majority concluded that the complainant had consented to the sexual activity, and so the real question was whether that consent had been vitiated by fraud, as in *Cuerrier* and *Mabior*.]

[67] As we have seen, "fraud" for the purposes of consent has two elements: (1) dishonesty, which can include the non-disclosure of important facts; and (2) deprivation or risk of deprivation in the form of serious bodily harm which results from the dishonesty: *Cuerrier*. Did the Crown prove that no consent was obtained by virtue of fraud?

[68] The dishonesty in this case is evident and admitted. Mr. Hutchinson obtained the complainant's consent to sexual intercourse only by failing to disclose the critical fact that he had sabotaged the condoms and thereby compromised their contraceptive value. The only remaining issue is whether there was a sufficient deprivation to establish fraud.

[69] Mr. Hutchinson argues that the universal threshold for deprivation under s. 265(3)(c) post-*Cuerrier* is a "significant risk of serious bodily harm", and that the Crown did not establish that here. The Crown argues that a new trial is required to determine whether the risk of pregnancy caused by the sabotaged condoms constituted a "significant risk of serious bodily harm". These arguments over-read *Cuerrier*. The Court in *Cuerrier* was addressing the specific risk of sexually transmitted diseases. It did not foreclose the possibility that other types of harm may amount to equally serious deprivations and therefore suffice to establish the requirements of fraud under s. 265(3)(c).

[70] The concept of "harm" does not encompass only bodily harm in the traditional sense of that term; it includes at least the sorts of profound changes

in a woman's body — changes that may be welcomed or changes that a woman may choose not to accept — resulting from pregnancy. Depriving a woman of the choice whether to become pregnant or increasing the risk of pregnancy is equally serious as a "significant risk of serious bodily harm" within the meaning of *Cuerrier*, and therefore suffices to establish fraud vitiating consent under s. 265(3)(c).

[71] We conclude that where a complainant has chosen not to become pregnant, deceptions that deprive her of the benefit of that choice by making her pregnant, or exposing her to an increased risk of becoming pregnant by removing effective birth control, may constitute a sufficiently serious deprivation for the purposes of fraud vitiating consent under s. 265(3)(c).

[72] This application of "fraud" under s. 265(3)(c) is consistent with *Charter* values of equality and autonomy, while recognizing that not every deception that induces consent should be criminalized. To establish fraud, the dishonest act must result in a deprivation that is equally serious as the deprivation recognized in *Cuerrier* and in this case. For example, financial deprivations or mere sadness or stress from being lied to will not be sufficient.

[The majority in *Hutchinson* indicated that they were guided by being consistent with *Cuerrier* and *Mabior*. However, note that the test they adopted in fact extends the *Cuerrier* approach, and allows consent to be vitiated by fraud based on criteria other than those in that case.]

PROBLEM

The accused is charged with sexual assault. He testified that he met the complainant on a street corner in the early morning hours and had agreed to pay her $100 for sexual intercourse. He conceded that he had driven the complainant to an underground parking lot and that he had sexual relations with her to which she consented. In the course of his testimony he stated that he never had intended to pay her $100 for sexual services and that he had offered to pay $100 only because he wanted to have some sexual activity. Result? Compare *R. v. P.* (1987), 58 C.R. (3d) 320, 35 C.C.C. (3d) 528 (B.C. C.A.).

In *R. v. Williams*, [2003] 2 S.C.R. 134 the accused had unprotected sexual relations with the complainant during their 18-month relationship. Five months into the relationship the accused learned that he had recently tested positive for HIV. He did not inform the complainant, who tested positive shortly thereafter. The Supreme Court held that he was wrongly convicted of aggravated assault on the principle that the *actus reus* and *mens rea* must coincide. There was no proof beyond reasonable doubt that he had infected the complainant at a time that he knew he was HIV positive. The Court substituted a conviction of attempted aggravated assault.

(e)   *De Minimis Non Curat Lex*

The most supportive consideration of the *de minimis* principle is to be found in the dissenting opinion of Justice Arbour in *Canadian Foundation for Children, Youth & the Law v. Canada (Attorney General)*, 16 C.R. (6th) 203, [2004] 1 S.C.R. 76, 180 C.C.C. (3d) 353. We have seen that in that decision a 6-3 majority upheld the constitutionality of the s. 43 defence allowing parents and teachers to use reasonable force in correction of children. In response to the concern that striking down s. 43 would criminalize acts of minor discipline Justice Arbour relied upon the *de minimis* doctrine (paras. 202-209). Reviewing the case law she noted that the issue was still open in the Supreme Court, and had not been widely used by courts due to charge screening by police and Crown. In her view it existed as a common law defence preserved by s. 8(3) of the *Criminal Code*. In her view *de minimis* does not mean that the act is justified; it remains unlawful but on account of its triviality goes unpunished. The doctrine:

(1)   ... reserves the application of the criminal law to serious misconduct;
(2)   protects an accused from the stigma of a criminal conviction and from the imposition of serious penalties for relatively trivial conduct; and
(3)   ... saves courts from being swamped by enormous number of trivial cases (para. 204).

In her majority judgment in *Canadian Foundation* Chief Justice McLachlin did not deny the existence of the *de minimis* doctrine, simply saying that it was "equally or more vague and difficult in application than the reasonableness defence offered by s. 43".

Lower courts are often resistant, especially Courts of Appeal:

R. v. KUBASSEK

(2004), 25 C.R. (6th) 340, 2004 CarswellOnt 3425, 188 C.C.C. (3d) 307
(C.A.)

CATZMAN J.A. (WEILER and MACPHERSON JJ.A. concurring): —

The Background

1 In *Halpern v. Canada (Attorney General)* (2003), 65 O.R. (3d) 161, this court held that the common law definition of marriage as a union between a man and a woman violated the Canadian *Charter of Rights and Freedoms* and that it should be reformulated as "the voluntary union for life of two persons to the exclusion of all others". The result was that, in Ontario, same-sex couples were entitled to marry.

2 One of the parties to the proceedings in Halpern was the Metropolitan Community Church, whose senior pastor, Rev. Brent Hawkes, had published the banns of marriage for two same-sex couples on three consecutive Sundays

and officiated at their weddings on January 14, 2001. The two couples whose marriage he celebrated were also parties to the proceedings in Halpern.

3 Erica Kubassek holds very strong views about same-sex marriages. She considers such marriages to be a falling away from God's truth. She believes herself to be a Christian servant of the Lord, endowed with the spiritual gifts of revelation and prophesy.

4 The Metropolitan Community Church had announced that the two same-sex marriages referred to above would be celebrated on Sunday afternoon, January 14, 2001. That Sunday morning, Ms. Kubassek, who was not a congregant of the Metropolitan Community Church, believed that she received a message from the Lord to go to the church, there to speak out for truth and to explain the word of the Lord. She drove from her home in Cambridge to Toronto, where she attended the church's 11:00 a.m. Sunday morning service. At a point in the service when Rev. Hawkes asked the congregation to come forward for anointing for healing, she went to the front, turned around and began to address the congregation. She quoted scripture, saying that homosexuality was an abomination and a sin in God's eyes. Rev. Hawkes went around her, faced her with his back to the congregation and asked her to stop. In response, she pushed or shoved him with her right hand. As a result, Rev. Hawkes stumbled backwards, towards the congregation, and almost fell over a pew that was two or three feet behind him. He did not fall and he was not injured in the incident. He turned to the congregation and asked everyone to sing. A security officer escorted Ms. Kubassek, who was screaming and throwing biblical pamphlets in the air, out of the church.

5 Ms. Kubassek was charged with assault. The trial judge found that she had intended to push Rev. Hawkes, but he dismissed the charge against her on the basis of the principle *de minimis non curat lex*: the law does not concern itself with trifles. The Crown appealed her acquittal to the summary conviction appeal court. The summary conviction appeal court judge agreed that the push had been intentional, but concurred with the trial judge that the *de minimis* principle applied. He affirmed Ms. Kubassek's acquittal.

6 The Crown now seeks leave to appeal and, if granted, to appeal from the decision of the summary conviction appeal court. For the reasons that follow, I would grant leave, allow the appeal, enter a finding of guilt and direct an absolute discharge.

De Minimis Non Curat Lex

17 The Crown's position on this appeal reduces itself to two basic submissions. The first is that the principle *de minimis non curat lex* has no application as a defence in criminal law. The second is that, even if can be raised as a defence

in criminal proceedings, the principle was not available in the circumstances of this case.

18 I agree with the Crown's second submission and do not find it necessary to decide the first.

19 The principle *de minimis non curat lex* is of considerable antiquity. The first record of the principle in the law reports is found in *Taverner v. Dominum Cromwell* (1594), 78 E.R. 601. Over two centuries later, the meaning of the expression was amplified in a case involving the seizure of a British ship for breach of British revenue laws by exporting logwood from Jamaica to the United States, which prohibited its importation: *The Reward* (1818), 2 Dods. 265, 165 E.R. 1482. In rejecting an invitation by the owners of the ship to reverse its condemnation because of the relative insignificance of the amount of logwood in issue, Sir Walter Scott (later Lord Stowell) said, at 269-270 Dods., 1484 E.R.:

> The court is not bound to a strictness at once harsh and pedantic in the application of statutes. The law permits the qualification implied in the ancient maxim, *de minimis non curat lex*. Where there are irregularities of very slight consequence, it does not intend that the infliction of penalties should be inflexibly severe. If the deviation were a mere trifle, which, if continued in practice, would weigh little or nothing on the public interest, it might properly be overlooked.

20 Within the last decade, the Supreme Court of Canada has touched upon, but not resolved, the question whether the *de minimis* principle provides a defence to a criminal charge. In *R. v. Hinchey*, [1996] 3 S.C.R. 1128, 111 C.C.C. (3d) 353 (S.C.C.), which involved a charge of corruption of a government employee, L'Heureux-Dubé J., writing for the majority of the court, acknowledged the possibility that the *de minimis* principle might operate as a defence to criminal culpability, but specifically left the question open. She said in obiter, at para. 69[1]:

> [A]ssuming that situations could still arise which do not warrant a criminal sanction, there might be another method to avoid entering a conviction: the principle of *de minimis non curat lex*, that "the law does not concern itself with trifles". This type of solution to cases where an accused has "technically" violated a Code section has been proposed by the Canadian Bar Association, in *Principles of Criminal Liability* (Ottawa: The Association, 1992), and others. see Professor Stuart, *Canadian Criminal Law*, 3rd ed. (Scarborough, Ont.: Carswell, 1995) at pp. 542-46. I am aware, however, that this principle's potential application as a defence to criminal culpability has not yet been decided by this court, and would appear to be the subject of some debate in the courts below. Since a resolution of this issue is not strictly necessary to decide this case, I would prefer to leave this issue for another day.

21 In *Canadian Foundation for Children, Youth and the Law v. Canada (Attorney General)*, [2004] 1 S.C.R. 76, 180 C.C.C. (3d) 353, the Supreme Court upheld the constitutionality of s. 43 of the *Criminal Code*, which provided that schoolteachers, parents or persons standing in the place of a parent were justified in using force by way of correction of a child under their care if the force did

not exceed what was reasonable in the circumstances. The decision of the majority was rendered by McLachlin C.J.C. Binnie, Arbour and Deschamps JJ. each wrote dissenting reasons. In Arbour J.'s dissent, she expressed the view that *de minimis non curat lex* does exist as a common law defence: see paras. 200-208. But all that McLachlin C.J.C., speaking for the majority of the court, said on the subject, at para. 44, was:

> Arbour J. argues that parents who face criminal charges as a result of corrective force will be able to rely on the defences of necessity and "*de minimis*". The defence of necessity, I agree, is available, but only in situations where corrective force is not in issue, like saving a child from imminent danger. As for the defence of *de minimis*, it is equally or more vague and difficult in application than the reasonableness defence offered by s. 43.

22 Like L'Heureux-Dubé J. in Hinchey and McLachlin C.J.C. in *Canadian Foundation*, I do not find it necessary to determine in the present case whether the *de minimis* principle operates as a defence in criminal law. I say that because even assuming, for the purpose of disposition of this appeal, that it does, the application of the label "trifling" to Ms. Kubassek's conduct constituted an error of law that is amenable to correction by this court.

The Present Case

23 In reaching the conclusion that Ms. Kubassek's conduct was not trivial, I have considered both the assault itself and the context in which it took place.

24 Ms. Kubassek's act of pushing or shoving Rev. Hawkes was intentional. Although he suffered no injury, he did fall backwards and almost tripped over a pew that was behind him. It is instructive to recall the circumstances in which the assault took place. The respondent chose to come to Metropolitan Community Church that Sunday morning. She chose to come to the front of the church for a purpose unconnected with the invitation extended to the congregation. She chose to deliver a message that she knew would fall on unreceptive ears. She chose to ignore the request of the senior pastor of the church not to interrupt the service. She chose to push or shove him to the side so that she could finish what she had to say. That he tripped, but did not fall or suffer injury, was purely fortuitous. She could fully have expected (as the trial judge found) that to go up to the front and preach to the congregants in terms she knew would be offensive could cause a disturbance. Against this backdrop, the push or shove that she intentionally applied to Rev. Hawkes cannot appropriately be characterized as an "irregularit[y] of very slight consequence ... a mere trifle, which, if continued in practice, would weigh little or nothing on the public interest" (*The Reward* (1818), 2 Dods. 265, 165 E.R. 1482: see para. 19). To minimize the assault by ascribing to it the designation "trifling" or "trivial" is to ignore the realities of what transpired between Ms. Kubassek and Rev. Hawkes that Sunday morning.

25 In the result, I conclude that the facts in the present case cannot be said to fall within the ambit of the defence (assuming it to be a defence available at law) of *de minimis non curat lex* and that the Crown's appeal must succeed.

Disposition

26 During the course of the argument, the court suggested to counsel that, if the Crown's appeal were to succeed, it might be appropriate at the penalty stage that Ms. Kubassek be given an absolute discharge. Neither counsel resisted that suggestion, and I consider it to be fair and reasonable.

27 Accordingly, I would grant the Crown's application for leave to appeal and would allow the appeal. I would set aside the respondent's acquittal, enter a finding of guilt, and order that she be discharged absolutely.

. . . .

Do you agree with the trial judge or the Ontario Court of Appeal? The Court of Appeal decides on the remedy of an absolute discharge. The suggested advantage of a judicial power to acquit (or stay) on the basis that the matter is too trivial is that it would be a vehicle for using the criminal sanction with restraint. There would be no criminal record. In contrast the legal effect of a discharge under the *Criminal Code* is that the accused is deemed not to have been convicted. Under the *Criminal Records Act*, R.S.C. 1985, c. C-47, s. 6.1(1) records are maintained and may be disclosed to anyone for a year. After the year disclosure to the police is still allowed: s. 6.2.

The suggested disadvantage to a *de minimis* defence is that it is the role of the Crown, not the judge, to decide whether charges should be laid: the judge's job is to decide whether all the elements of the offence have been proven, not whether he or she approves of the prosecution being brought. To allow a judge to refuse to convict a person where the elements of the offence have been proven can be said to undermine the rule of law.

Earlier in *R. v. Carson* (2004), 185 C.C.C. (3d) 541 (Ont. C.A.), leave to appeal refused (2004), 187 C.C.C. (3d) vi (S.C.C.) the Court, with very little analysis, held that the *do minimis* principle had no application to cases involving "the use of force or domestic violence" (at 549). In *H. v. Gale*, 2010 CarswellNfld 427, [2010] N.J. No. 5 (Prov. Ct.), Gorman J. decided that no such defence should be recognized in Canada as it was uncertain. However, this view was rejected in *R. v. Murphy* (2010), 367 N.B.R. (2d) 133, 946 A.P.R. 133 (Prov. Ct.) (accused with beer in hand dancing momentarily in aisle of theatre with female manager of theatre was acquitted of assault) and *R. v. Smale* (2016), 27 C.R. (7th) 83 (Alta. Prov. Ct.) (owner of residential cleaning business touching hips of co-worker in getting access to wall plug to detach vacuum hose acquitted of sexual assault and assault). The judge in *Smale* refers to a number of lower court decisions in favour of the *de minimis* principle and notes such a provision is in the Model Penal Code. Colton Fehr, "Reconceptualizing *De Minimis Non Curat Lex*" (2017) 64 Crim. L.Q. 200 supports the doctrine not as an individual defence under s. 8(3) but under the grossly disproportionate principle recognized under s. 7 of the *Charter.*

3.   OMISSIONS — LEGAL DUTIES TO ACT

(a)   Moral and Legal Duties

As observed earlier, the strong tendency of the criminal law is to require an act on the part of the accused before criminal liability can attach. There are explicit exceptions to this rule, however, in which omissions are made criminal. Under s. 21(1)(b), for example, a party to an offence is someone who:

> does or omits to do anything for the purpose of aiding any person to commit it.

In other cases the situation is less clear. Section 446.1, for example, makes the owner of an animal guilty of an offence if he or she "wilfully permits [the animal] to be caused unnecessary pain". The general rule is that positive action is required for liability, but the language of "permitting" might imply that an omission is sufficient in this case.

Often, in cases where an omission is explicitly criminalized, it is done so on the basis that an accused had a duty to act. See, for example, the definition of criminal negligence in s. 219, which deals in part with the behaviour of a person:

> (a) in doing anything, or

> (b) in omitting to do anything that it is his duty to do.

The general common law principle is that criminal responsibility for omissions is limited to cases where there is a legal and not merely a moral duty to act. A failure to fulfil the moral duty to stop a blind man walking over a cliff, or an animal drowning in a pool, or a person being stabbed is therefore insufficient to attract the criminal sanction. The vital question of whether there is a legal duty to act is, however, a difficult one to answer with any precision.

BUCH v. AMORY MORTGAGE CO.

(1898), 44 A. 809 at 810 (N.H. S.C.)

CARPENTER C.J.: —

. . . .

With purely moral obligations the law does not deal. For example, the priest and Levite who passed by on the other side were not, it is supposed, liable at law for the continued suffering of the man who fell among thieves, which they might, and morally ought to have, prevented or relieved. Suppose A., standing close by a railroad, sees a two year old babe on the track, and a car approaching.

He can easily rescue the child, with entire safety to himself, and the instincts of humanity require him to do so. If he does not, he may, perhaps, justly be styled a ruthless savage and a moral monster; but he is not liable in damages for the child's injury, or indictable under the statute for its death.

H.R.S. RYAN, CRIMINAL RESPONSIBILITY FOR OMISSIONS

(1967), Study Note

In the debate between Bentham (1781) and Macaulay (1873) — at long range, at the distance of two generations — the former would impose on everybody a duty to act to save another from harm when he can do so without prejudicing himself. So, we may note, would Bracton, writing in mid-13th century.

Bentham used the following examples:

(1) A woman's headdress catches fire;
(2) A drunken man falls face down into a puddle of water;
(3) A man with a lighted candle in his hand is about to enter a room in which gunpowder is lying scattered about.

In each case, somebody who is present and aware of the danger can easily prevent harm without the slightest danger to himself but omits to act and harm follows as a consequence.

"Who is there," asks Bentham, "That in these cases would think punishment misapplied?"

Livingstone, the American early 19th-century theorist and code maker, in his draft *Criminal Code* for Louisiana, proposed to constitute an offence of criminal homicide consisting of death following upon an omission to save life if the accused could have saved the life without personal danger or pecuniary loss.

But Macaulay, the draftsman of the *Indian Penal Code*, rejected this theory and the proposals based on it. He based his rejection on the great difficulty, if not impossibility of defining the conditions and limitations of guilt. His reasoning followed these lines:

(a) Suppose I have refused food to a beggar who must die unless I gave it to him and who has died. Am I guilty of criminal homicide? You cannot answer, "Yes", in all circumstances.

What if I myself am a beggar and have barely a crust between me and starvation?

What if my wife and children are hungry and wish to eat the food?

Are these two cases the same as if I am rich and need too much?

It may seem clear that I am not guilty in the first case. What about the second?

You can imagine an infinite number of readily possible cases in which the answer must be in doubt.

(b) Again, suppose I am a physician coming upon the scene of an accident and finding a victim bleeding to death and refuse to look after him. Am I guilty of criminal homicide?

What if I am on my way to treat a family all of whom are in danger of death from poison accidently taken?

What if I have been on duty for 48 hours at the scene of a disaster and am exhausted?

(c) If I am a surgeon and refuse to operate to save a life, will it make a difference whether I would have to walk a block to do it, or go to Barrifield? Or to Napanee? Or Belleville? Or Windsor?

(d) How far should I travel to give warning of an impending flood? 50 yards? Half a mile? Ten miles?

Many of Macaulay's examples clearly fall outside Bentham's limitation "without prejudicing himself" and Livingstone's "without personal danger or pecuniary loss" but he demonstrates the difficulty in practice of defining the limits of an offence based on an omission. It is, however, arguable that the offence could be so defined as to include only situations in which it is clearly demonstrated beyond question that the actor could have acted without in any way prejudicing himself personally or in property.

In Macaulay's draft *Code*, it was provided that an omission should be illegal if it had caused and had been intended to cause harm or was known to be likely to cause harm or was on other grounds illegal, that is, an offence in itself or a breach of some direction of law, or such a wrong as would be a good ground for a civil action.

He said that any further duty to act must be moral and not legal, enforced by public opinion and by teaching precepts of religion and morality.

As Jerome Hall points out, Macaulay and the English courts of the 18th and early 19th century had reached the same position.

Stephen, the draftsman of the *English Draft Code of 1878* on which the departmental draftsmen of the *Canadian Criminal Code of 1892* drew heavily, accepted Macaulay's position, and it appears in our present *Code*.

QUEBEC CHARTER OF HUMAN RIGHTS AND FREEDOMS

R.S.Q. 1980, c. C-12

2. Every human being whose life is in peril has a right to assistance. Every person must come to the aid of anyone whose life is in peril either personally or calling for aid, by giving him the necessary and immediate physical assistance, unless it involves danger to himself or a third person, or he has another valid reason.

For an assertion that this provision in the Quebec *Charter* has had a marked educative effect on the medical profession see S. Rodgers, "The Right to Emergency Medical Assistance in the Province of Quebec" (1980), 40 R. du B. 373.

FRENCH PENAL CODE

Article 63, translated by G. Hughes in "Criminal Omissions"
(1958), 67 Yale L.J. 590 at 632

Whoever is able to prevent by his immediate action, without risk to himself or others, the commission of a serious crime or offence against the person, and voluntarily neglects to do so shall be liable to imprisonment from one month to three years and a fine of 24,000 to 1,000,000 francs, or one of these penalties only.

The same punishments are applicable to one who voluntarily neglects to give to a person in peril assistance which he could render without risk to himself or others whether by his personal action or by procuring aid.

Should there be a criminal offence for failing to assist another whose safety is threatened?

(b)   What is an Omission?

O.W. HOLMES, THE COMMON LAW

Howe, ed., (1963), 218-219

Although a man has a perfect right to stand by and see his neighbor's property destroyed, or, for the matter of that, to watch his neighbor perish for want of his help, yet if he once intermeddles he has no longer the same freedom. He cannot withdraw at will. To give a more specific example, if a surgeon from benevolence cuts the umbilical cord of a newly-born child, he cannot stop there and watch the patient bleed to death. It would be murder wilfully to allow death to come to pass in that way, as much as if the intention had been entertained at the time of cutting the cord. It would not matter whether the wickedness began with the act, or with the subsequent omission.

FAGAN v. COMMISSIONER OF METROPOLITAN POLICE

[1968] 3 All E.R. 442 (C.A.)

July 31. LORD PARKER C.J.: — I will ask James J. to read the judgment which he has prepared, and with which I entirely agree.

JAMES J.: — The appellant, Vincent Martel Fagan, was convicted by the Willesden magistrates of assaulting David Morris, a police constable, in the execution of his duty on August 31, 1967. He appealed to quarter sessions. On October 25, 1967, his appeal was heard by Middlesex Quarter Sessions and was dismissed. This matter now comes before the court on appeal by way of case stated from that decision of quarter sessions.

The sole question is whether the prosecution proved facts which in law amounted to an assault.

On August 31, 1967, the appellant was reversing a motor car in Fortunegate Road, London, N.W.10, when Police Constable Morris directed him to drive the car forwards to the kerbside and standing in front of the car pointed out a suitable place in which to park. At first the appellant stopped the car too far from the kerb for the officer's liking. Morris asked him to park closer and indicated a precise spot. The appellant drove forward towards him and stopped it with the offside wheel on Morris's left foot. "Get off my foot," said the officer. "Fuck you, you can wait," said the appellant. The engine of the car stopped running. Morris repeated several times "Get off my foot." The appellant said reluctantly "Okay man, okay," and then slowly turned on the ignition of the vehicle and reversed it off the officer's foot. The appellant had either turned the ignition off to stop the engine or turned it off after the engine had stopped running.

The justices at quarter sessions on those facts were left in doubt as to whether the mounting of the wheel on the officer's foot was deliberate or accidental. They were satisfied, however, beyond all reasonable doubt that the appellant "knowingly, provocatively and unnecessarily allowed the wheel to remain on the foot after the officer said 'Get off, you are on my foot'." They found that on those facts an assault was proved.

Mr. Abbas for the appellant relied upon the passage in Stone's Justices' Manual (1968), Vol. 1, p. 651, where assault is defined. He contends that on the finding of the justices the initial mounting of the wheel could not be an assault and that the act of the wheel mounting the foot came to an end without there being any *mens rea*. It is argued that thereafter there was no act on the part of the appellant which could constitute an *actus reus* but only the omission or failure to remove the wheel as soon as he was asked. That failure, it is said, could not in law be an assault, nor could it in law provide the necessary *mens rea* to convert the original act of mounting the foot into an assault.

Mr. Rant for the respondent argues that the first mounting of the foot was an *actus reus* which act continued until the moment of time at which the wheel was removed. During that continuing act, it is said, the appellant formed the necessary intention to constitute the element of *mens rea* and once that element was added to the continuing act, an assault took place. In the alternative, Mr. Rant argues that there can be situations in which there is a duty to act and that in such situations an omission to act in breach of duty would in law amount to an assault. It is unnecessary to formulate any concluded views on this alternative.

In our judgment the question arising, which has been argued on general principles, falls to be decided on the facts of the particular case. An assault is any act which intentionally — or possibly recklessly — causes another person to apprehend immediate and unlawful personal violence. An assault may be committed by the laying of a hand upon another, and the action does not cease to be an assault if it is a stick held in the hand and not the hand itself which is laid on the person of the victim. So for our part we see no difference in principle between the action of stepping on to a person's toe and maintaining that position and the action of driving a car on to a person's foot and sitting in the car whilst its position on the foot is maintained.

To constitute the offence of assault some intentional act must have been performed: a mere omission to act cannot amount to an assault. Without going into the question whether words alone can constitute an assault, it is clear that the words spoken by the appellant could not alone amount to an assault: they can only shed a light on the appellant's action. For our part we think the crucial question is whether in this case the act of the appellant can be said to be complete and spent at the moment of time when the car wheel came to rest on the foot or whether his act is to be regarded as a continuing act operating until the wheel was removed. In our judgment a distinction is to be drawn between acts which are complete — though results may continue to flow — and those acts which are continuing. Once the act is complete it cannot thereafter be said to be a threat to inflict unlawful force upon the victim. If the act, as distinct from the results thereof, is a continuing act there is a continuing threat to inflict unlawful force.

For an assault to be committed both the elements of *actus reus* and *mens rea* must be present at the same time. The "*actus reus*" is the action causing the effect on the victim's mind (see the observations of Park B. in *Regina v. St. George*). The "*mens rea*" is the intention to cause that effect. It is not necessary that *mens rea* should be present at the inception of the *actus reus*; it can be superimposed upon an existing act. On the other hand the subsequent inception of *mens rea* cannot convert an act which has been completed without *mens rea* into an assault.

In our judgment the Willesden magistrates and quarter sessions were right in law. On the facts found the action of the appellant may have been initially unintentional, but the time came when knowing that the wheel was on the officer's foot the appellant (1) remained seated in the car so that his body through the medium of the car was in contact with the officer, (2) switched off the ignition of the car, (3) maintained the wheel of the car on the foot and (4) used words indicating the intention of keeping the wheel in that position. For our part we cannot regard such conduct as mere omission or inactivity.

There was an act constituting a battery which at its inception was not criminal because there was no element of intention but which became criminal from the moment the intention was formed to produce the apprehension which was flowing from the continuing act. The fallacy of the appellant's argument is that it seeks to equate the facts of this case with such a case as where a motorist has accidentally run over a person and, that action having been completed, fails to assist the victim with the intent that the victim should suffer.

We would dismiss this appeal.

BRIDGE J.: — I fully agree with my Lords as to the relevant principles to be applied. No mere omission to act can amount to an assault. Both the elements of *actus reus* and *mens rea* must be present at the same time, but the one may be superimposed on the other. It is in the application of these principles to the highly unusual facts of this case that I have, with regret, reached a different conclusion from the majority of the court. I have no sympathy at all for the appellant, who behaved disgracefully. But I have been unable to find any way of regarding the facts which satisfies me that they amounted to the crime of assault. This has not been for want of trying. But at every attempt I have encountered the inescapable question: after the wheel of the appellant's car had accidentally come to rest on the constable's foot, what was it that the appellant did which constituted the act of assault? However the question is approached, the answer I feel obliged to give is: precisely nothing. The car rested on the foot by its own weight and remained stationary by its own inertia. The appellant's fault was that he omitted to manipulate the controls to set it in motion again.

Neither the fact that the appellant remained in the driver's seat nor that he switched off the ignition seem to me to be of any relevance. The constable's plight would have been no better, but might well have been worse, if the appellant had alighted from the car leaving the ignition switched on. Similarly I can get no help from the suggested analogies. If one man accidentally treads on another's toe or touches him with a stick, but deliberately maintains pressure with foot or stick after the victim protests, there is clearly an assault. But there is no true parallel between such cases and the present case. It is not, to my mind, a legitimate use of language to speak of the appellant "holding" or "maintaining" the car wheel on the constable's foot. The expression which corresponds to the reality is that used by the justices in the case stated. They say, quite rightly, that he "allowed" the wheel to remain.

With a reluctantly dissenting voice I would allow this appeal and quash the appellant's conviction.

Appeal dismissed.

(c) How Do Legal Duties Arise?

Sometimes by statute. For example, consider these provisions of the *Criminal Code*:

215. (1) Every one is under a legal duty

   (*a*) as a parent, foster parent, guardian or head of a family, to provide necessaries of life for a child under the age of 16 years;
   (*b*) to provide necessaries of life to their spouse or common-law partner; and
   (*c*) to provide necessaries of life to a person under his charge if that person

      (i) is unable, by reason of detention, age, illness, mental disorder or other cause, to withdraw himself from that charge, and
      (ii) is unable to provide himself with necessaries of life.

216. Every one who undertakes to administer surgical or medical treatment to another person or to do any other lawful act that may endanger the life of another person is, except in cases of necessity, under a legal duty to have and to use reasonable knowledge, skill and care in so doing.

217. Every one who undertakes to do an act is under a legal duty to do it if an omission to do the act is or may be dangerous to life.

217.1 Every one who undertakes, or has the authority, to direct how another person does work or performs a task is under a legal duty to take reasonable steps to prevent bodily harm to that person, or any other person, arising from that work or task. [added by S.C.2003, c.21. s.3]

Can the courts create legal duties? Is this desirable? Remember s. 9 of the *Criminal Code*.

R. v. MILLER

[1983] 1 All E.R. 978, [1983] A.C. 161 (H.L.)

LORD DIPLOCK: — My Lords, the facts which give rise to this appeal are sufficiently narrated in the written statement made to the police by the appellant Miller. That statement, subject to two minor orthographical corrections, reads:

> Last night I went out for a few drinks and at closing time I went back to the house where I have been kipping for a couple of weeks. I went upstairs into the back bedroom where I've been sleeping. I lay on my mattress and lit a cigarette. I must have fell to sleep because I woke up to find the mattress on fire. I just got up and went into the next room and went back to sleep. Then the next thing I remember was the police and fire people arriving. I hadn't got anything to put the fire out with so I just left it.

He was charged on indictment with the offence of 'arson contrary to s. 1(1) and (3) of the *Criminal Damage Act, 1971*'; the particulars of offence were that he —

> on a date unknown between the 13th and 16th days of August 1980, without lawful excuse damaged by fire a house known as No. 9 Grantham Road, Sparkbrook, intending to do damage to such property or recklessly as to whether such property would be damaged.

He was tried in the Crown Court at Leicester before a recorder and a jury. He did not give evidence, and the facts as set out in his statement were not disputed. He was found guilty and sentenced to six months' imprisonment.

From his conviction he appealed to the Court of Appeal on the ground, which is one of law alone, that the undisputed facts did not disclose any offence under s. 1 of the *Criminal Damage Act 1971*. The appeal was dismissed (see [1982] 2 All E.R. 386), but leave to appeal to your Lordships' House was granted by the Court of Appeal, which certified that the following question of law of general public importance was involved:

> Whether the *actus reus* of the offence of arson is present when a Defendant accidentally starts a fire and thereafter, intending to destroy or damage property belonging to another or being reckless as to whether any such property would be destroyed or damaged, fails to take any steps to extinguish the fire or prevent damage to such property by that fire?

The question speaks of '*actus reus*'. This expression is derived from Coke's brocard (3 Co. Inst. ch. 1, fo. 10), '*Actus non facit reum, nisi mens sit rea*,' by converting incorrectly into an adjective the word *reus* which was there used correctly in the accusative case as a noun. As long ago as 1889 in *R. v. Tolson*, [1886-90] All E.R. Rep. 26 at 36-37 Stephen J. when dealing with a statutory offence, as are your Lordships in the instant case, condemned the phrase as likely to mislead, though his criticism in that case was primarily directed to the use of the expression '*mens rea*'. In the instant case, as the argument before this House has in my view demonstrated, it is the use of the expression '*actus reus*' that is liable to mislead, since it suggests that some positive act on the part of the accused is needed to make him guilty of a crime and that a failure or omission to act is insufficient to give rise to criminal liability unless some express provision in the statute that creates the offence so provides.

My Lords, it would I think be conducive to clarity of analysis of the ingredients of a crime that is created by statute, as are the great majority of criminal offences today, if we were to avoid bad Latin and instead to think and speak (as did Stephen J. in those parts of his judgment in *R. v. Tolson* to which I referred at greater length in *Sweet v. Parsley* [1969] 1 All E.R. 347 at 361) about the conduct of the accused and his state of mind at the time of that conduct, instead of speaking of *actus reus* and *mens rea*.

. . . .

The recorder, in his lucid summing up to the jury (they took 22 minutes only to reach their verdict), told them that the accused, having by his own act started a fire in the mattress which, when he became aware of its existence, presented an obvious risk of damaging the house, became under a duty to take some action to put it out. The Court of Appeal upheld the conviction, but its *ratio decidendi* appears to be somewhat different from that of the recorder. As I understand the judgment, in effect it treats the whole course of conduct of the accused, from the moment at which he fell asleep and dropped the cigarette onto the mattress until the time the damage to the house by fire was complete, as a continuous act of the accused, and holds that it is sufficient to constitute the statutory offence of arson if at any stage in that course of conduct the state of mind of the accused, when he fails to try to prevent or minimise the damage which will result from his initial act, although it lies within his power to do so, is that of being reckless whether property belonging to another would be damaged.

My Lords, these alternative ways of analysing the legal theory that justifies a decision which has received nothing but commendation for its accord with common sense and justice have, since the publication of the judgment of the Court of Appeal in the instant case, provoked academic controversy. Each theory has distinguished support. Professor J.C. Smith espouses the 'duty theory' (see [1982] Crim. L.R. 526 at 528); Professor Glanville Williams who, after the decision of the Divisional Court in *Fagan v. Metropolitan Police Comr.*, [1968] 3 All E.R. 442 appears to have been attracted by the duty theory, now prefers that of the continuous act (see: [1982] Crim. L.R. 773). When applied to cases where a person has unknowingly done an act which sets in train events that, when he becomes aware of them, present an obvious risk that property belonging to another will be damaged, both theories lead to an identical result; and, since what your Lordships are concerned with is to give guidance to trial judges in their task of summing up to juries, I would for this purpose adopt the duty theory as being the easier to explain to a jury; though I would commend the use of the word 'responsibility', rather than 'duty' which is more appropriate to civil than to criminal law since it suggests an obligation owed to another person, *i.e.*, the person to whom the endangered property belongs, whereas a criminal statute defines combinations of conduct and state of mind which render a person liable to punishment by the state itself.

While, in the general run of cases of destruction or damage to property belonging to another by fire (or other means) where the prosecution relies on the recklessness of the accused, the direction recommended by this House in *R. v. Caldwell* is appropriate, in the exceptional case (which is most likely to be one of arson and of which the instant appeal affords a striking example), where the accused is initially unaware that he has done an act that in fact sets in train events which, by the time the accused becomes aware of them, would make it obvious to anyone who troubled to give his mind to them that they present a risk that property belonging to another would be damaged, a suitable direction to the jury would be that the accused is guilty of the offence under s. 1(1) of the 1971 Act if, when he does become aware that the events in question have happened as a result of his own act, he does not try to prevent or reduce the risk of damage by his own efforts or if necessary by sending for help from the fire brigade and the reason why he does not is either because he has not given any thought to the possibility of there being any such risk[1] or because having recognized that there was some risk involved he has decided not to try to prevent or reduce it.

So, while deprecating the use of the expression '*actus reus*' in the certified question, I would answer that question Yes and would dismiss the appeal.

MOORE v. R.

[1979] 1 S.C.R. 195, 5 C.R. (3d) 289, 43 C.C.C. (2d) 83,
1978 CarswellBC 500, 1978 CarswellBC 559

SPENCE J. (MARTLAND, RITCHIE, PIGEON and BEETZ JJ. concurring): —
This is an appeal from the judgment of the Court of Appeal for British Columbia pronounced on June 7, 1977.

The appellant had been acquitted after his trial before His Honour Judge Millward and a jury upon an indictment charging him:

> THAT at the City of Victoria, County of Victoria, Province of British Columbia, on the 19th day of April, 1976, he did unlawfully and wilfully obstruct a Peace Officer, to wit, Constable Sutherland, in the execution of his duty as such Peace Officer, contrary to the *Criminal Code* of Canada.

The appellant was acquitted by a verdict directed by the learned trial judge at the close of the Crown's case. The facts are outlined in an admission by counsel for Moore which I quote:

> If it please, your Honour, I have certain admission of facts to make to expedite matters. Firstly, I am instructed to admit that on or about the 19th of April 1976, at or about 9:10 a.m., the Accused, Richard Harvey Moore, was southbound on Government Street at Pandora and at that intersection proceeded through a light which had not yet turned green and was, in fact red when he proceeded through on his ten-speed bicycle. That is the extent of my admission of fact.

and are further dealt with by Carrothers J.A., in his reasons for judgment as follows [36 C.C.C. (2d) 481 at p. 489, 40 C.R.N.S. 93]:

> Constable Sutherland, a peace officer with the Victoria City Police, in uniform and on a motorcycle, observed this infraction on the part of Moore and set about to "ticket" Moore. The constable and Moore proceeded side by side on their respective cycles, with Moore sometime taking elusive action by riding his bicycle on the sidewalk, with the constable repeatedly requesting Moore to "pull over and stop" and Moore lewdly rebuffing each such request with an obscene demand to leave him alone as he was in a hurry. I attach no importance to the particular salacious vulgarity used by Moore in rejecting the policeman's request to stop as it has been used by the unimaginative so excessively and indiscriminately as to have lost its literal quality, but there is no doubt that it constituted flat refusals on the part of Moore to stop as requested by the policeman.

---

1 We will see when we discuss the meaning of the word "recklessnees" in Chapter 3 that this statement would not be consistent with the definition of the term as it is used in Canadian jurisprudence.

As a result of this occurrence, Moore was charged upon an indictment, as I have said above, but he was not charged with failing to stop at a stop light only with obstructing a peace officer in the performance of his duty. The obstruction which the Crown put forward as constituting the offence was the failure of the appellant to give his name when requested to do so by the police constable.

The relevant sections of the provincial statutes with which I shall deal hereafter are as follows: first, the *Motor-vehicle Act*, R.S.B.C. 1960, c. 253. Section 2 contains definitions of "motor-vehicle" and "vehicle", as follows:

> "motor-vehicle" means a vehicle, not run upon rails, that is designed to be self-propelled or propelled by electric power obtained from overhead trolley-wires;

> . . . .

> "vehicle" means a device in, upon, or by which a person or thing is or may be transported or drawn upon a highway, except a device designed to be moved by human power or used exclusively upon stationary rails or tracks. [enacted 1963, c. 27, s. 2(c)]

Section 58 of the said *Motor-vehicle Act* provides:

> 58. Every person driving or operating or in charge of a motor-vehicle on any highway who refuses or fails
>
> > (a) to stop his motor-vehicle when signalled or requested to stop by any police officer or constable who is in uniform or who displays his police badge conspicuously on the outside of his outer coat; or
> >
> > (b) to state correctly his name and address and the name and address of the owner of the motor-vehicle when requested by any peace officer or constable to state the same
>
> is guilty of an offence.

It will be seen plainly that a bicycle is neither a "motor-vehicle" nor a "vehicle" of any kind under the provisions of the aforesaid definition. A bicycle is plainly not self-propelled and, therefore, cannot be a "motor-vehicle" and it is a device designed to be moved by human power and, therefore, it cannot be a "vehicle" at all. Much argument was spent in the Court of Appeal for British Columbia and in this court in an attempt to say that although a bicycle was neither a "motor-vehicle" nor a "vehicle" s. 58 of the *Motor-vehicle Act* applied thereto because of other sections with which I shall deal hereafter. As the courts below, I am quite unable to accept any such submission and I have come to the conclusion, with respect, that the Court of Appeal for British Columbia was quite correct in holding that the respondent was not in breach of s. 58 of the *Motor-vehicle Act* when he refused to give his name to the constable.

. . . .

After detailed consideration of statutory powers, Spence J. continued:

The constable, therefore, in requesting the appellant Moore to identify himself, was carrying out the duty of enforcing the law of the Province in this summary conviction matter by attempting to identify the accused person so that he might proceed to lay an information or take the more modern form permitted under the said *Summary Convictions Act* of British Columbia of issuing a ticket.

I am of the opinion that the Court of Appeal of British Columbia was correct in finding that when the appellant Moore refused to accede to the constable's request for his identification he was obstructing that constable in the performance of his duties. As did the members of the Court of Appeal, I am confining my consideration of this matter to the actual circumstances which occurred, that is, that a constable on duty observed the appellant in the act of committing an infraction of the statute and that that constable had no power to arrest the accused for such offence unless and until he had attempted to identify the accused so that he might be the subject of summary conviction proceedings.

I also agree, with respect, with the learned members of the Court of Appeal that this conclusion in no way opposes or ignores the judgment of the Queen's Bench in *Rice v. Connolly*, [1966] 2 All E.R. 649. In that case, the appellant was seen by police officers behaving suspiciously. On being questioned, he refused to say where he was going or where he had come from. He refused to give his full name and address, although he did give a name and the name of a road which were not untrue. He refused to accompany the police to a police box for identification purposes saying, "if you want me, you will have to arrest me". He was acquitted by the Court of Appeal upon a charge of obstructing the police. It is paramount to note that the appellant there had not committed any offence in the presence or view of a police officer. He had simply been acting in what the constable regarded as a suspicious manner. I view the situation very differently when a person is actually seen by the constable committing an offence.

Therefore, for the reasons which I have outlined above, I am of the opinion that the officer was under a duty to attempt to identify the wrongdoer and the failure to identify himself by the wrongdoer did constitute an obstruction of the police officer in the performance of his duties.

I add that in coming to this conclusion I have not forgotten the provisions of the *Canadian Bill of Rights* nor the topic of individual freedom generally but I am of the opinion that there is not even minimal interference with any freedom of a citizen who is seen committing an infraction by a police constable in the police constable simply requesting his name and address without any attempt to obtain from that person any admission of fault or any comment whatsoever. On the other hand, the refusal of a citizen to identify himself under such circumstances causes a major inconvenience and obstruction to the police in carrying out their proper duties. So that if anyone were engaged in any balancing of interest, there could be no doubt that the conclusion to which I have come would be that supported by the overwhelming public interest.

I would dismiss the appeal.

DICKSON J. (dissenting) (ESTEY J. concurring): — These proceedings originated in a minor traffic infraction in the City of Victoria, British Columbia. The issue raised, however, is an important one having to do with police power of interrogation and the right of citizens to remain silent. That right has always been regarded as absolute and as being firmly anchored to two fundamental common-law principles: the presumption of innocence and the privilege against self-incrimination. Explicit statutory provisions may impose a duty upon a person to identify himself to police officers in certain situations, but in this appeal the court is being asked to impose such a duty in the absence of any statutory underpinning whatever. In more stark terms, the question is whether a person committing a petty traffic offence exposes himself to a criminal charge of "obstructing" and a maximum penalty of two years' imprisonment, if he refuses to give his name and address to a police officer.

. . . .

The general principle

Any duty to identify oneself must be found in either common law or statute, quite apart from the duties of the police. A person is not guilty of the offence of obstructing a police officer merely by doing nothing, unless there is legal duty to act. Omission to act in a particular way will give rise to criminal liability only where a duty to act arises at common law or is imposed by statute: 11 Hals., 4th ed., p. 15, para. 9. This idea was expressed by Mr. Justice Schroeder in *R v. Patrick*, 128 C.C.C. 263 at p. 267, [1960] O.W.N. 206, 32 C.R. 338 at p. 343 (Ont. C.A.):

> Counsel for the appellant submitted that to sustain a charge of obstructing a peace officer in the execution of his duty, it was necessary for the Crown to prove either a positive act of interference, or a refusal to perform some act required to be done by a statute. . . . It not having been shown that the appellant was under any duty or obligation to communicate to the peace officer the information required of him under the provisions of either s. 221(2) of the Cr. Code, or s. 110(1) of the *Highway Traffic Act*, the Crown has failed to bring home to the appellant the commission of a criminal offence. This is sufficient to dispose of the appeal.
> . . .

The point under discussion is dealt with at some length by Dr. Glanville Williams in an article entitled "Demanding Name and Address" appearing in 66 *L.Q.R.* 465 (1950). The general principle of the common law is stated:

> neither a private person nor a constable has any effective power to demand the name and address of a person on the ground that he has committed an offence or is under a civil liability.

Dr. Williams refers to the case of *Hatton v. Treeby*, [1897] 2 Q.B. 452 as an illustration of this principle. The head note reads:

> A constable who sees a person riding a bicycle at night without a proper light, contrary to the provisions of s. 85 of the *Local Government Act, 1888*, has no power to stop him for the purpose of ascertaining his name and address.

The constable in that case called on the rider to stop, in order to ascertain his name and address. On the rider failing to do so, the constable caught hold of the handlebar of the bicycle, whereby the rider was thrown to the ground. The rider summoned the constable for assault. The Justices found that the constable did not know the name or address of the rider, and could not have ascertained his name or address in any other way than by stopping him, and that in so stopping him he used no more force than was necessary. They were of opinion that, as the rider was committing an offence punishable on summary conviction within view of the constable, the latter was justified in stopping him as he did in order to prevent a continuance of the offence and to ascertain his name and address. They accordingly dismissed the complaint, subject to a case for the opinion of the court. The appellate court held that the constable had no power to stop the bicycle rider at common law and the only question was whether he had statutory authority to do so. It was found that there was no statutory authority for the constable acting as he did. In the result the constable was convicted of assault.

No statutory duty

It appears to me impossible to extract from the statutory provisions of the British Columbia *Motor-vehicle Act*, R.S.B.C. 1960, c. 253, a duty on a cyclist, caught riding through a red light, to identify himself. Section 58 of the Act specifically places a duty on a person driving a "motor-vehicle" to state correctly his name and address when requested to do so by a peace officer. This in itself appears to recognize the absence of any such duty where there is no statutory requirement. Section 58 does not apply to persons operating either "vehicles" (as defined in s. 2) or bicycles, and there is no other provision in the *Motor-vehicle Act*, or any other relevant statute, placing such a duty on a cyclist caught committing a summary conviction offence under the *Motor-vehicle Act*.

I have had the advantage of reading the reasons of Mr. Justice Spence and I am in full agreement, for the reasons stated by him and by the Court of Appeal of British Columbia, that the accused was not in breach of s. 58 of the *Motor-vehicle Act*, when he refused to give his name and address to the constable.

. . . .

Power of arrest

. . . .

Constable Sutherland could have arrested the accused for the offence of proceeding against a red light if it were necessary to establish his identity. However, with great respect, I cannot agree that, as a consequence, the accused was guilty of the further, and much more serious, offence of obstructing the constable in the performance of his duties by refusing to divulge his name and address.

No common law duty

There is no duty at common law to identify oneself to police. As was stated by Lord Parker in *Rice v. Connolly*, [1966] 2 All E.R. 649 at p. 652 (Q.B.D.):

> It seems to me quite clear that though every citizen has a moral duty or, if you like, a social duty to assist the police, there is no legal duty to that effect, and indeed the whole basis of the common law is the right of the individual to refuse to answer questions put to him by persons in authority, and a refusal to accompany those in authority to any particular place, short, of course, of arrest.

The case stands for the proposition that refusal to identify oneself to the police could not constitute obstruction of the police. The court distinguished a refusal to answer, which is legal, from a "cock and bull" story to the police, which might constitute obstruction. No other distinction was made. Lord Parker said:

> In my judgment there is all the difference in the world between deliberately telling a false story, something which on no view a citizen has a right to do, and silence or refusing to answer, something which he has every right to do.

In *Ingleton v. Dibble*, [1972] 1 All E.R. 275 (Q.B.D.), a distinction was drawn between a refusal to act, on the one hand, and the doing of some positive act, on the other. Bridge J. (with whom Lord Widgery C.J. and Ashworth J. concurred), said, at p. 279:

> In a case, as in *Rice v. Connolly*, where the obstruction alleged consists of a refusal by the defendant to do the act which the police constable has asked him to do — to give information, it might be, or to give assistance to the police constable — one can see readily the soundness of the principle, if I may say so with respect, applied in *Rice v. Connolly*, that such a refusal to act cannot amount to a wilful obstruction under s. 51 unless the law imposes on the person concerned some obligation in the circumstances to act in the manner requested by the police officer.

The legal position in England and Wales has been described in these terms in *Police Powers in England and Wales* (1975), by Leigh, at p. 195:

> and in general it still remains the rule that a citizen has a right to be as unco-operative as he pleases, provided that he does not impede the course of justice by knowingly giving false information to the police.

In the Ontario case of *R. v. Carroll* (1959), 126 C.C.C. 19, 31 C.R. 315 (Ont. C.A.), the facts, as disclosed in the headnote, were these. The accused was charged with unlawfully and wilfully obstructing a police constable while engaged in his duties as a peace officer, contrary to s. 110(*a*) of the *Criminal Code*, 1953-54 (Can.), c. 51. The accused, in company with three other men, was proceeding along a highway at an early hour in the morning. The constable heard them whistling and yelling and he advised them to be quiet and go home. Three of the party followed his advice. The accused remained. The constable asked him to produce his identification but the accused refused to do so and proceeded on his way. The constable caught up to him and again asked accused to identify himself. An argument and struggle followed and the accused was arrested. He was later charged with obstructing a police officer and was convicted. He appealed. The conviction was quashed. It was held that under the circumstances, the accused was not under any duty to identify himself as requested.

The Crown conceded in this court that no such obligation was to be found in the common law. From whence then comes such a duty? Where does one find the legal compulsion to answer? A person cannot "obstruct" by refusing to answer a question unless he is under a legal duty to answer.

An "implied" or "reciprocal" duty?

It was strongly urged in argument before us that because a duty rested upon constables to investigate crime and enforce provincial laws, an "implied" or "reciprocal" duty rested upon a person, suspected of an infraction, to give his name and address, and refusal to do so amounted to such frustration as to constitute the offence of obstructing the police in the execution of their duty.

The Crown perforce had to fall back upon the proposition that because there was a duty upon the police officer to enquire before exercising the power to arrest under s. 450 [rep. & sub. R.S.C. 1970, c. 2, (2nd Supp.), s. 5] of the *Code*, there was a reciprocal duty upon the alleged culprit to respond. The alleged duty, as I understand the argument, is to be limited to divulging name and address, when caught in the commission of an offence and prior to arrest.

. . . .

A limited obligation to respond, effective only when the policeman is an eye witness, introduces into the criminal law, which should rest upon "broad, plain, intelligible" principles a qualification unsound in principle and unworkable in practice.

The fact that a police officer has a duty to identify a person suspected of, or seen committing, an offence says nothing about whether the person has the duty to identify himself on being asked. Each duty is entirely independent. Only if the police have a lawful claim to demand that a person identify himself, does the person have a corresponding duty to do so. As McFarlane J.A. said in *R. v. Bonnycastle*, [1969] 4 C.C.C. 198 at p. 201, 7 C.R.N.S. 37 (B.C. C.A.), the duty of a peace officer to make enquiries must not be confused with the right of a person to refuse to answer questions in circumstances where the law does not require him to answer.

The Legislature deliberately imposed a duty to identify upon the drivers of motor vehicles — perhaps because of their more lethal nature — but chose not to impose such duty on the drivers of other vehicles such as bicycles. The Legislature must be taken to have intended to relieve bicycle riders of the duty. To require the riders of bicycles to give their names and addresses would be tantamount to amending the *Motor-Vehicle Act*. It would also appear that Parliament, in providing in ss. 450(2) and 452(1)(*f*)(i) [rep. & sub. R.S.C. 1970, c. 2 (2nd Supp.), s. 5] of the *Criminal Code* for arrest and detention for the purpose of establishing identity, did not recognize a duty to identify oneself existing apart from statute, breach of which would expose the offender to a charge of "obstructing". Examples from English legislation of statutory obligation to disclose identity to police constables, unnecessary if the obligation existed otherwise, are to be found in the *Protection of Birds Act*, 1954 (U.K.), c. 30, s. 12(i)(*a*); *Dangerous Drugs Act*, 1965 (U.K.), c. 15, s. 15; *Representation of the People Act*, 1949 (U.K.), c. 68, s. 84(3); *Road Traffic Act*, 1960 (U.K.), c. 16, s. 228; *Prevention of Crime Act*, 1953 (U.K.), c. 14, s. 1(3).

The criminal law is no place within which to introduce implied duties, unknown to statute and common law, breach of which subjects a person to arrest and imprisonment.

The "reciprocal duty" argument advanced by the Crown in this case was considered by Dr. Glanville Williams in the article to which I have referred. Dr. Williams effectively disposed of the argument in words which I should like to adopt, pp. 473-4:

> The question may be asked whether the power of the police to demand name and address is in effect generalised by the statutes creating the offence of obstructing the police in the execution of their duty — so that refusal to comply with the demand amounts to an obstruction. At first sight it would seem that a good case could be made out for an affirmative answer. Although it is not the duty of the police to prosecute every crime, it can be said to be their duty to make inquiries into crimes with a view to prosecution. The courts have held that interference with the police when they are collecting evidence of an offence constitutes an obstruction. Moreover, it has been decided that an obstruction may take place merely by a nonfeasance, where there is a refusal to comply with the lawful orders of the police. Notwithstanding these authorities, it is submitted that the refusal by an offender to give his name and address does not constitute an obstruction, for at least two reasons. First, if it were

an obstruction, all the statutes making it an offence to refuse to give name and address in specific situations would have been unnecessary. When, for example, Parliament passed the *Public Order Act* in 1936, it must have been thought that the police had no general power to demand name and address. Secondly, it is a fundamental principle of English law that an accused person cannot be interrogated or at least cannot be forced to answer questions under a legal penalty if he refuses; this principle is absolute, and does not admit of exception even for a demand of name and address, unless a statute has expressly created an exception. To say that the police have a duty to gather evidence, and therefore that a criminal's refusal to give his name and address is an obstruction, is far too wide, because the same premise would yield the conclusion that a criminal's refusal to confess to the crime is an obstruction.

The views expressed by Dr. Williams were adopted in the New Zealand case of *Elder v. Evans*, [1951] N.Z.L.R. 801 at p. 806 (N.Z.S.C.).

I would allow the appeal, set aside the judgment of the Court of Appeal and restore the judgment at trial.

Appeal dismissed.

Section 252(1) of the *Criminal Code* makes it an offence for anyone in charge of a vehicle who is involved in an accident who, with intent to escape civil or criminal liability, fails to stop, give his or her name and address or offer assistance to any person who has been injured or appears to require assistance.

R. v. THORNTON

(1991), 3 C.R. (4th) 381, 1990 CarswellOnt 73 (Ont. C.A.)

The accused donated blood to the Red Cross. At that time the accused knew that he had twice tested positive for HIV antibodies and that he was therefore infectious. The Red Cross screening process detected the contaminated blood and it was put aside. The accused was charged that he did commit a common nuisance contrary to s. 180 of the *Criminal Code*. This section provides that every one commits a common nuisance who does an unlawful act or fails to discharge a legal duty and thereby endangers the lives, safety or health of the public. He was convicted and sentenced to a term of 15 months' imprisonment. At the trial the Crown did not argue an unlawful act but rather a failure to discharge a legal duty. The trial judge expressed concern with the Crown's position because it seemed to the Court that the facts in the case might define and constitute an unlawful act. The trial judge said the conduct of the accused was conduct evidencing marked disregard for the safety of others. Nevertheless the trial judge proceeded on the basis that there was an omission. The trial judge found a duty within s. 216 of the *Criminal Code* which provides:

> Everyone who undertakes to administer surgical or medical treatment to another person or to do any other lawful act that may endanger the life of another person is, except in cases of necessity, under a legal duty to have and to use reasonable knowledge, skill and care in so doing.

The trial judge decided that by donating blood to the Red Cross and knowing the purpose for which such donations are collected the accused was involved in a medical procedure. The accused appealed conviction and sentence. One of the grounds of appeal was that the accused's conduct, though reprehensible, did not amount to an offence known to the law. The appeals from conviction and sentence were dismissed.

GALLIGAN J.A. (BROOKE and DOHERTY JJ.A. concurring): —

... For the purposes of this appeal, I am prepared to assume the correctness of Mr. Greenspon's cogent argument that the words "unlawful act" must be taken to mean conduct which is specifically proscribed by legislation. The *Code* does not make it an offence to donate contaminated blood. Counsel were unable to refer the court to any other statutory provision, federal or provincial, which does so. On the assumption, therefore, that the appellant's conduct could not constitute an "unlawful act", I will examine whether it amounted to a failure to discharge a "legal duty".

I am unable to find any provision in the *Code*, or any other statute which I can read, as specifically imposing a legal duty upon a person to refrain from donating contaminated blood. The immediate issue therefore is two-fold. Can a "legal duty" within the meaning of s. 180(2) be one which arises at common-law, or must it be one found in a statute? Is there a "legal duty" arising at common law the breach of which, assuming the other essential elements of the offence were proved, could be the basis of an offence under s. 180?

There are no cases deciding whether the "legal duty" in s. 180(2) must be a duty imposed by statute or whether it can be a duty according to common law. However, the "duty imposed by law" which forms part of the definition of criminal negligence set out in s. 219 of the *Code* has been held to be either a duty imposed by statute or a duty arising at common law.

. . . .

In *R. v. Coyne* (1958), 31 C.R. 335, 124 C.C.C. 176, the New Brunswick Supreme Court, Appeal Division, considered the criminal negligence provisions of the *Code* in relation to a hunting accident. Speaking for that court, Ritchie J.A. held at pp. 179-180 [C.C.C., p. 338 C.R.]:

> The "duty imposed by law" may be a duty arising by virtue of either the common law or by statute. Use of a firearm, in the absence of proper caution, may readily endanger the lives or safety of others. Under the common law anyone carrying such a dangerous weapon as a rifle is under the duty to take such precaution in its use as, in the circumstances, would be observed by a reasonably careful man. If he fails in that duty and his behaviour is of such a character as to show or display a wanton or reckless disregard for the lives or safety of other persons, then, by virtue of s. 191, his conduct amounts to criminal negligence.

In *R. v. Popen* (1981), 60 C.C.C. (2d) 232, this court also had occasion to consider the nature of the "duty imposed by law" contained in the definition of criminal negligence. It was a child abuse case. In giving the judgment of the court, Martin J.A. said at p. 240 [C.C.C.]:

> [A] parent is under a legal duty at common law to take reasonable steps to protect his or her child from illegal violence used by the other parent or by a third person towards the child which the parent foresees or ought to foresee.

The effect of that judgment is to hold that the common law duty, which was there described, was a "duty imposed by law" within the meaning of s. 219 because the court held that its breach could amount to criminal negligence.

These decisions lead me to the opinion that it is well settled that, for the purpose of defining criminal negligence, a "duty imposed by law" includes a duty which arises at common law.

While the words "legal duty" in s. 180(2) are not the same as a "duty imposed by law" used in s. 219, they have exactly the same meaning. It follows therefore that the meaning given to a "duty imposed by law" in s. 219 should also be given to the "legal duty" contained in s. 180(2). Thus, I am of the opinion that the legal duty referred to in s. 180(2) is a duty which is imposed by statute or which arises at common law. It becomes necessary, then, to decide whether at common law there is a duty which would prohibit the donating of blood known to be HIV-contaminated to the Red Cross.

While this is not a civil case and the principles of tort law are not directly applicable to it, the jurisprudence on that subject is replete with discussions about the legal duties of one person to another which arise at common law. The jurisprudence is constant that those duties are legal ones: that is, they are ones which are imposed by law. Throughout this century and indeed since much earlier times, the common law has recognized a very fundamental duty, which while it has many qualifications, can be summed up as being a duty to refrain from conduct which could cause injury to another person.

This is not the place to make a detailed examination of the jurisprudence on the subject of tort law but a few references to authority are in order.

. . . .

In the course of his oft-quoted speech in the famous case of *M'Alister or (Donoghue) v. Stevenson*, [1932] A.C. 562 (H.L.), Lord Atkin said at p. 580 [A.C.]:

> The rule that you are to love your neighbour becomes, in law, you must not injure your neighbour.

. . . .

That brief reference to jurisprudence in civil matters shows that there is deeply embedded in the common law a broad fundamental duty which, although subject to many qualifications, requires everyone to refrain from conduct which could injure another. It is not necessary to decide in this case how far that duty extends. At the very least, however, it requires everyone to refrain from conduct which it is reasonably foreseeable could cause serious harm to other persons. Accepting, as I have said, that a "legal duty" within the meaning of that term in s. 180(2) includes a duty arising at common law, I think that the common law duty to refrain from conduct which it is reasonably foreseeable could cause serious harm to other persons is a "legal duty" within the meaning of that term in s. 180(2).

Donating blood which one knows to be HIV-contaminated to an organization whose purpose is to make the blood available for transfusion to other persons, clearly constitutes a breach of the common law duty to refrain from conduct which one foresees could cause serious harm to another person. It is thus a failure to discharge a "legal duty" within the contemplation of s. 180(2). It is therefore my conclusion that the indictment which alleges the commission of a nuisance by the donation of blood which the appellant knew to be HIV-contaminated does allege an offence known to law. The first argument made by counsel for the appellant cannot be accepted.

. . . .

In the light of the findings of the trial judge on the issue of credibility, and in the light of all of the other evidence, there can be no doubt that this appellant had personal knowledge that he should not donate his blood, that it was possible for it to get through the testing screen, and that it could cause serious damage to the life and health of members of the public. It follows that he knew that, by giving his blood to the Red Cross, he was endangering the lives and health of other members of the public. ... This appellant knew personally the danger to which the public was subjected by his donation of blood. He clearly had *mens rea*. ...

It is my opinion that the appellant was properly convicted of the offence under s. 180. Accordingly, I would dismiss the appeal from conviction.

With respect to sentence, the trial judge did not impose the maximum sentence prescribed by law. The maximum sentence must be reserved for the worst offender committing the worst category of the offence. The sentence imposed took into account that, because of his prior good record, the appellant would not fall into the category of the worst offender. The offence, however, can certainly be categorized as among the worst offences. The appellant's conduct verges on the unspeakable. It cried out for a sentence which would act as a deterrent to others and which would express society's repudiation of what he did. One must have great compassion for this man. He faces a terrible future. Nevertheless, the sentence demonstrates no error in principle and is one that is eminently fit.

The important issue of principle of whether a criminal omission can be based on a common law duty, in apparent violation of s. 9(a) of the *Criminal Code*, was unfortunately avoided when *Thornton* reached the Supreme Court.

THORNTON v. R.

[1993] 2 S.C.R. 445, 21 C.R. (4th) 215, 82 C.C.C. (3d) 530,
1993 CarswellOnt 98, 1983 CarswellOnt 982

LAMER C.J. (for a unanimous nine-person court, orally): — Section 216 imposed upon the [accused] a duty of care in giving his blood to the Red Cross. This duty of care was breached by not disclosing that his blood contained HIV antibodies. This common nuisance obviously endangered the life, safety and health of the public.

The above is the complete judgment of the Court. The Court appears to read s. 216 literally to impose a duty of care on those doing lawful acts which endanger others' lives. This seems to establish a new wide measure of criminal responsibility for omissions.

Do you prefer the interpretation of the trial judge, the Court of Appeal or the Supreme Court? Justify your preference.

See, more generally, Winnie Holland, "HIV/AIDS and the Criminal Law" (1994) 36 Crim. L.Q. 279.

R. v. BROWNE

(1997), 116 C.C.C. (3d) 183, 1997 CarswellOnt 1715 (Ont. C.A.),
leave to appeal refused (1997), 225 N.R. 396 (note) (S.C.C.)

The accused and the deceased were partners in drug dealing. The deceased swallowed a plastic bag of crack cocaine to avoid detection when they were strip-searched by police. She tried unsuccessfully to vomit it up. Later that night the accused found her shaking and sweating. He said he would take her to hospital. He called for a cab which took 10 minutes to arrive and a further 15 minutes to get her to hospital. She had no pulse or heartbeat and was pronounced dead shortly after arrival.

ABELLA J.A. (CATZMAN and LABROSSE JJ.A. concurring): —

. . . .

The statement found by the trial judge to constitute an "undertaking" by Browne is underlined.

He called her name a couple of times and she did not answer at first, but then she said yes. He said, "*I'm going to take you to the hospital.*" He helped her up the stairs. He asked her if she could get up and there was no response. She sat up and she put her arm around him and he put his arm around her waist and they walked up the stairs. She could not walk on her own. He called a taxi. He testified she got heavy and he laid her on the floor by the front door and waited 10 to 15 minutes for the taxi. She was still sweating, shaking, and was mumbling. The taxi arrived and he could not pick her up and asked his brother to help him take her to the taxi.

. . . .

On her arrival at the hospital, Greiner had no pulse and no heartbeat. She was pronounced dead at 3:10 a.m.

The trial judge found that the appellant told Ms. Greiner at about 2:00 a.m. that he would take her to the hospital and "immediately thereafter embarked on that act". She concluded that this statement was an "undertaking" within the meaning of s. 217 of the *Criminal Code*.

The circumstances giving rise to a legal duty were summarized by the trial judge in the following passages:

> By taking charge of Audrey Greiner after he knew that she had ingested crack, Dexter Browne undertook to care for her while the crack was in her body. That undertaking included rendering assistance to her which required taking her to the hospital immediately. On this basis, the legal duty to Audrey Greiner within the meaning of section 217 arose just after 11:30 when the accused knew that Audrey Greiner had not vomited the crack cocaine.

> Although Dexter Browne testified that he did not say to Audrey Greiner that he would take care of her if something bad happened, he did admit that he would take care of her if she sold to someone who tried to rob her or anything like that.

. . . .

Using a taxi instead of calling 911 reflected, according to the trial judge, a "wanton and reckless disregard" for Audrey Greiner's life contrary to s. 219(1) of the *Criminal Code*.

Analysis

The charge of criminal negligence against the appellant was particularized as follows, mirroring the language found in s. 217 of the *Criminal Code*:

> . . . that he . . . failed to render assistance to Audrey Greiner by failing to take her immediately to the hospital after undertaking to render such assistance and did thereby cause the death of Audrey Greiner . . .

The particularization of the charge in this way meant that to find a legal duty, there had first to be a finding of an undertaking. This flows from the language of s. 217 which states that everyone "who *undertakes* to do an act is under a legal duty to do it if an omission to do the act is or may be dangerous to life". In other words, the legal duty does not flow from the relationship between the parties, as it does in s. 215, which creates legal duties between spouses, between parents and children, and between dependants and their caregivers. Under s. 217, there is no pre-existing relationship or situation that creates a legal duty; there must be an undertaking before a legal duty is introduced into the relationship. The relationship or context is relevant only to the determination of whether the breach reflected a "wanton or reckless disregard" under s. 219(1), not to whether there was an undertaking under s. 217.

What kind of an undertaking gives rise to a legal duty within the meaning of s. 217, the breach of which can result in criminal culpability? In my view, the ordinary dictionary definition of "undertaking" is of little assistance. There is no doubt that the definition embraces an interpretive continuum ranging from an assertion to a promise. But it seems to me that when we are deciding whether conduct is caught by the web of criminal liability, the threshold definition we apply must justify penal sanctions. A conviction for criminal negligence causing death carries a maximum penalty of life imprisonment. The word "undertaking" in s. 217 must be interpreted in this context. The threshold definition must be sufficiently high to justify such serious penal consequences. The mere expression of words indicating a willingness to do an act cannot trigger the legal duty. There must be something in the nature of a commitment, generally, though not necessarily, upon which reliance can reasonably be said to have been placed.

Any other interpretation of "undertaking" imports theories of civil negligence, rendering individuals who breach civil standards of care susceptible to imprisonment. The criminal standard must be — and is — different and higher. Before someone is convicted of recklessly breaching a legal duty generated by his or her undertaking, that undertaking must have been clearly made, and with binding intent. Nothing short of such a binding commitment can give rise to the legal duty contemplated by s. 217.

The trial judge found that the relationship between Dexter Browne and Audrey Greiner as partners in drug dealing gave rise to an implicit undertaking by Browne that he would take Audrey Greiner to the hospital whenever she swallowed cocaine. The fundamental error made by the trial judge was in reversing the analytical steps under s. 217 by starting her analysis with whether a duty of care existed, finding that it did, and then basing her finding of an undertaking on the existence of a legal duty. The inquiry should have begun with whether there was an undertaking. Only if there was an undertaking in the nature of a binding commitment could a legal duty have arisen under s. 217, regardless of the nature of the relationship between the appellant and Audrey Greiner.

In my view, the evidence does not disclose any undertaking of a binding nature. These were two drug dealers who were used to swallowing bags of drugs to avoid detection by the police. There was no evidence that the appellant knew that Audrey Greiner was in a life-threatening situation until 2:00 a.m., when he immediately phoned for a taxi. His words to her at that time — "I'll take you to the hospital" — hardly constitute an undertaking creating a legal duty under s. 217. He said he would take her to the hospital when he saw the severity of her symptoms, and he did. There is no evidence either that a 911 call would have resulted in a significantly quicker arrival at the hospital at that hour, or even that had she arrived earlier, Audrey Greiner's life could have been saved.

There being no undertaking within the meaning of s. 217 of the *Criminal Code*, there can be no finding of a legal duty. There being no duty, there can be no breach contrary to s. 219 of the *Code*.

. . . .

Accordingly, I would allow the appeal, set aside the conviction, and enter an acquittal.

R. v. PETERSON

[2005] O.J. No. 4450, 2005 CarswellOnt 5093, 201 C.C.C. (3d) 220 (C.A.), leave to appeal refused (2006), 2006 CarswellOnt 1198, 2006 CarswellOnt 1199 (S.C.C.)

1 WEILER J.A. (ARMSTRONG J.A. concurring).:— This appeal requires us to consider when a parent is under the charge of a child thereby requiring the child to provide necessaries of life to that parent pursuant to s. 215 of the *Criminal Code*. The relevant portion of s. 215 states:

(1) Every one is under a legal duty

. . . .

(c) to provide necessaries of life to a person under his charge if that person

(i) is unable, by reason of detention, age, illness, mental disorder or other cause, to withdraw himself from that charge, and

(ii) is unable to provide himself with necessaries of life.

(2) Every one commits an offence who, being under a legal duty within the meaning of subsection (1), fails without lawful excuse, the proof of which lies upon him,[2] to perform that duty, if

. . . .

(b) with respect to a duty imposed by paragraph (1)(c), the failure to perform the duty

---

2 At trial, it was accepted by counsel that the reverse onus is unconstitutional and that the onus is on the Crown to prove the essential elements of the charge beyond a reasonable doubt.

endangers the life of the person to whom the duty is owed or causes or is likely to cause the health of that person to be injured permanently.

(3) Every one who commits an offence under subsection (2) is guilty of

(a) an indictable offence and is liable to imprisonment for a term not exceeding two years; or

(b) an offence punishable on summary conviction.

2 Because several members of the affected family have the same last name, where it is not possible to use the last name to identify the person, the first name has been used. No disrespect is intended by this practice.

3 On September 20, 2002, Dennis Peterson was convicted of failing to provide the necessaries of life to his father, Arnold Peterson, thereby endangering Arnold's life. Dennis was sentenced to six months imprisonment, two years probation, and one hundred hours community service on November 15, 2002. He appeals from his conviction, seeks leave to appeal his sentence, and, if leave is granted, appeals his sentence.

4 Dennis appeals his conviction on two bases. He submits that the reasons of the trial judge fail to satisfy the functional need to know the basis on which the conviction was entered and, accordingly, a new trial is necessary. Alternatively, Dennis submits that the evidence does not support a finding that Arnold was under his charge. Dennis also submits that the sentence was harsh and excessive in the circumstances.

5 For the reasons that follow I would dismiss the appeal from both conviction and sentence.

Factual Background

6 For over forty years, Arnold, who was approximately eight-four years old in 2000, lived in his three-story house in Toronto. For a period of time, Arnold lived with his adult son, Dennis; daughter, Linda Peterson; grandson, Derek Joyce; and the grandson's girlfriend, Laura Scriver. At that time the house was "open" in the sense that it was not divided into apartments. Linda moved out in January 1999. At the time of the events in question, the house was divided into apartments. Arnold occupied the first floor and the basement. Dennis lived on the second floor and occupied a living room on the first floor. Joyce lived on the third floor. An internal staircase linked the apartments. Dennis kept the doors to the upstairs apartments and to the main floor living room locked.

7 Arnold's living quarters were in disrepair to the point that the kitchen did not function. It had no drywall and the floorboards were lifting. It was also filled with dead cockroaches. Dirty dishes were stacked on the counter and in the sink,

and the cupboards were bare. Linda confirmed that this kitchen had not been used for a couple of years and she assumed that her father was eating upstairs with Dennis. However, Scriver, the former girlfriend of Arnold's grandson, testified she never saw Arnold on the second floor and that it was always locked. Arnold would sometimes go to the convenience store to buy bread, chips, or cookies, which he ate on the porch. However, he had not been seen buying groceries since before his deterioration in 1999. A neighbour estimated that over the winter and spring of 2000 Arnold lost up to thirty pounds.

8 There was no bathroom on the main floor where Arnold's apartment was located. There was a broken cistern toilet in the basement and a bathroom on the second floor. The broken dirt floor of the basement was covered in dog feces. The neighbours and Scriver did not see Arnold using the upstairs washroom. Arnold's bedroom was messy and there were no sheets on the bed.

9 Arnold would rake leaves and do repair jobs for the neighbours, including Catherine Raven and Ana Michalsky, until the spring of 2000. Raven or Michalsky would give him meals when he came over. He could not dress himself appropriately and often wore winter clothes in the summer and vice versa. Because of his weight loss, his clothes did not fit. He would wear pants without a belt or zipper and would pin the waist to keep them from falling down. He did not wear underwear. He stopped shaving and began to smell. His clothes became dirty.

10 Raven found Arnold locked out of the house at least a dozen times in the eight months before the police first had contact with the family. He would wait on Raven's porch and she would let him stay in her house until Dennis returned home, usually around midnight. Raven would not go to bed without checking to see if Arnold was locked out.

11 Raven and Scriver testified that the appellant would yell at Arnold, tease him about the Germans (Arnold had lost family in WWII), or ignore him and speak as if he was not there.

12 On April 30, 2000, Officer Houston responded to a call claiming that an old man "sat down rather heavily" in front of someone's house. It is Arnold, who was exhausted. The police helped him to his feet and drove him home. Dennis was not home so Michalsky offered to let Arnold stay with her until Dennis came home.

13 One week later, P.C. Cutmore visited the house. Dennis said it was hard to look after Arnold because he would go for long walks and get lost. P.C. Cutmore explained about community agencies that could help. Dennis did not call these agencies.

14 On June 7, 2000, a man flagged Officer Houston down to help Arnold, who had collapsed on the street close to where he had been found on April 30. He found Arnold sitting on a planter, reclining back on an elbow, looking filthy and exhausted. He was weaker than he had been before and required assistance to stand and walk. He smelled very badly and it appeared he had not showered for some time. He was not answering questions promptly and, other than recognising his name, Officer Houston did not think that Arnold knew what was asked of him. He needed to be reminded where he lived although he recognized the house as his home. No one answered the door when P.C. Houston knocked and, because Arnold could not move on his own, P.C. Houston took Arnold to St. Joseph's Hospital where he was admitted and given a place to lie down. P.C. Houston telephoned the address where Arnold lived and advised Dennis that his father was at the hospital. Arnold was released shortly thereafter.

15 On June 9, 2000, Officer Worth received a call from a gas company employee making meter checks who told him he had found a dead dog at the residence of a confused, elderly man. Officer Worth went to the address in question and found Arnold sitting on the front porch. Arnold was very dirty; his clothes were filthy and did not fit. His pants were too large and he had to hold them up with his hands. The fly was down or broken and he was wearing no underwear. The pants were dirty and wet in the crotch area. There was a very strong odour coming from him and it was obvious that he had not bathed in a number of days. He was quite thin, although he was a big man, and his cheeks were sunken in and unshaven. It was obvious to Officer Worth that Arnold had not eaten in a while. Arnold did not complain about Dennis or his grandson. He did say he was hungry. Officer Worth asked him when was the last time he had eaten and was told that it had been a few days and that his son gave him an apple the day before.

16 Officer Worth apprehended Arnold under the *Mental Health Act*, R.S.O. 1990, c. M.7. Officer Worth did not believe that Arnold was able to care for himself and apprehended him for his safety. He took him to St. Joseph's Hospital where he was admitted. Linda signed the forms to transfer him from St. Joseph's Hospital to a nursing home and he was admitted to Fairview Nursing Home on June 10.

17 Linda described her father as fiercely independent and contrary. He was very stubborn and would do the opposite of what Dennis told him to do. She stated that Arnold would not listen to anyone and that it was not uncommon for him to wear dirty clothes. When she and Dennis bought clothes for their father, it was very hard to get him to wear them. Linda testified that Dennis was concerned about their father and said that Dennis had always been good to him. Besides buying Arnold clothes, Dennis did his laundry, and cut his hair. He was never physically abusive towards his father. Arnold was adamant that he would not

go into a nursing home. Linda left the family home in January 1999. She and Dennis did not discuss who would take care of Arnold as they all "helped out". Arnold had a key that he wore around his neck but the last time Linda saw it was in June 1999. She had not been in the house for six months prior to June 7, 2000.

18 On February 28, 2000, Linda and Dennis asked a lawyer to draft two powers of attorney with the two of them acting as joint attorneys: one addressed financial affairs, the other, Arnold's personal care. They thought that if anything happened to Arnold, someone should be able to take care of his financial affairs and "everything".

19 After February 28, 2000, she and Dennis did not discuss their father's welfare and who should take care of him. Dennis never called her to say that their father's health was deteriorating.

20 Dr. Lam, a general practitioner who works at the nursing home, examined Arnold. He found him to be a little underweight for his height and build but not emaciated. Although he was pleasant and cooperative, Arnold seemed confused. He did not know where he was and was not able to tell Dr. Lam his home address when asked. Further testing to determine the extent of Arnold's cognitive impairment led Dr. Lam to the conclusion that Arnold was in the early stages of Alzheimer's dementia and that this dementia could have been going on for six months to two years. In Dr. Lam's opinion, given how Arnold was acting in the fall and winter of 1999 and the spring of 2000, he was likely suffering from some dementia process.

21 On admission, Arnold was incontinent in terms of urine. Dr. Lam doubted that Arnold would bathe himself without being reminded to do so. He would also need direction and assistance. Further, he would probably need supervision in terms of dressing and would not know how to dress appropriately for the weather. Arnold was able to feed himself, but he needed supervision, guidance, and direction. At the nursing home, he had to be taken to the dining hall when the meal was served and have it placed in front of him. Dr. Lam stated that Arnold would probably forget to eat if he were not called down to the dining hall.

22 Dr. Lam opined that Arnold's living situation was a totally unsafe environment for him. He was in danger of falling and the environment was very non-hygienic. The state of the rooms meant that Arnold probably could not take care of himself at all and that it was likely that Arnold was not even aware of the environment he was in. Arnold should have had supervision by a person who saw him at least once every half hour so that he could not wander off or fall and break a hip.

. . . .

The Issues

28 The appellant's first submission is that the trial judge failed "to explain the basis upon which he arrived at his conclusion that Arnold was in the Appellant's charge" and therefore the reasons fail to satisfy the basis upon which the conviction was entered in accordance with *R. v. Sheppard*, [2002] 1 S.C.R. 869. His second submission is that "the evidence does not support a finding beyond a reasonable doubt that Mr. Peterson was in the care of the appellant". The appellant further submits that there is at least a reasonable doubt that Arnold was not in Dennis's care having regard to the following factors:

* Arnold was energetic, physically active, and walked the neighbourhood on a regular basis.

* Arnold was fiercely independent, very stubborn, and would never look to anyone for help nor listen to his children.

* Linda Peterson testified that she and Dennis did not consider invoking their power of attorney because their father was well and there was no reason to think he would need care.

29 I propose to deal with the appellant's submissions together...

The Meaning of "Under His Charge"

33 This appears to be the first case to reach an appellate court in which the meaning of the phrase "under his charge" in s. 215(1)(c) as between an adult child and his or parent is in issue. That said, the section must be read and interpreted as a whole.

34 Section 215(1)(c) differs from section s. 215(1)(a), which imposes a duty on a "parent, foster parent, guardian or head of a family" to provide necessaries "for a child under the age of sixteen years", and from s. 215(1)(b), which imposes a duty on spouses and common-law partners to provide necessaries of life to their spouses and partners. Section 215(1)(c) makes it clear that the duty to provide necessaries is not limited to these relationships but can arise in other circumstances. The duty arises when one person is under the other's charge, is unable to withdraw from that charge, and is unable to provide himself or herself with necessaries of life. The phrase "necessaries of life" includes not only food, shelter, care, and medical attention necessary to sustain life but also appears to include protection of the person from harm: *R. v. Popen* (1981), 60 C.C.C. (2d) 232 (Ont. C.A.) at 240. Thus, s. 215(1)(c) obligations are driven by the facts and the context of each case.

35 Subsection 215(2) imposes liability on an objective basis. The offence is made out by conduct showing a marked departure from the conduct of a reasonably prudent person having the charge of another in circumstances where it is objectively foreseeable that failure to provide necessaries of life would risk danger to life or permanent endangerment of the health of the person under the charge of the other. The personal characteristics of the accused, falling short of capacity to appreciate the risk, are not a relevant consideration. The use of the word "duty" is indicative of a societal minimum that has been established and is aimed at establishing a uniform minimum level of care: *R. v. Naglik*, [1993] 3 S.C.R. 122 at paras. 37, 51 and 33 respectively.

36 The objective basis of liability includes an assessment of whether the person in charge could have acted other than as he or she did. For example, in *Naglik* at para. 36, a "crucial consideration" was that the evidence indicated the services of a public health nurse were made available to *Naglik* to help her in caring for her child, given her age, education, and lack of experience with children. She refused to accept any assistance.

37 The words "without lawful excuse" in s. 215(2) provide a defence and serve to prevent the punishment of the morally innocent. The obligation to provide necessaries is not absolute and may be excused, for example, where there is financial inability: *Naglik, supra*, and *R. v. Yuman* (1910), 17 C.C.C. 474 (Ont. C.A.).

38 On the other hand, I note that contributory negligence by the victim is not a defence for an accused charged with criminal negligence unless the injuries incurred are attributable solely to the victim: see Eugene G. Ewaschuk, *Criminal Pleadings and Practice in Canada*, 2d ed. looseleaf (Aurora: Canada Law Book, 1987) at para. 28:180, citing *R v Lesuk*, [2000] 7 W.W.R. 462 (Man. C.A.) at para. 31 and other appellate decisions from Alberta, Saskatchewan, Nova Scotia, and Prince Edward Island.

39 Section 215(2)(b) indicates that the failure to provide necessaries includes not only a failure to do a discrete act but also includes a failure to act in an ongoing relationship over a period of time: see *Naglik, supra*, at para. 36 in relation to section 215(2)(a)(ii), which is similar in wording to s. 215(2)(b).

40 In addition to the foregoing, I would make the following observations. First, the relationship of the parties to each other is among the factors to consider in determining whether a person is in the charge of another. The dependency of the parent under a disability on an independent adult child is justified not only by their past course of dealing in which the parent supported the child but also by their relationship to one another in which an element of trust will usually be present. The history of the section supports the interpretation that the section was intended to require certain minimal standards in relation to dependants such

as wives and children and was later broadened: see *R. v. Middleton*, [1997] O.J. No. 2758, at paras. 10-14. The mere breach of a federal or provincial statute, such as s. 32 of *the Family Law Act*, which imposes a duty on a child to support a parent, does not constitute a crime. It is nevertheless proper for the trier of fact to consider legislation governing the accused in order to determine whether the accused's actions or inactions show a "marked departure" from the conduct expected: see by analogy *R. v. Leblanc*, [1977] 1 S.C.R. 339, *R. v. Bergeron* (1999), 132 C.C.C. (3d) 45 (Que. C.A.).

41 Second, the word "charge" is not unknown to the criminal law in other contexts involving adults. In the impaired driving context, the court characterized having "care, charge or control" of a vehicle as requiring "a kind of domination as in the master-servant relationship and as in the parent-child or teacher-beginner relationship": *R. v. Slessor*, [1970] 1 O.R. 664 at 674. The court did not restrict the meaning of charge too far, however, stating, "'Charge', too, is a word of broad comprehension. One speaks of a person who is fixed with responsibility of supervision as one who is in 'charge'". The Ontario Environmental Appeal Board also considered the meaning of the word charge in *Re Karge* (1996), 21 C.E.L.R. (N.S.) 5 at para. 68-69. It referred to the dictionary meanings of the word and concluded essentially that it means to have the responsibility to take care of someone, something, or somewhere.

42 Used in these contexts the word "charge" connotes, among other things, the duty or responsibility of taking care of a person or thing. Similarly, one of the definitions of charge in *Black's Law Dictionary*, 8th ed. (St. Paul, Minneapolis: West Publishing, 2004) is "to entrust with responsibilities or duties e.g. to charge the guardian with the ward's care". What the definitions have in common is the exercise of an element of control by one person and a dependency on the part of the other.

43 In assessing whether one person is in the charge of another, the relative positions of the parties and their ability to understand and appreciate their circumstances is a factor to consider. A parent who is not in full possession of his or her faculties may not appreciate that he or she cannot provide himself or herself with the necessaries of life and may not have the capacity to understand that he or she is in an unsafe or unhealthy environment that is likely to cause permanent injury. Just as some contributory negligence by the victim is not a defence to a charge of criminal negligence, the inability of the victim to appreciate his or her need for necessaries and the victim's unwillingness to cooperate is not a defence for an accused charged with failure to provide necessaries. If the parent is otherwise in the child's charge and the child cannot care for the parent due to the parent's refusal to accept care, the child is obliged to seek the help of a community agency. See *Regina v. Stone & Dobinsons*, [1977] Q.B. 354 at 361.

44 A further consideration in determining whether a person is in the charge of another is whether one person has explicitly assumed responsibility for the other, for example, by obtaining a power of attorney for personal care or by publicly acknowledging to others in the community by words or conduct an assumption of responsibility.

45 The non-exhaustive criteria below illuminate the trial judge's findings and the path he took to his conclusion that Arnold was in the charge of the appellant:

1. Arnold was dependent: The trial judge found that in his state of dementia, Arnold was unable to provide himself with the necessaries of life. As he never cooked, had no food in the apartment, and sometimes went days without food, he was dependent on someone else to provide him with food. The trial judge also accepted Dr. Lam's evidence that Arnold needed assistance in choosing appropriate clothing to wear as well as assistance with his personal grooming.

2. The appellant had a familial relationship with Arnold and was aware of his father's dependency. The trial judge found that Dennis was fully aware that his father was in need of the necessaries of life. It was manifestly obvious, particularly because Arnold lost up to thirty pounds during the winter and spring of 2000.

3. The appellant controlled Arnold's living conditions and kept him in an unsafe environment. The trial judge found that the appellant had free access to Arnold's rooms but kept all of the rooms he occupied locked when he was not there. The logical inference is that Dennis prevented Arnold from having access to the only working kitchen, bathing facilities, and properly working toilet in the house. The trial judge also found that the toilet in the basement had no seat, was filthy, worked poorly, and the environment in which it was located was unsafe because the stairs to the basement were poorly lit and had no handrail until near the bottom. The trial judge further found that the kitchen was unsafe even for a fit person.

4. The appellant had control over Arnold's personal care. The appellant took steps to obtain the power to make decisions respecting Arnold's personal care and had the ability to make decisions about his personal care. Put another way, at the request of Dennis and his sister, Arnold entrusted them with the ability to make decisions respecting his personal care. Quite apart from the power of attorney, when Dennis came home and Arnold was locked out, as frequently happened, the appellant took Arnold into his charge from the neighbours. Thus, both legally and publicly Dennis assumed responsibility for Arnold.

5. The appellant chose not to make decisions that would result in Arnold receiving the necessaries of life. Dennis was made aware of community services that could assist him with the care of his father. He took no steps pursuant to Const. Cutmore's suggestions. (One suggestion, as revealed in the evidence, was to contact a church across the street that operated an extensive Meals-on-Wheels program.)

6. Arnold was incapable of withdrawing himself from the appellant's "charge" due to age and illness. He was too old, feeble, and senile to withdraw himself from the appellant's charge.

46 When the trial judge's reasons are considered in this manner, they disclose why the trial judge found that Arnold was under the appellant's charge as well as why Arnold was unable to withdraw from his son's charge. Thus, the reasons disclose why the trial judge convicted Arnold and satisfy the requirements of *Sheppard*, *supra*.

47 With respect to the third element of the offence, namely, the failure to provide Arnold with the necessaries of life, the appellant relied on Linda's evidence as contradicting the evidence that Dennis failed to provide Arnold with the necessaries of life and was under his charge. The appellant submits that the trial judge was required to resolve the conflict in the evidence. However, as Linda had not entered the house for at least six months prior to Arnold being apprehended, she was not in a position to testify about whether Dennis failed to provide Arnold with the necessaries of life. Her evidence did not raise a conflict that necessitated resolution by the trial judge. Thus the trial judge correctly found that the evidence was not really in dispute.

48 Insofar as the legal test for determining when a person is under the charge of another is concerned, the evidence that Arnold did not wish to bathe or change his clothes does not negate the appellant's having charge of him. The evidence simply supports the conclusion that Arnold had a mental disability that prevented him from exercising sound judgment to provide himself with the necessaries of life. This disability cannot be used by Dennis as a defence for failing to provide Arnold with the necessaries of life. Dennis could have called a community agency for help and did not. Further, there was no evidence that Arnold ever refused food yet, Dennis did not provide him with food regularly.

49 The trial judge's reasons are sufficient to permit his decision to be reviewed and do not disclose any error in law. Accordingly, I would dismiss the conviction appeal.

. . . .

The majority upheld the trial judge's sentence of 6 months' imprisonment followed by 2 years' probation and 100 hours of community service. Borins J.A.

would have upheld the sentencing portion of the appeal, substituting a conditional sentence, on the basis that failure to provide necessaries cases involving children were not sufficiently analogous. He agreed with the majority's conclusions on guilt, however, making the following comments:

BORINS J.A. (dissenting in part):—

66 In my view, contemporary legislation is required to deal with the issue of parent/child role reversal, which is one of the results of human longevity. An estimated 22.4 million households in the United States - nearly one in four - are providing care to a relative or friend aged fifty or older according to a 1997 survey by the National Alliance for Caregiving and the American Association of Retired Persons. It is likely that adults born between 1946 and 1965 will spend more years caring for a parent than for their children. As Susan Dominus pointed out in an article in *The New York Times Magazine*: "The philosophical impact [of human longevity] on family dynamics will be profound, as parents continue to lean on children long past retirement themselves, and people in their 80's learn what it means, at that age, to still be somebody's child." ("Life in The Age of Old, Old Age", *The New York Times Magazine*, February 22, 2004.)

67 In an article, "Longer Lives Reveal the Ties That Bind Us" (*The New York Times*, October 2, 2005), David Brooks points out that between now and 2050, the percentage of the population above age eighty-five is expected to quadruple. Brooks quotes Dr. Leon Kass, the former Chairman of the President's Council on Bioethics, as stating: "The defining characteristic of our time seems to be that we are both younger longer and older longer." To which Brooks adds:

> Parents have to spend more time preparing their children for the new economy and children have to spend a lot more time caring for their parents when they are old.

In other words, technology, which was supposed to be liberating, actually creates more dependence. We spend more of our lives while young and old dependent upon others, and we spend more time in between caring for those who depend on us.

68 Although these data and comments apply to the United States, there is little doubt that they also apply to Canada. This is why it is no longer satisfactory to rely on legislation designed for another purpose in another era to define what contemporary society requires of its members who have aging parents in need of care. Children of aging parents no doubt accept that their parents require some form of care, be it in respect to financial affairs or personal care. As the elderly lose their ability to remain self-sufficient, their adult children are gradually required to assume caregiving responsibilities. As a result of rising life expectancy, the child who becomes his or her parent's caregiver, is often well within the "senior citizen" age category. In addition, given that the age at which children are conceived is rising, the expectation is that there will be a sizeable

group of children who will face a double "necessaries" duty in respect to both their children and their parents, raising, perhaps, the need to chose between the welfare of their children and their parents. It is, therefore, of critical importance that if the duty to care for an aging population continues to be within the ambit of the criminal law, that care is taken to clearly define what constitutes criminal neglect or penal negligence.

69 Unlike its role in shaping the duty to provide care for very young children, which is easily defined and recognized, and which is governed by s. 215(1)(a) of the *Criminal Code*, the challenge for government is to address the issue of the child caregiver of an aging parent in a way that clearly defines the circumstances in which criminal liability will be imposed. Determining the level of responsibility that an adult child should bear for an elder parent together with defining the appropriate standard of care are difficult and challenging issues. Indeed, one may ask whether they should continue to be governed by criminal law. Useful contemporary legislative models may be found in several states in the United States that have enacted specific laws related to elder abuse and elder care, entrenching a defined duty of care. I refer, in particular, to legislation in California, Massachusetts and Illinois. The Massachusetts legislation is especially instructive in its comprehensive definition of "caretaker" in defining appropriate boundaries for criminal liability.

This decision is useful for beginning to analyze the question of when an elderly parent should be taken to be in the "charge" of an accused, thereby placing the accused under a duty to provide necessaries of life.* As Borins J.A. notes in his dissent, the demographics of the Canadian population make this an issue likely to arise more frequently in the future than it has in the past. More complete presentation by counsel of social sciences research into the issue of elder abuse and neglect would be helpful in allowing later decisions to flesh out these criteria even more fully.

The Supreme Court has regularly noted that it is important to avoid reliance on unsupported stereotypical thinking in legal reasoning: this has affected their reasoning around equality rights and around sexual assault, for example. There are a number of stereotypes about the elderly in society: that the typical elderly person is frail and dependent, for example. In fact, most elderly persons remain healthy and competent to make decisions for most of their lives: see, for instance, N. Chappel et al., *Aging in Contemporary Canada* (Toronto: Prentice Hall, 2003). Similarly, it is often supposed that the typical victim of "elder abuse" is dependent on the abuser. In fact, research suggests that more typically it is the abuser who is dependent on the victim in some way: see L. McDonald and A. Collins, *Abuse and Neglect of Older Adults: A Discussion Paper* (Ottawa: National Clearinghouse

---

* This note originally appeared in the *Criminal Reports* as an annotation to the *Peterson* decision: see Steve Coughlan, *R. v. Peterson*: Annotation, 34 C.R. (6th) 120.

on Family Violence, Health Canada, 2000). Similarly, the elderly are often presumed typically to refuse services due to incompetence. Again this assumption is false. Competent older people most often refuse services because they see those services as a threat to their independence, their privacy, their ability to remain in their own homes, or even their ability to continue a relationship with the "abuser": see J. Aronson and S. Naismith, "Manufacturing Social Exclusion in the Home Care Market" (2001) 27(2) Canadian Public Policy 151-164.

These stereotypes can be seen to have affected some social services legislation in various provinces. Although some provinces avoid relying on these stereotypes by making the wishes of the adult a primary consideration, others do not. The four Atlantic provinces, for instance, have all adopted versions of an "Adult Protection Act". This approach in essence assumes that the elderly are like children, and is modelled quite closely on child protection legislation. Generally speaking, these statutes give little or no weight to the wishes of the adult, and rather require courts to decide based on what a third party thinks are the adult's "best interests". The fact that an adult in need of protection might not (as the father in this case did not) wish to be placed in a nursing home would be of no consequence.

It is important that a proper understanding of the situation and attitudes of the elderly be incorporated into a full understanding of when an elderly person can be said to be in the "charge" of someone else. Here, the Court is content to limit discussion of the father's refusal to enter a nursing home to the issue of whether contributory negligence is a defence to criminal negligence. The majority hold at para. 43:

> If the parent is otherwise in the child's charge and the child cannot care for the parent due to the parent's refusal to accept care, the child is obliged to seek the help of a community agency.

The issue is not pursued at length, but there is the danger here that the parent's wishes are being treated merely as an obstacle, not as a legitimate consideration to be taken into account. Similarly the Court notes at para. 48:

> Insofar as the legal test for determining when a person is under the charge of another is concerned, the evidence that Arnold did not wish to bathe or change his clothes does not negate the appellant's having charge of him. The evidence simply supports the conclusion that Arnold had a mental disability that prevented him from exercising sound judgment to provide himself with the necessaries of life.

In the adult protection context, particularly in cases of "self-neglect", this same catch-22 situation reduces the likelihood of an adult's wishes being respected: those very wishes are taken as evidence to justify overriding the adult's wishes. We do not generally take this approach with other people, who are assumed to be entitled to make potentially foolish and hazardous decisions, like taking part in extreme skiing, eating live insects on a reality show, or investing in high-risk ventures. Similarly, if a 30-year-old ceases to bathe often enough, we try not to sit next to him or her on the bus: if the person is 70, we try to place him or her in a nursing home. Treating older adults differently seems like a natural approach if we stereotype them as like children. The ultimately negative impact this approach actually has on the elderly whom the law aims to "protect" has been noted and criticized: see Joan Harbison et al., *Mistreating Elderly People: Questioning the*

Legal Response to Elder Abuse and Neglect (Halifax: Dalhousie University Health Law Institute, 1995).

If courts too readily assume that care for the elderly involves a "parent/child role reversal" (para. 66), it is likely that the elderly will, in this context as well, be treated like children rather than like adults. In this criminal context, those stereotypes are likely to work to the detriment of those associated with the elderly, and who might be found to have failed to provide necessaries in circumstances where the accused might have thought he or she was simply recognizing the adult's independence and respecting his or her right to make decisions.

PROBLEM

In a controversial old United States decision in *People v. Beardsley,* 113 N.W. 1128 (Mich. S.C., 1907) the trial judge convicted the accused of manslaughter in the following circumstances:

"He was a married man living at Pontiac, and at the time the facts herein narrated occurred, he was working as a bartender and clerk at the Columbia Hotel. He lived with his wife in Pontiac, occupying two rooms on the ground floor of a house. Other rooms were rented to tenants, as was also one living room in the basement. His wife being temporarily absent from the city, respondent arranged with a woman named Blanche Burns, who at the time was working at another hotel, to go to his apartments with him. He had been acquainted with her for some time. They knew each other's habits and character. . . . On the evening of Saturday, March 18, 1905, he met her at the place where she worked, and they went together to his place of residence. They at once began to drink and continued to drink steadily, and remained together, day and night, from that time until the afternoon of the Monday following, except when respondent went to his work on Sunday afternoon. There was liquor at these rooms, and when it was all used they were served with bottles of whiskey and beer by a young man who worked at the Columbia Hotel, and who also attended respondent's fires at the house. . . . On Monday afternoon, about one o'clock, the young man went to the house to see if anything was wanted. . . . During this visit to the house the woman sent the young man to a drug store to purchase, with money she gave him, camphor and morphine tablets. He procured both articles. There were six grains of morphine in quarter-grain tablets. She concealed the morphine from respondent's notice, and was discovered putting something into her mouth by him and the young man as they were returning from the other room after taking a drink of beer. She in fact was taking morphine. Respondent struck the box from her hand. Some of the tablets fell on the floor, and of these, respondent crushed several with his foot. She picked up and swallowed two of them, and the young man put two of them in the spittoon. Altogether it is probable she took from three to four grains of morphine. The young man went away soon after this. Respondent called him by telephone about an hour later, and after he came to the house requested him to take the woman into the room in the basement which was occupied by a Mr. Skoba. She was in a stupor and did not rouse when spoken to. Respondent was too intoxicated to be of any assistance and the young man proceeded to take her downstairs. While doing this Skoba arrived, and together they put her in his room on the bed. Respondent requested Skoba to look after her and let her out the back way when she waked up. Between nine and ten o'clock in the evening Skoba became alarmed at her condition. He at once called the city marshal and a doctor. An examination by them disclosed that she was dead."

On appeal the accused was acquitted on the basis that there had been no legal duty to act. How would that issue be decided under current Canadian law as reviewed in preceding pages?

4. VOLUNTARINESS

(a) Defining Conduct That Is Not "Voluntary"

R. v. KING

[1962] S.C.R. 746 at 749, 38 C.R. 52, 133 C.C.C. 1,
1962 CarswellOnt 18 (S.C.R.)

TASCHEREAU J.: — It is my view that there can be no *actus reus* unless it is the result of a willing mind at liberty to make a definite choice or decision, or in other words, there must be a willpower to do an act whether the accused knew or not that it was prohibited by law.

RABEY v. R.

[1980] 2 S.C.R. 513, 54 C.C.C. (2d) 1, 15 C.R. (3d) 225 at 232, 235, 255,
1980 CarswellOnt 35, 1980 CarswellOnt 71

RITCHIE J.: —

. . . .

Automatism is a term used to describe unconscious, involuntary behaviour, the state of a person who, though capable of action, is not conscious of what he is doing. It means an unconscious involuntary act, where the mind does not go with what is being done.

DICKSON J.: —

. . . .

Although the word "automatism" made its way but lately to the legal state, it is basic principle that absence of volition in respect of the act involved is always a defence to a crime. A defence that the act is involuntary entitles the accused to a complete and unqualified acquittal. That the defence of automatism exists as a middle ground between criminal responsibility and legal insanity is beyond question. Although spoken of as a defence, in the sense that it is raised by the accused, the Crown always bears the burden of proving a voluntary act. . . . [A] . . . principle, fundamental to our criminal law, which governs this appeal is that no act can be a criminal offence unless it is done voluntarily. Consciousness is a *sine qua non* to criminal liability.

R. v. PARKS

[1992] 2 S.C.R. 871, 15 C.R. (4th) 289, 75 C.C.C. (3d) 287,
1992 CarswellOnt 107, 1992 CarswellOnt 996

LA FOREST J.: —
Automatism occupies a unique place in our criminal law system. Although spoken of as a "defence", it is conceptually a subset of the voluntariness requirement, which in turn is part of the *actus reus* component of criminal liability.

R. v. STONE

[1999] 2 S.C.R. 290, 24 C.R. (5th) 1, 134 C.C.C. (3d) 353,
1999 CarswellBC 1064, 1999 CarswellBC 1065

BASTARACHE J.: — I . . . prefer to define automatism as a state of impaired consciousness, rather than unconsciousness, in which an individual, though capable of action, has no voluntary control over that action. . . .

. . . .

[V]oluntariness, rather than consciousness, is the key legal element of automatistic behaviour since a defence of automatism amounts to a denial of the voluntariness component of the *actus reus*.

Note

In *Stone*, Bastarache, for a 5-4 majority, also held that accused had to prove any defence of automatism on a balance of probabilities.

The leading decisions in *Rabey* (disassociated state), *Parks* (sleepwalking) and *Stone* will be considered much later after a consideration of the defence of insanity when voluntariness is re-visited under the heading of automatism.

In *R. v. Ruzic* (2001), 41 C.R. (5th) 1 (S.C.C.) (considered later under duress), the court distinguished the issue of physical voluntariness required for proof of the *actus reus* from the issue of moral involuntariness arising in the case of justifications and excuses. The physical voluntariness requirement applies to any offence, and is distinct from any issue of fault. There is here no reference to a reverse onus, as compared to the onus of proof the majority placed on the accused for the defence of automatism in *Stone*.

COBB, FOUNDATIONS OF NEUROPSYCHIATRY

(1958), 117-18, quoted by S.J. Fox, "Physical Disorder Consciousness and Criminal Liability" (1963), 63 Col. L. Rev. 645 at 651

When the human organism is working well, functioning as a whole, there is probably the highest degree of consciousness, and a feeling of well being and capability. In such a state attention is usually directed to certain objects with neglect of others. Therefore there is never a state that could be called full consciousness. . . . When tired, bored, or slightly poisoned by alcohol, we are suffering from a partial loss of consciousness. From the excited state of great efficiency under stress, through normal work-a-day moods, to states of dullness, coma and stupor, there is a continuous series of states where consciousness is less and less active. . . . Only in deep sleep is the cortex inactive, as judged by the electroencephalograph. There are different degrees of consciousness in sleep. Persons lightly asleep can differentiate between ordinary noises and sounds that may mean danger. Dreaming is a form of consciousness. A sense of time may be carried through hours of sleep, allowing one to wake at a desired hour.

(b) Why Have a Voluntary Requirement for the *Actus Reus*?

H.L.A. HART, ACTS OF WILL AND RESPONSIBILITY

Punishment and Responsibility, (1968), 104-106

The General Doctrine Reconstructed.

Most people, lawyers and laymen alike, would I think agree that in our list of examples of involuntary conduct (conscious and unconscious), some radical defect is present, and some vital component of normal action is absent, even if Austin's terminology of "desire" or muscular movement or volitions misdescribes it. For the cases do not seem to be a *mere* list without any unifying feature to justify treating them alike as cases where conduct is not voluntary. If it is the policy of the law to mark these cases off, there seems some good factual basis for this policy. Is it then possible to give a more adequate account than that of the traditional theory? Or must we leave the dark phrases "not governed by the will", "no act of will", "involuntary", "no operation of the will" etc. unexplained?

In fact, I think it would not be difficult to construct an account which would explain and justify the intuitive feeling that, in all these cases, there is some more fundamental defect than lack of knowledge or foresight. By a "more adequate" account I mean one which involves no fictions; which is better fitted to the facts of ordinary experience; and which could be used by the courts in order to identify a range of cases where the minimum mental element required for responsibility is not satisfied. Such an account could cover both the conscious and unconscious examples suggested in the books, but it would necessarily differ from the kind of general explanation given there in two main ways. First it would be disassociated from any claim that the ordinary way of talking about actions was inferior, or less accurate than the definition of acts as muscular contractions. Secondly, omissions would have to be treated separately from positive interventions. Granted these two things, we could then characterise involuntary movements such as those made in epilepsy, or in a stroke, or mere reflex actions to blows or stings, as movements of the body which occurred although they were not appropriate, *i.e.* required for any action (in the ordinary sense of action) which the agent believed himself to be doing. This, I think, reproduces what is in fact meant by ordinary people when they say a man's bodily movements are uncontrolled, as in the case of a reflex or St. Vitus dance. Such movements are "wild" or not "governed by the will" in the sense that they are not subordinated to the agent's conscious plans of action: they do not occur as part of anything the agent takes himself to be doing. This is the feature which the Austinian theory represents in a distorted form by identifying the involuntary movements as those which are not caused by a desire for them.

In the unconscious cases, *e.g.* of epilepsy, automatism, etc. the same test can be used. Here too, the movements which we call involuntary are not part of any action the agent takes himself to be doing, because, being unconscious, he does not take himself to be doing any action. This test, it should be noted, preserves the distinction between involuntary conduct and mere lack of knowledge of circumstances or foresight of consequences, and so reproduces the sense that we have in involuntary movements a different and more fundamental defect. For one who merely fails to foresee that the gun he fires will harm someone still makes voluntary muscular movements, *i.e.* movements appropriate to the action of firing the gun, which he knows he is doing; whereas the involuntary tremors of the palsied man, who breaks a glass, are appropriate to no action which he believes himself to be doing.

Omissions must, I think, be catered for separately, though this can and should be done in a way which reveals that their voluntary or involuntary character depends on the same general principle as positive interventions. When a man fails to do some positive action demanded by the law, his failure to act is involuntary if he is unconscious and so *unable* to do any conscious action, or if, though conscious, he is *unable* to make the particular muscular movements required for the performance of actions demanded by the law.

I.H. PATIENT, SOME REMARKS ABOUT THE ELEMENT OF VOLUNTARINESS IN OFFENCES OF ABSOLUTE LIABILITY

(1968) Crim. L. Rev. 23 at 25-26

It is important at this stage to stress that involuntariness goes beyond lack of *mens rea*. A series of examples may show this.

Case 1: A shoots B meaning to kill him and B is indeed killed. A kills intentionally.

Case 2: A is not sure whether the shape in the distance is a human being or a tree, he nevertheless shoots. It was in fact B, who was killed by the shot. A kills recklessly.

Case 3: A is convinced he is shooting at a tree trunk. In fact it is B. A reasonable man would have realised it was a human being. B is killed by A's shot. A kills negligently.

Case 4: A shoots in a pistol club at a target. Suddenly B falls from the spectator's gallery into A's line of fire. He is killed. Even a reasonable man could not foresee this. A kills with blameless inadvertence, *i.e.*, accidentally.

In all four cases A's shooting was voluntary.

Case 5: A has an epileptic fit. One of his movements causes a gun which is lying beside him on a table to go off and kill B.
or:
A is aiming at a target. The physically stronger X takes hold of A's hand and forces him to point the gun at B and to pull the trigger. B is hit and killed.
or:
A is aiming at a target. He is attacked by a swarm of bees. His defensive reflex movement causes the gun to go off in B's direction and B is killed.

In all these cases there was a lack of voluntariness. There was no act on A's part. A cannot be said to have "shot" B. He caused his death, just as lightning can cause a man's death. Since there was no act neither was there an *actus reus*. To bring out the difference between involuntariness and *mens rea*, cases 4 and 5 have to be compared. In case 4, A kills accidentally, *i.e.*, without *mens rea*. Though there was no *mens rea* with regard to the killing, there was nonetheless a voluntary act. A did shoot. Moreover, he implemented the full *actus reus* of homicide, he killed a human being. If homicide were an offence of strict liability, *i.e.*, an offence which makes you liable even without *mens rea*, then A would be guilty of homicide in case 4. As the law stands he luckily will not be so liable. In case 5, however, there is not even an *actus reus*. An *actus reus* presupposes an act. There was no such act. A's movements were causal in bringing about B's death, but A did not "shoot" B. The defect in case 5 is therefore more fundamental than the defect in case 4. Even if homicide were an offence of strict liability, A would nevertheless not be liable in case 5. For strict [absolute] liability means liability without *mens rea*. In case 5 there is more than lack of *mens rea*. There is not even an *actus reus*.

O.W. HOLMES, THE COMMON LAW

Howe, ed., (1963), 46

The reason for requiring an act is, that an act implies a choice, and that it is felt to be impolitic and unjust to make a man answerable for harm, unless he might have chosen otherwise. But the choice must be made with a chance of contemplating the consequence complained of, or else it has no bearing on responsibility for that consequence. If this were not true, a man might be held answerable for everything which would not have happened but for his choice at some past time. For instance, for having in a fit fallen on a man, which he would not have done had he not chosen to come to the city where he was taken ill.

H.L. PACKER, THE LIMITS OF THE CRIMINAL SANCTION

(1968), 76-77

Conduct must be, as the law's confusing term has it, "voluntary." The term is one that will immediately raise the hackles of the determinist, of whatever persuasion. But, once again, the law's language should not be read as plunging into the deep waters of free will vs. determinism, Cartesian duality, or any of a half-dozen other philosophic controversies that might appear to be invoked by the use of the term "voluntary" in relation to conduct. The law is not affirming that some conduct is the product of the free exercise of conscious volition; it is excluding, in a crude kind of way, conduct that in any view is not. And it does so primarily in response to the simple intuition that nothing would more surely undermine the individual's sense of autonomy and security than to hold him to account for conduct that *he* does not think he can control. He may be deluded, if the determinists are right, in his belief that such conduct differs significantly from any other conduct in which he engages. But that is beside the point. *He* thinks there is a difference, and that is what the law acts upon.

(c)   Examples Not Associated with Mental Disorder

R. v. LUCKI

(1955), 17 W.W.R. 446, 1995 CarswellSask 72 (Sask. Pol. Ct.)

GOLDENBERG Q.C., P.M. — The charge against the accused is as follows:

[O]n the 22nd day of November, A.D., 1955, at the City of Saskatoon in the said Province did operate a motor vehicle, to wit, an automobile bearing Saskatchewan License Number 139-212 on a public highway in the said City of Saskatoon, to wit, Saskatchewan Crescent, and did fail to keep to the right half of the said highway, and did thereby inconvenience other persons using the said highway, contrary to the provisions of Section 125 (9) of *The Vehicles Act* of the Province of Saskatchewan.

The facts are not in dispute. The accused operated a car on 17th Street in the city of Saskatoon at a speed of from 10 to 15 miles per hour. He had proceeded on 17th Street a distance of only about 150 feet, and made a right turn onto Saskatchewan Crescent East. While doing so, his car skidded over onto the left or north side of the road, and as a result he collided with another car which was proceeding in an opposite direction.

It is clear that his car was not on the right half of the road and that another car was inconvenienced thereby. It is clear to me that he got onto the wrong side of the road by an involuntary act, caused by the condition of the road, and I cannot say upon the evidence before me that it was his faulty driving that placed him in the position where he ended up. I think it was an involuntary act, for which he is not to blame.

Do these facts render him guilty of an offence under sec. 125 (9) of *The Vehicles Act*, R.S.S., 1953, ch. 344 [amended by 1955, ch. 82, sec. 27 (3)]? There are many sections under that Act that require no *mens rea*. Is this one of them? I do not think so. Were it otherwise some grave injustices would arise.

I can think of a case where a person drives a car carefully and a drunken driver runs into him and pushes his car over on to the left side of the road. I do not believe that the legislature intended such a person to be convicted under the section in question. And yet, if *mens rea* was not an essential ingredient of this offence, he would be guilty of it, since he did drive on the left side of the road.

No general rule can be formulated beyond stating that a person who by an involuntary act for which he is not to blame gets onto the wrong side of the road is not guilty under the section in question.

I find the accused not guilty.

R. v. WOLFE

(1975), 20 C.C.C. (2d) 382 (Ont. C.A.)

The judgment of the court was delivered orally by GALE C.J.O.: — The appellant was found guilty following a trial on a charge of assault causing bodily harm. After the finding of guilt was registered, the trial judge granted the appellant a conditional discharge. The appellant now appeals from the finding of guilt and this court is unanimously of the opinion that the appeal ought to be allowed, the finding of guilt set aside and a verdict of acquittal entered.

The appellant is a part-owner of a hotel in Kingston. On previous occasions, the complainant had been told, for good reason, that he was not to enter the hotel premises. On the evening in question, despite that prohibition, he entered the hotel. The appellant, using discretion and restraint, ordered him to leave. The complainant would not leave. The appellant then went to the telephone and while he was calling the police for the purpose of having him removed, the complainant punched the appellant who turned quickly and hit the complainant on the head with the telephone receiver. The complainant had a rather serious cut on his forehead, but that was really all that happened.

In giving judgment the learned trial judge said:

> Now, there is evidence that Mr. Brown-Keay hit the accused Mr. Wolfe and then in a reflex action (if you can call it that) Mr. Wolfe, who was calling the police, hit Mr. Brown-Keay on the forehead and caused a four-inch cut on his forehead. . . .

If, as it would seem to us, the trial judge regarded the action by the accused as being the result of a reflex action then no offence was committed because some intent is a necessary ingredient in an assault occasioning bodily harm.

Mr. Campbell argues, not very vigorously, however, that, because of the limitation in brackets in the above quotation, the trial judge did not regard the action of the appellant as resulting from his reflexes. However, that was in fact what the judge said and we see no reason to depart from his conclusion.

In any event, the encounter was a trifling one and we have come to the conclusion that the appeal ought to be allowed and the finding of guilt set aside, as I have already indicated. The appeal will therefore be allowed.

Appeal allowed.

R. v. SWABY

44 C.R. (5th) 1, 155 C.C.C. (3d) 235, 2001 CarswellOnt 2160 (Ont. C.A.)

Acting on a confidential tip, police officers followed a car driven by the accused in which J. was a passenger. The car stopped and J. ran into a nearby backyard. The accused drove off. Both men were arrested shortly thereafter. The police found a loaded, unregistered, restricted handgun in the backyard. J., the main Crown witness at the accused's trial, had pleaded guilty to possession of the handgun and received a sentence of time served (42 days). J. had a significant criminal record and was the subject of immigration proceedings. The accused was tried before a judge and jury on an indictment containing eight counts. He was convicted of being an occupant in a vehicle knowing there was present an unlicensed, restricted weapon contrary to s. 91(3) of the *Criminal Code*, but acquitted on all other counts. According to J.'s testimony the gun was the accused's and he gave it to J. to dispose of. According to the accused the gun was J.'s and he only learned of it after the arrest. The accused appealed his conviction.

The majority of the Ontario Court of Appeal allowed the accused's appeal, set aside the conviction and ordered a new trial.

Per SHARPE J.A. (FELDMAN J.A. concurring): —

. . . .

The charging provision under which the appellant was convicted was s. 91(3) of the *Criminal Code*, R.S.C. 1985, c. C-46:

91(3) Every one who is an occupant of a motor vehicle in which he knows there is a restricted weapon is, unless some occupant of the motor vehicle is the holder of a permit under which he may lawfully have that weapon in his possession in the vehicle, or he establishes that he had reason to believe that some occupant of the motor vehicle was the holder of such permit,

(a) guilty of an indictable offence and liable to imprisonment for a term not exceeding five years; or

(b) guilty of an offence punishable on summary conviction.

. . . .

To establish guilt on this count, the Crown had to prove the coincidence of the two essential elements of the offence as defined by s. 91(3), namely occupancy of the vehicle and the appellant's knowledge of the weapon. In my view, it is implicit as well that the Crown had to prove that the coincidence of occupancy and knowledge was attributable to something amounting to voluntary conduct on the part of the appellant. Although the section under which the appellant was charged contained no explicit defence in the terms of the present s. 94(3), it must be interpreted so as to exclude the possibility of conviction for what would amount to an involuntary act.

Voluntary conduct is a necessary element for criminal liability: see A.W. Mewett & M. Manning, *Mewett & Manning on Criminal Law*, 3rd ed. (Toronto, Butterworths: 1994) at pp. 129-32; Glanville Williams, *Textbook of Criminal Law*, 2nd ed. (London, Stevens & Sons: 1983) at pp. 146-54. The requirement for voluntary conduct applies even if the provision creating the offence does not expressly require one: see D. Stuart, *Canadian Criminal Law: A Treatise*, 3rd ed. (Toronto, Carswell: 1995) at p. 94: "There is no general Code stipulation that the guilty act be voluntary. The requirement exists by virtue of judicial reasoning . . .". As explained by McLachlin J. in *R. v. Théroux*, [1993] 2 S.C.R. 5, 79 C.C.C. (3d) 449 at p. 17 S.C.R., p. 458 C.C.C.: ". . . the act must be the voluntary act of the accused for the *actus reus* to exist."

If one acquires knowledge of an illegal weapon while travelling in a moving vehicle, it surely cannot be the law that criminal liability instantly attaches. There must be some period of time, however short, afforded to the person who has acquired that knowledge to deal with the situation. If a passenger tells the driver that the passenger has a gun, it cannot be the case that the driver is immediately guilty. Should the driver immediately stop the vehicle and tell the passenger to leave, the driver would have known of the gun while he was an occupant of the vehicle, but he would have done all the law could expect. The driver's occupancy of the vehicle would have coincided with his knowledge of the gun, but it could not be said that the coincidence of knowledge and occupancy amounted to voluntary conduct on the part of the driver. It is the conduct of the driver following the coincidence of occupancy and knowledge that counts, and if the driver acts with appropriate dispatch to get either the gun or himself out of the vehicle, there is no voluntary act for the criminal law to punish.

Accordingly, it is my view that if the appellant acquired knowledge of the weapon while the vehicle was in motion, he would have to be given a reasonable opportunity to either remove himself or to see that the weapon was removed from the vehicle. If the appellant only acquired knowledge of the weapon at the point when J. was leaving the vehicle, he would be entitled to an acquittal.

. . . .

It is my view that the appellant was entitled to a fuller explanation from the trial judge of the necessary elements of this offence dealing more thoroughly with the circumstances in which guilt would follow if knowledge of the weapon were acquired after the vehicle was set in motion. For these reasons, I would allow the appeal, set aside the conviction, and order a new trial.

. . . .

Per MACPHERSON J.A. (dissenting): — The appellant testified that at no time until after charges were laid did he know that there was a gun in his car. In spite of this testimony, the appellant now contends that, in response to the jury's questions, the trial judge should have given a broad answer that would have included an instruction on a scenario in which there was no evidence — namely, that the appellant became aware that J. had a gun at some point during their ride together in the car. In such a circumstance, I do not think that the trial judge erred by answering the jury's questions within the context of the evidence they had heard:

> He must know of the existence of the weapon. You must be satisfied on the evidence you have heard in total throughout the trial but with respect to this particular question that you have asked, it must be proven by the Crown to have known of the existence of that weapon in that vehicle while both he and Mr. J. were in it.

In my view, this was a precise and, in light of the evidence (especially the appellant's position at trial), appropriate response to the jury's questions.

R. v. RYAN

(1967), 40 A.L.J.R. 488 (Aus. H.C.)

The accused, aged 20, read a novel in which the hero, feeling obliged to his parents, decided to rob a service station to obtain money to "invest" in the Irish sweepstake. In the book, the hero, armed with a gun, tied up the garage attendant's hands behind his back after having obtained his money. He subsequently won the lottery, repaid the owner of the service station handsomely and gave the balance of his winnings to his parents.

The accused, as an act of bravado and for excitement and self-aggrandizement, decided to emulate his hero. On arrival at the service station where he intended the drama to occur he left his companion outside and went in armed with a sawn-off rifle, loaded and cocked. He demanded money from the sole attendant, threatening him with the weapon. The attendant produced some money. The accused then told him to put his hands behind his back, and went to tie them together with a piece of cord he had brought with him for that purpose. At this point, according to the accused, the attendant made a sudden movement and the gun accidentally discharged, killing the attendant. It was clear that slight pressure by the accused's finger had caused the gun to discharge. The jury dismissed the defence of accident and convicted of murder. The accused was sentenced to life imprisonment.

On appeal the accused argued that the jury ought to have been instructed on the issue of Involuntariness which, if accepted, would have resulted in an acquittal. The firing of the gun was a reflex response to a sudden movement by the victim and was unwilled action on his part. The police had conducted several re-enactments of this scenario and on each occasion the actor had pulled the trigger. However, the Australian High Court unanimously rejected the view that the jury ought to have been so instructed.

WINDEYER J. (one of four judgments delivered): —

The essential that the act be a voluntary act is .... generally spoken of as a necessary quality of a criminal act; but it is perhaps more accurately regarded as a mental quality or attribute of the actor....

That an act is only punishable as a crime when it is the voluntary act of the accused is a statement satisfying in its simplicity. But what does it mean? What is a voluntary act? The answer is far from simple, partly because of ambiguities in the word "voluntary" and its supposed synonyms, partly because of imprecise, but inveterate, distinctions which have long dominated men's ideas concerning the working of the human mind. These distinctions, between will and intellect, between voluntary and involuntary action, may be unscientific and too simple for philosophy and psychology today. However that may be, the difficulty of expressing them in language is obvious and may be illustrated. The word "involuntary" is sometimes used as meaning an act done seemingly without the conscious exercise of the will, an "unwilled" act: sometimes as meaning an act done "unwillingly", that is by the conscious exercise of the will, but reluctantly or under duress so that it was not a "wilful" act. Words and phrases such as involuntary, unintentional, inadvertent, accidental, unmeditated, unthinking, not deliberate, unwilled and so forth are used by different writers. Their connotations often depend upon their context, and they are used in discussions which seem to drift easily off into psychological questions of consciousness, sanity and insanity and philosophical doctrines of free-will and of events uncontrolled by will. There is a discussion of some aspects of this subject in the American work, *Reflex Action, a Study in the History of Physiological Psychology*. I mention it, not because I profess any knowledge in this field, but because of the readiness with which the phrase "reflex action" was used in the course of the argument as a presumably exculpatory description of the act of the applicant when he pressed the trigger of the firearm.

The conduct which caused the death was of course a complex of acts all done by the applicant — loading the rifle, cocking it, presenting it, pressing the trigger. But it was the final act, pressing the trigger of the loaded and levelled rifle, which made the conduct lethal. When this was said to be a reflex action, the word "reflex" was not used strictly in the sense it ordinarily has in neurology as denoting a specific muscular reaction to a particular stimulus of a physical character. The phrase was, as I understood the argument, used to denote rather the probable but unpredictable reaction of a man when startled. He starts. In doing so he may drop something which he is holding, or grasp it more firmly. Doctor Johnson in his Dictionary — and his definition has been in substance repeated by others — said that "to start" means "to feel a sudden and involuntary twitch or motion of the animal frame on the apprehension of danger". The Oxford Dictionary speaks of a start as "a sudden involuntary movement of the body occasioned by surprise, terror, joy or grief ... ". But assume that the applicant's act was involuntary, in the sense in which the lexicographers use the word, would that, as a matter of law, absolve him from criminal responsibility for its consequences? I do not think so. I do not think that, for present purposes, such an act bears any true analogy to one done under duress, which, although done by an exercise of the will, is said to be involuntary because it was compelled. Neither does it, I think, bear any true analogy to an act done in convulsions or an epileptic seizure, which is said to be involuntary because by no exercise of the will could the actor refrain from doing it. Neither does it, I think, bear any true analogy to an act done by a sleepwalker or a person for some other reason rendered unconscious whose action is said to be involuntary because he knew not what he was doing.

Such phrases as "reflex action" and "automatic reaction" can, if used imprecisely and unscientifically, be, like "blackout", mere excuses. They seem to me to have no real application to the case of a fully conscious man who has put himself in a situation in which he has his finger on the trigger of a loaded rifle levelled at another man. If he then presses the trigger in immediate response to a sudden threat or apprehension of danger, as is said to have occurred in this case, his doing so is, it seems to me, a consequence probable and foreseeable of a conscious apprehension of danger, and in that sense a voluntary act. The latent time is no doubt barely appreciable, and what was done might not have been done had the actor had time to think. But is an act to be called involuntary merely because the mind worked quickly and impulsively? I have misgivings in using any language descriptive of psychological processes and phenomena, especially as I doubt whether all those skilled in this field employ their descriptive terms uniformly. Guided however by what has been said in other cases and by writers on criminal law whose works I have read, and especially by the judgments in the House of Lords in *Bratty v. Attorney-General for Northern Ireland*, [1963] A.C. 386, I have come to the conclusion that if the applicant, being conscious of the situation in which he had put himself, pressed the trigger as a result, however spontaneous, of the man whom he was threatening making some sudden movement, it could not be said that his action was involuntary so as to make the homicide guiltless. The act which caused the death was. ... an act of the accused. The question for the jury was whether it was an act done by him in such a way as to make the resulting homicide murder. This was the issue submitted to the jury. The application for special leave to appeal must I consider be refused.

KILBRIDE v. LAKE

[1962] N.Z.L.R. 590 (S.C.)

WOODHOUSE J.: — On Thursday, 15 June 1961, the appellant drove his wife's car into Queen Street in the City of Auckland where he left it parked. He returned to it a short time later to find stuck to the inside of the windscreen a traffic offence notice drawing his attention to the fact that a current warrant of fitness was not displayed in terms of Reg. 52 of the Traffic Regulations 1956 (S.R. 1956/217). It was agreed before me that the warrant had been in its correct position when he left the vehicle, but that it could not be found upon his return. It was further agreed that during the period of his absence from the car the warrant had become detached from the windscreen in some way and been lost, or it had been removed by some person unknown. The fact that it was a current warrant was proved conclusively by records showing that on 13 April it had been issued by the Auckland Municipal Motor Vehicle Testing Station under No. 4513, and in respect of voucher No. 115456. Thus it had been issued for only two months, and four months would elapse before it required to be renewed. Despite a written explanation to this general effect which he had forwarded on the same day, a prosecution followed and he was convicted before Justices on an information alleging that he "did operate a motor vehicle . . . and did fail to display in the prescribed manner a current warrant of fitness". The proceedings were defended, but no note of the evidence was taken and no reasons for the decision were given. In these circumstances the appeal was argued on agreed facts as I have summarised them.

So far as it is applicable the regulation reads:

> (1) . . . No person shall operate a motor vehicle . . . unless there is carried on the vehicle a current warrant of fitness as described in subclause (2) of this Regulation.

Subclause (2) provides that in the case of a vehicle fitted with a windscreen the warrant shall be affixed to the inside of the windscreen. The word "operate" is defined in Reg. 3 as meaning

> to use or drive or ride, or cause or permit to be driven or ridden, or to permit to be on any road whether the person operating is present in person or not.

The appeal was argued on the basis that the appellant operated the vehicle by permitting it to be on the road, and the facts do not support any wider application of the word "operate". Accordingly the regulation under review may be written, for the present purpose, as follows:

> No person shall permit a motor vehicle to be on a road whether the person operating it is present or not unless there is carried on the vehicle a current warrant of fitness.

The case for the appellant was that if he could show an absence of *mens rea*, then he could not be convicted, and he had succeeded in doing this as the warrant had disappeared without his knowledge during his absence from the car. On the other hand it was claimed for the respondent that this statutory offence was one which excluded *mens rea* as an ingredient to be proved. On this basis it was submitted that the offence was one of strict liability, and therefore the knowledge or the intention of the appellant was irrelevant. The issue thus raised on these simple facts directly poses the important question as to whether something done perfectly lawfully by the appellant could become an offence on his part by reason of an intervening cause beyond his influence or control, and which produced an effect entirely outside his means of knowledge.

It has long been established, of course, that if there is an absolute prohibition, and the prohibited act is done by the defendant, then the absence of *mens rea* affords no defence. This principle derives its justification from the general public interest, and any consequential injustice which might seem to follow in individual cases has necessarily been accepted. In the present case the respondent has conceded that the appellant had no opportunity of dealing with the situation which arose. But, it is said, however unfair a conviction might be to him personally, this offence has been made one of absolute liability as it is essential to put strong pressure on drivers of motor vehicles to do their whole duty. He permitted the car to be on the road, it was found there without a warrant, and accordingly he is guilty of the offence. With all respect to the arguments of both counsel, however, I am of the opinion that the emphasis which has been put on the matter of *mens rea* has obscured the real issue in this case.

It is fundamental that quite apart from any need there might be to prove *mens rea*,

> a person cannot be convicted of any crime unless he has committed an overt act prohibited by the law, or has made default in doing some act which there was a legal obligation upon him to do. The act or omission must be voluntary. (*10 Halsbury's Laws of England*, 3rd ed., 272.)

He must be shown to be responsible for the physical ingredient of the crime or offence. This elementary principle obviously involves the proof of something which goes behind any subsequent and additional inquiry that might become necessary as to whether *mens rea* must be proved as well. Until that initial proof exists arguments concerning *mens rea* are premature. If the first decision to be made is that the offence excludes *mens rea*, then that finding is likely to disguise the fact that there is an absence of proof showing that the accused has done all that is charged against him, should this in fact be the case. The missing link in the chain of causation, if it is noticed at all, appears to be provided by notions of absolute liability. But it is impossible, of course, to prove the one ingredient by eliminating the need to prove another. It appears to me that this confusion has arisen in this case. The primary question arising on this appeal, in my opinion, is whether or not the physical element in the offence was produced by the appellant. This physical element may be described by the convenient term *actus reus*, in contrast to the mental element or *mens rea* which is also an ingredient of a crime or offence, unless expressly excluded by its statutory definition.

In considering whether the *actus reus* can be attributed to a defendant, it is important to recognize that this is something which occurs following acts or omissions. It is not the line of conduct which produces the prohibited event, but it is the event itself. It is an occurrence brought about by some activity or inactivity, or by both. The crime therefore (excluding for the moment the possible ingredient of *mens rea*) is constituted by the event, and not by the discrete acts or omissions which preceded it: *Russell on Crime*, 11th ed., pp. 25, *et seq*. Accordingly it is not sufficient to show by some single act or omission that the accused produced the event. It is this fact which produces difficulties of causation when attempting to attribute responsibility for the *actus reus* to a given person. It is easy to do this when the *actus reus* can result from a single act, as, for example, a death by shooting. When it depends, however, upon supervening acts, and particularly when omissions are added to them, then the difficulties tend to multiply. Of course, when *mens rea* is an ingredient to be proved against an accused person, all these difficulties disappear as soon as they arise, because he usually cannot be proved to have intended acts done by others. He is thereupon acquitted on that ground. As *mens rea* is so frequently an ingredient of crimes and offences, this is a problem which rarely arises, and for that reason is not always recognized.

In the present case the definition of the offence takes the form of a prohibition followed by an exception. The prohibited event, however, in the sense of the term *actus reus* is not merely to permit a vehicle to be on a road. It is the doing of that act accompanied by an omission to observe the obligation to carry the current warrant of fitness. The *actus reus* occurs only when the second of these factual ingredients co-exists with the first. There must be the presence of the car combined with the absence of the warrant. Did this appellant produce that prohibited event, or did he merely set the stage?

There can be no doubt that the appellant permitted the vehicle to be on the road, and his conduct in this respect was a continuing act which did not end when he left the vehicle. Nevertheless, at this latter point of time the warrant was on the car, and there was no unlawful situation. Only when some extraneous cause subsequently removed the warrant did the event occur which the regulation is directed to prevent. If he is to be regarded as responsible for that *actus reus*, therefore, the decision must be made on the basis that he omitted immediately to replace the warrant.

It is, of course, difficult to demonstrate that an omission to act was not, in a causal sense, an omission which produced some event. All omissions result from inactivity, and in this matter of the warrant the appellant was necessarily inactive. But, in my opinion, it is a cardinal principle that, altogether apart from the mental element of intention or knowledge of the circumstances, a person cannot be made criminally responsible for an act or omission unless it was done or omitted in circumstances where there was some other course open to him. If this condition is absent, any act or omission must be involuntary, or unconscious, or unrelated to the forbidden event in any causal sense regarded by the law as involving responsibility. See for example *Salmond on Jurisprudence*, 11th ed. 401, *Causation in the Law* by Hart and Honore 292, *et seq*., and the passage in *10 Halsbury's Laws of England*, 3rd ed., 272 cited above. In my opinion a correct emphasis is now given by this last paragraph to the need for the act or omission making up the *actus reus* to be voluntary, whereas in the corresponding paragraph of the second edition this distinction was blurred in discussion of *mens rea*. Naturally the condition that there must be freedom to take one course or another involves free and conscious exercise of will in the case of an act, or the opportunity to choose to behave differently in the case of omissions. But this mental stimulus required to promote acts or available to promote omissions if the matter is adverted to, and consequently able to produce some forbidden condition, is entirely distinct from the mental element contained in the concept of *mens rea*. The latter is the intention or the knowledge behind or accompanying the exercise of will, while the former is simply the spark without which the *actus reus* cannot be produced at all. In the present case there was no opportunity at all to take a different course, and any inactivity on the part of the appellant after the warrant was removed was involuntary and unrelated to the offence. In these circumstances I do not think it can be said that the *actus reus* was in any sense the result of his conduct, whether intended or accidental. There was an act of the appellant which led up to the prohibited event (the *actus reus*), and that was to permit the car to be on the road. The second factual ingredient was not satisfied until the warrant disappeared during his absence. The resulting omission to carry the warrant was not within his conduct, knowledge, or control: on these facts the chain of causation was broken.

For the foregoing reasons I am of the opinion that the physical ingredient of this charge was not proved against the appellant. Accordingly, I express no opinion on the submission that *mens rea* is excluded as an ingredient of the offence. On the view I have taken of the case the point does not arise.

Appeal allowed.

5. ACTING THROUGH INNOCENT AGENT

R. v. MICHAEL

(1840), 9 C. & P. 356 (C.C.C.R.)

The prisoner was indicted for the wilful murder of George Michael. She was also charged on the coroner's inquisition with the same offence.

The indictment stated, that the prisoner, contriving and intending to kill and murder George Michael on the 31st day of March, in the third year of the reign of her present Majesty, upon the said George Michael feloniously, &c., did make an assault, and that the prisoner, a large quantity, to wit, half an ounce weight, of a certain deadly poison called laudanum, feloniously, &c., did give and administer unto the said George Michael, with intent that he should take and swallow the same down into his body (she then and there well knowing the said laudanum to be a deadly poison), and the said George Michael the said laudanum so given and administered unto him by the said Catherine Michael as aforesaid, did take and swallow down into his body; by reason and by means of which said taking and swallowing down the said laudanum into his body, as aforesaid, the said George Michael became and was mortally sick and distempered in his body, of which said mortal sickness and distemper the said George Michael from &c. till &c. did languish, &c., and died; and concluding in the usual form, as in cases of murder.

It appeared that the deceased was a child between nine and ten months old, and that the prisoner was its mother, and was a single woman living in service as wet nurse at Mrs. Kelly's, in Hunter Street, Brunswick Square. The child was taken care of by a woman named Stevens, living at Paddington, who received five shillings a week from the prisoner for its support. A few days before its death the prisoner told Mrs. Stevens that she had an old frock for the child, and a bottle of medicine, which she gave her, telling her it would do the baby's bowels good. Mrs. Stevens said the baby was very well, and did not want medicine; but the prisoner said it had done her mistress's baby good, and it would do her baby good, and desired Mrs. Stevens to give it one teaspoonful every night. Mrs. Stevens did not open the bottle, or give the child any of its contents, but put the bottle on the mantel-piece, where it remained till Tuesday, the 31st of March, on which day, about half-past four in the afternoon, Mrs. Stevens went out, leaving the prisoner's child playing on the floor with her children, one of whom, about five years of age, during the absence for about ten minutes of his elder sister, gave the prisoner's child about half the contents of the bottle, which made it extremely ill, and in the course of a few hours it died. The bottle was found to contain laudanum. The prisoner said that a young man, an assistant of Dr. Reid's, had given the bottle by mistake. This was proved to be untrue; and Dr. Reid stated, that in the course of a conversation he had with the prisoner, she used these remarkable words, speaking of the death of the child, and the probability of an inquest being held upon the body: — "If I am hanged for it, I could not support the child on my wages." It was also proved that the prisoner purchased the laudanum at the chemist's in Tavistock Place, Russell Square, saying that it was for her mistress, Mrs. Kelly, who was in the habit of taking it, being a bad sleeper. One of the medical men examined at the trial said, that a teaspoonful administered to a child of the age of the deceased would be sure to destroy life.

Alderson, B., in his summing up, told the jury, that if the prisoner delivered the laudanum to Sarah Stevens with the intention that she should administer it to the child, and thereby produce its death, and the quantity so directed to be administered was sufficient to cause death, and while the prisoner's original intention continued, the laudanum was administered by an unconscious agent, the death of the child, under such circumstances, would sustain the charge of murder against the prisoner. His Lordship added, that if the teaspoonful of laudanum was sufficient to produce death, the administration by the little boy of a much larger quantity would make no difference.

The jury found the prisoner guilty. The judgment was respited, that the opinion of the Judges might be taken, whether the facts above stated constituted an administering of the poison by the prisoner to the deceased child.

Ryland, for the prosecution.

Ballantine, for the prisoner.

At a subsequent Session, Mr. Baron Alderson, in passing sentence upon the prisoner, said, that the Judges were of opinion that the administering of the poison by the child of Mrs. Stevens, was, under the circumstances of the case, as much, in point of law, an administering by the prisoner as if the prisoner had actually administered it with her own hand. They therefore held that she was rightly convicted.

Would it have made any difference if the laudanum had been administered by a conscious agent who acted for his own purposes?

For Canadian authority applying the "doctrine of acting through an innocent agent" see *R. v. MacFadden* (1971), 5 C.C.C. (2d) 204, 16 C.R.N.S. 251 (N.B. C.A.) at 253; *R. v. Berryman* (1990), 78 C.R. (3d) 376, 57 C.C.C. (3d) 375, (B.C. C.A.); *R. v. Ali* (1990), 79 C.R. (3d) 382 (Ont. Prov. Ct.); and *R. v. Toma* (2000), 147 C.C.C. (3d) 252 (B.C. C.A.).

In *R. v. Devgan* (2007) 53 C.R. (6th) 104 (Ont. S.C.J.) Justice Ducharme held that a doctor could be guilty of trafficking drugs as the acts of the pharmacist unaware of the illegal scheme could be considered his acts even though he exercised independent judgment. Under the doctrine the instigator is deemed to be the actual perpetrator even though the agent's acts were non-criminal specific to the agent, such as the absence of *mens rea*, a defence, mental disorder or infancy. Requiring that the innocent agent cannot exercise independent judgment would lead to undesirable results.

The doctrine of acting through an agent has been relied on to confer some criminal responsibility as a perpetrator for injuries committed through animals (e.g., getting a dog to attack a person). We shall see much later under Parties to an Offence that there is also wide criminal responsibility in Canadian law beyond the actual perpetrator to those who merely assist or facilitate.

6. CAUSATION

(a) *Criminal Code*

In the case of some but not all offences the *actus reus* requires the causing of certain consequences. These offences include all homicides (s. 222), wilful damage to property (s. 430), arson (s. 433), and causing bodily harm (s. 221) or death (s. 220) by criminal negligence. The latter two offences illustrate that graver consequences may attract a higher maximum penalty — life imprisonment in the case of death and 10 years' imprisonment in the case of bodily harm. Since 1985 the maximum penalty of 5 years for the offence of dangerous operation of a vehicle increases to 10 years where that conduct causes bodily harm and to 14 years where death results (s. 249(3) and (4)) and see similarly for impaired driving (s. 255(2) and (3)).

Our *Code* contains no general principles concerning causation but only a number of special rules concerning homicide: see ss. 222 and 224-228.

B.C. ELECTRIC RY. v. LOACH

[1916] 1 A.C. 719 at 727-728 (P.C.)

LORD SUMNER: —

. . . .

It is surprising how many epithets eminent judges have applied to the cause, which has to be ascertained for this judicial purpose of determining liability, and how many more to other acts and incidents, which for this purpose are not the cause at all. or effective cause," "real cause," "proximate cause," "direct cause," "decisive cause," "immediate cause," "causa causans," on the one hand, as against, on the other, "causa sine qua non," "occasional cause," "remote cause," "contributory cause," "inducing cause," "condition," and so on. No doubt in the particular cases in which they occur they were thought to be useful or they would not have been used, but the repetition of terms without examination in other cases has often led to confusion, and it might be better, after pointing out that the inquiry is an investigation into responsibility, to be content with speaking of the cause of the injury simply and without qualification.

(b)   Common Law

SMITHERS v. R.

[1978] 1 S.C.R. 506, 40 C.R.N.S. 79, 34 C.C.C. (2d) 427,
1977 CarswellOnt 25, 1977 CarswellOnt 479F

DICKSON J.: — This is an appeal from a judgment of the Court of Appeal for Ontario dismissing an appeal brought by the appellant from his conviction by judge and jury on a charge of manslaughter. The indictment alleges that the appellant did unlawfully kill Barrie Ross Cobby by kicking him.

On February 18, 1973, a hockey game was played between the Applewood Midget Team and the Cooksville Midget Team at the Cawthra Park Arena in the Town of Mississauga. The leading player on the Applewood team was the deceased, Barrie Cobby, 16 years of age; the leading player on the Cooksville team was the appellant. The game was rough, the players were aggressive and feelings ran high. The appellant, who is black, was subjected to racial insults by Cobby and other members of the Applewood team. Following a heated and abusive exchange of profanities, the appellant and Cobby were both ejected from the game. The appellant made repeated threats that he was going to "get" Cobby. Cobby was very apprehensive and left the arena at the end of the game, some 45 minutes later, accompanied by eight or ten persons including friends, players, his coach and the team's manager. The appellant repeated his threats and challenges to fight as the group departed. Cobby did not take up the challenge. Instead, he hurried toward a waiting car. The appellant caught up with him at the bottom of the outside steps and directed one or two punches to Cobby's head. Several of Cobby's team mates grabbed the appellant and held him. Cobby, who had taken no steps to defend himself, was observed to double up and stand back while the appellant struggled to free himself from those holding him. While Cobby was thus bent over, and approximately two to four feet from the appellant, the appellant delivered what was described as a hard, fast kick to Cobby's stomach area. Only seconds elapsed between the punching and the kick. Following the kick, Cobby groaned, staggered towards his car, fell to the ground on his back, and gasped for air. Within five minutes he appeared to stop breathing. He was dead upon arrival at the Mississauga General Hospital.

Doctor David Brunsdon, who performed an autopsy, testified that in his opinion death was due to the aspiration of foreign materials present from vomiting. He defined aspiration as the breathing, or taking in, of foreign material through the windpipe into the lungs. It appears from the medical evidence that aspiration is generally due to barbiturate overdosage, alcohol intoxication, motor vehicle accidents or epilepsy. One medical witness testified to the possibility of spontaneous aspiration, whereby foreign material may be aspirated without any precipitating cause. This witness had seen three such cases out of the 900 to 1,000 cases of aspiration which he had experienced. In none of the three cases was the aspiration preceded by a blow. The consensus among the doctors was that spontaneous aspiration was a rare and unusual cause of death in the case of a healthy teenager such as Cobby. Normally, when a person vomits the epiglottis folds over to prevent the regurgitated stomach contents from entering the air passage. In the instant case this protective mechanism failed.

. . . .

The ground of dissent in the Ontario Appeal Court forms the first ground of appeal in this court. Counsel for the appellant submits that the trial judge, in emphasizing the act of assault as a constituent element in the crime of manslaughter, did not make it clear to the jury that the act of assault must also cause the death of the deceased and, secondly, that in giving his summation of the Crown and defence theories, the trial judge referred to the issue of causation as defence counsel's argument that the cause of death had not been proven beyond a reasonable doubt. It is contended that the effect of these remarks was to minimize this issue in the minds of the jury. The jury was never instructed, it is said, that as a matter of law one of the issues on which they had to be satisfied beyond a reasonable doubt was that the kick caused the vomiting.

. . . .

I agree with the majority view in the Ontario Court of Appeal that the issue as to the cause of death was properly and sufficiently delineated by the trial judge. It was not an unduly complicated issue. The assault by the appellant upon the deceased boy was undoubtedly an unlawful act. The principal issue was whether the appellant had committed homicide by directly or indirectly, by any means, causing the death of Cobby and whether such homicide was culpable for the reason that it was caused by an unlawful act. The Crown quite properly chose to establish causation principally through medical evidence and the doctors, men of high professional standing, understandably were disinclined to speak in absolute terms.

Doctor Brunsdon testified as to the effect of a sudden blow in the abdominal area. He said:

> I couldn't say always, but it certainly I think, would be predisposed to regurgitation. I am certainly not going to say it would happen in every case, but I think it could be predisposed to.

During cross-examination, Dr. Brunsdon used the expressions "very possible" and "very probable" to describe the cause and effect of the kick and the vomiting. As to the relationship of the kick and aspiration, he said: "I can amplify that a bit. It is a rare condition, but the kick would have made it more likely to aspirate." The following passage appears in the testimony of Dr. Hillsdon Smith, Professor of Forensic Pathology at the University of Toronto:

> I have already given in evidence that fear by itself can cause vomiting, a kick by itself can cause vomiting. The two together have simply a greater effect than either of those singly.

The jury was not limited to the evidence of the medical experts. In considering the issue of causation the jury had the benefit of uncontradicted evidence of a number of lay witnesses to the effect that the appellant kicked the deceased boy in the stomach area, that the kick was followed by immediate distress, and that the death occurred within minutes. This was cogent evidence to which the jury could apply common sense in considering the issue of causality. In my opinion, the first ground of appeal cannot be maintained.

The second ground, not unrelated to the first ground, is that the Court of Appeal erred in holding that there was evidence on the basis of which the jury was entitled to find that it had been established beyond a reasonable doubt that the kick caused the death. This broad question is unfortunately phrased, in that it leaves doubt whether the issue raised is one of sufficiency of evidence, a question of fact to which the jurisdiction of this court does not extend, or an entire absence of evidence upon which a finding could be made that the kick caused the death, a question of law. The appellant's factum tends to remove the uncertainty by subsuming, within the broad question, three narrower questions. The first of these is whether the jury was restricted to a consideration of the expert medical evidence in making its determination on the issue of causation. It is conceded that the jury was entitled to consider all of the evidence, expert and lay, in its deliberations with respect to the issue of causation but on the precise question of whether or not the kick caused the vomiting or the aspiration, it is contended the jury was restricted to the medical evidence. It seems to me to be a novel proposition, subversive of the usual jury procedure, that on a particular issue the jury should be denied the evidence of certain witnesses. I have difficulty also in reconciling the concession that the jury is entitled to consider all of the evidence on the issue of causation but something less than all the evidence when considering the only causative questions in the case, namely, whether the kick caused the vomiting and whether the kick caused the aspiration.

It is important in considering the issue of causation in homicide to distinguish between causation as a question of fact and causation as a question of law. The factual determination is whether A caused B. The answer to the factual question can only come from the evidence of witnesses. It has nothing to do with intention, foresight or risk. In certain types of homicide jurors need little help from medical experts. Thus, if D shoots P or stabs him and death follows within moments, there being no intervening cause, jurors would have little difficulty in resolving the issue of causality from their own experience and knowledge.

Expert evidence is admissible, of course, to establish factual cause. The work of expert witnesses in an issue of this sort, as Glanville Williams has pointed out ("Causation in Homicide", [1957] *Crim. L.R.* 429 at p. 431), is "purely diagnostic and does not involve them in metaphysical subtleties"; it does not require them to distinguish between what is a "cause", *i.e.*, a real and contributing cause of death, and what is merely a "condition", *i.e.*, part of the background of the death. Nor should they be expected to say, where two or more causes combine to produce a result, which of these causes contributes the more.

In the case at bar, the Crown had the burden of showing factual causation, that beyond a reasonable doubt the kick caused the death. In my view, the trial judge did not err in failing to instruct the jury that in determining that issue they could consider only the medical evidence. The issue of causation is for the jury and not the experts. The weight to be given to the evidence of the experts was entirely for the jury. In the search for truth, the jury was entitled to consider all of the evidence, expert and lay, and accept or reject any part of it. Non-medical testimony is available to both the Crown and the accused, and in the instant case, lay evidence was vital to the defence raised by the appellant. That evidence tended to show that all the circumstances preceding the kick were such as to create in the deceased boy a highly emotional state which might well have given rise to spontaneous vomiting, unassociated with the kick.

The second sub-question raised is whether there was evidence on the basis of which the jury was entitled to find that it had been established beyond a reasonable doubt that the kick caused the death. In answer to this question it may shortly be said that there was a very substantial body of evidence, both expert and lay, before the jury indicating that the kick was at least a contributing cause of death, outside the *de minimis* range, and that is all that the Crown was required to establish. It is immaterial that the death was in part caused by a malfunctioning epiglottis to which malfunction the appellant may, or may not, have contributed. No question of remoteness or of incorrect treatment arises in this case.

I should like to adopt two short passages from a case note on *R. v. Larkin* (1942), 29 Cr. App. R. 18, by G.A. Martin, as he then was, which appeared in 21 *Can. Bar Rev.* 503 at pp. 504-5 (1943):

> There are many unlawful acts which are not dangerous in themselves and are not likely to cause injury which, nevertheless if they cause death, render the actor guilty of culpable homicide, *e.g.*, the most trivial assault, if it should, through some unforeseen weakness in the deceased, cause death, will render the actor guilty of culpable homicide.
>
> . . . .
>
> In the case of so-called intentional crimes where death is an unintended consequence the actor is always guilty of manslaughter at least. The act of the accused in *R. v. Larkin* fell within the class of intentional crimes because he was engaged in committing an assault upon Nielsen, and the fact that he caused a different type of harm to that which he intended did not free him from criminal responsibility.

The Crown was under no burden of proving intention to cause death or injury. The only intention necessary was that of delivering the kick to Cobby. Nor was foreseeability in issue. It is no defence to a manslaughter charge that the fatality was not anticipated or that death ordinarily would not result from the unlawful act.[*]

In *R. v. Cato et al.* (1975), 62 Cr. App. R. 41, the act supporting the manslaughter conviction was the injection by the accused into another person of morphine which the accused had unlawfully taken into his possession. Attention was directed to causation, and the link alleged to exist between the injection of morphine and the death. The appellant's argument based on the

---

[*] Editors' note: This statement of the fault requirement for manslaughter was expressly overruled in *DeSousa*, which was followed by the full Court in *Creighton*, a case we consider later in Chapter 3, "The Fault Requirement (*Mens Rea* or Negligence)".

medical evidence of causation and the rejection of that argument by the Court of Appeal are to be found in the following passage, pp. 44-5:

> First of all, he invited us to look at the evidence of causation, and he pointed out that the medical evidence did not at any point say "This morphine killed Farmer"; the actual link of that kind was not present. The witnesses were hesitant to express such a view and often recoiled from it, saying it was not for them to state the cause of death. It is perfectly true, as Mr. Blom-Cooper says, that the expert evidence did not in positive terms provide a link, but it was never intended to do so. The expert witnesses here spoke to factual situations, and the conclusions and deductions therefore were for the jury. The first question was: was there sufficient evidence upon which the jury could conclude, as they must have concluded, that adequate causation was present?

The third sub-question is whether there was evidence from which the jury was entitled to find that it had been established beyond a reasonable doubt that the kick caused the aspiration. It is contended that the burden on the Crown was to prove beyond a reasonable doubt that the kick caused both the vomiting and the aggravated condition of aspiration. I do not agree. A person commits homicide, according to s. 205(1) of the *Code*, when directly or indirectly, by any means, he causes the death of a human being. Once evidence had been led concerning the relationship between the kick and the vomiting, leading to aspiration of stomach contents and asphyxia, the contributing condition of a malfunctioning epiglottis would not prevent conviction for manslaughter. Death may have been unexpected, and the physical reactions of the victim unforeseen, but that does not relieve the appellant.

In *R. v. Garforth*, [1954] Crim. L.R. 936, a decision of the Court of Criminal Appeal of England, the accused, aged 16, and another young man, S, quarrelled with the deceased, aged 18, outside a dance-hall. S kicked the deceased and when he doubled up stabbed him in the neck and heart, then the accused kicked him on the body and legs and S kicked him on the head. S was found guilty of murder and the accused was found guilty of manslaughter. The accused appealed against his conviction on the ground there was no evidence that what he did was a cause of death. It was held, dismissing the appeal, that there was clear evidence that the accused unlawfully assaulted the deceased and inflicted minor injuries which contributed to the death. Had the jury found that the accused intended to do grievous bodily harm, he would have been guilty of murder.

It is a well-recognized principle that one who assaults another must take his victim as he finds him. An extreme example of the application of the principle will be found in the English case of *R. v. Blaue*, [1975] 1 W.L.R. 1411, in which the court upheld a conviction for manslaughter where the victim's wounds were only fatal because of her refusal, on religious grounds, to accept a blood transfusion. The court rejected the argument that the victim's refusal had broken the chain of causation between the stabbing and the death.

Although causation in civil cases differs from that in a criminal case, the "thin skulled man" may appear in the criminal law as in the civil law. The case of *R. v. Nicholson* (1926), 47 C.C.C. 113, 59 N.S.R. 323, will serve as an illustration. In that case, the accused dealt the deceased man two heavy blows. The man who was struck was in poor physical condition. His heart was abnormally small and he was suffering from Bright's disease. An eminent medical specialist was asked if the blow or blows could cause death, given the condition of the body which was described, and he said it was possible. The blow might be one of the causes. Over-indulgence in alcohol, bad health, and the blow and tussle combined, in his opinion, to account for the result. The appeal from conviction was dismissed. Even if the unlawful act, alone, would not have caused the death, it was still a legal cause so long as it contributed in some way to the death. I myself presided at a jury trial in which the accused, one Alan Canada, following an argument, struck his brother lightly on the head with a piece of firewood as a result of which the brother died some time later without regaining consciousness. The medical evidence showed that the bony structure of his skull was unusually thin and fragile. The accused, on the advice of counsel, pleaded guilty to a charge of manslaughter and I have never considered that he was wrong in doing so.

I would conclude this point by saying that although Dr. Hillsdon Smith thought that once vomiting had been induced, aspiration in these circumstances was no more than an accident, both Dr. Brunsdon and Dr. Butt acknowledged that the kick may have contributed to the epiglottal malfunction.

That brings me to the third and final ground of appeal, namely, whether the trial Judge's charge to the jury on the issue of self-defence amounted to misdirection. Although undoubtedly much upset by the actions and language of Cobby during the first ten minutes of play, thereafter the appellant alone was the aggressor. He relentlessly pursued Cobby some 45 minutes later for the purpose of carrying out his threats to "get" Cobby. Despite the frail factual underpinning for such a defence, the trial judge charged fully on self-defence and in a manner which, in my opinion, was not open to criticism.

I would dismiss the appeal.

Appeal dismissed.

PROBLEM

At 9:30 p.m. the accused went to the nearby residence of the victim, angry that his cat had apparently been injured by the victim's cat. The accused stood on the porch of the victim's residence and threatened the cat and the victim, provoking the victim into agreeing to fight with the accused outside. The victim was barefoot and went downstairs to get his shoes. The victim's wife asked the accused to stop and twice pointed out that her husband had had strokes. The victim, who appeared emotionally upset, fetched his shoes and ran or walked quickly some 65 feet to the sidewalk in front of his house. In a very brief physical encounter, the victim was put or thrown down to the ground by the accused. A short while later that evening the victim suffered an acute heart attack and died at about 11:30 p.m.

The victim had a long history of medical illness. He had diabetes, high blood pressure, a history of strokes, and had suffered at least one prior heart attack. He had triple coronary disease, with high-grade calcification and obstruction in all three arteries. He was on disability leave, was inactive and overweight. A stress test had revealed that he was unable to do fundamental tasks such as vacuuming or taking out the garbage.

At the accused's trial on a charge of manslaughter before judge alone, prosecution medical evidence was led that an acute plaque rupture in the right coronary artery ultimately led to the blockage of blood to the victim's heart and, as a result, his death. According to the medical evidence emotional or physical stress or a combination of both may trigger a plaque rupture. It is often difficult to isolate specific triggering events. In cross-examination the cardiologist testified that there was an 80 to 90 percent probability that the plaque rupture may have occurred even if the physical assault had never taken place. As he put it, "I don't think that the actual dropping of the body, the actual fall, the trauma of the fall, had much bearing on the matter".

The trial judge found the accused guilty of unlawful act manslaughter. He found beyond a reasonable doubt that the unlawful act of physical assault, alone, was a contributing cause of death outside the *de minimis* range. The trial judge imposed a sentence of six years' imprisonment, emphasizing the need for specific and general deterrence. Do you agree with this ruling and sentence? Compare *R. v. Shanks* (1997), 4 C.R. (5th) 79 (Ont. C.A.) and accompanying annotation by David Tanovich.

The Supreme Court has adopted a stricter approach to causation for the purposes of first degree murder under s. 231(5):

R. v. HARBOTTLE

[1993] 3 S.C.R. 306, 24 C.R. (4th) 137, 84 C.C.C. (3d) 1,
1993 CarswellOnt 992, 1993 CarswellOnt 121

The accused together with a companion forcibly confined a young woman. After his companion brutally sexually assaulted her while the accused watched, the accused and his companion discussed ways of killing her. The accused held the victim's legs to prevent her from continuing to kick and struggle while his companion strangled her. The accused was convicted of murder in the first degree. The conviction was upheld at the Court of Appeal where it was conceded that the accused was a party to the murder while participating in her forcible confinement and sexual assault. At issue in the Supreme Court of Canada was whether the accused's participation was such that he could be found guilty of first degree murder pursuant to s. 214(5) [s. 231(5)] of the *Criminal Code*. The Court dismissed the accused's appeal.

CORY J.: —

. . . .

Object of the Section

In order to provide the appropriate distinctions pertaining to causation that must exist for the different homicide offences, it is necessary to examine the sections in their context while taking into account their aim and object.

At the outset, it is important to remember that when s. 214(5) comes into play it is in essence a sentencing provision. First degree murder is an aggravated form of murder and not a distinct substantive offence. See *R. v. Farrant*, [1983] 1 S.C.R. 124. It is only to be considered after the jury has concluded that the accused is guilty of murder by causing the death of the victim. An accused found guilty of second degree murder will receive a mandatory life sentence. What the jury must then determine is whether such aggravating circumstances exist that they justify ineligibility for parole for a quarter of a century. It is at this point that the requirement of causation set out in s. 214(5) comes into play. The gravity of the crime and the severity of the sentence both indicate that a *substantial and high* degree of blameworthiness, above and beyond that of murder, must be established in order to convict an accused of first degree murder.

Substantial Cause Test

Accordingly, I suggest a restrictive test of substantial cause should be applied under s. 214(5). That test will take into account the consequences of a conviction, the present wording of the section, its history and its aim to protect society from the most heinous murderers.

The consequences of a conviction for first degree murder and the wording of the section are such that the test of causation for s. 214(5) must be a strict one. In my view, an accused may only be convicted under the subsection if the Crown establishes that the accused has committed an act or series of acts which are of such a nature that they must be regarded as a substantial and integral cause of the death. A case which considered and applied a substantial cause test from Australia is *R. v. Hallett*, [1969] S.A.S.R. 141 (S.C. In Banco). In that case, the victim was left beaten and unconscious by the sea and was drowned by the incoming tide. The court formulated the following test of causation, at p. 149, which I find apposite:

> The question to be asked is whether an act or a series of acts (in exceptional cases an omission or series of omissions) consciously performed by the accused is or are so connected with the event that it or they must be regarded as having a sufficiently substantial causal effect which subsisted up to the happening of the event, without being spent or without being in the eyes of the law sufficiently interrupted by some other act or event.

The substantial causation test requires that the accused play a very active role — usually a physical role — in the killing. Under s. 214(5), the actions of the accused must form an essential, substantial and integral part of the killing of the victim. Obviously, this requirement is much higher than that described in *Smithers v. The Queen*, [1978] 1 S.C.R. 506, which dealt with the offence of manslaughter. There it was held at p. 519 that sufficient causation existed where the actions of the accused were "a contributing cause of death, outside the *de minimis* range". That case demonstrates the distinctions in the degree of causation required for the different homicide offences.

The majority of the Court of Appeal below expressed the view that the acts of the accused must physically result in death. In most cases, to cause physically the death of the victim will undoubtedly be required to obtain a conviction under s. 214(5). However, while the intervening act of another will often mean that the accused is no longer the substantial cause of the death under s. 214(5), there will be instances where an accused could well be the substantial cause of the death without physically causing it. For example, if one accused with intent to kill locked the victim in a cupboard while the other set fire to that cupboard, then the accused who confined the victim might be found to have caused the death of the victim pursuant to the provisions of s. 214(5). Similarly an accused who fought off rescuers in order to allow his accomplice to complete the strangulation of the victim might also be found to have been a substantial cause of the death.

Therefore, an accused may be found guilty of first degree murder pursuant to s. 214(5) if the Crown has established beyond a reasonable doubt that:

(1) the accused was guilty of the underlying crime of domination or of attempting to commit that crime;
(2) the accused was guilty of the murder of the victim;
(3) the accused participated in the murder in such a manner that he was a substantial cause of the death of the victim;
(4) there was no intervening act of another which resulted in the accused no longer being substantially connected to the death of the victim; and
(5) the crimes of domination and murder were part of the same transaction; that is to say, the death was caused while committing the offence of domination as part of the same series of events.

It would be appropriate to charge a jury in those terms.

At face value the *Harbottle* substantial cause test only applies to constructive first degree murder under what is now s. 231(5). See Watt J. (as he then was) in *R. v. Fatima* (2006), 42 C.R. (6th) 239 (Ont. S.C.J.). The *Harbottle* test has been held to be applicable to a person who is guilty of murder under s. 231(5) as a party rather than as the actual killer: *R. v. Ferrari* (2012), 287 C.C.C. (3d) 503, 95 C.R. (6th) 169 (Ont. C.A.).

The approach of *Smithers* was applied as the test for second degree murder but the majority also re-calibrated the *de minimis* language:

R. v. NETTE

[2001] 3 S.C.R. 488, 46 C.R. (5th) 197, 158 C.C.C. (3d) 486, 2001 CarswellBC 2481, 2001 CarswellBC 2482 (S.C.C.)

The accused was charged with first degree murder arising from the death of a 95-year-old widow, who had been the victim of robbery. Her house was entered and her hands and feet bound up. Some clothing was wrapped around her head. She was left on the bed. Some 24 to 48 hours later she died of asphyxiation due to upper airway obstruction. By the time of her death, her dentures had come loose in her mouth and the clothing wrapped around her head had become tightly wound around her neck. She had fallen from the bed.

During an R.C.M.P. undercover sting operation, the accused told a police officer that he had been involved in the robbery and death. The accused was charged with first degree murder under s. 231(5) of the *Criminal Code* — murder while committing the offence of unlawful confinement — and tried before a judge and jury. At trial, he claimed that he had fabricated the admission. He testified that he had gone alone to the victim's house only with intent to break and enter, that the back door to the house was open as though someone already had broken into the home, and that he left after finding the victim already dead in her bedroom. The accused was convicted of second degree murder. He appealed, on the basis that the jury was misdirected as to the test of causation applicable to second degree murder.

The Supreme Court dismissed the accused's appeal.

ARBOUR J. (IACCOBUCCI, MAJOR, BINNIE, and LeBEL JJ. concurring): —

In determining whether a person can be held responsible for causing a particular result, in this case death, it must be determined whether the person caused that result both in fact and in law. Factual causation, as the term implies, is concerned with an inquiry about how the victim came to his or her death, in a medical, mechanical, or physical sense, and with the contribution of the accused to that result. Where factual causation is established, the remaining issue is legal causation.

Legal causation, which is also referred to as imputable causation, is concerned with the question of whether the accused person should be held responsible in law for the death that occurred. It is informed by legal considerations such as the wording of the section creating the offence and principles of interpretation. These legal considerations, in turn, reflect fundamental principles of criminal justice such as the principle that the morally innocent should not be punished: see *Re B.C. Motor Vehicle Act*, [1985] 2 S.C.R.

486, at p. 513; *R. v. Vaillancourt*, [1987] 2 S.C.R. 636, at p. 652-53; *R. v. Stinchcombe*, [1991] 3 S.C.R. 326, at p. 336; *R. v. Creighton*, [1993] 3 S.C.R. 3, at p. 17; *Cribbin, supra*, at p. 568. In determining whether legal causation is established, the inquiry is directed at the question of whether the accused person should be held criminally responsible for the consequences that occurred. The nature of the inquiry at the stage of determining legal causation is expressed by G. Williams as follows in his *Textbook of Criminal Law* (2nd ed. 1983), at pp. 381-82, quoted in *Cribbin*, at p. 568:

> When one has settled the question of but-for causation, the further test to be applied to the but-for cause in order to qualify it for legal recognition is not a test of causation but a moral reaction. The question is whether the result can fairly be said to be imputable to the defendant. . . . If the term "cause" must be used, it can best be distinguished in this meaning as the "imputable" or "responsible" or "blamable" cause, to indicate the value-judgment involved. The word "imputable" is here chosen as best representing the idea. Whereas the but-for cause can generally be demonstrated scientifically, no experiment can be devised to show that one of a number of concurring but-for causes is more substantial or important than another, or that one person who is involved in the causal chain is more blameworthy than another.

In a given case, the jury does not engage in a two-part analysis of whether both factual and legal causation have been established. Rather, in the charge to the jury, the trial judge seeks to convey the requisite degree of factual and legal causation that must be found before the accused can be held criminally responsible for the victim's death.

While causation is a distinct issue from *mens rea*, the proper standard of causation expresses an element of fault that is in law sufficient, in addition to the requisite mental element, to base criminal responsibility. The starting point in the chain of causation which seeks to attribute the prohibited consequences to an act of the accused is usually an unlawful act in itself. When that unlawful act is combined with the requisite mental element for the offence charged, causation is generally not an issue. For example, in the case of murder, where an accused intends to kill a person and performs an act which causes or contributes to that person's death, it is rare for an issue to arise as to whether the accused caused the victim's death. As I discussed in *Cribbin, supra*, where the jury is faced with a charge of murder and is satisfied that the accused intended to kill or intended to cause bodily harm that he knew was likely to cause death and was reckless as to whether death occurred, it will rarely be necessary for the trial judge to charge the jury on the standard of causation. In such a case, the *mens rea* requirement generally resolves any concerns about causation. It would be rare in a murder case where the intention to kill or to cause bodily harm likely to cause death is proven for the accused to be able to raise a doubt that, while he intended the result that occurred, he did not cause the intended result. Where it is established that the accused had the subjective foresight of death or serious bodily harm likely to cause death required to sustain a murder conviction, as opposed to the lower manslaughter requirement of objective foreseeability of serious bodily harm, it would be unusual for an issue of causation to arise. Assuming a case arose where intention was established but causation was not proven, a proper verdict might be attempted murder: *Cribbin*, at p. 564.

The law of causation is in large part judicially developed, but is also expressed, directly or indirectly, in provisions of the *Criminal Code*. For example, s. 225 of the *Code* provides that where a person causes bodily injury that is in itself dangerous and from which death results, that person causes the death notwithstanding that the immediate cause of death is proper or improper treatment. Similarly, ss. 222(5)(c) and 222(5)(d) provide that a person commits culpable homicide where he causes the death of a person by causing that person, by threats, fear of violence or by deception, to do anything that causes his death or by wilfully frightening a child or sick person. These statutory provisions and others like them in the *Code* preempt any speculation as to whether the act of the accused would be seen as too remote to have caused the result alleged, or whether the triggering of a chain of events was then interrupted by an intervening cause which serves to distance and exonerate the accused from any responsibility for the consequences. Where the factual situation does not fall within one of the statutory rules of causation in the *Code*, the common law general principles of criminal law apply to resolve any causation issues that may arise.

In light of the statutory rules mentioned above, and in light of general principles of criminal responsibility, the civil law of causation is of limited assistance. The criminal law does not recognize contributory negligence, nor does it have any mechanism to apportion responsibility for the harm occasioned by criminal conduct, except as part of sentencing after sufficient causation has been found. In the same way it provides for the possibility of attributing responsibility through the law of attempt, which has no equivalent in the civil context. As a result, I do not find the appellant's submissions relating to the civil standard of causation to be helpful in elucidating the applicable criminal standard.

. . . .

In oral argument, the appellant submitted that the *Smithers* test applies to all culpable homicide but that the *Smithers* test should be reformulated and "crystallized" to the specific standard of "significant" or "substantial" rather than using the *Smithers* terminology of "beyond *de minimis*" or "more than trivial". The "crystallized" test of "significant" or "substantial" cause simply clarifies the language of causation so that the jury can properly focus on the correct standard, in the appellant's submission, and does not raise the threshold of causation required. The alleged errors made by the trial judge are first that the jury was instructed on the *Smithers* standard of "more than a trivial cause" rather than the "crystallized" test of "significant" or "substantial" and, second, that the trial judge twice erred in expressing the *Smithers* standard of "more than a trivial cause" by describing it instead as a "slight or trivial cause". The appellant submits that, as a result of these errors, the trial judge incorrectly explained the standard of causation for second degree murder to the jury and the jury may therefore have failed to understand the correct standard of causation.

The position of the respondent and the intervener Attorney General of Ontario is that *Harbottle* did establish an elevated causation threshold with the use of the terminology of "substantial cause" but that this elevated standard only applies to the offence of first degree murder pursuant to s. 231(5) of the *Criminal Code* and possibly also s. 231(6) of the *Code*. With respect to second degree murder and manslaughter, the respondent and intervener submit that the *Smithers* standard continues to apply.

There appears to be an inconsistency in the appellant's argument in the present case. On the one hand, he is arguing that the "substantial cause" terminology of *Harbottle* does not represent a higher standard of causation than the *Smithers* standard and that using the terminology of "substantial cause" in relation to all homicide offences would not raise the causation threshold. On the other hand, however, he is arguing that Wilkinson J.'s use of the *Smithers* terminology instead of the *Harbottle* terminology in charging the jury on second degree murder was an error of law so serious that it justifies overturning the conviction for second degree murder and ordering a new trial. If, as the appellant submits, "substantial cause" is not a higher standard of causation than the *Smithers* formulation of "beyond *de minimis*", it would seem to follow that using the *Smithers* terminology instead of the *Harbottle* terminology could not be an error of law, much less an error so serious that it should result in a new trial.

I agree with the appellant that what *Harbottle* really stresses is not solely or even primarily a higher causation requirement to raise murder to first degree murder under s. 231(5) of the *Code*, but rather the increased degree of participation required before the accused may be convicted of first degree murder under s. 231(5). However, I do not agree that the terminology of "substantial cause" should be used to describe the requisite degree of causation for all homicide offences.

. . . .

Once the jury concludes that the accused has committed murder, *Harbottle* indicates that the jury should then move on to consider whether aggravating circumstances exist that justify the increased sentence and stigma of a first degree murder conviction under s. 231(5). The additional "causation" requirement under s. 231(5) does not refer to factual causation but rather to an increased degree of legal causation. In other words, once the jury has determined that the accused committed murder, which entails a finding that the accused caused the victim's death in both factual and legal terms, it is then necessary to consider whether the moral culpability of the accused, as evidenced by his role in the killing, justifies a verdict of first degree murder. As Cory J. states in *Harbottle*, "[t]he gravity of the crime and the severity of the sentence both indicate that a substantial and high degree of blameworthiness, above and beyond that of murder, must be established in order to convict an accused of first degree murder". Such a high degree of blameworthiness would only be established where the actions of the accused were found to be "an essential, substantial and integral part of the killing of the victim". The terminology of "substantial cause" is used to indicate a higher degree of legal causation but it is a standard that only comes into play at the stage of deciding whether the accused's degree of blameworthiness warrants the increased penalty and stigma of first degree murder.

It is clear from a reading of *Harbottle* that the "substantial cause" test expresses the increased degree of moral culpability, as evidenced by the accused person's degree of participation in the killing, that is required before an accused can be found guilty under s. 231(5) of the *Criminal Code* of first degree murder. The increased degree of participation in the killing, coupled with a finding that the accused had the requisite *mens rea* for murder, justifies a verdict of guilty under s. 231(5) of the *Code*.

· · · ·

D. Explaining the Standard of Causation to the Jury

As I discussed earlier, it is important to distinguish between what the legal standard of causation is and how that standard is conveyed to the jury. The difference between these two concepts has been obscured somewhat in the present case by the parties' focus on the terminology used to describe the standard of causation. I agree with the appellant's submission that there is only one standard of causation for all homicide offences, whether manslaughter or murder. However, I do not agree with the appellant that the standard must be expressed for all homicide offences, including second degree murder, as one of "substantial cause" as stated in *Harbottle*. Nor must the applicable standard be expressed with the terminology of "beyond *de minimis*" used in the *Smithers* standard.

· · · ·

The causation standard expressed in *Smithers* is still valid and applicable to all forms of homicide. In addition, in the case of first degree murder under s. 231(5) of the *Code*, *Harbottle* requires additional instructions, to which I will return. The only potential shortcoming with the *Smithers* test is not in its substance, but in its articulation. Even though it causes little difficulty for lawyers and judges, the use of Latin expressions and the formulation of the test in the negative are not particularly useful means of conveying an abstract idea to a jury. In order to explain the standard as clearly as possible to the jury, it may be preferable to phrase the standard of causation in positive terms using a phrase such as "significant contributing cause" rather than using expressions phrased in the negative such as "not a trivial cause" or "not insignificant". Latin terms such as "*de minimis*" are rarely helpful.

In deciding how the applicable standard of causation should be articulated to the jury, trial judges have a discretion in choosing the terminology they wish to use to explain the standard. Causation issues are case-specific and fact-driven. For that reason, it is important to afford a trial judge with the flexibility to put issues of causation to the jury in an intelligible fashion that is relevant to the circumstances of the case, including whether or not there are multiple accused persons or parties. As I discussed in *Cribbin, supra*, at pp. 565-66, while different terminology has been used to explain the applicable standard in Canada, Australia and England, whether the terminology used is "beyond *de minimis*", "significant contribution" or "substantial cause", the standard of causation which this terminology seeks to articulate, within the context of causation in homicide, is essentially the same. . . . To the extent that trial judges may find it more useful to express the standard of causation in *Smithers* in a more direct and affirmative fashion, they may find it preferable to express the standard positively as a "significant contributing cause", to use the terminology of Lambert J.A. in the present appeal.

In light of *Harbottle*, where the jury must be instructed on first degree murder under s. 231(5) of the *Code* in addition to manslaughter or second degree murder, the terminology of "substantial cause" should be used to describe the applicable standard for first degree murder so that the jury understands that something different is being conveyed by the instructions concerning s. 231(5) of the *Code* with respect to the requisite degree of participation of the accused in the offence. In such cases, it would make sense to instruct the jury that the acts of the accused have to have made a "significant" contribution to the victim's death to trigger culpability for the homicide while, to be guilty of first degree murder under s. 231(5), the accused's actions must have been an essential, substantial and integral part of the killing of the victim.

E. Is Causation an Issue on the Facts of the Present Appeal?

. . . .

As I mentioned earlier, causation issues rarely arise in murder offences. Thus, in the usual case, it will be unnecessary for the trial judge to explain the applicable standard of causation to the jury in relation to either second degree murder or first degree murder. Causation issues arise more frequently in manslaughter cases, in which the fault element resides in a combination of causing death by an unlawful act, or by criminal negligence, and mere objective foreseeability of death. As the cases illustrate, causation issues tend to arise in factual situations involving multiple parties (e.g. *Harbottle*), thin skull victims (e.g. *Smithers*), intervening events (e.g. *Hallett*) or some combination of these factors.

. . . .

Given that the jury found the accused guilty of second degree murder, we must conclude that the jury found that the appellant had the requisite intent for the offence of murder, namely subjective foresight of death. In light of the jury's conclusion with respect to intent, which in my view could not have been affected by the instructions on causation, it is clear that no reasonable jury could have had any doubt about whether the appellant's actions constituted a significant, operative cause of the victim's death. What is not clear from the verdict is the basis for the acquittal on the charge of first degree murder. The appellant suggests that the jury acquitted on first degree murder because it had a reasonable doubt as to whether the accused caused the victim's death on the *Harbottle* standard of causation, but convicted of second degree murder because it was satisfied the accused caused death on the lower *Smithers* standard. In my view, the conviction for second degree murder was amply supported on the evidence and the jury was correctly charged on the applicable legal requirements of causation. The jury was entitled to have a doubt as to whether the degree of participation of the accused in the underlying offence of unlawful confinement, combined with the need for his substantial contribution to the death of the victim, was sufficient to elevate the murder to first degree. Whatever the jury's reasons for acquitting the appellant of first degree murder, the jury's verdict of second degree murder is unimpeachable.

. . . .

L'HEUREUX-DUBÉ J. (concurring in the result), (MCLACHLIN C.J.C., GONTHIER and BASTARACHE JJ. concurring): — I had the benefit of reading my colleague Madam Justice Arbour's reasons and while I concur in the result she reaches, I do not agree with her suggestion to rephrase the standard of causation for culpable homicide set out by this court in *R. v. Smithers*, [1978] 1 S.C.R. 506, 34 C.C.C. (2d) 427, 75 D.L.R. (3d) 321.

. . . .

In her reasons, my colleague also refers to the English translation of the *Smithers* test when she writes: "Since *Smithers*, the terminology of 'beyond *de minimis*' or 'more than a trivial cause' has been used interchangeably with 'outside the *de minimis* range' to charge juries as to the relevant standard of causation for all homicide offences, be it manslaughter or murder".

. . . .

Having said so, my colleague suggests reformulating the *Smithers* beyond *de minimis* test, i.e., "a contributing cause [of death] that is not trivial or insignificant" in the language of a "significant contributing cause". Evidently, my colleague considers that this rephrasing is merely a matter of semantics and, in her view, it does not alter the current test. I respectfully disagree. In my opinion, this issue is a matter of substance, not semantics. There is a meaningful difference between expressing the standard as "a contributing cause that is not trivial or insignificant" and expressing it as a "significant contributing cause". Changing the terminology of the *Smithers* test in this manner would drastically change its substance. On this point, I share Professor S. Yeo's view in his article "Giving Substance to Legal Causation" (2000), 29 C.R. (5th) 215 at p. 219:

> I submit that there is a material difference between describing something as "not an insignificant cause" on the one hand, and as "a significant cause" on the other. To ignore this difference is to ignore the reason for the use of a double negative in the first place. While the former description focuses the inquiry at the lower end of the scale of degrees of causation, the latter does not invoke such a focus. Using another set of words to illustrate my argument, when Mary says that she does not dislike John, she means, at most, that she is impartial towards him rather than that she likes him.

To claim that something not unimportant is important would be a sophism. Likewise, to consider things that are not dissimilar to be similar would amount to an erroneous interpretation. In the same vein, a substantial difference exists between the terms "not insignificant" and "significant", and there is no doubt in my mind that to remove the double negative formulation from the *Smithers* causation test would effect a radical change to the law. I therefore agree with the position of both the respondent and the intervener that a "significant contributing cause" calls for a more direct causal relationship than the existing "not insignificant" or "non trivial" test, thus raising the standard from where it currently stands.

. . . .

In conclusion, I reiterate that the causation test in *Smithers* remains the law and to rephrase it in the language of a "significant contributing cause", as my colleague suggests, would draw the line at a different place, thus drastically changing the law. I have found no legitimate reason to reformulate the *Smithers* test, rather it is my opinion that such alteration should be strenuously proscribed since it will elevate the threshold of causation. As a result, I consider the current language of "a contributing cause [of death] that is not trivial or insignificant" to be the correct formulation that trial judges should use when expressing to the jury the standard of causation for all homicide offences.

For comments on *Nette* see Stuart, "*Nette*: Confusing Cause in Reformulating the *Smithers* Test" (2002), 46 C.R. (5th) 230 and Sanjeev Anand, "Determining Causal Standards for First Degree Murder in the Wake of *Nette*: When Does the Substantial Cause Test Apply?" (2002) 46 Crim. L.Q. 282. Anand argues that the substantial cause test of *Harbottle* should, as a matter of policy, be applied to all first degree categories. See too, Lisa Dufraimont in a C.R. annotation to *Fatima*. Earlier writers had argued for that test for all murder charges: Allan Manson, "Rethinking Causation: The Implications of *Harbottle*" (1994), 24 C.R. (4th) 153 and David Tanovich and James Lockyer, "Revisiting *Harbottle*: Does the 'Substantial Cause' Test Apply to All Murder Offences?" (1996) 38 Crim. L.Q. 322.

R. v. TALBOT

(2007), 44 C.R. (6th) 176, 2007 CarswellOnt 627, 217 C.C.C. (3d) 415 (C.A.)

In the course of an appeal following a jury acquittal following an altercation outside a restaurant, an issue arose as to whether the initial blow or subsequent kick caused the death. In the course of determining that the issue was not necessary to decide the appeal the Court reviewed the law since *Nette*.

DOHERTY J.A. (LASKIN and ARMSTRONG J.A. concurring): —

[79] .... Causation in the criminal law has a factual and legal component. The former is concerned with the physical or medical cause of death. A "but for" inquiry answers the factual causation question in most, but not all situations. If the victim would not have died when he or she died but for the act of the accused, that act is a factual cause of death: see Isabel Grant, Dorothy Chunn & Christine Boyle, *The Law of Homicide* (Toronto: Carswell, 1994) at 3-21 to 3-29; Glanville Williams, *Textbook of Criminal Law*, 2d ed. (Agincourt, Ont.: Carswell, 1983) at 380-81; Wayne R. LaFave, *Substantive Criminal Law*, 2d ed. (Eagan, Minn.: Thomson/West, 2003) vol. 1 at 467-68.

[80] Legal causation requires a normative inquiry. It asks who among those who have factually caused a death should be held liable for causing that death in the eyes of the criminal law: see *R. v. Nette*, [2001] 3 S.C.R. 488 at paras. 44-45.

[81] Juries are not asked to determine factual and legal causation separately. Instead, the two inquiries are joined and the jury is asked to decide whether the accused's actions significantly contributed to the victim's death: see *R. v. Nette*, *supra*, at paras. 46-73. A contributing cause can be a cause that exacerbates an existing fatal condition, thereby accelerating death: see *R. v. Munro and Munro* (1983), 8 C.C.C. (3d) 260 at 290-91 (Ont. C.A.); *Criminal Code*, s. 226.

[82] If the Crown sought to rely on the kick as a contributing cause of death, it was incumbent on the Crown to prove beyond a reasonable doubt that the kick was a contributing cause within the meaning of *R. v. Nette*, *supra*. The evidence adduced by the Crown went no further than to suggest there was some unquantifiable possibility that was less than a likelihood that the kick exacerbated the internal head injuries.

This pithy analysis on legal cause cuts through ambiguities left by the Supreme Court in *Nette*. Arbour J. for the majority expressed a preference for the language of "significant contributing cause" but left it open for a trial judge to use the original *Smithers* language of outside the *de minimis* range. In *Nette*, L'Heureux-Dubé dissented on the basis that the language of significant cause would unnecessarily raise the *Smithers* standard. In *Talbot*, the Ontario Court of Appeal rests content with significance being the sole test. This should provide welcome clarity for trial judges, at least in Ontario.

Another ambiguity arising from both *Smithers* and *Nette* is the distinction between factual cause and the normative issue of legal cause. In essence, Justice Doherty boils down these cause inquiries into the one key test of significant contributing cause. Whether this test will deal satisfactorily with more difficult cause cases, such as those involving other intervening acts and multiple actors, left open by Arbour J. in *Nette* and Dickson J. in *Smithers*, remains to be seen.

(c)   *Charter*

The Supreme Court in *Nette* did not address *Charter* issues. Prior to *Nette* in *R. v. Cribbin* (1994), 28 C.R. (4th) 137 (Ont. C.A.) Justice Arbour had determined, when on the Ontario Court of Appeal, that causation is embedded in the s. 7 principle of fundamental justice that moral innocence should not be punished. The law should refrain from holding a person responsible for consequences that should not be attributed to the accused. Criminal causation was a legal rule based on concepts of moral responsibility. The morally innocent would be wrongly punished if criminal causation were reduced to a simple *sine qua non* test. However, she dismissed arguments that the *Smithers* test was too vague or too broad. She indicated that cases where an independent actor intervened to make matters worse raised more difficult issues. For criticism of *Cribbin* see Jill Presser, "All for a Good Cause: The Need for Overhaul of the *Smithers* Test of Causation" (1984), 28 C.R. (4th) 178.

R. v. F. (D.L.)

(1989), 73 C.R. (3d) 391, 1989 CarswellAlta 195 (Alta. C.A.)

McCLUNG J.A.: — As a result of a pedestrian injury accident in Calgary on December 2, 1986, the respondent, a youth, was tried on a multiple count information which included allegations that he:

1. Did unlawfully operate a motor vehicle within the said city while his ability to operate a motor vehicle was impaired by alcohol or a drug and did thereby cause bodily harm to Alex Primeau, contrary to the *Criminal Code.*
2. Having consumed alcohol in such a quantity that the concentration thereof in his blood exceeded 80 milligrams of alcohol in 100 millilitres of blood, did unlawfully operate a motor vehicle, contrary to the *Criminal Code.*

3. Did unlawfully operate a motor vehicle on a highway within the said city in a manner dangerous to the public, having regard to all the circumstances including the nature, condition and use of such place and the amount of traffic that at the time was or might reasonably be expected to be on such place, and did thereby cause bodily harm to Alex Primeau, contrary to the *Criminal Code*.

D.L.F. was acquitted on all counts by the trial judge after his review of the blameworthy aspects of D.L.F.'s driving as well as his physical condition. That review, which need not be set out in full, satisfied the trial judge that the driving pattern of the accused was dangerous within the meaning assigned by s. 249(1) of the *Code*. However, he was acquitted. The acquittal was gained, and this appeal taken, from the judge's conclusion that there was no culpable connection established between D.L.F.'s driving deficiencies and the bodily harm sustained by a pedestrian who was injured when he was struck by D.L.F.'s vehicle. The acquittal on the count alleging dangerous driving causing bodily harm is all that is under appeal by the Crown.

The trial judge felt that he was obligated to analyze each circumstance alleged by the Crown which, in their totality, were said to establish dangerous driving. The judge did so under the focus of what acts of negligence could be said to be traceable, and therefore contributory to, the bodily harm suffered by the pedestrian. The judge refused any connection arising from the accused's failure to wear corrective lenses to help his driving vision. He rejected any causal relationship arising from speed in excess of the posted limit and the accident. He rejected evidence of inefficient brakes. He rejected the failure of the accused to accommodate his driving to a narrowing of the road at the point of impact. The judge concluded that none of these facts were instrumental in the collision and the injuries that were suffered. He held that the sole factual connection joining the driving conduct and the accident was D.L.F.'s failure to see the pedestrian, who was jaywalking, before the impact. The judge credited this to inattention, not to dangerous driving.

. . . .

We think we are not only bound by, but fully agree with, the trial judge's finding that the driving pattern disclosed in the evidence was dangerous within the prohibition of s. 249(1), the definition section. The nature, condition and use of the highway by the accused and the pedestrian traffic that should have been anticipated, all support the judge's conclusion. However, the trial judge seems to have erred in attempting to analyze each blameworthy facet of the accused's driving pattern and attempting to determine whether those individual components, under separate examination, were an effective cause of the accident.

. . . .

Under the additional responsibility of determining whether bodily injury was *thereby caused* to any person by the dangerous driving (s. 249(3)), other considerations arise. Sections 249(3) and 249(4) codify aggravated acts of dangerous driving. That aggravation is supplied by proof that the accused's unlawful driving caused harm or death to others. The offence becomes indictable and the exposure to gaol, in the case of s. 249(3), is doubled as the maximum sentence becomes ten years. The words "thereby causes" demand some examination of the factual connection between the dangerous driving and the injury or fatality. That, of course, is an inquiry that is not required in prosecutions brought under s. 249(1), a lesser and included offence.

The approach suggested by Rick Libman of the Ontario Crown Attorney Office in his article, "The Requirements of Causation in the New Offences of Impaired Driving Causing Bodily Harm or Death" (1985), 48 M.V.R. 21, in terms of simplicity, has proved to be a useful and orderly guide for the trial of these aggravated driving cases. Mr. Libman suggests that in cases under s. 249(3) and s. 249(4), the trial court should:

1. Determine whether the driving conduct in question has been proven to be driving in a dangerous manner within the definition assigned by s. 249(1).
2. Determine whether the injuries complained of meet the test of "bodily harm" defined by s. 267(2) — ". . . bodily harm means any hurt or injury to the complainant that interferes with his or her health or comfort and that is more than merely transient or trifling in nature".
3. Where the preceding questions have been answered adversely to the accused, determine what correlative link exists between the dangerous driving and the bodily harm proven.

The difficult question remains: when is bodily harm or death "*thereby caused*" in s. 249(3) or s. 249(4) prosecutions? In my view the words "*thereby caused*" must demand, at least, that the unlawful operation of the accused's vehicle be proven to be a real and truly contributing cause of any ensuing injury or death and the trial court should be chary of allowing speculative inferences alone to stand as the causative link between the driving and the injury accident solely because of the target of the statute. The unlawful driving must still demonstrably influence the actual injury accident beyond serving as its backdrop. Mr. Libman (and Mr. MacDonald for the Crown here), invokes *R. v. Smithers*, [1978] 1 S.C.R. 506, 34 C.C.C. (2d) 427, and urges that the level of proof is "did the activities of the accused contribute in some way to the injury?" That was the Crown's proof commitment in culpable homicide cases, now statutorily defined by s. 222(*a*) of the *Criminal Code*. In *Smithers*, a kicking-death manslaughter prosecution demanding proof of general intent alone, the causation hurdle was described as proof that the unlawful act ". . . was at least a contributing cause of death, outside the *de minimis* range". The "outside *de minimis*" test has been recited in at least four appellate aggravated driving cases since and is now authoritative. *R. v. Laroque* (1988), 5 M.V.R. (2d) 221 (Ont. C.A.); *R. v. Singhal* (1988), 5 M.V.R. (2d) 172 (B.C. C.A.); *R. v. Halkert*, unreported, December 15/88, #4281 (Sask. C.A.) and *R. v. Pinske* (1988), 6 M.V.R. (2d) 19, appeal to S.C.C. dismissed October 12, 1989. Nonetheless, I confess to some difficulty with its fairness in all aggravated driving prosecutions.

I do not wish to flounder in semantics but the application of the "outside *de minimis*" test, as proposed by Mr. Libman, is not easily reconciled with the common understanding of the statutory words "thereby cause". In everyday usage, the latter words convey "resulting in" or "create by that means" — something more, and more onerous, than a mere identifiable contribution which I understand the "outside *de minimis*" test to imply.

The difficulty is twofold; the verb "cause" is particularly troublesome when found in penal statutes requiring full *mens rea* or even none at all. *R. v. Sault Ste. Marie* (1978), 85 D.L.R. (3d) 161, 183 (S.C.C.). Beyond that, a standard of proof related at all to the concept of "*de minimis*" would normally find little philosophical communion within the criminal law.

The distinction would not be a real issue in the majority of s. 249(3) or 249(4) prosecutions but in cases involving parallel or competing causes of an injury accident, one of which may be quite external to the conduct of the accused, it can arise. Two or three car collisions come to mind. See *R. v. Ewart*, Appeal No. 8803-0334-A (Alta. C.A.). Where the facts disclose the preponderant cause of an accident to be divorced from the conduct of the accused, the accused may be substantially blameless for that accident but snared under the criminality of the "outside *de minimis*" rule. In such cases, a finding that the accident which resulted in injury or death was inevitable, whatever the driving deficiencies of the accused, has been taken. *Singhal* (*supra*).

With all respect, there will be cases where it could be argued that the "outside *de minimis*" test is in conflict with the fundamental justice predicate of s. 7 of the *Canadian Charter of Rights and Freedoms*. It is a test of sweeping accountability. In *Smithers* the unlawful link that caused death involved nothing, on even a standard of objective awareness, suggesting the foreseeability of the victim's death. Statutory interpretations, at least those guiding the criminal process, that align with *Charter* values should now prevail. *Hills v. Atty. Gen. of Canada*, [1988] 1 S.C.R. 513. Nonetheless until the Supreme Court chooses to reconsider the matter the broader "outside *de minimis*" rule will govern. For this court the matter is presently resolved by *R. v. Pinske* (*supra*).

These concerns do not arise under the facts of this case and I do not apply them to resolve this appeal. They are only raised under a review of the stages of the approach suggested by Mr. Libman. This prosecution is, I think, determined by the judge's conclusion that there was dangerous driving including the fact that while the pedestrian was jaywalking, D.L.F. should have seen him but did not. In Judge Fitch's assessment of the evidence:

> He should have seen him, and there certainly is a direct causal connection between failing to observe the pedestrian jaywalking and the accident.

> If the charge before me was merely dangerous driving, the section in the *Code* prior to the 1985 amendments, and in the absence of the case law connecting dangerous driving and consequences, my conclusion would be, yes the accused's driving was dangerous within the meaning of the *Code*.

Under those findings a s. 249(3) offence was proven. I would allow the Crown's appeal and direct the entry of a conviction under the third Count of the Information which alleged dangerous driving causing bodily harm contrary to s. 249(3). The respondent is directed to appear, on a date to be forthwith fixed, for sentencing, before the Family and Youth Division of the Provincial Court of Alberta at Calgary.

(d) Cases of Intervening Cause

The Supreme Court in *Smithers*, *Nette* and *Harbottle* expressly recognize there might be more difficult causation issues especially where new actors intervene. Little guidance is offered as to the approach to be taken.

Note first the four statutory homicide rules where intervening causes are stated not to break the chain of causation: ss. 222(5)(c), 224, 225 and 226. The only way around these rules would be a successful *Charter* challenge.

In other cases, courts are left to struggle. Consider the following approaches, the first two adopted in the U.K. and Australia.

R. v. SMITH

[1959] 2 All E.R. 193 (Cts.-Man. App. Ct.)

THE LORD CHIEF JUSTICE: — The appellant in this case was convicted by a General Court-Martial in Germany of murder and was sentenced to imprisonment for life. The matter arose in this way: the appellant was a private soldier in the King's Regiment. At the material time a company of the King's Regiment was sharing barracks with a company of the Gloucestershire Regiment, and on the night of April 13, 1958, a fight developed. As a result of that fight three members of the Gloucesters were stabbed with a bayonet and one of them, Private Creed, subsequently died. It was for his murder that the appellant was convicted.

. . . .

The second ground concerns a question of causation. The deceased man in fact received two bayonet wounds, one in the arm and one in the back. The one in the back, unknown to anybody, had pierced the lung and caused haemorrhage. There followed a series of unfortunate occurrences. A fellow member of his company tried to carry him to the medical reception station. On the way he tripped over a wire and dropped the deceased man. He picked him up again, went a little further, and fell apparently a second time causing the deceased man to be dropped on the ground. Thereafter he did not try a third time, but went for help and ultimately the deceased man was brought into the reception station. There, the medical officer, Captain Millward, and his orderly were trying to cope with a number of other cases, two serious stabbings and some minor injuries, and it is clear that they did not appreciate the seriousness of the deceased man's condition or exactly what had happened. A transfusion of saline solution was attempted and failed. When his breathing seemed impaired, he was given oxygen and artificial respiration was applied, and in fact he died after he had been in the station about an hour, which was about two hours after the original stabbing. It is now known that, having regard to the injuries which the man had in fact suffered, his lung being pierced, the treatment that he was given was thoroughly bad and might well have affected his chances of recovery. There was evidence that there is a tendency for a wound of this sort to heal and for the haemorrhage to stop. No doubt his being dropped on the ground and having artificial respiration applied would halt or at any rate impede the chances of healing. Further, there were no facilities whatsoever for blood transfusion, which would have been the best possible treatment. There was evidence that, if he had received immediate and different treatment, he might not have died. Indeed, had facilities for blood transfusion been available and been administered, Dr. Camps, who gave evidence for the defence, said that his chances of recovery were as high as 75 percent.

In these circumstances Mr. Bowen urges that not only was a careful summing-up required, but that a correct direction to the court would have been that they must be satisfied that the death of Private Creed was a natural consequence and the sole consequence of the wound sustained by him and flowed directly from it. If there was, says Mr. Bowen, any other cause whether resulting from negligence or not, or if, as he contends here, something happened which impeded the chance of the deceased recovering, then the death did not result from the wound. The court is quite unable to accept that contention. It seems to the court that if at the time of death the original wound is still an operating cause and a substantial cause, then the death can properly be said to be the result of the wound, albeit that some other cause of death is also operating. Only if it can be said that the original wounding is merely the setting in which another cause operates can it be said that the death does not result from the wound. Putting it in another way, only if the second cause is so overwhelming as to make the original wound merely part of the history can it be said that the death does not flow from the wound.

There are a number of cases in the law of contract and tort on these matters of causation, and it is always difficult to find a form of words when directing a jury or, as here, a court, which will convey in simple language the principle of causation. It seems to the court enough for this purpose to refer to one passage in the judgment of Lord Wright in *The Oropesa*, reported in [1943] P. 32, where he says (at p. 39):

> To break the chain of causation it must be shown that there is something which I will call ultroneous, something unwarrantable, a new cause which disturbs the sequence of events, something which can be described as either unreasonable or extraneous or extrinsic.

To much the same effect was a judgment on the question of causation given by Denning J., as he then was, in *Minister of Pensions v. Chennel* in [1947] K.B. 250.

Mr. Bowen placed great reliance on a case decided in this court, *Jordan* (1956), 40 Cr. App. R. 152, and in particular on a passage in the headnote which says:

> *Semble*, that death resulting from any normal treatment employed to deal with a felonious injury may be regarded as caused by the felonious injury, but that the same principle does not apply where the treatment employed is abnormal.

Reading those words into the present case, Mr. Bowen says that the treatment that this unfortunate man received from the moment that he was struck to the time of his death was abnormal. The court is satisfied that *Jordan* (*supra*) was a very particular case depending upon its exact facts. It incidentally arose in this court on the grant of an application to call further evidence, and, leave having been obtained, two well-known medical experts gave evidence that in their opinion death had not been caused by the stabbing, but by the introduction of terramycin after the deceased had shown that he was intolerant to it and by the intravenous introduction of abnormal quantities of liquid. It also appears that at the time when that was done the stab wound which had penetrated the intestine in two places had mainly healed. In those circumstances the court felt bound to quash the conviction, because they could not say that a reasonable jury, properly directed, would not have been able on that to say that there had been a break in the chain of causation; the court could only uphold the conviction in that case if they were satisfied that no reasonable jury could have come to that conclusion.

In the present case it is true that the Judge-Advocate did not, in his summing-up, go into the refinements of causation. Indeed, in the opinion of this court, he was probably wise to refrain from doing so. He did leave the broad question to the court whether they were satisfied that the wound had caused the death in the sense that the death flowed from the wound, albeit that the treatment he received was in the light of after-knowledge a bad thing. In the opinion of this court, that was on the facts of the case a perfectly adequate summing-up on causation; I say "on the facts of the case," because in the opinion of the court they can only lead to one conclusion. A man is stabbed in the back, his lung is pierced and haemorrhage results; two hours later he dies of haemorrhage from that wound; in the interval there is no time for a careful examination and the treatment given turns out in the light of subsequent knowledge to have been inappropriate and, indeed, harmful. In those circumstances no reasonable jury or court could, properly directed, in our view possibly come to any other conclusion than that the death resulted from the original wound. Accordingly, the court dismisses this appeal.

Appeal dismissed.

R. v. BLAUE

[1975] 1 W.L.R. 1411 (C.A.)

July 16. LAWTON L.J. read the following judgment of the court. On October 17, 1974, at Teesside Crown Court after a trial before Mocatta J. the defendant was acquitted of the murder of Jacolyn Woodhead but was convicted of her manslaughter on the ground of diminished responsibility (count 1). He was also convicted of wounding her with intent to do her grievous bodily harm (count 2) and of indecently assaulting her (count 3). He pleaded guilty to indecently assaulting two other women (counts 4 and 5). He was sentenced to life imprisonment on counts 1 and 2 and to concurrent sentences of 12 months' imprisonment on counts 3, 4 and 5.

The defendant appeals with the leave of this court against his conviction on count 1 and, if his appeal is successful, he applies for leave to appeal against his sentence on count 2.

The victim was aged 18. She was a Jehovah's Witness. She professed the tenets of that sect and lived her life by them. During the late afternoon of May 3, 1974, the defendant came into her house and asked her for sexual intercourse. She refused. He then attacked her with a knife inflicting four serious wounds. One pierced her lung. The defendant ran away. She staggered out into the road. She collapsed outside a neighbour's house. An ambulance took her to hospital, where she arrived at about 7.30 p.m. Soon after she was admitted to the intensive care ward. At about 8.30 p.m. she was examined by the surgical registrar who quickly decided that serious injury had been caused which would require surgery. As she had lost a lot of blood, before there could be an operation there would have to be a blood transfusion. As soon as the girl appreciated that the surgeon was thinking of organising a blood transfusion for her, she said that she should not be given one and that she would not have one. To have one, she said, would be contrary to her religious beliefs as a Jehovah's Witness. She was told that if she did not have a blood transfusion she would die. She said that she did not care if she did die. She was asked to acknowledge in writing that she had refused to have a blood transfusion under any circumstances. She did so. The prosecution admitted at the trial that had she had a blood transfusion when advised to have one she would not have died. She did so at 12.45 a.m. the next day. The evidence called by the prosecution proved that at all relevant times she was conscious and decided as she did deliberately, and knowing what the consequences of her decision would be. In his final speech to the jury, Mr. Herrod for the prosecution accepted that her refusal to have a blood transfusion was *a* cause of her death. The prosecution did not challenge the defence evidence that the defendant was suffering from diminished responsibility.

Towards the end of the trial and before the summing up started counsel on both sides made submissions as to how the case should be put to the jury. Counsel then appearing for the defendant invited the judge to direct the jury to acquit the defendant generally on the count of murder. His argument was that her refusal to have a blood transfusion had broken the chain of causation between the stabbing and her death. As an alternative he submitted that the jury should be left to decide whether the chain of causation had been broken. Mr. Herrod submitted that the judge should direct the jury to convict, because no facts were in issue and when the law was applied to the facts there was only one possible verdict, namely, manslaughter by reason of diminished responsibility.

When the judge came to direct the jury on this issue he did so by telling them that they should apply their common sense. He then went on to tell them they would get some help from the cases to which counsel had referred in their speeches. He reminded them of what Lord Parker C.J. had said in *Reg. v. Smith*, [1959] 2 Q.B. 35, 42 and what Maule J. had said 133 years before in *Reg. v. Holland* (1841), 2 Mood. & R. 351, 352. He placed particular reliance on what Maule J. had said. The jury, he said, might find it "most material and most helpful." He continued:

> This is one of those relatively rare cases, you may think, with very little option open to you but to reach the conclusion that was reached by your predecessors as members of the jury in *Reg. v. Holland*, namely, "yes" to the question of causation that the stab was still, at the time of this girl's death, the operative cause of death — or a substantial cause of death. However, that is a matter for you to determine after you have withdrawn to consider your verdict.

Mr. Comyn has criticized that direction on three grounds: first, because *Reg. v. Holland* should no longer be considered good law; secondly, because *Reg. v. Smith*, when rightly understood, does envisage the possibility of unreasonable conduct on the part of the victim breaking the chain of causation; and thirdly, because the judge in reality directed the jury to find causation proved although he used words which seemed to leave the issue open for them to decide.

In *Reg. v. Holland*, 2 Mood. & R. 351, the defendant in the course of a violent assault, had injured one of his victim's fingers. A surgeon had advised amputation because of the danger to life through complications developing. The advice was rejected. A fortnight later the victim died of lockjaw. Maule J. said, at p. 352: "the real question is, whether in the end the wound inflicted by the prisoner was the cause of death." That distinguished judge left the jury to decide that question as did the judge in this case. They had to decide it as juries always do, by pooling their experience of life and using their common sense. They would not have been handicapped by a lack of training in dialectic or moral theology.

Maule J.'s direction to the jury reflected the common-law's answer to the problem. He who inflicted an injury which resulted in death could not excuse himself by pleading that his victim could have avoided death by taking greater care of himself: see *Hale's Pleas of the Crown* (1800 ed.), pp. 427-428. The common-law in Sir Matthew Hale's time probably was in line with contemporary concepts of ethics. A man who did a wrongful act was deemed *morally* responsible for the natural and probable consequences of that act. Mr. Comyn asked us to remember that since Sir Matthew Hale's day the rigour of the law relating to homicide has been eased in favour of the accused. It has been — but this has come about through the development of the concept of intent, not by reason of a different view of causation. Well known practitioner's textbooks, such as *Halsbury's Law's of England*, 3rd ed., vol. 10 (1955), p. 706 and *Russell on Crime*, 12th ed. (1964), vol. 1, p. 30 continue to reflect the common-law approach. Textbooks intended for students in jurisprudence have queried the common-law rule: see Hart and Honoré, *Causation in Law* (1959), pp. 320-321 and Smith and Hogan, *Criminal Law*, 3rd ed. (1973), p. 214.

. . . .

Mr. Comyn tried to overcome this line of reasoning by submitting that the jury should have been directed that if they thought the deceased's decision not to have a blood transfusion was an unreasonable one, then the chain of causation would have been broken. At once the question arises — reasonable by whose standards? Those of Jehovah's Witnesses? Humanists? Roman Catholics? Protestants of Anglo-Saxon descent? The man on the Clapham omnibus? But he might well be an admirer of Eleazar who suffered death rather than eat the flesh of swine (2 Maccabees, ch. 6, vv. 18-31) or of Sir Thomas More who, unlike nearly all his contemporaries, was unwilling to accept Henry VIII as Head of the Church in England. Those brought up in the Hebraic and Christian traditions would probably be reluctant to accept that these martyrs caused their own deaths.

As was pointed out to Mr. Comyn in the course of argument, two cases, each raising the same issue of reasonableness because of religious beliefs, could produce different verdicts depending on where the cases were tried. A jury drawn from Preston, sometimes said to be the most Catholic town in England, might have different views about martyrdom to one drawn from the inner suburbs of London. Mr. Comyn accepted that this might be so: it was, he said, inherent in trial by jury. It is not inherent in the common law as expounded by Sir Matthew Hale and Maule J. It has long been the policy of the law that those who use violence on other people must take their victims as they find them. This in our judgment means the whole man, not just the physical man. It does not lie in the mouth of the assailant to say that his victim's religious beliefs which inhibited him from accepting certain kinds of treatment were unreasonable. The question for decision is what caused her death. The answer is the stab wound. The fact that the victim refused to stop this end coming about did not break the causal connection between the act and death.

If a victim's personal representatives claim compensation for his death the concept of foreseeability can operate in favour of the wrongdoer in the assessment of such compensation: the wrongdoer is entitled to expect his victim to mitigate his damage by accepting treatment of a normal kind: see *Steele v. R. George & Co. (1937) Ltd.*, [1942] A.C. 497. As Mr. Herrod pointed out, the criminal law is concerned with the maintenance of law and order and the protection of the public generally. A policy of the common law applicable to the settlement of tortious liability between subjects may not be, and in our judgment is not, appropriate for the criminal law.

The issue of the cause of death in a trial for either murder or manslaughter is one of fact for the jury to decide. But if, as in this case, there is no conflict of evidence and all the jury has to do is to apply the law to the admitted facts, the judge is entitled to tell the jury what the result of that application will be. In this case the judge would have been entitled to have told the jury that the defendant's stab wound was an operative cause of death. The appeal fails.

Appeal dismissed.

THE QUEEN v. BINGAPORE

(1974-5), 11 S.A.S.R. 469 (S. Aus. S.C.)

The court (BRIGHT, SANGSTER and JACOBS JJ.) delivered the following judgment: —

This is in part an appeal as of right pursuant to s. 352(*a*) of the *Criminal Law Consolidation Act* 1935-1972 and in part an application for leave to appeal pursuant to placitum (*c*) of the same section and is wholly against the appellant's conviction for murder.

. . . .

The appellant was, admittedly, involved in an assault on the victim, McMillan.

About 11.45 a.m. a business man parked his car in Angas Street near the unoccupied premises; he noticed a man, slumped against the railings outside the unoccupied premises, appearing to be dazed and holding what appeared to be a red coloured rag against his head; that man then moved off towards Police Headquarters further west along Angas Street. Somewhere about that time McMillan arrived at Police Headquarters, was seen to be bleeding profusely, an ambulance was called and McMillan was taken to the Royal Adelaide Hospital and admitted.

. . . .

At the Royal Adelaide Hospital, McMillan's condition was found to include a profusely bleeding wound to the head and, after some trouble, an artery was sutured and the bleeding stopped; internal head injuries were suspected; he was kept at the hospital overnight. On the Saturday at about 12.30 p.m. conversations took place between a resident medical officer, McMillan, and Mrs. McMillan, the brief effect of which was that the medical officer warned both the McMillans of the danger involved in McMillan leaving the hospital, namely the danger of death, notwithstanding which McMillan signed a "risk form" and the McMillans left the hospital. They walked to the new lodgings at McLaren Street and some six hours or thereabouts later Mr. McMillan was brought back to the Royal Adelaide Hospital by ambulance, was seen to be in need of urgent attention, and within four and a half hours was operated on, but unsuccessfully, and he died the next day from brain damage caused by subdural haemorrhage which, in turn, was described in evidence as consistent with trauma to the head within a range of times which included the Friday morning.

. . . .

Three challenges were made to the learned trial judge's directions on causation. On causation we need look no further than *Reg. v. Bristow*, at p. 217 (citing *Reg. v. Smith*) and, in turn, cited with approval in *Reg. v. Hallett*: —

> It seems to the court that, if at the time of death the original wound is still an operating cause and a substantial cause, then the death can properly be said to be the result of the wound, albeit that some other cause of death is also operating. Only if it can be said that the original wounding is merely the setting in which another cause operates can it be said that the death does not result from the wound.

Counsel for the appellant contended that we should add to the law (as it is at present found in the authorities) a new proposition that where the gross negligence/unreasonable conduct/some degree of negligence more than mere negligence, (counsel used all three expressions without limiting his contentions to any one of them) contributed to the death of the victim, the chain of causation was broken. Alternatively, he contended, the learned trial judge's direction that causation was sufficiently established if the acts of the accused was "a" cause, should have been cut down to "the" cause, or alternatively "the most substantial" cause. In so far as we are able to follow his contentions we do not agree with them. In any case, on the evidence as the jury must have viewed it, the chain of causation was violence by the appellant to the victim, subdural haemorrhage from that violence, and death from that subdural haemorrhage, a short and direct chain. The appellant's only complaint is that had an operation on the victim been performed earlier it might have saved him, and that the victim's wanton departure from hospital (to which he was returned at his wife's instance about six hours later) denied him any opportunity for such an earlier operation. That complaint, of course, relates not to a break in the chain of causation, not to a new cause, but to the loss of a possible opportunity of avoiding death from a still operating cause, namely the violence inflicted by the appellant. The act of the appellant causing injuries from which the victim dies does not cease to be a causative act because the victim thereafter acts to his detriment or because some third party is negligent. The case of *Reg. v. Jordan* to which we were referred, is clearly distinguishable, for there the victim did not die from injuries caused by the act of the prisoner, but from some other cause for which the prisoner could not be held responsible.

. . . .

Appeal dismissed.

R. v. MAYBIN

2012 SCC 24, 92 C.R. (6th) 221, [2012] 2 S.C.R. 30

Three accused were charged with unlawful act manslaughter. Two brothers assaulted the victim in a bar. The victim had touched a ball on their pool table. TM punched the victim in the face and head while MM assisted in the attack. As a result the victim was left unconscious on a pool table. The third accused, BG, was a doorman at the bar. He came over to the commotion and saw the victim lying on the pool table. A patron indicated that the victim had started the fight. BG punched the victim in the head and then carried him outside. The victim was taken to hospital where he died. The medical evidence called by the Crown and the accused indicated that the subarachnoid haemorrhage which resulted in the victim's death might have been caused by the blows struck by TM, the blow struck by BG, or an accumulation of both. The trial judge found that the attack on the victim was not a single transaction and that there were two separate assaults: the first by TM, to which MM was a party, and the second by BG. He held that the medical evidence was equivocal and did not establish beyond a reasonable doubt either that the first assault was the cause of the victim's death or that the second assault was the cause of the victim's death. As a result he acquitted all three accused of manslaughter. The Crown appealed.

The B.C. Court of Appeal was unanimous that the assaults by TM and MM factually contributed to the death. The majority (Ryan J.A., Huddart J.A. concurring) held that the action of the bouncer was not an intervening cause. It was open to a trier of fact to find it reasonably foreseeable that their assault could attract the intervention of others, including bar staff, with the possibility of resulting bodily harm. A new trial was ordered. Finch C.J. dissented. An accused should not be held responsible for the intentional actions of a third party acting independently. Even if TM and MM could be held responsible for reasonably foreseeable actions, there was no evidence on the record for the claim that it was objectively foreseeable that bar staff would become involved in the altercation.

With regard to BG, the B.C. Court of Appeal was unanimous that the medical evidence left room for reasonable doubt about whether that blow was a contributing cause of death and so the appeal from the acquittal was dismissed. TM and MM appealed.

The Supreme Court of Canada dismissed the appeal and for the first time directly addressed the issue of intervening cause.

KARAKATSANIS J. (for the Court)

[The B.C. Court of Appeal had correctly concluded that the accused's actions were a factual cause of the death. Factual causation is not limited to the direct and immediate cause nor is it limited to the most significant cause. The brothers' assault was either the direct medical cause of the death or it rendered the victim vulnerable to the bouncer's assault. But for their attack the death would not have occurred.]

3. Factual Causation

[18] In this case all three judges of the Court of Appeal were satisfied that the appellants had factually caused the victim's death. As a result, the issue of factual causation was not strictly within the scope of this appeal. In oral submissions before this Court however, counsel for the appellants argued that factual causation was not established because the trial judge had a reasonable doubt as to who delivered the lethal blow. Counsel suggested that in such circumstances, it would be anomalous if the bouncer was acquitted and the appellants were convicted.

[19] As noted by the majority of Court of Appeal, the bouncer was not in the same position as the Maybin brothers: the bouncer's assault was at the end of the chain of events leading to the victim's death (para. 46). Given the uncertainty of the medical evidence, the trial judge had a reasonable doubt about whether the bouncer's blow contributed to the death. As a result, he could not find that the actions of the bouncer were a factual cause of death (para. 51 of the Court of Appeal reasons). The court therefore dismissed the appeal from the acquittal of the bouncer for manslaughter.

[20] On the other hand, the appellants' unlawful acts not only seriously injured the victim, but also rendered him unconscious on the pool table where he was subsequently assaulted by the bouncer. Given these facts, the Court of Appeal concluded that even if the appellants' actions were not the direct and immediate cause of the victim's death, "but for" their actions, the victim would not have died. I agree. As *Smithers* and *Nette* made clear, factual causation is not limited to the direct and immediate cause, nor is it limited to the most significant cause. The Maybin brothers' assault was either the direct medical cause of death or it rendered the victim vulnerable to the bouncer's assault.

[21] For these reasons, I agree with the Court of Appeal that the trial judge erred in the factual causation inquiry in this case. He stopped with his assessment of the medical cause of death and did not consider the contribution of the appellants to that result by asking whether the deceased would have died "but for" the actions of the appellants. As Arbour J. noted in *Nette* (para. 77):

The difficulty in establishing a single, conclusive medical cause of death does not lead to the legal conclusion that there were multiple operative causes of death. In a homicide trial, the question is not what caused the death or who caused the death of the victim but rather did the accused cause the victim's death. The fact that other persons or factors may have contributed to the result may or may not be legally significant in the trial of the one accused charged with the offence.

[22] The fact that the bouncer's act may have been a *novus actus interveniens*, or an intervening act, is part of the analysis of whether *legal* causation has been established and whether the appellants should be held legally accountable for the death.

4. Legal Causation — Intervening Act

[23] The doctrine of intervening acts is used, when relevant, for the purpose of reducing the scope of acts which generate criminal liability. As Cromwell J.A. stated in *R. v. Tower*, 2008 NSCA 3, 261 N.S.R. (2d) 135, "the law recognizes that other causes may intervene to 'break the chain of causation' between the accused's acts and the death. This is the concept of an 'intervening cause', that some new event or events result in the accused's actions not being a significant contributing cause of death" (para. 25).

[24] Jurisprudence in Canada and in other common law jurisdictions and academic scholarship have given rise to efforts to formulate a principle to deal with intervening acts. Professor Stanley Yeo describes many of them:

> Several efforts . . . may be gleaned from the case authorities. They include statements to the effect that a defendant is relieved of causal blame if the intervening event was "abnormal", "an unreasonable act", a "coincidence", "not a natural consequence", comprised the "voluntary conduct of the intervener" or "was not reasonably foreseeable". ("Blamable Causation" (2000), 24 *Crim.L.J.* 144, at p. 151)

[25] The difficulty in formulating one test to determine when an intervening cause interrupts the chain of causation lies in the vast range of circumstances in which this issue arises. As mentioned, the majority and the dissent in the court below focussed on two different approaches to explain when an intervening act breaks the chain of causation.

[26] The first approach, applied by the majority, looks to whether the intervening act was objectively or reasonably foreseeable (see *R. v. Shilon* (2006), 240 C.C.C. (3d) 401 (Ont. C.A.)). The majority asked whether the risk of harm caused by the intervening actor was reasonably foreseeable to the appellants at the time they were committing the unlawful acts. It concluded that a trier of fact could find that it was reasonably foreseeable to the appellants that their assault on the victim, which occurred in a crowded bar, late at night, would provoke the intervention of others, perhaps the bar staff, with resulting non-trivial harm.

[27] The second approach, applied by the dissent, considers whether the intervening act is an independent factor that severs the impact of the accused's actions, making the intervening act, in law, the sole cause of the victim's death (see *R. v. Pagett* (1983), 76 Cr. App. R. 279 (C.A.); *R. v. Smith*, [1959] 2 Q.B. 35 (C.-M.A.C.)). The dissent held that the bouncer's assault was just such an independent factor.

[28] In my view, both these approaches are analytical aids — not new standards of legal causation. I agree with the intervener, the Attorney General of Ontario, that while such approaches may be helpful, they do not create new tests that are dispositive. Neither an unforeseeable intervening act nor an independent intervening act is necessarily a sufficient condition to *break* the chain of legal causation. Similarly, the fact that the intervening act was reasonably foreseeable, or was not an independent act, is not necessarily a sufficient condition to *establish* legal causation. Even in cases where it is alleged that an intervening act has interrupted the chain of legal causation, the causation test articulated in *Smithers* and confirmed in *Nette* remains the same: Were the dangerous, unlawful acts of the accused a significant contributing cause of the victim's death?

[29] Depending on the circumstances, assessments of foreseeability or independence may be more or less helpful in determining whether an accused's unlawful acts were still a *significant contributing* cause at the time of death. Any assessment of legal causation should maintain focus on whether the accused should be held legally responsible for the consequences of his actions, or whether holding the accused responsible for the death would amount to punishing a moral innocent.

5. Reasonable Foreseeability

[30] An intervening act that is reasonably foreseeable will usually not break or rupture the chain of causation so as to relieve the offender of legal responsibility for the unintended result. This approach posits that an accused who undertakes a dangerous act, and in so doing contributes to a death, should bear the risk that other foreseeable acts may intervene and contribute to that death. Because the issue is whether the actions and consequences were reasonably foreseeable prospectively, at the time of the accused's objectively dangerous and unlawful act, it accords with our notions of moral accountability. This approach addresses the question: Is it fair to attribute the resulting death to the initial actor?

[31] Courts have sometimes couched the principle of foreseeability in different terms, asking whether the intervening act is so "extraordinary" or "unusual" that the accused should not be held responsible for the consequences of that act. In *R. v. Sinclair*, 2009 MBCA 71, 240 Man. R. (2d) 135 the accused beat the deceased and left him motionless in the roadway where he was struck by a

passing motorist. The Manitoba Court of Appeal held that, in order for *novus actus interveniens* to apply to sever legal causation, the intervening act had to be, in some way, "extraordinary" or "unusual". In *R. v. Hallett*, [1969] S.A.S.R. 141 (S.C. *in banco*), the victim was left unconscious on a beach; the Supreme Court of South Australia held that a natural event may break the chain of causation if it is "extraordinary" (a tidal wave), but not if it is the ordinary operation of natural forces (the tides).

[32] Objective foreseeability has thus been a useful tool in determining whether an intervening act severs the chain of legal causation. The more difficult question in applying such an approach is the scope of what has to be reasonably foreseeable. In this case, the parties disagree about whether the intervening act — the blow delivered by the bouncer — was reasonably foreseeable. While both the majority and dissent opinions apply a reasonable foreseeability framework, they arrive at different conclusions. This result is driven by their different views regarding what precisely must be reasonably foreseeable. Is it the specific assault by the intervening actor? Is it simply the risk of further bodily harm? Or is it the general nature of intervening acts and the accompanying risk of harm?

[33] The dissent took the narrow view that the specific scenario — the unprovoked assault by a bouncer of an unconscious patron — had to be reasonably foreseeable. The majority cast the net more broadly by concluding "that it was reasonably foreseeable that the appellants' assault would provoke the intervention of others, perhaps the bar staff, with resulting non-trivial harm" (para. 43).

[34] In my view, the chain of causation should not be broken only because the specific subsequent attack by the bouncer was not reasonably foreseeable. Because the time to assess reasonable foreseeability is at the time of the initial assault, rather than at the time of the intervening act, it is too restrictive to require that the precise details of the event be objectively foreseeable. In some cases, while the general nature of the ensuing acts and the risk of further harm may be reasonably likely, the specific manner in which it could occur may be entirely unpredictable. From the perspective of moral responsibility, it is sufficient if the general nature of the intervening act and the risk of non-trivial harm are objectively foreseeable at the time of the dangerous and unlawful acts.

[38] ... I conclude that it is the general nature of the intervening acts and the accompanying risk of harm that needs to be reasonably foreseeable. Legal causation does not require that the accused must objectively foresee the precise future consequences of their conduct. Nor does it assist in addressing moral culpability to require merely that the risk of some non-trivial bodily harm is reasonably foreseeable. Rather, the intervening acts and the ensuing non-trivial harm must be reasonably foreseeable in the sense that the acts and the harm that

actually transpired flowed reasonably from the conduct of the appellants. If so, then the accused's actions may remain a significant contributing cause of death.

[39] In this case, the appellants submit that the bouncer's assault of the unconscious victim was not reasonably foreseeable at all, unlike further injury to the victim by another patron joining in the fight or by bar staff attempting to impose order.

[40] I do not agree. If the physical intervention of the bar staff, with its risk of non-trivial harm was objectively foreseeable, then the specific details of that intervention did not themselves need to be foreseen. Focussing on the fact that the subsequent act was committed by a bouncer, as opposed to another patron, misplaces the focus on the actor, as opposed to the nature of the intervening act.

[41] While the majority of the Court of Appeal framed their approach broadly as the risk of harm, the judges ultimately based their conclusion on the foreseeability of the general nature of the intervening acts and the potential for non-trivial harm. They concluded that the trial judge could have found that, in the context of an escalating bar fight, it was reasonably foreseeable that further non-trivial harm would be caused by the interventions of other patrons and bar staff. This conclusion was supported by the trial judge's findings of fact. The appellants initiated an assault in a crowded bar, late at night, with drinking patrons and bar security staff nearby. It was open to the trial judge to conclude that it was reasonably foreseeable that the fight would escalate and other patrons would join or seek to end the fight or that the bouncers would use force to seek to gain control of the situation. It was further open to the trial judge to conclude that Matthew Maybin himself was aware of the risk of the escalation of the fight when he enlisted the support of another patron in advance because "there might be a fight . . . so I figured I'd grab another guy just in case" (para. 33 of the trial judge's decision).

[42] In this case, the fight did escalate, with other patrons joining in, others calling for a bouncer, and bar staff hurrying to the area. Moreover, the bouncer in this case testified that he thought he *was* trying to impose order ("When asked to explain why he had punched [the victim], [the bouncer] said that the man had been identified to him as being the instigator of the fight and so he hit him to shock and disorient him, so as to gain control of the situation" (para. 131 of the trial judge's decision)). It was open to the trial judge to conclude that the risk of intervention by patrons and the bouncer was objectively foreseeable when the appellants commenced a one-sided fight in a crowded bar. Accordingly, I agree with the majority of the Court of Appeal that it was open to the judge to find that the intervening act was reasonably foreseeable in the circumstances of this case.

[43] One final point on this issue. The majority of the Court of Appeal stated that the reasonable foreseeability test is determinative on the issue of legal causation (para. 35):

> . . . the law will not hold someone legally responsible if the ordinarily circumspect person would not have seen the outcome as likely to result from his or her act. In my view, this principle explains the purpose of the *novus actus interveniens* rule. The application of the rule provides a way of ensuring that a person will not be held responsible for objectively unforeseeable consequences.

[44] The Court of Appeal in effect elevated this analytical approach to a new causation rule. I do not agree. The reasonable foreseeability approach is a useful tool and directly incorporates the notion of blameworthiness. However, as noted above, there may be other helpful analytical tools to assess whether legal responsibility should be imputed to the accused and whether the accused's acts were a significant contributing cause of death as required in *Smithers* and *Nette*.

6. Independent Acts

[45] In dissent, Finch C.J.B.C. agreed that "a person should not be held responsible for objectively unforeseeable consequences" and concluded that the actions of the bouncer were not reasonably foreseeable. He continued:

> However, persons should similarly not be held responsible for intentional actions of a third party acting independently. This was articulated by the Ontario Court of Appeal in *R v. J.S.R.* (2008), 239 O.A.C. 42; 2008 ONCA 544, at para. 31:
>
>> [D]espite the existence of factual causation, it is said to be unfair to impute legal liability for the death to a person whose actions have been effectively overtaken by the more immediate causal action of another party acting independently . . .[The bouncer's] intentional conduct in striking the unconscious [victim] constitutes an intervening act in this case. He is an independent third party and the Maybin brothers should not be held morally or legally responsible for his acts, in the absence of a conclusion that the blows of Timothy Maybin and [the bouncer] in conjunction were the cause of death. [Emphasis in original; paras. 72-73.]

[46] Whether the effects of an accused's actions are "effectively overtaken by the more immediate causal action of another party acting independently" involves an assessment of the relative weight of the causes, looking retrospectively from the death.

[47] Courts have sought to articulate when the first cause ought to be overlooked because of the nature and effect of the subsequent causes, quite apart from whether or not the subsequent causes may have been foreseeable. In *R. v. Smith*, the victim died in hospital after being stabbed by the accused. It was later discovered that the victim had been improperly treated. When deciding whether the actions of medical staff constituted an intervening cause, the English Courts Martial Appeal Court declared that an intervening cause shields the accused from

responsibility only if the accused's act is "merely the setting in which another cause operates" (p. 43). Or, put another way, only if the intervening cause "is so overwhelming as to make the original wound merely part of the history" leading to the victim's death (p. 43). Ultimately, the court articulated the standard as: ". . . if at the time of death the original wound is still an operating cause and a substantial cause, then the death can properly be said to be the result of the wound"(pp. 42-43). In *R. v. Hallett* when faced with the death of a man left unconscious on a beach who drowned as a result of "the ordinary operations of the tides" (p. 150), the court asked whether the original unlawful act was "so connected with the event that it . . . must be regarded as having a sufficiently substantial causal effect which subsisted up to the happening of the event" (p. 149).

[48] In *R. v. Shilon*, the Ontario Court of Appeal accepted that "independent voluntary human intervention in events started by an accused may break the chain of causation" but concluded that it was the accused who "created and continued the highly charged situation" and "provoked" the third party's dangerous driving, which was therefore "directly linked" to the accused's actions (para. 43).

[49] Whether an intervening act is independent is thus sometimes framed as a question of whether the intervening act is a response to the acts of the accused. In other words, did the act of the accused merely set the scene, allowing other circumstances to (coincidentally) intervene, or did the act of the accused trigger or provoke the action of the intervening party?

[50] When the intervening acts are natural events, they are more closely tied to the theory of foreseeability, and the courts ask whether the event was "extraordinary", as in *R. v. Hallett*. When the intervening acts are those of a person, exercising his or her free will, the focus is often on the independence of the actions.

[51] The academic community has also sought to explain when the actions of another person will interrupt the chain of causation. Glanville Williams argues that while people are subject to the "causes" of nature, they have control over their actions and a voluntary act starts a new chain of causation, regardless of what has happened before. He explains how this accords with our ideas of moral responsibility and just punishment:

> The first actor who starts on a dangerous or criminal plan will often be responsible for what happens if no one else intervenes; but a subsequent actor who has reached responsible years, is of sound mind, has full knowledge of what he is doing, and is not acting under intimidation or other pressure or stress resulting from the defendant's conduct, replaces him as the responsible actor. Such an intervening act is thought to break the moral connection that would otherwise have been perceived between the defendant's acts and the forbidden consequence. ("*Finis* for *Novus Actus*?" (1989), 48 *Cambridge L.J.* 391, at p. 392)

[52] An intervening act by another person does not always sever the causal connection between the accused's act and the result: as mentioned, ss. 224 and 225 of the *Criminal Code* provide that the chain of causation is not broken if death could otherwise have been prevented by resorting to proper means (s. 224), or if the immediate cause of death is proper or improper treatment that is applied in good faith (s. 225). In addition, in this case, I need not consider the actions of a third party who acts in good faith, or under mistake, intimidation or similar pressure, or whose actions are not voluntary. Here, the bouncer criminally assaulted the unconscious victim causing bodily harm.

[53] What then, is the nature and degree of independence that may absolve the original actors of legal responsibility for the consequences of their actions? Turning to this case, was the act of the bouncer so independent of the actions of the appellants that his act should be regarded in law as the sole cause of the victim's death to the exclusion of the acts of the appellants?

[54] The appellants submit that it should because (1) the appellants were not aiders of the bouncer's assault; (2) they were not involved in a joint activity; and (3) the appellants could only be said to have contributed to the victim's death by leaving him in the position the bouncer found him when he took it upon himself to assault the unconscious man.

[55] I agree with the respondent that the inquiry as to whether an intervening act is independent is distinct from the inquiry of whether the accused and the intervening actor are parties acting in concert or with common purpose pursuant to s. 21 of the *Criminal Code*. If they are parties, each is responsible for the acts of the other. In the legal causation analysis, their respective acts remain separate. Legal causation focusses on the connection (or independence) between the actions of the individuals and the effect of those actions, not on the connection between the actors.

[56] Thus, the finding by the trial judge of independence for the purposes of accessorial liability under s. 21 would not affect a finding that the actions of the appellants triggered or provoked the actions of the intervening actor. Similarly, the fact that the bouncer was an independent third party does not, as suggested in the dissent, end the legal causation analysis. Their respective *actions* must be sufficiently independent for legal causation purposes.

[57] Was the bouncer's intentional assault an independent act? The answer depends upon whether the intervening act was so connected to the appellants' actions that it cannot be said to be independent. If the intervening act is a direct response or is directly linked to the appellants' actions, and does not by its nature overwhelm the original actions, then the appellants cannot be said to be morally innocent of the death.

[58] While the trial judge found the actions of the Maybin brothers and the actions of the bouncer to be separate and independent assaults, he also found these actions to be "an interrelated series of events" (para. 209). He found that the assaults took place in the same location and in the same manner, and from Timothy Maybin's first punch to the bouncer's blow, the elapsed time was less than a minute (see paras. 295-96 of the trial judge' reasons).

[59] In this case, then, the trial judge could have found that the bouncer acted in direct and virtually immediate reaction to what the appellants did; that the bouncer acted after asking who had started the fight; and that his act was responsive and not coincidental conduct. It was open to the trial judge to find that the bouncer's act was closely connected in time, place, circumstance, nature and effect with the appellants' acts and that the effects of the appellants' actions were still "subsisting" and not "spent" at the time the bouncer acted (*R. v. Tower*, at para. 26). The evidence could support the conclusion that the blow delivered by the bouncer was not so "overwhelming" as to make the effect of the original assaults merely part of the history so that it can be said that the original assaults were not "operative" at the time of death (*R. v. Smith*). I conclude that it was open to the trial judge to find that the assault of the bouncer was not independent of the appellants' unlawful acts and that the appellants' actions remained a significant contributing cause of the victim's death. Arguably, the dangerous and unlawful acts of the appellants were not so remote to suggest that they were morally innocent of the death.

7. Conclusion

[60] Courts have used a number of analytical approaches to determine when an intervening act absolves the accused of legal responsibility for manslaughter. These approaches grapple with the issue of the moral connection between the accused's acts and the death; they acknowledge that an intervening act that is reasonably foreseeable to the accused may well not break the chain of causation, and that an independent and intentional act by a third party may in some cases make it unfair to hold the accused responsible. In my view, these approaches may be useful tools depending upon the factual context. However, the analysis must focus on first principles and recognize that these tools do not alter the standard of causation or substitute new tests. The dangerous and unlawful acts of the accused must be a significant contributing cause of the victim's death.

[61] I agree with the majority of the Court of Appeal that based upon the trial judge's findings of fact, it was open to him to conclude that the general nature of the intervening act and the accompanying risk of harm were reasonably foreseeable; and that the act was in direct response to the appellants' unlawful actions. The judge could have concluded that the bouncer's assault did not necessarily constitute an intervening act that severed the link between Timothy and Matthew Maybins' conduct and the victim's death, such that it would

absolve them of moral and legal responsibility. The trial judge could have found that the appellants' actions remained a significant contributing cause of the death.

[62] For these reasons, I agree with the majority of the Court of Appeal that in the circumstances of this case, it was open to the trial judge to find that the appellants caused the death. I would dismiss the appeal.

Do you agree with the result reached by the Supreme Court in this case? Has the proper approach to intervening causes been satisfactorily identified for application in other cases?

Benjamin Snow, "A Cause for Concern: Incoherence in the Doctrine of Intervening Cause" (2012), 92 C.R. (6th) 241, suggests the approach is too uncertain and prefers the approach of the Manitoba Court of Appeal in *R. v. Sinclair* (2009), 69 C.R. (6th) 163 (Man. C.A.), that an accused not be accountable for an "extraordinary outcome" outside the ambit of risk created by the initial cause.

In murder cases where there is arguably an intervening cause leading to death it seems likely that most cases will turn not on *Maybin* respecting cause but on the *mens rea* requirement of knowledge of the likely risk of death. Gerry Ferguson, "Causation and the *Mens Rea* for Manslaughter" (2013), 99 C.R. (6th) 351, suggests that the much lower fault requirement for manslaughter and *Maybin* risks far too wide criminal responsibility for manslaughter, pointing also to the rigidity of the thin skull rule.

The Supreme Court has yet to address *Charter* issues respecting causation of some of the very old *Criminal Code* rules declaring responsibility despite intervening causes such as medical mistreatment applied in good faith (s. 225). The *Maybin* focus on the test of a "significant cause" at least makes it clear that criminal responsibility is unlike the tort law of negligence which normally rests on the wide "but for" test (*Clements (Litigation Guardian of) v. Clements*, 2012 SCC 32, [2012] 2 S.C.R. 181).

PROBLEM

The accused were charged with manslaughter. Three young men had assaulted a fourth and left him injured at night in the middle of the road. He was struck by a car 10 minutes later by someone driving a vehicle with poor lights and brakes. The pathologist could not say whether the death was caused by the assault or the driving.

Compare *R v. Sinclair* (2009), 69 C.R. (6th) 163 (Man. C.A.).

PROBLEM

The two accused were part of a large group of partying and drinking young people. An argument resulted in a physical altercation where a person was rendered unconscious. Other members of the group attempted to resuscitate him and took him to the hospital rather than wait for the ambulance. The uncontradicted expert evidence was that the death had occurred because the attempts at resuscitation had first caused the victim to vomit, which led him to aspirate the vomit into his lungs, leading him to asphyxiate. The accused used a sleeper hold. Had the others done nothing the victim might have recovered.

Compare *R. v. Reid* (2003), 18 C.R. (6th) 282 (N.S. C.A.).

PROBLEM

The accused struck a pedestrian while driving on the 401 highway shortly after midnight: the pedestrian's body was then run over by other vehicles, and she died as a result. The pedestrian had been drinking heavily and had been ejected from a taxi at the side of the road after an argument with the taxi driver minutes earlier. She was unsteady on her feet, wandering along the side of the highway and into live lanes of traffic when she was hit by the accused. There was breathalyzer and blood sample evidence that, despite some weaknesses, established that the accused had a blood alcohol level over .08, and was also sufficient to allow the conclusion that the accused was impaired. The accused was charged with driving while "over 80" causing death and with impaired driving causing death.

Compare *R. v. Phan* (2015), 19 C.R. (7th) 66 (Ont. S.C.J.) and *R. v. Gentles* (2016), 335 C.C.C. (3d) 82, 26 C.R. (7th) 414 (B.C. C.A.).

PROBLEM

The accused was charged with dangerous driving causing death and dangerous driving causing bodily harm. He admitted to having been involved in a street race with another vehicle. The other racer lost control and swerved into the oncoming lane, hitting another car: the racer was killed and the driver of the oncoming vehicle was seriously injured.

Compare *R. v. O'Leary* (2017), 36 C.R. (7th) 80 (Ont. C.A.) and *R. v. Menezes* (2002), 50 C.R. (5th) 343 (Ont. S.C.J.).

Chapter 3

THE FAULT REQUIREMENT
(MENS REA OR NEGLIGENCE)

1. INTRODUCTION

J.F. STEPHEN, A HISTORY OF THE CRIMINAL LAW OF ENGLAND

Vol. 2, (1883), 94-95

The maxim, *actus non facit reum nisi mens sit rea*, is sometimes said to be the fundamental maxim of the whole criminal law; but I think that, like many other Latin sentences supposed to form part of the Roman law, the maxim not only looks more instructive than it really is, but suggests fallacies which it does not precisely state.

It is frequently though ignorantly supposed to mean that there cannot be such a thing as legal guilt where there is no moral guilt, which is obviously untrue, as there is always a possibility of a conflict between law and morals.

It also suggests the notion that there is some state of mind called a *mens rea*, the absence of which, on any particular occasion, deprives what would otherwise be a crime of its criminal character. This also is untrue. There is no one such state of mind, as any one may convince himself by considering the definitions of dissimilar crimes. A pointsman falls asleep, and thereby causes a railway accident and the death of a passenger; he is guilty of manslaughter. He deliberately and by elaborate devices produces the same result; he is guilty of murder; if in each case there is a *mens rea*, as the maxim seems to imply, *mens rea* must be a name for two states of mind, not merely differing from but opposed to each other, for what two states of mind can resemble each other less than indolence and an active desire to kill?

The truth is that the maxim about *mens rea* means no more than that the definition of all or nearly all crimes contains not only an outward and visible element, but a mental element, varying according to the different nature of different crimes. Thus, in reference to murder, the *mens rea* is any state of mind which comes within the description of malice aforethought. In reference to theft the *mens rea* is an intention to deprive the owner of his property permanently, fraudulently and without claim of right. In reference to forgery the *mens rea* is anything which can be described as an intent to defraud. Hence the only means of arriving at a full comprehension of the expression *mens rea* is by a detailed examination of the definitions of particular crimes, and therefore the expression itself is unmeaning.

W.S. GILBERT, THE MIKADO, (1885)

That's the pathetic part of it. Unfortunately the fool of an Act says, 'Compassing the death of the heir apparent.' There's not a word about mistake, or not knowing, or having no notion, or not being there. There should be, of course, but there isn't. That's the slovenly way in which these Acts are drawn.

G. MUELLER, ON COMMON LAW MENS REA

(1957-58), 42 Minn. L. Rev. 1043 at 1055, 1061

There has crept into our thinking the idea that there is no singular concept of *mens rea* but that, since every crime has a different *mens rea* requirement, one should talk of *mentes reae* rather than *mens rea*. This is a misconception and it is false to conclude, as some do, that there is no unifying *mens rea* concept. Just as all cars have different wheels, little cars little wheels and big cars big wheels, and we are justified in referring to them collectively under the unifying concept wheels, so all crimes have a different *mens rea* and yet the concept of *mens rea* must be regarded as a unifying concept of various possible frames of mind.

Mens rea, then, is not the mere psychic relation between act and actor, it is, rather, the ethico-legal *negative* value of the deed (appearing in various legally prescribed forms), i.e., it is a *community value of which the perpetrator at the time of the deed knows the existence and that it will materialize when the deed becomes known.*

G.L. WILLIAMS, CRIMINAL LAW: THE GENERAL PART

2nd ed. (1961), 30-31

It may be said that any theory of criminal punishment leads to a requirement of some kind of *mens rea*. The deterrent theory is workable only if the culprit has knowledge of the legal sanction; and if a man does not foresee the consequence of his act he cannot appreciate that punishment lies in store for him if he does it. The retributive theory presupposes moral guilt; incapacitation supposes social danger; and the reformative aim is out of place if the offender's sense of values is not warped.

However, the requirement as we have it in the law does not harmonise perfectly with any of these theories. It does not quite fit the deterrent theory, because a man may have *mens rea* although he is ignorant of the law, . . . Again, the requirement does not quite conform to the retributive theory, because the *mens rea* of English law does not necessarily connote an intention to engage in moral wrongdoing. . . . There are similar difficulties with incapacitation and reform.

What, then, does legal *mens rea* mean? It refers to the mental element necessary for the particular crime, and this mental element may be either *intention* to do the immediate act or bring about the consequence or (in some crimes) *recklessness* as to such act or consequence. . . . Some crimes require intention and nothing else will do, but most can be committed either intentionally or recklessly. Some crimes require particular kinds of intention or knowledge.

Outside the class of crimes requiring *mens rea* there are some that do not require any particular state of mind but do require negligence. Negligence in law is not necessarily a state of mind; and thus these crimes are best regarded as not requiring *mens rea*. However, negligence is a kind of legal fault, and in that respect they are akin to crimes requiring *mens rea*.

Yet other crimes do not even require negligence. They are crimes of strict or vicarious responsibility, and, like crimes of negligence, they constitute exceptions to the adage *Actus non facit reum nisi mens sit rea*.

In the Canadian context, we shall discover that there is a constitutional requirement of fault for any offence threatening the liberty interest. Almost always the only real issue is what the fault requirement actually entails. Jurisprudence on fault is a matter of common law, statutory interpretation and *Charter* standards and is still in a state of flux. There is considerable ambiguity and confusion about definition. Although there is a common law presumption in favour of the subjective approach, which governs most of the time and indeed is constitutionally required in some cases, debate continues over the extent to which objective fault also plays a role.

2. SUBJECTIVE/OBJECTIVE DISTINCTION

The Supreme Court of Canada judgments in *R. v. Creighton*, [1993] 3 S.C.R. 3, 23 C.R. (4th) 189, 83 C.C.C. (3d) 346 and *R. v. Hundal*, [1993] 1 S.C.R. 867, 19 C.R. (4th) 169, 79 C.C.C. (3d) 97, accept that there should be a clear distinction between the subjective standard of whether the accused was actually aware of a risk and the objective standard of whether the accused failed to measure up to the external standard of the reasonable person, irrespective of awareness. On the subjective standard all of the accused's individual factors are taken into account. The objective standard is now clearly much tougher given the ruling by the majority in *Creighton*, to be fully discussed later, that on the objective standard no personal factors, such as age, race, gender, poverty and experience, can be taken into account except where they relate to incapacity. **Should such factors be considered before State punishment?**

How do we determine the accused's state of mind?

"The thought of man is not triable for the devil alone knoweth the thought of man." (Brian C.J., (1477), Year Books, Pasch Ed. IV Fi pl.2.)

"The state of man's mind is as much a fact as the state of his digestion." (Bowen L.J. in *Edington v. Fitzmaurice* (1885), 29 Ch.D. 459.)

The important distinction between a subjective substantive standard and the objective approach to proof is emphasized in the following judgments:

R. v. HUNDAL

[1993] 1 S.C.R. 867, 19 C.R. (4th) 169, 79 C.C.C. (3d) 97, 1993 CarswellBC 489, 1993 CarswellBC 1255

The Court was called on to determine the fault requirement for the crime of dangerous driving.

CORY J. (for the majority): —

A truly subjective test seeks to determine what was actually in the mind of the particular accused at the moment the offence is alleged to have been committed. In his very useful text, Professor Stuart puts it in this way in *Canadian Criminal Law* (2nd ed.) at pp. 123-24 and at p. 125:

> What is vital is that *this accused* given his personality, situation and circumstances, actually intended, knew or foresaw the consequence and/or circumstance as the case may be. Whether he "could", "ought" or "should" have foreseen or whether a reasonable person would have foreseen is not the relevant criterion of liability.

> . . . .

> In trying to ascertain what was going on in the accused's mind, as the subjective approach demands, the trier of fact may draw reasonable inferences from the accused's actions or words at the time of his act or in the witness box. The accused may or may not be believed. To conclude that, considering all the evidence, the Crown has proved beyond a reasonable doubt that the accused "must" have thought in the penalized way is no departure from the subjective substantive standard. Resort to an objective substantive standard would only occur if the reasoning became that the accused "must have realized it if he had thought about it". [Emphasis in original.]

On the other hand, the test for negligence is an objective one requiring a marked departure from the standard of care of a reasonable person. There is no need to establish the intention of the particular accused. The question to be answered under the objective test concerns what the accused "should" have known.

R. v. THÉROUX

[1993] 2 S.C.R. 5, 19 C.R. (4th) 194, 79 C.C.C. (3d) 449,
1993 CarswellQue 5, 1993 CarswellQue 156

The Court was called on to discuss the fault requirement for the crime of fraud. Justice McLachlin spoke for the majority:

This brings us to the *mens rea* of fraud. What is the guilty mind of fraud? At this point, certain confusions inherent in the concept of *mens rea* itself become apparent. It is useful initially to distinguish between the mental element or elements of a crime and the *mens rea*. The term *mens rea*, properly understood, does not encompass all of the mental elements of a crime. The *actus reus* has its own mental element; the act must be the voluntary act of the accused for the *actus reus* to exist. *Mens rea*, on the other hand, refers to the guilty mind, the wrongful intention, of the accused. Its function in criminal law is to prevent the conviction of the morally innocent — those who do not understand or intend the consequences of their acts. Typically, *mens rea* is concerned with the consequences of the prohibited *actus reus*. Thus in the crimes of homicide, we speak of the consequences of the voluntary act — intention to cause death, or reckless and wilfully blind persistence in conduct which one knows is likely to cause death. In other offences, such as dangerous driving, the *mens rea* may relate to the failure to consider the consequences of inadvertence.

This brings me to the question of whether the test for *mens rea* is subjective or objective. Most scholars and jurists agree that, leaving aside offences where the *actus reus* is negligence or inadvertence and offences of absolute liability, the test for *mens rea* is subjective. The test is not whether a reasonable person would have foreseen the consequences of the prohibited act, but whether the accused subjectively appreciated those consequences at least as a possibility. In applying the subjective test, the court looks to the accused's intention and the facts as the accused believed them to be: G. Williams, *Textbook of Criminal Law* (2nd ed. 1983), at pp. 727-28.

Two collateral points must be made at this juncture. First, as Williams underlines, this inquiry has nothing to do with the accused's system of values. A person is not saved from conviction because he or she believes there is nothing wrong with what he or she is doing. The question is whether the accused subjectively appreciated that certain consequences would follow from his or her acts, not whether the accused believed the acts or their consequences to be moral. Just as the pathological killer would not be acquitted on the mere ground that he failed to see his act as morally reprehensible, so the defrauder will not be acquitted because he believed that what he was doing was honest.

The second collateral point is the oft-made observation that the Crown need not, in every case, show precisely what thought was in the accused's mind at the time of the criminal act. In certain cases, subjective awareness of the consequences can be inferred from the act itself, barring some explanation casting doubt on such inference. The fact that such an inference is made does not detract from the subjectivity of the test.

R. v. MULLIGAN

(1974), 26 C.R.N.S. 179, 18 C.C.C. (2d) 270,
1974 CarswellOnt 11 (Ont. C.A.)

MARTIN J.A.: —

. . . .

The central issue in this case was whether the accused, when he caused the death of his wife by repeatedly stabbing her, meant to cause her death or meant to cause her bodily harm that he knew was likely to cause her death, and was reckless whether death ensued and thereby committed the crime of murder as defined by the *Criminal Code*, R.S.C. 1970, c. C-34, s. 212(*a*)(i), (ii). The accused's intention was a fact in issue and like any other fact in issue it fell to be determined by a consideration of all the evidence including his acts, his utterances and any other circumstances which might shed light on his state of mind. As previously observed, the accused did not testify with respect to his state of mind at the relevant time. Such evidence would have been relevant and admissible. *Rex v. Fitzpatrick* (1926), 19 Cr. App. R. 91; Wigmore on Evidence, 3rd ed., Vol. II, pp. 714-15.

The jury would, of course have been entitled to reject his evidence and conclude that the circumstances were consistent only with the existence of the necessary intent. Although the accused did not testify on his own behalf, the statements made by him to the police contained an assertion that he did not mean to kill the deceased. The jury was properly charged with respect to the use that they could make of those statements and it is perhaps unnecessary to add that the jury was entitled, if it saw fit, to reject his assertion that he did not mean to kill the deceased.

In *Vallance v. The Queen*, [1961] 108 C.L.R. 56, Windeyer J. said at pp. 82-83:

> What a man does is often the best evidence of the purpose he had in mind. The probability that harm will result from a man's act may be so great, and so apparent, that it compels an inference that he actually intended to do that harm. Nevertheless, intention is a state of mind. The circumstances and probable consequences of a man's act are no more than evidence of his intention. For this reason this court has often said that it is misleading to speak of a man

being presumed always to intend the natural and probable consequences of his acts. And this, I do not doubt is so.

and at p. 83 said:

> A man's own intention is for him a subjective state, just as are his sensations of pleasure or of pain. But the state of another man's mind, or of his digestion, is an objective fact. When it has to be proved, it is to be proved in the same way as other objective facts are proved. A jury must consider the whole of the evidence relevant to it as a fact in issue. If an accused gives evidence of what his intentions were, the jury must weigh his testimony along with whatever inference as to his intentions can be drawn from his conduct or from other relevant facts. References to a "subjective test" could lead to an idea that the evidence of an accused man as to his intent is more credible than his evidence of other matters. It is not: he may or may not be believed by the jury. Whatever he says, they may be able to conclude from the whole of the evidence that beyond doubt he had a guilty mind and a guilty purpose. But always the questions are what did *he* in fact know, foresee, expect, intend.

R. v. ORTT

(1968), 6 C.R.N.S. 233, [1970] 1 C.C.C. 223,
1968 CarswellOnt 29 (Ont. C.A.)

On appeal from a conviction of non-capital murder, the main ground was that the charge of the trial judge suggested there was an onus on the accused to prove his incapacity to have the specific intent necessary. The trial judge had said to the jury:

> The intention of a person *can* be judged by what he says or what he does. *In our law a person is presumed to have intended the natural consequences of his act.* Where a person deliberately strikes another with a lethal weapon an intention to kill will be *presumed* or, at least, an intention to cause bodily harm which is likely to result in death will be *presumed*. If a person strikes another with a knife in the region of the heart, in the region of the abdomen, various parts of the body, as was done to this woman, there would be a *presumption* that the person inflicting those wounds intended to cause the death of that woman or intended to cause bodily harm to her which he knew was likely to cause death and that he was reckless whether death would ensue or not. Where a person does acts calculated to kill a person and does kill that person, that is evidence of intent.

While the appeal was dismissed on the basis that the charge as a whole made it clear that the Crown had the onus of proof on the issue of intent, the Court noted:

> It has been held by this court that it is error in law to tell a jury it is a presumption of law that a person intends the natural consequences of his acts: *R. v. Giannotti* (1956), 115 C.C.C. 203, 23 C.R. 259. Moreover the word

"presumption" alone creates a difficulty in that it may suggest an onus on the accused. I agree with the comment of the authors of *Martin's Annual Criminal Code* (1968), p. 195:

> The difficulty would not arise if the use of the word "presumption" were avoided. A presumption requires that a certain conclusion must be drawn, unless the accused takes steps to make that conclusion unwarranted. An inference, however, is no more than a matter of common sense and merely indicates that a certain conclusion may be drawn if warranted by the evidence.

As was said by Denning L.J. in *Hosegood v. Hosegood* (1950), 66 T.L.R. 735 at p. 738:

> The presumption of intention is not a proposition of law but a proposition of ordinary good sense. It means this: that, as a man is usually able to foresee what are the natural consequences of his acts, so it is, as a rule, reasonable to infer that he did foresee them and intend them. But, while that is an inference which may be drawn, it is not one which must be drawn. If on all the facts of the case it is not the correct inference, then it should not be drawn.

In my opinion, therefore, the word "presumption" is to be avoided in this context and juries simply told that generally it is a reasonable inference that a man intends the natural consequences of his acts so that when, for instance, a man points a gun at another and fires it the jury may reasonably infer that he meant either to cause his death or to cause him bodily harm that he knew was likely to cause death reckless of whether death ensued or not.

Recall that in *Woolmington* the House of Lords found that the trial judge had erred by instructing the jury that they *must* conclude that the accused intended to kill his wife. It was wrong to say the jury *must* presume intent. That does not mean the jury would not, on the facts of the case, have been *permitted* to reach the conclusion that Woolmington did have that intent. Juries are permitted to make the "common sense inference" that a sane and sober person intends the natural and probable consequences of his or her actions, as the Supreme Court explains in the following case:

R. v. WALLE

2012 SCC 41, 284 C.C.C. (3d) 153, 94 C.R. (6th) 296, [2012] 2 S.C.R. 438

MOLDAVER J.:

63 In my view, instructing a jury on the common sense inference serves a useful purpose. It provides the jury with a marker against which to measure the rather amorphous concept of intent. A proper instruction also sounds a cautionary note. The jurors are admonished that the inference is permissive, not presumptive, and that before acting on it, they must carefully consider the evidence that points away from it. That is important. Left to its own devices, a jury might too readily turn to common sense for an answer, especially in cases like the present one, where common sense might suggest that anyone who fires a gun into a person's chest at close range would surely be aware of the consequences.

64 That said, I do not mean to suggest that the common sense inference instruction should be tied to a rigid formula. Thus, by way of example, while trial judges may choose to refer to the "sane and sober" person when instructing a jury on the common sense inference, they need not do so. A simple instruction along the lines that "a person usually knows what the predictable consequences of his or her actions are, and means to bring them about", would suffice. (See Canadian Judicial Council, *Model Jury Instructions* (2012) (online), at *Homicide*, Offence 229.a, at para. 6.)

65 In the end, what is critical is that the jury be made to understand, in clear terms, that in assessing the specific intent required for murder, it should consider the whole of the evidence that could realistically bear on the accused's mental state at the time of the alleged offence. The trial judge should alert the jury to the pertinent evidence. How detailed that recitation should be will generally be a matter for the trial judge, in the exercise of his or her discretion.

The following detailed consideration of the current law on fault will reveal that a low-level objective standard is pervasive for public welfare offences and that, while the subjective approach is still required for most crimes, for a significant number of crimes there are now less-demanding standards of fault.

3. FAULT FOR PUBLIC WELFARE (REGULATORY) OFFENCES

(a) Common Law

Until the pivotal decision in *Sault Ste. Marie*, in the case of some offences that were argued to be not truly criminal the choice for the courts was between requiring the Crown to establish full subjective *mens rea* in the actor or absolute liability. Absolute liability, at that time also called strict liability, rested merely on proof of an act with no requirement of any form of fault. Consider how the Supreme Court made this choice in a still-controlling 1957 decision:

BEAVER v. R.

[1957] S.C.R. 531, 26 C.R. 193, 118 C.C.C. 129, 1957 CarswellOnt 10

The accused was appealing convictions on counts of selling and possessing diacetylmorphine.

CARTWRIGHT J. (RAND and LOCKE JJ. concurring): —

. . . .

It is not necessary to set out the facts in detail. There was evidence on which it was open to the jury to find (i) that Max Beaver sold to a police officer, who was working under cover, a package which in fact contained diacetylmorphine, (ii) that the appellant was a party to the sale of the package, (iii) that while the appellant did not have the package on his person or in his physical possession he and Max Beaver were acting jointly in such circumstances that the possession which the latter had of the package was the possession of both of the accused, and (iv) that the appellant had no knowledge that the substance contained in the package was diacetylmorphine and believed it to be sugar of milk.

I do not mean to suggest that the jury would necessarily have made the fourth finding but there was evidence on which they might have done so, or which might have left them in a state of doubt as to whether or not the appellant knew that the package contained anything other than sugar of milk.

The learned trial judge, against the protest of the appellant, charged the jury, in effect, that if they were satisfied that the appellant had in his possession a package and sold it, then, if in fact the substance contained in the package was diacetylmorphine, the appellant was guilty on both counts, and that the questions (i) whether he had any knowledge of what the substance was, or (ii) whether he entertained the honest but mistaken belief that it was a harmless substance were irrelevant and must not be considered. Laidlaw J.A. who delivered the unanimous judgment of the Court of Appeal, [116 Can. C.C. 231], was of opinion that this charge was right in law and that the learned trial judge was bound by the decision in *R. v. Lawrence*, 102 Can. C.C. 121, to direct the jury as he did. The main question on this appeal is whether this view of the law is correct.

The problem is one of construction of the *Opium and Narcotic Drug Act*, R.S.C. 1952, c. 201, and particularly the following sections, which at the date of the offences charged read as follows:

> 4(1) Every, person who . . .
> (*d*) has in his possession any drug save and except under the authority of a licence from the Minister first had and obtained, or other lawful authority; . . .
> (*f*) manufactures, sells, gives away, delivers or distributes or makes any offer in respect of any drug, or any substance represented or held out by such person to be a drug, to any person without first obtaining a licence from the Minister, or without other lawful authority;
> . . .
> is guilty of an offence, and is liable
> (i) upon indictment, to imprisonment for any term not exceeding seven years and not less than six months, and to a fine not exceeding one thousand dollars and not less than two hundred dollars, and, in addition, at the discretion of the judge, to be whipped; or
> (ii) upon summary conviction, to imprisonment with or without hard labour for any term not exceeding 18 months and not less than six months, and to a fine not exceeding one thousand dollars and not less than two hundred dollars.

. . . .

The judgment in appeal is supported by earlier decisions of Appellate Courts in Ontario, Quebec and Nova Scotia, but a directly contrary view has been expressed by the Court of Appeal for British Columbia. While this conflict has existed since 1948, this is the first occasion on which the question has been brought before this court.

It may be of assistance in examining the problem to use a simple illustration. Suppose X goes to the shop of Y, a druggist, and asks Y to sell him some baking soda. Y hands him a sealed packet which he tells him contains baking soda and charges him a few cents. X honestly believes that the packet contains baking soda but in fact it contains heroin. X puts the package in his pocket, takes it home and later puts it in a cupboard in his bathroom. There would seem to be no doubt that X has had actual manual and physical possession of the package and that he continues to have possession of the package while it is in his cupboard. The main question raised on this appeal is whether, in the supposed circumstances, X would be guilty of the crime of having heroin in his possession?

. . . .

In *Reynolds v. G.H. Austin & Sons Ltd.*, [1951] 2 K.B. 135, Devlin J. says at pp. 147-8:

> It has always been a principle of the common law that *mens rea* is an essential element in the commission of any criminal offence against the common law. In the case of statutory offences it depends on the effect of the statute. In *Sherras v. De Rutzen*, [1895] 1 Q.B. 918, 921, Wright, J., in his well-known judgment, laid it down that there was a presumption that *mens rea* was an essential ingredient in a statutory offence, but that that presumption was liable to be displaced either by the words of the statute creating the offence or by the subject-matter with which it dealt. . . . Kennedy, L.J., in *Hobbs v. Winchester Corporation*, [1910] 2 K.B. 471, 483, thought that in construing a modern statute this presumption as to *mens rea* did not exist. In this respect, as he said, he differed from Channell, J., in the court below. But the view of Wright, J., in *Sherras v. De Rutzen* has consistently been followed. I need refer only to the dictum of Lord Goddard, C.J., in *Harding v. Price*, [1948] 1 K.B. 695, 700, "The general rule applicable to criminal cases is *actus non facit reum nisi mens sit rea*, and I venture to repeat what I said in *Brend v. Wood* (1946), 62 T.L.R. 462, 463, 'It is of the utmost importance for the protection of the liberty of the subject that a court should always bear in mind that, unless a statute either clearly or by necessary implication rules out *mens rea* as a constituent part of a crime, the court should not find a man guilty of an offence against the criminal law unless he has a guilty mind.' "

In *R. v. Tolson* (1889), 23 Q.B.D. 168 at p. 188, Stephen J. says:

> "I think it may be laid down as a general rule that an alleged offender is deemed to have acted under that state of facts which he in good faith and on reasonable grounds believed to exist when he did the act alleged to be an offence. I am unable to suggest any real exception to this rule, nor has one ever been suggested to me.

And adds at p. 189:

> Of course, it would be competent to the legislature to define a crime in such a way as to make the existence of any state of mind immaterial. The question is solely whether it has actually done so in this case.

I adhere to the opinion which, with the concurrence of my brother Nolan, I expressed in *R. v. Rees*, 115 Can. C.C. 1 at p. 11, [1956] S.C.R. 640 at p. 651 that the first of the statements of Stephen J. quoted above should now be read in the light of the judgment of Lord Goddard C.J., concurred in by Lynskey and Devlin JJ. in *Wilson v. Inyang*, [1951] 2 All E.R. 237, which, in my opinion, rightly decides that the essential question is whether the belief entertained by the accused is an honest one and that the existence or non-existence of reasonable grounds for such belief is merely relevant evidence to be weighed by the tribunal of fact in determining that essential question.

In *Watts & Gaunt v. The Queen*, 105 Can. C.C. 193 at p. 199, [1953], 1 S.C.R. 505 at p. 511, Estey J. says:

> While an offence of which *mens rea* is not an essential ingredient may be created by legislation, in view of the general rule a section creating an offence ought not to be so construed unless Parliament has, by express language or necessary implication, disclosed such an intention.

. . . .

When the decisions as to the construction of the *Opium and Narcotic Drug Act* on which the respondent relies are examined it appears that two main reasons are assigned for holding that *mens rea* is not an essential ingredient of the offence created by s. 4(1)(*d*), these being (i) the assumption that the subject-matter with which the Act deals is of the kind dealt with in the cases of which *Hobbs v. Winchester Corp.*, [1910] 2 K.B. 471, is typical and which are sometimes referred to as "public welfare offence cases", and (ii) by implication from the wording of s. 17 of the Act.

As to the first of these reasons, I can discern little similarity between a statute designed, by forbidding the sale of unsound meat, to ensure that the supply available to the public shall be wholesome, and a statute making it a serious crime to possess or deal in narcotics; the one is to ensure that a lawful and necessary trade shall be carried on in a manner not to endanger the public health, the other to forbid altogether conduct regarded as harmful in itself. As a necessary feature of his trade, the butcher holds himself out as selling meat fit for consumption; he warrants that quality; and it is part of his duty as trader to see that the merchandise is wholesome. The statute simply converts that civil personal duty into a public duty.

. . . .

Has X possession of heroin when he has in his hand or in his pocket or in his cupboard a package which in fact contains heroin but which he honestly believes contains only baking soda? In my opinion that question must be answered in the negative. The essence of the crime is the possession of the forbidden substance and in a criminal case there is in law no possession without knowledge of the character of the forbidden substance. Just as in *R. v. Ashwell* (1885), 16 Q.B.D. 190, the accused did not in law have possession of the complainant's sovereign so long as he honestly believed it to be a shilling so in my illustration X did not have possession of heroin so long as he honestly believed the package to contain baking soda. The words of Lord Coleridge C.J. in *R. v. Ashwell* at p. 225, quoted by Charles J. delivering the unanimous judgment of the Court of Criminal Appeal in *R. v. Hudson* (1943), 29 Cr. App. R. 65 at p. 71:

> "In good sense it seems to me he did not take it till he knew what he had got; and when he knew what he had got, that same instant he stole it."

might well be adapted to my illustration to read: "In good sense it seems to me he did not have possession of heroin till he knew what he had got."

. . . .

If the matter were otherwise doubtful I would be drawn to the conclusion that Parliament did not intend to enact that *mens rea* should not be an essential ingredient of the offence created by s. 4(1)(*d*) by the circumstance that on conviction a minimum sentence of six months' imprisonment plus a fine of $200 must be imposed. Counsel informed us that they have found no other statutory provision which has been held to create a crime of strict responsibility, that is to say, one in which the necessity for *mens rea* is excluded, on conviction for which a sentence of imprisonment is mandatory. The legislation dealt with in *Hobbs v. Winchester, supra,* provided that a sentence of imprisonment might, not must, be imposed on a convicted person.

. . . .

It would, of course, be within the power of Parliament to enact that a person who, without any guilty knowledge, had in his physical possession a package which he honestly believed to contain a harmless substance such as baking soda but which in fact contained heroin, must on proof of such facts be convicted of a crime and sentenced to at least six months' imprisonment; but I would refuse to impute such an intention to Parliament unless the words of the statute were clear and admitted of no other interpretation. To borrow the words of Lord Kenyon in *Fowler v. Padget* (1798), 7 Term R. 509 at p. 514, 101 E.R. 1103: "I would adopt any construction of the statute that the words will bear, in order to avoid such monstrous consequences as would manifestly ensue from the construction contended for by the defendant."

The conclusion which I have reached on the main question as to the proper construction of the word possession makes it unnecessary for me to consider the other points raised by Mr. Dubin in his argument as to the construction of s. 4(1)(d). For the above reasons I would quash the conviction on the charge of having possession of a drug.

As to the charge of selling, as is pointed out by my brother Fauteux, the appellant's version of the facts brings his actions within the provisions of s. 4(1)(f) since he and his brother jointly sold a substance represented or held out by them to be heroin; and I agree with the conclusion of my brother Fauteux that the conviction on the charge of selling must be affirmed.

. . . .

FAUTEUX J. (dissenting), ABBOTT J. (concurring): —

. . . .

The plain and apparent object of the Act is to prevent, by a rigid control of the possession of drugs, the danger to public health, and to guard society against the social evils which an uncontrolled traffic in drugs is bound to generate. The scheme of the Act is this: The importation, exportation, sale, manufacture, production and distribution of drugs are subject to the obtention of a licence which the Minister of National Health and Welfare may issue, with the approval of the Governor-General in Council, and in which the place where such operations may be carried on is stated. Under the same authority are indicated ports and places in Canada where drugs may be exported or imported, the manner in which they are to be packed and marked for export, the records to be kept for such export, import, receipt, sale, disposal and distribution. The Act also provides for the establishment of all other convenient and necessary regulations with respect to duration, terms and forms of the several licences therein provided. Without a licence, it is an offence to import or export from Canada and an offence for any one who, not being a common carrier, takes or carries, or causes to be taken or carried from any place in Canada to any other place in Canada, any drug. Druggists, physicians, dentists and veterinary surgeons stand, of course, in a privileged class; but even their dealings in drugs for medicinal purposes are the object of a particular control. Under penalties of the law, some of them have to keep records of their operations, while others have the obligation to answer inquiries in respect thereto. Having in one's possession drugs without a licence or other lawful authority, is an offence. In brief, the principle underlying the Act is that possession of drugs covered by it is unlawful; and where any exception is made to the principle, the exceptions themselves are attended with particular controlling provisions and conditions.

The enforcement sections of the Act manifest the exceptional vigilance and firmness which Parliament thought of the essence to forestall the unlawful traffic in narcotic drugs and cope effectively with the unusual difficulties standing in the way of the realization of the object of the statute. Substantive and procedural principles generally prevailing under the *Criminal Code* in favour of the subject are being restricted or excepted. The power to search by day or by night, either premises or the person, is largely extended under s. 19. Special writs of assistance are provided for under s. 22. The consideration of the provisions of ss. 4 and 17 being deferred for the moment, the burden of proof is either alleviated or shifted to persons charged with violations under ss. 6, 11, 13, 16 and 18. Minimum sentences are provided or are made mandatory, under ss. 4 and 6. Deportation of aliens found guilty is also mandatory and this notwithstanding the provisions of the *Immigration Act* [R.S.C. 1952, c. 325] or any other Act, under s. 26. And the application of the *Identification of Criminals Act* [R.S.C. 1952, c. 144], ordinarily limited to the case of indictable offences, is, by s. 27, extended to any offence under the Act.

All of these provisions are indicative of the will of Parliament to give the most efficient protection to public health against the danger attending the uncontrolled use of drugs as well as against the social evils incidental thereto, by measures generally centred and directed to possession itself of the drugs covered by the Act. The subject-matter, the purpose and the scope of the Act are such that to subject its provisions to the narrow construction suggested on behalf of appellant would defeat the very object of the Act.

. . . .

This case, amongst others, such as *R. v. Thomas Wheat, R. v. Marion Stocks*, [1921] 2 K.B. 119, is a clear authority supporting the proposition that the presumption that *mens rea* is an ingredient to an offence, as well as the defence flowing from an honest belief as to the existence of a state of facts may, by reason of the subject-matter of the Act or of the language of its provisions, or of both, cease to obtain. The *Opium and Narcotic Drug Act* comes, in my view, within these classes of Acts referred to by Wright J. in *Sherras v. De Rutzen*, *supra*.

. . . .

On the plain, literal and grammatical meaning of the words of this section, there is an absolute prohibition to be in possession of drugs, whatever be the various meanings of which the word possession may be susceptible, unless the possession is under the authority of a licence from the Minister, first had and obtained, or under other lawful authority. . . .

Appeal from conviction for possession of drug allowed; appeals from conviction for sale of a drug and finding of being an habitual criminal dismissed.

Although the majority in *Beaver* was only 3-2 it has since been accepted that all drug offences require subjective *mens rea*. In the case of offences based on possession, s. 4(3) of the *Criminal Code* now expressly requires knowledge.

R. v. CITY OF SAULT STE. MARIE

[1978] 2 S.C.R. 1299, 3 C.R. (3d) 30, 40 C.C.C. (2d) 353,
1978 CarswellOnt 24, 1978 CarswellOnt 594

DICKSON J.: — In the present appeal the court is concerned with offences variously referred to as "statutory", "public welfare", "regulatory", "absolute liability", or "strict responsibility", which are not criminal in any real sense, but are prohibited in the public interest: *Sherras v. De Rutzen*, [1895] 1 Q.B. 918. Although enforced as penal laws through the utilization of the machinery of the criminal law, the offences are in substance of a civil nature and might well be regarded as a branch of administrative law to which traditional principles of criminal law have but limited application. They relate to such everyday matters as traffic infractions, sales of impure food, violations of liquor laws, and the like. In this appeal we are concerned with pollution.

The doctrine of the guilty mind expressed in terms of intention or recklessness, but not negligence, is at the foundation of the law of crimes. In the case of true crimes there is a presumption that a person should not be held liable for the wrongfulness of his act if that act is without *mens rea*: *R. v. Prince* (1875), L.R. 2 C.C.R. 154; *R. v. Tolson* (1889), 23 Q.B.D. 168; *R. v. Rees*, 115 C.C.C. 1, [1956] S.C.R. 640; *Beaver v. The Queen*, 118 C.C.C. 129, [1957] S.C.R. 531, 26 C.R. 193; *R. v. King*, 133 C.C.C. 1, [1962] S.C.R. 746. Blackstone made the point over two hundred years ago in words still apt: "to constitute a crime against human laws, there must be, first, a vicious will; and secondly, an unlawful act consequent upon such vicious will . . .": see *Commentaries on the Laws of England* (1809), Book IV, 15th ed., c. 15, p. 21. I would emphasize at the outset that nothing in the discussion which follows is intended to dilute or erode that basic principle.

. . . .

The City of Sault Ste. Marie was charged that it did discharge, or cause to be discharged, or permitted to be discharged, or deposited materials into Cannon Creek and Root River, or on the shore or bank thereof, or in such place along the side that might impair the quality of the water in Cannon Creek and Root River, between March 13, 1972 and September 11, 1972. The charge was laid under s. 32(1) of the *Ontario Water Resources Act*, R.S.O. 1970, c. 332, [formerly *Ontario Water Resources Commission Act*, renamed by 1972, c. 1, s. 70(1)] which provides, so far as relevant, that every municipality or person that discharges, or deposits, or causes, or permits the discharge or deposit of any material of any kind into any water course, or on any shore or bank thereof, or in any place that may impair the quality of water, is guilty of an offence and, on summary conviction, is liable on first conviction to a fine of not more than $5,000 and on each subsequent conviction to a fine of not more than $10,000, or to imprisonment for a term of not more than one year, or to both fine and imprisonment.

Although the facts do not rise above the routine, the proceedings have to date had the anxious consideration of five courts. The City was acquitted in Provincial Court (Criminal Division), but convicted following a trial *de novo* on a Crown appeal. A further appeal, by the City, to the Divisional Court was allowed and the conviction quashed. The Court of Appeal for Ontario on yet another appeal directed a new trial. Because of the importance of the legal issues, this court granted leave to the Crown to appeal and leave to the City to cross-appeal.

To relate briefly the facts, the City on November 18, 1970, entered into an agreement with Cherokee Disposal and Construction Co. Ltd., for the disposal of all refuse originating in the City. Under the terms of the agreement, Cherokee became obligated to furnish a site and adequate labour, material and equipment. The site selected bordered Cannon Creek which, it would appear, runs into the Root River. The method of disposal adopted is known as the "area", or "continuous slope" method of sanitary land fill, whereby garbage is compacted in layers which are covered each day by natural sand or gravel.

Prior to 1970, the site had been covered with a number of fresh-water springs that flowed into Cannon Creek. Cherokee dumped material to cover and submerge these springs and then placed garbage and wastes over such material. The garbage and wastes in due course formed a high mound sloping steeply toward, and within 20 ft. of, the creek. Pollution resulted. Cherokee was convicted of a breach of s. 32(1) of the *Ontario Water Resources Act*, the section under which the City has been charged. The question now before the court is whether the City is also guilty of an offence under that section.

In dismissing the charge at first instance, the judge found that the City had had nothing to do with the actual disposal operations, that Cherokee was an independent contractor and its employees were not employees of the City. On the appeal *de novo* Judge Vannini found the offence to be one of strict liability and he convicted. The Divisional Court in setting aside the judgment found that the charge was duplicitous. As a secondary point, the Divisional Court also held that the charge required *mens rea* with respect to causing or permitting a discharge. When the case reached the Court of Appeal that court held that the conviction could not be quashed on the ground of duplicity, because there had been no challenge to the information at trial. The Court of Appeal agreed, however, that the charge was one requiring proof of *mens rea*. A majority of the court (Brooke and Howland JJ.A.) held there was not sufficient evidence to establish *mens rea* and ordered a new trial. In the view of Mr. Justice Lacourcière, dissenting, the inescapable inference to be drawn from the findings of fact of Judge Vannini was that the City had known of the potential impairment of waters of Cannon Creek and Root River and had failed to exercise its clear powers of control.

The divers, and diverse, judicial opinions to date on the points under consideration reflect the dubiety in these branches of the law.

. . . .

The mens rea point

The distinction between the true criminal offence and the public welfare offence is one of prime importance. Where the offence is criminal, the Crown must establish a mental element, namely, that the accused who committed the prohibited act did so intentionally or recklessly, with knowledge of the facts constituting the offence, or with wilful blindness toward them. Mere negligence is excluded from the concept of the mental element required for conviction. Within the context of a criminal prosecution a person who fails to make such inquiries as a reasonable and prudent person would make, or who fails to know facts he should have known, is innocent in the eyes of the law.

In sharp contrast, "absolute liability" entails conviction on proof merely that the defendant committed the prohibited act constituting the *actus reus* of the offence. There is no relevant mental element. It is no defence that the accused was entirely without fault. He may be morally innocent in every sense, yet be branded as a malefactor and punished as such.

Public welfare offences obviously lie in a field of conflicting values. It is essential for society to maintain, through effective enforcement, high standards of public health and safety. Potential victims of those who carry on latently pernicious activities have a strong claim to consideration. On the other hand, there is a generally held revulsion against punishment of the morally innocent.

Public welfare offences evolved in mid-19th century Britain (*R. v. Woodrow* (1846), 15 M. & W. 404, and *R. v. Stephens* (1866), L.R. 1 Q.B. 702) as a means of doing away with the requirement of *mens rea* for petty police offences. The concept was a judicial creation, founded on expediency. That concept is now firmly embedded in the concrete of Anglo-American and Canadian jurisprudence, its importance heightened by the ever-increasing complexities of modern society.

Various arguments are advanced in justification of absolute liability in public welfare offences. Two predominate. Firstly, it is argued that the protection of social interests requires a high standard of care and attention on the part of those who follow certain pursuits and such persons are more likely to be stimulated to maintain those standards if they know that ignorance or mistake will not excuse them. The removal of any possible loophole acts, it is said, as an incentive to take precautionary measures beyond what would otherwise be taken, in order that mistakes and mishaps be avoided. The second main argument is one based on administrative efficiency. Having regard to both the difficulty of proving mental culpability and the number of petty cases which daily come before the courts, proof of fault is just too great a burden in time and money to place upon the prosecution. To require proof of each person's individual intent would allow almost every violator to escape. This, together with the glut of work entailed in proving *mens rea* in every case would clutter the docket and impede adequate enforcement as virtually to nullify the regulatory acts statutes. In short, absolute liability, it is contended, is the most efficient and effective way of ensuring compliance with minor regulatory legislation and the social ends to be achieved are of such importance as to override the unfortunate by-product of punishing those who may be free of moral turpitude. In further justification, it is urged that slight penalties are usually imposed and that conviction for breach of a public welfare offence does not carry the stigma associated with conviction for a criminal offence.

Arguments of greater force are advanced against absolute liability. The most telling is that it violates fundamental principles of penal liability. It also rests upon assumptions which have not been, and cannot be, empirically established. There is no evidence that a higher standard of care results from absolute liability. If a person is already taking every reasonable precautionary measure, is he likely to take additional measures, knowing that however much care he takes, it will not serve as a defence in the event of breach? If he has exercised care and skill, will conviction have a deterrent effect upon him or others? Will the injustice of conviction lead to cynicism and disrespect for the law, on his part and on the part of others? These are among the questions asked. The argument that no stigma attaches does not withstand analysis, for the accused will have suffered loss of time, legal costs, exposure to the processes of the criminal law at trial and, however one may downplay it, the opprobrium of conviction. It is not sufficient to say that the public interest is engaged and, therefore, liability may be imposed without fault. In serious crimes, the public interest is involved and *mens rea* must be proven. The administrative argument has little force. In sentencing, evidence of due diligence is admissible and therefore the evidence might just as well be heard when considering guilt. Additionally, it may be noted that s. 198 of the *Alberta Highway Traffic Act*, R.S.A. 1970, c. 169, provides that upon a person being charged with an offence under this Act, if the Judge trying the case is of the opinion that the offence (a) was committed wholly by accident or misadventure and without negligence, and (b) could not by the exercise of reasonable care or precaution have been avoided, the Judge may dismiss the case. See also s. 230(2) [am. 1976, c. 62, s. 48] of the Manitoba *Highway Traffic Act*, R.S.M. 1970, c. H60, which has a similar effect. In these instances at least, the Legislature has indicated that administrative efficiency does not foreclose inquiry as to fault. It is also worthy of note that historically the penalty for breach of statutes enacted for the regulation of individual conduct in the interests of health and safety was minor, $20 or $25; today, it may amount to thousands of dollars and entail the possibility of imprisonment for a second conviction. The present case is an example.

Public welfare offences involve a shift of emphasis from the protection of individual interests to the protection of public and social interests: see F.B. Sayre, "Public Welfare Offenses", 33 *Columbia Law Rev.* 55 (1933); Hall, *General Principles of Criminal Law* (1947), c. 13, p. 427; R.M. Perkins, "Civil Offense", 100 *U. of Pa. L. Rev.* 832 (1952); Jobson, "Far From Clear", 18 *Crim. L.Q.* 294 (1975-76). The unfortunate tendency in many past cases has been to see the choice as between two stark alternatives: (i) full *mens rea*; or (ii) absolute liability. In respect of public welfare offences (within which category pollution offences fall) where full *mens rea* is not required, absolute liability has often been imposed. English jurisprudence has consistently maintained this dichotomy: see "Criminal Law, Evidence and Procedure", 11 Hals., 4th ed., pp. 20-2, para. 18. There has, however, been an attempt in Australia, in many Canadian Courts, and indeed in England, to seek a middle position, fulfilling the goals of public welfare offences while still not punishing the entirely blameless. There is an increasing and impressive stream of authority which holds that where an offence does not require full *mens rea*, it is nevertheless a good defence for the defendant to prove that he was not negligent.

Dr. Glanville Williams has written: "There is a half-way house between *mens rea* and strict responsibility which has not yet been properly utilized, and that is responsibility for negligence" (*Criminal Law: General Part*, 2nd ed. (1961), p. 262.) Morris and Howard, in *Studies in Criminal Law* (1964), p. 200, suggest that strict responsibility might with advantage be replaced by a doctrine of responsibility for negligence strengthened by a shift in the burden of proof. The defendant would be allowed to exculpate himself by proving affirmatively that he was not negligent. Professor Howard ("Strict Responsibility in the High Court of Australia", 76 *L.Q.R.* 547 (1960)) offers the comment that English law of strict responsibility in minor statutory offences is distinguished only by its irrationality, and then has this to say in support of the position taken by the Australian High Court, at p. 548:

> Over a period of nearly sixty years since its inception the High Court has adhered with consistency to the principle that there should be no criminal responsibility without fault, however minor the offence. It has done so by utilizing the very half-way house to which Dr. Williams refers, responsibility for negligence.

In his work, "Public Welfare Offenses", at p. 78, Professor Sayre suggests that if the penalty is really slight involving, for instance, a maximum fine of $25, particularly if adequate enforcement depends upon wholesale prosecution, or if the social danger arising from violation is serious, the doctrine of basing liability upon mere activity rather than fault, is sound. He continues, however, at p. 79:

> On the other hand, some public welfare offenses involve a possible penalty of imprisonment or heavy fine. In such cases it would seem sounder policy to maintain the orthodox requirement of a guilty mind but to shift the burden of proof to the shoulders of the defendant to establish his lack of a guilty intent if he can. For public welfare offenses defendants may be convicted by proof of the mere act of violation; but, if the offense involves a possible prison penalty, the defendant should not be denied the right of bringing forward affirmative evidence to prove that the violation was the result of no fault on his part.

and at p. 82:

> It is fundamentally unsound to convict a defendant for a crime involving a substantial term of imprisonment without giving him the opportunity to prove that his action was due to an honest and reasonable mistake of fact or that he acted without guilty intent. If the public danger is widespread and serious, the practical situation can be met by shifting to the shoulders of the defendant the burden of proving a lack of guilty intent.

The doctrine proceeds on the assumption that the defendant could have avoided the *prima facie* offence through the exercise of reasonable care and he is given the opportunity of establishing, if he can, that he did in fact exercise such care.

The case which gave the lead in this branch of the law is the Australian case of *Proudman v. Dayman* (1941), 67 C.L.R. 536, where Dixon J., said, at p. 540:

> It is one thing to deny that a necessary ingredient of the offence is positive knowledge of the fact that the driver holds no subsisting licence. It is another to say that an honest belief founded on reasonable grounds that he is licensed cannot exculpate a person who permits him to drive. As a general rule an honest and reasonable belief in a state of facts which, if they existed, would make the defendant's act innocent affords an excuse for doing what would otherwise be an offence.

This case, and several others like it, speak of the defence as being that of reasonable mistake of fact. The reason is that the offences in question have generally turned on the possession by a person or place of an unlawful status, and the accused's defence was that he reasonably did not know of this status: *e.g.*, permitting an unlicensed person to drive, or lacking a valid licence oneself, or being the owner of property in a dangerous condition. In such cases, negligence consists of an unreasonable failure to know the facts which constitute the offence. It is clear, however, that in principle the defence is that all reasonable care was taken. In other circumstances, the issue will be whether the accused's behaviour was negligent in bringing about the forbidden event when he knew the relevant facts. Once the defence of reasonable mistake of fact is accepted, there is no barrier to acceptance of the other constituent part of a defence of due diligence.

The principle which has found acceptance in Australia since *Proudman v. Dayman, supra,* has a place also in the jurisprudence of New Zealand: see *The Queen v. Strawbridge,* [1970] N.Z.L.R. 909; *The King v. Ewart* (1905), 25 N.Z.L.R. 709.

. . . .

[The Court then reviewed a number of Canadian decisions.]

We have the situation therefore in which many courts of this country, at all levels, dealing with public welfare offences favour (i) *not* requiring the Crown to prove *mens rea*, (ii) rejecting the notion that liability inexorably follows upon mere proof of the *actus reus*, excluding any possible defence. The courts are following the lead set in Australia many years ago and tentatively broached by several English Courts in recent years.

It may be suggested that the introduction of a defence based on due diligence and the shifting of the burden of proof might better be implemented by legislative act. In answer, it should be recalled that the concept of absolute liability and the creation of a jural category of public welfare offences are both the product of the judiciary and not of the Legislature. The development to date of this defence, in the numerous decisions I have referred to, of courts in this country as well as in Australia and New Zealand, has also been the work of judges. The present case offers the opportunity of consolidating and clarifying the doctrine.

The correct approach, in my opinion, is to relieve the Crown of the burden of proving *mens rea*, having regard to *Pierce Fisheries* and to the virtual impossibility in most regulatory cases of proving wrongful intention. In a normal case, the accused alone will have knowledge of what he has done to avoid the breach and it is not improper to expect him to come forward with the evidence of due diligence. This is particularly so when it is alleged, for example, that pollution was caused by the activities of a large and complex corporation. Equally, there is nothing wrong with rejecting absolute liability and admitting the defence of reasonable care.

In this doctrine it is not up to the prosecution to prove negligence. Instead, it is open to the defendant to prove that all due care has been taken. This burden falls upon the defendant as he is the only one who will generally have the means of proof. This would not seem unfair as the alternative is absolute liability which denies an accused any defence whatsoever. While the prosecution must prove beyond a reasonable doubt that the defendant committed the prohibited act, the defendant must only establish on the balance of probabilities that he has a defence of reasonable care.

I conclude, for the reasons which I have sought to express, that there are compelling grounds for the recognition of three categories of offences rather than the traditional two:

1. Offences in which *mens rea*, consisting of some positive state of mind such as intent, knowledge, or recklessness, must be proved by the prosecution either as an inference from the nature of the act committed, or by additional evidence.

2. Offences in which there is no necessity for the prosecution to prove the existence of *mens rea*; the doing of the prohibited act *prima facie* imports the offence, leaving it open to the accused to avoid liability by proving that he took all reasonable care. This involves consideration of what a reasonable man would have done in the circumstances. The defence will be available if the accused reasonably believed in a mistaken set of facts which, if true, would render the act or omission innocent, or if he took all reasonable steps to avoid the particular event. These offences may properly be called offences of strict liability. Mr. Justice Estey so referred to them in *Hickey's* case.

3. Offences of absolute liability where it is not open to the accused to exculpate himself by showing that he was free of fault.

Offences which are criminal in the true sense fall in the first category. Public welfare offences would, *prima facie*, be in the second category. They are not subject to the presumption of full *mens rea*. An offence of this type would fall in the first category only if such words as "wilfully", "with intent", "knowingly", or "intentionally" are contained in the statutory provision creating the offence. On the other hand, the principle that punishment should in general not be inflicted on those without fault applies. Offences of absolute liability would be those in respect of which the Legislature had made it clear that guilt would follow proof merely of the proscribed act. The over-all regulatory pattern adopted by the Legislature, the subject-matter of the legislation, the importance of the penalty, and the precision of the language used will be primary considerations in determining whether the offence falls into the third category.

Ontario Water Resources Act, s. 32(1)

Turning to the subject-matter of s. 32(1) — the prevention of pollution of lakes, rivers and streams   it is patent that this is of great public concern. Pollution has always been unlawful and, in itself, a nuisance: *Groat v. City of Edmonton*, [1928] 3 D.L.R. 725, [1928] S.C.R. 522. A riparian owner has an inherent right to have a stream of water "come to him in its natural state, in flow, quantity and quality": *Chasemore v. Richards* (1859), 7 H.L. Cas. 349 at p. 382. Natural streams which formerly afforded "pure and healthy" water for drinking or swimming purposes become little more than cesspools when riparian factory owners and municipal corporations discharge into them filth of all descriptions. Pollution offences are undoubtedly public welfare offences enacted in the interests of public health. There is thus no presumption of a full *mens rea*.

There is another reason, however, why this offence is not subject to a presumption of *mens rea*. The presumption applies only to offences which are "criminal in the true sense", as Ritchie J., said in *the Queen v. Pierce Fisheries, supra*, at p. 199 C.C.C., p. 597 D.L.R., p. 13 S.C.R. The *Ontario Water Resources Act* is a provincial statute. If it is valid provincial legislation (and no suggestion was made to the contrary), then it cannot possibly create an offence which is criminal in the true sense.

The present case concerns the interpretation of two troublesome words frequently found in public welfare statutes: "cause" and "permit". These two words are troublesome because neither denotes clearly either full *mens rea* nor absolute liability. It is said that a person could not be said to be permitting something unless he knew what he was permitting. This is an over-simplification. There is authority both ways, indicating that the courts are uneasy with the traditional dichotomy. Some authorities favour the position that "permit" does not import *mens rea*; see *Millar v. The Queen* (1954), 107 C.C.C. 321, 17 C.R. 293; *R. v. Royal Canadian Legion* (1971), 4 C.C.C. (2d) 196; *R. v. Teperman & Sons Ltd.*, [1968] 4 C.C.C. 67; *R. v. Jack Cewe Ltd.* (1975), 23 C.C.C. (2d) 237; *Browning v. J.W.H. Watson (Rochester) Ltd.*, [1953] 1 W.L.R. 1172; *Lyons v. May*, [1948] 2 All E.R. 1062; *Korten v. West Sussex County Council* (1903) , 72 L.J.K.B. 514. For a *mens rea* construction see *James & Son Ltd. v. Smee*, [1955] 1 Q.B. 78; *Somerset v. Hart* (1884), 12 Q.B.C. 360; *Grays Haulage Co. Ltd. v. Arnold*, [1966] 1 All E.R. 896; Smith & Hogan, *Criminal Law*, 3rd ed. (1973), p. 87; Edwards, *Mens Rea and Statutory Offences* (1955), pp. 98-119. The same is true of "cause". For a non-*mens rea* construction, see *R. v. Peconi* (1907), 1 C.C.C. (2d) 213; *Alphacell Ltd. v. Woodward*, [1972] A.C. 824; *Sopp v. Long*, (1969) 1 All E.R. 855; *Laird v. Dobell*, [1906] 1 K.B. 131; *Korten v. West Sussex County Council, supra*; *Shave v. Rosner*, [1954] 2 W.L.R. 1057. Others say that "cause" imports a requirement for a *mens rea*: see *Lovelace v. D.P.P.*, [1954] 3 All E.R. 481; *Ross Hillman Ltd. v. Bond*, [1974] 2 All E.R. 287; Smith and Hogan, *Criminal Law*, pp, 89-90.

The Divisional Court of Ontario relied on these latter authorities in concluding that s. 32(1) created a *mens rea* offence.

The conflict in the above authorities, however, shows that in themselves the words "cause" and "permit" fit much better into an offence of strict liability than either full *mens rea* or absolute liability. Since s. 32(1) creates a public welfare offence, without a clear indication that liability is absolute, and without any words such as "knowingly" or "wilfully" expressly to import *mens rea*, application of the criteria which I have outlined above undoubtedly places the offence in the category of strict liability.

Proof of the prohibited act *prima facie* imports the offence, but the accused may avoid liability by proving that he took reasonable care. I am strengthened in this view by the recent case of *R. v. Servico Ltd.* (1977), 2 Alta. L.R. (2d) 388, in which the Appellate Division of the Alberta Supreme Court held that an offence of "permitting" a person under 18 years to work during prohibited hours was an offence of strict liability in the sense which I have described. It also will be recalled that the decisions of many lower courts which have considered s. 32(1) have rejected absolute liability as the basis for the offence of causing or permitting pollution, and have equally rejected full *mens rea* as an ingredient of the offence.

New trial ordered.

The distinction between crimes and regulatory offences was central to the decision in *Sault Ste. Marie (City)*. It was revisited by Mr. Justice Cory in a minority concurring judgment in *Wholesale Travel Group Inc.* That decision's complex rulings on the issue of fault and reverse onus for regulatory offences will soon be revisited in these materials.

Do you find Mr. Justice Cory's approach to distinguishing regulatory offences persuasive?

R. v. WHOLESALE TRAVEL GROUP INC.

[1991] 3 S.C.R. 154, 8 C.R. (4th) 145, 67 C.C.C. (3d) 193,
1991 CarswellOnt 117, 1991 CarswellOnt 1029

The accused corporation, a travel agency, was charged with various counts of misleading advertising contrary to what is now s. 60(2) of the *Competition Act*. Although that offence carries a sentence on conviction on indictment to a fine in the discretion of the court and to imprisonment for five years or to both and on summary conviction to a fine of $25,000 or to imprisonment for one year or both, Mr. Justice Cory nevertheless characterized it as a regulatory offence as follows:

CORY J. (L'HEUREUX-DUBÉ J. concurring): —

. . . .

The Rationale for the Distinction

It has always been thought that there is a rational basis for distinguishing between crimes and regulatory offences. Acts or actions are criminal when they constitute conduct that is, in itself, so abhorrent to the basic values of human society that it ought to be prohibited completely. Murder, sexual assault, fraud, robbery and theft are all so repugnant to society that they are universally recognized as crimes. At the same time, some conduct is prohibited, not because it is inherently wrongful, but because unregulated activity would result in dangerous conditions being imposed upon members of society, especially those who are particularly vulnerable.

The objective of regulatory legislation is to protect the public or broad segments of the public (such as employees, consumers and motorists, to name but a few) from the potentially adverse effects of otherwise lawful activity. Regulatory legislation involves a shift of emphasis from the protection of individual interests and the deterrence and punishment of acts involving moral fault to the protection of public and societal interests. While criminal offences are usually designed to condemn and punish past, inherently wrongful conduct, regulatory measures are generally directed to the prevention of future harm through the enforcement of minimum standards of conduct and care.

It follows that regulatory offences and crimes embody different concepts of fault. Since regulatory offences are directed primarily not to conduct itself but to the consequences of conduct, conviction of a regulatory offence may be thought to import a significantly lesser degree of culpability than conviction of a true crime. The concept of fault in regulatory offences is based upon a reasonable care standard and, as such, does not imply moral blameworthiness in the same manner as criminal fault. Conviction for breach of a regulatory offence suggests nothing more than that the defendant has failed to meet a prescribed standard of care.

That is the theory, but, like all theories, its application is difficult. For example, is the single mother who steals a loaf of bread to sustain her family more blameworthy than the employer who, through negligence, breaches regulations and thereby exposes his employees to dangerous working conditions, or the manufacturer who, as a result of negligence, sells dangerous products or pollutes the air and waters by its plant? At this stage it is sufficient to bear in mind that those who breach regulations may inflict serious harm on large segments of society. Therefore, the characterization of an offence as regulatory should not be thought to make light of either the potential harm to the vulnerable or the responsibility of those subject to regulation to ensure that the proscribed harm does not occur. It should also be remembered that, as social values change, the degree of moral blameworthiness attaching to certain conduct may change as well.

Nevertheless there remains, in my view, a sound basis for distinguishing between regulatory and criminal offences. The distinction has concrete theoretical and practical underpinnings and has proven to be a necessary and workable concept in our law. Since *Sault Ste. Marie*, this court has reaffirmed the distinction. Most recently, in *Thomson Newspapers Ltd. v. Canada (Director of Investigation and Research*, [1990] 1 S.C.R. 425, 76 C.R. (3d) 129, 54 C.C.C. (3d) 417, at pp. 510-511 [S.C.R., p. 209 C.R.], Justice La Forest adopted the following statement of the Law Reform Commission of Canada (Criminal Responsibility for Group Action, Working Paper No. 16 1976, at p. 12):

> [The regulatory offence] is not primarily concerned with values, but with results. While values necessarily underlie all legal prescriptions, the regulatory offence really gives expression to the view that it is expedient for the protection of society and for the orderly use and sharing of society's resources that people act in a prescribed manner in prescribed situations, or that people take prescribed standards of care to avoid risks of injury. The object is to induce compliance with rules for the overall benefit of society.

B. The Fundamental Importance of Regulatory Offences in Canadian Society

Regulatory measures are the primary mechanisms employed by governments in Canada to implement public policy objectives. What is ultimately at stake in this appeal is the ability of federal and provincial governments to pursue social ends through the enactment and enforcement of public welfare legislation.

Some indication of the prevalence of regulatory offences in Canada is provided by a 1974 estimate by the Law Reform Commission of Canada. The commission estimated that there were, at that time, approximately 20,000 regulatory offences in an average province, plus an additional 20,000 regulatory offences at the federal level. By 1983, the commission's estimate of the federal total had reached 97,000. There is every reason to believe that the number of public welfare offences at both levels of government has continued to increase.

Statistics such as these make it obvious that government policy in Canada is pursued principally through regulation. It is through regulatory legislation that the community seeks to implement its larger objectives and to govern itself and the conduct of its members. The ability of the government effectively to regulate potentially harmful conduct must be maintained.

It is difficult to think of an aspect of our lives that is not regulated for our benefit and for the protection of society as a whole. From cradle to grave, we are protected by regulations; they apply to the doctors attending our entry into this world and to the morticians present at our departure. Every day, from waking to sleeping, we profit from regulatory measures which we often take for granted. On rising, we use various forms of energy whose safe distribution and use are governed by regulation. The trains, buses and other vehicles that get us to work are regulated for our safety. The food we eat and the beverages we drink are subject to regulation for the protection of our health.

In short, regulation is absolutely essential for our protection and well-being as individuals, and for the effective functioning of society. It is properly present throughout our lives. The more complex the activity, the greater the need for and the greater our reliance upon regulation and its enforcement. For example, most people would have no idea what regulations are required for air transport or how they should be enforced. Of necessity, society relies on government regulation for its safety.

II. The Offence in the Present Case

Competition legislation generally

The offence of misleading advertising with which Wholesale Travel is charged is found in the *Competition Act* (the "Act"). This Act, like its predecessor, the *Combines Investigation Act*, is aimed at regulating unacceptable business activity. In *General Motors of Canada Ltd. v. City National Leasing*

Ltd., [1989] 1 S.C.R. 641, Dickson C.J.C. held that the Act embodied a complex scheme of economic regulation, the purpose of which is to eliminate activities that reduce competition in the marketplace.

The nature and purpose of the Act was considered in greater detail in *Thomson Newspapers*, *supra*. La Forest J. pointed out that the Act is aimed at regulating the economy and business with a view to preserving competitive conditions which are crucial to the operation of a free market economy. He observed that the Act was not concerned with "real crimes" but with regulatory or public welfare offences. He put the position this way, at p. 510 [S.C.R., pp. 199-200 C.R.]:

> At bottom, the Act is really aimed at the regulation of the economy and business, with a view to the preservation of the competitive conditions which are crucial to the operation of a free market economy. This goal has obvious implications for Canada's material prosperity. It also has broad political overtones in that it is aimed at preventing concentration of power ... It must be remembered that private organizations can be just as oppressive as the state when they gain such a dominant position within their sphere of operations that they can effectively force their will upon others.
>
> *The conduct regulated or prohibited by the Act is not conduct which is by its very nature morally or socially reprehensible. It is instead conduct we wish to discourage because of our desire to maintain an economic system which is at once productive and consistent with our values of individual liberty. It is, in short, not conduct which would be generally regarded as by its very nature criminal and worthy of criminal sanction. It is conduct which is only criminal in the sense that it is in fact prohibited by law.* One's view of whether it should be so proscribed is likely to be functional or utilitarian, in the sense that it will be based on an assessment of the desirability of the economic goals to which combines legislation is directed or its potential effectiveness in achieving those goals. *It is conduct which is made criminal for strictly instrumental reasons.* [Emphasis added.]

These decisions make it clear that the *Competition Act* in all its aspects is regulatory in character.

The Offence of False or Misleading Advertising

Is the offence of false or misleading advertising regulatory in nature? It seems to me that the fact that the provision is located within a comprehensive regulatory framework would ordinarily be sufficient to demonstrate its regulatory nature. Several other considerations point to the same conclusion.

The offence of misleading advertising has existed in Canada since 1914. It is not without significance that it was, in 1969, transferred from the *Criminal Code* to the *Combines Investigation Act*, a step which confirms the regulatory nature of the offence. The provision was amended in 1975 to provide for a defence of due diligence, converting the offence from absolute to strict liability.

It is true that the availability of imprisonment as a sanction for breach of a statute might be taken to indicate that the provision is criminal in nature. However, this fact is not itself dispositive of the character of an offence. Rather, one must consider the conduct addressed by the legislation and the purposes for which such conduct is regulated. This view was most recently expressed by La Forest J. in *Thomson Newspapers, supra,* at p. 509 [S.C.R., p. 129 C.R.]. He noted that many regulatory offences provide for imprisonment in order to ensure compliance with the terms of the statute and thereby achieve the regulatory goal.

The appellant has argued that conviction for the offence of false advertising carries a stigma of dishonesty, with the inference that the accused falsely advertised for the purposes of obtaining economic advantage. It is said that nothing could be more damaging to a business than the implication that it has made dishonest representations. In my view, however, the offence does not focus on dishonesty but rather on the harmful consequences of otherwise lawful conduct. Conviction suggests only that the defendant has made a representation to the public which was in fact misleading, and that the defendant was unable to establish the exercise of due diligence in preventing the error. This connotes a fault element of negligence rather than one involving moral turpitude. Thus, any stigma that might flow from a conviction is very considerably diminished.

In summary, the offence of false advertising possesses the essential characteristics which distinguish regulatory offences from those which are truly criminal. Accordingly, it should be considered to be a regulatory offence rather than a crime in the ordinary sense.

. . . .

[His Lordship further held that the contextual approach to *Charter* interpretation required that regulatory and criminal offences be treated differently for the purposes of *Charter* review.]

Before proceeding to the substantive analysis, however, it is necessary to consider the justifications for differential treatment. They are two-fold: the first relates to the distinctive nature of regulatory activity, while the second acknowledges the fundamental need to protect the vulnerable through regulatory legislation.

1. *The Licensing Justification*

Those who argue against differential treatment for regulatory offences assert that there is no valid reason to distinguish between the criminal and regulatory accused. Each, it is said, is entitled in law to the same procedural and substantive protections. This view assumes equality of position between criminal and regulatory defendants; that is to say, it assumes that each starts out from a position of equal knowledge, volition and "innocence". The argument against differential treatment further suggests that differentiating between the regulatory and criminal defendants implies the subordination and sacrifice of the regulatory accused to the interests of the community at large. Such a position, it is argued, contravenes our basic concern for individual dignity and our fundamental belief in the importance of the individual. It is these assumptions which the licensing justification challenges.

Criminal law is rooted in the concepts of individual autonomy and free will and the corollary that each individual is responsible for his or her conduct. It assumes that all persons are free actors, at liberty to choose how to regulate their own actions in relation to others. The criminal law fixes the outer limits of acceptable conduct, constraining individual freedom to a limited degree in order to preserve the freedom of others. Thus, the basis of criminal responsibility is that the accused person has made a deliberate and conscious choice to engage in activity prohibited by the *Criminal Code*. The accused person who is convicted of an offence will be held responsible for his or her actions, with the result that the opprobrium of society will attach to those acts and any punishment imposed will be considered to be deserved.

The licensing argument is directed to this question of choice. Thus, while in the criminal context, the essential question to be determined is whether the accused has made the choice to act in the manner alleged in the indictment, the regulated defendant is, by virtue of the licensing argument, assumed to have made the choice to engage in the regulated activity. The question then becomes not whether the defendant chose to enter the regulated sphere but whether, having done so, the defendant has fulfilled the responsibilities attending that decision. Professor Genevra Richardson puts the position this way in "Strict Liability for Regulatory Crime: the Empirical Research," [1987] Crim. L.R. 295, at pp. 295-296:

> [I]t can be argued that the strict liability regulatory offender is not a "blameless innocent". By indulging in the regulated activity she has voluntary adopted the risks of regulatory infraction and her supposed "innocence" flows from the law's traditional tendency to view the criminal act "only in the context of its immediate past".

The licensing concept rests on the view that those who choose to participate in regulated activities have, in doing so, placed themselves in a responsible relationship to the public generally and must accept the consequences of that responsibility. Therefore, it is said, those who engage in regulated activity should, as part of the burden of responsible conduct attending participation in the regulated field, be deemed to have accepted certain terms and conditions applicable to those who act within the regulated sphere. Foremost among these implied terms is an undertaking that the conduct of the regulated actor will comply with and maintain a certain minimum standard of care.

The licensing justification is based not only on the idea of a conscious choice being made to enter a regulated field, but also on the concept of control. The concept is that those persons who enter a regulated field are in the best position to control the harm which may result, and that they should therefore be held responsible for it. A compelling statement of this view is found in the decision of the United States Supreme Court in *Morissette v. United States*, 342 U.S. 246, 72 S.Ct. 240 (Mich., 1952), where the court stated, at p. 256 [U.S.]:

The accused, if he does not will the violation, usually is in a position to prevent it with no more care than society might reasonably expect and no more exertion than it might reasonably exact from one who assumed his responsibilities.

The licensing justification may not apply in all circumstances to all offenders. That is, there are some cases in which the licensing argument may not apply so as to permit the imputation to an accused of choice, knowledge and implied acceptance of regulatory terms and conditions. This may occur, for instance, where the nature of the regulated conduct is so innocuous that it would not trigger in the mind of a reasonable person the possibility that the conduct was regulated.

The nature of the regulated conduct will itself go far to determining whether the licensing argument applies. It is useful to distinguish between conduct which, by virtue of its inherent danger or the risk it engenders for others, would generally alert a reasonable person to the probability that the conduct would be regulated, from that conduct which is so mundane and apparently harmless that no thought would ordinarily be given to its potentially regulated nature. In the latter circumstances, the licensing argument would not apply.

. . . .

2. *The Vulnerability Justification*

The realities and complexities of a modern industrial society, coupled with the very real need to protect all of society and particularly its vulnerable members, emphasize the critical importance of regulatory offences in Canada today. Our country simply could not function without extensive regulatory legislation. The protection provided by such measures constitutes a second justification for the differential treatment, for *Charter* purposes, of regulatory and criminal offences.

This court has on several occasions observed that the *Charter* is not an instrument to be used by the well-positioned to roll back legislative protections enacted on behalf of the vulnerable. This principle was first enunciated by Dickson C.J.C. for the majority in *R. v. Videoflicks Ltd.*, (sub nom. *R. v. Edwards Books & Art Ltd.*), [hereinafter "*Edwards Books*"], [1986] 2 S.C.R. 713, 55 C.R. (3d) 193, 30 C.C.C. (3d) 385. He wrote, at p. 779 [S.C.R., p. 241 C.R.]:

In interpreting and applying the *Charter* I believe that the courts must be cautious to ensure that it does not simply become an instrument of better situated individuals to roll back legislation which has as its object the improvement of the condition of less advantaged persons.

The same principle has been repeated and emphasized in *Irwin Toy Ltd. v. Quebec (Attorney General)*, [1989] 1 S.C.R. 927, at p. 993, and in *Slaight Communications Inc. v. Davidson*, [1989] 1 S.C.R. 1038, at p. 1051. This principle recognizes that much government regulation is designed to protect the vulnerable. It would be unfortunate indeed if the *Charter* were used as a weapon to attack measures intended to protect the disadvantaged and comparatively powerless members of society. It is interesting to observe that in the United States, courts struck down important components of the program of regulatory legislation known as "the New Deal". This so-called *"Lochner* era" is now almost universally regarded by academic writers as a dark age in the history of the American Constitution.

Regulatory legislation is essential to the operation of our complex industrial society; it plays a legitimate and vital role in protecting those who are most vulnerable and least able to protect themselves. The extent and importance of that role has increased continuously since the onset of the Industrial Revolution. Before effective workplace legislation was enacted, labourers — including children — worked unconscionably long hours in dangerous and unhealthy surroundings that evoke visions of Dante's *Inferno*. It was regulatory legislation with its enforcement provisions which brought to an end the shameful situation that existed in mines, factories and workshops in the nineteenth century. The differential treatment of regulatory offences is justified by their common goal of protecting the vulnerable.

The importance of the vulnerability concept as a component of the contextual approach to *Charter* interpretation has been recognized in the employer/employee field in *Edwards Books, supra,* and *Slaight Communications, supra,* and in the sphere of commercial advertising in *Irwin Toy, supra.* The same considerations should apply whenever regulatory legislation is subject to *Charter* challenge.

In *Wholesale Travel* the Supreme Court points to the presence of moral blameworthiness as a crucial consideration in deciding whether an offence is a crime as opposed to a regulatory offence. Recall that in *Reference re Firearms Act (Canada)*, [2000] 1 S.C.R. 783, 34 C.R. (5th) 1, the Supreme Court found that moral content is not always a necessary criterion for a matter to be "criminal law". These findings are not inconsistent. In the *Firearms Reference* the Court was deciding whether the federal government, as a matter of division of powers, had the jurisdiction to create the legislation in question. The fact that a piece of legislation is "criminal law" within the meaning of s. 91(27) does not automatically mean that it creates criminal offences as opposed to regulatory offences. Indeed, the predecessor legislation to the *Competition Act* (which in *Wholesale Travel* is found to create the regulatory offence of false advertising) was the *Combines Investigation Act*, and that Act was found as a matter of division of powers to fall within federal jurisdiction as criminal law under s. 91(27): *Canadian National Transportation Ltd. v. Canada (Attorney General)*, [1983] 2 S.C.R. 206, 38 C.R. (3d) 97.

In *R. v. Stucky* (2009), 240 C.C.C. (3d) 141 (Ont. C.A.) the Court noted that in 1999 Parliament had made false or misleading advertising a *mens rea* offence under s. 52 of the federal *Competition Act* by expressly requiring knowledge or recklessness. The distinction between regulatory offences and crimes had blurred and in this case criminal law principles applied.

R. v. CHAPIN

[1979] 2 S.C.R. 121, 7 C.R. (3d) 225, 45 C.C.C. (2d) 333,
1979 CarswellOnt 39, 1979 CarswellOnt 1316

Dickson J.: —

The Facts

Mrs. Loise Chapin went duck hunting in the Balmoral marsh, near Chatham, one windy afternoon in mid-October 1976. She was accompanied by a friend whom she had not seen for some time. As they walked through the marsh they were, she testified, talking a lot and not paying attention to anything but the beautiful day. They reached a dyke road and walked along it a short distance, then along some "duck boards", five or six inches in width, placed over water and leading to a duck blind from which Mrs. Chapin intended to shoot.

Some time, and two ducks, later, Mrs. Chapin was arrested by a conservation officer of the Ontario Ministry of Natural Resources. He had been in the area and heard shots. Leaving his car, he proceeded on foot through two gates, down through a small canal gully, over scrub land and across a corn field, and finally arrived at a road leading to a small pond. The road over which Mrs. Chapin and her friend had passed earlier was approximately 12 feet in width and composed of a mixture of mud and gravel. As the conservation officer approached the pond, he observed, in the centre of the road and about ten feet from the water's edge, a small pile of soy beans, weed seeds and wheat, like the gleanings from a harvesting operation on a farm. The officer said that he was practically on top of the pile before he noticed it. It was a small pile, about a foot to a foot and a half in length, three inches wide and approximately two inches in depth. The blind from which Mrs. Chapin had been shooting was located some distance out from the edge of the pond and about 50 yards from the pile. The officer also noted grain in the water on either side of the boardwalk.

Mrs. Chapin testified that she was unaware of the presence of the grain. It was a very windy day and many things were flying around the marsh. When she walked along the duck boards, in hip waders and carrying a gun, her sole concern was to avoid falling into the water. It seems to be generally accepted that Mrs. Chapin did not know that the grain was there until it was pointed out to her by the conservation officer. Even then, she did not know what it was. She was shooting on private property belonging to the Balmoral Hunt Club, of which her husband was part owner. During the trial, there was vague reference by defence counsel to "spite baiting", but no evidence adduced to indicate by whom or in what circumstances the grain had been deposited.

The Migratory Birds Regulations

Now, it is unlawful to hunt for migratory birds within 1/4 mile of a place where bait has been deposited. Section 14 [am. SOR/73-509; SOR/75-436] of the *Migratory Birds Regulations*, SOR/71-376, reads:

> 14. (1) Subject to subsection (2), no person shall hunt for migratory game birds within one-quarter mile of any place where bait has been deposited.
>
> (2) Subsection (1) does not apply to a place where bait had been deposited, if
>
> (*a*) a game officer inspects that place and declares that it is clear of bait, and
>
> (*b*) seven days have elapsed since the inspection referred to in paragraph (*a*).
>
> (3) Where bait is deposited in a place after an inspection referred to in subsection (2), that subsection ceases to apply to that place for the remainder of the open season.
>
> (4) No person shall deposit bait in any place during the period commencing seven days before the open season applicable in that place and ending on the day immediately following the last day of the open season in that place unless that person, at least thirty days prior to placing the bait,
>
> (*a*) obtains the consent in writing of
>
> (i) every landowner and every lessee or tenant whose land is located within one-quarter mile of that place, and
>
> (ii) the Director and the Chief Game Officer of a province, and
>
> (*b*) posts in that place signs of a type and wording satisfactory to, and in a location designated by, the Director,
>
> (5) A consent obtained pursuant to paragraph (4)(*a*) is valid only in respect of the open season in respect of which it was obtained.
>
> (6) Subsection (4) does not apply to the holder of a permit referred to in section 19 or 20 who places bait
>
> (*a*) in a confined area specified in his permit, or
>
> (*b*) at a distance of not less than one-quarter mile from an area where the hunting of migratory birds is permitted for the sole purpose of feeding migratory birds lawfully in his possession.
>
> (7) For the purpose of subsection (1), any area
>
> (*a*) of standing crops, whether flooded or not,
>
> (*b*) of harvested crop land that is flooded,
>
> (*c*) where crops are properly shocked in the field where they grow, or
>
> (*d*) where grain is scattered solely as a result of normal agricultural or harvesting operations shall not be regarded as a place where bait has been deposited.

Section 12(1) of the *Migratory Birds Convention Act*, R.S.C. 1970, c. M-12, provides:

> 12. (1) Every person who violates this Act or any regulation is, for each offence, liable upon summary conviction to a fine of not more than three hundred dollars and not less than ten dollars, or to imprisonment for a term not exceeding six months, or to both fine and imprisonment.

. . . .

The case has now, by leave, reached this court. There are two preliminary observations. First, the judicial history of the case, all before the judgment of this court in *R. v. Sault Ste. Marie* (1978), 3 C.R. (3d) 30, 40 C.C.C. (2d) 353, provides an interesting example of the courts attempting to come to grips with the classic sort of regulatory offence. The three courts which have dealt with the matter to date have characterized the offence in three different ways. Walker J. P. treated it as an offence of strict liability, to which the accused could plead that she committed the offence under an honest and reasonable mistake of fact. Beardall Co. Ct. J. considered it to be one of absolute liability. The court of Appeal majority regarded it as a *mens rea* offence, while Houlden J.A. regarded it as one of absolute liability.

In *Sault Ste. Marie* at pp. 53-54, this court recognized three categories of offences.

. . . .

The Crown argues that the offence is one of absolute liability or, in the alternative, strict liability. The respondent contends that it is one requiring full *mens rea* or, if not, a strict liability offence.

Not a Mens Rea Offence

One would be hard pressed to characterize the offence created by s. 14(1) of the *Migratory Birds Regulations* as a "crime in the true sense". Violation is punishable upon summary conviction, and not by indictment. One must note the absence of the usual signals connoting *mens rea*, such as "wilfully" or "with intent". In contrast, to take an example, s. 10 of the *Migratory Birds Convention Act* commences:

> 10. Any person who wilfully refuses to furnish information or wilfully furnishes false information to a game officer. . . .

The *Migratory Birds Convention Act* is a regulatory statute enacted by the Parliament of Canada for the general welfare of the Canadian public, not to mention the welfare of the ducks. The purpose of the legislation is expressed in the preamble to the Migratory Birds Convention, which has been sanctioned, ratified and confirmed by s. 2 of the Act, and which reads in part as follows:

> Whereas many species of birds in the course of their annual migrations traverse certain parts of the Dominion of Canada and the United States; and
>
> Whereas many of these species are of great value as a source of food or in destroying insects which are injurious to forests and forage plants on the public domain, as well as to agricultural crops, in both Canada and the United States, but are nevertheless in danger of extermination through lack of adequate protection during the nesting season or while on their way to and from their breeding grounds:
>
> His Majesty the King of the United Kingdom of Great Britain and Ireland and of the British dominions beyond the seas, Emperor of India, and the United States of America, being desirous of saving from indiscriminate slaughter and of insuring the preservation of such

migratory birds as are either useful to man or are harmless, have resolved to adopt some uniform system of protection which shall effectively accomplish such objects.

Article I of the Convention, attached as a schedule to the Act, describes the migratory game birds included in the terms of the Convention. Article II provides for closed seasons, "during which no hunting shall be done except for scientific or propagating purposes under permits issued by proper authorities". Article III provides for a continuous close season on certain migratory game birds. Article IV provides for special protection to be given the wood duck and the eider duck. Article V provides for the prohibition of the taking of nests or eggs, and Art. VI for the prohibition of the shipment or export of migratory birds or their eggs during the continuance of the close season. Finally, Art. VII provides for the issuance of permits to kill migratory birds which, under extraordinary conditions, may become seriously injurious to the agricultural or other interests in any particular community.

The *Migratory Birds Convention Act* authorizes the making of *Migratory Birds Regulations* for the purpose of effecting the public welfare goals of the Migratory Birds Convention. Section 4 of the Act provides, in part:

> 4.(1) The Governor in Council may make such regulations as are deemed expedient to protect the migratory game, migratory insectivorous and migratory nongame birds that inhabit Canada during the whole or any part of the year.
> (2) Subject to the provisions of the Convention, the regulations may provide . . .
> (b) for limiting the number of migratory game birds that may be taken by a person in any specified time during the season when the taking of such birds is legal, and providing the manner in which such birds may then be taken and the appliances that may be used therefor.

It seems clear that the offence of hunting for migratory game birds within 1/4 mile of any place where bait has been deposited contrary to s. 14(1) of the *Migratory Birds Regulations* and s. 12(1) of the *Migratory Birds Convention Act* is legislation designed to protect migratory birds from indiscriminate slaughter for the general welfare of the public. It seems equally clear that s. 14(1) of the *Migratory Birds Regulations* creates a public welfare offence which is not criminal in the true sense, and it is therefore not subject to the presumption of full *mens rea*. Section 14(1) is thus not creating a new crime, but in the public interest is prohibiting an act under a penalty: *Sherras v. De Rutzen*, [1895] 1 Q.B. 918 (D.C.).

Not an Absolute Liability Offence

The language of the offence is straightforward: "No person shall. . . ." Yet there is not a strict prohibition on hunting, rather a hunt controlled within certain limits as to season, methods, and types and numbers of species taken. Nor can one ignore the controls on shipment and export of game, not the stricter controls in certain prescribed geographic areas "for the control and management of such area".

Accepting that this is a public welfare or regulatory offence, neither party mentions the approach taken by this court in *Sault Ste. Marie*, *supra*, that "public welfare offences would *prima facie* be in the second category" of strict liability. The Crown merely lists the factors suggested as relevant in *Sault Ste. Marie*, *viz.*, the overall regulatory pattern, the subject matter of the legislation, the importance of the penalty and the precision of the language, in order to move the offence out of the second category and into the third.

The Crown suggests that "the summary conviction nature of the penalty" should carry some weight. Summary conviction it may be, but one could hardly term the penalties minimal. Rather than a "small monetary fine" alone, we find a number of serious consequences upon conviction. Section 12(1) of the Act lays down a minimum fine of $10 and a maximum fine of $300, or up to six months' imprisonment, or both. (The County Court Judge imposed a fine of $100 in this case.) Other serious consequences ensue. Section 22(1) provides for a mandatory prohibition upon conviction of either holding or applying for a migratory game bird hunting permit for a period of one year from date of conviction. Further, as the respondent points out, the court may, under s. 88(2) of the *Game and Fish Act*, R.S.O. 1970, c. 186, cancel "any licence to hunt" — not just a game bird licence — and may further order no obtaining of, or application for, a hunting licence "during the period stated in the order". Nor is that all. The most serious potential consequence comes in s. 7 of the *Migratory Birds Act* itself, permitting the justice of the peace to make an order of forfeiture of the gun and any other equipment used in violation of the Act or Regulations. While the respondent employs these penalties in support of her full *mens rea* position, they certainly support the *prima facie* classification of strict liability.

The best the Crown can do to shift this offence into the category of absolute liability is to suggest that the availability of a defence of reasonable care would considerably weaken the enforcement of the legislation. This may be true, but, as Weatherston J.A. observed, the problems that may be encountered in the administration of a statute or regulation are a very unsure guide to its proper interpretation. Difficulty of enforcement is hardly enough to dislodge the offence from the category of strict liability, particularly when regard is had to the penalties that may ensue from conviction. I do not think that the public interest, as expressed in the Convention, requires that s. 14 of the Regulations be interpreted so that an innocent person should be convicted and fined and also suffer the mandatory loss of his hunting permit and the possible forfeiture of his hunting equipment, merely in order to facilitate prosecution.

The Crown contends that a person found hunting within 1/4 mile of a place where bait is deposited is guilty of an offence, to which no defence is available. On the Crown's submission, proof of making all *reasonable* efforts to ascertain the presence of the bait would be unavailing, as would proof of all *possible* efforts. This, in my view, is an untenable position. Hunting being a permitted sport, it would be a practical impossibility for a hunter to search a circular area having a diameter of 1/2 mile for the presence of illegally deposited bait before hunting. One must bear in mind the nature of the terrain over which hunting is done, as the evidence in this case discloses, and the fact that many hunters hope to get into position before first light. Is one first expected to search through swamp, bog, creeks, corn fields, over land and in water in search of illegal bait?

The case of *R. v. Pierce Fisheries Ltd.*, [1971] S.C.R. 5, 12 C.R.N.S. 272, [1970] 5 C.C.C. 193, was cited, but I do not believe that it assists the Crown. In that case, care had not been taken to acquire knowledge of the facts constituting the offence. Ritchie J. said that it would not have been a difficult matter for some officer or responsible person of the accused company to acquire knowledge of the undersize lobsters, and failure to acquire that knowledge did not afford a defence. Nor does the decision of the Ontario Court of Appeal in *R. v. Hickey*, supra, assist, having regard to the many differences between the *Ontario Highway Traffic Act*, R.S.O. 1970, c. 202, and the legislation here under consideration.

In my view, subs. (1) and (4) of s. 14 of the Regulations must be read together. Together they speak of legal baiting, the obtaining of written consents and the posting of signs to give notice of the presence of bait. Anyone who hunts within such a posted area may be more readily taken to be knowingly or recklessly in breach of the Regulations. The Regulations do not seek to impose an absolute obligation upon a hunter who innocently hunts in an unposted area within 1/4 mile of bait which has been placed illegally by a person unknown. Parliament could not have intended to afford a person hunting within 1/4 mile of an illegally baited area any less protection than that afforded a person hunting within 1/4 mile of a legally baited area. Otherwise, as counsel for Mrs. Chapin argues, an activity which is legal is rendered illegal by the illegal act of someone over whom the accused has no control. We should not assume that punishment is to be imposed without fault.

These considerations incline me to the view that the offence here under study is not one of absolute liability.

Strict Liability Offence

In my view, the offence created by s. 14(1) is one of strict liability. It is a classic example of an offence in the second category delineated in the *Sault Ste. Marie* case, *supra*. An accused may absolve himself on proof that he took all the care which a reasonable man might have been expected to take in all the circumstances or, in other words, that he was in no way negligent.

Conclusion

It remains to consider whether to dispose of the case in this court or send it back for a new trial. The respondent has to date been subjected to two trials and two appeals. She lost her hunting privileges from April to November 1977. Her gun was seized and held under seizure for some time.

The following evidence is undisputed. The hunting was done at a private club, of which the husband of the respondent was part owner and to which she had been going for some eight years. The club had a permit from the Canadian Wildlife Service to bait at the proper season, but the club had never baited ponds. The respondent played no part in the management of the marsh. The day was windy, with matter of all kinds flying about. The pile of grain was not large. It looked like a gleaning after harvesting. It lay on a mud and gravel road. Mrs. Chapin had no reason to be looking down. The conservation officer did not notice the grain until he was practically on top of it. The other grain was in the water on either side of a narrow duck walk which Mrs. Chapin had to navigate to get to the blind. There were no signs indicating that this was a baited area.

After careful reading of all the evidence, I have arrived at the conclusion reached by this count in *Thibodeau v. R.*, [1955] S.C.R. 646, 21 C.R. 265, namely, that on the evidence in the record it would have been unreasonable to convict the respondent, and that we ought not to direct a new trial.

I would accordingly dismiss the appeal. Pursuant to the terms under which leave to appeal was granted, the respondent is entitled to costs on a solicitor-and-client basis.

Appeal dismissed.

(b)   *Charter* Standards

Within a mere three years from the date of the entrenchment of the *Canadian Charter of Rights and Freedoms,* the *Sault Ste. Marie* compromise of allowing a due diligence defence for regulatory offences with a reverse onus became a minimum constitutional standard of fault for any offence which threatens the liberty interest.

REFERENCE RE SECTION 94(2) OF THE
MOTOR VEHICLE ACT (B.C.)

[1985] S.C.R. 486, 48 C.R. (3d) 289, 23 C.C.C.(3d) 289,
1985 CarswellBC 398, 1985 CarswellBC816

LAMER J. (DICKSON C.J.C., BEETZ, CHOUINARD and LE DAIN JJ.
concurring): —

The Facts

On August 16, 1982, the Lieutenant-Governor in Council of British
Columbia referred the following question to the Court of Appeal of that province,
by virtue of s. 1 of the *Constitutional Question Act*, R.S.B.C. 1979, c. 63.:

> Is s. 94(2) of the *Motor Vehicle Act*, R.S.B.C. 1979, as amended by the *Motor Vehicle
> Amendment Act, 1982*, consistent with the *Canadian Charter of Rights and Freedoms*?

On February 3, 1983, the Court of Appeal handed down reasons in answer
to the question in which it stated that s. 94(2) of the Act is inconsistent with the
Canadian Charter of Rights and Freedoms: (1983), 4 C.C.C. (3d) 243, 33 C.R.
(3d) 22. The Attorney General for British Columbia launched an appeal to this
court.

The Legislation

Motor Vehicle Act, R.S.B.C. 1979, c. 288, s. 94, as amended by the *Motor
Vehicle Act Amendment Act, 1982*, S.B.C. 1982 c. 36, s. 19:

> 94.(1) A person who drives a motor vehicle on a highway or industrial road while
>> (a) he is prohibited from driving a motor vehicle under sections 90, 91, 92 or 92.1, or
>> (b) his driver's licence or his right to apply for or obtain a driver's licence is suspended
>> under s. 82 or 92 as it was before its repeal and replacement came into force pursuant
>> to the *Motor Vehicle Amendment Act, 1982*,
> commits an offence and is liable,
>> (c) on a first conviction, to a fine of not less than $300 and not more than $2000 and
>> to imprisonment for not less than seven days and not more than six months, and
>> (d) on a subsequent conviction, regardless of when the contravention occurred, to a fine
>> of not less than $300 and not more than $2000 and to imprisonment for not less than 14
>> days and not more than one year.
>
> (2) Subsection (1) creates an absolute liability offence on which guilt is established by proof
> of driving, whether or not the defendant knew of the prohibition or suspension.

Canadian Charter of Rights and Freedoms: Constitution Act, 1982:

> S.1 The *Canadian Charter of Rights and Freedoms* guarantees the rights and freedoms
> set out in it subject only to such reasonable limits prescribed by law as can be
> demonstrably justified in a free and democratic society.

S.7 Everyone has the right to life, liberty and security of the person and the right not to be deprived thereof except in accordance with the principles of fundamental justice.

. . . .

Section 7

. . . .

The concerns with the bounds of constitutional adjudication explain the characterization of the issue in a narrow and restrictive fashion, *i.e.*, whether the terms "principles of fundamental justice" have a substantive or merely procedural content. In my view, the characterization of the issue in such fashion preempts an open-minded approach to determining the meaning of "principles of fundamental justice".

The substantive/procedural dichotomy narrows the issue almost to an all-or-nothing proposition. Moreover, it is largely bound up in the American experience with substantive and procedural due process. It imports into the Canadian context American concepts, terminology and jurisprudence, all of which are inextricably linked to problems concerning the nature and legitimacy of adjudication under the U.S. Constitution. That Constitution, it must be remembered, has no s. 52 nor has it the internal checks and balances of sections 1 and 33. We would, in my view, do our own Constitution a disservice to simply allow the American debate to define the issue for us, all the while ignoring the truly fundamental structural differences between the two constitutions. Finally, the dichotomy creates its own set of difficulties by the attempt to distinguish between two concepts whose outer boundaries are not always clear and often tend to overlap. Such difficulties can and should, when possible, be avoided.

. . . .

The task of the court is not to choose between substantive or procedural content *per se* but to secure for persons "the full benefit of the *Charter's* protection" (Dickson C.J.C. in *R. v. Big M Drug Mart Ltd.*, [1985] 1 S.C.R. 295 at 344), under s. 7, while avoiding adjudication of the merits of public policy. This can only be accomplished by a purposive analysis and the articulation (to use the words in *Curr v. The Queen*, [1972] S.C.R. 889, at p. 899) of "objective and manageable standards" for the operation of the section within such a framework.

A number of courts have placed emphasis upon the Minutes of the Proceedings and Evidence of the Special Joint Committee of the Senate and of the House of Commons on the Constitution in the interpretation of "principles of fundamental justice". . .

In particular, the following passages dealing with the testimony of federal civil servants from the Department of Justice have been relied upon:

Mr. Strayer (Assistant Deputy Minister, Public Law):

> Mr. Chairman, it was our belief that the words "fundamental justice" would cover the same thing as what is called procedural due process, that is the meaning of due process in relation to requiring fair procedure. However, it in our view does not cover the concept of what is called substantive due process, which would impose substantive requirements as to policy of the law in question.
>
> This has been most clearly demonstrated in the United States in the area of property, but also in other areas such as the right to life. The term due process has been given the broader concept of meaning both the procedure and substance. Natural justice or fundamental justice in our view does not go beyond the procedural requirements of fairness.

. . . .

> Mr. Strayer: The term "fundamental justice" appears to us to be essentially the same thing as natural justice.

Mr. Tassé (Deputy Minister) also said of the phrase "principles of fundamental justice" in testimony before the committee:

> We assume that the court would look at that much like a court would look at the requirements of natural justice, and the concept of natural justice is quite familiar to courts and they have given a good deal of specific meaning to the concept of natural justice. We would think that the court would find in that phraseology principles of fundamental justice a meaning somewhat like natural justice or inherent fairness.
>
> Courts have been developing the concept of administrative fairness in recent years and they have been able to give a good deal of consideration, certainly to these sorts of concepts and we would expect they could do the same with this.

The Honourable Jean Chrétien, then federal Minister of Justice, also indicated to the Committee that, while he thought "fundamental justice marginally more appropriate than natural justice" in s. 7, either term was acceptable to the government.

. . . .

[T]he simple fact remains that the *Charter* is not the product of a few individual public servants, however distinguished, but of a multiplicity of individuals who played major roles in the negotiating, drafting and adoption of the *Charter*. How can one say with any confidence that within this enormous multiplicity of actors, without forgetting the role of the provinces, the comments of a few federal civil servants can in any way be determinative?

. . . .

Another danger with casting the interpretation of s. 7 in terms of the comments made by those heard at the Special Joint Committee Proceedings is that, in so doing, the rights, freedoms and values embodied in the *Charter* in effect become frozen in time to the moment of adoption with little or no possibility of growth, development and adjustment to changing societal needs.

. . . .

The main sources of support for the argument that "fundamental justice" is simply synonymous with natural justice have been the Minutes of the Proceedings and Evidence of the Special Joint Committee on the Constitution and the *Bill of Rights* jurisprudence. In my view, neither the Minutes nor the *Bill of Rights* jurisprudence are persuasive or of any great force. The historical usage of the term "fundamental justice" is, on the other hand, shrouded in ambiguity. Moreover, not any one of these arguments, taken singly or as a whole, manages to overcome in my respectful view the textual and contextual analyses.

Consequently, my conclusion may be summarized as follows:

The term "principles of fundamental justice" is not a right, but a qualifier of the right not to be deprived of life, liberty and security of the person; its function is to set the parameters of that right.

Sections 8 to 14 address specific deprivations of the "right" to life, liberty and security of the person in breach of the principles of fundamental justice, and as such, violations of s. 7. They are therefore illustrative of the meaning, in criminal or penal law, of "principles of fundamental justice"; they represent principles which have been recognized by the common law, the international conventions and by the very fact of entrenchment in the *Charter*, as essential elements of a system for the administration of justice which is founded upon a belief in the dignity and worth of the human person and the rule of law.

Consequently, the principles of fundamental justice are to be found in the basic tenets and principles, not only of our judicial process, but also of the other components of our legal system.[1]

We should not be surprised to find that many of the principles of fundamental justice are procedural in nature. Our common law has largely been a law of remedies and procedures and, as Frankfurter J. wrote in *McNabb v. U.S.* 318 U.S. 332 (1942) at p. 347, "the history of liberty has largely been the history of observance of procedural safeguards". This is not to say, however, that the principles of fundamental justice are limited solely to procedural guarantees. Rather, the proper approach to the determination of the principles of fundamental justice is quite simply one in which, as Professor Tremblay has written, "future growth will be based on historical roots". ((1984), 18 U.B.C.L. Rev. 201 at 254).

Whether any given principle may be said to be a principle of fundamental justice within the meaning of s. 7 will rest upon an analysis of the nature, sources,

---

1 Editors' note. Recall that the majority in *Malmo-Levine* later decided that a principle of fundamental justice must be a legal principle for which there is societal consensus and of sufficient precision to be workable in practice.

rationale and essential role of that principle within the judicial process and in our legal system, as it evolves.

Consequently, those words cannot be given any exhaustive content or simple enumerative definition, but will take on concrete meaning as the courts address alleged violations of s. 7.

I now turn to such an analysis of the principle of *mens rea* and absolute liability offences in order to determine the question which has been put to the court in the present Reference.

Absolute Liability and Fundamental Justice in Penal Law

It has from time immemorial been part of our system of laws that the innocent not be punished. This principle has long been recognized as an essential element of a system for the administration of justice which is founded upon a belief in the dignity and worth of the human person and on the rule of law. It is so old that its first enunciation was in Latin *actus non facit reum nisi mens sit rea*.

One of the many judicial statements on the subject worth mentioning is of the highest authority, *per* Goddard C.J. in *Harding v. Price*, [1948] 1 K.B. 695 at p. 700, where he said:

> The general rule applicable to criminal cases is *actus non facit reum nisi mens sit rea*, and I venture to repeat what I said in *Brend v. Wood* (1946), 62 T.L.R. 462, 463: 'It is of the utmost importance for the protection of the liberty of the subject that a court should always bear in mind that, unless a statute either clearly or by necessary implication rules out *mens rea* as a constituent part of a crime, the court should not find a man guilty of an offence against the criminal law unless he has a guilty mind'.

This view has been adopted by this court in unmistakable terms in many cases, amongst which the better known are *Beaver v. The Queen*, [1957] S.C.R. 531, and the most recent and often quoted judgment of Dickson J. (as he then was), writing for the court in *R. v. City of Sault Ste. Marie, supra*.

This court's decision in the latter case is predicated upon a certain number of postulates one of which, given the nature of the rules it elaborates, has to be to the effect that absolute liability in penal law offends the principles of fundamental justice. Those principles are, to use the words of Dickson J., to the effect that "there is a generally held revulsion against punishment of the morally innocent". He also stated that the argument that absolute liability "violates fundamental principles of penal liability" was the most telling argument against absolute liability and one of greater force than those advanced in support thereof.

In my view it is because absolute liability offends the principles of fundamental justice that this court created presumptions against legislatures having intended to enact offences of a regulatory nature falling within that category. This is not to say, however, and to that extent I am in agreement with the Court of Appeal, that, as a result, absolute liability *per se* offends s. 7 of the *Charter*.

A law enacting an absolute liability offence will violate s. 7 of the *Charter* only if and to the extent that it has the potential of depriving of life, liberty, or security of the person.

Obviously, imprisonment (including probation orders) deprives persons of their liberty. An offence has that potential as of the moment it is open to the judge to impose imprisonment. There is no need that imprisonment, as in s. 94(2), be made mandatory.

I am therefore of the view that the combination of imprisonment and of absolute liability violates s. 7 of the *Charter* and can only be salvaged if the authorities demonstrate under s. 1 that such a deprivation of liberty in breach of those principles of fundamental justice is, in a free and democratic society, under the circumstances, a justified reasonable limit to one's rights under s. 7.

As no one has addressed imprisonment as an alternative to the non-payment of a fine, I prefer not to express any views in relation to s. 7 as regards that eventuality as a result of a conviction for an absolute liability offence; nor do I need to address here, given the scope of my finding and the nature of this appeal, minimum imprisonment, whether it offends the *Charter per se* or whether such violation, if any, is dependent upon whether it be for a *mens rea* or strict liability offence. Those issues were not addressed by the court below and it would be unwise to attempt to address them here. It is sufficient and desirable for this appeal to make the findings I have and no more, that is, that no imprisonment may be imposed for an absolute liability offence, and, consequently, given the question put to us, an offence punishable by imprisonment cannot be an absolute liability offence.

. . . .

Administrative expediency, absolute liability's main supportive argument, will undoubtedly under s. 1 be invoked and occasionally succeed. Indeed, administrative expediency certainly has its place in administrative law. But when administrative law chooses to call in aid imprisonment through penal law, indeed sometimes criminal law and the added stigma attached to a conviction, exceptional, in my view, will be the case where the liberty or even the security of the person guaranteed under s. 7 should be sacrificed to administrative expediency. Section 1 may, for reasons of administrative expediency, successfully come to the rescue of an otherwise violation of s. 7, but only in cases arising out of exceptional conditions, such as natural disasters, the outbreak of war, epidemics, and the like.

Section 94(2)

I do not take issue with the fact that it is highly desirable that "bad drivers" be kept off the road. I do not take issue either with the desirability of punishing severely bad drivers who are in contempt of prohibitions against driving. The bottom line of the question to be addressed here is: whether the Government of British Columbia has demonstrated as justifiable that the risk of imprisonment of a few innocent is, given the desirability of ridding the roads of British Columbia of bad drivers, a reasonable limit in a free and democratic society. That result is to be measured against the offence being one of strict liability open to a defence of due diligence, the success of which does nothing more than let those few who did nothing wrong remain free.

As did the Court of Appeal, I find that this demonstration has not been satisfied, indeed, not in the least.

McIntyre and Wilson JJ. gave separate concurring judgments.

In *R. v. Pontes* (1995), 41 C.R. (4th) 201, 100 C.C.C. (3d) 353, [1995] 3 S.C.R. 44, the Supreme Court reconsidered the constitutionality of the offence of driving while prohibited under s. 94 of the B.C. *Motor Vehicle Act*. This time the Court held that the offence was constitutional. A 5-4 majority classified the offence as one of absolute liability but held there was no violation of the right to life, liberty and security of the person as there was no longer any risk of imprisonment. By amendments to the B.C. *Offence Act* a person is no longer liable to imprisonment and non-payment of a fine would not result in imprisonment. The majority did, however, leave open for future consideration the issue of an absolute liability offence punishable by a fine with the possibility of imprisonment for non-payment where the legislation provided a means test for the imposition and collection of any fine. For a critical review of this complex decision see Anne-Marie Boisvert, "Innocence Morale, Diligence Raisonnable et Erreur de Droit" (1995), 41 C.R. (4th) 243 and Jill Presser, "Absolute Liability and Mistakes of Law in the Regulatory Context: *Pontes* Disappoints and Confuses" (1995), 41 C.R. (4th) 249. See also *R. v. Transport Robert*, below.

In *Lévis (Ville) c. Tétreault*, [2006] 1 S.C.R. 420, 36 C.R. (6th) 215, 207 C.C.C. (3d) 1, the Supreme Court held that regulatory vehicle offences of failure to pay registration and licence fees by the due date under the *Quebec Highway Safety Code* were properly classified as strict liability.

In writing for a unanimous court of seven justices, Justice LeBel noted that the sections in question did not place the burden of proving *mens rea* on the prosecution and included no expression of the legislature's intent to create an absolute liability offence. Applying the court's approach in *R. v. Sault Ste. Marie*, there was common law presumption that they should be characterized as strict rather than absolute, thereby affording the accused the chance of proving a due diligence defence. Absolute liability offences still exist, but they have become, said LeBel J. for the Court, an exception requiring clear proof of legislative intent.

In deciding between strict and absolute liability LeBel J. expressly rejected the inquiry added by Cory J. in *R. v. Pontes*, [1995] 3 S.C.R. 44 of asking whether the legislature intended to make a due diligence defence available. LeBel J. indicated this made the approach "harder to apply" and it was better to return to the clear framework of *Sault Ste. Marie*.

On the facts the due diligence defence raised had not been made out. Justice LeBel reasoned that the concept of diligence is based on the acceptance of a citizen's civic duty to take action to find out what his or her obligations are. Passive ignorance is not a valid defence. T did no more than state that he expected to receive a renewal notice for his licence and that he had confused the licence expiry date with the due date for paying the fees required to keep the licence valid. He proved no action or attempt to obtain information. The same was true of the company, which did nothing, even though it was aware of the date when the fees relating to the registration of its vehicle would be due. It could and should have been concerned when it did not receive a notice. Christine Boyle and Sam de Groot, "The Responsible Citizen in the City of Levis: Due Diligence and Officially Induced Error" C.R. *ibid.* at 249, suggest that this gloss will make it harder for the defence of due diligence to succeed.

The Supreme Court's strong preference for strict liability for regulatory offences is thus alive and well. There has been a tendency in recent jurisprudence for this classification issue to focus more on the *Charter* guarantee of a due diligence defence applying only where there is a risk of imprisonment. For example, in its brief endorsement judgment in *Corporation of the City of London v. Polewsky* (2005), 202 C.C.C. (3d) 257, the Ontario Court of Appeal rejected the possibility of a due diligence defence for speeding charges on the basis that there were no good policy reasons against absolute liability and that the chance of going to jail in default of payment of a fine was too remote. This decision needs to be reconsidered in light of the Supreme Court's emphasis in *City of Lévis* on the common law presumption of strict liability. Compare *R. v. Williams* (1992), 14 C.R. (4th) 218 (N.S.C.A.), where speeding offences in Nova Scotia were held to be properly classified as strict to allow for due diligence defences in appropriate cases.

In *R. v. Cancoil Thermal Corp.* (1986), 52 C.R. (3d) 188 (Ont. C.A.) the Ontario Court of Appeal considered the provincial *Occupational Health and Safety Act*, and specifically charges under s. 14 of that Act. The Court noted that the statute included a due diligence defence for ss. 14(1)(b), (c) and (d), but not for s. 14(1)(a). They took that omission to indicate that the legislature intended s. 14(1)(a) to be an absolute liability offence. However, since imprisonment was available as a penalty, s. 14(1)(a) had to be read as a strict liability offence despite the legislature's intention, in order to avoid a s. 7 *Charter* violation.

R. v. WHOLESALE TRAVEL GROUP INC.

[1991] 3 S.C.R. 154, 8 C.R. (4th) 145, 67 C.C.C. (3d) 193,
1991 CarswellOnt 117, 1991 CarswellOnt 1029

In a most complex ruling the Court determined that a due diligence defence was all that could constitutionally be required in the case of the offence of false advertising under what is now s. 52(1)(a) of the *Competition Act*, R.S.C. 1985, c. C-34.

The Court also unanimously ruled that the due diligence defence could not be watered down by a more rigorous requirement than that of reasonable care. The Court struck down the *Competition Act's* express requirement that there had to have been a prompt retraction of the advertisement before an accused could subsequently successfully rely on the due diligence defence.

The Court's conclusion on these issues is found in the judgment of Chief Justice Lamer:

Counsel for Wholesale Travel argued that the stigma attaching to a conviction of false/misleading advertising is akin to the stigma of dishonesty which attaches to a conviction of theft. Given that the stigma attaching to theft was explicitly contemplated in *Vaillancourt* as one which may well necessitate a subjective *mens rea*, it was argued that the offence of false/misleading advertising also requires an element of subjective *mens rea* in order to comply with the principles of fundamental justice. In my view, while a conviction for false/misleading advertising carries some stigma, in the sense that it is not morally neutral behaviour, it cannot be said that the stigma associated with this offence is analogous to the stigma of dishonesty which attaches to a conviction for theft. A conviction for false/misleading advertising will rest on a variety of facts, many of which will not reveal any dishonesty but, rather, carelessness and the conviction of same does not brand the accused as being dishonest. In my opinion, the same cannot be said for a conviction for theft.

Thus, while it is clear that there are some offences for which the special stigma attaching to conviction is such that subjective *mens rea* is necessary in order to establish the moral blameworthiness which justifies the stigma and sentence, the offence of false/misleading advertising is not such an offence. . .

Therefore, an element of subjective *mens rea* is not required by s. 7 of the *Charter* and the provisions in question are not inconsistent with s. 7 on the basis that they do not require intent or knowledge on the part of an accused. I turn now to the question posed above: namely, do paras. (a) through (d) of s. 37.3(2) provide an accused with a defence of due diligence?[2]

---

2 The defence read as follows:

    37.3(2) No person shall be convicted of an offence under section 36 or 36.1, if he establishes that,

        (a) the act or omission giving rise to the offence with which he is charged was the result of error;

        (b) he took reasonable precautions and exercised due diligence to prevent the occurrence of such error;

        (c) he, or another person, took reasonable measures to bring the error to the attention of the class of

Section 37.3(2) (a) through (d) sets out the only defence, under the Act, to false/misleading advertising, once it has been established that the advertisement is objectively false or misleading (i.e., once the actus reus is established). It is clear from the inclusion of the word "and" after s. 37.3(2)(c) that all four components of s. 37.3(2) must be established in order for the accused to be acquitted. While the Crown has suggested that, in certain circumstances, only paras. (a) and (b) must be fulfilled (relying on certain dicta of the Ontario Court of Appeal in *R. v. Consumers Distributing Co.*, *supra*, it is my respectful view that this is an incorrect interpretation of the provision.

Thus, the question becomes whether a situation could arise where an accused would be unable to establish all four components of s. 37.3(2) but would nonetheless be duly diligent (i.e., not negligent). If the answer to this question is yes, it means that the constitutionally required element of negligence is not fulfilled by the statutory defence contained in s. 37.3(2).

The Crown has conceded that the statutory defence afforded by s. 37.3(2) is "more restricted" than the common law defence of due diligence, but nonetheless argues that the limited nature of the statutory defence does not render it unconstitutional. Although paras. (a) and (b) of s. 37.3(2) refer specifically to an "error" and to the exercise of due diligence to prevent an "error", they, in my view, largely correspond to the usual due diligence defence. In other words, paras. (a) and (b) operate so as to provide a defence to an accused who has taken reasonable precautions to prevent false/misleading advertising and who has been duly diligent in ensuring that advertising is not false or misleading in nature. However, the additional requirement of "timely retraction" embodied in paras. (c) and (d) means that the statutory defence is considerably more narrow than the common law defence of due diligence.

An accused who did not realize, and could not reasonably have been expected to realize, that the representation in question was false or misleading until it was too late to comply with paras. (c) and (d) or who was, for some reason, unable to comply with paras. (c) and (d), but who had nonetheless taken reasonable precautions and who had exercised due diligence in preventing false/misleading advertising, would not fall within the statutory defence and would be convicted of false/misleading advertising. I agree with the majority of the Ontario Court of Appeal that paras. (c) and (d) of s. 37.3(2) could have the effect of depriving an accused of the defence of due diligence and could therefore require the conviction of an accused who was not negligent. Paragraphs (c) and (d) make the failure to undertake corrective advertising (a component of the offence of false/misleading advertising) an "offence" of absolute liability. Consequently, the constitutionally required fault level is not present in the false/misleading advertising provisions.

---

persons likely to have been reached by the representation or testimonial; and
(d) the measures referred to in paragraph (c) . . . were taken forthwith after the representation was made or the testimonial was published.

In light of the above discussion, I agree with the majority of the Court of Appeal that it is the presence of paras. (c) and (d) alone which offends s. 7 of the *Charter*. Thus, unless the limitation on s. 7 can be upheld under s. 1 of the *Charter*, these two paragraphs must be held to be of no force or effect, pursuant to s. 52(1) of the *Constitution Act*, 1982.

[The Court held that paragraphs (c) and (d) could not be upheld under s. 1. The Court accepted, under the *Oakes* test, that the legislation had a sufficiently important objective. Under the proportionality aspect of the *Oakes* test, however, the Court was not convinced that the minimal impairment branch was satisfied.]

It is not necessary to convict of false/misleading advertising those who did not undertake corrective advertising because they did not realize (and ought not to have realized) that the advertisement was false/misleading, in order to achieve the objectives set out above. If Parliament wished to encourage corrective advertising in order to meet the objectives set out above, it could have:

(a) enacted a separate offence of "failure to correct false/misleading advertising" under which an accused who discovers or who ought to have discovered that an advertisement was false or misleading is required to be duly diligent in taking the corrective measures set out in paras. (c) and (d) in order to come within the statutory defence to this offence;

or

(b) maintained the component of "failure to correct false/misleading advertising" within the existing statutory defence to false advertising, but worded paras. (c) and (d) in such a way that the requirement for corrective advertising would arise upon the accused's discovery that the advertisement was false or misleading (or upon a finding that the accused ought to have discovered that the advertisement was false/misleading).

In my view, either of these alternative means would, without convicting the innocent, achieve the objective of encouraging advertisers to undertake corrective advertising and would therefore achieve the dual objectives of protecting consumers from the effects of false advertising and of preventing advertisers from benefiting from false/misleading representations. Given that these two alternatives were clearly open to Parliament, it can be seen that the existing paragraphs are unnecessarily intrusive on constitutional rights.

While an absolute liability component to the offence of false advertising would perhaps be more effective in facilitating convictions than would the alternatives proposed above, the simple answer to this contention is that Parliament could have retained the absolute liability component and, at the same time, infringed *Charter* rights to a much lesser extent, had it not combined this absolute liability with the possibility of imprisonment. In this sense, removing the possibility of imprisonment and leaving paras. (c) and (d) unchanged was a further less intrusive means which was available to Parliament.

In a complex division, a 5-4 majority of the Court upheld the reverse legal onus associated with the due diligence defence, although no single set of reasons attracted majority support. Four judges found that the reverse legal onus violated s. 11(d) of the *Charter* and was not saved under s. 1, two judges found that it did not violate s. 11(d) in the first place, and three judges found that it violated s. 11(d) but was saved under s. 1.

LAMER C.J.C. (SOPINKA, MCLACHLIN and LA FOREST JJ. concurring) (dissenting on this point): —

. . . .

2. *As Little as Possible*

While the imposition of a persuasive burden is rationally connected to the objective, it does not, in my view, infringe constitutionally protected rights as little as is reasonably possible. The Crown has not established that it is necessary to convict those who were duly diligent in order to "catch" those accused who were *not* duly diligent.

Parliament clearly had the option of employing a mandatory presumption of negligence (following from proof of the *actus reus*) which could be rebutted by something *less* than an accused's establishing due diligence on a balance of probabilities. This option was, in fact, recommended by the Ontario Law Reform Commission in its *Report on the Basis of Liability for Provincial Offences* (Toronto, 1990). The Commission stated (at p. 48):

> With respect to the burden of proof for strict liability offences, the Commission proposes a compromise solution that balances the fundamental rights of the accused with the need for effective law enforcement. We recommend the enactment of a mandatory presumption rather than a reverse onus. In other words, *in the absence of evidence to the contrary, negligence will be presumed. The Crown will continue to bear the burden of establishing the physical element or actus reus beyond a reasonable doubt. However, in a strict liability case, it will be necessary that evidence of conduct capable of amounting to reasonable care be adduced, either by the testimony of the accused, through the examination or cross-examination of a Crown or defence witness, or in some other way. The accused will merely have an evidentiary burden and will no longer be required to satisfy the persuasive burden of establishing, on a balance of probabilities, that he was not negligent. Where evidence of reasonable care has been adduced, thereby rebutting the presumption, in order to secure a conviction the prosecution should be required to establish the accused's negligence beyond a reasonable doubt.* [Emphasis added.]

. . . .

In light of the alternative means open to Parliament, I am of the view that the use of a persuasive burden in s. 37.3(2) cannot be justified under the proportionality part of the *Oakes* test.

In summary, it is my view that the words "he establishes that" contained in s. 37.3(2) limit s. 11(*d*) of the *Charter* and cannot be upheld as a reasonable limit under s. 1. Consequently, the words "he establishes that" must be held to be of no force or effect, pursuant to s. 52(1) of the *Constitution Act, 1982*.

CORY J. (L'HEUREUX-DUBÉ J. concurring): —

. . . .

It is difficult to conceive of a situation in which a regulated accused would not be able to adduce *some* evidence giving rise to the possibility that due diligence was exercised. For instance, an environmental polluter would often be able to point to *some* measures it had adopted in order to prevent the type of harm which ultimately resulted. This might raise a reasonable doubt that it had acted with due diligence, no matter how inadequate those measures were for the control of a dangerous situation. Similarly, a wholly inadequate effort to ensure that an advertisement was true might nevertheless succeed in raising a reasonable doubt as to due diligence.

To impose such a limited onus is inappropriate and insufficient in the regulatory context. Criminal offences have always required proof of guilt beyond a reasonable doubt; the accused cannot, therefore, be convicted where there is a reasonable doubt as to guilt. This is not so with regulatory offences, where a conviction will lie if the accused has failed to meet the standard of care required. Thus, the question is not whether the accused has exercised *some* care, but whether the degree of care exercised was sufficient to meet the standard imposed. If the false advertiser, the corporate polluter and the manufacturer of noxious goods are to be effectively controlled, it is necessary to require them to show on a balance of probabilities that they took reasonable precautions to avoid the harm which actually resulted. In the regulatory context, there is nothing unfair about imposing that onus; indeed, it is essential for the protection of our vulnerable society.

. . . .

As with the s. 7 challenge, licensing considerations support the conclusion that strict liability does not violate s. 11(*d*) of the *Charter*. The licensing argument attributes to the regulated actor knowledge and acceptance, not only of the standard of reasonable care itself, but also of the responsibility to establish on a balance of probabilities the exercise of reasonable care. Acceptance of this burden is an implied term and a precondition of being allowed to engage in activity falling within the regulated sphere. Regulated actors are taken to understand that, should they be unable to discharge this burden, an inference of negligence will be drawn from the fact that the proscribed result has occurred.

I wish to emphasize, however, that the difference in the scope and meaning of s. 11(*d*) in the regulatory context does not imply that the presumption of innocence is meaningless for a regulated accused. The Crown must still prove the *actus reus* of regulatory offences beyond a reasonable doubt. Thus, the Crown must prove that the accused polluted the river, sold adulterated food, or published a false advertisement. However, once having established this beyond a reasonable doubt, the Crown is presumptively relieved of having to prove anything further. Fault is presumed from the bringing about of the proscribed result, and the onus shifts to the defendant to establish reasonable care on a balance of probabilities.

For these reasons, I conclude that the presumption of innocence as guaranteed in s. 11(*d*) of the *Charter* is not violated by strict liability offences as defined in *Sault Ste. Marie*. The imposition of a reverse persuasive onus on the accused to establish due diligence on a balance of probabilities does not run counter to the presumption of innocence, notwithstanding the fact that the same reversal of onus would violate s. 11(*d*) in the criminal context.

IACOBUCCI J. (GONTHIER and STEVENSON JJ. concurring): — [Agreeing with the result of Justice Cory's judgment, and therefore making up the majority judgment.]

· · · ·

With respect to the second requirement of *Oakes*, I agree that there is a rational connection between the desired objective and the means chosen to attain the objective. Removing the burden on the Crown to prove lack of due diligence beyond a reasonable doubt, and instead requiring the accused to establish due diligence on a balance of probabilities, is without a doubt a rational and logical way of attaining the legislative objective.

However, it is with respect to the third requirement of the *Oakes* analysis, that I respectfully disagree with the conclusions of Lamer C.J.C. This step requires a consideration of whether the means chosen impair the right or freedom in question *no more than is necessary to accomplish the desired objective*. Lamer C.J.C. is of the opinion that the use of a persuasive burden in s. 37.3(2) of the *Competition Act* cannot pass this third step of the *Oakes* analysis because of the presence of an alternative means open to Parliament that would be less intrusive on s. 11(*d*) of the *Charter* and would "go a long way" in achieving the objective. The alternative in question is the use of a "mandatory presumption of negligence" (following from the proof of the *actus reus*) which could be rebutted by something less than an accused establishing due diligence on a balance of probabilities, *i.e.*, by raising a reasonable doubt as to due diligence. With respect, I cannot agree that such a means would achieve the stated objective as effectively, nor would it go a long way in achieving it. Such a means would shift to the accused the burden of simply raising a reasonable doubt as to due diligence, and would not thereby allow the effective pursuit of the regulatory objective. It would leave the Crown the legal burden of proving facts largely within the peculiar knowledge of the accused.

For the reasons given by Cory J. in the context of his s. 11(*d*) analysis, such an alternative would in practice make it virtually impossible for the Crown to prove public welfare offences such as the one in question, and would effectively prevent governments from seeking to implement public policy through prosecution. It would also not provide effective inducement for those engaged in regulated activity to comply strictly with the regulatory scheme, including adopting proper procedures and record-keeping and might even have a contrary effect. Though such a result would be clearly advantageous to an accused, it would not be effective in avoiding the loss of convictions because the Crown could not prove facts within the particular knowledge of the accused. In sum, taking into account the particular circumstances described by Cory J. in his reasons, Parliament could *not* "reasonably have chosen an alternative means which would have achieved the identified objective as effectively": *R. v. Chaulk*, [1990] 3 S.C.R. 1303, 2 C.R. (4th) 1, 62 C.C.C. (3d) 193, at p. 1341, [S.C.R., p. 31 C.R.] per Lamer C.J.C. for the majority.

It has not yet been determined whether the majority's ruling on the question of onus can also apply to the burden of proving due diligence defences in the case of some *Criminal Code* offences. In the context of the following regulatory offence, which was accepted to be one of strict liability, consider whether it was wise that the Supreme Court decided that the accused should bear a persuasive and not merely evidentiary burden of proving due diligence:

> An elevator installation worker, employed by the elevator installation subcontractor, fell down an elevator shaft to his death at a building under construction. He had apparently arrived earlier than expected, unfastened a barrier to the shaft, and either climbed or jumped down to a wooden structure a few feet below the level of the 13th floor. The structure had been temporarily supported but was not sufficiently strong to support a person's weight. Charges were laid under the *Occupational Health and Safety Act*, R.S.O. 1980, c. 321, against the general contractor for failing to ensure that the safety measures set out in the regulations were carried out on its project, and also against the project's superintendent for failing to ensure that workers acted in accordance with the safety measures.

Compare *R. v. Ellis-Don Ltd.* (1990), 2 C.R. (4th) 118 (Ont. C.A.), in which the majority held that the accused should merely have an evidentiary burden. This ruling was reversed without full reasons by the Supreme Court of Canada, applying *Wholesale Travel* (1992), 71 C.C.C. (3d) 63 (S.C.C.). Unlike *Wholesale Travel*, the Court had here been presented with full evidence of enforcement patterns seeking to show that the reverse onus was unnecessary.

R. v. TRANSPORT ROBERT,
R. v. WILLIAM CAMERON TRUCKING
(sub. nom. R. v. 1260448 ONTARIO INC.)

(2003), 16 C.R. (6th) 136, 180 C.C.C. (3d) 254 (Ont. C.A.),
leave to appeal refused (2004), 330 N.R. 197 (note) (S.C.C.)

By the Court (McMURTRY C.J.O., ROSENBERG and MOLDAVER JJ.A.): —

The issue in these two appeals is whether it is open to the Legislature to create an absolute liability offence where there is no possibility of imprisonment or probation if the defendant is convicted. Section 84.1(1) of the *Highway Traffic Act*, R.S.O. 1990, c. H.8 (*HTA*) provides that the owner and operator of a commercial motor vehicle are guilty of an offence where a wheel becomes detached from the vehicle while it is on a highway. Subsection (5) provides that it is no defence to the charge that the defendant exercised due diligence to avoid or prevent the detaching of the wheel. The penalty for the offence is a fine of not less than $2,000 and not more than $50,000, but the defendant is not liable to imprisonment or probation as a result of the conviction or for default in payment of the fine resulting from the conviction (subsection (4)).

The defendants submit that notwithstanding the only possible penalty for this offence is a monetary one, the creation of this absolute liability offence violates the guarantee to security of the person in s. 7 of the *Canadian Charter of Rights and Freedoms* and the presumption of innocence in s. 11(d) of the *Charter*. For the following reasons we have concluded that there is no violation of s. 7 or s. 11(d). We therefore allow the Crown appeal in the *Transport Robert* case and dismiss the appeal by *William Cameron Trucking*.

In view of our conclusion on the constitutional issue, it is unnecessary to review the facts of either prosecution in any great deal. Most of the evidence adduced at the trials was led in an attempt to explain how the wheels became detached and why the defendants nevertheless acted with due diligence.

. . . .

Analysis

Section 11(d)

The argument based on s. 11(d) of the *Charter* can be dealt with quickly. As Professor Hogg points out in *Constitutional Law of Canada*, (Carswell, Toronto, 1997) vol. 2, p. 48-17, while s. 11(d) prohibits the reversal of the burden of proof of a fact that is an element of the offence, that subsection says nothing about elimination of an element. If the offence as drafted includes certain elements or if s. 7 mandates proof of a certain element as a matter of fundamental justice, placing the burden of proof of such elements on the defence may be an unconstitutional violation of s. 11(d) subject to the Crown establishing that the reversal is a reasonable limit under s. 1. However, there is no violation of s. 11(d) because the legislature has defined an offence so as to eliminate an element, or as here, a possible common law defence.

The real and only constitutional issue in this case then is whether, despite the wording of s. 84.1 of the *HTA*, s. 7 mandates that the defendants be able to defend the case on the basis of due diligence. We therefore turn to that issue.

Although the rights guaranteed by s. 7 can only be enjoyed by human beings, a corporation has standing to challenge the constitutionality of a penal provision on the basis that the provision violates the s. 7 rights of a human being: *R. v. Wholesale Travel Group Inc.*, [1991] 3 S.C.R. 154. Thus, it is open to these corporate defendants to challenge the constitutionality of s. 84.1 of the *HTA*.

As the law now stands, a defendant alleging a violation of s. 7 must establish both a violation of the right to life, liberty or security of the person and that the deprivation of that right does not accord with the principles of fundamental justice. The defendants properly concede that since there is no possibility that an individual convicted of the offence can be either imprisoned or placed on probation, s. 84.1 of the *HTA* does not violate any liberty interest protected by s. 7. They do submit, however, that the provision infringes the security of the person of an individual because it allows for the conviction of a person who is without fault. Their submission of an infringement of the security of the person is primarily based on the effect of the stigma attached to a conviction together with the large possible monetary penalty, the highest in the *HTA*.

. . . .

Security of the person and absolute liability

As indicated, the defendants submit that as a result of the combination of the high maximum fine and the stigma attached to the s. 84.1 of the *HTA* offence, a conviction for that offence results in the deprivation of security of the person. They point out that s. 84.1 was enacted in response to a number of highly publicized incidents and recommendations from inquests following the deaths of motorists when wheels came loose from commercial vehicles. They argue that a person convicted of this offence is stigmatized as someone who has exposed innocent motorists or pedestrians to the risk of serious injury or death. They also point out that the offence should be considered, not from the point of view of a large trucking company, but that of an individual, possibly an owner/operator with one commercial vehicle.

In considering the constitutionality of s. 84.1, it is necessary to take into account certain contextual factors. The section applies only to owners and operators of commercial vehicles. These persons operate for profit in a highly regulated industry. In *R. v. Ladouceur* (1990), 56 C.C.C. (3d) 22 at 39 (S.C.C.), Cory J. for the majority of the Supreme Court explained that driving is a privilege and not a right: "[I]t is fitting that governmental action be taken to prevent or at least to lessen this carnage on our highways. Proper laws and regulations are necessary to regulate the privilege of driving a motor vehicle on public thoroughfares."

Although s. 84.1 provides for a maximum fine of $50,000 and a minimum fine of $2,000, under s. 59(2) of the *Provincial Offences Act*, R.S.O. 1990, c. P.33, in exceptional circumstances, the court may impose a fine that is less than the minimum or suspend the sentence. The Crown points out that s. 84.1 has received a narrow interpretation from this court in *Ontario (Minister of Transport) v. Ryder Truck Rental Canada Ltd.* (2000), 47 O.R. (3d) 171 at para. 16 (C.A.), where it was held that the offence only applies if a wheel becomes detached and does not apply where the entire axle, hub, wheel and tire assembly comes off in one piece. The Crown also concedes that although due diligence is not available as a defence, certain other *actus reus* "defences" would be available as where the wheel became detached in a collision caused by a third party.

While the courts have not fully defined the limits of security of the person in s. 7, there are certain propositions established by the cases. In *Blencoe v. British Columbia (Human Rights Commission)*, [2000] 2 S.C.R. 307 at para. 57, Bastarache J., speaking for the majority held that, "[N]ot all state interference with an individual's psychological integrity will engage s. 7. Where the psychological integrity of a person is at issue, security of the person is restricted to 'serious state-imposed psychological stress' ". Thus, "[N]ot all forms of psychological prejudice caused by government will lead to automatic s. 7 violations." Further, there is no "generalized right to dignity, or more specifically, a right to be free from stigma" (para. 57) and, "[d]ignity and reputation are not self-standing rights. Neither is freedom from stigma" (para. 80).

In *Blencoe*, the concern was with the lengthy delay in dealing with a human rights complaint, a proceeding that according to the respondent *Blencoe*, had ruined his reputation. Bastarache J. held at para. 83 that it would only be in "exceptional cases where the state interferes in profoundly intimate and personal choices of an individual that state-caused delay in human rights proceedings could trigger the s. 7 security of the person interest . . . they would not easily include the type of stress, anxiety and stigma that result from administrative or civil proceedings."

There are admittedly distinctions between the *Blencoe* context and the context of these cases. In particular, the defendants here are charged with quasi-criminal offences and required to appear in open court to face the charges. We also take the point that this offence was enacted in response to a serious public safety issue "in the wake of several serious incidents of 'flying truck wheels' ". See *Ryder Truck Rental, supra*, at para. 1.

However, we are not convinced that a prosecution for the s. 84.1 offence engages the kind of exceptional state-induced psychological stress, even for an individual, that would trigger the security of the person guarantee in s. 7. The offence does not create a true crime, and like most regulatory offences, it focuses on the harmful consequences of otherwise lawful conduct rather than any moral turpitude. Thus, in *Wholesale Travel, supra*, at p. 224, Cory J. rejected the accused's claim that conviction for false advertising carried the stigma of dishonesty. In that case, where due diligence was available, the court characterized the fault element as one of "negligence rather than one involving moral turpitude" and thus, "any stigma that might flow from a conviction is very considerably diminished." The same can be said in this case. The s. 84.1 offence focuses on the unintended but harmful consequences of the commercial trucking industry. We reject the proposition that a defendant charged with this offence is stigmatized as a person operating in a wanton manner, heedless of the extreme dangers to life and limb posed by his or her operation. Conviction for the offence at most implies negligence and like the misleading advertising offence considered in *Wholesale Travel*, any stigma is very considerably diminished.

The diminished stigma attached to the s. 84.1 offence is not sufficient to trigger the security interest in s. 7 even when coupled with the possibility of a significant fine. This is simply not the kind of serious state-imposed psychological stress that is intended to be covered by security of the person. It is qualitatively different than the kinds of stresses that have been recognized in the cases. A review of those cases demonstrates a concern with state action that intrudes in an intimate and profound way as in *New Brunswick (Minister of Health and Community Services) v. G.(J.)*, [1999] 3 S.C.R. 46 (attempt to take a child away from its parents); *Rodriguez v. British Columbia (Attorney General)*, [1993] 3 S.C.R. 519 (criminal prohibition on assisting suicide for a desperately ill patient) and *R. v. Morgentaler*, [1988] 1 S.C.R. 30 (regulating abortion).

The right to security of the person does not protect the individual operating in the highly regulated context of commercial trucking for profit from the ordinary stress and anxieties that a reasonable person would suffer as a result of government regulation of that industry. As Lamer C.J.C. said in *G. (J.)* at para 59, "[I]f the right were interpreted with such broad sweep, countless government initiatives could be challenged on the ground that they infringe the right to security of the person, massively expanding the scope of judicial review, and, in the process, trivializing what it means for a right to be constitutionally protected."

Accordingly, s. 84.1 of the *HTA* does not violate s. 7. It is therefore unnecessary to consider whether any violation could be saved by s. 1.

Disposition

The appeal by the defendant William Cameron Trucking is dismissed. The appeal by the Crown in *Transport Robert* is allowed, the order for a new trial set aside and a conviction entered. Particularly in light of the evidence led by the defendant concerning its attempts at preventing the loss of wheels, we agree with the Crown that the proper disposition would be imposition of the minimum fine of $2,000. The defendant will have 30 days to pay the fine.

Is there a a danger that law and order legislatures will now jump on the strategy used in s. 84.1 in Ontario or in B.C. generally to avoid the due diligence *Charter* standard? Will they now routinely expressly impose absolute liability and expressly avoid the possibility of imprisonment even in default?

There are important policy questions to consider. **Is, for example, absolute liability good penal policy for the high-profile offence that led to the special s. 84.1 regime?** There are certainly arguments of law enforcement expediency here relied on by the Ontario Court of Appeal. **But what of the fundamental choice of policy asserted by the Supreme Court in *Sault Ste. Marie*?** If owners and operators of commercial vehicles can prove reasonable maintenance standards for a vehicle that has nevertheless lost a wheel on the highway even at great risk to others, punishment is NOT justly imposed. On the other hand, if due diligence cannot be established, punishment is indeed fully deserved and one wonders why it is limited to a fine, even one as large as $50,000. A large fine would be rational if the offence targeted only corporations but that is not necessarily so considering it could ensnare an individual using his own vehicle for commercial reasons.

See further Stuart, "Is the *Sault Ste. Marie* Approach in Regulatory Offences About to Disappear?" (2004), 16 C.R. (6th) 147.

See also the decision of the Ontario Court of Appeal in *R. v. Michaud*, 2015 ONCA 585. That case dealt with s. 68.1 of the Ontario *Highway Traffic Act*, which requires commercial motor vehicles (primarily trucks) to be equipped with a speed-limiting device preventing them from going faster than 105 kph (that is, 5 kph over the speed limit). The section is punishable only by fine and so did not infringe the accused's liberty. However, the evidence showed that, although braking or steering was the way to avoid an accident 98% of the time, in 2% of cases accelerating would be the better choice, and that in some portion of that 2% of cases the vehicle would already be at its maximum speed. The Ontario Court of Appeal felt compelled to conclude that this meant there was a breach of security of the person, on the basis that *R. v Bedford*, (2013) SCC 72 had established that a negative impact on a single person was sufficient to establish a s. 7 breach. They made clear that they saw this as an undesirable result, restating the concern expressed in *Transport Robert* that this raised the spectre of trivializing constitutional protection. They also went on to save the violation under s. 1: see the discussion in Chapter 1 under "*Oakes* test for section 1".

PROBLEMS

1. A fishing packaging company is charged with being in possession of lobsters less than three and three-sixteenth inches from length of eye socket to the rear of the body, contrary to the minimum length specified in Lobster Fishery Regulations passed under the *Fisheries Act*, R.S.C. 1952, as amended. Inspectors found 26 short lobsters amongst the 50,000 or 60,000 lbs. of lobsters on the premises. The penalty is a fine. Company officials deny any knowledge of the undersized lobsters. Should the offence be defined as absolute or strict liability? Should the company be convicted? What of fisherman who caught them?

Compare *R. v. Pierce Fisheries Ltd.*, [1969] 4 C.C.C. 163 (N.S. C.A.), reversed (1970), [1971] S.C.R. 5, 12 C.R.N.S. 272, 5 C.C.C. 193.

2. The accused shot and killed a black bear and three grizzly bears. They had obtained the appropriate hunting licence for each type of bear. A week earlier, after an abortive hunt, they had shot and killed an ailing horse and left it in the area. The bears had been attracted to the carcass. The accused were charged with the offence of using bait for the purpose of hunting big game, contrary to s. 50(1)(b) of the *Alberta Wildlife Act*, R.S.A. 1980, c. W-9, which reads: "No person shall for the purpose of hunting or taking big game set out, use or employ . . . any bait of any kind." The penalty is a fine of not less than $100 and not more than $1,500 and, in default of payment, imprisonment for a term of not more than six months.

How should the offence be classified?

Compare *R. v. Brown* (1982), 29 C.R. (3d) 107, 69 C.C.C. (2d) 301 (Alta. C.A.), leave to appeal to S.C.C. refused (1982), 46 N.R. 85.

3. The accused was charged with wilfully having evaded or attempted to evade the payment of moneys, contrary to s. 62(d) of the *Quebec Revenue Department Act*, S.Q. 1972, c. 22. At trial, counsel for the accused admitted all the facts charged except that he had acted "wilfully". The prosecution then declared its case closed. Counsel for the accused moved for non-suit, alleging absence of proof of intent, this being a *mens rea* offence.

Rule on the motion

(1) where "wilfully" appears in the section, and

(2) where it does not.

Compare *Pichette v. Quebec (Deputy Minister of Revenne)* (1982), 29 C.R. (3d) 129 (Que. C.A.).

4. The accused, while hunting, shot a deer, then realized that he had left his deer tag at home. He returned home to get his deer tag, but in the meantime a Lands and Forests Officer found the untagged deer. The accused was charged with failing to tag deer contrary to the Deer Regulations made pursuant to the *Nova Scotia Lands and Forests Act*, R.S.N.S. 1967, c. 163. The regulations declare that a licensed hunter on killing a deer "shall immediately affix and securely lock" his tag to the carcass. The penalty is a fine of not less than $100 nor more than $300.

Is the offence absolute or strict? Is it constitutional?

Compare *R. v. Maidment* (1984), 37 C.R. (3d) 387, 10 C.C.C. (3d) 512 (N.S. C.A.).

5. The accused was charged under s. 5(1) of the *Food and Drugs Act*, R.S.C. 1970, c. F-27, which provides:

> 5.(1) No person shall label, package, treat, process, sell or advertise any food in a manner that is false, misleading or deceptive or is likely to create an erroneous impression regarding its character, value, quantity, composition, merit or safety.

An inspector of the Federal Department of Consumer and Corporate Affairs went to the accused's meat market to discuss the purchase of a side of beef. He requested that, after packaging, all bone and trim be returned to him. Subsequent analysis indicated a weight discrepancy of some 15 pounds. Reconstructing the side of beef indicated both the sirloin tip and a sirloin steak were missing. Also, extraneous portions of bone and fat were found that could not have been part of the side purchased. The accused testified that he was not in the store on the day the side was butchered. His employee, who could not specifically recollect the sale, stated that the store was very busy that day. The employee and the accused both testified that no meat was ever deliberately left out of an order but occasionally meat was forgotten or inadvertently left in the freezer. When those incidents occurred and the store was notified the mistakes were always rectified. Section 29 of the Act only provides a defence to any individual dealing with *pre-packaged* material if he can establish that he could not with reasonable diligence ascertain the quality of the goods. Give judgment. Compare *R. v. Grottoli* (1978), 43 C.C.C. (2d) 158 (Ont. C.A.).

6. The possibility of a leakage from the MacMillan Bloedel Ltd.'s underground pipes at its Skidegate operation in the Queen Charlotte Islands came to the company's attention in 1993 when it received a complaint from the Ministry of the Environment. At that time the pipes, which had been installed in the 1960s, were dug up and tested. No leakage was discovered. The company's equipment supervisor and its manager were of the opinion that the pipes were sound. In September 1995 an environmental inspector with the company's environmental services department prepared a comprehensive report. Amongst other things, the report identified the use of underground fuel lines by the company, including those at Skidegate, as a significant environmental problem. He recommended that the pipes either be installed above ground or in a secondary sleeve to allow early detection of leaks. Company personnel reviewed the report. Underground lines at some locations were replaced as a result. The company had replaced underground lines at some of its operations prior to receiving the report. There was some evidence that where pipes were replaced, they were found to be in good condition. The Skidegate pipes were regarded as low on the company's list of environmental concerns. There was no evidence as to when any action was intended to be taken with respect to them.

On May 16, 1997, diesel fuel was observed by a fisheries officer in Crabapple Creek, adjacent to the Skidegate operation. The accused was charged with an offence contrary to the *Fisheries Act* of depositing or permitting to be deposited a deleterious substance in water frequented by fish contrary to s. 36(3) of the *Fisheries Act* of Canada. At trial it was common cause that the discharge had occurred as a result of a fuel leakage from pipes at the accused's Skidegate facility. The company tendered the opinion of a metallurgical expert that the cause was microbiologically influenced corrosion likely brought about in 1993 by the evacuation of the fuel lines. Has the accused company established the defence of due diligence?

Compare *R. v. MacMillan Bloedel Ltd.* (2002), 5 C.R. (6th) 129 (B.C. C.A.), discussed by Bruce Pardy, "*MacMillan Bloedel*: Progress on Due Diligence" (2002), 5 C.R. (6th) 146.

7. The accused was driving his two sons, aged 12 and 8, to school on April 8, 2004. He was stopped by a police constable and charged with violating s. 106(6) of the *Highway Traffic Act*; under what is now s. 106(4) of the *HTA*:

> No person shall drive on a highway a motor vehicle in which there is a passenger who is under sixteen years of age and occupies a seating position for which a seat belt assembly has been provided unless that passenger is wearing the complete seat belt assembly and it is properly adjusted and securely fastened.

The accused testified that he had ensured that both boys were wearing their seat belts when he left the family home. He was not aware that his younger son, seated in the back seat, had unfastened his seat belt during the drive. Should the offence be classified as absolute or strict? If the latter should the accused be acquitted on the basis of due diligence?

Compare *R. v. Kanda* (2008), 53 C.R. (6th) 331, 227 C.C.C. (3d) 417 (Ont. C.A.) and *R. v. Wilson* (2014), 308 C.C.C. (3d) 350 (Ont. C.A.).

8. On April 29, 2008, the accused was driving westbound on Highway 7, a two-lane highway. The speed limit was 80 km/ h. She drove up behind a large tractor trailer that was moving at about 90 km/h and pulled out to pass the truck. She testified that as she attempted to pass the tractor trailer, it seemed longer than it had when she pulled out into the passing lane and the truck seemed to pick up speed as she attempted to pass it. She indicated that she became afraid, and sped up to get around the truck and back into the westbound lane. The police officer who was operating the radar from a police car behind the accused's car testified that there was nothing unsafe or remarkable about her driving apart from the speed. He clocked the accused at between 129 km/h and 131 km/h as she passed the truck. She slowed to about 110 km/h after she had passed the truck. Based on the single radar reading of 131 km/h, which was 51 km/h over the speed limit, the officer elected to charge the accused with stunt driving contrary to s. 172 of the Ontario *Highway Traffic Act* as amended in 2007. The penalty is a fine of not less than $2,000 and not more than $10,000, imprisonment of

up to six months, or both a fine and a term of imprisonment. In addition to these sanctions, the driver's licence may be suspended for up to two years on a first conviction and for up to ten years on a subsequent conviction. A person charged under s. 172 is required to surrender his or her licence to the police officer at the scene, is subject to an automatic seven-day administrative licence suspension and the vehicle must be impounded for seven days at the cost of and risk to its owner. Does the accused have a defence? See *R. v. Raham* (2010), 74 C.R. (6th) 96 (Ont. C.A.).

(c) Summary

Regulatory Offences

Express fault requirements	Strict liability	Absolute liability
Crown must prove act and fault.	Crown proves act. Accused must prove due diligence.	Crown proves act.

It would appear that all provincial offences, and federal offences which do not incorporate *Criminal Code* standards, may be safely characterized as regulatory. In such cases the approach to fault seems clear. Courts should give full expression to any express legislative fault requirement whether this be subjective *mens rea*, negligence or statutory due diligence defences. In the case of all other regulatory offences, as a matter of common law presumption or constitutional requirement, where the liberty interest is engaged, the court should read in a defence of due diligence. Under this state of the law absolute liability offences should be very rare unless the legislature, as in B.C., chooses not to enact a penalty of imprisonment, not even in default of payment of a fine.

A few provincial offences expressly invoke subjective *mens rea*. For example the Ontario *Highway Traffic Act*, s. 134(3):

> Where signs or traffic control devices have been posted or placed under subsection (2), no person shall drive or operate a vehicle on the closed highway or part thereof in intentional disobedience of the signs or traffic control devices.

In such cases the due diligence compromise is irrelevant. That was the ruling in *R. v. Edwards* (2007), 56 C.R. (6th) 192 (Ont. C.J.) respecting a charge of "knowingly" having a false insurance card contrary to s. 13.1(1)(a) of the *Compulsory Automobile Insurance Act* of Ontario. The card, obtained by the accused's friend, was false but the trial judge, Fairgrieve J., acquitted. The Crown had not proved that the accused had knowledge or was wilfully blind that it was false.

Another example of an express fault requirement in a regulatory statute is the objective test required for provincial offences of careless driving. Typical wording is that found in the *Highway Traffic Act*, R.S.O. 1990, c. H.8, s. 130:

> Every person is guilty of an offence of driving carelessly who drives a vehicle or street car on a highway without due care and attention and without reasonable consideration for other persons using the highway and on conviction is liable to a fine of not less than $200 and not more than $1,000 or to imprisonment for a term of not more than six months, or to both, and in addition his licence or permit may be suspended for a period of not more than two years.

R. v. BEAUCHAMP

(1953), 16 C.R. 270, 106 C.C.C. 6, 1953 CarswellOnt 11 (Ont. C.A.)

The accused was convicted of careless driving. The accused had driven his bus out onto the street from the parking garage. At this time there were no other cars on the street. The accused waited for another bus to leave the garage and then proceeded to back very slowly into a parking position on the street. Unfortunately, in the interim, another car had come down the street and parked in that position. The accused testified he checked his inside mirror, also looked through the back window, but found his outside mirror was loose and, because of the vibration, of no use. The bus crumpled the other car's bumper, grille and fender. The Court of Appeal allowed the accused's appeal.

MACKAY J.A.: —

. . . .

My conclusions are that, while the same facts may, and in many cases do, give rise to both civil and criminal proceedings, nevertheless there is no necessity, in dealing with criminal or quasi-criminal conduct in relation to the operation of motor vehicles, for entering into a discussion or consideration of the negligence that would support a civil action. It is also clear that there are different degrees of criminal or quasi-criminal negligence.

Section 29(1) of *The Highway Traffic Act* creates a statutory offence that is quasi-criminal in its nature: *Rex v. Van Leishout* (1943), 80 C.C.C. 361.

A crime is defined in 9 Halsbury, 2nd ed. 1933, p. 9, para. 1, as follows:

> A crime is an unlawful act or default which is an offence against the public, and renders the person guilty of the act or default liable to legal punishment. While a crime is often also an injury to a private person, who has remedy in a civil action, it is as an act or default contrary to the order, peace, and well-being of society that a crime is punishable by the State. A civil proceeding has for its object the recovery of money or other property, or the enforcement of a right for the advantage of the person suing, while a criminal proceeding has for its object the punishment of a public offence.

To support a charge under s. 29(1) of *The Highway Traffic Act*, the evidence must be such as to prove beyond reasonable doubt that the accused drove in the manner prohibited by the subsection, namely, without due care and attention or without reasonable consideration for others. The standard of care and skill to be applied has been long established and is not that of perfection. It is, I think, correctly stated in Mazengarb, *op cit.*, at pp. 176-7, as follows:

> The law does not require of any driver that he should exhibit "perfect nerve and presence of mind, enabling him to do the best thing possible." It does not expect men to be more than ordinary men. Drivers of vehicles cannot be required to regulate their driving as if in constant fear that other drivers who are under observation, and apparently acting reasonably and properly, may possibly act at a critical moment in disregard of the safety of themselves and other users of the road.
>
> But the law does insist upon a reasonable amount of skill in the handling of a vehicle which is a potential source of danger to other users of the road. . . . The question always is "What would an ordinary prudent person in the position of the plaintiff have done in relation to the event complained of?" (Pollock on Torts uses the term "average man".)

Motor vehicles are now in general use as a common means of transportation and pleasure. If too high a standard of care and skill were demanded, those people who are not capable of attaining such a standard would be deprived of the privilege of driving motor vehicles, and their use would be confined to experts, and even persons who might become experts might well be prevented from qualifying as such by experience. It must also be borne in mind that the test, where an accident has occurred, is not whether, if the accused had used greater care or skill, the accident would not have happened. It is whether it is proved beyond reasonable doubt that this accused, in the light of existing circumstances of which he was aware or of which a driver exercising ordinary care should have been aware, failed to use the care and attention or to give to other persons using the highway the consideration that a driver of ordinary care would have used or given in the circumstances? The use of the term "due care", which means care owing in the circumstances, makes it quite clear that, while the legal standard of care remains the same in the sense that it is what the average careful man would have done in like circumstances, the factual standard is a constantly shifting one, depending on road, visibility, weather conditions, traffic conditions that exist or may reasonably be expected, and any other conditions that ordinary prudent drivers would take into consideration. It is a question of fact, depending on the circumstances in each case.

In this case, and in some of the cases to which I have referred, evidence has been admitted to show that the accused had a good record as a careful driver. Such evidence is not relevant on the issue of guilt or innocence. As was said by Lord Hewart C.J. in *McCrone v. Riding, supra,* at p. 158: "That standard is an objective standard, impersonal and universal, fixed in relation to the safety of other users of the highway. It is in no way related to the degree of proficiency or degree of experience attained by the individual driver."

There is a further important element that must also be considered, namely, that the conduct must be of such a nature that it can be considered a breach of duty to the public and deserving of punishment. This further step must be taken even if it is found that the conduct of the accused falls below the standard set out in the preceding paragraphs. This principle may be somewhat difficult to apply, but I think it might be illustrated by the common example of a motorist attempting to park at the curb in a space between two other parked vehicles. Frequently one or other of the parked vehicles is bumped in the process. Damage seldom arises, because cars are equipped with bumpers, but if damage were caused it might well give rise to a civil action for damages, but it could hardly be said to be such a lack of care or attention as would be considered to be deserving of punishment as a crime or quasi-crime.

The added *Beauchamp* requirement in Ontario that careless driving be deserving of punishment has often resulted in acquittals. In *R. v. Ereddia* (2006), 42 C.R. (6th) 180 (Ont. C.J.) the accused was acquitted for a minor error of judgment in cracking a mirror of a parked garbage truck. This *Beauchamp* requirement was rejected in *R. v. Jacobsen* (1964), 44 C.R. 24 (B.C. C.A.).

Given that the legislature has expressly stated a fault requirement for careless driving without reference to a reverse onus one might have expected that there is no reverse onus on the accused to establish due diligence. Such a reverse onus is, however, frequently required: see especially *R. v. Skorput* (1992), 72 C.C.C. (3d) 294 (Ont. Prov. Div.).

4.   FAULT FOR CRIMES

(a)   Murder and the *Charter*

(i)   Murder under ss. 229(a)(i) and (ii)

SIMPSON v. R.

(1981), 20 C.R. (3d) 36 at 61-64, 58 C.C.C. (2d) 122 (Ont. C.A.),
1981 Carswell 40

MARTIN J.A.: —

Following the argument of the appeal, and while the decision of the court was under reserve, the court requested counsel to submit argument with respect to the effect of a passage in the judge's charge defining the intent requisite for attempted murder, to which no objection was taken at the trial and which was not a ground of appeal. The court reconvened on 12th February 1981 and heard argument with respect to the passage in question.

The learned trial judge charged the jury as follows:

> Under the *Criminal Code*, anyone who attempts by any means to commit murder is guilty of an indictable offence. In this case, neither victim died, most fortunately. So the charge isn't murder, but attempted murder. What is murder? It is defined in s. 212 of the *Criminal Code*, in part, as follows:
> "Culpable homicide is murder
>> (*a*) where the person who causes the death of a human being
>> (i) means to cause his death, or
>> (ii) means to cause him bodily harm that he knows is likely to cause his death and is reckless whether death ensues or not".
>
> Now, "culpable" means "blameworthy". Culpable homicide is death of a human being for which some person may be blamed in law. The definition that I have just read to you, then, is one of murder, and the charge we are dealing with here is attempt to murder. I have earlier told you that proof of the intention of the accused is an essential element in the offence of attempt to murder. The Crown must satisfy you beyond a reasonable doubt that the accused stabbed the victim and that he did so intending to cause the death, or intending to cause the victim bodily harm that he knew or ought to have known was likely to cause death and was reckless whether death ensued or not. I repeat the second part of that definition: If the Crown has, on the evidence, satisfied you beyond a reasonable doubt that the accused was the stabber and that in stabbing he intended to cause bodily harm that he knew or ought to have known was likely to cause death and was reckless whether death ensued or not, then the offence of attempted murder has been proved.

It has now been authoritatively decided that either of the intents specified in s. 212(*a*)(i) and (ii) [now ss. 229(*a*)(i) and (ii)] suffices to constitute the intent required for the offence of attempted murder: see *Lajoie v. R.*, [1974] S.C.R. 399, 20 C.R.N.S. 360; *R. v. Ritchie*, (1970), 16 C.R.N.S. 287, [1970] 5 C.C.C. 336 (C.A.). Unfortunately, the learned trial judge, in paraphrasing the intent specified in s. 212(*a*)(ii) — namely, an intention to cause bodily harm that the offender *knows* is likely to cause death — substituted for the requisite intent an intention to cause bodily harm that the offender knows or *ought to know* is likely to cause death. This incorrect summary of the provision of s. 212(*a*)(ii) constituted a serious error. Liability under s. 212(*a*)(ii) is subjective, and the requisite *knowledge* that the intended injury is likely to cause death must be brought home to the accused subjectively. To substitute for that state of mind an intention to cause bodily harm that the accused knows or *ought* to know is likely to cause death is to impose liability on an objective basis. An intention to cause bodily harm that the offender *ought* to have known was likely to cause death is merely evidence from which, along with all the other circumstances, the jury *may* infer that the accused actually had the requisite intention and knowledge required by s. 212(*a*)(ii). It does not, however, constitute the requisite state of mind.

The effect of the misdirection is magnified by the fact that the incorrect statement of the intention required to be proved was repeated twice in the passage above reproduced. Although the learned trial judge had read the provisions of s. 212(*a*)(i) and (ii) just before the impugned passage, the jury was more likely to remember his clear-cut summary than the provisions of the *Code*: see *R. v. Harrison* (1945), 84 C.C.C. 78 at 82-83 (C.A.).

The error was never corrected by the learned trial judge. It is true that, in putting the case for the Crown, he said:

> The Crown suggests to you that, if you are satisfied that Simpson was the attacker, you should in the circumstances have no doubt that he intended to kill or cause bodily harm knowing that it might result in death and being reckless as to whether death ensued or not.

It is to be observed that even this passage is not entirely correct, as it refers to an intention to cause bodily harm knowing that it *might* result in death, as distinct from an intention to inflict bodily harm that the offender knows is *likely* to cause bodily harm. In any event, the jury would rely on the judge's instruction, as they had previously been told they must, with respect to the elements of the offence of attempted murder.

In my view, the seriousness of the error requires a new trial, unless it is proper to invoke the curative provisions of s. 613(1)(*b*)(iii). In *R. v. Smith* (1977), 33 C.C.C. (2d) 172 (Ont. C.A.), the trial judge, in instructing the jury as to the definition of murder, had on a number of occasions incorrectly summarized the provisions of s. 212(*a*)(ii) by omitting from the definition of the necessary intent the requirement that the person who means to cause bodily harm knows that the bodily harm is likely to cause death. The court in that case was satisfied, in view of the clear direction with respect to this requirement by the trial judge on so many occasions during his charge, that in the context in which the slips occurred they did not result in a substantial wrong or miscarriage of justice. In *R. v. Reynolds* (1978), 44 C.C.C. (2d) 129 (C.A.), the trial judge, in instructing the jury as to the elements of murder under s. 212(*a*)(ii), had made a similar error on a number of occasions in his charge, but on the error being brought to his attention he gave the jury an emphatic and correct instruction which, in the opinion of the court, nullified the earlier errors.

I have not been persuaded, even by Mr. Watt's able argument, that it is appropriate to invoke the provisions of s. 613(1)(*b*)(iii) in relation to the conviction of the appellant on count 2, relating to Cathy Wagenaar. I am not satisfied that a reasonable jury, properly instructed, having found that the appellant was Cathy Wagenaar's assailant, would inevitably have found that he intended to kill her or intended to inflict an injury upon her that he *knew* was likely to kill her. Although it would be open to a properly instructed jury to conclude that the requisite intent to constitute attempted murder had been established, the accompanying circumstances and the assailant's utterances are not such as to inevitably require a reasonable jury to reach that conclusion.

. . . .

New trial ordered.

R. v. EDELENBOS

(2004), 23 C.R. (6th) 350, 187 C.C.C. (3d) 465,
2004 CarswellOnt 2701 (Ont. C.A.)

The accused was charged with first degree murder of E.C. He admitted he had gone to her home and had sexually assaulted and strangled her. His defence to murder was one of intention. His defence was that he strangled her to stop her from screaming and that he did not intend to kill her, and should therefore be convicted of manslaughter. The jury returned a verdict of first degree murder. The accused appealed his conviction *inter alia* on the basis that the trial judge erred in defining the word "likely" in his jury charge regarding the intent requirement for murder; the Ontario Court of Appeal dismissed his appeal.

LANG J.A.: —

[12] For the most part, the trial judge's charge to the jury followed the accepted pattern regarding the intent required for murder, and the difference between murder and manslaughter. However, the trial judge gave the jury a novel explanation of the meaning in s. 229 of "likely" in the clause "means to cause him bodily harm that he knows is likely to cause his death".

[13] As applicable in this case, the current Ontario Specimen Jury Instructions (Criminal) (Toronto: Carswell, 2002), prepared by Watt J. of the Ontario Superior Court of Justice (the "Watt Charges"), would have had the judge tell the jury:

> The crime of murder requires proof of a particular state of mind. For an unlawful killing to be murder, Crown counsel must prove that Mr. Edelenbos meant either to kill Ms. Coffey or meant to cause Ms. Coffey bodily harm that Mr. Edelenbos *knew* was likely to kill Ms. Coffey, and was reckless whether Ms. Coffey died or not. The Crown does *not* have to prove *both*. One is enough. All of you do *not* have to agree on the same state of mind, as long as everyone is sure that one of the required states of mind has been proven beyond a reasonable doubt.
>
> If Mr. Edelenbos did *not* mean to do either, Mr. Edelenbos committed manslaughter. (Emphasis in original)

Although the Watt Charges were not distributed until 2002, the charge often used in 2000 was similar in content. It is relevant to observe that the Watt Charges contain no definition of "likely".

[14] Instead of using the standard charge however, the trial judge gave the following definition of "likely":

> Likely means more than a possibility. It involves a substantial degree of probability. However, it does not mean more likely than not in the mathematical sense of 51 percent. The phrase is meant to convey the notion of a substantial or real chance, as distinct from a mere possibility. Likely to cause death means could well cause death. A fine calculation that the odds were against death, although the risk was plainly there, is no defence. By using the word "likely"

the legislators were trying to get at killings where the risk was subjectively so appreciable that to engage in the conduct would be seen as a virtual equivalent of an intentional killing. A likelihood is a real risk, a substantial risk or something that might well happen.

[15] In choosing this definition, the trial judge relied on Isabel Grant, Dorothy Chunn, and Christine Boyle in *The Law of Homicide*, looseleaf (Scarborough: Carswell, 1994). They argue, at pp. 4-44 to 4-46 that, in some circumstances, the difference between knowing that death is "likely" and that death is "possible" distinguishes murder from manslaughter. They look to foreign case law to support this approach, particularly the New Zealand Court of Appeal decision in *R. v. Piri*, [1987] N.Z.L.R. 66.

[16] No Canadian cases were brought to our attention that discuss the meaning of "likely" in the context of s. 229. It would seem that the need for such a discussion has probably not arisen. In my view, the need did not arise in this case. It was unnecessary and potentially confusing to the jury for the trial judge to engage in a nuanced discussion of the precise meaning of "likely" in the circumstances of this trial. The facts simply did not call for an analysis of where "likely" stands on the spectrum from possible to probable. The jury in this case would have given the word "likely" its common sense plain language meaning, as other juries have across Canada.

[17] The purpose of the Ontario Specimen Criminal Jury Trial Project, chaired by Watt J., was to help judges draft jury instructions in plain language. The resulting Watt Charges do not include a definition of "likely" in the standard murder instructions. In my view, this is because juries are able to apply "likely", in accordance with its established ordinary meaning, to the particular context.

[18] Where the jury does not need an analysis of a commonplace everyday word, the trial judge should avoid entering into the possible shades of its meaning. I recognize, however, that there may be cases where the trial judge may feel that the circumstances call for elaboration or definition. If so, before providing such an elaboration or definition, particularly one that has apparently not been used in a Canadian context, the trial judge should so advise counsel during the pre-charge conference. Each counsel should then be given an opportunity to make submissions.

[19] No such opportunity was given in this case. The trial judge did not advise counsel about his research in the area or his intention to depart from the standard charge. At the conclusion of the charge, defence counsel objected to the instruction on the meaning of "likely". The trial judge then explained his reasoning. While defence counsel, at that time, did not persist with his objection, he simply was not given an adequate opportunity to consider and research the matter. In any event, the absence of an objection is not fatal to an appeal.

[20] As I have said, the circumstances of this case did not require an analysis of the meaning of "likely"; indeed, in my view, it would be a most exceptional situation that would ever require such an analysis. The issue here, therefore, is whether the definition given by the judge to the jury operated to the prejudice of the defence. I conclude that it did not, for five reasons.

[21] First, the challenged instruction must be considered in context. It comprised three-quarters of a page in a succinct 45-page charge. The jury was not given a copy of the jury charge to take with them into their deliberations. Accordingly, the jury would not have laboured over the precise words of the instruction. Rather, it would have been left with an impression of the judge's definition of "likely".

[22] Second, in the course of his instruction, the judge referred to "likely" as being a "substantial degree of probability", not a "mere possibility", a "substantial risk", and on two occasions, as "something that might well happen". While he spoke of a "real chance" or "real risk", he also said murder was conduct virtually "equivalent to an intentional killing", a definition consistent with the authorities: see *R. v. Cooper*, [1993] 1 S.C.R. 146, 78 C.C.C. (3d) 289.

[23] Third, during the charge, a copy of the relevant provision of the *Criminal Code* was projected onto a screen for the jury, including its reference to "likely" to cause death. That provision does not include a definition of "likely". The trial judge provided the jury with a copy of s. 229 when they retired for their deliberations, while he did not give them a copy of his jury charge.

[24] Fourth, the trial judge himself used the word "likely" repeatedly in his charge, showing that he assumed the term did not need repeated or complex analysis. After he provided the definition of "likely", the trial judge referred simply to "likely" to cause death on 12 further occasions. As well, immediately after the definition, the trial judge instructed the jury that "recklessness" was "redundant" or "almost an afterthought". He said that, "if the Crown establishes the first two elements beyond a reasonable doubt—that an accused person intended to cause bodily harm and that he or she knew that it would likely cause death then this by itself, or these two elements by themselves, meet the test for recklessness."

[25] Finally, the trial judge's instructions following the definition of "likely" made the Crown's burden with respect to intent very clear. The trial judge instructed the jury that the critical issue was whether the Crown had established beyond a reasonable doubt that Mr. Edelenbos meant to cause Ms. Coffey's death or meant to cause her bodily harm that he knew was "likely" to cause her death. He canvassed the evidence of the effect of Mr. Edelenbos's inebriation on the capacity to form intent and the need for the Crown to prove Mr. Edelenbos's appropriate level of subjective intent.

[26] Quite rightly, he omitted the part of the standard jury charge that says it may be inferred, as a matter of common sense, that a sane and sober person usually intends to cause predictable consequences. There was evidence that Mr. Edelenbos had been drinking. The trial judge said:

The critical issue in this trial is whether or not the prosecutor has established beyond a reasonable doubt that Martin Edelenbos either meant to cause the death of Eileen Coffey, or meant to cause her bodily harm that he knew was likely to cause her death. The intoxicating effect of alcohol is well known. Intoxication which causes a person to cast off restraint and act in a manner in which he or she would not have acted if sober affords no excuse for the commission of an offence while in that state if he or she had the intent required to constitute the offence. A drunken intent is nonetheless an intent. The offence of murder is not committed if the accused lacked the intent to either cause the death of Eileen Coffey, or to cause her bodily harm that he knew was likely to cause her death. Intoxication could compromise the formation of:

1. The intent to cause death;

2. The intent to cause bodily harm; or

3. The appreciation that the intended bodily harm was likely to cause death.

The Crown is entitled to prove either intent beyond a reasonable doubt. If the intent to cause bodily harm for the second type of murder has been so proved, then the Crown must go on and also prove beyond a reasonable doubt that he knew that such bodily harm was likely to cause death. In considering whether the Crown has proved beyond a reasonable doubt either of these scenarios you should take into account Mr. Edelenbos's consumption of alcohol, along with the other facts which throw light on his state of mind at the time the offence was allegedly committed.

[27] The trial judge reviewed the evidence about alcohol consumption and said:

Once he assaulted Ms. Coffey he only meant to stop her screaming when he put his hands, or hand on her throat. He denies either intending to kill her, or intending to cause her bodily harm. He denies any appreciation that his assault was likely to cause her death. He swore that the lethal nature of his assault was not evident to him because of the extent of his intoxication. He insists that the only intent he had was to stop her from screaming, despite his concession in the sober confines of this courtroom that the obvious purpose of putting one's hands around another's throat is to stop them from breathing.

To prove either the intent to cause death, or the intent to cause bodily harm that Mr. Edelenbos knew was likely to cause death, the Crown relies on [expert evidence].

[28] The judge went on to describe the expert evidence about the severity of the injuries to Ms. Coffey and the evidence that Mr. Edelenbos was in sufficient control to carry out a thorough clean-up after the killing.

[29] Taking into consideration the instructions given by the trial judge after the definition of "likely", and reading the charge as a whole, I conclude that the jury would have appreciated that the Crown was obliged to prove Mr.

Edelenbos's subjective intent to cause bodily harm that was likely to cause Ms. Coffey's death.

Has the Ontario Court of Appeal phrased the test correctly in para. 29?

See further *R. v. Czibulka* (2005), 24 C.R. (6th) 152, 189 C.C.C. (3d) 199 (Ont. C.A.); *R. v. Patterson* (2006), 205 C.C.C. (3d) 171 (Ont. C.A.); *R. v. Moo* (2009), 247 C.C.C. (3d) 34 (Ont. C.A.); *R. v. Brar* (2009), 250 C.C.C. (3d) 198 (B.C. C.A.); *R. v. MacDonald* (2008), 236 C.C.C. (3d) 269 (Ont. C.A.); and *R. v. Kahnapace* (2010), 76 C.R. (6th) 38 (B.C. C.A.) (instructions referring to foresight of danger or risk rather than likelihood amounting to error). See the further analysis of Gary Trotter, "Instructing Juries on Murder and Intent" (2005), 24 C.R. (6th) 178.

(ii)   Constructive murder: ss. 229(c) and 230

VAILLANCOURT v. R.

[1987] 2 S.C.R. 636, 60 C.R. (3d) 289, 39 C.C.C. (3d) 118,
1987 CarswellQue 18, 1987 CarswellQue 98

LAMER J. (DICKSON C.J.C. and WILSON J. concurring): —

INTRODUCTION

Vaillancourt was convicted of second degree murder following a trial before a Sessions Court judge and jury in Montreal. He appealed to the Quebec Court of Appeal, arguing that the Judge's charge to the jury on the combined operation of ss. 213(*d*) [now s. 230(*d*)] and 21(2) of the *Criminal Code*, R.S.C. 1970, c. C-34, was incorrect. His appeal was dismissed and the conviction was affirmed [31 C.C.C. (3d) 75]. Before this court, he has challenged the constitutional validity of s. 213(*d*), alone and in combination with s. 21(2), under the *Canadian Charter of Rights and Freedoms*.

THE FACTS

For the purposes of this appeal, the Crown does not contest the following statement of the facts.

The appellant and his accomplice committed an armed robbery in a pool hall. The appellant was armed with a knife and his accomplice with a gun. During the robbery, the appellant remained near the front of the hall while the accomplice went to the back. There was a struggle between the accomplice and a client. A shot was fired and the client was killed. The accomplice managed to escape and has never been found. The appellant was arrested at the scene.

In the course of his testimony, the appellant said that he and his accomplice had agreed to commit this robbery armed only with knives. On the night of the robbery, however, the accomplice arrived at their meeting place with a gun. The appellant said that he objected because on a previous armed robbery his gun had discharged accidentally, and he did not want that to happen again. He insisted that the gun be unloaded. The accomplice removed three bullets from the gun and gave them to the appellant. The appellant then went to the bathroom and placed the bullets in his glove. The glove was recovered by the police at the scene of the crime and was found at trial to contain three bullets. The appellant testified that at the time of the robbery he was certain that the gun was unloaded.

CONSTITUTIONAL QUESTIONS

Before this court, the following constitutional questions were formulated:

> 1. Is s. 213(d) of the *Criminal Code* inconsistent with the provisions of either s. 7 or s. 11(d) of the *Canadian Charter of Rights and Freedoms* and, therefore, of no force or effect?
> 2. If not, is the combination of s. 21 and 213(d) of the *Criminal Code* inconsistent with the provisions of either s. 7 or s. 11(d) of the *Canadian Charter of Rights and Freedoms* and is s. 21 of the *Criminal Code* therefore of no force or effect in the case of a charge under s. 213(d) of the *Criminal Code*?

THE LAW

Narrowing the issue

The appellant has framed his attack on s. 213(d) of the *Code* in very wide terms. He has argued that the principles of fundamental justice require that, before Parliament can impose any criminal liability for causing a particular result, there must be some degree of subjective *mens rea* in respect of that result. This is a fundamental question with far-reaching consequences. If this case were decided on that basis, doubt would be cast on the constitutional validity of many provisions throughout our *Criminal Code*, in particular s. 205(5)(a) [now s. 222(5)(a)], whereby causing death by means of an unlawful act is culpable homicide, and s. 212(c) [now s. 229(c)], whereby objective foreseeability of the likelihood of death is sufficient for a murder conviction in certain circumstances.

However, the appellant was convicted under s. 213(d) and the constitutional question is limited to this provision. In my opinion, the validity of s. 213(d) can be decided on somewhat narrower grounds. In addition, the Attorney General of Canada has seen fit not to intervene to support the constitutionality of s. 213(d), which is clearly in jeopardy in this case, though he might have intervened to support ss. 205(5)(a) and 212(c) and other similar provisions. I will thus endeavour not to make pronouncements the effect of which will be to predispose in *obiter* of other issues more properly dealt with if and when the constitutionality of the other provisions is in issue. I do, however, find it virtually impossible to make comments as regards s. 213(*d*) that will not have some effect on the validity of the rest of s. 213 or that will not reveal to some extent my views as regards s. 212(*c*). However, the validity of those sections and of subs. (*a*) to (*c*) of s. 213 is not in issue here and I will attempt to limit my comments to s. 213(*d*).

The appellant has also challenged the combined operation of ss. 21(2) and 213(*d*). Given my decision on the validity of s. 213(*d*), and in view of the importance of s. 21(2) and the absence of the Attorney General of Canada, I do not find it necessary or advisable to deal with s. 21(2) in this appeal.

Analysis of s. 213(d)

Section 213(*d*) in the context of the murder provisions

It is first necessary to analyze s. 213(*d*) in the context of the other murder provisions in the *Code* in order to determine its true nature and scope. Murder is defined as a culpable homicide committed in the circumstances set out at ss. 212 and 213 of the *Code*. There is a very interesting progression through s. 212 to s. 213 with respect to the mental state that must be proven.

The starting point is s. 212(*a*)(i), which provides:

212. Culpable homicide is murder

(*a*) where the person who causes the death of a human being

(i) means to cause his death . . .

This clearly requires that the accused have actual subjective foresight of the likelihood of causing the death, coupled with the intention to cause that death. This is the most morally blameworthy state of mind in our system.

There is a slight relaxation of this requirement in s. 212(*a*)(ii), which provides:

212. Culpable homicide is murder

(*a*) where the person who causes the death of a human being . . .

(ii) means to cause him bodily harm that he knows is likely to cause his death, and is reckless whether death ensues or not . . .

Here again the accused must have actual subjective foresight of the likelihood of death. However, the Crown need no longer prove that he intended to cause the death, but only that he was reckless whether death ensued or not. It should also be noted that s. 212(*a*)(ii) is limited to cases where the accused intended to cause bodily harm to the victim.

Section 212(*c*) provides:

212. Culpable homicide is murder. . .

(*c*) where a person, for an unlawful object, does anything that he knows or ought to know is likely to cause death, and thereby causes death to a human being, notwithstanding that he desires to effect his object without causing death or bodily harm to any human being.

In part, this is simply a more general form of recklessness, and thus the logical extension of s. 212(*a*)(ii), in that it applies when the accused "does *anything* . . . he knows . . . is likely to cause death" (emphasis added). However, there is also a further relaxation of the mental element required for murder, in that it is also murder where the accused "does *anything that he . . . ought to know* is likely to cause death" (emphasis added). This eliminates the requirement of actual subjective foresight and replaces it with objective foreseeability or negligence.

The final relaxation in the definition of murder occurs at s. 213:

213. Culpable homicide is murder where a person causes the death of a human being while committing or attempting to commit high treason or treason or an offence mentioned in section 52 (sabotage), 76 (piratical acts), 76.1 (hijacking an aircraft), 132 or subsection 133(1) or sections 134 to 136 (escape or rescue from prison or lawful custody), 143 or 145 (rape or attempt to commit rape), 149 or 156 (indecent assault), subsection 246(2) (resisting lawful arrest), 247 (kidnapping and forcible confinement), 302 (robbery), 306 (breaking and entering) or 389 or 390 (arson), whether or not the person means to cause death to any human being and whether or not he knows that death is likely to be caused to any human being, if

(*a*) he means to cause bodily harm for the purpose of
(i) faclitating the commission of the offence, or
(ii) facilitating his flight after committing or attempting to commit the offence, and the death ensues from the bodily harm;

(*b*) he administers a stupefying or overpowering thing for a purpose mentioned in paragraph (*a*), and the death ensues therefrom;

(*c*) he wilfully stops, by any means, the breath of a human being for a purpose mentioned in paragraph (*a*), and the death ensues therefrom; or

(*d*) he uses a weapon or has it upon his person
(i) during or at the time he commits or attempts to commit the offence, or
(ii) during or at the time of his flight after committing or attempting to commit the offence, and the death ensues as a consequence.

Under this provision, it is murder if the accused causes the victim's death while committing or attempting to commit one of the enumerated offences if he performs one of the acts in subss. (*a*) to (*d*). Proof that the accused performed one of the acts in subss. (*a*) to (*d*) is substituted for proof of any subjective foresight, or even objective foreseeability, of the likelihood of death.

I should add that there appears to be a further relaxation of the mental state when the accused is a party to the murder through s. 21(2) of the *Code*, as in this case. However, as I have said, it is sufficient to deal with 213(*d*) in order to dispose of this appeal.

The historical development of s. 213

Although the concept of felony murder has a long history at common law, a brief review of the historical development of s. 213 indicates that its legitimacy is questionable.

In the early history of English criminal law, "murdrum", or murder, referred to a secret killing, or the killing of a Dane, or later a Norman, by an Englishman, and to the fine levied on the township where the killing occurred. By the early 14th century, the fines had been abandoned and murder had come to be the name used to describe the worst kind of homicide. The expression "malice aforethought" was subsequently adopted to distinguish murder from manslaughter, which denoted all culpable homicides other than murder. Malice aforethought was not limited to its natural and obvious sense of premeditation, but would be implied whenever the killing was intentional or reckless. In these instances, the malice was present and it is the premeditation which was implied by law.

Coke took this one step further and implied both the malice and the premeditation in cases where the death occurred in the commission of an unlawful act. He wrote in the Third Part of the Institutes of the Laws of England (1817), London, W. Clarke and Sons, at p. 56:

> *Unlawful.* If the act be unlawful it is murder. As if A. meaning to steale a deere in the park of B., shooteth at the deer, and by the glance of the arrow killeth a boy that is hidden in a bush: this is murder, for that the act was unlawfull, although A. had no intent to hurt the boy, nor knew not of him. But if B. the owner of the park had shot at his own deer, and without any ill intent had killed the boy by the glance of his arrow, this had been homicide by misadventure and no felony.
>
> So if one shoot at any wild fowle upon a tree, and the arrow killeth any reasonable creature afar off, without any evill intent in him, this is *per infortunium*: for it was not unlawfull to shoot at the wilde fowle: but if he had shot at a cock or hen, or any tame fowle of another mans, and the arrow by mischance had killed a man, this had been murder, for the act was unlawfull.

Coke's statement of the unlawful act murder rule has been much criticized. Stephen demonstrated that Coke's statement was not supported by the authorities cited: History of the Criminal Law of England (1883), vol. 3, pp. 57-58. Further, a recent author has suggested that Coke's statement was just "a slip of the quill" and that Coke intended to say that accidental killing by an unlawful act was manslaughter: see D. Lanham, "Felony Murder — Ancient and Modern" (1983), 7 Crim. L.J. 90, at pp. 92-94. Other 17th century writers (Dalton, Countrey Justice (1619), pp. 225-26, and Hale, History of the Pleas of the Crown (1736), vol. 1, at p. 475) and cases (*Chichester's Case* (1647), Aleyn 12, and *Hull's Case* (1664), Kel. 40) rejected the unlawful act murder rule as set out by Coke.

Despite all of this, Coke's doctrine seems to have been accepted by the writers and the cases in the 18th century, and their only contribution was to limit it to killings in the course of felonies: see *R. v. Plummer* (1702), Kel. 109, 84 E.R. 1103 at 1107; Hawkins Pleas of the Crown (1716), vol. 1, c. 29, s. 11; *R. v. Woodburne* (1722), 16 St. Tr. 53; Foster, Crown Law (1762), p. 258; East, Pleas of the Crown (1803), vol. 1, at p. 255. Of course, at that time both the underlying felony and the murder were punishable by death, so the definition of a homicide in the course of a felony as a murder had little practical effect.

In the 19th century, the felony murder rule was accepted as part of the common law: see *Stephen's Digest of the Criminal Law*, 9th ed. (1950), art. 264(*c*). However, the rule was strongly criticized by Stephen, who labelled it "cruel" and "monstrous": *History of the Criminal Law*, vol. 3, p. 75.

Despite the rule's questionable origins and the subsequent criticisms, s. 175 of the *English Draft Code of 1879* included a restricted form of felony murder, which was subsequently adopted in the first *Canadian Criminal Code*, in 1892. Through subsequent amendments this provision has been widened, and it is now s. 213. It is more restricted than the common-law rule, in that it is limited to deaths occurring in the commission of certain enumerated offences and it requires that the accused have committed one of the acts set out in subss. (*a*) to (*d*).

Section 213 and its predecessors in the *Code* have long been subject to academic criticism: see J. Willis, Comment on *Rowe v. R.* (1951), 29 Can. Bar Rev. 784, at pp. 794-96; J. Ll. J. Edwards, "Constructive Murder in Canadian and English Law" (1961), 3 Cr. L.Q. 481, at pp. 506-509; A. Hooper, "Some Anomalies and Developments in the Law of Homicide" (1967), 3 Univ. of B.C. L. Rev. 55, at pp. 75-77; P. Burns and R.S. Reid, "From Felony Murder to Accomplice Felony Attempted Murder: The Rake's Progress Compleat?" (1977), 55 Can. Bar Rev. 75, at pp. 103-105; G. Parker, *An Introduction to Criminal Law* (1977), pp. 145-48; D. Stuart, *Canadian Criminal Law: A Treatise* (1982), pp. 222-25; I. Grant and A.W. Mackay, "Constructive Murder and the Charter: In Search of Principle" (1987), 25 Alta. L. Rev. 129; cf. A.W. Mewett and M. Manning, Criminal Law, 2nd ed. (1985), p. 545. It has also been subject to judicial criticism. In *R. v. Farrant*, [1983] 1 S.C.R. 124, 32 C.R. (3d) 289, 4 C.C.C. (3d) 354, Dickson J. (as he then was) wrote that s. 213 seemed harsh (p. 130). In *R. v. Ancio*, [1984] 1 S.C.R. 225, 39 C.R. (3d) 1, 10 C.C.C. (3d) 385, dealing with the *mens rea* of attempted murder, McIntyre J. wrote at pp. 250-51 [S.C.R.]:

> It was argued, and it has been suggested in some of the cases and academic writings on the question, that it is illogical to insist upon a higher degree of *mens rea* for attempted murder, while accepting a lower degree amounting to recklessness for murder. I see no merit in this argument. The intent to kill is the highest intent in murder and there is no reason in logic why an attempt to murder, aimed at the completion of the full crime of murder, should have any lesser intent. *If there is any illogic in this matter, it is in the statutory characterization of unintentional killing as murder.* [Emphasis added.]

Finally, the Law Reform Commission of Canada criticized s. 213 in its working paper 33, Homicide (1984), at pp. 47-51, and excluded the notion of constructive murder from its *Draft Criminal Code* in its report 30, Recodifying Criminal Law (1986), s. 6(3), p. 54.

Felony murder in other jurisdictions

Felony murder is a peculiarly common-law concept which appears to be unknown outside a small circle of common-law jurisdictions, and it has not fared well in those jurisdictions. In the United Kingdom, where the rule originated, it was abolished by the *Homicide Act*, 1957 (5 & 6 Eliz. 2, c. 11). The rule is still quite widespread in the United States, though it is said to be in decline: R.W. Perkins and R.N. Boyce, *Criminal Law*, 3rd ed. (1982), p. 70. The rule has been abolished by statute or by the courts in several jurisdictions (see *People v. Aaron; People v. Thompson; People v. Wright*, 299 N.W. 2d 304, 409 Mich. 672, 13 A.L.R. 4th 1180 (S.C. 1980), and *State v. Doucette*, 470 A. 2d 676 (S.C. Vt., 1983)), and it has been downgraded to manslaughter in others. In addition, the courts and the legislatures have limited the scope of the common-law rule by limiting the felonies to which it is applicable, requiring some degree of *mens rea* with respect to the death, establishing affirmative defences or limiting the punishments available. The rule also exists in New Zealand and certain Australian states, but it is narrower, and abolition has been recommended in some jurisdictions.

Section 213(d) and the Charter

This appeal calls into play two principles of fundamental justice.

The First Principle: The essential elements of certain crimes and s. 7 of the *Charter*

Prior to the enactment of the *Charter*, Parliament had full legislative power with respect to "The Criminal Law" (*Constitution Act, 1867*, s. 91(27)), including the determination of the essential elements of any given crime. It could prohibit any act and impose any penal consequences for infringing the prohibition, provided only that the prohibition served "a public purpose which can support it as being in relation to criminal law": *Ref. re S. 5(a) of the Dairy Indust. Act*, [1949] S.C.R. 1 at 50, affirmed (sub nom. *Cdn. Fed. of Agriculture v. Can. (A.G.)*) [1951] A.C. 179 (P.C.). Once the legislation was found to have met this test, the courts had very little power to review the substance of the legislation. For example, in *R. v. Sault Ste. Marie (City)*, [1978] 2 S.C.R. 1299, 3 C.R. (3d) 30, 40 C.C.C. (2d) 353 [Ont.], Dickson J. (as he then was) held that, when an offence was criminal in the true sense, there was a presumption that the prosecution must prove the *mens rea*. However, it was always open to Parliament expressly to relieve the prosecution of its obligation to prove any part of the *mens rea*, as it is said to have done in s. 213 of the *Criminal Code* with respect to the foreseeability of the death of the victim. It is thus clear that, prior to the enactment of the *Charter*, the validity of s. 213 could not have been successfully challenged.

However, federal and provincial legislatures have chosen to restrict through the *Charter* this power with respect to criminal law. Under s. 7, if a conviction, given either the stigma attached to the offence or the available penalties, will result in a deprivation of the life, liberty or security of the person of the accused, then Parliament must respect the principles of fundamental justice. It has been argued that the principles of fundamental justice in s. 7 are only procedural guarantees. However, in *Ref. re S. 94(2) of Motor Vehicle Act*, [1985] 2 S.C.R. 486, 48 C.R. (3d) 289, 23 C.C.C. (3d) 289, this court rejected that argument and used s. 7 to review the substance of the legislation. As a result, while Parliament retains the power to define the elements of a crime, the courts now have the jurisdiction and, more important, the duty, when called upon to do so, to review that definition to ensure that it is in accordance with the principles of fundamental justice.

This court's decision in *Re Motor Vehicle Act* stands for the proposition that absolute liability infringes the principles of fundamental justice, such that the combination of absolute liability and a deprivation of life, liberty or security of the person is a restriction on one's rights under s. 7 and is *prima facie* a violation thereof. In effect, *Re Motor Vehicle Act* acknowledges that, whenever the state resorts to the restriction of liberty, such as imprisonment, to assist in the enforcement of a law, even, as in *Re Motor Vehicle Act*, a mere provincial regulatory offence, there is, as a principle of fundamental justice, a minimum mental state which is an essential element of the offence. It thus elevated *mens rea* from a presumed element in *Sault Ste. Marie, supra*, to a constitutionally-required element. *Re Motor Vehicle Act* did not decide what level of *mens rea* was constitutionally required for each type of offence, but inferentially decided that even for a mere provincial regulatory offence *at least* negligence was required, in that *at least* a defence of due diligence must *always* be open to an accused who risks imprisonment upon conviction. In *Sault Ste. Marie*, Dickson J. stated at pp. 1309-10:

> Where the offence is criminal, the Crown must establish a mental element, namely, that the accused who committed the prohibited act did so intentionally or recklessly, with knowledge of the facts constituting the offence, or with wilful blindness toward them. Mere negligence is excluded from the concept of the mental element required for conviction. Within the context of a criminal prosecution a person who fails to make such enquiries as a reasonable and prudent person would make, or who fails to know facts he should have known, is innocent in the eyes of the law.

It may well be that, as a general rule, the principles of fundamental justice require proof of a subjective *mens rea* with respect to the prohibited act, in order to avoid punishing the "morally innocent". It must be remembered, however, that

Dickson J. was dealing with the *mens rea* to be presumed in the absence of an express legislative disposition, and not the *mens rea* to be required in all legislation providing for a restriction on the accused's life, liberty or security of the person. In any event, this case involves criminal liability for the result of an intentional criminal act, and it is arguable that different considerations should apply to the mental element required with respect to that result. There are many provisions in the *Code* requiring only objective foreseeability of the result or even only a causal link between the act and the result. As I would prefer not to cast doubt on the validity of such provisions *in this case*, I will assume, but only for the purposes of this appeal, that something less than subjective foresight of the result may sometimes suffice for the imposition of criminal liability for causing that result through intentional criminal conduct.

But, whatever the minimum *mens rea* for the act or the result may be, there are, though very few in number, certain crimes where, because of the special nature of the stigma attached to a conviction therefor or the available penalties, the principles of fundamental justice require a *mens rea* reflecting the particular nature of that crime. Such is theft, where, in my view, a conviction requires proof of some dishonesty. Murder is another such offence. The punishment for murder is the most severe in our society, and the stigma that attaches to a conviction for murder is similarly extreme. In addition, murder is distinguished from manslaughter only by the mental element with respect to the death. It is thus clear that there must be some special mental element with respect to the death before a culpable homicide can be treated as a murder. That special mental element gives rise to the moral blameworthiness which justifies the stigma and sentence attached to a murder conviction. I am presently of the view that it is a principle of fundamental justice that a conviction for murder cannot rest on anything less than proof beyond a reasonable doubt of subjective foresight. Given the effect of this view on part of s. 212(c), for the reasons I have already given for deciding this case more narrowly, I need not and will not rest my finding that s. 213(d) violates the *Charter* on this view, because s. 213(d) does not, for reasons I will set out hereinafter, even meet the lower threshold test of objective foreseeability. I will therefore, for the sole purpose of this appeal, go no further than to say that it is a principle of fundamental justice that, absent proof beyond a reasonable doubt of at least objective foreseeability, there surely cannot be a murder conviction.

Section 1

Finding that s. 213 of the *Criminal Code* infringes ss. 7 and 11(d) of the *Charter* does not end the inquiry on the constitutional validity of s. 213. Any or all of subss. (a) to (d) of s. 213 can still be upheld as a reasonable limit "demonstrably justified in a free and democratic society" under s. 1 of the *Charter*.

In this case and at this stage of the inquiry, we need only consider subs. (*d*) of s. 213. The criteria to be assessed under s. 1 have been set out by this court in several cases, particularly *R. v. Big M Drug Mart Ltd.*, [1985] 1 S.C.R. 295, 18 C.C.C. (3d) 385, and *R. v. Oakes, supra*. First, the objective which the measures are designed to serve must be "of sufficient importance to warrant overriding a constitutionally protected right or freedom": *Big M Drug Mart*, at p. 352 [S.C.R.]. Through s. 213(*d*) of the *Code*, Parliament intended to deter the use or carrying of a weapon in the commission of certain offences, because of the increased risk of death. In my view, it is clear that this objective is sufficiently important.

In addition, the measures adopted must be reasonable and demonstrably justified. The measures adopted appear to be rationally connected to the objective: indiscriminately punishing for murder all those who cause a death by using or carrying a weapon, whether the death was intentional or accidental, might well be thought to discourage the use and the carrying of weapons. I believe, however, that the measures adopted would unduly impair the rights and freedoms in question: see *Big M Drug Mart* at p. 352 [S.C.R.]. It is not necessary to convict of murder persons who did not intend to foresee the death and who could not even have foreseen the death in order to deter others from using or carrying weapons. If Parliament wishes to deter the use or carrying of weapons, it should punish the use or carrying of weapons. A good example of this is the minimum imprisonment for using a firearm in the commission of an indictable offence under s. 83 of the *Criminal Code*. In any event, the conviction for manslaughter which would result instead of a conviction for murder is punishable by from a day in jail to confinement for life in a penitentiary. Very stiff sentences when weapons are involved in the commission of the crime of manslaughter would sufficiently deter the use or carrying of weapons in the commission of crimes. But stigmatizing the crime as murder unnecessarily impairs the *Charter* right.

In my view, therefore, s. 213(*d*) is not saved by s. 1.

CONCLUSION

As a result of the foregoing, I would answer the first constitutional question in the affirmative, as s. 213(*d*) violates both s. 7 and s. 11(*d*) of the *Charter*, and I would declare s. 213(*d*) of the *Criminal Code* to be of no force or effect. I would, for the reasons which I have given, decline to answer the second constitutional question. It follows that the appeal must be allowed, the appellant's conviction for murder set aside, and a new trial ordered.

Short concurring opinions of three justices and the dissenting opinion of McIntyre J. are here omitted.

For views on *Vaillancourt*, see the Criminal Reports Forum in (1988), 60 C.R. (3d) 332-345. See also Stuart, "Progress on the Constitutional Requirement of Fault" (1988), 64 C.R. (3d) 352.

In *Martineau* Lamer C.J. went further, finding a majority for the view that under s. 7 of the *Charter* objective foresight is not enough to establish murder. There must be subjective foresight of the likelihood of death.

R. v. MARTINEAU

[1990] 2 S.C.R. 633, 79 C.R. (3d) 129, 58 C.C.C. (3d) 353,
1990 CarswellAlta 143, 1990 CarswellAlta 657

The accused and a companion, armed with a pellet pistol and a rifle respectively, set out to commit a crime. The accused testified that he thought it would only be a break and enter. They forced their way into a trailer and tied up two of its occupants, James and Ann McLean. The companion shot and killed the two people after robbing them and their home. The accused testified that as soon as he heard the first shot, he realized that James McLean had been shot. He testified that he then "said or thought, 'Lady, say your prayers'". As they left, the accused asked his companion why he killed them and the companion answered "They saw our faces". The accused responded "But they couldn't see mine 'cause I had a mask on". The accused was convicted of second degree murder. The trial judge charged the jury on s. 213(a) and (d) (now s. 230(a) and (d)) and on s. 21(1) and (2) of the *Criminal Code*. The Court of Appeal held that s. 213(a) was inconsistent with ss. 7 and 11(d) of the *Charter* for reasons given in *R. v. Vaillancourt* and that it was not saved by s. 1 of the *Charter*. The Court ordered a new trial and the Crown appealed.

Per LAMER C.J.C. (DICKSON C.J.C. and WILSON, GONTHIER and CORY JJ. concurring): —

This is the first of a series of appeals that raises the constitutionality of s. 213(*a*) of the *Criminal Code*, R.S.C. 1970, c. C-34, (now s. 230(*a*), *Criminal Code*, R.S.C., 1985, c. C-46).

. . . .

In *Vaillancourt* I analyzed a number of matters, including s. 213 of the *Code* in the context of the other murder provisions, the historical development of s. 213, felony murder provisions in other jurisdictions, the essential elements of certain crimes at common law, and the principles of fundamental justice under the *Charter* and their application to s. 213 of the *Code*. As a result of this analysis I concluded that objective foreseeability of death was the minimum threshold test before a conviction for murder could be sustained. I went on to state, however, that it was my view that the principles of fundamental justice require more; they demand that a conviction for murder requires proof beyond a reasonable doubt of subjective foresight of death. The Chief Justice, Estey and Wilson JJ. agreed with that position. I am still of that view today, and indeed, while I agree with the Alberta Court of Appeal and could dispose of this appeal on the basis of objective foreseeability, it is on the basis of the principle of subjective foresight of death that I choose to dispose of this appeal. I choose this route because I would not want this case, a very serious matter, to return to this court once again on the grounds that there is some doubt as to the validity of the portion of s. 212(*c*) of the *Code* that allows for a conviction for murder if the accused "ought to know" that death is likely to result. I need not, therefore, repeat the analysis from *Vaillancourt* here, except to add some brief observations as regards s. 213(*a*) and the principle of fundamental justice that subjective foresight of death is required before a conviction for murder can be sustained.

Section 213(*a*) of the *Code* defines culpable homicide as murder where a person causes the death of a human being while committing or attempting to commit a range of listed offences, whether or not the person means to cause death or whether or not he or she knows that death is likely to ensue if that person means to cause bodily harm for the purpose of facilitating the commission of the offence or flight after committing or attempting to commit the offence. The introductory paragraph of the section, therefore, expressly removes from the Crown the burden of proving beyond a reasonable doubt that the accused had subjective foresight of death. This section stands as an anomaly as regards the other murder provisions, especially in light of the common-law presumption against convicting a person of a true crime without proof of intent or recklessness: *R. v. Sault Ste. Marie (City)*, [1978] 2 S.C.R. 1299 at 1309-10, 3 C.R. (3d) 30, 40 C.C.C. (2d) 353, [Ont.], per Dickson J., (as he then was).

A conviction for murder carries with it the most severe stigma and punishment of any crime in our society. The principles of fundamental justice require, because of the special nature of the stigma attached to a conviction for murder, and the available penalties, a *mens rea* reflecting the particular nature of that crime. The effect of s. 213 is to violate the principle that punishment must be proportionate to the moral blameworthiness of the offender, or as Professor Hart puts it in *Punishment and Responsibility* (1968), at p. 162, the fundamental principle of a morally based system of law that those causing harm intentionally be punished more severely than those causing harm unintentionally. The rationale underlying the principle that subjective foresight of death is required before a person is labelled and punished as a murderer is linked to the more general principle that criminal liability for a particular result is not justified except where the actor possesses a culpable mental state in respect of that result: see *R. v. Bernard*, [1988] 2 S.C.R. 833, 67 C.R. (3d) 113, 45 C.C.C. (3d) 1, per McIntyre J.; and *R. v. Buzzanga* (1979), 49 C.C.C. (2d) 369 (C.A.), per Martin J.A. In my view, in a free and democratic society that values the autonomy and free will of the individual, the stigma and punishment attaching to the most serious of crimes, murder, should be reserved for those who choose to intentionally cause death or who choose to inflict bodily harm that they know is likely to cause death. The essential role of requiring subjective foresight of death in the context of murder is to maintain a proportionality between the stigma and punishment attached to a murder conviction and the moral blameworthiness of the offender. Murder has long been recognized as the "worst" and most heinous of peace time crimes. It is, therefore, essential that to satisfy the principles of fundamental justice, the stigma and punishment attaching to a murder conviction must be reserved for those who either intend to cause death or who intend to cause bodily harm that they know will likely cause death. In this regard, I refer to the following works as support for my position, in addition to those cited in *Vaillancourt*: Cross, "The Mental Element in Crime" (1967), 83 L.Q. Rev. 215; Ashworth, "The Elasticity of *Mens Rea*" in Crime, Proof and Punishment (1981); Williams, The Mental Element in Crime (1965); and Williams, "Convictions and Fair Labelling" [1983] 42 C.L.J. 85.

In sum then, I am of the view that a special mental element with respect to death is necessary before a culpable homicide can be treated as murder. That special mental element gives rise to the moral blameworthiness that justifies the stigma and punishment attaching to a murder conviction. For all the foregoing reasons, and for the reasons stated in *Vaillancourt*, I conclude that it is a principle of fundamental justice that a conviction for murder cannot rest on anything less than proof beyond a reasonable doubt of subjective foresight of death. That was my position when *Vaillancourt* was decided, and that is my position today. Therefore, since s. 213 of the *Code* expressly eliminates the requirement for proof of subjective foresight, it infringes ss. 7 and 11(*d*) of the *Charter*.

As regards s. 1 of the *Charter*, there is no doubt that the objective of deterring the infliction of bodily harm during the commission of certain offences because of the increased risk of death is of sufficient importance to warrant overriding a *Charter* right. Further, indiscriminately punishing for murder all those who cause death irrespective of whether they intended to cause death might well be thought to discourage the infliction of bodily harm during the commission of certain offences because of the increased risk of death. But it is not necessary in order to achieve this objective to convict of murder persons who do not intend or foresee the death. In this regard the section unduly impairs the *Charter* rights. If Parliament wishes to deter persons from causing bodily harm during certain offences, then it should punish persons for causing the bodily harm. Indeed, the conviction for manslaughter that would result instead of a conviction for murder is punishable by, from a day in jail, to confinement for life. Very stiff sentences for the infliction of bodily harm leading to death in appropriate cases would sufficiently meet any deterrence objective that Parliament might have in mind. The more flexible sentencing scheme under a conviction for manslaughter is in accord with the principle that punishment be meted out with regard to the level of moral blameworthiness of the offender. To label and punish a person as a murderer who did not intend or foresee death unnecessarily stigmatizes and punishes those whose moral blameworthiness is not that of a murderer, and thereby unnecessarily impairs the rights guaranteed by ss. 7 and 11(*d*) of the *Charter*. In my view then, s. 213(*a*), indeed all of s. 213, cannot be saved by s. 1 of the *Charter*.

The fact that I have based my reasons on the principle of subjective foresight casts serious if not fatal doubt on the constitutionality of part of s. 212(*c*) of the *Code*, specifically the words "ought to know is likely to cause death". The validity of s. 212(*c*) of the *Code* has not been directly attacked in this appeal, but the court has had the benefit of hearing argument from the Attorney General of Canada and from the Attorneys General for Alberta, British Columbia, Ontario, Quebec, and Manitoba, who chose to intervene, on the issue of whether subjective foresight or objective foreseeability of death is the constitutionally required minimum *mens rea* for murder. In my view, subjective foresight of death must be proven beyond a reasonable doubt before a conviction for murder can be sustained, and as a result, it is obvious the part of s. 212(*c*) of the *Code* allowing for a conviction upon proof that the accused ought to have known that death was likely to result violates ss. 7 and 11(*d*) of the *Charter*. I find further support for this view in the following passage from Professor Stuart's treatise *Canadian Criminal Law: A Treatise*, at pp. 217-18, dealing specifically with the objective element of s. 212(*c*) of the *Code* and the principle of subjective foresight:

> This is a clear instance where our legislation has not kept up with developments in other jurisdictions. We have seen that a similar objective test for murder resorted to by the House of Lords in the notorious decision in *Director of Public Prosecutions v. Smith* (1960) [[1961] A.C. 290 (H.L.)] was rejected by the British Legislature and by the Australian High Court. Very few jurisdictions, including those in the United States, resort to anything but the subjective approach in defining murder. The only direct parallels to our section 212(*c*) are to be found in the codes of Queensland, Tasmania, and New Zealand. The wording in these provisions is almost identical to ours except that in New Zealand the words "or ought to have known" were deleted as a result of a quick and firm rejection of *Smith*. The New Zealand section now reads in part:

> ... if the offender for any unlawful object does an act that he knows to be likely to cause death, and thereby kills any person, though he may have desired that his object should be effected without hurting anyone.

Indeed, Lord Goff in his article "The Mental Element in the Crime of Murder" (1988), 104 L.Q. Rev. 30, at p. 36, had this to say about the *Smith* decision and about objective foreseeability as a test for murder:

> This decision was very much criticised, by Judge and jurist alike. What they disliked about it was that it imposed an objective instead of a subjective test for ascertaining the existence of the relevant mental element for the crime of murder. In due course, it was reversed by statute; later, on an appeal from a jurisdiction where that statute did not apply at the relevant time, *Smith* was, in effect, held by the Judicial Committee of the Privy Council to have been wrongly decided (see *Frankland and Moore v. R.*), [[1987] 2 W.L.R. 1251]). *So the objective test was never part of the common law, properly understood; and we can now forget about it.* [Emphasis added.]

Although it would be open to save that part of s. 212(c) under s. 1 of the *Charter*, it seems to me that the attempt would fail for the reasons I have given in respect of the attempt to similarly save s. 213 of the *Code*. I would therefore answer the constitutional questions as follows:

> Q: Does s. 213(a) of the *Criminal Code* infringe or deny the rights or freedoms guaranteed by s. 7 and/or s. 11(d) of the *Canadian Charter of Rights and Freedoms*?
>
> A: Yes, the section infringes both ss. 7 and 11(d) of the *Charter*.
>
> Q: If the answer to question 1 is affirmative, is s. 213(a) justified by s. 1 of the *Canadian Charter of Rights and Freedoms*, and therefore not inconsistent with the *Constitution Act, 1982*?
>
> A: No.

The only remaining issue is the potential application of s. 613(1)(b)(iii) of the *Criminal Code*. The Court of Appeal for Alberta declined to invoke the section and enter a conviction for the following reason, at p. 279:

> The jury in this case was not instructed on any portion of s. 212. I am unable to say that a properly instructed jury must necessarily have found that the appellant had, at some point, the requisite intention under that section rather than being carried along by events.

I agree. In the present case, the respondent was convicted pursuant to a combination of ss. 213 and 21 of the *Code*. Since in this case the jury was left only with s. 213 which has been declared to be inoperative, a new trial must be ordered. Accordingly, the Court of Appeals decision quashing the convictions and directing a new trial is affirmed. The appeal is, therefore, dismissed.

L'HEUREUX-DUBÉ J. (dissenting): —

. . . .

My colleague concludes that s. 213(a) is unconstitutional because it violates ss. 7 and 11(d) of the *Charter* and cannot be saved by s. 1. In his opinion, the principles of fundamental justice demand that subjective foresight of death be proven beyond a reasonable doubt before a conviction for murder can be secured. I reach a contrary conclusion on the basis that subjective foresight is not the only appropriate standard that can be applied to conform to ss. 7 and 11(d) of the *Charter*. My reasons are as follows: the test of objective foreseeability of death for the crime of murder does not offend the principles of fundamental justice; this Court's decisions, including *R. v. Vaillancourt*, [1987] 2 S.C.R. 636, 60 C.R. (3d) 289, 39 C.C.C. (3d) 118 [Que.], do not commend such a result; the exclusive standard of subjective foresight of death for the crime of murder has found no parallel in other common law jurisdictions; and there are significant policy considerations in favour of upholding the existing legislation.

. . . .

The above analysis indicates that tests of subjective foresight and objective foreseeability cannot be seen as static or distinct concepts. They are certainly not mutually exclusive. In most instances, and certainly in those limited circumstances delineated by s. 213(*a*), discussed below, death will be both objectively and subjectively foreseeable. There is a profound interrelationship between the two, especially when dealing with a crime committed during the execution of a predicate crime. The validity of a provision should not be evaluated on a strict "either-or" approach, and a fastidious adherence to prescribed labels becomes particularly obdurate when gauging the constitutionality of Parliamentary legislation.

. . . .

Vaillancourt held that s. 213(*d*) of the *Criminal Code* violated ss. 7 and 11(*d*) of the *Canadian Charter of Rights and Freedoms*, and could not be saved by s. 1. Paragraph 213(*a*) of the *Criminal Code* is completely different — in its historical development, in its consistency with the objective foreseeability of death test established in *Vaillancourt*, and in the parallel provisions adopted in other common law jurisdictions.

. . . .

(b)   *Section 213(a) Passes the Objective Foreseeability Test*

An exacting combination of factors *must* be proven, all beyond a reasonable doubt, before the accused can be found guilty of murder under this paragraph. The offender must:

(1) cause the death by means of the commission of a "culpable homicide";

(2) cause the death while committing or attempting to commit one of a limited number of very serious crimes all of which are, by their very nature, inherently dangerous;

(3) intentionally inflict bodily harm while committing one of these inherently dangerous offences, all of which are specific intent crimes;

(4) inflict the bodily harm purposefully in order to perpetrate the dangerous underlying crime or for the purpose of facilitating his flight; and

(5) the death must ensue from the bodily harm intentionally inflicted.

It should be noted that in the present case the underlying offence was committed, and the intent to inflict bodily harm was clear. Moreover, this amalgamation of indispensable prerequisites establishes that this crime, as phrased by Lamer J. in *Vaillancourt* is "tantamount to one which has objective foreseeability as an essential element, and, if objective foreseeability is sufficient, then it would not be in violation of s. 7 or s. 11(*d*) in doing so in that way". I am of the view that in light of these requirements, the test of objective foreseeability is sufficient, and that if that test has been met, then no *Charter* violation has taken place. The above list requires that the accused specifically intend to, and actually commit the underlying offence, and specifically intend to, and actually inflict bodily harm. In my view, the inexorable conclusion is that the resulting death is objectively foreseeable.

Those who are critical of all forms of the "felony-murder" rule base their denunciation on the premise that *mens rea* is the exclusive determinant of the level of "stigma" that is properly applied to an offender. This appears to me to confuse some very fundamental principles of criminal law and ignores the pivotal contribution of *actus reus* to the definition and appropriate response to proscribed criminal offences. If both components, *actus reus* as well as *mens rea*, are not considered when assessing the level of fault attributable to an offender, we would see manslaughter and assault causing bodily harm as no more worthy of condemnation than an assault. Mere attempts would become as serious as full offences. The whole correlation between the consequences of a criminal act and its retributive repercussions would become obscured by a stringent and exclusive examination of the accused's own asserted intentions.

As stated in Crump and Crump, "In Defense of the Felony Murder Doctrine" (1985), 8 Harv. J. of L. and P.P. 359, at p. 366:

> Scholarly criticisms of felony murder have tended to neglect its relationship to proportionality and grading. The criticisms erroneously tend to regard *mens rea* as the only legitimate determinant of the grade of a homicide resulting from a felony. This reasoning sometimes leads modern writers into the same rigid formalism, divorced from policy, that they rightly reject in historical justifications of the rule. *Mens rea is not a "unified field theory" of homicide, and while such a theory might make the subject artificially "logical" or "consistent", it does not reflect our society's more complex understanding of the nature, function, and purpose of the criminal law. The fallacy of this approach is its denigration of actus reus and its failure to include the result of defendant's conduct as a determinant of just disposition.* [Emphasis added.]

. . . .

(c) *A Comparative Analysis*

This sudden introduction of a subjective foresight standard for the crime of murder is most novel, and finds no parallel in Great Britain, Australia, New Zealand or the United States. While each of these jurisdictions imposes different requirements for the crime of murder, none has adopted the requirement of subjective foresight of death.

. . . .

IV. POLICY CONSIDERATIONS

During the 27-year period from 1961-87, the evidence reveals that 2,177 homicide offences occurred during the commission of another criminal act. The percentage of homicide offences committed during the commission of another criminal act has varied from 11.9 percent in 1965 to 28.4 percent in 1970. The annual average for the period was 16.7 percent. "Homicide in Canada: Offences Committed During the Commission of Another Criminal Act", statistics provided by R.C.M.P. for the period 1961-87. The homicide offences committed during another criminal act are divided into four categories:

Robbery: includes robbery, theft, and break and enter offences. 1315 victims; 61.7 percent of all homicide offences committed during another criminal act.

Sexual Assault & Rape: includes all sexual attacks on either males or females. 483 victims; 22.3 percent of all homicide offences committed during another criminal act.

Escape: involves attempts to escape from correctional institutions or lawful custody, to avoid arrest, or to escape detection as a parole or probation violator. 346 victims; 14.2 percent of all homicide offences committed during another criminal act.

Other: includes other types of criminal acts such as arson, assault, kidnapping, etc. 33 victims; 1.8 percent of all homicide offences committed during another criminal act.

These statistics reflect a matter of critical public concern, and sustain the Legislature's compulsion to deliver an appropriate response. It is constitutionally permissible under the *Canadian Charter of Rights and Freedoms* to define the mental element required for murder with reference to an intention by the perpetrator to harm or injure the victim, with death resulting. How that harm or injury is to be defined, and what level of harm or injury is required are matters for Parliament to consider and decide.

. . . .

The fact that the principles embraced by s. 213(*a*) have existed for over 300 years is in itself relevant, though not necessarily determinative, of whether or not a rule of "fundamental justice" has been breached by virtue of their adoption by the Parliament of Canada. In my view, while the guarantee entrenched in s. 7 of the *Charter* is to have broad application, it cannot go so far as to grant the courts judicial licence to modify or strike down legislation in the absence of a constitutional violation.

. . . .

Section 213(*a*) is intended to carve out certain killings and place them in a category of the most serious culpable homicides, murder. This is a designation which Parliament is entitled to ascribe pursuant to its responsibility for the protection of those under its dominion. This legislative objective can be anchored in Parliament's legitimate attempt to deter persons from conduct which falls within s. 213(*a*). In particular, Parliament is attempting to deter those who commit crimes from intentionally inflicting actual bodily harm on their victims in order to achieve their unlawful purpose. The killings subsumed within s. 213(*a*) are regarded as sufficiently heinous to warrant being placed in the category of the gravest culpable homicides. Parliament felt that this was the appropriate manner to ensure that the criminal law is in accordance with social values as to the gravity of such killings, and that this was an effective method to preserve the lives and safety of Canadians.

In *R. v. Arkell* (1988), 43 C.C.C. (3d) 402, 64 C.R. (3d) 340 (B.C. C.A.), affirmed 79 C.R. (3d) 207, 59 C.C.C. (3d) 65, [1990] 2 S.C.R. 695, at pp. 412-13, McLachlin J.A. (now of this court) considered the validity of s. 214(5) (now s. 231(5)). Writing for the British Columbia Court of Appeal – this court's decision in *Arkell* is being rendered concurrently with the present one – she held that:

> ... it must be recognized that many factors other than the accused's degree of moral blameworthiness must be considered by Parliament in establishing a sentencing scheme. General deterrence, the degree of perceived danger to the public and the prevalence of certain types of offences are only some of the other considerations which Parliament may properly consider. It follows that the mere fact that a harsher sentence may be imposed for one offence than for another offence which is arguably more blameworthy, does not mean that the scheme that permits the sentence violates s. 7 of the *Charter*.
>
> . . . .
>
> Many factors enter into the determination of an appropriate penalty for a particular offence; the degree of blameworthiness is only one. *The question is one of policy, to be determined by Parliament. So long as Parliament does not act irrationally or arbitrarily or in a manner otherwise inconsistent with the fundamental principles of justice, its choice must be upheld.* [Emphasis added.]

I agree completely, and find that the test applies to s. 213(a) as well. If Parliament chooses to label a crime "murder" and attach commensurate penalties, so long as a *mens rea* requirement is imposed, as it is here, this court should not lightly interfere with that legislative decision. Mewett & Manning, writing before this court's decision in *Vaillancourt*, acknowledged at pp. 544-45 that:

> Section 213 [now section 230] and the concept of constructive murder have been much criticized and, in fact, abolished in many jurisdictions. The criticism is that it imposes liability for murder in situations where death was not intended nor even, in some cases, foreseen. *But murder is a legal concept; it does not have to be defined in terms of intentional killing, and even under s. 212 [now s. 229] the definition is not this narrow. The policy behind s. 213 is to put the risk of killing a victim during the course of the commission of certain offences upon the offender to a higher degree than if it were merely classified as manslaughter.* In any case, with the present distinction between murder punishable by death and murder punishable by life imprisonment now abolished, much of the criticism loses its force. It was the thought of

someone being executed for a non-intended homicide that led to the feeling that the definition of murder should somehow be limited to the old common law concept of "murder with malice aforethought". [Emphasis added.]

Parliament can abrogate s. 213 in its entirety and pioneer a strict subjective standard for the crime of murder, but the Constitution does not require that it do so. As McIntyre J. said, dissenting in *Vaillancourt*, at p. 663:

The principal complaint in this case is not that the accused should not have been convicted of a serious crime deserving of severe punishment, but simply that Parliament should not have chosen to call that crime "murder". No objection could be taken if Parliament classified the offence as manslaughter or a killing during the commission of an offence, or in some other manner. . . While it may be illogical to characterize an unintentional killing as murder, *no principle of fundamental justice is offended only because serious criminal conduct, involving the commission of a crime of violence resulting in the killing of a human being, is classified as murder and not in some other manner.* [Emphasis added.]

In *R. v. Smith*, [1987] 1 S.C.R. 1045, 34 C.C.C. (3d) 97, 58 C.R. (3d) 193, Lamer J. cited numerous examples of curial deference to Parliamentary enactments. My colleague then adopted, at p. 1070, the following passage of Borins Dist. Ct. J. from *R. v. Guiller*, Ont. Dist. Ct., Sept. 23, 1985, unreported:

It is not for the court to pass on the wisdom of Parliament with respect to the gravity of various offences and the range of penalties which may be imposed upon those found guilty of committing the offences. *Parliament has broad discretion in proscribing conduct as criminal* and in determining proper punishment. While the final judgment as to whether a punishment exceeds constitutional limits set by the *Charter* is properly a judicial function the court should be reluctant to interfere with the considered views of Parliament and then only in the clearest of cases where the punishment prescribed is so excessive when compared with the punishment prescribed for other offences as to outrage standards of decency. [Emphasis added.]

In the present appeal, my colleague's justification for insisting on the narrowest of all possible definitions for the crime of murder is that [pp. 106-107]:

A conviction for murder carries with it the most severe stigma and punishment of any crime in our society. . . . [and] should be reserved for those who choose to intentionally cause death or who choose to inflict bodily harm that they know is likely to cause death.

The menacing component of "stigma" was discussed in *Vaillancourt* as well. As Lindsay pointed out in "The Implications of *R. v. Vaillancourt*: Much Ado About Nothing?" (1989), 47 U. of Toronto Fac. L. Rev. 465, at p. 472:

It should also be noted that Lamer J. justified a requirement of a "special mental element" based on *either* the stigma associated with a crime or the penalties available. A murder conviction qualified on both grounds. However, theft can involve penalties as low as an absolute discharge. *Thus, the inclusion of theft in Lamer J.'s list of crimes requiring a "special mental element" must have been based on stigma rather than available penalties.* [Emphasis added.]

I find this concentration on social "stigma" to be overemphasized, and in the great majority of cases, completely inapplicable. The facts in the present appeals reveal the truly heinous nature of the criminal acts at issue. The concern that these offenders not endure the Mark of Cain is, in my view, an egregious example of misplaced compassion. If the apprehension is that the offenders in question will suffer from their "murderer" label, I suspect they will fare little better tagged as "manslaughterers". Accidental killings cannot, after *Vaillancourt*, result in murder prosecutions. Only killings resulting from circumstances in which death is, at a minimum, objectively foreseeable will be prosecuted under s. 213(*a*). Furthermore, the duration of imprisonment, if at all different, will not attenuate the "stigma". To the extent that any such "stigma" can be said to exist, it is at least as palpable upon release to the outside world as it is within the prison environment itself.

. . . .

Section 213(*a*) does not deal with accidental killings, but rather with killings that are objectively foreseeable as a result of the abominable nature of the predicate crimes, committed with specific intent, coupled with the intentional infliction of bodily harm. Given the dual subjective requirement already in place, the deterrence factor is most cogent in these circumstances. Whatever the competing arguments may be with respect to deterring the merely negligent, here we are dealing with those who have already expressly acted with the intent to commit at least two underlying serious crimes. If deterrence is to ever have any application to the criminal law, and in my view it should, this is the place.

Deterrence can neither be analyzed in the abstract nor in isolation from the context of the provision in question. Section 213(*a*) deals with one who has already proven to be a "hijacker", a "kidnapper", a "rapist", or an "arsonist". Furthermore, this person has already proven willing to cause bodily harm to commit the offence or to enable himself to escape after having committed the offence. In these circumstances, it is certainly appropriate for Parliament to put this person on notice, that if these purposeful acts result in death, you will be charged as a "murderer" as well.

This notion of Parliamentary autonomy cannot be displaced unless a *Charter* violation has occurred. In my view that has not taken place here. Repeating my colleagues own test, as articulated in *Vaillancourt* at p. 657, if the legislation is "tantamount to one which has objective foreseeability as an essential element, and, if objective foreseeability is sufficient, then it would not be in violation of s. 7 or s. 11(*d*) in doing so in that way."

V. Conclusion

Policy considerations in Canada as well as in other jurisdictions have inspired legislation that considers objective foreseeability sufficient as the minimum *mens rea* requirement for murder. While it may not be the very best test for all cases, it is certainly a constitutionally valid one. Parliament did not have to enact s. 213(*a*), but that is not the question before this court. The issue is whether it could. In my view, the answer rests on what level of foreseeability will be required before a conviction for murder can be returned. Based on this court's precedents, and the principles of fundamental justice, I believe that the objective foreseeability of death test for the crime of murder is constitutionally valid. The additional mandatory elements demanded by s. 213(*a*) lend even greater force to this conclusion.

Striking down the legislation simply because some other scheme may be preferable would be an unwarranted intrusion into Parliament's prerogative, and would undermine the means it has chosen to protect its citizens. The *Charter* is not designed to allow this court to substitute preferable provisions for those already in place in the absence of a clear constitutional violation. Such a task should be reserved for the Law Reform Commission or other advisory bodies. This court's province is to pronounce upon the constitutionality of those provisions properly before it. The *Charter* does not infuse the courts with the power to declare legislation to be of no force or effect on the basis that they believe the statute to be undesirable as a matter of criminal law policy. For the aforementioned reasons, I do not believe that s. 213(*a*) offends the *Canadian Charter of Rights and Freedoms*.

. . . .

SOPINKA J. (concurring in the result): — I have had the advantage of reading the reasons of Lamer C.J.C. and L'Heureux-Dubé J. [appeal from (1988), 43 C.C.C. (3d) 417]. I agree with Lamer C.J.C. that there must be a new trial in this case. I would give the same answers to the constitutional questions as Lamer C.J.C. but, with respect, I cannot agree with his reasons.

In my view, the issue of subjective foresight of death should be addressed only if it is necessary to do so in order to decide this case or if there is an overriding reason making it desirable to do so. Overbroad statements of principle are inimical to the tradition of incremental development of the common law. Likewise, the development of law under the *Canadian Charter of Rights and Freedoms* is best served by deciding cases before the courts, not by anticipating the results of future cases.

The first inquiry is whether ruling on the issue of subjective foresight is necessary for the disposition of this case. In my view, the case at bar is governed by the reasons given in this court's decision in *R. v. Vaillancourt*, [1987] 2 S.C.R. 636, 60 C.R. (3d) 289, 39 C.C.C. (3d) 118 [Que.]. The court need go no further.

For diverging comments on *Martineau* see Stuart, "Further Progress on the Constitutional Requirement of Fault, But Stigma is Not Enough" (1990), 79 C.R.

(3d) 247 and Rosemary Cairns Way, "Constitutionalizing Subjectivism: Another View" (1990), 79 C.R. (3d) 260.

In *R. v. Sit* (1991), 9 C.R. (4th) 126 (S.C.C.), the Supreme Court made it clear that the constructive murder category under what was s. 213(c) [later s. 230(c)] was also unconstitutional since it resorts to a test of objective foresight and therefore does not involve proof beyond a reasonable doubt that the accused had subjective foresight of the death of the victim.

For over ten years after *Vaillancourt*, prosecutors appeared reluctant to test the possible interpretation that the unlawful object murder category under s. 229(c) was still partially constitutional. However, in *Meiler* (1999), 25 C.R. (5th) 161, 136 C.C.C. (3d) 11 (Ont. C.A.), the Ontario Court of Appeal confirmed a murder conviction where a trial judge had instructed the jury it could convict on the basis of s. 229(c) if it found that the accused for an unlawful object did anything knowing that it was likely to cause someone's death. The decision can be criticized for not adopting a narrower interpretation limiting s. 229(c) to a person who had a subjective awareness of the likelihood of the actual victim's death: see, further, R.J. Delisle, "Unlawful Object Murder Is Alive and Well" (1995), 25 C.R. (5th) 179. In *Meiler*, on the accused's evidence, he was carrying a loaded and cocked shotgun with intent to kill a particular person and the gun discharged during a struggle and accidentally killed another. The particular application of s. 229(c) in *Meiler* appears to resurrect a type of constructive murder the Supreme Court had declared unconstitutional.

R. v. SHAND

80 C.R. (6th) 199, 266 C.C.C. (3d) 137, 2011 CarswellOnt 14 (C.A.), leave to appeal refused (2012), 432 N.R. 391 (note) (S.C.C.)

The accused and two others went to the home of a local drug dealer planning to steal marijuana. The drug dealer indicated that he did not have the quantity of marijuana they were asking for. They noticed the dealer's girlfriend holding a bag of marijuana and pursued her into the basement. There was disputed evidence as to what occurred there. It was clear that the accused pulled out a gun and that it discharged killing a male, F. The dispute was as to whether the gun was discharged accidentally or deliberately. On the second degree murder charge the trial judge directed the jury on s. 229(a)(i), 229(a)(ii) and also s. 229(c). The defence objected to an instruction on s. 229(c) arguing that liability under that section was incompatible with an accidental discharge. The jury convicted of second degree murder.

On appeal the accused, supported by intervenors, challenged the constitutionality of s. 229(c) on the basis that s. 7 of the *Charter* demanded a minimum *mens rea* of intent to cause serious bodily harm to the victim to found a conviction for murder and, in the alternative, that the section violated s. 7 on the basis of vagueness and overbreadth.

ROULEAU J.A.: —

[Before considering whether s. 229(c) is constitutional, Justice Rouleau found it first necessary to determine the proper interpretation and application of the section. Though its wording had undergone little change in over 100 years, its context had changed greatly. There have been amendments to the *Criminal Code*, the phrase "ought to know" was read out of s. 229(c) by the Supreme Court in *R. v. Martineau* [1990] 2 S.C.R. 633 and the Supreme Court held that constructive murder provisions in s. 230 which permitted conviction with objective foresight of death were unconstitutional. The new context dictated a narrower reading of s. 229(c), clearly focused on the requirement that, when the act causing the death is carried out, the accused subjectively foresaw that some person's death is likely. It was important that s. 229(c) be given a meaning distinct from ss. 229(a)(i) and (ii) (para. 129)].

138. In *DeWolfe* [(1976) 130 O.R. (2d) 302 (Ont.C.A.)] , this court commented that courts must be careful about engaging in the unrealistic dissection of the unlawful object in order to fit the facts of the case into s. 229(c). This will arise in situations in which the accused commits an act or series of acts with one general purpose, and the fundamental question facing the trier of fact is whether or not the accused intended to kill or to cause grievous bodily harm to the victim. In these cases, decision makers should be careful not to search out additional and tenuous unlawful objects that the accused carried out, in order to apply s. 229(c)

141. As gatekeeper, the trial judge must be cautious not to instruct juries on s. 229(c) in situations which fit squarely within ss. 229(a) or (b). The unlawful object must be a genuine object, and not simply one aspect of the same "general purpose" of causing death or bodily harm that is likely to cause death.

142. This caution also addresses the concern that section 229 (c) might be used by the Crown as a substitute to ss. 229(a) or (b), in an attempt to somehow lessen the burden of proving intent. . .

3) THE CONSTITUTIONALITY OF s. 229(c)

155 Relying largely on *Vaillancourt* and *Martineau*, the appellant and interveners contend that it is unconstitutional to label an unintentional killing "murder". They argue that s. 229(c) imposes an impermissibly low mens rea requirement for murder, the most serious offence in the *Criminal Code*. In their submission, nothing short of intentionally killing or causing bodily harm knowing that it is likely to cause death, is sufficient to meet the constitutional minimum for murder. Harm caused unintentionally should not be dealt with as harshly as these intentional acts.

156 The appellant and interveners argue that in *Martineau*, the Supreme Court of Canada did not rule on the constitutionality of s. 229(c). In their submission, *Martineau* should be read as establishing the principle that subjective foresight of death is a necessary, but not a sufficient condition to meet the constitutional minimum for murder.

. . . .

158 The Crown submits that, based on existing Supreme Court jurisprudence, the constitutional issue raised by the appellant and interveners has already been decided. A proper reading of Martineau and its companion cases, as well as subsequent decisions of that court, establishes subjective foresight of death as a sufficient constitutional standard of mens rea for murder. The respondent argues that s. 229(c) is, in substance, no different from s. 229(a)(ii). Neither provision requires an intention to cause death. Section 229(a)(ii) requires an intent to cause bodily harm and the subjective foresight of death, while s. 229(c) simply replaces the intent to cause bodily harm with an intent to pursue another unlawful object.

159 The respondent contends that an accused who, engaged in an unlawful pursuit, chooses to commit a dangerous act knowing that another person is likely to die as a result, is as morally blameworthy as the person who intends to cause death or to cause bodily harm knowing that death is likely.

160 In my view, the issue as to whether the *mens rea* for murder under s. 229(c) is constitutionally sufficient has been resolved in past Supreme Court jurisprudence. As I will explain, I agree with the respondent's submission that, in *Martineau* and its companion cases, the Supreme Court of Canada decided the issue, and found s. 229(c) to be constitutional.

. . . .

4) APPLYING THE PRINCIPLES TO THE FACTS OF THIS CASE

188 As explained earlier, s. 229(c) will be satisfied where the following elements are present:

(a) the accused must pursue an unlawful object other than to cause the death of the victim or bodily harm to the victim knowing that death is likely;

(b) the unlawful object must itself be an indictable offence requiring *mens rea* [applying *R. v. Vasil* [1981] 1 S.C.R. 459;

(c) in furtherance of the unlawful object, the accused must intentionally commit a dangerous act;

(d) the dangerous act must be distinct from the unlawful object, but as stated above, only in the sense that the unlawful object must be something other than the likelihood of death, which is the harm that is foreseen as a consequence of the dangerous act;

(e) the dangerous act must be a specific act, or a series of closely related acts, that in fact results in death, though the dangerous act need not itself constitute an offence; and

(f) when the dangerous act is committed, the accused must have subjective knowledge that death is likely to result.

189 In applying the principles outlined above to the facts of this case, the unlawful object was robbery. Although the appellant carried a gun to the robbery, and this is also unlawful, this was not his purpose or goal, so it is not an unlawful object in the sense used in s. 229(c). In all probability, the appellant was hoping to carry out the theft with little violence and no likelihood of death.

190 In identifying the dangerous act, as explained earlier, it is important not to frame the dangerous act too broadly. A broad and vague characterization of what constitutes the dangerous act does not fit well into the causation framework and may skew the subsequent mens rea analysis.

191 It would, for example, be wrong to frame the dangerous act as entering a home with a loaded gun or engaging in a home invasion with a gun. Although these "acts", in a sense, led to the events in the basement bedroom, they were not the acts that actually caused the death.

192 When Brisbois fled to the basement with the marijuana and the appellant and J.B. pursued her, the situation changed significantly.

193 In my view, it is upon entering the basement bedroom that the appellant committed the dangerous act. The act was drawing and using his gun in an attempt to subdue the occupants of the room. This act was clearly done in furtherance of the unlawful object, being the robbery. Whether the gun was intentionally or accidently discharged, it was the choice to use the gun in order to subdue the occupants that caused the death.

194 The critical issue, then, is whether the appellant possessed the necessary mens rea at the time that he committed the dangerous act. If, when he pulled out the gun and used it in the confined space of the basement bedroom, the appellant knew that it was likely to cause death, but did so nonetheless in pursuance of the theft, this would satisfy the mens rea component of s. 229(c).

195 If, however, he did not then know that death was likely, the necessary mens rea would be absent. It is critical that the appellant's state of mind at this particular point in time is ascertained. That determination is a subjective one. The question is not what he ought to have known. The question is what he actually knew and foresaw. Surrounding facts, including the appellant's prior conduct, can be considered to determine what the appellant actually knew. What his state of mind may have been before or after committing the dangerous act is not determinative.

196 In determining the appellant's subjective knowledge, relevant facts could include: the appellant's knowledge of whether the gun was loaded and whether the safety of the gun was on or off; the appellant's knowledge of the presence and location of a person or persons who could be hurt if the gun discharged; whether the appellant was acting in panic or out of fear; the conduct of the appellant as observed by others; whether the appellant drew the gun or had already drawn it; and whether the appellant was using the gun to press or force others to submit or using it in an attempt to extricate himself from a dangerous situation. All of these facts may shed light on the mental state of the appellant at the critical moment in time.

197 The appellant argues that s. 229(c) had no application to the facts of this case, as it requires that there be a dangerous act distinct from the unlawful object. At trial, the theory of the defence was that the appellant brought the gun in order to carry out the robbery and that it discharged accidently, killing the victim. On the appellant's view, there was no dangerous act separate and distinct from the unlawful object of robbery, as the gun and its use were an integral part of the robbery. In other words, this was a robbery gone wrong.

198 As I explained earlier, the dangerous act need not be distinct in the sense of being unrelated to the acts carrying out the unlawful object. In fact, as the text of s. 229(c) requires that the dangerous act be committed for or in pursuance of the unlawful object, the dangerous act must be associated with the unlawful object to fall within the provision. In the present case, the dangerous act was the choice to draw and use the gun in order to subdue the occupants of the basement bedroom and take the bag of marijuana. The fact that the gun may have discharged accidently while being used to that end does not remove these facts from the ambit of s. 229(c).

199 In my view, therefore, there was an adequate factual basis for the trial judge to charge the jury on s. 229(c).

The *Shand* court, in its re-evaluation of s. 229(c) since the *Charter* rulings in *R v. Martineau*, [1990] 2 S.C.R. 633, makes a strong case through meticulous analysis of Supreme Court jurisprudence that the constitutionality of s. 229(c) purged of the object foresight limb has already been decided by the Supreme Court.

Key aspects of the re-evaluation of s. 229(c) in *Shand* are the emphasis that the dangerous act be intentional, that the act cause the death and that there be subjective foresight of the likelihood of death. These requirements are important and welcome vehicles for restraint, remembering that murder carries a mandatory sentence of life imprisonment. This restraint is not as evident in *R. v. S. (J.)* (2008), 237 C.C.C. (3d) 305 (Ont. C.A.), where the Court of Appeal (per Doherty, Moldaver and Watt JJ.A.) decided that s. 229(c) but not the transferred intent s.

229(b) could be applied to convict of murder one who shot over the heads of a Boxing Day sale crowd in a public street at a rival gang member whose return shot killed an innocent bystander aged 15. The *Shand* court at various points goes out of its way to ensure that trial judges do not unduly stretch the ambit of s. 229(c) and indeed do not instruct on it where the issue should focus on whether the accused meant to cause death or bodily harm to the victim and knew of the likelihood of death.

There are, however, some troubling aspects. In its ruling on the facts in *Shand* the Court of Appeal finds that s. 229(c) was applicable even if the discharge of the gun was accidental. This is difficult to square with the Court's strong assertion that the dangerous act must be intentional and that the key mental element is subject foresight of the likelihood of death, not just of a possibility or a danger of death. In this application we appear to be back to a form of constructive murder held unconstitutional in *Martineau*.

Professor Kent Roach, "The Problematic Revival of Murder under Section 229(c) of the Criminal Code" (2010) 47 Alta. L. Rev. 675 shows how the resurgent use of s. 229(c) since *R. v. Meiler* (1999), 25 C.R. (5th) 161 (Ont. C.A.), especially in Ontario, has resulted in accidental killings being held to constitute s. 229(c) murder. He is especially critical of several arson cases. The Court in *Shand* does try to avoid this result in its discussion of arson examples where it emphasizes the requirement of knowledge of the likelihood of death. Roach questions the judicial reluctance to resort to the transferred intent provision in s. 229(b) in cases like *J.S.R.* and questions whether the approach in *J.S.R.* is consistent with the *Charter* standard in *Martineau* that intentional conduct must be punished more severely than negligent conduct. Neither of these issues was addressed in *Shand*.

Although the Court in *Shand* has tried hard to achieve clarity, the six elements it requires for s. 229(c) liability are hugely complex and a nightmare to try to explain to juries; even more so where they have to be combined with a charge on party liability such as under s. 21(2). Where there has been a fatal attack on a person who died as a result, pragmatic judges may wish to keep matters relatively simple and take the Court of Appeal's hint in *Shand* to stick to directions on s. 229(a)(i) and (ii).

There is also a real danger that the Court's reference to a "dangerous act" requirement for s. 229(c) will be hard for the judge or jury to distinguish from unlawful act manslaughter, which presently only requires a dangerous unlawful act and normally no marked departure from the objective norm (*R. v. Creighton*, [1993] 3 S.C.R. 3).

Parliament has not got around to deleting the unconstitutional objective "ought to have foreseen" element from s. 229(c). On three occasions embarrassing for the justice system, s. 229(c) in its unconstitutional form was left with juries. This necessitated new trials in B.C, Ontario and New Brunswick (see the detailed discussion by Roach). In *R. v. Townsend*, 2010 BCCA 400, Justice Chiasson speaking for the Court said:

> I cannot leave these reasons without wondering why steps have not been taken to amend the Criminal Code to conform to the now 20-year-old decision of the Supreme Court of Canada in *Martineau* determining that language in s. 229(c) is unconstitutional. The law that is recorded in the statute, on which every citizen is entitled to rely, is not the law of the land. An issue such as arose in this case should not occur. It creates the risk of a miscarriage of justice and the potential

> need to incur significant costs addressing an error in an appellate court with the possible costs of a new trial, assuming one is practical. In my view, failure to deal appropriately with such matters by updating the *Criminal Code* to remove provisions that have been found to offend the Constitution is not in the interests of justice. [para. 43]

A similar error occurred in September 2016 where a trial judge in Alberta relied on the long-declared unconsitutional constructive murder provision s. 230, to convict Travis Vader of murder. Bill C-39 before Parliament would remove *Criminal Code* provisions declared unconstitutional.

The Ontario Court of Appeal adopted a strict approach to the fault element for s. 229(c) in the arson case of *R. v. Roks* (2011), 87 C.R. (6th) 144 (Ont. C.A.), additional reasons (2011), 284 C.C.C. (3d) 510 (Ont. C.A.). The accused was guilty of a conspiracy to commit arson of a building to defraud insurers. The conspirators had hired expert arsonists but they had used too much gasoline and one of the arsonists had died in the explosion. Justice Watt decided the trial judge had reached an unreasonable verdict in finding the accused guilty of murder under s. 229(c). Considering the requirements set out in *Shand,* the unlawful object was fraud on the insurers and the act of setting the store premises on fire was a dangerous, unlawful act committed intentionally that was distinct from the unlawful object. However, the evidence did not support the conclusion that the accused knew that the death of a human being would likely occur. Justice Watt defined the requisite fault element as follows:

> The accused must know that the death of a human being is a *likely* consequence of the dangerous act. The term "likely" refers to the probability of a consequence. Proof that an accused was aware of the risk, possibility, danger or chance of death as a consequence of a dangerous act is inadequate to establish the mental or fault element in s. 229(c). [para. 134]

Justice Watt noted that the accused was not involved in the setting of the fire and knew that the fire was to be set on Christmas Eve to minimize the risk to others. Foresight of death was not enough. At points the trial judge wrongly spoke of foresight of harm. She also proceeded backwards from the fact that someone died to the conclusion the accused must have known someone would die. She relied heavily on the "common sense proposition" that "harm or death is a natural and even likely consequence of spreading accelerants in a building then setting fire to them". Her analysis essentially substituted a test of objective foreseeability, which was constitutionally infirm. A verdict of manslaughter was substituted and a ten-year sentence later imposed: (2011), 284 C.C.C. (3d) 510 (Ont. C.A.).

Roks was a judge-alone case where we see the trier of fact's reasoning process. Justice Watt decided that knowledge of likelihood is to be interpreted as knowledge of a probability. We have seen that courts have long not required that gloss to be automatically included in jury directions on the meaning of knowledge of likelihood of death for s. 229(a)(ii) purposes. That view should now be reconsidered for reasons of consistency and proper jury comprehension. The meaning of likelihood is not self-evident. Jury instructions on the meaning of reasonable doubt have long found it important to explain distinctions between possibilities, probabilities and certainty.

(iii)   First degree murder: s. 231

The punishment for both first and second degree murder is fixed at life imprisonment. The significance of the distinction relates to parole eligibility: see s. 745.

R. v. SMITH

(1979), 51 C.C.C. (2d) 381, 1979 CarswellSask 193 (Sask. C.A.)

CULLITON C.J.S.: — Gerald Thomas Smith was charged that he, on July 9, 1978, at the Edenwold District, Saskatchewan, did cause the death of Darryl Wayne Skwarchuk and thereby commit first degree murder contrary to s. 218 [now s. 231] [rep. & sub. 1974-75-76, c. 93, s. 5] of the *Criminal Code*.

After a jury trial presided over by MacLeod J., he was found guilty as charged and was sentenced to life imprisonment without eligibility for parole until he has served 25 years of his sentence.

While he has appealed in respect of conviction and sentence, his counsel conceded both at the trial and on the appeal that there were only three verdicts open to the jury, namely, guilty of first degree murder, guilty of second degree murder or guilty of manslaughter. I am satisfied the evidence fully supported that position.

The argument that a verdict of manslaughter was open to the jury was founded on the plea of provocation. That defence was rejected by the jury and, in my view, rightly so. Thus, the sole question on the appeal is simply whether or not there was evidence of planning and deliberation upon which the jury could properly find the appellant guilty of first degree murder.

For the court to consider this question, it is not necessary to review all of the evidence adduced at trial. The evidence upon which the Crown relied in its contention that a finding of first degree murder was a proper finding, was the evidence of William Mitchel Massier. I think it is evident the jury accepted his evidence and it is the only evidence in respect of the actual killing.

Massier was a young man 18 years of age, who, at the time he gave evidence, was also charged with the murder of Skwarchuk. He said he knew Smith and first met him in October, 1977, while working at MacDonald's. He said, he also knew Skwarchuk and met him in November, 1977, while Skwarchuk was working at a laundromat. He said that he, Smith and Skwarchuk became friends. He said they partied together and jointly engaged in a number of breaking and entering offences in the spring of 1978. He said from time to time they went hunting together and probably did so some 20 or 25 times. They always went north of the city and usually had a rented car or Skwarchuk's car. On occasion he said they had a friend's car.

Massier said that on July 9, 1978, he had a .12 gauge shot-gun. He said he had possessed that gun for three or four months having obtained it from an apartment which they broke and entered. He said Skwarchuk also had a .22 gun and that Smith owned a .22 semi-automatic rifle and a pellet gun.

Smith lived at 201 Branew Apts. at the corner of St. John St. and Victoria Ave. Massier testified they used to party there. These parties consisted of drinking liquor and at times smoking marijuana and taking pills. Skwarchuk lived on Osler St.

On Sunday, July 9, 1978, at about 11:00 or 11:30 a.m., Massier said Smith telephoned to him and asked if they should keep the rented car that day. According to Massier, Smith had possession of a car which they had rented the previous day. He told Smith to keep the car.

About 12 noon, Smith arrived at Massier's place in the car accompanied by Skwarchuk. Massier said he went out and was told they were going hunting and he said he would go with them. They then went to Smith's apartment and picked up a .22 ruger with a scope, a .12 gauge shot-gun and a pellet pistol. The shot-gun had been sawed off and was owned by Massier. Smith also brought some shot-gun shells. They then went to Skwarchuk's and obtained 50 rounds of .22 ammunition.

After this, they drove to MacDonald's where they had something to eat. According to Massier, Smith and Skwarchuk were taking valium pills. After eating, they returned to Massier's place and picked up some tools and a pair of gloves. According to Massier, they obtained the tools and gloves because Smith said he wanted to break into a drug store. At the same time, they picked up more .22 ammunition.

Following this, they drove north on Highway 6. After travelling some 10 or 15 miles they turned west off of the highway. Massier said, from time to time, thereafter, they stopped to shoot birds, ducks and mail boxes. Finally they arrived at an abandoned farmhouse and stopped there. Smith shot off the door knob with the shot-gun.

According to the evidence of Massier, while driving from Regina, Smith had consumed the best part of a mickey of rye. He said during the drive there was considerable conversation about girl friends but no unfriendliness was shown by anyone.

After Smith had shot off the door knob, Massier said he broke down the inside door and they all went into the house. He said Smith and Skwarchuk were shooting up the house and windows with the shot-gun and he smashed a couple of windows with a beer bottle. He said he also shot a few rounds with the .22.

Massier said after about 15 minutes, Smith and Skwarchuk said they wanted to leave. They then all left the house. He said they went to the car and there he obtained a pair of leather gloves. He said he put the gloves on and returned to the house and started smashing windows with a board. He said he smashed two front windows and then smashed a window on the west side. He jumped through this window and was then at the back of the house. He broke two more windows there and then went around the corner where he saw Smith and Skwarchuk and heard an argument between them.

Massier said he was some distance away and could not understand exactly what they were saying. He said it seemed to him Smith was telling Skwarchuk to put down his gun and he would do the same. He said Smith had the shot-gun and Skwarchuk the .22 and they were pointing the guns at each other.

Massier said he did not think the situation was serious so he returned to his window breaking activity. He said he was on the east side of the house when he heard a shot. He testified he then immediately came to the front of the house and saw Smith standing at the front of the car, on the driver's side, and Skwarchuk was about three yards from the rear bumper on the passenger side. He saw Smith with the shot-gun in his hand and Skwarchuk's gun was on the ground. He said Skwarchuk had been shot in the left elbow, and his arm was hanging and blood was squirting on the ground. He said Skwarchuk was running away; that he ran some distance, stopped and faced the car. Massier testified Skwarchuk was screaming and yelling and said he was bleeding to death and should be taken to a hospital.

When Skwarchuk stopped, Massier said he went to the car and asked Smith what was going on and Smith told him to shut up. He said he asked Smith if he was going to shoot Skwarchuk and Smith did not answer. He said he then asked Smith if he was going to shoot him and Smith told him to shut up and get behind him. According to Massier, this episode lasted from one to three minutes. During this time, Smith reloaded the shot-gun. He put in five shells. According to Massier, Smith then called Skwarchuk's name. Following this Skwarchuk took a step towards the car and when Smith pumped the shell into the chambers of the gun, Skwarchuk turned and ran. He said Smith shot from long range and he could not tell whether Skwarchuk had been hit. He said Smith shot again. It appeared some pellets hit Skwarchuk in the back. Massier said Skwarchuk continued to run but before he stopped, Smith shot him again and he fell down and stayed down.

According to Massier, Smith then walked up to Skwarchuk who was sitting with his knees up and his head resting on his knees. He said Smith held the gun three or four inches from the back of Skwarchuk's head and then fired the same. Skwarchuk fell back and appeared to be dead. Massier said this episode took about 30 seconds.

After this, Massier said he asked Smith if he was going to shoot him, to which Smith replied: "No, you are my friend: don't worry about it". Massier testified Smith told him to go back to the car and get the .22. He said he went to the car and was followed by Smith. Massier said when he went to load the .22, the clip was not in the gun. He said Smith gave him the clip which he loaded with four shells and gave it to Smith. Smith put the clip in the gun. When asked by Massier what he was going to do, Smith answered he was going to shoot Skwarchuk with the .22 and that would be his insurance: if he got caught, he would say Massier shot him. Massier testified he followed Smith who went to where Skwarchuk was lying and shot him in the head three times.

According to Massier, he was told to take Skwarchuk's watch; that he did so and threw it into a pond. They heard a truck approach and Smith said that they should take off. Smith put the .22 and the shot-gun in the car and they returned to the city. They were subsequently arrested and charged with the murder of Skwarchuk.

Section 214(2) [rep. & sub. 1974-75-76, c. 105, s. 4] of the *Code* reads:

214(2) [now s. 231(2)] Murder is first degree murder when it is planned and deliberate.

In *More v. The Queen*, [1963] 3 C.C.C. 289, [1963] S.C.R. 522, the Supreme Court of Canada considered the meaning of the words "planned" and "deliberate". The court made it clear that the accused could not be found guilty of first degree murder unless it was proved beyond a reasonable doubt, not only that the murder was planned but also that it was deliberate. Fauteux J. (later C.J.C.), accepted as a meaning of "planned" — "arranged beforehand".

In so far as the word "deliberate" is concerned Cartwright J. (later C.J.C.). said at p. 291 C.C.C., p. 534 S.C.R.:

The learned trial judge also rightly instructed the jury that the word "deliberate", as used in s. 202A(2)(*a*), means "considered, not impulsive".

Other meanings of the adjective given in the Oxford Dictionary are "not hasty in decision", "slow in deciding" and "intentional". The word as used in the subsection cannot have simply the meaning "intentional" because it is only if the accused's act was intentional that he can be guilty of murder and the subsection is creating an additional ingredient to be proved as a condition of an accused being convicted of capital murder.

Similar views were expressed by the Supreme Court in *McMartin v. The Queen*, [1965] 1 C.C.C. 142, [1964] S.C.R. 484. In *R. v. Mitchell*, [1965] 1 C.C.C. 155, 43 C.R. 391, Spence J., in delivering the majority judgment of the Supreme Court, after referring to *More v. The Queen, supra*, and *McMartin v. The Queen, supra*, said at p. 162 C.C.C., pp. 393-4 C.R.:

I am of the opinion that the judgment in these two cases have as their *ratio decidendi* the principle that in determining whether the accused committed the crime of capital murder in that it was "planned and deliberate on the part of such person" the jury should have available and should be directed to consider all the circumstances including not only the evidence of the accused's actions but of his condition, his state of mind as affected by either real or even imagined insults and provoking actions of the victim and by the accused's consumption of alcohol. There is no doubt this is a finding of fact. The questions which the jury must decide and decide beyond reasonable doubt before they may convict the accused of capital murder under the relevant subsection — s. 202A(2)(*a*) — are: Was the murder which he committed planned and was it deliberate? I separate the jury's problem in that form because I am in complete agreement with Whittaker J.A., when he said [[1964] 2 C.C.C. at p. 16]: "It is possible to imagine a murder to some degree planned and yet not deliberate." Therefore, to determine whether the charge to the jury delivered by the learned trial Judge was adequate in submitting to them the issue of planning and deliberation the charge must be examined with some care.

In *R. v. Widdifield*, Gale J. (later C.J.O.), in charging the jury on planned and deliberate, as reported in 6 *Crim. L.Q.* 152 at p. 153 (1963-64), said:

> I think that in the Code "planned" is to be assigned, I think, its natural meaning of a calculated scheme or design which has been carefully thought out, and the nature and consequences of which have been considered and weighed. But that does not mean, of course, to say that the plan need be a complicated one. It may be a very simple one, and the simpler it is perhaps the easier it is to formulate.

The foregoing direction was approved by the Ontario Court of Appeal in *R. v. Reynolds* (1978), 44 C.C.C. (2d) 129. See particulary the comments of Martin J.A., speaking for the court at p. 137.

I realize it is both difficult and unwise to attempt to give an exhaustive meaning to the word "planned". It is a common word and to it should be attributed its meaning as understood in everyday life. Clearly, planning must not be confused with intention as the planning would only occur after the intent to murder had been formed. There must be some evidence the killing was the result of a scheme or design previously formulated or designed by the accused and the killing was the implementation of that scheme or design. It is obvious a murder committed on a sudden impulse and without prior consideration, even though the intent to kill is clearly proven, would not constitute a planned murder.

In the present case, there is not the slightest evidence the appellant had given any consideration to the murder of Skwarchuk until after he and Skwarchuk had left the house. In instructing the jury, the learned trial judge said:

> So without beating it more than that, the Crown must establish to establish first degree murder that the accused caused the death, he intended to do so and that he planned and deliberated. Now, I think you can say without any doubt that there was no plan to kill prior to arriving at the farm. There's no evidence of that, nor any suggestion of that. Equally there was no plan or intention to kill the first while at the farm. If the accused planned to kill, deliberated this, it must have been started, at the earliest, about the time of the altercation. There is no evidence that it would have started earlier than that, and then the question that you must weigh and consider is did he have the time to deliberate under the circumstances; did he have time to plan, and if so, did he? If you can say beyond a reasonable doubt that from the circumstances that you see and the facts that you find that it was planned and deliberate, then you should return a verdict of guilty of first degree murder. If you have a reasonable doubt about any of those things, then you should not bring a verdict of first degree murder.

To the foregoing instruction, no objection was taken by counsel either for the Crown or for the appellant. As a matter of fact, learned counsel for the Crown, in his address to the jury relied entirely on the evidence of Massier to establish "planned" and "deliberate".

I am satisfied there was no evidence whatever to support the conclusion that the actions of the appellant, cruel and sadistic as they were, in killing Skwarchuk was the implementation of a previously determined design or scheme. I think it is obvious his actions were the result of a sudden impulse. It would be pure speculation to try and determine what triggered that impulse.

It may well be that the killing was deliberate. However, even if it was, there could only be a verdict of first degree murder if the evidence established as well that the murder was planned.

Whether or not there was evidence the murder was planned was a question of law for the judge. In my respectful view, as there was no such evidence, the learned trial judge erred in law in instructing the jury there was evidence upon which a verdict of first degree murder could be found. In these circumstances, therefore, I direct that the verdict of first degree murder be set aside and a conviction of second degree murder be substituted therefore.

In *R. v. Travers* (2007), 51 C.R. (6th) 105 (Que. S.C.) Champagne J. required first degree murder to be well-ordered and based on consideration, prudence and reflection. In *R. v. K. (M.M.)* (2006), 213 C.C.C. (3d) 538 (Alta. C.A.) it was held that the trial judge had wrongly equated wilful with deliberation, which required more.

In *R. v. Banwait*, 276 C.C.C. (3d) 385, [2011] 3 S.C.R. 533, the Court was unanimous in approving the use by a trial judge of the following direction from the Watt Pattern Instructions, coupled with an application to the relevant facts of the case:

MCLACHLIN C.J.C.:

A planned murder is one that is committed as a result of a scheme or plan that has been previously formulated or designed. It is the implementation of that scheme or design. A "murder" committed on a sudden impulse and without prior consideration, even with an intention to kill is not a planned murder.

"Deliberate" is not a word that we often use when speaking to other people. It means "considered, not impulsive", "carefully thought out, not hasty or rash", "slow in deciding", "cautious".

A deliberate act is one that the actor has taken time to weigh the advantages and disadvantages of. The deliberation must take place before the act of murder, that is, before the verbal confrontation with the deceased at the Albion Mall started. A murder committed on a sudden impulse and without prior consideration, even with an intention to kill is not a deliberate murder.

R. v. NYGAARD AND SCHIMMENS

(1989), 72 C.R. (3d) 257, 51 C.C.C. (3d) 417,
1989 CarswellAlta 621, 1989 CarswellAlta 152 (S.C.C.)

M bought a car stereo from the accused N for $100. Payment was made by means of a cheque signed jointly by T and H. The cheque bounced. N came to M's motel and told him that, if the matter was not cleared up that day, M could expect trouble. Later that day N, the accused S, and another man, went to the apartment. S struck M several times on the forehead with a baseball bat and broke his arm, which was raised to protect his face. S then asked who had signed the cheque. When told it was H, he proceeded to attack H with the bat, hitting him three times between the eyes with full two-handed swings. H died in hospital of multiple skull fractures. S and N were charged with first degree murder. Following trial before judge and jury they were convicted.

When the matter reached the Supreme Court of Canada a new trial was ordered respecting a misdirection on a point of evidence. In the course of the judgment the Court unanimously held that the trial judge had not erred in directing the jury that they could return a verdict of first degree murder on the basis of a combination of ss. 229(a)(ii) and 231(2):

CORY J.: —

Throughout history the idea that one human being could cold-bloodedly plan and deliberate upon the killing of another has been repugnant to all civilized societies and has tended to be considered as the most reprehensible of violent crimes. In *Droste v. R.*, Dickson C.J.C. noted that it is the element of planning and deliberation of the murder which makes the crime of murder in the first degree more culpable and justifies the harsher sentence.

It remains then to consider what is the specific *mens rea* required by s. 212(*a*)(ii) to which the element of planning and deliberation must be related. The section requires that the Crown prove that the accused meant to cause the victim such bodily harm that he knew that it was likely to cause the death of the victim and was reckless whether death ensued or not as a result of causing that bodily harm. The essential element is that of intending to cause bodily harm of such a grave and serious nature that the accused knew that it was likely to result in the death of the victim. The aspect of recklessness is almost an afterthought insofar as the basic intent is concerned.

In *Sansregret v. R.*, [1985] 1 S.C.R. 570, 45 C.R. (3d) 193, 18 C.C.C. (3d) 223, recklessness was defined as being the attitude of one who was aware of the danger the prohibited conduct could bring about yet nevertheless persisted in that conduct despite the knowledge of the risk. Thus the section requires the accused to intend to cause the gravest of bodily harm that is so dangerous and serious that he knows it is likely to result in death and to persist in that conduct despite the knowledge of the risk.

In my view, the vital element of the requisite intent is that of causing such bodily harm that the perpetrator knows that it is likely to cause death and yet persists in the assault. There can be no doubt that a person can plan and deliberate to cause terrible bodily harm that he knows is likely to result in death. Nothing is added to the aspect of planning and deliberation by the requirement that the fatal assault be carried out in a reckless manner, that is to say, by heedlessly proceeding with the deadly assault in the face of the knowledge of the obvious risks. The planning and deliberation to cause the bodily harm which is likely to be fatal must of necessity include the planning and deliberating to continue and to persist in that conduct despite the knowledge of the risk. The element of recklessness does not exist in a vacuum as a sole *mens rea* requirement, but rather it must act in conjunction with the intentional infliction of terrible bodily harm. I therefore conclude that planning and deliberation may well be coupled with the *mens rea* requirements of s. 212(*a*)(ii) and that a first degree murder conviction can be sustained by virtue of the combined operation of ss. 214(2) and 212(*a*)(ii). This ground of appeal must therefore fail.

As well, the appellant argued it was wrong to label an offence under s. 212(*a*)(ii) as murder. It was said that the requisite *mens rea* is such that it is not as grave a crime as that defined in s. 212(*a*)(i), where the requisite intent is to cause the death of someone. I cannot accept that contention. The variation in the degree of culpability is too slight to take into account. Let us consider the gravity of the crime described by s. 212(*a*)(ii) in the light of three examples which, pursuant to the section, would be murder. First, an accused forms the intent to inflict multiple stab wounds in the abdomen and chest of a person knowing that the wounds are likely to kill the victim and, heedless of the known probable result, proceeds with the stabbing. Second, an accused forms the intent to shoot a former associate in the chest knowing that death is likely to ensue and, uncaring of the result, shoots the victim in the chest. Third, two accused form the intent to repeatedly and viciously strike a person in the head with a baseball bat realizing full well that the victim will probably die as a result. Nonetheless they continue with the bone-splintering, skull-shattering assault. The accused in all these examples must have committed as grave a crime as the accused who specifically intends to kill. Society would, I think, find the drawing of any differentiation in the degree of culpability an exercise in futility. The difference in the calibration on the scale of culpability is too minute to merit a distinction. I would conclude that the crime defined in s. 212(*a*)(ii) can properly be described as murder and on a "culpability scale" it varies so little from s. 212(*a*)(i) as to be indistinguishable.

I find some support for this position in *R. v. Vaillancourt*, [1987] 2 S.C.R. 636, 60 C.R. (3d) 289, 39 C.C.C. (3d) 118 [Que.]. There Lamer J., giving the reasons for the court, stated at pp. 644-45:

> There is a very interesting progression through s. 212 to s. 213 with respect to the mental state that must be proven.
>
> The starting point is s. 212(*a*)(i) . . .
> This clearly requires that the accused have actual subjective foresight of the likelihood of causing the death coupled with the intention to cause that death. This is the most morally blameworthy state of mind in our system.
>
> There is a slight relaxation of this requirement in s. 212(*a*)(ii) . . .
> Here again the accused must have actual subjective foresight of the likelihood of death. However, the Crown need no longer prove that he intended to cause the death but only that he was reckless whether death ensued or not. It should also be noted that s. 212(*a*)(ii) is limited to cases where the accused intended to cause bodily harm to the victim.

He went on to note that there is still a greater relaxation of the requisite mental element in s. 212(*c*), a provision which "eliminates the requirement of actual subjective foresight and replaces it with objective foreseeability or negligence" (pp. 645-46). It is clear from these observations that the court in that case concluded that there was but a slight relaxation of the requisite intent in s. 212(*a*)(ii) from that required by s. 212(*a*)(i). Section 212(*a*)(ii) demands a highly subjective mental element to be present, that of the intent to cause the gravest of bodily injuries that are known to the accused to be likely to cause death to the victim. It is to this intent that the s. 214(2) requirement of planning and deliberation can be properly applied.

For comment on *Nygaard* see Stuart (1989), 72 C.R. (3d) 259-261.

It has not yet been decided whether there can be a planned and deliberate s. 229(c) murder.

R. v. COLLINS

69 C.R. (3d) 235, 48 C.C.C. (3d) 343, 1989 CarswellOnt 83 (Ont. C.A.)

Goodman J.A.: —

. . . .

There can be no doubt that the onus was on the Crown to establish beyond a reasonable doubt the *actus reus* and *mens rea* of the substantive offence of murder under s. 212. I am of the view, however, that under s. 214(4)(*a*) [now s. 231(4)(*a*)] there is an onus on the Crown to establish beyond a reasonable doubt that the victim was a person who falls within the designation of the occupations set forth in that subsection acting in the course of his duties to the knowledge of the accused or with recklessness on his part as to whether the victim was such a person so acting.

In my opinion there is no binding authority to the contrary. It seems clear to me that the object of the classification of first degree murder in s. 214 is to require a more severe punishment for the offence of murder in circumstances that involve an added degree of moral culpability or to act as a more effective deterrent in the prevention of the murder of persons engaged in the preservation, prevention of infringement and enforcement of the law or of persons who have fallen under the domination of an offender.

It is my view that s. 214(4)(*a*) should be interpreted in such a manner that requires proof of the facts which give rise to the added moral culpability or which would act as an additional deterrent. It is clear to me that to fulfil such interpretation it is necessary that the Crown prove that the murderer had knowledge of the identity of the victim as one of the persons designated in the subsection and that such person was acting in the course of his duties or was reckless as to such identity and acts of the victim.

The section could, of course, be interpreted to simply require that the Crown prove that the occupation of the victim was one of those set forth in the subsection and that the person was acting in the course of his duties without proof of knowledge thereof on the part of the murderer. The subsection does not refer to proof of such knowledge.

I am satisfied that if the latter interpretation is adopted, it would offend s. 7 of the *Charter*: If, for example, a gunman sees two persons on the street dressed in plain clothes of whom one is a merchant walking home and the other is a detective on his way to investigate or in the process of investigating a break-in, and if the gunman decides without planning and deliberation to shoot and kill one of them and does, so he would be guilty of murder no matter which person he killed. In the case of the killing of the ordinary citizen he would be guilty of second degree murder with a sentence of life imprisonment with a possibility of parole eligibility after 10 years but in the case of the killing of the detective he would be guilty of first degree murder with a sentence of life imprisonment with a possibility of parole in no less than 25 years, being the minimum period before parole eligibility (subject of course to the provisions of s. 745 of the *Code* (formerly s. 672)).

Although the crime of murder is deserving of the heavy sentence involved, it seems to me that there would be no difference in moral culpability in the example set forth above no matter which person was the victim, nor would there be any additional deterrent provided under s. 214(4)(*a*) in those circumstances if proof of knowledge that the detective was indeed a detective acting in the course of his duty were not required. There would then be no rational or logical reason for imposing a heavier penalty in the case where the murderer killed the person whom he did not know and had no reason to know was a police officer acting in the course of his duties.

On the other hand, if s. 214(4)(*a*) is interpreted to require proof of such knowledge before the murder can be classified as first degree murder, then a heavier sentence can be justified on the basis of added moral culpability or as additional deterrent on the grounds of public policy. In such event, it is my opinion that the subsection would not contravene the provisions of s. 7 of the *Charter*.

I am of the opinion that, where a statutory provision is open to two interpretations, one of which will contravene the *Charter* and the other of which will not, the provision should be interpreted in such a manner as will not contravene the *Charter*: see *R. v. Corbett*, [1988] 1 S.C.R. 670, 64 C.R. (3d) 1 at 23, 41 C.C.C. (3d) 385, per Beetz J.

I conclude that the onus was on the Crown to prove that the appellant knew that the victim was a police officer who was acting in the course of his duty and I find, accordingly, that the provisions of s. 214(4)(*a*) do not contravene s. 7 of the *Charter*. In the present case the trial judge charged the jury in accordance with this conclusion. There was evidence to support a finding of knowledge on the part of the appellant. (And see *R. v. Prevost* (1988), 64 C.R. (3d) 188, 42 C.C.C. (3d) 314 at 318 (C.A.).) This ground of appeal, therefore, fails.

R. v. ARKELL

[1990] 2 S.C.R. 695, 79 C.R. (3d) 207, 59 C.C.C. (3d) 65,
1990 CarswellBC 197, 1990 CarswellBC 758

The accused was convicted, pursuant to now s. 231(5), of first degree murder. It was the theory of the Crown that the victim was killed while he attempted to sexually assault her. One of the the the constitutional questions for the Court was whether s. 231(5) contravened s. 7 of the *Charter*.

LAMER C.J.C. (DICKSON C.J.C. and WILSON, GONTHIER and CORY JJ. concurring): —

The main argument of the appellant, as regards his constitutional challenge of the section, is that it is arbitrary and irrational and thereby offends s. 7 of the *Charter*.

. . . .

The argument of the appellant suggests that the sentencing scheme is flawed and in violation of s. 7 of the *Charter* because it results in the punishment of individuals that is not proportionate to the seriousness of the offences giving rise to the sentences. First, I must note that as a result of this court's decision in *Martineau*, released concurrently, it can no longer be said that s. 214(5) has the potential to classify unintentional killings as first degree murder. A conviction for murder requires proof beyond a reasonable doubt of subjective foresight of death. Therefore, when we reach the stage of classifying murders as either first or second degree, we are dealing with individuals who have committed the most serious crime in our *Criminal Code*, and who have been proven to have done so with the highest level of moral culpability, that of subjective foresight. Section 214(5) represents a decision by Parliament to impose a more serious punishment on those found guilty of murder while committing certain listed offences.

This leads me to a second point, namely, a consideration of the underlying rationale of s. 214(5). Again, I refer to the decision of this court in *R. v. Paré*, [1987] 2 S.C.R. 618, at pp. 632-33:

All murders are serious crimes. Some murders, however, are so threatening to the public that Parliament has chosen to impose exceptional penalties on the perpetrators. One such class of murders is that found in s. 214(5), murders done while committing a hijacking, a kidnapping and forcible confinement, a rape, or an indecent assault. . .

The offences listed in s. 214(5) are all offences involving the unlawful domination of people by other people. Thus an organizing principle for s. 214(5) can be found. This principle is that where a murder is committed by someone already abusing his power by illegally dominating another, the murder should be treated as an exceptionally serious crime. Parliament has chosen to treat these murders as murders in the first degree.

I can find no principle of fundamental justice that prevents Parliament, guided by the organizing principle identified by this court in *Paré*, from classifying murders done while committing certain underlying offences as more serious, and thereby attaching more serious penalties to them. In the case of the distinction between first and second degree murder, the difference is a maximum extra 15 years that must be served before one is eligible for parole. This distinction is neither arbitrary nor irrational. The section is based on an organizing principle that treats murders committed while the perpetrator is illegally dominating another person as more serious than other murders. Further, the relationship between the classification and the moral blameworthiness of the offender clearly exists. Section 214 only comes into play when murder has been proven beyond a reasonable doubt. In light of *Martineau*, this means that the offender has been proven to have had subjective foresight of death. Parliament's decision to treat more seriously murders that have been committed while the offender is exploiting a position of power through illegal domination of the victim accords with the principle that there must be a proportionality between a sentence and the moral blameworthiness of the offender and other considerations such as deterrence and societal condemnation of the acts of the offender. Therefore, I conclude that in so far as s. 214(5) is neither arbitrary nor irrational, it does not infringe upon s. 7 of the *Charter*.

L'Heureux-Dubé J. and Sopinka J. concurred in the result.

For critical comments, see Allan Manson, "The Easy Acceptance of Long Term Confinement In Canada" (1990), 79 C.R. (3d) 265.

In *R. v. Strong* (1990), 2 C.R. (4th) 239 (Alta. C.A.), the Court held that first degree murder under s. 231(5) did not include murder in the course of robbery. Not all offences involving illegal domination of one person by another had been included in the list of offences. However, in *R. v. Pritchard* (2008), 61 C.R. (6th) 254 (S.C.C.) the Supreme Court held that killing in the course of unlawful confinement met the requirement even if this was for purpose of robbery.

Doesn't this make the section arbitrary, contrary to s. 7 of the *Charter*?

(b)   Subjective Awareness Guaranteed by *Charter* for Few Crimes

When the Supreme Court struck down the constructive murder rule in s. 230(d) of the *Criminal Code* in *Vaillancourt*, Justice Lamer left the impression that the Court might one day decide that subjective *mens rea* was constitutionally required for all crimes. It is now clear that the Supreme Court is only likely to declare such a requirement for a very few offences. At present the Supreme Court has required subjective fault for murder (e.g., *Martineau*); attempted murder (*R. v. Logan*, [1990] 2 S.C.R. 731, 79 C.R. (3d) 169, 58 C.C.C. (3d) 391); accessory liability to an offence constitutionally requiring a subjective test (*Logan*); war crimes and crimes against humanity (*R. v. Finta*, [1994] 1 S.C.R. 701, 28 C.R. (4th) 265, 88 C.C.C. (3d) 417); and organized crime offences (*R. c. Venneri*, 2012 SCC 33, [2012] 2 S.C.R. 211, 93 C.R. (6th) 223). There is also *obiter* recognition in *Vaillancourt* and *Martineau* that theft requires subjective awareness.

It is important to be clear what this *Charter* rule means, and what it does not mean. That only a few crimes are *guaranteed* subjective fault does not displace the common law presumption from *R. v. Beaver*, [1957] S.C.R. 531, 26 C.R. 193, 118 C.C.C. 129 and strongly reaffirmed in *R. v. H. (A.D.)*, 2013 SCC 28, [2013] 2 S.C.R. 269, 295 C.C.C. (3d) 376, 2 C.R. (7th) 1, that all crimes as a matter of fact have subjective fault unless Parliament has clearly expressed a contrary intention. What the *Martineau* rule establishes is that for a few crimes, even if Parliament *does* clearly express a contrary intention, the offence must have subjective fault nonetheless. See the further discussion of this point under subheading 5(a)(i) Common Law Presumption.

The *Charter* analysis is still turning on the unruly criterion of stigma criticized by most commentators as unreliable and potentially circular. See, for example, Isabel Grant and Christine Boyle, "Equality, Harm and Vulnerability: Homicide and Sexual Assault Post-*Creighton*" (1993), 23 C.R. (4th) 252 at 258-259 and Rosemary Cairns Way, "Constitutionalizing Subjectivism: Another View" (1990), 79 C.R. (3d) 260. The Supreme Court has decided that the stigma necessary to require subjective *mens rea* does not follow from a conviction of the *Criminal Code* offences of unlawful act causing bodily harm (*R. v. DeSousa*, [1992] 2 S.C.R. 944, 15 C.R. (4th) 66, 76 C.C.C. (3d) 124); dangerous driving (*R. v. Hundal*, [1993] 1 S.C.R. 867, 19 C.R. (4th) 169, 79 C.C.C. (3d) 97; manslaughter (*R. v. Creighton*, [1993] 3 S.C.R. 3, 23 C.R. (4th) 189, 83 C.C.C. (3d) 346); failing to provide necessaries of life (*R. v. Naglik*, [1993] 3 S.C.R. 122, 23 C.R. (4th) 335, 83 C.C.C. (3d) 526); and careless use of a firearm (*R. v. Finlay*, [1993] 3 S.C.R. 103, 23 C.R. (4th) 321, 83 C.C.C. (3d) 513 and *R. v. Gosset*, [1993] 3 S.C.R. 76, 23 C.R. (4th) 280, 83 C.C.C. (3d) 494).

Provincial Courts of Appeal have also been unreceptive to *Charter* arguments to entrench subjective tests. Challenges have been rejected for offences of causing bodily harm in committing assault (*R.v. Brooks* (1988), 64 C.R. (3d) 322, 41 C.C.C. (3d) 157 (B.C. C.A.)); criminal negligence (*R. v. Nelson* (1990), 75 C.R. (4th) 70, 54 C.C.C. (3d) 285 (Ont. C.A.) and *R. v. Gingrich* (1991), 6 C.R. (4th) 197, 65 C.C.C. (3d) 188 (Ont. C.A.)); and arson (*R. v. Peters* (1991), 11 C.R. (4th) 48, 69 C.C.C. (3d) 461 (B.C. C.A.)).

5. THREE TYPES OF FAULT FOR CRIMES SINCE *CREIGHTON*

Given *Creighton*, *Criminal Code* offences are, for the determination of fault, divided into three categories as follows:

Fault for Crimes

Subjective *mens rea*	Objective negligence	Offences based on predicate offences
aware of risk, all individual factors	marked departure from objective norm, no individual factors short of incapacity	objective foresight of harm, no individual factors, no marked limit,except for predicate offences of negligence
e.g., murder, assault, break and enter, theft, possession offences	*e.g.*, dangerous driving, careless firearms, failure to provide necessaries	*e.g.*, unlawful act man-slaughter, unlawfully causing bodily harm, aggravated assault

(a) Crimes Requiring Subjective Awareness

(i) Common law presumption

Subjective *mens rea* is guaranteed by the *Charter* for only a few offences. Nonetheless, the common law has long dictated a presumption of subjective fault for crimes, and this rule applies whether the *Charter* guarantee is applicable or not. The Supreme Court held in *R. v. Beaver*, [1957] S.C.R. 531, 26 C.R. 193, 118 C.C.C. 129 that all crimes as a matter of fact have subjective fault unless Parliament has clearly expressed a contrary intention. Sometimes offences contain clear *mens rea* words, such as "intentionally", "wilfully" or "knowingly". Even in the absence of *mens rea* words, however, the Court has held that offences should be interpreted to require subjective fault, unless there is some clear indication that the offence was intended to be one of objective fault.

Examples of cases where the Court has interpreted offences to require subjective fault in accordance with this presumption include *R. v. Pappajohn*, [1980] 2 S.C.R. 120, 52 C.C.C. (2d) 481 and *R. v. Sansregret*, [1985] 1 S.C.R. 570, 45 C.R. (3d) 193 (both concerning the former offence of rape), *R. c. Théroux*, [1993] 2 S.C.R. 5, 19 C.R. (4th) 194 (fraud), *R. v. Clemente*, [1994] 2 S.C.R. 758, 31 C.R. (4th) 28 (uttering threats), *R. c. Boulanger*, [2006] 2 S.C.R. 49, 39 C.R. (6th) 1 (breach of trust) or *R. v. Levkovic*, 1 C.R. (7th) 223, [2013] 2 S.C.R. 204,

296 C.C.C. (3d) 457 (intentionally concealing a child that dies before birth knowing that the fetus was likely to be born alive).

Beyond those specific examples, the common law rule is that crimes are presumed to have subjective fault. This presumption was hotly debated but maintained by a 5-2 majority in:

R. v. H. (A.D.)

2013 SCC 28, 2 C.R. (7th) 1, [2013] 2 S.C.R. 269, 295 C.C.C. (3d) 376

The accused was charged with abandoning a child contrary to s. 218 of the *Criminal Code* and thereby endangering life after she gave birth in a Wal-Mart store washroom cubicle and left the newborn in the toilet. She was in the store no more than 15 minutes. The baby was found in the toilet by customers, who alerted store staff. The baby was resuscitated and survived completely healthy. She testified that she did not know she was pregnant and that the baby was blue and appeared to be dead. She testified that she left the store in a state of panic and shock. As soon as she heard media reports that the infant was alive, she contacted police and identified herself as the mother.

There was expert evidence at trial that a baby born after a precipitous birth might appear dead to untrained observers. The bystanders who saw the baby in the toilet said they thought he was dead until they saw his arm move. The defence expert also testified that approximately 1 in 2,500 pregnancies is undetected. The Crown's theory was that H knew she was pregnant but was trying to conceal the pregnancy because her boyfriend was not the father.

Under s. 218:

> Everyone who unlawfully abandons or exposes a child who is under the age of ten years, so that its life is or is likely to be endangered or its health is or is likely to be permanently injured
>
> (a) Is guilty of an indictable offence and liable to imprisonment for a term not exceeding five years; or
>
> (b) Is guilty of an offence punishable on summary conviction and liable to imprisonment for a term not exceeding eighteen months

The trial judge noted that the accused acknowledged that she had left her child in the toilet, thereby committing the *actus reus* of the s. 218 offence. The trial judge decided that subjective fault was required and found that the Crown had not proven beyond a reasonable doubt that the accused intended to abandon her child or did so recklessly with full knowledge of the facts and circumstances, or was wilfully blind to them. The trial judge accordingly found the accused not guilty and dismissed the charge. A majority of the Saskatchewan Court of Appeal dismissed the appeal. The Crown appealed.

The Supreme Court unanimously dismissed the appeal and confirmed the acquittal. But the two judgments markedly diverged in their reasons.

CROMWELL J. (MCLACHLIN C.J.C. and FISH, ABELLA, and KARAKATSANIS JJ. concurring):

[According to the majority, although the text of s. 218 of the *Criminal Code* does not expressly set out a fault requirement, read in light of its full context, it supports the conclusion that subjective fault is required.]

[23] An important part of the context in which we must interpret s. 218 is the presumption that Parliament intends crimes to have a subjective fault element. The Court has stated and relied on this interpretative principle on many occasions: see, e.g., *Watts v. The Queen*, [1953] 1 S.C.R. 505, at p. 511; *R. v. Rees*, [1956] S.C.R. 640, at p. 652; *Beaver v. The Queen*, [1957] S.C.R. 531, at pp. 542-43; *R. v. Sault Ste. Marie*, [1978] 2 S.C.R. 1299, at pp. 1303 and 1309-10; *R. v. Prue*, [1979] 2 S.C.R. 547, at pp. 551 and 553; *R. v. Bernard*, [1988] 2 S.C.R. 833, at p. 871; *R. v. Martineau*, [1990] 2 S.C.R. 633, at p. 645; *R. v. Théroux*, [1993] 2 S.C.R. 5, at p. 18; *R. v. Lucas*, [1998] 1 S.C.R. 439, at para. 64. Perhaps the classic statement is that of Dickson J. (as he then was) for the Court in *Sault Ste. Marie*:

> In the case of true crimes there is a presumption that a person should not be held liable for the wrongfulness of his act if that act is without *mens rea* . . . .
>
> . . . . Where the offence is criminal, the Crown must establish a mental element, namely, that the accused who committed the prohibited act did so intentionally or recklessly, with knowledge of the facts constituting the offence, or with wilful blindness toward them. Mere negligence is excluded from the concept of the mental element required for conviction. Within the context of a criminal prosecution a person who fails to make such enquiries as a reasonable and prudent person would make, or who fails to know facts he should have known, is innocent in the eyes of the law. [Citations omitted; pp. 1303 and 1309-10.]

[24] Notwithstanding these many statements, the Crown in effect submits that there is no such presumption of legislative intent because it has not always been applied. The Crown notes that there are many offences in the *Code* that do not require subjective fault and further that there is no absolute rule requiring complete symmetry between the fault element and the prohibited consequences of the offence. In my view, however, these points do not negate the existence of the presumption of legislative intent. They show merely that the presumption does not invariably determine the outcome of a full contextual and purposive interpretation of a particular provision.

[25] Presumptions of legislative intent are not self-applying rules. They are instead principles of interpretation. They do not, on their own, prescribe the outcome of interpretation, but rather set out broad principles that ought to inform it. As Professor Sullivan has observed, presumptions of legislative intent, such as this one, serve as a way in which the courts recognize and incorporate important values into the legal context in which legislation is drafted and should be interpreted. These values both inform judicial understanding of legislation

and play an important role in assessing competing interpretations: R. Sullivan, *Sullivan and Driedger on the Construction of Statutes* (4th ed. 2002), at p. 365.

[26] Professor Côté has described how these presumptions may inform the legal context in which legislation is drafted. He put it this way: "In some sense, presumptions of intent form part of the enactment's context, as they reflect ideas which can be assumed to have been both present in the mind of the legislature and sufficiently current as to render their explicit mention unnecessary": P.A. Côté, in collaboration with S. Beaulac and M. Devinat, *The Interpretation of Legislation in Canada* (4th ed. 2011), at p. 470; see also R. Cross, *Statutory Interpretation* (3rd ed. 1995), by J. Bell and G. Engle, at pp. 165-67, and K. Roach, "Common Law Bills of Rights as Dialogue Between Courts and Legislatures" (2005), 55 *U.T.L.J.* 733. Parliament must be understood to know that this presumption will likely be applied unless some contrary intention is evident in the legislation.

[27] As for the role of the presumption of subjective fault in assessing competing interpretations, it sets out an important value underlying our criminal law. It has been aptly termed one of the "presumptive principles of criminal justice": *R. v. Beatty*, 2008 SCC 5, [2008] 1 S.C.R. 49, *per* Charron J., at paras. 22-23. While the presumption must — and often does — give way to clear expressions of a different legislative intent, it nonetheless incorporates an important value in our criminal law, that the morally innocent should not be punished. This has perhaps never been better expressed than it was by Dickson J. in *Pappajohn*, at pp. 138-39:

> There rests now, at the foundation of our system of criminal justice, the precept that a man cannot be adjudged guilty and subjected to punishment, unless the commission of the crime was voluntarily directed by a willing mind. . . . Parliament can, of course, by express words, create criminal offences for which a guilty intention is not an essential ingredient. Equally, *mens rea* is not requisite in a wide category of statutory offences which are concerned with public welfare, health and safety. Subject to these exceptions, *mens rea*, consisting of some positive states of mind, such as evil intention, or knowledge of the wrongfulness of the act, or reckless disregard of consequences, must be proved by the prosecution.

[28] Viewed in this way, the presumption of subjective fault is not an outdated rule of construction which is at odds with the modern approach to statutory interpretation repeatedly endorsed by the Court. On the contrary, the presumption forms part of the context which the modern approach requires to be considered.

[29] As I will explain, there is nothing in the text or context of the child abandonment offence to suggest that Parliament intended to depart from requiring subjective fault. In fact, the text, scheme and purpose of the provision support the view that subjective fault is required. To the extent that the

Parliament's intent is unclear, the presumption of subjective fault ought to have its full operation in this case.

[After lengthy analysis the majority concluded that viewed in the light of the broad scope of potential liability under s. 218 of the *Criminal Code*, the requirement for subjective fault serves an important purpose of ensuring that the reach of the criminal law does not extend too far. While the conduct and people that fall within s. 218 are broadly defined, the requirement for subjective fault ensures that only those with a guilty mind are punished. The words "abandon", "expose" and "unlawfully" all suggested a subjective fault requirement. The use of the word "likely" in both ss. 214 and 218 does not suggest an objective fault requirement given that it is simply aimed at criminalizing the creation of risk and the fault element may require knowledge of that risk. The text of s. 218 did not contain any of the language typically employed by Parliament when it intends to create an offence of objective fault.]

MOLDAVER J. (Rothstein J. concurring):

[Section 218 is child protection legislation. The presumption that Parliament intends crimes to have a subjective fault element had to be kept in its proper perspective.]

[96] Once it is accepted that in enacting s. 218 Parliament intended to guard against dangerous conduct that any reasonable person would foresee is likely to endanger a child's life or expose it to permanent injury, I fail to see why Parliament would turn around and provide accused persons with a host of defences based on their individual characteristics. Doing so would effectively defeat the provision's purpose of imposing a societal minimum standard of conduct, since crimes of subjective fault require an assessment of personal characteristics to the extent that they tend to prove or disprove an element of the offence (*Creighton*, at p. 63). Age, temperament, mental development, experience, sophistication and education would all factor into the determination of whether a particular accused appreciated the risk of harm resulting from the inherently dangerous conduct of abandoning or exposing a helpless child. Of particular concern, such an approach would provide a defence to the errant parent or irresponsible caregiver who, by virtue of intoxication, could not or did not foresee the likely consequences of his or her dangerous conduct, whether it be locking a child in a car on a hot summer's day or exposing a child to the elements on a cold winter's night.

[97] I do not accept that Parliament, in enacting s. 218, contemplated such a self-defeating regime. Common sense suggests that Parliament would not treat the lives and safety of innocent children with such indifference.

[Moldaver J. concluded that the s. 218 offence is a duty-based offence as is the offence of failing to provide necessaries of life under s. 215. Like s. 215, the level of fault required is penal negligence. The Crown must establish that a reasonable person would have foreseen that his or her conduct placed or was likely to place the child at risk of death or permanent injury and that the accused's conduct constitutes a marked departure from that expected of a reasonable person in the circumstances. In this case, the trial judge found that the accused honestly believed that her child was dead at birth and that this was reasonable in the context of the situation. She was entitled to be acquitted.]

Which judgment do you agree with and why? For comment see Stuart, "*H.A.D.*: The Supreme Court Strongly Reaffirms the Presumption of Subjective Fault for Crimes" (2013), 2 C.R. (7th) 64.

Given that there is a presumption the Crown must prove the accused's subjective state of mind, it is important to be clear exactly what that entails, or in some cases, does *not* entail. The next four subheadings – Motive, Desire/Purpose, Intention or Knowledge, and Recklessness or Wilful Blindness – elaborate on that issue. We will discover that our courts have often been inconsistent.

(ii)   Motive

"Motive" has been described as "the reason, or at least one of the reasons, that a person chooses to engage in conduct" (*R. v. Khawaja*, 97 C.R. (6th) 223, [2012] 3 S.C.R. 555). A motive is not usually one of the elements of a criminal offence, and so in general the Crown is not required to prove *why* the accused chose to perform the *actus reus*. That said, proving that the accused had a motive might often be helpful for the Crown in proving things it is required to prove. For example, if there is a question as to whether an application of force was intentional or not, the presence or absence of a motive might sway the trier of fact in one direction or the other. Similarly, if identity were at issue and only two people had the opportunity to commit the offence, we might be interested to know whether either person had a motive to commit it.

The general rules around motive were summarized by the Supreme Court of Canada in *R. v. Lewis*, [1979] 2 S.C.R. 821, 47 C.C.C. (2d) 24:

(1) As evidence, motive is always relevant and hence evidence of motive is admissible.

. . . .

(2) Motive is no part of the crime and is legally irrelevant to criminal responsibility. It is not an essential element of the prosecution's case as a matter of law.

. . . .

(3) Proved absence of motive is always an important fact in favour of the accused and ordinarily worthy of note in a charge to the jury.

. . . .

(4) Conversely, proved presence of motive may be an important factual ingredient in the Crown's case, notably on the issues of identity and intention, when the evidence is purely circumstantial.

. . . .

(5) Motive is therefore always a question of fact and evidence and the necessity of referring to motive in the charge to the jury falls within the general duty of the trial Judge not only to outline the theories of the prosecution and defence but to give the jury matters of evidence essential in arriving at a just conclusion.

. . . .

(6) Each case will turn on its own unique set of circumstances. The issue of motive is always a matter of degree.

. . . .

The Court says in *Lewis* that motive is not an essential element of the Crown's case. However, we will see that criminal law sometimes distinguishes between two types of intent: general intent and specific intent. "General intent" simply means that the accused performed an action intentionally, as opposed to accidentally; specific intent, however, is sometimes described as "ulterior intention", in the sense of the reason *why* the accused performed the action. Most crimes only require the Crown to show general intent, but some require specific intent. The statement in *Lewis* that motive is no part of an offence is best understood as applying only to general intent crimes. The Ontario Court of Appeal explained this point in *Khawaja*:

90 For example, the offence of break and enter with intent to steal can be described as requiring proof of the reason or motive that precipitated the break-in— an intention to steal. However, if one wishes to avoid using the word "motive" to describe an element of the *mens rea*, one can refer to the intention to steal as the burglar's ulterior intention and describe the burglar's motive as his or her desire for financial gain, a state of mind that is irrelevant to criminal culpability.

91 The aphorism that "motive is no part of a crime" does not express a criminal law principle referable to the permitted scope of criminal liability, much less a principle of fundamental justice protected by s. 7 of the Charter. The aphorism refers to the interpretive rule that, ordinarily, when interpreting the mens rea required for criminal culpability, and absent statutory language to the contrary, the reason or reasons that cause an accused to engage in prohibited conduct or to choose to bring about a prohibited consequence are irrelevant to culpability: *United States of America v. Dynar*, [1997] 2 S.C.R. 462, at pp. 496-97.

92 Nor do we accept that treating motive as relevant to criminal culpability is foreign to Canadian criminal law. Motive plays a part in many aspects of the substantive criminal law, including the definition of the fault component of some crimes and the definition of exculpatory justifications and excuses: M. Plaxton, "Irruptions of Motive in the War on Terror" (2007) 11 Can. Crim. L.R. 233; Colvin & Anand, at pp. 192-93. For example, there are many Criminal Code offences that require that the prohibited conduct be done for a specified purpose that is ulterior to the conduct component of the crime (e.g., s. 23(1) (accessory after the fact), s. 51 (intimidating Parliament or the legislature), s. 52 (sabotage), s. 53 (inciting to mutiny), s. 57(2) (false statement in relation to passport), s. 151 (sexual interference), s. 152 (invitation to sexual touching)). The requirement that the Crown prove "purpose" can refer to different states of mind, including the requirement of proof of the reason that precipitated the conduct that brought about the intended consequence. When purpose is used in this sense, it is effectively indistinguishable from the concept of motive: *R. v. Hibbert*, [1995] 2 S.C.R. 973, at para. 27; *R. v. Kerr*, [2004] 2 S.C.R. 371, at paras. 26-27.

The Ontario Court of Appeal has itself earlier found it useful to distinguish motive from intent in its decision in *R. v. Priestap* (2006), 39 C.R. (6th) 391 (Ont. C.A.). The offence of prowling at night was held to have been introduced to criminalize "peeping tom" conduct and the Crown did not have to prove motive or an underlying specific evil purpose.

(iii) Desire/Purpose

R. v. HIBBERT

[1995] 2 S.C.R. 973, 40 C.R. (4th) 141, 99 C.C.C. (3d) 193,
1995 CarswellOnt 117, 1995 CarswellOnt 530

In the context of a major ruling on duress (considered later), Chief Justice Lamer for the Court considered the meaning of the word "purpose" in s. 21(1)(b) of the *Code*. That section imposes criminal liability for an offence on anyone who "does or omits to do anything for the purpose of aiding any person to commit it". The Court held that purpose is not the same as desire. In an earlier ruling, *R. v. Paquette* (1976), [1977] 2 S.C.R. 189, 39 C.R.N.S. 257, 30 C.C.C. (2d) 417, the Court had concluded that a person who, out of fear, assisted another person to commit a crime did not have a "common intention" with that person, and so would not be liable as a party under s. 21(2). In *Hibbert* the Court decides not to adopt that same approach to s. 21(1)(b), and indeed to abandon it with regard to s. 21(2).

LAMER C.J.: —

. . . .

It is impossible to ascribe a single fixed meaning to the term "purpose". In ordinary usage, the word is employed in two distinct senses. One can speak of an actor doing something "on purpose" (as opposed to by accident) thereby equating purpose with "immediate intention". The term is also used, however, to indicate the ultimate ends an actor seeks to achieve, which imports the idea of "desire" into the definition. This dual sense is apparent in the word's dictionary definition. For instance, the Oxford English Dictionary (2nd ed., 1989), defines "purpose" alternatively as "[t]hat which one sets before oneself as a thing to be done or attained; the object which one has in view" and as "[t]he action or fact of intending or meaning to do something; intention, resolution, determination". The first of these definitions reflects the notion of one's "purpose" as relating to one's ultimate object or desire, while the latter conveys the notion of "purpose" as being synonymous with "intention".

Commentators who have considered the meaning of "purpose" in definitions of criminal offences have come to differing conclusions on the question of which of these alternate meanings is more appropriate in this context. Professor E.

Colvin, for instance, argues on behalf of the "purpose as desire" interpretation in his text *Principles of Criminal Law*, 2nd ed. (Toronto: Carswell, 1991). He states (at pp. 121-22):

> The terms "direct intention" and "desire" are sometimes used instead of purpose. The latter term, however, best describes the relevant state of mind. In ordinary language descriptions of action, the concept of purpose usually refers to an actor's *reasons* for doing what he did . . . [Emphasis in original.]

According to Colvin, "an actor's purpose was to accomplish something if the prospect of its occurrence played a causal role in his decision to do what he did" (p. 122). The actor's knowledge that his actions will result in the occurrence, however, is not determinative. As Colvin states (at p. 123):

> If it is to be concluded that an actor's purpose in doing something did not include an outcome which was foreseen, then the actor must have been genuinely opposed or indifferent to it. Purpose is not negated where an actor *chose* to bring about the outcome as a means of attaining some further objective. [Emphasis in original.]

Other commentators, however, have questioned this equation of "purpose" with "desire", arguing instead that a person who consciously performs an act knowing the consequences that will (with some degree of certainty) flow from it "intends" these consequences or causes them "on purpose", regardless of whether he or she *desired* them. As Mewett and Manning state:

> . . . the distinction between purpose/intent and knowledge/intent does not work, because if there is, given an awareness of the consequences of an act, a freedom of choice as to whether one acts or not, by choosing to act those consequences have been chosen. If intent is the choosing of consequences, it does not make any difference to the existence of the intent whether the accused wants those consequences to follow or merely knows that they will follow, without necessarily desiring them to do so.
>
> "Intent", is not a very descriptive word. *Mens rea* connotes volition on the part of the accused, that is to say, given an awareness that certain consequences will follow (or will probably follow) if he acts, an accused who chooses to act when he has the alternative of not acting "intends" those consequences in the sense of choosing to bring them about. It seems not only unnecessary but positively misleading to attempt to distinguish between purpose/intent and knowledge/intent.

(*Criminal Law* (2nd ed., 1985), at p. 113.)

A similar argument is made by the English authors J. C. Smith and B. Hogan:

> . . . person may know that he cannot achieve his purpose, A, without bringing about some other result, B. If he is to bring about A, he knows he must also, at the same time or earlier, bring about B. It may be that, in any other circumstances, he would much rather B did not happen, indeed its occurrence may be abhorrent to him. But, the choice being between going without A and having A and B, he decides to have A and B. It seems fair to say that he intends to cause B as well as A.

(*Criminal Law* (7th ed., 1992), at p. 55.)

As this debate reveals, the term "purpose" is capable of bearing two distinct meanings, both of which can be supported by reasoned arguments. In a case, such as this one, where an interpretation of the term in a specific statutory context is required, the court's task is to determine which of the two possible meanings best accords with Parliament's intention in drafting the particular statutory provision at issue. In other words, our task in the present case is to consider the meaning of "purpose" as it is employed in s. 21(1)(*b*) of the *Code* in light of the Parliamentary objective underlying the subsection. It must be emphasized, however, that the word "purpose" is employed in many different sections of the *Criminal Code*, in a number of distinct contexts. My conclusions in the present case on the proper interpretation of the word "purpose" as it is employed in s. 21(1)(*b*) of the *Code* are thus restricted to this particular subsection. It may well be that in the context of some other statutory provision a different interpretation of the term will prove to be the most appropriate.

. . . As I will explain, I am of the view that in the context of s. 21(1)(*b*) of the *Code*, the second of the two meanings of "purpose" discussed above — that is, the interpretation that equates "purpose" with "intention" — best reflects the legislative intent underlying the subsection. In contrast, adopting the first interpretation of "purpose" (the "purpose" equals "desire" interpretation) to describe the mens rea for aiding in s. 21(1)(*b*) would, in my view, create a number of theoretical and practical difficulties that Parliament is unlikely to have envisioned or intended.

The problems associated with the "purpose equals desire" interpretation are several. First, incorporating the accused's feelings about the desirability of the commission of an offence by the principal into the definition of the mens rea for "aiding" can result in distinctions being made which appear arbitrary and unreasonable in light of the policy underlying s. 21(1)(*b*). As Professor Colvin notes, under the "purpose equals desire" interpretation a person would not be guilty of aiding in the commission of an offence if he or she were "genuinely opposed or indifferent to it" (p. 123). The reason for the aider's indifference or opposition would be immaterial. The perverse consequences that flow from this are clearly illustrated by the following hypothetical situation described by Mewett and Manning:

> If a man is approached by a friend who tells him that he is going to rob a bank and would like to use his car as the getaway vehicle for which he will pay him $100, when that person is . . . charged under s. 21 for doing something for the purpose of aiding his friend to commit the offence, can he say "My purpose was not to aid the robbery but to make $100"? His argument would be that while he knew that he was helping the robbery, his desire was to obtain $100 and he did not care one way or the other whether the robbery was successful or not.

(*Criminal Law*, *supra*, at p. 112.)

I agree with the authors' conclusion that "[t]hat would seem an absurd result" (p. 112). As I noted in *McIntosh, supra,* at pp. 704-5, "[a]bsurdity is a factor to consider in the interpretation of ambiguous statutory provisions". That is, to quote the words of La Forest J.A. (as he then was) in *Re Estabrooks Pontiac Buick Ltd.* (1982), 44 N.B.R. (2d) 201, at p. 210, "[t]he fact that the words as interpreted would give an unreasonable result . . . is certainly ground for the courts to scrutinize a statute carefully to make abundantly certain that those words are not susceptible of another interpretation". In my view, the absurdity that would flow from the equation of "purpose" with "desire" cannot legitimately be ascribed to Parliamentary intention. This serves to cast considerable doubt on the correctness of this interpretation of the word "purpose" in this context, especially when one recalls that there exists an alternative interpretation of the word that can just as accurately be said to reflect its "plain meaning", under which this absurdity would be avoided.

. . . .

Finally, I am satisfied that the interpretation of the mens rea for liability under s. 21(1)(*b*) that I am proposing will not result in unjust convictions in cases involving coercion by threats of death or bodily harm, since in these cases the common law defence of duress will remain available to the accused. As I will explain shortly, this defence, properly understood, provides an excuse to persons who assist in the commission of offences as a result of threats of serious violence. On the other hand, interpreting "purpose" as equivalent to "desire" in s. 21(1)(*b*) would result in the introduction of unnecessary complication into the law. Under such an interpretation, juries in duress cases would have to be provided with extremely complex instructions that would, in the end, have very little, if any, impact on the final determination of guilt or innocence. As a matter of logic, the issue of whether an accused can invoke an excuse or justification arises only after the Crown has proven the existence of all the elements of the offence, including mens rea. Thus, if "purpose" were understood as incorporating "desire", and hence as being susceptible to "negation" by duress, trial judges would have to instruct juries accordingly. This would require judges, and juries, to delve into the arcane issue of whether a person who intentionally commits an offence in order to save his or her own skin commits the offence "on purpose" — a question of some philosophical significance, perhaps, but no easy matter for a judge to explain succinctly, or for a jury to comprehend readily.

Furthermore, as was the case with s. 21(1)(b), the interpretation of s. 21(2)'s *mens rea* requirement that was adopted by the court in *Paquette* is not essential as a means of ensuring the avoidance of unjust convictions in duress cases, since here, as in cases involving s. 21(1)(b), accused persons who act under duress have recourse to the protection from criminal liability provided by the common law defence of duress. At the same time, it can be seen that the interpretation of s. 21(2) adopted in *Paquette* significantly complicates the law of duress, in so far as it requires juries to be instructed on both the manner in which duress might "negate" *mens rea* and on the common law defence of duress itself, notwithstanding the fact that both cover essentially the same ground. This problem would be exacerbated if the interpretation of s. 21(2) in *Paquette* was preserved alongside the interpretation of s. 21(1)(b) that we are adopting in the present appeal. In a significant number of cases, the two subsections will be presented to the jury as alternative bases for liability. In such cases, a trial judge who was required to follow both the holding in this case and *Paquette* would have to instruct the jury that the accused's subjective view as to the desirability of the commission of the offence was not relevant to s. 21(1)(b), but that it was relevant to s. 21(2), and that the existence of duress might "negate" *mens rea* under the latter (but not the former) provision. He or she would then have to go on to charge the jury, in the alternative, on the common law defence of duress. While complex jury instructions are sometimes unavoidable if justice is to be done, I am of the view that unnecessary complexity is something that courts should strive to avoid. The Canadian justice system places considerable faith in jurors' ability to follow the trial judge's instructions. In exchange, I believe it is incumbent on the courts to do what they can to ease, rather than add to, the difficult burden we call upon jurors to bear, subject, of course, to the overriding imperative that trial fairness be preserved.

(iv)   Intention or knowledge

Our *Code* uses a variety of terms to capture this concept: e.g., "means to" (murder: s. 229(a)), "intentionally" (assault: s. 265), "with intent" (theft: s. 322), "purpose" (possessing weapon for a purpose dangerous to the public peace: s. 88) and "knowingly" (possessing: s. 4(3)).

In modern Criminal Codes, such as those found in the United States, such terms are statutorily defined. Since 1892, our *Criminal Code* has left this task of general definition to judges. Our courts have been heavily influenced by the writings of Professor Glanville Williams of Cambridge University. When our courts invoke subjective *mens rea* we shall see below that they are now usually satisfied with *mens rea* in any of the forms of intent, knowledge, recklessness or wilful blindness.

However, there is uncertain jurisprudence that limits the *mens rea* required for certain offences to intent rather than allowing extensions to recklessness or wilful blindness. The leading decision is that in *Buzzanga and Durocher*, which is also the leading authority on the definition of intent as conscious purpose or foresight of a certainty:

R. v. BUZZANGA and DUROCHER

(1979), 49 C.C.C. (2d) 369 (Ont. C.A.)

The defendants were active in promoting the construction of a French language high school in Essex County. They caused to be printed and circulated the following document:

WAKE UP CANADIANS

YOUR FUTURE IS AT STAKE!

IT IS YOUR TAX DOLLARS THAT SUBSIDIZE THE ACTIVITIES OF THE FRENCH MINORITY OF ESSEX COUNTY.

DID YOU KNOW THAT THE ASSOCIATION CANADIAN FRANCAIS DE L'ONTARIO HAS INVESTED SEVERAL HUNDREDS OF THOUSANDS OF DOLLARS OF YOUR TAX MONEY IN QUEBEC?

AND THAT NOW THEY ARE STILL DEMANDING 5 MILLION MORE OF YOUR TAX DOLLARS TO BUILD A FRENCH LANGUAGE HIGH SCHOOL?

YOU ARE SUBSIDIZING SEPARATISM WHETHER IN QUEBEC OR ESSEX COUNTY.

IF WE GIVE THEM A SCHOOL, WHAT WILL THEY DEMAND NEXT . . . INDEPENDENT CITY STATES? CONSIDER THE ETHNIC PROBLEM OF THE UNITED STATES AND TAKE HEED.

DID YOU KNOW THAT THOSE OF THE FRENCH MINORITY WHO SUPPORT THE BUILDING OF THE FRENCH LANGUAGE HIGH SCHOOL ARE IN FACT A SUBVERSIVE GROUP AND THAT MOST FRENCH CANADIANS OF ESSEX COUNTY ARE OPPOSED TO THE BUILDING OF THAT SCHOOL?

WHO WILL RID US OF THIS SUBVERSIVE GROUP IF NOT OURSELVES?

WE MUST STAMP OUT THE SUBVERSIVE ELEMENT WHICH USES HISTORY TO JUSTIFY ITS FREELOADING ON THE TAXPAYERS OF CANADA, NOW.

THE BRITISH SOLVED THIS PROBLEM ONCE BEFORE WITH THE ACADIANS, WHAT ARE WE WAITING FOR . . . ?

MARTIN J.A.: —

. . . .

The statement was composed by the appellant Durocher whose facility with the English language was greater than that of Buzzanga.

The appellant Durocher testified that the francophone community seemed to be "fed up" with the issue of the French-language high school and was becoming apathetic. He said that although economics was the stated reason for not building the school, this was merely an excuse and the real reason was prejudice. The appellant Buzzanga shared Durocher's feeling in this respect.

Both appellants testified as to their purpose in preparing and distributing the pamphlet. The appellant Durocher testified that his purpose was to show the prejudice directed towards French Canadians and expose the truth about the real problem that existed with respect to the French-language school. He said that the statement was largely composed from written material he had seen and from experiences he had had, although the paragraph: "WHO WILL RID US OF THIS SUBVERSIVE GROUP, IF NOT OURSELVES?" was pure theatrics and has its origin in the quotation "Who will rid me of this meddlesome priest", attributed to Henry II. He testified in some detail as to the origin of various parts of the document and endeavoured to show that it reflected statements contained in such sources as letters to the editor of the Windsor Star, a document alleged to have been circulated by a member of the Essex County Ratepayers Association, a paid advertisement published in several newspapers, a book entitled "Bilingual Today, French Tomorrow", and the like. He said that he thought the pamphlet would be a catalyst that would bring a quick solution to the problem of the French-language school by provoking a Government reaction and thereby put pressure on the school board. He thought that by stating these things people would say: "This is ridiculous." A fair reading of his evidence is that he did not want to promote hatred against the "French people", for to do so would be to promote hatred against himself.

The appellant Buzzanga, too, said that he wanted to expose the situation, to show the things that were being said so that intelligent people could see how ridiculous they were. The pamphlet was intended as a satire. He wanted to create a furor that would reach the "House of Commons" and compel the Government to do something that would compel the opposing factions on the school question to reopen communications. He said it was not his intention "to raise hatred towards anyone".

The appellant Buzzanga arranged for the printing and distribution of the document. He placed the order for the printing of the document in the name of Wilfred Fortowsky, the president of the Essex County Ratepayers Association, but asked the printer to delete the name of Mr. Fortowsky when he picked up the material, leaving, however, the name of the Essex County Ratepayers Association on the order form. Neither Mr. Fortowsky nor the Essex County Ratepayers Association were, of course, aware that their names had been so used.

. . . .

The threshold question to be determined is the meaning of "wilfully" in the term "wilfully promotes hatred" in s. 281.2(2) [now s. 319(2)] of the *Criminal Code*. It will, of course, be observed that the word "wilfully" modifies the words "promotes hatred", rather than the words "communicating statements".

The word "wilfully" has not been uniformly interpreted and its meaning to some extent depends upon the context in which it is used. Its primary meaning is "intentionally", but it is also used to mean "recklessly": see Glanville Williams, *Criminal Law, The General Part*, 2nd ed. (1961), pp. 51-2; Glanville Williams, *Text book of Criminal Law* (1978), p. 87; Smith and Hogan, *Criminal Law*, 4th ed. (1978), pp. 104-5. The term "recklessly" is here used to denote the subjective state of mind of a person who foresees that his conduct may cause the prohibited result but, nevertheless, takes a deliberate and unjustifiable risk of bringing it about: see Glanville Williams, *Textbook of Criminal Law*, pp. 70 and 76; Smith and Hogan, *Criminal Law*, 4th ed., pp. 52-3.

The word "wilfully" has, however, also been held to mean no more than the accused's act is done intentionally and not accidentally. In *R. v. Senior*, [1899] 1 Q.B. 283, Lord Russell of Killowen C.J., in interpreting the meaning of the words "wilfully neglects" in s. 1 of the *Prevention of Cruelty to Children Act*, 1894 (U.K.), c. 41, said at pp. 290-1: " 'Wilfully' means that the act is done deliberately and intentionally, not by accident or inadvertence, but so that the mind of the person who does the act goes with it."

On the other hand, in *Rice v. Connolly*, [1966] 2 Q.B. 414, where the accused was charged with wilfully obstructing a constable in the execution of his duty, Lord Parker L.C.J., said at p. 419: "'Wilful' in this context not only in my judgment means 'intentional' but something which is done without lawful excuse. . .".

In *Willmott v. Atack*, [1976] 3 All E.R. 794, the appellant was convicted on a charge of wilfully obstructing a peace officer in the execution of his duty. A police officer, acting in the execution of his duty, arrested a motorist who struggled and resisted. The appellant, who knew the motorist, intervened with the intention of assisting the officer but, in fact, his conduct obstructed the officer. The Queen's Bench Divisional Court quashed the conviction and held that it was not sufficient to prove the appellant intended to do what he did, and which resulted in an obstruction, but that the prosecution must prove that the appellant intended to obstruct the officer.

The judgment of the Court of Criminal Appeal of Queensland in *R. v. Burnell*, [1966] Qd. R. 348, also illustrates that, depending on its context, the word "wilfully" may connote an intention to bring about a proscribed consequence. In that case the appellant was charged with arson in having set fire to a shed. Section 461 of the Queensland *Criminal Code* provides that ". . . any person who wilfully and unlawfully sets fire to . . . any building or structure is guilty of a crime. . .". The accused had deliberately set fire to some mattresses in a shed whereby the shed was set on fire. The trial Judge instructed the jury that "wilfully" connoted no more than a willed and voluntary act as distinguished from the result of an accident or mere negligence. The Queensland Court of Criminal Appeal, in setting aside the conviction, held that in the context of the section "wilfully" required proof that the accused did an act which resulted in setting fire to the building with the intention of bringing about that result. Gibbs J. (with whom Douglas J. concurred), said at p. 356:

> Under s. 461 it is not enough that the accused did the act which resulted in setting fire to the building foreseeing that his act might have that effect but recklessly taking the risk; it is necessary that the accused did the act which resulted in setting fire to the building with the intention of bringing about that result.

Mr. Manning conceded that in some cases the element of wilfulness is supplied by recklessness but he contended that in its context in s. 281.2(2) of the *Criminal Code* "wilfully" means with the intention of promoting hatred. In the course of his argument, Mr. Manning stressed the definition of "wilfully" contained in s. 386(1) [now s. 429(1)] of the *Code*, which reads:

> 386(1) Every one who causes the occurrence of an event by doing an act or by omitting to do an act that it is his duty to do, knowing that the act or omission will probably cause the occurrence of the event and being reckless whether the event occurs or not, shall be deemed, for the purposes of this Part, wilfully to have caused the occurrence of the event.

Mr. Manning emphasized that s. 386(1) provides that wilfully is to have the meaning specified in that section for the purposes of Part IX [now Part XI] of the *Code*. He argued with much force that the state of mind specified in s. 386(1) is recklessness and that where Parliament intends to extend the meaning of wilfully to include recklessness it does so expressly. In *R. v. Rese*, [1968] 1 C.C.C. 363 at p. 366, 2 C.R.N.S. 99, Laskin J.A. (as he then was), referred to the definition now contained in s. 386(1) as an extended meaning of "wilfully".

As previously indicated, the word "wilfully" does not have a fixed meaning, but I am satisfied that in the context of s. 281.2(2) it means with the intention of promoting hatred, and does not include recklessness. The arrangement of legislation proscribing the incitement of hatred, in my view, leads to that conclusion.

Section 281.2(1), unlike s. 281.2(2), is restricted to the incitement of hatred by communicating statements in a public place where such incitement is likely to lead to a breach of the peace. Although no mental element is expressly mentioned in s. 281.2(1), where the communication poses an immediate threat to public order, *mens rea* is, none the less, required since the inclusion of an offence in the *Criminal Code* must be taken to import *mens rea* in the absence of a clear intention to dispense with it: see *R. v. Prue; R. v. Baril* (1979), 46 C.C.C. (2d) 257 at pp. 260-1, 96 D.L.R. 577 at pp. 580-1, 8 C.R. (3d) 68 at p. 73. The general *mens rea* which is required and which suffices for most crimes where no mental element is mentioned in the definition of the crime, is either the intentional or reckless bringing about of the result which the law, in creating the offence, seeks to prevent and, hence, under s. 281.2(1) is either the intentional or reckless inciting of hatred in the specified circumstances.

The insertion of the word "wilfully" in s. 281.2(2) was not necessary to import *mens rea* since that requirement would be implied in any event because of the serious nature of the offence: see *R. v. Prue, supra*. The statements, the communication of which are proscribed by s. 281.2(2), are not confined to statements communicated in a public place in circumstances likely to lead to a breach of the peace and they, consequently, do not pose such an immediate threat to public order as those falling under s. 281.2(1); it is reasonable to assume, therefore, that Parliament intended to limit the offence under s. 281.2(2) to the intentional promotion of hatred. It is evident that the use of the word "wilfully" in s. 281.2(2), and not in s. 281.2(1), reflects Parliament's policy to strike a balance in protecting the competing social interests of freedom of expression on the one hand, and public order and group reputation on the other hand.

Having concluded that proof of an intention to promote hatred is essential to constitute the offence: under s. 281.2(2), it is necessary to consider the mental attitude which must be established to constitute an intention to promote hatred. The state of mind connoted by "intention", where an intention to bring about a certain result is an element of the offence, has been the subject of much discussion, and writers on jurisprudence, as well as Judges, have not always been in agreement as to its meaning.

. . . .

There are cases which appear to provide support for the proposition that where an intention to produce a particular consequence is essential to constitute the offence, an act is not done with intent to produce the prohibited consequence unless it is the actor's conscious purpose to bring it about, and that the actor's foresight of the certainty of the consequence is not synonymous with an intention to produce it: see *R. v. Miller* (1959), 125 C.C.C. 8 at p. 30, 31 C.R. 101; *R. v. Ahlers*, [1915] 1 K.B. 616; *Sinnasamy Selvanayagam v. The King*, [1951] A.C. 83; *R. v. Steane*, [1947] 1 K.B. 997. Most of these cases are subjected to critical examination by Dr. Glanville Williams in *Criminal Law, The General Part*, 2nd ed. (1961), pp. 40-2.

There is, however, substantial support for the proposition that in the criminal law a person intends a particular consequence not only when his conscious purpose is to bring it about, but also when he foresees that the consequence is certain or substantially certain to result from his conduct: see Glanville Williams, *Criminal Law, The General Part*, 2nd ed. (1961), p. 38; Walter Wheeler Cook, *Act, Intention, and Motive in the Criminal Law* (1916-17), 26 Yale L.J. 645 at pp. 654-8; Rollin Perkins, *A Rationale of Mens Rea*, 52 Harv. L. Rev. 905 at pp. 910-1 (1938-39).

Smith and Hogan, the learned authors of *Criminal Law*, 4th ed., state at p. 51, that the authorities referred to by them:

> suggest that in the criminal law generally, though not universally, a person intends a consequence if it is his purpose to achieve it or if he knows that the achievement of some other purpose is certain, or "morally" certain, to produce the consequence in question.

In *R. v. Lemon; R. v. Gay News Ltd.*, *supra*, Lord Diplock, however, defined intention in much wider terms. He said that where intention to produce a particular result is a necessary element of an offence, no distinction is to be drawn in law between the state of mind of one who does an act because he desires to produce that particular result, and the state of mind of one who, when he does the act, is aware that it is likely to produce that result but is prepared to take the risk that it may do so in order to achieve some other purpose. He considered that the law has been settled by *Hyam v. Director of Public Prosecutions*, *supra*, "that both states of mind constitute 'intention' in the sense in which that expression is used in the definition of a crime whether at common law or in a statute" (at p. 905).

Hyam v. Director of Public Prosecutions, *supra*, was concerned with the mental element required to constitute "malice aforethought". It may well be that either an intention to kill or cause serious bodily harm, or foresight that death or serious bodily harm is a highly probable consequence of an act done for some other purpose, is a sufficient *mens rea* for murder at common law. I do not consider, however, that the actor's foresight that a consequence is highly probable, as opposed to substantially certain, is the same thing as an intention to bring it about: see *Hyam v. Director of Public Prosecutions*, *supra*, *per* Lord Hailsham at p. 75; *R. v. Belfon*, [1976] 3 All E.R. 46; Smith and Hogan, *Criminal Law*, 4th ed., pp. 47-51; Commentary on *R. v. Lemon et al.*, [1979] Crim. L.R. 311 at p. 314. In my view, the mental attitude described by Lord Diplock is a form of recklessness.

I agree, however (assuming without deciding that there may be cases in which intended consequences are confined to those which it is the actor's conscious purpose to bring about), that, as a general rule, a person who foresees that a consequence is certain or substantially certain to result from an act which he does in order to achieve some other purpose, intends that consequence. The actor's foresight of the certainty or moral certainty of the consequence resulting from his conduct compels a conclusion that if he, none the less, acted so as to produce it, then he decided to bring it about (albeit regretfully), in order to achieve his ultimate purpose. His intention encompasses the means as well as to his ultimate objective.

I conclude, therefore, that the appellants "wilfully" (intentionally) promoted hatred against the French Canadian community of Essex County only if: (a) their conscious purpose in distributing the document was to promote hatred against that group, or (b) they foresaw that the promotion of hatred against that group was certain or morally certain to result from the distribution of the pamphlet, but distributed it as means of achieving their purpose of obtaining the French-language high school.

Whether the trial judge misdirected himself as to the meaning of wilfully?

The learned trial judge in comprehensive reasons first considered whether the document objectively promoted hatred and concluded that the cumulative effect of the document rendered it a communication that promoted hatred against the French-speaking community of Essex County. He then said:

> It is, however, incumbent upon the Crown to prove beyond a reasonable doubt that the two accused wilfully promoted such hatred. In other words, has the Crown established the necessary element of *mens rea*. In considering the meaning to be given to the word "wilfully" in this section the court must distinguish between what has been described by learned writers as primary and secondary intent; or to phrase it in a more understanding way, the distinction between intent and motive. I have earlier discussed the purpose or motive as explained by the accused themselves. They wished to create a situation that would require the intervention of senior levels of Government and result in the construction of the high school. It is in evidence that the handbill was, in fact, shown to a mediator representing the Minister of Education who was in this area attempting to resolve the school issue. It is, of course, a matter of judicial notice that the Province did pass special legislation requiring the construction of the school. It is extremely doubtful, however, that this document played any part in the formulation of that decision. It was also their desire to unify the French Canadian community. As Father Vincent stated, opposition from outside often cements an ethnic group and tends to strengthen people rather than weaken them.
>
> This is what the court would refer to as the purpose or motive of the accused.
>
> Wilful in this section, however, means intentional as opposed to accidental. Miss Susan Moylan who testified for the accused was involved in the early discussions between the accused in the preparation of the handbill. She testified that the document was not to create strong feelings but to create strong actions and strong reactions. How one can do the latter without the former is beyond the comprehension of this court. The accused themselves testified they wished to create controversy, furor and an uproar. What better way of describing active dislike, detestation, enmity or ill will. The motives of the accused may or may not be laudable. The means chosen by the accused was the wilful promotion of hatred.

. . . .

I am not persuaded that the learned trial judge fell into the error of detaching the word "wilfully" from the words "promotes hatred" and applied it only to the distribution of the pamphlet. I am of the view, however, that the learned trial judge erred in holding that "wilfully" means only "intentional as opposed to accidental". Although, as previously indicated, "wilfully" has sometimes been used to mean that the accused's act, as distinct from its consequences, must be intended and not accidental (as in *R. v. Senior*, [1899] 1 Q.B. 283), it does not have that meaning in the provisions under consideration.

The learned trial judge's view of the meaning of "wilfully" inevitably caused him to focus attention on the intentional nature of the appellants' conduct, rather than on the question whether they actually intended to produce the consequence of promoting hatred.

. . . .

In some cases the inference from the circumstances that the necessary intent existed may be so strong as to compel the rejection of the accused's evidence that he did not intend to bring about the prohibited consequence. The learned trial judge did not, however, state that he disbelieved the appellants' evidence that they did not intend to promote hatred. He appears to have treated the appellants' testimony that they wished to create "controversy, furor and an uproar" as a virtual admission that they had the state of mind requisite for guilt.

I am, with deference to the learned trial judge, of the view that an intention to create "controversy, furor and an uproar" is not the same thing as an intention to promote hatred, and it was an error to equate them. I would, of course, agree that if the appellants intentionally promoted hatred against the French-speaking community of Essex County as a means of obtaining the French-language high school, they committed the offence charged. The appellants' evidence, if believed, does not, however, as the learned trial judge appears to have thought, inevitably lead to that conclusion. The learned trial judge, not having disbelieved the appellants' evidence, failed to give appropriate consideration to their evidence on the issue of intent and, in the circumstances, his failure so to do constituted self-misdirection.

In view of the conclusion which I have reached it is necessary to refer only briefly to the other grounds of appeal which we regard as requiring discussion.

. . . .

Conclusion

I have concluded that the self-misdirection with respect to the meaning of the word "wilfully", and the failure to appreciate the significance of the appellants' evidence on the issue of intent requires a new trial. The outrageous conduct of the appellants in preparing and distributing this deplorable document was evidence to be weighed in determining their intent, but in the peculiar circumstances of this case I am not satisfied that the inferences to be drawn from it are such as to inevitably lead to a conclusion that they had the requisite intent or that the trial judge would inevitably have reached that conclusion but for his self-misdirection.

In the result, I would allow the appeal, set aside the convictions and order new trials.

Appeal allowed; new trial ordered.

This interpretation was later adopted by the Supreme Court in *R. v. Keegstra*, [1990] 3 S.C.R. 697, 1 C.R. (4th) 129, 61 C.C.C. (3d) 1, a decision holding that s. 319(2) was constitutional. Although the offence violated freedom of expression guaranteed by s. 2(b) of the *Charter* the limit was held to be demonstrably justified as a reasonable limit under s. 1. One of the reasons given by Chief Justice Dickson for the majority was that:

> The interpretation of "wilfully" in *Buzzanga* has great bearing upon the extent to which s. 319(2) limits the freedom of expression. This mental element, requiring more than merely negligence or recklessness as to result, significantly restricts the reach of the provision, and thereby reduces the scope of the targeted expression (at 193).

In *R. v. Harding* (2001), 48 C.R. (5th) 1 (Ont. C.A.), the Court, after referring to *Buzzanga*, nevertheless decided that "wilfully" in s. 319(2) should be extended to the subjective concept of wilful blindness.

In two high-profile wilful obstruction of justice charges, lack of proof of intent was the basis for acquittals. In *Kirkham* (1998), 17 C.R. (5th) 250, 126 C.C.C. (3d) 397 (Sask. Q.B.), a Crown Attorney had arranged for a police questionnaire to obtain information about the background of potential jurors for a mercy killing murder trial, *Latimer*, which he did not disclose to defence counsel. In *Murray* (2000), 34 C.R. (5th) 290, 144 C.C.C. (3d) 289 (Ont. S.C.J.), a defence counsel in the double murder case of *Bernardo* had withheld incriminating videotapes of sexual abuse of murder victims by his client and co-accused for 17 months. Such a definitional quagmire concerning so basic a crime as obstruction of justice speaks volumes about a need for a General Part with clear fault definitions.

R. v. Chartrand (1994), 31 C.R. (4th) 1 (S.C.C.), concerning the crime of abduction of a child under 14, is now strong authority for the view that where an offence has an express "with intent" element this requires proof of intent or actual foresight of certainty. Madam Justice L'Heureux-Dubé for the Court relied on *Buzzanga*. The Court implicitly decided recklessness would not do but there is no discussion of why this should be so.

We have seen that the Supreme Court has limited the offence of threatening to proof of an intent to intimidate or an intent to be taken seriously. Intent has been held to extend, as in *Buzzanga*, to a subjective foresight of a certainty but not to recklessness: *R. v. Armstrong* (2012), 95 C.R. (6th) 46 (B.C. C.A.), leave to appeal refused (2013), 452 N.R. 400 (note) (S.C.C.).

In the case of so-called incomplete or inchoate crimes (see Chapter 9) Canadian courts have usually limited the *mens rea* to intent and not extended to recklessness and wilful blindness; see, for example, *Ancio* (1984), 39 C.R. (3d) 1 (S.C.C.) (attempts), but in *R. v. Hamilton*, [2005] 2 S.C.R. 432, 198 C.C.C. (3d) 1, 30 C.R. (6th) 243 a 6-3 majority extended the offence of counselling an offence that was not committed to recklessness. See Chapter 9

Even if the word "knowing" is not included in a criminal provision, the Crown must prove knowledge of the relevant circumstance. Further, the presence of the word "knowing" in a criminal provision can sometimes point to the existence of a corresponding external element. In *United States v. Dynar*, [1997] 2 S.C.R. 462 (which will also be considered below under "Attempts") the accused was charged with laundering money "knowing" that it was the proceeds of crime. The money in question was provided by the FBI as part of a "sting" operation and was not, in fact, the proceeds of crime. The Supreme Court held that this meant the accused could not be found guilty; the requirement in the statute that he "know" the money was the proceeds of crime (as opposed to simply believing that) meant that the money had to actually be the proceeds of crime:

> 41 Because it is not possible to know what is false, no one who converts money that is not in fact the proceeds of crime commits these offences. This is clear from the meaning of the word "know". In the Western legal tradition, knowledge is defined as true belief: "The word 'know' refers exclusively to true knowledge; we are not said to 'know' something that is not so" (Glanville Williams, *Textbook of Criminal Law* (2nd ed. 1983), at p. 160).

Although use of the word "knowing" points to the presence of a corresponding external element, use of the word "intent" or similar language does not necessarily have the same effect. There are many offences in the *Criminal Code* which require that the accused have a particular intent, but where it is irrelevant whether the accused succeeds in this attempt. See, for example, s. 348(1):

> 348. (1) Every one who
>   (*a*) breaks and enters a place with intent to commit an indictable offence therein,
>   (*b*) breaks and enters a place and commits an indictable offence therein. . .
> is guilty [of an offence].

Under s. 348(1)(b) it would be necessary to show that the accused actually committed an indictable offence; under s. 348(1)(a) it is only necessary to show the intent to do so.

The term most often associated with such a "free-floating" fault element is "with intent to". That is not the only possible language, however, and so it is a matter of reading the provision grammatically to determine what is intended. See, for example, s. 249.1:

> 249.1 (1) Every one commits an offence who, operating a motor vehicle while being pursued by a peace officer operating a motor vehicle, fails, without reasonable excuse and *in order to evade the peace officer*, to stop the vehicle as soon as is reasonable in the circumstances.

So, too, the offence of using a computer to communicate with a person believed to be under 16 for the commission of a sexual offence has been interpreted not to require proof of an intent to meet the child in person: *R. v. Legare*, 70 C.R. (6th) 1, [2009] 3 S.C.R. 551. See C.R. annotation by Janine Benedet.

R. v. THÉROUX

[1993] 2 S.C.R. 5, 19 C.R. (4th) 194, 79 C.C.C. (3d) 449,
1993 CarswellQue 5, 1993 CarswellQue 156

The accused, the directing mind of a company involved in residential construction, was charged with fraud. The company entered into contracts and received deposits on the basis of a false representation by the company that the deposits were insured. The company became insolvent, the project was not completed and most of the depositors lost their money. The trial judge found that the accused, as directing mind of the company, was responsible for the misrepresentations that the deposits were guaranteed. The accused knew at the time that the insurance was not in place but nevertheless made misrepresentations to induce potential home purchasers to sign a contract and give a deposit. The trial judge also found that the accused sincerely believed that the residential project would be completed and hence that the deposits would not be lost. The accused was convicted of fraud pursuant to s. 380(1)(a) of the *Criminal Code* and the Court of Appeal upheld the conviction. The issue for the Supreme Court was whether the fact that the accused honestly believed that the project would be completed negated the *mens rea* of the offence of fraud.

McLACHLIN J.: —

There is no doubt that the appellant deliberately practised a deceitful act, constituting the *actus reus* of the offence of fraud. The issue is whether the fact that he honestly believed that the projects would be completed negates the guilty mind or *mens rea* of the offence. This requires this court to examine the question of what constitutes the *mens rea* for the offence of fraud.

. . . .

The prohibited act is deceit, falsehood, or some other dishonest act. The prohibited consequence is depriving another of what is or should be his, which may, as we have seen, consist in merely placing another's property at risk. The *mens rea* would then consist in the subjective awareness that one was undertaking a prohibited act (the deceit, falsehood or other dishonest act) which could cause deprivation in the sense of depriving another of property or putting that property at risk. If this is shown, the crime is complete. The fact that the accused may have hoped the deprivation would not take place, or may have felt there was nothing wrong with what he or she was doing, provides no defence. To put it another way, following the traditional criminal-law principle that the mental state necessary to the offence must be determined by reference to the external acts which constitute the *actus* of the offence (see Williams, *supra*, c. 3), the proper focus in determining the *mens rea* of fraud is to ask whether the accused intentionally committed the prohibited acts (deceit, falsehood, or other dishonest act) knowing or desiring the consequences proscribed by the offence (deprivation, including the risk of deprivation). The personal feeling of the accused about the morality or honesty of the act or its consequences is no more relevant to the analysis than is the accused's awareness that the particular acts undertaken constitute a criminal offence.

This applies as much to the third head of fraud, "other fraudulent means", as to lies and acts of deceit. Although other fraudulent means have been broadly defined as means which are "dishonest", it is not necessary that an accused personally consider these means to be dishonest in order that he or she be convicted of fraud for having undertaken them. The "dishonesty" of the means is relevant to the determination whether the conduct falls within the type of conduct caught by the offence of fraud; what reasonable people consider dishonest assists in the determination whether the *actus reus* of the offence can be made out on particular facts. That established, it need only be determined that an accused knowingly undertook the acts in question, aware that deprivation, or risk of deprivation, could follow as a likely consequence.

I have spoken of knowledge of the consequences of the fraudulent act. There appears to be no reason, however, why recklessness as to consequences might not also attract criminal responsibility. Recklessness presupposes knowledge of the likelihood of the prohibited consequences. It is established when it is shown that the accused, with such knowledge, commits acts which may bring about these prohibited consequences, while being reckless as to whether or not they ensue.

These doctrinal observations suggest that the *actus reus* of the offence of fraud will be established by proof of:

1. the prohibited act, be it an act of deceit, a falsehood or some other fraudulent means; and

2. deprivation caused by the prohibited act, which may consist in actual loss or the placing of the victim's pecuniary interests at risk.

Correspondingly, the *mens rea* of fraud is established by proof of:

1. Subjective knowledge of the prohibited act; and

2. Subjective knowledge that the prohibited act could have as a consequence the deprivation of another (which deprivation may consist in knowledge that the victim's pecuniary interests are put at risk).

Where the conduct and knowledge required by these definitions are established, the accused is guilty whether he actually intended the prohibited consequence or was reckless as to whether it would occur.

The inclusion of *risk* of deprivation in the concept of deprivation in *Olan* requires specific comment. The accused must have subjective awareness, at the very least, that his or her conduct will put the property or economic expectations of others at risk. As noted above, this does not mean that the Crown must provide the trier of fact with a mental snapshot proving exactly what was in the accused's mind at the moment the dishonest act was committed. In certain cases, the inference of subjective knowledge of the risk may be drawn from the facts as the accused believed them to be. The accused may introduce evidence negating that inference, such as evidence that his deceit was part of an innocent prank, or evidence of circumstances which led him to believe that no one would act on his lie or deceitful or dishonest act. But in cases like the present one, where the accused tells a lie knowing others will act on it and thereby puts their property at risk, the inference of subjective knowledge that the property of another would be put at risk is clear.

R. v. BOULANGER

(2006), 39 C.R. (6th) 1, [2006] 2 S.C.R. 49, 210 C.C.C. (3d) 1, 2006
CarswellQue 5739, 2006 CarswellQue 5740 (S.C.C.)

The accused was charged with breach of trust under s. 122 of the *Criminal Code*. The accused was director of public security for a municipality, and his daughter was involved in an automobile accident. After a report had been filed the accused ordered a subordinate officer to prepare a supplementary accident report on the accident. The supplementary report concluded that his daughter was not at fault; the accused forwarded the report to his insurance company and as a result did not have to pay the insurance deductible of $250.

Justice McLachlin, for a unanimous Court, observed that the offence of breach of trust had existed at common law and had been in the *Criminal Code* since 1892, but that nonetheless the elements of the offence remained uncertain. She concluded, after a thorough review, that the Crown was required to prove the following elements:

1. The accused is an official;

2. The accused was acting in connection with the duties of his or her office;

3. The accused breached the standard of responsibility and conduct demanded of him or her by the nature of the office;

4. The conduct of the accused represented a serious and marked departure from the standards expected of an individual in the accused's position of public trust; and

5. The accused acted with the intention to use his or her public office for a purpose other than the public good, for example, for a dishonest, partial, corrupt or oppressive purpose.

It is the Court's discussion of the final element, the *mens rea* for the offence, which is important to us here. Is the Court's approach here to the relevance of the accused's subjective purpose consistent with their approach in *Theroux*?

2.4.2 *Mens Rea*

55 In the early common law cases, the mental element of misfeasance in public office was imprecise and varied from case to case. However, common law judges consistently insisted on the presence of some variant of nefarious or dishonest intent. This was described using different terms: dishonesty, corruption, partiality and oppression. All reflected a central concern: that public officials, entrusted with duties for the benefit of the public, carry out those duties honestly and for the benefit of the public, and that they not abuse their offices for corrupt or improper purposes.

56 Consistent with fundamental criminal law principles, the bar for mental culpability for the offence of public misfeasance was an elevated one. Mistakes did not suffice. Nor did errors of judgment. To quote Abbott C.J. in *Borron*:

> ... the question has always been, not whether the act done might, upon full and mature investigation, be found strictly right, but from what motive it had proceeded; whether from a dishonest, oppressive, or corrupt motive, under which description, fear and favour may generally be included, or from mistake or error. In the former case, alone, they have become the objects of punishment. [pp. 721-22]

In principle, the *mens rea* of the offence lies in the intention to use one's public office for purposes other than the benefit of the public. In practice, this has been associated historically with using one's public office for a dishonest, partial, corrupt or oppressive purpose, each of which embodies the non-public purpose with which the offence is concerned.

57 As with any offence, the *mens rea* is inferred from the circumstances. An attempt by the accused to conceal his or her actions may often provide evidence of an improper intent: *Arnoldi*. Similarly, the receipt of a significant personal benefit may provide evidence that the accused acted in his or her own interest rather than that of the public. However, the fact that a public officer obtains a benefit is not conclusive of a culpable *mens rea*. Many legitimate exercises of public authority or power by a public servant confer incidental advantages on the actor. As Widgery J. (as he then was) stated in *R. v. Llewellyn-Jones* (1966), 51 Cr. App. R. 4, at p. 7:

> ... I would not be prepared to say that it would be misconduct for this purpose for a registrar to make a decision which did affect his personal interests, merely because he knew that his interests were so involved, if the decision was made honestly and in a genuine belief that it was a proper exercise of his jurisdiction so far as the beneficiaries and other persons concerned came into it. [Cited by Widgery L.C.J. in *Dytham*, at p. 394.]

Conversely, the offence may be made out where no personal benefit is involved.

· · · ·

63 I turn first to *mens rea*. The question is whether the evidence establishes an intention to use his public office for a purpose other than the public good, for example, for a dishonest, partial, corrupt or oppressive purpose. The trial judge found that the evidence supported the good faith of both Mr. Boulanger and Constable Stephens (para. 100). Specifically, she concluded that the report accorded with the preponderance of evidence relating to the accident, that it was not falsified, and that the accused did not ask or obtain a supplementary report with the intent of misleading the insurance company (paras. 97-99). Indeed, she expressly labelled Mr. Boulanger's conduct as an error in judgment (para. 108). Moreover, as Dalphond J.A. noted, the facts as found demonstrate no attempt whatsoever to conceal.

64 It is true that Mr. Boulanger knew that he would benefit from Constable Stephens' report. This alone does not, however, establish a culpable state of mind. For example, as discussed, it is not misconduct to make a decision knowing it furthers one's personal interests, if the decision is made honestly and in the belief that it is a proper exercise of the public power the official enjoys: *Dytham*. Mr. Boulanger's private purpose did not seek to undermine the public good. Had Mr. Boulanger instructed Constable Stephens to put a particular content into the report, that might have amounted to using his office in a way that betrayed the public trust. But Mr. Boulanger did not do this. Constable Stephens testified that the report contained his own opinion about the responsibility of Alexandra Boulanger for the accident (trial judgment, at para. 51). He further testified that he never felt any pressure or obligation to write the report (trial judgment, at para. 52). As noted, the trial judge concluded that the report accorded with the preponderance of evidence relating to the accident, that it was not falsified, and that Mr. Boulanger did not ask or obtain a supplementary report with the intent of misleading the insurance company (paras. 97-99). In these circumstances, it is not clear that Mr. Boulanger's intention was to betray the public trust reposed in him.

65 As a check, it may be asked whether Mr. Boulanger's intention rose to the level of culpability traditionally required by the common law for the offence of breach of trust — for example, whether he acted for a dishonest, partial, corrupt or oppressive purpose. Dishonesty, corruption and oppression were clearly not made out. Nor, arguably, was partiality. "Partiality" denotes an "unfair bias in favour of one thing . . . compared with another": *The New Oxford Dictionary of English* (1998), at p. 1352. Mr. Boulanger's intention was to have Constable Stephens make a complete report, not to skew it in one direction or another.

66 I conclude that the facts as found raise a reasonable doubt that the *mens rea* necessary for conviction under s. 122 of the *Criminal Code* was established.

(v)   *Recklessness or wilful blindness*

There are occasions where our *Criminal Code* expressly relies on recklessness as fault.

1.   murder under s. 229(a)(ii);

2.   "wilful" as defined in s. 429 for all Part XI offences (mostly property offences such as mischief, damage to property and arson);

3.   criminal harassment (s. 264); and

4.   offences based on criminal negligence (s. 219) (considered separately as *sui generis* later).

There are no examples where Parliament has expressly resorted to wilful blindness, a concept invented by Glanville Williams.

Whether or not there is an express extension to recklessness or wilful blindness our courts usually extend subjective *mens rea* beyond actual intent or knowledge to recklessness and wilful blindness. The central concept is actual awareness of risk in one of these forms.

SANSREGRET v. R.

[1985] 1 S.C.R. 570, 45 C.R. (3d) 193, 18 C.C.C. (3d) 223,
1985 CarswellMan 176, 1985 CarswellMan 380

Sansregret is a leading decision on the crime of rape, to be considered later in the chapter on "Sexual Assault". During the course of his unanimous judgment for the Supreme Court, Mr. Justice McIntyre authoritatively defined and distinguished the concepts of recklessness and wilful blindness as follows:

. . . .

The concept of recklessness as a basis for criminal liability has been the subject of much discussion. Negligence, the failure to take reasonable care, is a creature of the civil law and is not generally a concept having a place in determining criminal liability. Nevertheless, it is frequently confused with recklessness in the criminal sense and care should be taken to separate the two concepts. Negligence is tested by the objective standard of the reasonable man. A departure from his accustomed sober behaviour by an act or omission which reveals less than reasonable care will involve liability at civil law but forms no basis for the imposition of criminal penalties. In accordance with well-established principles for the determination of criminal liability, recklessness, to form a part of the criminal *mens rea*, must have an element of the subjective. It is found in the attitude of one who, aware that there is danger that his conduct could bring about the result prohibited by the criminal law, nevertheless persists, despite the risk. It is, in other words, the conduct of one who sees the risk and who takes the chance. It is in this sense that the term "recklessness" is used in the criminal law and it is clearly distinct from the concept of civil negligence.

. . . .

The idea of wilful blindness in circumstances such as this has been said to be an aspect of recklessness. While this may well be true, it is wise to keep the two concepts separate because they result from different mental attitudes and lead to different legal results. A finding of recklessness in this case could not override the defence of mistake of fact. The appellant asserts an honest belief that the consent of the complainant was not caused by fear and threats. The trial judge found that such an honest belief existed. In the facts of this case, because of the reckless conduct of the appellant, it could not be said that such a belief was reasonable but, as held in *Pappajohn*, the mere honesty of the belief will support the "mistake of fact" defence, even where it is unreasonable. On the other hand, a finding of wilful blindness as to the very facts about which the honest belief is now asserted would leave no room for the application of the defence because, where wilful blindness is shown, the law presumes knowledge on the part of the accused, in this case knowledge that the consent had been induced by threats.

Wilful blindness is distinct from recklessness because, while recklessness involves knowledge of a danger or risk and persistence in a course of conduct which creates a risk that the prohibited result will occur, wilful blindness arises where a person who has become aware of the need for some inquiry declines to make the inquiry because he does not wish to know the truth. He would prefer to remain ignorant. The culpability in recklessness is justified by consciousness of the risk and by proceeding in the face of it, while in wilful blindness it is justified by the accused's fault in deliberately failing to inquire when he knows there is reason for inquiry. Cases such as *Wretham v. R.* (1971), 16 C.R.N.S. 124 (Ont. C.A.); *R. v. Blondin* (1971), 2 C.C.C. (2d) 118, affirmed [1971] S.C.R. v, 4 C.C.C. (2d) 566; *R. v. Currie* (1976), 24 C.C.C. (2d) 292 (Ont. C.A.); *R. v. McFall* (1976), 26 C.C.C. (2d) 181 (B.C. C.A.); *R. v. Aiello* (1978), 38 C.C.C. (2d) 485 (Ont. C.A.); *Taylor's Central Garages (Exeter) Ltd. v. Roper*, [1951] 2 T.L.R. 284 (Div. Ct.), among others, illustrate these principles. The textwriters have also dealt with the subject, particularly Glanville Williams, *Criminal Law: The General Part*, 2nd ed. (1961), at pp. 157-60. He says, at p. 157:

> Knowledge, then, means either personal knowledge or (in the licence cases) imputed knowledge. In either event there is someone with actual knowledge. To the requirement of actual knowledge there is one strictly limited exception. Men readily regard their suspicions as unworthy of them when it is to their advantage to do so. To meet this, the rule is that if a party has his suspicion aroused but then deliberately omits to make further enquiries, because he wishes to remain in ignorance, he is deemed to have knowledge.

He then referred to the words of Lord Sumner in *Re The Zamora*, [1921] 1 A.C. 801 at 811-12 (P.C.), which was a case wherein a ship and cargo were condemned in the Prize Court as contraband. The managing director of the shipping company denied knowledge of the contraband carried by the ship, and on this subject Lord Sumner said, at pp. 811-12:

> Lord Sterndale [the president of the Prize Court] thus expressed his final conclusion: "I think the true inference is that, if Mr. Banck did not know this was a transaction in contraband, it was because he did not want to know, and that he has not rebutted the presumption arising from the fact of the whole cargo being contraband."
>
> Their Lordships have been invited to read this as saying that Mr. Banck is not proved to have known the contraband character of the adventure; that if he did not know, because he did not want to know, he was within his rights and owed no duty to the belligerents to inform himself; and that the *Zamora* is condemned contrary to the passage above cited from *The Hakan* upon a legal presumption arising solely and arbitrarily from the fact that the whole

cargo was contraband. It may be that in his anxiety not to state more than he found against Mr. Banck, the learned President appeared to state something less, but there are two senses in which a man is said not to know something because he does not want to know it. A thing may be troublesome to learn, and the knowledge of it, when acquired, may be uninteresting or distasteful. To refuse to know any more about the subject or anything at all is then a wilful but a real ignorance. On the other hand, a man is said not to know because he does not want to know, where the substance of the thing is borne in upon his mind with a conviction that full details or precise proof may be dangerous, because they may embarrass his denials or compromise his protests. In such a case he flatters himself that where ignorance is safe, 'tis folly to be wise, but there he is wrong, for he has been put upon notice and his further ignorance, even though actual and complete, is a mere affectation and disguise.

Glanville Williams, however, warns that the rule of deliberate blindness has its dangers and is of narrow application. He says, at p. 159:

> The rule that wilful blindness is equivalent to knowledge is essential, and is found throughout the criminal law. It is, at the same time, an unstable rule, because Judges are apt to forget its very limited scope. A court can properly find wilful blindness only where it can almost be said that the defendant actually knew. He suspected the fact; he realised its probability; but he refrained from obtaining the final confirmation because he wanted in the event to be able to deny knowledge. This, and this alone, is wilful blindness. It requires in effect a finding that the defendant intended to cheat the administration of justice. Any wider definition would make the doctrine of wilful blindness indistinguishable from the civil doctrine of negligence in not obtaining knowledge.

This subject is also dealt with by Professor Stuart in *Canadian Criminal Law* (1982), at p. 130 et seq., where its relationship to recklessness is discussed.

In *R. v. Hamilton*, [2005] 2 S.C.R. 432, 198 C.C.C. (3d) 1, 30 C.R. (6th) 243 (a case on counselling, considered later under Chapter 9, Incomplete Crimes) Fish J. for the majority remarked as follows:

> Finally, a brief word on *R. v. Sansregret*, [1985] 1 S.C.R. 570, 45 C.R. (3d) 193, 18 C.C.C. (3d) 223. The court in that case defined recklessness as the conduct of "one who, aware that there is danger that his conduct could bring about the result prohibited by the criminal law, nevertheless persists, despite the risk. . . . in other words, the conduct of one who sees the risk and who takes the chance" (p. 582). The court, in *Sansregret*, did not set out the degree of risk required to attract criminal sanction. As Don Stuart points out, courts have arbitrarily endorsed varying standards: "certainty, probability, likelihood [and] possibility" - and, in some instances, "probability" and "possibility" in the very same case (*Canadian Criminal Law: A Treatise* (4th ed. 2001), at pp. 225-26).
>
> We have not been invited in this case to revisit *Sansregret* or to consider afresh the governing principles of recklessness as a fault element under the criminal law of Canada. And I should not be taken to have done so.

In *R. v. Jorgensen* (1996), 43 C.R. (4th) 137 (S.C.C.) Jorgensen was the sole officer of a company which owns and operates an adult video store in Scarborough, Ontario. Undercover police officers bought eight videotapes from that store. Jorgensen and the company were charged with eight counts of knowingly selling obscene material without lawful justification or excuse contrary to s. 163(2)(a) of the *Criminal Code*. The trial judge found that three of the eight videos were obscene within the meaning of s. 163(8) of the *Criminal Code* due to their portrayal of sex coupled with violence and coercion, or subordination which created the risk of harm. The Ontario Court of Appeal upheld the convictions: (1993) 26 C.R. (4th) 75 (Ont. C.A.) (reported *sub. nom. R. v. Ronish*).

On appeal the Supreme Court substituted an acquittal. Sopinka J. spoke for the Court on the issue of *mens rea*. The Court struck a middle position. The Crown had argued that to prove that the accused "knowingly" sold obscene material it should be sufficient to prove that the accused knew that he was selling sex films. The Court rejected this argument, since this would amount to convicting the accused of a crime when the only intent proven was to do something legal:

> 88 Having reviewed these cases, I would suggest that the jurisprudence supports the conclusion that for the Crown to convict on a charge of "knowingly" selling obscene materials, it must show more than that the accused had a general knowledge of the nature of the film as a sex film. Although the cases have been few and are by no means clear on this point, cases such as *McFall* and *Metro News* illustrate that courts have looked for some indication that the seller of the obscene material was aware of the relevant facts that made the material obscene. In the case of displaying paintings or posters, it could be inferred that the person selling these paintings or posters had knowledge of what made them obscene. The obscene material is plainly in view and its contents and knowledge of the specific nature of its contents can be assumed "known". The same cannot be said concerning films, videos and other media involving a collection of images and where it takes some time and active steps to observe and "know" the contents. In the case of pornographic films and videos, it cannot be easily inferred that those selling these materials "know" their contents. As noted above, it may be inferred that the retailer is aware that the materials are erotic or pornographic and deal with the exploitation of sex. But selling films which deal with the exploitation of sex is not an illegal activity in itself. There must be something in the material that transports it into the realm of obscenity. Not only must the dominant characteristic of the material be the exploitation of sex, but the exploitation of sex must be undue.

But although the Crown is required to prove more than the sexual nature of the films, it is not required to prove that the retailer actually knows that the films meet the legal definition of obscenity:

> 97 This is not, of course, to suggest that a retailer must know that the materials being sold were obscene in law. If the retailer says he viewed the films and saw the particular spanking or noticed the underlying degradation but thought that it was harmless and inoffensive, this will not provide a defence. The retailer will not be immune from charges merely because he or she does not know how the law defines obscenity. Nor will a retailer be immune from conviction because he or she is unaware that there are any laws against selling obscene material. This would amount to the defence of mistake of law and it is well established that ignorance of the law is no defence. What is required is that the Crown prove beyond a reasonable doubt the retailer's knowledge that the materials being sold have the qualities or contain the specific scenes which render such materials obscene in law.

Canadian courts generally draw a clear line between objectively determined negligence and the subjective test for recklessness or wilful blindness; for example in decisions that negligence is not enough to convict for failing to appear offences: *Weishar* (2003), 13 C.R. (6th) 59 (Ont. S.C.J.) and *Mullin* (2003), 13 C.R. (6th) 54 (Y.T. Terr. Ct.).

R. v. BRISCOE

[2010] 1 S.C.R. 411, 2010 CarswellAlta 589, 2010 CarswellAlta 588, 73 C.R.
(6th) 224, 253 C.C.C. (3d) 140

In a very disturbing case on the facts, the issue was whether the accused had aided in the first degree murder of two teenage girls by driving them to a secluded location where they were raped and killed by others. We will return to that issue under "Parties". Here we consider the ruling that the requirement of "knowledge of the likelihood of death" can be satisfied by wilful blindness. *Briscoe* is now the controlling authority defining wilful blindness as "deliberate ignorance".

CHARRON J.: —

21 Wilful blindness does not define the mens rea required for particular offences. Rather, it can substitute for actual knowledge whenever knowledge is a component of the mens rea. The doctrine of wilful blindness imputes knowledge to an accused whose suspicion is aroused to the point where he or she sees the need for further inquiries, but deliberately chooses not to make those inquiries. See *Sansregret v. The Queen*, [1985] 1 S.C.R. 570, and *R. v. Jorgensen*, [1995] 4 S.C.R. 55. As Sopinka J. succinctly put it in *Jorgensen* (at para. 103), "[a] finding of wilful blindness involves an affirmative answer to the question: Did the accused shut his eyes because he knew or strongly suspected that looking would fix him with knowledge?"

22 Courts and commentators have consistently emphasized that wilful blindness is distinct from recklessness. The emphasis bears repeating. As the Court explained in *Sansregret* (at p. 584):

> . . . while recklessness involves knowledge of a danger or risk and persistence in a course of conduct which creates a risk that the prohibited result will occur, wilful blindness arises where a person who has become aware of the need for some inquiry declines to make the inquiry because he does not wish to know the truth. He would prefer to remain ignorant. The culpability in recklessness is justified by consciousness of the risk and by proceeding in the face of it, while in wilful blindness it is justified by the accused's fault in deliberately failing to inquire when he knows there is reason for inquiry. [Emphasis added.]

23 It is important to keep the concepts of recklessness and wilful blindness separate. Glanville Williams explains the key restriction on the doctrine:

> The rule that wilful blindness is equivalent to knowledge is essential, and is found throughout the criminal law. It is, at the same time, an unstable rule, because judges are apt to forget its very limited scope. A court can properly find wilful blindness only where it can almost be said that the defendant actually knew. He suspected the fact; he realised its probability; but he refrained from obtaining the final confirmation because he wanted in the event to be able to deny knowledge. This, and this alone, is wilful blindness. It requires in effect a finding that the defendant intended to cheat the administration of justice. Any wider definition would make the doctrine of wilful blindness indistinguishable from the civil doctrine of negligence in not obtaining knowledge. [Emphasis added.]

(Criminal Law: The General Part (2nd ed. 1961), at p. 159 (cited in *Sansregret* at p. 586.)

24 Professor Don Stuart makes the useful observation that the expression "deliberate ignorance" seems more descriptive than "wilful blindness", as it connotes "an actual process of suppressing a suspicion". Properly understood in this way, "the concept of wilful blindness is of narrow scope and involves no departure from the subjective focus on the workings of the accused's mind" *(Canadian Criminal Law: A Treatise* (5th ed. 2007), at p. 241). While a failure to inquire may be evidence of recklessness or criminal negligence, as for example, where a failure to inquire is a marked departure from the conduct expected of a reasonable person, wilful blindness is not simply a failure to inquire but, to repeat Professor Stuart's words, "deliberate ignorance".

How far does an accused have to go in making inquiries?

R. v. LAGACE

(2003), 181 C.C.C. (3d) 12, 2003 CarswellOnt 4509 (Ont. C.A)

DOHERTY J.A. (for the Court): —

27 Counsel for the appellant also argues that as a matter of law, the doctrine of wilful blindness could not operate against the appellant because he made an inquiry after his suspicion was aroused.

28 I disagree. Culpability on the basis of wilful blindness rests on a finding of deliberate ignorance. An accused who suspects that property is stolen but declines to make the inquiries that will confirm that suspicion, preferring instead to remain ignorant is culpable. Where an accused makes some inquiry, the question remains whether that accused harboured real suspicions after that inquiry and refrained from making further inquiries because she preferred to remain ignorant of the truth. Where some inquiry is made, the nature of that inquiry will be an important consideration in determining whether the accused remained suspicious and chose to refrain from further inquiry because she preferred to remain deliberately ignorant of the truth. For example, a finding that an accused took all reasonable steps to determine the truth would be inconsistent with the conclusion that the accused was wilfully blind: *R. v. Maru*, [1997] 2 S.C.R. 630 at para. 51.

29 I, of course, do not suggest that there is any onus on the accused to demonstrate that all reasonable steps were taken. In any case where the Crown relies on the doctrine of wilful blindness and some inquiry has been made, the trier of fact will have to decide whether the Crown has proved beyond a reasonable doubt that despite that inquiry the accused remained suspicious and refrained from making any further inquiry because she preferred to remain

ignorant of the truth. As I read the trial judge's reasons, he held that the appellant's inquiry did not remove his suspicion and that no further inquiry was made because the appellant chose not to confirm his suspicion, preferring ignorance over the truth.

R. v. BLONDIN

(1971), 2 C.C.C. (2d) 118, 1970 CarswellBC 72 (B.C. C.A.)

ROBERTSON J.A.: — The respondent ("Blondin") was charged:

that he . . . between the 27th day of August A.D. 1969 and the 29th day of August A.D. 1969, at the Municipality of Richmond, in the County of Vancouver, in the Province of British Columbia, did unlawfully import into Canada a narcotic, to wit: Cannabis resin, contrary to the provisions of the *Narcotic Control Act*.

He was tried by a judge and jury in the County Court and was found not guilty. Against that acquittal the Crown has appealed. Blondin did not give evidence.

Having returned to Canada from Japan, Blondin went to the premises of Canadian Pacific Air Lines in the air terminal in Richmond to collect baggage that he had shipped from Japan, namely, a scuba-diving outfit. The weight of the tank that was part of the outfit aroused suspicion. At one time while it was being examined there were present, among others, Blondin, a Customs official named Montgomery and a constable of the R.C.M.P. named Kennedy. Kennedy was not in uniform and at that time did not identify himself to Blondin as a member of the R.C.M.P. Attempts to remove the valve stem from the tank having proved fruitless, Blondin voluntarily accompanied Montgomery and Kennedy to the Aquatic Shop in Vancouver to try to have the valve stem removed from the tank. At the Aquatic Shop the valve stem was removed, but not much could be seen inside the tank. In the course of the operation the harness was removed from the tank and this revealed that the tank had been cut in half and that the two halves had been put together again; they were kept together by a sleeve inside. When the two halves were separated, Kennedy saw inside a number of brown wafer-like objects; he immediately had the tank closed. Later analysis showed that the objects were cannabis resin, or hashish; they weighed about 23 lbs. After the tank was closed Kennedy, who had not yet made it known to Blondin that he was a police officer, approached Blondin. As Kennedy approached him, Blondin volunteered "I guess I am in for it". Kennedy then identified himself and gave the usual warning. I shall refer to these exchanges as the first conversation. Kennedy then took Blondin, Montgomery and the tank to the R.C.M.P. barracks in Montgomery's car. In the car what I shall call the second conversation occurred. Kennedy asked Blondin if he was aware of what was in the tank and Blondin replied that he did not know. Blondin then asked Kennedy what was in the tank and Kennedy replied that it was hashish. Kennedy asked Blondin if he knew what hashish was and Blondin replied that he did not. On arrival at the barracks Blondin, Montgomery and Kennedy went upstairs to the drug squad office, where a third conversation took place. Kennedy asked Blondin if he was aware that the tank contained narcotics and Blondin said that he knew that there was something in the tank and that it was illegal. He went on to say that he had been paid to bring the tank over. Kennedy asked him who had paid him and Blondin replied that he did not think it was right for him to say. Kennedy asked Blondin to whom he was delivering the tank, and Blondin replied that he did not wish to say.

I am of the respectful opinion that the learned trial judge erred when he instructed the jury that, in order to find Blondin guilty, they must find that he knew that the substance in the tank was cannabis resin. It would be sufficient to find, in relation to a narcotic, *mens rea* in its widest sense.

It remains to decide whether the judge could properly instruct the jury that, if they were satisfied beyond a reasonable doubt that Blondin knew that it was illegal to import the substance in the tank, they might find him guilty, even though he did not know that the substance was a narcotic. I am not prepared so to hold. An essential ingredient of the offence is the importation of a narcotic and I do not consider that *mens rea qua* that offence is proven by an intention to commit an offence which, so far as Blondin's admitted knowledge went, might have been one against the *Customs Act*, R.S.C. 1952, c. 58.

These reasons will, I fear, dispose of this case inadequately if I do not indicate how I think the jury could properly have found *mens rea* in the circumstances of this case. They could have done so if they had found that Blondin had been paid to smuggle a substance illegally into Canada and either was reckless about what it was or wilfully shut his eyes to what it was, inferring therefrom that he suspected that it might be a narcotic. It follows that the learned judge ought to have told the jury that they might convict if they found that Blondin brought the substance into Canada from Japan and knew that it was a narcotic. He should also have instructed the jury that they might convict if they found that he had brought the substance into Canada illegally and had either been reckless about what it was or wilfully shut his eyes to what it was, and then drew the inference that he suspected that it might be a narcotic.

I would allow the appeal, set aside the verdict and order a new trial.

MacFarlane J.A.: —

I agree with my brother Robertson that the learned trial judge was wrong in instructing the jury that the Crown must prove beyond reasonable doubt that the respondent knew the substance was cannabis resin. I agree also it would be wrong to instruct the jury that proof of knowledge that the substance was one which it would be unlawful to import is itself sufficient to support a conviction. The offence of smuggling goods which may be imported lawfully on disclosure and payment of customs duty is, for this purpose, I think, essentially different from that of importing a narcotic, which Parliament has declared to be a serious offence. I refer to the statement by Cartwright J., as he then was, in *Beaver v. The Queen*, [1957] S.C.R. 531 at 539, 26 C.R. 193, 118 C.C.C. 129, that Parliament regards dealing in narcotics as conduct "harmful in itself". The importation of narcotics has been forbidden except by licence issued under authority of the Governor in Council pursuant to s. 12 of the statute [the *Narcotic Control Act*, 1960-61 (Can.), c. 35].

I therefore agree with my brother Robertson that the jury should have been instructed that the onus on the Crown was to prove beyond reasonable doubt that the respondent knew the substance was a narcotic, although not necessarily cannabis resin.

In *Beaver v. The Queen*, *supra*, the Supreme Court was dealing with a case of unlawful possession of a narcotic. Delivering the judgment of the majority of the court, Cartwright J. (as he then was) said at p. 541:

> The essence of the crime is the possession of the forbidden substance and in a criminal case there is in law no possession without knowledge of the character of the forbidden substance. . . .
>
> In my view the law is correctly stated in the following passage in the judgment of O'Halloran J.A., with whom Robertson J.A. concurred, in *Rex v. Hess* (1949) 8 C.R. 42, 94 C.C.C. 48 at 50-1 (B.C. C.A.):
>
>> "To constitute 'possession' within the meaning of the criminal law it is my judgment that where, as here, there is manual handling of a thing, it must be co-existent with knowledge of what the thing is, and both these elements must be co-existent with some act of control (outside public duty). When those three elements exist together, I think it must be conceded that under sec. 4(1)(*d*) it does not then matter if the thing is retained for an innocent purpose."

I think that on a fair interpretation I must treat this decision as being applicable to a case of importing a narcotic. It follows that knowledge that the substance being imported is a narcotic is an essential ingredient of that offence.

As to proof of knowledge, I think the following extract from the speech of Lord Reid in *Warner v. Metropolitan Police Commissioner*, [1969] 2 A.C. 256 at 279-80 (a possession case) is apt and I respectfully adopt it:

> The object of this legislation is to penalise possession of certain drugs. So if mens rea has not been excluded what would be required would be the knowledge of the accused that he had prohibited drugs in his possession: it would be no defence, though it would be a mitigation, that he did not intend that they should be used improperly. And it is a commonplace that, if the accused had a suspicion but deliberately shut his eyes, the court or jury is well entitled to hold him guilty. Further it would be pedantic to hold that it must be shown that the accused knew precisely which drug he had in his possession. Ignorance of the law is no defence and in fact virtually everyone knows that there are prohibited drugs. So it would be quite sufficient to prove facts from which it could properly be inferred that the accused knew that he had a prohibited drug in his possession. That would not lead to an unreasonable result. In a case like this Parliament, if consulted, might think it right to transfer the onus of proof so that an accused would have to prove that he neither knew nor had any reason to suspect that he had a prohibited drug in his possession. But I am unable to find sufficient grounds for imputing to Parliament an intention to deprive the accused of all right to show that he had no

knowledge or reason to suspect that any prohibited drug was in his premises or in a container which was in his possession.

I accordingly agree that it would be correct to instruct a jury that the existence of that knowledge may be inferred as a fact, with due regard to all the circumstances, if the jury finds that the accused has recklessly or wilfully shut his eyes or refrained from inquiry as to the nature of the substance he imports.

I would, therefore, allow the appeal, set the verdict of acquittal aside and order a new trial.

The brief concurring judgment of Davey J.A. is omitted.

A further appeal to the Supreme Court of Canada was dismissed without reasons (1972), 4 C.C.C. (2d) 566 (S.C.C.).

(b)   Crimes of Objective Fault

The *Criminal Code* has long contained a wide variety of offences which expressly adopt an objective standard such as "ought to", "reasonable care", "good reason", "reasonable ground", "reasonably expected" or "reasonable steps". Such offences included, until declared unconstitutional by the Supreme Court, unlawful object murder. The current list includes the doctrine of common intent for accessories (s. 21(2)); careless use of firearms or ammunition (s. 86(2)); and a strange assortment of other offences including counselling another to be a party to an offence (s. 22(2)); treason (s. 46(2)(b)); failure to use reasonable care to prevent injury from an explosive substance (ss. 79-80); bigamy as a result of a mistaken and unreasonable belief that a spouse is dead (s. 290); publishing defamatory material (s. 303); and criminal breach of trust (s. 422). Another important example is Parliament's declaration that there can be no mistaken belief in consent defence to a sexual assault charge unless reasonable steps were taken: see Chapter 4 "Rape and Sexual Assault". The anomalous list of offences clearly indicates a haphazard approach.

Sometimes our courts have resorted to an objective standard for a *Criminal Code* offence where such an approach is not expressly required. Sometimes courts read in objective fault where the crime involves a duty to act, as in the case of failing to provide necessaries of life (see *Naglik*). This has long been the approach for unlawful act manslaughter, discussed *infra*, and also respecting offences requiring "criminal negligence". The jurisprudence respecting the latter has been conflicting and complex and requires separate treatment.

(i)   Criminal negligence: s. 219

Since 1955 the *Criminal Code* has provided:

219.(1) Every one is criminally negligent who
    (a) in doing anything, or
    (b) in omitting to do anything that it is his duty to do,
shows wanton or reckless disregard for the lives or safety of other persons.
(2) For the purposes of this section, "duty" means a duty imposed by law.

220. Every person who by criminal negligence causes death to another person is guilty of an indictable offence and liable

    (a) where a firearm is used in the commission of the offence, to imprisonment for life and to a minimum punishment of imprisonment for a term of four years; and
    (b) in any other case, to imprisonment for life.

221. Every one who by criminal negligence causes bodily harm to another person is guilty of an indictable offence and liable to imprisonment for a term not exceeding ten years.

222.(1) A person commits homicide when, directly or indirectly, by any means, he causes the death of a human being.
(2) Homicide is culpable or not culpable.
(3) Homicide that is not culpable is not an offence.
(4) Culpable homicide is murder or manslaughter or infanticide.
(5) A person commits culpable homicide when he causes the death of a human being,
    (a) by means of an unlawful act;
    (b) by criminal negligence;
    (c) by causing that human being, by threats or fear of violence or by deception, to do anything that causes his death; or
    (d) by wilfully frightening that human being, in the case of a child or sick person.

. . . .

234. Culpable homicide that is not murder or infanticide is manslaughter.

. . . .

236. Every person who commits manslaughter is guilty of an indictable offence and liable
    (a) where a firearm is used in the commission of the offence, to imprisonment for life and to a minimum punishment of imprisonment for a term of four years; and
    (b) in any other case, to imprisonment for life.

O'GRADY v. SPARLING

[1960] S.C.R. 804, 33 C.R. 293, 128 C.C.C. 1 at 808, 1960 CarswellMan 41

The appellant, charged with careless driving contrary to provincial legislation, argued that such legislation was inoperative as being in relation to criminal law and also because Parliament had occupied the field by its enactment (s. 233(1) of the *Criminal Code*, repealed in 1985) proscribing criminally negligent driving. For the majority, Judson J. dismissed the appeal, in part on the basis that criminal negligence according to what is now s. 219 of the *Criminal Code* is a form of recklessness which connotes advertence. The Court adopted the following passage from Kenny's *Outlines of Criminal Law*, 17th ed.:

> The difference between recklessness and negligence is the difference between advertence and inadvertence; they are opposed and it is a logical fallacy to suggest that recklessness is a degree of negligence. The common habit of lawyers to qualify the word "negligence" with some moral epithet such as "wicked", "gross", or "culpable" has been most unfortunate since it has inevitably led to great confusion of thought and of principle.

There was, however, an overwhelming tendency for provincial courts to ignore *O'Grady* in adopting an objective standard for criminal negligence under s. 219. Many, however, assert a requirement of a gross departure from the objective norm.

R. v. TUTTON and TUTTON

[1989] 1 S.C.R. 1392, 69 C.R. (3d) 289, 48 C.C.C. (3d) 129,
1989 CarswellOnt 959, 1989 CarswellOnt 84

The accused were charged with manslaughter respecting the death of their five-year-old son. The charge and particulars alleged that they had caused the death of their son by criminal negligence through omitting to provide him necessaries of life, in failing to provide insulin and to obtain timely medical assistance. Their son had been diagnosed as a diabetic more than two years earlier. At the time, his parents were advised of his need to have insulin on a daily basis for the rest of his life and thorough instructions were given as to what was required for his care. For some time, both parents followed the instructions for the administration of insulin and observed the necessary dietary controls. They were members of a religious sect which believed in faith healing, believing that God can perform miracles and cure ailments in response to prayer. The sect was not opposed to seeking medical advice and taking medicine, but believed that God can cure ailments which are beyond the purview of medical science. The parents' primary concern was for a cure for their son which would relieve him of the necessity of a lifetime daily intake of insulin. On one occasion the mother ceased administering insulin because she firmly believed that her son was being healed through the power of the Holy Spirit. His health immediately failed and he was taken to hospital, where the parents were strongly advised to continue with the insulin. They did so, but later the mother received a further vision from God which she believed advised her that her son was in fact cured of diabetes and no longer required insulin treatment. As a result of this the mother, with the agreement of the father, stopped the insulin "by God's authority". The son rapidly became ill. He died shortly after being admitted to hospital, his death being attributed to complications of diabetic hyperglycemia. Following a trial by judge and jury, the accused were convicted of manslaughter. On appeal, the Ontario Court of Appeal set aside the conviction and ordered a new trial. The Court held that there had been a reversible error as the trial judge had not clearly explained to the jury that the reverse onus in respect of proving a lawful excuse on a balance of probabilities applied only in the case of the included offence of failing to provide the necessaries of life under s. 197(2) [now s. 215(2)] of the *Criminal Code*. The Court further held that, although in some cases criminal negligence consisted of a marked and substantial departure from the standard of a reasonable person in the circumstances, in this case of criminal negligence through omission the jury had to be satisfied that the accused knew that there was a risk to the life or safety of their son and unjustifiably took that risk or closed their minds to any such risk with disregard for either his life or his safety. The Crown appealed.

After reserving for some 18 months, the Supreme Court of Canada unanimously confirmed the order of a new trial on the basis that there had been a reversible error in the charge respecting onus of proof. The Court also took the opportunity to consider the test for criminal negligence. On this issue, there was an inconclusive 3-3 split.

MCINTYRE J. (L'HEUREUX-DUBÉ J. concurring): —

. . . .

In reaching a conclusion as to whether the conduct of an accused person has shown, within the meaning of s. 202 [now s. 219] of the *Criminal Code*, wanton or reckless disregard for the lives or safety of other persons, the authorities dictate an objective test: see the review of the authorities on this subject by Cory J.A. for the Court of Appeal in *R. v. Waite* (1986), 52 C.R. (3d) 355, 28 C.C.C. (3d) 326, approved in this court (judgment given concurrently) [post, p. 323]. Indeed, in the Court of Appeal, Dubin J.A. accepted the objective test as one of general application, but made an exception in cases where the conduct complained of consisted of an act or acts of omission, as opposed to those of commission. In such cases, it was his view that occasions would arise where a subjective test would be required where acts of omission were under consideration. He considered that this was such a case. It is my view, however, that no such distinction as Dubin J.A. would adopt may be made. I am wholly unable to see any difference in principle between cases arising from an omission to act and those involving acts of commission. Indeed, the words of s. 202 of the *Criminal Code* make it clear that one is criminally negligent who, *in doing anything* or *in omitting to do anything* that it is his duty to do, shows wanton or reckless disregard for the lives or safety of other persons. The objective test must, therefore, be employed where criminal negligence is considered, for it is the conduct of the accused, as opposed to his intention or mental state, which is examined in this inquiry.

Our concept of criminal culpability relies primarily upon a consideration of the mental state which accompanies or initiates the wrongful act, and the attribution of criminal liability without proof of such a blameworthy mental state raises serious concerns. Nonetheless, negligence has become accepted as a factor which may lead to criminal liability and strong arguments can be raised in its favour. Section 202 of the *Criminal Code* affords an example of its adoption. In choosing the test to be applied in assessing conduct under s. 202 of the *Criminal*

Code, it must be observed at once that what is made criminal is negligence. Negligence connotes the opposite of thought-directed action. In other words, its existence precludes the element of positive intent to achieve a given result. This leads to the conclusion that what is sought to be restrained by punishment under s. 202 of the *Code* is conduct, and its results. What is punished, in other words, is not the state of mind but the consequence of mindless action. This is apparent, I suggest, from the words of the section, which make criminal conduct which *shows* wanton or reckless disregard. It may be observed as well that the words "wanton or reckless" support this construction, denying as they do the existence of a directing mental state. Nor can it be said that criminal negligence, as defined in s. 202, imports in its terms some element of malice or intention. This point was made in the Crown's factum in para. 41, which provided, in part:

> The plain and ordinary meaning of the terms "wanton" and "reckless" when used in connection with the concept of negligence would seem to include a state of being heedless of apparent danger. Section 202(1) does not use the term "reckless" as an extended definition of intention or malice, but rather employs the term as part of a definition of conduct which amounts to "negligence" in a criminal context.

In my view, then, an objective standard must be applied in determining this question because of the difference between the ordinary criminal offence, which requires proof of a subjective state of mind, and that of criminal negligence. In criminal cases, generally, the act coupled with the mental state or intent is punished. In criminal negligence, the act which exhibits the requisite degree of negligence is punished. If this distinction is not kept clear, the dividing line between the traditional *mens rea* offence and the offence of criminal negligence becomes blurred. The difference, for example, between murder and manslaughter, both unlawful killings, is merely one of intent. If the question of an accused's intent had to be considered and separately proved in offences under s. 202 of the *Criminal Code*, the purpose of the section would be defeated because intentional conduct would perforce be considered under other sections of the *Code* and s. 202, aimed at mindless but socially dangerous conduct, would have no function. For these reasons, the objective test should be employed and, in my view, the Court of Appeal was in error in concluding in this case that a subjective test would be required. The test is that of reasonableness, and proof of conduct which reveals a marked and significant departure from the standard which could be expected of a reasonably prudent person in the circumstances will justify a conviction of criminal negligence.

In reaching this conclusion, I am not overlooking the comments I made in *Sansregret v. R.*, [1985] 1 S.C.R. 570 at 581-82, 45 C.R. (3d) 193, 23 C.C.C. (3d) 223, which were cited by counsel for the appellant. In *Sansregret*, I expressed the view that "recklessness, to form a part of the criminal *mens rea*, must have an element of the subjective." I then went on to say that "It is in this sense that the term 'recklessness' is used in the criminal law and it is clearly distinct from the concept of civil negligence." It was argued upon the basis of these words and later comments on the nature of negligence in relation to the criminal law that a subjective test should therefore be applied in considering the existence of criminal negligence under s. 202 of the *Code*. I would reject that argument on the basis that the concept of recklessness there described is not applicable in a case under s. 202 of the *Code*. Sansregret was charged with rape, a crime which involves positive mind-directed conduct on the part of the accused which aims at the accom plishment of a specific result. It is a traditional *mens rea* offence and a mental state must be proved, in that case an intention to persist with his purpose despite the fact that the complainant's consent has been extorted by threats and fear. Recklessness on his part forms a part of the *mens rea* (the blameworthy state of mind) and has to be proved on a subjective basis as part of the mental element of the offence. In this sense, the words in *Sansregret* are apposite. Section 202, on the other hand, has created a separate offence; an offence which makes negligence — the exhibition of wanton or reckless behaviour — a crime in itself and has thus defined its own terms. As noted by Cory J.A. in *R. v. Waite*, s. 202 of the *Criminal Code* was enacted in its present form as a codification of the offence which had emerged in Canadian jurisprudence, and in respect of which the necessary *mens rea* may be inferred on an objective basis from the acts of the accused.

The application of an objective test under s. 202 of the *Criminal Code*, however, may not be made in a vacuum. Events occur within the framework of other events and actions and, when deciding on the nature of the questioned conduct, surrounding circumstances must be considered. The decision must be made on a consideration of the facts existing at the time and in relation to the accused's perception of those facts. Since the test is objective, the accused's perception of the facts is not to be considered for the purpose of assessing malice or intention on the accused's part but only to form a basis for a conclusion as to whether or not the accused's conduct, in view of his perception of the facts, was reasonable. This is particularly true where, as here, the accused have raised the defence of mistake of fact. If an accused under s. 202 has an honest and reasonably held belief in the existence of certain facts, it may be a relevant consideration in assessing the reasonableness of his conduct. For example, a welder, who is engaged to work in a confined space, believing on the assurance of the owner of the premises that no combustible or explosive material is stored nearby, should be entitled to have his perception, as to the presence or absence of dangerous materials, before the jury on a charge of manslaughter when his welding torch causes an explosion and a consequent death.

As noted earlier, the Tuttons raised the defence of mistake of fact at trial. They argued that the failure to supply insulin was based upon the belief that the child had been cured by divine intervention and that the failure to provide medical care in timely fashion was based upon the belief that the child was not seriously ill, so medical assistance was not necessary. The trial Judge, it was argued, was in error in telling the jury that for any such belief to be effective as a defence it must have been reasonably held. It was held in this court in

Pappajohn v. R., [1980] 2 S.C.R. 120, 14 C.R. (3d) 243, 19 C.R. (3d) 97, 52 C.C.C. (2d) 481 [B.C.], that an honest, though mistaken, belief in the existence of circumstances which, if present, would make the questioned conduct non-culpable would entitle an accused to an acquittal. It was also held in *Pappajohn* that the honest belief need not be reasonable, because its effect would be to deny the existence of the requisite *mens rea*. The situation would be different, however, where the offence charged rests upon the concept of negligence, as opposed to that of the guilty mind or blameworthy mental state. In such case, an unreasonable though honest belief on the part of the accused would be negligently held. The holding of such a belief could not afford a defence when culpability is based on negligent conduct. I would therefore conclude that the trial Judge made no error in charging the jury to the effect that any mistaken belief which could afford a defence in a charge of criminal negligence would have to be reasonable.

In the case at bar, then, the assertion of the Tuttons that they believed a cure had been effected by divine intervention and that insulin was not necessary for the preservation of the child's life would have to be considered by the jury. The jury would have to consider whether such belief was honest and whether it was reasonable. In this, they would be required to consider the whole background of the case. They would have to take into account the experience of the Tuttons with the child's illness; the fact that they had seen the result of the withdrawal of insulin on one occasion and that they had been informed of its necessity for the continued care of the child; and the fact that Mrs. Tutton had received some formal instruction or training in dealing with diabetes and diabetics. They would, as well, have to consider whether the belief in a miraculous cure leading to the conclusion that insulin and medical care were not required, though honest, was reasonable. Upon these facts and all others concerning the matter which were revealed in the evidence, the jury would be required to decide whether the refusal of insulin and medical attention represented a marked and significant departure from the standard to be observed by reasonably prudent parents.

I would dismiss the appeal and confirm the direction for a new trial.

LAMER J.: — I have read the reasons of my colleague, Mr. Justice McIntyre, and I am in agreement with them, subject to the following remarks. I am of the view that, when applying the objective norm set out by Parliament in s. 202 [now s. 219] of the *Criminal Code* [R.S.C. 1970, c. C-34; now R.S.C. 1985, c. C-46], there must be made "a generous allowance" for factors which are particular to the accused, such as youth, mental development and education: see Don Stuart, *Canadian Criminal Law: A Treatise*, 2nd ed. (1987), Toronto, Carswell, p. 194; see also Toni Pickard, "Culpable Mistakes and Rape: Relating *Mens Rea* to the Crime" (1980), 30 Univ. of Toronto L.J. 75. When this is done, as we are considering conduct which is likely to cause death, that is, high risk conduct, the adoption of the subjective or of an objective test will, in practice, nearly if not always produce the same result: see Eric Colvin, "Recklessness and Criminal Negligence" (1982), 32 Univ. of Toronto L.J. 345.

I should note that Parliament, when enacting s. 202, did not purport to determine the nature of the negligence which is required when grounding criminal liability thereupon. My understanding of s. 202 is that Parliament has in that section simply defined the expression "criminal negligence" whenever used in the *Criminal Code*.

I should finally mention that in this case the constitutionality of s. 205(5)(*b*) [now s. 222(5)(*b*)] was not in issue. Indeed, assuming without now deciding that it is a principle of fundamental justice that knowledge of a likely risk or deliberate ignorance thereof (foresight or wilful blindness) is an essential element of the offence of manslaughter, the issue as to whether proof of the substituted element of "criminal negligence" as defined by Parliament and interpreted by this court satisfies the test set out in *R. v. Vaillancourt*, [1987] 2 S.C.R. 636, 60 C.R. (3d) 289, 39 C.C.C. (3d) 118 [Que.], does not arise. I therefore do not by my concurrence feel precluded or limited when addressing such a constitutional challenge, of course, if and when called upon to do so.

WILSON J. (DICKSON C.J.C. and LAFOREST J. concurring): —

. . . .

I do not, however, agree with my colleagues' conclusion that criminal negligence under s. 202 [now s. 219] of the *Criminal Code*, R.S.C. 1970, c. C-34 [now R.S.C. 1985, c. C-46], consists only of conduct in breach of an objective standard and does not require the Crown to prove that the accused had any degree of guilty knowledge. I also have reservations concerning the approach my colleagues suggest is available in order to relieve against the harshness of the objective standard of liability which they find in s. 202 and to ensure that the morally innocent are not punished for the commission of serious criminal offences committed through criminal negligence.

. . . .

I wish to deal first with the implications of my colleagues' approach in this case. By concluding that s. 202 of the *Criminal Code* prohibits conduct and the consequences of mindless action absent any blameworthy state of mind, they have, in effect, held that the crime of criminal negligence is an absolute liability offence. Conviction follows upon proof of conduct which reveals a marked and substantial departure from the standard expected of a reasonably prudent person in the circumstances regardless of what was actually in the accused's mind at the time the act was committed.

. . . .

This court made clear in *Sault Ste. Marie* and other cases that the imposition of criminal liability in the absence of proof of a blameworthy state of mind, either as an inference from the nature of the act committed or by other evidence, is an anomaly which does not sit comfortably with the principles of penal liability and fundamental justice.

. . . .

This is particularly so in the case of offences carrying a substantial term of imprisonment which by their nature, severity and attendant stigma are true criminal offences aimed at punishing culpable behaviour as opposed to securing the public welfare. In the absence of clear statutory language and purpose to the contrary, this court should, in my view, be most reluctant to interpret a serious criminal offence as an absolute liability offence.

. . . .

Section 202 of the *Criminal Code* is, in my view, notorious in its ambiguity. Since its enactment in its present form in the 1955 amendments to the *Criminal Code* it has bedevilled both courts and commentators who have sought out its meaning. The interpretation put upon it usually depends upon which words are emphasized. On the one hand, my colleague's judgment demonstrates that emphasizing the use of the words "shows" and "negligence" can lead to the conclusion that an objective standard of liability was intended and that proof of unreasonable conduct alone will suffice. On the other hand, if the words "wanton or reckless disregard for the lives or safety of other persons" are stressed along with the fact that what is prohibited is not negligence simpliciter but "criminal" negligence, one might conclude that Parliament intended some degree of advertence to the risk to the lives or safety of others to be an essential element of the offence. When faced with such fundamental ambiguity, it would be my view that the court should give the provision the interpretation most consonant not only with the text and purpose of the provision but also, where possible, with the broader concepts and principles of the law: see also *R. v. Paré*, [1987] 2 S.C.R. 618, 60 C.R. (3d) 346, 38 C.C.C. (3d) 97.

. . . .

The expression *wanton* disregard for the lives and safety of others is perhaps less clear. The word *wanton* taken in its acontextual sense could signal an element of randomness or arbitrariness more akin to an objective standard but, given the context in which it appears, coupled with the adjective "reckless", and its clear use to accentuate and make more heinous the already serious matter of disregard for the lives or safety of others, I would think that the preferable interpretation is that the word "wanton" was intended to connote wilful blindness to the prohibited risk: see P.J.T. O Hearn, "Criminal Negligence: An Analysis in Depth — Part II" (1965), 7 Cr. L.Q. 407, at p. 411.

In short, the phrase "wanton or reckless disregard for the lives or safety of other persons" signifies more than gross negligence in the objective sense. It requires some degree of awareness or advertence to the threat to the lives or safety of others or alternatively a wilful blindness to that threat which is culpable in light of the gravity of the risk that is prohibited.

. . . .

As I have suggested above, the words of the section can reasonably bear an interpretation which leaves room for the mental element of awareness or advertence to a risk to the lives or safety of others or wilful blindness to such risk. Conduct which shows a wanton or reckless disregard for the lives and safety of others will by its nature constitute *prima facie* evidence of the mental element, and in the absence of some evidence that casts doubt on the normal degree of mental awareness, proof of the act and reference to what a reasonable person in the circumstances must have realized will lead to a conclusion that the accused was aware of the risk or wilfully blind to the risk.

. . . .

I would add that the importance of what the reasonable person would have foreseen to the determination of whether a particular accused would have become aware or wilfully blind to the prohibited risk will vary with the context. For example, in the case of a licensed driver engaging in high-risk motoring, I am in general agreement with Morden J.A. in *R. v. Sharp* (1984), 39 C.R. (3d) 367, 12 C.C.C. (3d) 428 at 434-35 (C.A.), that it is open to the jury to find the accused's blameworthy state of mind from driving which shows wanton or reckless disregard for the lives or safety of others, subject to an explanation in the evidence which would account for the deviant conduct, such as a sudden mechanical malfunction or a bee sting or other accident beyond the accused's control. I would think that in the driving context, where risks to the lives and safety of others present themselves in a habitual and obvious fashion, the accused's claim that he or she gave no thought to the risk or had simply a negative state of mind would in most, if not all, cases amount to the culpable positive mental state of wilful blindness to the prohibited risk.

The minimal nature of the requirement of a blameworthy state of mind and the relevance of the objective standard as a rebuttable mode of proof suggests to me that a holding that s. 202 requires proof of the mental element of advertence to the risk or wilful blindness to the risk will not undermine the policy objectives of the provision. The loss in terms of deterrence and social protection would seem to be negligible when the retention of a subjective standard would at most offer protection for those who due to some peculiarity or unexpected accident commit conduct which, although it shows a reckless or wanton disregard for the lives or safety of others, can be explained as inconsistent with any degree of awareness of or wilful blindness to such a risk.

Should social protection require the adoption of an objective standard it is open to Parliament to enact a law which clearly adopts such a standard. In my respectful view this court should not do it for them.

. . . .

In recognition of the harshness of a uniform application of an objective standard of criminal liability, much of the recent work in criminal jurisprudence has canvassed the possibility of introducing a subjective dimension into the objective standard in order to relieve the harshness of imposing an objective standard on those who, because of their peculiar characteristics, could not fairly be expected to live up to the standard set by the reasonable person. H.L.A. Hart was perhaps the first to explore this possibility, in his essay "Negligence, *Mens Rea* and Criminal Responsibility" in Oxford Essays in Jurisprudence (1961), c. 2. He recognized the dangers of the use of an objective standard at p. 47:

> If our conditions of liability are invariant and not flexible *i.e.* if they are not adjusted to the capacities of the accused, then some individuals will be held liable for negligence though they could not have helped their failure to comply with the standard. In *such* cases, indeed, criminal responsibility will be made independent of any "subjective element": since the accused could not have conformed to the required standard.

In response to this most legitimate fear, Professor Hart proposed the following two-pronged test for criminal negligence:

> (i) Did the accused fail to keep those precautions which any reasonable man with normal capacities would in the circumstances have taken?
>
> (ii) Could the accused, given his mental and physical capacities, have taken those precautions?

A similar approach has been taken by the criminal law theorist George Fletcher. Professor Fletcher also proposed that criminal liability for negligent conduct be determined in a two-step process, the first being the determination of wrongdoing, which in the case of the prohibition of negligence would proceed on the basis of breach of an objective standard, and the second being the process by which the court determines whether it would be fair to hold a particular accused responsible for the act of wrongdoing. Professor Fletcher notes in *Rethinking Criminal Law* (1978), at p. 511:

> If the law ignored the question of attribution, namely, the question whether individuals were properly held accountable for their wrongful acts, the criminal law undoubtedly would generate some unjust decisions. If it were true that the only relevant norms of the legal system were those of wrongdoing, injustice would be inescapable in cases in which individuals could not but violate the law.

See also G. Fletcher, "The Theory of Criminal Negligence: A Comparative Analysis" (1971), 119 Univ. of Pa. L. Rev. 401; A. Stalker, "Can George Fletcher Help Solve The Problem of Criminal Negligence?" (1981), 7 Queen's

L.J. 274. Professor Toni Pickard has also adopted an approach to this issue similar to that of Professors Hart and Fletcher. She proposes in "Culpable Mistakes and Rape? Relating *Mens Rea* to the Crime" (1980), 30 Univ. of Toronto L.J. 75, at p. 79, to modify an objective standard of unreasonableness so that "the relevant characteristics of the particular actor, rather than those of the ordinary person" will be "the background against which to measure the reasonableness of certain conduct or beliefs". Professor Pickard elaborates:

> This individualized standard is neither "subjective" nor "objective". It partakes of the subjective position because the inquiry the fact finder must conduct is about the defendant himself, not about some hypothetical ordinary person. It partakes of the objective position because the inquiry is not limited to what was, in fact, in the actor's mind, but includes an inquiry into what could have been in it, and a judgment about what ought to have been in it.

In their judgments in this case my colleagues McIntyre and Lamer JJ. seem to have adopted variations of the above developments. McIntyre J., for example, states [pp. 302-303]:

> The application of an objective test under s. 202 of the *Criminal Code*, however, may not be made in a vacuum. Events occur within the framework of other events and actions and, when deciding on the nature of the questioned conduct, surrounding circumstances must be considered. The decision must be made on a consideration of the facts existing at the time and in relation to the accused's perception of those facts. Since the test is objective, the accused's perception of the facts is not to be considered for the purpose of assessing malice or intention on the accused's part but only to form a basis for a conclusion as to whether or not the accused's conduct, in view of his perception of the facts, was reasonable.

My colleague then, however, goes on to suggest that the factual perceptions of the accused must be not only honest but reasonable in order to be factored into the assessment of the objective standard. For example, he suggests that the appellants in this case should not be held to the standard of honest but mistaken belief in circumstances which would render their conduct not culpable, as set out in *Pappajohn*, *supra*, but rather that their beliefs and perceptions in order to be considered must not be negligently or unreasonably held. To my mind, when the offence charged is criminal negligence the distinction from *Pappajohn* lies not in the introduction of an overriding standard of reasonableness, as this in effect holds the accused simply to the standards of what would be expected from the reasonable person, but rather in the degree of guilty knowledge that must be proven. Although a person may have an honest yet unreasonable view of the circumstances which would render him or her in the large sense blameless, this would not necessarily decide the relevant question of whether he or she had any awareness of the prohibited risk or at some time during the relevant transaction wilfully blinded him or herself to an otherwise obvious risk. To require, as does my colleague, that all misperceptions be reasonable will, in my view, not excuse many of those who through no fault of their own cannot fairly be expected to live up to the standard of the reasonable person.

My colleague Justice Lamer takes a somewhat different approach. He suggests [at p. 304] that courts when applying the objective standard in s. 202 should make " 'a generous allowance' for factors which are particular to the accused, such as youth, mental development and education". I do not doubt that an expansive application of this approach could relieve some of the harshness of applying an objective standard to those who could not fairly be expected to meet the standard and I am cautiously sympathetic to attempts to integrate elements of subjective perception into criminal law standards that are clearly objective: see *R. v. Vasil*, [1981] 1 S.C.R. 469, 20 C.R. (3d) 193, 58 C.C.C. (2d) 97 [Ont.]; *R. v. Hill*, [1986] 1 S.C.R. 313, 51 C.R. (3d) 97, 25 C.C.C. (3d) 322. Despite this, the test proposed by my colleague suffers, in my respectful view, from the various degrees of over- and underinclusiveness that would be expected from a test which is only a rough substitute for a finding of a blameworthy state of mind in each case. For example, an instruction to the trier of fact that they are to hold a young accused with modest intelligence and little education to a standard of conduct that one would expect from the reasonable person of tender years, modest intelligence and little education sets out a fluctuating standard which in my view undermines the principles of equality and individual responsibility which should pervade the criminal law. It tells the jury simply to lower the standard of conduct expected from such people regardless of whether in the particular case the accused attained the degree of guilty knowledge that I have set out above. Professor Fletcher in "The Theory of Criminal Negligence: A Comparative Analysis" has termed the decision whether to make the standard of liability more or less objective by including or excluding specific personal characteristics a "policy question", "a low visibility device for adjusting the interests of competing classes of litigants", and I respectfully agree with the following criticism he makes of this process at pp. 407-408:

> The question in the criminal context is not one of adjusting the interests of competing classes of litigants, but of justifying the state's depriving an individual of his liberty.

Professor Fletcher's solution to this problem, the introduction of a comprehensive range of individualized excuses, is in my view far from realization in Canadian criminal law jurisprudence and, as such, the concern he identifies of the culpability of the individual is still, in my view, best served by continued adherence to subjective standards of liability.

One problem with attempts to individualize an objective standard is that regard for the disabilities of the particular accused can only be applied in a general fashion to alter the objective standard. It seems preferable to me to continue to address the question of whether a subjective standard (a standard, I might add, that in its form is applied equally to all and consistent with individual responsibility) has been breached in each case than to introduce varying standards of conduct which will be only roughly related to the presence or absence of culpability in the individual case. Varying the level of conduct by factoring in some personal characteristics may be unavoidable if the court is faced with a clearly objective standard but it should, in my opinion, be avoided if the more exacting subjective test is available as a matter of statutory interpretation. I have no doubt that factors such as the accused's age and mental development will often be relevant to determining culpability, but under a subjective test they will be relevant only as they relate to the question of whether the accused was aware of or wilfully blind to the prohibited risk and will not have to be factored in wholesale in order to adjust the standard of conduct that is expected from citizens.

Attempts to introduce subjective elements into objective standards not only risk being overinclusive in the sense that they mandate a lowering of the objective standard of liability on a characteristic by characteristic basis, they also risk the danger of being underinclusive for those accused who have idiosyncracies that cannot be articulated ex ante into the necessarily limited list of personal characteristics which can be grafted on to an objective standard. For example, the characteristics listed by my colleague Lamer J. would not relieve the harshness of the application of an objective standard for a driver who, because of a sudden injury or ailment, drove a motor vehicle in a fashion which showed a reckless or wanton disregard for the lives and safety of others. It would not matter that the particular accused was not capable of adverting or wilfully closing his or her eyes to the prohibited risk; the conduct in itself would have breached the objective standard.

The limited range of personal characteristics which can be imported into a modified objective standard is often justified by the notion that a thoroughly subjective approach will allow those who deprive themselves of normal awareness through voluntary intoxication or fits of temper to be exempted from criminal liability. My answer to this (it was also my answer in the cases of *Bernard*, *supra*, and *R. v. Quin*, [1988] 2 S.C.R. 825, 67 C.R. (3d) 162, 44 C.C.C. (3d) 570) is that greater attention must be paid to the minimal levels of guilty knowledge that are required for conviction of many offences of violence under the *Criminal Code*. It is, in my respectful view, perfectly permissible for the trier of fact to reason from an objective standard and ask the question: must not the accused have had the minimal awareness of what he or she was doing? The important point is that this question is rebuttable and leaves room for acquitting an accused who, for whatever reason, lacked the minimal awareness that would normally accompany the commission of high-risk or violent acts.

I am in complete agreement with what my colleague Justice Lamer has to say concerning the issue of constitutionality.

WAITE v. R.

[1989] 1 S.C.R. 1436, 69 C.R. (3d) 323, 48 C.C.C. (3d) 1,
1989 CarswellOnt 85, 1989 Carswell 960

The accused, who had been drinking, struck and killed four young people taking part in a hayride and injured a fifth. The hayride involved three tractors each towing a wagon with bales of hay along a public road. Four or five of the young people had been running alongside the wagons or had been running from one wagon to another when the accused came upon the hayride. The accused drove behind the hayride, passed it, turned around and deliberately approached the hayride at high speed on the wrong side of the road. The accused testified that he had said to his companions, "Let's see how close we can get". Estimates of the speed varied from 50 to 90 m.p.h. He was driving without headlights.

Following trial before a judge and jury, the accused was found not guilty of four counts of causing death by criminal negligence and one count of causing bodily harm by criminal negligence, but guilty of five counts of the included offence of dangerous driving. The charge to the jury did not specifically mention the objective test for criminal negligence but did convey that the *mens rea* required for proof of the commission of the offence could be found in the accused's conduct. While the jury were deliberating, they returned to ask the judge the difference between dangerous driving and criminal negligence. The judge advised them that in dangerous driving they should look objectively at the manner of driving but that in the case of criminal negligence they had to look at a subjective element and find a "deliberate and wilful assumption of the risk involved in driving in the manner in which he was driving". The Ontario Court of Appeal allowed the Crown's appeal. It held that where allegations of criminal negligence are based upon the manner of driving or some other act of commission, the test is the objective one of whether the driving or the act of commission constitutes a marked and substantial departure from the conduct expected of a reasonable man in the same circumstances. A new trial was directed on the criminal negligence charges. The accused appealed.

The accused's appeal to the Supreme Court was heard at the same time as *Tutton*. The Court unanimously dismissed the accused's appeal. The objective McIntyre wing repeated their views in *Tutton* justifying an objective test of a marked and substantial departure from the standard of behaviour expected of reasonably prudent persons in the circumstances. In agreeing to dismiss the appeal, the subjective wing reasoned as follows:

WILSON J.: —

In my view the trial judge's final instruction to the jury was in error as to the degree of *mens rea* required under s. 202 [now s. 219] of the *Criminal Code*, R.S.C. 1970, c. C-34 [now R.S.C. 1985, c. C-46]. When the jury asked the trial Judge to explain the moral difference between dangerous driving and causing death by criminal negligence, the trial judge instructed the jury that the subjective element in criminal negligence was "a deliberate and wilful assumption of the risk involved in driving in the manner in which he was driving". Later in his reply to the jury he repeated that the subjective element in criminal negligence was "assumption and deliberate assumption of the risk". Although I believe there is a subjective element to criminal negligence, the Judge in this case placed much too high an onus on the Crown to prove elements of deliberation and wilfulness. For the reasons I gave in *Tutton* I am of the view that the mental element in criminal negligence is the minimal intent of awareness of the prohibited risk or wilful blindness to the risk.

The trial judge's erroneous instructions to the jury were given near the close of the trial and they were crucial because they were in response to a question from the jury. The facts of the case also suggest that, had the jury been instructed as to the minimal intent requirements of awareness or wilful blindness to the prohibited risk, they would not necessarily have returned the verdict of acquittal on the charges of causing death by criminal negligence: see *Vézeau v. R.*, [1977] 2 S.C.R. 277, 34 C.R.N.S. 309, 28 C.C.C. (2d) 81 [Que.].

Is this a proper application of the subjective test? Compare Stuart, "Criminal Negligence: Deadlock and Confusion in the Supreme Court" (1989), 69 C.R. (3d) 331.

R. v. ANDERSON

[1990] 1 S.C.R. 265, 75 C.R. (3d) 50, 53 C.C.C. (3d) 481, 1990 CarswellMan 190, 1990 CarswellMan 375

The accused was charged with criminal negligence causing death. He had been thinking of something else, ran a red light and a passenger in the car he hit died as a result of injuries suffered in the accident. There was no evidence of any erratic driving apart from driving through the red traffic light. The accused, although legally impaired, showed little sign of impairment. The trial judge found that the Crown had failed to prove the charge beyond a reasonable doubt. During the course of his reasons the trial judge stated that neither the *mens rea* nor the consequences of the manner of driving were material in making a decision as to guilt or innocence. An appeal was allowed by the Court of Appeal. The accused appealed. The sole issue was whether the trial judge's comments relating to the relevance of consequences and intention affected the outcome.

The judgment of the seven-person court was delivered by SOPINKA J.: —

. . . .

In approaching the critique of a trial judgment dealing with a charge of criminal negligence, one can only have profound sympathy for the plight of the trial judge. This area of the law, both here and in other common law countries, has proved to be one of the most difficult and uncertain in the whole of the criminal field. The sections of the *Criminal Code*, R.S.C. 1970, c. C-34, under consideration here are relatively simple.

The use of the word "negligence" suggests that the impugned conduct must depart from a standard objectively determined. On the other hand, the use of the words "wanton and reckless disregard" suggests that an ingredient of the offence includes a state of mind or some moral quality to the conduct which attracts the sanctions of the criminal law. The section makes it clear that the conclusion that there is a wanton or reckless disregard is to be drawn from the conduct which falls below the standard. The major disagreement in the cases centers around the manner in which this conclusion is to be drawn.

On the one hand, there are the cases that hold that it is to be done on an objective basis. If the conduct is a marked departure from the norm, then, based on the standard of an ordinary prudent individual, the accused ought to have known that his actions could endanger the lives or safety of others. On the other hand, there are cases that apply a subjective standard and require some degree of advertence to the risk to be proved. This may be done by inferring advertence from the nature of the conduct in the context of the surrounding circumstances. A refinement on the latter view is that a marked departure constitutes a *prima facie* case of negligence. The trier of fact may but it is not obliged to infer the necessary mental element from the conduct which is found to depart substantially from the norm.

In both the objective and subjective approaches, the court is determining foreseeability of consequences. In a civil negligence case concerned with adjustment of losses, the connection between conduct and consequences is often quite tenuous. The mythical reasonable man has been equipped with a great deal of clairvoyance in order to compensate the innocent victim. Often the defendant will not, in fact, have foreseen the consequences of his negligent acts for which he is held accountable on an objective basis. In a criminal case the connection must be more substantial. To establish recklessness, the consequences must be more obvious. That is the rationale for the requirement of a marked departure from the norm. The greater the risk created, the easier it is to conclude that a reasonably prudent person would have foreseen the consequences. Equally, it is easier to conclude that the accused must have foreseen the consequences. It is apparent, therefore, that as the risk of harm increases, the significance of the distinction between the objective and subjective approaches decreases. The ultimate in this process of reasoning is reached when the risk is so high that the consequences are the natural result of the conduct creating the risk. The conduct in such circumstances can be characterized as intentional.

A finding that the impugned conduct is a marked departure from the standard is, accordingly, central to both the objective and subjective approaches. In *R. v. Tutton*, [1989] 1 S.C.R. 1392, this court was divided as to which approach is correct.

. . . .

Criminal Negligence — Application to This Case

In this case as in most of these cases there is no direct evidence of the state of mind of the appellant. The conclusion that he had a wanton or reckless disregard for the lives and safety of others must be drawn from the conduct which is alleged to be a marked departure from the norm. If an objective standard is employed, this will be determined on the basis of the state of mind of an ordinary prudent person in the circumstances. If the subjective standard or its refinement are applied, then the conclusion, if drawn, must be drawn from the conduct of the appellant.

The conduct relied on in this case is (a) the combination of drinking and driving, and (b) the breach of a traffic light regulation. Clearly the trial judge considered both. He concluded that the conduct was not a marked departure from the norm. That being the case, a conclusion that the appellant had a wanton or reckless disregard for the lives and safety of others could not be drawn on either a subjective or objective basis.

The trial judge specifically addressed the question of the drinking and driving. The Court of Appeal agreed that this was so. Nevertheless he was not prepared to find that this, together with the traffic violation, was sufficient. It left him in a state of doubt. No doubt setting out to drive after drinking in some circumstances may be sufficient to conclude either objectively or subjectively that there is a wanton or reckless disregard for the lives and safety of others. It will not be so, however, in every case. The contrary conclusion would render redundant subss. (2) and (3) of s. 237 [now s. 255] of the *Criminal Code* which provides specific penalties for causing death or bodily harm through the operation of a motor vehicle while impaired. The decision, however, in each case is one of fact, and in this case the trial judge was not prepared to so conclude.

Was this finding affected by the reference to intention? The statement in context is as follows: "nor is *mens rea*, or the intention required to be proved by the Crown. It matters not what the man's intention was when he entered the automobile to put it into use." I do not read this statement to mean that the evidence that the appellant chose to drive his car knowing he had been drinking was not relevant. Such an interpretation would constitute too microscopic an approach to the trial judge's reasons. Clearly, the trial judge went on to consider the relevance of this evidence. What the trial judge was dealing with here was the Crown's obligation. Intention need not be proved by the Crown. From the Crown's point of view, it did not matter that the appellant intended to drive safely when he entered the automobile. The sentence following the above-quoted passage emphasizes that this is the context in which the statement is made: "Nevertheless, of course, the Crown must carry its burden. . . ."

The trial judge's statement that the consequences are not relevant must also be dealt with in the context in which it was made. This reference is undoubtedly one to the tragic death of the passenger in the other vehicle involved in the collision. The death of the passenger was a necessary ingredient of the *actus reus*. It was not otherwise relevant unless a conclusion could be drawn from it with respect to whether there was a wanton and reckless disregard for the lives and safety of other persons. It was not suggested by the Crown that it was a circumstance from which such a conclusion could be drawn either on an objective or subjective basis.

In the circumstances of this case, the unfortunate fact that a person was killed added nothing to the conduct of the appellant. The degree of negligence proved against the appellant by means of the evidence that he drove after drinking and went through a red light was not increased by the fact that a collision occurred and death resulted. If driving and drinking and running a red light was not a marked departure from the standard, it did not become so because a collision occurred. In some circumstances, perhaps, the actions of the accused and the consequences flowing from them may be so interwoven that the consequences may be relevant in characterizing the conduct of the accused. That is not the case here.

In my opinion, the trial Judge came to the conclusion on the evidence that there was a reasonable doubt that the conduct of the accused constituted criminal negligence. He was entitled to do so on the facts. Although he made some general remarks that perhaps should not have been made without elaboration, I am satisfied that no error of law resulted. In any event, the statements to which I have alluded did not affect the outcome. The respondent has not satisfied me that the verdict would not necessarily have been the same. The Court of Appeal ought not to have set aside the acquittal.

In view of this conclusion, it is unnecessary to deal with the appellant's submissions with respect to *R. v. Caldwell*, [1981] All E.R. 961, nor the appellant's submissions that the judgment of the Manitoba Court of Appeal is inconsistent with the principle in *R. v. Vaillancourt* (1987), 39 C.C.C. (3d) 118.

Disposition

In the result, the appeal is allowed, the judgment of the Court of Appeal set aside and the acquittal restored.

See comment by Patrick Healy, "*Anderson:* Marking Time or a Step Back on Criminal Negligence?" (1990), 75 C.R. (3d) 58.

We shall see in the next section that eventually, after 20 years, the Supreme Court in *F. (J.)* resolved the division in *Tutton* in favour of the objective standard. However, we shall see that they added a requirement of a marked *and substantial* departure from the objective norm for offences based on "criminal negligence".

(ii) *Marked departure test*

In *Tutton*, Justice Lamer argued that the objective test should include a generous allowance for characteristics particular to the accused. Justice Wilson (preferring to adopt a subjective approach to *mens rea*) expressed concerns over such a "modified objective" test, arguing that it could be both over-inclusive and under-inclusive. The Court continued the debate over whether an objective test ought to set a uniform standard or be a modified objective test in *R. v. Hundal*, [1993] 1 SCR 867.

R. v. HUNDAL

[1993] 1 S.C.R. 867, 79 C.C.C. (3d) 97, 19 C.R. (4th) 169

The accused was charged with dangerous driving causing death. He was driving an overloaded dump truck in busy Vancouver traffic in wet conditions. He drove through an intersection after his light had turned red, honking his horn to indicate he was doing so, and struck a car that was proceeding legally: the driver of the car was killed instantly. A witness testified that this was the second red light the accused had driven through, and estimated that he was going 50 – 60 km/h at the time of the collision.

The first issue was the nature of the fault element: the Court unanimously concluded that this was an objective fault crime. Justice Cory wrote for five judges on this point:

18 The nature of driving offences suggests that an objective test, or more specifically a modified objective test, is particularly appropriate to apply to dangerous driving. I say that for a number of reasons.

(a) The Licensing Requirement

19 First, driving can only be undertaken by those who have a licence. The effect of the licensing requirement is to demonstrate that those who drive are mentally and physically capable of doing so. Moreover, it serves to confirm that those who drive are familiar with the standards of care which must be maintained by all drivers. There is a further aspect that must be taken into consideration in light of the licensing requirement for drivers. Licensed drivers choose to engage in the regulated activity of driving. They place themselves in a position of responsibility to other members of the public who use the roads.

20 As a result, it is unnecessary for a court to establish that the particular accused intended or was aware of the consequences of his or her driving. The minimum standard of physical and mental well-being coupled with the basic knowledge of the standard of care required of licensed drivers obviate that requirement. As a general rule, a consideration of the personal factors, so essential in determining subjective intent, is simply not necessary in light of the fixed standards that must be met by licensed drivers.

(b) The Automatic and Reflexive Nature of Driving

21 Second, the nature of driving itself is often so routine, so automatic that it is almost impossible to determine a particular state of mind of a driver at any given moment. Driving motor vehicles is something that is familiar to most adult Canadians. It cannot be denied that a great deal of driving is done with little conscious thought. It is an activity that is primarily reactive and not contemplative. It is every bit as routine and familiar as taking a shower or going to work. Often it is impossible for a driver to say what his or her specific intent was at any moment during a drive other than the desire to go from A to B.

22 It would be a denial of common sense for a driver, whose conduct was objectively dangerous, to be acquitted on the ground that he was not thinking of his manner of driving at the time of the accident.

(c) The Wording of Section 233 (now Section 249)

23 Third, the wording of the section itself which refers to the operation of a motor vehicle "in a manner that is dangerous to the public, having regard to all the circumstances" suggests that an objective standard is required. The "manner of driving" can only be compared to a standard of reasonable conduct. That standard can be readily judged and assessed by all who would be members of juries.

24 Thus, it is clear that the basis of liability for dangerous driving is negligence. The question to be asked is not what the accused subjectively intended but rather whether, viewed objectively, the accused exercised the appropriate standard of care. It is not overly difficult to determine when a driver has fallen markedly below the acceptable standard of care. There can be no doubt that the concept of negligence is well understood and readily recognized by most Canadians. Negligent driving can be thought of as a continuum that progresses, or regresses, from momentary lack of attention giving rise to civil responsibility through careless driving under a provincial Highway Traffic Act to dangerous driving under the *Criminal Code*.

(d) Statistics

25 Fourth, the statistics which demonstrate that all too many tragic deaths and disabling injuries flow from the operation of motor vehicles indicate the need to control the conduct of drivers. The need is obvious and urgent. Section 233 (now s. 249) seeks to curb conduct which is exceedingly dangerous to the public. The statistics on car accidents in Canada indicate with chilling clarity the extent of the problem. The number of people killed and injured each year in traffic accidents is staggering. Data from Transport Canada shows that, in 1991, the number of deaths related to traffic accidents in Canada was 3,654. In 1990, there were 178,423 personal injury traffic accidents, 630,000 property damage accidents and 3,442 fatal accidents. These figures highlight the tragic social cost which can and does arise from the operation of motor vehicles. There is therefore a compelling need for effective legislation which strives to regulate the manner of driving vehicles and thereby lessen the carnage on our highways. It is not only appropriate but essential in the control of dangerous driving that an objective standard be applied.

26 In my view, to insist on a subjective mental element in connection with driving offences would be to deny reality. It cannot be forgotten that the operation of a motor vehicle is, as I have said so very often, automatic and with little conscious thought. It is simply inappropriate to apply a subjective test in determining whether an accused is guilty of dangerous driving.

[On the objective test, Justice LaForest wrote:]

La Forest J.:

36 I am in substantial agreement with what Justice Cory has to say about the mens rea required for the offence of dangerous driving and I would, therefore, dispose of the appeal in the manner proposed by him. I would simply add that both in its wording and object (it is a quasi-regulatory offence), this provision differs from the general offence of criminal negligence which, concurring with Wilson J., I concluded required subjective mens rea; see *R. v. Tutton*, [1989] 1 S.C.R. 1392 and *R. v. Waite*, [1989] 1 S.C.R. 1436.

[Having decided the test was an objective one, the Court then turned to the nature of that test. Justice Cory said that it should be judged on a modified objective standard.]

40 A modified objective test was aptly described by McIntyre J. in *R. v. Tutton*, *supra*, at p. 1413. Although he was dealing with criminal negligence, his words, at p. 1432, are apt in considering the dangerous driving section which is essentially concerned with negligent driving that constitutes a marked departure from the norm:

> The application of an objective test under s. 202 of the *Code*, however, may not be made in a vacuum. Events occur within the framework of other events and actions and when deciding on the nature of the questioned conduct surrounding circumstances must be considered. The decision must be made on a consideration of the facts existing at the time and in relation to the accused's perception of those facts. Since the test is objective, the accused's perception of the facts is not to be considered for the purpose of assessing malice or intention on the accused's part but only to form a basis for a conclusion as to whether or not the accused's conduct, in view of his perception of those facts, was reasonable. If an accused under s. 202 has an honest and reasonably held belief in the existence of certain facts, it may be a relevant

consideration in assessing the reasonableness of his conduct. For example, a welder, who is engaged to work in a confined space believing on the assurance of the owner of the premises that no combustible or explosive material is stored nearby, should be entitled to have his perception, as to the presence or absence of dangerous materials, before the jury on a charge of manslaughter when his welding torch causes an explosion and a consequent death.

Justice McLachlin (Chief Justice Lamer concurring) agreed with the substance of the majority's conclusion about how to judge whether an accused was guilty of dangerous driving, but expressed doubts about their use of terminology:

6 This brings me to the modified objective test. The label "modified objective test" might be taken to suggest an amalgam of objective and subjective factors; a test that looks at what ought to have been in the accused's mind, but goes on to consider what was actually there or not there. If this is what it means, it runs afoul of Professor Stuart's sensible admonition that jurists should be very clear about whether they are convicting on the basis of the subjective test or the objective test. On the objective test, the Crown is not required to establish what was in the accused's mind as a matter of fact.

7 Consideration of the context in which the term has been used suggests that the phrase "modified objective test" was introduced in an effort to ensure that jurists applying the objective test take into account all relevant circumstances in the events surrounding the alleged offence and give the accused an opportunity to raise a reasonable doubt as to what a reasonable person would have thought in the particular situation in which the accused found himself or herself. Thus Cory J. in discussing the modified objective test at p. 883 stresses that "personal factors" may be raised and affirms at p. 886 that "it will remain open to the accused to raise a reasonable doubt that a reasonable person would have been aware of the risks in the accused's conduct". He goes on to say, "The test must be applied with some measure of flexibility. That is to say the objective test should not be applied in a vacuum but rather in the context of the events surrounding the incident."

8 If, as my colleague suggests, McIntyre J. was describing a modified objective test in *R. v. Tutton*, [1989] 1 S.C.R. 1392, at p. 1432, the language and example used indicate that his concern too was to ensure that in applying the objective test all relevant circumstances, including those personal to the accused be considered. He reaffirms the objective test by asserting that only "an honest and reasonably held belief" can exonerate the accused. In other words, it is no defence to say, on the subjective level, "I was being careful", or "I believed I could do what I did without undue risk". The defence arises only if that belief was reasonably held. McIntyre J. goes on to offer the example of a welder who is engaged to work in a confined space believing on the assurance of the owner of the premises that no combustible or explosive material is nearby. The welder charged in connection with a subsequent explosion, McIntyre J. asserts, should

532 THE FAULT REQUIREMENT

be allowed to introduce evidence that he believed there were no combustible or explosive materials on the premises. This is an objective test; the fact that the welder had been told there were no combustible or explosive materials on the site is one of the circumstances which a jury should take into account in determining what a reasonable person would have thought and done. Was it reasonable for the welder in these circumstances to turn his torch on in the enclosed space? The answer, on the objective test, is "of course".

9 Nor does Cory J.'s example of "a totally unexpected heart attack, epileptic seizure or detached retina" (at p. 886), which renders an accused unable to control his or her motor vehicle, require the introduction of an element of subjectivity. The better analysis, in my view, is that the onset of a "disease or disability" makes the act of losing control of the motor vehicle involuntary, with the result that there is no *actus reus*. Thus we do not reach the question of what a reasonable person would have been thinking or adverting to as the car goes off the road, much less what the accused was in fact thinking or not thinking. Alternatively, if the *actus reus* were taken as established in these examples, the heart attack or epileptic seizure might be viewed as a circumstance which negates the ordinary inference of want of care which flows from the fact of having lost control of a motor vehicle.

The Supreme Court in *Creighton* and its companion cases adopted a new approach to the interpretation of all objective crimes. The Court was unanimous in requiring a marked departure from the standard of care of a reasonable person. The Court, however, divided 5:4 over the question whether personal factors could be considered in applying an objective standard. McLachlin J. for the majority decided that no individual factors short of incapacity could be considered. **Which opinion do you prefer?**

R. v. CREIGHTON

[1993] 3 S.C.R. 3, 23 C.R. (4th) 189, 83 C.C.C. (3d) 346,
1993 CarswellOnt 115, 1993 CarswellOnt 989

On a charge of manslaughter, defence counsel conceded at trial that the injection into the deceased's body of cocaine constituted trafficking within the definition set out in s. 4(1) of the *Narcotic Control Act*. The Crown argued that the accused was guilty of manslaughter as the death was the direct consequence of that unlawful act, contrary to s. 222(5)(a) of the *Criminal Code*. The accused was convicted, and the Court of Appeal upheld the conviction. The common law had decided that where the accused had committed an unlawful act, objective foreseeability of the risk of bodily harm which is neither trivial nor transitory was sufficient and foreseeability of the risk of death was not required. The Supreme Court was called on to determine whether the common law definition of unlawful act manslaughter contravened s. 7 of the *Charter*. In deciding that it did not, the Court expressed some thoughts on the meaning of negligence in the criminal law.

LAMER C.J. (SOPINKA, IACOBUCCI and MAJOR JJ. concurring): — The Crown bears the burden of proving beyond a reasonable doubt that a reasonable person in the context of the offence would have foreseen the risk of death created by his or her conduct. As I explain in more detail in *R. v. Gosset*, S.C.C., No. 22523, released this same day, the reasonable person will be invested with any enhanced foresight the accused may have enjoyed by virtue of his or her membership in a group with special experience or knowledge related to the conduct giving rise to the offence. For example, in *Gosset* the accused police officer's experience and training in the handling of firearms is relevant to the standard of care under s. 86(2) of the *Criminal Code* concerning the careless use of firearms. In the present case, the reasonable person should be deemed to possess Mr. Creighton's considerable experience in drug use. Once the Crown has established beyond a reasonable doubt that this reasonable person in the context of the offence would have foreseen the risk of death created by his or her conduct, the focus of the investigation must shift to the question of whether a reasonable person in the position of the accused would have been capable of foreseeing such a risk. The objective test cannot, to reiterate, relieve the accused of criminal liability simply because he or she did not, in fact, foresee creating the risk of death. I wish to reiterate that the standard of care remains uniform and unchanging irrespective of the particular accused — the prosecution must demonstrate a marked departure from the standard of a reasonable person; rather, it is in the determination of what is reasonable that the skill and expertise of the accused may be considered.

The objective test can be best understood when stated as a "checklist" for the trier of fact to apply to the accused's conduct in a particular case. Where the accused is charged with the offence of unlawful act manslaughter, the trier of fact must ask:

(1) Would a reasonable person in the same circumstances have been aware that the likely consequences of his or her unlawful conduct would create the risk of death?

This question provides the threshold to the objective test. If the answer to this question is No, then the accused must be acquitted. If the answer is Yes, however, the trier must then ask:

(2) Was the accused unaware

(a) because he or she did not turn his or her mind to the consequences of the conduct and thus to the risk of death likely to result; or

(b) because he or she lacked the capacity to turn his or her mind to the consequences of the conduct and thus to the risk of death likely to result, due to human frailties?

If the answer is (a), the accused must be convicted, since the criminal law cannot allow the absence of actual awareness to be an excuse to criminal liability. An important distinction must be maintained within the objective test between the capacity to decide to turn one's mind to a risk, and the decision not to turn one's mind to it. As Colvin, *Principles of Criminal Law* (2nd ed. 1991), notes, at p. 155:

> As long as attention is directed to the individual's own capabilities, a judgment of fault can be made on the ground that there was a fair opportunity to have recognized the risks and harm of conduct.

A key element of the objective test is that of the control an accused could have exercised over the frailty which rendered him or her incapable of acting as the reasonable person would in the same circumstances. The notion of control is related to that of moral responsibility; if one is able to act prudently and not endanger the life of others, one will be held liable for failing to do so. One must be morally — and criminally — responsible to act according to his or her capacities not to inflict harm, even unintentional harm. By contrast, the inability to control a particular frailty which resulted in the creation of the risk may offer a moral excuse for having brought about that risk. Therefore, if the answer to the second branch of the objective test is (b), the third and final stage of the inquiry is required:

> (3) In the context of the particular offence, would the reasonable person with the capacities of the accused have made him or herself aware of the likely consequences of the unlawful conduct and the resulting risk of death?

In this inquiry, the accused's behaviour is still measured against the standard of the reasonable person, but the reasonable person is constructed to account for the accused's particular capacities and resulting inability to perceive and address certain risks. This test is similar to that advocated by Hart, in "Negligence, *Mens Rea* and Criminal Responsibility", *supra*, at p. 154:

> (i) Did the accused fail to take those precautions which any reasonable man with normal capacities would in the circumstances have taken?

> (ii) Could the accused, given his mental and physical capacities, have taken those precautions?

It must be emphasized that this is not a subjective test: if a reasonable person with the frailties of the accused would nevertheless have appreciated the risk, and the accused did not in fact appreciate the risk, the accused must be convicted.

The rationale of incorporating capacity into the objective determination of fault is analogous to the rationale underlying the defence of mistake of fact in criminal law, where an accused who has an honest and reasonably held belief in an incorrect set of facts, and acts on the basis of those facts, is excused from punishment for the resulting harm. Human frailties which may affect the capacity of an accused to recognize the risks of unlawful conduct must be considered, however, not because they result in the accused believing in an incorrect set of facts, but rather because they render the accused incapable of perceiving the correct set of facts. It is, however, only those human frailties which relate to an accused's capacity to appreciate the risk in question that may be considered in this inquiry.

I shall now turn to elaborating what "human frailties" may factor into the objective test. It is perhaps best to begin by stating clearly what is not included. Intoxication or impairment through drug use which occurs as a result of voluntary consumption cannot serve to vitiate liability for the risks created by the negligent conduct of an accused. Additionally, a sudden and temporary incapacity to appreciate risk due to exigent circumstances (an emergency which diverts one's attention from an activity, for example) is not properly considered under the third part of the test, but may well result in an acquittal under the first part of the test, that is, would a reasonable person's attention in the same circumstances of the accused have been diverted from that activity.

Human frailties encompass personal characteristics habitually affecting an accused's awareness of the circumstances which create risk. Such characteristics must be relevant to the ability to perceive the particular risk. For example, while illiteracy may excuse the failure to take care with a hazardous substance identifiable only by a label, as the accused may be unable, in this case, to apprehend the relevant facts, illiteracy may not be relevant to the failure to take care with a firearm. This attention to the context of the offence and the nature of the activity is explored in greater detail below.

It should be emphasized that the relevant characteristics must be traits which the accused could not control or otherwise manage in the circumstances. For example, while a person with cataracts cannot be faulted for having reduced vision, he or she may be expected to avoid activity in which that limitation will either create risk or render him or her unable to manage risk which is inherent in an activity (driving, for example). The reasonable person is expected to compensate for his or her frailties, to the extent he or she is conscious of them and able to do so.

This general discussion is not intended to set out an exhaustive definition, but rather to lay the groundwork for examining the different factual contexts which may arise. Two central criteria in this regard are (1) the gravity of the offence, and (2) the inherent purposefulness of the conduct involved. With respect to the gravity of the offence, there may be a significant gulf between neglecting to safely store a bottle containing a prescription drug, and neglecting to unload a firearm and return it to its cabinet. In these different contexts, the behaviour of the reasonable person who possesses all of the accused's limitations may be very different, and therefore the answer to the third question regarding the ability of an accused to control or compensate for his or her frailties may be different as well.

McLACHLIN   J.   (L'HEUREUX-DUBÉ,   GONTHIER   and   CORY   JJ. concurring): —

The Nature of the Objective Test

I respectfully differ from the Chief Justice on the nature of the objective test used to determine the *mens rea* for crimes of negligence. In my view, the approach advocated by the Chief Justice personalizes the objective test to the point where it devolves into a subjective test, thus eroding the minimum standard of care which Parliament has laid down by the enactment of offences of manslaughter and penal negligence.

By way of background, it may be useful to restate what I understand the jurisprudence to date to have established regarding crimes of negligence and the objective test. The *mens rea* of a criminal offence may be either subjective or objective, subject to the principle of fundamental justice that the moral fault of the offence must be proportionate to its gravity and penalty. Subjective *mens rea* requires that the accused has intended the consequences of his or her acts, or that knowing of the probable consequences of those acts, the accused has proceeded recklessly in the face of the risk. The requisite intent or knowledge may be inferred directly from what the accused said or says about his or her mental state, or indirectly from the act and its circumstances. Even in the latter case, however, it is concerned with "what was actually going on in the mind of this particular accused at the time in question": L'Heureux-Dubé J. in *R. v. Martineau, supra*, at p. 655, quoting Stuart, *Canadian Criminal Law* (2nd ed. 1987), at p. 121.

Objective *mens rea*, on the other hand, is not concerned with what the accused intended or knew. Rather, the mental fault lies in failure to direct the mind to a risk which the reasonable person would have appreciated. Objective *mens rea* is not concerned with what was actually in the accused's mind, but with what should have been there, had the accused proceeded reasonably.

It is now established that a person may be held criminally responsible for negligent conduct on the objective test, and that this alone does not violate the principle of fundamental justice that the moral fault of the accused must be commensurate with the gravity of the offence and its penalty: *R. v. Hundal*, [1993] 1 S.C.R. 867.

However, as stated in *Martineau*, it is appropriate that those who cause harm intentionally should be punished more severely than those who cause harm inadvertently. Moreover, the constitutionality of crimes of negligence is also subject to the caveat that acts of ordinary negligence may not suffice to justify imprisonment: *R. v. City of Sault Ste. Marie*, [1978], 2 S.C.R. 1299; *R. v. Sansregret*, [1985] 1 S.C.R. 570. To put it in the terms used in *Hundal*: The negligence must constitute a "marked departure" from the standard of the reasonable person. The law does not lightly brand a person as a criminal. For this reason, I am in agreement with the Chief Justice in *R. v. Finlay, supra*, that the word "careless" in an underlying firearms offence must be read as requiring a marked departure from the constitutional norm.

It follows from this requirement, affirmed in *Hundal*, that in an offence based on unlawful conduct, a predicate offence involving carelessness or negligence must also be read as requiring a "marked departure" from the standard of the reasonable person. As pointed out in *DeSousa*, the underlying offence must be constitutionally sound.

To this point, the Chief Justice and I are not, as I perceive it, in disagreement. The difference between our approaches turns on the extent to which personal characteristics of the accused may affect liability under the objective test. Here we enter territory in large part uncharted. To date, debate has focused on whether an objective test for *mens rea* is ever available in the criminal law; little has been said about how, assuming it is applicable, it is to be applied. In *R. v. Hundal, supra*, it was said that the *mens rea* of dangerous driving should be assessed objectively in the context of all the events surrounding the incident. But the extent to which those circumstances include personal mental or psychological frailties of the accused was not explored in depth. In these circumstances, we must begin with the fundamental principles of criminal law.

1. Underlying Principles

The debate about the degree to which personal characteristics should be reflected in the objective test for fault in offences of penal negligence engages two fundamental concepts of criminal law.

The first concept is the notion that the criminal law may properly hold people who engage in risky activities to a minimum standard of care, judged by what a reasonable person in all the circumstances would have done. This notion posits a uniform standard for all persons engaging in the activity, regardless of their background, education or psychological disposition.

The second concept is the principle that the morally innocent not be punished (*Re B.C. Motor Vehicle Act*, [1985] 2 S.C.R. 486, at p. 513; *R. v. Gosset*, S.C.C., No.22523, reasons of Lamer C.J. at p. 20). This principle is the foundation of the requirement of criminal law that the accused must have a guilty mind, or *mens rea*.

I agree with the Chief Justice that the rule that the morally innocent not be punished in the context of the objective test requires that the law refrain from holding a person criminally responsible if he or she is not capable of appreciating the risk. Where I differ from the Chief Justice is in his designation of the sort of educational, experiential and so-called "habitual" factors personal to the accused which can be taken into account. The Chief Justice, while in principle advocating a uniform standard of care for all, in the result seems to contemplate a standard of care which varies with the background and predisposition of each accused. Thus an inexperienced, uneducated, young person, like the accused in

R. v. Naglik, S.C.C., Nos. 22490 and 22636, September 9, 1993, could be acquitted, even though she does not meet the standard of the reasonable person (reasons of the Chief Justice, at p. 24). On the other hand, a person with special experience, like Mr. Creighton in this case, or the appellant police officer in *R. v. Gosset*, S.C.C., No. 22523 (reasons released concurrently), will be held to a higher standard than the ordinary reasonable person.

I must respectfully dissent from this extension of the objective test for criminal fault. In my view, considerations of principle and policy dictate the maintenance of a single, uniform legal standard of care for such offences, subject to one exception: incapacity to appreciate the nature of the risk which the activity in question entails.

This principle that the criminal law will not convict the morally innocent does not, in my view, require consideration of personal factors short of incapacity. The criminal law, while requiring mental fault as an element of a conviction, has steadfastly rejected the idea that a person's personal characteristics can (short of incapacity) excuse the person from meeting the standard of conduct imposed by the law.

. . . .

The Chief Justice relies on Professor H.L.A. Hart in support of importing what Wilson J. calls "individualized excusing conditions" into the objective test for offences of manslaughter and penal negligence. In fact, Professor Hart sees the principle of preventing the punishment of the morally innocent as dictating only that people should not be punished when they lacked the capacity to appreciate the consequences of their conduct. He reasons that no one should be held blameworthy and punished for criminal conduct if he or she acted without free will (H. Hart, *Punishment and Responsibility* (1968), at pp. 35-40). He states that "the need to inquire into the 'inner facts' is dictated . . . by the moral principle that no one should be punished who could not help doing what he did" (p. 39) (emphasis added).

In summary, I can find no support in criminal theory for the conclusion that protection of the morally innocent requires a general consideration of individual excusing conditions. The principle comes into play only at the point where the person is shown to lack the capacity to appreciate the nature and quality or the consequences of his or her acts. Apart from this, we are all, rich and poor, wise and naive, held to the minimum standards of conduct prescribed by the criminal law. This conclusion is dictated by a fundamental proposition of social organization. As Justice Oliver Wendell Holmes wrote in *The Common Law* (1881), at p. 108: "when men live in society, a certain average of conduct, a sacrifice of individual peculiarities going beyond a certain point, is necessary to the general welfare."

It may be that in some cases educational deficiencies, such as illiteracy on the part of a person handling a marked bottle of nitroglycerine in the Chief

Justice's example, may preclude a person from being able to appreciate the risk entailed by his or her conduct. Problems of perception may have the same effect; regardless of the care taken, the person would have been incapable of assessing the risk, and hence been acquitted. But, in practice, such cases will arise only exceptionally.

. . . .

This is not to say that the question of guilt is determined in a factual vacuum. While the legal duty of the accused is not particularized by his or her personal characteristics short of incapacity, it is particularized in application by the nature of the activity and the circumstances surrounding the accused's failure to take the requisite care. As McIntyre J. pointed out in *R. v. Tutton*, [1989] 1 S.C.R. 1392, the answer to the question of whether the accused took reasonable care must be founded on a consideration of all the circumstances of the case. The question is what the reasonably prudent person would have done in all the circumstances. Thus a welder who lights a torch causing an explosion may be excused if he has made an enquiry and been given advice upon which he was reasonably entitled to rely, that there was no explosive gas in the area. . . .

The matter may be looked at in this way. The legal standard of care is always the same—what a reasonable person would have done in all the circumstances. The *de facto* or applied standard of care, however, may vary with the activity in question and the circumstances in the particular case.

. . . .

A person may fail to meet an elevated *de facto* standard of care in either of two ways. First, the person may undertake an activity requiring special care when he or she is not qualified to give that care. Absent special excuses like necessity, this may constitute culpable negligence. An untrained person undertaking brain surgery might violate the standard in this way. Second, a person who is qualified may negligently fail to exercise the special care required by the activity. A brain surgeon performing surgery in a grossly negligent way might violate the standard in this second way. The standard is the same, although the means by which it is breached may differ.

Just as the adoption of a uniform standard of care which is blind to personal characteristics of the accused short of incapacity precludes lowering the standard for deficiencies of experience and temperament, so it precludes raising the standard for special experience or training. Since the criminal law is concerned with setting minimum standards for human conduct, it would be inappropriate to hold accused persons to a higher standard of care by reason of the fact that they may be better informed or better qualified than the person of reasonable prudence. Some activities may impose a higher de facto standard than others; brain surgery requires more care than applying an antiseptic. But as discussed earlier, this flows from the circumstances of the activity, not from the expertise of the actor.

. . . .

LA FOREST J.: —

. . . .

There are important educative and psychological differences between the two approaches that have led me to prefer the subjective view of *mens rea*. That view underlines that no one will be punished for anything he or she did not intend or at least advert to, and its use supports one's feeling that a morally innocent person will not be punished.

The objective view, however qualified, does not fully serve these ends. It is true that the qualified objective view would theoretically protect some of the individuals the subjective view would protect, but by no means all; see *Tutton*, *supra*, per Wilson J., at p. 1419. And it does not respond to the educative and psychological ends sought to be attained by those advocating subjective *mens rea*. Indeed, it introduces a differentiation between individuals in criminal proceedings that, however well-meant, seems foreign to our law. What is more, the qualified objective approach loses most of the practical advantages sought to be attained by the objective approach. Indeed, some of the difficulties that have been perceived to result from the adoption of the subjective view would be exacerbated. I think, in particular, of the difficulties of instructing a jury. On this question, too, I find McLachlin J.'s reasons more persuasive.

Creighton stands firmly against any development of a cultural defence: see Charmaine M. Wong, "Good Intentions, Troublesome Applications: The Cultural Defence and Other Uses of Cultural Evidence in Canada" (1999), 42 Crim. L.Q. 367. The author fully explores the possibilities and drawbacks to such a defence but, surprisingly, makes no mention of *Creighton*. See, too, Stephen Coughlan, "The Omission of Provocation from a General Part" in Stuart, Delisle and Manson (eds.), *Towards a Clear and Just Criminal Law* (1999), 243 at 244-245, who argues against the defence and suggests debate seems to exist only in the United States. See also Jennifer Choi, "The Viability of a 'Cultural Defence' in Canada" (2003), 8 Can. Crim. L.R. 93.

As to the issue of incapacity, it has been held that severe mental retardation can be taken into account for criminal negligence, *Ubhi* (1994), 27 C.R. (4th) 332 (B.C. C.A.), leave to appeal refused (1994), 31 C.R. (4th) 405 (note) (S.C.C.), but not religious beliefs in an exorcism case involving the death of an infant, *Canhoto* (1999), 140 C.C.C. (3d) 321, 29 C.R. (5th) 170 (Ont. C.A.).

Creighton was seemingly ignored on the issue of no individual factors in *Brocklebank* (1996), 106 C.C.C. (3d) 234 (Can. Ct. Martial App. Ct.). The standard for negligent performance of military duty was adjusted to take into account accused's rank, degree of responsibility and exigencies of operation.

In *R. v. L. (J.)* (2006), 204 C.C.C. (3d) 324 (Ont. C.A.) a conviction for criminal negligence causing death was overturned in part because the trial judge had not taken into account the factor of youthfulness.

R. v. BEATTY

54 C.R. (6th) 1, 2008 CarswellBC 307, 2008 CarswellBC 308, [2008] 1 S.C.R. 49, 228 C.C.C. (3d) 225

The accused was charged with three counts of dangerous operation of a motor vehicle causing death under s. 249(4) of the *Criminal Code*. The accused's pick up truck, for no apparent reason, suddenly crossed the solid centre line into the path of an oncoming vehicle, killing all three occupants. Witnesses driving behind the victims' car observed the accused's vehicle being driven in a proper manner prior to the accident. An expert inspection concluded that the accused's vehicle had not suffered from mechanical failure. Intoxicants were not a factor. The accused stated that he was not sure what happened but that he must have lost consciousness or fallen asleep due to heat stroke from working in the sun all day. The trial judge concluded that these few seconds of negligent driving could, without more, fall within the continuum that would attract civil negligence but could not support a finding of a marked departure from the standard of care of a reasonably prudent driver for a conviction.

The British Columbia Court of Appeal set aside the acquittals and ordered a new trial. The accused's conduct of crossing the centre line into the path of oncoming traffic at 90 kilometres per hour on a well-travelled road could only be viewed as objectively dangerous and a "marked departure" from the requisite standard of care.

In the Supreme Court, although three separate opinions were delivered, the Court was unanimous in the result in deciding that the appeal should be allowed and the acquittals restored.

CHARRON J. (BASTARACHE, DESCHAMPS, ABELLA, and ROTHSTEIN JJ. concurring):

[20] It is well established that dangerous driving is based on a form of negligent conduct. [The court reviewed the rationale established in *Hundal*. In that decision the Court had decided that dangerous driving was an objective fault crime for four reasons: driving requires a license, it is an "automatic and reflexive" activity which normally does not involve subjective thought, the language of the section ("in a manner") suggested objective fault, and the urgent need to curb conduct which was exceedingly dangerous to the public.]

. . . .

3.3.2 First Modification to the Objective Test: The Marked Departure

[33] The court in *Hundal*, however, made it clear that the requisite *mens rea* may only be found when there is a "marked departure" from the standard of care expected of a reasonable person in the circumstances of the accused. This modification to the usual civil test for negligence is mandated by the criminal setting. It is only when there is a "marked departure" that the conduct demonstrates sufficient blameworthiness to support a finding of penal liability. One aspect of driving, "the automatic and reflexive nature of driving," particularly highlights the need for the "marked departure" requirement in a criminal setting. Cory J. described this aspect as follows (at p. 884-85):

> Second, the nature of driving itself is often so routine, so automatic that it is almost impossible to determine a particular state of mind of a driver at any given moment. Driving motor vehicles is something that is familiar to most adult Canadians. It cannot be denied that a great deal of driving is done with little conscious thought. It is an activity that is primarily reactive and not contemplative. It is every bit as routine and familiar as taking a shower or going to work. Often it is impossible for a driver to say what his or her specific intent was at any moment during a drive other than the desire to go from A to B.

[34] Therefore, as noted by Cory J., the difficulty of requiring positive proof of a particular subjective state of mind lends further support to the notion that *mens rea* should be assessed by objectively measuring the driver's conduct against the standard of a reasonably prudent driver. In addition, I would note that the automatic and reflexive nature of driving gives rise to the following consideration. Because driving, in large part, is automatic and reflexive, some departures from the standard expected of a reasonably prudent person will inevitably be the product, as Cory J. states, of "little conscious thought". Even the most able and prudent driver will from time to time suffer from momentary lapses of attention. These lapses may well result in conduct that, when viewed objectively, falls below the standard expected of a reasonably prudent driver. Such automatic and reflexive conduct may even pose a danger to other users of the highway. Indeed, the facts in this case provide a graphic example. The fact that the danger may be the product of little conscious thought becomes of concern because, as McLachlin J. (as she then was) aptly put it in *R. v. Creighton*, [1993] 3 S.C.R. 3, at p. 59: "The law does not lightly brand a person as a criminal." In addition to the largely automatic and reflexive nature of driving, we must also consider the fact that driving, although inherently risky, is a legal activity that has social value. If every departure from the civil norm is to be criminalized, regardless of the degree, we risk casting the net too widely and branding as criminals persons who are in reality not morally blameworthy. Such an approach risks violating the principle of fundamental justice that the morally innocent not be deprived of liberty.

[35] In a civil setting, it does not matter how far the driver fell short of the standard of reasonable care required by law. The extent of the driver's liability

depends not on the degree of negligence, but on the amount of damage done. Also, the mental state (or lack thereof) of the tortfeasor is immaterial, except in respect of punitive damages. In a criminal setting, the driver's mental state does matter because the punishment of an innocent person is contrary to fundamental principles of criminal justice. The degree of negligence is the determinative question because criminal fault must be based on conduct that merits punishment.

[36] For that reason, the objective test, as modified to suit the criminal setting, requires proof of a marked departure from the standard of care that a reasonable person would observe in all the circumstances. As stated earlier, it is only when there is a marked departure from the norm that objectively dangerous conduct demonstrates sufficient blameworthiness to support a finding of penal liability. With the marked departure, the act of dangerous driving is accompanied with the presence of sufficient *mens rea* and the offence is made out. The court, however, added a second important qualification to the objective test — the allowance for exculpatory defences.

3.3.3 Second Modification to the Objective Test: The Allowance for Exculpatory Defences

[37] The underlying premise for finding fault based on objectively dangerous conduct that constitutes a marked departure from the norm is that a reasonable person in the position of the accused would have been aware of the risk posed by the manner of driving and would not have undertaken the activity. However, there will be circumstances where this underlying premise cannot be sustained because a reasonable person in the position of the accused would not have been aware of the risk or, alternatively, would not have been able to avoid creating the danger. Of course, it is not open to the driver to simply say that he or she gave no thought to the manner of driving because the fault lies in the failure to bring to the dangerous activity the expected degree of thought and attention that it required. As Cory J. explained (at p. 885 of *Hundal*):

> It would be a denial of common sense for a driver, whose conduct was objectively dangerous, to be acquitted on the ground that he was not thinking of his manner of driving at the time of the accident.

However, because the accused's mental state is relevant in a criminal setting, the objective test must be modified to give the accused the benefit of any reasonable doubt about whether the reasonable person would have appreciated the risk or could and would have done something to avoid creating the danger. On these occasions, even when the manner of driving viewed objectively will clearly be dangerous, the accused cannot be convicted. Cory J., in *Hundal*, gave some useful examples (at p. 887):

> Take for example a driver who, without prior warning, suffers a totally unexpected heart attack, epileptic seizure or detached retina. As a result of the sudden onset of a disease or physical disability the manner of driving would be dangerous yet those circumstances could provide a complete defence despite the objective demonstration of dangerous driving. Similarly, a driver who, in the absence of any warning or knowledge of its possible effects, takes a prescribed medication which suddenly and unexpectedly affects the driver in such a way that the manner of driving was dangerous to the public, could still establish a good defence to the charge although it had been objectively established.

[38] We can readily appreciate the injustice of branding the driver in each of these examples as a criminal. In the same vein, a reasonably held mistake of fact may provide a complete defence if, based on the accused's reasonable perception of the facts, the conduct measured up to the requisite standard of care. It is therefore important to apply the modified objective test in the context of the events surrounding the incident. In *Tutton*, McIntyre J. provided the following useful example in the context of a criminal negligence charge (at p. 1432, repeated in *Hundal*, at pp. 887-88):

> If an accused under s. 202 has an honest and reasonably held belief in the existence of certain facts, it may be a relevant consideration in assessing the reasonableness of his conduct. For example, a welder, who is engaged to work in a confined space believing on the assurance of the owner of the premises that no combustible or explosive material is stored nearby, should be entitled to have his perception, as to the presence or absence of dangerous materials, before the jury on a charge of manslaughter when his welding torch causes an explosion and a consequent death.

[39] It is important however not to confuse the personal characteristics of the accused with the context of the events surrounding the incident. In the course of the earlier debate on whether to adopt a subjective or objective test, Lamer J. favoured an objective approach but, in an attempt to alleviate its potential harshness, he would have made generous allowances for factors particular to the accused, such as youth, mental development and education: see for example, *Tutton*, at p. 1434. Under this approach, the young and inexperienced driver's conduct would be measured against the standard expected of a reasonably prudent but young and inexperienced driver. This approach, however, was not favoured by other members of the court. As Wilson J. stated in *Tutton*, this individualized approach 'sets out a fluctuating standard which in my view undermines the principles of equality and individual responsibility which should pervade the criminal law" (p. 1418).

3.4 Restatement of the Test in *Hundal*

[41] In *Hundal*, Cory J. summarized the analytical framework for applying the modified objective test in the following oft-quoted passage (at pp. 888-89):

> It follows then that a trier of fact may convict if satisfied beyond a reasonable doubt that, viewed objectively, the accused was, in the words of the section, driving in a manner that was "dangerous to the public, having regard to all the circumstances, including the nature, condition and use of such place and the amount of traffic that at the time is or might reasonably be expected to be on such place". In making the assessment, the trier of fact should be satisfied that the conduct amounted to a marked departure from the standard of care that a reasonable person would observe in the accused's situation.

Next, if an explanation is offered by the accused, such as a sudden and unexpected onset of illness, then in order to convict, the trier of fact must be satisfied that a reasonable person in similar circumstances ought to have been aware of the risk and of the danger involved in the conduct manifested by the accused.

[42] In reviewing a number of cases that have applied this test, I have observed two common difficulties. First, there appears to be some confusion on the distinction, if any, between "objectively dangerous driving" on one hand, and "a marked departure from the standard of care" on the other. This difficulty is quite understandable because some departures from the reasonable standard of care may not be "marked" or "significant" but are nonetheless undeniably dangerous. As we shall see, this case is one example. Second, there appears to be much uncertainty in the case law on how to deal with evidence about the accused's mental state. In particular, when is evidence about the accused's actual mental state relevant? Is it relevant in determining whether the conduct constitutes a "marked departure" from the norm or, as the courts below in this case have done, should it be considered only as part of a distinct analysis on potential exculpatory defences?

[43] As we have seen, the requisite *mens rea* for the offence of dangerous driving was the sole issue before the court in *Hundal*, and the test was expressed accordingly. In order to clarify the uncertainties I have mentioned, it may assist to restate the summary of the test in terms of both the *actus reus* and the *mens rea* of the offence. I respectfully disagree with the Chief Justice that the test for the *actus reus* is defined in terms of a marked departure from the normal manner of driving (para. 67). The *actus reus* must be defined, rather, by the words of the enactment. Of course, conduct that is found to depart markedly from the norm remains necessary to make out the offence because nothing less will support the conclusion that the accused acted with sufficient blameworthiness, in other words with the requisite *mens rea*, to warrant conviction. In addition, it may be useful to keep in mind that while the modified objective test calls for an objective assessment of the accused's manner of driving, evidence about the

accused's actual state of mind, if any, may also be relevant in determining the presence of sufficient *mens rea*. I would therefore restate the test reproduced above as follows:

(a) The Actus reus

The trier of fact must be satisfied beyond a reasonable doubt that, viewed objectively, the accused was, in the words of the section, driving in a manner that was "dangerous to the public, having regard to all the circumstances, including the nature, condition and use of the place at which the motor vehicle is being operated and the amount of traffic that at the time is or might reasonably be expected to be at that place".

(b) The Mens rea

The trier of fact must also be satisfied beyond a reasonable doubt that the accused's objectively dangerous conduct was accompanied by the required *mens rea*. In making the objective assessment, the trier of fact should be satisfied on the basis of all the evidence, including evidence about the accused's actual state of mind, if any, that the conduct amounted to a marked departure from the standard of care that a reasonable person would observe in the accused's circumstances. Moreover, if an explanation is offered by the accused, then in order to convict, the trier of fact must be satisfied that a reasonable person in similar circumstances ought to have been aware of the risk and of the danger involved in the conduct manifested by the accused.

[44] I wish to elaborate on certain aspects of this test before applying it to the facts of this case.

3.4.1 Determining the Actus reus

[45] I deal firstly with the *actus reus*. The offence is defined by the words of the legislative provision, not by the common law standard for civil negligence. In order to determine the *actus reus*, the conduct must therefore be measured as against the wording of s. 249. Although the offence is negligence-based, this is an important distinction. As we have seen, conduct that constitutes dangerous operation of a motor vehicle as defined under s. 249 will necessarily fall below the standard expected of a reasonably prudent driver. The converse however is not necessarily true – not all negligent driving will constitute dangerous operation of a motor vehicle. If the court is satisfied beyond a reasonable doubt that the manner of driving was dangerous to the public within the meaning of s. 249, the *actus reus* of the offence has been made out. Nothing is gained by adding to the words of s. 249 at this stage of the analysis.

[46] As the words of the provision make plain, it is the manner in which the motor vehicle was operated that is at issue, not the consequence of the driving. The consequence, as here where death was caused, may make the offence a more serious one under s. 249(4), but it has no bearing on the question whether the offence of dangerous operation of a motor vehicle has been made out or not. Again, this is also an important distinction. If the focus is improperly placed on the consequence, it almost begs the question to then ask whether an act that killed someone was dangerous. The court must not leap to its conclusion about the manner of driving based on the consequence. There must be a meaningful inquiry into the manner of driving. The consequence, of course, may assist in assessing the risk involved, but it does not answer the question whether or not the vehicle was operated in a manner dangerous to the public. This court explained this distinction in *R. v. Anderson*, [1990] 1 S.C.R. 265, as follows:

> In the circumstances of this case, the unfortunate fact that a person was killed added nothing to the conduct of the appellant. The degree of negligence proved against the appellant by means of the evidence that he drove after drinking and went through a red light was not increased by the fact that a collision occurred and death resulted. *If driving and drinking and running a red light was not a marked departure from the standard, it did not become so because a collision occurred.* In some circumstances, perhaps, the actions of the accused and the consequences flowing from them may be so interwoven that the consequences may be relevant in characterizing the conduct of the accused. That is not the case here. [Emphasis added; p. 273.]

3.4.2 Determining the Mens rea

[47] In determining the question of *mens rea*, the court should consider the totality of the evidence, including evidence, if any, about the accused's actual state of mind. As discussed at length above, the *mens rea* requirement for the offence of dangerous driving will be satisfied by applying a modified objective test.[3] This means that, unlike offences that can only be committed if the accused possesses a subjective form of *mens rea*, it is not necessary for the Crown to prove that the accused had a positive state of mind, such as intent, recklessness or wilful blindness. Of course, this does not mean that the actual state of mind of the accused is irrelevant. For example, if proof is made that a driver purposely drove into the path of an oncoming vehicle in an intentionally dangerous manner for the purpose of scaring the passengers of that vehicle or impressing someone in his own vehicle with his bravado, the requirement of *mens rea* will easily be met. One way of looking at it is to say that the subjective *mens rea* of intentionally creating a danger for other users of the highway within the meaning of s. 249 of the *Criminal Code* constitutes a "marked departure" from the

---

3 This reference to a "modified objective test" is not meant to reverse the rejection of such a test in *Creighton*. Rather, it is an unfortunate ambiguity, and is merely intended to refer to the fact that the objective test in this context is a marked departure from the norm, not merely a departure, and that the relevant circumstances are to be taken into account.

standard expected of a reasonably prudent driver. Doherty J.A. similarly equates such deliberate action with a "marked and substantial" departure from the norm in the context of a criminal negligence charge in *R. v. Willock* (2006), 210 C.C.C. (3d) 60 (Ont. C.A.), where he states, at para. 32:

> I think the appellant's conduct during the two or three seconds in issue could only reasonably be said to constitute a marked and substantial departure from the conduct expected of a reasonable driver if the appellant deliberately jerked the steering wheel to cause the vehicle to swerve, presumably to either show off or frighten his young passengers. If that finding was reasonably open on the evidence, then the appellant could properly have been convicted of criminal negligence, as he was unable to retain control of the vehicle before it crossed the median and collided with the westbound vehicle. As indicated, I read the trial judge as making that finding. With respect, I do not think that finding was reasonably available on the totality of the evidence.

I agree with the Chief Justice (at para. 75 of her reasons) that the analysis in *Willock* does not have the effect of imposing on the Crown the burden of proving the subjective intention of the accused in order to make out the offence. Doherty J.A. specifically held at para. 31 that "conduct occurring in a two to three second interval can amount to a marked departure from the standard of a reasonable person and demonstrate a wanton or reckless disregard for the life or safety of others." Doherty J.A. simply recognizes, as I do, that evidence about the actual intention of an accused is relevant to a court's objective assessment of whether or not conduct constitutes a marked departure from the norm.

[48] However, subjective *mens rea* of the kind I have just described need not be proven to make out the offence because the mischief Parliament sought to address in enacting s. 249 encompasses a wider range of behaviour. Therefore, while proof of subjective *mens rea* will clearly suffice, it is not essential. In the case of negligence-based offences such as this one, doing the proscribed act with the absence of the appropriate mental state of care may instead suffice to constitute the requisite fault. The presence of objective *mens rea* is determined by assessing the dangerous conduct as against the standard expected of a reasonably prudent driver. If the dangerous conduct constitutes a "marked departure" from that norm, the offence will be made out. As stated earlier, what constitutes a "marked departure" from the standard expected of a reasonably prudent driver is a matter of degree. The lack of care must be serious enough to merit punishment. There is no doubt that conduct occurring in a few seconds can constitute a marked departure from the standard of a reasonable person. Nonetheless, as Doherty J.A. aptly remarked in *Willock*, "conduct that occurs in such a brief time frame in the course of driving, which is otherwise proper in all respects, is more suggestive of the civil rather than the criminal end of the negligence continuum" (para. 31). Although *Willock* concerned the offence of criminal negligence, an offence which is higher on the continuum of negligent driving, this observation is equally apt with respect to the offence of dangerous operation of a motor vehicle.

[49] If the conduct does not constitute a marked departure from the standard expected of a reasonably prudent driver, there is no need to pursue the analysis. The offence will not have been made out. If, on the other hand, the trier of fact is convinced beyond a reasonable doubt that the objectively dangerous conduct constitutes a marked departure from the norm, the trier of fact must consider evidence about the actual state of mind of the accused, if any, to determine whether it raises a reasonable doubt about whether a reasonable person in the accused's position would have been aware of the risk created by this conduct. If there is no such evidence, the court may convict the accused.

4. Application to this Case

[50] First, did Mr. Beatty commit the *actus reus* of the offence? Did he operate his motor vehicle "in a manner that is dangerous to the public, having regard to all the circumstances, including the nature, condition and use of the place at which the motor vehicle is being operated and the amount of traffic that at the time is or might reasonably be expected to be at that place"? I repeat here the Court of Appeal's analysis of the circumstances for convenience:

> However, the evidence showed that there was only one lane for travel in each direction, the traffic was proceeding at or near the posted speed limit of 90 kilometres per hour, the highway was well-travelled, there was limited visibility approaching the curve, and the collision occurred within a split second of the respondent's crossing onto the oncoming lane of traffic.
>
> Viewed objectively, the respondent's failure to confine his vehicle to its own lane of travel was in "all the circumstances" highly dangerous to other persons lawfully using the highway, and in particular those approaching in a westerly direction on their own side of the road. [paras. 23, 24]

[51] Up to this point in the analysis, I would agree with the Court of Appeal. In all the circumstances, Mr. Beatty's failure to confine his vehicle to his own lane of traffic was dangerous to other users of the highway. Further, no suggestion was made at trial that Mr. Beatty was in a state of non-insane automatism at the time. However, this conclusion only answers the *actus reus* part of the offence. The more difficult question is whether Mr. Beatty had the necessary *mens rea*. There is no evidence here of any deliberate intention to create a danger for other users of the highway that could provide an easy answer to that question. Indeed, the limited evidence that was adduced about the actual state of mind of the driver suggested rather that the dangerous conduct was due to a momentary lapse of attention. Hence, the trial judge was correct in finding that the question of *mens rea* in this case turns on whether Mr. Beatty's manner of driving, viewed on an objective basis, constitutes a marked departure from the norm.

[52] In my respectful view, the Court of Appeal erred in faulting the trial judge for addressing her attention to Mr. Beatty's "momentary lack of attention" and his "few seconds of lapsed attention". The trial judge appropriately focussed her

analysis on Mr. Beatty's manner of driving in all the circumstances. She noted that there was no evidence of improper driving before the truck momentarily crossed the centre line and that the "few seconds of clearly negligent driving" was the only evidence about his manner of driving (para. 36). She appropriately considered the totality of the evidence in finding that "the only reasonable inference" was that "he experienced a loss of awareness" that caused him to drive straight instead of following the curve in the road (para. 36). In her view, this momentary lapse of attention was insufficient to found criminal culpability. She concluded that there was "insufficient evidence to support a finding of a marked departure from the standard of care of a prudent driver" (para. 37).

[53] Based on the totality of the evidence, I see no reason to interfere with the trial judge's assessment of Mr. Beatty's conduct in this case and her conclusion on Mr. Beatty's criminal liability. By contrast, it is my respectful view that the Court of Appeal leaped too quickly to the conclusion that the requisite *mens rea* could be made out from the simple fact of the accident occurring, leaving no room for any assessment of Mr. Beatty's conduct along the continuum of negligence.

[54] For these reasons, I would allow the appeal and restore the acquittals.

Chief Justice McLachlin (Binnie and LeBel JJ. concurring) would have preferred the analysis that the "marked departure" requirement applies to both the *actus reus* and the *mens rea* of the offence of dangerous operation of a motor vehicle. She added that a momentary lapse of attention without more cannot establish the *actus reus* and *mens rea* of the offence of dangerous driving. The heavy sanctions and stigma that follow from a criminal offence should not be visited upon a person for a momentary lapse of attention. Provincial regulatory offences appropriately and adequately deal with this sort of conduct. However, additional evidence might show that a momentary lapse is part of a larger pattern that, considered as a whole, establishes the marked departure from the norm required for the offence of dangerous driving.

In a separate opinion Fish J. expressed the view that the *mens rea* for dangerous driving could be established in two ways. In rare cases, the prosecution would be able to establish that the accused drove in a deliberately dangerous manner. In such cases it was not necessary to establish that the conduct was a marked departure from the norm. The fault element can be established, and generally is, by demonstrating that the accused failed to meet the objective standard of a reasonable person in the circumstances. In such cases, the fault element was not the marked departure from the norm of a reasonably prudent driver, but the fact that a reasonably prudent driver in the accused's circumstances would have been aware of the risk of that conduct, and if able to do so, would have acted to avert it.

Reviewing the ruling in *Beatty*

This major ruling on dangerous driving is written in language which applies to any crime requiring objective fault where there is a risk of imprisonment. For such crimes the Court holds that, in contrast to civil liability for negligence or the due diligence standard for regulatory offences, principles of fundamental justice under s. 7 of the *Charter* require proof of a marked departure from the objective norm. A uniquely Canadian *Charter* standard is now firmly in place for crimes based on objective fault. The Court also determines that sometimes it may be necessary to consider the accused's mental state to decide whether the reasonable person would have been aware of the risk. **Do you agree with the court's approach?**

Do you agree with the decision in *Beatty* that causing three deaths on the basis of a momentary lack of attention was not a marked departure from the objective norm? Given *Beatty* expect defences of momentary inattention to be frequently advanced against dangerous driving charges. It should be remembered, though, that in *Beatty* there was no evidence of any other bad driving.

However, most major vehicle accidents happen in a flash and proof of a pattern of bad driving that day will often be hard to come by with witnesses long gone down the highway. Given the lenient ruling on the facts one can expect that many serious accidents on highways, even those involving fatalities, will now almost always have to be dealt with by charges of careless driving under provincial laws where the maximum penalties are typically as low as six months' imprisonment. Dangerous driving acquittals resulted in *R. v. McCaughan* (2009), 65 C.R. (6th) 360 (Man. C.A.), *R. v. Desbiens* (2010), 73 C.R. (6th) 97 (Que. C.A.) and *R. v. Delorey* (2011), 78 C.R. (6th) 66 (N.S. C.A.) (tire conditions of loaner vehicle from car dealership causing accident). See too *R. v. Jiang* (2007), 48 C.R. (6th) 49 (B.C. C.A.) (medical evidence of chronic sleep disorder), *R. v. De Ciantis* (2011), 90 C.R. (6th) 219 (B.C. C.A.) (speeding trucker changing lanes and striking pedestrians walking in slow lane) and *R. v. Adams* (2012), 289 C.C.C. (3d) 339 (P.E.I. C.A.) (accused losing control while avoiding oncoming vehicle while passing). However, there were convictions in *R. v. Settle* (2010), 261 C.C.C. (3d) 45 (B.C. C.A.) (evidence of prior drinking), *R. v. Relkie* (2011), 278 C.C.C. (3d) 469 (B.C. C.A.), leave to appeal refused (2012), 435 N.R. 387 (note) (S.C.C.) (deliberately moving into oncoming traffic to pass), *R. v. Gould* (2012), 297 C.C.C. (3d) 277 (Alta. C.A.) (street racing causing serious injury), *R. c. Truchon* (2016), 32 C.R. (7th) 420 (C.A. Que.) (sports vehicle travelling at almost twice speed limit colliding with vehicle signaling right at intersection but making left turn, killing driver and injuring passenger) and *R. v. Burger* (2017), 35 C.R. (7th) 183 (Ont. C.A.) (accused fully depressed accelerator while reversing into store entrance, killing two bystanders). The Supreme Court of Canada applied *Beatty* to acquit in *R. v. Roy*, 93 C.R. (6th) 1, [2012] 2 S.C.R. 60 (crossing snow-covered highway in foggy conditions and striking tractor-trailer). However, the highest Court restored a conviction in *R. c. Bélanger*, 299 C.C.C. (3d) 417, [2013] 1 S.C.R. 401 (passing on double line).

The Court decides that no personal factors can be considered on an objective fault test on the basis that this had been determined in *R. v. Creighton*, [1993] 3

S.C.R. 3, 23 C.R. (4th) 189, 83 C.C.C. (3d) 346. We shall see in later chapters that the Court itself has consistently decided since that decision that, in the context of defences such as self-defence, necessity and duress, the objective approach must be modified to require that individual factors be considered so that the reasonable person is considered in the context of the accused's situation and experience. In the law of the tort of negligence the Court has no problem taking into account personal factors. In establishing the tort of negligent investigation in *Hill v. Hamilton-Wentworth (Regional Municipality) Police Services Board*, 50 C.R. (6th) 279, [2007] 3 S.C.R. 129 Chief Justice McLachlin writing for the 6-3 majority observes that:

> The general rule is that the standard of care in negligence is that of the reasonable person in similar circumstances. In cases of professional negligence, this rule is qualified by an additional principle: the defendant must "live up to the standards possessed by persons of reasonable skill and experience in that calling". (para. 69)

Why then are we not to take into account the experience and situation of the driver in a dangerous driving case? Are we, for example, to hold a driver of a large transport truck, or a police officer at the wheel of a cruiser, criminally responsible for bad driving only on the standard of the average, reasonable driver? The approach appears quite unrealistic and will likely be ignored in trial courts with live witnesses, as has been the case with this aspect of the *Creighton* ruling. Can a trier of fact really overlook such obvious factors as age and experience? In *R. v. Tayfel* (2009), 72 C.R. (6th) 45 (Man. C.A.) the Court took into account the experience of bush pilots in deciding upon the amount of fuel needed. The accused miscalculated the amount of fuel in his tanks and did not use the flight standard for non-visual flying. He ran out of fuel and crash-landed near Winnipeg, injuring four persons and killing a passenger. The Court of Appeal found him guilty of dangerous operation of an aircraft but not guilty of criminal negligence charges.

For various views on *Beatty* see Stuart "*Beatty*: *Charter* Standard of Marked Departure for All Crimes of Negligence" (2008), 54 C.R. (6th) 33; David Tanovich, "The Implications of *Beatty* for Criminal Negligence" (2008), 54 C.R. (6th) 38; and Hamish Stewart, "*Beatty*: Towards a Coherent Law of Penal Negligence" (2008), 54 C.R. (6th) 45.

At one point in *Beatty* the Court speaks of the offence of criminal negligence under s. 216 as an offence "higher on the continuum of negligent driving" (para. 48). There is no longer a specific crime of negligent driving but a motorist could still be charged with criminal negligence causing bodily harm, criminal negligence causing death or manslaughter. We have seen that the Court was infamously equally divided in *R. v. Tutton*, [1989] 1 S.C.R. 1392, 69 C.R. (3d) 289, 48 C.C.C. (3d) 129 on what to make of this special fault element of "criminal negligence" requiring proof of conduct showing wanton or reckless disregard for lives or safety. Most provincial courts before and after *Tutton* have applied the marked departure from the objective norm test. Yet some courts insist that this a form of fault higher than dangerous driving (see *R. c. Palin* (1999), 135 C.C.C. (3d) 119 (Que. C.A.), leave to appeal refused (1999), 243 N.R. 196 (note) (S.C.C.) and *R. v. L. (J.)* (2006), 204 C.C.C. (3d) 324 (Ont. C.A.)).

It took a stunning period of some 20 years for the Supreme Court to resolve the impasse in *Tutton* respecting the meaning of criminal negligence under s. 219:

R. v. F. (J.)

(2008), 60 C.R. (6th) 205, 2008 CarswellOnt 6339, 2008 CarswellOnt 6340, 236 C.C.C. (3d) 421 (S.C.C.)

The split verdict in *Tutton* has since seemingly been resolved by the Court in *F. (J.)*, though that decision was actually considering a technical appeal based on inconsistent jury verdicts rather than directly addressing the issue of the fault requirement for criminal negligence. In the course of that decision Justice Fish for a majority of the Court stated:

[7] The fault element required for conviction at trial was essentially common to both counts of manslaughter. On count 1, the requisite fault element was that of the underlying offence of criminal negligence; on count 2, the requisite fault element was that of failure to provide the necessaries of life. Neither criminal negligence nor failure to provide the necessaries of life requires proof of intention or actual foresight of a prohibited consequence. Under both counts, the jury was required to determine not what the respondent knew or intended, but what he ought to have foreseen.

[8] On the count alleging failure to provide necessaries, the Crown was bound to establish that the respondent's failure to protect his foster child represented "a *marked departure* from the conduct of a reasonably prudent parent in circumstances where it was objectively foreseeable that the failure to provide the necessaries of life would lead to a *risk* of danger to the life, or a *risk* of permanent endangerment to the health, of the child": *R. v. Naglik*, [1993] 3 S.C.R. 122, at p. 143 (emphasis added). It will later become apparent why I have emphasized the word "risk" in this description of the offence by the Chief Justice, speaking for the court on this point.

[9] On the count alleging criminal negligence, the Crown was bound to show that the respondent's very same omission represented a marked and substantial departure (as opposed to a marked departure) from the conduct of a reasonably prudent parent in circumstances where the accused either recognized and ran an obvious and serious risk to the life of his child or, alternatively, gave no thought to that risk: *R. v. Tutton*, [1989] 1 S.C.R. 1392, at pp. 1430-31, *R. v. Sharp* (1984),12 C.C.C. (3d) 428 (Ont. C.A.)

Note that in this passage Justice Fish has done more than decide that criminal negligence in s. 222(5)(b) is based on objective fault. He has also distinguished between a "marked and substantial" departure from the required level of care, which is required for a conviction of criminal negligence, as opposed to a mere "marked departure" from that standard, required as a *Charter* standard for other objective fault crimes. As a practical matter, this is likely to be a hard line for courts to draw. This normative distinction between degrees of gross negligence seems likely to confuse and cause head-scratching by lawyers, judges and jurors. Be that as it may, until otherwise advised there are now three degrees of objective fault requirements:

1. Due diligence with the onus reversed for regulatory offences (as a matter of common law presumption under *Sault Ste. Marie* or as a *Charter* standard where there is a risk of imprisonment) .This is a standard of simple negligence like that long applied for the tort of negligence.

2.   A marked departure from the objective norm as a *Charter* standard for crimes with objective fault requirements (*Beatty*) (gross negligence).

3.   A marked and substantial departure from the objective norm for offences bases on criminal negligence under s. 219 *F. (J.)* (worse than gross negligence)

It may have been preferable for the Court to have rested content with the notion that the fault requirements for criminal negligence and failing to provide necessities of life are essentially the same: a marked departure from the objective norm, and then to have pointed to the higher stigma and especially the higher penalties declared by Parliament for criminal negligence. So jurors could then in future have been advised that criminal negligence is the more serious offence carrying a larger penalty. The particular problem here making *F. (J.)* a hard case is that the two counts charged were both forms of manslaughter where the maximum penalty of life is the same whatever the underlying offence. It is not clear why the Crown chose to complicate matters by charging the two counts.

The majority in *F. (J.)* confirmed, as did the majority in *Beatty*, that negligence is a form of fault, not *actus reus*. This is consistent with the definition of forms of fault in modern *Criminal Codes*, and also with the *Charter* standard that intentional conduct must be punished more than negligent conduct: *R. v. Martineau.*

PROBLEMS

1. The accused was charged with criminal negligence causing bodily harm. He had attempted to circumcise his four-year-old son in observance of an upcoming religious holiday. The accused was recently converted and decided that following the laws of Moses "would make things right with God". No medical professional would perform the procedure. The accused had researched circumcision but had no medical training. The procedure caused bodily harm which had to be remedied in a hospital.

Compare *R. v. W. (D.J.)* (2011), 282 C.C.C. (3d) 352 (B.C. C.A.), leave to appeal allowed (2012), 435 N.R. 394 (note) (S.C.C.), affirmed [2012] 3 S.C.R. 396, 294 C.C.C. (3d) 480.

2. The accused was charged with criminal negligence causing death after a 22-month-old boy in her care drowned in a bathtub. The deceased was one of five toddler-age foster children living with the accused, her husband and their nine-year-old daughter. On the evening in question, the accused placed the deceased in the bathtub in 1-2 inches of water with the taps off. He was able to sit upright, stand and even climb out of the bathtub by himself, and had never in the past turned on the taps in the bathtub. She left the bathroom and stepped into the kitchen for a few minutes. While she was gone, the infant turned on the hot water tap and drowned in the scalding hot water. He had never turned on the taps before.

Compare *R. v. Wudrich* (2013), 100 C.R. (6th) 381 (Sask. Q.B.).

3. The accused was charged with criminal negligence causing bodily harm. He took his dog off leash in an empty, confined area and the dog bit

an eleven-year-old boy who jumped into the area. The dog had no history of aggression. The accused had extensive experience in training dogs.

Compare *R. v. Vantroba* (2015), 19 C.R. (7th) 92 (Ont. S.C.J.).

4. The accused was charged with two counts of criminal negligence causing death. He was the officer of the watch in sole control of operating and navigating a passenger ferry, *The Queen of the North*, en route from Prince Rupert to Port Hardy. At the time the accused was alone on the bridge as the officer of the watch with a female helmsman. They had recently mutually terminated a six-month affair. Both testified as to very little communication between them at the time and only brief small talk. The ferry failed to make the normal course change, continued at full cruising speed of just over 17 knots for 12 to 14 minutes, and then struck an island and sank. Two passengers died. Relying on a model direction suggested by the Canadian Judicial Council the trial judge instructed the jury that the Crown must prove that the accused's conduct showed a marked and substantial departure from the conduct of a reasonable person in the circumstances but also that "[i]n deciding what a reasonable person would have done or foreseen, you must not take into account [the accused's] individual characteristics or experience". However the Crown was permitted to cross-examine the accused to the effect that no mariner with his experience, training and qualifications would have performed as he testified.

Compare *R. v. Lilgert* (2014), 318 C.C.C. (3d) 30, 16 C.R. (7th) 346 (B.C. C.A.) at para. 29, leave to appeal refused 2015 CarswellBC 1285, 2015 CarswellBC 1286 (S.C.C.).

(c) Crimes Based on Predicate Offences

On the authority of *Creighton* and *DeSousa* there are some offences based on predicate offences where the fault requirement regarding the consequence of the underlying offence is much reduced but constitutional. The problem will be how to identify them. Thus far there are three recognized by the Supreme Court: *DeSousa* concerns the offence of unlawful act causing harm (s. 269); *Creighton* the manslaughter category of unlawful act causing death (s. 222(5)(a)); and *R. v. Godin*, [1994] 2 S.C.R. 484, 31 C.R. (4th) 33, 89 C.C.C. (3d) 574, aggravated assault (s. 268). In each case the unlawful act is interpreted to require objective foresight of harm. *DeSousa* also held that the unlawful act must be a provincial or federal offence, that the fault for the predicate offence must be proved and that this cannot be absolute liability. There is no requirement of a marked departure from the objective norm beyond proof of the underlying offence. However, where the predicate or underlying offence is one of negligence the gross departure limit must be applied to it. See *R. v. Gosset* (1993), 23 C.R. (4th) 280 (S.C.C.) at 284.

Beatty requires a marked departure for all objective crimes. Logically, this should include those based on predicate offences given the reduced fault requirement of an objectively dangerous act. On this view the offence of unlawful act manslaughter, for example, may well now always require a marked departure from the norm. See further L. Wilson, "Too Many Manslaughters" (2007) 52 Crim.

L.Q. 433 and "*Beatty, J.F.* and the Law of Manslaughter" (2010) 47 Alberta L. Rev. 651. In the view of the majority in *F. (J.)* manslaughter by criminal negligence would require a marked and substantial departure from the objective norm.

R. v. DeSOUSA

[1992] 2 S.C.R. 944, 15 C.R. (4th) 66, 76 C.C.C. (3d) 124,
1992 CarswellOnt 100, 1992 CarswellOnt 1006F

A fight broke out at a New Year's Eve party. The accused was involved in the fight. A bystander was injured on the arm when a bottle, allegedly thrown by the accused, broke against a wall and a glass fragment struck the bystander. The accused was charged with unlawfully causing bodily harm contrary to s. 269 of the *Criminal Code*. At the outset of the trial, before any evidence was heard, the accused brought a motion to have s. 269 declared of no force or effect on the ground that it violated s. 7 of the *Charter*. The trial judge granted the motion and quashed the indictment. He found that s. 269 created criminal responsibility for causing bodily harm by way of an unlawful act. The unlawful act could be a violation of a federal or provincial statute, including an offence of absolute liability. Since the section also allowed the possibility of imprisonment, it contravened s. 7 of the *Charter* and was not justified under s. 1. On appeal, the Court of Appeal overturned the motion judgment and set aside the order quashing the indictment. The accused appealed. Notice that an assault is not an essential element of the offence charged in this case; if an assault caused bodily harm the accused would be culpable under s. 267(1)(b).

SOPINKA J. (CORY, GONTHIER, MCLACHLIN, and IACOBUCCI JJ. concurring):

. . . .

B. Section 269 of the *Criminal Code* —

To be brought within the ambit of s. 269, an accused must have committed an underlying unlawful offence (otherwise referred to as the predicate offence) and have caused bodily harm to another person as a result of committing that underlying offence. For liability to be imposed for unlawfully causing bodily harm, the harm caused must have sufficient causal connection to the underlying offence committed (see *R. v. Wilmot*, (1940), 74 C.C.C. 1 (Alta. C.A.), at pp. 17 and 26-27 [C.C.C.], appeal dismissed for want of jurisdiction [1941] S.C.R. 53, 75 C.C.C. 161. The requirement of an underlying "unlawful" offence includes at its most general, and subject to the restrictions discussed below, only offences prohibited by federal or provincial legislation.

. . . .

(1)   The Mental Element Requirement of Section 269

The major issue raised in this appeal concerns the mental element required by s. 269 of the *Code*. After delineating the statutorily required mental element, the question of the constitutional sufficiency of this element will then be addressed to determine whether it passes constitutional muster.

It is axiomatic that in criminal law there should be no responsibility without personal fault. A fault requirement was asserted to be a fundamental aspect of our common law by this court in *R. v. Sault Ste. Marie (City)*, [1978] 2 S.C.R. 1299, 3 C.R. (3d) 30, 40 C.C.C. (2d) 353, and as a matter of constitutional law under s. 7 of the *Charter* in *Reference re s. 94(2) of the Motor Vehicle Act (British Columbia)*, [1985] 2 S.C.R. 486, 48 C.R. (3d) 289, 23 C.C.C. (3d) 289, (sub nom. *Constitutional Question Act, R.S.B.C. 1979, Chap. 63*) [1986] D.L.Q. 90 (headnote) [hereafter *Re B.C. Motor Vehicle Act.*] As a matter of statutory interpretation, a provision should not be interpreted to lack any element of personal fault unless the statutory language mandates such an interpretation in clear and unambiguous terms. Unlike most offences, the mental element of s. 269 is composed of two separate requirements. The first requirement is that the mental element of the underlying offence of s. 269 be satisfied. The second requirement is that the additional fault requirement supplied by the wording of s. 269, discussed more fully, *infra*, also be satisfied.

(a)   *The mental element of the underlying offence*

To be convicted under s. 269, the prosecution must first satisfy the mental element requirement of the underlying offence. In interpreting the ambit of the underlying offences covered by s. 269 it is important to recognize the abhorrence of the criminal law for offences of absolute liability. While not all underlying offences will have a possibility of imprisonment and despite the fact that s. 269 has a fault requirement in addition to that supplied by the underlying offence, as a matter of statutory interpretation, underlying offences of absolute liability are excluded from forming the basis for a prosecution under s. 269. For the reasons given by this court in *Sault Ste. Marie, supra*, and *Re B.C. Motor Vehicle Act, supra*, s. 269 should not be interpreted so as to bootstrap underlying offences of absolute liability into the criminal law. The criminal law is based on proof of personal fault and this concept is jealously guarded when a court is asked to interpret criminal provisions, especially those with potentially serious penal consequences. This statutory conclusion is mandated by the general presumption in the interpretation of criminal statutes against absolute liability and the absence of clear words to the contrary to rebut this presumption. Thus, the concept of "unlawful" as it is used in s. 269 does not include any underlying offence of absolute liability. The inclusion of such offences would be contrary to the general canons of criminal interpretation quite apart from any *Charter* considerations (see particularly *R. v. Baril*, [1979] 2 S.C.R. 547, 8 C.R. (3d) 68, 46 C.C.C. (2d)

257, at p. 553 [S.C.R.], and *Beaver v. R.*, [1957] S.C.R. 531, 26 C.R. 193, 118 C.C.C. 129, at pp. 537-538 and 542-543 [S.C.R.]). Although not relying on constitutional requirements in foreclosing the possibility of absolute liability offences forming the predicate offences of s. 269, certainly principles of fundamental justice require no less.

In addition to satisfying the statutorily required mental element of the underlying offence, the mental element of the underlying offence must also be constitutionally sufficient in its own right. If the underlying offence contains a constitutionally insufficient mental element, it is of no force or effect and thus cannot form the basis for a prosecution under s. 269. The underlying offence must be valid in law on its own before it can be used to support a charge under s. 269.

(b) *The meaning of "unlawful" in section 269*

In addition to the mental element required by the underlying offence, the wording of s. 269, and particularly the case law interpreting the term "unlawfully", imports an additional aspect to the mental element of s. 269. The case law interpreting the use of this term in similar provisions has focused on the offence most commonly known as unlawful act manslaughter. While manslaughter is not the offence at issue in this appeal, the case law which seeks to interpret the term "unlawful" in that context is instructive.

The leading English authority on the issue of the meaning of "unlawful" in this area is *R. v. Larkin* (1942), 29 Cr. App. R. 18, where the Court of Criminal Appeal held that:

> Where the act which a person is engaged in performing is unlawful, then if at the same time it is a dangerous act, that is, an act which is likely to injure another person, and quite inadvertently the doer of the act causes the death of that other person by that act, then he is guilty of manslaughter. (At p. 23 [Cr. App. R.].)

English authority has consistently held that the underlying unlawful act required by its manslaughter offence requires proof that the unlawful act was "likely to injure another person" or in other words put the bodily integrity of others at risk. . . . This position has also been adopted by most Canadian courts. [citations omitted.]

. . . .

Despite ample authority that the underlying act must be objectively dangerous in order to sustain a conviction under what is now s. 222(5)(*a*), the law in this area is not entirely free from doubt. In *R. v. Smithers*, [1978] 1 S.C.R. 506, 40 C.R.N.S. 79, 34 C.C.C. (2d) 427, Dickson J. (as he then was) adopted certain comments made by G. Arthur Martin (later Martin J.A.) in a short case note on the English *Larkin* case. The adopted comments included the following:

There are many unlawful acts which are not dangerous in themselves and are not likely to cause injury which, nevertheless if they cause death, render the actor guilty of culpable homicide...

. . . .

In the case of so-called intentional crimes where death is an unintended consequence the actor is always guilty of manslaughter at least.

("Criminal Law — Voluntary and Involuntary Manslaughter — Lawful and Unlawful Acts" (1943), 21 Can. Bar. Rev. 503, at pp. 504-505; cited in *Smithers, supra*, at p. 519. [S.C.R.])

This passage appears to raise doubt as to whether the "unlawful act" must be inherently dangerous to sustain a manslaughter conviction. This issue was not addressed in *Smithers*, however, as the assault which occurred in that case was clearly an intentional, dangerous, act. As well, *Smithers* was a case concerned with the issue of causation and not the meaning to be given to the term "unlawful act". Finally, *Smithers* was not argued under the *Charter*. In the absence of a more definitive statement or a more extensive analysis of the issue, I am reluctant to freeze the meaning of "unlawful" for the purposes of s. 269 based on the 1943 comments of even as persuasive a source as G. Arthur Martin. More telling, and also more considered, authority was provided by Martin J.A. in *Tennant, supra*, which predates *Smithers* but was not discussed by Dickson J. in the latter decision. In *Tennant*, a Court of Appeal panel composed of Gale C.J.O. and Brooke and Martin JJ.A. rendered a *per curiam* judgment which concluded that:

When death is accidentally caused by the commission of an unlawful act which any reasonable person would inevitably realize must subject another person to, at least, the risk of some harm resulting therefrom, albeit not serious harm, that is manslaughter. (At p. 96 [C.C.C., p. 19 C.R.N.S.].)

The court later noted that:

... if death was caused by the *accidental discharge* of the fire-arm in the commission of such unlawful act and if the jury were satisfied beyond a reasonable doubt that the *unlawful act* was such as any reasonable person would inevitably realize must subject another to the risk of, at least, some harm, albeit not serious harm, the death would amount to manslaughter. [Emphasis in original.] (At p. 96 [C.C.C., p. 19 C.R.N.S.].)

The court thus substantially adopted the English position as articulated in *Larkin*.

In accordance with the English law and in furtherance of the developing Canadian case law, the most principled approach to the meaning of "unlawful" in the context of s. 269 is to require that the unlawful act be at least objectively dangerous. This conclusion is both supported by the meaning given to the word "unlawful act" by virtually all of the lower courts and also is in accord with the emerging jurisprudence of this court in regard to personal fault.

Objective foresight of bodily harm should be required for both criminal and non-criminal unlawful acts which underlie a s. 269 prosecution. I can see no reason why there should be a difference between the two categories of acts. There is no need to differentiate between criminal and non-criminal unlawful acts when one unifying concept is available. Thus the test is one of objective foresight of bodily harm for all underlying offences. The act must be both unlawful, as described above, *and* one that is likely to subject another person to danger of harm or injury. This bodily harm must be more than merely trivial or transitory in nature and will in most cases involve an act of violence done deliberately to another person. In interpreting what constitutes an objectively dangerous act, the courts should strive to avoid attaching penal sanctions to mere inadvertence. The contention that no dangerousness requirement is required if the unlawful act is criminal should be rejected. The premise on which this proposition is based is that most, if not all, criminal acts are inherently dangerous. This premise is an overstatement inasmuch as a large part of the criminal law is concerned with offences against property and other interests which are not inherently dangerous. But, even if this premise were accepted, the difference between the two positions would be simply one of semantics. To maintain the correct focus it is preferable to inquire whether a reasonable person would inevitably realize that the underlying unlawful act would subject another person to the risk of bodily harm rather than getting sidetracked on a question regarding the classification of the offence.

(2) Constitutional Sufficiency

The mental element of s. 269 has two separate aspects. The first aspect of the mental element is the requirement that an underlying offence with a constitutionally sufficient mental element has been committed. Additionally, s. 269 requires that the prosecution prove that the bodily harm caused by the underlying unlawful act was objectively foreseeable. This latter requirement insures that all prosecutions under s. 269 contain *at least* a fault requirement based on an objective standard. As this court has not indicated that fundamental justice requires fault based on a subjective standard for all offences, the mental element required by s. 269 passes constitutional muster unless s. 269 is one of those few offences which due to its stigma and penalty require fault based on a subjective standard. I agree with the respondent and intervenors that s. 269 has neither the stigma nor criminal sanction to require a more demanding mental element than it already has. The criminal sanction is flexible and thus can be tailored to suit the circumstances of the case. The stigma associated with conviction will generally reflect the degree of opprobrium which the underlying offence attracts. The stigma attached to the underlying offence will in turn influence the minimum mental requirement for that offence.

Unless a minimum mind state of subjective intention in regard to consequences is constitutionally required, the test discussed above satisfies the dictates of s. 7 of the *Charter*. I will now consider that issue.

C. Foresight of Consequences

Although I have concluded by means of statutory interpretation that s. 269 requires objective foresight of the consequences of an accused's unlawful act, the appellant argues that s. 7 of the *Charter* requires subjective foresight of all consequences which comprise part of the *actus reus* of an offence. The appellant notes that in *R. v. Martineau*, [1990] 2 S.C.R. 633, 79 C.R. (3d) 129, 58 C.C.C. (3d) 353, Lamer C.J.C., speaking for the majority of the court, discussed a:

> general principle that criminal liability for a particular result is not justified except where the actor possesses a culpable mental state in respect of that result: . . . At p. 645 [S.C.R.].)

The appellant also relies on *R. v. Metro News Ltd.* (1986), 53 C.R. (3d) 289, 29 C.C.C. (3d) 35 (C.A.), leave to appeal refused, [1986] 2 S.C.R. viii, 64 C.R. (3d) xxx (note), 29 C.C.C. (3d) 35n, for a similar proposition that:

> The minimum and necessary mental element required for criminal liability for most crimes is knowledge of the circumstances which make up the *actus reus* of the crime and foresight or intention with respect to any consequence required to constitute the *actus reus* of the crime. (At pp. 54-55 [C.C.C.], p. 309 C.R.].)

The appellant submits that this authority supports a requirement that the minimum mental element required by s. 7 of the *Charter* for s. 269 includes an intention to cause bodily harm. In isolation, it is true that the language used in some earlier decisions of this court could be interpreted as suggested by the appellant. This proposition draws additional support from statements such as those of Wilson J. in *R. v. Docherty*, [1989] 2 S.C.R. 941, 72 C.R. (3d) 1, 51 C.C.C. (3d) 1, where she infers that proof of intention is required in regard to *each* of the elements of the *actus reus*. Wilson J. states:

> A full *mens rea* offence under the *Criminal Code* demands that the accused have an intent to perform the acts that constitute the *actus reus* of the offence. (At p. 958 [S.C.R.].)

As one of the elements of the *actus reus* in this appeal is that bodily harm be produced, it is arguable that the case law of this court has implied that foresight of the consequences of an act must be proved when such consequences constitute an essential element of the offence. This argument, however, misconstrues and overgeneralizes the language used by this court in these earlier judgments (see also *R. v. Rees*, [1956] S.C.R. 640, 24 C.R. 1, 115 C.C.C. 1, and *R. v. Pappajohn*, [1980] 2 S.C.R. 120, 14 C.R. (3d) 243, 19 C.R. (3d) 97, 52 C.C.C. (2d) 481, at p. 139 [S.C.R.]). In the circumstances of *Docherty*, the offence definition itself required intention in regard to all aspects of the *actus reus* and thus this proposition was not meant to be set down as an overriding principle of criminal law. Equally, in *Martineau* it was only as a result of the stigma and penal consequences of a murder conviction that subjective foresight of death was required. Here again, it was not meant to be stated as a general principle of criminal law. As far back as Blackstone's *Commentaries*, it was recognized that criminal guilt did not always require foresight of the consequences of an unlawful act:

> If a man be doing any thing *unlawful*, and a consequence ensues which he did not foresee or intend, as the death of a man or the like, his want of foresight shall be no excuse; for, being guilty of one offence, in doing antecedently what is in itself unlawful, he is criminally guilty of whatever consequence may follow the first misbehaviour.

(Blackstone, *Commentaries on the Laws of England* (1769), Book IV, at p. 27.)

In *R. v. Nguyen*, [1990] 2 S.C.R. 906, 79 C.R. (3d) 332, (sub nom. *R. v. Nguyen; R. v. Hess*) 59 C.C.C. (3d) 161 [hereinafter *Hess*], the court concluded that a meaningful mental element was required in regard to a *blameworthy* element of the *actus reus*. Provided that there is a sufficiently blameworthy element in the *actus reus* to which a culpable mental state is attached, there is no additional requirement that any other element of the *actus reus* be linked to this mental state or a further culpable mental state. As inferred by Blackstone, *supra*, provided that the actor is already engaged in a culpable activity, foresight of consequences is not required in order to hold that actor responsible for the results of his or her unlawful activity. Lamer C.J.C. stated in *Martineau* that "[i]f Parliament wishes to deter persons from causing bodily harm during certain offences, then it should punish persons for causing the bodily harm" (p. 647 [S.C.R.]). This is exactly what s. 269 attempts to do. In this particular provision the mental element requirement is composed of both the mental element of the underlying unlawful act *and* the additional requirement of objective foresight of bodily harm. There is, however, no constitutional requirement that intention, either on an objective or a subjective basis, extend to the consequences of unlawful acts in general.

The absence of a constitutional requirement that intention extend to all aspects of an unlawful act was discussed by Wilson J. in *R. v. Bernard*, [1988] 2 S.C.R. 833, 67 C.R. (3d) 113, 45 C.C.C. (3d) 1, at pp. 888-889 [S.C.R.], where she concludes that the minimal element of the application of force is sufficient for a conviction for sexual assault causing bodily harm. She inferentially confirms that s. 7 of the *Charter* does not mandate intention in regard to all of the consequences required by the offence. The contrary position, that intention must extend to all of the required consequences of an offence, is not supported by the case law and should not be adopted as a constitutional requirement.

There are many provisions where one need not intend all of the consequences of an action. As was pointed out in *Hess*, *supra*, there must be an element of personal fault in regard to a culpable aspect of the *actus reus*, but not necessarily in regard to each and every element of the *actus reus*. The requirement of fault in regard to a meaningful aspect of the *actus reus* is necessary to prevent punishing the mentally, and morally innocent and is in keeping with a long line of cases of this court including *Rees*, *supra*, and *Pappajohn*, *supra*. In many offences, such as assault or dangerous driving, the offence is made out regardless of the consequences of the act but the consequences can be used to aggravate liability for the offence. For example, both assault and assault causing bodily harm have identical *mens rea* requirements and the element of causing bodily harm is merely used to classify the offence. No principle of fundamental justice prevents Parliament from treating crimes with certain consequences as more serious than crimes which lack those consequences.

A number of *Criminal Code* offences call for a more serious charge if certain consequences follow. To require intention in relation to each and every consequence would bring a large number of offences into question including manslaughter (s. 222(5)), criminal negligence causing bodily harm (s. 221), criminal negligence causing death (s. 220), dangerous operation causing bodily harm (s. 249(3)), dangerous operation causing death (s. 249(4)), impaired driving causing bodily harm (s. 255(2)), impaired driving causing death (s. 255(3)), assault causing bodily harm (s. 267(1)(*b*)), aggravated assault (s. 268), sexual assault causing bodily harm (s. 272(*c*)), aggravated sexual assault (s. 273), mischief causing danger to life (s. 430(2)) and arson causing bodily harm (s. 433(*b*)). As noted by Professor Colvin, "[i]t would, however, be an error to suppose that *actus reus* and *mens rea* always match in this neat way" (E. Colvin, *Principles of Criminal Law*, 2nd ed. (Toronto: Carswell, 1991), at p. 55).

Conduct may fortuitously result in more or less serious consequences depending on the circumstances in which the consequences arise. The same act of assault may injure one person but not another. The implicit rationale of the law in this area is that it is acceptable to distinguish between criminal responsibility for equally reprehensible acts on the basis of the harm that is actually caused. This is reflected in the creation of higher maximum penalties for offences with more serious consequences. Courts and legislators acknowledge the harm actually caused by concluding that in otherwise equal cases a more serious consequence will dictate a more serious response.

There appears to be a general principle in Canada and elsewhere that, in the absence of an express legislative direction, the mental element of an offence attaches only to the underlying offence and not to the aggravating circumstances (Colvin, *supra*, at p. 57). This has been confirmed by this court in a number of cases including those which have held that sexual assault requires intention simply in relation to the assault and not any aggravating circumstance (see *R. v. Chase*, [1987] 2 S.C.R. 293, 59 C.R. (3d) 193, 37 C.C.C. (3d) 97, and *R. v. Bernard*, *supra*, at pp. 888-889) [S.C.R.]. To require fault in regard to each consequence of an action in order to establish liability for causing that consequence would substantially restructure current notions of criminal responsibility. Such a result cannot be founded on the constitutional aversion to punishing the morally innocent. One is not morally innocent simply because a particular consequence of an unlawful act was unforeseen by that actor. In punishing for unforeseen consequences the law is not punishing the morally innocent but those who cause injury through avoidable unlawful action. Neither basic principles of criminal law, nor the dictates of fundamental justice require, by necessity, intention in relation to the consequences of an otherwise blameworthy act.

DISPOSITION

On a proper interpretation of s. 269 of the *Code*, the concept of an unlawful act as it is used in that section includes only federal and provincial offences. Excluded from this general category of offences are any offences which are based on absolute liability and which have constitutionally insufficient mental elements on their own. Additionally, the term "unlawfully", as it is used in this section requires an act which is at least objectively dangerous. Interpreted in this way s. 269 complies with the requirements of s. 7 of the *Charter*. In the absence of a violation of s. 7, there is no violation of s. 11(*d*).

For a critical comment on *DeSousa* see Stuart, "The Supreme Court Drastically Reduces the Constitutional Requirement of Fault: A Triumph of Pragmatism and Law Enforcement Expediency" (1992), 15 C.R. (4th) 88.

R. v. CREIGHTON

[1993] 3 S.C.R. 3, 23 C.R. (4th) 189, 83 C.C.C. (3d) 346,
1993 CarswellOnt 115, 1993 CarswellOnt 989

The Court divided 5-4 on the issue of whether the objective test for unlawful act manslaughter required reasonable foresight of death (Lamer C.J. for the minority) or merely reasonable foresight of bodily harm (McLachlin J. for the majority).

LAMER C.J. (SOPINKA, IACOBUCCI and MAJOR JJ. concurring): —

18 It is now well established that there is a group of offences, albeit a small group, that requires a subjectively determined culpable mental state in relation to the prohibited result.

. . . .

20 The only basis upon which subjective foresight of death or the risk of death could be found to be constitutionally required in the case of unlawful act manslaughter, therefore, would be to find that the offence is one of those crimes for which "because of the special nature of the stigma attached to a conviction therefore or the available penalties, the principles of fundamental justice require a *mens rea* reflecting the particular nature of that crime": see *R. v. Vaillancourt*, per Lamer J., at p. 653.

21 There are two main branches to the analysis of social stigma. First the court must look to the conduct being punished to determine if it is of sufficient gravity to import significant moral opprobrium on the individual found guilty of engaging in such conduct. In the case of manslaughter under s. 222(5)(a), the conduct in question consists of killing someone as a consequence of committing an unlawful act. In this respect, there may well be no difference between the *actus reus* of manslaughter and that of murder; arguably both give rise to the stigma of being labelled by the state and the community as responsible for the wrongful death of another. Clearly, there can be no conduct in our society more grave than taking the life of another without justification.

22 The second branch of the stigma test concerns the moral blameworthiness not of the offence, but of the offender found guilty of committing it. As a general proposition, more stigma will attach to those who knowingly engage in wrongful conduct than to those who recklessly or inadvertently engage in the same conduct. . .

23 In my view, the stigma which attaches to a conviction for unlawful act manslaughter is significant, but does not approach the opprobrium reserved in our society for those who knowingly or intentionally take the life of another. It is for this reason that manslaughter developed as a separate offence from murder at common law.

[Chief Justice Lamer then went on to hold that although objective fault was sufficient, the stigma associated with manslaughter required symmetry between the external and fault elements:]

29 Thus, as I stated, unlawful act manslaughter falls into the class of offences where a mental element in relation to the consequence must be established, but in any event, I find the stigma attached to a conviction for culpable homicide, albeit culpable homicide which is not murder, to be significant enough to require, at a minimum, objective foresight of the risk of death in order for the offence to comply with s. 7 of the *Charter*.

McLACHLIN J. (L'HEUREUX-DUBÉ, GONTHIER and CORY JJ. concurring) (and LAFOREST concurring separately): — The *Criminal Code* defines three general types of culpable homicide. There is murder, the intentional killing of another human being. There is infanticide, the intentional killing of a child. All other culpable homicides fall into the residual category of manslaughter.

Manslaughter is a crime of venerable lineage. It covers a wide variety of circumstances. Two requirements are constant: (1) conduct causing the death of another person; and (2) fault short of intention to kill. That fault may consist either in committing another unlawful act which causes the death, or in criminal negligence. The common-law classification of manslaughter is reflected in the definition of culpable homicide in s. 222(5) of the *Criminal Code*.

. . . .

The structure of the offence of manslaughter depends on a predicate offence of an unlawful act or criminal negligence, coupled with a homicide. It is now settled that the fact that an offence depends upon a predicate offence does not render it unconstitutional, provided that the predicate offence involves a dangerous act, is not an offence of absolute liability, and is not unconstitutional: *R. v. DeSousa*, [1992] 2 S.C.R. 944. But a further objection is raised in this case. It is said that the offence of manslaughter is unconstitutional because it requires only foreseeability of the risk of bodily harm and not foreseeability of death, and that the trial judge erred in requiring only foreseeability of bodily harm.

The cases establish that in addition to the *actus reus* and *mens rea* associated with the underlying act, all that is required to support a manslaughter conviction is reasonable foreseeability of the risk of bodily harm. While s. 222(5)(*a*) does not expressly require foreseeable bodily harm, it has been so interpreted: see *R. v. DeSousa*, *supra*. The unlawful act must be objectively dangerous, that is likely to injure another person. The law of unlawful act manslaughter has not, however, gone so far as to require foreseeability of death. The same is true for manslaughter predicated on criminal negligence; while criminal negligence, *infra*, requires a marked departure from the standards of a reasonable person in all the circumstances, it does not require foreseeability of death.

. . . .

In more recent times, the prevailing view has been that foreseeability of bodily harm is required for manslaughter. In England, it was said in *R. v. Larkin*, [1943] 1 All E.R. 217 (C.A.), at p. 219, that the act must be "a dangerous act, that is, an act which is likely to injure another person". In *R. v. Tennant* (1975), 23 C.C.C. (2d) 80, at p. 96, the Ontario Court of Appeal stated that the unlawful act must be "such as any reasonable person would inevitably realize must subject another to the risk of, at least, some harm, albeit not serious harm". Similarly, in *R. v. Adkins* (1987), 39 C.C.C. (3d) 346 (B.C. C.A.), at p. 348, Hutcheon J.A. wrote, "the unlawful act was such as any reasonable person would inevitably realize must subject another to the risk of at least some harm."

This court in *R. v. DeSousa*, *supra*, confirmed that a conviction for manslaughter requires that the risk of bodily harm have been foreseeable. After referring to the statement in *Larkin*, *supra*, that a "dangerous act" is required, Sopinka J. stated that English authority has consistently held that the underlying unlawful act required for manslaughter requires "proof that the unlawful act was 'likely to injure another person' or in other words put the bodily integrity of others at risk" (at p. 959). Moreover, the harm must be more than trivial or transitory. The test set out by Sopinka J. (at p. 961) for the unlawful act required by s. 269 of the *Criminal Code* is equally applicable to manslaughter:

> ... the test is one of objective foresight of bodily harm for all underlying offences. The act must be both unlawful, as described above, *and* one that is likely to subject another person to danger of harm or injury. This bodily harm must be more than merely trivial or transitory in nature and will in most cases involve an act of violence done deliberately to another person. In interpreting what constitutes an objectively dangerous act, the courts should strive to avoid attaching penal sanctions to mere inadvertence. The contention that no dangerousness requirement is required if the unlawful act is criminal should be rejected. [Emphasis in original.]

So the test for the *mens rea* of unlawful act manslaughter in Canada, as in the United Kingdom, is (in addition to the *mens rea* of the underlying offence) objective foreseeability of the risk of bodily harm which is neither trivial nor transitory, in the context of a dangerous act. Foreseeability of the risk of death is not required. The question is whether this test violates the principles of fundamental justice under s. 7 of the *Charter*.

. . . .

2. Constitutionality of the "Foresight of Bodily Harm" Test for Manslaughter

Before venturing on analysis, I think it appropriate to introduce a note of caution. We are here concerned with a common-law offence virtually as old as our system of criminal law. It has been applied in innumerable cases around the world. And it has been honed and refined over the centuries. Because of its residual nature, it may lack the logical symmetry of more modern statutory offences, but it has stood the practical test of time. Could all this be the case, one asks, if the law violates our fundamental notions of justice, themselves grounded in the history of the common law? Perhaps. Nevertheless, it must be with considerable caution that a 20th century court approaches the invitation which has been put before us: to strike out, or alternatively, rewrite, the offence of manslaughter on the ground that this is necessary to bring the law into conformity with the principles of fundamental justice.

As I read the reasons of the Chief Justice, his conclusion that the offence of manslaughter as it stands is unconstitutional, rests on two main concerns. First, it is his view that the gravity or seriousness of the offence of manslaughter, and in particular the stigma that attaches to it, requires a minimum *mens rea* of foreseeability of death. Second, considerations of symmetry between the element of mental fault and the consequences of the offence mandate this conclusion. I will deal with each concern in turn.

(a)   *Gravity of the Offence*

A number of concepts fall under this head. Three of them figure among the four factors relevant to determining the constitutionality of a *mens rea* requirement, as set out by this court in *R. v. Martineau*, [1990] 2 S.C.R. 633:

1. The stigma attached to the offence, and the available penalties requiring a *mens rea* reflecting the particular nature of the crime;

2. Whether the punishment is proportionate to the moral blameworthiness of the offender; and

3. The idea that those causing harm intentionally must be punished more severely than those causing harm unintentionally.

The Chief Justice in his reasons places considerable emphasis on the first factor of stigma. He argues that "there may well be no difference between the *actus reus* of manslaughter and murder; arguably both give rise to the stigma of being labelled by the state and the community as responsible for the wrongful death of another" (p. 11). But later in his reasons (at p. 12) he concedes that "the stigma which attaches to a conviction for unlawful act manslaughter", while "significant, . . . does not approach the opprobrium reserved in our society for those who *knowingly* or *intentionally* take the life of another" (emphasis is original). The Chief Justice goes on to observe that "[i]t is for this reason that manslaughter developed as a separate offence from murder at common law." Nevertheless, in the end the Chief Justice concludes that the "constitutional imperative", taken with other factors, requires a minimum *mens rea* of foreseeability of the risk of death, suggesting that stigma may remain an important factor in his reasoning.

To the extent that stigma is relied on as requiring foreseeability of the risk of death in the offence of manslaughter, I find it unconvincing. The most important feature of the stigma of manslaughter is the stigma which is not attached to it. The *Criminal Code* confines manslaughter to non-intentional homicide. A person convicted of manslaughter is not a murderer. He or she did not intend to kill someone. A person has been killed through the fault of another, and that is always serious. But by the very act of calling the killing manslaughter the law indicates that the killing is less blameworthy than murder. It may arise from negligence, or it may arise as the unintended result of a lesser unlawful act. The conduct is blameworthy and must be punished, but its stigma does not approach that of murder.

To put it another way, the stigma attached to manslaughter is an appropriate stigma. Manslaughter is not like constructive murder, where one could say that a person who did not in fact commit murder might be inappropriately branded with the stigma of murder. The stigma associated with manslaughter is arguably exactly what it should be for an unintentional killing in circumstances where risk of bodily harm was foreseeable.

. . . .

It would shock the public's conscience to think that a person could be convicted of manslaughter absent any moral fault based on foreseeability of harm. Conversely, it might well shock the public's conscience to convict a person who has killed another only of aggravated assault — the result of requiring foreseeability of death — on the sole basis that the risk of death was not reasonably foreseeable. The terrible consequence of death demands more. In short, the *mens rea* requirement which the common law has adopted — foreseeability of harm — is entirely appropriate to the stigma associated with the offence of manslaughter. To change the *mens rea* requirement would be to risk the very disparity between *mens rea* and stigma of which the appellant complains.

I come then to the second factor mentioned in *Martineau*, the relationship between the punishment for the offence and the *mens rea* requirement. Here again, the offence of manslaughter stands in sharp contrast to the offence of murder. Murder entails a mandatory life sentence; manslaughter carries with it no minimum sentence. This is appropriate. Because manslaughter can occur in a wide variety of circumstances, the penalties must be flexible. An unintentional killing while committing a minor offence, for example, properly attracts a much lighter sentence than an unintentional killing where the circumstances indicate an awareness of risk of death just short of what would be required to infer the intent required for murder. The point is, the sentence can be and is tailored to suit the degree of moral fault of the offender. It follows that the sentence attached to manslaughter does not require elevation of the degree of *mens rea* for the offence.

. . . .

This brings me to the third factor relating to the gravity of the offence set out in *Martineau*, the principle that those causing harm intentionally must be punished more severely than those causing harm unintentionally. As noted, this principle is strictly observed in the case of manslaughter. It is by definition an unintentional crime. Accordingly, the penalties imposed are typically less than for its intentional counterpart, murder.

I conclude that the standard of *mens rea* required for manslaughter is appropriately tailored to the seriousness of the offence.

b)   *Symmetry Between the Element of Fault and the Consequences of the Offence*

The Chief Justice correctly observes that the criminal law has traditionally aimed at symmetry between the *mens rea* and the prohibited consequences of the offence. The *actus reus* generally consists of an act bringing about a prohibited consequence, *e.g.*, death. Criminal-law theory suggests that the accompanying *mens rea* must go to the prohibited consequence. The moral fault of the accused lies in the act of bringing about that consequence. The Chief Justice reasons from this proposition that since manslaughter is an offence involving the prohibited act of killing another, a *mens rea* of foreseeability of harm is insufficient; what is required is foreseeability of death.

The conclusion that the offence of manslaughter is unconstitutional because it does not require appreciation of the consequential risk of death rests on two propositions: (1) that risk of bodily harm is appreciably different from risk of death in the context of manslaughter; and (2) that the principle of absolute symmetry between *mens rea* and each consequence of a criminal offence is not only a general rule of criminal law, but a principle of fundamental justice which sets a constitutional minimum. In my view, neither of these propositions is free from doubt.

I turn first to the distinction between appreciation of the risk of bodily harm and the risk of death in the context of manslaughter. In my view, when the risk of bodily harm is combined with the established rule that a wrong-doer must take his victim as he finds him and the fact that death did in fact occur, the distinction disappears. The accused who asserts that the risk of death was not foreseeable is in effect asserting that a normal person would not have died in these circumstances, and that he could not foresee the peculiar vulnerability of the victim. Therefore, he says, he should be convicted only of assault causing bodily harm or some lesser offence. This is to abrogate the thin-skull rule that requires that the wrong-doer take his victim as he finds him. Conversely, to combine the test of reasonable foreseeability of bodily harm with the thin-skull rule is to mandate that in some cases, foreseeability of the risk of bodily harm alone will properly result in a conviction for manslaughter.

What the appellant asks us to do, then, is to abandon the "thin-skull" rule. It is this rule which, on analysis, is alleged to be unjust. Such a conclusion I cannot accept. The law has consistently set its face against such a policy. It decrees that the aggressor must take his victim as he finds him. Lord Ellenborough C.J. discussed the principle nearly two centuries ago:

> He who deals in a perilous article must be wary how he deals; otherwise, if he observe not proper caution, he will be responsible . . . It is a universal principle that, when a man is charged with doing an act, of which the probable consequence may be highly injurious, the intention is an inference of law, resulting from the doing of the act. (*R. v. Dixon* (1814), 3 M. & S. 11; approved, per Blackburn J., *R. v. Hicklin* (1868), L.R. 3 Q.B. 375, and per Amphlett J., *R. v. Aspinall* (1876), 2 Q.B.D. 48, 65).

Stephen J. illustrated the principle in similar fashion in *R. v. Serné* (1887), 16 Cox 311, at p. 313:

> ... when a person began doing wicked acts for his own base purposes, he risked his own life as well as that of others. That kind of crime does not differ in any serious degree from one committed by using a deadly weapon, such as a bludgeon, a pistol, or a knife. If a man once begins attacking the human body in such a way, he must take the consequences if he goes further than he intended when he began.

The principle that if one engages in criminal behaviour, one is responsible for any unforeseen actions stemming from the unlawful act, has been a well-established tenet for most of this century in Canada, the U.S. and U.K. . . . . In *Smithers v. The Queen*, [1978] 1 S.C.R. 506 at pp. 521-22, Dickson J., writing for a unanimous court, confirmed this principle:

> It is a well-recognized principle that one who assaults another must take his victim as he finds him. . . .
> Although causation in civil cases differs from that in a criminal case, the "thin-skulled man" may appear in the criminal law as in the civil law . . . Even if the unlawful act, alone, would not have caused the death, it was still a legal cause so long as it contributed in some way to the death.

The thin-skull rule is a good and useful principle. It requires aggressors, once embarked on their dangerous course of conduct which may foreseeably injure others, to take responsibility for all the consequences that ensue, even to death. That is not, in my view, contrary to fundamental justice. Yet the consequence of adopting the amendment proposed by the Chief Justice would be to abrogate this principle in cases of manslaughter.

In fact, when manslaughter is viewed in the context of the thin-skull principle, the disparity diminishes between the *mens rea* of the offence and its consequence. The law does not posit the average victim. It says the aggressor must take the victim as he finds him. Wherever there is a risk of harm, there is also a practical risk that some victims may die as a result of the harm. At this point, the test of harm and death merge.

The second assumption inherent in the argument based on symmetry between *mens rea* and each consequence of the offence is that this is not only a general rule of criminal law, but a principle of fundamental justice — a basic constitutional requirement. I agree that as a general rule the *mens rea* of an offence relates to the consequences prohibited by the offence. As I stated in *R. v. Théroux*, [1993] 2 S.C.R. 5, at p. 17, "[t]ypically, *mens rea* is concerned with the consequences of the prohibited *actus reus*." Yet our criminal law contains important exceptions to this ideal of perfect symmetry. The presence of these exceptions suggests that the rule of symmetry is just that — a rule — to which there are exceptions. If this is so, then the rule cannot be elevated to the status of a principle of fundamental justice which must, by definition, have universal application.

It is important to distinguish between criminal law theory, which seeks the ideal of absolute symmetry between *actus reus* and *mens rea*, and the constitutional requirements of the *Charter*. As the Chief Justice has stated several times, "the Constitution does not always guarantee the 'ideal'" (*R. v. Lippé*, [1991] 2 S.C.R. 114 at p. 142; *R. v. Wholesale Travel Group Inc.*, [1991] 3 S.C.R. 154, at p. 186; *R. v. Finlay*, S.C.C. No. 22596, released concurrently, at p. 12).

I know of no authority for the proposition that the *mens rea* of an offence must always attach to the precise consequence which is prohibited as a matter of constitutional necessity. The relevant constitutional principles have been cast more broadly. No person can be sent to prison without *mens rea*, or a guilty mind, and the seriousness of the offence must not be disproportionate to the degree of moral fault. Provided an element of mental fault or moral culpability is present, and provided that it is proportionate to the seriousness and consequences of the offence charged, the principles of fundamental justice are satisfied.

. . . .

Thus when considering the constitutionality of the requirement of foreseeability of bodily harm, the question is not whether the general rule of symmetry between *mens rea* and the consequences prohibited by the offence is met, but rather whether the fundamental principle of justice is satisfied that the gravity and blameworthiness of an offence must be commensurate with the moral fault engaged by that offence. Fundamental justice does not require absolute symmetry between moral fault and the prohibited consequences. Consequences, or the absence of consequences, can properly affect the seriousness with which Parliament treats specified conduct.

The trial judge properly found that Mr. Creighton committed the unlawful act of trafficking in cocaine. He also found that he was guilty of criminal negligence, using the standard which I view as correct, the standard of the reasonable person. The only remaining question, on the view I take of the law, was whether the reasonable person in all the circumstances would have foreseen the risk of bodily harm. I am satisfied that the answer to this question must be affirmative. At the very least, a person administering a dangerous drug like cocaine to another has a duty to inform himself as to the precise risk the injection entails and to refrain from administering it unless reasonably satisfied that there was no risk of harm. That was not the case here, as the trial judge found.

The issue of symmetry between *actus reus* and *mens rea* was in issue in an unsuccessful *Charter* challenge to Parliament's criminal harassment offence in s. 264.

R. v. KRUSHEL

(2000), 31 C.R. (5th) 295, 142 C.C.C. (3d) 1,
2000 CarswellOnt 325 (Ont. C.A.)

CATZMAN J.A. (CARTHY and WEILER JJ.A. concurring): —

. . . .

All three appellants were convicted of criminal harassment under s. 264 of the *Criminal Code*. That section provides, in relevant part:

264.(1) No person shall, without lawful authority and knowing that another person is harassed or recklessly as to whether the other person is harassed, engage in conduct referred to in subsection (2) that causes that other person reasonably, in all the circumstances, to fear for their safety or the safety of anyone known to them.

(2) The conduct mentioned in subsection (1) consists of

(a) repeatedly following from place to place the other person or anyone known to them;

(b) repeatedly communicating with, either directly or indirectly, the other person or anyone known to them;

(c) besetting or watching the dwelling-house, or place where the other person, or anyone known to them, resides, works, carries on business or happens to be; or

(d) engaging in threatening conduct directed at the other person or any member of their family.

. . . .

The appellant Krushel was convicted of criminal harassment under s. 264 by engaging in the conduct referred to in s. 264(2)(c) The victim was his former common law spouse. He was sentenced to 90 days, to be served intermittently, and two years probation.

. . . .

(i) Section 7

Counsel for Krushel submitted that s. 264 infringed s. 7 of the *Charter* for two reasons: first, that the section was impermissibly vague in that it fails to give sufficient notice of what conduct is prohibited; and second, that it allows the morally innocent to be punished, specifically, in its failure to require that the accused have the intention to cause the victim to fear for their safety or the safety of anyone known to them (the "constructive liability argument").

The constructive liability argument was considered by the Alberta Court of Appeal in *R. v. Sillipp* (1997), 120 C.C.C. (3d) 384 (Alta. C.A.), leave to appeal to S.C.C. refused (1998), 219 A.R. 107 (S.C.C.). In that case, as in this, the appellant argued that s. 264 allowed the morally innocent to be punished because it lacked a *mens rea* requirement attaching to the consequence of reasonable fear. That court concluded that s. 7 was not infringed by the provisions of s. 264. At pp. 397-398, Berger J.A., speaking for the court, described the operation of the section in the following terms:

> In my view, the *actus reus* of the offence of criminal harassment is constituted by volitional subsection (2) conduct which meets discernible standards of nature, cause and effect, with the *mens rea* requirement being that of an intention to engage in that conduct or, at minimum, recklessness or wilful blindness, relative to that conduct.
>
> That which is prohibited is a person engaging in subsection (2) conduct with knowledge (reckless or wilful blindness) that *such conduct* is causing the complainant to be harassed. The *mens rea* of the offence is the intention to engage in the prohibited conduct with the knowledge that the complainant is thereby harassed.
>
> . . . .
>
> A conviction under s. 264 requires that the accused have "known" that his subsection (2) conduct was causing the complainant to be harassed, or that he was aware of such risk and was reckless or wilfully blind as to whether or not the person was harassed. The Appellant's "morally innocent accused" who honestly believed that his subsection (2) behaviour was not known to the complainant, and who was not reckless or wilfully blind, would escape criminal liability.

In the result, Berger J.A. concluded, at p. 399:

> The Appellant's argument that it is a matter of constitutional necessity that the element of mental culpability be linked to the prohibited consequence of causing actual fear in the complainant is unfounded. Clearly Parliament has created a new kind of culpable activity — subsection (2) conduct which, by objective standards (as described earlier in this judgment), is of a nature and extent as to reasonably cause fear. Such conduct is deemed by s. 264 to be criminal activity. Thus, in accordance with the principle set out in *DeSousa (supra)*, given that there is in s. 264 a sufficiently blameworthy element in the *actus reus* to which the culpable mental state attaches, foresight of the prohibited consequence of causing actual fear is not required in order to hold the accused responsible for the results of his or her unlawful activity.

In reaching this conclusion, Berger J.A. noted (at pp. 396-398) that the contention that there must be symmetry between *mens rea* and each consequence of an offence had been expressly rejected by McLachlin J. in *R. v. Creighton* (1993), 83 C.C.C. (3d) 346 (S.C.C.) and (at p. 399) that there need only be a sufficiently blameworthy element in the *actus reus* to which the culpable mental state attaches: *R. v. DeSousa* (1992), 76 C.C.C. (3d) 124 (S.C.C.). I agree with Berger J.A., and I would reject the constructive liability argument.

The argument that s. 264 is impermissibly vague was not considered by the Alberta Court of Appeal. However, in an earlier challenge to s. 264, the Alberta Court of Queen's Bench rejected that argument: *R. v. Sillipp* (1995), 99 C.C.C.

(3d) 394 (Alta. Q.B.). In that proceeding, Murray J. dismissed an application to declare s. 264 to be of no force and effect, finding, *inter alia*, that the section did not suffer from vagueness. His reasons on this point appear at p. 406:

> In my opinion, s. 264 does not suffer from vagueness. Certainly there are many facets of it that will have to be interpreted by the court. I have no doubt that as time progresses it will be given a constant and settled meaning. I have no problem interpreting s. 264 so as to understand that certain conduct is subject to legal restrictions and the area of risk is set out, namely, if you intentionally behave in certain ways knowing that by doing so you are harassing another person, then if your conduct causes that person to reasonably fear for his or her safety, you run the risk of being criminally sanctioned. I would think that anyone reading the section would receive that message loud and clear. I do not believe that it has the effect of permitting a "standardless sweep" so as to allow the police, or for that matter, the judiciary, to simply use its discretion in how they interpret it or apply its provisions which was the concern of Lamer C.J.C. in *Morales, supra*. I have listened to argument by Crown and defence counsel and I am satisfied that the legislation permits the framing of a meaningful legal debate with respect to the objectives contained in the legislation. In my view, it provides "an adequate basis for reaching a conclusion as to its meaning by reasoned analysis applying legal criteria".

I agree with Murray J., and I would reject the appellant's argument that s. 264 violates s. 7 because it is impermissibly vague.

On the above state of the law, do you think that the following accused, each charged with manslaughter, should be convicted?

1. The accused pointed a rifle at his friend and discharged it, killing him. The accused and the victim were friends who had been hunting the day before. The accused had, only moments before, pulled the trigger and the gun had not discharged. He thought that the gun was not loaded and that it would not discharge. There was evidence that the firing mechanism on the gun was faulty. Note that under s. 87(1) of the *Criminal Code* it is an offence to point a firearm at another whether or not it is loaded.
Compare R v Jakubowych (1968), 66 W.W.R. 755 (Alta. S.C.).

2. During a hunting trip a woman shot and killed her husband, mistaking him for a bear. The shooting occurred after it was no longer fully daylight, but the Crown did not show that it occurred after hunting was still legally permitted or that it was too dark to permit an appropriate method of identification of a target. The accused would have been expecting her husband to be with a guide, who was not in fact walking beside the deceased. The deceased was walking on uneven ground, which would have required him to be walking bent over to some degree, and would have caused him to appear to be bobbing up and down. The deceased was dressed in dark clothing and was walking in an area of tall grass, which would have made him appear to be shorter than he actually was. The deceased did not signal in any way, though he knew that the accused might be expecting game to be flushed out in the area where he was walking. The accused expected that there would be a bear in the area of the shooting, and she knew what a bear looked like and how it moved. She was originally

unable to identify the object she saw appear, but after looking at it for a short period of time she determined it was a bear, based on its rounded shape and what she perceived to be its head. She thought it was clear that it was a bear and shot it from 200 feet, which was not a long shot.

Compare *R. v. Harshbarger* (2010), 79 C.R. (6th) 373 (N.L. T.D.).

3. The accused had intravenously injected a quantity of prescription asthma pills mixed with water into a friend's arm. That friend later bought a large quantity of pyribenzamine pills and requested the accused to crush six of them and mix them with water and inject them as before. He did not want to but she insisted, so he did so. In a short time she lapsed into unconsciousness and underwent convulsive spasms. She encountered difficulty in breathing. The accused summoned an ambulance only when she seemed to stop breathing. She was already dead. Pyribenzamine can be lawfully purchased at any drug store without a prescription.

Compare *R. v. Davis* (1978), 37 C.C.C. (2d) 114 (Sask. C.A.).

4. Justice Ewaschuk of the Ontario Superior Court found the following:

"In 1980 the accused's mother died of cancer, leaving him an orphan. As a result he lived with his grandmother.

On 20th October 1983 the grandmother left Hamilton to visit friends. She left her then 16-year-old grandson in the charge of his aunt. The accused later lied to his aunt and told her that he would be staying at the home of Roberto Fidanza, a fellow classmate. Instead these two, and others, on Saturday, 22nd October 1983, met at the grandmother's home to party and have a general good time.

Initially, in fact, at about 7:00 p.m. that evening, three other male friends dropped over with a case of beer, which was eventually drunk. At about 8:00 p.m. two more male friends, among them the deceased, Roberto Fidanza, 16 years old, arrived with two girlfriends and another case of beer, also eventually consumed.

Between 10:30 and 11:00 p.m., Fidanza and another male teenager came up from downstairs, where they had been with the two girls. The two young girls remained downstairs. The accused, Barron, suggested that the boys "streak" the girls by disrobing themselves. All declined to do so except Fidanza and Barron, the author of the escapade.

The deceased and the accused thereupon undressed themselves to their underwear. The deceased eventually reached the landing above the downstairs with the accused directly behind him, when the deceased apparently changed his mind. He hesitated and said, , I don't want to do it." The accused then stated, "Come on, Roberto, let's go," and with that statement gave the deceased a slight push on the back.

Unfortunately the push or shove was substantial enough for the deceased to lose his balance and fall down the stairs to his eventual death.

In fact, he died on 1st November 1983 of a pneumonic infection of his lungs brought on as a direct result of the head injuries suffered from the fall. The blood-alcohol reading of this rather small 120-pound boy proved to be 131 milligrams at the time of his death.

The events that followed the fall proved bizarre. Seemingly out of character, the accused panicked and acted callously. He struck a friend who tried to telephone for an ambulance. He then ordered everyone out of his grandmother's home, compelling the others to carry his unconscious classmate outside. In fact, the deceased never regained consciousness. Eventually, the other teenagers were able to get an ambulance and hail down a police car.

The accused himself fled the scene. Eventually he returned but denied pushing his friend. It was not until the police told him that one of the other boys claimed that the accused pushed the deceased that he admitted it. However, even then he falsely claimed that someone else pushed him from behind."

Compare *R. v. Barron* (1984), 39 C.R. (3d) 379 (Ont. H.C.), reversed (1985), 48 C.R. (3d) 334, 23 C.C.C. (3d) 544 (Ont. C.A.).

5. A group of friends spent the night stealing cars and joyriding. K, aged 13 at the time, while standing on a boulevard, threw a metal shovel at a car three or four times, as the driver of the car deliberately drove past him. On the last throw the shovel hit a 14-year-old youth, who was then hanging half out of the car window. The car was going at 80-90 kilometers per hour. The boy was hit and killed by the blow.

Compare *R. v. T. (K.)* (2003), 31 C.R. (6th) 187 (Man. C.A.).

One would have expected that since *Creighton* the Supreme Court would be applying *DeSousa* with caution, especially in the case of a very serious crime such as that of aggravated assault. The crime of aggravated assault under what is now s. 268(1) is the most serious form of assault and carries a maximum penalty of 14 years' imprisonment. Under s. 268(1):

> Every one commits an aggravated assault who wounds, maims, disfigures or endangers the life of the complainant.

Prior to *DeSousa* and *Creighton* most Courts of Appeal had interpreted the offence of aggravated assault to merely require proof of an intent to assault and of an act which in fact caused the aggravated consequences complained of. See *Leclerc* (1991), 7 C.R. (4th) 282 (Ont. C.A.), *Lucas* (1987), 34 C.C.C. (3d) 28 (Que. C.A.), *Carriere* (1987), 56 C.R. (3d) 57 (Alta. C.A.) and *Scharf* (1988), 42 C.C.C. (3d) 378 (Man. C.A.). This meant a form of absolute liability respecting that consequence. Only the New Brunswick Court of Appeal in *Parish* (1990), 60 C.C.C. (3d) 350 (N.B. C.A.) had related the intent to the consequences prohibited in their determination that the Crown would have to prove not just an intent to assault but an intent to wound, maim, disfigure or endanger life.

In *Godin* (1993), 22 C.R. (4th) 265 (N.B. C.A.), Angers J.A. for the majority of the New Brunswick Court of Appeal persisted with this approach. He persuasively pointed out that the offence was distinguishable from the offence of unlawfully causing bodily harm at issue in *DeSousa* in that it was not defined as wounding, maiming, etc. in the course of assault nor expressly as an offence which caused certain consequences. It followed that there would have to be subjective foresight of the forbidden acts. The majority pointed out that a life might be endangered without the commission of an assault. When *Godin* reached the Supreme Court, [1994] 2 S.C.R. 484, 31 C.R. (4th) 33, 89 C.C.C. (3d) 574, the Court took but a few lines in an oral endorsement to reverse the New Brunswick Court of Appeal. The Court did not fully justify its position. It merely remarked that the section "pertains to an assault that has the consequence of wounding, maiming or disfiguring". Intent was not required respecting those consequences and the fault element was objective foresight of bodily harm. This was said to flow from *DeSousa* and *Creighton*. On the above analysis of *Creighton* can this be correct? The reference to "bodily harm" may have been a slip of the tongue. The express *mens rea* required for an assault under s. 265(1) is applying force intentionally and there is no mention of bodily harm. However, the *Godin* test has now been applied in *R. v. Williams* (see earlier under Commission of an Unlawful Act.)

The Supreme Court in *Godin* did not consider *L. (S.R.)* (1992), 16 C.R. (4th) 311, 76 C.C.C. (3d) 502 (Ont. C.A.), in which there was a careful attempt by the Ontario Court of Appeal to apply *DeSousa* to aggravated assault. This necessitated a reversal of that court's previous decision in *Leclerc*. The crime of aggravated assault was now to be interpreted, per Justice Doherty for the Court, as requiring not only proof of the *mens rea* required for assault, applying force intentionally, but also objective foresight of the risk of wounding, maiming, disfiguring or endangering life. The Ontario Court saw that the further pronouncement in *DeSousa* that a fault element need not relate to the consequence was *obiter* and decided not to follow it. Compare *Reyat* (1993), 20 C.R. (4th) 149 (B.C. C.A.).

The Ontario Court of Appeal's interpretation was most welcome, and had the Supreme Court accepted it, would have done much to undo the Supreme Court's unnecessary and unprincipled attempt to separate the fault requirement from its factual context. However, especially since *Creighton*, there is even more to be said for the approach of the New Brunswick Court of Appeal which sought to keep objective tests out of the law of assault and to apply the usual principle of relating fault to the prohibited consequence. The effect of *Godin* is that the crime of aggravated assault has been added to the uncertain list of so-called predicate offences for which the fault requirement is much reduced.

At present the *Criminal Code* attempts through its maximum penalties to distinguish in seriousness between assault, assault with a weapon or causing bodily harm and aggravated assault. Not surprisingly, given the inconsistency and confusion in the Supreme Court, Courts of Appeal are in disarray as to how *DeSousa, Creighton* and *Godin* are to determine the *mens rea* required for assault causing bodily harm. The Saskatchewan Court of Appeal, *Swenson* (1994), 91 C.C.C. (3d) 541 (Sask. C.A.), merely requires the basic assault element of intent to apply force. There is no requirement of foresight of bodily harm. Criminal responsibility for the more serious offence of assault causing bodily harm will result even if bodily harm resulted in an unforeseen or unforeseeable way. This amounts to absolute liability as to the consequence. This is even less of a requirement than the objective foresight of harm *DeSousa* required for unlawfully causing bodily harm. In contrast the Ontario Court of Appeal, *Nurse* (1993), 83

C.C.C. (3d) 546 and *Emans* (2000), 35 C.R. (5th) 386, (*sub nom. R. v. E. (A.)*) 146 C.C.C. (3d) 449 (Ont. C.A.), and the Alberta Court of Appeal, *Dewey* (1998), 21 C.R. (5th) 232, 132 C.C.C. (3d) 348 (Alta. C.A.), assert for assault causing bodily harm a test of reasonable foresight of harm but not the specific type of harm. In *R. v. Zhao* (2013), 297 C.C.C. (3d) 533, 3 C.R. (7th) 95 (Ont. C.A.) the Ontario Court of Appeal held that where the charge is sexual assault causing bodily harm consent is a defence except where, under *Jobidon*, the harm was intended; see criticism by Janine Benedet in the C.R.s at 96.

Our law of assault is in urgent need of rethinking by the Supreme Court or Parliament. Crimes of assault should be based on actual foresight of the type of harm caused or risked and should carry higher penalties than those crimes based on a failure to reasonably foresee the risk, such as the present crime of criminal negligence causing bodily harm. It would be more workable to distinguish between only two types of assault based on the seriousness of the harm caused or risked. So too with crimes of criminal negligence.

6. NORMATIVE THEORIES

G.P. FLETCHER, RE-THINKING CRIMINAL LAW

(1978), 367

When used normatively, "criminal" refers to the type of person who by virtue of his deeds deserves to be branded and punished as a criminal. When used descriptively, as in the phrase "criminal act" it may refer simply to any act that the legislature has declared to be "criminal".

G.P. FLETCHER, THE THEORY OF CRIMINAL NEGLIGENCE: A COMPARATIVE ANALYSIS

(1970-71), 119 U. of Penn. L. Rev. 401 at 414-415

We require *mens rea* as an essential condition for criminal liability, not because we suppose that mental states are essential to criminality, but because we realize intuitively that the condemnatory sanctions should apply only to those who are justly condemned for their conduct. And men are not justly condemned and deprived of their liberty unless they are personally culpable in violating the law. That is the point of Coke's saying: the act is not culpable under the law (*actus non facit reum*) unless the actor is culpable for acting as he did (*nisi mens sit rea*).

The proper construction of Coke's embezzlement case is that if the actor lacks the intent required by the law as it existed in the 17th century, he is not culpable for violating the law: there is neither an act prohibited by the law nor personal culpability for engaging in the prohibited act. It does not follow, inversely, that if the actor intended to steal at the time he received possession of the goods that the maxim *actus facit reum nisi mens sit rea* would be satisfied. The actor might be *non compos mentis*, and Coke demonstrably would say that he lacked *mens rea* even though he intentionally took the goods of another. Similarly, the actor might have performed the act under duress or necessity, and in these situations, his conduct should be treated the same as the conduct of an actor *non compos mentis*. In all of these cases, the actor acts with the subjective state prohibited by law, namely, the intention to take the goods of another. But he is not personally culpable — he lacks *mens rea* — if he is insane, or if his conduct is rendered involuntary by duress or necessity.

. . . .

Once the normative status of *mens rea* comes into focus, the problem of negligence as a form of *mens rea* is tractable. If *mens rea* refers not to a specific subjective state, but to the actor's moral culpability in acting as he does, then there might logically be a way to establish personal culpability without referring to a state of mind. In the normal case of intentional conduct, where the actor is sane and his conduct is not excused by duress or necessity, it might be sufficient in establishing *mens rea* to show that the actor acted intentionally. But surely it does not follow that intentional conduct, or something like it, is a necessary condition for criminal culpability. Structural differences between negligence and intentional conduct do not preclude treating negligence as a form of *mens rea*. Nor is the issue settled by the characteristic externality of negligent conduct. Whether negligence constitutes *mens rea* depends on whether negligent conduct is a ground for justly blaming another.

ANNE STALKER, CAN GEORGE FLETCHER HELP SOLVE THE PROBLEM OF CRIMINAL NEGLIGENCE?

(1982), 7 Queen's L.J. 274 at 291-292

A normative test is one that applies directly to the underlying policy, without translating it into measurable and consistent components. A descriptive test, on the other hand, would specify identifiable elements that are consistent from case to case. The problem with a normative test is that it is discretionary and can change from judge to judge and day to day. The problem with a descriptive test is that it is rigid and may not accurately reflect the underlying principle or policy in every situation.

For strong criticism of the pervasive descriptive approach to fault in Canadian law see James Stribopoulos, "The Constitutionalization of 'Fault' in Canada: A Normative Critique" (1999) 42 Crim. L.Q. 227.

J.M. WEILER, R. V. KUNDEUS: THE SAGA OF TWO SHIPS PASSING IN THE NIGHT

(1976), 14 Osgoode Hall L.J. 457 at 470

[Brett] asks whether there is any reason for holding the accused free from blame, rather than whether the prosecution has proved the mental element of the crime. He rejects the latter approach since he does not believe that it is possible to identify in advance all of the possible excuses that might serve to absolve the accused from blame. In his judgment, the search for the conditions of imputability which requires a precise *a priori* analysis of *mens rea* is never successful.

Something is always left out. We cannot anticipate and enumerate all of the conditions of blameworthiness in advance: better not to try. Instead we can recognize blame when we see it, and should have no need for an *a priori* definition.

ROSEMARY CAIRNS WAY, THE CHARTER, THE SUPREME COURT AND THE INVISIBLE POLITICS OF FAULT: A CRITICAL ANALYSIS OF THE CONSTITUTIONALIZATION OF FAULT

LL.M. thesis for the Faculty of Law, Queen's University, October 1992.

The political nature of subjectivism however, remains largely unexamined in the court's judgments. Although I am concerned about the implications of subjectivism, this thesis is not an argument for objectivism. It is a plea for a multidimensional, contextualized approach to fault, and it questions whether such an approach is possible or likely within a constitutionalized discourse of rights. A great deal of energy in criminal law theory is devoted to the objective/ subjective debate, which is understood as one of the fundamental conundrums of the criminal law. In my view, the current construction of the objective/ subjective debate as irreconcilable polarities submerges the complexity of the question of blame. The risk of unidimensional, decontextualized approaches to law is magnified when complex concepts like fault are elevated to constitutional status. The implications of a decision to view constitutional culpability through the lens of objectivism, although different in kind from those which flow from a commitment to subjectivism would be equally grave.

· · · ·

Decisions about responsibility should invoke a rich and multifaceted debate about the nature and appropriate allocation of blame, the assumption of free will and the efficacy of the criminal law as a mechanism of social control. To act without engaging in this debate is at once to impoverish our jurisprudence about the criminal law and to limit the possibilities for change.

TONI PICKARD AND PHIL GOLDMAN,
DIMENSIONS OF CRIMINAL LAW

(1992), 402-405.

The basis in fairness for an objective standard. An "objective" standard presupposes the possibility of agreeing on what is reasonable or natural in any given situation. That possibility, in turn, presupposes both shared understandings, perceptions, and values among the fact finders, and shared understandings between those who are finding facts and the population subject to the law. (Remember that, in law, whether a belief is reasonable or not is conceived to be a question of fact, not a choice of values or perspectives.)

. . . .

Loss of centre and the problem of fairness. Whatever may be true of distant cultures, people in Canada, though differently situated and subject to marked disparities in power, do seem to share at least some understandings across the divisions. Indeed, if we did not think people in our culture shared some understandings, we would hardly be able to use phrases like "our culture" meaningfully. There is, however, a growing acknowledgment that people of different classes, races, ages, genders, religions, sexual orientations, ethnic backgrounds, physical abilities, political visions, and so on, not only have different and sometimes conflicting values, but that their perceptions of facts, of cause and effect, of what is natural, and of what is meant by certain words and gestures are significantly shaped by those differing and sometimes conflicting values.

Increasingly, people believe that facts (even scientific facts) and (more obviously) meanings are not out there in the world in any absolute sense, independent of the observer (that is, objectively), but that, on the contrary, a fact or a meaning — even whether something is perceived as a fact, or heard as a meaning — is in large part a function of the observer's beliefs (and hence, of social place). This insight seriously undermines our ability to believe that the way a decision maker or fact finder sees things is in fact "how things are" or "objectively true". Still more radically affected is our sense that it is fair to impose some people's judgments of what is reasonable on others.

7. GENERAL REVIEW QUESTIONS

1. Emotions are running high outside a courthouse. A crowd of student protestors is awaiting the outcome of a controversial trial of acquaintance rape charges alleged to have occurred on campus.

The group is chanting "Justice for women". One member of the group, Andrew, is challenged by another student, Bob, a supporter of the accused.

Bob shouts "Vigilantes go home". At this point Andrew shakes a clenched fist at Bob and says "Let's sort it out". Bob promptly lands a blow on Andrew's jaw. The punch is hard enough to knock Andrew off balance. He falls over, hits his forehead on a granite pillar of the courthouse steps and loses consciousness. He quickly comes to and is unharmed. A nearby police officer asks Bob for his name and address. Bob gives his name but is so flustered he can't remember the number of his temporary apartment. He gives it as No. 314 Portsmouth House. It is in fact No. 217. The officer indicates Bob will be charged with assault.

At this point, Andrew's friends take him to an ambulance stationed in the courthouse parking lot. The ambulance driver, Chris, aged 60, agrees to take Andrew to be checked at the Hotel Dieu. Chris has been an ambulance driver for 30 years. This is his very last shift and he is tired. He drives down West Street with his emergency lights and siren activated. It is cold but roads are dry and visibility is fine. As he approaches an intersection the traffic signal turns red. He slows to about 5 k.p.h. but proceeds through the intersection. He collides with a Pyke milk truck which enters the intersection on a green light at about 30 k.p.h. Neither driver saw the other vehicle until it was too late. Both vehicles were damaged. Furthermore, Andrew was jolted from the stretcher and broke his leg. He was attended to in the hospital where he was pronounced fit except for the broken bone. It healed satisfactorily within six weeks.

You are serving your articles with a 65-year-old judge who is to preside over the upcoming trial arising from these events. She asks you for a legal memorandum identifying viable legal issues and their possible resolution. She requests careful reference to appropriate case and statutory authority.

There are three charges to consider.

Bob is charged with:
1. assault causing bodily harm to Andrew (to wit, a broken leg) contrary to s. 267(1)(b) of the *Criminal Code*, and
2. wilful obstruction of a police officer, by giving a false address contrary to s. 129(a) of the *Criminal Code*.

Chris is charged with:
3. failing to stop at a red light contrary to s. 124(16) of the *Highway Traffic Act* of Ontario.

Respecting this third charge, note that under s. 124:

(16) Every driver approaching a traffic control signal showing a circular red indicator and facing the indication shall stop his vehicle and shall not proceed until a green indication is shown.

(18) Notwithstanding subsection (16), a driver of an emergency vehicle, after stopping the vehicle, may proceed without a green indication being shown if it is safe to do so.

Pursuant to s. 188(1) of the Act, anyone convicted of an offence under s. 124 is subject to a minimum fine of $60 and a maximum fine of $500.

2. Hemophilia is a hereditary disorder that interferes with blood clotting in about one male in 5,000. Until the early 1970s the accepted treatment was blood transfusions. The development of blood-factor concentrates allowed

patients to receive treatment quickly at home by simple injection. In Canada, it has always been necessary to import a large quantity of such concentrates from the United States. Each sample injected will come from a number of separate donors.

In 1982, following the death of four hemophiliacs from AIDS in the United States, the Canadian Blood Committee, a committee of civil servants appointed from each province to implement the policy of blood distribution, were warned of the "theoretical risk" that an unknown transmissible agent present in blood-factor concentrates might cause AIDS. The Committee decided that this was too speculative a risk to cause them to change their policy and such concentrates were continued to be used. In 1984, it was widely reported that a United States agency had confirmed that there was an AIDS risk from contaminated blood and that it could be eliminated by a high-heat treatment of the blood product. The Canadian Blood Committee decided, after consultation with doctors, users and manufacturers, to use up existing inventory and phase in heat-treated blood over an eight-month period ending in July 1984.

In October 1992, Alex, a hemophiliac, dies after a debilitating illness. His wife of 20 years, Barbara, only learned that he died from AIDS from the coroner, who asked her whether the cause was contaminated blood. Barbara is devastated. Doctor Cain has been the family physician for both Alex and Barbara since 1975. Neither Doctor Cain nor Alex ever told her that Alex had the HIV virus. Doctor Cain says he was bound by a professional oath of confidentiality and, anyhow, Alex insisted that he did not trouble his wife with the bad news. Alex and Barbara never used a condom. Barbara now has her blood tested and is found to have the HIV virus herself. The HIV virus will usually lead to full-blown AIDS within six to seven years. Thereafter death will occur within three years. Barbara is 100 percent sure that Alex got the virus from contaminated blood he started to inject in January of 1984 and that the only way she could have got the virus herself is from Alex.

She consults a Crown Attorney who lays three charges.

Each member of the Blood Committee is charged, based on the Committee's delay in stopping the distribution of contaminated blood in 1984, with criminal negligence causing death of Alex and criminal negligence causing bodily harm to Barbara contrary, respectively, to ss. 220 and 221 of the *Criminal Code*. Dr. Cane is charged, based on his failure to warn Barbara of Alex's AIDS, with criminal negligence causing her bodily harm contrary to s. 221 of the *Criminal Code*.

The Crown Attorney asks you for a legal memorandum in which you discuss, with reference to appropriate authority, possible defences to each charge assessing the chances of her obtaining convictions. Indicate what further evidence, if any, may be useful in the upcoming trials.

3. The accused, Cain, is charged, pursuant to s. 221 of the *Criminal Code*, with causing bodily harm by criminal negligence. Cain is also

charged with a violation of s. 8 of the *Explosives Act* of Ontario. That section provides:

> 8. Every one who allows explosives to be stored in a manner which endangers the lives or safety of others is guilty of an offence punishable by a fine of up to $25,000 or imprisonment of six months or both.

Cain, aged 40, has just been promoted to foreman for a construction company charged with the task of excavating for a new library being erected by the University. The construction site is immediately opposite the building housing the law faculty. The task has proved more difficult than expected and Cain is finding his new job quite stressful. On the evening of December 1, 1992, the accused placed a case of explosives in a storage container on the construction site. For the last several weeks of blasting he had assumed the container was one of the type that automatically locks when the lid is closed. That was the sort of container in use at his former job. Unfortunately the container was not of that type and the explosives were left accessible to anyone who cared to lift the lid. Cain had previously delegated the storage of explosives to a particular worker. On the day in question that worker had caused trouble and Cain had told him to leave the site. Cain remembers being angry and preoccupied with that altercation. He did not notice a padlock on the container.

Arthur Able, a young law student, was disappointed with the quality of instruction in his criminal law class and also with the underground classrooms where he gained such instruction. On the evening of December 1 he decided to bury the classrooms. He climbed the fence and found the explosives left by the accused. He fashioned a crude demolition device and set the time for the beginning of the Criminal Law class. The blast destroyed the premises and the learned law professor was injured as a result.

Write a legal memorandum advising, with reference to appropriate authority, as to all the possible defences to the two charges against Cain.

4. Alec is a large, athletic young man. He always wears a Hells Angels biker jacket and has many visible tattoos. During a routine medical check-up it is discovered that he is HIV positive. When the young Public Health nurse, Betty, advises him of the results he immediately says "No problem, they have this thing licked, right?" Betty knows that her medical protocol is to clearly and strongly advise him that he should register for treatment and to inform all his sexual partners, past, present or future, as to his HIV status and to now always use a condom. However, Betty is scared of him and is also exhausted after a very long shift. She says nothing. Driving herself home she is preoccupied by the thought that she did not do the right thing. She approaches an intersection with traffic lights. She believes the green light has turned orange and she slides through. In fact the orange light was malfunctioning and she has gone through a red light. There is a minor "fender bender" accident as she collides with someone commencing on green. No one is injured.

Alec later has unprotected sexual intercourse with a new partner, Claire. He told Claire he is HIV positive but before he said anything more, she said

"No problem. Don't bother with a condom. I don't like them". Two months later she tests HIV positive. She has had no sexual relations with anyone since that one occasion with Alec. A year later she develops full blown AIDS. She proves severely allergic to anti-AIDS drugs and is in the process of dying.

You are articled to a Crown Attorney who asks you for a legal memorandum. He wants to go for broke. He is contemplating six charges and wants your advice on the legal issues that he might anticipate arising on those charges and advice as to his chances of obtaining convictions.

The six contemplated charges are as follows:

In the case of Alec,

> 1. aggravated assault endangering life contrary to s. 268.1 of the *Criminal Code*, and
> 2. if Claire dies, second degree murder or
> 3. first degree murder.

In the case of Betty,

> 4. aggravated assault endangering life contrary to s. 268.1 of the *Criminal Code*, and
> 5. "failing to stop at an intersection" contrary to s. 125A of the Ontario *Highway Traffic Act*, and
> 6. careless driving contrary to s. 130 of the Ontario *Highway Traffic Act*.

The penalty for the s. 125A traffic offence is a fixed $200 fine. For s. 130 it is a fine of not less than $200 and not more than $1000 or to imprisonment of not more than six months or both. Both could result in a license suspension.

5. The accused, Don, aged 24, has lived in Ottawa all his life. In his early childhood he was socially inept, quiet and brooding. He was so troublesome at school that his mother Pam, a single mother living alone, had to do her best to home school him. By the age of 12 Don became very withdrawn. He has no real friends. He is addicted to violent video games, heavy metal music, marijuana, and is a paranoid gun aficionado. His mother knows that he has become increasingly bitter about authority and bureaucracy of any sort, including social workers who he regards as evil agents of the evil government. He usually sleeps in the basement of his mother's house. He is obsessed with watching a video of the man recently shooting a soldier at the War Memorial and trying to go after politicians in the Parliament Building. His mother is aware that he is making something scary in her basement but he won't tell her what this is. She is fearful of what he is planning but does not dare to interfere. All he says is that "I want to leave my own mark".

One afternoon Don heads to the War Memorial with three homemade incendiary devices in a bag and holding a loaded handgun. When he arrives,

Peter, one of the unarmed soldiers on duty at the Memorial, sees the gun and runs at Don to stop him from doing something. However, Don pulls the detonator from one of his devices and tries to lob the contraption over the oncoming soldier towards the Memorial. He later admits he was trying to destroy the Memorial. The device explodes before there is any damage to the Memorial but Peter is badly wounded by the explosion. Don is quickly taken into custody by a uniformed police officer. Before an ambulance arrives a bystander, a nurse recently back from service in West Africa, attends to Peter. She tries for some 10 minutes to staunch the profuse bleeding. Peter is taken to hospital where he undergoes surgery. Within a week he is recovering well. Tragically, and unknown to the nurse at the time, she had contracted the Ebola virus which she passed on to Peter. Both the nurse and Peter died within a few weeks.

War veterans and the public are outraged and shocked by this second tragedy at the War Memorial. A search of Pam's house reveals a cupboard in the basement full of guns, bullets, homemade bombs and detonators. Don had padlocked that cupboard. Pam admits that she was worried about what was in that cupboard but was too scared to confront her son.

The defence counsel acting for both Don and Pam asks you for a legal brief as to possible defences to the charges laid. Identify applicable legal authorities and assess the chances of getting your clients acquitted.

Don is charged with:

1. first degree murder contrary to the *Criminal Code*.
   [Ignore the issue of a lesser verdict of manslaughter as the Crown is adamantly seeking the toughest approach possible] and
2. using explosives contrary to s. 81(1)(a) of the *Criminal Code*.

Under s. 81(1)(a) it is an offence subject to imprisonment for a maximum of life to "do anything with intent to cause an explosion of an explosive substance that is likely to cause serious bodily harm or death to persons or is likely to cause serious damage to property". Section 2 defines "explosive substance" under the *Criminal Code* as "anything intended to be used to make an explosive substance".

Pam is charged with possession of an explosive substance contrary to s. 82(1) of the *Criminal Code*.

Under s. 82(1) it is an offence punishable for a term not exceeding five years for "Every person [to have] ... in possession ... an explosive substance".

Chapter 4

RAPE AND SEXUAL ASSAULT

1. RAPE LAWS IN CONTEXT[1]

Sexual violence is about power and control, not sexual desire. It is about exerting power and aggression over someone else.[2]

It is submitted that sexual assault is an equality issue. Children are singled out for sexual assault because of their age and sex, that is, because of their vulnerability, accessibility, powerlessness, and lack of credibility. Women are singled out for sexual assault and their accusations of sexual assault are systematically disbelieved because of their gender, that is, because they are relegated to an inferior social status as female, including being socially defined as appropriate targets for forced sex. As a result of these perceptions, women are made vulnerable to sexual assault.[3]

Sexual assault is endemic. According to the Badgley Committee's Report,[4] about one in two females and one in three males have been subjected to unwanted sexual acts. About four in five of these incidents first happened when these persons were children.[5]

Sexual assault is a highly gendered crime that is disproportionately perpetrated by men against women. According to 2007 police-reported data, rates of sexual victimization were more than five times higher for women than for men.[6] Further, although men are responsible for most violent crime in any case (82% overall) that percentage is even greater in the case of sexual assault (98%).[7]

---

1 We acknowledge with thanks the updating of this introduction by Pam Hrick, while she was a second-year law student at Queen's.

2 Ontario, *Changing Attitudes, Changing Lives: Ontario's Sexual Violence Action Plan* (Toronto: Ontario Women's Directorate, 2011) at 4 <http://www.citizenship.gov.on.ca/owd/english/women/svap2011.pdf>.

3 Affidavit filed to gain intervener status in the Supreme Court of Canada for the Legal Education and Action Fund (LEAF) in the case of *Seaboyer v. R.*, on appeal from the Ontario Court of Appeal.

4 *Sexual Offences Against Children* (Ottawa: Minister of Supply and Services, 1984) vol. 1 at 175, 186.

5 A thorough discussion of child sexual abuse is beyond the scope of this chapter. However, for further comment, see Nicholas Bala, "Double Victims: Child Sexual Abuse and the Canadian Criminal Justice System" (1980), 15 Queen's L.J. 3 and Institute for the Prevention of Child Abuse, Update Child Sex Abuse and the Law (1992).

6 Shannon Brennan & Andrea Taylor-Butts, *Sexual Assault in Canada 2004 and 2007* (Ottawa: Statistics Canada, Canadian Centre for Justice Statistics, 2008) at 12-13.

7 Statistics Canada, "Cases completed in adult criminal court, by type of offence and sex of the accused, Canada, 2014/2015", *Juristat*, April 27 2017 <http://www.statcan.gc.ca/pub/85-002-x/2017001/article/14699/tbl/tbl06-eng.htm>.

Almost 40% of women report having experienced some kind of sexual violence since the age of 16.[8]

Women in marginalized demographics often experience a higher rate of sexual violence. For example, it is estimated that 83% of women with disabilities will be sexually assaulted in their lifetime.[9] This issue is particularly serious for Aboriginal women, for whom the annual victimization rate is more than three times that for non-Aboriginal women. This disproportion is reduced but not eliminated when other risk factors for victimization (a generally younger population, a higher rate of a history of homelessness, and so on) are taken into account.[10]

The myth that the "worst rapes" are committed by strangers, should be dispelled. The danger is that only these types of sexual assaults will be taken seriously by the police and eventually the courts. In reality, many women experience sexual violence in intimate partner relationships or at the hands of individuals known to them. Only 18% of sexual assaults conform to the stereotype of the accused being a stranger in an alleyway, while 31% are committed by family members and 28% are committed by acquaintances.[11]

A brutal violation by a stranger may be less devastating than a brutal violation by one who the survivor loved and trusted. LEAF points out the very real harm that women who have been sexually violated suffer. They experience "the dissolution of the foundations, values and pleasures which previously gave their life meaning and stability. . .and can include trust in relationships, a sense of security in one's home and one's bedroom . . . control over one's physical and emotional functions, self-confidence",[12] etc. The myth about the identity of perpetrators is probably based on the notion that once consent has been given it cannot be withdrawn. This is clearly offensive. The devastation of those who are sexually assaulted can be significant.

Notwithstanding the frequency of this crime, it is estimated that fewer than 10% of sexual assaults are reported to the police. Sexual offences are less likely to be cleared by police than other types of violent crimes, with charges being laid in just over a third of sexual assault cases as compared to almost half of other types of violent offences. Conviction rates for sexual assault are lower than for most other violent crimes. The conviction rate for sexual assault is 43%, compared to 52% for major non-sexual assaults, and 49% for violent offences

---

8 Canadian Panel on Violence Against Women, *Changing the Landscape: Ending Violence – Achieving Equality* (Ottawa: Minister of Supply and Services, 1993). For controversial views in both Canada and the U.K. that research on the extent of violence against women and children is based on faulty methodologies and has exaggerated the problem, see John Fekete, *Moral Panic: Biopolitics Rising* (1994) and Christina Hoff Sommers, *Who Stole Feminism? How Women Have Betrayed Women* (1994).

9 Liz Stimpson & Margaret C. Best, "Courage Above All: Sexual Assault Against Women with Disabilities" (Toronto: DisAbled Women's Network, 1991) cited in Ontario, *Sexual Assault: Dispelling Myths* (Toronto: Ontario Women's Directorate, 2009) <http://www.citizenship.gov.on.ca/owd/english/resources/publications/ dispelling/dispellingthemyth.pdf>.

10 Statistics Canada, "Criminal Victimization in Canada, 2014", by Samuel Perreault, in *Juristat*, Catalogue No. 85-002-X (Ottawa: 23 November 2015), online: <http://www.statcan.gc.ca/pub/85-002-x/2015001/article/ 14241-eng.htm>.

11 *Supra* note 6 at 13.

12 *Supra* note 3 at 13.

generally.[13] The majority of sexual assault survivors never report the assault because of mistrust of the system that is trying them, not their attackers:

> Our files are filled with poignant examples of women who are twice punished. They have lived through the violation of a sexual assault and then the violation of the courtroom experience, where often they – the victims – are put on trial. These women undergo the humiliating and painful process of relating the story of their assault to a room full of strangers, of reliving the trauma, their responses directed by questions over which they have no control. Their reward often is to see their assaulter acquitted.[14]

The crime of sexual assault is unique in that it is overwhelmingly perpetrated against women and children. The law has responded to these groups in a particular way due to their unique role in society. Historically, women were considered chattels and the law responded to crimes against women from this viewpoint. Consider the following roots of our sexual assault laws, as they formed part of the Laws from Alfred, King of the West Saxons, 871-900:

> If anyone seizes by the breast a young woman belonging to the commons, he shall pay her 5 shillings compensation.
>
> s. 1. If he throws her down but does not lie with her, he shall pay [her] 10 shillings compensation
>
> s. 2. If he lies with her, he shall pay [her] 60 shillings compensation.
>
> s. 3. If another man has previously lain with her, then the compensation shall be half this [amount].
>
> s. 4. If she is accused [of having previously lain with a man], she shall clear herself by [an oath of] 60 hides, or lose half the compensation due to her.
>
> s. 5. If this [outrage] is done to a woman of higher birth, the compensation to be paid shall increase according to the wergeld.[15]

The underlying rationale behind such laws is clearly rooted in viewing women as possessions.

> Rape was originally seen as a crime of theft of sexual property. A rapist would often have to pay money in damages to the woman's husband or father because the woman was seen as having lost the value of a marriageable daughter or of a pure wife.[16]

This point of view — of women as sexual possessions — has been reflected in certain aspects of Canadian criminal law. For example, until 1983 it was not

---

13 Statistics Canada, "Cases completed in adult criminal court, by type of offence and decision, Canada, 2014/ 2015", *Juristat* (Ottawa: 27 April 2017), online: <http://www.statcan.gc.ca/pub/85-002-x/2017001/article/ 14699/tbl/tbl04-eng.htm>.

14 Pat Marshall, "Sexual Assault, The Charter and Sentencing Reform" (1988), 63 C.R. (3d) 216 at 217.

15 The Laws of the Earliest English Kings, 71 (F.L. Altenborough trans. & ed., 1922).

16 Megan Ellis, *Surviving Procedures After a Sexual Assault* (Vancouver: Press Gang Publishers, 1985) at 4. See, too, Constance Backhouse, "Nineteenth Century Canadian Rape Law: 1800-1892" in David Flaherty, *Essays in the History of the Criminal Law* (1983, Osgoode Soc.), vol. II at 200.

an offence under the *Criminal Code* for a man to rape his wife. Attitudes toward the crime of rape developed from these roots and produced pernicious myths:

> Many people believed that if a woman got raped it was her own fault. They thought that only certain kinds of women got raped. These attitudes meant that women who were raped did not want to tell people because they were afraid of being blamed. Because women did not tell, many people thought that rape did not happen very often.[17]

Other myths concerned women who did report their rape. Often they were not believed and were suspected of having provoked the attack. Again, the attitude was that women were at fault. These propositions were not held in isolation, but were also reflected in many powerful segments of society, including within the criminal justice system, which accepted a number of harmful propositions, such as:

> A (good) woman cannot be raped against her will, and will mount fierce resistance before yielding her virtue. She should have injuries to corroborate her claims of having been forced. . .Absent overt resistance that is recognized as such by a sexual aggressor and by the trier of fact, silence can be taken as a yes; no may mean yes; drinking or dancing with, humouring, accepting a ride or working late with, faking sleep, rolling over in one's sleep, wearing particular clothes or few clothes or sex-appropriate clothes, being unescorted by a man – all may mean yes if a man who wants sex wants it to mean yes or can persuade a judge or jury that there is some air of reality to the logic by which his wish becomes her desire.[18]

Such attitudes were reflected in the way courts treated rape cases and the clearly discriminatory evidentiary rules which were fashioned regarding women who were raped. Women were often questioned about their past sexual history for two reasons. There was the belief that sexual history or reputation was clearly relevant to the issue of consent, as well as being related to whether or not the woman was telling the truth. Also, if the woman had not reported the rape immediately, it was suggested that in the interim she had fabricated the charge of rape. In rape prosecutions the jury was warned that it was dangerous to convict on the evidence of the woman alone if there was not other corroborating evidence, independent of her, implicating the accused. In other instances the statute provided that no conviction could be had without corroboration even if the jury was satisfied of guilt beyond a reasonable doubt.

(a) Prior Sexual History

Courts have long focused on the previous sexual history of the primary witness in a sexual assault case as relevant to the outcome of the trial. Unchastity was considered relevant both to the issue of consent and to the credibility of the testimony of the witness. It was not uncommon to read judicial expressions such as that "no impartial mind can resist the conclusion that a female who had been in the recent habit of illicit intercourse with others will not be so likely to resist

---

17 Ellis, *ibid.* at 5.
18 Sheila McIntyre, "Tracking and Resisting Backlash Against Equality Gains in Sexual Offence Law" (2000) 20(3) *Canadian Woman Studies* 72 at 73.

as one spotless and pure."[19] Even Wigmore believed that such information was relevant. A sexually active victim was suspect since "[t]he unchaste ... mentality finds incidental but direct expression in the narration of imaginary sex incidents of which the narrator is the heroine or the victim".[20] An unrestricted right to cross-examine a rape victim as to her previous sexual history with others was perhaps the practice that was most responsible for trials being seen as trials of the victim rather than trials of the accused.

(b)   Doctrine of Recent Complaint

The doctrine of recent complaint was embodied in the common law. It meant that a complaint by a victim of a sexual assault had to be made at the first reasonable opportunity and it had to be made spontaneously.[21] This was an exception to the general common law rule that a witness' previous statements are inadmissible since they constitute self-confirmation of one's own version of the event.[22]

The justification for the fresh-complaint rule was clearly due to the distrust of women. As was stated in the Model Penal Code, the "requirement of prompt complaint springs in part from a fear that unwanted pregnancy or bitterness at a relationship gone sour might convert a willing participant in sexual relations into a vindictive complainant".[23] This was the "logic" behind the doctrine of recent complaint.

Such views were integral in the judicial consideration of sexual assault charges, and resulted in the establishment of certain presumptions. As was held by one court, it "is so natural as to be almost inevitable that a female upon whom the crime has been committed will make immediate complaint".[24] Since the presumption existed that a sexual assault would lead immediately to a complaint, judges often commented on the absence of a complaint at the first reasonable opportunity, inviting juries to draw an adverse or negative inference about the victim's credibility.[25]

(c)   Corroboration

The requirement for corroboration of a woman's evidence in sexual matters was established by early authorities and "justified" by writers. As Wigmore stated:

> Modern psychiatrists have amply studied the behaviour of errant young girls and women coming before the courts in all sorts of cases. Their psychic complexes are multifarious, distorted partly

---

19 *Lee v. State* (1915), 132 Tenn. 655, 179 S.W. 145 at 658 [Tenn.].

20 John Henry Wigmore, *Evidence in Trials at Common Law*, rev. ed. James H. Chadbourn (Boston: Little, Brown, 1970), vol. 3A, sec. 924a at 736 (originally published in 1904).

21 *R. v. Lillyman* (1896), 2 L.R. 167; *R. v. Osbourne*, [1905] 1 K.B. 551 (C.C.R.); *Thomas v. The Queen*, [1952] 2 S.C.R. 344; *R. v. Kulak* (1979), 46 C.C.C. (2d) 30 (Ont. C.A.).

22 *Cross on Evidence*, 6th ed. (1979) at 258.

23 *Model Penal Code and Commentaries* (The American Law Institute, 1985) s. 213.6, Comment 5, p. 421.

24 *State v. Connelly* (1894), 57 Minn. 482, 59 N.W. 479 at 481 [N.W.].

25 See *R. v. Kistendey* (1975), 29 C.C.C. (2d) 382 (Ont. C.A.); *R. v. Boyce* (1974), 28 C.R.N.S. 336 (Ont. C.A.).

by inherent defects, partly by diseased derangements or abnormal instincts, partly by bad social environment, partly by temporary physiological or emotional conditions. One form taken by these complexes is that of contriving false charges of sexual offences by men.... The real victim, however, too often in such cases is the innocent man ... (and) a plausible tale by an attractive, innocent-looking girl may lead to a life-sentence for the accused, because the rules of Evidence (and the Judge's unacquaintance with modern psychiatry) permit no adequate probing of the witness' veracity.... No Judge should ever let a sex-offence charge go to the jury unless the female complainant's social history and mental make-up have been examined and testified to by a qualified physician.[26]

The justification for this rule was very explicitly laid out in the *Columbia Law Review*:

Surely the simplest, and perhaps the most important reason not to permit conviction for rape on the uncorroborated word of the prosecutrix is that that word is very often false ... Since stories of rape are frequently lies or fantasies, it is reasonable to provide that such a story, in itself, should not be enough to convict a man of a crime.[27]

This view was also reflected in court decisions. Without a corroboration requirement, "every man is in danger of being prosecuted and convicted on the testimony of a base woman, in whose testimony there is no truth".[28] And as a court quoting Glanville Williams found, "sexual cases are particularly subject to the danger of deliberately false charges, resulting from sexual neurosis, fantasy, jealousy, spite, or simply a girl's refusal to admit that she consented to an act of which she is now ashamed".[29] This reflects the state the common law was in.

While in this day and age the propositions Wigmore espoused seem patently unreasonable, no one can doubt the influence that Wigmore had and does have in law. For this reason, it seems important to examine his assumptions:

Wigmore ... omitted material from ... case histories which might undermine or contradict his hypothesis that young girls who report sexual assault or abuse are lying about the charge....

Wigmore's unequivocal assertion that young girls who complain of sexual assault are likely to be lying is not supported by recent clinical experience or by survey research data. Surveys conducted during the period of the 1950's through the 1970's suggest that a significant portion of the female population has had some type of childhood sexual encounter with an adult male, many with relatives....

Historically, the Wigmore doctrine has survived because it appealed to society's traditional distrust and general hostility towards women, which was embodied in the law ... . When Wigmore passionately expressed his view about the threatening nature of complaints of sexual assault made by female children, he articulated and memorialized an attitude which was apparently widely shared. By documenting his case, however, he has allowed later readers to discover the inherent flaw — or call it a 'blind spot' — which lay behind his ostensibly objective presentation of scientific evidence.[30]

---

26 *Supra* note 20 at sec. 924a, p. 736-7.
27 "Corroborating Charges of Rape" (1967), 67 Colum. L. Rev. 1137-1138.
28 *Davis v. State* (1904), 120 Ga. 433, 48 S.E. 180 at 181 [S.E.].
29 *State v. Anderson* (1965), 272 Minn. 384, 137 N.W. 2d 781 at 783 [N.W.], quoting Glanville Williams, "Corroboration — Sexual Cases" October 1962, Crim. L. Rev. 662-671.
30 L.B. Bienen, "A Question of Credibility: John Henry Wigmore's Use of Scientific Authority" (1983), 19 Cal. Western L. Rev. 235 at 253.

ALAN N. YOUNG, WHEN TITANS CLASH:
THE LIMITS OF CONSTITUTIONAL ADJUDICATION
(1995), 44 C.R. (4th) 152 at 153-155

In a comment on the Supreme Court's controversial decision in *R. v. O'Connor* (1995), 44 C.R. (4th) 1, 103 C.C.C. (3d) 1, [1995] 4 S.C.R. 411, which set out a two-part procedure for determining defence access to therapeutic and medical records of sexual assault complainants, Professor Alan Young described the following "battlefield":

In the last five years we have seen an ever-increasing defence strategy of requesting production of psychiatric and therapeutic records relating to sexual assault complainants. Stripped of its ideological and political context, this phenomena is no different than the flurry of breathalyzer production requests which followed upon the *Bourget* decision in 1987. Ultimately, the breathalyzer production strategy faded into oblivion as the courts imposed an "air of reality" restriction on the applications and indicated that they would not be inclined to order stays of proceedings for failure to produce alcohol standard solutions, representative ampoules and breathalyzer mouthpieces.

Unlike the breathalyzer experience, the issue of producing sensitive and confidential records of complainants is animated by deeply held ideological and political beliefs, and, as such, this issue would not fade into oblivion notwithstanding the "likely to be relevant" threshold restriction which the courts placed upon these applications for production. In this context, battle lines appeared to be carved in stone with little incentive to adopt a compromise settlement. In fact, complainants and custodians of sensitive records have appeared willing to disregard court orders. Beyond the unprofessional conduct of the Crown in *R. v. O'Connor*, reported *ante*, p. 1, in failing to properly comply with an order of production, we have seen cases in which the records have been destroyed and shredded in an attempt to thwart the request for production. To date, the courts have turned a blind eye to this extra-legal obstruction and have concluded that a stay of proceeding is not warranted upon proof of an intent to obstruct but is only warranted if the obstruction truly impaired full answer and defence in a material way.

[Since Professor Young wrote this piece the Supreme Court of Canada has ordered a stay when documents were shredded on the basis that they might have been helpful to the accused. See *R. v. Carosella*, (1997), 112 C.C.C. (3d) 289 (S.C.C.).]

To understand the intensity of this battle one must recognize that, historically, sexual assault victims have been re-victimized by an insensitive and patriarchal criminal justice system. Fuelled by Freud's assertion that women and children are hysterical by nature, we find countless examples of statutory and common law evidentiary rules which treated the evidence of sexual assault victims with great suspicion and skepticism. In *Wigmore's Treatise on Evidence*, the eminent commentator noted that "no judge should ever let a sexual offence charge go to the jury unless the female complainant's social history and mental makeup have been examined and testified to by a qualified physician."

The ghosts of the past still haunt the criminal justice system, and, as Madam Justice L'Heureux-Dubé, noted, "uninhibited disclosure of complainants' private lives indulges the discriminatory suspicion that women and children's reports of sexual victimization are uniquely likely to be fabricated." Therefore, it is not surprising that complainants and custodians of sensitive records would view almost all production requests as a form of character assassination which is premised upon the dangerous Freudian and Wigmorian stereotype of half the population being prone to fabrication.

On the other hand, we have a defence lawyer poised for battle because his/her client has denied the accusation. In most cases of sexual assault, there is an absence of confirmatory evidence and independent witnesses, and this raises the spectre of false accusations. This fear of false accusation is somewhat supported by a recent study by the Canadian Centre for Justice Statistics which revealed that the "unfounded"[31] rate for sexual assault was 14 per cent, 9 per cent and 14 per cent for sexual assault level I (s. 271), level II (s. 272) and level III (s. 273) respectively. These figures were compared to the unfounded rate for non-sexual assault which varied from 8 per cent with respect to assault level I (s. 266) to 3 per cent with respect to assault level II and III (ss. 267 and 268).[32] Furthermore, a recent study by an American sociologist demonstrated that 40 per cent of all rape charges investigated by city police turned out to be false as determined by recantation by the accuser and supported by other evidence.[33] Although it is conceded that further study must be given in order to explain this high unfounded rate, it is not surprising that defence counsel will search for whatever effective tools may be available to fully explore an accusation of sexual assault in order to ensure that his or her client is in the category of the unfounded complaint.

There are other offences which have higher unfounded rates than sexual assault (arson — 23.8 per cent; trespass at night — 14.3 per cent; abduction of person under 14 - 42.3 per cent),[34] yet we do not see the mad rush to impeach the credibility of Crown witnesses in these cases by resort to psychiatric and therapeutic records. This apparent inconsistency in defence strategy may suggest that defence lawyers still cling to and believe in the Wigmorian assessment of sexual assault complainants. However, it is equally plausible that the reliance

---

31 "Unfounded" does not necessarily mean frivolous or false. It is defined as follows: "if the preliminary enquiry conducted by the police reveals that a reported crime has not been committed, this incident is to be classified as unfounded."

32 *Juristat*, "Canadian Justice Processing of Sexual Assault Cases" (Ottawa: Centre for Justice Statistics, March 1994), vol. 14, no. 7 at 10.

33 E. Kanin, *False Rape Accusations (1994) Archives of Sexual Behavior* (New York: Plenum Press, 1994) at 81-92.

34 Statistics Canada, *Canadian Crime Statistics 1993* (Ottawa: Centre for Justice Statistics, 1993).

on production requests in sexual assault trials is more a reflection of the nature of these trials, which turn largely on credibility battles without the luxury of independent evidence of a confirmatory nature. Regardless of which explanation is correct, it is apparent that both sides to this battle view the other with much suspicion and some disdain.

2. DEFINITION OF THE CRIME OF RAPE

Until it was replaced by the crime of sexual assault in 1982 [S.C. 1980-81-82, c. 125, s. 19], the offence of rape was defined by what was then s. 143 of the *Criminal Code* as follows:

> A male person commits rape when he has sexual intercourse with a female person who is not his wife,
>
> (a) without her consent, or
> (b) with her consent if the consent
>> (i) is extorted by threats or fear of bodily harm,
>> (ii) is obtained by personating her husband, or
>> (iii) is obtained by false and fraudulent representations as to the nature and quality of the act.

Note the absolute immunity for the man who raped his wife. Note also the requirement of proof of sexual intercourse, defined elsewhere to be "penetration to even the slightest degree". This aspect often became the focal point of the trial and the reason why a prosecution might fail despite it being clear that a forced sexual encounter had occurred.

Section 143 contained no express *mens rea* requirement. That requirement and the possibility of a defence of mistaken belief was the issue in the controversial cases of *Pappajohn* and *Sansregret* which follow.

PAPPAJOHN v. R.

[1980] 2 S.C.R. 120, 14 C.R. (3d) 243, 52 C.C.C. (2d) 481,
1980 CarswellBC 446, 1980 CarswellBC 546

McINTYRE J. (PIGEON, BEETZ and CHOUINARD JJ. concurring): — The appellant appeals his rape conviction, which was affirmed in the Court of Appeal for British Columbia [5 C.R. (3d) 193, 45 C.C.C. (2d) 67] with one dissent, upon the ground that the trial Judge failed to put to the jury the defence of mistake of fact. That ground is expressed in the appellant's factum in these words:

> Did the learned trial Judge err in failing to instruct the jury on the question of honest belief by the accused that the Complainant consented to intercourse and thus on the facts of

this case, failed to put properly before the jury a defence, such failure being a non-direction amounting to mis-direction?

A consideration of the facts of the case is vital to a resolution of the problem it poses. The complainant was a real estate saleswoman employed by a well-known and well-established real estate firm in Vancouver. She was successful in her work. The appellant is a businessman who was anxious to sell his home in Vancouver, and he had listed it for sale with the real estate firm with which the complainant was associated. She was to be responsible for the matter on her firm's behalf. On 4th August 1976 at about 1:00 p.m. she met the appellant by appointment at a downtown restaurant for lunch. The purpose of the meeting was to discuss the house sale. The lunch lasted until about 4:00 or 4:30 p.m. During this time a good deal of liquor was consumed by both parties. The occasion became convivial, the proprietor of the restaurant and his wife joined the party and estimates of the amount of alcohol consumed varied in retrospect, as one would expect. It does seem clear, however, that, while each of the parties concerned had a substantial amount to drink, each seemed capable of functioning normally.

At about 4:00 p.m. or shortly thereafter they left the restaurant. The appellant drove the complainant's car while she sat in the front passenger seat. They went to the appellant's house, the one which was listed for sale, to further consider questions arising in that connection. Up to the time of arrival at the home, at about 4:30 or 5:00 p.m., there is no significant variation in their accounts of events. From the moment of arrival, however, there is a complete divergence. She related a story of rape completely against her will and over her protests and struggles. He spoke of an amorous interlude involving no more than a bit of coy objection on her part and several acts of intercourse with her consent. Whatever occurred in the house, there is no doubt that at about 7:30 p.m. the complainant ran out of the house naked with a man's bow tie around her neck and her hands tightly tied behind her back with a bathrobe sash. She arrived at the door of a house nearby and demanded entry and protection. The occupant of the house, a priest, admitted her. She was in an upset state and exhibited great fear and emotional stress. The police were called, and these proceedings followed. More detailed reference to the facts will be made later.

When the defence closed its case, and before the trial Judge commenced his charge, the jury was excluded while counsel for the appellant argued that, on the facts of the case as it appeared from the evidence, the trial Judge should have put the defence of mistake of fact to the jury. He contended that the appellant was entitled to have the Judge tell the jury that, if the appellant entertained an honest though mistaken belief that the complainant was consenting to the acts of intercourse as they occurred, the necessary *mens rea* would not be present and the appellant would be entitled to an acquittal. Reliance for this proposition was placed upon *D.P.P. v. Morgan*; *D.P.P. v. McDonald*; *D.P.P. v. McLarty*; *D.P.P. v. Parker*, [1976] A.C. 182 (H.L.), and *R. v. Plummer* (1975), 31 C.R.N.S.

220, 24 C.C.C. (2d) 497 (Ont. C.A.). The trial judge refused to accede to defence counsel's request and, in disposing of the motion, had this to say:

> In this case, the complainant has testified that the accused had intercourse with her during a three-hour period some five times without her consent. The accused has testified that the acts of intercourse that he had with the complainant were all with her consent and that the only resistance to his amorous advances was of a token variety, and that orally, along the lines of; "Oh George, what are you doing?"
> There are many conflicts in the evidence during the critical period of time when the acts of sexual intercourse took place, and the jury will have to be directed to accept either the complainant's or the accused's version of the facts.
> The essence of the case, as I see it, is essentially: Has the Crown negatived the complainant's consent?

. . . .

In the Court of Appeal this ruling found support in the majority judgment of Farris C.J.B.C., with whom Craig J.A. agreed. The majority adopted the view that the issue emerging from the evidence was a simple one of consent or no consent. In a dissenting judgment, Lambert J.A. was of the opinion that there was sufficient evidence to put the defence to the jury. He would have directed the jury that the accused was entitled to an acquittal if the jury found that he entertained an honest and *reasonably held* mistaken belief in the existence of consent. This is a view which I cannot share, in view of the pronouncement in this court in *Beaver v. R.*, [1957] S.C.R. 531 at 538, 118 C.C.C. 129.

It is well-established that it is the duty of a trial judge, in giving directions to a jury, to draw to their attention and to put before them fairly and completely the theory of the defence. In performing this task, it is also clear that the trial judge must put before the jury any defences which may be open to the accused upon the evidence, whether raised by the accused's counsel or not. He must give all necessary instructions on the law relating to such defences, review the relevant evidence and relate it to the law applicable. This, however, does not mean that the trial judge becomes bound to put every defence suggested to him by counsel. Before any obligation arises to put defences, there must be in the evidence some basis upon which the defence can rest, and it is only where such an evidentiary basis is present that a trial judge must put a defence. Indeed, where it is not present he should not put a defence, for to do so would only be to confuse.

. . . .

McIntyre J. then reviewed the evidence in greater detail and continued:

In summary, then, this was the state of evidence when the trial judge was called upon to make his ruling. It became his task to apply the rule enunciated above. In assessing his resolution of the matter, we must consider the situation as it presented itself to him at the time. Speculation as to what the jury did, or would have done after being charged, is not relevant here.

With that thought in mind, and bearing in mind that the object of the judicial search must be evidence of a mistaken but honest belief in the consent of the complainant, one must first ask the question "Where is this evidence to be found?" It cannot be found in the evidence of the complainant. She denies actual consent, and her evidence cannot provide any support for a mistaken belief in consent. Her conduct, according to her description, is that of a terrified, hysterical, non-consenting woman who resisted the appellant's advances, albeit unsuccessfully, and when able fled from his house in search of assistance. Turning then to the evidence of the appellant, it immediately becomes apparent that his evidence speaks of actual consent, even co-operation, and leaves little, if any, room for the suggestion that she may not have been consenting but he thought she was. The two stories are, as has been noted before, diametrically opposed on this vital issue. It is not for the trial judge to weigh them and prefer one to the other. It is for him in this situation, however, to recognize the issue which arises on the evidence for the purpose of deciding what defences are open. In this situation the only realistic issue which can arise is the simple issue of consent or no consent. In my opinion, the trial judge was correct in concluding that there simply was not sufficient evidence to justify the putting of the defence of mistake of fact to the jury. He left the issue of consent, and that was the only one arising on the evidence.

In reaching this conclusion, I am not unmindful of the evidence of surrounding circumstances which were said to support the appellant's contention. I refer to the absence of serious injury suffered by the complainant and the absence of damage to clothing, as well as to the long period of time during which the parties remained in the bedroom. These matters may indeed be cogent on the issue of actual consent but, in my view, they cannot by themselves advance a suggestion of a mistaken belief. The finding of the clothes at the foot of the bed and the necklace and the keys in the living room are equally relevant on the issue of actual consent and, in my view, cannot affect the issue, which was clearly framed by the opposing assertions of consent and non-consent.

It would seem to me that, if it is considered necessary in this case to charge the jury on the defence of mistake of fact, it would be necessary to do so in all cases where the complainant denies consent and an accused asserts it. To require the putting of the alternative defence of mistaken belief in consent, there must be, in my opinion, some evidence beyond the mere assertion by counsel for the appellant of belief in consent. This evidence must appear from or be supported by sources other than the appellant in order to give it any air of reality. In *R. v. Plummer, supra*, Evans J.A. (as he then was), speaking for the Ontario Court of Appeal, considered that there was such evidence as far as Brown was concerned, and directed a new trial because the defence had not been put. In that case, the complainant had gone to Plummer's "pad", where she had been raped by Plummer. Brown entered the room where the rape occurred after Plummer had gone. Apparently he had arrived at the house separately from Plummer. It was open on the evidence to find that he was unaware then that Plummer had threatened the complainant and terrorized her into submission. He had intercourse with her, and she said that because of continuing fear from Plummer's threats, she submitted without protest. In these special circumstances the defence was required. The facts clearly established at least an air of reality to Brown's defence. In *Morgan, supra*, there was evidence of an invitation by the complainant's husband to have intercourse with his wife and his assurance that her show of resistance would be a sham. In other words, there was evidence explaining, however preposterous the explanation might be, a basis for the mistaken belief. In the case at bar, there is no such evidence.

Where the complainant says rape and the accused says consent, and where on the whole of the evidence, including that of the complainant, the accused and the surrounding circumstances, there is a clear issue on this point, and where, as here, the accused makes no assertion of a belief in consent, as opposed to an actual consent, it is unrealistic, in the absence of some other circumstance or circumstances, such as are found in the *Plummer* and *Morgan* cases, *supra*, to consider the judge bound to put the mistake of fact defence. In my opinion, the trial judge was correct in refusing to put the defence on the evidence before him.

I might add that I have had the advantage of reading the reasons of my brother Dickson and, while it is apparent that I am unable to accept his view on the evidentiary question, I am in agreement with that part of his judgment dealing with the availability as a defence to a charge of rape in Canada of what is generally termed the defence of mistake of fact. I would dismiss the appeal.

[Martland J. concurred with McIntyre J. but held that the mistaken belief would have to be honest and reasonable.]

DICKSON J. (dissenting) (ESTEY J. concurring): —

. . . .

It will be convenient to identify the pivotal issues on which the appellant's case turns:

(1) What is the *mens rea* of rape?

(2) Is a mistaken belief in consent available in defence to the charge of rape?

(3) If so, does mistake afford a defence only where the mistake is one which is held both honestly *and on reasonable grounds*?

(4) Did the trial judge err in the case at bar in ruling that there was not sufficient basis of fact to justify leaving the defence of mistake of fact to the jury?

I

Mens Rea

There rests now, at the foundation of our system of criminal justice, the precept that a man cannot be adjudged guilty and subjected to punishment unless the commission of the crime was voluntarily directed by a willing mind. Blackstone spoke of a "vicious act" consequent upon a "vicious will" (Commentaries on the Laws of England (1765), vol. 4, p. 21). Proof of the mental element is an essential and constituent step in establishing criminal responsibility. Parliament can, of course, by express words, create criminal offences for which a guilty intention is not an essential ingredient. Equally, *mens rea* is not requisite in a wide category of statutory offences which are concerned with public welfare, health and safety. Subject to these exceptions, *mens rea*, consisting of some positive state of mind, such as evil intention or knowledge of the wrongfulness of the act or reckless disregard of consequences, must be proved by the prosecution. The mental element may be established by inference from the nature of the act committed, or by additional evidence.

The *mens rea* which is required, and its nature and extent, will vary with the particular crime; it can be determined only by detailed examination of the *actus reus* of the offence. Speaking generally, at least where the circumstance is not "morally indifferent", the mental element must be proved with respect to all circumstances and consequences that form part of the *actus reus*. It follows that, in a case of alleged rape, where a fact or circumstance is not known to, or is misapprehended by, the accused, leading to a mistaken but honest belief in the consent of the woman, his act is not culpable in relation to that element of the offence: Glanville Williams, *Criminal Law, The General Part*, 2nd ed. (1961), p. 52:

> For if the *actus reus* includes surrounding circumstances, it cannot be said to be intentional unless *all its elements*, including those circumstances, are known. (The italics are mine.)

Taking these principles, then, what is the mental element required under s. 143 of the *Criminal Code*, R.S.C. 1970, c. C-34, on a charge of rape? This crime was historically regarded as an offence of physical violence. Blackstone defined rape as "the carnal knowledge of a woman forcibly and against her will" (Commentaries, p. 210). A more comprehensive definition of rape at common law is found in Archbold, *Pleading, Evidence and Practice in Criminal Cases*, 38th ed. (1973), para. 2871:

> Rape consists in having unlawful sexual intercourse with a woman without her consent by force, fear or fraud [citing East's Pleas of the Crown (1803), vol. 1, p. 434, and Hale's Pleas of the Crown (1736), vol. 1, p. 627].

Section 143 of our *Code*, in brief, defines rape as an act of sexual intercourse with a female person without her consent, or with consent if that consent is extorted by threats or fear of bodily harm. It will be seen that the statutory definition does not depart in any significant way from the common law definition. For all practical purposes, the *Criminal Code* merely codifies the common law. The essence of the crime consists in the commission of an act of sexual intercourse where a woman's consent, or genuine consent, has been withheld.

. . . .

In summary, intention or recklessness must be proved in relation to all elements of the offence, including absence of consent. This simply extends to rape the same general order of intention as in other crimes.

II

Mistake of Fact

Belief by an accused in a mistaken set of facts has not always afforded an answer to a criminal charge. By the early criminal law, the only real defence that could be raised was that an act had not been voluntary and therefore could not be imputed to the accused. Thus it was possible in some cases to excuse a man who had acted under a mistake by the argument that his conduct was not truly voluntary: Russell On Crime, 12th ed. (1964), vol. 1, p. 71. In the 17th century, Hale wrote: "But in some cases *ignorantia facti* doth excuse, for such an ignorance many times makes the act itself morally involuntary." (Pleas of the Crown (1736), vol. 1, p. 42).

The leading English cases on mistake of fact are, of course, *R. v. Prince* (1875), 13 Cox C.C. 138 (C.C.R.), and *R. v. Tolson* (1889), 23 Q.B.D. 168 (C.C.R.). In the *Prince* decision (p. 152), Brett J. cited from Blackstone's Commentaries, p. 27:

> *Ignorance or mistake* is another defect of will, when a man, intending to do a lawful act, does that which is unlawful. For here, the deed and the will acting separately, there is not that conjunction between them which is necessary to form a criminal act.

Brett J. held that mistake as a defence applies whenever facts are present, in which an accused believes and has reasonable ground to believe, which if true would render his act innocent and not a crime. The *Tolson* case, following *Prince*, considered the extent to which a mistaken, though honest and reasonable, belief that the first spouse was dead could afford a defence to a charge of bigamy. The classic statement is that of Cave J. (p. 181):

> At common law an honest and reasonable belief in the existence of circumstances, which, if true, would make the act for which the prisoner is indicted an innocent act has always been held to be a good defence.

An honest and reasonable mistake of fact is on the same footing as the absence of a reasoning faculty, as with infants, or impairment of the faculty, as in lunacy (*Tolson*, p. 181). Culpability rests upon commission of the offence with knowledge of the facts and circumstances comprising the crime. If, according to an accused's belief concerning the facts, his act is criminal, then he intended the offence and can be punished. If, on the other hand, his act would be innocent, according to facts as he believed them to be, he does not have the criminal mind and ought not to be punished for his act. (See E.R. Keedy, "Ignorance and Mistake in the Criminal Law" (1908), 22 Harvard L. Rev. 75, p. 82).

As stated by Dixon J., as he then was, in *Thomas v. R.*, 59 C.L.R. 279 at 299-300 (H.C.):

> States of volition are necessarily dependant upon states of fact, and a mistaken belief in the existence of circumstances cannot be separated from the manifestation of the will which it prompts ... the nature of an act of volition may be of an entirely different description if it is based on mistake of fact. The state of facts assumed must often enter into the determination of the will. It would be strange if our criminal law did not contain this principle and treat it as fundamental.

Mistake is a defence, then, where it prevents an accused from having the *mens rea* which the law requires for the very crime with which he is charged. Mistake of fact is more accurately seen as a negation of guilty intention than as the affirmation of a positive defence. It avails an accused who acts innocently, pursuant to a flawed perception of the facts, and nonetheless commits the *actus reus* of an offence. Mistake is a defence, though, in the sense that it is raised as an issue by an accused. The Crown is rarely possessed of knowledge of the subjective factors which may have caused an accused to entertain a belief in a fallacious set of facts.

If I am correct that: (i) s. 143 of the *Criminal Code* imports a *mens rea* requirement; and (ii) the *mens rea* of rape includes intention, or recklessness as to non-consent of the complainant, a mistake that negatives intention or recklessness entitles the accused to an acquittal. Glanville Williams notes in *Criminal Law, The General Part*, para. 65, p. 173:

> It is impossible to assert that a crime requiring intention or recklessness can be committed although the accused laboured under a mistake negativing the requisite intention or recklessness. Such an assertion carries its own refutation.

Howard (Criminal Law, 3rd ed. (1977)), points out that rape is aimed at the protection of women from forcible subjection to non-marital sexual intercourse, but that the facts of life not infrequently impede the drawing of a clean line between consensual and non-consensual intercourse (p. 149):

> it is easy for a man intent upon his own desires to mistake the intentions of a woman or girl who may herself be in two minds about what to do. Even if he makes no mistake it is not unknown for a woman afterwards either to take fright or for some other reason to regret what has happened and seek to justify herself retrospectively by accusing the man of rape.

I do not think the defence of mistaken belief can be restricted to those situations in which the belief has been induced by information received from a third party. That was the situation in the *Morgan* case, *supra*. In *Morgan*, the belief in consent was induced by information related by the complainant's husband, who spoke of his wife's sexual propensities. The foundation for the defence, incredible as it turned out to be, in view of the violence, was the misinformation of the husband. Had the defendants believed that information and had the wife's overt conduct been relatively consistent with it, the defendants would have had a defence. That is the effect of the dicta of the House of Lords in the *Morgan* case.

In principle, the defence should avail when there is an honest belief in consent or an absence of knowledge that consent has been withheld. Whether the mistake is rooted in an accused's mistaken perception or is based upon objective but incorrect facts confided to him by another should be of no consequence. The kind of mistaken fact pleaded by the *Morgan* defendants, however, is more likely to be believed than a bald assertion of mistaken belief during a face-to-face encounter. In any event, it is clear that the defence is available only where there is sufficient evidence presented by an accused, by his testimony or by the circumstances in which the act occurred, to found the plea.

III

Honest and Reasonable Mistake

The next question which must be broached is whether a defence of honest, though mistaken, belief in consent must be based on reasonable grounds.

. . . .

In Canada, the *Tolson* rule has already been rejected by this court in favour of the honest belief standard. Unless this court wishes to overrule *Beaver v. R.*, [1957] S.C.R. 531, 118 C.C.C. 129, it is difficult to see how the minority in *Morgan* can decide this appeal.

In *R. v. Rees*, [1956] S.C.R. 640, 24 C.R. 1, 115 C.C.C. 1, the issue was whether there is *mens rea* for the offence of knowingly or wilfully contributing to juvenile delinquency. Cartwright J. set out the *Tolson* test and then held as follows (p. 11 C.R.):

> The first of the statements of Stephen J. quoted above should now be read in the light of the judgment of Lord Goddard C.J., concurred in by Lynskey and Devlin JJ. in *Wilson v. Inyang* [*supra*], which, in my opinion, rightly decides that the essential question is whether the belief entertained by the accused is an honest one and that the existence or non-existence of reasonable grounds for such belief is merely relevant evidence to be weighed by the tribunal of fact in determining such essential question.

One year later, in *Beaver v. R.*, *supra*, a narcotics case, the opinion of Cartwright J. was accepted by a majority of the court. He adopted the paragraph quoted above from *Rees*. *Beaver* has since been regarded as an authoritative contribution to the law as to mental element, and mistaken belief, in true crimes.

It is not clear how one can properly relate reasonableness (an element in offences of negligence) to rape (a "true crime" and not an offence of negligence). To do so, one must, I think, take the view that the *mens rea* goes only to the physical act of intercourse and not to non-consent, and acquittal comes only if the mistake is reasonable. This, upon the authorities, is not a correct view, the intent in rape being not merely to have intercourse but to have it with a non-consenting woman. If the jury finds that mistake, whether reasonable or unreasonable, there should be no conviction. If, upon the entire record, there is evidence of mistake to cast a reasonable doubt upon the existence of a criminal mind, then the prosecution has failed to make its case. In an article by Professor Colin Howard, "The Reasonableness of Mistake in the Criminal Law" (1961), 4 University of Queensland L.J. 45, the following is offered (p. 47):

> To crimes of *mens rea*, or elements of a crime which requires *mens rea*, mistake of fact *simpliciter* is a defence; to crimes of negligence, or elements of an offence which requires only negligence, mistake of fact is a defense only if the mistake was in all the circumstances a reasonable one to make.

The same analysis is expressed by Glanville Williams, *Criminal Law, The General Part*, para. 71, p. 202.

. . . .

. . . With respect, there is no compelling reason for extending to rape the misapprehension, having its genesis in *Tolson* and now endemic in English law, that makes bigamy a crime of negligence and would have a like effect if applied to statutory rape.

Lambert J.A. recognized that, while his conclusion was directed by precedent rather than logic, he also found it to be supported, in relation to rape, by policy and practical sense [p. 212]:

> Why should a woman who is sexually violated by such a man have to defend herself by screams or blows in order to indicate her lack of consent, or have to consent through fear, for a charge of rape to be sustained? Surely a firm oral protest, sufficient to deny any reasonable grounds for belief in consent, should be a sufficient foundation in these circumstances for a charge of rape.

I am not unaware of the policy considerations advanced in support of the view that if mistake is to afford a defence to a charge of rape it should, at the very least, be one of a reasonable man might make in the circumstances. There is justifiable concern over the position of the woman who alleges that she has been subjected to a non-consensual sexual act; fear is expressed that subjective orthodoxy should not enable her alleged assailant to escape accountability by advancing some cock-and-bull story. The usual response of persons accused of rape is: "She consented." Are such persons now to be acquitted simply by saying: "Even if she did not consent, I believed she consented"? The concern is legitimate and real. It must, however, be placed in the balance with other relevant considerations. First, cases in which mistake can be advanced in answer to a charge of rape must be few in number. People do not normally commit rape per incuriam. An evidential case must exist to support the plea. Second, if the woman in her own mind withholds consent but her conduct and other circumstances lend credence to belief on the part of the accused that she was consenting, it may be that it is unjust to convict. I do not think it will do to say that in those circumstances she in fact consented. In fact, she did not, and it would be open to a jury to so find. Third, it is unfair to the jury and to the accused to speak in terms of two beliefs, one entertained by the accused, the other by a reasonable man, and to ask the jury to ignore an actual belief in favour of an attributed belief. The mind with which the jury is concerned is that of the accused. By importing a standard external to the accused, there is created an incompatible mix of subjective and objective factors. If an honest lack of knowledge is shown, then the subjective element of the offence is not proved. The following passage from the Heilbron Report is, however, apposite:

> 66. *Morgan's* case did not decide, as some critics seem to have thought, than an accused person was entitled to be acquitted, however ridiculous his story might be, nor did it decide that the reasonableness or unreasonableness of his belief was irrelevant. Furthermore it is a mistaken assumption that a man is entitled to be acquitted simply because he asserts this belief, without more.

Perpetuation of fictions does little for the jury system or the integrity of criminal justice. The ongoing debate in the courts and learned journals as to whether mistake must be reasonable is conceptually important in the orderly development of the criminal law, but, in my view, practically unimportant, because the accused's statement that he was mistaken is not likely to be believed unless the mistake is, to the jury, reasonable. The jury will be concerned to consider the reasonableness of any grounds found, or asserted to be available, to support the defence of mistake. Although "reasonable grounds" is not a precondition to the availability of a plea of honest belief in consent, those grounds determine the weight to be given the defence. The reasonableness or otherwise of the accused's belief is only evidence for or against the view that the belief was actually held and the intent was therefore lacking.

Canadian juries, in my experience, display a high degree of common sense and an uncanny ability to distinguish between the genuine and the specious.

The words of Dixon J. in *Thomas*, *supra*, at p. 309, bear repeating:

> a lack of confidence in the ability of a tribunal correctly to estimate evidence of states of mind and the like can never be sufficient ground for excluding from inquiry the most fundamental element in a rational and humane criminal code.

In *Textbook Of Criminal Law* (1978), p. 102, Professor Glanville Williams states the view, with which I am in agreement, that it is proper for the trial Judge to tell the jury "that if they think the alleged belief was unreasonable, that may be one factor leading them to conclude that it was not really held; but they must look at the facts as a whole". It will be a rare day when a jury is satisfied as to the existence of an unreasonable belief. If the claim of mistake does not raise a reasonable doubt as to guilt and all other elements of the crime have been proved, then the trier of fact will not give effect to the defence. But if there is any evidence that there was such an honest belief, regardless of whether it is reasonable, the jury must be entrusted with the task of assessing the credibility of the plea.

To apply the reasonable standard in this appeal, the court, in my view, would have to: (a) accept the minority decision in *Morgan*, *supra*; (b) overrule *Beaver*, *supra*, or find a means of distinguishing the offence of rape; and (c) defy accepted and sound principles of criminal law.

IV

The Plea and the Evidence

I come now to what is perhaps the most difficult part of this case, namely, whether there was an evidential base sufficient to require the trial judge to place before the jury the defence of mistaken belief in consent.

. . . .

Leaving aside the possibility of post-bondage intercourse, the jury could have reached any one of three alternative conclusions: (1) the appellant was telling the truth and the complainant did consent; (2) he was not telling the truth, she did not consent and he was aware of that fact or reckless to it; or (3) though he did not plead mistake, he believed she was consenting, notwithstanding token resistance. His defence of consent is rejected and that of honest belief accepted. I think there was sufficient evidence to put that third alternative to the jury.

Because the case turns on evidential matters, detailed reference thereto is unavoidable.

. . . .

There is circumstantial evidence supportive of a plea of belief in consent: (1) Her necklace and car keys were found in the living room. (2) She confirmed his testimony that her blouse was neatly hung in the clothes closet. (3) Other items of folded clothing were found at the foot of the bed. (4) None of her clothes were damaged in the slightest way. (5) She was in the house for a number of hours. (6) By her version, when she entered the house the appellant said he was going to break her. She made no attempt to leave. (7) She did not leave while he undressed. (8) There was no evidence of struggle. (9) She suffered no physical injuries, aside from three scratches.

The Heilbron Report contains the following observations which seem pertinent to the case at bar. The crime of rape involves an act — sexual intercourse — which is not in itself either criminal or unlawful and can indeed be both desirable and pleasurable; whether it is criminal depends on complex considerations, since the mental states of both parties and the influence of each upon the other, as well as their physical interaction, have to be considered and are sometimes difficult to interpret — all the more so since normally the act takes place in private; there can be many ambiguous situations in sexual relationships; hence, however precisely the law may be stated it cannot always adequately resolve these problems; in the first place, there may well be circumstances where each party interprets the situation differently, and it may be quite impossible to determine with any confidence which interpretation is right.

Toy J. gave a full, fair and accurate summary of the testimony by the complainant and appellant. There can be no criticism of the instructions in this respect. He did not, however, charge the jury on the defence of mistaken belief, as he earlier ruled that there was not "in the evidence any sufficient basis of fact to leave the defence of mistake of fact to this jury".

In my view, with respect, the judge erred in failing to instruct the jury: (a) that, as to pre-bondage intercourse, the issues were consent and belief in consent; and (b) that, as to post-bondage intercourse, the issue was whether an act of intercourse occurred or not. If the answer to (b) was negative, a conviction could not be founded upon the post-bondage period. If the answer was in the affirmative, a conviction would almost of necessity follow, because there was admittedly no consent or belief in consent after the "bondage". That the case gave the jury difficulty is clear from the fact that the charge was delivered about noon on a Friday and the verdict was not rendered until about 5:00 p.m. on Saturday.

I am mindful of the comment of Pigeon J. in *Leary*, *supra*, that consideration should be given to the plight of a complainant, who should not be subjected to the humiliation of having to testify again unless justice makes it imperative. The possibility of a mistaken belief in consent in the pre-bondage phase was an issue that should have been placed before the jury; the judge's failure to do so makes it imperative, in my opinion, in the interests of justice, that there be a new trial. It was open to the jury to find only token resistance prior to the "bondage"incident, which the appellant may not have perceived as withholding of consent. The accused was convicted of that which, perhaps, he did not intend to do had he known of no consent. It does not follow that, by simply disbelieving the appellant on consent, in fact, the jury thereby found that there was no belief in consent and that the appellant could not reasonably have believed in consent.

I would allow the appeal, set aside the judgment of the British Columbia Court of Appeal and direct a new trial.

Appeal dismissed.

For a view that mistaken beliefs in consent are mistakes of law rather than fact, see Lucinda Vandervort, "Mistake of Law and Sexual Assault: Consent and *Mens Rea*" (1987-88), 2 C.J.W.L. 233.

ROBIN WEINER, SHIFTING THE COMMUNICATION BURDEN: A MEANINGFUL CONSENT STANDARD IN RAPE

(1983), 6 Harv. Women's L.J. 143 at 147, 149

Robin Weiner has commented on the potential difficulties of applying an objective approach:

> If women and men always communicated their sexual interests and desires in the same manner, or if they understood each other's communications, they could, in fact, be represented by the same hypothetical person.... Behavior is not so accurately perceived, however; a gender gap in sexual communications exists.

. . . .

> Courts do not clarify the perspective from which the 'reasonableness' standard should be applied. They vary dramatically in what must be reasonable — the perpetrator's behavior, the victim's fear, or the perpetrator's perception of the victim's behavior as an indication of lack of consent.

SANSREGRET v. R.

[1985] 1 S.C.R. 570, 45 C.R. (3d) 193, 18 C.C.C. (3d) 223,
1985 CarswellMan 176, 1985 CarswellMan 380

McINTYRE J.: — This appeal [from (1984), 37 C.R. (3d) 45, 10 C.C.C. (3d) 164] raises once more the issue of the application of the defence of mistake of fact in a rape case. On this occasion its relevance on a charge laid under s. 143(*b*)(i) of the *Criminal Code*, now repealed but in force when this case arose, is questioned. In view of the significant changes made in this branch of the law by the amendments in 1980-81-82-83 (Can.), c. 125, it may be thought that this question has become of minor importance, but it would appear that similar cases involving similar defence claims may well arise under the new *Code* provisions and the applicable principles will still require consideration.

The appellant, a man in his early 20s, and the complainant, a woman of 31 years, had lived together in the complainant's house for about a year before the events of 15th October 1982. Their relationship had been one of contention and discord with violence on the part of the appellant: "slappings" or "roughing up" in his description, "blows" in hers. The appellant had left the house for short periods and in September 1982 the complainant decided to end the affair. She told the appellant to leave and he did.

On 23rd September 1982, some days after his dismissal, the appellant broke into the house at about 4:30 a.m. He was "raging" at her and furious because of his expulsion. He terrorized her with a file-like instrument with which he was armed. She was fearful of what might occur, and in order to calm him down she held out some hope of a reconciliation and they had intercourse. A report was made to the police of this incident, the complainant asserting she had been raped, but no proceedings were taken. The appellant's probation officer became involved and there was evidence than he had asked the complainant not to press the matter, presumably because it would interfere with the appellant's probation.

On 15th October 1982, again at about 4:30 a.m., the appellant broke into the complainant's house through a basement window. She was alone, and awakened by the entry she seized the bedroom telephone in an effort to call the police. The appellant picked up a butcher knife in the kitchen and came into the bedroom. He was furious and violent. He accused her of having another boyfriend; pulled the cord of the telephone out of the jack and threw it into the living room; threatened her with the knife and ordered her to take off her nightdress and made her stand in the kitchen doorway, naked save for a jacket over her shoulders, so he could be sure where she was while he repaired the window to conceal his entry from the police, should they arrive. He struck her on the mouth with sufficient force to draw blood, and on three occasions rammed the knife blade into the wall with great force, once very close to her. He told her that if the police came he would put the knife through her, and added that if he had found her with a boyfriend he would have killed them both. At one point he tied her hands behind her back with a scarf. The complainant said she was in fear for her life and sanity.

By about 5:30 a.m., after an hour of such behaviour by the appellant, she tried to calm him down. She pretended again that there was some hope of a reconciliation if the appellant would settle down and get a job. This had the desired effect. He calmed down and after some conversation he joined her on the bed and they had intercourse. The complainant swore that her consent to the intercourse was solely for the purpose of calming him down, to protect herself from further violence. This, she said, was something she had learned from earlier experience with him. In her evidence she said:

> I didn't consent at any time.
>
> I was very afraid. My whole body was trembling. I was sure I would have a nervous breakdown. I came very, very close to losing my mind. All I knew was I had to keep this man calm or he would kill me.

At about 6:45 a.m., after further conversation with the appellant, she got dressed and prepared to leave for work. She had a business appointment at 8:00 a.m. She drove the appellant to a location which he chose, and in the course of the journey he returned her keys and some money that he had taken from her purse upon his arrival in the early morning. Upon dropping him off she drove immediately to her mother's home, where she made a complaint of rape. The police were called and the appellant was arrested that evening.

The appellant was charged with rape, unlawful confinement, robbery, breaking and entering with intent to commit an indictable offence, and possession of a weapon. At trial, before Krindle Co. Ct. J. in the County Court of Winnipeg without a jury, he was acquitted on the charge of rape but was convicted of breaking and entering and unlawful confinement [34 C.R. (3d) 162]. The Court of Appeal (Matas, Huband and Philp JJ.A., Philp J.A. dissenting) allowed the Crown's appeal on the charge of rape and entered a conviction as well as imposing a sentence of five years' imprisonment. The unlawful confinement count was held to be subsumed in the rape. The appellant appealed to this Court asserting that the defence of mistake of fact, in this case a belief by the appellant that the complainant consented to intercourse, is open to an accused under s. 143(b)(i) of the *Criminal Code* as well as under subs. (a), and that it is the honesty of such belief that is determinative in considering the defence, not its reasonableness. Reliance was placed on *Pappajohn v. R.*, [1980] 2 S.C.R. 120, 14 C.R. (3d) 243, 19 C.R. (3d) 97, 52 C.C.C. (2d) 481.

The indictment set out the rape count in these terms:

> 1. THAT he, the said John Henry Sansregret, a male person, on or about the fifteenth day of October, in the year of our Lord one thousand nine hundred and eighty-two, at the City of Winnipeg in the Eastern Judicial District in the Province of Manitoba, did unlawfully have sexual intercourse with [T.W.], a female person who was not his wife, with her consent, which consent was extorted by threats or fear of bodily harm.

It clearly falls within s. 143(*b*)(i) of the *Criminal Code*. On the facts of this case, briefly summarized above, at first glance it may appear strange indeed that a defence of mistake of fact could be suggested, let alone made out. To appreciate how the issue arises, reference must be made to the findings of fact made at trial and to the judgments given in the Court of Appeal.

The trial judge described the complainant as a bright, sophisticated woman, articulate, capable, and well-employed. She considered that the appellant was neither particularly intelligent nor "verbal" and expressed surprise that any intimate relationship had ever arisen between them. She described the events of 23rd September 1982, a month before the events in question, and she considered that there was no evidence that the appellant knew she had complained of rape as a result of that incident. Comment will be made on this question later. She then referred to the defence of mistake of fact, and said [at p. 164]:

> If there were any evidence before me that the accused was aware on 15th October that the complainant had considered the sexual relations of 23rd September 1982 to have been non-consensual, I would have rejected this defence out of hand. There is no such evidence. I can speculate, but that is not proof.

She described in detail the events of 15th October and said that she accepted the complainant's version insofar as it differed from the appellant's, but she observed that in many respects his evidence confirmed hers. She continued [at p. 166):

> I am satisfied beyond any doubt that the accused broke and entered the complainant's residence on 15th October motivated primarily by jealousy and I do not doubt for a moment that, had the complainant had a man there, the knife would have been used aggressively. Having not found another man, he was bound and determined to make the complainant hear what he had to say to her by confining her unlawfully. He certainly broke and entered the dwelling-house with the intent to commit an indictable offence therein, and he certainly took possession of the butcher knife for purposes dangerous to the public peace.
>
> Having entered the house and discovering that the complainant was on the telephone, being unsure about whether or not she had called the police, two things became paramount. One was to cover up the evidence of his break-in so that it would not be visible from the street, and to cover up his presence in the house by reducing it to darkness. The second was to prevent the escape of the complainant, or her use of the telephone, particularly probable events while he was outside putting the basement window back on the house. What better way to confine her than to take her car keys, her house keys and her money, to strip her naked, to bind her hands and to force her to stand by the back door and whistle so he could hear where she was.
>
> I find that the accused forced the complainant to strip and tied her hands, not by way of preliminaries to an intended rape, but by way of confining the complainant. I similarly find the forced taking of her keys and money to part of the unlawful confinement.

She said that once the appellant became satisfied that the police would not come he set out to convince the complainant to reconcile. She accepted the evidence of the complainant that she was absolutely terrified, and that her consent was given solely to protect herself from further violence or death. She told him the things he wanted to hear regarding reconciliation, and she assured him that no other man was of interest to her. Then the trial judge continued [at pp. 167-68]:

> As I said, no rational person could have been under any honest mistake of fact. However, people have an uncanny ability to blind themselves to much that they do not want to see, and to believe in the existence of facts as they would wish them to be. The accused says that, notwithstanding the reign of terror which preceded their chat, notwithstanding that he held a knife while they talked, notwithstanding that he did most of the talking and that the complainant's answers were clearly equivocal, he presumed and believed that everything between them was peachy, this notwithstanding that three weeks earlier, on a replay of the same sort of evening, his probation officer became involved and the complainant moved out of her house. Very honestly, despite my confidence in the ability of people to blind themselves to reality, and even if the accused had not lied about other parts of his testimony, I would have been hard pressed to credit the honesty of his belief.
>
> However, his honest belief finds support in the testimony of the complainant. She knows him and, in her opinion, notwithstanding all the objective facts to the contrary, he did believe that everything was back to normal between them by the time of the sexual encounter. His subsequent behaviour as well attests to that fact.
>
> I do not like the conclusion which this leads me to. There was no real consent. There was submission as a result of a very real and justifiable fear. No one in his right mind could have believed that the complainant's dramatic about-face stemmed from anything other than fear. But the accused did. He saw what he wanted to see, heard what he wanted to hear, believed what he wanted to believe.
>
> The facts in *R. v. Pappajohn*, [1980] 2 S.C.R. 120, 14 C.R. (3d) 243, 19 C.R. (3d) 97, 52 C.C.C.(2d) 481, are quite dissimilar to those in this case. The dictum of the Supreme Court of Canada, however, is clear and broad and in no way seems to limit itself to the peculiar circumstances of that case. Perhaps the Crown will appeal this decision to obtain some direction from the Supreme Court on whether it was that court's intention to cover situations where an accused who demonstrates the clarity and shrewdness this accused showed in securing his own safety at the outset can turn around and, because it does not suit his wishes, can go wilfully blind to the obvious shortly thereafter. In any event, the ratio of *Pappajohn* is clear and it leaves me no alternative but to acquit.

To summarize, the trial judge found that the appellant did not enter the house with intent to make a sexual assault on the complainant; that the complainant consented to intercourse only because of the fear engendered by the threats of the appellant and to save herself, and that the appellant honestly believed that the complainant was giving a free and genuine consent to intercourse. She found as well that the complainant, who knew the appellant, also believed in the honesty of his belief.

. . . .

Rape, as defined in s. 143(*a*) of the *Criminal Code*, is of course the act of having sexual intercourse without consent. The issue with which we are concerned arises directly in a charge under subs. (*a*). The question will be: Did the accused have an honest belief that the woman gave her consent? It is in this form that the issue arose in *Pappajohn*, in *Morgan*, *supra*, and in *R. v. Plummer* (1975), 31 C.R.N.S. 220, 24 C.C.C. (2d) 497 (Ont. C.A.). While those cases provide authority for the existence of the defence and for its application where the consent is in issue, in my view they do not cover a charge under s. 143(*b*)(i) where consent is assumed from the outset. In other words, the existence of the consent is established and only its nature, that is, whether it was freely given or procured by threats, is in issue. Where the accused in a case arising under s. 143(*b*)(i) asserts an honest belief in consent, the honest belief must encompass more than the fact of consent. It must include a belief that it has been freely given and not procured by threats. I agree in this respect with Huband J.A. The defence would apply then, subject to what is said later about wilful blindness, in favour of an accused who had an honest belief that the consent was not the result of threats but one freely given.

. . . .

I would conclude then that the *mens rea* for rape under s. 143(*a*) of the *Code* must involve knowledge that the woman is not consenting, or recklessness as to whether she is consenting or not, and, for s. 143(*b*)(i), knowledge that the consent was given because of threats or fear of bodily harm, or recklessness as to its nature. It would follow, as has been held by the majority of this court in *Pappajohn*, that an honest belief on the part of the accused, even though unreasonably held, that the woman was consenting to intercourse freely and voluntarily and not because of threats would negate the *mens rea* under s. 143(*b*)(i) of the *Code* and entitle the accused to an acquittal.

The concept of recklessness as a basis for criminal liability has been the subject of much discussion. Negligence, the failure to take reasonable care, is a creature of the civil law and is not generally a concept having a place in determining criminal liability. Nevertheless, it is frequently confused with recklessness in the criminal sense and care should be taken to separate the two concepts. Negligence is tested by the objective standard of the reasonable man. A departure from his accustomed sober behaviour by an act or omission which reveals less than reasonable care will involve liability at civil law but forms no basis for the imposition of criminal penalties. In accordance with well-established principles for the determination of criminal liability, recklessness, to form a part of the criminal *mens rea*, must have an element of the subjective. It is found in the attitude of one who, aware that there is danger that his conduct could bring about the result prohibited by the criminal law, nevertheless persists, despite the risk. It is, in other words, the conduct of one who sees the risk and who takes the chance. It is in this sense that the term "recklessness" is used in the criminal law and it is clearly distinct from the concept of civil negligence.

On the face of it, one would have thought that a man who intimidates and threatens a woman and thereafter obtains her consent to intercourse would know that the consent was obtained as a result of the threats. If specific knowledge of the nature of the consent was not attributable to him in such circumstances, then one would think that at the very least recklessness would be. It might be said then that this case could have been disposed of on the basis of recklessness. The trial judge, however, did not do so because of her application of the "mistake of fact" defence.

There was indeed an abundance of evidence before the trial judge upon which a finding of recklessness could have been made. After a stormy period of cohabitation, the complainant dismissed the appellant from her house in September 1982, thus demonstrating her rejection of him. He broke into the house on 23rd September and there went through a performance which led to an act of intercourse with a consent given by the complainant out of fear for her life. This incident led to a report to the police and the involvement of the appellant's probation officer. In the early morning hours of 15th October he again broke into the house and repeated his earlier performance, which provided the basis for the present charges.

There was also evidence from which the clear inference can be drawn that the appellant knew a complaint of rape had been made in respect of the first incident. Though the complainant complained to the police about that incident, no charges were laid. She was persuaded not to pursue the matter by the appellant's probation officer, who had approached her and told her that he would find a job for Sansregret if she did not press the charges. A police officer testified as to a conversation which occurred between himself and Sansregret after the latter's arrest. In response to a question as to why he ran from the police when they approached him on the evening of 16th October, the appellant replied: "From before, that time she phoned the police on me before."This reply was confirmed by Sansregret on direct examination but then denied on cross-examination. Sansregret admitted that he knew his probation officer had called the complainant with respect to the September incident and that he knew that he was not welcome in her house. There was then evidence that the appellant knew of her attitude towards him; knew that she had complained to the police with respect to the 23rd September incident; and knew that it was only the intervention of his parole officer which prevented charges from being laid after that incident. I therefore disagree with the trial Judge, who, in my opinion, was in error in not drawing the inference that the appellant knew that the complainant had complained of rape as a result of the incident on 23rd September.

It is evident that the trial judge would have convicted the appellant of rape had it not been for the defence of mistake of fact. She considered that the belief in the consent expressed by the appellant was an honest one and therefore on the basis of *Pappajohn*, *supra*, even if it were unreasonably held, as it is clear she thought it was, he was entitled to his acquittal. This application of the defence of mistake of fact would be supportable were it not for the fact that the trial judge found in addition that the appellant had been wilfully blind to reality in his behaviour on 15th October. Such a finding would preclude the application of the defence and lead to a different result. It is my opinion then that the trial Judge erred in this matter in that, though she made the requisite findings of fact that the appellant was wilfully blind to the consequences of his acts, she did not apply them according to law.

The idea of wilful blindness in circumstances such as this has been said to be an aspect of recklessness. While this may well be true, it is wise to keep the two concepts separate because they result from different mental attitudes and lead to different legal results. A finding of recklessness in this case could not override the defence of mistake of fact. The appellant asserts an honest belief that the consent of the complainant was not caused by fear and threats. The trial judge found that such an honest belief existed. In the facts of this case, because of the reckless conduct of the appellant, it could not be said that such a belief was reasonable but, as held in *Pappajohn*, the mere honesty of the belief will support the "mistake of fact" defence, even where it is unreasonable. On the other hand, a finding of wilful blindness as to the very facts about which the honest belief is now asserted would leave no room for the application of the defence because, where wilful blindness is shown, the law presumes knowledge on the part of the accused, in this case knowledge that the consent had been induced by threats.

Wilful blindness is distinct from recklessness because, while recklessness involves knowledge of a danger or risk and persistence in a course of conduct which creates a risk that the prohibited result will occur, wilful blindness arises where a person who has become aware of the need for some inquiry declines to make the inquiry because he does not wish to know the truth. He would prefer to remain ignorant. The culpability in recklessness is justified by consciousness of the risk and by proceeding in the face of it, while in wilful blindness it is justified by the accused's fault in deliberately failing to inquire when he knows there is reason for inquiry. Cases such as *Wretham v. R.* (1971), 16 C.R.N.S. 124 (Ont. C.A.); *R. v. Blondin*, 2 C.C.C. (2d) 118, affirmed [1971] S.C.R. v, 4 C.C.C. (2d) 566; *R. v. Currie* (1976), 24 C.C.C. (2d) 292 (Ont. C.A.); *R. v. McFall* (1976), 26 C.C.C. (2d) 181 (B.C.C.A.); *R. v. Aiello* (1978), 38 C.C.C. (2d) 485 (Ont. C.A.); *Taylor's Central Garages (Exeter) Ltd. v. Roper*, [1951] 2 T.L.R. 284 (Div. Ct.), among others, illustrate these principles. The textwriters have also dealt with the subject, particularly Glanville Williams, *Criminal Law: The General Part*, 2nd ed. (1961), at pp. 157-60. He says, at p. 157:

> Knowledge, then, means either personal knowledge or (in the licence cases) imputed knowledge. In either event there is someone with actual knowledge. To the requirement of actual knowledge there is one strictly limited exception. Men readily regard their suspicions as unworthy of them when it is to their advantage to do so. To meet this, the rule is that if a party has his suspicion aroused but then deliberately omits to make further enquiries, because he wishes to remain in ignorance, he is deemed to have knowledge.

He then referred to the words of Lord Sumner in *Re The Zamora*, [1921] 1 A.C. 801 at 811-12 (P.C.), which was a case wherein a ship and cargo were condemned in the Prize Court as contraband. The managing director of the shipping company denied knowledge of the contraband carried by the ship, and on this subject Lord Sumner said, at pp. 811-12:

> Lord Sterndale [the president of the Prize Court] thus expressed his final conclusion: "I think the true inference is that, if Mr. Banck did not know this was a transaction in contraband, it was because he did not want to know, and that he has not rebutted the presumption arising from the fact of the whole cargo being contraband."
>
> Their Lordships have been invited to read this as saying that Mr. Banck is not proved to have known the contraband character of the adventure; that if he did not know, because he did not want to know, he was within his rights and owed no duty to the belligerents to inform himself; and that the *Zamora* is condemned contrary to the passage above cited from *The Hakan* upon a legal presumption arising solely and arbitrarily from the fact that the whole cargo was contraband. It may be that in his anxiety not to state more than he found against Mr. Banck, the learned President appeared to state something less, but there are two senses in which a man is said not to know something because he does not want to know it. A thing may be troublesome to learn, and the knowledge of it, when acquired, may be uninteresting or distasteful. To refuse to know any more about the subject or any, thing at all is then a wilful but a real ignorance. On the other hand, a man is said not to know because he does not want to know, where the substance of the thing is borne in upon his mind with a conviction that full details or precise proofs may be dangerous, because they may embarrass his denials or compromise his protests. In such a case he flatters himself that where ignorance is safe, 'tis folly to be wise, but there he is wrong, for he has been put upon notice and his further ignorance, even though actual and complete, is a mere affectation and disguise.

Glanville Williams, however, warns that the rule of deliberate blindness has its dangers and is of narrow application. He says, at p. 159:

> The rule that wilful blindness is equivalent to knowledge is essential, and is found throughout the criminal law. It is, at the same time, an unstable rule, because judges are apt to forget its very limited scope. A court can properly find wilful blindness only where it can almost be said that the defendant actually knew. He suspected the fact; he realised its probability; but he refrained from obtaining the final confirmation because he wanted in the event to be able to deny knowledge. This, and this alone, is wilful blindness. It requires in effect a finding that the defendant intended to cheat the administration of justice. Any wider definition would make the doctrine of wilful blindness indistinguishable from the civil doctrine of negligence in not obtaining knowledge.

This subject is also dealt with by Professor Stuart in *Canadian Criminal Law* (1982), at p. 130 et seq., where its relationship to recklessness is discussed.

This case reveals, in my view, an appropriate set of circumstances for the application of the "wilful blindness" rule. I have outlined the circumstances which form the background. I have referred to the findings of the trial Judge that the appellant blinded himself to the obvious and made no inquiry as to the nature of the consent which was given. If the evidence before the court was limited to the events of 15th October, it would be difficult indeed to infer wilful blindness. To attribute criminal liability on the basis of this one incident would come close to applying a constructive test to the effect that he should have known she was consenting out of fear. The position, however, is changed when the evidence reveals the earlier episode and the complaint of rape which it caused, knowledge of which, as I have said, had clearly reached the accused. Considering the whole of the evidence, then, no constructive test of knowledge is required. The appellant was aware of the likelihood of the complainant's reaction to his threats. To proceed with intercourse in such circumstances constitutes, in my view, self-deception to the point of wilful blindness.

In my view, it was error on the part of the trial judge to give effect to the "mistake of fact" defence in these circumstances where she had found that the complainant consented out of fear and the appellant was wilfully blind to the existing circumstances, seeing only what he wished to see. Where the accused is deliberately ignorant as a result of blinding himself to reality the law presumes knowledge, in this case knowledge of the nature of the consent. There was therefore no room for the operation of this defence.

This is not to be taken as a retreat from the position taken in *Pappajohn*, *supra*, that the honest belief need not be reasonable. It is not to be thought that any time an accused forms an honest though unreasonable belief he will be deprived of the defence of mistake of fact. This case rests on a different proposition. Having wilfully blinded himself to the facts before him, the fact that an accused may be enabled to preserve what could be called an honest belief, in the sense that he has no specific knowledge to the contrary, will not afford a defence because, where the accused becomes deliberately blind to the existing facts, he is fixed by law with actual knowledge and his belief in another state of facts is irrelevant.

I would dismiss this appeal.

A. MANSON, ANNOTATION

(1985), 45 C.R. (3d) 194

McIntyre J. clarifies much of the confusion apparent in the lower court judgments by accurately characterizing the issue as whether the accused believed, not just in the existence of consent, but that the consent had been freely given and not procured by threats. The trial judge found as a fact that "the appellant honestly believed that the complainant was giving a free and genuine consent to intercourse" (p. 200). McIntyre J. states at p. 206 that a "finding of recklessness in this case could not override the defence of mistake of fact". However, he ultimately concludes (p. 208) that the accused's mistaken honest belief cannot exonerate him, since he "was wilfully blind to the existing circumstances, seeing only what he wished to see". In so doing, McIntyre J. seems to misunderstand the relationship between recklessness, wilful blindness and mistaken honest belief when knowledge of some factual element is an essential issue. In the result, he effectively reverses the finding of fact made by the trial judge.

Let us assume that a case involves as an essential element the issue of whether the accused knew that a thing was black or white. The accused would be guilty if he knew that the thing was black. If the offence can be committed recklessly, then the accused would be reckless as to this essential element if he recognized that it was a question whether the thing was black or white but acted in the face of this issue without resolving it. The accused would be wilfully blind if he had a strong suspicion that the thing was black and had steps available which would confirm the suspicion, but deliberately chose not to take the steps. In other words, where knowledge is an element, wilful blindness is tantamount to knowledge, in that the accused virtually knows but insulates himself from perfect knowledge. By comparison, an accused could be said to have an honest but mistaken belief only if he in fact believed that the thing was white. A finding of recklessness as to the colour, or wilful blindness about blackness cannot coexist with a finding that the accused had an honest belief in whiteness. Regardless of the reasonableness of the conclusion, a finding of honest belief can arise only if the accused has resolved the question of colour, albeit erroneously. Of course, the question is not answered simply by listening to the accused's version of what he knew or believed, but by examining and weighing all of the evidence. At the end of the day, however, if the trial judge finds that the accused honestly believed that the thing was white, then there is no room any longer for a question of wilful blindness or recklessness.

Rape is committed when the accused intentionally acts without the free consent of the complainant or is reckless as to the issue of consent. Thus, both knowledge of non-consent and recklessness as to this element would result in a conviction. Because knowledge is incorporated into the calculus, then wilful blindness is necessarily also applicable, since it is tantamount to knowledge. McIntyre J. may be correct when he assesses the evidence and indicates that there was substantial support for a finding of wilful blindness given the antecedent relations between the accused and the complainant. Nonetheless, as a matter of fact, the trial judge found an honest belief in freely given consent. An exculpatory mistake of fact requires a finding of honest belief, which cannot coexist with a concomitant conclusion that the accused was wilfully blind as to the element in issue. The former is an honest but mistaken belief in whiteness, while the latter is a strong suspicion — deliberately unconfirmed — of blackness.

McIntyre J. obviously doubts whether the accused in fact had an honest belief in freely given consent. That, however, was the trial judge's finding (p. 168): "No one in his right mind could have believed that the complainant's dramatic about-face stemmed from anything other than fear. *But the accused did*." (The italics are mine.) The question of the accused's belief in the impact of the threats was clearly within the trial judge's contemplation. In the circumstances, the finding certainly appears dubious. However, the Crown did not dispute it, nor did the Manitoba Court of Appeal reverse it: see 36 C.R. (3d) 45.

The jurisdiction of the Supreme Court of Canada is limited to questions of law alone: see *R. v. Warner*, [1960] S.C.R. 144, 34 C.R. 246, 128 C.C.C. 366; *Hobbins v. R.*, [1982] 1 S.C.R. 553, 27 C.R. (3d) 289, 66 C.C.C. (2d) 289 at 291. In the absence of a power to reverse the finding of fact, the appeal should have been allowed.

3. CRIMES OF SEXUAL ASSAULT (1983)

In 1983 the crime of rape was replaced by a three-tier structure of sexual assault offences, now ss. 271, 272 and 273. The aim was to reflect the violent rather than the sexual nature of the offence. Heavy reliance was placed on the study by L. Clark and D. Lewis, *Rape: The Price of Coercive Sexuality*.[35] The House of Commons Debates reflect the impetus and the result of ten years of protest from rape crisis centres, women's groups and many others:

> [T]he current laws relating to rape and indecent assault are being changed to emphasize the violence as opposed to the sexual aspects to these crimes. In other words, we will no longer have the term 'rape' in law.
>
> This legislation has a long history. Individual women and groups of women all across the country have been pushing for years to change the rape laws. It was apparent that this section of the *Criminal Code* cried out for reform. The number of reported rape cases was far below the actual number of offences. It has been estimated that only one in ten cases of rape was reported. That was due largely to the stigma which surrounded the rape victim — the idea that nice girls do not get raped and the belief that she must have asked for it.... The conviction rate for rape has traditionally been much lower than the conviction rate for other serious crimes — only 52 percent conviction rate for rape, compared with an 82 percent conviction rate in the case of other indictable offences. As a result, women's groups such as the National Action Committee on the Status of Women and the National Council of Women began calling for a complete removal of the existing rape sections from the *Criminal Code*. They wanted, instead, the enactment of a new offence dealing with rape as a type of assault.
>
> The government responded with Bill C-52 some four years ago, and that had one major beneficial effect. It brought together all women's groups calling for four basic principles which they wanted to see embodied in the law: treatment of rape as a type of assault, creating tiers of sexual assault to parallel existing assault offences, abolishing spousal immunity, and limiting admissibility of past sexual history ....
>
> We now have a bill which provides that the assault and sexual assault structure of the *Criminal Code* will have three tiers. The Minister has outlined those three tiers. The women's groups which appeared before the committee were unanimous in their desire that the new law would be modeled on existing assault provisions in the *Criminal Code*, so that there would be a firm foundation for the new sexual assault provisions. This was the reason our party insisted in committee on three tiers of assault and sexual assault....
>
> I know the bill before us is not perfect, but indeed it is a great step forward and it is of particular significance to women. I believe this piece of legislation will mark a new beginning in the way society views coercive sexual acts.[36]

Along with this new, gender-neutral definition of the offence came the abolition of spousal immunity, restrictions on the cross-examination of the primary witness as to her previous sexual history, ss. 276-277, the abrogation of the doctrine of

---

35 (Toronto: The Women's Press, 1977).
36 Hon. Flora MacDonald, reported in *House of Commons Debates*, Official Reporter Vol. XVII, First Session, *Thirty-Second Parliament* (Quebec: Supply and Services Canada) at 20041 (4 August, 1982).

recent complaint, s. 275, (see *R. v. Page* (1984), 40 C.R. (3d) 85, 12 C.C.C. (3d) 250 (Ont. H.C.) and accompanying Annotation criticizing the same) and the repeal of corroboration requirements and warnings, s. 274. It is clear that these legislative changes have answered some of the complaints of legal bias against victims of sexual assault. To what extent *attitudes* have changed remains to be seen.

Since "rape" was replaced with the term "sexual assault", there has been some confusion over the definition of the crime since Parliament did not define the term in the *Criminal Code*. The Supreme Court of Canada had to grapple with the issue in the following case.

R. v. CHASE

[1987] 2 S.C.R. 293, 59 C.R. (3d) 193, 37 C.C.C. (3d) 97,
1987 CarswellNB 25, 1987 CarswellNB 315

McIntyre J.: — This appeal concerns the meaning of the term 'sexual assault', as it is used in ss. 244 and 246.1 of the *Criminal Code*.

. . . .

The facts may be briefly described. The respondent, Chase, was a neighbour of the complainant, a 15-year-old girl. They lived in a small hamlet near Fredericton, New Brunswick. On October 22, 1983, Chase entered the home of the complainant without invitation. The complainant and her 11-year-old brother were in the downstairs portion of the house, playing pool. Their 83-year-old grandfather was upstairs sleeping. Their parents were absent. The respondent seized the complainant around the shoulders and arms and grabbed her breasts. When she fought back, he said: "Come on dear, don't hit me, I know you want it." The complainant said at trial that: "He tried to grab for my private, but he didn't succeed because my hands were too fast." Eventually, the complainant and her brother were able to make a telephone call to a neighbour and the respondent left. Prior to leaving, he said that he was going to tell everybody that she had raped him. The whole episode lasted little more than half an hour. The respondent was charged with the offence of sexual assault and was found guilty after trial in the Provincial Court. He appealed to the Court of Appeal for New Brunswick where his appeal was dismissed, a verdict of guilty of the included offence of common assault under s. 245(1) of the *Criminal Code* was substituted, and a sentence of six months' imprisonment was imposed.

. . . .

In the Court of Appeal, Angers J.A., speaking for a unanimous Court (Stratton C.J.N.B., Ryan and Angers JJ.A.), expressed the view that the principles developed with respect to rape and indecent assault were of little assistance in approaching the question of sexual assault. In his view, the modifier "sexual" should be taken to refer to parts of the body, particularly the genitalia. He considered that a broader definition of the term could lead to absurd realities if it encompassed other portions of the human anatomy described as having "secondary sexual characteristics". He also expressed the view that sexual assault did not require or involve a specific intent. Because there was no contact with the complainant's genitals, the conviction at trial was set aside and a conviction for common assault substituted. It becomes evident from the recital of these facts that the only question arising on the appeal is that of the definition of the offence of sexual assault.

The new sexual assault provisions of the *Criminal Code* were enacted in the *Act to amend the Criminal Code in relation to sexual offences and other offences against the person and to amend certain other Acts in relation thereto or in consequence thereof*, S.C. 1980-81-82-83, c. 125. They replace the previous offences of rape, attempted rape, sexual intercourse with the feeble-minded, and indecent assault on a female or male. It is now for the courts to endeavour to develop a realistic and workable approach to the construction of the new sections. The key sections are 244 and 246.1 [now ss. 265 and 271], *supra*. Section 246.1 creates the offence of sexual assault, an expression nowhere defined in the *Criminal Code*. To determine its nature, we must first turn to the assault section 244(1), where an assault is defined in terms similar, if not identical, to the concept of assault at common law. Section 244(2) provides that the section applies to sexual assaults. It was suggested in argument by the respondent that paras. (a), (b) and (c) of s. 244(1) are to be read disjunctively so that only para. (a) could be applicable to the offence of sexual assault. This, it was said, must have been the position taken by the New Brunswick Court of Appeal because, in its consideration of s. 244, it dealt only with para. (a), apparently considering that contact was necessary to complete a sexual assault. I would dispose of this argument by simply referring to the specific words of s. 244(2) which make the section applicable to sexual assaults. In my view, however sexual assault may be defined, its definition cannot be limited to the provisions of s. 244(1)(a).

Since judgment was given in this case in the New Brunswick Court of Appeal, other appellate courts have dealt with the problem. As far as I am able to determine, none has followed the approach of the Court of Appeal in this case. In *R. v. Alderton* (1985), 49 O.R. (2d) 257, the matter was presented to the Ontario Court of Appeal. In that case, the accused gained entry to an apartment building at night, wearing a face mask. He entered the apartment of the complainant who was alone and asleep in her bedroom. He seized her and forced her back upon the pillows but after a struggle she managed to escape. The Court of Appeal dismissed an appeal from a conviction of sexual assault made at trial. Martin J.A., speaking for a unanimous court (Martin, Lacourcière and Finlayson JJ.A.), said at p. 263:

> We are, with the greatest deference, unable to accept the views of the court expressed in that case [*Chase*]. Without in any way attempting to give a comprehensive definition of a "sexual assault" we are all satisfied that it includes an assault with the intention of having sexual intercourse with the victim without her consent, or an assault made upon a victim for the purpose of sexual gratification.
>
> We are all of the view that in the circumstances of the present case, there was ample evidence upon which the jury could find that the appellant committed a sexual assault upon the complainant and, indeed, we think the evidence did not permit of any other conclusion.

As he said, in these words, Martin J.A. was not attempting a comprehensive definition of sexual assault, nor was he saying that the concept of sexual assault was limited to an assault with the intention of having sexual intercourse or for the purposes of sexual gratification. His view was that, where these elements were present, it would be sufficient to categorize the assault as sexual. They do not constitute the sole basis for a finding of sexual assault, nor may this reference to them be taken as a finding that a specific intent is required for the completion of the offence.

In *R. v. Taylor* (1985), 44 C.R. (3d) 263, the matter was considered in the Alberta Court of Appeal. The accused, in seeking to discipline a teenage girl placed in his care, tied the girl's wrists to an overhead metal support and made her stand naked for periods of ten to fifteen minutes and, on one occasion, administered several blows with a wooden paddle on the buttocks. There were no other acts which could have been described as sexual in nature. The accused was acquitted at trial. The Crown's appeal was allowed and a new trial was ordered. Laycraft C.J.A., for a unanimous court (Laycraft C.J.A., Haddad and Belzil JJ.A.), said, at p. 268:

> The new provisions do not define "sexual assault". However, "assault" is defined and thus the new offences are an assault with some additional meaning required by the modifier "sexual". In the offences which were replaced this was also true of "indecent assault", a term which gave no difficulty in judicial interpretation. For decades, juries were charged that indecent assault was an assault in circumstances of indecency (*R. v. Louie Chong* (1914), 32 O.L.R. 66, 23 C.C.C. 250 (C.A.); *R. v. Quinton*, [1947] S.C.R. 234, 3 C.R. 6, 88 C.C.C. 231). Though this approach was susceptible to the comment that it was simply an assertion that an assault is indecent if it is indecent, it was nevertheless an approach perfectly understandable by generations of juries, and eminently practicable in the administration of the criminal law.

He then went on to discuss various authorities and rejected the *Chase* approach with its reliance on the specific involvement of areas of body and the dictionary definitions of the term "sexual". He noted that all the decisions he discussed rejected the *Chase* approach and he spoke approvingly of the position of Martin J.A. in the Ontario Court of Appeal in *Alderton, supra*, saying, at p. 269:

> Without joining a battle of dictionaries, it is my view that these words were intended to comprehend a wide range of forcible acts within the definition of "assault" to which, in the circumstances disclosed by the evidence, there is a carnal aspect. "Sexual assault" is therefore an act of force in circumstances of sexuality as that can be seen in the circumstances. Like Martin J.A. I would not attempt a comprehensive definition of "sexual assault". The term includes, however, an act which is intended to degrade or demean another person for sexual gratification. Nothing in the new sections of the *Code* in my view restricts the carnal or sexual aspect only to acts of force involving the sexual organs and I respectfully disagree with the restricted meaning expressed in *R. v. Chase, supra*.

It was his view that the carnal aspect was to be judged objectively: "Viewed in the light of all the circumstances, is the sexual or carnal context of the assault visible to a reasonable observer?"

In the British Columbia Court of Appeal, the matter was considered in *R. v. Cook* (1985), 20 C.C.C. (3d) 18. In this case, on facts which clearly revealed conduct which would qualify as sexual assaults, the *Chase* approach was again rejected. Lambert J.A. did not attempt to give a precise definition of sexual assault where Parliament had declined to do so, but he did consider that the characteristic which made a simple assault into a sexual assault was not solely a matter of anatomy. He considered that a real affront to sexual integrity and sexual dignity may be sufficient.

It will be seen from this brief review of the cases that the approach taken by the New Brunswick Court of Appeal in the case at bar has found little, if any, support. All the cases cited have recognized the need for a broader approach and all have recognized the difficulty in formulating one. While I would agree that it is difficult and probably unwise to attempt to develop a precise and all-inclusive definition of the new offence of sexual assault at this stage in its development, it seems to me to be necessary to attempt to settle upon certain considerations which may be of assistance to the courts in developing on a case-to-case basis a workable definition of the offence.

To begin with, I agree, as I have indicated, that the test for the recognition of sexual assault does not depend solely on contact with specific areas of the human anatomy. I am also of the view that sexual assault need not involve an attack by a member of one sex upon a member of the other; it could be perpetrated upon one of the same sex. I agree as well with those who say that the new offence is truly new and does not merely duplicate the offences it replaces. Accordingly, the definition of the term "sexual assault" and the reach of the offence it describes is not necessarily limited to the scope of its predecessors. I would consider as well that the test for its recognition should be objective.

While it is clear that the concept of a sexual assault differs from that of the former indecent assault, it is nevertheless equally clear that the terms overlap in many respects and sexual assault in many cases will involve the same sort of conduct that formerly would have justified a conviction for an indecent assault. The definitional approach to indecent assault also an offence not defined in the *Criminal Code*, therefore offers a guide in our approach to the new offence, as recognized by Laycraft C.J.A. After many years of dealing with the concept of indecent assault, the courts developed the definition, "an assault in circumstances of indecency". This, of course, was in imprecise definition but everyone knew what an indecent assault was. The law in that respect was reasonably clear and there was little difficulty with its enforcement. In my view then, a similar approach may be adopted in formulating a definition of sexual assault.

Applying these principles and the authorities cited, I would make the following observations. Sexual assault is an assault within any one of the definitions of that concept in s. 244 (1) of the *Criminal Code* which is committed in circumstances of a sexual nature, such that the sexual integrity of the victim is violated. The test to be applied in determining whether the impugned conduct has the requisite sexual nature is an objective one: "Viewed in the light of all the circumstances, is the sexual or carnal context of the assault visible to a reasonable observer" (*Taylor, supra*, per Laycraft C.J.A., at p. 269). The part of the body touched, the nature of the contact, the situation in which it occurred, the words and gestures accompanying the act, and all other circumstances surrounding the conduct, including threats which may or may not be accompanied by force will be relevant (see S.J. Usprich, "A New Crime in Old Battles: Definitional Problems with Sexual Assault" (1987), 29 Crim. L.Q. 200, at p. 204) The intent or purpose of the person committing the act, to the extent that this may appear from the evidence, may also be a factor in considering whether the conduct is sexual. If the motive of the accused is sexual gratification, to the extent that this may appear from the evidence, it may be a factor in determining whether the conduct is sexual. It must be emphasized, however, that the existence of such a motive is simply one of many factors to be considered, the importance of which will vary depending on the circumstances.

Implicit in this view of sexual assault is the notion that the offence is one requiring a general intent only. This is consistent with the approach adopted by this court in cases such as *Leary v. The Queen*, [1978] 1 S.C.R. 29, and *Swietlinski v. The Queen*, [1980] 2 S.C.R. 956, where it was held that rape and indecent assault were offences of general intent. I am unable to see any reason why the same approach should not be taken with respect to sexual assault. The factors which could motivate sexual assault are said to be many and varied (see C. Boyle, *Sexual Assault* (1984), at p. 74). To put upon the Crown the burden of proving a specific intent would go a long way toward defeating the obvious purpose of the enactment. Moreover, there are strong reasons in social policy which would support this view. To import an added element of specific intent in such offences, would be to hamper unreasonably the enforcement process. It would open the question of the defence of drunkenness, one which has always been related to the capacity to form a specific intent and which has generally been excluded by law and policy from offences requiring only the minimal intent to apply force (see *R. v. Bernard* (1985), 18 C.C.C. (3d) 574 (Ont. C.A., per Dubin J.A.)) For these reasons, I would say that the offence will be one of general rather than specific intent.

Turning to the case at bar I have no difficulty in concluding, on the basis of the principles I have discussed above, that there was ample evidence before the trial Judge upon which he could find that sexual assault was committed. Viewed objectively in the light of all the circumstances, it is clear that the conduct of the respondent in grabbing the complainant's breasts constituted an assault of a sexual nature. I would therefore allow the appeal, set aside the conviction of common assault recorded by the Court of Appeal and restore the conviction of sexual assault made at trial. The sentence of six months should stand.

Appeal allowed.

PROBLEM

The accused is charged with sexually assaulting his three-year-old son. He admits that he grabbed his son's testicles on three occasions as a disciplinary response to the child having engaged in similar activity with others, including the accused. He wanted to show him how much it hurt. There is evidence of bruising. Has the accused committed a sexual assault?

Compare *R. v. V. (K.B.)* (1993), 22 C.R. (4th) 86, 82 C.C.C. (3d) 382, [1993] 2 S.C.R. 857.

PROBLEM

The accused is charged with sexual assault. He was operating a residential cleaning business. He came up behind a female co-worker and briefly placed his hands on her hips to move her so he could detach a vacuum from a wall plug. He went on vacuuming but she was distressed and left to call the police. The accused testified he touched her in order to move her and that while he did not ask for permission he assumed it was okay to touch her.

Compare *R. v. Smale* (2016), 27 C.R. (7th) 83 (Alta. Prov. Ct.). See C.R. comment by Janine Benedet at 84.

In the 1983 amendments, Parliament changed the provisions concerning coerced consent (s. 265(3), considered earlier in Chapter 2). It also codified for the first time a defence of mistake as to consent applicable to all assaults, including sexual assaults. See s. 265(4). **Does the section continue the *Pappajohn* interpretation?**

R. v. BULMER

[1987] 1 S.C.R. 782, 58 C.R. (3d) 48, 33 C.C.C. (3d) 385,
1987 CarswellBC 702, 1987 CarswellBC 149

On the trial of the accused on charges of rape, attempted rape and indecent assault, the evidence indicated that the complainant, a prostitute, agreed to provide her services to the accused L. for a certain price. She testified that they went to a hotel room and, on entering, she discovered the two other accused, B. and I., and objected to their presence. I. sought to engage her services. She quoted her price and told him to come back in 20 minutes. B. and I. then left, but returned shortly after. A discussion followed, and I. told the complainant that she would have to provide her services without payment. Frightened, she performed various sexual acts with all three. She denied giving consent and receiving payment. There was no physical violence other than the various sexual acts. B. did not give evidence. L. and I. testified that price was discussed with the complainant after B. and I. returned to the room and that she finally agreed to have sex with them for $20 each. No threats were made. The occupant of an adjoining room testified that he heard two persons leave and return. He also heard a woman complaining about their presence. Her voice seemed normal at first, but as time passed it took on a whining, wheedling tone. There was also discussion about price.

In defence, the accused took the position that the complainant had consented to the acts. Counsel made the alternative submission that L. had held an honest but mistaken belief in consent. The trial judge left the defence to the jury and told them that all three could rely upon the defence. The jury returned verdicts of guilty of rape against both L. and I. B. was acquitted of rape, but convicted of indecent assault. The majority of the British Columbia Court of Appeal having dismissed their appeals, the accused appealed further.

The Supreme Court agreed that there was evidence of the mistake defence fit to go to the jury but ordered a new trial on the basis that the trial judge had wrongly instructed, in his supplementary charge, that the belief had to be both honest and reasonable.

McINTYRE J. (DICKSON C.J., WILSON, LE DAIN, and LA FOREST JJ. concurring): —

In discussing the application of the "air of reality" test in the *Pappajohn* case, I said, at p. 133:

> To require the putting of the alternative defence of mistaken belief in consent, there must be, in my opinion some evidence beyond the mere assertion of belief in consent by counsel for the appellant. This evidence must appear from or be supported by sources other than the appellant in order to give it any air of reality.

These words appear, on occasion, to have been misunderstood, but I do not withdraw them. There will not be an air of reality about a mere statement that "I thought she was consenting" not supported to some degree by other evidence or circumstances arising in the case. If that mere assertion were sufficient to require a trial Judge to put the "mistake of fact" defence, it would be a simple matter in any rape case to make such an assertion and, regardless of all other circumstances, require the defence to be put. It must be remembered that at this stage of the proceedings the trial judge is not in any way concerned with the question of guilt or innocence. He is not concerned with the weight of evidence or with the credibility of evidence. The question he must answer is this. In all the circumstances of this case, is there any reality in the defence? To answer this question, he must consider all the evidence, all the circumstances. The statement of the accused alleging a mistaken belief will be a factor but will not by itself be decisive, and even in its total absence, other circumstances might dictate the putting of the defence. This view finds support in the passage from the Heilbron Report (Great Britain, Report of the Advisory Group on the Law of Rape (1975)) referred to by Dickson J., at p. 155 in *Pappajohn*, in these terms:

> 66. *Morgan's* case did not decide, as some critics seem to have thought, that an accused person was entitled to be acquitted, however ridiculous his story might be, nor did it decide that the reasonableness or unreasonableness of his belief was irrelevant. *Furthermore it is a mistaken assumption that a man is entitled to be acquitted simply because he asserts his belief, without more.* [Emphasis added.]

When the defence of mistake of fact — or for that matter any other defence — is raised, two distinct steps are involved. The first step for the trial judge is to decide if the defence should be put to the jury. It is on this question, as I have said, that the "air of reality" test is applied. It has nothing to do with the jury and is not a factor for its consideration. If it is decided to put the defence, the second step requires the trial judge to explain the law to the jury, review the relevant evidence, and leave the jury with the issue of guilt or innocence. The jury must consider all the evidence, and they must be satisfied beyond a reasonable doubt in the case of a rape charge that there was no consent before they may convict. Where they find there was consent or honest belief in consent or if they have a doubt on either issue, they must acquit. They should be told as well that the belief, if honestly held, need not be based on reasonable grounds. Before going further, it should be observed that since the decision of this court in *Pappajohn*, the *Criminal Code* has been amended by the addition of s. 244(4) [now s. 265(4)], which provides:

> (4) Where an accused alleges that he believed that the complainant consented to the conduct that is the subject-matter of the charge, a Judge, if satisfied that there is sufficient evidence and that, if believed by the jury, the evidence would constitute a defence, shall instruct the jury, when reviewing all the evidence relating to the determination of the honesty of the accused's belief, to consider the presence or absence of reasonable grounds for that belief.

This section, in my view, does not change the law as applied in *Pappajohn*. It does not require that the mistaken belief be reasonable or reasonably held. It simply makes it clear than in determining the issue of the honesty of the asserted belief, the presence or absence of reasonable grounds for the belief are relevant factors for the jury's consideration. This approach was, I suggest, foreshadowed in *Pappajohn* by Dickson J., at pp. 155-56, where he said:

> Perpetuation of fictions does little for the jury system or the integrity of criminal justice. The ongoing debate in the courts and learned journals as to whether mistake must be reasonable is conceptually important in the orderly development of the criminal law, but in my view, practically unimportant because the accused's statement that he was mistaken is not likely to be believed unless the mistake is, to the jury, reasonable. The jury will be concerned to consider the reasonableness of any grounds found, or asserted to be available, to support the defence of mistake. Although "reasonable grounds" is not a precondition to the availability of a plea of honest belief in consent, those grounds determine the weight to be given the defence. The reasonableness, or otherwise, of the accused's belief is only evidence for, or against, the view that the belief was actually held and the intent was, therefore, lacking.

The jury should then be instructed, in accordance with s. 244(4) of the *Code*, that when considering all the evidence relating to the question of the honesty of the accused's asserted belief in consent they must consider the presence or absence of reasonable grounds for that belief.

. . . .

LAMER J. — I have read the reasons for judgment of my colleague Justice McIntyre and, for the reasons he sets out, I agree that this appeal should succeed. I wish to add, however, the following qualifications to certain statements made in his reasons.

I agree with McIntyre J. that "a trial judge is not bound to put every defence suggested by counsel in the absence of some evidentiary base" (at p. 789), and that "to put a wholly unsupported defence would only cause confusion" (at p. 790) amongst the jurors. In addition I do not take issue with the "air of reality" test referred to in *Pappajohn v. The Queen*, [1980] 2 S.C.R. 120 by McIntyre J.

With respect, however, I have difficulties with his application of the "air of reality" test. In *Pappajohn*, he said, at p. 133:

> To require the putting of the alternative defence of mistaken belief in consent, there must be, in my opinion, some evidence beyond the mere assertion of belief in consent by counsel for the appellant. This evidence must appear from or be supported by sources other than the appellant in order to give it any air of reality.

In his reasons in this case, he says (at p. 790):

> These words [air of reality] appear, on occasion, to have been misunderstood, but I do not withdraw them. There will not be an air of reality about a mere statement that "I thought she was consenting" not supported to some degree by other evidence or circumstances arising in the case. If that mere assertion were sufficient to require a trial judge to put the mistake of fact defence, it would be a simple matter in any rape case to make such an assertion and, regardless of all other circumstances, require the defence to be put.

If this means that the trial judge is not required to put the defence to the jury merely because the accused's lawyer has referred to the defence in argument, then I agree. There must be some evidence supporting the defence before it is to be put to the jury. However, I must respectfully take issue with the "air of reality" norm if it is to be understood as going so far as enabling the trial judge to choose not to leave the defence of honest belief with the jury even in a case where the accused has taken the stand and asserted under oath that he or she honestly believed in consent. An accused's oath to the effect that he or she honestly believed in consent is always some evidence, and its probative value in any given case belongs to the jury and not to the trial judge. It is, of course, open to the trial Judge to comment on the probative value of the evidence, but the jury remains the master of the facts. The trial judge must not usurp the role of the jury by removing the evidence from the jury's consideration on the ground that, in his or her view, the defence lacks an "air of reality".

. . . .

The old common-law rule in sexual assault cases that the trial judge must instruct the jury that it is unsafe to convict in the absence of corroboration of the complainant's testimony (which was abolished by s. 246.4 of the *Criminal Code*) would in effect be replaced by a rule requiring corroboration of the accused's testimony. Such a requirement will often work an injustice to the accused. Clearly the best, and quite often the only, evidence of the accused's subjective belief will be his or her testimony, and there is no basis in law or in principle for requiring corroboration. In addition, this court decided in *Pappajohn* that the accused's belief must be honest but need not be reasonable. As a result, there clearly cannot be a requirement that the accused's belief be supported by the circumstances before it can be submitted to the jury. As Dickson J., as he then was, wrote, at p. 156:

> It will be a rare day when a jury is satisfied as to the existence of an unreasonable belief. If the claim of mistake does not raise a reasonable doubt as to guilt, and all other elements of the crime have been proved, then the trier of fact will not give effect to the defence. But, it there is any evidence that there was such an honest belief, regardless of whether it is reasonable, the jury must be entrusted with the task of assessing the credibility of the plea.

I should, in passing, add that in my view the issue of mistaken belief in consent should also be submitted to the jury in all cases where the accused testifies at trial that the complainant consented. The accused's testimony that the complainant consented must be taken to mean that he believed that the complainant consented. As a result, if the jury believes the complainant and concludes that the complainant did not consent, that does not end the matter, for the accused's assertion cannot be disposed of completely unless consideration is then given to his or her being honestly mistaken in believing that the complainant consented.

Finally, I wish to add that I do not believe that this view of the "air of reality" test will open the floodgates to claims of honest mistake as to consent in sexual assault cases. An accused who wishes to raise the defence in the absence of any other evidence supporting an honest mistake will be required to take the stand and will run the risks of cross-examination. In addition, I do not think that the jury will be fooled by false claims of the defence. Juries are constantly assessing and then discarding defences because they lack an air of reality and do not raise a reasonable doubt. Sexual offence cases are no different.

Subject to these reservations, I agree with McIntyre J.'s reasons and would accordingly allow the appeal and direct a new trial.

Appeal allowed and new trial ordered.

In *R. v. Reddick*, [1991] 1 S.C.R. 1086, 5 C.R. (4th) 389, 64 C.C.C. (3d) 257, the majority adopted and applied the *Pappajohn* requirement of sources other than the accused. It seems clear that this special "air of reality" ruling in *Pappajohn* accounted for the reality that the mistaken belief defence has rarely been put to juries. Since *Pappajohn* there have been very few decisions with written reasons where an acquittal has been based on a mistaken belief defence and only one such acquittal confirmed by a Court of Appeal; see *R. v. Weaver* (1990), 80 C.R. (3d) 396 (Alta. C.A.).

The pattern seemed likely to change with the decision in *R. v. Osolin*, [1993] 4 S.C.R. 595, 26 C.R. (4th) 1, 86 C.C.C. (3d) 481. The Court in *Osolin* unanimously decided that the air of reality test declared in s. 265(4) did not violate the presumption of innocence of s. 11(d) of the *Charter* nor the right to trial by jury under s. 11(f). Mr. Justice Cory reached this conclusion by changing or reading down. He expressly rejected the McIntyre view that there must be a source of evidence other than the accused:

> In my view, this proposition cannot be correct. There is no requirement that there be evidence independent of the accused in order to have the defence put to the jury. However, the mere assertion by the accused that "I believed she was consenting" will not be sufficient. What is required is that the defence of mistaken belief be supported by evidence beyond the mere assertion of a mistaken belief.

The Court was unanimous on this point. McLachlin J. expressly adopted Cory J.'s "resolution of the confusion which existed in the earlier cases". This is as close as Her Ladyship gets to acknowledging that her previous position for the Court in *Reddick* has changed.

The Court in *Osolin* did not accept all of the Lamer position in *Bulmer*. The mistaken belief defence need not always be put where the accused testifies as to mistaken belief. Like any other defence, the trial judge must assess whether there is an evidentiary basis for the defence to be considered by the jury.

In a complex series of split opinions the Supreme Court has now reached further agreement on this issue of air of reality. This was summarized by Chief Justice Lamer for a unanimous court in *Davis*.

R. v. DAVIS

[1999] 3 S.C.R. 759, 29 C.R. (5th) 1, 139 C.C.C. (3d) 193,
1999 CarswellNfld 291, 1999 CarswellNfld 292

LAMER C.J.C. (L'HEUREUX-DUBÉ, GONTHIER, CORY, MCLACHLIN, MAJOR and BINNIE JJ. concurring): —

. . . .

The defence of honest but mistaken belief in consent is simply a denial of the *mens rea* of sexual assault: *R. v. Ewanchuk*, [1999] 1 S.C.R. 330 (S.C.C.) at para. 43; *R. v. Pappajohn*, [1980] 2 S.C.R. 120 (S.C.C.) at p. 148. The *actus reus* of sexual assault requires a touching, of a sexual nature, without the consent of the complainant. The *mens rea* requires the accused to intend the touching and to know of, or to be reckless or wilfully blind as to the complainant's lack of consent: *Ewanchuk, supra,* at paras. 25 and 42. In some circumstances, it is possible for the complainant not to consent to the sexual touching but for the accused to honestly but mistakenly believe that the complainant consented. In these circumstances, the *actus reus* of the offence is established, but the *mens rea* is not.

Before the defence can be considered, there must be sufficient evidence for a reasonable trier of fact to conclude that (1) the complainant did not consent to the sexual touching, and (2) the accused nevertheless honestly but mistakenly believed that the complainant consented: see *R. v. Osolin*, [1993] 4 S.C.R. 595 (S.C.C.) at p. 648, per McLachlin J. In other words, given the evidence, it must be *possible* for a reasonable trier of fact to conclude that the *actus reus* is made out but the *mens rea* is not. In these circumstances, the defence is said to have an "air of reality", and the trier of fact, whether a judge or jury, must consider it. Conversely, where there is no air of reality to the defence, it should not be considered, as no reasonable trier of fact could acquit on that basis: see *R. v. Park*, [1995] 2 S.C.R. 836 (S.C.C.) at para. 11.

In determining whether there is an air of reality to the defence, the trial judge should consider the totality of the evidence: see *Osolin, supra,* at p. 683, per Cory J.; *Park, supra,* at para. 16. The role of the judge in making this determination was set out by Major J. in *Ewanchuk, supra,* at para. 57. He held that the judge should make "no attempt to weigh the evidence". The sole concern is "with the facial plausibility of the defence", and the judge should "avoid the risk of turning the air of reality test into a substantive evaluation of the merits of the defence". Care should be taken not to usurp the role of the trier of fact. Whenever there is a possibility that a reasonable trier of fact could acquit on the basis of the defence, it must be considered.

It is not necessary for the accused to specifically assert a belief that the complainant consented. By simply asserting that the complainant consented, either directly under oath or through counsel, the accused is also asserting a *belief* that the complainant consented: see *Park, supra*, at para. 17. However, the accused's mere assertion will not give the defence an air of reality: see *R. v. Bulmer*, (*sub nom. R. v. B.*) [1987] 1 S.C.R. 782 (S.C.C.) at p. 790.

While this is evidence of a belief in consent, it is not sufficient evidence of an *honest but mistaken* belief in consent. Sexual assault is not a crime that is generally committed by accident: see *Pappajohn*, at p. 155, *per* Dickson J.; *Osolin*, at pp. 685-86, *per* Cory J. In most cases, the issue will be simply one of "consent or no consent", and there will be only one of two possibilities. The first is that the complainant consented, in which case there is no *actus reus*. The second is that the complainant did not consent, and the accused had subjective knowledge of this fact. Here, the *actus reus* is made out, and the *mens rea* follows straightforwardly.

For example, suppose the complainant and the accused relay diametrically opposed stories. The complainant alleges a brutal sexual assault and vigorous resistance, whereas the accused claims consensual intercourse. Suppose further that it is impossible to splice together the evidence to create a third version of events in which the accused honestly but mistakenly believed the complainant consented. In such circumstances, the trial becomes, essentially, a pure question of credibility. If the complainant is believed, the *actus reus* is made out and the *mens rea* follows straightforwardly. If the accused is believed, or if there is a reasonable doubt as to the complainant's version of events, there is no *actus reus*. There is no third possibility of an honest but mistaken belief in consent, notwithstanding the accused's assertion that the complainant consented: *Park, supra*, at paras. 25-26.

Although the accused's mere assertion that the complainant consented will not be sufficient evidence to raise the defence, the requisite evidence may nevertheless come from the accused: see *Park, supra*, at pp. 852-53, paras. 19-20, per L'Heureux-Dubé J.; *Osolin, supra*, at pp. 686-87, *per* Cory J., and pp. 649-50, *per* McLachlin J. It may also come from the complainant, other sources, or a combination thereof. In *R. v. Esau*, [1997] 2 S.C.R. 777 (S.C.C.). McLachlin J., dissenting in the result, accurately conveyed the nature of this evidence at para. 63:

> There must be evidence not only of non-consent and belief in consent, but in addition evidence capable of explaining how the accused could honestly have mistaken the complainant's lack of consent as consent. Otherwise, the defence cannot reasonably arise. There must, in short, be evidence of a situation of ambiguity in which the accused could honestly have misapprehended that the complainant was consenting to the sexual activity in question.

Finally, the court has held that there will be no air of reality where the evidence shows that the accused was reckless or wilfully blind as to whether the complainant consented. In those circumstances, the accused has subjectively adverted to the absence of consent, and therefore cannot have an *honest* but mistaken belief that the complainant consented.

I note that the appellant was charged with offences allegedly committed prior to the introduction of s. 273.2 in August of 1992. Consequently, the statutory amendments to the defence of honest but mistaken belief in consent do not apply to this appeal.

PROBLEM

The accused was charged with the sexual assault of V, a 15-year-old girl. V and her young friend, T, had willingly gone with the accused and another man, both aged 28. The men had picked them up in the accused's car at 1:30 a.m. The accused drove to a parking lot where the four consumed some beer. The other man kissed V in the back seat. They then went to a second parking lot, where the two girls exchanged seats at the request of the other man. They drove to a third lot, where the accused had sexual intercourse with V. The accused then drove the two girls to T's home. V testified that she resisted the accused throughout. She said she told him no during intercourse and tried to push him away. She testified that, although the accused was not violent and the windows were open and the doors unlocked, she was afraid to scream. V stated that when they arrived at T's apartment, the accused hugged her. V said that it was possible that she had hugged him back, before saying "bye". When asked by counsel for the accused why, on returning to T's apartment building, she didn't run into the apartment with T to escape, she stated that she didn't because she didn't want the men "to know that anything was wrong". The accused testified that V had been a willing partner while they mutually kissed and touched each other and that he climbed over the gear shift onto her side of the car after she touched his leg and penis. He stated that V hugged him before she left the car. The accused stated that he gave a slip of paper to T on which he had written his name and telephone number before she and V switched places in the car. He also argued that, in light of V's denial that she had consented, circumstances were such that he had entertained an honest but mistaken belief in consent. The trial judge put both defences to the jury. The accused was acquitted.

Was there an air of reality to the mistaken belief defence? Compare *Livermore*, [1995] 4 S.C.R. 123, 43 C.R. (4th) 1, 102 C.C.C. (3d) 212 (S.C.C.) and *Esau*, [1997] 2 S.C.R. 777, 7 C.R. (5th) 357, 116 C.C.C. (3d) 289 (S.C.C.).

In *Livermore* a new trial was ordered on the basis of misdirections on the issue of consent. In sole dissent on this point, Major J. concluded as follows:

> The circumstances giving rise to the complaint were decisive in this case. The alleged sexual assault took place in the bucket seat of a sports car. The cramped quarters were such that on the facts of this case some co-operation, if not the consent, of the complainant was necessary for the alleged offence to have occurred. This was consistent with the accused's testimony and inconsistent with that of the complainant. The errors of the trial judge such as they were would not have changed the result.

What do you think of Major J.'s reasoning?

SUSAN ESTRICH, TEACHING RAPE LAW

(1992), 102 Yale L.J. 509

I know many students, and even a few professors, who believe that the women are always right and the men are always wrong; that if she didn't consent fully and voluntarily, it is rape, no matter what she said or did, or what he did or did not realize. Everything about his past should be admitted, and nothing about hers. And that's what they want to hear in class.

This kind of orthodoxy is not only bad educationally but, in the case of rape, it also misses the point. Society is not so orthodox in its views. There is a debate going on in courthouses and prosecutors' offices, and around coffee machines and dinner tables, about whether Mike Tyson was guilty or not, and whether William Kennedy Smith ever should have been prosecuted; about when women should be believed, and what counts as consent. There's a debate going on in America as to what is reasonable when it comes to sex. Turn on the radio and you will hear it. To silence that debate in the classroom is to remove the classroom from reality, and to make ourselves irrelevant. It may be hard for some students, but ultimately the only way to change things — and that's usually the goal of those who find the discussions most difficult — is to confront the issues squarely, not to pretend that they don't exist. Besides, the purpose of education, in my classes anyway, is to prepare our students to participate in the controversies that animate the law, not to provide them with a shelter from reality.

. . . .

When I first started teaching rape, the hard questions were whether and when "no means yes," whether nonconsent meant more than saying no, and whether force required more than a push onto the bed and a heavy caress. In those days, it was possible to argue that both the man and the woman in a typical acquaintance rape case were telling the truth: that she said no and did not consent, and that he thought he was engaging in consensual intercourse. The question was not just who to believe, but what standard to apply — male or female, objective or subjective — and how to define it. Is the reasonable man the average man, or the man most reasonable women would like to date? And who is the reasonable woman?

Today, the old questions seem a little easier, but there is a new set that is, in many respects, even more difficult. In the William Kennedy Smith trial, for example, the defense lawyers took pains to point out that they were not arguing that no means yes, or that necking constitutes presumptive consent or even that going to a man's house in the middle of the night entitles him to make any assumptions. Rather, they argued that the complainant said yes.

The Smith defence strategy, I think, reflects an accurate assumption that judges and juries these days are less inclined to accept male conduct that only a few years ago was tolerated as understandably macho. I don't find as many students in my classes these days who believe that a man has the right to ignore the fact that a woman is saying no. And I don't think the reason for this change is that feminists have defined what is "politically correct" in the classroom; I think instead that most of my students, male and female, actually believe that a man should listen to a woman's words, and take her at her word.

This shift in our thinking about the elements of culpability leaves credibility as the only defense game in town. After all, rapes rarely take place in front of witnesses. If no doesn't mean yes, if bruises aren't necessary, and if no unusual force is required, then in many cases there's not going to be much physical evidence to rely on. She gives her version and he gives his. If you are the defense attorney, your job is to convince the jury not to believe what she says — which means that the only way to defend may be to destroy the credibility of the victim.

The key question in many acquaintance rape cases today thus becomes not what counts as rape but rather what we need to know about the victim, and the defendant, in order to decide who is telling the truth.

. . . .

It is one thing to exclude evidence of a woman's sexual past or of psychiatric treatment when she has been beaten and burned; it is easy to argue there that admitting such evidence does almost nothing except to deter legitimate prosecutions and to victimize the victim. But it is surely a harder case when there have been no weapons and no bruises, and when the man's liberty depends on convincing a jury not to believe a woman who appears at least superficially credible.

Many of the traditional rules of rape liability were premised on the notion that women lie; Wigmore went so far as to view rape complainants as fundamentally deranged. I don't buy that for a moment nor, I expect, do most of my students. Yet even if only one of a hundred men, or one of a thousand, is falsely accused, the question is still how we can protect that man's right to disprove his guilt. Assume for a moment, I tell my students, that it was you, or your brother, or your boyfriend or your son, who was accused of rape by a casual date with a history of psychiatric problems, or by a woman he met in a bar who had a history of one-night stands. Would you exclude that evidence? What else can the man do to avoid a felony conviction and a ruined life? Where do you draw the line? But if you don't exclude the evidence, will some women as a result become unrapable, at least as a matter of law? That is, will women who have histories of mental instability or of "promiscuity" ever be able to convince

juries who know those histories that they really were raped? Similar issues arise
with respect to the man's credibility. The first question many people asked when
Anita Hill charged that Clarence Thomas had harassed her was whether there
were other women who had been similarly mistreated. The first significant ruling
in the Smith case, indeed the decisive ruling, was the judge's pretrial decision
to exclude the testimony of three other women who claimed that they had been
sexually abused by the defendant. If the testimony of only one woman cannot
be believed — unless she is a Sunday school teacher, camera in hand, as Desiree
Washington was, and the defendant is a black man who has made a host of
inconsistent statements, as Mike Tyson did — is it fair to exclude the testimony
of the other women? And if the testimony is not excluded, do we risk convicting
a defendant for being a bad man, indeed being a rapist, rather than committing
the particular act charged?

One answer is to say that we need symmetry: exclude all the evidence about
both of them. That's the approach the judge followed in the William Kennedy
Smith case. On the surface, it is neat and appealing. The only problem is that
it's a false symmetry that is being enforced. After all, evidence that a man has
abused other women is much more probative of rape than evidence that a woman
has had consensual sex with other men is probative of consent. Most women
have had sexual experiences, and unless those experiences fall into some kind
of unusual pattern, the mere fact that a woman has had lovers tells us almost
nothing about whether she consented on the particular occasion that she is
charging as rape. But won't we all look at a defendant differently if three other
women have also come forward to say they were abused? The danger with such
evidence is not that it proves so little, but that it may prove too much. Symmetry
won't get you out of this hole, at least not in my classroom.

Thus, even if most students can agree these days that no means no, and that
force can be established if you push a woman down, there's very little agreement
about what we need to know about her or him before deciding whether she in
fact said yes or no, and whether he actually pushed her down or just lay down
with her. The consensus on what counts as rape is more apparent than real.
These days, society's continued ambivalence towards acquaintance rape is
increasingly being expressed in evidentiary rules and standards of credibility
rather than in the definitions of force and consent. The questions have shifted;
answering them is no easier.

R. v. SEABOYER; R. v. GAYME

[1991] 2 S.C.R. 577, 7 C.R. (4th) 117, 66 C.C.C. (3d) 321,
1991 CarswellOnt 1022, 1991 CarswellOnt 109

The rape shield provisions inserted into the *Criminal Code* in 1983 were ss.
276 and 277. The former section dealt with evidence of the complainant's sexual
activity as referable to the issue of consent and the latter as referable to the

credibility of the complainant. The Court, by a majority of 7:2, decided s. 277 was constitutional but not s. 276.

MCLACHLIN J. (LAMER C.J.C., LAFOREST, SOPINKA, CORY, STEVENSON and IACOBUCCI JJ. concurring): — These cases raise the issue of the constitutionality of ss. 276 and 277 of the *Criminal Code*, R.S.C. 1985, c. C-46 (formerly ss. 246.6 and 246.7), commonly known as the "rape-shield" provisions. The provisions restrict the right of the defence on a trial for a sexual offence to cross-examine and lead evidence of a complainant's sexual conduct on other occasions. The question is whether these restrictions offend the guarantees accorded to an accused person by the *Canadian Charter of Rights and Freedoms*.

My conclusion is that one of the sections in issue, s. 276, offends the *Charter*. While its purpose — the abolition of outmoded, sexist-based use of sexual conduct evidence — is laudable, its effect goes beyond what is required or justified by that purpose. At the same time, striking down s. 276 does not imply reversion to the old common law rules, which permitted evidence of the complainant's sexual conduct even though it might have no probative value to the issues on the case and, on the contrary, might mislead the jury. Instead, relying on the basic principles that actuate our law of evidence, the courts must seek a middle way that offers the maximum protection to the complainant compatible with the maintenance of the accused's fundamental right to a fair trial.

· · · ·

I deal first with *Seaboyer*. The accused was charged with sexual assault of a woman with whom he had been drinking in a bar. On the preliminary inquiry the judge refused to allow the accused to cross-examine the complainant on her sexual conduct on other occasions. The appellant contends that he should have been permitted to cross-examine as to other acts of sexual intercourse which may have caused bruises, and other aspects of the complainant's condition which the Crown had put in evidence. While the theory of the defence has not been detailed at this early stage, such evidence might arguably be relevant to consent, since it might provide other explanations for the physical evidence tendered by the Crown in support of the use of force against the complainant.

The *Gayme* case arose in different circumstances. The complainant was 15, the appellant 18. They were friends. The Crown alleges that the appellant sexually assaulted her at his school. The defence, relying on the defences of consent and honest belief in consent, contends that there was no assault and that the complainant was the sexual aggressor. In pursuance of this defence, the appellant at the preliminary inquiry sought to cross-examine and present evidence of prior and subsequent sexual conduct of the complainant.

· · · ·

It should be noted that the admissibility of the evidence sought to be tendered in the two cases is not at issue. In neither case did the preliminary inquiry judge consider whether the evidence would have been relevant or admissible in the absence of ss. 276 or 277 of the *Criminal Code*.

RELEVANT LEGISLATION

Criminal Code, s. 276:

276. (1) In proceedings in respect of an offence under section 271, 272 or 273, no evidence shall be adduced by or on behalf of the accused concerning the sexual activity of the complainant with any person other than the accused unless
> (*a*) it is evidence that rebuts evidence of the complainant's sexual activity or absence thereof that was previously adduced by the prosecution;
> (*b*) it is evidence of specific instances of the complainant's sexual activity tending to establish the identity of the person who had sexual contact with the complainant on the occasion set out in the charge; or
> (*c*) it is evidence of sexual activity that took place on the same occasion as the sexual activity that forms the subject-matter of the charge, where that evidence relates to the consent that the accused alleges he believed was given by the complainant.

(2) No evidence is admissible under paragraph (1)(*c*) unless
> (*a*) reasonable notice in writing has been given to the prosecutor by or on behalf of the accused of his intention to adduce the evidence together with particulars of the evidence sought to be adduced; and
> (*b*) a copy of the notice has been filed with the clerk of the court.

(3) No evidence is admissible under subsection (1) unless the judge, provincial court judge or justice, after holding a hearing in which the jury and the members of the public are excluded and in which the complainant is not a compellable witness, is satisfied that the requirements of this section are met.

Criminal Code, s. 277:

277. In proceedings in respect of an offence under section 271, 272 or 273, evidence of sexual reputation, whether general or specific, is not admissible for the purpose of challenging or supporting the credibility of the complainant.

. . . .

Everyone, under s. 7 of the *Charter*, has the right to life, liberty and security of person and the right not to be deprived thereof except in accordance with the principles of fundamental justice.

. . . .

The real issue under s. 7 is whether the potential for deprivation of liberty flowing from ss. 276 and 277 takes place in a manner that conforms to the principles of fundamental justice.

. . . .

All the parties agree that the right to a fair trial — one which permits the trier of fact to get at the truth and properly and fairly dispose of the case — is a principle of fundamental justice. Nor is there any dispute that encouraging reporting of sexual offences and protection of the complainant's privacy are legitimate goals, provided they do not interfere with the primary objective of a fair trial. Where the parties part company is on the issue of whether ss. 276 and 277 of the *Criminal Code* in fact infringe the right to a fair trial. The supporters of the legislation urge that it furthers the right to a fair trial by eliminating evidence of little or no worth and considerable prejudice. The appellants, on the other hand, say that the legislation goes too far and in fact eliminates relevant evidence which should be admitted notwithstanding the possibility of prejudice.

. . . .

This court has affirmed the trial judges' power to exclude Crown evidence the prejudicial effect of which outweighs its probative value in a criminal case, but a narrower formula than that articulated by McCormick has emerged. In *Wray, supra*, at p. 293, [[1971] S.C.R.] the court stated that the judge may exclude only "evidence gravely prejudicial to the accused, the admissibility of which is tenuous, and whose probative force in relation to the main issue before the court is trifling". More recently, in *R. v. Sweitzer*, [1982] 1 S.C.R. 949, at p. 953, an appeal involving a particularly difficult brand of circumstantial evidence offered by the Crown, the court said that "admissibility will depend upon the probative effect of the evidence balanced against the prejudice caused to the accused by its admission." In *Morris, supra*, at p. 193 [[1983] 2 S.C.R.], the court without mentioning *Sweitzer* cited the narrower *Wray* formula. But in *R. c. Potvin*, [1989] 1 S.C.R. 525, 68 C.R. (3d) 193, 47 C.C.C. (3d) 289, La Forest J. (Dickson C.J.C. concurring) affirmed in general terms "the rule that the trial Judge may exclude admissible evidence if its prejudicial effect substantially outweighs its probative value" (p. 531 [S.C.R.]).

I am of the view that the more appropriate description of the general power of a judge to exclude relevant evidence on the ground of prejudice is that articulated in *Sweitzer* and generally accepted throughout the common law world.

. . . .

The Canadian cases cited above all pertain to evidence tendered by the Crown against the accused. The question arises whether the same power to exclude exists with respect to defence evidence. Canadian courts, like courts in most common-law jurisdictions, have been extremely cautious in restricting the power of the accused to call evidence in his or her defence, a reluctance founded in the fundamental tenet of our judicial system that an innocent person must not be convicted. It follows from this that the prejudice must substantially outweigh the value of the evidence before a judge can exclude evidence relevant to a defence allowed by law.

. . . .

Section 277 excludes evidence of sexual reputation for the purpose of challenging or supporting the credibility of the plaintiff. The idea that a complainant's credibility might be affected by whether she has had other sexual experience is today universally discredited. There is no logical or practical link between a woman's sexual reputation and whether she is a truthful witness. It follows that the evidence excluded by s. 277 can serve no legitimate purpose in the trial. Section 277, by limiting the exclusion to a purpose which is clearly illegitimate, does not touch evidence which may be tendered for valid purposes, and hence does not infringe the right to a fair trial.

I turn then to s. 276. Section 276, unlike s. 277, does not condition exclusion on use of the evidence for an illegitimate purpose. Rather, it constitutes a blanket exclusion, subject to three exceptions — rebuttal evidence, evidence going to identity, and evidence relating to consent to sexual activity on the same occasion as the trial incident. The question is whether this may exclude evidence which is relevant to the defence and the probative value of which is not substantially outweighed by the potential prejudice to the trial process. To put the matter another way, can it be said a priori, as the Attorney-General for Ontario contends, that any and all evidence excluded by s. 276 will necessarily be of such trifling weight in relation to the prejudicial effect of the evidence that it may fairly be excluded?

In my view, the answer to this question must be negative. The Canadian and American jurisprudence affords numerous examples of evidence of sexual conduct which would be excluded by s. 276 but which clearly should be received in the interests of a fair trial, notwithstanding the possibility that it may divert a jury by tempting it to improperly infer consent or lack of credibility in the complainant.

Consider the defence of honest belief. It rests on the concept that the accused may honestly but mistakenly (and not necessarily reasonably) have believed that the complainant was consenting to the sexual act. If the accused can raise a reasonable doubt as to his intention on the basis that he honestly held such a belief, he is not guilty under our law and is entitled to an acquittal. The basis of the accused's honest belief in the complainant's consent may be sexual acts performed by the complainant at some other time or place. Yet s. 276 would preclude the accused leading such evidence.

Another category of evidence eliminated by s. 276 relates to the right of the defence to attack the credibility of the complainant on the ground that the complainant was biased or had motive to fabricate the evidence. In *State v. Jalo*, 27 Or. App. 845, 557 P.2d 1359 (1976), a father accused of sexual acts with his young daughter sought to present evidence that the source of the accusation was his earlier discovery of the fact that the girl and her brother were engaged in intimate relations. The defence contended that when the father stopped the relationship, the daughter, out of animus toward him, accused him of the act. The father sought to lead this evidence in support of his defence that the charges were a concoction motivated by animus. Notwithstanding its clear relevance, this evidence would be excluded by s. 276. The respondent submits that the damage caused by its exclusion would not be great, because all that would be forbidden would be evidence of the sexual activities of the children, and the father could still testify that his daughter was angry with him. But surely the father's chance of convincing the jury of the validity of his defence would be greatly diminished if he were reduced to saying, in effect, "My daughter was angry with me, but I can't say why or produce any corroborating evidence." As noted above, to deny a defendant the building blocks of his defence is often to deny him the defence itself.

Other examples abound. Evidence of sexual activity excluded by s. 276 may be relevant to explain the physical conditions on which the Crown relies to establish intercourse or the use of force, such as semen, pregnancy, injury or disease — evidence which may go to consent. . . . In the case of young complainants, where there may be a tendency to believe their story on the ground that the detail of their account must have come from the alleged encounter, it may be relevant to show other activity which provides an explanation for the knowledge.

. . . .

Even evidence as to pattern of conduct may on occasion be relevant. Since this use of evidence of prior sexual conduct draws upon the inference that prior conduct infers similar subsequent conduct, it closely resembles the prohibited use of the evidence and must be carefully scrutinized. . . . Yet such evidence might be admissible in non-sexual cases under the similar fact rule. Is it fair, then, to deny it to an accused, merely because the trial relates to a sexual offence?

. . . .

These examples leave little doubt that s. 276 has the potential to exclude evidence of critical relevance to the defence. Can it honestly be said, as the Attorney-General for Ontario contends, that the value of such evidence will always be trifling when compared with its potential to mislead the jury? I think not. The examples show that the evidence may well be of great importance to getting at the truth and determining whether the accused is guilty or innocent under the law — the ultimate aim of the trial process. They demonstrate that s. 276, enacted for the purpose of helping judges and juries arrive at the proper and just verdict in the particular case, overshoots the mark, with the result that it may have the opposite effect of impeding them in discovering the truth.

. . . .

2.   Is s. 276 Saved by s. 1 of the *Charter*?

Is s. 276 of the *Criminal Code* justified in a free and democratic society, notwithstanding the fact that it may lead to infringements of the *Charter*?

The first step under s. 1 is to consider whether the legislation addresses a pressing and substantial objective.

. . . .

The second requirement under s. 1 is that the infringement of rights be proportionate to the pressing objective. . . . In creating exceptions to the exclusion of evidence of the sexual activity of the complainant on other occasions, Parliament correctly recognized that justice requires a measured approach, one which admits evidence which is truly relevant to the defence notwithstanding potential prejudicial effect. Yet Parliament at the same time excluded other evidence of sexual conduct which might be equally relevant to a legitimate defence and which appears to pose no greater danger of prejudice than the exceptions it recognizes. To the extent the section excludes relevant defence evidence whose value is not clearly outweighed by the danger it presents, the section is overbroad.

I turn finally to the third aspect of the proportionality requirement — the balance between the importance of the objective and the injurious effect of the legislation. The objective of the legislation, as discussed above, is to eradicate the erroneous inferences from evidence of other sexual encounters that the complainant is more likely to have consented to the sexual act in issue or less likely to be telling the truth. The subsidiary aims are to promote fairer trials and increased reporting of sexual offences and to minimize the invasion of the complainant's privacy. In this way the personal security of women and their right to equal benefit and protection of the law are enhanced. The effect of the legislation, on the other hand, is to exclude relevant defence evidence, the value of which outweighs its potential prejudice. As indicated in the discussion of s. 7, all parties agree that a provision which rules out probative defence evidence which is not clearly outweighed by the prejudice it may cause to the trial strikes the wrong balance between the rights of complainants and the rights of the accused. The line must be drawn short of the point where it results in an unfair trial and the possible conviction of an innocent person. Section 276 fails this test.

I conclude that s. 276 is not saved by s. 1 of the *Charter*.

. . . .

4.   What Follows From Striking Down s. 276?

The first question is whether the striking down of s. 276 revives the old common-law rules of evidence permitting liberal and often inappropriate reception of evidence of the complainant's sexual conduct.

. . . .

The answer to this question is no. The rules in question are common-law rules. Like other common-law rules of evidence, they must be adapted to conform to current reality. As all counsel on these appeals accepted, the reality in 1991 is that evidence of sexual conduct and reputation in itself cannot be regarded as logically probative of either the complainant's credibility or consent. Although they still may inform the thinking of many, the twin myths which s. 276 sought to eradicate are just that — myths — and have no place in a rational and just system of law. It follows that the old rules which permitted evidence of sexual conduct and condoned invalid inferences from it solely for these purposes have no place in our law.

The inquiry as to what the law is in the absence of s. 276 of the *Code* is thus remitted to consideration of the fundamental principles governing the trial process and the reception of evidence. Harking back to Thayer's maxim, relevant evidence should be admitted, and irrelevant evidence excluded, subject to the qualification that the value of the evidence must outweigh its potential prejudice to the conduct of a fair trial. Moreover, the focus must be not on the evidence itself, but on the use to which it is put. As Professor Galvin puts it, our aim is "to abolish the outmoded, sexist-based use of sexual conduct evidence while permitting other uses of such evidence to remain": at p. 809 [70 Minn. L. Rev.].

This definition of the problem suggests an approach which abolishes illegitimate uses and inferences, while preserving legitimate uses. There is wide agreement that the approach of a general exclusion supplemented by categories of exceptions is bound to fail because of the impossibility of predicting in advance what evidence may be relevant in a particular case: see Galvin, Doherty, and Elliott. On the other hand, judges are not free to act on whim. As Professor Vivian Berger puts it in her article "Man's Trial, Woman's Tribulation: Rape Cases in the Courtroom" (1977), 77 Colum. L. Rev. 1, at p. 69:

> The problem is to chart a course between inflexible legislative rules and wholly untrammelled judicial discretion: The former threatens the rights of defendants; the latter may ignore the needs of complainants.

Professor Galvin, after a comprehensive review of the various approaches to rape-shield legislation which have been adopted in different jurisdictions, proposes a prohibition on illegitimate uses of the evidence, combined with case-by-case judgment exercised with the aid of guidelines.

. . . .

Galvin's proposal, with some modification, reflects an appropriate response to the problem of avoiding illegitimate inferences from evidence of the complainant's sexual conduct, while preserving the general right to a fair trial. It is, moreover, a response which is open to trial judges in the absence of legislation. It reflects, in essence, an application of the fundamental common-law notions which govern the reception of evidence on trials. The general prohibition on improper use of evidence of sexual conduct reflects the fact that it is always open to a judge to warn against using a particular piece of evidence for an inference on an issue for which that evidence has no probative force. Similarly, the mandate to the judge to determine when the evidence may be properly receivable is a reflection of the basic function of the trial judge of determining the relevance of evidence and whether it should be received, bearing in mind the balance between its probative value and its potential prejudice.

As for the procedures which should govern the determination of whether the sexual conduct evidence should be admitted, Galvin proposes a written motion followed by an *in camera* hearing (p. 904). The devices of a preliminary affidavit and an *in camera* hearing are designed to minimize the invasion of the complainant's privacy. If the affidavit does not show the evidence to be relevant, it will not be heard at all. Where this threshold is met, the evidence will be heard *in camera* so that, in the event the judge finds its value is outweighed by its potential prejudice, it will not enter the public domain. Such procedures do not require legislation. It has always been open to the courts to devise such procedures as may be necessary to ensure a fair trial. The requirements of a *voir dire* before a confession can be admitted, for example, is judge-made law.

While accepting the premise and the general thrust of Galvin's proposal, I suggest certain modifications. There seems little purpose in having separate rules for the use of sexual conduct evidence for illegitimate inferences of consent and credibility in the Canadian context. Again, I question whether evidence of other sexual conduct with the accused should automatically be admissible in all cases; sometimes the value of such evidence might be little or none. The word "complainant" is more compatible with the presumption of innocence of the accused than the word "victim". Professor Galvin's reference to the defence of reasonable belief in consent must be adapted to meet Canadian law, which does not require reasonableness. And the need to warn the jury clearly against improper uses of the evidence should be emphasized, in my view.

In the absence of legislation, it is open to this court to suggest guidelines for the reception and use of sexual conduct evidence. Such guidelines should be seen for what they are — an attempt to describe the consequences of the application of the general rules of evidence governing relevance and the reception of evidence — and not as judicial legislation cast in stone.

In my view, the trial judge under this new regime, shoulders a dual responsibility. First, the judge must assess with a high degree of sensitivity whether the evidence proffered by the defence meets the test of demonstrating a degree of relevance which outweighs the damages and disadvantages presented by the admission of such evidence. The examples presented earlier suggest that while cases where such evidence will carry sufficient probative value will exist, they will be exceptional. The trial judge must ensure that evidence is tendered for a legitimate purpose, and that it logically supports a defence. The fishing expeditions which unfortunately did occur in the past should not be permitted. The trial judge's discretion must be exercised to ensure that neither the *in camera* procedure nor the trial become forums for demeaning and abusive conduct by defence counsel.

The trial judge's second responsibility will be to take special care to ensure that, in the exceptional case where circumstances demand that such evidence be permitted, the jury is fully and properly instructed as to its appropriate use. The jurors must be cautioned that they should not draw impermissible inferences from evidence of previous sexual activity. While such evidence may be tendered for a purpose logically probative of the defence to be presented, it may be important to remind jurors that they not allow the allegations of past sexual activity to lead them to the view that the complainant is less worthy of belief, or was more likely to have consented for that reason. It is hoped that a sensitive and responsive exercise of discretion by the judiciary will reduce and even eliminate the concerns which provoked legislation such as s. 276, while at the same time preserving the right of an accused to a fair trial.

I would summarize the applicable principles as follows:

1. On a trial for a sexual offence, evidence that the complainant has engaged in consensual sexual conduct on other occasions (including past sexual conduct with the accused) is not admissible solely to support the inference that the complainant is by reason of such conduct:
   (a) more likely to have consented to the sexual conduct at issue in the trial;
   (b) less worthy of belief as a witness.

2. Evidence of consensual sexual conduct on the part of the complainant may be admissible for purposes other than an inference relating to the consent or credibility of the complainant, where it possesses probative value on an issue in the trial and where that probative value is not substantially outweighed by the danger of unfair prejudice flowing from the evidence.

By way of illustration only, and not by way of limitation, the following are examples of admissible evidence:

(A) Evidence of specific instances of sexual conduct tending to prove that a person other than the accused caused the physical consequences of the rape alleged by the prosecution;
(B) Evidence of sexual conduct tending to prove bias or motive to fabricate on the part of the complainant;

(C) Evidence of prior sexual conduct, known to the accused at the time of the act charged, tending to prove that the accused believed that the complainant was consenting to the act charged (without laying down absolute rules, normally one would expect some proximity in time between the conduct that is alleged to have given rise to an honest belief and the conduct charged);

(D) Evidence of prior sexual conduct which meets the requirements for the reception of similar act evidence, bearing in mind that such evidence cannot be used illegitimately merely to show that the complainant consented or is an unreliable witness.

(E) Evidence tending to rebut proof introduced by the prosecution regarding the complainant's sexual conduct;

3. Before evidence of consensual sexual conduct on the part of a victim is received, it must be established on a *voir dire* (which may be held *in camera*) by affidavit or the testimony of the accused or third parties, that the proposed use of the evidence of other sexual conduct is legitimate.

4. Where evidence that the complainant has engaged in sexual conduct on other occasions is admitted on a jury trial, the judge should warn the jury against inferring from the evidence of the conduct itself, either that the complainant might have consented to the act alleged, or that the complainant is less worthy of credit.

. . . .

L'HEUREUX-DUBÉ J. (GONTHIER J. concurring) (dissenting in part): —

[She agreed to allow the appeal on jurisdictional grounds but held that, in any event, there had been no *Charter* violation and that any violation could have been justified under s. 1.]

. . . .

Sexual assault is not like any other crime. In the vast majority of cases the target is a woman and the perpetrator is a man. . . . Unlike other crimes of a violent nature, it is for the most part unreported. Yet, by all accounts, women are victimized at an alarming rate, and there is some evidence that an already frighteningly high rate of sexual assault is on the increase. The prosecution and conviction rates for sexual assault are among the lowest for all violent crimes. Perhaps more than any other crime, the fear and constant reality of sexual assault affects how women conduct their lives and how they define their relationship with the larger society. Sexual assault is not like any other crime.

. . . .

There are a number of reasons why women may not report their victimization: fear of reprisal, fear of a continuation of their trauma at the hands of the police and the criminal justice system, fear of a perceived loss of status and lack of desire to report due to the typical effects of sexual assault such as depression, self-blame or loss of self-esteem. Although all of the reasons for failing to report are significant and important, more relevant to the present inquiry are the numbers of victims who choose not to bring their victimization to the attention of the authorities due to their perception that the institutions, with which they would have to become involved, will view their victimization in a stereotypical and biased fashion.

The woman who comes to the attention of the authorities has her victimization measured against the current rape mythologies, *i.e.*, who she should be in order to be recognized as having been, in the eyes of the law, raped; who her attacker must be in order to be recognized, in the eyes of the law, as a potential rapist; and how injured she must be in order to be believed. If her victimization does not fit the myths, it is unlikely that an arrest will be made or a conviction obtained. As prosecutors and police often suggest, in an attempt to excuse their application of stereotype, there is no point in directing cases toward the justice system if juries and judges will acquit on the basis of their stereotypical perceptions of the "supposed victim" and her "supposed" victimization.

. . . .

More specifically, police rely in large measure upon popular conceptions of sexual assault in order to classify incoming cases as "founded" or "unfounded". It would appear as though most forces have developed a convenient shorthand regarding their decisions to proceed in any given case. This shorthand is composed of popular myth regarding rapists (distinguishing them from men as a whole), and stereotype about women's character and sexuality. Holmstrom and Burgess, at pp. 174-199, conveniently set out and explain the most common of these myths and stereotypes:

1. *Struggle and Force: Woman as Defender of Her Honour.* There is a myth that a woman cannot be raped against her will, that if she really wants to prevent a rape she can.

The prosecution attempts to show that she did struggle, or had no opportunity to do so, while the defence attempts to show that she did not.

Women know that there is no response on their part that will assure their safety. The experience and knowledge of women is borne out by the *Canadian Urban Victimization Survey: Female Victims of Crime* (1985). At p. 7 of the report, the authors note:

> Sixty percent of those who tried reasoning with their attackers, and 60 percent of those who resisted actively by fighting or using weapon [sic] were injured. Every sexual assault incident is unique and so many factors are unknown (physical size of victims and offenders, verbal or physical threats, etc.) that no single course of action can be recommended unqualifiedly.

2. *Knowing the Defendant: The Rapist as a Stranger.* There is a myth that rapists are strangers who leap out of bushes to attack their victims. . . . [T]he

view that interaction between friends or between relatives does not result in rape is prevalent.

The defence uses the existence of a relationship between the parties to blame the victim. . . .

3. *Sexual Reputation: The Madonna-Whore Complex*. . . . [W]omen . . . are categorized into one-dimensional types. They are maternal or they are sexy. They are good or they are bad. They are madonnas or they are whores.

The legal rules use these distinctions.

4. *General Character: Anything Not 100 Percent Proper and Respectable*. . . . Being on welfare or drinking or drug use could be used to discredit anyone, but where women are involved, these issues are used to imply that the woman consented to sex with the defendant or that she contracted to have sex for money.

5. *Emotionality of Females*. Females are assumed to be "more emotional" than males. The expectation is that if a woman is raped, she will get hysterical during the event and she will be visibly upset afterward. If she is able to "retain her cool," then people assume that "nothing happened".

6. *Reporting Rape*. Two conflicting expectations exist concerning the reporting of rape. One is that if a woman is raped she will be too upset and ashamed to report it, and hence most of the time this crime goes unreported. The other is that if a woman is raped, she will be so upset that she will report it. Both expectations exist simultaneously.

7. *Woman as Fickle and Full of Spite*. Another stereotype is that the feminine character is especially filled with malice. Woman is seen as fickle and as seeking revenge on past lovers.

8. *The Female Under Surveillance: Is the Victim Trying to Escape Punishment?* . . . It is assumed that the female's sexual behaviour, depending on her age, is under the surveillance of her parents or her husband, and also more generally of the community. Thus, the defense argues, if a woman says she was raped, it must be because she consented to sex that she was not supposed to have. She got caught, and now she wants to get back in the good graces of whomever's surveillance she is under.

9. *Disputing That Sex Occurred*. That females fantasize rape is another common stereotype. Females are assumed to make up stories that sex occurred when in fact nothing happened. . . . Similarly, women are thought to fabricate the sexual activity not as part of a fantasy life, but out of spite.

10. *Stereotype of the Rapist*. One stereotype of the rapist is that of a stranger who leaps out of the bushes to attack his victim and later abruptly leaves her. . . .

[S]tereotypes of the rapist can be used to blame the victim. She tells what he did. And because it often does not match what jurors *think* rapists do, his behaviour is held against her.

. . . .

This list of stereotypical conceptions about women and sexual assault is by no means exhaustive. Like most stereotypes, they operate as a way, however flawed, of understanding the world and, like most such constructs, operate at a level of consciousness that makes it difficult to root them out and confront them directly. This mythology finds its way into the decisions of the police regarding their "founded"/"unfounded" categorization, operates in the mind of the Crown when deciding whether or not to prosecute, influences a judge's or juror's perception of guilt or innocence of the accused and the "goodness" or "badness" of the victim, and finally, has carved out a niche in both the evidentiary and substantive law governing the trial of the matter.

. . . .

Absolutely pivotal to an understanding of the nature and purpose of the provisions and constitutional questions at issue in this case is the realization of how widespread the stereotypes and myths about rape are, notwithstanding their inaccuracy.

The appellants argue that we, as a society, have become more enlightened, that prosecutors, police, judges and jurors can be trusted to perform their tasks without recourse to discriminatory views about women manifested through rape myth. Unfortunately, social science evidence suggests otherwise. Rape myths still present formidable obstacles for complainants in their dealings with the very system charged with discovering the truth. Their experience in this regard is illustrated by the following remarks of surprisingly recent vintage:

> Women who say no do not always mean no. It is not just a question of saying no, it is a question of how she says it, how she shows and makes it clear. If she doesn't want it she has only to keep her legs shut and she would not get it without force and there would be marks of force being used.

> (Judge David Wild, Cambridge Crown Court, 1982, quoted in Elizabeth Sheehy, "Canadian Judges and the Law of Rape: Should the *Charter* Insulate Bias?" (1989) 21 Ottawa L. Rev. 741, at p. 741.)

> Unless you have no worldly experience at all, you'll agree that women occasionally resist at first but later give in to either persuasion or their own instincts.

> (Judge Frank Allen, Manitoba Provincial Court, 1984, quoted in Sheehy at p. 741.)

> [I]t is easy for a man intent upon his own desires to mistake the intentions of a woman or girl who may herself be in two minds about what to do. Even if he makes no mistake it is not

unknown for a woman afterwards either to take fright or for some other reason to regret what has happened and seek to justify herself retrospectively by accusing the man of rape.

(Colin Howard, *Criminal Law*, 3d ed. (Sydney: Law Book Co., 1977), at p. 149.)

Modern psychiatrists have amply studied the behaviour of errant young girls and women coming before the courts in all sorts of cases. Their psychic complexes are multifarious, distorted partly by inherent defects, partly by diseased derangements or abnormal instincts, partly by bad social environment, partly by temporary physiological or emotional conditions. One form taken by these complexes is that of contriving false charges of sexual offenses by men.

(J.H. Wigmore, *Evidence in Trials at Common Law*, Vol. 3A, rev. J.H. Chadbourn (Boston: Little, Brown, 1970), at p. 736.)

Regrettably, these remarks demonstrate that many in society hold inappropriate stereotypical beliefs, and apply them when the opportunity presents itself.

. . . .

It is thus clear that, from the making of the initial complaint down to the determination of the issue at trial, stereotype and mythology are at work, lowering the number of reported cases, influencing police decisions to pursue the case, thereby decreasing the rates of arrest, and, finally, distorting the issues at trial and necessarily, the results. Professor Catharine MacKinnon asserts that in the United States:

It is not only that women are the principal targets of rape, which by conservative definition happens to almost half of all women at least once in their lives. It is not only that over one-third of all women are sexually molested by older trusted male family members or friends or authority figures as an early, perhaps initiatory, interpersonal sexual encounter. . . . All this documents the extent and terrain of abuse and the effectively unrestrained and systematic sexual aggression by less than one-half of the population against the other more than half. It suggests that it is basically allowed.

(Catharine MacKinnon, *Toward a Feminist Theory of the State* (Cambridge, Mass.: Harvard, University Press, 1989), at pp. 142-143.)

. . . .

Under the guise of a principled application of the legal concept of relevance, the common law allowed the accused to delve at great length into the moral character of the complainant by adducing "relevant" sexual history. The prejudicial impact of such an inquiry has already been discussed at length. The true nature and purpose of the inquiry into sexual history is revealed by the resulting prejudice and by the fact that these concepts were only applicable in respect of sexual offences and, in addition, were not deemed relevant to the credibility of the male accused.

Application of the relevance concept was not the only way in which the common law integrated stereotype and myth into trials of sexual offences. Also part of the unique body of evidentiary law surrounding sexual offences were, among other things, the doctrine of recent complaint and corroboration rules. These evidentiary concepts were also based upon stereotypes of the female complainant requiring independent evidence to support her evidence and, in addition, evidence that she raised a "hue and cry" after her assault. It is noteworthy that both recent complaint and corroboration rules formed exceptions to general rules of evidence.

. . . .

Relevance and Admissibility at Common Law and Under the Legislative Provisions

Like many of the other legal rules and principles that are brought to bear in trials of persons charged with sexual offences, the concept of relevance has been imbued with stereotypical notions of female complainants and sexual assault. That this is so is plain from the common law, which held that evidence of "unchasteness" was relevant to both consent and credibility. Any connection between the evidence sought to be adduced and the fact or matter of which it was supposedly probative must be bridged by stereotype (that "unchaste" women lie and "unchaste" women consent indiscriminately), otherwise the propositions make no sense. While some may think that these represent egregious examples of the use of stereotype, it is well to remember that relevancy determinations such as this are still being made, though the myth which drives the particular determination may be better obscured or, due to the entrenchment of these beliefs, more automatically made.

Traditional definitions of what is relevant include "whatever accords with common sense" (Peter K. McWilliams, *Canadian Criminal Evidence*, 3d ed. (Aurora, Ont.: Canada Law Book, 1990), at p. 35); "'relevant' means that any two facts to which it is applied are so related to each other that according to the common course of events one either taken by itself or in connection with other facts proves or renders probable the past, present or future existence or non-existence of the other" (Sir James Fitzjames Stephen's *Digest of the Law of Evidence* 12th ed. (London: Macmillan, 1936), art. 1), and finally Thayer's "logically probative" test with relevance as an affair of logic and not of law, a test adopted by this court in *Morris*.

. . . .

Whatever the test, be it one of experience, common sense or logic, it is a decision particularly vulnerable to the application of private beliefs. Regardless of the definition used, the content of any relevancy decision will be filled by the particular judge's experience, common sense and/or logic. For the most part there will be general agreement as to that which is relevant, and the determination will not be problematic. However, there are certain areas of inquiry where experience, common sense and logic are informed by stereotype and myth. As I have made clear, this area of the law has been particularly prone to the utilization of stereotype in determinations of relevance and, again, as was demonstrated earlier, this appears to be the unfortunate concomitant of a society which, to a large measure, holds these beliefs. It would also appear that recognition of the large role that stereotype may play in such determinations has had surprisingly little impact in this area of the law.

. . . .

Once the mythical bases of relevancy determinations in this area of the law are revealed (discussed at greater length later in these reasons), the irrelevance of most evidence of prior sexual history is clear. Nevertheless, Parliament has provided broad avenues for its admissibility in the setting out of the exceptions to the general rule in s. 246.6 (now s. 276). Moreover, *all* evidence of the complainant's previous sexual history with the accused is *prima facie* admissible under those provisions. Evidence that is excluded by these provisions is simply, in a myth- and stereotype-free decision-making context, irrelevant.

For comments on *Seaboyer* see Christine Boyle and Marilyn MacCrimmon, "*R. v. Seaboyer*: A Lost Cause?" (1992), 7 C.R. (4th) 225 and a reply by Anthony Allman in (1992), 10 C.R. (4th) 153.

Most would agree that receiving evidence of the complainant's previous sexual history on a trial of sexual assault will so prejudice the trial that the same should rarely be admitted. **Has the Court drawn the proper line?**

While striking down the complainant's statutory protection, the Court recognized the possibility that the then-existing common law rules could permit the inappropriate reception of evidence of the complainant's sexual conduct and the majority therefore changed the common law. The majority said it was suggesting "guidelines for the reception of sexual conduct evidence" and these were not to be seen as "judicial legislation cast in stone". Rather they were "an attempt to describe the consequences of the application of the general rules of evidence governing relevance and the reception of evidence". While the majority wrote that it was not legislating but only offering "guidelines", if the "guidelines" are the Supreme Court of Canada's thoughts on the common law of today, their expression differs little from the exercise of legislating. There will surely be no different result waiting for the trial judge who decides not to follow the guidelines.

The new regime announced in *Seaboyer* offers greater protection to the complainant than did the legislative provision that was struck down. The old s. 276 forbade the introduction of evidence "concerning the sexual activity of the complainant with *any person other than the accused*". The common law had always recognized that previous sexual conduct with the accused was relevant to the issue of whether the complainant consented on the occasion under review.

CRIMES OF SEXUAL ASSAULT (1983) 655

The majority's opinion "question(ed) whether evidence of other sexual conduct with the accused should automatically be admissible in all cases; sometimes the value of such evidence might be little or none". While sometimes the value of such evidence will be little or none the majority decided to exclude it in all cases: "evidence that the complainant has engaged in consensual sexual conduct on other occasions (*including past sexual conduct with the accused*) is not admissible solely to support the inference that (she) was more likely to have consented".

Suppose A and B have been living together for a year. The evidence is clear and undisputed that the parties regularly engaged in consensual sexual intercourse. On the evening brought into question before the Court sexual intercourse occurred. A says it was consensual and B says it was not. The Court in *Seaboyer* says that evidence of the previous consensual activity is not admissible. Such evidence cannot come in if the sole purpose is to show consent. No one, of course, would suggest that such previous conduct would be determinative of the issue, but is it relevant and at least worth considering along with the other evidence?

The commonly accepted meaning of relevance, we noted earlier, bespeaks a very low threshold: does the evidence offered render the desired inference more probable than it would be without the evidence? Consider the absolute nature of the prohibition which operates regardless of whether the probative value of the evidence outweighs the potential prejudice to the proper outcome of the trial. There is no discretion in the trial judge to receive the evidence if, in his or her opinion, the probative value outweighs the prejudice.

The majority in *Seaboyer* cited frequently and quoted heavily from Professor Galvin's article, "Shielding Rape Victims in the State and Federal Courts: A Proposal for the Second Decade".[37] Galvin's proposed rape shield law, however, was confined to the exclusion of evidence of sexual conduct with persons other than the accused. The majority in *Seaboyer* wrote "Galvin's proposal, with some modification, reflects an appropriate response to the problem".[38] One "modification" eliminates the distinction regarding sexual conduct with the accused. This is a major modification. Professor Galvin wrote:

> Even the most ardent reformers acknowledged the high probative value of past sexual conduct in at least two instances. The first is when the defendant claims consent and establishes prior consensual relations between himself and the complainant. . . . Although the evidence is offered to prove consent, its probative value rests on the nature of the complainant's specific mindset toward the accused rather than on her general unchaste character. . . . All 25 statutes adopting the Michigan approach (to rape shield laws) allow the accused to introduce evidence of prior sexual conduct between himself and the complainant. The high probative value and minimal prejudicial effect of this evidence have been discussed.[39]

---

37 (1986), 70 Minn. L. Rev. 763.
38 *Seaboyer* at 156.
39 *Supra* note 37 at 807-880.

Another article quoted by the majority in *Seaboyer* is Professor Vivian Berger's *"Man's Trial, Woman's Tribulation"*.[40] Professor Berger justified the reception of evidence of sexual conduct with the accused in this way:

> The inference from past to present behaviour does not, as in cases of third party acts, rest on highly dubious beliefs about "women who do" and "women who don't" but rather relies on common sense and practical psychology. Admission of the proof supplies the accused with a circumstance making it probable that he did not obtain by violence what he might have secured by persuasion.[41]

Another *major* modification to Galvin's proposal is with respect to so-called similar fact evidence. Galvin proposed that "evidence of a pattern of sexual conduct so distinctive and so closely resembling the accused's version of the alleged encounter with the victim as to tend to prove that the victim consented to the act charged" could be received. The majority in *Seaboyer* wrote that "similar fact evidence ... cannot be used illegitimately merely to show that the complainant consented" and where evidence of sexual conduct on other occasions is admitted, the trial judge should warn the jury against this prohibited use. Why? This major modification of Galvin's proposal is not explained unless we are to take it as a given that previous sexual conduct of the complainant can never be indicative of a propensity, a disposition, a willingness, to have sexual intercourse, from which a trier could infer that she acted in conformity with that character.

Suppose the evidence is that the accused and complainant met in Sam's Bar one Saturday night and left to go to her apartment. It's agreed that sexual intercourse occurred but the parties disagree on the issue of consent. The accused's evidence is that he was sitting at the bar when the complainant approached him, offered him a drink and propositioned him. Should the accused be able to call Sam to testify that every Saturday night for the previous four weeks the complainant came into his bar, offered a stranger a drink, propositioned him and left in his company?

On the issue of receiving similar fact evidence tendered by the accused, Professor Berger wrote:

> What if the accused were offering to show that the victim habitually goes to bars on Saturday nights, picks up strangers and takes them home to bed with her, and that over the past 12 months she has done so on more than 20 occasions. Now could one assert with assurance that this particular sexual record does not substantially reinforce the defendant's version of the night's events? And if it does, should he not be permitted as a matter of constitutional right to place this evidence before the jury?[42]

---

40 (1977), 77 Colum. L. Rev. 1.
41 *Ibid.* at 58-59.
42 *Ibid.*

4. PARLIAMENT'S RESPONSE TO *SEABOYER* (1992)

(a) Rape Shield

Seaboyer produced an immediate outcry on the basis that it would mean that women and children would be even less likely to pursue charges of sexual assault given that there would be unrestricted cross-examination of their prior sexual history. Such comments were quite unfair to the majority of the Supreme Court of Canada. For the majority, Madam Justice McLachlin had been quite alive to the dangers of leaving this crucial issue to unfettered judicial discretion and had crafted what she considered to be careful guidelines as to the admissibility of such evidence. She had also extended the protection to prior sexual conduct *with the accused*. One of the sources of the vehement reaction was that the majority took but a line to hold that, although victims might have equality rights, these had to give way to the accused's right to make full answer and defence.

The response from the Minister of Justice, the Honourable Kim Campbell, was swift. She announced that Parliament would better respond to protect women and children. She called a meeting of national and regional women's groups and thereafter worked very closely with them in drafting and revising a bill.[43] The coalition of some 60 women's groups reached unanimity at each point and agreed to oppose any attempt to water down the bill.

Bill C-49 was tabled on December 12, 1991. It was referred to committee after second reading on April 16, 1992. It quickly passed through the House of Commons and Senate and received Royal Assent on June 23, 1992. Bill C-49 was proclaimed to be in force on August 15, 1992.

The new s. 276, regarding the admissibility of evidence of the complainant's sexual activity, provides:

> 276. (1) In proceedings in respect of an offence under section 151, 152, 153, 155 or 159, subsection 160(2) or (3) or section 170, 171, 172, 173, 271, 272 or 273, evidence that the complainant has engaged in sexual activity, whether with the accused or with any other person, is not admissible to support an inference that, by reason of the sexual nature of that activity, the complainant
>
> > (a) is more likely to have consented to the sexual activity that forms the subject-matter of the charge; or
> > (b) is less worthy of belief.
>
> (2) In proceedings in respect of an offence referred to in subsection (1), no evidence shall be adduced by or on behalf of the accused that the complainant has engaged in sexual activity other than the sexual activity that forms the subject-matter of the charge, whether with the accused or with any other person, unless the judge, provincial court judge or justice determines, in accordance with the procedures set out in sections 276.1 and 276.2, that the evidence
>
> > (a) is of specific instances of sexual activity;
> > (b) is relevant to an issue to be proved at trial; and
> > (c) has significant probative value that is not substantially outweighed by the danger of prejudice to the proper administration of justice.

---

43 *Proceedings of the Standing Senate Committee on Legal and Constitutional Affairs*, 3rd Sess., 34 Parl. 1991-92 (June 22, 1992): 29-31. See, too, Sheila McIntyre, "Redefining Reformism: The Consultations that Shaped Bill C-49" in J. Roberts & R. Mohr, eds., *Confronting Sexual Assault. A Decade of Legal and Social Change* (1994), ch. 12.

(3) In determining whether evidence is admissible under subsection (2), the judge, provincial court judge or justice shall take into account
  (a) the interests of justice including the right of the accused to make a full answer and defence;
  (b) society's interest in encouraging the reporting of sexual assault offences;
  (c) whether there is a reasonable prospect that the evidence will assist in arriving at a just determination in the case;
  (d) the need to remove from the fact-finding process any discriminatory belief or bias;
  (e) the risk that the evidence may unduly arouse sentiments of prejudice, sympathy or hostility in the jury;
  (f) the potential prejudice to the complainant's personal dignity and right of privacy;
  (g) the right of the complainant and of every individual to personal security and to the full protection and benefit of the law; and
  (h) any other factor that the judge, provincial court judge or justice considers relevant.

The new s. 276.1 imposes a requirement of written notice for a hearing to determine admissibility under s. 276(2). Section 276.2 provides for the exclusion of the public at the hearing and the non-compellability of the complainant. The new s. 276.4 requires the trial judge to instruct the jury as to the proper use of the evidence received.

Does the new legislation give more or less discretion to judges than did *Seaboyer*? What are the differences?

Section 276(1) seems to contain an express blanket prohibition on what is commonly referred to as the "twin myths" reasoning. It prohibits the use of prior sexual history of the complainant on the issue of consent or to show that the complainant was less worthy of belief. This seemed to make it unconstitutional because *Seaboyer* had called for discretion (see Delisle, "Potential Charter Challenges to the New Rape Shield Law" (1992), 13 C.R. (4th) 309).

However, Professor David Paciocco, "The New Rape Shield Provision Should Survive Charter Challenge" (1993), 21 C.R. (4th) 223, suggested that the legislation could be read down. Section 276(1) only prohibited general stereotypical inferences. Evidence of prior sexual history with the accused could be admitted under s. 276(2) where the defence could establish that a specific inference can be drawn from such evidence to an issue relevant in the trial. In *Charter* challenges in lower courts the Paciocco position carried the day and was increasingly relied on as the proper interpretation.

When the Supreme Court finally considered the constitutionality of the "new" statutory scheme in *Darrach* a unanimous court had little difficulty in declaring the "new" rape shield provisions constitutional.

R. v. DARRACH

[2000] 2 S.C.R. 443, 36 C.R. (5th) 223, 148 C.C.C. (3d) 97,
2000 CarswellOnt 3321, 2000 CarswellOnt 3322

The accused was charged with sexual assault and, at his trial, attempted to introduce evidence of the complainant's sexual history. He unsuccessfully challenged the constitutionality of s. 276.1(2)(a) of the *Criminal Code* (which requires that the affidavit contain "detailed particulars" about the evidence), ss. 276(1) and 276(2)(c) (which govern the admissibility of sexual conduct evidence generally), and s. 276.2(2) (which provides that the complainant is not a compellable witness at the hearing determining the admissibility of evidence of prior sexual activity). After a *voir dire*, the trial judge refused to allow the accused to adduce the evidence of the complainant's sexual history. The accused was convicted and the Court of Appeal dismissed the accused's appeal, concluding that the impugned provisions did not violate the accused's right to make full answer and defence, his right not to be compelled to testify against himself or his right to a fair trial as protected by ss. 7, 11(c) and 11(d) of the *Canadian Charter of Rights and Freedoms*. Here we consider the accused's argument that s. 276(1) was unconstitutional.

GONTHIER J. (MCLACHLIN C.J.C., L'HEUREUX-DUBÉ, IACOBUCCI, MAJOR, BASTARACHE, BINNIE, ARBOUR and LEBEL J.J. concurring): —

. . . .

The current s. 276 categorically prohibits evidence of a complainant's sexual history only when it is used to support one of two general inferences. These are that a person is more likely to have consented to the alleged assault and that she is less credible as a witness by virtue of her prior sexual experience. Evidence of sexual activity may be admissible, however, to substantiate other inferences.

. . . .

The current version of s. 276 is carefully crafted to comport with the principles of fundamental justice. It protects the integrity of the judicial process while at the same time respecting the rights of the people involved. The complainant's privacy and dignity are protected by a procedure that also vindicates the accused's right to make full answer and defence. The procedure does not violate the accused's s. 7 *Charter* right to a fair trial nor his s. 11(c) right not to testify against himself or his s. 11(d) right to a fair hearing.

. . . .

[T]he court's jurisprudence . . . has consistently held that the principles of fundamental justice enshrined in s. 7 protect more than the rights of the accused.

. . . .

One of the implications of this analysis is that while the right to make full answer and defence and the principle against self-incrimination are certainly core principles of fundamental justice, they can be respected without the accused being entitled to "the most favourable procedures that could possibly be imagined" (*R. v. Lyons*, [1987] 2 S.C.R. 309 (S.C.C.) at p. 362; cited in *Mills*, *supra*, at para. 72). Nor is the accused entitled to have procedures crafted that take only his interests into account. Still less is he entitled to procedures that would distort the truth-seeking function of a trial by permitting irrelevant and prejudicial material at trial.

In *Seaboyer*, the court found that the principles of fundamental justice include the three purposes of s. 276 identified above: protecting the integrity of the trial by excluding evidence that is misleading, protecting the rights of the accused, as well as encouraging the reporting of sexual violence and protecting "the security and privacy of the witnesses" (p. 606). This was affirmed in *Mills*, *supra*, at para. 72. The court crafted its guidelines in *Seaboyer* in accordance with these principles, and it is in relation to these principles that the effects of s. 276 on the accused must be evaluated.

The court in *Mills* upheld the constitutionality of the provisions in the *Criminal Code* that control the use of personal and therapeutic records in trials of sexual offences. The use of these records in evidence is analogous in many ways to the use of evidence of prior sexual activity, and the protections in the *Criminal Code* surrounding the use of records at trial are motivated by similar policy considerations. L'Heureux-Dubé J. has warned that therapeutic records should not become a tool for circumventing s. 276: "[w]e must not allow the defence to do indirectly what it cannot do directly" (*R. v. O'Connor*, [1995] 4 S.C.R. 411 (S.C.C.), at para. 122, and *R. v. Osolin*, [1993] 4 S.C.R. 595, at p. 624). Academic commentators have observed that the use of therapeutic records increased with the enactment of s. 276 nonetheless (see K. Kelly, "'You must be crazy if you think you were raped': Reflections on the Use of Complainants' Personal and Therapy Records in Sexual Assault Trials" (1997), 9 *C.J.W.L.* 178, at p. 181).

. . . .

[T]he test for admissibility in s. 276(2) requires not only that the evidence be relevant but also that it be more probative than prejudicial. *Mills* dealt with a conflict among the same three *Charter* principles that are in issue in the case at bar: full answer and defence, privacy and equality (at para. 61). The court defined these rights relationally: "the scope of the right to make full answer and defence must be determined in light of privacy and equality rights of complainants and witnesses" (paras. 62-66 and 94). The exclusionary rule was upheld. The privacy and equality concerns involved in protecting the records justified interpreting the right to make full answer and defence in a way that did not include a right to all relevant evidence.

. . . .

In the case at bar, I affirm the reasons in *Seaboyer* and find that none of the accused's rights are infringed by s. 276 as he alleges. *Seaboyer* provides a basic justification for the legislative scheme in s. 276, including the determination of relevance as well as the prejudicial and probative value of the evidence. *Mills* and *White* show how the impact of s. 276 on the principles of fundamental justice relied on by the accused should be assessed in light of the other principles of fundamental justice that s. 276 was designed to protect. The reasons in *Mills* are apposite because they demonstrate how the same principles of equality, privacy and fairness can be reconciled. I shall show below how the procedure created by s. 276 to protect the trial process from distortion and to protect complainants is consistent with the principles of fundamental justice. It is fair to the accused and properly reconciles the divergent interests at play, as the court suggested in *Seaboyer.*

. . . .

Section 276(1) — The Exclusionary Rule

The accused objects to the exclusionary rule itself in s. 276(1) on the grounds that it is a "blanket exclusion" that prevents him from adducing evidence necessary to make full answer and defence, as guaranteed by ss. 7 and 11(*d*) of the *Charter*. He is mistaken in his characterization of the rule. Far from being a "blanket exclusion", s. 276(1) only prohibits the use of evidence of past sexual activity when it is offered to support two specific, illegitimate inferences. These are known as the myths", namely that a complainant is more likely to have consented or that she is less worthy of belief "by reason of the sexual nature of the activity" she once engaged in.

This section gives effect to McLachlin J.'s finding in *Seaboyer* that the "twin myths" are simply not relevant at trial. They are not probative of consent or credibility and can severely distort the trial process. Section 276(1) also clarifies *Seaboyer* in several respects. Section 276 applies to all sexual activity, whether with the accused or with someone else. It also applies to non-consensual as well as consensual sexual activity, as this court found implicitly in *R. v. Crosby*, [1995] 2 S.C.R. 912 (S.C.C.), at p. 924. Although the *Seaboyer* guidelines referred to "consensual sexual conduct" (pp. 634-35), Parliament enacted the new version of s. 276 without the word "consensual". Evidence of non-consensual sexual acts can equally defeat the purposes of s. 276 by distorting the trial process when it is used to evoke stereotypes such as that women who have been assaulted must have deserved it and that they are unreliable witnesses, as well as by deterring people from reporting assault by humiliating them in court. The admissibility of evidence of non-consensual sexual activity is determined by the procedures in s. 276. Section 276 also settles any ambiguity about whether the "twin myths" are limited to inferences about "unchaste" women in particular; they are not (as discussed by C. Boyle and M. MacCrimmon, "The Constitutionality of Bill C-49: Analyzing Sexual Assault As If Equality Really Mattered" (1998), 41 *Crim. L.Q.* 198, at pp. 231-32).

The *Criminal Code* excludes all discriminatory generalizations about a complainant's disposition to consent or about her credibility based on the *sexual nature* of her past sexual activity on the grounds that these are improper lines of reasoning. This was the import of the court's findings in *Seaboyer* about how sexist beliefs about women distort the trial process. The text of the exclusionary rule in s. 276(1) diverges very little from the guidelines in *Seaboyer*. The mere fact that the wording differs between the court's guidelines and Parliament's enactment is itself immaterial. In *Mills, supra,* the court affirmed that "[t]o insist on slavish conformity" by Parliament to judicial pronouncements "would belie the mutual respect that underpins the relationship" between the two institutions (para. 55). In this case, the legislation follows the court's suggestions very closely.

The phrase "by reason of the sexual nature of the activity" in s. 276 is a clarification by Parliament that it is inferences from the *sexual nature* of the activity, as opposed to inferences from other potentially relevant features of the activity, that are prohibited. If evidence of sexual activity is proffered for its non-sexual features, such as to show a pattern of conduct or a prior inconsistent statement, it may be permitted. The phrase "by reason of the sexual nature of the activity" has the same effect as the qualification "solely to support the inference" in *Seaboyer* in that it limits the exclusion of evidence to that used to invoke the "twin myths" (p. 635).

. . . .

An accused has never had a right to adduce irrelevant evidence. Nor does he have the right to adduce misleading evidence to support illegitimate inferences: "the accused is not permitted to distort the truth-seeking function of the trial process" (*Mills, supra,* at para. 74). Because s. 276(1) is an evidentiary rule that only excludes material that is not relevant, it cannot infringe the accused's right to make full answer and defence. Section 276(2) is more complicated, and I turn to it now.

Section 276(2) — "Significant Probative Value"

If evidence is not barred by s. 276(1) because it is tendered to support a permitted inference, the judge must still weigh its probative value against its prejudicial effect to determine its admissibility. This essentially mirrors the common law guidelines in *Seaboyer* which contained this balancing test (at p. 635). The accused takes issue with the fact that s. 276(2)(*c*) specifically requires that the evidence have "significant probative value". The word "significant" was added by Parliament but it does not render the provision unconstitutional by raising the threshold for the admissibility of evidence to the point that it is unfair to the accused.

. . . .

The context of the word "significant" in the provision in which it occurs substantiates this interpretation. Section 276(2)(*c*) allows a judge to admit evidence of "*significant* probative value that is not *substantially* outweighed by the danger of prejudice to the proper administration of justice" (emphasis added). The adverb "substantially" serves to protect the accused by raising the standard for the judge to exclude evidence once the accused has shown it to have significant probative value. In a sense, both sides of the equation are heightened in this test, which serves to direct judges to the serious ramifications of the use of evidence of prior sexual activity for all parties in these cases.

In light of the purposes of s. 276, the use of the word "significant" is consistent with both the majority and the minority reasons in *Seaboyer*. Section 276 is designed to prevent the use of evidence of prior sexual activity for improper purposes. The requirement of "significant probative value" serves to exclude evidence of trifling relevance that, even though not used to support the two forbidden inferences, would still endanger the "proper administration of justice". The court has recognized that there are inherent "damages and disadvantages presented by the admission of such evidence" (*Seaboyer*, *supra*, at p. 634). As Morden A.C.J.O. puts it, evidence of sexual activity must be significantly probative if it is to overcome its prejudicial effect. The *Criminal Code* codifies this reality.

By excluding misleading evidence while allowing the accused to adduce evidence that meets the criteria of s. 276(2), s. 276 enhances the fairness of trials of sexual offences. Section 11(*d*) guarantees a fair trial. Fairness under s. 11(*d*) is determined in the context of the trial process as a whole (*R. v. Stoddart* (1987), 37 C.C.C. (3d) 351 (Ont. C.A.), at pp. 365-66). As L'Heureux-Dubé J. wrote in *Crosby*, *supra*, at para. 11, "[s]ection 276 cannot be interpreted so as to deprive a person of a fair defence." At the same time, the accused's right to make full answer and defence, as was held in *Mills*, *supra*, at para. 75, is not "automatically breached where he or she is deprived of relevant information." Nor is it necessarily breached when the accused is not permitted to adduce relevant information that is not "significantly" probative, under a rule of evidence that protects the trial from the distorting effects of evidence of prior sexual activity.

. . . .

Thus the threshold criteria that evidence be of "significant" probative value does not prevent an accused from making full answer and defence to the charges against him. Consequently his *Charter* rights under ss. 7 and 11(*d*) are not infringed by s. 276(2)(*c*).

The Procedural Sections to Determine Relevance: The Affidavit and Voir Dire

The constitutionality of the procedure that must be followed to introduce evidence of prior sexual activity has also been challenged. It requires that whoever seeks to introduce it "by or on behalf of the accused" must present an affidavit and establish on a *voir dire* that the evidence is admissible in accordance with the criteria in the *Criminal Code*.

[The Court determined that the procedural provisions were not violative of the accused's constitutional rights. In the course of its analysis the Court later commented on relevance and probative value of evidence of previous sexual activity.]

Although the Supreme Court has determined the issue of constitutionality, it seems very likely that *Darrach* has not resolved the question of the proper application of ss. 276(1) and (2), especially in the context of prior sexual history with the accused where the issue is consent. We have seen that the Court in *Darrach* at one point says that such evidence is not relevant, then in the next breath it says it may be admitted. Towards the end of the judgment this is put in yet another way:

> Evidence of prior sexual activity will rarely be relevant to support a denial that sexual activity took place or to establish consent (C.R., para. 58).

That judges have different views on the issue of the relevance and probative value of evidence of prior sexual history with the accused on the issue of consent is reflected in the views of the Ontario Court of Appeal in the Court below in *Darrach*, which were not addressed in the Supreme Court. According to Morden A.C.J.O. for the Court (1998), 13 C.R. (5th) 283, 122 C.C.C. (3d) 225 (Ont. C.A.), (Osborne and Doherty JJ.A. concurring):

> It will likely be that evidence of previous sexual activity with the accused will satisfy the requirements of admissibility in s. 276(2) more often than that relating to sexual activity with others. This does not mean that this evidence should always be admitted (C.R. at 299).

Trial judges appear to regularly admit evidence of a prior or ongoing relationship where there is a viable issue of consent. That is not to say that such evidence is determinative. Otherwise the trial would be devoid of context and potentially unfair to accused. See, for example, *Termertzoglou* (2002), 11 C.R. (6th) 179 (Ont. S.C.J.) and *Strickland* (2007), 45 C.R. (6th) 183 (Ont. S.C.J.). But see strong criticism by Elaine Craig, "Section 276 Misconstrued: The Failure to Properly Interpret and Apply Canada's Rape Shield Provisions" (2016) 94 Can. Bar Rev. 45.

Most of the rape shield provisions in the United States allow the admission of prior sexual history with the accused. In the U.K. the House of Lords in *R. v. A. (No. 2)*, [2001] 3 All E.R. 1 decided, referring to *Darrach*, that a new U.K. rape shield law should not be applied to preclude evidence of prior sexual history with the accused. This would violate the right to a fair trial under the European Convention of Human Rights.

(b) Consent

The new s. 273.1 seeks to define consent in the case of sexual assault but, consistent with *R. v. Jobidon*, is expressly not exhaustive:

> 273.1(1) Subject to subsection (2) and subsection 265(3), "consent" means, for the purposes of sections 271, 272 and 273, the voluntary agreement of the complainant to engage in the sexual activity in question.

> (2) No consent is obtained, for the purposes of sections 271, 272 and 273, where
>   (a) the agreement is expressed by the words or conduct of a person other than the complainant;
>   (b) the complainant is incapable of consenting to the activity;
>   (c) the accused induces the complainant to engage in the activity by abusing a position of trust, power or authority;
>   (d) the complainant expresses, by words or conduct, a lack of agreement to engage in the activity; or
>   (e) the complainant, having consented to engage in sexual activity, expresses, by words or conduct, a lack of agreement to continue to engage in the activity.

> (3) Nothing in subsection (2) shall be construed as limiting the circumstances in which no consent is obtained.

These provisions clearly set out to give courts better guidance as to situations in which consent can be held to have been not genuine and therefore not consent in law. Subsections (b), (c) and (e) were amended as the bill passed through committee. The amendments were largely inconsequential, merely clarifying rather than changing the original intent. Subsection (b) had read that the complainant was incapable of consenting to the activity "by reason of intoxication or other condition". The provision was criticized as being vague, especially in its reference to "other condition". Parliament clearly decided to leave the matter to the discretion of trial judges while preserving the common law principle that one incapable of giving consent cannot be considered to have consented.

These new consent provisions seem adequately drafted and a welcome assertion of the "No Means No" philosophy. With the exception of s. (c), which requires judicial interpretation, the provisions appear to merely restate existing legal principles.

Some interpreted s. (d) as preserving the existing common law that consent can be express or implied. A suggestion by the women's coalition that consent should be limited to unequivocal expressions[44] was rejected. Critics of Bill C-49 suggested that in future written consent will be needed in advance for any sexual

---

44 The Coalition's rejected proposal of November 27, 1991 had the following definition: "For the purposes of sections 271, 272 and 273 consent shall be sought and obtained and shall mean words or gestures which unequivocally express or manifest voluntary agreement to the sexual activity": see, further, Sheila McIntyre, "Redefining Reformism: The Consultations that Shaped Bill C-49" in J. Roberts & R. Mohr, eds., *Sexual Assault: A Decade of Legal and Social Change* (1994), ch. 12.

conduct, that there is an onus of proof on the accused[45] or that Bill C-49 criminalizes seduction.[46]

(c) Mistaken Belief in Consent

While Bill C-49 does not remove a belief in consent defence to a charge of sexual assault it substantially restricts it. Under s. 273.2 belief in consent is not a defence to any sexual assault charge where

    (a) the accused's belief arose from the accused's
        (i) self-induced intoxication, or
        (ii) recklessness or wilful blindness; or

    (b) the accused did not take reasonable steps, in the circumstances known to the accused at the time, to ascertain that the complainant was consenting.

Sections 273.1 and 273.2 were authoritatively interpreted by the Supreme Court.

R. v. EWANCHUK

[1999] 1 S.C.R. 330, 22 C.R. (5th) 1, 131 C.C.C. (3d) 481,
1999 CarswellAlta 99, 1999 CarswellAlta 100

The accused initiated a number of touching incidents, each progressively more intimate although the complainant clearly said "no" on each occasion. He stopped each time she said "no" but persisted shortly afterwards. The accused was charged with sexual assault.

At a trial before a judge of the Alberta Court of Queen's Bench the accused did not testify, leaving only the complainant's evidence as to what took place between them. The accused was acquitted. The trial judge found that the complainant was a credible witness. He found that in her mind she had not consented to any of the sexual touching which took place, that she had been fearful throughout the encounter, that she didn't want the accused to know she was afraid and that she had actively projected a relaxed and unafraid visage. He concluded that the failure of the complainant to communicate her fear, including her active efforts to the contrary, rendered her subjective feelings irrelevant. He characterized the defence as one of "implied consent". On the totality of the evidence, provided solely by the Crown's witnesses, the trial judge concluded that the Crown had not proven the absence of consent beyond a reasonable doubt and acquitted the accused.

---

45 This was the position of an editorial in *The Globe and Mail*, May 19, 1992: "An assault on the law, not to say common sense", effectively rebutted by the Minister of Justice in a letter published in *The Globe and Mail*, May 27, 1992.

46 *Ibid*. Kim Campbell wrote: "The definition does not purport to constrain or reform the sexual relationships of ordinary Canadians. It does not, for example, require that the consent be overt, or unequivocal, or given in advance. Rather it accepts that consensual sexual matters will unfold as they will, in a variety of ways as infinite as the numbers of sexual encounters."

A majority of the Alberta Court of Appeal dismissed the Crown appeal. Each of the three justices of the Court of Appeal issued separate reasons. McClung and Foisy JJ.A. both dismissed the appeal on the basis that it was a fact-driven acquittal from which the Crown could not properly appeal. In addition, McClung J.A. concluded that the Crown had failed to prove beyond a reasonable doubt that the accused had intended to commit an assault upon the complainant. Fraser C.J. delivered a lengthy dissent.

The Supreme Court allowed the Crown appeal, substituting a conviction and remitting the matter for sentence.

MAJOR J. (LAMER C.J., CORY, IACOBUCCI, BASTARACHE and BINNIE JJ. concurring): —

. . . The trial judge relied on the defence of implied consent. This was a mistake of law as no such defence is available in assault cases in Canada. This mistake of law is reviewable by appellate courts . . .

1. Facts

The complainant was a 17-year-old woman living in the city of Edmonton. She met the accused respondent Ewanchuk on the afternoon of June 2, 1994, while walking through the parking lot of the Heritage Shopping Mall with her roommate. The accused, driving a red van towing a trailer, approached the two young women. He struck up a conversation with them. He related that he was in the custom wood-working business and explained that he displayed his work at retail booths in several shopping malls. He said that he was looking for staff to attend his displays, and asked whether the young women were looking for work. The complainant's friend answered that they were, at which point the accused asked to interview her friend privately. She declined, but spoke with the accused beside his van for some period of time about the sort of work he required, and eventually exchanged telephone numbers with the accused.

The following morning the accused telephoned the apartment where the complainant and her friend resided with their boyfriends. The complainant answered the phone. She told the accused that her friend was still asleep. When he learned this, the accused asked the complainant if she was interested in a job. She indicated that she was, and they met a short time later, again in the Heritage Mall parking lot. At the accused's suggestion, the interview took place in his van. In the words of the complainant, a "very business-like, polite" conversation took place. Some time later, the complainant asked if she could smoke a cigarette, and the accused suggested that they move outside since he was allergic to cigarette smoke. Once outside the van, he asked the complainant if she would like to see some of his work, which was kept inside the trailer attached to his van, and she indicated that she would.

The complainant entered the trailer, purposely leaving the door open behind her. The accused followed her in, and closed the door in a way which made the complainant think that he had locked it. There is no evidence whether the door was actually locked, but the complainant stated that she became frightened at this point. Once inside the trailer, the complainant and the accused sat down side-by-side on the floor of the trailer. They spoke and looked through a portfolio of his work. This lasted 10 to 15 minutes, after which the conversation turned to more personal matters.

During the time in the trailer the accused was quite tactile with the complainant, touching her hand, arms and shoulder as he spoke. At some point the accused said that he was feeling tense and asked the complainant to give him a massage. The complainant complied, massaging the accused's shoulders for a few minutes. After she stopped, he asked her to move in front of him so that he could massage her, which she did. The accused then massaged the complainant's shoulders and arms while they continued talking. During this mutual massaging the accused repeatedly told the complainant to relax, and that she should not be afraid. As the massage progressed, the accused attempted to initiate more intimate contact. The complainant stated that, "he started to try to massage around my stomach, and he brought his hands up around — or underneath my breasts, and he started to get quite close up there, so I used my elbows to push in between, and I said, "No".

The accused stopped immediately, but shortly thereafter resumed non-sexual massaging, to which the complainant also said, "No". The accused again stopped, and said, "See, I'm a nice guy. It's okay."

The accused then asked the complainant to turn and face him. She did so, and he began massaging her feet. His touching progressed from her feet up to her inner thigh and pelvic area. The complainant did not want the accused to touch her in this way, but said nothing as she said she was afraid that any resistance would prompt the accused to become violent. Although the accused never used or threatened any force, the complainant testified that she did not want to "egg [him] on". As the contact progressed, the accused laid himself heavily on top of the complainant and began grinding his pelvic area against hers. The complainant testified that the accused asserted, "that he could get me so horny so that I would want it so bad, and he wouldn't give it to me because he had self-control".

The complainant did not move or reciprocate the contact. The accused asked her to put her hands across his back, but she did not; instead she lay "bone straight". After less than a minute of this the complainant asked the accused to stop. "I said, Just please stop. And so he stopped". The accused again told the complainant not to be afraid, and asked her if she trusted that he wouldn't hurt her. In her words, the complainant said, "Yes, I trust that you won't hurt me." On the stand she stated that she was afraid throughout, and only responded to the accused in this way because she was fearful that a negative answer would provoke him to use force.

After this brief exchange, the accused went to hug the complainant and, as he did so, he laid on top of her again, continuing the pelvic grinding. He also began moving his hands on the complainant's inner thigh, inside her shorts, for a short time. While still on top of her the accused began to fumble with his shorts and took out his penis. At this point the complainant again asked the accused to desist, saying, "No, stop."

Again, the accused stopped immediately, got off the complainant, smiled at her and said something to the effect of, "It's okay. See, I'm a nice guy, I stopped." At this point the accused again hugged the complainant lightly before opening up his wallet and removing a $100 bill, which he gave to the complainant. She testified that the accused said that the $100 was for the massage and that he told her not to tell anyone about it. He made some reference to another female employee with whom he also had a very close and friendly relationship, and said that he hoped to get together with the complainant again.

Shortly after the exchange of the money the complainant said that she had to go. The accused opened the door and the complainant stepped out. Some further conversation ensued outside the trailer before the complainant finally left and walked home. On her return home the complainant was emotionally distraught and contacted the police.

At some point during the encounter the accused provided the complainant with a brochure describing his woodwork and gave her his name and address, which she wrote on the brochure. The investigating officer used this information to locate the accused at his home, where he was arrested.

B. The Components of Sexual Assault

A conviction for sexual assault requires proof beyond reasonable doubt of two basic elements, that the accused committed the *actus reus* and that he had the necessary *mens rea*. The *actus reus* of assault is unwanted sexual touching. The *mens rea* is the intention to touch, knowing of, or being reckless of or wilfully blind to, a lack of consent, either by words or actions, from the person being touched.

(1) *Actus Reus*

The crime of sexual assault is only indirectly defined in the *Criminal Code*, R.S.C., 1985, c. C-46. The offence is comprised of an assault within any one of the definitions in s. 265(1) of the *Code*, which is committed in circumstances of a sexual nature, such that the sexual integrity of the victim is violated: see *R. v. S. (P.L.)*, [1991] 1 S.C.R. 909.

. . . .

The *actus reus* of sexual assault is established by the proof of three elements: (i) touching, (ii) the sexual nature of the contact, and (iii) the absence of consent. The first two of these elements are objective. It is sufficient for the Crown to prove that the accused's actions were voluntary. The sexual nature of the assault is determined objectively; the Crown need not prove that the accused had any *mens rea* with respect to the sexual nature of his or her behaviour: see *R. v. Litchfield*, [1993] 4 S.C.R. 333, and *R. v. Chase*, [1987] 2 S.C.R. 293.

The absence of consent, however, is subjective and determined by reference to the complainant's subjective internal state of mind towards the touching, at the time it occurred: see *R. v. Jensen* (1996), 106 C.C.C. (3d) 430 (Ont. C.A.), at pp. 437-38, aff'd [1997] 1 S.C.R. 304, *R. v. Park*, [1995] 2 S.C.R. 836, at p. 850, per L'Heureux-Dubé J., and D. Stuart, Canadian Criminal Law (3rd ed. 1995), at p. 513.

. . . .

While the complainant's testimony is the only source of direct evidence as to her state of mind, credibility must still be assessed by the trial judge, or jury, in light of all the evidence. It is open to the accused to claim that the complainant's words and actions, before and during the incident, raise a reasonable doubt against her assertion that she, in her mind, did not want the sexual touching to take place. If, however, as occurred in this case, the trial judge believes the complainant that she subjectively did not consent, the Crown has discharged its obligation to prove the absence of consent.

. . . .

(a) "Implied Consent"

Counsel for the respondent submitted that the trier of fact may believe the complainant when she says she did not consent, but still acquit the accused on the basis that her conduct raised a reasonable doubt. Both he and the trial judge refer to this as "implied consent". It follows from the foregoing, however, that the trier of fact may only come to one of two conclusions: the complainant either consented or not. There is no third option. If the trier of fact accepts the complainant's testimony that she did not consent, no matter how strongly her conduct may contradict that claim, the absence of consent is established and the third component of the *actus reus* of sexual assault is proven. The doctrine of implied consent has been recognized in our common law jurisprudence in a variety of contexts but sexual assault is not one of them. There is no defence of implied consent to sexual assault in Canadian law.

(b) Application to the Present Case

In this case, the trial judge accepted the evidence of the complainant that she did not consent. That being so, he then misdirected himself when he considered the actions of the complainant, and not her subjective mental state, in determining the question of consent. As a result, he disregarded his previous finding that all the accused's sexual touching was unwanted. Instead he treated what he perceived as her ambiguous conduct as a failure by the Crown to prove the absence of consent.

As previously mentioned, the trial judge accepted the complainant's testimony that she did not want the accused to touch her, but then treated her conduct as raising a reasonable doubt about consent, described by him as "implied consent". This conclusion was an error. See D. Stuart, Annotation on *R. v. Ewanchuk* (1998), 13 C.R. (5th) 330, where the author points out that consent is a matter of the state of mind of the complainant while belief in consent is, subject to s. 273.2 of the *Code*, a matter of the state of mind of the accused and may raise the defence of honest but mistaken belief in consent.

The finding that the complainant did not want or consent to the sexual touching cannot co-exist with a finding that reasonable doubt exists on the question of consent. The trial judge's acceptance of the complainant's testimony regarding her own state of mind was the end of the matter on this point.

. . . .

(c) Effect of the Complainant's Fear

To be legally effective, consent must be freely given. Therefore, even if the complainant consented, or her conduct raises a reasonable doubt about her non-consent, circumstances may arise which call into question what factors prompted her apparent consent. The *Code* defines a series of conditions under which the law will deem an absence of consent in cases of assault, notwithstanding the complainant's ostensible consent or participation. As enumerated in s. 265(3), these include submission by reason of force, fear, threats, fraud or the exercise of authority, and codify the longstanding common law rule that consent given under fear or duress is ineffective: see G. Williams, *Textbook of Criminal Law* (2nd ed. 1983), at pp. 551-61.

. . . .

The words of Fish J.A. in *Saint-Laurent v. Hétu*, [1994] R.J.Q. 69 (C.A.), at p. 82, aptly describe the concern which the trier of fact must bear in mind when evaluating the actions of a complainant who claims to have been under fear, fraud or duress:

> "Consent" is . . . stripped of its defining characteristics when it is applied to the submission, non-resistance, non-objection, or even the apparent agreement, of a deceived, unconscious or compelled will.

In these instances the law is interested in a complainant's reasons for choosing to participate in, or ostensibly consent to, the touching in question. In practice, this translates into an examination of the choice the complainant believed she faced. The courts' concern is whether she freely made up her mind about the conduct in question. The relevant section of the *Code* is s. 265(3)(b), which states that there is no consent as a matter of law where the complainant believed that she was choosing between permitting herself to be touched sexually or risking being subject to the application of force.

. . . The trier of fact has to find that the complainant did not want to be touched sexually and made her decision to permit or participate in sexual activity as a result of an honestly held fear. The complainant's fear need not be reasonable, nor must it be communicated to the accused in order for consent to be vitiated. While the plausibility of the alleged fear, and any overt expressions of it, are obviously relevant to assessing the credibility of the complainant's claim that she consented out of fear, the approach is subjective.

Section 265(3) identifies an additional set of circumstances in which the accused's conduct will be culpable. The trial judge only has to consult s. 265(3) in those cases where the complainant has actually chosen to participate in sexual activity, or her ambiguous conduct or submission has given rise to doubt as to the absence of consent. If, as in this case, the complainant's testimony establishes the absence of consent beyond a reasonable doubt, the *actus reus* analysis is complete, and the trial judge should have turned his attention to the accused's perception of the encounter and the question of whether the accused possessed the requisite *mens rea*.

(2) *Mens Rea*

Sexual assault is a crime of general intent. Therefore, the Crown need only prove that the accused intended to touch the complainant in order to satisfy the basic *mens rea* requirement. See *R. v. Daviault*, [1994] 3 S.C.R. 63.

However, since sexual assault only becomes a crime in the absence of the complainant's consent, the common law recognizes a defence of mistake of fact which removes culpability for those who honestly but mistakenly believed that they had consent to touch the complainant. To do otherwise would result in the injustice of convicting individuals who are morally innocent: see *R. v. Creighton*, [1993] 3 S.C.R. 3. As such, the *mens rea* of sexual assault contains two elements: intention to touch and knowing of, or being reckless of or wilfully blind to, a lack of consent on the part of the person touched. See *Park*, supra, at para. 39.

The accused may challenge the Crown's evidence of *mens rea* by asserting an honest but mistaken belief in consent. The nature of this defence was described in *Pappajohn v. The Queen*, [1980] 2 S.C.R. 120, at p. 148, by Dickson J. (as he then was) (dissenting in the result):

> Mistake is a defence . . . where it prevents an accused from having the mens rea which the law requires for the very crime with which he is charged. Mistake of fact is more accurately seen as a negation of guilty intention than as the affirmation of a positive defence. It avails an accused who acts innocently, pursuant to a flawed perception of the facts, and nonetheless commits the actus reus of the offence. Mistake is a defence though, in the sense that it is raised as an issue by an accused. The Crown is rarely possessed of knowledge of the subjective factors which may have caused an accused to entertain a belief in a fallacious set of facts.

The defence of mistake is simply a denial of *mens rea*. It does not impose any burden of proof upon the accused (see *R. v. Robertson*, [1987] 1 S.C.R. 918, at p. 936) and it is not necessary for the accused to testify in order to raise the issue. Support for the defence may stem from any of the evidence before the court, including the Crown's case-in-chief and the testimony of the complainant. However, as a practical matter, this defence will usually arise in the evidence called by the accused.

(a) Meaning of "Consent" in the Context of an Honest but Mistaken Belief in Consent

As with the *actus reus* of the offence, consent is an integral component of the *mens rea*, only this time it is considered from the perspective of the accused. Speaking of the *mens rea* of sexual assault in *Park*, supra, at para. 30, L'Heureux-Dubé J. (in her concurring reasons) stated that:

> . . . the mens rea of sexual assault is not only satisfied when it is shown that the accused knew that the complainant was essentially saying "no", but is also satisfied when it is shown that the accused knew that the complainant was essentially not saying "yes".

In order to cloak the accused's actions in moral innocence, the evidence must show that he believed that the complainant communicated consent to engage in the sexual activity in question. A belief by the accused that the complainant, in her own mind wanted him to touch her but did not express that desire, is not a defence. The accused's speculation as to what was going on in the complainant's mind provides no defence.

For the purposes of the *mens rea* analysis, the question is whether the accused believed that he had obtained consent. What matters is whether the accused believed that the complainant effectively said "yes" through her words and/or actions. The statutory definition added to the *Code* by Parliament in 1992 is consistent with the common law:

> 273.1 (1) Subject to subsection (2) and subsection 265(3), "consent" means, for the purposes of sections 271, 272 and 273, the voluntary agreement of the complainant to engage in the sexual activity in question.

There is a difference in the concept of "consent" as it relates to the state of mind of the complainant vis-à-vis the *actus reus* of the offence and the state of mind of the accused in respect of the *mens rea*. For the purposes of the *actus reus*, "consent" means that the complainant in her mind wanted the sexual touching to take place.

In the context of *mens rea* — specifically for the purposes of the honest but mistaken belief in consent — "consent" means that the complainant had affirmatively communicated by words or conduct her agreement to engage in sexual activity with the accused. This distinction should always be borne in mind and the two parts of the analysis kept separate.

(b) Limits on Honest but Mistaken Belief in Consent

Not all beliefs upon which an accused might rely will exculpate him. Consent in relation to the *mens rea* of the accused is limited by both the common law and the provisions of ss. 273.1(2) and 273.2 of the *Code.*

. . . .

For instance, a belief that silence, passivity or ambiguous conduct constitutes consent is a mistake of law, and provides no defence: see *R. v. M. (M.L.)*, [1994] 2 S.C.R. 3. Similarly, an accused cannot rely upon his purported belief that the complainant's expressed lack of agreement to sexual touching in fact constituted an invitation to more persistent or aggressive contact. An accused cannot say that he thought "no meant yes". As Fraser C.J. stated at p. 272 of her dissenting reasons below:

> One "No" will do to put the other person on notice that there is then a problem with "consent". *Once a woman says "No" during the course of sexual activity, the person intent on continued sexual activity with her must then obtain a clear and unequivocal "Yes" before he again touches her in a sexual manner.* [Emphasis in original.]

I take the reasons of Fraser C.J. to mean that an unequivocal "yes" may be given by either the spoken word or by conduct.

Common sense should dictate that, once the complainant has expressed her unwillingness to engage in sexual contact, the accused should make certain that she has truly changed her mind before proceeding with further intimacies. The accused cannot rely on the mere lapse of time or the complainant's silence or equivocal conduct to indicate that there has been a change of heart and that consent now exists, nor can he engage in further sexual touching to "test the waters". Continuing sexual contact after someone has said "No" is, at a minimum, reckless conduct which is not excusable. In *R. v. Esau*, [1997] 2 S.C.R. 777, at para. 79, the court stated:

> An accused who, due to wilful blindness or recklessness, believes that a complainant . . . in fact consented to the sexual activity at issue is precluded from relying on a defence of honest but mistaken belief in consent, a fact that Parliament has codified: Criminal Code, s. 273.2(a)(ii).

(c) Application to the Facts

In this appeal the accused does not submit that the complainant's clearly articulated "No's" were ambiguous or carried some other meaning. In fact, the accused places great reliance on his having stopped immediately each time the complainant said "no" in order to show that he had no intention to force himself upon her. He therefore knew that the complainant was not consenting on four separate occasions during their encounter.

. . . .

As the accused did not testify, the only evidence before the court was that of the complainant. She stated that she immediately said "NO" every time the accused touched her sexually, and that she did nothing to encourage him. Her evidence was accepted by the trial judge as credible and sincere. Indeed, the accused relies on the fact that he momentarily stopped his advances each time the complainant said "NO" as evidence of his good intentions. This demonstrates that he understood the complainant's "NO's" to mean precisely that. Therefore, there is nothing on the record to support the accused's claim that he continued to believe her to be consenting, or that he re-established consent before resuming physical contact. The accused did not raise nor does the evidence disclose an air of reality to the defence of honest but mistaken belief in consent to this sexual touching.

The trial record conclusively establishes that the accused's persistent and increasingly serious advances constituted a sexual assault for which he had no defence. But for his errors of law, the trial judge would necessarily have found the accused guilty. In this case, a new trial would not be in the interests of justice.

In her reasons, Justice L'Heureux-Dubé makes reference to s. 273.2(b) of the Code. Whether the accused took reasonable steps is a question of fact to be determined by the trier of fact only after the air of reality test has been met. In view of the way the trial and appeal were argued, s. 273.2 (b) did not have to be considered.

. . . .

Cases involving a true misunderstanding between parties to a sexual encounter infrequently arise but are of profound importance to the community's sense of safety and justice. The law must afford women and men alike the peace of mind of knowing that their bodily integrity and autonomy in deciding when and whether to participate in sexual activity will be respected. At the same time, it must protect those who have not been proven guilty from the social stigma attached to sexual offenders.

L'HEUREUX-DUBÉ (GONTHIER J. concurring): —

. . . So pervasive is violence against women throughout the world that the international community adopted in December 18, 1979 (Res. 34/180), in addition to all other human rights instruments, the Convention on the Elimination of All Forms of Discrimination Against Women, Can. T.S. 1982 No. 31, entered into force on September 3, 1981, to which Canada is a party, which has been described as "the definitive international legal instrument requiring respect for and observance of the human rights of women."(R. Cook, "Reservations to the

Convention on the Elimination of All Forms of Discrimination Against Women" (1990), 30 Va. J. Int'l L. 643, at p. 643).

. . . .

Our *Charter* is the primary vehicle through which international human rights achieve a domestic effect (see *Slaight Communications Inc. v. Davidson*, [1989] 1 S.C.R. 1038; *R. v. Keegstra*, [1990] 3 S.C.R. 697). In particular, s. 15 (the equality provision) and s. 7 (which guarantees the right to life, security and liberty of the person) embody the notion of respect of human dignity and integrity.

. . . .

I have had the benefit of the reasons of Justice Major in this appeal and I agree generally with his reasons on most issues and with the result that he reaches. However, I wish to add some comments and discuss some of the reasoning of the trial judge and of the majority of the Court of Appeal.

. . . .

This case is not about consent, since none was given. It is about myths and stereotypes . . .

The trial judge believed the complainant and accepted her testimony that she was afraid and he acknowledged her unwillingness to engage in any sexual activity. In addition, there is no doubt that the respondent was aware that the complainant was afraid since he told her repeatedly not to be afraid. The complainant clearly articulated her absence of consent: she said no. Not only did the accused not stop, but after a brief pause, as Fraser C.J. puts it, he went on to an "increased level of sexual activity" to which twice the complainant said no. What could be clearer?

. . . .

In the circumstances of this case, it is difficult to understand how the question of implied consent even arose. Although he found the complainant credible, and accepted her evidence that she said "no" on three occasions and was afraid, the trial judge nonetheless did not take "no" to mean that the complainant did not consent. Rather, he concluded that she implicitly consented and that the Crown had failed to prove lack of consent. This was a fundamental error. As noted by Professor Stuart in Annotation on *R. v. Ewanchuk* (1998), 13 C.R. (5th) 330, at p. 330:

> Both the trial judgment and that of Justice McClung do not make the basic distinction that consent is a matter of the state of mind of the complainant and belief in consent is, subject to s. 273.2 of the Criminal Code, a matter of the state of mind of the accused.

This error does not derive from the findings of fact but from mythical assumptions that when a woman says "no" she is really saying "yes," "try again," or "persuade me." To paraphrase Fraser C.J. at p. 263, it denies women's sexual autonomy and implies that women are "walking around this country in a state of constant consent to sexual activity".

In the Court of Appeal, McClung J.A. compounded the error made by the trial judge. At the outset of his opinion, he stated at p. 245 that "it must be pointed out that the complainant did not present herself to Ewanchuk or enter his trailer in a bonnet and crinolines." He noted, at pp. 245-46, that "she was the mother of a six-month-old baby and that, along with her boyfriend, she shared an apartment with another couple".

Even though McClung J.A. asserted that he had no intention of denigrating the complainant, one might wonder why he felt necessary to point out these aspects of the trial record. Could it be to express that the complainant is not a virgin? Or that she is a person of questionable moral character because she is not married and lives with her boyfriend and another couple? These comments made by an appellate judge help reinforce the myth that under such circumstances, either the complainant is less worthy of belief, she invited the sexual assault, or her sexual experience signals probable consent to further sexual activity. Based on those attributed assumptions, the implication is that if the complainant articulates her lack of consent by saying "no," she really does not mean it and even if she does, her refusal cannot be taken as seriously as if she were a girl of "good" moral character. "Inviting" sexual assault, according to those myths, lessens the guilt of the accused . . .

McClung J.A. writes, at p. 247:

> There is no room to suggest that Ewanchuk knew, yet disregarded, her underlying state of mind as he furthered his *romantic intentions*. He was not aware of her true state of mind. Indeed, his ignorance about that was what she wanted. The facts, set forth by the trial judge, provide support for the overriding trial finding, couched in terms of consent by implication, that the accused had no proven preparedness to assault the complainant to get what he wanted. [Emphasis added.]

On the contrary, both the fact that Ewanchuk was aware of the complainant's state of mind, as he did indeed stop each time she expressly stated "no," and the trial judge's findings reinforce the obvious conclusion that the accused knew there was no consent. These were two strangers, a young 17-year-old woman attracted by a job offer who found herself trapped in a trailer and a man approximately twice her age and size. This is hardly a scenario one would characterize as reflective of "romantic intentions." It was nothing more than an effort by Ewanchuk to engage the complainant sexually, not romantically.

The expressions used by McClung J.A. to describe the accused's sexual assault, such as "clumsy passes" (p. 246) or "would hardly raise Ewanchuk's stature in the pantheon of chivalric behaviour" (p. 248), are plainly inappropriate in that context as they minimize the importance of the accused's conduct and the reality of sexual aggression against women.

McClung J.A. also concluded that "the sum of the evidence indicates that Ewanchuk's advances to the complainant were far less criminal than hormonal" (p. 250) having found earlier that "every advance he made to her stopped when she spoke against it" and that "[t]here was no evidence of assault or even its threat" (p. 249). According to this analysis, a man would be free from criminal responsibility for having non-consensual sexual activity whenever he cannot control his hormonal urges. Furthermore, the fact that the accused ignored the complainant's verbal objections to any sexual activity and persisted in escalated sexual contact, grinding his pelvis against hers repeatedly, is more evidence than needed to determine that there was an assault.

Finally, McClung J.A. made this point: "In a less litigious age going too far in the boyfriend's car was better dealt with on site — a well-chosen expletive, a slap in the face or, if necessary, a well directed knee" (p. 250). According to this stereotype, women should use physical force, not resort to courts to "deal with" sexual assaults and it is not the perpetrator's responsibility to ascertain consent, as required by s. 273.2(b), but the women's not only to express an unequivocal "no," but also to fight her way out of such a situation. In that sense, Susan Estrich has noted that "rape is most assuredly not the only crime in which consent is a defense; but it is the only crime that has required the victim to resist physically in order to establish nonconsent" ("Rape" (1986), Yale L.J. 1087, at p. 1090).

. . . .

This case has not dispelled any of the fears I expressed in *Seaboyer*, supra, about the use of myths and stereotypes in dealing with sexual assault complaints (see also Bertha Wilson, "Will Women Judges Really Make a Difference?" (1990), 28 Osgoode Hall L.J. 507). Complainants should be able to rely on a system free from myths and stereotypes, and on a judiciary whose impartiality is not compromised by these biased assumptions. The *Code* was amended in 1983 and in 1992 to eradicate reliance on those assumptions; they should not be permitted to resurface through the stereotypes reflected in the reasons of the majority of the Court of Appeal. It is part of the role of this court to denounce this kind of language, unfortunately still used today, which not only perpetuates archaic myths and stereotypes about the nature of sexual assaults but also ignores the law.

. . . .

I agree entirely with Chief Justice Fraser that, unless and until an accused first takes reasonable steps to assure that there is consent, the defence of honest but mistaken belief does not arise (see *R. v. Daigle*, [1998] 1 S.C.R. 1220; *Esau*, supra, per McLachlin J. dissenting; and J. McInnes and C. Boyle, "Judging

Sexual Assault Law against a Standard of Equality" (1995), 25 U.B.C. L. Rev. 341). In this case, the accused proceeded from massaging to sexual contact without making any inquiry as to whether the complainant consented. Obviously, interpreting the fact that the complainant did not refuse the massage to mean that the accused could further his sexual intentions is not a reasonable step. The accused cannot rely on the complainant's silence or ambiguous conduct to initiate sexual contact. Moreover, where a complainant expresses non-consent, the accused has a corresponding escalating obligation to take additional steps to ascertain consent. Here, despite the complainant's repeated verbal objections, the accused did not take any step to ascertain consent, let alone reasonable ones. Instead, he increased the level of his sexual activity. Therefore, pursuant to s. 273.2(b) Ewanchuk was barred from relying on a belief in consent.

. . . .

McLACHLIN J.: — I agree with the reasons of Justice Major. I also agree with Justice L'Heureux-Dubé that stereotypical assumptions lie at the heart of what went wrong in this case. The specious defence of implied consent (consent implied by law), as applied in this case, rests on the assumption that unless a woman protests or resists, she should be "deemed" to consent (see L'Heureux-Dubé J.). On appeal, the idea also surfaced that if a woman is not modestly dressed, she is deemed to consent. Such stereotypical assumptions find their roots in many cultures, including our own. They no longer, however, find a place in Canadian law.

———————

L'Heureux-Dubé J.'s rebuke to McLung J. led him to protest in press statements. These in turn were the subject of a formal complaint to the Canadian Judicial Council. On May 9, 1999, a panel chaired by Constance Glube, Chief Justice of Nova Scotia, issued a report expressing strong disapproval of the judge's conduct. It did not recommend his removal from office.

What do you think of each of the new limits the court imposes on the mistaken belief defence?

For a critical review see Stuart, *Canadian Criminal Law: A Treatise* (7th ed., 2014) Chapter 4. See too Deborah Hatch, "Culpability and Capitulation: Sexual Assault and Consent in the Wake of *R. v. Ewanchuk*" (1999) 43 Crim. L.Q. 551.

The Supreme Court in *Ewanchuk* substituted a conviction of sexual assault and remitted the matter back for sentencing. The sentencing judge rejected the Crown submission for a five-year sentence. Noting the accused's prior criminal record of four convictions for sexual offences, including rape, the judge nevertheless held that this offence was not flagrant and the accused was now in a stable relationship. The judge imposed a sentence of one year's imprisonment. On the further Crown appeal the sentence was increased to two years less one day: (2003), 6 C.R. (6th) 88 (Alta. C.A.).

The acid test of the new *Ewanchuk* tests will be in borderline cases. A rapist does not have consent and makes no mistake. So, too, with any other sexual predator. But the key question is how the assault doctrines of consent and mistake work out when the situation between the two parties was ambiguous and there is a real issue of whether a sexual assault occurred.

In *Ewanchuk*, Major J. expressed the opinion that ambiguous situations are rare in sexual assault cases:

> Cases involving a true misunderstanding between parties to a sexual encounter infrequently arise but are of profound importance to the community's sense of safety and justice (para. 66).

This assessment may be contrasted with that of Justice Casey Hill of the Ontario Court of Justice, General Division, who wrote in an unreported judgment in *T.S.*, [1999] O.J. No. 268, (January 25, 1999), Doc. Brampton 2084/98 (Ont. Gen. Div.) as follows:

> Ordinarily, people communicate things like consent or no-consent simply and effectively: *The Queen v. Esau*, per McLachlin J. Be that as it may, however, we have also acknowledged "the complex and diverse nature of consent" (*The Queen v. Currier*, per McLachlin J.) and that the dynamics of a sexual encounter are not infrequently far from simple. In *Regina v. Welch* (1995), 25 O.R. (3d) 665 (C.A.) at 674, Griffiths J.A. referred to "the varying and private nature of sexual relations". As Dickson J. stated in dissent in *Pappajohn v. The Queen* (1980), 52 C.C.C. (2d) 481 (S.C.C.) at 505, there can be many "ambiguous situations" in sexual relationships and there may well be circumstances where each party interprets the situation differently. It has been said that it is difficult to draw clear bright lines in defining human relations particularly those of a consenting sexual nature: *The Queen v. Currier*, per Cory J. at para. 102.

It has always seemed obvious that extending the reach of sexual assault laws to include such conduct as unwanted touching would inevitably embroil trial courts in deciding whether to criminalize conduct where the parties actually miscommunicated. This is especially likely in situations where there was first consensual conduct and later, according to the complainant, a withdrawal of consent. The acquittal rates for sexual assault are unknown but widely believed to be relatively high. This also suggests triers of fact are finding ambiguity.

It is strange that the duty to take reasonable steps in s. 273.2(b) was not considered when *Darrach* reached the Supreme Court or by the majority in *Ewanchuk*. There are undoubted difficulties in interpreting s. 273.2(b), which clearly has subjective and objective elements and was drafted to demand that reasonable steps be taken but not necessarily all steps that could be imagined. In *Malcolm* (2000), 35 C.R. (5th) 365, 147 C.C.C. (3d) 34 (Man. C.A.), Madam Justice Helper, speaking for the Manitoba Court of Appeal, recently carefully reviewed case law and writings on s. 273.2(*b*) and arrived at a commendably clear test:

> Section 273.2(b) requires the court to apply a quasi-objective test to the situation. First, the circumstances known to the accused must be ascertained. Then, the issue which arises is, if a reasonable man was aware of the same circumstances, would he take further steps before proceeding with the sexual activity? If the answer is yes, and the accused has not taken further steps, then the accused is not entitled to the defence of honest belief in consent. If the answer is no, or even maybe, then the accused would not be required to take further steps and the defence will apply. (C.R. at 373, para. 24.)

The Court held that a new trial had to be ordered where a trial judge had acquitted on the basis of a mistaken belief defence without considering the reasonable steps requirement. After a night of partying and drinking, without any invitation to so do, the accused entered the complainant's bedroom while she was sleeping, knowing that she was married to a close friend. He did not engage in any conversation with her. He stated that by her conduct, he believed she wanted to have sexual intercourse with him. Surely in such a situation, the Court would need to be satisfied that the accused took reasonable steps to ascertain that the complainant was consenting to that sexual activity.

R. v. CORNEJO

(2003), 18 C.R. (6th) 124, 181 C.C.C. (3d) 206 CarswellOnt 4679
(Ont. C.A.), leave to appeal refused (2004), 2004 CarswellOnt 4086,
2004 CarswellOnt 4087 (S.C.C.)

The accused was charged with sexual assault. The jury acquitted and the Crown appealed, arguing that the trial judge erred in leaving the defence of honest but mistaken belief in consent for the jury's consideration when there was no air of reality to that defence.

Per ABELLA J.A. (CATZMAN and GILLESE JJ.A. concurring): —

The complainant and Luis Cornejo were co-workers. They appeared to have a moderately friendly casual relationship which included bantering with a sexual aspect . . . [She had twice said no to his sexual advances.] . . . . On the day of the events that gave rise to the charges, both the complainant and Mr. Cornejo were at a company golf tournament. They did not speak to each other at the tournament and left separately. They had both been drinking.

Mr. Cornejo testified that he called the complainant at home at about 12:30 a.m. and that she sounded as if she had been sleeping. He spoke to her very briefly, during which time she told him she wanted to get off the telephone because she was expecting a telephone call from her boyfriend. Several minutes later, Mr. Cornejo called the complainant again and was informed that her boyfriend had not called so she needed the line to call her boyfriend. Mr. Cornejo called a third time, and asked what had occurred between the complainant and her boyfriend. The complainant told him that her boyfriend was not coming over. Mr. Cornejo said he asked if he could come over, and the complainant's response, according to the transcript, was "mm-hmm". Mr. Cornejo testified that he took this to be an affirmative response to his request.

He arrived at the complainant's apartment at about 1:30 a.m. When he got no response after knocking on her door, he tried the door, found it unlocked and entered the apartment. The complainant had left the door unlocked for her boyfriend. The complainant was sleeping on her couch. Mr. Cornejo testified that he said "hello" to the complainant, at which point the complainant woke up and asked "What the hell are you doing here?" He then sat beside her on the couch, ran his fingers through her hair, and kissed her on the forehead and on her mouth. He testified that she put her finger on his mouth and said "no, not on the mouth". He asked "why not" and she responded "because I don't love you". He then began kissing her on the neck and removed the blanket that was covering her.

His evidence was that she did not touch him in return, and that she remained lying on the couch with her eyes closed throughout the entire encounter. Mr. Cornejo said that when he tried to take her jeans off, she lifted her pelvis. Shortly thereafter, he took her underwear off and indicated that once again she had lifted her pelvis. When he tried to position the complainant for intercourse, she said "no". Mr. Cornejo sat up and said "I thought that you wanted it". She told him to get out. He then noticed he had blood on his hand and asked her if she had her period. She did not respond. He went to the washroom. She told him that she wanted him to leave, at which point he left.

According to the complainant, although she rarely drank, on the day of the golf tournament she drank nine beers and was very drunk. She fell asleep on her couch at home and awoke to find Mr. Cornejo on top of her, naked and attempting to penetrate her. Her underwear and pants had been removed. She tried unsuccessfully to push him off and asked him repeatedly what he was doing. She was explicit in asserting that she did not consent to the sexual activity. She does not remember any of the facts that Mr. Cornejo relies on, and has no memory of him entering the apartment or telephoning her that night. She was wearing a tampon when Mr. Cornejo attempted to penetrate her.

When ruling on whether the air of reality threshold was met, the trial judge relied solely on the pelvic movements of the complainant as evidence satisfying the air of reality threshold:

> And with respect to the summation of the decision in *Ewanchuk*, it states that a belief that one, silence; two, facility; or three, ambiguous conduct constitutes consent is not the defence.
>
> It would seem to me that, if the accused's testimony is believed, there is conduct on the complainant's part that goes beyond any of those three listed items, and would constitute unambiguous consent and that is co-operation in the removal of clothing. And that I take to be the gist of part of the accused's testimony.
>
> Therefore, I think that there is sufficient evidence to permit this defence to go to the jury.

With respect, I believe that the trial judge erred in concluding in these circumstances that the movements of the complainant's pelvis were a sufficient evidentiary basis to allow the defence to go to the jury.

Analysis

In *R. v. Cinous*, [2002] 2 S.C.R. 3, the Supreme Court of Canada discussed the air of reality test, albeit not in the context of a sexual assault. This judgment confirmed that a trial judge has a duty to keep from the jury any defences lacking an evidentiary foundation or an air of reality. As explained by McLachlin C.J.C. at p. 29, the "test is whether there is evidence on the record upon which a properly instructed jury acting reasonably could acquit". Further, the trial judge must consider the "totality of the evidence" and assume the evidence relied upon by the accused to be true.

In *R. v. Livermore*, [1995] 4 S.C.R. 123 at 135, McLachlin J. explained that the defence of honest but mistaken belief in consent "involves two elements: (1) that the accused *honestly believed* the complainant consented; and (2) that the accused have been *mistaken* in this belief" [original emphasis].

In *Ewanchuk*, [1999] 1 S.C.R. 330 at p. 354, Major J. stated:

> In order to cloak the accused's action in moral innocence, the evidence must show that he believed that the complainant *communicated consent to engage in the sexual activity in question*. A belief by the accused that the complainant in her own mind, wanted him to touch her, but did not express desire, is not a defence . . . . What matters is whether the accused believed that the complainant effectively said "yes" through words and/or actions [original emphasis].

He also observed, at p. 356, that "belief that silence, passivity or ambiguous conduct constitutes consent is a mistake of law, and provides no defence".

In my view, based on Mr. Cornejo's own testimony, the evidence points to an absence of consent on the complainant's part and a giant leap of imagination on his. The lifting of her pelvis by a woman who has been drinking, is asleep, and, as Mr. Cornejo well knew, is totally uninterested in any kind of intimate relationship, cannot give rise to an assumption that the woman is consenting to sexual activity. In these circumstances, I cannot, with respect, see any air of reality to Mr. Cornejo's assertion that he honestly believed the complainant was consenting to his presence in her apartment, let alone to the sexual activity he engaged in with her there.

In these circumstances, other than Mr. Cornejo's assertion that he believed the complainant was consenting and the movement of her pelvis significantly after he had already initiated the sexual activity, there was overwhelming evidence that she either did not consent or was incapable of consenting. Mr. Cornejo took advantage of a passive and unclear response.

During his testimony, Mr. Cornejo explained that the complainant's eyes were closed while he was kissing her and while he removed her clothing, and admitted that it was possible that she was asleep during the encounter. He testified that when she said "no", she suddenly seemed very awake and there was a big difference in the way she was acting.

The facts do not provide an evidentiary foundation for the assertion that when Mr. Cornejo commenced sexual activity with the complainant, he believed she was consenting. After entering a person's home, late at night without permission, an individual cannot commence sexual activity with a person who has been drinking and was asleep, and then rely on the mistake defence solely on the basis that at one point late in the encounter, the woman moved her body. The trial judge failed to make reference to any facts other than the movement of the complainant's body after the sexual activity had begun. In these circumstances, the movement of the complainant's pelvis was simply an insufficient basis to allow the defence to go the jury.

These circumstances called for Mr. Cornejo to take reasonable steps to ascertain consent, and as he took no steps, s. 273.2(b) statutorily bars the defence. As explained by Don Stuart in *Canadian Criminal Law*, (6th ed.) (Scarborough: Carswell, 2011) at p. 295:

> The accused still has to pass the air of reality test for a mistake of defence . . . . He now will never have the defence open where his mistaken belief arose from self-induced intoxication, recklessness or wilful blindness, or, more importantly, where he did not take reasonable steps in the circumstances known to him to ascertain that the complainant was consenting.

Therefore, given Mr. Cornejo's failure to take any steps, in the words of McLachlin J. in *Cinous* at p. 31, there was no 'real issue' for the jury to decide.

. . . .

The requirement to provide evidence of reasonable steps being taken is explained by Professor Kent Roach in *Criminal Law*, 2nd ed. (Toronto: Irwin Law, 2000) at pp. 157-158 as follows:

> The denial in section 273.2(b) of the mistake of fact unless the accused takes reasonable steps in the circumstances known to him at the time to ascertain whether the complainant was consenting to the activity in question combines subjective and objective fault elements in a novel and creative manner. . . . The accused's obligation to take reasonable steps is only based on what he subjectively knows at the time. On the other hand, section 273.2(b) requires the accused to act as a reasonable person would in the circumstances by taking reasonable steps to ascertain whether the complainant was consenting. Much will depend on the court's view of what reasonable steps are necessary to ascertain consent. Some judges may find that positive steps are required in most, if not all, situations regardless of the accused's subjective perception of the circumstances. Others may only require such steps if the complainant has indicated resistance or lack of consent in some way that is subjectively known to the accused.[47]

---

47 It is indeed now clear that judges differ as to what reasonable steps are required. See, for example, *R. v. Williams* (2009), 67 C.R. (6th) 363 (Ont. S.C.J.) (no positive steps required to ascertain consent in face of passive behaviour where parties were friends; criticized in C.R. annotation by Janine Benedet) and see *R. v. Millar*, (2008), 59 C.R. (6th) 39 (Ont. S.C.J.) (accused acquitted on basis of mistaken belief where intoxicated complainant allowed accused to touch and kiss her). However, courts found failures to take reasonable steps where an identical twin initiated sexual intercourse with the sleeping complainant, who co-operated until she found out he wasn't her partner (*R. v. Crangle* (2010), 256 C.C.C. (3d) 234 (Ont. C.A.), leave to appeal refused [2010] 3 S.C.R. v (note)) or where a massage therapist who obtained consent to massage the patient's chest then proceeded to massage her breasts (*R. v. Zacher* (2009), 71 C.R. (6th) 141 (Alta. Prov. Ct.), confirmed on appeal). Courts of Appeal have sometimes found an air of reality where the complainant did and said things that led the accused to believe she was consenting and she was not so severely intoxicated as to be incapable of consent (*R. v. Howe* (2015), 328 C.C.C. (3d) 546, 23 C.R. (7th) 63 (N.S. C.A.)) and where the accused claimed to believe the woman sleeping in the trailer was his wife (*R. v. Walsh* (2015), 320 C.C.C. (3d) 313,

. . . .

They did not speak at the golf tournament that day, and she had given him no indication that she was interested in seeing him, let alone engaging in sexual activity with him. On the night in question, Mr. Cornejo telephoned the complainant three times after midnight. Knowing that the complainant had been waiting for her boyfriend to visit her, Mr. Cornejo decided to drive to her apartment on the strength of what can only be described as an ambiguous groan on her part. When he arrived, he knocked on the door and she did not answer. Mr. Cornejo testified that he had no right to enter her apartment that night and that the complainant was sound asleep when he arrived. When he awoke the complainant, she asked, "What the hell are you doing here", an unambiguous comment and a clear reflection that she had not agreed to his coming to her apartment.

The only words Mr. Cornejo said the complainant expressed were "what the hell are you doing here", "no, not on the mouth", and "because I don't love you". Either in isolation or taken together, these are phrases of rejection. They are not ambiguous. It is hard to see how these statements could be interpreted as enticement entitling Mr. Cornejo to assume that he could proceed with his sexual activity. These were circumstances crying out for reasonable steps to ascertain consent. The complainant's prior rejections of his sexual advances, his apology to her in the past for his inappropriate sexual advances, her request to him that he hang up during the first two telephone calls so she could speak to her boyfriend, her ambiguous response to his third phone call, her failure to answer the door, his entering the apartment without permission and finding the complainant sleeping and shocked by his presence, all required that he take reasonable steps to clarify whether she was consenting to sexual activity. She never touched him, her eyes were closed, he knew she had been drinking that day, and every rejection by her that evening, even according to his own evidence, resulted in more aggressive sexual conduct on his part.

Mr. Cornejo's counsel pointed to the following as reasonable steps taken to ascertain consent: he ran his fingers through her hair; he kissed her on the forehead; he kissed her on the mouth; the complainant lifted her pelvis when he removed her clothing. But this is a submission that permits Mr. Cornejo to transform his own acts into reflections of consent. In these circumstances, Mr. Cornejo ought to have taken steps before he engaged in any sexual activity to ascertain whether she was consenting. In *R. v. Darrach* (1998), 122 C.C.C. (3d) 225 (Ont. C.A.), affirmed [2002] 2 S.C.R. 443, Morden A.C.J.O. explained at para. 90 that s. 273.2(b) requires that "a person about to engage in sexual activity take reasonable steps . . . to ascertain that the complainant was consenting." In my view, no steps of any kind, let alone reasonable ones, were taken.

---

17 C.R. (7th) 196 (N.L. C.A.), leave to appeal refused 2015 CarswellNfld 188, 2015 CarswellNfld 189 (S.C.C.)), criticized by Janine Benedet in her C.R. comment.

On the basis of Mr. Cornejo's own evidence, the complainant said no and physically stopped him from kissing her on the mouth. This could not be interpreted as a reasonable step in ascertaining consent to sexual activity or as providing him with confidence that he had thus secured her consent to proceed further. Any reasonable person in Mr. Cornejo's position, who was aware of these same circumstances, would have taken further steps to ascertain consent before proceeding with sexual activity. No reasonable person, on the other hand, when being told that someone was uninterested in being kissed because she did not love him, would assume that she would, in the alternative, be interested in having her clothes removed and engaging in sexual intercourse.

As a result, the trial judge erred in leaving the defence of honest but mistaken belief in consent with the jury. Accordingly, I would allow the appeal, set aside the acquittals, and direct a new trial.

In the U.K. the recent Canadian *Criminal Code* amendments have had a direct impact in the decision of the U.K. Parliament to finally reverse the subjective approach required by *D.P.P. v. Morgan*: see The Home Office Document "Setting the Boundaries: Reforming the law on sex offences": <http://www.homeoffice.gov.uk/docs/vol1main/pdf>. The new *Sexual Offences Act* of 2003, in force as of May, 2004, limits the mistaken belief defence to a reasonable belief to be determined having regard to all the circumstances, including any steps taken to ascertain consent. By requiring that the belief be reasonable, the U.K. position is tougher than the subjective/objective compromise in s. 273.2(b) in Canada.

To assess whether the Supreme Court has got the balance right consider the *Ewanchuk* tests in the following problems.

PROBLEMS

1. Two teenagers, Jack and Jill, have their first date at the movies. After the movies they go to Jack's apartment for coffee. They talk. Jill tells Jack that she has a boyfriend but also that she is an open, friendly, and affectionate person, and that she often likes to touch people. Jack tells her that he is an open, friendly, and affectionate person and that he often likes to touch people. They talk more. They touch each other; they hug. At some point Jack kisses Jill. Jack thinks she has responded positively to his sexual advance although nothing was said. Jill did not welcome the kiss and felt she did nothing to encourage Jack. She was not scared of him. She admits that at that point she opened two buttons of her blouse but this was because she felt claustrophobic and nothing else. Jack felt he was being encouraged by her action and touched her breasts. Jill slapped him.

2. The same as problem 1, except that it was Jill who kissed Jack.

3. The accused is charged with sexual assault. The accounts of the complainant and the accused varied significantly. The complainant was 15 years old, a ward of the Children's Aid Society and living in a group home. The accused was 23 years old, and lived in a bachelor apartment. They met at a bus stop, chatted briefly and then agreed to walk to the accused's apartment and drink beer together. On the way from the beer store the accused made flirtatious and sexually suggestive remarks. When the two returned to the apartment, they sat and drank beer for some time. The complainant testified that she became increasingly withdrawn and uncomfortable as the evening progressed and that this frustrated the accused. The accused denied this.

At one point, the complainant got up to go to the bathroom, and when she returned she found the accused lying on the bed. At his urging she joined him on the bed, although she said she felt awkward. The accused testified that the complainant had gone to get massage oil and then allowed him to massage her, which the complainant denied. The accused then began to play with the complainant's hair, and used his hand to lay her down on the bed. They then began to have intercourse and, at some time during that intercourse, he asked her whether he should use a condom, and, according to the accused, the complainant said that that would be a good idea. He then went into the bathroom to put on a condom and returned. However, on his account, he had difficulty sustaining an erection and no further intercourse took place. He then manually stimulated himself and he and the complainant went to sleep. The complainant testified that there was an initial brief period of intercourse, followed by her becoming quiet and withdrawn, followed by a second encounter. On cross-examination, the accused acknowledged that at some time the complainant had said "No", but he took that as meaning "No" without a condom. The accused also testified that he told the complainant, at some point, that he knew when a woman said no, she meant no. The complainant testified that she said "No" on the earlier occasion as the accused was trying to take her pants off, but the accused testified that she took off her own pants. The trial judge found that "it is common ground that she did say 'No' at one stage, although, on the evidence, it is not clear to me just when that was said and under what circumstances". The trial judge found that the complainant was not an active participant in the sexual activity and that in her mind, she had decided she didn't want to have sexual relations with the accused that night. Compare *O. (M.)* (2000), 36 C.R. (5th) 258 (S.C.C.).

4. The accused is charged with sexual assault. The accused and the complainant went to a birthday party at a private residence.

The complainant arrived at the party at about 12:30 a.m. with a male friend. At around 4 a.m. she felt she was intoxicated and unable to drive. She decided to stay the night and lay down on a couch in the living-room. She testified she later "woke up to intercourse". The person with whom she was having intercourse was behind her. At first she thought it was the friend with whom she had come to the party and with whom she had a relationship. When she turned round and saw it was the accused, she was in shock. She got up and left. She testified that when she awoke her pants and underwear had been pulled down. She was unable to provide an explanation as to how this had occurred or whether she had assisted.

The accused testified that he too tried to go to sleep on the couch at about 4 a.m. He testified that the complainant, some time after daylight, started to rub herself against him. He asked her if she wanted to have sex and she said "yes". According to the accused she pulled down her clothes and consented to intercourse. He was surprised she got up and left the house without saying anything.

Is there an air of reality to the accused's alternative defences of consent and mistaken belief? If so, should the defence or defences succeed? Are you satisfied with the result?

Compare *R. v. Osvath* (1996), 46 C.R. (4th) 124 (Ont. C.A.), appeal quashed by the majority of the Supreme Court on the basis that the decision did not involve an error of law: (1997), 5 C.R. (5th) 329 (S.C.C.).

5. The accused was charged with sexual assault after he and another man publicly fondled the breasts of an unconscious woman. Early one afternoon, the two men were lying on a sidewalk in downtown Edmonton with the woman between them. A passing motorist observed the sexual touching and called police. The men, who were intoxicated but able to answer questions, were still touching the woman's breasts when police arrived. The complainant was taken to hospital. The police left before she regained consciousness and she was never interviewed.

At trial, the Crown called the driver and the two attending officers. The woman was not called as a witness, and the defence called no evidence. There was no evidence about how the woman came to be lying between the men or about anything she might have said or done before losing consciousness. Is the accused guilty of sexual assault?

Compare *R. v. Ashlee* (2006), 40 C.R. (6th) 125, 212 C.C.C. (3d) 477 (Alta. C.A.), leave to appeal refused (2006), 404 W.A.C. 396 (note) (S.C.C.) and see annotation by Janine Benedet, C.R. *ibid.* at 126-127.

6. In *R. v. V. (R.)* (2004), 20 C.R. (6th) 346 (Ont. S.C.J.) a husband had persisted in sexual advances on three occasions over a weekend although his wife had clearly said no. He did not proceed to the point of sexual intercourse. The trial judge acquitted on the basis of a mistaken belief in consent. He went as far as to say:

> Within the confines of a viable marriage, the Crown must prove beyond a reasonable doubt that the conduct of the accused was subjectively outside the norms of tolerated sexual behaviour in that particular couple's sexual relationship within their marriage...[The] Crown must establish not that the complainant said "no" on that particular occasion, but that in the context of the parties' entire marital relationship, and in the context of the particular situation, her saying "no" differed from the way they historically interacted for a sexual purpose and that the accused , thereby, should have known from such different behaviour that her "no" or her rejection of the accused's advances in fact was different from the way the parties interacted sexually in the past (at 2612).

After deliberating well over a year, the summary conviction appeal judge, Thomas J. of the Ontario Superior Court, dismissed the Crown appeal. He rejected the Crown position that a criminal assault occurred once there was physical touching without express consent of his wife in advance. The Crown's position was held to be wrong in law, erroneous in principle and offending common sense. Do you agree with the Crown or Justice Thomas? See Christine Boyle, "Sexual Assault as Foreplay: Does *Ewanchuk* Apply to Spouses?" (2004), 20 C.R. (6th) 359-367. The Ontario Court of Appeal dismissed the appeal in a brief endorsement judgement. It was an error to find a mistaken belief defence nor was there implied consent. However, the trial judge had made inconsistent findings so there was no proof beyond reasonable doubt: (2004) CarswellOnt 5287 (Ont. C.A.).

Compare *R. v. T. (W.A.)* (2011), 86 C.R. (6th) 125 (Alta. Q.B.) and C.R. comment by Janine Benedet.

A 6-3 majority of the Supreme Court recently re-asserted its *Seaboyer* and *Ewanchuk* principles in the course of a controversial ruling that a person cannot validly consent to sexual activity in advance:

R. v. A. (J.)

2011 CarswellOnt 3515, 2011 CarswellOnt 3516, 84 C.R. (6th) 1, 271 C.C.C. (3d) 1, [2011] 2 S.C.R. 440

One evening, in the course of sexual relations, J.A. placed his hands around the throat of his long-term partner, K.D., and choked her until she was unconscious. At trial, K.D. estimated that she was unconscious for "less than three minutes". She testified that she consented to J.A. choking her, and understood that she might lose consciousness. She stated that she and J.A. had experimented with erotic asphyxiation, and that she had lost consciousness before. When K.D. regained consciousness, she was on her knees with her hands tied behind her back, and J.A. was inserting a dildo into her anus. K.D. gave conflicting testimony about whether this was the first time J.A. had inserted a dildo in her anus. K.D. testified that J.A. removed the dildo 10 seconds after she regained consciousness. The two then had vaginal intercourse. When they finished, J.A. cut K.D.'s hands loose.

K.D. made a complaint to the police two months later and stated that while she consented to the choking, she had not consented to the sexual activity that had occurred. She later recanted her allegation, claiming that she made the complaint because J.A. threatened to seek sole custody of their young son. The trial judge found that K.D. had consented to being choked into unconsciousness but had not suffered bodily harm. However, she found that K.D. had not consented to the insertion of a dildo and convicted J.A. of sexual assault. In the alternative she could not legally consent to sexual activity while unconscious.

The Ontario Court of Appeal allowed the appeal, set aside the conviction and dismissed the charges against J.A. The Court was unanimous that there had not been proof beyond reasonable doubt that K.D. had not consented to the insertion of the dildo in advance of unconsciousness. A 2-1 majority (per Simmons J.A., Juriancz J.A. concurring, LaForme J.A. dissenting) further decided that such consent would have been legally valid. The Crown appealed.

A 6-3 majority of the Supreme Court allowed the appeal and restored the conviction for sexual assault.

McLachlin C.J. (Deschamps, Abella, Charron, Rothstein and Cromwell JJ. concurring): —

[3] Our task on this appeal is to determine whether the *Criminal Code* defines consent as requiring a conscious, operating mind throughout the sexual activity. I conclude that the *Code* makes it clear that an individual must be conscious throughout the sexual activity in order to provide the requisite consent. Parliament requires ongoing, conscious consent to ensure that women and men are not the victims of sexual exploitation, and to ensure that individuals engaging in sexual activity are capable of asking their partners to stop at any point.

. . . .

[21] The only question before this Court is whether consent for the purposes of sexual assault requires the complainant to be conscious throughout the sexual activity. This is because the Crown appeals to this Court as of right on the basis of "any question of law on which a judge of the court of appeal dissents": *Criminal Code*, s. 693(1)(*a*). Accordingly, whether the complainant consented in fact or suffered bodily harm are not at issue; nor is the Court of Appeal's holding that for reasons of procedural fairness, the Crown in this case cannot rely on bodily harm to vitiate consent since it did not formally allege that bodily harm occurred. Since the issue of bodily harm is not before this Court, I take no position on whether or in which circumstances individuals may consent to bodily harm during sexual activity. In my view, it would be inappropriate to decide the matter without the benefit of submissions from interested groups.

B. *Framework of Sexual Assault*

[22] Before turning to the issue in this case, it is useful to consider the framework of the law of sexual assault.

[23] A conviction for sexual assault under s. 271(1) of the *Criminal Code* requires proof beyond a reasonable doubt of the *actus reus* and the *mens rea* of the offence. A person commits the *actus reus* if he touches another person in a sexual way without her consent. Consent for this purpose is actual subjective consent in the mind of the complainant at the time of the sexual activity in

question: *Ewanchuk*. As discussed below, the *Criminal Code*, s. 273.1(2), limits this definition by stipulating circumstances where consent is not obtained.

[24] A person has the required mental state, or *mens rea* of the offence, when he or she knew that the complainant was not consenting to the sexual act in question, or was reckless or wilfully blind to the absence of consent. The accused may raise the defence of honest but mistaken belief in consent if he believed that the complainant communicated consent to engage in the sexual activity. However, as discussed below, ss. 273.1(2) and 273.2 limit the cases in which the accused may rely on this defence. For instance, the accused cannot argue that he misinterpreted the complainant saying "no" as meaning "yes" (*Ewanchuk*, at para. 51).

[25] The issue in this case is whether the complainant consented, which is relevant to the *actus reus*; the Crown must prove the absence of consent to fulfill the requirements of the wrongful act. However, the provisions of the *Criminal Code* with respect to the *mens rea* defence of honest but mistaken belief also shed light on the issue of whether consent requires the complainant to have been conscious throughout the duration of the sexual activity.

[26] The relevant provisions of the *Criminal Code* are ss. 265, 273.1 and 273.2.

C. *The Concept of Consent under the Criminal Code*

[31] The foregoing provisions of the *Criminal Code* indicate that Parliament viewed consent as the conscious agreement of the complainant to engage in every sexual act in a particular encounter.

[32] The proper approach to statutory interpretation was summarized in *Canada Trustco Mortgage Co. v. Canada*, 2005 SCC 54, [2005] 2 S.C.R. 601: "The interpretation of a statutory provision must be made according to a textual, contextual and purposive analysis to find a meaning that is harmonious with the Act as a whole." The Court emphasized that while "[t]he relative effects of ordinary meaning, context and purpose on the interpretive process may vary, . . . in all cases the court must seek to read the provisions of an Act as a harmonious whole" (para 10).

[33] It follows that we must seek to interpret the provisions that deal with consent in a harmonious way. Applying this approach, we see that Parliament defined consent in a way that requires the complainant to be conscious throughout the sexual activity in question. The issue is not whether the Court should identify a new exception that vitiates consent to sexual activity while unconscious (see Fish J., at para. 95), but whether an unconscious person can qualify as consenting under Parliament's definition.

[34] Consent for the purposes of sexual assault is defined in s. 273.1(1) as "the voluntary agreement of the complainant to engage in the sexual activity in question". This suggests that the consent of the complainant must be specifically directed to each and every sexual act, negating the argument that broad advance consent is what Parliament had in mind. As discussed below, this Court has also interpreted this provision as requiring the complainant to consent to the activity "at the time it occur[s]" (*Ewanchuk*, at para. 26).

[35] Section 273.1(2) provides a non-exhaustive list of circumstances in which no consent is obtained. These examples shed further light on Parliament's understanding of consent.

[36] Section 273.1(2)(*b*) provides that no consent is obtained if "the complainant is incapable of consenting to the activity". Parliament was concerned that sexual acts might be perpetrated on persons who do not have the mental capacity to give meaningful consent. This might be because of mental impairment. It also might arise from unconsciousness: see *R. v. Esau*, [1997] 2 S.C.R. 777; *R v. Humphrey* (2001), 143 O.A.C. 151, at para. 56, *per* Charron J.A. (as she then was). It follows that Parliament intended consent to mean the conscious consent of an operating mind.

[37] The provisions of the *Criminal Code* that relate to the *mens rea* of sexual assault confirm that individuals must be conscious throughout the sexual activity. Before considering these provisions, however, it is important to keep in mind the differences between the meaning of consent under the *actus reus* and under the *mens rea*: *Ewanchuk*, at paras. 48-49. Under the *mens rea* defence, the issue is whether the accused believed that the complainant *communicated consent*. Conversely, the only question for the *actus reus* is whether the complainant was subjectively consenting in her mind. The complainant is not required to *express* her lack of consent or her revocation of consent for the *actus reus* to be established.

[38] With this caution in mind, I come to the three provisions that relate to the *mens rea* that are relevant to the issue in this case: s. 273.1(2)(*d*), s. 273.1(2)(*e*) and s. 273.2(*b*).[39] Section 273.1(2)(*d*) provides that there can be no consent if the "complainant expresses, by words or conduct, a lack of agreement to engage in the activity". Since this provision refers to the expression of consent, it is clear that it can only apply to the accused's *mens rea*. The point here is the linking of lack of consent to any "activity". This suggests a present, on-going conception of consent, rather than advance consent to a suite of activities.

[40] Section 273.1(2)(*e*) establishes that it is an error of law for the accused to believe that the complainant is still consenting after she "expresses . . . a lack of agreement [to continue] to engage in the activity". Since this provision refers to the expression of consent, it is clear that it can only apply to the accused's *mens*

rea. Nonetheless, it indicates that Parliament wanted people to be capable of revoking their consent at any time during the sexual activity. This in turn supports the view that Parliament viewed consent as the product of a conscious mind, since a person who has been rendered unconscious cannot revoke her consent. As a result, the protection afforded by s. 273.1(2)(*e*) would not be available to her.

[41] According to my colleague, Fish J., s. 273.1(2)(*e*) "suggests that the complainant's consent *can* be given in advance, and remains operative unless and until it is subsequently revoked" (para. 104 (emphasis in original)). With respect, I cannot accept this interpretation. The provision in question establishes that the accused must halt all sexual contact once the complainant expresses that she no longer consents. This does not mean that a failure to tell the accused to stop means that the complainant must have been consenting. As this Court has repeatedly held, the complainant is not required to express her lack of consent for the *actus reus* to be established. Rather, the question is whether the complainant subjectively consented in her mind: *Ewanchuk*; *R. v. M. (M.L.)*, [1994] 2 S.C.R. 3.

[42] Section 273.2 sheds further light on Parliament's conception of consent. Section 273.2 (*b*) states that a person wishing to avail himself of the *mens rea* defence must not only believe that the complainant communicated her consent (or in French, "*l'accusé croyait que le plaignant avait consenti*"), but must also have taken reasonable steps to ascertain whether she "was consenting" to engage in the sexual activity in question at the time it occurred. How can one take reasonable steps to ascertain whether a person is consenting to sexual activity while it is occurring if that person is unconscious? Once again, the provision is grounded in the assumption that the complainant must consciously consent to each and every sexual act. Further, by requiring the accused to take reasonable steps to ensure that the complainant "was consenting", Parliament has indicated that the consent of the complainant must be an ongoing state of mind.

[43] The question in this case is whether Parliament defined consent in a way that extends to advance consent to sexual acts committed while the complainant is unconscious. In my view, it did not. J.A.'s contention that advance consent can be given to sexual acts taking place during unconsciousness is not in harmony with the provisions of the *Code* and their underlying policies. These provisions indicate that Parliament viewed consent as requiring a "capable" or operating mind, able to evaluate each and every sexual act committed. To hold otherwise runs counter to Parliament's clear intent that a person has the right to consent to particular acts and to revoke her consent at any time. Reading these provisions together, I cannot accept the respondent's contention that an individual may consent in advance to sexual activity taking place while she is unconscious.

[46] The only relevant period of time for the complainant's consent is while the touching is occurring: *Ewanchuk*, at para. 26. The complainant's views towards the touching before or after are not directly relevant. An offence has not occurred if the complainant consents at the time but later changes her mind (absent grounds for vitiating consent). Conversely, the *actus reus* has been committed if the complainant was not consenting in her mind while the touching took place, even if she expressed her consent before or after the fact.

[47] The jurisprudence of this Court also establishes that there is no substitute for the complainant's actual consent to the sexual activity at the time it occurred. It is not open to the defendant to argue that the complainant's consent was implied by the circumstances, or by the relationship between the accused and the complainant. There is no defence of implied consent to sexual assault: *Ewanchuk,* at para. 31.

[57] . . .. In the case of non-sexual assaults, consent may, where appropriate, be implied at common law: *R. v. Cuerrier*, [1998] 2 S.C.R. 371, *per* McLachlin J. (as she then was), at para. 52; *R. v. Jobidon*, [1991] 2 S.C.R. 714, *per* Gonthier J., at p. 743. This Court, applying the common law, has recognized cases in which the social setting and the relationship between the parties implies consent to non-sexual touching, such as shaking hands at a business meeting or colliding with a hockey player on the ice. Conversely, in interpreting the provisions of the *Criminal Code* that relate to sexual assault, this Court has expressly rejected the notion of implied consent: *Ewanchuk*, at para. 31.

[58] The respondent also argues that requiring conscious consent to sexual activity may result in absurd outcomes. He cites the example of a person who kisses his sleeping partner. In that situation, he argues, the accused would be guilty of sexual assault unless he is permitted to argue that his sleeping partner consented to the kiss in advance.

[59] The first difficulty with altering the definition of consent to deal with the respondent's hypothesis is that it would only provide a defence where the complainant specifically turns her mind to consenting to the particular sexual acts that later occur before falling asleep. The respondent's position is that there is no sexual assault in this case because the complainant consented to both being rendered unconscious and to engaging in the sexual activity that occurred while she was unconscious. If a hypothetical complainant did not expect her partner to kiss her — or whatever other acts are at issue — while she was asleep, the respondent's approach would not provide a defence.

[60] The second difficulty is the risk that the unconscious person's wishes would be innocently misinterpreted by his or her partner. Sexual preferences may be very particular and difficult for individuals to precisely express. If the accused fails to perform the sexual acts precisely as the complainant would have wanted

— by neglecting to wear a condom for instance — the unconscious party will be unintentionally violated. In addition to the risk of innocent misinterpretation, the respondent's position does not recognize the total vulnerability of the unconscious partner and the need to protect this person from exploitation. The unconscious partner cannot meaningfully control how her person is being touched, leaving her open to abuse: *R. v. Osvath* (1996), 46 C.R. (4th) 124 (Ont. C.A.), *per* Abella J.A. (as she then was), dissenting.

[61] A third difficulty is evidentiary. If the complainant is unconscious during the sexual activity, she has no real way of knowing what happened, and whether her partner exceeded the bounds of her consent. Only one person really knows what happened during the period of unconsciousness, leaving the unconscious party open for exploitation. The complainant may never discover that she was in fact the victim of a sexual assault. Fish J. correctly points out that in some cases, there may be forensic evidence that establishes conclusively that the accused exceeded the bounds of the consent given. However, if the complainant never suspects that a sexual assault has occurred, no forensic evidence will be gathered. Moreover, many acts of sexual assault leave no forensic evidence.

[62] A fourth difficulty is jurisprudential. Recognizing exceptions to the requirement of conscious consent would not only run counter to the definition of consent in the *Criminal Code*, but would impose on the courts the task of determining how consent to unconscious sexual activity can be proven. The respondent suggests that the court could ask if the complainant consented before losing consciousness to the sexual acts that subsequently occurred — pre-unconsciousness authorization. This would require the court to determine what the unconscious party wanted just prior to going unconscious, and then assess if this is what indeed occurred. This inquiry would be objective, contrary to the subjective inquiry required by the *Criminal Code*. The only other option — post-unconsciousness determination of consent where the complainant decides when she regains consciousness if she would have consented to all the acts that occurred — is also problematic. A *post facto* determination runs contrary to the rule that the complainant's post-act sentiments are irrelevant; if a complainant consents to sexual activity while it is taking place, but later decides that she should not have, the accused should be acquitted on the *actus reus* of the offence.

[63] The Crown suggested that this Court could allow for mild sexual touching that occurs while a person is unconscious by relying on the *de minimis* doctrine, based on the Latin phrase "*de minimis non curat lex*", or the "law does not care for small or trifling things": *Canadian Foundation for Children, Youth and the Law v. Canada (Attorney General)*, 2004, SCC 4, [2004] 1 S.C.R. 76, at para. 200, *per* Arbour J., dissenting. Without suggesting that the *de minimis* principle has no place in the law of sexual assault, it should be noted that even mild non-

consensual touching of a sexual nature can have profound implications for the complainant.

[64] Running through the arguments in favour of carving out particular circumstances as exceptions to the conscious consent paradigm of the *Criminal Code* is the suggestion that the strict approach Parliament has adopted toward consent in the context of sexual assault has no place in relationships of mutual trust, like marriage. However, accepting this view would run counter to Parliament's clear rejection of defences to sexual assault based on the nature of the relationship. The *Criminal Code* does not establish a different inquiry into consent depending on the relationship between the accused and the complainant. Their relationship may be evidence for both the *actus reus* and the *mens rea,* but it does not change the nature of the inquiry into whether the complainant consented, as conceived by the *Criminal Code*.

[65] In the end, we are left with this. Parliament has defined sexual assault as sexual touching without consent. It has dealt with consent in a way that makes it clear that ongoing, conscious and present consent to "the sexual activity in question" is required. This concept of consent produces just results in the vast majority of cases. It has proved of great value in combating the stereotypes that historically have surrounded consent to sexual relations and undermined the law's ability to address the crime of sexual assault. In some situations, the concept of consent Parliament has adopted may seem unrealistic. However, it is inappropriate for this Court to carve out exceptions when they undermine Parliament's choice. In the absence of a constitutional challenge, the appropriate body to alter the law on consent in relation to sexual assault is Parliament, should it deem this necessary.

IV. Summary

[66] The definition of consent for sexual assault requires the complainant to provide actual active consent throughout every phase of the sexual activity. It is not possible for an unconscious person to satisfy this requirement, even if she expresses her consent in advance. Any sexual activity with an individual who is incapable of consciously evaluating whether she is consenting is therefore not consensual within the meaning of the *Criminal Code*.

FISH J. (BINNIE and LEBEL JJ. concurring) (dissenting)

[68] It is a fundamental principle of the law governing sexual assault in Canada that no means "no" and only yes means "yes".

[69] K.D., the complainant in this case said yes, not no. She consented to her erotic asphyxiation by the respondent, J.A., her partner at the time. Their shared purpose was to render K.D. unconscious and to engage in sexual conduct while

she remained in that state. It is undisputed that K.D.'s consent was freely and voluntarily given — in advance and while the conduct was still in progress. Immediately afterward, K.D. had intercourse with J.A., again consensually.

[70] K.D. first complained to the police nearly two months later when J.A. threatened to seek sole custody of their two-year-old child. She later recanted.

[71] We are nonetheless urged by the Crown to find that the complainant's *yes in fact* means *no in law*. With respect for those who are of a different view, I would decline to do so.

[72] The provisions of the *Criminal Code*, R.S.C. 1985, c. C-46, regarding consent to sexual contact and the case law (including *R. v. Ewanchuk* [1999] 1 S.C.R. 330) relied on by the Crown were intended to protect women against abuse by others. Their mission is not to "protect" women *against themselves* by limiting their freedom to determine autonomously when and with whom they will engage in the sexual relations of their choice. Put differently, they aim to safeguard and enhance the sexual autonomy of women, and not to make choices for them.

[73] The Crown's position, if adopted by the Court, would achieve exactly the opposite result. It would deprive women of their freedom to engage by choice in sexual adventures that involve no proven harm to them or to others. That is what happened here.

[74] Adopting the Crown's position would also require us to find that cohabiting partners across Canada, including spouses, commit a sexual assault when either one of them, *even with express prior consent*, kisses or caresses the other while the latter is asleep. The absurdity of this consequence makes plain that it is the product of an unintended and unacceptable extension of the *Criminal Code* provisions upon which the Crown would cause this appeal to rest.

[75] Lest I be misunderstood to suggest otherwise, I agree that consent will be vitiated where the contemplated sexual activity involves a degree of bodily harm or risk of fatal injury that cannot be condoned under the common law, or on grounds of public policy. Asphyxiation to the point of unconsciousness may well rise to that level, but the contours of this limitation on consent have not been addressed by the parties. Nor has the matter been previously considered by the Court. For procedural reasons as well, the issue of bodily harm must be left for another day.

[76] I agree as well that prior consent affords no defence where it is later revoked or where the ensuing conduct does not comply with the consent given.

[77] Applying these principles here, I would dismiss the appeal.

[78] Finally, I think it helpful to set out succinctly the issue on this appeal.

[79] According to the Chief Justice, the question is "whether an unconscious person can qualify as consenting [to sexual activity]" (at para. 33). With respect, that is not the question at all: *No one* has suggested in this case that an unconscious person can validly consent to sexual activity.

[80] Rather, the question is whether a *conscious* person can freely and voluntarily consent in advance to agreed sexual activity that will occur while he or she is briefly and consensually rendered unconscious. My colleague would answer that question in the negative; I would answer that question in the affirmative, absent a clear prohibition in the *Criminal Code*, absent proven bodily harm that would vitiate consent at common law, and absent any evidence that the conscious partner subjected the unconscious partner to sexual activity beyond their agreement.

[81] In this case, J.A. engaged with K.D. in sexual activity to which K.D. freely consented while conscious. The Chief Justice would nonetheless convict J.A. of sexual assault, a serious crime. I oppose this result. In my respectful view, it is unwarranted as a matter of statutory interpretation, prior decisions of the Court, or considerations of policy. And it is wrong on the facts of this case.

[82] That is what divides us. The rest is commentary.

[95] The Chief Justice finds that Parliament has created a statutory exception to the well-established general principle that the complainant's genuine consent precludes a finding of sexual assault. In my colleague's view, the purpose and effect of this perceived exception is to vitiate consent to "unconscious sexual activity" — that is, sexual contact that is expected to occur while the consenting adult is asleep or unconscious. With respect, nothing in the *Criminal Code* indicates that Parliament has considered, let alone adopted, an exception of this sort.

[96] Section 273.1(1) of the *Code* defines consent for the purposes of the sexual assault provisions as "the voluntary agreement of the complainant to engage in the sexual activity in question". Nothing in this definition refers to the timing of consent or otherwise excludes advance consent to unconscious sexual contact. And it is important to remember that, on this appeal, neither the voluntariness nor the specificity of the complainant's consent is in issue before us.

[97] On the contrary, as the Court of Appeal found, there is no basis in the evidence to support a finding that the complainant did not freely and consciously consent to "the sexual activity in question": erotic asphyxiation involving anal penetration during the contemplated period of transitory unconsciousness, followed by vaginal intercourse.

[101] Section 273.1(2)(*b*) provides that "[n]o consent is obtained . . . where . . . the complainant is incapable of consenting to the activity". I agree that unconsciousness qualifies as "incapa[city]" within the meaning of this provision. But it is apparent from the ordinary meaning of the words used by Parliament and from their context that s. 273.1(2)(*b*) has no application here. It simply confirms that consent cannot be *obtained* from a person who is at the time incapable of consenting. It does not contemplate consent given in advance at a time when the complainant, as in this case, was *capable* — not *incapable* — of giving her free and knowing consent.

[102] Section 273.1(2)(*e*), the second exception invoked by the Crown, provides that no consent is obtained where "the complainant, having consented to engage in sexual activity, expresses, by words or conduct, a lack of agreement to continue to engage in the activity". The Crown submits, and the Chief Justice accepts, that this provision is inconsistent with the possibility of advance consent to unconscious sexual touching because Parliament intended people engaged in sexual activity to have the right to revoke consent at any time during the activity and "[a] person who has been rendered unconscious cannot revoke her consent" (reasons of the Chief Justice, at para. 40).

[103] I agree that prior consent to sexual activity can later be revoked. And I agree that a person cannot while unconscious consent or revoke consent. It hardly follows, in my respectful view, that consenting adults cannot, as a matter of law, willingly and consciously agree to engage in a sexual practice involving transitory unconsciousness — on the ground that, during the brief period of that consensually induced mental state, they will be unable to consent to doing what they have already consented to do.

[104] If anything, the wording of s. 273.1(2)(*e*) suggests that the complainant's consent *can* be given in advance, and remains operative unless and until it is subsequently revoked: It provides that "the complainant, having consented to engage in sexual activity", may later revoke his or her consent. I agree with the respondent that revocation is a question of fact. In this regard, I again mention that the complainant, upon regaining consciousness, did not revoke her prior consent to the sexual conduct in issue — which was then still ongoing. And it has not been suggested that she had earlier revoked her consent by words or conduct, or even in her own mind.

[105] With respect, there is no factual or legal basis for holding that K.D.'s prior consent, otherwise operative throughout, was temporarily rendered inoperative during the few minutes of her voluntary unconsciousness. In my view, it was not suspended by the fact that she had rendered herself incapable of revoking the consent she had chosen, freely and consciously, *not to revoke* either immediately before or immediately after the brief interval of her unconsciousness. Nothing in s. 273.1(2)(*e*) creates a legal requirement, or a

binding legal fiction, that warrants convicting the complainant's partner of sexual assault in these circumstances.

[106] Finally, the Chief Justice relies on s. 273.2(*b*), which precludes a defence of honest but mistaken belief in consent where "the accused did not take reasonable steps, in the circumstances known to the accused at the time, to ascertain that the complainant was consenting". The Chief Justice finds that, "by requiring the accused to take reasonable steps to ensure that the complainant 'was consenting', Parliament has indicated that the consent of the complainant must be an ongoing state of mind" (para. 42).

[107] With respect, I read s. 273.2 differently. It provides that a belief in consent is not a defence where "the accused believed that the complainant consented to the activity [in question]" and failed to take reasonable steps "to ascertain that the complainant was consenting". Any doubt whether "was consenting" and "consented" refer to prior consent is dispelled by the corresponding French text of the provision: "*Ne constitue pas un moyen de défense . . . le fait que l'accusé croyait que le plaignant avait consenti à l'activité à l'origine de l'accusation . . . [et] n'a pas pris les mesures raisonnables . . . pour s'assurer du consentement.*"

[108] Lest I be misunderstood in this regard, I hasten to add that K.D.'s prior consent to the "activity in question" constituted a valid consent only to the contemplated activity. In the absence of any evidence that J.A.'s conduct exceeded the scope of K.D.'s consent, I am unable to find in the mentioned provisions of the *Criminal Code* any basis for concluding that K.D.'s consent in fact was not a valid consent in law.

[In particular, the minority held that the right of women to make decisions about their bodies, and whether to engage in sexual activity, was better respected by allowing advance consent, not by forbidding it.]

IV

[110] First, the provisions in question were enacted to address policy concerns that are entirely different from those before us here. The preamble to Bill C-49 and the Parliamentary debates preceding its enactment demonstrate that the consent provisions were intended to protect women from sexual violence and to protect and enhance their freedom to choose when, and with whom, they will engage in sexual relations of their choice.

[111] The dominant theme throughout the debates was that women have "the right to make decisions about their bod[ies], including whether or not to engage in sexual activity" and that "[n]o in every conceivable circumstance means no" (*House of Commons Debates*, vol. VIII, 3rd Sess., 34th Parl., April 8, 1992, at p. 9507, and vol. IX, June 15, 1992, at p. 12045). Legislative changes were

required to ensure that a woman who previously said "yes" to sexual activity could subsequently say "no" and be taken seriously, first by her sexual partner and, failing that, by the police and the courts.

[112] These policy concerns are simply not engaged on the facts before us: *This is not a case about a woman who said no — at any time*. Rather, the complainant described herself as a willing and enthusiastic participant throughout all stages of the sexual activity in question. She consented to the sexual activity leading up to her unconsciousness and to the unconsciousness itself. The Court of Appeal found, as we have seen, that nothing in the record supports a finding that she did not consent to the sexual activity that occurred while she was unconscious.

[113] Moreover, we have no idea how long the anal penetration had gone on when she awoke — she may in fact have awoken as soon as it began — but we do know that she did not ask the accused to stop when she was awake and knew exactly what was going on.

[114] I am unable to conclude that Parliament, in protecting the right to say no, restricted the right of adults, female or male, consciously and willingly to say yes to sexual conduct in private that neither involves bodily harm nor exceeds the bounds of the consent freely given. The right to make decisions about one's own body clearly comprises both rights.

[115] Although this right to choose is not absolute, I agree that private, consensual sexual behaviour "should only give rise to criminal sanctions where there is a compelling principle of fundamental justice that constitutes a reasonable limit on the right to personal and sexual autonomy" (D. M. Tanovich, "Criminalizing Sex At The Margins" (2010), 74 C.R. (6th) 86 at p. 90.). I agree as well that "it would be a significant limit on the sexual autonomy of each individual to say that, as a matter of law, no-one can consent in advance to being sexually touched while asleep or unconscious" (Hamish Stewart, *Sexual Offences in Canadian Law* (loose-leaf), at p. 3-25.

[116] Respect for the privacy and sexual autonomy of consenting adults has long been embraced by Parliament as a fundamental social value and an overarching statutory objective: "Keeping the state out of the bedrooms of the nation" is a legislative policy, and not just a political slogan.

[117] The approach advocated by the Chief Justice would also result in the criminalization of a broad range of conduct that Parliament cannot have intended to capture in its definition of the offence of sexual assault. Notably, it would criminalize kissing or caressing a sleeping partner, however gently and affectionately. The absence of contemporaneous consent, and therefore the *actus reus*, would be conclusively established by accepted evidence that the complainant was asleep at the time. Prior consent, or even an explicit request

— "kiss me before you leave for work" — would not spare the accused from conviction....

[119] The Crown acknowledges that, on its view of the law, anyone who engages in amorous expressions of affection while his or her partner is asleep would be guilty of sexual assault. In response to the implausibility of the suggestion that Parliament intended to criminalize such conduct, the Crown has identified only two safeguards, more aptly characterized as palliatives that should give us little comfort: prosecutorial discretion and the doctrine of *de minimis non curat lex* (the law is not concerned with trifling matters).

[120] As for prosecutional discretion, I think it is sufficient to recall that this Court, in dealing with the delicate issue of nullifying consent at law, has in the past demonstrated a "healthy reluctance to endorse the exercise of prosecutorial discretion as a legitimate means of narrowing the applicability of a criminal section" (*R. v. Cuerrier*, [1998] 2 S.C.R. 371, at para. 136, *per* Cory J.). And Justice McLachlin (as she then was), in agreement on this point, made clear that "[p]rosecutorial deference cannot compensate for overextension of the criminal law; it merely replaces overbreadth and uncertainty at the judicial level with overbreadth and uncertainty at both the prosecutorial level and the judicial level" (para. 53).

[121] And, as for reliance on the *de minimis* doctrine, I do not view sexual assault of any kind as a trifling matter. It is a serious crime with serious consequences both for the complainant and for an accused. I agree with the Chief Justice (at para. 63) that "even mild non-consensual touching of a sexual nature can have profound implications for the complainant". For public policy reasons, the Ontario Court of Appeal has held that it would be inappropriate to apply this principle in the context of domestic assaults (*R. v. Carson* (2004), 185 C.C.C. (3d) 541, at para. 25).

[122] Finally, even if one accepts that s. 273.1(3) "authorizes the courts to identify additional cases in which no consent is obtained" (reasons of the Chief Justice, at para. 29), identifying a *new* exception in this case would go well beyond what *Jobidon* permits.

[127] Nor is the rejection of the defence of implied consent in *Ewanchuk* dispositive of the issue before us. We are not asked by the respondent to *infer* the complainant's consent. Her actual subjective consent w*as established through her own testimony. Ewanchuk* decided that if the complainant testifies that she did *not* subjectively consent — and she is believed — then the *actus reus* will be made out regardless of her outward conduct. That is not our case.

[128] As we shall presently see, this Court has stressed that consent should only be vitiated by judges in limited circumstances and on a case-by-case basis. The

broad nullification of consent now proposed by my colleague can hardly be said to have been decided in *Ewanchuk*, a case in which the possibility of advance consent to unconscious sexual touching was not even remotely in issue.

. . . .

V

[129] In *Jobidon*, this Court stressed that "[t]he law's willingness to vitiate consent on policy grounds is <u>significantly limited</u>" (at p. 766 (emphasis added)). As Gonthier J. took care to explain, the Court's decision in that case was narrowly restricted to situations in which adults intentionally apply force to each other during the course of a fist fight or brawl and serious hurt or non-trivial bodily harm is both intended and caused.

[130] Since *Jobidon* was decided, the vitiation of consent on grounds of public policy has been limited to situations in which actual bodily harm was both intended *and* caused. In *R. v. Paice*, 2005 SCC 22, [2005] 1 S.C.R. 339, the majority of the Court insisted that both constraints remain operative. To remove either requirement, the Court held, would risk the criminalization — "by judicial fiat" — of "numerous activities that were never intended by Parliament to come within the ambit of the assault provisions" (para. 12).

[131] The policy concerns identified by the Crown do not warrant the extension of the "significantly limited" principle invoked in *Jobidon* to a situation in which bodily harm was neither intended nor caused. As I have explained, the record before us does not permit us to revisit the issue of bodily harm addressed in the courts below. Our mandate is circumscribed by the question of law before us, which is whether unconsciousness *alone* is sufficient to nullify consent.

[145] For all of these reasons, I would affirm the judgment of the Court of Appeal and dismiss the present appeal to this Court.

With which position do you agree? Identify policy considerations favouring each side. Do you think that consent and mistaken belief principles in the *Criminal Code* and *Ewanchuk* should apply equally to cases where there was prior consensual sexual conduct? Do you think that the doctrine of *de minimis non curat lex* has any application to sexual assault cases? For markedly divergent views see Janine Benedet, "*J.A.*: Consent to Sexual Activity Cannot Be Irrevocable" (2011), 84 C.R. (6th) 35; Don Stuart, "*J.A.*: Asserting Dogma Over Reality" (2011), 84 C.R. (6th) 38; and Elaine Craig, "Capacity to Consent to Sexual Risk (2014) 17 New Criminal Law Review 103 (preferring an approach based on assessing risk rather than morality). For criticism of the Ontario Court of Appeal ruling see Hilary Young, "*R. v. A. (J.)* and the Risks of Advance Consent to Unconscious Sex", (2010) 14 Can. Crim. L. Rev. 253 but see the response by Joshua Sealy-Harrington, "Tied Hands? A Doctrinal and Policy Argument for the Validity of Advance Consent" (2014) 18 Can. Crim. L. Rev. 119.

Much of the debate in *J.A.* focuses around the possibility of the morally innocent being charged with sexual assault for kissing a sleeping spouse. The majority opinion seems to mean that such a person would in fact be guilty. On the one hand it seems counterintuitive that such behaviour should be criminal, but on the other hand it seems unlikely that any charges would ever be laid in such circumstances. **To what extent should the law worry about conceptual purity as opposed to crafting a law which is in fact applied fairly?**

For example, the decision in *Ewanchuk* was criticized on the grounds that it had the potential to criminalize the behaviour of morally innocent people who were engaged in typical sexual overtures. Elaine Craig, "Ten Years After *Ewanchuk* The Art of Seduction is Alive and Well: An Examination of the Mistaken Belief in Consent Defence" (2009) 13 Can. Crim. L. Rev. 3 has published a comprehensive review of reported and unreported mistaken belief decisions since *Ewanchuk*. She argues that situations of ambiguity arising from harmless sexual overtures do not in fact result in criminal charges: rather, a claim of mistaken belief in consent is most typically argued in cases where the complainant is unconscious and intoxicated.

> 'Ambiguity' arises in these cases not from a pubescent and gendered confusion over the complainant's (lack of) sexual interest but rather from a sleeping or barely conscious complainant who moans, rolls over or lifts her hips slightly while the accused is disrobing, fondling or penetrating her.

She suggests that the fear of over-criminalization has been misplaced and that, properly applied, *Ewanchuk* can reach fair results in cases of ambiguous communications. She applauds the courts for applying these principles to respect the sexual integrity of the intoxicated party-goer but suggests that they have not been properly applied to protect wives and girlfriends where consensual sexual acts have escalated and exceeded the initial consent.

A contrary view is that the judicial record suggests that *Ewanchuk* principles too often result in the mistaken belief issue having no air of reality to be considered by judge or jury. Especially where there was a prior sexual relationship, trial judges sometimes find the *Seaboyer* and *Ewanchuk* principles unjust and won't apply their full rigour. Where both accused and complainant were heavily intoxicated, *Charter* issues have not been resolved (see below).

PROBLEM

The complainant agreed to sexual activity with H, insisting that he use a condom in order to prevent conception. Unknown to her, H had poked holes in the condom hoping that she became pregnant, which she did. She ended the relationship, terminated the pregnancy and suffered complications for two weeks. H was charged with aggravated sexual assault. The trial judge found that the accused had not endangered the life of the complainant but that she had not consented to unprotected sex. He convicted H of sexual assault.

When the matter reached the Supreme Court, the Court of seven justices agreed that the accused had been properly convicted. Four justices (McLachlin C.J. and Cromwell J. with Rothstein and Wagner JJ. concurring) found guilt under s. 265(3)(c) of the *Criminal Code* as consent vitiated by fraud and resulting in serious deprivation. Three justices (Abella and Moldaver JJ. with Karakatsanis J. concurring) found guilt under s. 273.1 because of lack of consent to the sexual activity in question. Assuming you also favour conviction which cohort's solution do you prefer?

Compare *R. v. Hutchinson*, 2014 SCC 19, [2014] 1 S.C.R. 346, 308 C.C.C. (3d) 413, 8 C.R. (7th) 255 (see earlier under "Consent Making Act Lawful" for extracts from the judgments).

R v. BARTON

(2017), 38 C.R. (7th) 316, 2017 CarswellAlta 1167 (Alta. C.A.)

The accused was charged with first degree murder in the death of G. She was found dead in the bathtub in a hotel room occupied by the accused. She died from blood loss from a perforation of her vaginal wall.

The Crown's theory was that, on the evening of June 21, 2011, G was incapacitated because of a blood alcohol level of 340 milligrams per hundred millilitres of blood, more than four times the legal limit. The accused used a sharp object to cut G's vaginal wall. When G began to bleed heavily, B carried her to the bathroom and put her into the bathtub. Alternatively, the Crown argued that even if the jury had a reasonable doubt whether the accused cut G's vaginal wall with a sharp object, the accused was nevertheless still guilty of unlawful act manslaughter on the basis that he caused G's death in the course of a sexual assault.

The accused testified that he had sexual relations with G the night before on June 20, for which he had agreed to pay her $60 for "everything", which he defined as "intercourse, sex". This included forceful use of his fist. He did not testify as to any such conversation on June 21 and said only that he and G agreed to the same price and he believed she knew what she was coming for. On this occasion when he saw that she was bleeding he said he decided not to have intercourse and told her to wash up and leave. He denied carrying her to the bathtub. He found her lifeless in the bathtub when he woke in the morning. He admitted causing G's death but claimed this was an accident resulting from consensual sexual activity and should not result in criminal liability.

Expert evidence was divided about the nature and cause of the fatal wound B inflicted. The Crown's two experts said the perforation was a cut caused by a sharp instrument. The defence expert said the perforation was a laceration, not a cut, and it was the result of blunt force trauma.

A jury found him not guilty of first degree murder and not guilty of the lesser included offence of unlawful act manslaughter. The Crown appealed.

The Alberta Court of Appeal (Fraser C.J., Watson and Martin JJ.A.), after nine months of deliberation, issued a very lengthy judgment. The Court set aside the acquittals and ordered a new first degree murder trial.

The Court found that there had been multiple legal errors in the charge to the jury, many of them due to reliance on outdated pattern jury instructions.

Per curiam:

[5] We have . . . concluded the time has come to push the reset button for jury charges in this country for cases involving an alleged sexual assault. First, there exists an imperative need to align jury charges in use nationally with changes to the law on sexual assault adopted years ago. Key provisions in some jury charges have fossilized concepts Parliament sought to remove a quarter century ago. Second, there is a requirement to ensure that jury charges communicate the present law correctly and effectively to jurors – and to judges who often use jury charges for self-instruction on judge-alone trials. Third, despite efforts to thwart them, myths and stereotypes continue to stalk the halls of justice in cases involving sexual offences, enabled sometimes by inadequate jury charges. Fourth, these persistent presumptions and problematic jury charges reduce the entitlement of individuals to the equal recognition and protection of the law. This inequality falls most heavily on women since sexual assault has been, and continues to be, largely a gender-based crime. The vast majority of victims are female, and the vast majority of perpetrators male.

The Court proposed a number of model jury instructions dealing with the strict interpretation of the rape shield provision in s. 276, the meaning of consent and the limits to the mistaken belief defence imposed at common law and by the *Criminal Code*.

The Court also addressed the issue of prejudice that arose from the start of the trial with the complainant repeatedly referred to as a "Native prostitute";

Per curiam:

b. Calling Gladue a "Prostitute" and "Native Woman"

[116] The Crown, defence and trial judge all referred to Gladue as a "prostitute" in front of the jury at various points in the proceedings.

[117] The joint interveners, the Women's Legal Education and Action Fund and the Institute for the Advancement of Aboriginal Women, argued that the Crown's labelling of Gladue, in its opening statement, as a "prostitute" who had "struck a working relationship" with Barton was inadmissible sexual conduct evidence. They argued that s 276 creates a categorical prohibition on the admission of sexual history evidence to support one of the twin myths, regardless of which party seeks to introduce that evidence. They submitted that the trial judge did not ask the Crown to address the relevance, probative value or prejudicial effect of characterizing Gladue as a prostitute. Nor did the trial judge caution the jury as to the inferences it could – and could not – draw from that

characterization. Moreover, they contended that in the final instructions, the trial judge wrongly said a factor important to consent was that Gladue was a prostitute.

[118] The interveners also argued that these errors were compounded by the references to Gladue as a "Native girl" or "Native woman"; these were prejudicial both independently and in combination with calling her a prostitute. They asserted that the jurors were invited or permitted to draw the prohibited inference that because Gladue was presented as a "Native" prostitute, she was even more likely to have consented to the sexual activity that was the subject of the charge. In their view, because of widespread racial bias against Aboriginal people, specific and detailed instructions were required beyond the generic caution provided to ensure the jurors acted fairly and impartially.

[119] To those who would immediately say, "of course it is relevant that she was a prostitute", our answer is this. A decision that sexual conduct evidence is admissible requires compliance with s. 276. Parliament has called for a careful consideration of underlying assumptions according to a set of stated factors. Given the limits of s. 276 in its current form, it is open to an accused to apply to introduce evidence of a complainant's prostitution. This is so notwithstanding that, as early as *Seaboyer*, L'Heureux-Dubé J (in dissent but not on this point) observed that "[e]vidence of prior acts of prostitution or allegations of prostitution ... is never relevant and, besides its irrelevance, is hugely prejudicial." However, whether an accused will succeed in opening this generally prejudicial door is another question: *R v Nepinak* (2010), 82 CR (6th) 362; *R v Ingman* (2004), 246 Sask R 305; *R v Roper* (1997), 98 OAC 225, 32 OR (3d) 204 (CA).

[120] Section 276 was intended to replace quick conclusions based on false logic and discriminatory thinking about who consents, who tells the truth and what is relevant with a careful and structured analytical process designed to balance evidence in the search for the truth, notably by excluding misleading evidence in support of illegitimate inferences. Everyone in Canada, including sex trade workers, is entitled to that protection.

[121] To put this issue in context, the evidence is that on June 20, Barton asked a man in the parking lot, Steve, if he knew of any "lady friends" Barton could have sex with. Later that first evening, Steve introduced Gladue to Barton. According to Barton, he and Gladue discussed how much it would cost him. She asked for $100.00, and he negotiated the price down to $60. Barton said he agreed to pay this amount on both nights. On the second night when Barton and Atkins were in the hotel bar drinking with Gladue, Barton again met Steve. Steve was concerned that there were two of them, but Barton assured Steve that Gladue would only be with him. Barton told Steve not to worry, "you know me" and gave him $5. Later when walking back to his hotel room, Barton offered Atkins

"a piece" of Gladue. From that evidence, all that is known is that on two occasions, Gladue agreed to accept money for having sex with Barton.

[122] Expressly referring to Gladue as a prostitute conveyed that she was a female sex trade worker who made her living by routinely and habitually performing sexual activities for money. Prostitution is largely a gendered practice. Most prostitutes are female; most buyers are male. Calling someone a prostitute is a form of sexual conduct evidence caught by s. 276 if advanced by the defence, and governed by *Seaboyer* if advanced by the Crown. Since it is not evidence of a specific instance of sexual activity as required under s 276(2)(a), it is, by itself, inadmissible. It also amounts to evidence of sexual reputation which is separately prohibited under s 277, regardless of who seeks to tender it.

[123] This one word – prostitute – had the effect of ushering in Gladue's prior sexual conduct with all the others, real or imaginary, who may have paid her for sex. Gladue was referred to as a prostitute at least 25 times during the trial. Where a participant in sexual activity is a prostitute, a litany of unjust stereotypes about autonomy and consent persist in our society. That is so regardless of the label used to describe the person who sells sex for money. At the top of the list is that a prostitute will consent to anything for money. Linked to this is another improper belief, namely that once a prostitute has agreed to sell sex for money, the prostitute has given "implied consent" to any and all sexual acts to which the prostitute is then subjected. And perhaps worse yet, labelling someone a prostitute signals to the jurors that the prostitute is "deserving" of harm sustained on the job because prostitutes "choose" to engage in a risky profession: *Bedford*, *supra* at para 80.

[124] To compound this problem, the jurors were repeatedly told that Gladue was a "Native girl" or "Native woman". In particular, she was referred to as "Native" approximately 26 times throughout the trial by witnesses, defence counsel and Crown counsel. In one instance, the witness was directly asked to describe Gladue's ethnicity. In other circumstances, witnesses introduced and used the term "Native" or "Native woman" as a descriptor of Gladue and defence counsel, and Crown counsel continued to use that descriptor while questioning the witness.

[125] The defence argued there was no evidence before this Court to support the Interveners' submission that widespread racism against Aboriginal peoples was likely to negatively influence jurors. It suggested a commission of inquiry or parliamentary committee would be required to properly evaluate the Interveners' submission. We reject this argument.

[126] Courts in this country have long recognized that the potential for racial prejudice against visible minorities in the justice system is a notorious social

fact not capable of reasonable dispute: *R v Spence*, at para 5, [2005] 3 SCR 458 [*Spence*]. Jurors may consciously or subconsciously consider certain people less worthy and this bias can shape the information received during the trial to conform with the bias: see *R v Parks* (1993), 84 CCC (3d) 353 at 372 (Ont CA); *Spence* (inter-racial crime); *R v Find*, [2001] 1 SCR 863 (nature of the charges); and *R v Kokopenace*, [2015] 2 SCR 398 (representativeness in juries and impartiality). Hence, beginning almost two decades ago in *R v Williams*, [1998] 1 SCR 1128 [*Williams*], Canadian courts moved from a "hands-off" approach to the recognition that courts could, *and should*, take proactive steps to prevent racism from compromising trials.

[127] In this case, the trial judge ought to have addressed the repeated references to Gladue as a "Native" girl and "prostitute" to overcome the real risk of reasoning prejudice. And yet, the only caution given to this jury was this limited generic one typically offered in every jury trial:

> When examining the evidence, you must do so without sympathy or prejudice for or against anyone involved in these proceedings. That means you must now make good on your promise to put aside whatever biases or prejudices you may hold or feel. It also means that sympathy can have no place in your deliberations.

[128] This standard caution in the final instructions was not wrong in itself. But it was inadequate to counter the stigma and potential bias and prejudice that arose from the repeated references to Gladue as a "prostitute", "Native girl" and "Native woman". Those references implicitly invited the jury to bring to the fact-finding process discriminatory beliefs or biases about the sexual availability of Indigenous women and especially those who engage in sexual activity for payment. What was at play here, given the way in which the evidence unfolded, was the intersection of assumptions based on gender (woman), race (Aboriginal) and class (sex trade worker). We emphasize that we are not suggesting that counsel or the trial judge sought to insinuate improper thinking into the minds of this jury. Nevertheless, without a sufficient direction to the jury, the risk that this jury might simply have assumed that Barton's money bought Gladue's consent to whatever he wanted to do was very real, indeed inescapable. Add to this the likely risk that because Gladue was labelled a "Native" prostitute – who was significantly intoxicated – the jury would believe she was even more likely to have consented to whatever Barton did and was even less worthy of the law's protection. This is the very type of thinking that s 276 was introduced to eradicate.

[129] Prior consent to sexual activity is not a blanket authorization, or for that matter, any authorization, for future sexual activity. Decades ago, Parliament jettisoned the marital rape exception to rape and the idea that a wife was legally obliged to submit to sexual activity at the behest of her husband. Today, we recognize that each person's entitlement to human autonomy, especially in

sexual matters, is essential to the bodily integrity and security of that person. Our law does not abide discriminating against sex trade workers by depriving them of the rights accorded to every citizen in this country merely because they are sex trade workers. Juries need to understand this as a matter of law. Just as it is improper to impose "implied consent" to sexual activity on a spouse or person in an intimate relationship, a jury needs to be told that a sex trade worker does not give her "implied consent" to whatever sexual acts the client decides to do and still less to whatever degree of force the client inflicts upon her incidental to the sexual acts. Canadian law does not recognize "implied consent" to sexual activity, and this protection extends to everyone in our society.

[130] The jury charge here was further skewed by the trial judge's acting on a defence request to warn the jury that they could draw no negative inference *against Barton* for being the type of person who used prostitutes. That such a caution was requested and considered necessary clearly shows that the trial judge accepted the defence position that Gladue's being a prostitute would likely have a negative impact on the jury's thinking. The sting of this warning was that if Barton's actions were somehow viewed as discrediting Barton, it was because prostitutes, including Gladue, should be regarded as discreditable. That was the message left with this jury. It was false and prejudicial. To caution the jury on the stigma and potential prejudice only from the perspective of Barton's character and reputation did not counter the stigma and potential prejudice to Gladue's rights to equality and privacy and the state's interests in a fair trial from Gladue's being labelled a prostitute.

[131] One very real consequence of not conducting the analysis required under s. 276 is that the trial judge never addressed whether prostitution generally, or the alleged sexual activity between Gladue and Barton the prior night, was relevant to any issue in the trial. Nor did the trial judge address the further question whether the evidence had significant probative value that was not substantially outweighed by its prejudicial effect. Most important, had s 276 been followed, the trial judge would have been obligated to set out in the required ruling what use the jury could – and could not – make of the admissible evidence. The trial judge's failure to reflect on the scope of admissibility of this evidence may well have influenced other contents of his charge to the jury as well.

[132] Finally, even if it were determined that the commercial context of the sexual relationship between Barton and Gladue on the night she died was relevant for certain purposes, that would not require repeatedly labelling Gladue a prostitute, and still less a Native prostitute, any more than it would require labelling Barton a john.

For differing views on *Barton* see D. Stuart, "Barton: Assault Trials Must be

Fair Not Fixed" (2017), 38 C.R. (7th) 438 and Janine Benedet, "*Barton.* 'She knew what she was coming for'. Sexual Assault, Prostitution and the Meaning of Consent" (2017), 38 C.R. (7th) 445.

Two Views on the Acquittal of Jian Ghomeshi: (2016), 27 C.R. (7th) 17 (Ont. C.J.)

The accused was charged with the sexual assault of three women and with choking one of them. The accused was a popular radio host who met the complainants through his work. In each case, the complainants testified that they found the accused charming and attractive but that he attacked them physically as part of sexual gratification. C1 testified that the accused hit her in the head and pulled her hair. C2 and C3 testified that they were choked by the accused. The complainants came forward after a public appeal by police for victims of the accused, after media reports linking him to violent sexual misconduct with another woman from his place of employment.

Each complainant admitted in cross-examination that she had further contact or communication with the accused after the alleged offences, in many cases contradicting evidence that she had given in her testimony-in-chief. The contact included communications that were flirtatious or had sexual overtones. C3 also acknowledged a further sexual act with the accused after the alleged assault. C1 maintained the truth of certain details of the accused's car and of her appearance that had been conclusively disproven. C2 and C3 had extensive communications after the charges were laid in which they expressed a strong desire to see the accused punished and in which C2 indicated that the case would benefit her career as an actress. The accused did not testify.

The accused was acquitted on March 23, 2016.

Justice Horkins held that the evidence of each complainant failed to satisfy the standard of proof beyond a reasonable doubt. Each complainant had shown a willingness to disregard the truth and had not been completely honest with the court. Complainants 2 and 3 had worked together to tailor their evidence to further their deep animosity toward the accused. While Justice Horkins was not deciding whether the sexual assaults had in fact taken place, he could not accept the complainants' evidence because of their disregard for the importance of telling the truth.

JANINE BENEDET, GHOMESHI: TELLING THE WHOLE TRUTH MIGHT NOT HAVE CHANGED THE RESULT
(2017), 27 C.R. (7th) 47

Ghomeshi can be read as an unremarkable sexual assault case that does not raise any new issues of law and simply applies well-established principles of the presumption of innocence and the standard of proof beyond a reasonable doubt to the evidence of witnesses who were shown to be unreliable, selective and, in the case of two of them, communicating with each other to strategize how to "take down" the accused.

At another level, however, it cannot be ignored that the case has generated extensive public debate about whether sexual assault trials, as currently constructed, are fair to victims of sexual assault. The large number of victims who came forward publicly to report sexual violence and harassment by the accused left members of the public wondering how he could have been acquitted. The admonition by justice system participants that we should not try individuals by social media and instead leave it to the courts can seem unfair to laypersons when the judge can reach a verdict without having to decide if the sexual assaults actually took place.

While *Ghomeshi* is legally straightforward, and the acquittals entirely unsurprising given how the evidence unfolded, it does present an opportunity to consider other questions about how we try sexual assault cases. First, the decision raises the relevance of sexual activity or communications between the complainant and the accused after the event. If the complainants had been entirely forthcoming about these additional encounters, would this have been held against them anyway, not as going to their credibility generally but instead as making it less likely that the earlier encounters were non-consensual or violent? Is that why the accused saved some of this material for over a decade? Judges and juries may be unaware that some victims of sexual assault continue to date their assailant while they come to terms with what happened to them, in the hope of making things "normal". The evidence of the first complainant also raised questions about our assumptions regarding the way memory works after a traumatic event. Once again, there is a body of social science evidence that makes clear that we may splice details into the surrounding fabric of traumatic memories, so that we are sure that the yellow car we saw the accused driving months later was the one he was driving on the night of the assault. This does not mean that the traumatic event itself did not happen.

A second issue worth considering is how we deal with evidence of animosity by a complainant toward an accused. The communications between two of the complainants were problematic inasmuch as they could be read as one complainant dominating and directing the other in ways that may have affected her testimony. However, we should consider whether we treat animosity by sexual assault victims differently than we would for a victim of another crime. If the teller who is terrified by a bank robbery, or the pedestrian who is hit by a drunk driver, wants the court to lock the offender up and throw away the key, do we find this reaction suspicious or destructive of her credibility, or just one of the many reactions that someone who is harmed may legitimately display? It may be that this response is portrayed as vindictiveness only in the context of women who accuse men of sexual assault.

It is important that the criminal process for sexual assault charges provides the accused with a fair trial in accordance with the presumption of innocence and the right to remain silent. It is also important that we not draw conclusions or make assumptions about sexual assault complainants that are not visited on other witnesses or that are rooted in flawed "common sense" that may not accord with reality.

DON STUART, GHOMESHI: DANGERS IN OVERREACTING TO THIS HIGH-PROFILE ACQUITTAL
(2017), 27 C.R. (7th) 45

Much of the public reaction in the media to this high-profile acquittal in *R. v. Ghomeshi* has been negative. Major concerns include that the decision will further discourage victims from reporting sexual assaults to the police and prosecutors, that it was outrageous that the accused did not testify and face cross-examination, that the complainants were vilified in cross-examination, and that "survivors must be believed".[48]

It is unfortunate that few recognized the reality that "he said/ she said" sexual assault trials in our courts are very rarely resolved with the accused exercising the right to remain silent. Of course the key to understanding this case, as carefully pointed out by the trial judge, Justice Horkins, is that all three complainants chose not to disclose their subsequent relationships with the accused until just before the trial. The trial judge understandably concluded that this made it impossible to determine the truth given their prior denial of any subsequent relationship with the accused. There was also a major problem of collusion amongst the complainants.

Commendably few critics are calling for the reversal of the burden on the Crown to prove guilt beyond a reasonable doubt. Our criminal justice system is proudly based on the presumption of innocence and a rigorous process of trying to determine the truth through cross-examination.

Some have called for complainants to have separate legal representation independent of the Crown. The irony here is that each of the three complainants did have separate legal representation. Those lawyers may have failed their clients in not advising them to tell the whole truth and to hold nothing back. Don't blame the Crown Attorney. He was caught completely off guard by the complainants' failure to give timely disclosure of information highly pertinent to a full and fair assessment of their credibility.

Some are now calling for a tougher rape law protection to ensure that post-charge conduct of the complainant is automatically inadmissible. If such a rule had been in place in this trial the accused would surely have had an unfair trial. Our rape shield laws are already amongst the toughest in the Western legal

---

48 In *R. v. Nyznik*, 2017 ONSC 4392 the trial judge acquitted three Toronto police officers charged with sexual assault. In the course of a lengthy judgment finding reasonable doubt on the issue of consent Justice Molloy said

> Although the slogan "Believe the victim" has become popularized of late, it has no place in a criminal trial. To approach a trial with the assumption that the complainant is telling the truth is the equivalent of imposing a presumption of guilt on the person accused of sexual assault and then placing a burden on him to prove his innocence. That is antithetical to the fundamental principles of justice enshrined in our constitution and the values underlying our free and democratic society. [para. 17].

systems especially in their application not only to sexual conduct with others but also sexual conduct *with the accused*. In this respect Canada's approach was expressly rejected by the Law Lords in *R. v. A.*, [2001] 2 W.L.R. 1546 (U.K. H.L.).

Some suggest a greater resort to civil actions for sexual assault because of the lower burden of proof on a balance of probabilities. That is true but the difference can be exaggerated. According to the Supreme Court in *C. (R.) v. McDougall*, (*sub nom.* F.H. v. McDougall) [2008] 3 S.C.R. 41, 61 C.R. (6th) 1 that standard is one that does not change commensurate with the circumstances but the evidence must "always be sufficiently clear, convincing and cogent". There are also systemic issues with the civil process. Yes the accused would have no right to silence and would be forced to testify and be cross-examined. However plaintiffs are also much less protected with no applicable rape shield or *Charter* rights to limit cross-examination. Furthermore access to justice issues in the form of high costs would only allow a plaintiff with deep financial resources to sue and a plaintiff would only recover adequate compensation if the defendant were able to pay the damage award. Money awards rather than just punishment such as jail would likely often provide little or insufficient satisfaction to victims.

Some pin hopes on a "restorative justice" process. This concept is notoriously difficult to define. Advocates often have quite different aims in mind. In any event it is hard to imagine that effective reconciliation in any form between accused and victims could be contemplated or achieved unless the accused fully confesses without being coerced to do so.

On June 15, 2017, the government introduced Bill C-51, which will make a number of changes to the sexual assault provisions in the *Criminal Code*. The Backgrounder to the Bill explains the intended changes:

> In keeping with the Government's commitment to ensure that victims of sexual assault and gender-based violence are treated with the utmost compassion and respect, this legislation would make several amendments to clarify and strengthen the sexual assault provisions in the *Criminal Code*. Some of these proposed amendments reflect Supreme Court of Canada decisions and would address some misapplications of the current law. More specifically, the legislation would:
>
> - Amend section 273.1 to clarify that an unconscious person is incapable of consenting, which reflects the Supreme Court of Canada's decision in *R v J.A* (2011).
> - Amend section 273.2 to clarify that the defence of mistaken belief in consent is not available if the mistake is based on a mistake of law – for example, if the accused believed that the complainant's failure to resist or protest meant that the complainant consented. This would codify aspects of the Supreme Court of Canada's decision in *R v Ewanchuk* (1999).
> - Expand the "rape shield" provisions to include communications of a sexual nature or communications for a sexual purpose. These provisions provide that evidence of a complainant's prior sexual history cannot be used to support an inference that the complainant was more likely to have consented to the sexual activity at issue, or that the complainant is less worthy of belief (referred to as the "twin myths").

- Provide that a complainant has a right to legal representation in rape shield proceedings.
- Create a regime to determine whether an accused can introduce a complainant's private records at trial that are in their possession. This would complement the existing regime governing an accused's ability to obtain a complainant's private records when those records are in the hands of a third party.

Some of these changes are, as indicated, intended to codify rules that had already become part of the common law, though one might question whether they are successful in doing so. For example the Bill will amend s. 273.1(2) to say:

No consent is obtained . . . where (a.1) the complainant is unconscious.

This is presented as having been decided in *A. (J.)*, which is arguably inaccurate. There was no question that a person who "is unconscious" cannot give consent: *A. (J.)* addressed whether a conscious person could give consent that would operate after she became unconscious.

Other parts of the Bill create new rules, and might have been motivated by the *Ghomeshi* trial and similar ones. For example, there is a statutory scheme governing applications by an accused to obtain private records relating to the complainant (see ss. 278.1*ff*), but that scheme had been found not to apply to records that were already in the hands of the accused (see *R. v. Shearing*, 2002 SCC 58, [2002] 3 S.C.R. 33, 165 C.C.C. (3d) 225, 2 C.R. (6th) 213). In the *Ghomeshi* trial (as in many others) part of the evidence introduced on behalf of the accused included communications from complainants to the accused after the alleged incident. Those communications were introduced by the accused in an attempt to show doubt about the complainants' version of events, and in particular about their mental state at the time. Under Bill C-51, such communications in the possession or control of the accused made before or after the alleged assault will not be automatically admissible. Rather, an accused must apply to the judge to introduce them, and the complainant is entitled both to take part in that hearing and to be represented by counsel. Admissibility will be determined in a special hearing essentially governed by rape shield principles.

5.   *CHARTER* ARGUMENTS

After *Creighton*, challenges based on assertion of a constitutional requirement of fault now seem far less likely to succeed. There would nevertheless appear to be at least four possible *Charter* challenges to Bill C-49's substantive regime. Of course, given the seriousness of the problem of sexual violence, if any of these challenges were accepted the Court might well wish to consider saving Parliament's scheme as a demonstrably justified reasonable limit under s. 1.

(1) Section 273.2's exclusion of any intoxication defence imposes absolute liability which threatens the liberty interest.

It is quite clear that any penal law that imposes absolute liability will violate s. 7 of the *Charter* and be declared of no force and effect where there is a potential deprivation of the liberty interest. Absolute liability occurs where a conviction can be based on mere proof of the act without any necessity to prove any form of fault on the part of the accused. Absolute liability seems to occur where the extreme drunkenness of the accused is said to be irrelevant but that of the victim determinative. Such a challenge succeeded in the controversial decision of the Supreme Court in *Daviault*, considered later under the defence of intoxication.

(2) Sexual assault is one of those few offences requiring a minimum degree of mens rea in the form of subjective foresight.

The Supreme Court has identified a few offences which have a constitutional requirement of subjective foresight. It placed considerable emphasis on the special nature of the stigma attached and the penalties available. Thus far the list of offences is short. The criterion of stigma has been often criticized as an inadequate and unreliable test but if it remains the discriminating factor, is sexual assault an offence calling for such special treatment?

(3) The duty to take reasonable steps in s. 273.2 is an objective standard which is unconstitutional because the legislation does not require a marked departure from the objective norm.

This argument flows from *Creighton* and *Beatty*. Of course, the offence could be read down as requiring the marked departure standard. There could also be a strong argument that one engaging in sexual conduct without taking reasonable steps to ascertain whether there was consent has necessarily markedly departed from the expected norm. Furthermore, the section refers to "in the circumstances known to the accused at the time" and this would appear to allow for some individual factors and thus be a less severe objective standard than that imposed by the majority in *Creighton*.

(4) Section 273.2 is unconstitutional because it violates the constitutional principle that those causing harm intentionally must be punished more severely than those causing harm unintentionally.

This principle, acknowledged and applied in *Creighton*, is sound and should be boldly asserted by all judges. In *Creighton*, the flexible penalty for manslaughter was held to satisfy the *Charter* requirement. This suggests that the new sexual assault scheme will also survive. However, there may be a difference. While the maximum penalty for sexual assault remains the same, Parliament has criminalized, in the same prohibition carrying the same penalty, one who is deliberately aware of a risk and one who was acting unreasonably. The new sexual assault scheme could be struck down or at least read down to ensure that these fundamental principles are respected. The key determination of whether the actor was deliberate or negligent should be made at trial and not left to the uncertain exercise of sentencing.

Do you think that any of these *Charter* arguments should succeed?

Prior to *Ewanchuk,* the Ontario Court of Appeal interpreted s. 273.2(b) and held it to be constitutional:

R. v. DARRACH

(1998), 122 C.C.C. (3d) 225, 13 C.R. (5th) 283, 1998 CarswellOnt 684 (Ont. C.A.), affirmed [2000] 2 S.C.R. 443, 36 C.R. (5th) 223, 148 C.C.C. (3d) 97, 2000 CarswellOnt 3321, 2000 CarswellOnt 3322

MORDEN A.C.J.O. (OSBORNE and DOHERTY JJ.A. concurring): —

With respect to the challenge [to s. 273.2(b)] based on s. 7, I am far from satisfied that sexual assault is one of those "very few" offences (*R. v. Vaillancourt,* [1987] 2 S.C.R. 636 (S.C.C.), at 653) which carries such a stigma that its *mens rea* component must be one of subjectivity. See Hogg, *Constitutional Law of Canada* (1992), loose-leaf ed., Vol. 2 at pp. 44-34 to 44-35. I say this because: it is an offence of general intent; it can be prosecuted by way of summary conviction; it is a generic offence which covers a broad range of conduct, some of which may be very minor compared to other offences; there is no minimum penalty, the maximum penalty is 10 years, and within this range the sentence can be tailored to reflect the moral opprobrium of both the offence and the offender. See *R. v. Creighton,* [1993] 3 S.C.R. 3 (S.C.C.), particularly at pp. 48-49, with respect to the offence of manslaughter. Further, I accept that the stigma characterization has been fairly criticized as being a most unstable one for making important constitutional decisions on the applicability of s. 7 of the *Charter* to the substantive elements of offences. See, for example, Hogg, *Constitutional Law of Canada* (1992) loose-leaf ed., at p. 44-35 and Stuart, *Charter Justice in Canadian Criminal Law,* 2nd ed. (1996) at p. 74.

Notwithstanding the foregoing reservations, I am prepared to decide this issue on the basis that the offence of sexual assault carries with it a sufficient social stigma as to require a subjective fault requirement on the part of the accused person. In my view, notwithstanding s. 273.2(b), the offence is still largely one based on subjective fault — at least to a level that would satisfy constitutional requirements.

No doubt, the provision can be regarded as introducing an objective component into the mental element of the offence but it is one which, in itself, is a modified one. It is personalized according to the subjective awareness of the accused at the time. The accused is to "take reasonable steps, *in the circumstances known to the accused at the time,* to ascertain that the complainant was consenting". In other words, the accused is not under an obligation to determine all the relevant circumstances — the issue is what he actually knew, not what he ought to have known.

In addition, while the provision requires reasonable steps, it does not require that *all* reasonable steps be taken, as it did in the first version of the bill (Bill

C-49, s. 1) that resulted in s. 273.2 and as does s. 150.1(4) of the *Criminal Code*, which is referred to in the judgment of the Supreme Court of Canada in *R. v. Nguyen*, [1990] 2 S.C.R. 906 (S.C.C.) at 922 and 925. Clearly, "all reasonable steps" imposes a more onerous burden than that in s. 273.2(b). I, of course, do not intend to express any view on the constitutionality of s. 150.1(4).

The subjective *mens rea* component of the offence remains largely intact. The provision does not require that a mistaken belief in consent must be reasonable in order to exculpate. The provision merely requires that a person about to engage in sexual activity take "reasonable steps . . . to ascertain that the complainant was consenting." Were a person to take reasonable steps, and nonetheless make an unreasonable mistake about the presence of consent, he or she would be entitled to ask the trier of fact to acquit on this basis.

The extent to which the provision alters principles of liability underlying the offence of sexual assault is indicated in the reasons of McLachlin J. in *R. v. Esau* (1997), 116 C.C.C. (3d) 289 (S.C.C.) at 314. Although the statement is in a dissenting judgment I do not think that there is any proposition in the majority judgment of Major J. at variance with it. McLachlin J. said:

> A person is not entitled to take ambiguity as the equivalent of consent. If a person, acting honestly and without wilful blindness, perceives his companion's conduct as ambiguous or unclear, his duty is to abstain or obtain clarification on the issue of consent. This appears to be the rule at common law. In this situation, to use the words of Lord Cross of Chelsea in *Morgan, supra*, [[1976] A.C. 182] at p. 203, "it is only fair to the woman and not in the least unfair to the man that he should be under a duty to take reasonable care to ascertain that she is consenting to the intercourse and be at risk of a prosecution if he fails to take such care". As Glanville Williams, *Textbook of Criminal Law* (London: Stevens & Sons, 1978), at p. 101, put it: "the defendant is guilty if he realized the woman might not be consenting and took no steps to find out".

Following this quotation, she said at pp. 314-15:

> I note that Parliament has affirmed this common sense proposition in enacting s. 273.2 of the *Criminal Code* of Canada which states that "[i]t is not a defence to a charge [of sexual assault] that the accused believed that the complainant consented to the activity that forms the subject-matter of the charge, where . . . the accused did not take reasonable steps, in the circumstances known to the accused at the time, to ascertain that the complainant was consenting". See also *R. v. Darrach* (1994), 17 O.R. (3d) 481 (Prov. Div.) [the judgment under appeal before this court]. The question is whether the defendant at bar, properly attentive to the issue of consent (i.e., not wilfully blind), could have, in light of the ambiguity, honestly concluded that the complainant had the capacity and was consenting to the sexual activity.

Finally, having regard to the basic rationale underlying constitutionally mandated fault requirements that it is wrong to punish a person who is "morally innocent" (*Reference re s. 94(2) of the Motor Vehicle Act (British Columbia)* (1985), 23 C.C.C. (3d) 289 (S.C.C.) at 311), it is difficult to contemplate that a man who has sexual intercourse with a woman who has not consented is morally innocent if he has not taken reasonable steps to ascertain that she was consenting.

. . . .

This *Charter* issue was not brought before the Supreme Court of Canada when the decision was appealed.

In its controversial decision in *R. v. O'Connor* (1995), 44 C.R. (4th) 1, 103 C.C.C. (3d) 1, [1995] 4 S.C.R. 411, respecting defence access to medical records of sexual assault complaints, the Court unanimously decided that the right of the accused to full answer and defence should be weighed against the privacy rights of complainants which were constitutionally protected under ss. 7 and 8 of the *Charter*. However, a 5-4 majority refused to recognize s. 15 equality rights for such complainants. Parliament, in Bill C-49, and in Bill C-72 in response to *Daviault*, see later, and in its bill in response to *O'Connor* which introduced ss. 276.1-278.91 into the *Criminal Code*, invokes in aid in preambles, equality rights of women and children.

Recognition of equality rights for sexual assault complainants came with a revised composition of the Court in *Mills*, [1999] 3 S.C.R. 668, 28 C.R. (5th) 207, 139 C.C.C. (3d) 321 (S.C.C.). When it came to establish a s. 15 right to equality, the Court proceeded by mere assertion. Particularly stunning is the lack of any reference to the ten-part test for judging s. 15 claims established in *Law v. Canada (Minister of Human Resources Development)*, [1999] 1 S.C.R. 497 (S.C.C.), by Justice Iacobucci J. for a unanimous court, only a few month earlier. The Court in *Law* set out to describe basic principles under which courts are to analyze claims of discrimination under s. 15. The essence of the *Law* test is that there is in fact no *Charter* guarantee of equality *per se*. The guarantee is against discrimination within the meaning of s. 15. This is set out in part 3 of *Law* as follows:

> (3) Accordingly, a court that is called upon to determine a discrimination claim under s. 15(1) should make the following three broad inquiries:
>
> A. Does the impugned law (a) draw a formal distinction between the claimant and others on the basis of one or more personal characteristics, or (b) fail to take into account the claimant's already disadvantaged position within Canadian society resulting in substantively differential treatment between the claimant and others on the basis of one or more personal characteristics?
>
> B. Is the claimant subject to differential treatment based on one or more enumerated and analogous grounds?
>
> and
>
> C. Does the differential treatment discriminate, by imposing a burden upon or withholding a benefit from the claimant in a manner which reflects the stereotypical application of presumed group or personal characteristics, or which otherwise has the effect of perpetuating or promoting the view that the individual is less capable or worthy of recognition or value as a human being or as a member of Canadian society, equally deserving of concern, respect, and consideration? (para. 88).

The Court in *Law* also requires careful identification of "one or more relevant comparators", discrimination on an enumerated or analogous ground and a consideration of context. Why, then, did the Court in *Mills* not apply any of this careful analysis? In *Law*, Iacobucci J. did indicate that they were guidelines for analysis and not to be interpreted as a rigid test. He certainly didn't suggest they could be ignored. It would clearly be an error of law for lower courts to do so. Is the comparator group in *Mills* all other victims of crime or is it male victims of sexual assault? It surely couldn't be the accused given that the context is a criminal trial where the issue is punishment rather than compensation. Is the violation discrimination by gender or age or is it an analogous ground because complainants in sexual assault cases have been discriminated against through myths and stereotypical views?

The implications of an enforceable s. 15 claim for complainants in sexual assault cases is left unexplored. The policy issues are far wider than establishing rights for protection of therapeutic and other records of complainants. Can complainants now seek status to be represented throughout a sexual assault trial? How about rights to cross-examine the accused, to challenge the similar fact evidence rule or to reverse the presumption of innocence?

See, further, Stuart, *Charter Justice in Canadian Criminal Law* (6th ed., 2014) Chapters 1 and 10.

In *R. v. Shearing* (2002), 2 C.R. (6th) 213 (S.C.C.), a case involving multiple sexual offence charges, the defence counsel had been given the diary of one of the complainants. The trial judge allowed him to cross-examine on the inconsistencies between that document and her present testimony. The trial judge, however, refused to permit cross-examination on the failure by the complainant to mention anything about sexual abuse by the accused. When the matter reached the Supreme Court, a 7-2 majority ordered a new trial to allow such cross-examination. Binnie J., writing for the majority, saw the issue as one of the right to cross-examine rather than production. *Seaboyer* was the controlling authority. The majority also speaks of equality "interests" rather than equality rights. L'Heureux-Dubé J. (Gonthier J. concurring) dissented on the basis that the defence should hand back the diary and seek production under the *Criminal Code* provisions. She also considered that the majority had wrongly returned to the doctrine of recent complaint. For a comment on *Shearing* see Stuart, "*Shearing*: Admitting Similar Fact Evidence and Re-asserting the Priority of Rights of Accused in Sexual Assault Trials" (2002), 2 C.R. (6th) 268.

In *R. v. Kapp*, 2008 SCC 41, 58 C.R. (6th) 1 (S.C.C.), a decision on the affirmative action clause s. 15(2), the Court was unanimous in backing away from the *Law* tests. Chief Justice McLachlin and Justice Abella, speaking for the Court, re-emphasized its approach in *Andrews v. Law Society of British Columbia*, [1989] 1 S.C.R. 143. In particular the Court now holds that dignity of the person is no longer a test of discrimination and that the *Law* factors need not be slavishly followed. The Court cites but does not analyze numerous scholarly criticisms of the *Law* test, which in general suggest that the approach in *Law* was too complicated, too confusing and made s. 15 claims much harder to establish. The exact significance of the court's retreat remains to be seen in future cases but its promise of a new and simpler path will likely be widely applauded.

That the Court remains divided in their approach to s. 15 is clear from the Court's decision in *Quebec (Attorney General) v. A.*, [2013] 1 S.C.R. 61. The Court was asked to consider the constitutionality of several spousal support and property division provisions in the *Civil Code of Quebec,* which provide protection to spouses in formal unions but not to *de facto* spouses (the Quebec equivalent of common-law spouses). A former *de facto* spouse for ten years sued for alimony and child support to claim a portion of her former partner's fortune as the billionaire founder of Cirque du Soleil. In a 5-4 split the Court found that the provisions did discriminate contrary to s. 15 on the grounds of marital status. Justice Abella wrote for the majority (McLachlin C.J.C., and Deschamps, Cromwell and Karakatsanis JJ. concurring) and Justice LeBel dissented, joined by Fish, Rothstein and Moldaver JJ. However, McLachlin C.J.C. found that the infringement was a reasonable limit prescribed by law that could be demonstrably justified in a free and democratic society under s. 1 of the *Charter.* She saw the object of the Quebec legislature as promoting choice and autonomy. This tipped the balance, and in the result a differently composed 5-4 majority found the provisions concerning the partition of property constitutionally valid. This decision gives little protection to the 31.5 percent of Quebeckers who are living in *de facto* spousal relationships (Sue Montgomery, "Eric v. Lola", *Gazette Justice Reporter,* January 25, 2013, quoting 2011 statistics) and less protection than similarly situated common-law spouses in other provinces.

Despite the ultimate result of the case, Justice Abella's judgment in *A* remains the controlling test for discrimination under s. 15(1). Her judgment for the majority on s. 15(1) cautions against requiring s. 15 claimants to prove that a distinction will perpetuate prejudicial or stereotypical attitudes towards them. "What is relevant is not the *attitudinal* progress towards [the claimant], but the continuation of their discriminatory *treatment.*"

LeBel J., writing for the minority on s. 15(1) and in the majority in result, disagrees. Instead, he argues that in stressing the importance of the perpetuation of prejudice and stereotyping in *Kapp* and later cases, the Court made them crucial to the identification of discrimination and to the application of the analytical framework for s. 15(1).

6.   OTHER SUBSTANTIVE OPTIONS

Would it have been preferable for Parliament to have created a separate offence of negligent sexual assault penalizing unreasonable behaviour in a sexual context with a maximum penalty of five years' imprisonment? Would the possibility of guilty pleas to this lesser offence be an advantage? Should the distinction between deliberate and negligent conduct be left to sentencing? Should it make a difference?

For the case for a separate negligent sexual assault offence see Stuart, "Sexual Assault Substantive Issues Before and After Bill C-49" (1993) 35 Crim. L.Q. 1. and Helen Power, "Towards a Redefinition of the Mens Rea of Rape" (2003) 23 Oxford J. Legal Stud. 381.

Some commentators express concern that placing rape in the same category as sexual touching, including an unwanted kiss, has trivialized rape. Some view rape as more than a crime of violence:

CATHERINE MCKINNON, FEMINISM, MARXISM AND THE STATE: TOWARDS FEMINIST JURISPRUDENCE

(1983), 8 Signs: Journal of Women in Culture and Society 635 at 646-647

Feminists have reconceived rape as central to women's condition in two ways. Some see rape as an act of violence, not sexuality, the threat of which intimidates all women. Others see rape, including its violence, as an expression of male sexuality, the social imperatives of which define all women. . . . The more feminist view to me, one which derives from victims' experiences, sees sexuality as a social sphere of male power of which forced sex is paradigmatic. Rape is not less sexual for being violent: to the extent that coercion has become integral to male sexuality, rape may be sexual to the degree that, and because, it is violent.

The point of defining rape as "violence not sex" or "violence against women" has been to separate sexuality from gender in order to affirm sex (heterosexuality) while rejecting violence (rape). The problem remains what it has always been: telling the difference. The convergence of sexuality with violence, long used at law to deny the reality of women's violation, is recognized by rape survivors, with a difference: where the legal system has seen the intercourse in rape, victims see the rape in intercourse. The uncoerced context for sexual expression becomes as elusive as the physical acts come to feel indistinguishable. Instead of asking, what is the violation of rape, what if we ask, what is the nonviolation of intercourse? To tell what is wrong with rape, explain what is right about sex. If this, in turn, is difficult, the difficulty is as instructive as the difficulty men have in telling the difference when women see one. Perhaps the wrong of rape has proven so difficult to articulate because the unquestionable starting point has been that rape is definable as distinct from intercourse, when for women it is difficult to distinguish them under conditions of male domination.

KATIE ROIPHE, RAPE HYPE BETRAYS FEMINISM

New York Times Magazine, June 13, 1993

People have asked me if I have ever been date-raped. And thinking back on complicated nights, on too many glasses of wine, on strange and familiar beds, I would have to say yes. With such a sweeping definition of rape, I wonder how many people there are, male or female, who haven't been date-raped at one point or another. People pressure and manipulate and cajole each other into all sorts of things all of the time.

With their expansive version of rape, rape-crisis feminists are inventing a kinder, gentler sexuality. Beneath the broad definition of rape, these feminists are endorsing their own utopian vision of sexual relations: sex without struggle, sex without power, sex without persuasion, sex without pursuit. If verbal coercion constitutes rape, then the word rape itself expands to include any kind of sex a woman experiences as negative.

Experience since 1983 suggests that rape prosecutions are now routinely prosecuted at the lowest level of sexual assault, as sexual assault *simpliciter*. The problem is that the second category under s. 272 requires proof of bodily harm, a threat or the use of a weapon. This may be difficult to prove in many acquaintance-rape situations where there may be no physical injury such as bruises.

In *B. (W.P.)* (1992), 13 C.R. (4th) 281 (Ont. Prov. Ct.), Judge Cole decided on his own motion to commit an accused charged with sexual assault *simpliciter* to trial on the more serious offence of sexual assault causing bodily harm. He utilized the ruling in *R. v. McCraw*, [1991] 3 S.C.R. 72, where the Supreme Court of Canada interpreted bodily harm to include psychological injury. Judge Cole recognizes that *McCraw* was reached in the different context of s. 264.1(1)(a), involving the crime of threatening serious bodily harm, but holds that the Supreme Court clearly intended to make a general pronouncement.

There would appear to be dangers in the approach of Judge Cole. He holds that judges at preliminary inquiries and at trial must be satisfied that there is evidence of psychological harm and that it is non-trivial. This may well have the indirect effect of compelling victims to testify as to the consequences of the assault and to be submitted to cross-examination as to the extent of injury. In this sense, the victim will be back on trial once again. Another problem is that it is difficult to see how any form of sexual assault will not involve at least some psychological harm. If this is true, sexual assault *simpliciter* will have ceased to exist by judicial fiat.

Should any form of attempted penetration of any orifice become a new category placed in the second level of sexual assault, where the maximum penalty is raised from 10 to 14 years? What shall the offence be called?

The amendment would emphasize the seriousness of all rapes and make it unnecessary and indeed irrelevant to hear evidence as to the consequences for the victim. If rapists were again singled out for special legal treatment it would be much easier to track and assess responses to rape. At present rape statistics are not separated from those for other types of sexual assault.

From the point of view of accused it seems unjust that anyone convicted of sexual assault is automatically put on the sexual offender registry. A sexual assault conviction for an unwanted kiss of a girl under 16 could also now result in a mandatory jail sentence. The Registry entry will not indicate the less serious nature of the sexual offence.

Chapter 5

MISTAKE

1. MISTAKE OF FACT

(a) General Principles

On the issue of whether a mistake of fact is a defence, *Pappajohn v. R.* (see previous chapter) is still the leading decision. Chief Justice Dickson there decided for the majority that a mistake of fact defence constitutes a denial that the Crown has proved the fault element. It follows that, in the absence of statutory wording to the contrary:

1. Where there is a subjective *mens rea* requirement the mistake need merely be honestly held with reasonableness only relevant to assessment of credibility;
2. Where the fault element requires objective negligence, the mistake must be both honest and reasonable;
3. Where there is a due diligence defence, the mistake must be both honest and reasonable, with an onus of proof on the accused in the case of regulatory offences; and
4. Where the offence is one of absolute liability, mistake of fact is not a defence.

(b) *Charter* Standards

The fourth situation may raise a constitutional challenge.

Until repealed in 1988 it was an offence, often known as statutory rape, to have sexual intercourse with a girl under 14 even if she consented or, indeed, even if she was the initiating partner. The provision was as follows:

> 146. (1) Every male person who has sexual intercourse with a female person who
>   (*a*) is not his wife, and
>   (*b*) is under the age of 14 years,
> whether or not he believes that she is 14 years of age or more, is guilty of an indictable offence and is liable to imprisonment for life. [am. 1972, c. 13, s. 70]

The express exclusion of the defence of mistake as to age of the victim was challenged under s. 7 of the *Charter*.

R. v. HESS; R. v. NGUYEN

[1990] 2 S.C.R. 906, 79 C.R. (3d) 332, 59 C.C.C. (3d) 161,
1990 CarswellMan 223, 1990 CarswellMan 437

H and N were both charged with sexual intercourse with a female person under the age of 14 under what was then s. 146(1) of the *Criminal Code* (since repealed). In the case of H, the trial judge quashed the indictment on the ground that s. 146(1) violated s. 15 of the *Charter*. The Ontario Court of Appeal reversed the decision and ordered a new trial. In the case of N, the trial judge convicted. The conviction was upheld by the Manitoba Court of Appeal, which found that there had been no violation of s. 15 and that, although s. 146(1) breached s. 7 of the *Charter*, that breach was saved by s. 1. The accused appealed and the appeals were heard together.

Complex divisions in the Supreme Court resulted in 5-2 rulings that s. 146(1) constituted absolute liability contrary to s. 7 and could not be saved under s. 1 and that there was no unconstitutional violation of s. 15 equality standards.

WILSON J. (LAMER C.J.C., LA FOREST and L'HEUREUX-DUBÉ JJ. concurring): — I have had the advantage of reading the reasons of my colleague Justice McLachlin. While I agree that s. 146(1) of the *Criminal Code of Canada* (as it read in May 1985) infringes s. 7 of the *Canadian Charter of Rights and Freedoms*, in my view the impugned provision is not saved by s. 1 of the *Charter*. I am also of the view that s. 146(1) does not trigger s. 15(1) of the *Charter*.

. . . .

Section 146(1) of the *Code* makes it an indictable offence punishable by a maximum of life imprisonment for a man to have sexual intercourse with a female under the age of 14 who is not his wife. The provision expressly removes the defence that the accused bona fide believed that the female was 14 years of age or older. An accused may not resort to the defence of mistake of fact, a defence which the principles set out in *R. v. Sault Ste. Marie (City)* . . . and *Pappajohn v. R.* . . ., make clear would normally be available. These cases provide that absent a legislative decision to eliminate the *mens rea* requirement, where one is dealing with a "true" criminal offence as opposed to a "public welfare" offence of the kind seen in *Sault Ste. Marie*, the Crown must prove *mens rea* (*i.e.*, "some positive state of mind such as intent, knowledge or recklessness") either by an inference from the nature of the act committed or by additional evidence (per Dickson J. (as he then was) in *Sault Ste. Marie*, at p. 1325).

. . . .

[I]t seems to me particularly important to reiterate that long before the *Charter* was enacted our system of law had a profound commitment to the principle that the innocent should not be punished.

Even the most cursory review of the history of the doctrine of *mens rea* confirms this observation and reveals that the doctrine is an integral and indispensable feature of our criminal law.

. . . .

The doctrine of *mens rea* reflects the conviction that a person should not be punished unless that person knew that he was committing the prohibited act or would have known that he was committing the prohibited act if, as Stroud put it, "he had given to his conduct, and to the circumstances, that degree of attention which the law requires, and which he is capable of giving".

Our commitment to the principle that those who did not intend to commit harm and who took all reasonable precautions to ensure that they did not commit an offence should not be imprisoned stems from an acute awareness that to imprison a "mentally innocent" person is to inflict a grave injury on that person's dignity and sense of worth. Where that person's beliefs and his actions leading up to the commission of the prohibited act are treated as completely irrelevant in the face of the state's pronouncement that he must automatically be incarcerated for having done the prohibited act, that person is treated as little more than a means to an end. That person is in essence told that because of an overriding social or moral objective he must lose his freedom even although he took all reasonable precautions to ensure that no offence was committed.

Prior to the *Charter*, Parliament had to use express statutory language in order to displace the requirement that the prosecutor prove *mens rea*. With the advent of the *Charter*, Parliament must now be prepared to show that a provision that purports to make it unnecessary for the Crown to prove *mens rea* and that does not provide an accused, at a minimum, with a due diligence defence is a reasonable limit that can be demonstrably justified in a free and democratic society. I therefore turn to s. 1 of the *Charter*.

. . . .

(iii) *Minimal Impairment and Proportionality*

When the respondents turn to the question whether the impugned provision impairs the right as little as possible, they assert that the defence of due diligence or reasonable belief would not provide as effective a deterrent to men who might wish to engage in sexual intercourse with a female under 14 as the removal of all defences based on the accused's lack of knowledge of the victim's age. They also submit that the fact that Parliament has chosen to replace s. 146(1) with a provision that allows for a due diligence defence does not mean that one cannot justify s. 146(1) as a reasonable limit on s. 7 of the *Charter*. I note that Justice McLachlin not only accepts these submissions but that she is also of the view that in those instances where an accused is truly mentally innocent this factor may be taken into account in the sentence [p. 327]: "if . . . persuaded that the accused was truly morally blameless, he may be set free: see s. 663 (now s. 737) of the *Criminal Code*".

I think it useful to consider these arguments under three separate headings.

(a) The Deterrence Argument

The respondents place a great deal of weight on arguments about deterrence in their analysis of whether the impugned provision is rationally connected to the legislative objective and in their submissions with respect to the proportionality test set out in *Oakes*. . . . [T]he premise on which the deterrence arguments are based is not a strong one since it assumes that before having sexual intercourse with a young girl the accused, including a teen-aged accused, will in fact address his mind to a fairly obscure provision of the *Code*.

But if I am wrong in this, it seems to me that any deterrence value that s. 146(1) might have would only protect a narrow sub-set of the group that s. 146(1) addresses. Whatever deterrence value the fear of making a mistake might have would only protect that group of young females close enough to the age of 14 that a mistake as to whether they were under or over 14 was a realistic possibility.

. . . .

More importantly, the deterrent effect of the rule cannot readily be documented and the respondents have not submitted *any* evidence to support their deterrence argument. Where one is dealing with the potential for life imprisonment it is not good enough, in my view, to rely on intuition and speculation about the potential deterrent effect of an absolute liability offence. We need concrete and persuasive evidence to support the argument.

. . . .

The respondents contend that all that a person need do to avoid the risk of conviction is to refrain from having sex with a young girl unless he is sure that she is over fourteen. But this begs the question: what if he is sure that she is over 14 but turns out to be wrong? This argument boils down to the proposition that all that a person who has made a mistake of fact needs to do to avoid the risk of conviction is to make sure that he is not making a mistake of fact. The argument would appear to be somewhat circular.

This point leads me to another, more fundamental, problem with the deterrence argument, one that Dickson J. identified in *Sault Ste. Marie*. I noted in connection with my s. 7 analysis that the criminal law has come to recognize that punishing the mentally innocent with a view to advancing particular objectives is fundamentally unfair. It is to use the innocent as a means to an end. While utilitarian reasoning may at one time have been acceptable, it is my view that when we are dealing with the potential for life imprisonment it has no place in a free and democratic society. Thus, even if there were some substance to the premise on which the deterrence argument is based, the argument would still, in my opinion, lead to a fundamentally unfair state of affairs.

(b) Sentencing

Justice McLachlin recognizes that there *is* something troubling about subjecting someone who has made a genuine mistake of fact to life imprisonment. She feels that mental innocence may be taken into account when sentencing the accused. It seems to me that her discomfort with the idea of incarcerating the mentally innocent for as extended a period as the mentally guilty is entirely natural. But in my view, rather than work in favour of s. 146(1), this serves to highlight the weaknesses of arguments upholding the linking of life imprisonment to an absolute liability offence. Indeed, it seems to me that my colleague implicitly accepts that there *should* be some correlation between moral blame and punishment.

But one cannot leave questions of mental innocence to the sentencing process. The legislature must take into account the implications of the distinction between the mentally innocent and the mentally guilty when drafting legislation. Any flaws in the provision cannot be justified by arguments that ask us to have faith that the prosecutor and judge will take these flaws into account when deciding how the accused will be punished. Reliance on prosecutorial or judicial discretion to mitigate the harshness of an unjust law will provide little comfort to the mentally innocent and cannot, in my view, serve to justify a fundamentally unsound provision.

(c) Section 150.1(4) of the *Criminal Code*, R.S.C., 1985, c. C 46

In 1987, Parliament repealed s. 146(1) and put in place a series of measures that include a provision that allows a person who would previously have been charged under s. 146(1) the defence of due diligence [An Act to amend the *Criminal Code* and the *Canada Evidence Act*, R.S.C. 1985, c. 19 (3rd Supp.)]. Sections 151 and 152 of the current *Code* create the new substantive offences of sexual interference and invitation to sexual touching. Both of these provisions apply to sexual conduct with a person under the age of 14. Section 150.1(4) limits the range of defences available to an accused charged under these sections, removing the defence of consent but allowing a due diligence defence:

150.1 . . .

(4) It is not a defence to a charge under section 151 or 152, subsection 160(3) or 173(2), or section 271, 272 or 273 that the accused believed that the complainant was fourteen years of age or more at the time the offence is alleged to have been committed *unless the accused took all reasonable steps to ascertain the age of the complainant.* [Emphasis added.]

. . . .

Sections 151 and 152 seek to protect young people from a broad range of sexual activity. These provisions continue to protect young females from the physical and emotional trauma of premature sexual intercourse. . . . Parliament has concluded that it can effect its objective of protecting young females from the undesirable consequences of premature sexual intercourse in a manner that does not restrict an accused's right as much as s. 146(1).

I am therefore of the view that s. 146(1) does not satisfy the proportionality test set out in *Oakes*. The potential benefits flowing from the retention of absolute liability are far too speculative to be able to justify a provision that envisages the possibility of life imprisonment for one who is mentally innocent. At a minimum the provision must provide for a defence of due diligence.

. . . .

While it is not, strictly speaking, necessary for me to consider s. 15(1) of the *Charter*, it may be useful to address the question whether in addition to a s. 7 violation there is also a s. 15(1) violation, particularly since I cannot agree with Justice McLachlin's conclusion that s. 146(1) of the *Code* infringes s. 15(1) of the *Charter*.

The appellants Hess and Nguyen submit that s. 146(1) of the *Code* creates a distinction that violates s. 15(1) of the *Charter*. They say that s. 146(1) distinguishes between potential accused on the basis of a ground enumerated in s. 15(1) of the *Charter* in that only men may be charged under the provision. They point out, moreover, that the provision clearly envisages that only females may be complainants. The question arises therefore whether it is open to the Legislature to create an offence that applies only to accused of one sex and to victims of one sex.

. . . .

In these appeals we are asked to consider when a distinction drawn on the basis of sex may legitimately be made and when it may not. In the context of the criminal law it seems to me that the answer to this question will depend on the nature of the offence in issue. If the impugned provision creates an offence that can, as a matter of fact, be committed by either sex but goes on to specify that it is only an offence when committed by one sex, then there may well be an infringement of s. 15(1) that would have to be justified under s. 1 of the *Charter*.

. . . .

It seems to me that the first question that we face in these appeals is whether s.146(1) addresses an offence that as a matter of biological fact can only be committed by males.

I note that s. 3(6) of the *Code* states:

> (6) For the purposes of this Act, sexual intercourse is complete upon penetration to even the slightest degree, notwithstanding that seed is not emitted.

In addition, s. 147 states that only males over 14 may commit the offence envisaged in s. 146, a provision that reflects the common law's rather artificial assumption that boys under 14 are not physically capable of sexual intercourse. . . . When s. 146(1) is read in light of ss. 147 and 3(6), it becomes clear that the legislature was of the opinion that, because only males over a certain age were physically capable of penetrating another person, only they needed to be listed as potential accused. . . . In my view, we are therefore dealing with an offence that involves an act that as a matter of biological fact only men over a certain age are capable of committing. And given that only men may be the penetrators, it is as absurd to suggest that the provision discriminates against males because it does not include women in the category of potential offenders as it is to suggest that a provision that prohibits self-induced abortion is discriminatory because it does not include men among the potential class of offenders.

. . . .

[I]t is appropriate to issue a declaration to the effect that the words in s. 146(1) "whether or not he believes that she is 14 years of age or more" are of no force and effect. The section shorn of its offensive words therefore reads:

> 146. (1) Every male person who has sexual intercourse with a female person who
> (*a*) is not his wife, and
> (*b*) is under the age of 14 years,
>
> is guilty of an indictable offence and is liable to imprisonment for life.

MCLACHLIN J. (dissenting) (GONTHIER J. concurring): —

. . . .

An accused can be convicted under s. 146(1) although he lacks a guilty mind. He clearly must intend to have intercourse. But that is not an offence. Without wishing to commit the crime or intending to commit the crime of having intercourse with a girl of less than 14 years, an accused may stand convicted. It follows from the principles laid down by this in *Re B.C. Motor Vehicle Act* and *Vaillancourt* that s. 146(1) violates s. 7 of the *Charter*.

2. *Does s. 146(1) of the Criminal Code violate s. 15 of the Charter?*

It is argued that s. 146(1) violates s. 15 of the *Charter* in two ways.

The first is that only men can be convicted under s. 146(1). Men are thus deprived of a benefit or advantage enjoyed by women. The second is that only young women are protected by s. 146(1). Thus males of 14 years or less are not given the same benefit as females.

Two requirements must be met to establish infringement of s. 15 of the *Charter*. First, an inequality or distinction in the treatment of members of groups must be established. Second, this distinction must constitute discrimination: *Andrews v. Law Soc. of B.C.*, [1989] 1 S.C.R. 143.

The alleged violations of s. 15 raised in this case both involve distinctions on the basis of sex, one of the categories enumerated in s. 15. Thus the first condition for a violation of s. 15 is met. The question is whether the second requirement, discrimination, is established.

. . . .

In my view, the essential requirements for discrimination under s. 15 remain as set forth in *Andrews*.

Applying that test, I find that s. 146(1) constitutes discrimination under s. 15 of the *Charter*. It makes distinctions on the enumerated ground of sex. It burdens men as it does not burden women. It offers protection to young females which it does not offer to young males. It is discriminatory.

. . . .

3. *Are the violations of ss. 7 and 15 saved under s. 1 of the Charter?*

(a) Is the Breach of s. 7 Saved by s. 1 of the *Charter*?

(i) *The objective of the proposed limit*

. . . .

Section 146(1) represents the Canadian equivalent of a provision which is known throughout the western democratic world. The offence has long been part of the criminal law of England which we in Canada inherited. It has survived innumerable constitutional challenges in the United States. . . . It is not an exaggeration to say that the offence of "statutory rape", as it is commonly referred to, is embedded in our social consciousness.

These facts attest to the importance of the objective served by the offence.

. . . .

What then is the objective of s. 146(1)? It has two aspects. The first is the protection of female children from the harms which may result from premature sexual intercourse and pregnancy. The second is the protection of society from the impact of the social problems which sexual intercourse with children may produce.

. . . .

[T]he protection of children from the evils of intercourse is multi-faceted and so obvious as not to require formal demonstration. Children merit this protection for three primary reasons. The first is the need to protect them from the consequences of pregnancies with which they are ill-equipped to deal from the physical, emotional and economic point of view. The second is the need to protect them from the grave physical and emotional harm which may result from sexual intercourse at such an early age. The third is the need to protect them from exploitation by those who might seek to use them for prostitution and related nefarious purposes.

. . . .

I conclude that the objectives of s. 146(1) of the *Criminal Code* are of great importance — sufficient importance to justify overriding a constitutionally protected right.

(ii) *Are the means chosen to effect the objective reasonable and demonstrably justified in a free and democratic society?*

A. Rational Connection

Is there a rational connection between the imposition of strict liability and deterrence of men from intercourse with young girls? In my view, there is. Were the defence of reasonable belief available, a man could escape conviction simply by saying that he believed the girl to be older than 14. The defence of due diligence would require him to make inquiries to avoid conviction, but still leaves open the possibility that the girl may lie as to her age or even produce false identification, not an uncommon practice in the world of juvenile prostitution.

The imposition of strict liability eliminates these defences. In doing so, it effectively puts men who are contemplating intercourse with a girl who might be under 14 years of age on guard. They know that if they have intercourse without being certain of the girl's age, they run the risk of conviction, and many conclude that they will not take the chance. That wisdom forms part of the substratum of consciousness with which young men grow up, as exemplified by terms such as "jailbait". There can be no question but that the imposition of absolute liability in s. 146(1) has an additional deterrent effect.

B. Degree of Impairment

The limit should impair the right or freedom "as little as possible" . . . The infringement would not extend beyond what is reasonably necessary to achieve the legislative objective. This is because a measure which infringes more than necessary is to that extent infringing a right without justification. That is inconsistent with s. 1 of the *Charter*.

In dealing with this point, I find it useful to ask whether there is another way the same objective could be achieved without infringement of the right or with a lesser infringement of the right. In the case of s. 146(1), the answer to this question must be negative for the reasons I discussed under A. Rational Connection.

. . . .

I cannot leave this aspect of the analysis without adverting to the fact that Parliament has repealed s. 146(1) and adopted a provision allowing the defence of due diligence. In my opinion, the fact that Parliament has chosen to do this does not establish that the objectives of s. 146(1) can be accomplished with a lesser infringement of the accuseds rights. An equally viable explanation is that Parliament has chosen, for whatever reasons, to reduce its objective.

. . . .

C. Proportionality Between the Effect of the Limit and the Objective

We arrive at the point where we must weigh the impact of the infringement of the accused's constitutional right against the importance of what is achieved by the legislation. In the case at bar, what hangs in the balance is the public and private interest in protecting very young girls from intercourse on the one hand, and on the other the right of a person charged with an offence not to be convicted if he did not intend to commit the offence.

In the abstract, both considerations are of high importance.

. . . .

The question in the case at bar is whether deviation from the principle which requires *mens rea* can *ever* be tolerated in our society. The submission put before us was essentially that in no case could a measure which violated the requirement for *mens rea* be justified under s. 1 of the *Charter*.

. . . .

I cannot accept this submission.

As a matter of construction, to hold that s. 1 can never as a matter of law be applicable to *Charter* rights falling within certain categories is to rewrite the *Charter*. The framers of the *Charter* expressly subjected all the rights and freedoms which it guarantees to the override of s. 1.

. . . .

I therefore proceed on the premise that important as the right not to be convicted in the absence of *mens rea* is, one must nevertheless proceed to s. 1 of the *Charter* to determine if s. 146(1) can be saved as a reasonable measure justified in a free and democratic society.

The first point is that many societies which we would regard as free and democratic, such as England and the United States, consider the offence of statutory rape to be both reasonable and justifiable notwithstanding its elimination of *mens rea*.

. . . .

The second is that the elimination of *mens rea* from s. 146(1) of the *Criminal Code* may be viewed as less offensive than, for example, the elimination of *mens rea* from the offence of murder.

. . . .

Although one may postulate the case of a "morally blameless" person being convicted under s. 146(1), however rare that case may be, one must also remember that all that a person need do to avoid the risk of this happening is to refrain from having sex with girls of less than adult age unless he knows for certain that they are over 14. Viewed thus, the infringement on the freedom imposed by s. 146(1) of the *Criminal Code* does not appear unduly Draconian, considering the great harms to which the section is directed.

. . . .

The actual effect of the absence of *mens rea* in s. 146(1) is much less serious than it may be in other cases.

. . . .

These considerations, coupled with the fact that the lack of *mens rea* in s. 146(1) is less intrusive of the accused's rights than is the case in other absolute liability offences, lead me to conclude that the intrusion on the accused's right not to be convicted in the absence of a guilty mind represented by s. 146(1) is reasonable and demonstrably justifiable in a free and democratic society.

(b) Is the breach of s. 15 saved by s. 1 of the *Charter*?

. . . .

I need not expatiate further on the objective of s. 146(1); it is clearly capable of overriding other *Charter* rights, provided the means used are appropriate and proportionate. The rational link between the objective and the measure and impairment to a minimum degree are likewise established. The only question is whether the infringement of s. 15 is justified, given the objectives of s. 146(1).

I am satisfied that the means represented by s. 146(1) are proportionate and justified when weighed against the seriousness of the infringement of the rights of equality of accused persons and victims under s. 15 of the *Charter*. The singling out of males as the only offenders is justified given the fact that only males can cause pregnancies, one of the chief evils addressed by s. 146(1). The protection of female children to the exclusion of male children may be justified on the same ground; only females are likely to become pregnant.

Justice Sopinka agreed with the majority that the section contravened s. 7 and could not be saved by s. 1. He also agreed with the minority that the section infringed s. 15 of the *Charter* but he believed it was saved by s. 1.

For commentary, see William Black and Isabel Grant, "Equality and Biological Differences" (1990), 79 C.R. (3d) 372.

In the 28 years that have passed since *Hess and Nguyen,* Parliament has created a number of new offences to protect against abuse directed at the young and vulnerable, and has also raised the age of protection to 16 and 18 in the case of the offences of obtaining sexual services. In most cases the accused is given a mistaken belief in age defence but only if the accused took *all* reasonable steps to find out the complainant's age. The internet luring offence requires reasonable steps but does not specify a requirement of taking "all" reasonable steps: s. 171.1(4) of the *Criminal Code.* The defence rarely succeeds as shown in decisions in cases of internet luring. See *R. v. Legare,* 70 C.R. (6th) 1, [2009] 3 S.C.R. 551 and *R. v. Levigne,* 77 C.R. (6th) 1, [2010] 2 S.C.R. 3 (in absence of evidence to contrary provision not shifting burden of proof). See too *R. v. Alicandro,* 63 C.R. (6th) 330 (Ont. C.A.), leave to appeal refused (2010), 410 N.R. 383 (note) (S.C.C.) and *R. v. Dragos* (2012), 95 C.R. (6th) 406 (Ont. C.A.). But see *R. v. Thain* (2009), 243 C.C.C. (3d) 230 (Ont. C.A.) (new trial ordered); *R. v. Hoffart* (2010), 76 C.R. (6th) 182 (Alta. Prov. Ct.) (acquittal); and *R. v. Pengelley* (2010), 261 C.C.C. (3d) 93 (Ont. S.C.J.) (acquittal). So too in cases of child pornography (*R. v. Morelli,* 72 C.R. (6th) 208, [2010] 1 S.C.R. 253); sexual interference where the complainant is under age (*R. v. Mastel* (2011), 84 C.R. (6th) 405 (Sask. C.A.) and *R. v. O. (J.M.)* (1992), 17 C.R. (4th) 350 (Nfld. C.A.), but see *R. v. P. (L.T.)* (1997), 113 C.C.C. (3d) 42 (B.C. C.A.) and *R. v. O.D.* (2017), 36 C.R. (7th) (Ont. S.C.)); and obtaining sexual services from someone under 18 (*R. v. Slater* (2005), 31 C.R. (6th) 112 (Sask. C.A.)).

PROBLEM

At the time of the alleged offences of sexual assault and sexual interference, the accused was 43 years old and the complainant was 15. They had known each other for about two years. Their interactions were limited to the local hockey arena, where the complainant had tickets in the "kids zone". The two would often talk at the rink or outside in the smoking area. The complainant testified that she never lied about her age, that the accused knew that she was in middle school when they met and that she was in grade 10 at the time of the sexual activity giving rise to the charge. The complainant snuck away from a friend's home and met the accused at his house at midnight. He gave her three or four vodka coolers. He refused to provide the complainant with his last name when asked. He asked her to go into the bedroom and they had sexual intercourse. The friend who picked her up testified that she appeared drunk and upset.

The accused testified that the complainant looked older than 15, that she always dressed in high heels and low cut shirts, and that she had once told him she was 17, although he could provide no details of when that occurred. He also testified that the complainant told him she had a part-time job and that she took birth control pills.

The trial judge acquitted. While he rejected the accused's evidence that the complainant had told him she was 17, he found that the accused believed the complainant to be 16 years or older and that he had taken all reasonable steps in the circumstances to ascertain her age. Should this decision be reversed?

Compare *R. v. Mastel* (2011), 84 C.R. (6th) 405 (Sask. C.A.); *R. v. Clarke* (2016), 338 C.C.C. (3d) 83, 31 C.R. (7th) 101 (Sask. C.A.); and *R. v. Chapman* (2016), 337 C.C.C. (3d) 269, 28 C.R. (7th) 335 (Ont. C.A.), leave to appeal refused 2016 CarswellOnt 16185, 2016 CarswellOnt 16186 (S.C.C.).

In her C.R. comment Janine Benedet suggests that any

"visual observation" standard is of particular concern since it can amount to relying on signs of early sexualisation that may itself be the result of abuse, so as to justify further sexual exploitation. Girls who develop physically at an earlier age and who conform to cultural expectations to dress in a sexualized way are at particular risk under this approach. Given the magnitude of the potential harm and the reference to "all" reasonable steps in the subsection, the approach of the Newfoundland Court of Appeal in *R. v. Osborne* (1992) 17 C.R. (4th) 350 is to be preferred. There the court noted that the requirement is "more than a casual requirement. There must be an earnest inquiry or some other *compelling* factor that obviates the need for an inquiry." [emphasis added] Smoking and high heels are not compelling factors. Where, as here, the accused knows that the complainant is an adolescent, the need for active inquiry is overwhelming.

Should there be a successful *Charter* challenge on the basis that the "all steps" requirement is placing a limit on the minimum *Charter* fault standard of due diligence? The Supreme Court in *Wholesale Travel*, considered earlier, held that that standard cannot be limited, even for regulatory offences.

We have seen that Parliament did not require that high standard for the mistaken belief defence to sexual assault.

(c) As to Nature of Offence

The remainder of this chapter addresses the issue of how courts determine whether a mistake of fact exonerates, and whether it should be thought of as a "defence" or not.

On the one hand one might think of "mistake of fact" as just a failure on the part of the Crown to prove an element of the offence. That is the approach adopted by Justice Dickson in *R. v. Pappajohn,* who indicated it was wrong to view the mistaken belief in consent issue as a defence; it was rather a denial of proof of *mens rea.* In *R. v. Beaver*, [1957] S.C.R. 531 the Supreme Court established that one cannot knowingly possess something without knowledge of the character of the substance possessed. More simply, what of an accused who takes an item mistaking it for his or her own? That mistake would seem to mean that the Crown cannot prove an element of the offence (that the accused knew the property belonged to another) and so the accused should be found not guilty.

On the other hand, "mistake of fact" is also sometimes spoken of in the case law as a defence.

A particularly difficult issue arises where on the accused's version of the facts he (or she) is committing a particular offence but, had he not been mistaken, he would be guilty of another offence. May the fault for the other offence be transferred to find guilt? Courts have not been consistent. The traditional approach is from the old English case of *R. v. Tolson* (1889), 23 Q.B.D. 168 (Eng. Q.B.), which only allows the defence if, on the accused's view, he was innocent of any offence whatsoever. On that approach, an accused who believes he is committing a relatively less serious offence (trafficking in mescaline) could be found guilty of a more serious offence (trafficking in L.S.D.) despite his mistake: see *R. v. Kundeus*, below. However, other cases seem to apply the rule that the accused can be guilty of an offence despite a mistake of fact only if, on the accused's view, he was committing an offence of equal seriousness: see *R. v. Blondin* (1971), 2 C.C.C. (2d) 118 (B.C. C.A.).

These different approaches can lead to different results on the same facts.

PROBLEM

A plainclothes police officer intervenes to stop a fight between two youths. An onlooker, not knowing that he is a police officer, tries to pull him away telling him to mind his own business. The officer punches the onlooker in the nose and the onlooker punches him back. The officer then draww his revolver and gains control of the situation. The onlooker is charged with assault of a police officer contrary to s. 270 of the *Criminal Code*. This offence carries a maximum penalty on indictment of 5 years imprisonment. The maximum penalty for assault under s. 266 is the same although in practice the offence of assault of a police officer is considered

more serious and attracts a higher penalty. Consider whether the mistake defence should succeed on the *Tolson* and *Beaver* tests. Which result do you prefer and why?

Compare *R. v. McLeod* (1954), 20 C.R. 281 (B.C. C.A.) and *R. v. Collins* (1989), 69 C.R. (3d) 235, 48 C.C.C. (3d) 343 (Ont. C.A.).

What test was applied in the following two decisions. Do you agree with the results?

R. v. LADUE

[1965] 4 C.C.C. 264, 45 C.R. 287, 1965 CarswellYukon 2 (Y.T. C.A.)

DAVEY J.A.: — Ladue either copulated or attempted to copulate with a dead woman and was convicted under s. 167(*b*) [now s. 182(*b*)] of the *Criminal Code* of indecently interfering with a dead human body. The material part of the section reads as follows:

167. Every one who

. . . .

(*b*) improperly or indecently interferes with or offers any indignity to a dead human body or human remains, whether buried or not,

is guilty of an indictable offence and is liable to imprisonment for five years.

The only point of substance in Ladue's appeal against his conviction is whether the learned trial judge was right in holding that it was not open to the appellant to contend that he was not guilty because he did not know the woman was dead. There was considerable evidence upon which the learned judge might have held, if he had not considered the defence untenable in law, that while Ladue knew what he was doing physically, he was so intoxicated that he did not realize the woman was dead. Subject to what I have to say later that would have been a good defence.

In his oral reasons the learned trial judge, in dealing with the effect of intoxication upon the appellant's understanding, said this:

What does the argument amount to? The only way you can make it, the only way in which you could make this argument — certainly I don't know. She was dead. He thought she was unconscious. Because she was dead? No. That is about it. At the time of the incident can a person be heard to say "that it didn't occur to me she was dead, and I am therefore innocent." I will tell you, I will not listen to such an argument. That would be an admission he was having intercourse with a person.

It is a fundamental principle of criminal law that, unless excluded by statute, *mens rea*, that is guilty intention, is necessary to constitute a crime, and that a person doing an act is not guilty of a crime if his mind be innocent: *R. v. Prince* (1875), L.R. 2 C.C.R. 154; *R. v. Tolson* (1889), 23 Q.B.D. 168, *per* Willis J., at pp. 171-2. I see nothing in s. 167(*b*) to exclude that principle. Accordingly it was open to the appellant to attempt to rebut the inference of *mens rea* flowing from what he deliberately did to the body by proving that he did not know the woman was dead.

But in attempting to defend himself in that way the appellant runs into the insuperable difficulty alluded to by the learned trial judge. The appellant could not have failed, even in his drunken state, to perceive that the woman was unconscious, and incapable of giving her consent to copulation. Indeed the appellant does not suggest that he thought he had her consent to the act. So if the woman was alive he was raping her. Therefore it is impossible for him to argue that, not knowing her to be dead, he was acting innocently. An intention to commit a crime, although not the precise crime charged, will provide the necessary *mens rea* under a statute in the form of s. 167(*b*): *R. v. Tolson per* Willis J., at p. 172, Stephen J., at pp. 189-90; *R. v. Prince, per* Brett J., at pp. 169-170, because in those circumstances an accused cannot contend he was acting lawfully or innocently.

It follows that in my respectful opinion the learned trial judge was right in the particular circumstances of this case in saying that he would not entertain an argument that appellant was innocent because he did not know the woman was dead.

. . . .

The nature of the offence under s. 167(*b*) and the language of that section would not seem to require knowledge that the body is dead as a specific ingredient of an offence under that section, because in most cases that fact would be clear, and proof of a deliberate act improperly or indecently interfering with a body that was in fact dead would be sufficient proof of a criminal intention or *mens rea*. It would be only in the most exceptional case where the offender might have any doubt whether a body was quick or dead, and in such a case he might defend himself by showing that he did not know the body was dead and that according to his understanding he was acting lawfully and innocently. That is what the appellant cannot show in this case, because if the woman was alive he was raping her.

I would dismiss the appeal.

Appeal dismissed.

R. v. KUNDEUS

[1976] 2 S.C.R. 272, 32 C.R.N.S. 129 at 135, 24 C.C.C. (2d) 276,
1975 CarswellBC 181, 1975 CarswellBC 285

26th June 1975. DE GRANDPRÉ J. (MARTLAND, JUDSON, RITCHIE, PIGEON,
DICKSON and BEETZ JJ. concurring): — With leave of this Court, the Crown
appeals the unanimous judgment of the British Columbia Court of Appeal, ante
p. 133, setting aside the conviction of respondent. In the words of the indictment,
Kundeus was charged that he did:

> on the 24th day of August A.D. 1972, unlawfully traffic in a restricted drug, to wit: Lysergic
> Acid Diethylamide (LSD), contrary to the provisions of the *Food and Drugs Act*.

The facts are stated in the reasons for judgment of the trial judge [p. 132]:

> Police Constable MacKay-Dunn testified that on 24th August 1972 at about 10:15 p.m.,
> the constable, acting undercover in the Gastown area, and the accused were at a table in the
> Travellers Hotel, 57 West Cordova in the City of Vancouver. The police constable testified
> the accused was calling out, "Speed, acid, MDA or hash" to passers-by in the beer parlor.
> The police constable asked for hash or acid. The accused said they were all sold out. The
> accused offered mescaline at $2. The police constable accepted the offer, requested two "hits"
> and paid $4 to the accused for same. The accused left, returned in about five minutes, and
> handed two capsules, Ex. 1, to the police constable. Exhibit 1 was, in fact, two capsules of
> L.S.D. (see Ex. 2).

The trial judge adds that [p. 132]: "The accused elected not to adduce any
evidence in defence."

After having stated that the sole issue was *mens rea*, the trial judge examined
the relevant parts of the *Food and Drugs Act*, R.S.C. 1970, c. F-27, and the
regulations thereunder, as well as the cases of *Regina v. Blondin* (1971), 2 C.C.C.
(2d) 118, affirmed (1972), 4 C.C.C. (2d) 566n (Can.); *Regina v. Burgess*, [1970]
3 C.C.C. 268 (Ont. C.A.); and *Regina v. Custeau*, 17 C.R.N.S 124, 6 C.C.C.
(2d) 179 (Ont. C.A.), and concluded:

> The court has considered the evidence in this trial and the able submissions of respective
> counsel.
> The court concludes that the prosecution has proved, beyond a reasonable doubt, the
> guilt of the accused.

Respondent inscribed an appeal alleging an error involving a question of
law upon the following ground:

> The learned trial judge misdirected himself in law in holding that if he was satisfied
> beyond a reasonable doubt that the accused knew it was illegal to sell the drug mescaline,
> although said drug is not a restricted drug as defined in the *Food and Drugs Act*, and in fact
> intended to sell the drug mescaline, he should convict the accused of trafficking in L.S.D., a
> restricted drug under the *Food and Drugs Act*, when the substance sold as mescaline was
> analyzed to be L.S.D., even if the accused did not know that the substance was in fact the
> restricted drug L.S.D.

The Court of Appeal disagreed with the conclusion reached by the trial judge and specifically refused to follow *Regina v. Custeau*. The conviction was consequently set aside.

Mens rea cannot, of course, be examined without reference to *Beaver v. The Queen*, 26 C.R. 193, [1957] S.C.R. 531, 118 C.C.C. 129.

. . . .

Our facts are different. They are very simple and uncontradicted. One reading of them is that Kundeus was offering L.S.D. for sale, actually sold L.S.D. and received payment therefor. On that reading, it is obvious that the conviction should have been affirmed.

Another reading is that adopted by the Court of Appeal and expressed by McFarlane J.A., speaking for the Court (*ante* p. 133):

> The evidence disclosed, and the trial judge found, that the appellant offered to sell mescaline at $2 to a police constable acting undercover. The constable accepted the offer and paid the appellant $4 for two "hits". The appellant left, returned in about five minutes and handed the constable two capsules which were found, on analysis, to contain L.S.D.
>
> I think I must interpret the reasons for judgment of the trial judge as a finding that although the appellant did in fact sell L.S.D. he thought he was selling, and intended to sell, mescaline and that the constable also thought he was purchasing mescaline.

Assuming that this reading of the trial judgment is the proper one, was the Court of Appeal right in holding that the necessary *mens rea* had not been proved? I do not believe so.

In *Regina v. Blondin*, *supra*, a case dealing with the importation of narcotics, the Crown succeeded on the following ground of its appeal [p. 6]:

> (e) THAT the learned trial Judge misdirected the jury in instructing it that the Crown was obliged to prove beyond a reasonable doubt that the accused knew that the contents of the scuba diving tank (Exhibit 1) was a narcotic drug as alleged in the Indictment herein, namely, Cannabis Resin.

After a full review of the authorities, Robertson J.A. concluded (pp. 13-14):

> Basing my opinion upon what I understand to be the principle enunciated in the several passages I have quoted, I am of the respectful opinion that the learned trial Judge erred when he instructed the jury that, in order to find Blondin guilty, they must find that he knew that the substance in the tank was cannabis resin. It would be sufficient to find, in relation to a narcotic, *mens rea* in its widest sense.

An appeal to this Court by the accused was dismissed by the full bench in the following terms: "We agree that the Court of Appeal rightly allowed the appeal and directed a new trial on ground (e) of the notice of appeal to that Court."

That judgment must be read with another decision of this Court, namely, *Regina v. King*, 38 C.R. 52, [1962] S.C.R. 746, 133 C.C.C. 1, where the facts, the question submitted to this Court and the holding are expressed in the [S.C.R.] headnote:

> The accused went to his dentist by appointment to have two teeth extracted. He was injected with a drug known as sodium pentothal, a quick-acting anaesthetic. Earlier, he had been required to sign a printed form containing a warning not to drive after the anaesthetic until his head had cleared. After he regained consciousness, the nurse in attendance, to whom he appeared to be normal, warned him not to drive until his head was "perfectly clear". He replied that he intended to walk. The accused said that he heard no such warning and did not remember signing any form containing a warning. He remembered getting into his car and that while driving he became unconscious. His car ran into the rear of a parked vehicle. Medical evidence was given that his mental and physical condition (he was staggering and his co-ordination was poor) was consistent with the after-effects of the drug in question which may induce a state of amnesia accompanied by a period during which the subject may feel competent to drive a car and in the next second be in a condition in which he would not know what was happening. The accused stated that he did not know anything about this drug.
>
> He was charged and convicted of the offence of driving a motor vehicle while his ability to do so was impaired by a drug, contrary to s. 223 of the *Criminal Code*. After a trial *de novo* before a County Court judge under s. 720 of the *Code*, his conviction was affirmed. The Court of Appeal granted him leave to appeal and quashed the conviction. The Crown was granted leave to appeal to this Court on the question as to whether *mens rea* relating to both the act of driving and to the state of being impaired was an essential element of the offence.

I refer particularly to a paragraph of the reasons of Ritchie J., speaking also for the Chief Justice and for Martland J., at p. 763:

> The existence of *mens rea* as an essential ingredient of an offence and the method of proving the existence of that ingredient are two different things, and I am of the opinion that when it has been proved that a driver was driving a motor vehicle while his ability to do so was impaired by alcohol or a drug, then a rebuttable presumption arises that his condition was voluntarily induced and that he is guilty of the offence created by s. 223 and must be convicted unless other evidence is adduced which raises a reasonable doubt as to whether he was, through no fault of his own, disabled when he undertook to drive and drove, from being able to appreciate and know that he was or might become impaired.

In the case at bar, such a rebuttable presumption has arisen. No evidence having been tendered by the accused, it is not possible to find that he had an honest belief amounting to a non-existence of *mens rea* and the Court of Appeal was in error in its conclusion.

The quality of respondent's conduct is not to be determined by the existence or non-existence of a binding civil agreement as to the purchase of L.S.D. between him and the constable. That is not the test. In *Poitras v. The Queen* (1973), 12 C.C.C. (2d) 337 (Can.), where the question was to determine the exact meaning of "trafficking" under the *Narcotic Control Act*, R.S.C. 1970, c. N-1, Dickson J., speaking for the majority, wrote at pp. 416-17:

> It was argued on behalf of the appellant that the words "to buy" do not appear in the definition of "trafficking" under the *Narcotic Control Act*; therefore, a mere purchaser does not traffic and an agent for the purchaser comes under the same protective umbrella. I do not agree. One cannot apply the civil law of "agency" in this context. "Agency" does not serve

to make non-criminal an act which would otherwise be attended by criminal consequences. Even if the appellant could be said to be the "agent" of Constable Arsenault for the purposes of civil responsibility, his acts may, none the less, amount to trafficking in narcotics or aiding in such trafficking. If, as the trial Judge would seem to have found, the evidence was consistent with the accused delivering or selling or trading in drugs or offering to do so, the fact that he may have been acting as an agent for Arsenault would not exculpate him.

In my view, the result in *Regina v. Custeau* was the proper one and this notwithstanding the error committed by the Court of Appeal of Ontario and underlined by the Court of Appeal of British Columbia in the case at bar, mescaline having been described as a controlled drug when it is a drug mentioned in the regulations under the Act which cannot be sold without a prescription.

I would allow the appeal, set aside the order of the Court of Appeal of British Columbia and restore the judgment at trial together with the sentence imposed thereat.

LASKIN C.J.C. (SPENCE J. concurring) (dissenting): —

. . . .

The scheme of the *Food and Drugs Act* is of considerable relevance in this case. Sections 40 and 42, on which the prosecution was based, are in Pt. IV of the Act dealing with "restricted drugs", which are those included in Sched. H, and L.S.D. is one of those mentioned. Part III of the Act deals with "controlled drugs" which are those included in Sched. G, and among them are amphetamine and methamphetamine.

. . . .

It is common ground that any offence under the Act or regulations relating to the sale of mescaline would be punishable under s. 26. On the other hand, this provision would have no application to controlled or restricted drugs in the face of the penalty provisions of ss. 34 and 42 which alone govern illegal dealing in them. A comparison of the respective penalty provisions governing mescaline and L.S.D. shows how much heavier the penalty is in respect of illegal dealing in the latter than in the former, both where the prosecution is on summary conviction and on indictment.

. . . .

It was the contention of the appellant Crown that the required proof of *mens rea* was furnished by evidence showing what Crown counsel called a general intention to traffic in drugs; and, this being shown, it was immaterial that the accused did not intend to traffic in the specific drug which was named in the charge but thought (as did his purchaser) that he was trafficking in another drug. Crown counsel thus takes the position to which I referred earlier in these reasons, and he stated in this connection that the accused could meet the case against him only by relying on mistake of fact which must be an honest mistake on reasonable grounds that the facts believed by him to be true would not attract culpability of any drug offence. That, according to Crown counsel, was not this case.

There are, in my opinion, three issues that stem from this submission. The first is whether mistake of fact arises at all as a separate defence for the accused in the face of the burden on the Crown to prove *mens rea* as an element of the offence charged. The offence charged was trafficking in a restricted drug, namely, L.S.D.; and although I would agree that proof of knowledge by the accused that he was trafficking in a drug of that class might be enough, even if it be not L.S.D., the question that must be faced is whether it is enough for the Crown to offer proof of trafficking in any drug or, as here, in a drug that is in a lower scale of prohibition and regulation.

Having regard to the evidence adduced at the trial and to the findings of fact on that evidence, I do not think it necessary in the present case to consider the relationship between the Crown's burden of proof, where *mens rea* is an element of the offence charged, and mistake of fact as an affirmative defence. Clearly enough, mistake of fact in that sense does not arise where proof of *mens rea* is an element of proof of the offence charged and the evidence adduced by the Crown does not establish it. If mistake is put forward in this context by evidence offered by or on behalf of the accused, it is only by way of meeting an evidentiary burden and raising a reasonable doubt that the Crown has met the persuasive burden of proof resting upon it. What we are concerned with here, on the record, is whether evidence by the Crown going to show that the accused intended to commit a lesser offence than that charged is enough to support the conviction entered after trial.

The second issue which arises on the Crown's submissions is whether the mistake of fact must be objectively reasonable or whether it is enough that it be based upon an honest belief. Leaving to one side cases of strict criminal liability (on which the judgment of Dixon J. in *Proudman v. Dayman* (1941), 67 C.L.R. 536 at 539-41, is specially instructive), where serious criminal charges are involved, this Court put the matter as follows in *Beaver v. The Queen, supra,* where Cartwright J. said this (at p. 538):

> the essential question is whether the belief entertained by the accused is an honest one and ... the existence or non-existence of reasonable grounds for such belief is merely relevant evidence to be weighed by the tribunal of fact in determining that essential question.

See also *D.P.P. v. Morgan*, [1975] 2 All E.R. 347.

The third issue, which is tied in with the first, is whether mistake of fact is shown on proof that, on the facts as the accused honestly believed them to be, he was innocent of the offence charged, albeit guilty of another offence, or whether he must show that he was innocent of any offence. This last matter invites consideration of a proposition advanced in *Regina v. Prince* (1875), L.R.

2 C.C.R. 154, by the one dissenting judge of the 16 who heard the case in the Court of Crown Cases Reserved. The majority of that court held that *mens rea* was not an essential ingredient of the offence charged, which was unlawfully taking any unmarried girl under age 16 out of the possession and against the will of her father or mother. (The word "knowingly" was not in the charge.) The accused reasonably believed that the girl he had abducted was over age 16. One of the points made by Brett J., who dissented on the ground that *mens rea* was an ingredient of the offence as it related to age, was that where *mens rea* must be proved it would suffice to show, if the facts were as the accused believed them to be, that he would still be guilty of a crime, albeit one of a lesser degree than that charged as a result of the *actus reus*.

I do not think that this view is any longer sustainable. The requirement that where the *actus reus* of an offence is proved there must also be proof of the *mens rea* of the same crime is now basic in our criminal law. Williams, *Criminal Law: The General Part*, 2nd ed. (1961), at p. 129, makes the point when dealing with the question of "transferred malice" as follows:

> The accused can be convicted where he both has the *mens rea* and commits the *actus reus* specified in the rule of law creating the crime, though they exist in respect of different objects. He cannot be convicted if his *mens rea* relates to one crime and his *actus reus* to a different crime, because that would be to disregard the requirement of an appropriate *mens rea*.

And again at p. 131:

> What are different crimes for the purpose of the rule depends primarily upon the arrangement of the statute; each section presumptively creates a different crime or group of crimes. It is possible for a single sentence of a section to create a number of different crimes, as is shown by the decisions on duplicity in pleading. If a section is thus held to create different crimes, it would not he possible to transfer the malice from one crime to another even within the same section.

See also Smith and Hogan, *Criminal Law*, 3rd ed. (1973), at pp. 49-51.

This is apt for the statutory situation which exists here and to which I have referred earlier in these reasons. Even if it be proper to describe trafficking in controlled drugs, whatever be the drug, or trafficking in restricted drugs, whatever be the drug, as being, in each case, a description of the same crime, I think it is impossible to bring mescaline within either category when it stands entirely outside the group of controlled or restricted drugs and is governed by other statutory provisions than those governing controlled or restricted drugs. I am unable to agree that where *mens rea* is an element of an offence, as it is here, it can be satisfied by proof of its existence in relation to another offence unless, of course, the situation involves an included offence of which the accused may be found guilty on his trial of the offence charged.

A different class of case, raising the question of *mens rea* referable to a more serious crime than that charged, is *Regina v. Ladue*, 45 C.R. 287, [1965]

4 C.C.C. 264, a judgment of the Yukon Territory Court of Appeal which is staffed by members of the British Columbia Court of Appeal. The charge was indecently interfering with a dead human body, and the evidence showed copulation or attempted copulation with a woman who was then dead, albeit the accused testified that by reason of his intoxication he did not know that she was dead. The Court held that knowledge that the woman was dead was not an ingredient of the offence and hence, I take it, not an element requiring proof by the Crown. The Court also appears to have held, somewhat inconsistently, that proof that he did not know the woman was dead could be offered in defence by the accused, but it added that here he would be in the dilemma of admitting to rape (there being no question of consent), a more serious offence than that charged. It does occur to me, however, that the facts being what they were, the proper charge ought to have been attempted rape.

Is any general principle deducible from the foregoing catalogue of instances? Certainly, it cannot be said that, in general, where *mens rea* is an ingredient of an offence and the *actus reus* is proved it is enough if an intent is shown that would support a conviction of another crime, whether more or less serious than the offence actually committed. Coming to the particular, to the case before this Court, where proof is made of an *actus reus* that, in a general sense, is common to a range or variety of offences which require *mens rea* but those offences differ as to gravity by reason of different classifications and different penalties, is a charge of a more serious offence established by proof only that the accused intended to commit and could have been found guilty of a less serious, a lesser offence? The matter, in terms of principle, depends on how strict an observance there should be of the requirement of *mens rea*. If there is to be a relaxation of the requirement, should it not come from Parliament, which could provide for the substitution of a conviction of the lesser offence, in the same way as provision now exists in our criminal law for entering a conviction on an included offence?

Kundeus is a pre-*Charter* decision. Given the proportionality requirement articulated in *R. v. Martineau,* would the same result be reached today?

2. MISTAKE OF LAW

(a) Policy Considerations

Section 19 of the *Criminal Code* declares:

> Ignorance of the law by a person who commits an offence is not an excuse for committing that offence.

O.W. HOLMES, THE COMMON LAW

Howe, ed., (1963), 40-41

Ignorance of the law is no excuse for breaking it. This substantive principle is sometimes put in the form of a rule of evidence, that every one is presumed to know the law. It has accordingly been defended by Austin and others, on the ground of difficulty of proof. If justice requires the fact to be ascertained, the difficulty of doing so is no ground for refusing to try. But every one must feel that ignorance of the law could never be admitted as an excuse, even if the fact could be proved by sight and hearing in every case. Furthermore, now that parties can testify, it may be doubted whether a man's knowledge of the law is any harder to investigate than many questions which are gone into. The difficulty, such as it is, would be met by throwing the burden of proving ignorance on the law-breaker.

The principle cannot be explained by saying that we are not only commanded to abstain from certain acts, but also to find out that we are commanded. For if there were such a second command, it is very clear that the guilt of failing to obey it would bear no proportion to that of disobeying the principal command if known, yet the failure to know would receive the same punishment as the failure to obey the principal law.

The true explanation of the rule is the same as that which accounts for the law's indifference to a man's particular temperament, faculties, and so forth. Public policy sacrifices the individual to the general good. It is desirable that the burden of all should be equal, but it is still more desirable to put an end to robbery and murder. It is no doubt true that there are many cases in which the criminal could not have known that he was breaking the law, but to admit the excuse at all would be to encourage ignorance where the law-maker has determined to make men know and obey, and justice to the individual is rightly outweighed by the larger interests on the other side of the scales.

P.K. RYU, H. SILVING, ERROR JURIS: A COMPARATIVE STUDY

(1957), 24 U. of Chic. L. Rev. 421 at 466-471

There is a noticeable trend toward increasing recognition of error of law as a defense in several legal systems.

. . . .

Within the concept of responsibility, conceived to imply a basic freedom of choice, knowledge of the law is essential for there can be no choice without knowledge. In answering the crucial question — For what is man responsible? — Binding, the most ardent advocate of the defense of legal error, stated that criminality was defiance of the legal prohibition, a contempt of the law or a rebellion against its commands. The idea that the essence of law violation is "rebellion against the law," however, implies that every lawbreaker is a revolutionary. We believe that in a free society the sanction of the community is imposed neither for "rebellion" nor for "disobedience" but simply for violation of a duty toward the community — the actor's duty, as a member of the community, to abide by its rules. To be subject to a sanction thus conceived, the actor, as a free agent, must know the rule which he violates.

The duty of free men, however, is not exhausted merely by compliance with known law. They must also exert their conscience to ascertain what the law is.

. . . .

Lastly, the difficulty of proving legal knowledge is not in itself greater than is the difficulty of showing the presence of any other mental element. When a man shoots another in broad daylight from a distance of five feet, he will not, in the absence of special circumstances, be heard to say that he believed the target to be a hare. Nor would any man — in legal systems which admit error of law as a defense — be heard to say that he did not know the killing of a human being to be unlawful. The problem of proof changes with circumstances. A man who shoots another might well be heard to say he thought the target a hare if he had shot, in a place reserved for hunting, at great distance and under unfavorable light conditions. So might a man be heard to say that he believed he did no wrong in abbreviating the life of a friend who had but a short time to live, in order to save him from extreme suffering. As in the case of the hunter it might be deemed significant that his companions shared his optical illusion, so in the case of the mercy killer it might be considered relevant that many other persons of his environment shared his legal illusion. Thus a significant question in judging a claim of legal error is: "Is he alone ignorant of that which everybody in the State knows?"

. . . .

The policy suggested in this article may be summarized thus: Any restraint imposed upon man is, in a sense, offensive to human dignity. The aim of free society is hence to reduce legal restraint to the minimum required in a given situation. Restraint is less undignified when imposed upon conscious nonconformance with law. Subjection of man to sanctions under a law which is unknown and unknowable to him and which he has no opportunity to accept or to reject expresses the view that he is a mere object of the law. We believe, however, that in a democratic society man is the ultimate end of the law.

R. v. ESOP

(1836), 173 E.R. 203

The prisoner was indicted for an unnatural offence, committed on board of an East India ship, lying in St. Katherine's Docks. It appeared that he was a native of Bagdad.

Chambers, for the prisoner. — In the country from which the prisoner comes, it is not considered an offence; and a person who comes into this country and does an act, believing that it is a perfectly innocent one, cannot be convicted according to the law of England. A party must know that what he does is a crime. This is the principle upon which infants, idiots, and lunatics are held not to be answerable. If a person is unconscious that he is doing a wrong act, or believes that it is a right or innocent act, he is exonerated. Where one man kills another under the persuasion that he is doing a good action, he is not liable to punishment, for he knows not the distinction between right and wrong, and upon that point is insane.

Bosanquet, J. — I am clearly of opinion that this is no legal defence.

Vaughan, J. — Where is the evidence that it is not a crime in the prisoner's own country? But if it is not a crime there, that does not amount to a defence here. Numbers have been most improperly executed if it is a defence.

The prisoner, after the examination of some witnesses on his behalf, from whose statements it appeared that the witnesses for the prosecution acted under the influence of spite and ill will, was found

Not guilty.

R. v. CAMPBELL AND MLYNARCHUK

21 C.R.N.S. 273, 10 C.C.C. (2d) 26, 1972 CarswellAlta 125 (Alta. Dist. Ct.)

KERANS D.C.J. (orally): — This is an appeal by Darlene Agatha Campbell from conviction and sentence.

. . . .

On a charge before the Summary Conviction Court that she did, between February 9, 1972, and February 21, 1972, at the City of Edmonton, in the Province of Alberta, unlawfully take part as a performer in an immoral performance at Chez Pierre's situated at 10615 Jasper Ave., Edmonton, contrary to s. 163(2) [now s. 167(2)] of the *Criminal Code*.

This matter, therefore, comes before me by way of a trial *de novo*. That section provides, in s-s. (2):

> (2) Everyone commits an offence who takes part or appears as an actor, performer, or assistant in any capacity, in an immoral, indecent or obscene performance, entertainment or representation in a theatre.

The facts before me are relatively straightforward. On the dates in question, at the place in question, the appellant danced on stage, before an audience. At the start of her performance, she was wearing some clothes. By the end of her performance, she was not wearing any clothes. The dance was described to me as a "go-go dance" which, I understand, is a violent movement of almost all parts of the body, more or less in time to strongly rhythmic music.

I have no doubt in coming to the conclusion that this is a performance within the meaning of the section, and that, in doing what she did, the appellant took part as a performer in that performance. On the question of whether or not the performance was immoral, both counsel have agreed that I am bound to follow the recent decision of the Appellate Division of the Supreme Court of Alberta in *R. v. Johnson (No. 1)*, 8 C.C.C. (2d) 1. This was a stated case before the learned Riley J. [(1972), 6 C.C.C. (2d) 462], and appealed from him to the Appellate Division.

In that case, McDermid J.A., speaking for the Court, said, after drawing attention to the fact that s. 170 of the *Criminal Code* makes it a crime for anyone to appear nude in a public place, that he understood the enactment of that offence, by the Parliament of Canada, and, I quote, "declared that it is a breach of a moral standard in Canada". And he goes on,

> We know of no better way of establishing a moral standard than a declaration by the Parliament of Canada, and so the Provincial Judge was justified in accepting this as his standard in finding that the dance by the respondent in the nude was an immoral performance.

I understand, therefore, that since, to be nude in a public place is itself an offence; to perform in the nude, therefore, is an immoral performance within the meaning of the charging section. Therefore, I must conclude that the performance here was immoral within the meaning of that section.

. . . .

The next argument raised on behalf of the appellant is that the appellant lacked the necessary *mens rea* for this offence. The facts in this respect were these: she engaged to do this performance, where, earlier, she had refused to engage to do this performance, because she relied upon the statement made to her, by Pierre Couchard, that he, in turn, had been informed that a Supreme Court Judge had, to use his words because he also gave evidence, "Ruled that we could go ahead with bottomless dancing." That decision arose out of a charge in the City of Calgary, of a business acquaintance of Couchard, who was the manager of the place where this performance took place. Ironically, the decision to which Couchard and the appellant referred is the decision at the Trial Division level in *R. v. Johnson (No. 1)*, to which I earlier referred, and which, the witnesses tell me, obtained some newspaper publicity. It was a decision then, that subsequently was reversed on appeal.

Mistake of fact is a defence to a criminal charge, where it can be said that the facts believed by the accused, if true, would have afforded him a defence. It is also said that a mistake of mixed fact and law is a defence. I understand that proposition to be correct, simply because, if there is a mistake of mixed fact and law, then there is a mistake of fact. In my view, there was no mistake of fact by the appellant here. What she was told had happened, in fact, did happen.

Her mistake, if she made any mistake, was in concluding that a statement of law, expressed by the learned Riley J., was the law. That is not a mistake of fact, that is a mistake of law. It is a mistake of law to misunderstand the significance of the decision of a judge, or of his reasons. It is also a mistake of law to conclude that the decision of any particular judge correctly states the law, unless that Judge speaks on behalf of the ultimate Court of Appeal.

This is not a situation like others, where a mistake of law can be a defence, not because a mistake of law is a defence, but because a mistake of law can negative a malicious intent required for that crime. Thus, for example, where the law requires that a person wilfully, or maliciously, or knowingly, does something wrong, it could conceivably be a defence as negativing intention, to show that, because of the mistake in the understanding of the law, there was no wilful intent or malice. This is not one of those situations, as no such special intention is required for this offence. The only *mens rea* required here is that the appellant intended to do that which she did. And there is no suggestion, for a moment, that she lacked that *mens rea*.

This statement, that mistake of law is no defence, is contained in the *Criminal Code*, in s. 19, under the old numbering, which says:

> 19. Ignorance of the law by a person who commits an offence is not an excuse for committing that offence.

Excuse, or legal justification, is a defence at law, and I understand that defence to mean that it is a defence to a criminal charge to show that the act complained of was authorized by some other law. Section 19 says that defence is not available, in effect, when a person has made a mistake as to whether or not this act is excused by another law or authorized by another law.

Properly understood, in my view, the section removing ignorance of the law as a defence, in criminal matters, is not a matter of justice, but a matter of policy. There will always be cases, not so complicated as this, where honest and reasonable mistakes as to the state of the law will be the explanation of the conduct of an accused. In such a circumstance, one cannot help but have sympathy for the accused. But that situation, traditionally, is not a defence. It is not a defence, I think, because the first requirement of any system of justice, is that it work efficiently and effectively. If the state of understanding of the law of an accused person is ever to be relevant in criminal proceedings, we would have an absurd proceeding. The issue in a criminal trial would then not be what the accused did, but whether or not the accused had a sufficiently sophisticated understanding of the law to appreciate that what he did offended against the law. There would be a premium, therefore, placed upon ignorance of the law.

Our courts, following the traditions of English jurisprudence, have closed that avenue from consideration in the criminal court-room. I respectfully disagree with the learned American judges in those cases cited by the counsel for the appellant.

The defence should not be allowed as a matter of public policy, contrary to the statement of those learned judges. Indeed, it cannot be allowed because of public policy. This is the case, notwithstanding the sympathy evoked by the situation of an accused person.

Kenny, in his book, *Outlines of Criminal Law*, and I am quoting from the first edition, said at p. 69:

> although mistakes of law, unreasonable or even reasonable, thus leave the offender punishable for the crime which he has blundered into, they may of course afford good grounds for inflicting on him a milder punishment.

That is the only relevance, in my view, of the situation in which the appellant finds herself.

I have given some consideration as to whether or not this position varies at all, because of the unique circumstances here, where the appellant relied upon a specific judgment of a very immediate in terms of time and place, as opposed to a solicitor's opinion or some understanding as to the law. There is no question that there is something of an anomaly here. Reliance on a specific order, of a specific judge, granted at a specific time and place, seems, at first sight, not to be ignorance of the law, but knowledge of the law. If it turns out that that judge is mistaken, then, of course, the reliance on that Judge's judgment is mistaken. The irony is this: people in society are expected to have a more profound knowledge of the law than are the Judges. I am not the first person to have made that comment about the law, and while it is all very amusing, it is really to no point.

The principle that ignorance of the law should not be a defence in criminal matters is not justified because it is fair, it is justified because it is necessary, even though it will, sometimes produce an anomalous result.

When this appellant relied on the decision of the learned trial judge, she relied on his authority for the law. As it turns out, that reliance was misplaced, as misplaced as reliance on any statement as to the law I might make. Less so, I am sure.

Like counsel, I have had difficulty finding any authorities on this point. I was referred to *Conway v. The King* (1943), 81 C.C.C. 189, by counsel for the appellant. I have read that case. This issue, in my view, is not discussed in that case.

I have also read *R. v. Brinkley* (1907), 12 C.C.C. 454, in which the matter is discussed, although not this specific situation. In that case, a man had received advice from his counsel that a decree of divorce, made by a foreign court, validly dissolved his marriage in the eyes of the courts of Canada, and that he was, therefore, free to remarry without fear of bigamy. That opinion was mistaken. He was charged with bigamy, and he was convicted, notwithstanding his reliance on that opinion.

I have also read *Kokoliades v. Kennedy* (1911), 18 C.C.C. 495, which, to me, comes as close as can be to the situation here. This was a case in the Quebec Supreme Court, and arose in 1911. In that case, the accused was charged in the City of Montreal, with selling candy on a Sunday, contrary to a provision in a federal statute. His defence was that he relied on a municipal by-law licensing him to sell candy on a Sunday.

It would appear that this strange situation arose because there was some doubt as to the validity of the federal legislation which had been removed from the revised statutes, although not repealed. Subsequently, the Province of Quebec and the City of Montreal passed regulatory legislation purporting to permit in certain cases sales on the Lord's Day forbidden in the federal statute. The magistrate hearing the trial heard argument from the Crown that the federal legislation was constitutionally valid, and the Montreal City by-law was constitutionally invalid, and therefore an excuse was not available to the accused because the law authorizing him to do what he did, and upon which he relied, although enacted by a Legislature, or under the authority of the Legislature, was *ultra vires*.

The learned magistrate in that case, found that the Montreal by-law was *ultra vires*, and the federal statute *intra vires*; a decision which, in another case, was subsequently confirmed by the Privy Council, as we all know.

The learned magistrate went on to say that, because the law upon which the accused relied was unconstitutional, it was no law at all. He had nothing to rely upon, and he was guilty. This matter was appealed to Quebec Supreme Court. The Supreme Court Judge said that a statute authorizing an act should give rise to the defence of excuse, even though that statute may be *ultra vires*, and that the defence of excuse should be available in such a situation until there has been a judgment declaring the statute to be *ultra vires* spoken by a Court of high jurisdiction "after the gravest consideration". That is a strange remark. I would have thought that courts of high or low jurisdiction give every case grave consideration.

The situation there is not unlike the situation here. The accused there, saw a city by-law, seemingly authorizing him to do what he did, and relied upon it. It turned out the by-law had no validity. But it would take sophistication in the law to appreciate that.

Similarly, here, the appellant relied upon a statement of law, by a Supreme Court Judge in Alberta. It would take the greatest of sophistication of knowledge of the law to conclude that he was or might be mistaken. In the first case, a judge, on appeal, held that the defence of excuse ought to be allowed.

I respectfully disagree with the judge in that case, for the reasons I have mentioned.

. . . .

I, therefore, conclude that the mistake of law of the appellant affords no defence to her on this charge. There being no other defences, and the facts necessary having been made out, the conviction of the below, in my opinion, was correct. The appeal as to conviction is dismissed.

. . . .

I should have been more careful in my language a moment ago, when I said the appeal as to conviction was dismissed. Under the new law, I should have more properly said that I find the appellant guilty of the charge, and will hear argument as to whether or not to allow or dismiss the appeal as to conviction.

. . . .

Well, I have already indicated, in a quotation from Kenny, that, in this awkward situation, the matter does not afford a defence, but should certainly be considered in mitigation of sentence. Indeed, there are several cases, not as awkward as this, in the law reports, involving a person who had an honest and reasonable mistake in belief as to the law, and for whom the courts expressed sympathy, and, in respect of whom, sentence was mitigated.

It is at this stage where the scales of justice are balanced. Clothed with very recent power to refuse to enter a conviction, I can now balance the scales of justice even more delicately. I have read a note in vol. 14 of the English and Empire Digest, at p. 51 of an old case, *R. v. Bailey* (1800), Russ & Ry. 1. It goes back to 1800. In that case, the Government of England had passed a statute, making something a crime which was not previously a crime. Subsequently, the accused did the forbidden act. The court found that, in fact, in the district in which this crime was committed, no news had yet reached anyone of the passage of this Act. Nor could any news have reached this district of the passage of this Act. And that the accused, therefore, had to be convicted of an offence which he did not and could not have known was an offence. And they said there that the proper way of dealing with the matter was to give a pardon, which I understand to be a conviction followed immediately by the wiping out of a conviction.

I have no power to give a pardon, but I do have power to give an absolute discharge. In my view, this is the proper case.

Ironically, the decision of Riley J. in *Johnson*, relied on by Campbell to her detriment, was later upheld on final appeal: *Johnson v. R.* (1974), 23 C.R.N.S. 273, 13 C.C.C. (2d) 402 (S.C.C.).

(b) Distinguishing Mistake of Law and Fact

R. v. PRUE; R. v. BARIL

[1979] 2 S.C.R. 547, 8 C.R. (3d) 68 , 46 C.C.C. (2d) 257,
1979 CarswellBC 689, 1979 CarswellBC 524 (S.C.C.)

LASKIN C.J. (SPENCE, DICKSON and ESTEY JJ. concurring): —

The facts relevant to the disposition of these two appeals are set out in the reasons prepared by my brother Ritchie which I have had the advantage of reading. The basic fact, common to both cases, is that the two accused suffered an automatic suspension of their driving licences under s. 86D of the Motor-vehicle Act, R.S.B.C. 1960, c. 253, as amended by 1976 (B.C.), c. 35, s. 20, and by 1977 (B.C.), c. 41, s.3. They thereafter drove motor vehicles notwithstanding such suspension, and were then charged not for a violation of the provincial statute under which the suspension was made but rather under s. 238(3) of the federal Criminal Code. There was a finding on the trials of this charge that neither accused knew that his licence to drive had been suspended. Despite this finding they were convicted at first instance, but on appeal by way of stated case, their convictions were set aside by Gould J. who held that proof of *mens rea* was essential to a conviction of an offence under s. 238(3). The British Columbia Court of Appeal affirmed. I hold the same view.

Section 238(3) [now s. 259(4)] of the *Criminal Code* is as follows:

(3) Every one who drives a motor vehicle in Canada while he is disqualified or prohibited from driving a motor vehicle by reason of the legal suspension or cancellation, in any province, of his permit or licence or of his right to secure a permit or licence to drive a motor vehicle in that province is guilty of

    (a) an indictable offence and is liable to imprisonment for two years; or

    (b) an offence punishable on summary conviction.

What Parliament has done is to create a criminal offence merely by reason of a violation of a provincial sanction against driving while one's licence is suspended, save that it applies its own sanction throughout Canada. It needs no extensive citation of authority to say that Parliament does not acquire legislative jurisdiction simply by making its legislation operative throughout Canada: see *Toronto Electric Commissioners v. Snider* [[1925] A.C. 396], at p. 401. There must be a substantive non-geographical basis for federal legislation, and where the criminal law is concerned, and especially where an offence is included in the Criminal Code, it is generally found in a requirement of proof of *mens rea*.

This Court expressed this general principle in *Beaver v. The Queen* [[1957] S.C.R. 531], and it was expressed many years ago in England in *Sherras v. De*

Rutzen [[1895] 1 Q.B. 918], at p. 921. If *mens rea* is not a requirement for proof of an offence under s. 238(3), I would have serious doubt as to its validity on the principle expressed in *Johnson v. Attorney-General of Alberta* [[1954] S.C.R. 127], namely, that just as it is not open to a Province to supplement by additional sanctions the provisions of the *Criminal Code*, it is not open to Parliament to add a sanction, without more, to a violation of a provincial penal statute.

Much of the argument in this Court by the Crown appellant proceeded on the basis that ignorance of the suspension was ignorance of law and not of fact, and hence there was no defence to the charge under s. 238(3). The effect, if this is a correct appraisal, is to make s. 238(3) an offence of absolute liability where the provincial suspension of a driving licence is automatic under the provincial enactment (proof of such suspension being made), but not if the provincial suspension does not take effect without a requirement of notice. In either case, the consequence is to govern the operation of the federal statute by what is prescribed by the provincial enactment, and hence to create a variable type of federal offence which may have a different operation in different provinces according to the character of the relevant provincial legislation.

This cannot be. Criminality under the *Criminal Code* must depend on what Parliament independently proscribes; it risks the vulnerability of its enactment if it simply applies a sanction to a violation of a provincial statute. In my opinion, the issue of ignorance of fact or ignorance of law is properly applicable to the enforcement of the provincial enactment under which the suspension from driving is made and not to the enforcement of s. 238(3) of the *Criminal Code*. Thus, in the present case reference should properly be made to the British Columbia *Motor-vehicle Act*, s. 18, as amended and to ss. 98 and 99, as amended, if it is to be invoked against persons who claim to be unaware of the suspension of their driving licences.

So far as the operation of s. 238(3) is concerned, the existence of a suspension from driving is a question of fact underlying the invocation of that provision, and so too is proof that an accused charged thereunder drove while his licence to do so was under suspension. That was the view taken by Culliton C.J.S. in *Regina v. Ooms* [[1973] 4 W.W.R. 767], by the Ontario Court of Appeal in *Regina v. Finn* [[1972] 3 O.R. 509], and earlier in Nova Scotia in *Regina ex rel. Ross v. Jollimore* [(1961), 131 C.C.C. 319]. I do not see how this position is affected by whether the provincial legislation operates to make a suspension automatic or whether it arises only upon some notice or other action to be taken thereunder. For the purpose of the *Criminal Code*, whether there has been an effective suspension is simply a question of fact. In my opinion, therefore, *Regina v. Villeneuve* [[1968] 1 C.C.C. 267], a judgment of O'Hearn Co.Ct.J. in Nova Scotia, was wrongly decided.

This brings me back to the essentiality of *mens rea* to found a conviction under s. 238(3). I should have thought that the fact that the offence may be prosecuted by indictment and carries in that respect a maximum two-year term of imprisonment would support the application of the general principle laid down in *Beaver v. The Queen, supra*. I need not repeat the constitutional consideration which I have mentioned earlier and which leads to the same conclusion. Indeed, the inclusion of an offence in the *Criminal Code* by that very fact must be taken to import *mens rea*, and there would have to be clear indication against it before a would be justified in denying its essentiality. The *Criminal Code* is a code of outright prohibitions, distinguishable from regulatory offences created by other kinds of federal legislation. In this last-mentioned class, it is understandable that there should be questions raised about the requirement of *mens rea*. The judgment of this Court in *Regina v. Pierce Fisheries Ltd.* [[1971] S.C.R. 5] is illustrative.

The encompassing judgment of my brother Dickson in *Regina v. City of Sault Ste. Marie* [[1978] 2 S.C.R. 1299], does not lead to a different conclusion in the present case. It must be remembered that in wrestling, as he so admirably did, with whether there were two or (as he concluded) three categories of offences, he was dealing with the operation of provincial legislation, namely, The *Ontario Water Resources Commission Act*, R.S.O. 1970, c. 332, and was not concerned with evaluating offences under the *Criminal Code*. Several passages in his reasons make clear that *mens rea* continued to be essential to prove commission of a *Criminal Code* offence. I refer particularly to the following passage (at p. 1309):

> The distinction between the true criminal offence and the public welfare offence is one of prime importance. Where the offence is criminal, the Crown must establish a mental element, namely, that the accused who committed the prohibited act did so intentionally or recklessly, with knowledge of the facts constituting the offence, or with wilful blindness toward them.

Justice Dickson's classification would be an appropriate reference point for assessing the thrust of the provincial *Motor-vehicle Act* in its effect upon a person who drove in the Province while his licence to do so was suspended, but I see no need here to go further than to say with him that s. 238(3) falls clearly within his first category of offences requiring *mens rea*.

I would dismiss the two appeals.

RITCHIE J. (PIGEON J. concurring) (dissenting): —

. . . It will be readily apparent that a wide difference exists between the case of a man who acts in ignorance of the provision for automatic suspension and is therefore acting under a mistake of law, and a man who resides in a province where the imposition of such a suspension can only be effected as the result of the intervention of some administrative act by the authorities. The latter situation is evidenced in jurisdictions where provision is made for the clerk of the court, the presiding magistrate or some other official giving notice to the accused of the suspension of his licence before that suspension can be effective. In the latter type of case when the requisite administrative step or steps have not been taken and the accused can show that he was therefore ignorant of the fact of his suspension, his ignorance is one of fact and not of law, and in this event it has been consistently held that he has a valid defence to the charge. The cases in support of this proposition are collected and form the subject of comment in the reasons for judgment of Mr. Justice Martin of the Court of Appeal of Ontario in *R. v. Lock* [(1974), 18 C.C.C. (2d) 477], and they are referred to with approval in the reasons for judgment of Mr. Justice Seaton in these cases. These cases turn on the finding that the failure to give notice or to take such other administrative step as is required is a question of fact and that the accused's failure to know of the suspension is not a mistake of law.

In the present cases the respondents' lack of knowledge of the suspension of their licences was not occasioned by any mistake of fact but rather by ignorance of the law attendant upon failure to be aware of the automatic suspension for which provision is made in s. 86D of the *Motor-vehicle Act* (*supra*). In this latter regard I share the view expressed by His Honour Judge Peter O'Hearn of the County Court in Nova Scotia, in *R. v. Villeneuve, supra*, where conviction under s. 221 of the *Criminal Code* (now s. 236) resulted in automatic revocation of the licence and the defence was advanced that the accused was ignorant of the fact that his licence had been revoked. Judge O'Hearn, in referring to *Regina ex rel. Ross v. Jollimore* [(1961), 131 C.C.C. 319], said of the charge before him (at pp. 270-1):

> Of what was he ignorant? In *Jollimore* it could be said that the defendant did not know whether the Magistrate had forwarded a record of the original conviction to the Registrar, or whether the Registrar had acted thereupon by revoking the licence. These are administrative acts; they are matters of fact. In the instant case, the accused was ignorant of the fact that his licence was revoked but this was a direct consequence of his ignorance of the legal effect of conviction under *Cr. Code* s. 221. That is, his ignorance of the fact of revocation is not independent of his ignorance of the law, but directly dependent upon it, and his ignorance is essentially ignorance of the law. There is no independent factual error to make it a mistake of mixed law and fact.

I am satisfied that the mistake made by the accused in the present cases is nothing more than a mistake as to the legal consequences of a conviction under s. 236 of the *Criminal Code* involving as they do the automatic suspension of the operator's licence under s. 86D of the *Motor-vehicle Act*.

Once the mistake is recognized as being founded in ignorance of the law the respondents are faced with the provisions of s. 19 of the *Criminal Code* which read as follows:

> 19. Ignorance of the law by a person who commits an offence is not an excuse for committing that offence.

What we have here is a plain statement of the law in British Columbia, as contained in s. 86D of the *Motor-vehicle Act*, requiring the automatic suspension of an operator's licence upon breach of certain sections of the *Criminal Code* dealing with the operation of motor vehicles and a disregard of the provisions of this section which involved the accused in a breach of s. 238 of the *Criminal Code*. There is no evidence that either of the respondents made any effort to determine whether their licences had been suspended or not and this is not a case involving ignorance of some regulation or technicality which might have been understandably unknown to the driving public and thus to the respondents.

For all these reasons I would allow these appeals, set aside the judgment of the Court of Appeal for British Columbia and direct the conviction of the two respondents for the offences with which they were charged.

[The dissenting judgment of Beetz J. has been omitted.]

Appeals dismissed.

R. v. MACDONALD

2014 SCC 3, [2014] 1 S.C.R. 37, 303 C.C.C. (3d) 113, 7 C.R. (7th) 229

LeBel J. :

C. Appeal of the Acquittal on the Charge Under Section 95 of the Code

[51] The Crown is appealing Mr. MacDonald's acquittal on the charge under s. 95 of the *Code*. It submits that the Court of Appeal erred in interpreting the *mens rea* requirement of the offence of possession of a loaded restricted firearm provided for in s. 95 and imposed a nearly insurmountable burden on the Crown which is inconsistent with the principle that ignorance of the law is no excuse. Mr. MacDonald takes the position that the Court of Appeal correctly interpreted the *mens rea* requirement of that offence and correctly held that the *mens rea* had not been made out. I agree with the Crown that the Court of Appeal made an error in requiring the Crown to prove, in order to secure a conviction under s. 95, that the accused knew his possession and acquisition licence and authorization to transport the firearm did not extend to the place where he unlawfully had it in his possession. As I will explain, such a requirement is inconsistent with the rule, codified in s. 19 of the *Code*, that ignorance of the law is no excuse.

[52] Section 95(1) of the *Code* reads as follows:

> 95. (1) Subject to subsection (3), every person commits an offence who, in any place, possesses a loaded prohibited firearm or restricted firearm, or an unloaded prohibited firearm or restricted firearm together with readily accessible ammunition that is capable of being discharged in the firearm, unless the person is the holder of
>
> > (a) an authorization or a licence under which the person may possess the firearm in that place; and

(b) the registration certificate for the firearm.

[53] In this Court, Mr. MacDonald's argument on his conviction under s. 95 relates to the *mens rea* of the offence. He does not dispute that he possessed a loaded restricted firearm in the unit. Nor does Mr. MacDonald deny that he possessed the firearm there without being the holder of an authorization or a licence that entitled him to possess it in that place. Rather, he argues that s. 95 is a *mens rea* offence and that, to secure a conviction, the Crown must show that he knew his possession of the firearm in the unit was unauthorized. This, Mr. MacDonald says, the Crown failed to do, whereas he testified at trial that he had a subjective belief that the authorization he had obtained in Alberta extended to his condominium in Halifax.

[54] In my view, the offence provided for in s. 95 is a *mens rea* offence. As this Court recognized in *Lévis (City) v. Tétreault*, 2006 SCC 12, [2006] 1 S.C.R. 420, at para. 16, classifying an offence as either a mens rea offence, a strict liability offence or an absolute liability offence is a question of statutory interpretation. The Crown agreed at the hearing of this case that the offence at issue is a *mens rea* offence, and in any event, we may validly rely on the presumption that an offence should be classified as a *mens rea* offence where, as here, nothing in the statute indicates a contrary intention (*The Queen v. Sault Ste. Marie*, [1978] 2 S.C.R. 1299, at pp. 1309-10; *Beaver v. The Queen*, [1957] S.C.R. 531).

[55] The *mens rea* the Crown is required to prove under s. 95(1) does not, however, include knowledge that possession in the place in question is unauthorized. Rather, knowledge that one possesses a loaded restricted firearm, together with an intention to possess the loaded firearm in that place, is enough. An individual who knowingly possesses a loaded restricted firearm in a particular place with an intention to do so will be liable to punishment for the offence provided for in s. 95(1) unless he or she holds an authorization or a licence under which the firearm may be possessed in that place. Thus, a proper authorization or licence serves to negate the *actus reus* of the offence, thereby allowing someone who legitimately possesses a restricted firearm in a given place to avoid liability.

[56] With respect, the Court of Appeal erred in law by improperly reading a defence of ignorance of the law into s. 95(1). In the majority's view, the Crown had to prove that Mr. MacDonald knew or was wilfully blind to the fact that his possession was unauthorized. Such a burden would compel the Crown to prove that an accused knew the conditions of his or her authorization or licence. This amounts to requiring the Crown to prove that the accused knew the law.

[57] The following example illustrates the point that an error made by an accused in interpreting his or her authorization or licence is a mistake of law and not one

of fact. Suppose the *Code* provided that restricted firearms could be possessed only in the province of Alberta, and nowhere else in Canada. Surely, if that were the case, there could be no dispute that Mr. MacDonald's possession of such a firearm in Halifax contravened this rule, and any suggestion that he thought he could lawfully possess it there would have to be considered a mistake of law and would therefore afford no defence to a charge of unlawful possession. For my part, I find no distinction when such a rule is expanded to an individual's authorization and the applicable section of the *Code* merely refers to such a document. Mr. MacDonald's subjective belief that he could possess the firearm in Halifax is therefore nothing other than a mistake of law.

[58] I therefore find that a requirement that an accused knew or was wilfully blind to the fact that his possession was unauthorized would be grounded on the acceptance of mistake of law as a defence to a charge under s. 95(1). It is trite law that, except in the case of an officially induced error, a mistake of law is no defence in our criminal justice system. Section 19 of the *Code* states:

> 19. Ignorance of the law by a person who commits an offence is not an excuse for committing that offence.

. . . .

[60] In sum, the Court of Appeal erred by treating Mr. MacDonald's mistake of law as a mistake of fact which exonerated him of the charge resulting from his actions. I would allow the Crown's appeal on this issue and restore the conviction under s. 95(1).

Where the mistake or ignorance relates to law, s. 19 must be applied. There are, however, two major exceptions — colour of right, which is a statutory exception applying to certain property offences, and officially induced error of law, a common law defence.

(c)   Colour of Right for Property Offences

The defence of colour of right is expressly a defence to theft under s. 322. The most significant other statutory colour of right exception to the rigid rule that ignorance or mistake of law is no defence is set out in s. 429(2) for Part XI offences. This allows, for those accused of offences in that Part, the defence of proving that they acted "with legal justification or excuse and with colour of right". Our courts have long relied on the determination that "and" before "colour of right" was a drafting error and should read "or": *R. v. Creaghan* (1982), 31 C.R. (3d) 277 (Ont. C.A.). The list of Part XI offences currently includes mischief, attacks on internationally protected premises, unauthorized recording of a movie, arson, raising a false fire alarm, injuring cattle, cruelty to animals and keeping a cockpit.

Parliament has not bothered to correct the drafting error or to address the obvious anomalies in the colour of right defences. In *R. v. Kingsbury* (2012), 99

C.R. (6th) 94 (B.C. C.A.) it was confirmed that although colour of right is a defence to theft it is not a defence to fraud. In the absence of a *Charter* challenge the Court had no choice but to apply that interpretation. As a matter of policy it makes little sense for there to be a generous honest belief in a legal right defence to theft in these circumstances but not to fraud. This is a good example of the urgent need for principled *Criminal Code* review and reform. **Should there, for example, be a general defence of honest and reasonable belief in a legal right?**

In *R. v. Simpson*, [2015] 2 S.C.R. 827, 327 C.C.C. (3d) 360, 21 C.R. (7th) 225 the Supreme Court held in *obiter* – as there was no air of reality to the defence on the evidence in the case at bar – that a colour of right defence "would appear to apply to other property-related offences, including breaking and entry" [para. 31].

This view – which allows for a colour of right defence in the absence of any statutory language making it available – appears to be in error. The Court refers to *Adgey v. R.* (1973), [1975] 2 S.C.R. 426, 13 C.C.C. (2d) 177 and *R. v. Charters*, 2007 NBCA 66 for that view. Those two early cases cannot be considered as establishing such a defence as the comments there made were in passing and in the context of entries where consent to enter had been clearly revoked. Authority in lower courts is consistent in holding that the colour of right defence if based on a mistake of law is an anomaly confined to statutory exceptions – currently only s. 429(2) for Part XI property offences, a few other property offences such as the various forms of theft in ss. 322, 342 and 342.1 and forcible detainer in s. 72(2).

R. v. DOROSH

20 C.R. (6th) 368, 183 C.C.C. (3d) 224, 2004 CarswellSask 55 (Sask. C.A.)

1   BAYDA C.J.S.: — The appellant (defendant) was charged with stealing a trailer, the property of Randy Zayshley of a value not exceeding $5,000, contrary to s. 334(b) of the *Criminal Code*. He was tried and convicted by a judge of the Provincial Court, whereupon, pursuant to s. 813 of the *Code*, he appealed from his conviction to the Court of Queen's Bench. His appeal was dismissed. Then, pursuant to s. 839(1) of the *Code*, he applied to this court for leave to appeal, and if leave be granted, he requested this court to hear his appeal. At the conclusion of the hearing, this court granted the application for leave, allowed the appeal and directed a new trial, with reasons to follow. These are those reasons.

2   The ground of appeal raised by the defendant before the Court of Queen's Bench, and before this Court, involved the question whether the learned Provincial Court judge (the trial judge) erred in his interpretation of the phrase "without colour of right" appearing in s. 322 of the *Code* and in his application of the law embodied by that phrase to the facts of this case.

3   The facts are essentially not in dispute. (Although the trial judge did not explicitly make findings of fact, it is implicit in his ruling that he accepted the testimonies of the defendant and the other witnesses and found no contradiction that required resolution.) The defendant purchased from Mr. Zayshley a "1988 Dodge Van with Carpet Cleaning Unit as is condition, no warranty's." No purchase price was stipulated in the bill of sale. Instead, the document contemplated as consideration for the sale, the delivery by the defendant to Mr. Zayshley of three items, namely, a cargo trailer, a roto tiller, and a power plant together with the payment to Mr. Zayshley of $1,200 cash and $1,300 "in thirty days." The document went on to state "All items as is and free and clear of all debts." The defendant delivered the three items to Mr. Zayshley and paid him the $1,200 cash. He has not paid the remaining $1,300.

4   Shortly after he acquired the van and cleaning unit, the defendant concluded that the cleaning unit "was not operational". He testified that Mr. Zayshley orally undertook that the van and unit were operational. The unit, he contends, needs "major repairs" estimated to cost "several thousand dollars." He went on to say that he "tried reaching Mr. Zayshley and could not get a hold of him." He became "suspicious" about the transaction and contacted his lawyer. The lawyer made a search of the Personal Property Registry and determined that there were writs of execution registered against Mr. Zayshley's name. (It turned out that the writs were actually registered against the name of Mr. Zayshley's son who happens to have the name: Randy Zayshley Jr.)

5   Based on the information he received from his lawyer, the defendant concluded that "there were liens against the van." In addition, the defendant felt that Mr. Zayshley failed to honour his undertaking to train the defendant in the use of the cleaning equipment. All of this put together lead the defendant to conclude that "the deal was dead." He went to Mr. Zayshley's home and picked up the trailer that he had originally delivered to Mr. Zayshley as part of the consideration for the purchase of the van. Mr. Zayshley was not at home at the time. The defendant in his testimony explained:

> I felt I was picking up my own trailer, and I tried reaching them to get a hold of them to tell them that, look, there was problems with the van, that - like I stressed so strongly, over and over to him, with the deal, the van had to be operational because I knew nothing about carpet cleaning; I needed help in the training. I stressed that very strongly and he agreed, and nothing, and nothing came through with the training or the van was not operational, that it needed major repairs, there were liens against it. Like it was - I felt like I was being rooked into this deal. [Transcript pp. 46, line 25 -47, line 9]

6   He then advertised the trailer for sale and sold it to a person by the name of Donald Heisler who responded to the advertisement. When asked in his examination-in-chief about his "state of mind" when he sold the trailer to Mr. Heisler, he testified:

Well as far as I was concerned, I hadn't - Mr. Zayshley, I tried repeatedly phoning Mr. Zayshley. In fact I had talked to his wife or girlfriend once on the phone and I told her to have Randy phone me back, there was a problem with the van. I got no replies back. And as far as I was concerned the deal was dead, and the trailer was mine. And this is like a month later, so I decided to resell the trailer. [Transcript p. 47, lines 13-20]

7   The police arranged to have the trailer returned to Mr. Zayshley and charged the defendant with theft.

. . . .

9   During the trial, in one of his exchanges with counsel, the trial judge referred to colour of right in these terms:

Like to me colour of right is when I say I'm going to sell this pen to you for a dollar and you say here's a dollar, I'll pick up the pen later, and now, unbeknownst to you there's pen number 2, and you come up and you get this pen. Now the pen that, you know, you thought you were buying is worth so much and the other pen is worth a totally different amount. And you thought you were taking the pen you bought, so now you thought you had a colour of right to take the pen that you picked up, when all of a sudden I say, no, no, this is the one that you bought. So that to me is the criminal law issue of colour of right. But to acknowledge an issue of colour of right when somebody is grabbing something because they think they have a civilly justifiable claim, that may well not hold water. [Transcript p. 29, lines 8-23]

. . . .

11   In my respectful view the trial judge neither properly interpreted the phrase "without colour of right" as used in s. 322 of the *Code*, nor properly applied the law embodied by that phrase to the facts of this case. The summary appellate court judge erred in failing to redress those errors.

12   The relevant provisions of s. 322 of the *Code* are subsections (1)(a), (2) and (3):

322. (1) Every one commits theft who fraudulently and without colour of right takes, or fraudulently and without colour of right converts to his use or to the use of another person, anything, whether animate or inanimate, with intent

(a) to deprive, temporarily or absolutely, the owner of it, or a person who has a special property or interest in it, of the thing or of his property or interest in it;

. . . .

(2) A person commits theft when, with intent to steal anything, he moves it or causes it to move or to be moved, or begins to cause it to become movable.

(3) A taking or conversion of anything may be fraudulent notwithstanding that it is effected without secrecy or attempt at concealment.

13   The *actus reus* of the offence charged consisted of the taking by the defendant of the trailer (an animate thing). There is no dispute that the Crown

established this element of the offence beyond a reasonable doubt. Indeed, the defendant admitted the taking.

14   The *mens rea* element is another matter. The Crown needed to prove, beyond a reasonable doubt, the three requirements of this element, namely, (i) a fraudulent intent on the part of the defendant at the time of the taking of the trailer; (ii) an absence of any colour of right asserted by the defendant, and (iii) an intent on the part of the defendant to deprive, temporarily or absolutely, the owner, Mr. Zayshley, of the trailer.

15   The parties and the trial judge focussed their attention on the second of these requirements and made no reference to the first or the third.

16   The jurisprudential history surrounding the phrase "colour of right" indicates that the meaning of the phrase has a certain quality of elusiveness (see *The Law of Theft and Related Offences* by Winifred H. Holland (Toronto: Carswell, 1998) at pp. 150-170). The definition of the phrase by Martin J.A., speaking for the Court (including Gale C.J.O. and Estey J.A.), in *R. v. DeMarco* (1973), 13 C.C.C. (2d) 369 (Ont. C.A.) at 372 may be taken to have settled many, if not all, of the contentious issues raised by earlier Canadian cases where the phrase was considered. He said:

> The term "colour of right" generally, although not exclusively, refers to a situation where there is an assertion of a proprietary or possessory right to the thing which is the subject-matter of the alleged theft. One who is honestly asserting what he believes to be an honest claim cannot be said to act "without colour of right", even though it may be unfounded in law or in fact: see *R. v. Howson*, [1966] 3 C.C.C. 348, 55 D.L.R. (2d) 582, [1966] 2 O.R. 63. The term "colour of right" is also used to denote an honest belief in a state of facts which, if it actually existed would at law justify or excuse the act done: *R. v. Howson*. The term when used in the latter sense is merely a particular application of the doctrine of mistake of fact.

17   Since *DeMarco* was decided, the Supreme Court of Canada has dealt with the "colour of right" issue in two cases: *R. v. Lilly*, [1983] 1 S.C.R. 794; and *R. v. Jones*, [1991] 3 S.C.R. 110. Nothing said in the judgments in either of those cases in any way detracts from Martin J.A.'s definition. If anything, the court's decision in *Lilly* may be said to impliedly support the definition. In two other cases, *R. v. Lafrance*, [1975] 1 S.C.R. 201 and *R. v. Milne*, [1992] 1 S.C.R. 697 the "colour of right" issue arose only incidentally and not as a principal issue. These judgments as well contain nothing that detracts from the DeMarco definition.

18   A colour of right can have its basis in either a mistake of civil law (a colour of right provides an exception to s. 19 of the *Code*; see: *The Law of Theft and Related Offences* p. 153) or in a mistake in a state of facts. The mistake in each case must give rise to either an honest belief in a proprietary or possessory right to the thing which is the subject matter of the alleged theft or an honest

belief in the state of facts which if it actually existed would at law justify or excuse the act done.

19   In my respectful view the trial judge erred when, in essence, he found that a colour of right can have a basis only in a mistake in a state of facts. The "pen" example he gave in his exchange with counsel during the course of the proceedings that I quoted earlier is a clear acknowledgement of his acceptance that a mistake in a state of facts can serve as a basis for a colour of right. But in that same exchange he essentially rejected a mistake of civil law as a basis when he said:

> But to acknowledge an issue of colour of right when somebody is grabbing something because they think they have a civilly justifiable claim that may well not hold water. [Emphasis added, Transcript p. 29, lines 20-23]

20   The judge obviously carried this thinking into his final ruling.

21   Even if it can be said that the judge did not reject the first basis - a mistake in civil law - as a basis for colour of right, then he clearly erred in applying to the facts of this case the law embraced by a properly defined colour of right concept. I say that for these reasons: The judge appears to have acknowledged that the defendant had a belief he had a claim to the trailer. But, instead of asking himself: Did the defendant have an honest belief in his claim even though the claim may be unfounded in law and in fact?, the judge, in effect, asked himself the question: Was the defendant's claim unfounded in law? The judge then proceeded to answer the latter question in the negative and on that premise concluded the defendant had no colour of right.

22   Parenthetically, I note that counsel (counsel for the Crown before us did not appear as counsel at trial) and the judge appeared to treat the absence of a colour of right not as a requirement of *mens rea* for the Crown to prove beyond a reasonable doubt, but as a defence for the defendant to establish. I again note that no attention - not even casual - was paid to the other two requirements of *mens rea*, namely, the fraudulent intent and the specific intent contemplated by clause 322(1)(a). I do not propose to deal with these aspects of the case as they were not argued before us.

. . . .

25   It is for these reasons that we directed a new trial.

An important point to recognize is that colour of right is limited to a mistaken belief about a *legal* right, and cannot rest on a view about the *morality* of the law in question. This point is illustrated by the difference in treatment of protestors in a pair of related cases, *R. v. Potts* and *R. v. Drainville*. Both protesters had taken part in a blockade of a parcel of land to prevent the construction of a road through what was claimed to be unceded land belonging to the Teme-Augama Anishnabai Nation, and both were charged with mischief under s. 430(1)(c). Potts was a chief of the Teme-Augama Anishnabai Nation, and testified (among other things) that he believed his people retained title to the land. In fact his people had lost a court decision, as Potts knew, but the Supreme Court of Canada had granted leave to appeal: Potts testified that despite the Ontario Court of Appeal ruling he believed that his people had the legal right to the land. At his trial, Potts was found to have colour of right on the basis of that honest (if unreasonable) mistaken belief, and was acquitted.

Drainville was a priest and a member of the provincial legislature, and he too took part in the blockade and was arrested. The trial judge concluded that Father Drainville's evidence showed him to have "a great and deep moral conviction as the basis for his belief that the Teme-Augama Anishnabai Nation has a good claim to the lands" but "an honest belief in a moral as opposed to legal right cannot constitute a colour of right defence". See the discussion of both cases in *R. v. Drainville* (1991), 5 C.R. (4th) 38 (Ont. Prov. Div.).

Drainville made a separate argument that – in the spirit of Mahatma Gandhi or Henry David Thoreau – his actions amounted to acts of civil disobedience, which should be seen as a defence for him:

[42] Another line of defence advanced on behalf of the accused is that his actions constitute at best passive resistance, a type of civil disobedience which ought not to result in his conviction. It is said that his involvement was indeed minimal, that his motives and intentions were noble and good, and that, in fact, he has contributed in his own small way to a just and honourable political solution. In referring to a "political solution", counsel is no doubt alluding to the memorandum of agreement dated April 23, 1990, entered into by the representatives of the Teme-Augama Anishnabai Nation and those of the Ontario Government.

The trial judge did not accept the fundamental premise behind this argument:

[49] In the unreported case of *R. v. Potts*, this Court made its views known with respect to civil disobedience. I had occasion to quote Mr. Chief Justice Howland, as he then was, when he addressed the government at the opening of courts ceremony, in Toronto, in January 1990. He said:

It is one of the fundamental principles of our democratic society that no one is above the law, and everyone is equal before the law. The rule of law is based on the fact that our current laws represent the will of the majority of the people. If a law no longer represents the will of the majority, then it should be changed but until it is changed by lawful means, it must be obeyed. Defiance of the law is not the answer.

[50] Finally, let me reiterate this Court's position. Is "civil disobedience" or even "passive resistance" such a small infraction, or such a minimal use of force, that the "*actus reus*" ought to be overlooked? Should such activity as obstructing a road be justified by some sort of approval by the courts on the grounds that the motives are good and noble, or that the situation is really a "political" one? In light of the existing circumstances of this case, where it seems a just and appropriate political solution appears to have been found, this might be a tempting proposition. But certainly that would be tantamount to a declaration that, in some instances, at the discretion of some judge, and irrespective of the "rule of law", there are times when "the ends justify the means." Even in this case, where it appears that the government of Ontario may be about to change its policies and perhaps admit to a previous error in judgment, where it appears that a memorandum of agreement termed a viable "political solution" is now in place and that those protesters may have been morally right, surely, the process of legitimizing previously unlawful

acts after the fact is an inherently dangerous concept which is simply not acceptable as an alternative to the "rule of law".

[51] To permit this process to replace the "rule of law" would be to grant permission to anyone to arrogate himself with the powers of a judge and determine for himself or herself, and from time-to-time, what is acceptable or just, and what is not, on behalf of the majority. As such anyone could adjudicate himself or herself above the law, and no one would be equal before the law. Such a situation would surely lead to anarchy, and very quickly so.

(d) Officially Induced Error of Law

LÉVIS (CITY) v. TÉTREAULT;
LÉVIS (CITY) v. 2629-4470 QUÉBEC INC.

[2006] 1 S.C.R. 420, 36 C.R. (6th) 215, 2006 SCC 12, 207 C.C.C. (3d) 1,
2006 CarswellQue 2911, 2006 CarswellQue 2912

In these two cases, the City of Lévis appealed acquittals entered by the Quebec Municipal Court on charges brought against T and a numbered company under the *Highway Safety Code*, R.S.Q., c. C-24.2. T was charged with driving a motor vehicle without a valid driver's licence contrary to s. 93.1. He raised the defence of due diligence, stating that he was unaware that the date appearing on his licence was the date the licence expired rather than a payment due date. The numbered company was charged with operating a motor vehicle for which the fees relating to its registration had not been paid contrary to s. 31.1. It raised the defences of due diligence and officially induced error, alleging that a representative of the Société de l'assurance automobile du Québec ("SAAQ") had had it pay registration fees corresponding to a 15-month period and had told it that a renewal notice would be sent to it before the period expired. Because of an error, the SAAQ sent the notice to the company with an incomplete address and the postal service returned it to the sender. The Municipal Court of the City of Lévis found that both offences were offences of strict liability. The defences of due diligence were accepted and the accused acquitted.

When the matter finally reached the Supreme Court, the Court confirmed that the offences were properly classified as strict liability. On the facts the Court however held that the defence of due diligence had not been established. Both accused had simply remained passive rather than attempting to discover the nature of their legal obligation to pay. The Supreme Court allowed the appeal, entered convictions and imposed minimum fines.

In the course of dismissing the appeals the Court also finally decided that the defence of officially induced error of law is available for any offence.

LeBel J.: —

. . . .

D. Defence of Officially Induced Error

20.   Because the respondent company argues that it was misled by erroneous information obtained from an SAAQ official regarding the procedure for paying the fees relating to the registration of its vehicle, we must now consider the nature and availability of the defence of officially induced error. This Court has never clearly accepted this defence, although several decisions by Canadian courts have recognized it to be relevant and legitimate.

21.   First of all, to place the nature and limits of this defence in the proper perspective, it should be noted that ignorance of the law is not accepted in Canadian criminal law as a means to erase or mitigate criminal liability, despite occasional criticism of the inflexibility of this rule (D. Stuart, *Canadian Criminal Law: A Treatise* (4th ed. 2001), at pp. 322-31). Section 19 of the *Criminal Code*, R.S.C. 1985, c. C-46, states that ignorance of the law is not an excuse for committing an offence. Pursuant to art. 60 C.P.P., this principle applies to regulatory offences created by Quebec legislation. As a result of art. 60, the rules and principles of Canadian criminal law relating to the definition and conduct of available defences against criminal charges apply in Quebec penal law (G. Létourneau and P. Robert, *Code de procédure pénale du Québec annoté* (6th ed. 2004), at pp. 8-9 and 88).

22.   This Court has firmly and consistently applied the principle that ignorance of the law is no defence. It has given effect to this principle not only in the context of the criminal law itself, but also in cases involving regulatory offences (*Molis v. The Queen*, [1980] 2 S.C.R. 356; *Pontes*). However, the inflexibility of this rule is cause for concern where the error in law of the accused arises out of an error of an authorized representative of the state and the state then demands, through other officials, that the criminal law be applied strictly to punish the conduct of the accused. In such a case, regardless of whether it involves strict liability or absolute liability offences, the fundamental fairness of the criminal process would appear to be compromised. Although the Court has not ruled on this point, Lamer C.J. responded to these concerns, in concurring reasons in *Jorgensen* (*R. v. Jorgensen*, [1995] 4 S.C.R. 55), by proposing to recognize the defence of officially induced error and attempting to define the conditions under which the defence would be allowed.

23.   In that case, which involved a charge of selling obscene material, Lamer C.J. carefully reviewed the development of this defence by the courts. He pointed out that the defence had surfaced gradually in criminal law and had been applied by trial and appeal courts to both crimes and regulatory offences: *Jorgensen*, at

paras. 12-24). He noted that the judges of this Court, including Ritchie J. in *R. v. MacDougall*, [1982] 2 S.C.R. 605, at p. 613, had at times appeared to acknowledge the appropriateness of such a defence (*Jorgensen*, at para. 17). Later, Gonthier J. too, discussed the framework and nature of the defence of officially induced error in his dissenting reasons in *Pontes*, at p. 88 (*Jorgensen*, at para. 23).

24.   In Lamer C.J.'s view, this defence constituted a limited but necessary exception to the rule that ignorance of the law cannot excuse the commission of a criminal offence:

> Officially induced error of law exists as an exception to the rule that ignorance of the law does not excuse. As several of the cases where this rule has been discussed note, the complexity of contemporary regulation makes the assumption that a responsible citizen will have a comprehensive knowledge of the law unreasonable. This complexity, however, does not justify rejecting a rule which encourages a responsible citizenry, encourages government to publicize enactments, and is an essential foundation to the rule of law. Rather, extensive regulation is one motive for creating a limited exception to the rule that *ignorantia juris neminem excusat*.

(*Jorgensen*, at para. 25)

25.   Lamer C.J. equated this defence with an excuse that has an effect similar to entrapment. The wrongfulness of the act is established. However, because of the circumstances leading up to the act, the person who committed it is not held liable for the act in criminal law. The accused is thus entitled to a stay of proceedings rather than an acquittal (*Jorgensen*, at para. 37).

26.   After his analysis of the case law, Lamer C.J. defined the constituent elements of the defence and the conditions under which it will be available. In his view, the accused must prove six elements:

(1) that an error of law or of mixed law and fact was made;
(2) that the person who committed the act considered the legal consequences of his or her actions;
(3) that the advice obtained came from an appropriate official;
(4) that the advice was reasonable;
(5) that the advice was erroneous; and
(6) that the person relied on the advice in committing the act.

(*Jorgensen*, at paras. 28-35).

27.   Although the Court did not rule on this issue in *Jorgensen*, I believe that this analytical framework has become established. Provincial appellate courts have followed this approach to consider and apply the defence of officially induced error (*R. v. Larivière* (2000), 38 C.R. (5th) 130 (Que. C.A.); *Maitland Valley Conservation Authority v. Cranbrook Swine Inc.* (2003), 64 O.R. (3d) 417 (C.A.)). I would also note that, in this appeal, neither the prosecution nor

the intervener, the Attorney General of Canada, has questioned the existence of this defence in Canadian criminal law as it presently stands. At most, the Attorney General of Canada has suggested another condition in addition to those enumerated by Lamer C.J., namely that the act was committed contemporaneously with the reception of the information. I do not think this addition is necessary. The Attorney General of Canada's concerns relate more to the need to demonstrate that the advice was reasonable and that the accused relied on it. It should be noted, as the Ontario Court of Appeal has done, that it is necessary to establish the objective reasonableness not only of the advice, but also of the reliance on the advice *(R. v. Cancoil Thermal Corp.* (1986), 27 C.C.C. (3d) 295; *Cranbrook Swine).* Various factors will be taken into consideration in the course of this assessment, including the efforts made by the accused to obtain information, the clarity or obscurity of the law, the position and role of the official who gave the information or opinion, and the clarity, definitiveness and reasonableness of the information or opinion (*Cancoil Thermal*, at p. 303). It is not sufficient in such cases to conduct a purely subjective analysis of the reasonableness of the information. This aspect of the question must be considered from the perspective of a reasonable person in a situation similar to that of the accused.

31.   In the case of the [accused company], a due diligence defence has not been made out, and it has not been demonstrated that all the conditions under which the defence of officially induced error is available have been met.

. . . .

33.   In my view, the respondent's allegations of fact do not show conduct that meets the standard of due diligence. The respondent was aware of the date when the fees relating to the registration of its vehicle would be due and, accordingly, the date when the registration would cease to be valid. It could and should have been concerned when it failed to receive a notice. Instead, it did nothing. It had a duty to do more. The acquittal was therefore unjustified.

34.   Nor has the respondent established that the conditions under which the defence or excuse of officially induced error is available have been met in this case and justified a stay of proceedings. The issues raised related at most to administrative practices, not to the legal obligation to pay the fees by the prescribed date. Two fundamental conditions that must be met for this defence to be available were therefore missing. In the circumstances, the respondent could not have considered the legal consequences of its conduct on the basis of advice from the official in question, nor could it have acted in reliance on that opinion, since no information regarding the nature and effects of the relevant legal obligations had been requested or obtained.

Do you agree with the Supreme Court that this defence should be established with a remedy of a judicial stay rather than an acquittal on the merits, as is the case with most defences?

In *Canada (Attorney General) v. Charles* (2005), 30 C.R. (6th) 316 (Sask. C.A.) farmers selling wheat in protest of the monopoly of the Canadian Wheat Board were held to have a defence of officially induced error of law to a charge of failing to report their export to customs officials. The customs officials had no legal basis for refusing to accept documentation other than the Wheat Board export license. However, in *R. v. Shiner* (2007), 46 C.R. (6th) 268 (N.L. C.A.) the defence did not succeed in the case of sealers catching blueback seal and selling their pelts. The fact that the ban against such hunting had not been enforced in previous years, and that a Department of Fisheries and Oceans Officer was present at the hunt and did nothing, was not a sufficient basis for the defence. Their acquittals were reversed.

Justice Wagner for a 6-1 majority in *Québec (Autorité des marchés financiers) c. Souveraine, cie d'assurance générale*, 6 C.R. (7th) 250, [2013] 3 S.C.R. 756, 305 C.C.C. (3d) 287 confirms that in the case of regulatory offences (in that case a charge against an insurance company selling products in Quebec contrary to provincial regulations) the defence of officially induced error of law and the defence of due diligence are to be kept distinct. Where the mistake is one of law alone the defence of due diligence is not available. The Court also confirms the ruling in *Lévis* that mere passivity will not satisfy either defence.

Christine Boyle and Sam de Groot, "The Responsible Citizen in the City of Lévis: Due Diligence and Officially Induced Error of Law" (2006), 30 C.R. (6th) 316 persuasively suggested that the Supreme Court view of passivity has made both defences unduly hard to establish. Only Justice Abella in dissent in *La Souveraine* was prepared to broaden the officially induced error of law exception. In the Quebec Court of Appeal in the Court below, Cournoyer J.C.A. (*ad hoc*) also points out that the accused was in part relying on legal advice from the broker's lawyers. Canadian courts have never accepted that such advice could ground the defence, presumably based on the fear that incompetent and/or corrupt lawyers could in effect provide erroneous advice which would exempt their clients from the law. Interestingly, Wagner J. does not close the door to this argument as Courts of Appeal have done:

> The appellant relied solely on the legal advice of professionals acting for a third party, Flanders, in Manitoba. A reasonable person would at least have sought an independent opinion from a member of the Barreau du Québec, preferably one who specializes in insurance law. Thus, the appellant in this case has not shown that it took all reasonable steps to avoid breaking the law. [para. 79]

For an argument that a rigid division of legally significant error into ignorance of law and mistake of fact is contrary to s. 7 of the *Charter*, see Hamish Stewart, "Mistake of Law Under the *Charter*" (1998), 34 Crim. L.Q. 476.

1. A motorist is stopped by the police and requested to provide a breathalyzer sample at the police station. At the police station he refuses to provide a sample and is charged with failing to provide a breath sample

without reasonable excuse contrary to the *Criminal Code*. Consider whether he has a defence

(1) If he refused because he had heard of a Provincial Court ruling that the breathalyzer provisions are unconstitutional. That decision was reversed by the Court of Appeal before the accused's trial on the refusal charge.

In *R. v. MacIntyre* (1983), 24 M.V.R. 67, leave to appeal to S.C.C. refused 2 O.A.C. 400, the Ontario Court of Appeal dismissed the defence without reasons being given.

(2) If the situation is the same but before the refusal a lawyer advised the accused, in error, that the provincial court judge's decision was still valid law.

Compare *R. v. Dunn* (1977), 21 N.S.R. (2d) 334 (C.A.) and *R. v. Whelan* (2002), 170 C.C.C.(3d) 151 (N.L.C.A.).

(3) Would your answer to (2) differ if the advice had been that of the Registrar of Motor Vehicles?

2. The accused were operating a laboratory in which they were manufacturing various chemicals. Unknown to the accused a police investigation discovered that one of these drugs was M.D.M.A., which was not an illegal drug under any of the schedules of the *Food and Drugs Act*, R.S.C. 1970, c. F-27. However, the police suspected it could be used in combination with others to produce illegal drugs. The police managed to have M.D.M.A. added to the schedule of restricted drugs under the *Food and Drugs Act*. This amendment was published in the *Canada Gazette*. The accused continued to produce M.D.M.A. and, two months later, were charged with trafficking in that drug. Can the accused rely on ignorance of the law?

Compare *Molis v. R.*, [1980] 2 S.C.R. 356, 55 C.C.C. (2d) 558.

3. The accused is charged with possession of a prohibited weapon contrary to s. 90(1) of the *Criminal Code*. When stopped by the police he was wearing a knife sheath attached to his belt. The officer examined the knife and, with a forceful downward motion of his arm and wrist, while holding the handle of the knife, was able to open its blade. The accused immediately indicated that he was unaware that the knife could be opened in this manner. Section 84(1)(b) of the *Criminal Code* defines a prohibited weapon in part as "any knife that has a blade that opens automatically by gravity or centrifugal force or by hand pressure applied to a button, spring or other device in or attached to the handle of the knife". Has the accused made a mistake of law or fact?

Compare *R. v. Archer* (1983), 6 C.C.C. (3d) 129 (Ont. C.A.).

4. The accused were charged with unlawfully conducting a bingo contrary to s. 206(1)(d) of the *Criminal Code*. The charges arose out of gaming operations on a reserve. The accused maintained that they were entitled to be acquitted by reason of a defence of colour of right. That right was the belief that s. 206 did not apply to their activities since they were carried out on a reserve which they thought was not subject to the laws of Canada relating to gaming. Is this a mistake of fact or law? Is there a colour of right defence?

Compare *R. v. Jones* (1991), 8 C.R. (4th) 137 (S.C.C.).

5. The accused relied on the information of a firearms officer that a permit was not required for a garage sale. He was charged with the *Criminal Code* offence of selling firearms without a permit.

Compare *R. v. Dubeau* (1993), 80 C.C.C. (3d) 54 (Ont. Gen. Div.).

6. The accused is charged with contravening a municipal by-law by using a family dwelling as a professional office. On first conviction the penalty is a fine of not more that $25,000. The accused, a registered denture therapist, and the co-accused, her husband, opened an office for some of her work at their place of residence. Before doing so the husband purchased a copy of the relevant by-law at the city offices and asked a city planner whether he could open a business in his place. The planner advised that his wife could open the office as she qualified as a drugless practitioner. Should there be a defence of officially induced error of law? Would it matter if the offence was one of absolute liability?

Compare *R. v. Bauman* (1994), 32 C.R. (4th) 176 (Ont. Prov. Ct.).

GENERAL REVIEW QUESTIONS

1. Al Capone is charged with speeding contrary to s. 109 of the *Highway Traffic Act*, R.S.O. 1980, c. 198, in that he drove a motor vehicle in excess of 50 k.p.h. in a 50 k.p.h. zone. If he is convicted the penalty is mandatory: a fine of $18.75.

The uncontested evidence is that the accused was driving at 65 k.p.h. in a 50 k.p.h. zone and that he was knowingly exceeding that speed limit as he genuinely believed he was in a 70 k.p.h. zone. The source of the mistake was a sign reading "70 k.p.h. limit ahead" which Al interpreted to immediately raise the speed limit, whereas this was in reality only achieved 300 metres further along the street, by a sign reading "70 k.p.h. limit". Al, a school principal, had been troubled about this ambiguity before and had telephoned the local police detachment. A sergeant had unambiguously informed him (in error) that the speed limit was raised by the first sign.

You are articled to the defence lawyer. She requests a memorandum discussing all possible defences and the authorities on which they would be based. In each case assess the likelihood of success.

2. Kevin owns a bar. A customer, Susan, comes into the bar and orders a double whisky. Kevin asks her how old she is, to which she answers in unambiguous terms that he should mind his own business. Kevin is pretty confident that she is about 16 years of age. The problem is that he is not sure whether the recent raising of the drinking age from 16 to 18 is in effect. He asks a lawyer in the bar who advises, "The Act comes into effect next week". Kevin serves Susan. Susan's seemingly younger companion, Gordon, then also orders whisky. Kevin, suspecting Gordon is underage, asks him for his driver's licence. Gordon produces the driver's licence of one Ross, whose age is shown as 18, Kevin is surprised but gives no thought to whether the licence is really that of the customer. He serves Gordon.

In fact the new provincial *Liquor Act* is already in force. Section 10 reads:

> Every one who supplies liquor to a person under the age of 18 is guilty of an offence and liable to a fine of not less than $300.

Kevin is facing two charges under s. 10 since Susan is 17 and Gordon 15. Write a legal memorandum on his possible defences, discussing appropriate authorities and assessing his chances of acquittal.

Chapter 6

INCAPACITY

1. AGE

Until 1982 the age of absolute exemption from criminal responsibility was set by the *Criminal Code* at seven. That a child under seven committed the *actus reus* with the requisite *mens rea* made no difference. Furthermore children over seven and under 14 were likewise exempt unless the prosecutor could show that the child was "competent to know the nature and consequence of his conduct and to appreciate that it was wrong". In 1982 this latter so-called *doli incapax* presumption was abolished and the age of criminal responsibility was raised from seven to 12 years in a new s. 13 [en. 1980-81-82, c. 110, s. 72] of the *Criminal Code*. The *Young Offenders Act*, S.C. 1980-81-82, c. 110 replaced the *Juvenile Delinquents Act*. It governed the trials of all children over the age of 11 but under the age of 18. The *Young Offenders Act* was itself replaced by the *Youth Criminal Justice Act*, S.C. 2002, c. 1, which came into force in April 1, 2003. Nick Bala, "When a Child Kills in Canada, There's No Sense of Justice", *Globe and Mail*, September 5, 2013, suggests that the age of criminal responsibility should be lowered to 10.

Consideration of the special procedural and dispositional alternatives dealt with in this new Act are beyond the scope of this book. For our purposes it is sufficient to observe that the substantive law principles that we are exploring apply equally in Youth Court. See, generally, Corrado, Bala, Linden and LeBlanc, *Juvenile Justice in Canada* (Butterworths, 1992); Nicholas Bala, *Young Offenders Law* (Irwin Law, 2nd ed., 2009); and Nicholas Bala and Sanjeev Anand, *Youth Criminal Justice Law* (Irwin Law, 3rd ed., 2012).

In *R. v. D. (D.)*, 2008 SCC 25, 231 C.C.C. (3d) 338, 56 C.R. (6th) 203, [2008] 2 S.C.R. 3 (S.C.C.) the Supreme Court recognized a new principle of fundamental justice that young people who engage in criminal conduct should be presumed to have less moral blameworthiness and culpability than adults. The majority constitutionalized a presumption of lower sentences for young offenders. Contrast the ruling in *Canadian Foundation for Children v. Canada (A.G.)*, [2004] 1 S.C.R. 76, 16 C.R. (6th) 203 (the spanking case considered in Chapter 1) that the common law principle of acting in the best interests of the child was not a principle of fundamental justice as there was insufficient consensus for that principle and it was not workable.

2. INSANITY (MENTAL DISORDER)

(a) Psychiatric Classification: Limited Truths

Psychiatric Classification of Mental Disorder

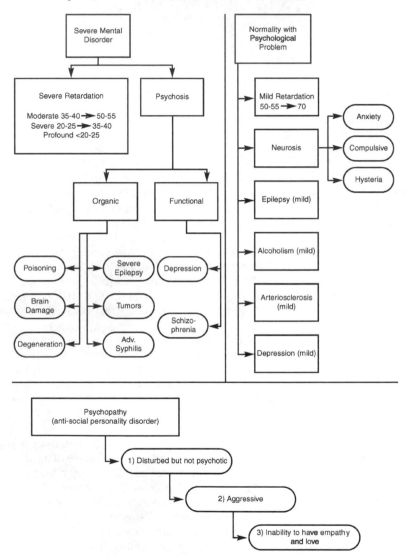

This diagram is derived from the work of Dr. N.D. Walker of Cambridge University, *Crime and Punishment in Britain* (1968) and DSM-5. Thanks to Adam Wygodny, a former Queen's law student, for the computer graphics.

There are problems inherent in any classifications that make expertise in diagnosis elusive in all but the most obvious cases. In particular, each psychiatric label is a shorthand expression of relative rather than absolute conditions which are difficult to define; any one individual can present the conditions more strongly at some times rather than others, and each individual can present symptoms of more than one psychiatric label at any one time.

These limits are recognized in the influential DSM-III classification announced by the American Psychiatric Association in 1980. The classification is now known as DSM-5 to reflect changes made up until 2013.[1] This divides "mental disorder" into, *inter alia*, "mental retardation", psychoses,[2] "anxiety disorders" and "personality disorders". It is, for example, stated at the outset of DSM-IV:

> In DSM-IV there is no assumption that each category of mental disorder is a completely discrete entity with absolute boundaries dividing it from other mental disorders or from no mental disorder.[3]

Clinicians are encouraged to assign more than one label whenever appropriate. The DSM-5 "personality disorder" label includes "Anti-social Personality Disorder"[4] as a form of mental disorder. This has also been known as the concept of "psychopathy" or "sociopathy". The label appears frequently in the criminal law and is highly controversial.

The classic description of "psychopathic syndrome" is provided by the McCords[5] in their exhaustive study:

> The psychopath is asocial. His conduct often brings him into conflict with society. The psychopath is driven by primitive desires and an exaggerated craving for excitement. In his self-centred search for pleasure, he ignores restrictions of his culture. The psychopath is highly impulsive. He is a man for whom the moment is a segment of time detached from all others. His actions are unplanned and guided by his whims. The psychopath is aggressive. He has learned few socialized ways of coping with frustration. The psychopath feels little, if any, guilt. He can commit the most appalling acts, yet view them without remorse. The psychopath has a warped capacity for love. His emotional relationships, when they exist, are meager, fleeting, and designed to satisfy his own desires. These last two traits, guiltlessness and lovelessness, conspicuously mark the psychopath as different from other men.[6]

The World Health Organization's 1978 International Classification of Diseases similarly describes a "personality disorder with predominantly sociopathic or asocial manifestation" as a:

> Personality disorder characterized by disregard for social obligations, lack of feeling for others, and impetuous violence or callous unconcern. There is a gross disparity between behaviour and the prevailing social norms. Behaviour is not readily modifiable by experience, including punishment. People with this personality are often affectively cold and may be abnormally

---

1 *Diagnostic and Statistical Manual of Mental Disorders*, 5th ed. (2013) (DSM-5).
2 The classification avoids the umbrella "psychosis" label but has a category of "psychotic disorders not elsewhere specified".
3 DSM-IV at xxii.
4 DSM-5 at 649-650.
5 W. McCord & J. McCord, *The Psychopath: An Essay on the Criminal Mind* (1964).
6 *Ibid.* at 16-17.

aggressive or irresponsible. Their tolerance to frustration is low; they blame others or offer plausible rationalizations for the behaviour which brings them into conflict with society.[7]

The DSM-5 classification avoids abstraction and instead identifies a host of "diagnostic criteria":

Diagnostic criteria for 301.7 Anti-social Personality Disorder

A. There is a pervasive pattern of disregard for and violation of the rights of others occurring since age 15 years, as indicated by three (or more) of the following:

  (1) failure to conform to social norms with respect to lawful behaviours as indicated by repeatedly performing acts that are grounds for arrest
  (2) deceitfulness, as indicated by repeated lying, use of aliases, or conning others for personal profit or pleasure
  (3) impulsivity or failure to plan ahead
  (4) irritability and aggressiveness, as indicated by repeated physical fights or assaults
  (5) reckless disregard for safety of self or others
  (6) consistent irresponsibility, as indicated by repeated failure to sustain consistent work behaviour or honor financial obligations
  (7) lack of remorse, as indicated by being indifferent to or rationalizing having hurt, mistreated, or stolen from another.

B. The individual is at least age 18 years.

C. There is evidence of Conduct Disorder ... with onset before age 15 years.

D. The occurrence of anti-social behaviour is not exclusively during the course of Schizophrenia or a Manic Episode.[8]

Conduct disorders are defined as involving repetitive and persistent patterns of violations of social norms falling into four categories: aggression to people and animals, destruction of property, deceitfulness or theft and serious violation of rules.[9]

The DSM guide highlights the glaring deficiencies of the label "psychopathic syndrome". Surely the criteria, based on consensus rather than being verified by research, are arbitrary, extremely ambiguous, overinclusive and, above all, circular. A startling example of the process occurred in 1973 where it took a vote of the trustees and a 60 percent vote of the membership by ballot to remove homosexuality from the Manual's list of mental disorders.[10] The criteria were even vaguer in the 1980 classification. In 1987 they were changed because in constructing questions for use by clinicians "it was found that many of those criteria were imprecise and in need of further specification". This label seems to be a ragbag description of a persistent recidivist who carries on committing crimes for no apparent reason. There is a strong body of opinion in England[11] but less

---

7 W.H.O., *Mental Disorders: Glossary and Guide to Their Classification in Accordance with the Ninth Revision of the International Classification of Diseases* (1978) point 301.7.

8 *Supra* note 1 at 649-650. Reproduced by permission of the American Psychiatric Association.

9 *Ibid.* at 85, 646.

10 See Eric H. Marcus, "Unbiased Medical Testimony: Reality or Myth?" (1985) 6 Am. J. For. Psych. 3.

11 See especially Walker, *Crime and Punishment in Britain*, rev. ed. (1968) at 82-8 and (with S. McCabe) *Crime and Insanity in England* (1973) vol. 2 ch. 10.

so in Canada[12] that the label "obliterates more information than it conveys".[13] It tells us nothing about causation, prognosis or treatment. Changing the label to "sociopath", "personality disorder", "character disorder" or the like will not address these criticisms.[14] With any psychiatric label, and this one in particular, lawyers should request that psychiatrists be as precise as possible in their descriptions of the actual behaviour of the individual before the court rather than hide behind imperfect abstractions. Clearly they are too imprecise for use as legal criteria of responsibility.

Some psychiatrists accept this perspective. Professor Orchard,[15] for example, recognizes that the issue of legal insanity,

> ultimately must be decided by the judge and jury. This conclusion is consistent with the important legal principle that expert opinion, including medical and psychiatric opinion, should be used to assist the court in arriving at a finding, but that the responsibility of making this finding is, and must remain, in the hands of the triers of fact. Doctors may not enjoy the obvious questioning of the validity of their diagnosis and opinions which this entails. However, as no one, not even a doctor, sad to say, is infallible, it is most important that any judge or jury look at all the evidence, including the psychiatric opinion and the data upon which it is based, with the utmost of careful scrutiny. In the light of the serious consequences that may ensue, this means vigorous examination and cross-examination are necessary.

T.S. SZASZ, PSYCHIATRY, ETHICS AND THE CRIMINAL LAW

(1958) 58 Col. L. Rev. 183 at 190

The controversial sceptic of psychology and author of *The Manufacture of Madness* and *The Myth of Mental Illness* displays his usual boisterous style in condemning the *Durham* rule:

According to the *Durham* decision, if the defence of insanity has been raised in a criminal trial, it is considered to be a "matter of fact" for the jury to decide whether the offender suffered from a "mental illness" at the time of the commission of the act with which he is charged.

This is unadulterated nonsense. It could come about only as a result of the great prestige which the medical profession commands in our present-day society, and is, in fact, an expression of that prestige. Disregarding even the most obvious doubt concerning exactly what the expression "mental illness" is supposed to denote, it denotes a *theory* (if it denotes anything) and not a fact. This would be true, of course, for any disease, and especially for a bodily disease,

---

12 J. Nemeth, "Psychopathic Personality. Its Relevance in the Correctional After-Care Agency" (1961), 3 Can. J. Corr. 128, but compare H.H.A. Cooper, "The Inadequate Psychopath: Some Medico-Legal Problems and a Clinical Profile" (1973) 21 Chitty's L.J. 325; R.D. Hare, *Manual for the Revised Checklist* (1991); and G.T. Harris, M.E. Rice & C.A. Cormier, "Psychopathy and Violent Recidivism" (1991) 15 *Law & Human Behaviour* at 625-637.

13 Walker, *supra*, note 11.

14 *Ibid.*, but see *contra* the *Report of the Butler Committee on Mentally Abnormal Offenders*, (1975) (Cmnd. 6244), which recommends the term "personality disorder".

15 B.C.L. Orchard, "Insanity — A Psychiatrist's View of the Recent Rulings of the Supreme Court of Canada" (1981) 2 Sup. Crt. L. Rev. 405.

after which the notion of "mental disease" is fashioned. Thus, it may be a fact that a patient is jaundiced, that is, that his skin appears to be yellow to the average observer. But being jaundiced is not the same as having a "disease". And whether this hypothetical patient with yellow skin has a gall stone, infectious hepatitis, or whatever, his "disease" is a *theory* which physicians (or others) form in order to explain his yellow skin. Accordingly, it would be a perversion of our language and thought to refer to a "disease" (or "illness", which I use as a synonym) as if it were a "fact".

To speak of "mental illness" is, epistemologically, very much worse than it is to speak of diseases of the body. Yet the jury is supposed to determine, as a matter of *fact*, whether the accused has or has not a "mental illness". Of course, it is quite possible for a group of people (a jury) to decide that someone is "crazy" or "mentally ill". But this is then *their theory* of why he has acted the way he did. It is no more — or less — a fact than it would be to assert that the accused is possessed by the devil; that is another "theory", now discarded. To believe that one's own theories are facts is considered by many contemporary psychiatrists as a "symptom" of schizophrenia. Yet this is what the language of the *Durham* decision does. It rectifies some of the shakiest and most controversial aspects of contemporary psychiatry (*i.e.*, those pertaining to what is "mental disease" and the classification of such alleged diseases) and by legal fiat seeks to transform inadequate theory into "judicial fact".

Further, *Durham* takes the notion of "mental illness" and requires the psychiatrist and the jury to determine whether the criminal act in question was committed as a result of such "illness". This, too, is supposed to be a "fact". Unfortunately, this not only cannot be a fact, but it cannot even be a theory. For, if the notion of "mental illness" means anything, it means that it is the theory by means of which we "explain" how the events in question might have occurred.

In 1999 the APA began work on its fifth revision of DSM. DSM-5 was published in 2013. Modern critics complain that the DSM categories are still not the subject of scientifically verified research, that they have grown exponentially, that psychiatrists too often tend to blindly rely on them to prescribe psychoactive drugs, and that psychiatrists have become too beholden to the pharmaceutical industry. See Marcia Angell. "The Illusions of Psychiatry", *The New York Review of Books* July 14, 2011.

DSM-5 has broadened diagnostic boundaries by including precursors of disorders such as "psychosis risk syndrome", "mild cognitive impairment", "unspecified disorder"; adding the term spectrum such as "autism spectrum disorder"; and adding new entities such as "hypersexual disorder", "restless leg syndrome" and " binge eating".

DSM-5 thankfully replaces the pejorative label of "mental retardation" with "intellectual disability" (p. 33) although it still uses the categories of mild, moderate, severe and profound. The guide emphasises that an IQ test is insufficient to fairly assess reasoning in real life situations and practical skills (p. 33).

DSM-5 expressly maintains the current approach from DSM-IV for personality disorders. Confusingly, the APA introduces a detailed new approach for further study stated to address "numerous shortcomings" of the present approach. To lawyers that sounds like double jeopardy.

Significantly, DSM-5 expressly provides a "Cautionary Statement for Forensic Use" (p. 25). The Manual notes that it does not provide treatment guidelines and expressly cautions nonclinical decision-makers that:

> a diagnosis does not carry any necessary implications regarding the etiology or causes of the individual's mental disorder or the individual's degree of control over behaviours that may be associated with the disorder (p. 25).

(b) Mental Disorder under *Criminal Code*

In February, 1992, Bill C-30 came into force. It enacted a new Part XXI of the *Criminal Code*, which declares a comprehensive legal regime to deal with accused who suffer from mental disorder. The law is sometimes concerned with the accused's state of mind at the time of his or her trial. The accused must be both mentally and physically present. There are detailed provisions in Part XXI relating to remands for observation and for determinations whether an accused is fit to stand trial. Our concern here, however, is with an accused who is fit to stand trial and who seeks a verdict under s. 672.45 of not criminally responsible on account of mental disorder. Such an inquiry relates to the accused's state of mind at the time of the alleged act.

Until Bill C-30, such a verdict had been called an acquittal on account of insanity. The key provisions were as follows:

> 16. (1) No person shall be convicted of an offence in respect of an act or omission on his part while he was insane.
>
> (2) For the purposes of this section a person is insane when he is in a state of natural imbecility or has disease of the mind to an extent that renders him incapable of appreciating the nature and quality of an act or omission or of knowing that an act or omission is wrong.
>
> (3) A person who has specific delusions, but is in other respects sane, shall not be acquitted on the ground of insanity unless the delusions caused him to believe in the existence of a state of things that, if it existed, would have justified or excused his act or omission.
>
> (4) Every one shall, until the contrary is proved, be presumed to be and to have been sane.

> . . . .

> 614. (1) Where, upon the trial of an accused who is charged with an indictable offence, evidence is given that the accused was insane at the time the offence was committed and the accused is acquitted,
>
> (a) the jury, or
>
> (b) the Judge or Magistrate, where there is no jury, shall find whether the accused was insane at the time the offence was committed and shall declare whether he is acquitted on account of insanity.
>
> (2) Where the accused is found to have been insane at the time the offence was committed, the Court, Judge or Magistrate before whom the trial is held shall order that he be kept in strict custody in the place and in the manner that the Court, Judge or Magistrate directs, until the pleasure of the lieutenant governor of the province is known.

Section 16 was a Canadian version of the famous *M'Naghten* rules, whose history is described in the following decision.

U.S. v. FREEMAN

(1966), 357 F. (2d) 606 (2nd. Circ.)

KAUFMAN J.: —

. . . .

M'Naghten and its antecedents can, in many respects, be seen as examples of the law's conscientious efforts to place in a separate category, people who cannot be justly held "responsible" for their acts. As far back as 1582, William Lambard of Lincolns' Inn set forth what can be viewed as the forerunner of the M'Naghten test as we know it: "If a man or a natural fool, or a lunatic in the time of his lunacy, or a child who apparently has no knowledge of good or evil do kill a man, this is no felonious act . . . for they cannot be said to have any understanding will." By 1724, the language had shifted from "good or evil" to the more familiar emphasis on the word "know." Thus, in *Rex v. Arnold*, 16 How. St. Tr. 695, 764 the "Wild Beast" test was enunciated. It provided for exculpation if the defendant "doth not *know* what he is doing, no more than . . . a wild beast." (Emphasis added.)

By modern scientific standards the language of these early tests is primitive. In the 18th century, psychiatry had hardly become a profession, let alone a science. Thus, these tests and their progeny were evolved at a time when psychiatry was literally in the Dark Ages.

In the pre-M'Naghten period, the concepts of phrenology and monomania were being developed and had significant influence on the right and wrong test. Phrenologists believed that the human brain was divided into 35 separate areas, each with its own peculiar mental function. The sixth area, for example, was designated "destructiveness." It was located, we are told, above the ear because this was the widest part of the skull of carnivorous animals. Monomania, on the other hand, was a state of mind in which one insane idea predominated while the rest of the thinking processes remained normal.

Of course, both phrenology and monomania are rejected today as meaningless medical concepts since the human personality is viewed as a fully integrated system. But, by an accident of history, the rule of M'Naghten's case froze these concepts into the common law just at a time when they were becoming obsolete. A discussion of M'Naghten's case will demonstrate how this came about. Daniel M'Naghten suffered from what now would be described as delusions of persecution. Apparently, he considered his major persecutor to be Robert Peel, then Prime Minister of England, for M'Naghten came to London with the intention of assassinating the chief of the Queen's government. His plan would have succeeded but for the fact that Peel chose to ride in Queen Victoria's carriage because of her absence from the city, while Drummond, his secretary, rode in the vehicle which normally would have been occupied by Peel. M'Naghten, believing that the Prime Minister was riding in his own carriage, shot and killed Drummond in error.

After a lengthy trial in 1843, M'Naghten was found "not guilty by reason of insanity." M'Naghten's exculpation from criminal responsibility was most significant for several reasons. His defense counsel had relied in part upon Dr. Isaac Ray's historic work, Medical Jurisprudence of Insanity which had been published in 1838. This book, which was used and referred to extensively at the trial, contained many enlightened views on the subject of criminal responsibility in general and on the weaknesses of the right and wrong test in particular. Thus, for example, the jury was told that the human mind is not compartmentalized and that a defect in one aspect of the personality could spill over and affect other areas. As Chief Judge Biggs tells us in his Isaac Ray lectures compiled in The Guilty Mind, the court was so impressed with this and other medical evidence of M'Naghten's incompetency that Lord Chief Justice Tindal practically directed a verdict for the accused.

For these reasons, M'Naghten's case could have been the turning point for a new approach to more modern methods of determining criminal responsibility. But the Queen's ire was raised by the acquittal and she was prompted to intervene. Mid-19th century England was in a state of social upheaval and there had been three attempts on the life of the Queen and one on the Prince Consort. Indeed, Queen Victoria was so concerned about M'Naghten's acquittal that she summoned the House of Lords to "take the opinion of the judges on the law governing such cases." Consequently, the 15 judges of the common-law courts were called in a somewhat extraordinary session under a not too subtle atmosphere of pressure to answer five prolix and obtuse questions on the status of criminal responsibility in England. Significantly, it was Lord Chief Justice Tindal who responded for 14 of the 15 judges, and thus articulated what has come to be known as the M'Naghten Rules or M'Naghten test. Rather than relying on Dr. Ray's monumental work which had apparently impressed him at M'Naghten's trial, Tindal, with the Queen's breath upon him, reaffirmed the old restricted right-wrong test despite its 16th century roots and the fact that it, in effect, echoed such uninformed concepts as phrenology and monomania.

Under s. 614(2) where an accused was acquitted on account of insanity, the trial judge had to order that the accused be kept in strict custody "until the pleasure of the lieutenant governor of the province is known". The trial judge had no discretion or power in this matter. In practice, it was up to provincial Mental Health Review Boards to decide if, when and how the accused should be detained. This amounted to indeterminant detention at the discretion of the mental health authorities.

In *R. v. Swain* (1991), 5 C.R. (4th) 253 (S.C.C.), the Supreme Court held that the mandatory detention of an insane acquittee under s. 614(2) without any chance of a hearing offended s. 7 of the *Charter* and also that detention without criteria constituted arbitrary detention under s. 9. Neither violation could be saved by s. 1. The Court ordered a six-month period of temporary validity for s. 614(2). The Minister of Justice obtained one extension. Finally, Bill C-30 was passed as a general reform package and also to respond to *Swain*.

The 1991 amendments abandoned the legalistic terminology of "insanity" in favour of "mental disorder" now used by most psychologists and psychiatrists. However, the change is not as significant as first appears given that s. 2 defines "mental disorder" as "a disease of the mind" and that the tests remain tests of legal irresponsibility derived from the M'Naghten rules. There is thus a descriptive advantage in continuing to refer to the defence of insanity at trial. It is clear that the issue is still not determined by modern psychology and psychiatry. The revised s. 16 reads as follows:

> 16. (1) No person is criminally responsible for an act committed or an omission made while suffering from a mental disorder that rendered the person incapable of appreciating the nature and quality of the act or omission or of knowing that it was wrong.
>
> (2) Every person is presumed not to suffer from a mental disorder so as to be exempt from criminal responsibility by virtue of subsection (1), until the contrary is proved on the balance of probabilities.
>
> (3) The burden of proof that an accused was suffering from a mental disorder so as to be exempt from criminal responsibility is on the party that raises the issue.

Parliament has made it clear that the accused has the burden of proving the exemption on a balance of probabilities. It will be recalled that in *Chaulk* (1991), 2 C.R. (4th) 1 (S.C.C.), the Supreme Court of Canada, over the sole dissent of Wilson J., held that this was the effect of the former presumption of sanity. The majority further ruled that the onus of proof on the accused could be demonstrably justified as a reasonable limit under s. 1.

The verdict is now "not criminally responsible on account of mental disorder" (s. 672.34). Following such a verdict the trial judge now has a discretion, and an obligation on application by the accused or the Crown, to hold a disposition hearing (s. 672.45). Such disposition may be an absolute or conditional discharge or detention in custody in a hospital (s. 672.54). See Laura Burt, "The Mental Disorder Provisions: Community Residence and Dispositions Under Section 672.54(c)" (1993) 36 Crim. L.Q. 40. Subject to such a court order, detention or release is in the jurisdiction of Provincial Review Boards, which are now mandatory and subject to detailed procedural requirements. See ss. 672.38-672.94 and see, generally, A.J.C. O'Marra, "*Hadfield* To *Swain*: The *Criminal Code* Amendments Dealing With the Mentally Disordered Accused" (1993) 36 Crim. L.Q. 49. This includes a right of appeal to a Court of Appeal. See *R. v. Peckham* (1994), 33 C.R. (4th) (C.A.), where the Court held that in applying the test of reasonableness the Court "must be cognizant of the Board's expertise and show that expertise appropriate curial deference". Parliament also enacted caps on detention such as life for first or second degree murder and ten years for certain designated offences and two years for other offences. Those capping provisions were not proclaimed along with the rest of the changes, and were eventually repealed without ever having been in force. Without caps there would appear to have been little change to the former reality of indeterminate detention especially as trial judges may wish to defer to mental health authorities.

The new legal regime survived *Charter* review in *Winko v. Forensic Psychiatric Institute*, [1999] 2 S.C.R. 625. For a court unanimous on the issues of constitutionality, McLachlin J. held that the provisions did not violate s. 7 protections. The scheme was premised on treatment and assessment, and balanced the rights of the offender and society. The offender found not criminally responsible by reason of mental disorder had to be discharged absolutely unless the Board or the Court found that the offender was a significant threat to public safety. This meant a real risk of physical or psychological harm beyond the trivial or annoying. The provisions were not vague or overbroad and did not impose a burden on the offender. The regime did not violate the equality guarantee under s. 15. Although there was differential treatment based on the personal characteristic of medical illness it was not discriminatory. At every stage of Part XX.1 the assessment was based on the individual's situation and needs and was subject to the overriding rule of the least restrictive avenue and annual review.

Regrettably, the Court in *Winko* did not address the significance of the non-proclamation of the capping provisions. This had prompted the Manitoba Court of Appeal to declare that ss. 672.54 and 672.81(1) violated s. 7 and were of no force or effect: *Hoeppner* (1999), 25 C.R. (5th) 91 (Man. C.A.), reconsideration refused (1999), 145 Man. R. (2d) 160 (note) (S.C.C.). In *Winko*, McLachlin J., in the course of deciding that the new scheme was not overbroad, indicated baldly that "I cannot agree with the contrary decision" in *Hoeppner* (at para. 71, C.R.).

Where the defence of lack of responsibility through mental disorder has not been raised or has been rejected, upon conviction the trial judge has the normal range of sentencing options. These powers do not include the jurisdiction to order the place and type of imprisonment although the prison regime can be determined by setting the length at two years or more (federal) or less than two years (provincial). The judge has no power to order psychiatric treatment in a prison or that the accused be transferred from a prison to a psychiatric facility; see *R. v. Deans* (1977), 37 C.C.C. (2d) 221 (Ont. C.A.); *R. v. Trecroce* (1980), 55 C.C.C. (2d) 202 (Ont. C.A.) at 218. Judicial recommendations do not have to be followed by prison authorities. There is no sentence alternative in Canada, as there is in England, of a hospital order where a judge may sentence directly to a mental institution. A power to order detention in a psychiatric facility for up to 60 days in acute cases was contained in the 1992 amendments, s. 736.11, but this provision has not been proclaimed. Provincial psychiatric hospitals appear reluctant to accept more mentally-disordered persons sent from the criminal justice system. In *R. v. Knoblauch* (2001), 37 C.R. (5th) 349 (S.C.C.), however, the Supreme Court decided that ss. 742.1 and 742.3 of the *Criminal Code* do not preclude a conditional sentence that requires all or part of a sentence to be served in a locked psychiatric unit with consent.

It would appear that even under the new *Criminal Code* regime there are limited dispositional options. A defence based on mental disorder will still likely result in indeterminate detention at the discretion of health authorities. The defence is therefore likely to be rare except in those cases where the accused faces the option of a long prison sentence and would prefer secure custody in a mental facility.

Concerns have been expressed about the realities of the NCRMD regime. Janet Leiper, "Cracks in the Façade of Liberty: The Resort to Habeas Corpus to Enforce Part XX.I of the Criminal Code" (2009) 55 Crim. L.Q. 134, documents that litigation in Ontario has found delays caused by lack of resources for NCRMD detainees in the forensic health care assessment processes which "revealed a problem of human suffering and a systemic failure to align lofty statements of principle with reality". However, in *Centre for Addiction and Mental Health v. R.*, 2014 SCC 60, (*sub nom. R. v. Conception*) [2014] 3 S.C.R. 82, 316 C.C.C. (3d) 182, 13 C.R. (7th) 317 a 5-4 majority decided that the *Criminal Code* requires that hospitals must consent to any admission pursuant to a court order. Hospitals are held to be entitled to refuse to consent to a "forthwith" treatment order. See criticism by Steve Coughlan in C.R. comment and C.R. article by Michael Davies and Meaghan McMahon, "Two Very Different Conceptions of Dealing with the Mentally Ill" (2014), 13 C.R. (7th) 360.

A concern of a quite different sort came from the Government of Canada in 2013. Concerned at some high-profile cases in which accused who had killed people were found to be NCRMD, the government introduced Bill C-54. It allowed for greater participation of victims and victims' families in dispositions and stated that public safety is the paramount concern. It also removed from s. 672.54 the requirement that a court or Review Board must make the disposition that is "the least onerous and least restrictive to the accused", replacing that with a requirement that the disposition be "necessary and appropriate in the circumstances". This was particularly problematic because the "least onerous" requirement was specifically relied on by the Supreme Court in *Winko* as its basis for finding that the legislation was not overbroad. Although one would expect that to have led to a renewed *Charter* challenge, in fact that was not what happened. Rather, Review Boards and courts concluded that the "necessary and appropriate" order *was* the one that was "the least onerous and least restrictive to the accused": see *Ranieri, Re*, 2015 ONCA 444. Accordingly, there was found to be no change in the standard despite the change in the language.

The bill also sets out an exceptional regime for NCR accused designated by judges as "high risk". Rebecca Sutton, "Canada's Not Criminally Responsible Reform Act: Mental Disorder and the Danger of Public Safety" (2013) 6 Crim. L.Q. 41, sees the new bill as violating the *Charter* standards declared in *Winko* and as counterproductive in ignoring rehabilitation and preventative responses to mental health.

It has been a long common law tradition in Canada that in a jury trial jurors should not be instructed as to the sentencing or other consequences of their verdicts on the basis that this might detract from their fact-finding function. In Quebec there is now conflicting authority in the case of the NCRMD verdict. In *R. c. Mailhot*, 2012 QCCA 964, leave to appeal allowed (2012), 445 N.R. 393 (note) (S.C.C.), reversed on other grounds 2013 SCC 17, [2013] 2 S.C.R. 96, 303 C.C.C. (3d) 27, the majority of the Quebec Court of Appeal held that the instruction as to consequences should be given as a general rule. However, in *R. c. Proulx* (2012), 95 C.R. (6th) 117 (C.A. Que.), leave to appeal refused (2013), 451 N.R.

400 (note) (S.C.C.) the same court held this should only be when the circumstances call for it. See Thierry Nadon, "Should We Tell Juries About The Consequences of an NCRMD Verdict? (2012), 95 C.R. (6th) 117.

The Ontario Court of Appeal in *R. v. Szostak* (2012), 94 C.R. (6th) 48 (Ont. C.A.) declared that a defence counsel is ethically entitled and "perhaps bound" to raise the issue of fitness but cannot raise the issue of criminal responsibility without the client's instructions. The wisdom of this bright line has been questioned: Paul Calarco "*R. v. Szostak*: Counsel's Ethical Duties and the Mentally Ill Client" (2012), 94 C.R. (6th) 78.

COOPER v. R.

(1979), [1980] 1 S.C.R. 1149, 13 C.R. (3d) 97, 51 C.C.C. (2d) 129, 1979 CarswellOnt 60, 1979 CarswellOnt 74

The accused was charged with the murder of a patient at a psychiatric hospital (the detailed facts and the accused's psychiatric history are considered below). At the trial the defence of insanity was not raised by the accused but the trial judge nevertheless put it to the jury. The accused's appeal to the Ontario Court of Appeal was dismissed. Only the dissenting judge, Dubin J.A., would have ordered a new trial on the ground of misdirection as to defence of insanity. The Supreme Court of Canada ordered a new trial, finding that the trial judge had not dealt with s. 16 properly. In particular, the Court discussed the meaning of the term "disease of the mind" and explained what is entailed by "appreciating" the nature and quality of an act or omission.

DICKSON J. (LASKIN C.J.C., BEETZ, ESTEY and McINTYRE JJ. concurring): — Issues fundamental to the design and range of the "insanity defence" and to notions of responsibility in our criminal justice system are before the court in this appeal.

The case opens up the broad and difficult question of the obligation of a trial Judge to charge on insanity in circumstances where an accused has a lengthy psychiatric history but the medical evidence is that he does not suffer from "disease of the mind".

The appellant, Gary Albert Cooper, was charged with the murder of one Denise Hobbs, at the time an in-patient at the Hamilton Psychiatric Hospital. The appellant was an out-patient at the same institution. There was evidence that the appellant had been drinking during the day of 8th October 1975. That evening he arrived at a regularly scheduled dance held at a nearby church for patients of the hospital, and there met Denise Hobbs, with whom he was acquainted. At his invitation, the two left the dance to seek a bottle of pop and cigarettes. Ultimately, after an unsuccessful attempt at sexual intercourse the appellant choked the deceased. The cause of death was asphyxiation by strangulation.

At trial, counsel for the defence directed argument to raising a doubt on the issue of intent, and did not plead the "defence" of insanity. Nonetheless, the trial judge, Van Camp J., charged the jury on insanity, though in a manner vigorously challenged in this appeal. The jury found the appellant guilty of non-capital murder, and an appeal was dismissed without written reasons, Dubin J.A. dissenting. At a later date Dubin J.A. delivered lengthy reasons in dissent [40 C.C.C. (2d) 145].

. . . .

I
DISEASE OF THE MIND

Let me say by way of commencement that, to date, the phrase "disease of the mind" has proven intractable and has eluded satisfactory definition by both medical and legal disciplines. It is not a term of art in either law or psychiatry. Indeed, Glanville Williams (*Textbook of Criminal Law* (1978), p. 592) says that the phrase is no longer in medical use. "It is a mere working concept, a mere abstraction, like sin" (Wily and Stallworthy, Mental Abnormality and the Law (1962), p. 20). Although the term expresses a legal concept, and a finding is made according to a legal test, psychiatric knowledge is directly linked to the legal conclusion, for medical testimony forms part of the evidence on which the trier of fact must reach its decision. But medical and legal perspectives differ.

. . . .

Recently, in Canada, the Ontario Court of Appeal contributed judicial direction in this area of the law in the cases of *R. v. Rabey* (1977), 40 C.R.N.S. 46, 37 C.C.C. (2d) 461, and *R. v. Simpson* (1977), 35 C.C.C. (2d) 337, both of which were decided subsequent to the trial of the appellant. Judgment in *Rabey* postdates the decision of the Court of Appeal in the case at bar, and is presently on appeal to this court on an issue unrelated to those raised herein. Martin J.A., who wrote for the court in both *Rabey* and *Simpson*, was not among the members of the court who heard the *Cooper* appeal.

Simpson has greater significance for the present appeal. There, the accused appealed the finding of not guilty by reason of insanity on two charges of attempted murder. The facts, which indicate two incidents of stabbing, are not remarkable. As framed by Martin J.A., the issue was whether a personality disorder is a disease of the mind within the meaning of s. 16 of the *Code*. He held that, notwithstanding the psychiatric evidence, the question raised must be resolved as a question of law. But the legal position, as I understand it, is properly expressed in the following passage (pp. 349-50):

The term "disease of the mind" is a legal concept, although it includes a medical component, and what is meant by that term is a question of law for the Judge. . . . It is the function of the psychiatrist to describe the accused's mental condition and how it is considered from the medical point of view. It is for the Judge to decide whether the condition described is comprehended by the term "disease of the mind."

As a matter of practice, the trial judge can permit the psychiatrist to be asked directly whether or not the condition in question constitutes a disease of the mind. Concerning the controversy over the classification of a "psychopathic personality", Martin J.A. found implicit recognition in Canadian and British authorities for the proposition that such a disorder can constitute a disease.

The general principles, not in issue on the further appeal to this court, were reiterated by Martin J.A. in *R. v. Rabey*. Disease of the mind is a legal term. It is within the province of the judge to determine what mental conditions are within the meaning of that phrase and whether there is any evidence that an accused suffers from an abnormal mental condition comprehended by that term. More importantly, he held that, if there is any evidence that the accused did suffer from such a disease, in legal terms, the question of fact must be left with the jury.

I think Dubin J.A. correctly characterizes the decision in *Simpson* as holding that "personality disorder" has been recognized as "being capable of constituting a 'disease of the mind' ". I share his view that "there is no reason to give a narrow or limited interpretation to the term 'disease of the mind' ". Admittedly, in *Simpson* both of the psychiatrists stated that the personality disorder there in question did or could constitute a disease of the mind. While Martin J.A. in that case had little difficulty finding evidence that the appellant suffered from a "disease of the mind", the case foundered upon the second segment of s. 16(2). It should also be kept in mind that *Simpson* presented an odd situation, in which the Crown successfully raised the insanity defence against the wishes of the accused, who appealed the verdict of not guilty by reason of insanity.

What is interesting in these two cases, for our purposes, is the maintenance of a clear distinction between the weight to be given medical opinions expressed in evidence, however relevant, and the task of the trial Judge to form an independent conclusion as to whether the mental condition falls within the legal concept.

In summary, one might say that, in a legal sense, "disease of the mind" embraces any illness, disorder or abnormal condition which impairs the human mind and its functioning, excluding, however, self-induced states caused by alcohol or drugs, as well as transitory mental states such as hysteria or concussion. In order to support a defence of insanity, the disease must, of course, be of such intensity as to render the accused incapable of appreciating the nature and quality of the violent act or of knowing that it is wrong.

Underlying all of this discussion is the concept of responsibility and the notion that an accused is not legally responsible for acts resulting from mental disease or mental defect.

II
APPRECIATE

In contrast to the position in England under the M'Naghten Rules, where the words used are "knows the nature and quality of his act", s. 16 of the *Code* uses the phrase "appreciating the nature and quality of an act or omission". The two are not synonymous. The draftsman of the *Code*, as originally enacted, made a deliberate change in language from the common-law rule in order to broaden the legal and medical considerations bearing upon the mental state of the accused and to make it clear that cognition was not to be the sole criterion. Emotional as well as intellectual awareness of the significance of the conduct is in issue. The Report of the Royal Commission on the Law of Insanity as a Defence in Criminal Cases (McRuer Report) (1956), contains a useful discussion on the point (p. 12):

> The word "appreciating", not being a word that is synonymous with "knowing", requires far-reaching legal and medical consideration when discussing Canadian law. It had its origin in the Stephen Draft Code. Not infrequently judicial reference is made to the New Oxford Dictionary for the definition of words used in Canadian statutes. The New Oxford Dictionary gives five different uses of the word 'appreciate", depending on the context. The one applicable to this statute is:
>
> "2. To estimate aright, to perceive the full force of.
> "b. esp. to be sensitive to, or sensible of, any delicate impression or distinction.
> " 'Until the truth of any thing . . . be appreciated, its error, if any, cannot be detected.' "
>
> An examination of the civil law of England and Canada shows that there is an important difference between "know" or "knowledge" on the one hand and "appreciate" or "appreciation" on the other when used and applied to a given set of circumstances. This is best illustrated by the principles of law underlying those cases in which the maxim *volenti non fit injuria* is involved. There is a clear distinction between mere knowledge of the risk and appreciation of both the risk and the danger.

To "know" the nature and quality of an act may mean merely to be aware of the physical act, while to "appreciate" may involve estimation and understanding of the consequences of that act. In the case of the appellant, as an example, in using his hands to choke the deceased he may well have known the nature and quality of that physical act of choking. It is entirely different to suggest, however, that in performing the physical act of choking he was able to appreciate its nature and quality, in the sense of being aware that it could lead to or result in her death. In the opinion of the medical expert who testified at the trial, the appellant could have been capable of intending bodily harm and of choking the girl, but not of having intended her death.

Our *Code* postulates an independent test, requiring a level of understanding of the act, which is more than mere knowledge that it is taking place; in short, a capacity to apprehend the nature of the act, and its consequences. The position in law is well expressed in the McRuer Report at p. 12:

Under the Canadian statute law a disease of the mind that renders the accused person incapable of an appreciation of the nature and quality of the act must necessarily involve more than mere knowledge that the act is being committed; there must be an appreciation of the factors involved in the act and a mental capacity to measure and foresee the consequences of the violent conduct.

It should be noted that the issue of appreciation of the nature and quality of the act was not before this court in *Schwartz v. R., supra*. The sole issue was the meaning of the word "wrong". The decision in *Schwartz* should not be taken as authority for the proposition that "appreciating" the nature and quality of an act is synonymous with "knowing" the physical character of that act.

The test proposed in the McRuer Report, which I would adopt (save for deletion of the "fully" in the fourth line) is this (p. 13):

The true test necessarily is, was the accused person at the very time of the offence — not before or after, but at the moment of the offence — by reason of disease of the mind, unable fully to appreciate not only the nature of the act but the natural consequences that would flow from it? In other words, was the accused person, by reason of disease of the mind, deprived of the mental capacity to foresee and measure the consequences of the act?

The legally relevant time is the time when the act was committed.

In *R. v. O'Brien, supra*, Ritchie J.A. referred to the McRuer Report and stated at pp. 301-302:

If an accused person is to be deprived of the protection of s. 16, he must, at the time of committing the offence, have had an *appreciation of the factors involved in his act and the mental capacity to measure and foresee the consequences of it.*

In the *Simpson* decision, *supra*, Martin J.A. offered the view that s. 16(2) exempts from liability an accused who, due to a disease of the mind, has no real understanding of the nature, character and consequences of the act at the time of its commission. I agree. With respect, I accept the view that the first branch of the test, in employing the word "appreciates", imports an additional requirement to mere knowledge of the physical quality of the act. The requirement, unique to Canada, is that of perception, an ability to perceive the consequences, impact and results of a physical act. An accused may be aware of the physical character of his action (*i.e.*, in choking) without necessarily having the capacity to appreciate that, in nature and quality, that act will result in the death of a human being. This is simply a restatement, specific to the defence of insanity, of the principle that *mens rea*, or intention as to the consequences of an act, is a requisite element in the commission of a crime.

III
EVIDENCE — NON-MEDICAL

It will now be convenient to turn to the evidence, because, as I understand him, counsel for the Crown concedes that, if there was sufficient evidence to go to the jury on the question of insanity, the trial judge failed to deal adequately with insanity in her charge and effectively withdrew the insanity defence from the jury.

It is important to observe at the outset that the trial judge did charge the jury on insanity, although, as I have stated, the defence was not raised by the appellant's counsel. The judge felt the evidence sufficient to warrant an instruction to the jury on the issue, whatever the posture of defence counsel. In my opinion, she was correct in doing so, having regard to the evidence upon this issue, which I will now endeavour to summarize.

The Crown adduced evidence that before 7:00 p.m. on the night in question a resident nursing assistant, present at the church where the dance was being held, addressed the appellant upon his arrival. The appellant had a "faraway", "dazed", "blank" look in his eyes, and appeared unresponsive. The appellant's father testified that he received a telephone call at approximately 8:15 p.m. from his son, who seemed excited and out of breath. The appellant, trying to speak quickly, was having difficulty "getting his words out". He told his father, "Hello dad, how are you doing? Dad I just killed somebody . . . on James Street Mountain steps . . . I was coming down the steps and thought somebody was following me . . . I jumped over the railing . . . I jumped out and grabbed hold of them." In response to the question "Is he dead'." the appellant said: "Yes. I felt for a heartbeat and a pulse. I dragged her out in the bushes."

Constable Slote of the Hamilton police force testified that he received a call at 8:39 p.m. from the appellant, who attested to having "just seen a murder". The conversation was recorded on the police dispatcher:

> I seen somebody kill a girl. I don't know if he dragged her in the bushes or not . . . I was just coming down the James Street stairs and I heard a screams [sic]; I don't know, I'd just turned around and seen somebody grab some girl and drag her into the bushes . . . I don't know, you know, if she's dead or alive or what.

Constable Slote considered it a crank call, as there was a lack of emotion in the caller's voice. A police cruiser dispatched to the telephone booth, and thereafter to Cooper's apartment, was unable to locate the appellant.

The deceased was discovered the following morning, 9th October, in the bushes near the James Street steps. Her upper body and part of her face were covered by her jacket, and her brassiere, unfastened, was in place. Her slacks, also unfastened, were about her hips. Soil and leaves adhered to her back. There was no evidence of sexual intercourse. However, she had been undressed and an attempt made to redress her. There was no evidence of struggle, and the deceased was neither battered nor badly bruised. Her strangulation was by hand, without the use of a rope or weapon.

At 11:35 a.m. that morning the appellant was apprehended and detained by police officers until 12:10 p.m., at which time an interrogation commenced. At the time he was true to his story of having seen a murder committed by another person. To both officers in attendance, the appellant appeared mentally slow and spoke slowly.

The officers left the appellant to continue the investigation and returned to the interview at 7:25 p.m. Upon their confronting him with additional facts and indicating that he would be charged with murder, the appellant said, "Hold it. Hold it. I didn't mean to kill her." The appellant offered to give a full statement (which I have paraphrased, except where in quotes):

> I went to the church and bumped into Denise Hobbs. . . . we went for a walk down the James Street stairs then I kissed her then she wanted to go back up then I grabbed her around the throat and choked her [with] my hands. Then I got scared and tried to feel for pulse or something and got none so I ran downstairs for a phone booth.
> ". . . we were in the bushes standing up, I kissed her and I grabbed her around the throat and choked her *I was afraid she would go back and tell them I was kissing her.*"(The italics are mine.)

The appellant did testify at trial. Defence counsel attempted to establish a lack of intention to commit the murder, supported by the evidence of the appellant's intoxication and susceptibility to abnormal behaviour.

The appellant was 31 years of age. His father, Albert Cooper, testified that, as a young boy, the appellant was subject to seizures, convulsions and sudden mood changes — he would quickly become very excited for no apparent reason and then quickly calm down. Often the appellant would seem to be "far away" and his "mind was elsewhere". Sometimes he would have blackouts and fall down. He heard things which were not there to be heard. His condition worsened as he got older. The appellant was first seen by psychiatrists at age 7. At age 10 or 12 he was treated for auditory hallucinations. He experienced a great deal of difficulty at school, and at age 16 had progressed only as far as Grade V at a trade school. He held a series of menial jobs, from which he was discharged after short periods of time. In his testimony the appellant stated that he had been admitted to the Hamilton Psychiatric Hospital in 1965 (it was in fact in 1962) and remained until 1971, after which time he was an out-patient and still had contact with the doctors at the hospital. He married in April 1972 (he had met his wife at the psychiatric hospital) and had two children. He returned to the hospital for a period of 15 days in 1974.

IV

EVIDENCE — MEDICAL

Medical evidence relating to the appellant's mental and behavioural problems is offered in testimony of Dr. Sim. I think it useful to break down his evidence, reorganized slightly from the sequence in which it was given at trial, as follows:

(a) *General history*

The hospital records indicated that the appellant was first seen at age 7, as he was failing at school and exhibited disturbing behaviour. A condition of borderline mental deficiency was diagnosed at that time. He was re-examined at age 8 and described as being wild and hyperactive and having a poor sense of reality. At 10, an abnormal E.E.G. reading was discovered upon examination for his problem of narcolepsy (sleep seizures). At 11, further I.Q. testing disclosed borderline deficiency, and at age 12 the appellant was treated by a psychiatrist for mental confusion and auditory hallucinations. He was admitted to the Hamilton Psychiatric Hospital as a young man and diagnosed as "without psychosis — borderline intelligence". In 1965 his condition was described as "psychosis with mental deficiency". Dr. Sim described "psychosis" in this way:

> Psychosis, basically, involves a break with reality in which the person may or may not be confused, and have other symptoms like hallucinations of his hearing, seeing, tasting, or smelling, feeling things that are not actually around, or can have such symptoms as delusions. And delusion is usually described as a false belief which cannot be changed by persuasion and/or reason.

In 1965 there was a bizarre episode wherein the appellant was reported to have swallowed part of a lighter, his belt buckle, buttons from his clothing and a zipper from his trousers. In 1967 he swallowed part of a disassembled cigarette lighter. In 1967 he was re-diagnosed as "mental deficiency without psychosis". Since, he has also been described medically as having "personality disorder, anti-social type with borderline mental retardation". Other evidence indicated that the appellant was released from the hospital in 1971 and returned subsequently in 1974 for a period of 15 days.

(b) *Electroencephalogram*

Dr. Sim reviewed the medical history of abnormal brainwave patterns (electrical discharges from the brain). All such tests (from March 1962 to June 1974) showed generalized abnormality, and in one or two of the E.E.G. tests there was abnormality in brainwaves from the temporal lobe. However, the E.E.G. tests were suggestive, at most, of an "epileptic diathesis" (tendency or propensity to epilepsy, without necessarily resulting in seizures). Dr. Sim could say only that it is possible that Cooper could experience epileptic seizures.

(c) *Intelligence*

The appellant's intellectual ability was measured on a number of occasions according to the full-scale intelligence quotient. His I.Q. ranged from 69 to 79 and was usually between 71 and 79. The normal I.Q. reading is in the region of 90 to 110. In Dr. Sim's opinion, the appellant is of borderline intelligence (*i.e.*, bordering on retardation or classification as an "outright mentally defective person"). The changeover is at an I.Q. of 70. To quote the doctor:

> In summary we are dealing with a male who has shown evidence of breaking with reality in the past. He has a long history of unstable, aggressive and inadequate behaviour. He was unable to adjust at school, academically, socially, economically, in his marriage. He has some brainwave abnormalities which could more readily make this man more irritable and aggresive by alcohol than a person without these abnormalities. He is also of limited intelligence, having a borderline to high-grade defective level of I.Q. Putting all this together, and bringing the stress — the fact that he was under stress financially and so forth, plus the alcohol and under the circumstances which are described as having occurred at the time, it would be my opinion that he would be in such a state of clouded consciousness that he would not be able to form the intent to kill.

Dr. Sim agreed with the diagnosis of other psychiatrists of 26th March 1976 that the appellant had "personality disorder, mixed type, showing schizoid, anti-social explosive and inadequate features, borderline mental retardation". However, on direct examination Dr. Sim was of the view that at the time of the offence the appellant was *not* suffering from a disease of the mind.

(d) *Intention*

Dr. Sim expressed the opinion that, although the appellant probably knew he was causing bodily harm, he was incapable of forming an intent to kill and he could not have known that any harm he was causing might result in death.

. . . .

VI
CONCLUSIONS

In my opinion, there was evidence sufficient to require the judge to fully instruct the jury on the issue of insanity. The judge was of the opinion that that issue should go to the jury. With respect, the trial judge erred:

(1) In treating Dr. Sim's reply to the judge's isolated question as virtually determinative of the issue of whether the appellant had a "disease of the mind". Although in practice it is often convenient to do so, in strictness a medical witness is not entitled to state that a particular condition is or is not a disease of the mind, since this is a legal question. Mental disease is not purely a matter of

psychiatric definition. It is for the jury, and not for medical men, of whatever eminence, to determine the issue: *R. v. Rivett* (1950), 34 Cr. App. R. 87 at 94 (C.A.). The entire psychiatric history, if accepted by the jury, was such as would have entitled the jury to hold that the accused suffered from a disease of the mind, within its legal meaning, regardless of whether one isolates the personality disorder. Personality disorders such as the appellant displayed at various stages in his life can constitute a disease of the mind. The real question before the jury was the extent to which the accused's appreciation of the nature and quality of his act was impaired. Included in the evidence on this point was the evidence of Dr. Sim that the appellant lacked the capacity to form the intent to cause death.

(2) In failing to review adequately the evidence bearing upon the insanity issue and in failing to relate the evidence of the accused's capacity to intend certain acts to the issue of insanity. The judge did not analyze the evidence of Dr. Sim or the other evidence as it may have related to the defence of insanity on the issue of whether the appellant appreciated the nature and quality of his act. Failure before the jury on the issues of intent and intoxication did not preclude success on the issue of insanity. The insanity question should have been put to the jury in such a way as to ensure their due appreciation of the value of the evidence: *R. v. Laycock*, [1952] O.R. 908, 15 C.R. 292, 104 C.C.C. 274 (C.A.).

(3) In concluding this portion of the charge in language which, to all intents, withdrew from the jury the essential determination of fact which it was its province to decide. If the issue was to go to the jury, then, in fairness to the accused, a much more careful charge was warranted. The issue should have been clearly left with the jury to decide. On a matter of such importance, and having regard to the strong evidence of personality disorder, s. 613 [am. 1974-75-76, c. 93, s. 75] of the *Code* should not be applied in this case.

I would allow the appeal and order a new trial.

[The dissenting judgment of Martland J., Pratte J. concurring, is omitted.]

Appeal allowed; new trial ordered.

The next two pragmatic decisions make it clear that psychopathy, although a disease of the mind, will not result in a finding of NCRMD:

KJELDSEN v. R.

[1981] 2 S.C.R. 617, 24 C.R. (3d) 289, 64 C.C.C. (2d) 161,
1981 CarswellAlta 311, 1981 CarswellAlta 94

McIntyre J., on behalf of the Court, held that psychopathy was a disease of the mind within the meaning of *Criminal Code* s. 16, and also adopted the further analysis of Martin J.A. in *R. v. Simpson* (1977), 35 C.C.C. (2d) 337 at 355 (Ont. C.A.):

Emotional disturbance caused by disease of the mind may be so severe as to deprive the accused of the use of his understanding at the time of the act, rendering him incapable of appreciating the nature and quality of the act or of knowing that it was wrong, and thus exempting him from liability under s. 16(2) of the *Code*: see *R. v. Gorecki* (1976), 32 C.C.C. (2d) 135, a judgment of this court . . . I do not, however, read the psychiatric evidence to be that the accused was by reason of emotional turmoil produced by disease of the mind incapable of understanding or realizing what he was doing, but rather that he lacked normal emotions and was therefore incapable of experiencing normal feelings concerning the acts assuming he committed them.

While I am of the view that s. 16(2) exempts from liability an accused who by reason of disease of the mind has no real understanding of the nature, character and consequences of the act at the time of its commission, I do not think the exemption provided by the section extends to one who has the necessary understanding of the nature, character and consequences of the act, but merely lacks appropriate feelings for the victim or lacks feelings of remorse or guilt for what he has done, even though such lack of feeling stems from "disease of the mind". Appreciation of the nature and quality of the act does not import a requirement that the act be accompanied by appropriate feeling about the effect of the act on other people: see *Willgoss v. R.* (1960), 105 C.L.R. 295 (Aust. H.C.); *R. v. Leech*, 21 C.R.N.S. 1, 10 C.C.C. (2d) 149 (Alta. T.D.); *R. v. Craig* (1975), 22 C.C.C. (2d) 212, affirmed 28 C.C.C. (2d) 311 (Alta. C.A.). No doubt the absence of such feelings is a common characteristic of many persons who engage in repeated and serious criminal conduct.

R. v. ABBEY

[1982] 2 S.C.R. 24, 29 C.R. (3d) 193, 68 C.C.C. (2d) 394,
1982 CarswellBC 230, 1982 CarswellBC740

The accused was charged with importing cocaine and unlawfully possessing cocaine for the purpose of trafficking. Upon his arrival at Vancouver International Airport from Lima, Peru, the accused's shoulder bag was searched and found to contain two plastic bags with 5.5 ounces of 50 percent pure cocaine. When asked what was in the bags, the accused answered, "Naturally, cocaine", and advised the police in a written statement about the events leading to his arrest. In his defence the accused raised insanity. The psychiatric evidence suggested that he suffered a disease of the mind which, although not rendering him incapable of appreciating the nature and quality of his act, involved a delusional belief that he was committed to a course of action, no harm would come to him and he would not be punished. The trial judge acquitted the accused by reason of insanity, ruling that he was insane within the meaning of *Code* s. 16(2) because he failed to appreciate the penal consequences of his act. When the matter reached the Supreme Court it was held that this was one of the errors necessitating a new trial.

DICKSON J.: —

. . . .

. . . . As the court observed in *Cooper, supra,* the requirement that the accused be able to perceive the consequences of a physical act is a restatement, specific to the defence of insanity, of the principle of *mens rea,* or intention as to the consequences of an act, as a requisite element in the commission of a crime. The mental element must be proved with respect to all circumstances, and consequences, that form part of the *actus reus.* As the Crown in this case correctly points out, "while punishment may be a *result* of the commission of a criminal act it is not an *element* of the crime itself". A delusion which renders an accused "incapable of appreciating the nature and quality of his act" goes to the *mens rea* of the offence and brings into operation the "first arm" of s. 16(2): he is not guilty by reason of insanity. A delusion which renders an accused incapable of appreciating that the penal sanctions attaching to the commission of the crime are applicable to him does not go to the *mens rea* of the offence, does not render him incapable of appreciating the nature and quality of the act, and does not bring into operation the "first arm" of the insanity defence.

Abbey was charged with importing and trafficking in cocaine. There is no dispute as to the fact that he carried cocaine into the country. In his statement to police, it was his admitted intention to import cocaine for the purposes of trafficking. In other words, Abbey appreciated that the *actus reus* of each of the offences charged was being committed. Both the psychiatrist called for the defence and the psychiatrist who testified on behalf of the Crown stated that Abbey appreciated the nature and quality of his act. The judge erred, in my view, in going on to say that a failure to appreciate the penal sanctions ("consequences of punishment") brought the accused within the ambit of the "first arm" of the insanity defence of s. 16(2).

The second arm of s. 16(2)

Should the question of "personal penal consequences" be relevant at all, it is more appropriately discussed within the context of the second arm of s. 16(2), *i.e.,* "knowing that an act is wrong". Glanville Williams in his *Criminal Law, The General Part,* at p. 478 says:

> "It has been determined that this phrase ['nature and quality'] refers to the physical character of the act, not its legal quality: legal right and wrong are cared for by the second question [citing *R. v. Codere, supra,* at p. 27]."

This court having decided in *Schwartz v. R., supra,* that "wrong" means wrong according to law, and it being established that Abbey knew his act was "wrong", his inability to "appreciate" the penal consequences is really irrelevant to the question of legal insanity. There seems to be no doubt on the evidence, and on the judge's findings, that Abbey knew that he was doing an act forbidden by law.

With respect, the trial judge homogenized the first and second arms of s. 16(2), collapsing the one into the other in, for example, the following passage from his judgment:

> "As I understand the evidence and the submissions of counsel, the accused had the capacity to appreciate the nature of the act of importing and of possessing the cocaine. He also had the capacity to appreciate the immediate consequences of those acts, that is to say, that they were illegal, that he should not commit them overtly . . ."

In *Schwartz v. R.,* [1977] I S.C.R. 673, 34 C.R.N.S. 138, 29 C.C.C. (2d) 1, Justice Martland, for a 5:4 majority of the Court, adopted the interpretation of the English Court of Criminal Appeal in *R. v. Windle,* [1952] 2 Q.B. 826, that "wrong" in s. 16(2) of the *Criminal Code* means "contrary to law". In fact the majority specified criminal law. The four dissenting judges, through Dickson J., would have adopted the opinion of the Australian High Court in *Stapleton v. R.* (1952), 86 C.L.R. 358, that "wrong" means morally wrong. In determining which interpretation of the word "wrong" should be adopted, the Court relied more on traditional legal sources than on assessment of the social policy considerations. Justice Martland was unwilling to acquit an insane person who knew that his or her act was illegal but considered it morally justifiable, pointing out that this would not acquit a sane person. He was also of the view that the interpretation of morally wrong required a subjective test of insanity which would be dangerous. Justice Dickson in dissent held that "moral wrong" was "not to be judged by the personal standards of the offender but by his awareness that society regards the act as wrong". Justice Dickson used an historical and contextual approach to statutory construction in reasoning that, if a wrong meant contrary to law, Parliament would have used the word "unlawful" as it had done elsewhere in the *Code,* that the law in 1843 dealt with insanity in terms of rightness and wrongness, and that the McRuer Report concluded that "wrong" means "something that would be condemned in the eyes of mankind".

R. v. CHAULK

[1990] 3 S.C.R. 1303, 2 C.R. (4th) 1, 62 C.C.C. (3d) 193,
1990 CarswellMan 385, 1990 CarswellMan 239

A 6-3 majority of the Supreme Court overruled *Schwartz*.

LAMER C.J.C. (DICKSON C.J.C. and WILSON, LA FOREST, GONTHIER and CORY JJ.): —

[I]t is plain to me that the term "wrong" as used in s. 16(2) must mean more than simply legally wrong. In considering the capacity of a person to know whether an act is one that he ought or ought not to do, the inquiry cannot terminate with the discovery that the accused knew that the act was contrary to the formal law. A person may well be aware that an act is contrary to law but, by reason of "natural imbecility" or disease of the mind, is at the same time incapable of knowing that the act is morally wrong in the circumstances according to the moral standards of society. This would be the case, for example, if the person suffered from a disease of the mind to such a degree as to know that it is legally wrong to kill but, as described by Dickson J. in *Schwartz*, kills "in the belief that it is in response to a divine order and therefore not morally wrong" (p. 678).

. . . .

[T]he insanity defence should not be made unavailable simply on the basis that an accused knows that a particular act is contrary to law and that he knows, generally, that he should not commit an act that is a crime. It is possible that a person may be aware that it is ordinarily wrong to commit a crime but, by reason of a disease of the mind, believes that it would be "right" according to the ordinary morals of his society to commit the crime in a particular context. In this situation, the accused would be entitled to be acquitted by reason of insanity.

In *R. v. Oommen*, [1994] 2 S.C.R. 507, 30 C.R. (4th) 195, 91 C.C.C. (3d) 8, the Court applied the *Chaulk* test in holding that an insanity defence had been wrongly rejected by the trial judge in a murder case. Late one night the accused shot and killed, without apparent motive, a young female friend at his apartment. He had long suffered from a mental disorder described as "a psychosis of a paranoid delusional type". His specific belief at the time of the shooting was that members of a local union had conspired to "destroy" him and that they had given a commission to the victim to kill him.

At his murder trial before judge alone the accused raised the defence of insanity. The trial judge rejected it. Although the accused had had a compulsive fear that the young girl would kill him, it was more probable than not that at the time of the killing the accused was capable of knowing that he was doing wrong according to moral standards of society. The evidence of medical witnesses was that his delusion would not prevent him from being aware of what he was doing in the sense that he knew his discharge of the firearm was a death-threatening act. His subjective belief that the act was not wrong would not, according to the trial judge, assist him.

The Supreme Court unanimously confirmed the Alberta Court of Appeal's order of a new trial. The Court confirmed that under s. 16(1) of the *Criminal Code* a person who lacks capacity to know that the act he is committing is wrong is exempt from criminal responsibility. The inquiry is to focus not on general capacity to know right from wrong but rather on the ability to know that a particular act was wrong in the circumstances. The question is whether the accused lacks the capacity to rationally decide whether the act is right or wrong and hence to make a rational choice about whether to do it or not. Does the accused possess the capacity present in the ordinary person to know that the act was wrong having regard to the everyday standards of the ordinary person? Since s. 16 is an independent condition of criminal responsibility the Supreme Court decided that it was not necessary to show that a defence such as self-defence would apply; this rejected the view of the Alberta Court of Appeal in the Court below (1993), 21 C.R. (4th) 117 (Alta. C.A.). The findings of the trial judge were consistent with the conclusion that the accused's mental disorder deprived him of the capacity to know his act was wrong by the standards of the ordinary person.

R. v. CAMPIONE

(2015), 321 C.C.C. (3d) 63, 17 C.R. (7th) 379 (Ont. C.A.)

The accused was a young woman with a history of mental illness who killed her two young daughters by drowning them. She then placed them in bed with rosary beads around their interlocked hands, and tried unsuccessfully to kill herself. At trial she had relied unsuccessfully on s. 16, but was convicted of two counts of first degree murder. The Ontario Court of Appeal dismissed her appeal, holding in particular that the jury had been properly instructed on the issue of whether the accused was capable of knowing that her act was wrong.

Blair J.A.:

[5] At trial, her defence was that she was not criminally responsible for her acts by reason of mental disorder ("NCR") because she was suffering from a psychotic disorder that rendered her incapable of making rational choices i.e., of knowing that her acts were morally wrong. The defence theory was that the killings were – from her perspective – an altruistic act driven by her psychotic delusions; she believed that the only way to save her children from harm at the hands of her estranged husband and his family was to send them to heaven where they would be safe in God's hands (and where she would be to protect them as well).

[6] The Crown's theory was that the killings were acts of vengeance directed against her estranged husband and family, and carried out in the midst of a bitter custody battle in which the appellant risked losing the children because her husband was manoeuvring to have the state of her mental health be revealed in court.

. . . .

[28] Section 16(1) of the *Criminal Code* states:

> No person is criminally responsible for an act committed or an omission made while suffering from a mental disorder that rendered the person incapable of appreciating the nature and quality of the act or omission or of knowing that it was wrong.

[29] The issue at trial was whether the appellant was incapable of knowing that her acts were wrong. As noted above, the experts agreed that she was capable of appreciating the nature and quality of her acts, and that she understood the killings were "legally wrong". They differed, however, on whether she had the capacity to understand that they were "morally wrong".

[30] The concept of "moral wrongfulness" in this context has been established by the Supreme Court of Canada in *R. v. Chaulk*, [1990] 3 S.C.R. 1303, *R. v. Oommen*, [1994] 2 S.C.R. 507, and their progeny. The focus is not on whether the accused lacks the general capacity to know right from wrong, but rather on whether he or she is deprived – by reason of a mental disorder (including, in some cases, delusions) – of the capacity to know that the particular act is right or wrong having regard to the everyday standards of reasonable people: *Oommen*, at pp. 516-20. It follows that not every mental illness or delusion-driven subjective view will qualify an accused for the s. 16 defence. As Lamer C.J.C. stated in *R. v. Ratti*, [1991] 1 S.C.R. 68, at p. 80:

> It is not sufficient to decide that the appellant's act was a result of his delusion. Even if the act was motivated by the delusion, the appellant will be convicted if he was capable of knowing, in spite of such delusion, that the act in the particular circumstances would have been morally condemned by reasonable members of society.

[31] Moral wrongfulness as contemplated in s. 16 is a slippery concept to apply. However, this Court very succinctly summarized the relevant considerations in *Ross*, at para. 27, when it stated that "a subjective belief by the accused that his conduct was justifiable will not spare him from criminal responsibility even if his personal views or beliefs were driven by mental disorder, as long as he retained the capacity to know that it was regarded as wrong on a societal standard": see also *R. v. Woodward*, [2009] O.J. No. 5484, at para. 5.

. . . .

[37] Ms. Dann [defence counsel] submits that the test is subjective in this sense: an accused who honestly believes that his or her actions are morally justifiable in line with normal societal standards, still qualifies for an NCR defence no matter how unreasonable that belief may be. The appellant's honest belief is not to be measured against what a reasonable person, suffering from the same delusions, would have done in the circumstances. In the context of this case, Ms. Dann submits that the question for the jury was "whether [the appellant's] delusions so affected her perception of reality that she honestly believed killing was the right thing to do, according to normal societal standards"

. . . .

[39] The ultimate issue for the jurors to determine was whether – in spite of her delusions and any honest belief in the justifiability of her actions – the appellant had the capacity to know that those actions were contrary to society's moral standards. The centrepiece of the inquiry is her *capacity to know and to make that choice*; it is not the level of honesty or unreasonableness with which she may have held her beliefs. Concentrating on the latter unduly complicates the inquiry for the very reason the appellant raises in support of her argument; it leads to the application of reasonableness considerations to the appellant's delusions and subjective belief.

. . . .

[41] In short, a subjective, but honest belief in the *justifiability* of the acts – however unreasonable that belief may be – is not sufficient, alone, to ground an NCR defence, because an individual accused's personal sense of justifiability is not sufficient. The inquiry goes further. The accused person's mental disorder must also render him or her *incapable* of knowing that the acts in question are morally wrong as measured against societal standards, and therefore incapable of making the choice necessary to act in accordance with those standards.

. . . .

[48] Accordingly, the jurors were made well aware that, if they accepted the appellant's version of the killings, they had to render a verdict of NCR. I see no basis for confusion on this issue. While the focus of the test is on the appellant's state of mind and her capacity for rationale choice, the question is not whether the appellant considered the acts justified according to her own moral code, but whether she was incapable of knowing that her actions were contrary to society's morality.

[49] I would not give effect to this ground of appeal.

(c)   Mental Disorder Negativing *Mens Rea*

In *R. v. Swain*, [1991] 1 S.C.R. 933, Mr. Justice Lamer, for the majority, held that the common law rule allowing the Crown to adduce evidence of insanity over and above the accused's wishes was not in accordance with principles of fundamental justice under s. 7 and could not be saved by s. 1. His Lordship referred to the relaxation of the *Oakes* test to require merely that the violation infringed rights as "little as is reasonably possible", but however determined that consideration of judicial deference had no place respecting common law violations for which only the "least intrusive" alternative would do. The majority went on to fashion a new common law rule which would only allow the Crown to independently raise the issue of insanity after the trier of fact had concluded that the accused was otherwise guilty. The issue of insanity would be tried after a finding of guilt, but before a conviction was entered. The Court also recognized that the Crown could adduce evidence of insanity during the trial, if the accused had put his or her mental state in issue.

The Court in *Swain* refers to evidence of mental impairment short of insanity negativing the requisite mental element, for example, planning and deliberation in the case of first degree murder or the specific intent required for murder. This ruling was *obiter* but was accepted as the law in *Jacquard* (1997), 113 C.C.C. (3d) 1 (S.C.C.), the Court dividing only on whether the judge's direction had been sufficiently clear. Thus the Supreme Court has recognized that evidence of mental disorder short of a full-blown defence under s.16 may be admitted on the issue of *mens rea*.

In *R. v. Reeves* (2017), 36 C.R. (7th) 133 (B.C. C.A.) a conviction of second degree murder was reduced to manslaughter on the basis the trial judge had erred in not allowing evidence that the accused stated he snapped and was suffering from mental delusions to be considered on the issue of intent. The Court held that the absence of expert evidence was not determinative.

3.   AUTOMATISM

R. v. RABEY

(1977), 40 C.R.N.S. 46, 37 C.C.C. (2d) 461,
1977 CarswellOnt 24 (Ont. C.A.)

The accused was charged with causing bodily harm with intent to wound and possessing a weapon for the purpose of committing an offence. The trial judge acquitted. On appeal the Ontario Court of Appeal ordered a new trial on the charge of wounding on the basis that the defence of sane automatism was not available. Any defence would be that of insanity or lack of *mens rea*. The acquittal on the weapons charge was confirmed on the basis of lack of proof of *mens rea*. On further appeal the majority of the Supreme Court adopted the approach of Martin J.A. in the Court of Appeal. Reproduced first is the review of the evidence in the Court of Appeal:

MARTIN J.A.: --

Factual background

On 1st March 1974 the respondent, Wayne Kenneth Rabey, then aged 20, was a third-year student at the University of Toronto at Erindale College where he was enrolled in the honours science course, majoring in geology. Miss X was also a third-year student at Erindale College.

An association between Miss X and the respondent began in September 1973 when, in their third year, they commenced to have most of their classes together. Along with two classmates, John Lund and Rick Hampel, they studied together in their spare periods, lunched together and went to the "pub" together.

Miss X and the respondent had also gone for walks together and visited each other's homes. During the Christmas holidays in 1973, along with John Lund they had gone with a group of students to Quebec to ski.

It is clear that the respondent was emotionally attached to Miss X, but his feelings were not reciprocated, and she described her relationship with the respondent as "just a friend". On Miss X's initiative, her association with the respondent lessened after their return from the trip to Quebec.

Miss X on 28th February 1974, during a lecture, wrote a letter to a girlfriend. She put the letter in her notebook which she placed in her locker. The letter referred to another student, a young man by whose sexual experience Miss X was impressed and in whom she expressed a sexual interest. The letter also stated that even though she insulted Wayne and Rick they still "bugged" her in class, and she implied that they were "nothings".

The respondent, whose evidence was accepted by the trial Judge, testified that he was sitting outside the library on the afternoon of 28th February when Miss X came out of the library and asked him to help her with some problems. He said that they went inside the library to work on the problems, and when flipping through Miss X's notebook to find some equations, during her absence for a few minutes, he came across the letter mentioned above. He read part of the letter, was interested in its contents, and put it in his pocket. The respondent read the letter that evening at home and underlined certain passages. He said that he was upset, confused and angry at the time.

The following day, 1st March 1974, the respondent went to the geology lab to review some problems posted on the board, and while there he took a piece of Galena rock, wrapped it in paper towelling and put it in his pocket. He testified that he intended to take the rock home to study it, as he had previously done with other samples of rock with the consent of his professor.

There was a class starting at 11:00 a.m. but the respondent decided not to take it as he wanted to study for an examination that he had in the afternoon. He testified that later that morning he met another student who said that he was going to be playing squash at 12:00 o'clock, and the respondent said he would go and watch him play. The respondent said that, quite by chance, while on the way to the squash courts, he met Miss X in the locker area. He said that when he first saw her he felt strange for a second but that this feeling passed. He invited Miss X to go with him to watch the game, and she accepted the invitation.

When they reached the observation gallery no one was playing in any of the squash courts. Miss X said the respondent seemed surprised to find the courts empty. They then returned downstairs; the respondent seemed his normal self. When they had reached the foot of the stairs he asked Miss X what she thought of "Gord", a mutual friend, and she replied that he was "just a friend". The respondent then asked her what she thought of him, referring to himself. She said he was a friend too. They then started to go through a set of fire doors located near the bottom of the stairs, which, being heavy, were hard to push open. Before Miss X could get the door on her side open she heard a crash and a "crumbling sound", and she thought something was falling down from the roof. She turned around to see what was happening, and the respondent grabbed her around the arms and struck her on the head twice. She then became unconscious, and when she recovered consciousness the respondent was on his knees, leaning forward and choking her. She asked him why he was doing this, and he yelled, "You bitch, you bitch", after which she again lost consciousness.

Kenneth Turner, a student at Erindale College, was walking down the stairs on his way to the gymnasium when he noticed the respondent crouched at the bottom of the stairs near some books and a red puddle. As Turner continued down the stairs, the respondent apparently noticed him and came up the stairs towards him. The respondent said there had been a terrible accident. Turner noticed the respondent was very pale, sweating, glassy-eyed and had a frightened expression, and Turner endeavoured to reassure him. Turner also noticed that there was a trail which led under the stairwell from the pool of blood which he had first noticed. He looked over the railing and saw Miss X's head, her body being under the stairs.

At this time the respondent said, "I've killed her and I am going to kill you too." The respondent then seized Turner, who freed himself and then went for assistance. Turner met Professor Houston in the hall and requested Professor Houston to accompany him. On the way to the area where Turner had seen Miss X they encountered the respondent, whom Professor Houston sought to restrain momentarily by placing his hand on the respondent's wrist. The respondent said he had to get a nurse, and continued on his way. Professor Houston noticed that the respondent was very pale and seemed bewildered.

The respondent appeared in the office of Mrs. Degutis, a nurse employed at the college health centre, and asked her to come quickly to help him; that he thought he had killed someone. Mrs. Degutis said he looked very upset and seemed filled with fear and anxiety. His pulse was very fast and was not strong; he had a limp, "clammy" appearance. As a result of her observation of the respondent she placed him in a room by himself. In subsequent contacts with the respondent after Miss X had been found, Mrs. Degutis was unable to convince him that Miss X was not dead.

In the meantime, Professor Houston had found Miss X in an unconscious condition "under" the stairwell. She soon recovered consciousness and was taken to the college health centre and then to a hospital. She was found to have three puncture wounds in her head in which fragments of rock were embedded and which required 20 stitches to close. She also had a reddish mark on her throat. She, however, made a complete recovery within a short time.

Two quantities of black rock, which fragmented easily, were found at two different sites in the area of the bottom of the stairwell. The largest piece of rock, some school books and a purse were found in the vicinity of a pool of blood near the foot of the stairwell. There was a smear of blood, some 14 feet long, leading from the pool of blood at the bottom of the stairwell to another pool of blood beside the stairwell. The physical findings support the inference that Miss X was struck near the foot of the stairs and then dragged to the position, partly underneath the stairs, where she was found.

William Huggett, Associate Dean of Erindale College, shortly after 12:00 o'clock on 1st March 1974, was requested to go to the nursing station, and on arriving there he found the respondent in an inner room. The respondent appeared depressed or dazed; he recognized Dean Huggett and said, "I don't know why I started or why I stopped", and also said that he "liked her better than anyone he had ever known".

Constable Pollitt arrived at the college shortly after 1:00 o'clock and went to the nursing station where he arrested the respondent at about 1:25 p.m. After being cautioned by Constable Pollitt the respondent said: "I did it, I know I did it, I just couldn't stop hitting her."

The letter written by Miss X the day before was found in the pocket of the respondent's jacket. Detective Price took a statement from the respondent between 4:30 and 4:45 p.m. The statement reads, in part, as follows:

> I was asking her about the ballet, then I asked her if she liked this guy Gord. She said something about just as a friend. Then I guess I hit her right then on the head. She was bleeding from the head and the next thing I remember it all happened so fast she was on the floor and I was sitting on top of her and choking her. I thought she was dead, there was blood everywhere. I just don't know what happened.

The respondent, of whom a number of character witnesses spoke highly, recounted how he obtained Miss X's letter, his chance meeting with her in the locker area and their fruitless visit to the squash courts, as previously outlined. He testified that he remembered asking Miss X what she thought of a mutual friend, and her replying that he was just a friend. The next thing he remembered was choking her; that her face was a "funny" colour. He remembered seeing a lot of blood and stopped choking her. The next thing he remembered was being on the bottom of the steps and seeing Turner coming down. He thought he remembered asking Turner to go for help, but he did not remember Turner answering. He remembered grabbing Turner but did not remember Turner running away; he was "just gone". He remembered seeing Turner's face and a lady's face; the next thing he remembered was being at the nurse's office and telling her that he had killed someone, or he thought that he had killed someone. He recalled talking to Dean Huggett and the nurse, calling his mother on the telephone and being arrested.

The psychiatric evidence

The respondent was admitted, on 5th March 1974, to the Lakeshore Psychiatric Hospital for psychiatric assessment on a warrant of remand by the Provincial Court, and was discharged on 1st April 1974. A detailed neurological examination of the respondent disclosed no neurological disease. Dr. Slyfield's report to the Provincial Court stated that if the respondent was telling the truth about his amnesia for most of the incident, then it was probable that his consciousness was dissociated at the time but that such a psychological mechanism need not indicate mental illness.

The medical reports of the Lakeshore Psychiatric Hospital with respect to the psychiatric assessment of the respondent were admitted in evidence by the consent of both counsel.

Dr. Orchard, assistant professor of psychiatry at the University of Toronto, examined the respondent on 18th May 1974.

Dr. Orchard testified that, in his opinion, the respondent entered into a complete dissociative state at the foot of the stairs. The dissociative state is a recognized diagnosis and is a disorder of consciousness which occurs as a result of part of the nervous system shutting off. Dr. Orchard said that a person in a severe dissociative state may be capable of performing physical actions without consciousness of such actions. In Dr. Orchard's opinion, when the respondent entered the dissociative state near the foot of the stairs his mind "shut off", and the return of consciousness was gradual; he returned to some awareness when he found his hands around Miss X's neck. The clouding of consciousness did not completely lift, however, until later when he spoke to his mother and the police.

Dr. Orchard said that the dissociative state which occurred was caused by a powerful emotional shock which resulted from the shattering of the respondent's image of Miss X; he was unable to tolerate seeing her as she revealed herself in the letter, and because the reality was not tolerable for him the dissociative state occurred as a psychological defence mechanism. The conversation at the foot of the stairs as to how she regarded "Gord" and himself, against the background of the letter, "triggered" the dissociative state. In Dr. Orchard's opinion the dissociative state which occurred was comparable to that produced by a physical blow; it was caused by a "psychological blow" which produced certain physical effects as observed by Turner, Professor Houston, Mrs. Degutis and Dean Huggett. Dr. Orchard did not consider that the subsequent statements made by the respondent, indicating that he was aware that he had struck Miss X, were inconsistent with the respondent being in a dissociative state that was total at the time he struck Miss X with the rock and, by a process of reconstruction, realizing what he had done when some awareness returned to him and he found himself choking Miss X while she was lying on the floor with blood around her.

Dr. Orchard said that the respondent was a young man of average health, or better than average health, with no pre-disposition to dissociate. Dr. Orchard distinguished between the dissociative state and dissociation which may occur as a result of a major pathological condition, such as schizophrenia, manic-depressive psychosis or injury to the brain. The severe dissociative state, such as the respondent suffered, usually occurs in persons within the category of normal people where the mind is unable to cope with stress in an area that is important to that individual, and it is more severe than the dissociation which occurs as a symptom of other conditions. He said that it is rare for the severe dissociative state not caused by some underlying pathology to recur, and that there was only a very slight possibility that the respondent would suffer from a recurrence of this disorder of consciousness.

Dr. Orchard said that he could find no evidence that the respondent suffered from any pathological condition which he defined as a "diseased condition or abnormally sick condition". He testified that the dissociative state itself is an occurrence, is not a mental illness and is not a "disease of the mind". There are three main groups of mental disorders, which he categorized as follows:

(1) The psychoses which are the major mental illnesses involving a loss of contact with reality.

(2) The neuroses which are the minor mental illnesses which do not involve loss of contact with reality.

(3) The personality or character disorders which are neither psychoses nor neuroses but are a "maladaptive pattern or life-style".

Dr. Orchard agreed that in the medical literature the dissociative state is included as one of the neuroses in the subdivision of hysteria. Although, in cross-examination, Dr. Orchard rejected as authoritative a number of textbooks on psychiatry to which he was referred, he acknowledged that in a textbook, which he accepted as generally authoritative, the dissociative state is classified as a neurosis. It was Dr. Orchard's view that the dissociative state is not "fully categorizable"; it is not a psychosis because there is no ongoing pathological condition, and it occurs without a pre-disposing personality; it is not a neurosis, which by definition is a minor mental illness without loss of contact with reality, since in the dissociative state there is a loss of contact with reality.

Dr. Rowsell, who, like Dr. Orchard, is a psychiatrist of eminence, examined the respondent on 16th May 1975. He had available to him, as Dr. Orchard had, the reports of the Lakeshore Psychiatric Hospital.

It was the opinion of Dr. Rowsell that the respondent did not go into a dissociative state; that he is a controlled young man who went into an extreme state of rage at that moment and while in that state, struck Miss X on the head and choked her; he had good reason to think from the amount of blood that he had killed her. Dr. Rowsell testified that, in his opinion, the respondent was aware that he was hitting Miss X, being then in a state of rage. Dr. Rowsell testified that if, contrary to his opinion, the respondent was in a dissociative state, he suffered from "disease of the mind". Dr. Rowsell said that consciousness is the distinguishing feature of mental life; the dissociative state is, by definition, a subdivision of hysterical neurosis, which is a definite mental illness. It is, by definition, a disorder of the mind.

Dr. Rowsell was of the opinion that the "blotting out" of parts of the incident by the respondent occurred after the event. Dr. Rowsell, unlike Dr. Orchard, was of the opinion that the respondent still had a psychiatric problem for which he required treatment to help him face up to what had occurred. He considered that the treatment would take six months to a year and could be undertaken on an out-patient basis. The prognosis was excellent.

RABEY v. R.

[1980] 2 S.C.R. 513, 15 C.R. (3d) 225, 54 C.C.C. (2d) 1,
1980 CarswellOnt 35, 1980 CarswellOnt 71

RITCHIE J. (MARTLAND, PIGEON and BEETZ JJ. concurring): —

. . . .

It should be observed also that the appellant was subjected to a number of interviews with psychiatrists, with the result that the courts have found themselves involved in the shadowy area of mental disorders, concerning which it is not surprising to find that there are wide differences in opinion amongst the "experts". The meaning of the word "automatism" — in any event so far as it is employed in the defence of non-insane automatism — has in my opinion been satisfactorily defined by Lacourcière J. (as he then was) of the Ontario High Court of Justice in the case of *R. v. K.* (1971), 3 C.C.C. (3d) 84 at 84:

> Automatism is a term used to describe unconscious, involuntary behaviour, the state of a person who, though capable of action, is not conscious of what he is doing. It means an unconscious, involuntary act, where the mind does not go with what is being done.

The defence of automatism, as used in the present case, of course involves a consideration of the provisions of s. 16.

. . . .

What is said here is that at the relevant time the appellant was in a state where, though capable of action, he was not conscious of what he was doing, and more particularly that he was not suffering from a disease of the mind and was therefore not insane. The central question in deciding any case involving the defence of automatism is whether or not the accused was suffering from a disease of the mind. The opinions of psychiatrists go no further than characterizing the condition in which the appellant was found as being "a dissociative state", but it is clear, at least since the case of *Bratty v. A.G. Northern Ireland*, [1963] A.C. 386, 46 Cr. App. R. 1, [1961] 3 All E.R. 523 (H.L.), that the question of whether or not such a state amounts to "a disease of the mind" is a question of law for the judge to determine. The general rule is that it is for the judge as a question of law to decide what constitutes a "disease of the mind", but that the question of whether or not the facts in a given case disclose the existence of such a disease is a question to be determined by the trier of fact. I think it would be superfluous for me to retrace the line of authorities in this area, as they have been so exhaustively discussed by my brother Dickson and also by Martin J.A. of the Court of Appeal and by the learned trial judge. I am satisfied in this regard to adopt the following passages from the reasons for judgment of Martin J.A. at pp. 62-63:

> In general, the distinction to be drawn is between a malfunctioning of the mind arising from some cause that is primarily internal to the accused, having its source in his psychological or emotional makeup, or in some organic pathology, as opposed to a malfunctioning of the mind, which is the transient effect produced by some specific external factor such as, for example, concussion. Any malfunctioning of the mind or mental disorder having its source primarily in some subjective condition or weakness internal to the accused (whether fully understood or not) may be a "disease of the mind" if it prevents the accused from knowing what he is doing, but transient disturbances of consciousness due to certain specific external factors do not fall within the concept of disease of the mind. (For an interesting and helpful discussion see "The Concept of Mental Disease In Criminal Law Insanity Tests" 33 University of Chicago L. Rev. 229, by Herbert Fingarette.) Particular transient mental disturbances may not, however, be capable of being properly categorized in relation to whether they constitute "disease of the mind" on the basis of a generalized statement and must be decided on a case-by-case basis.

The same learned judge later stated in the same judgment at p. 68:

> In my view, the ordinary stresses and disappointments of life which are the common lot of mankind do not constitute an external cause constituting an explanation for a malfunctioning of the mind which takes it out of the category of a "disease of the mind". To hold otherwise would deprive the concept of an external factor of any real meaning. In my view, the emotional stress suffered by the respondent as a result of his disappointment with respect to Miss X cannot be said to be an external factor producing the automatism within the authorities, and the dissociative state must be considered as having its source primarily in the respondent's psychological or emotional makeup. I conclude, therefore, that, in the circumstances of this case, the dissociative state in which the respondent was said to be constituted a "disease of the mind". I leave aside, until it becomes necessary to decide them, cases where a dissociative state has resulted from emotional shock without physical injury, resulting from such causes, for example, as being involved in a serious accident although no physical injury has resulted; being the victim of a murderous attack with an uplifted knife, notwithstanding that the victim has managed to escape physical injury; seeing a loved one murdered or seriously assaulted, and like situations. Such extraordinary external events might reasonably be presumed to affect the average normal person without reference to the makeup of the person exposed to such experience.

> For the above reasons I am of the opinion, with deference, that the learned trial Judge erred in holding that the so-called "psychological blow", which was said to have caused the dissociative state, was, in the circumstances of this case, an externally originating cause, and she should have held that if the respondent was in a dissociative state at the time he struck Miss X he suffered from "disease of the mind". A new trial must, accordingly, be had on count 2.

In my view a possible key to the cause of the malfunctioning of the appellant's mind at the time of the alleged assault is to be found in para. 5 of the agreed statement of facts, to which I have already referred, and where it is said of him:

> 5. The Appellant had never dated any other girl for any length of time, and had only a minimal amount of sexual experience. An introvert, he was infatuated with the attractive, outgoing. . . .

It seems to me that his infatuation with this young woman had created an abnormal condition in his mind, under the influence of which he acted unnaturally and violently to an imagined slight to which a normal person would not have reacted in the same manner.

It was contended on behalf of the appellant that a finding of disease of the mind and consequently of insanity in the present case would involve gross unfairess to the appellant, who could be subject to the provisions of s. 545 [re-en. 1972, c. 13, s. 45; am. 1974-75-76, c. 93, s. 69] of the *Criminal Code* and thus detained at the pleasure of the Lieutenant-Governor of the province. That such a result does not carry with it the hardship contended for is illustrated by the following passage from the reasons for judgment of Martin J.A. at p. 69:

> It would, of course, be unthinkable that a person found not guilty on account of insanity because of a transient mental disorder constituting a disease of the mind, who was not dangerous and who required no further treatment, should continue to be confined. The present provisions of s. 545(l)(*b*) [re-en. 1972, c. 13, s. 45], however, authorize the Lieutenant-Governor to make an order if, in his opinion, it would be in the best interest of the accused and not contrary to the interest of the public for the discharge of a person found not guilty on account of insanity, either absolutely or subject to such conditions as he prescribes. In addition to the periodic reviews required to be made by a board of review appointed pursuant to s. 547(1) of the *Code*, the Lieutenant-Governor under s. 547(6) of the *Code* may request the board of review to review the case of any person found not guilty on account of insanity, in which case the board of review is required to report forthwith whether such person has recovered and, if so, whether in its opinion it is in the interest of the public and of that person for the Lieutenant-Governor to order that he be discharged absolutely or subject to such conditions as the Lieutenant-Governor may prescribe.

For all these reasons, as well as for those expressed by Martin J.A. in the Court of Appeal for Ontario, I would dismiss the appeal and dispose of the matter in the manner proposed by him.

DICKSON J., dissenting (ESTEY and MCINTYRE JJ. concurring): — The automatism "defence" has come into considerable prominence in recent years.

Although the word "automatism" made its way but lately to the legal state, it is basic principle that absence of volition in respect of the act involved is always a defence to a crime. A defence that the act is involuntary entitles the accused to a complete and unqualified acquittal. That the defence of automatism exists as a middle ground between criminal responsibility and legal insanity is beyond question. Although spoken of as a defence, in the sense that it is raised by the accused, the Crown always bears the burden of proving a voluntary act.

The issue in this appeal is whether automatism resulting from a "psychological blow" is available to an accused in answer to a charge of causing bodily harm with intent to wound. The appellant, Wayne Kenneth Rabey, suddenly and without warning assaulted a fellow student and friend, causing her injury. The theory of the defence was that his behaviour was caused by a psychological blow, an intense emotional shock which induced a "dissociative state", during which, for a time, the appellant was neither conscious of nor able to control his conduct, so that it was involuntary. This is sometimes spoken of as non-insane automatism, to distinguish it from cases in which the state of automatism is attributable to disease of the mind.

At common law a person who engaged in what would otherwise have been criminal conduct was not guilty of a crime if he did so in a state of unconsciousness or semi-consciousness. Nor was he responsible if he was, by reason of disease of the mind or defect of reason, unable to appreciate the nature and quality of an act or that its commission was wrong. The fundamental precept of our criminal law is that a man is responsible only for his conscious, intentional acts. Devlin J. summed up the position in *R. v. Kemp*, [1956] 3 All E.R. 249 at 251:

> In the eyes of the common law if a man is not responsible for his actions he is entitled to be acquitted by the ordinary form of acquittal, and it matters not whether his lack of responsibility was due to insanity or to any other cause.

In order to protect the public from the dangerous criminally insane the common law was changed by statute, long ago. By the *Criminal Lunatics Act*, 1800 (39 & 40 Geo. 3), c. 94, and the *Trial of Lunatics Act*, 1883 (46 & 47 Vict.), c. 38, and in Canada by the *Criminal Code*, [now] R.S.C. 1970, c. C-34, a verdict of not guilty by reason of insanity results in committal to an institution. The purpose of the qualified verdict of acquittal is, of course, to ensure custody and treatment for those who might pose a continuing threat to society by reason of mental illness. In Canada, an accused who is acquitted on the ground of insanity is kept in strict custody in the place and in the manner that the court directs, until the pleasure of the Lieutenant-Governor of the province is known [s. 542(2) of the *Code*].

The term "automatism" first appeared in the cases and in the periodical literature about 30 years ago. It is seen with increasing frequency. The defence of automatism is successfully invoked in circumstances of a criminal act committed unconsciously, and, in the past, has generally covered acts done while sleepwalking or under concussional states following head injuries.

The defence of automatism is, in some respects, akin to that of insanity. In both instances, the issue is whether an accused had sufficient control over or knowledge of his criminal act to be held culpable. The two defences are, however, separate and distinct. As Professor J. Ll. J. Edwards observed in "Automatism and Criminal Responsibility" (1958), 21 Mod. L. Rev. 375 at 384:

> Both circumstances are concerned to prove mental irresponsibility, the essential difference . . . being that in the case of insanity the defect of the understanding must originate in a disease of the mind, whereas in the defence of automatism *simpliciter* the criminal law is not concerned with any question of the disease of the mind.

Although separate, the relationship between the two defences cannot be discounted. Automatism may be subsumed in the defence of insanity in cases in which the unconscious action of an accused can be traced to, or rooted in, a disease of the mind. Where that is so, the defence of insanity prevails. This is all felicitously expressed by Gresson P. in *R. v. Cottle*, [1958] N.Z.L.R. 999 at 1007 (C.A.):

> It would appear that automatism raised as a defence to a criminal charge may be something quite different and distinct from insanity. In a particular case, it may be that the automatism relied on is due to some "disease of the mind" but is not necessarily so. Automatism, which strictly means action without conscious volition, has been adopted in criminal law as a term to denote conduct of which the doer is not conscious — in short doing something without knowledge of it, and without memory afterwards of having done it — a temporary eclipse of consciousness that nevertheless leaves the person so affected able to exercise bodily movements. In such a case, the action is one which the mind in its normal functioning does not control. This may be due to some "disease of the mind" or it may not; it may happen with a perfectly healthy mind (*e.g.* in somnambulism which may be unaccompanied by an abnormality of mind), or it may occur where the mind is temporarily affected as the result of a blow, or by the influence of a drug or other intoxication. It may on the other hand be caused by an abnormal condition of the mind capable of being designated a mental disease. What are known as the M'Naghten Rules can have no application unless there is some form of "disease of the mind", which is not necessarily present in all cases of automatism.

· · · ·

This case raises interesting issues, and the judicial conclusion, in my view, should be guided by general principles of criminal responsibility. Before alluding to those principles, it is useful to recall s. 16(4) of the *Criminal Code*, which reads:

> (4) Every one shall, until the contrary is proved, be presumed to be and to have been sane.

In the usual case in which an accused pleads insanity, he has the burden of overcoming the presumption of sanity. In the present case the appellant is not seeking to establish that he was insane on 1st March 1974. The Crown is asserting the insanity in answer to the defence of automatism raised by the appellant. The presumption of sanity runs in the appellant's favour.

We turn to s. 16(2): a person is insane when he is in a state of natural imbecility or has a disease of the mind to an extent that renders him incapable of appreciating the nature and quality of an act or omission or of knowing that an act or omission is wrong. The important words, for present purposes, are "disease of the mind".

The first principle, fundamental to our criminal law, which governs this appeal is that no act can be a criminal offence unless it is done voluntarily. Consciousness is a sine qua non to criminal liability.

The prosecution must prove every element of the crime charged. One such element is the state of mind of the accused, in the sense that the act was voluntary. The circumstances are normally such as to permit a presumption of volition and mental capacity. That is not so when the accused, as here, has placed before the court, by cross-examination of Crown witnesses or by evidence called on his own behalf, or both, evidence sufficient to raise an issue that he was unconscious of his actions at the time of the alleged offence. No burden of proof is imposed upon an accused raising such defence beyond pointing to facts which indicate the existence of such a condition: *R. v. Berger* (1975), 27 C.C.C. (2d) 357 at 379, leave to appeal to the Supreme Court of Canada refused 27 C.C.C. (2d) 357n. Whether lack of consciousness relates to *mens rea* or to *actus reus* or both may be important in a case in which the offence charged is one of absolute liability, but the conceptual distinction does not concern us in the case at bar.

The second principle is that no person should be committed to a hospital for the criminally insane unless he suffers from disease of the mind in need of treatment or likely to recur.

The Ontario Court of Appeal held that the excusing factor was insanity. This finding was reached though the appellant exhibited no pathological symptoms indicative of a previously existing, or ongoing, psychiatric disorder. On medical evidence accepted by the trial judge, the prospect of a recurrence of dissociation is extremely remote. There was no finding that the appellant suffered from psychosis, neurosis or personality disorder. He does not have an organic disease of the brain. This was an isolated event. The appellant has already spent several weeks in a mental institution undergoing psychiatric, neurological and psychological assessment, the result of which did not indicate need for treatment.

There are undoubtedly policy considerations to be considered. Automatism as a defence is easily feigned. It is said the credibility of our criminal justice system will be severely strained if a person who has committed a violent act is allowed an absolute acquittal on a plea of automatism arising from a psychological blow. The argument is made that the success of the defence depends upon the semantic ability of psychiatrists, tracing a narrow path between the twin shoals of criminal responsibility and an insanity verdict. Added to these concerns is the in terrorem argument that the floodgates will be raised if psychological blow automatism is recognized in law.

There are competing policy interests. Where the condition is transient rather than persistent, unlikely to recur, not in need of treatment and not the result of self-induced intoxication, the policy objectives in finding such a person insane are not served. Such a person is not a danger to himself or to society generally.

The Ontario Court of Appeal in the present case focused upon "external cause". The "ordinary stresses and disappointments of life" were held not to constitute an external cause. The court considered that the "emotional stress" suffered by the appellant could not be said to be an external factor producing the automatism; the dissociative state had its source primarily in the psychological or emotional makeup of the appellant.

There is no evidence to support Martin J.A.'s statement attributing the dissociated state to the psychological or emotional makeup of the appellant. To exclude the defence of automatism it lay upon the Crown to establish that the appellant suffered from a disease of the mind at the time of the attack. The existence of the mental disease must be demonstrated in evidence. Here there is no such evidence from any of the expert or other witnesses with reference to the crucial period of the assault. Moreover, as earlier noted, s. 16(4) presumes sanity. The Court of Appeal's conclusion was directly contrary to the testimony of Dr. Orchard, accepted by the trial judge, and finds no support in the testimony of Dr. Rowsell.

Martin J.A. left open the question whether it is possible to dissociate as a result of emotional shock rather than physical injury. The effect of the appellate court judgment was to differ from the trial judge's finding that the dissociation was brought about by an externally operating cause. In the circumstances, I do not think it is open to this court to disturb the findings of fact at trial.

If the effect of the appellate court judgment is that, as a matter of law, emotional stress can never constitute an external factor then, with respect, I disagree. Indeed, in the passage quoted below the court seems to concede as much. If the controlling factor is one of degree of emotional stress, and the application of some form of quantitative test, then the question becomes one of fact for the trier of fact and not one of law for an appellate court.

It is not clear to me why, as a matter of law, an emotional blow — which can be devastating — should be regarded as an external cause of automatism in some circumstances and an internal cause in others, as the Court of Appeal would seem to propose in this passage [p. 68]:

> I leave aside, until it becomes necessary to decide them, cases where a dissociative state has resulted from emotional shock without physical injury, resulting from such causes, for example, as being involved in a serious accident although no physical injury has resulted; being the victim of a murderous attack with an uplifted knife, notwithstanding that the victim has managed to escape physical injury; seeing a loved one murdered or seriously assaulted, and the like stiuations. Such extraordinary external events might reasonably be presumed to

affect the average normal person without reference to the subjective makeup of the person exposed to such experience.

I cannot accept the notion that an extraordinary external event, *i.e.*, an intense emotional shock, can cause a state of dissociation or automatism if and only if all normal persons subjected to that sort of shock would react in that way. If I understood the quoted passage correctly, an objective standard is contemplated for one of the possible causes of automatism, namely, psychological blow, leaving intact the subjective standard for other causes of automatism, such as physical blow or reaction to drugs.

As in all other aspects of the criminal law (except negligence offences) the inquiry is directed to the accused's actual state of mind. It is his subjective mental condition with which the law is concerned. If he has a brittle skull and sustains a concussion which causes him to run amok, he has a valid defence of automatism. If he has an irregular metabolism which induced an unanticipated and violent reaction to a drug, he will not be responsible for his acts. If he is driven into shock and unconsciousness by an emotional blow, and was susceptible to that reaction but has no disease, there is no reason in principle why a plea of automatism should not be available. The fact that other people would not have reacted as he did should not obscure the reality that the external psychological blow did cause a loss of consciousness. A person's subjective reaction, in the absence of any other medical or factual evidence supportive of insanity, should not put him into the category of persons legally insane. Nor am I prepared to accept the proposition, which seems implicit in the passage quoted, that whether an automatic state is an insane reaction or a sane reaction may depend upon the intensity of the shock.

M.E. Schiffer, in his text *Mental Disorder and the Criminal Trial Process* (1978), states that psychological blow automatism is described as a reaction to a shock (p. 101):

> However, in cases where the psychological stress has taken the form of a sudden jolt or blow to the accused, the court may be more willing to treat a short-lived bout of automatism as sane. Because the automatism, in order to be a defence in itself, must be an "on the sudden" reaction to psychological stress, the defence of "psychological blow automatism" may be seen as somewhat analogous to the defence of provocation.

I agree with the requirement that there be a shock precipitating the state of automatism. Dissociation caused by a low stress threshold and surrender to anxiety cannot fairly be said to result from a psychological blow. In a recent decision of the British Columbia Court of Appeal, *R. v. MacLeod* (1980), 52 C.C.C. (2d) 193, Craig J.A. adopted the judgment of Martin J.A. in *Rabey*. The facts of *MacLeod* cannot be compared with those in the instant appeal. There, the accused absorbed four double drinks of liquor prior to entering the alleged state of dissociation. His loss of consciousness cannot be traced to an immediate emotional shock. He had been subject to ongoing stress for some time, which was heightened by his wife's recent departure. "Though unwilling to classify it a disease of the mind, the accused's medical witness described it as a "neurotic disorder" which could be induced by an "anxiety reaction". The Court of Appeal held that non-insane automatism was not available.

Dr. Glanville Williams' new book, *Textbook of Criminal Law* (1978), is helpful in this discussion, in particular c. 27. The author cites, as the main instances of automatism, "sleepwalking, concussion, some cases of epilepsy, hypoglycaemia and dissociative states". Williams says (pp. 608-609) that "automatism" has come to express "any abnormal state of consciousness (whether confusion, delusion or dissociation) that is regarded as incompatible with the existence of *mens rea*, while not amounting to insanity", adding:

> It would better be called "impaired consciousness", but the orthodox expression can be used if we bear in mind that it does not mean what it says.

And in a footnote [on p. 609]:

> Because automatism is a legal concept, a psychiatrist should be asked to testify to the mental condition as psychiatrically recognized, not to "automatism". It is for the Judge to make the translation. In most of the conditions referred to legally as automatism the psychiatrist would speak of an altered state of consciousness.

The *Parnerkar* case is discussed at some length and the following observations made with respect thereto [p. 613]:

> The decision illustrates the difficulty that can be caused to the courts by over-enthusiastic psychiatrists. If such evidence were regularly given and accepted a considerable breach would be made in the law of homicide. A medical witness who proclaims that the defendant, though awake, did not know that he was stabbing a person because of his dissociated state invites incredulity, particularly where it is shown that the defendant immediately afterwards telephoned for an ambulance and the police. Further, to assert that this medical condition amounts to insanity ignores the distinction that has been developed between sane and non-sane automatism. *If Parnerkar was in a state of automatism at all it was of the non-insane variety, since there was no evidence of psychosis or brain damage or continuing danger.* (The italics are mine.)

At the conclusion of the discussion on *Parnerkar*, Williams makes the following comment, particularly apt in the present case [p. 613]:

> It may also be remarked that commitment to hospital is inappropriate in a case of hysterical dissociation, since once the episode is over the patient does not need to be detained.

Under the heading "Insanity versus Automatism" Williams states that before the decision in *Quick, supra*, Lord Denning's view in *Bratty, supra*, was generally accepted. The test of insanity was the likelihood of recurrence of danger. In *Quick* the Court of Appeal adopted what might seem at first sight to be a different test for insane versus non-insane automatism. But the real question is whether the violence is likely to be repeated. Williams concludes that "on the whole, it would be much better if the courts kept to Lord Denning's plain rule; the rule in *Quick* adds nothing to it" (p. 615).

This view, which the Ontario Court of Appeal appears to have rejected, finds ample support in the legal literature. See S.M. Beck, "Voluntary Conduct: Automatism, Insanity and Drunkenness" (1966-67), 9 Cr. L.Q. 315 at 321: "The cause of the automatic conduct, and the threat of recurrence, are plainly factors that determine the line between sane and insane automatism"; F.A. Whitlock, *Criminal Responsibility and Mental Illness* (1963), p. 120: "The test of whether or not an episode of automatism is to be judged as sane or insane action seems to rest on the likelihood of its repetition"; Professor J. Ll J. Edwards, "Automatism and Criminal Responsibility", at p. 385: "Where evidence is available of recurrent attacks of automatism during which the accused resorts to violence . . . . [this] inevitably leads to consideration of the imposition of some restraint"; S. Prevezer, "Automatism and Involuntary Conduct", [1958] Crim. L.R. 440 at 441: "If . . . it can safely be predicted that his conduct is not likely to recur, having regard to the cause of the automatism, there can be no point in finding him insane and detaining him in Broadmoor"; G.A. Martin, "Insanity as a Defence" (1965-66), 8 Cr. L.Q. 240 at 253: "Perhaps the distinction lies in the likelihood of recurrence and whether the person suffering from it is prone to acts of violence when in that state."

In principle, the defence of automatism should be available whenever there is evidence of unconsciousness throughout the commission of the crime that cannot be attributed to fault or negligence on his part. Such evidence should be supported by expert medical opinion that the accused did not feign memory loss and that there is no underlying pathological condition which points to a disease requiring detention and treatment.

I would add only that s. 16 determines the consequences of the finding of "no consciousness" on the basis of a legal conclusion guided by the medical evidence of the day. What is disease of the mind in the medical science of today may not be so tomorrow. The court will establish the meaning of disease of the mind on the basis of scientific evidence as it unfolds from day to day. The court will find as a matter of fact in each case whether a disease of the mind, so defined, is present.

The circumstances in this case are highly unusual, uncomplicated by alcohol or psychiatric history. The real question in the case is whether the appellant should be confined in an institution for the criminally insane. The trial Judge negated an act of passion, lack of self-control or impulsiveness. The medical evidence negated a state of disease or disorder or mental disturbance arising from infirmity. Save what was said by Dr. Rowsell, whose evidence as to *ex post facto* hysterical amnesia was rejected by the trial judge, the medical experts gave the appellant a clean mental bill of health. I can see no possible justification for sending the case back for a new trial.

I would allow the appeal, set aside the judgment of the Ontario Court of Appeal and restore the verdict of acquittal.

Appeal dismissed.

At the new trial the sentence was a conditional discharge and 18 months probation.

R. v. PARKS

[1992] 2 S.C.R. 871, 15 C.R. (4th) 289, 75 C.C.C. (3d) 287,
1992 CarswellOnt 107, 1992 CarswellOnt 996

The accused was experiencing serious personal problems, including the loss of his job, which made it difficult for him to sleep. One night he fell asleep in the living room, but a few hours later he got up, put on a jacket and running shoes, grabbed his car keys and the keys to his in-laws' home and drove 23 kilometres to their home. Some of this distance is a multi-lane high-speed highway, and the trip takes 20 minutes in moderate traffic. He then parked in a somewhat confined underground parking area, took a tire iron from his car and entered the home. He got a knife from the kitchen and went to his in-laws' bedroom, where they were sleeping. He strangled his father-in-law until he was unconscious and at some stage inflicted cuts to his head and chest. The father-in-law was hospitalized but recovered. The accused repeatedly stabbed his mother-in-law and brutally beat her with a blunt instrument. She died. The accused then drove to a nearby police station, taking the knife with him. He arrived at the police station with badly cut hands. He was agitated and in great distress. He made various exclamations to the effect that he had just killed two people with his bare hands. He indicated that these people were his mother and father-in-law. The accused had previously had a good relationship with both of his wife's parents. He was charged with murder and attempted murder.

At his murder trial, he raised the defence of sleepwalking and was acquitted by a jury. The trial judge ruled that his defence should be left to the jury as non-insane automatism, entitling him to an acquittal, rather than as a form of the defence of insanity which, if accepted, would result in the special verdict of not guilty by reason of insanity. At the subsequent trial for attempted murder, the trial judge acquitted the accused on the basis that the doctrine of issue estoppel required him to accept the previous jury's determination that the defence of sleepwalking had been made out.

The Crown appealed these acquittals. The Ontario Court of Appeal [(1990) 78 C.R. (3d) 1] dismissed the appeals on the basis that there was no evidence of a disease of the mind and that, while the facts of the case stretched credulity, an appellate court had to guard against the temptation to usurp the jury's function. The Crown appealed further. The Supreme Court dismissed the appeal. The Court was in agreement that, on this evidence, the trial judge had not erred in leaving the jury the defence of automatism rather than that of insanity.

CHIEF JUSTICE LAMER (for the court on this point): —

This court has only ruled on sleepwalking in an *obiter dictum* in *R. v. Rabey*, [1980] 2 S.C.R. 513, 15 C.R. (3d) 225. The court found that sleepwalking was not a "disease of the mind" in the legal sense of the term and gave rise to a defence of automatism. Should the court maintain this position?

In *Black's Law Dictionary*, 5th ed. (St. Paul, Minn.: West Publishing Co., 1979) automatism is defined as follows:

> Behaviour performed in a state of mental unconsciousness or dissociation without full awareness, *i.e.*, somnambulism, fugues. Term is applied to actions or conduct of an individual apparently occurring without will, purpose, or reasoned intention on his part; a condition sometimes observed in persons who, without being actually insane, suffer from an obscuration of the mental faculties, loss of volition or of memory, or kindred affections. . . .

In *Rabey* this court affirmed the judgment of the Ontario Court of Appeal (1977), 40 C.R.N.S. 46, 37 C.C.C. (2d) 461, in which Martin J.A. defined the expression "disease of the mind" at pp. 472-473 [C.C.C., p. 57 C.R.N.S.]:

> "Disease of the mind" is a legal term, not a medical term of art; although a legal concept, it contains a substantial medical component as well as a legal or policy component.
>
> The legal or policy component relates to (a) the scope of the exemption from criminal responsibility to be afforded by mental disorder or disturbance, and (b) the protection of the public by the control and treatment of persons who have caused serious harms while in a mentally disordered or disturbed state. The medical component of the term, generally, is medical opinion as to how the mental condition in question is viewed or characterized medically. Since the medical component of the term reflects or should reflect the state of medical knowledge at a given time, the concept of "disease of the mind" is capable of evolving with increased medical knowledge with respect to mental disorder or disturbance.

As Martin J.A. pointed out at p. 477 [C.C.C., p. 62 C.R.N.S.], Canadian and foreign courts and authors have recognized that sleepwalking is not a disease of the mind:

> Sleepwalking appears to fall into a separate category. Unconscious behaviour in a state of somnambulism is non-insane automatism....

In Canada, see also *R. v. Hartridge* (1966), 48 C.R. 389, [1967] 1 C.C.C. 346 (Sask. C.A.).

In Britain, Lord Denning in *Bratty v. Attorney General for Northern Ireland*, [1963] A.C. 386 (H.L.), at p. 409, recognized that sleepwalking gave rise to a defence of automatism:

> No act is punishable if it is done involuntarily; and an involuntary act in this context — some people nowadays prefer to speak of it as "automatism" — means an act which is done by the muscles without any control by the mind, such as a spasm, a reflex action or a convulsion; or an act done by a person who is not conscious of what he is doing, such as an act done whilst suffering from concussion or whilst sleepwalking.

Other foreign decisions have recognized the same principle: *Ryan v. R.*, [1967] A.L.R. 577; *R. v. Cottle*, [1958] N.Z.L.R. 999; *R. v. Ngang*, [1960] 3 S.A.L.R. 363; *R. v. Tolson* (1889), 23 Q.B.D. 168 (C.C.R.); *H.M. Advocate v. Fraser* (1878), 4 Couper 70.

However, two British decisions seem to go against this line of authority: *R. v. Sullivan*, [1984] A.C. 156, [1983] 2 All E.R. 673 (H.L.), and *R. v. Burgess*, [1991] 2 Q.B. 92 (C.A.). The comment in *Sullivan* at p. 677 [All E.R.] was *obiter*, since the case concerned epilepsy:

> If the effect of a disease is to impair these faculties so severely as to have either of the consequences referred to in the latter part of the [*M'Naghten*] rules, it matters not whether the aetiology of the impairment is organic, as in epilepsy, or functional, or whether the impairment itself is permanent or is transient and intermittent, provided that it subsisted at the time of commission of the act.

Some writers have interpreted this *obiter* as an indication that future cases of sleepwalking would only lead to a defence of insanity:

> Although sleepwalkers have always received an absolute acquittal for what they do, no social inconvenience has hitherto resulted. There seems to be no recorded instance of a sleepwalker doing injury a further time after being acquitted. However, since the decision in *Sullivan*, to be discussed in the next section, it seems very likely that sleepwalkers will in future find themselves saddled with an insanity verdict. [Williams, *supra*, at p. 666.]

However, the evidence in the case at bar does not indicate the presence of an illness. Accordingly, I do not believe that this *obiter* can be applied to sleepwalking cases such as that of Mr. Parks. *Burgess* cannot be applied here for the same reason, but we will return to it later.

. . . .

In the case at bar the trial judge first reviewed the case law and scholarly analysis and said he did not intend to go against it:

> In *Rabey*, *supra*, Martin J.A. considered somnambulism or sleepwalking to be a special category or case of non-insane automatism, one that perhaps could not be justified in accordance with a strict application of principles invoked to determine whether a condition from which an accused suffers amounts to "a disease of the mind" within s-s. 16(2) of the *Criminal Code*. Quite simply put, and notwithstanding that the observations concerning the legal characterization of sleepwalking as a separate category of non-insane automatism would not appear to have been necessary to a decision of the issue on appeal in *Rabey*, *supra*, I am not prepared to depart from the pronouncement of such an eminent authority as Martin J.A. on matters concerning the scope of criminal responsibility. The statement there made is, as one might expect, amply supported by the jurisprudence and academic writings upon the issue.

He then considered the facts of the instant case:

> In the circumstances of the present case, it is doubtful whether the sleep disorder from which the accused suffers would constitute a disease of the mind under s-s. 16(2) in accordance with general principle.

I therefore propose to review the evidence in this matter. A large part of the defence evidence in this case was medical evidence. Five physicians were heard: Dr. Roger James Broughton, a neurophysiologist and specialist in sleep and sleep disorders, Dr. John Gordon Edmeads, a neurologist, Dr. Ronald Frederick Billings, a psychiatrist, Dr. Robert Wood Hill, a forensic psychiatrist, and finally, Dr. Frank Raymond Ervin, a neurologist and psychiatrist.

The medical evidence in the case at bar showed that the respondent was in fact sleepwalking when he committed the acts with which he is charged. All the expert witnesses called by the defence said that in their opinion Parks was sleepwalking when the events occurred. This is what Dr. Broughton said:

> Q. . . . assuming for a moment that Mr. Parks caused the death of Barbara Woods, did you, sir, reach an opinion as to his condition at the time he caused that death?
>
> A. Yes. My opinion is that he did it during a sleepwalking episode.

Though sceptical at the outset, the expert witnesses unanimously stated that at the time of the incidents the respondent was not suffering from any mental illness and that, medically speaking, sleepwalking is not regarded as an illness, whether physical, mental or neurological.

. . . .

They also unanimously stated that a person who is sleepwalking cannot think, reflect or perform voluntary acts.

. . . .

The evidence also disclosed that sleepwalking was very common, almost universal, among children, and that 2 to 2.5 percent of "normal" adults had sleepwalked at least once. Dr. Hill further noted that he found it significant that there were several sleepwalkers in the respondent's family:

> Thirdly, I think, as I indicated, it turns out, as enquiries are made more and more, that there is a significant history in the background family of Mr. Parks of difficulties, of bedwetting difficulties, of sleeptalking and sleepwalking, that is in keeping with what we know about the phenomena of sleepwalking. We know that there are often family members so affected and that was present.

Dr. Broughton, for his part, indicated that he had never known of sleepwalkers who had acted violently who had repeated this kind of behaviour:

> Q. Yes. Now, with respect to Mr. Parks, do you have any opinion, sir, as to the probability of a recurrence of an event of sleepwalking with serious aggression involving physical harm to others?
>
> A. I think the risk of that is infinitesimal, I don't think it would exceed the risk of the general population almost. He has the family predisposition to sleepwalk, but it would only be in the likelihood of all precipitating and extenuating and so forth factors that built up to this crisis that would theoretically have to almost reappear.
>
> Q. And even if they were to reappear, would there be any probability of another homicidal event?

A. It would still — As I say, there are no reported cases in the literature, so there is essentially — The probability of it occurring is not statistically significant. It is just absolutely improbable.

In cross-examination he also added that sleepwalking episodes in which violent acts are committed are not common:

Q. And does that, in fact, agree with your own experience with respect to people that you have dealt with at the sleep lab and have seen over the years, that the majority of sleepwalking episodes generally involve what you call trivial behaviour?

A. It is well known that aggression during sleepwalking is quite rare.

Q. How many cases of aggression during sleepwalking have you personally deal[t] with or been involved with at your sleep lab?

A. In the last — Perhaps a total of five or six. In the last five years we have seen three.

Further, on being questioned about a cure or treatment, Dr. Broughton answered that the solution was sleep hygiene, which involved eliminating factors that precipitated sleepwalking such as stress, lack of sleep and violent physical exercise.

. . . .

Three very important points emerge from this testimony: (1) the respondent was sleepwalking at the time of the incident; (2) sleepwalking is not a neurological, psychiatric or other illness — it is a sleep disorder very common in children and also found in adults; (3) there is no medical treatment as such, apart from good health practices, especially as regards sleep. It is important to note that this expert evidence was not in any way contradicted by the prosecution, which as the trial judge observed, did have the advice of experts who were present during the testimony given by the defence experts and whom it chose not to call.

I am of the view that in the instant case, based on the evidence and the testimony of the expert witnesses heard, the trial judge did not err in leaving the defence of automatism rather than that of insanity with the jury, and that the instant appeal should be dismissed. For a defence of insanity to have been put to the jury, together with or instead of a defence of automatism, as the case may be, there would have had to have been in the record evidence tending to show that sleepwalking was the cause of the respondent's state of mind. As we have just seen, that is not the case here. This is not to say that sleepwalking could never be a disease of the mind, in another case on different evidence.

LA FOREST J. (five justices concurring): — I have had the advantage of reading the reasons of the Chief Justice. I agree with him that the trial judge was correct in leaving only the defence of non-insane automatism with the jury. I am also in agreement with what the Chief Justice has to say on that issue, but I wish to add the following comments concerning the distinction in law between insane and non-insane automatism, particularly as it relates to somnambulism.

In his reasons, the Chief Justice finds that the evidence and expert testimony from the trial of the accused support the trial judge's decision to instruct the jury on non-insane automatism. I agree with this finding, but in my view that is not the end of the matter. In distinguishing between automatism and insanity the trial judge must consider more than the evidence; there are overarching policy considerations as well. Of course, the evidence in each case will be highly relevant to this policy inquiry.

Automatism occupies a unique place in our criminal law system. Although spoken of as a "defence", it is conceptually a subset of the voluntariness requirement, which in turn is part of the *actus reus* component of criminal liability. A useful introduction is found in the dissenting reasons of Dickson J. (as he then was) in *R. v. Rabey*, [1980] 2 S.C.R. 513, 15 C.R. (3d) 225, at p. 522 [S.C.R.]:

> Although the word "automatism" made its way but lately to the legal stage, it is basic principle that absence of volition in respect of the act involved is always a defence to a crime. A defence that the act is involuntary entitles the accused to a complete and unqualified acquittal. That the defence of automatism exists as a middle ground between criminal responsibility and legal insanity is beyond question. Although spoken as a defence, in the sense that it is raised by the accused, the Crown always bears the burden of proving a voluntary act.

One qualification to this statement should be noted. When the automatistic condition stems from a disease of the mind that has rendered the accused insane, then the accused is not entitled to a full acquittal, but to a verdict of insanity; see *Bratty v. Attorney General for Northern Ireland*, [1963] A.C. 386 (H.L.), at pp. 403-404 and 414 [A.C.]. The condition in that instance is referred to as insane automatism, and the distinction between it and non-insane automatism is the crucial issue in this appeal.

When a defence of non-insane automatism is raised by the accused, the trial judge must determine whether the defence should be left with the trier of fact. This will involve two discrete tasks. First, he or she must determine whether there is some evidence on the record to support leaving the defence with the jury. This is sometimes referred to as laying the proper foundation for the defence; see *Bratty, supra*, at pp. 405 and 413 [A.C.]. Thus an evidential burden rests with the accused, and the mere assertion of the defence will not suffice; see *Bratty*, at p. 414 [A.C.]. Dickson J. summarized the point in comprehensive fashion in the following passage in *Rabey*, at p. 545 [S.C.R.]:

> The prosecution must prove every element of the crime charged. One such element is the state of mind of the accused, in the sense that the act was voluntary. The circumstances are normally such as to permit a presumption of volition and mental capacity. That is not so when the accused, as here, has placed before the court, by cross-examination of Crown witnesses or by evidence called on his own behalf, or both, evidence sufficient to raise an issue that he was

unconscious of his actions at the time of the alleged offence. No burden of proof is imposed upon an accused raising such defence beyond pointing to facts which indicate the existence of such a condition.

If the proper foundation is present the judge moves to the second task: he or she must consider whether the condition alleged by the accused is, in law, non-insane automatism. If the trial judge is satisfied that there is some evidence pointing to a condition that is in law non-insane automatism, then the defence can be left with the jury; see *Rabey*, per Ritchie J., at p. 519 [S.C.R.]. The issue for the jury is one of fact: did the accused suffer from or experience the alleged condition at the relevant time? Because the Crown must always prove that an accused has acted voluntarily, the onus rests on the prosecution at this stage to prove the absence of automatism beyond a reasonable doubt.

In the present case, there is no question that the accused has laid the proper foundation for the defence of automatism. The expert testimony reviewed by the Chief Justice is more than adequate on that score. At issue here is the question of law: is sleepwalking properly classified as non-insane automatism, or does it stem from a disease of the mind, thereby leaving only the defence of insanity for the accused? When considering this question, s. 16(4) of the *Criminal Code*, R.S.C., 1985, c. C-46, should be recalled: "Every one shall, until the contrary is proved, be presumed to be and to have been sane." If the accused pleads automatism, the Crown is then entitled to raise the issue of insanity, but the prosecution then bears the burden of proving that the condition in question stems from a disease of the mind; see *Rabey*, *supra*, at pp. 544-545 [S.C.R.].

In Canada, the approach to distinguishing between insane and non-insane automatism was settled by this court's judgment in *Rabey*.

. . . .

In part because of the imprecision of medical science in this area, the legal community reserves for itself the final determination of what constitutes a "disease of the mind". This is accomplished by adding the "legal or policy component" to the inquiry.

A review of the cases on automatism reveals two distinct approaches to the policy component of the disease of the mind inquiry. These may be labelled the "continuing danger" and "internal cause" theories; see E. Colvin, *Principles of Criminal Law,* 2d ed. (Toronto: Carswell, 1991), at p. 293. At first glance these approaches may appear to be divergent, but in fact they stem from a common concern for public safety. This was recognized by Martin J.A. who referred to "protection of the public" as a focus of the policy inquiry. More recently, the Chief Justice had occasion to comment on this aspect of the insanity provisions of the *Criminal Code*, albeit in a division of powers context, in *R. v. Swain*, [1991] 1 S.C.R. 933, 5 C.R. (4th) 253, 63 C.C.C. (3d) 481, at p. 998 [S.C.R.]:

It is true that the dominant characteristic of these provisions is not punishment; however, neither is it treatment. The "pith and substance" of the legislative scheme dealing with individuals acquitted by reason of insanity is the protection of society from dangerous people who have engaged in conduct proscribed by the *Criminal Code* through the prevention of such acts in the future. While treatment may be incidentally involved in the process, it is not the dominant objective of the legislation.

The continuing danger theory holds that any condition likely to present a recurring danger to the public should be treated as insanity. The internal cause theory suggests that a condition stemming from the psychological or emotional makeup of the accused, rather than some external factor, should lead to a finding of insanity. The two theories share a common concern for recurrence, the latter holding that an internal weakness is more likely to lead to recurrent violence than automatism brought on by some intervening external cause.

It would appear that the internal cause approach has gained a certain ascendancy in both Canadian and English jurisprudence. The theory was the basis for deciding *Rabey*.

. . . .

The theory has also been adopted in England, first in *R. v. Quick*; *R. v. Paddison*, [1973] 3 All E.R. 347 (C.A.) [hereafter *R. v. Quick*], at p. 356 [All E.R.], and most recently in *R. v. Hennessy*, [1989] 2 All E.R. 9 (C.A.), where Lord Lane C.J. stated the approach as follows, at p. 13 [All E.R.]:

> The question in many cases, and this is one such case, is whether the function of the mind was disturbed on the one hand by disease or on the other hand by some external factor.

The judgments in both *Rabey* and *Hennessy* are careful to state that the internal cause theory is not a universal approach to the disease of the mind inquiry. Indeed Martin J.A., at p. 477 [C.C.C., p. 62 C.R.N.S.], appears to suggest that sleepwalking is one of those conditions that is not usefully assessed on this basis.

The internal cause approach has been criticized as an unfounded development of the law, and for the odd results the external/internal dichotomy can produce; see G. Williams, *Textbook of Criminal Law* 2d ed. (London: Sweet & Maxwell, 1983), at pp. 671-676; D. Stuart, *Canadian Criminal Law* 2d ed. (Toronto: Carswell, 1987), at pp. 92-94; Colvin, *supra*, at p. 291. These criticisms have particular validity if the internal cause theory is held out as the definitive answer to the disease of the mind inquiry. However, it is apparent from the cases that the theory is really meant to be used only as an analytical tool, and not as an all-encompassing methodology. As Watt J. commented in his reasons in support of his charge to the jury in this case, the dichotomy "constitutes a general, but not an unremitting or universal, classificatory scheme for 'disease of the mind'".

As Martin J.A. suggested in *Rabey*, somnambulism is an example of a condition that is not well suited to analysis under the internal cause theory. The poor fit arises because certain factors can legitimately be characterized as either internal or external sources of automatistic behaviour. For example, the Crown in this case argues that the causes of the respondent's violent sleepwalking were entirely internal, a combination of genetic susceptibility and the ordinary stresses of everyday life (lack of sleep, excessive afternoon exercise, and a high stress level due to personal problems). These "ordinary stresses" were ruled out as external factors by this court in *Rabey* (although by a narrow majority). However, the factors that for a waking individual are mere ordinary stresses can be differently characterized for a person who is asleep, unable to counter with his conscious mind the onslaught of the admittedly ordinary strains of life. One could argue that the particular amalgam of stress, excessive exercise, sleep deprivation and sudden noises in the night that causes an incident of somnambulism is, for the sleeping person, analogous to the effect of a concussion upon a waking person, which is generally accepted as an external cause of non-insane automatism; see Williams, *supra*, at p. 666. In the end, the dichotomy between internal and external causes becomes blurred in this context, and is not helpful in resolving the inquiry.

The continuing danger approach stems from an *obiter* comment of Lord Denning in *Bratty, supra*, where he proposes the following test for distinguishing between insane and non-insane automatism, at p. 412 [A.C.]:

> It seems to me that any mental disorder which has manifested itself in violence and is prone to recur is a disease of the mind. At any rate it is the sort of disease for which a person should be detained in hospital rather than be given an unqualified acquittal.

Lord Denning's causal proposition has not been universally accepted, although some elements of the theory remain today. It was questioned in *R. v. Quick, supra*, at pp. 351-352 [All E.R.], and legal academics have questioned the utility of the test; see Stuart, *supra*, at pp. 94-95; Colvin, *supra*, at p. 294. As well, medical authorities have doubted the ability of their profession to predict recurrent dangerousness; see Roth, "Modern Psychiatry and Neurology and the Problem of Responsibility", in S.J. Hucker, C. Webster and M. Ben-Aron, eds., *Mental Disorder and Criminal Responsibility* (Toronto: Butterworths, 1981), at pp. 104-109. In *Rabey*, Martin J.A. doubted the merit of Lord Denning's test, noting, at p. 476 [C.C.C., p. 60 C.R.N.S.], that the converse of Denning's proposition was surely not good law. He stated:

> It would be quite unreasonable to hold that a serious mental disorder did not constitute a disease of the mind because it was unlikely to recur. To so hold would be to exclude from the exemption from responsibility afforded by insanity, persons, who by reason of a severe mental disorder were incapable of appreciating the nature and quality of the act or of knowing that it was wrong, if such mental disorder was unlikely to recur.

The majority of this court approved these comments, and Dickson J. in dissent conceded the point, at p. 533 [S.C.R.]:

A test of proneness to recur does not entail the converse conclusion, that if the mental malady is not prone to recur it cannot be a disease of the mind. A condition, organic in nature, which causes an isolated act of unconscious violence could well be regarded as a case of temporary insanity.

Nonetheless, Dickson J. sought to revive Lord Denning's basic formulation...

. . . .

While Dickson J.'s views did not carry the day in *Rabey*, nothing in the majority judgment precludes the consideration of a continuing danger as a factor at the policy stage of the inquiry.

Since *Rabey*, the House of Lords has revisited the question of disease of the mind, in *R. v. Sullivan*, [1984] A.C. 156, Lord Diplock, speaking for a unanimous court, commented, at p. 172 [A.C.], as follows:

> The nomenclature adopted by the medical profession may change from time to time; Bratty was tried in 1961. But the meaning of the expression "disease of the mind" as the cause of "a defect of reason", remains unchanged for the purposes of the application of the M'Naghten Rules. I agree with what was said by Devlin J. in *Reg. v. Kemp* [1957] 1 Q.B. 399, 407, that "mind" in the M'Naghten Rules is used in the ordinary sense of the mental faculties of reason, memory and understanding. If the effect of a disease is to impair these faculties so severely as to have either of the consequences referred to in the latter part of the rules, it matters not whether the aetiology of the impairment is organic, as in epilepsy, or functional, or whether the impairment itself is permanent or is transient and intermittent, provided that it subsisted at the time of commission of the act. *The purpose of the legislation relating to the defence of insanity, ever since its origin in 1800, has been to protect society against recurrence of the dangerous conduct. The duration of a temporary suspension of the mental faculties of reason, memory and understanding, particularly if, as in Mr. Sullivan's case, it is recurrent, cannot on any rational ground be relevant to the application by the courts of the M'Naghten Rules*, though it may be relevant to the course adopted by the Secretary of State, to whom the responsibility for how the defendant is to be dealt with passes after the return of the special verdict of "not guilty by reason of insanity." [My emphasis.]

This passage, while not entirely clear, appears to endorse the consideration of recurrence as a non-determinative factor in the insanity inquiry. Lord Diplock states that the *duration* of the condition in question is not a relevant consideration: a disease of the mind can be temporary or permanent. He also suggests that the relative impermanence of a condition is particularly inconsequential *if the condition is prone to recur*. A necessary corollary of these statements is the more general proposition that recurrence suggests insanity, but the absence of recurrence does not preclude it. This view of the law was stated explicitly in *R. v. Burgess*, [1991] 2 All E.R. 769 (C.A.), at p. 774 [All E.R.]:

> It seems to us that if there is a danger of recurrence that may be an added reason for categorising the condition as a disease of the mind. On the other hand, the absence of the danger of recurrence is not a reason for saying that it cannot be a disease of the mind. Subject to that possible qualification, we respectfully adopt Lord Denning's suggested definition.

In my view, the Court of Appeal has properly stated the law on this point. Recurrence is but one of a number of factors to be considered in the policy phase of the disease of the mind inquiry. Moreover, the absence of a danger of recurrence will not automatically exclude the possibility of a finding of insanity.

In this case, then, neither of the two leading policy approaches determines an obvious result. It is clear from the evidence that there is almost no likelihood of recurrent violent somnambulism. A finding of insanity is therefore less likely, but the absence of a continuing danger does not mean that the respondent must be granted an absolute acquittal. At the same time, the internal cause theory is not readily applicable in this case. It is therefore necessary to look further afield.

In his dissenting reasons in *Rabey*, at p. 546, [S.C.R.] Dickson J. enumerates certain additional policy considerations that are relevant to the distinction between insanity and automatism:

> There are undoubtedly policy considerations to be considered. Automatism as a defence is easily feigned. It is said the credibility of our criminal justice system will be severely strained if a person who has committed a violent act is allowed an absolute acquittal on a plea of automatism arising from a psychological blow. The argument is made that the success of the defence depends upon the semantic ability of psychiatrists, tracing a narrow path between the twin shoals of criminal responsibility and an insanity verdict. Added to these concerns is the *in terrorem* argument that the floodgates will be raised if psychological blow automatism is recognized in law.

These factors are raised by Dickson J. as arguments against a finding of non-insane automatism. In the present case, however, none of these arguments is persuasive. It seems unlikely that the recognition of somnambulism as non-insane automatism will open the floodgates to a cascade of sleepwalking defence claims. First of all, the defence of somnambulism has been recognized, albeit in *obiter* discussion, in an unbroken line of cases stretching back at least a century, yet I am unaware of any current problem with specious defence claims of somnambulistic automatism. Indeed, this case and *Burgess* are among the few appellate decisions in which the status of somnambulism was a question to be decided. Moreover, it is very difficult to feign sleepwalking — precise symptoms and medical histories beyond the control of the accused must be presented to the trier of fact, and as in this case the accused will be subjected to a battery of medical tests. Finally, a comprehensive listing of the indicia of sleepwalking can be consulted by both the court and the medical experts; see P. Fenwick, "Somnambulism and the Law: A Review" (1987), 5 Behavioral Sciences and the Law 343, at p. 354.

It may be that some will regard the exoneration of an accused through a defence of somnambulism as an impairment of the credibility of our justice system. Those who hold this view would also reject insane automatism as an excuse from criminal responsibility. However, these views are contrary to certain fundamental precepts of our criminal law: only those who act voluntarily with the requisite intent to commit an offence should be punished by criminal sanction. The concerns of those who reject these underlying values of our system of criminal justice must accordingly be discounted.

In the end, there are no compelling policy factors that preclude a finding that the accused's condition was one of non-insane automatism. I noted earlier that it is for the Crown to prove that somnambulism stems from a disease of the mind; neither the evidence nor the policy considerations in this case overcome the Crown's burden in that regard. Committal under s. 614(2) of the *Criminal Code* is therefore precluded, and the accused should be acquitted.

As I noted at the outset, it is apparent that the medical evidence in this case is not only significant in its own right, but also has an impact at several stages of the policy inquiry. As such, I agree with the Chief Justice that in another case, on different evidence, sleepwalking might be found to be a disease of the mind. As Dickson J. commented in *Rabey*, at p. 552 [S.C.R.]:

> What is disease of the mind in the medical science of today may not be so tomorrow. The court will establish the meaning of disease of the mind on the basis of scientific evidence as it unfolds from day to day. The court will find as a matter of fact in each case whether a disease of the mind, so defined, is present.

R. v. STONE

[1999] 2 S.C.R. 290, 24 C.R. (5th) 1, 134 C.C.C. (3d) 353,
1999 CarswellBC 1064, 1999 CarswellBC 1065

The accused decided to visit his sons from a previous marriage. His current wife insisted on accompanying him and expressed her objections to the visit before and after the accused saw his sons for some 15 minutes. According to the accused his wife raised the issue of divorce, told him she had falsely reported to the police that he was abusing her and that they were ready to arrest him, that she would stay in the house and have him support her and their children, and that "she couldn't stand to listen to me whistle, that every time I touched her, she felt sick, that I was a lousy fuck and that I had a small penis and that she's never going to fuck me again". He testified he felt a "whoosh" sensation washing over him from his feet to his head. When his eyes focused again, he was staring straight ahead and felt something in his hand. He was holding a six-inch hunting knife. He looked over and saw his wife slumped over on the seat. She was dead. It was later established she had been stabbed 47 times. He put the body in his truck tool box, cleaned up, drove home, prepared a note for his stepdaughter, packed, checked into a hotel for a shower and shave, collected a debt, sold a car and flew to Mexico. While in Mexico, he awoke one morning to the sensation of having his throat cut. In trying to recall his dream, he remembered stabbing his wife twice in the chest before experiencing a "whooshing" sensation. On his return to Canada he surrendered to police and was charged with murder.

At his trial before judge and jury the accused admitted stabbing his wife. His defences were insane automatism, non-insane automatism, lack of intent, and alternatively, provocation. The trial judge found that there was evidence of unconsciousness throughout the commission of the crime but ruled the defence had laid a proper evidentiary foundation for insane but not non-insane automatism. Accordingly, he instructed the jury on insane automatism, intention in relation to second degree murder and provocation.

The accused was found guilty of manslaughter and sentenced to four years' imprisonment. In imposing this sentence, the trial judge took into account the 18-month pre-trial period as the equivalent of three years' imprisonment.

The Supreme Court accepted that this was a proper case for provocation to go to the jury and also dismissed the Crown appeal against sentence. The 5-4 division in the Court came on the issue of whether sane automatism should have been left with the jury. Justice Bastarache determined that the judge had been correct in not putting the defence to the jury. The majority also decided to reverse the onus of proof. Bastarache J. also offered detailed guidance on how this burden can be discharged and how to distinguish cases of sane automatism from those of insanity which are subsumed by the defence of mental disorder under s. 16.

BINNIE J., dissenting (LAMER C.J., IACOBUCCI and MAJOR JJ. concurring): — A fundamental principle of the criminal law is that no act can be a criminal offence unless it is performed or omitted voluntarily. In this case the appellant acknowledges that he killed his wife. He stabbed her 47 times with his knife in a frenzy. His defence was that he lost consciousness when his mind snapped under the weight of verbal abuse which the defence psychiatrist characterized as "exceptionally cruel" and "psychologically sadistic". The trial judge ruled in favour of the appellant that "there is evidence of unconsciousness throughout the commission of the crime", and the British Columbia Court of Appeal agreed ((1997), 86 B.C.A.C. 169, at p. 173) that "a properly instructed jury, acting reasonably, could find some form of automatism".

The appellant had elected trial by jury. He says he was entitled to have the issue of voluntariness, thus properly raised, determined by the jury. He says that there was no proper legal basis for the courts in British Columbia to deprive him of the benefit of an evidentiary ruling which put in issue the Crown's ability to prove the *actus reus* of the offence.

The trial judge ruled that the evidence of involuntariness was only relevant (if at all) to a defence of not criminally responsible by reason of mental disorder (NCRMD). This was upheld by the Court of Appeal. When it is appreciated that all of the experts agreed the appellant did not suffer from any condition that medicine would classify as a disease of the mind, it is perhaps not surprising that the jury found the accused to be sane. He was convicted of manslaughter. The contention of the appellant that the act of killing, while not the product of a mentally disordered mind, was nevertheless involuntary, was never put to the jury.

The appellant argues that the judicial reasoning that effectively took the issue of voluntariness away from the jury violates the presumption of his innocence and his entitlement to the benefit of a jury trial guaranteed by s. 11(*d*) and (*f*) and is not saved by s. 1 of the Canadian *Charter of Rights and Freedoms*.

. . . .

In my view, it follows from the concurrent findings in the courts below (that the appellant successfully put in issue his consciousness at the time of the offence) that he was entitled to the jury's verdict on whether or not his conduct, though sane, was involuntary. That issue having been withdrawn from the jury, and the Crown thereby having been relieved of the one real challenge to its proof, the appellant is entitled to a new trial.

. . . .

The jury in this case, for example, had before it the testimony of the Crown psychiatrist that the appellant's violent response to his wife's verbal attack was entirely too purposeful and the loss of memory entirely too convenient to be considered "involuntary". The members of the jury could, I think, have been counted on to exhibit powerful scepticism about such evidence. Anyone who thinks a jury of bus drivers, office workers and other practical people will be less sceptical than members of the bench or professors of law has perhaps spent insufficient time in buses or around office coffee machines.

(5) Conclusion on the Automatism Issue

In the result, I believe the appellant was entitled to have the plea of non-mental disorder automatism left to the jury in this case in light of the trial judge's evidentiary ruling that there was evidence the appellant was unconscious throughout the commission of the offence, for the following reasons.

Firstly, I do not accept the Crown's argument that a judge-made classification of situations into mental disorder automatism and non-mental disorder automatism can relieve the Crown of the obligation to prove all of the elements of the offence, including voluntariness. As stated, such an interpretation encounters strong objections under s. 7 and s. 11(d) of the *Charter*, and there has been no attempt in this case to provide a s. 1 justification.

Secondly, imposition of a persuasive burden of proof on the appellant to establish "involuntariness" on a balance of probabilities, in substitution for the present evidential burden, runs into the same *Charter* problems, and no attempt has been made in the record to justify it.

Thirdly, the "internal cause" theory, on which the Crown rested its argument, cannot be used to deprive the appellant of the benefit of the jury's consideration of the voluntariness of his action, once he had met the evidential onus, without risking a violation of s. 11(f) of the *Charter*. *Rabey*'s treatment of the internal cause theory has to be looked at in light of the decision of this court in *Parks*, *supra*, which signalled some serious reservations about the usefulness of the "internal cause" theory, except as an "analytical tool". *Rabey*, as clarified in *Parks*, does not impose a presumption that a lack of voluntariness must be attributed to the existence of a mental disorder any time there is no identification of a convincing external cause. Once the appellant in this case had discharged his evidential onus, he was entitled to have the issue of voluntariness go to the jury.

Fourthly, it was wrong of the courts to require the appellant to substitute for his chosen defence of involuntariness the conceptually quite different plea of insanity. One of the few points of agreement between the defence and Crown experts at trial was that the appellant did not suffer from anything that could be described medically as a disease of the mind. He was either unconscious at the time of the killing or he was not telling the truth at the time of the trial. This was a question for the jury. The statutory inquiry into whether he was "suffering from a mental disorder" that rendered him "incapable of appreciating the nature and quality of the act or omission or of knowing that it was wrong" are qualitative questions that are not really responsive to his allegation that he was not conscious of having acted at all.

Finally, the evidence established that there *are* states of automatism where perfectly sane people lose conscious control over their actions. At that point, it was up to the jury, not the judge, to decide if the appellant had brought himself within the physical and mental condition thus identified. As Dickson C.J. observed in *Bernard, supra,* at p. 848, the jurors were "perfectly capable of sizing the matter up".

BASTARACHE J. (L'HEUREUX-DUBÉ, GONTHIER, CORY, and MCLACHLIN JJ. concurring): — The present case involves automatism, and more specifically, "psychological blow" automatism. The appellant claims that nothing more than his wife's words caused him to enter an automatistic state in which his actions, which include stabbing his wife 47 times, were involuntary. How can an accused demonstrate that mere words caused him to enter an automatistic state such that his actions were involuntary and thus do not attract criminal law sanction? This is the issue raised in this appeal.

. . . .

Nature and Origin of the Burdens Applied in Cases Involving Claims of Automatism

This court has stated on many occasions that it is a fundamental principle of criminal law that only voluntary actions will attract findings of guilt. [Citations omitted.]

In *Parks, supra,* La Forest J. classified automatism as a sub-set of the voluntariness requirement, which he too recognized as part of the *actus reus* component of criminal responsibility. I agree and would add that voluntariness, rather than consciousness, is the key legal element of automatistic behaviour since a defence of automatism amounts to a denial of the voluntariness component of the *actus reus*.

The law presumes that people act voluntarily. Accordingly, since a defence of automatism amounts to a claim that one's actions were not voluntary, the accused must rebut the presumption of voluntariness. An evidentiary burden is thereby imposed on the accused. The nature of this evidentiary burden stems from the legal burden imposed in cases involving claims of automatism. Generally, the legal burden in such cases has been on the Crown to prove voluntariness, a component of the *actus reus*, beyond a reasonable doubt — hence Dickson J.'s contention in *Rabey* that an accused claiming automatism need only raise evidence sufficient to permit a properly instructed jury to find a reasonable doubt as to voluntariness in order to rebut the presumption of voluntariness. The Crown then has the legal burden of proving voluntariness beyond a reasonable doubt to the trier of fact. If the Crown fails to satisfy this burden, the accused will be acquitted.

. . . .

In her 1993 *Proposals to amend the Criminal Code (General Principles)*, the Minister of Justice recommended that the legal burden of proof in all cases of automatism be on the party that raises the issue on a balance of probabilities. This is the same legal burden that this court applied to a claim of extreme intoxication akin to a state of automatism in *Daviault, supra*. It is also the legal burden Parliament assigned to the defence of mental disorder in s. 16 of the *Code*, which, as mentioned above, is equally applicable to voluntary and involuntary actions stemming from a disease of the mind and therefore applies to mental disorder automatism.[16] As I explained above, different legal approaches to claims of automatism, whether based on the context in which the alleged automatism arose or on the distinction between mental disorder and non-mental disorder automatism, is problematic and should be avoided.

. . . .

An appropriate legal burden applicable to all cases involving claims of automatism must reflect the policy concerns which surround claims of automatism.

. . . .

The foregoing leads me to the conclusion that the legal burden in cases involving claims of automatism must be on the defence to prove involuntariness on a balance of probabilities to the trier of fact. This is the same burden supported

---

16 Elsewhere in his judgment, Justice Bastarache says "the terms 'mental disorder' automatism and 'non-mental disorder' automatism rather than 'insane' automatism and 'non-insane' automatism more accurately reflect the recent changes to s. 16 of the *Code*, and the addition of Part XX.1 of the *Code*."

by Lord Goddard, dissenting in *Hill v. Baxter*, [1958] 1 Q.B. 277, at pp. 282-83, and imposed in some American jurisdictions; see for example *State v. Caddell*, 215 S.E.2d 348 (N.C. 1975); *Fulcher v. State*, 633 P.2d 142 (Wyo. 1981); *Polston v. State*, 685 P.2d 1 (Wyo. 1984); *State v. Fields*, 376 S.E.2d 740 (N.C. 1989).

In *Chaulk* and *Daviault* this court recognized that although placing a balance of probabilities burden on the defence with respect to an element of the offence constitutes a limitation of an accused person's rights under s. 11(*d*) of the *Charter*, it can be justified under s. 1. In my opinion, the burden is also justified in the present case. The law presumes that people act voluntarily in order to avoid placing the onerous burden of proving voluntariness beyond a reasonable doubt on the Crown. Like extreme drunkenness akin to automatism, genuine cases of automatism will be extremely rare. However, because automatism is easily feigned and all knowledge of its occurrence rests with the accused, putting a legal burden on the accused to prove involuntariness on a balance of probabilities is necessary to further the objective behind the presumption of voluntariness. In contrast, saddling the Crown with the legal burden of proving voluntariness beyond a reasonable doubt actually defeats the purpose of the presumption of voluntariness. Thus, requiring that an accused bear the legal burden of proving involuntariness on a balance of probabilities is justified under s. 1. There is therefore no violation of the Constitution.

. . . .

To sum up, in order to satisfy the evidentiary or proper foundation burden in cases involving claims of automatism, the defence must make an assertion of involuntariness and call expert psychiatric or psychological evidence confirming that assertion. However, it is an error of law to conclude that this defence burden has been satisfied simply because the defence has met these two requirements. The burden will only be met where the trial judge concludes that there is evidence upon which a properly instructed jury could find that the accused acted involuntarily on a balance of probabilities. In reaching this conclusion, the trial judge will first examine the psychiatric or psychological evidence and inquire into the foundation and nature of the expert opinion. The trial judge will also examine all other available evidence, if any. Relevant factors are not a closed category and may, by way of example, include: the severity of the triggering stimulus, corroborating evidence of bystanders, corroborating medical history of automatistic-like dissociative states, whether there is evidence of a motive for the crime, and whether the alleged trigger of the automatism is also the victim of the automatistic violence. I point out that no single factor is meant to be determinative. Indeed, there may be cases in which the psychiatric or psychological evidence goes beyond simply corroborating the accused's version of events, for example, where it establishes a documented history of automatistic-like dissociative states. Furthermore, the ever advancing state of medical knowledge may lead to a finding that other types of evidence are also indicative of involuntariness. I leave it to the discretion and experience of trial judges to weigh all of the evidence available on a case-by-case basis and to determine whether a properly instructed jury could find that the accused acted involuntarily on a balance of probabilities.

Step 2: Determining Whether to Leave Mental Disorder or Non-Mental Disorder Automatism with the Trier of Fact

. . . .

The determination of whether mental disorder or non-mental disorder automatism should be left with the trier of fact must be undertaken very carefully since it will have serious ramifications for both the individual accused and society in general. As mentioned above, mental disorder automatism is subsumed by the defence of mental disorder as set out in the *Code*. Accordingly, a successful defence of mental disorder automatism will result in a verdict of not criminally responsible on account of mental disorder as dictated by s. 672.34 of the *Code*. Under s. 672.54, an accused who receives this qualified acquittal may be discharged absolutely, discharged conditionally or detained in a hospital. In contrast, a successful defence of non-mental disorder automatism will always result in an absolute acquittal.

. . . .

Taken alone, the question of what mental conditions are included in the term disease of the mind is a question of law. However, the trial judge must also determine whether the condition the accused claims to have suffered from satisfies the legal test for disease of the mind. This involves an assessment of the particular evidence in the case rather than a general principle of law and is thus a question of mixed law and fact. See *Southam, supra*, at paras. 35 and 36. The question of whether the accused actually suffered from a disease of the mind is a question of fact to be determined by the trier of fact. See *Rabey* (S.C.C.), *supra*, at p. 519, *per* Ritchie J.; *Parks, supra*, at p. 897, *per* La Forest J.; and *Bratty, supra*, at p. 412, *per* Lord Denning.

In response to the above-mentioned proposed revisions to the *Code* regarding automatism, the Canadian Psychiatric Association submitted a Brief to the House of Commons Standing Committee on Justice and the Solicitor General. In this brief, the Association, on behalf of its 2,400 members nationwide, suggested that from a medical perspective, all automatism necessarily stems from mental disorder. Accordingly, the Association recommended that non-mental disorder automatism be eliminated and all claims of automatism be classified as mental disorders.

Since mental disorder is a legal term, the opinion of the Canadian Psychiatric Association, while relevant, is not determinative of whether two distinct forms of automatism, mental disorder and non-mental disorder, should continue to be recognized at law. In my opinion, this court should not go so far as to eliminate the defence of non-mental disorder automatism as the Association suggests. However, I take judicial notice that it will only be in rare cases that automatism is not caused by mental disorder. Indeed, since the trial judge will have already concluded that there is evidence upon which a properly instructed jury could find that the accused acted involuntarily on a balance of probabilities, there is a serious question as to the existence of an operating mind by the time the disease of the mind issue is considered. The foregoing lends itself to a rule that trial judges start from the proposition that the condition the accused claims to have suffered from is a disease of the mind. They must then determine whether the evidence in the particular case takes the condition out of the disease of the mind category. This approach is consistent with this court's decision in *Rabey*, *supra*.

Determining Whether the Conditions the Accused Claims to Have Suffered from is a Disease of the Mind

In *Parks*, La Forest J. recognized that there are two distinct approaches to the disease of the mind inquiry: the internal cause theory and the continuing danger theory. He recognized the internal cause theory as the dominant approach in Canadian jurisprudence but concluded, at p. 902, that this theory "is really meant to be used only as an analytical tool, and not as an all-encompassing methodology". This conclusion stemmed from a finding that somnambulism, the alleged trigger of the automatism in *Parks*, raises unique problems which are not well-suited to analysis under the internal cause theory. I agree that the internal cause theory cannot be regarded as a universal classificatory scheme for "disease of the mind". There will be cases in which the approach is not helpful because, in the words of La Forest J., at p. 903, "the dichotomy between internal and external causes becomes blurred". Accordingly, a new approach to the disease of the mind inquiry is in order. As I will explain below, a more holistic approach, like that developed by La Forest J. in *Parks*, must be available to trial judges in dealing with the disease of the mind question. This approach must be informed by the internal cause theory, the continuing danger theory and the policy concerns raised in this court's decisions in *Rabey* and *Parks*.

[The Court then described the jurisprudence surrounding the Internal Cause Theory and the Continuing Danger Theory and concluded.]

In my opinion, trial judges should continue to consider the continuing danger theory as a factor in the determination of whether a condition should be classified as a disease of the mind. However, I emphasize that the continuing danger factor should not be viewed as an alternative or mutually exclusive approach to the internal cause factor. Although different, both of these approaches are relevant factors in the disease of the mind inquiry. As such, in any given case a trial judge may find one, the other or both of these approaches of assistance. To reflect this unified, holistic approach to the disease of the mind question, it is therefore more appropriate to refer to the internal cause factor and the continuing danger factor, rather than the internal cause theory and the continuing danger theory.

In their Case Comment on *R. v. Parks* (1993), 72 *Can. Bar Rev.* 224, I. Grant and L. Spitz point out that in assessing the likelihood of recurrence of violence, courts have been asking the wrong question. Courts have been focussing on whether the accused is likely to exhibit violent behaviour if he or she were again to encounter the alleged trigger of the current automatistic episode. According to Grant and Spitz, a more appropriate question is simply whether the alleged trigger is likely to recur. Grant and Spitz reason that there is no way of accurately predicting whether actual violence will recur. Indeed the likelihood of the initial automatistic violence would generally have been remote and thus difficult to predict. In contrast, the likelihood of recurrence of the circumstances which are alleged to have given rise to the automatism is more easily predicted (see pp. 235-36).

The logic of the reasoning of Grant and Spitz is difficult to deny. Indeed, it reveals that an assessment of the likelihood that the particular accused will again encounter the trigger alleged to have caused the current automatistic episode, or a similar one of at least equal severity, may assist a judge in assessing the continuing danger factor. The greater the anticipated frequency of the trigger in the accused's life, the greater the risk posed to the public and, consequently, the more likely it is that the condition alleged by the accused is a disease of the mind.

. . . .

(3) Other Policy Factors

There may be cases in which consideration of the internal cause and continuing danger factors alone does not permit a conclusive answer to the disease of the mind question. Such will be the case, for example, where the internal cause factor is not helpful because it is impossible to classify the alleged cause of the automatism as internal or external, and the continuing danger factor is inconclusive because there is no continuing danger of violence. Accordingly, a holistic approach to disease of the mind must also permit trial judges to consider other policy concerns which underlie this inquiry. As mentioned above, in *Rabey* and *Parks*, this court outlined some of the policy concerns which surround automatism. I have already referred to those specific policy concerns earlier in these reasons. I repeat that I do not view those policy concerns as a closed category. In any given automatism case, a trial judge may identify a policy factor which this court has not expressly recognized. Any such valid policy concern can be considered by the trial judge in order to determine whether the condition the accused claims to have suffered from is a disease of the mind. In determining this issue, policy concerns assist trial judges in answering the fundamental question of mixed law and fact which is at the centre of the disease of the mind inquiry: whether society requires protection from the accused and, consequently, whether the accused should be subject to evaluation under the regime contained in Part XX.1 of the *Code*.

Application to the Present Case

. . . .

Turning to the disease of the mind stage of the automatism analysis, I note that the evidence in this case raised *only one alleged cause* of automatism, Donna Stone's words. Based on this evidence, the trial judge found that only mental disorder automatism should be left with the jury. This conclusion was based primarily on a finding that the present case is indistinguishable from *MacLeod, supra*. Such reliance on precedent fails to reveal what effect, if any, the internal cause factor, the continuing danger factor and other policy factors had on the decision to leave only mental disorder automatism with the jury. This is not in accordance with the holistic approach to the disease of the mind question set out in these reasons. However, the internal cause factor and the continuing danger factor, as well as the other policy factors set out in this court's decisions in *Rabey* and *Parks* all support the trial judge's finding that the condition the appellant alleges to have suffered from is a disease of the mind in the legal sense. In particular, the trigger in this case was not, in the words of Martin J.A. quoted in this court's decision in *Rabey*, at p. 520, "extraordinary external events" that would amount to an extreme shock or psychological blow that would cause a normal person, in the circumstances of the accused, to suffer a dissociation in the absence of a disease of the mind. Accordingly, I find that the trial judge nevertheless reached the correct result on the disease of the mind question. As previously noted, in such a case, only mental disorder automatism must be put to the jury. There is no reason to go beyond the facts of this case in applying the rules discussed above.

In the end, I must conclude that no substantial wrong or miscarriage of justice occurred in the present case.

It is usually regarded as a wise proposition that a judge should not pronounce on matters that were not in issue between the parties and accordingly were not argued. Should the Court have considered reversing the onus of proof although the Crown and no intervenor addressed the issue? Are you satisfied with the majority's authority and justification of a presumption of voluntariness and requiring the accused to prove sane automatism on a balance of probabilities? What are the onus implications for other defences such as intoxication and self-defence? Wasn't the

presumption of innocence under s. 11(d) implicated? What of *Laba* concerning s. 1 justification? The Court in *Laba* held that an evidentiary burden should be considered before justifying a persuasive burden for an accused. See critical comments by Delisle, "*Stone:* Judicial Activism Gone Awry to Presume Guilt" (1999), 24 C.R. (5th) 91; David Paciocco, "Death by *Stone*-ing: The Demise of the Defence of Simple Automatism" (1999), 24 C.R. (5th) 273; and "Editorial, Rewriting Automatism" (1999) 4 Can. Crim. L. Rev. 119. See also the strong criticism of Frances Chapman, "The Presumption of Sanity, Automatism and *R. v. H.(S.):* Is it Insane to Have a Presumption of Insanity?" (2015) 62 Crim. L.Q. 168.

For the view that psychological blow automatism is not based on sound psychological assumptions, see James D. Livingston and Simon N. Verdun-Jones, "Sidebar Psychology: Discussing the Defence of Psychological-Blow Automatism" (2002) 47 Crim. L.Q. 79.

R. v. LUEDECKE

2008 ONCA 716, 61 C.R. (6th) 139, 236 C.C.C. (3d) 317, 2008 CarswellOnt 6024 (Ont. C.A.)

The accused and the complainant were guests at a large house party in Toronto where an annual croquet tournament was being held. The complainant attended the party with some friends. At around 2 a.m. she fell asleep on an L-shaped couch while waiting for her friends to depart. At about 5 a.m. she was awakened by a man who was having intercourse with her. He had pulled down her underwear and pushed up her skirt. She pushed him off her, shouted at him "Who are you, what are you doing?". She had no idea who he was. She screamed and pushed him away. He looked dazed and grabbed her belongings. When she came back to get her keys, she found the man still standing in the living room. When she asked who he was, he identified himself as "Jan". She did not recognize him. The complainant went to the hospital and later called police.

The accused, a landscaper, gave a voluntary videotaped statement to police. He stated that the day prior to the party he had been drinking and consuming magic mushrooms at a friend's cottage on Georgian Bay. He arose at dawn, swam, and then drove back to Toronto, where he attended the party. At the party he consumed eight to twelve beers, a couple of drinks of rum and Coke, and a couple of vodkas. By the time he fell asleep on the same couch as the complainant he was very drunk and had been awake for 22 hours. The next thing he remembered was being pushed off the couch by a woman onto the floor. He drove to his parents' house and fell asleep again. When he awoke he saw that he was wearing a condom, which he flushed down the toilet. He went back to sleep and awoke with a vague recollection that something had happened. The defence advanced the defence of non-insane automatism.

The accused testified that he had probably had sexual intercourse with the complainant without her consent, although he could not remember what had happened. The defence called a sleep disorder expert. The expert diagnosed the accused with parasomnia, a disorder in which a person experiences a sudden unexplained arousal from deep sleep, where people are not aware of what they are doing and behave in abnormal ways. He testified that this behaviour could include acts as simple as hand gestures, talking or walking and more rarely acts as complicated as eating, sexual acts or driving a car. He relied on the accused's past history of sleep problems, his statements that he had four prior incidents of what he termed "sexsomnia" with former girlfriends and brainwave measurements of the accused taken in a sleep laboratory. The defence expert also testified that physical activity, sleep deprivation, alcohol and stress increase the likelihood of triggering a parasomnistic episode. He further testified that the parasomnia was not a mental illness or disease of the mind. There was no cure but it could be controlled with good sleep habits, limiting alcohol consumption and medication.

A witness proffered by the Crown to give expert evidence on sleep disorders was not qualified by the Court and not permitted to testify. The Crown argued that the defence evidence was based on hearsay, and that the evidence of parasomnistic behaviour did not support a conclusion that the accused could carry out fine motor skills while asleep. This incident was an attack on a stranger and was therefore dissimilar to the alleged previous incidents which, if they occurred, took place in the context of consensual relationships. The Crown argued that the accused was not in a state of automatism when he removed his and the complainant's clothes, put on a condom, and sexually assaulted the complainant.

The trial judge, relying mainly on the uncontradicted evidence of the defence expert found that the accused's actions were involuntary, that he had no control over his actions and that they were not the product of a mental disorder. He acquitted. The Crown appealed.

DOHERTY J.A. (BORINS and LANG JJ.A. concurring): —

. . . .

E. ANALYSIS

[52]   Before testing the trial judge's characterization of the respondent's parasomnia as non-mental disorder automatism against the binding jurisprudence, I will sketch in the necessary legal background.

(i) Automatism Claims

[53]   Conduct that is not voluntary cannot be criminal: *Rabey*, per Ritchie J. (majority) at p. 6, per Dickson J. (dissenting on other grounds) at p. 26; *Parks*. The voluntariness requirement is a principle of fundamental justice protected by s. 7 and s. 11(d) of the *Charter*: *R. v. Daviault* (1994), 93 C.C.C. (3d) 21 (S.C.C.), at pp. 48-49, 69.

[54]   A claim by an accused that his or her conduct was involuntary and should result in an acquittal for that reason can arise in a variety of very different circumstances. Automatism is the legal term used to describe one specific kind

of involuntary action: see *Bratty v. Attorney General for Northern Ireland*, (1963) 3 All E.R. 523 (H.L.), per Lord Denning at pp. 408-409; *Parks*, per La Forest J. at p. 302. Automatism refers to involuntary conduct that is the product of a mental state in which the conscious mind is disassociated from the part of the mind that controls action. A person in a state of automatism may perform acts, sometimes complicated and apparently purposeful acts, but have no control over those actions: William Wilson, et al., "Violence, Sleepwalking and the Criminal Law: (2) The Legal Aspects" (2005) Crim. L.R. 614, at pp. 615-16. North P. put it this way in *R. v. Burr*, [1969] N.Z.L.R. 736 (C.A.), at p. 744:

> In my opinion then there is now clear judicial authority for the view that in order for a defence of automatism to succeed, *the person whose conduct is under review must be unconscious of what he was doing. In short that what he did was an unconscious involuntary act... [I]n my opinion, the evidence must be sufficient to lay a proper foundation for the plea that the accused person acted through his body and without the assistance of his mind, in the sense that he was not able to make the necessary decisions and to determine whether or not to do the act.*
> [Emphasis added.]

[55]   The disassociative state that is the hallmark of automatism can be caused by many things including disease, mental illness, concussion, drugs, and parasomnia. Each of these conditions can produce a condition in which an accused, while capable of complex, apparently goal-oriented conduct, is incapable of exercising any control over those actions. As will be discussed below, the cause of the automatism is an important consideration in characterizing the nature of the automatism.

[56]   The automatism "defence" is not a defence in the true sense but is a denial of the commission of the *actus reus* of the crime. Absent the commission of the prohibited act, there can be no crime and hence no criminal liability. A person who is unable to decide whether to perform an act and unable to control the performance of the act cannot be said, in any meaningful sense, to have committed the act. Nor can it be appropriate in a criminal justice system in which liability is predicated on personal responsibility to convict persons based on conduct which those persons have no ability to control: see *Stone*, per Bastarache J. at p. 417, per Binnie J. (dissent) at pp. 378-79; Don Stuart, *Canadian Criminal Law: A Treatise*, 5th ed. (Toronto: Carswell, 2007), at pp. 107-110; David Ormerod, *Smith & Hogan Criminal Law*, 11th ed. (New York: Oxford University Press, 2005), at pp. 44-46; Andrew Ashworth, *Principles of Criminal Law*, 5th ed. (New York: Oxford University Press, 2006), at pp. 98-100; Stanley Yeo, "Putting Voluntariness Back Into Automatism" (2001) 32 V.U.W.L.R. 15.

[57]   Automatism claims raise legitimate questions about an accused's mental status and his or her potential danger to the public. These claims are almost always advanced in cases where the accused has caused serious personal injury or at least put members of the public at serious risk. It hardly seems controversial that persons who engage in what would otherwise be regarded as serious criminal

conduct and claim to have had absolutely no control over that conduct should have their mental health and their right to remain at liberty scrutinized. Automatism claims, which by their very nature assert that the accused acted while in an abnormal and impaired mental state, inevitably bring into play the exemption to criminal liability created by s. 16 of the *Criminal Code*.

[58]   Section 16 exempts persons from criminal responsibility if, as a result of a "mental disorder", they were incapable of appreciating the nature and quality of their acts or of knowing that their acts were wrong. As Binnie J. observed in dissent in *Stone*, at paras. 78-83, s. 16 does not speak to the voluntariness of one's actions but instead addresses cognitive functions that assume voluntary conduct. It is, however, accepted in Canada, and throughout the Commonwealth, that a person whose conduct is involuntary because of a condition that is the product of a mental disorder falls exclusively within the purview of the "insanity" defence: see *R. v. Revelle* (1979), 48 C.C.C. (2d) 267 (Ont. C.A.), at p. 271, aff'd (1981), 61 C.C.C. (2d) 575; *Rabey* (Ont. C.A.), at p. 472, (S.C.C.), at p. 6; *Stone*, per Bastarache J., for the majority, at paras. 160-161; *Attorney-General's Reference* (No. 2 of 1992), [1994] Q.B. 91 (C.A.), at pp. 104-105; *R. v. Falconer* (1990), 171 C.L.R. 30 (H.C.); *The Queen v. Cottle*, [1958] N.Z.L.R. 999 (C.A.).

[59]   If an accused's automatism is rooted in a mental disorder, the accused will not be acquitted but will be found NCR-MD. Under Part XX.I of the *Criminal Code*, a person found NCR-MD is subject to a post-verdict disposition hearing before either the trial judge or a Review Board. Section 672.54 of the *Criminal Code* lists the dispositions available. These range from an absolute discharge to confinement in a hospital. A person found NCR-MD must be granted an absolute discharge if the court or review board is not satisfied that he or she poses a "significant risk": see *Winko v. British Columbia (Forensic Psychiatric Institute)* (1999), 135 C.C.C. (3d) 129 (S.C.C.).

[60]   The distinction between non-mental disorder automatism and mental disorder automatism depends on whether the automatistic state is the product of a "mental disorder". That term is defined in s. 2 of the *Criminal Code* as a "disease of the mind". That phrase, which is almost as old as the insanity defence itself, describes a legal and not a medical concept, the purpose of which is normative, not diagnostic: *Rabey*, per Martin J.A. at pp. 473-74; *Parks*, per La Forest J. at p. 304. I will use the two phrases interchangeably.

[61]   The broader the definition of mental disorder, the narrower the ambit of the "defence" of non-mental disorder automatism. Canadian courts have adopted a very broad definition. In *R. v. Cooper* (1980), 51 C.C.C. (2d) 129 (S.C.C.), at p. 144, Dickson J. said:

In summary, one might say that in a legal sense "disease of the mind" embraces any illness, disorder or abnormal condition which impairs the human mind and its functioning, excluding however, self-induced states caused by alcohol or drugs, as well as transitory mental states such as hysteria or concussion.

[62]   Professor Brudner has described the effect of this broad definition in these terms:

Clearly the definition of mental disease elaborated by the courts in the aforementioned cases bears little resemblance to any that a psychiatrist might proffer. *It is a legal rather than a medical definition – one carefully crafted with a view to a policy of controlling persons thought to be dangerous.* This definition ensures, first of all, that anyone accused of a crime who lacked conscious choice because of a dangerous and potentially recurrent disorder or event will not go free but will be subject to continued detention and confinement after acquittal. Obversely, it ensures that only those whose lack of conscious choice was caused by an external and probably non-recurrent event will have the benefit of a defence that leads to an absolute acquittal and a return to society. [Emphasis added.]

[63]   The broad definition of the term "mental disorder" has led to the channelling of most automatism claims into the NCR-MD pool. That trend reached its high water mark in *Stone*. Bastarache J., for the majority, went so far as to take judicial notice "that it will only be in rare cases that automatism is not caused by mental disorder". Bastarache J. further observed, at para. 199, that trial judges should start with the assumption that the condition constitutes a disease of the mind. Trial judges should then look to the evidence to determine whether that presumption has been rebutted. After *Stone*, many argue that successful claims of non-mental disorder automatism will be limited to those very rare "one off" cases in which an accused suffers a single incident of automatism, and where the accused can point to some specific external event that precipitated that event, can demonstrate that the event is unlikely to reoccur, and finally, can show that the event could have produced a disassociative state in an otherwise "normal" person.

. . . .

[90]   *Stone* alters the approach to the characterization of automatism as non mental disorder automatism or mental disorder automatism in at least two significant ways. First, after *Stone* the trial judge must begin from the premise that the automatism is caused by a disease of the mind and look to the evidence to determine whether it convinces him or her that the condition is not a "disease of the mind". This approach is in direct contrast with *Parks* where the non-mental disorder automatism claim succeeded because the Crown failed to prove that the condition was caused by a disease of the mind.

[91]   Second, although *Stone* accepts the multi-factored approach to the policy component of the characterization of the automatism set out in *Parks*, it refocuses the continuing danger aspect of that approach. After *Stone*, in

evaluating the risk of repetition and hence the danger to the public, trial judges must not limit their inquiry only to the risk of further violence while in an automatistic state. Rather, trial judges must examine the risk of the recurrence of the factors or events that triggered the accused's automatistic state. Commenting on this refinement of the continuing danger inquiry Professor Paciocco observes in "Death by *Stone*-ing: The Demise of the Defence of Simple Automatism" at p. 281:

> This part of the judgment effectively reverses *Parks*. The triggers for Parks' somnambulism or sleep-walking included stress, fatigue, insomnia and exercise. There is no point in speaking of the likelihood of such triggers being present in the future. It is a veritable certainty that they will be. *It is clear that had Parks been tried using the Stone test, the only defence that would have been left to the jury would be "mental disorder automatism"*. [Emphasis added.]

[92]   Professor Paciocco's prediction is largely borne out by the Canadian parasomnia cases that post-date Stone. I am aware of five including this case. In the other four cases, the automatistic states flowing from the parasomnia were held to constitute diseases of the mind: see *Canada v. Campbell* (2000), 35 C.R. (5th) 314 (Ont. S.C); *R. v. Balenko*, [2000] Q.J. No. 717 (C.Q. (Crim. Div.)); *R. v. Romas* (2002), 6 M.V.R. (5th) 101 (B.C. Prov. Ct.); and *R. v. Churchyard*, an unreported decision of Smith J. released November 19, 2003 (Ont. S.C.).

[93]   The majority position in *Stone* signals a strong preference for a finding of NCR-MD in cases where an accused establishes that he or she was in a disassociative state and acted involuntarily. Social defence concerns, inevitably present in such cases, must to a large degree drive the analysis in automatism cases after *Stone*.

[94]   The strong preference for an NCR-MD verdict expressed in *Stone* is explained in part by the very different treatment accorded those found NCR-MD compared to the historical treatment provided to those found not guilty by reason of insanity, as was the case at the time of the trial in *Parks*. Prior to 1991, persons found not guilty by reason of insanity were detained indefinitely at the pleasure of the Lieutenant Governor in Council. The provisions of Part XX.I of the *Criminal Code* not only disposed of the insanity nomenclature but completely changed the post-verdict treatment of those found NCR-MD: S.C. 1991, c. 43.

[95]   I do not think it is coincidental that *Stone* and *Winko*, the leading case on the interpretation of Part XX.I of the *Criminal Code*, were heard by the same nine judges about ten days apart, and decided about three weeks apart several months later. It is hard to resist the inference that *Stone* was written having in mind what the court would say three weeks later when it released its decision in *Winko*.

[96]   In *Winko*, McLachlin J. explained the operation of Part XX.I this way at para. 43:

> In summary, the purpose of Part XX.I is to replace the common law regime for the treatment of those who offend while mentally ill with a new approach emphasizing individualized assessment and the provision of opportunities for appropriate treatment. Under Part XX.I, the NCR accused is neither convicted nor acquitted. Instead, he or she is found not criminally responsible by reason of illness at the time of the offence. This is not a finding of dangerousness. *It is rather a finding that triggers a balanced assessment of the offender's possible dangerousness and of what treatment-associated measures are required to offset it. Throughout the process the offender is to be treated with dignity and accorded the maximum liberty compatible with Part XX.I's goals of public protection and fairness to the NCR accused.* [Emphasis added.]

[97]   *Winko* provides a detailed examination of s. 672.54, the provision governing the dispositions available with respect to persons found NCR-MD. As interpreted in *Winko*, s. 672.54 requires the absolute discharge of anyone found NCR-MD unless the court or the Review Board determines that the individual poses "a significant threat to the public". McLachlin J. said at para. 52:

> This interpretation of s. 672.54 eliminates any need for the NCR accused to prove lack of dangerousness and relieves him or her of any legal or evidentiary burden. If the evidence does not support the conclusion that the NCR accused is a significant risk, the NCR accused need do nothing; the only possible order is an absolute discharge.

[98]   The risk determination required by s. 672.54 cannot not be based on speculation or assumptions about how persons with mental disorders behave. There must be evidence establishing the significant risk. That risk must be a real risk of criminal conduct involving physical or psychological harm to individuals in the community. A risk of trivial harm or miniscule risk of significant harm will not suffice to deprive the individual of his or her liberty: *Winko*, at para. 57.

[99]   As explained in *Winko*, there are also significant procedural safeguards built into Part XX.I of the *Criminal Code*. A person found NCR-MD must receive a timely disposition hearing before either the court or the Review Board. He or she has full access to the bail provisions pending that hearing. The disposition hearing is not adversarial but provides for a full and wide-ranging inquiry into all factors relevant to the appropriate disposition. The disposition hearing allows for the input of medical professionals who will have had a chance to assess the person found NCR-MD and to develop opinions based on an up-to-date assessment of that person's condition. Where, as in most cases, the disposition hearing is before the Review Board, the panel will include a psychiatrist.

[100]   A combined reading of *Stone* and *Winko* yields a comprehensive response to automatism claims. At the pre-verdict stage, social defence concerns

dominate. Those concerns focus on the risk posed by the potential recurrence of the conduct in issue. Where that risk exists, the risk combined with the occurrence of the conduct that led to the criminal proceedings will almost always justify further inquiry into the accused's dangerousness so as to properly protect the public.

[101]   In the post-verdict stage, however, the emphasis shifts to an individualized assessment of the actual dangerousness of the person found NCR-MD. Where that personalized assessment does not demonstrate the requisite significant risk, the person found NCR-MD must receive an absolute discharge. Even where a significant risk exists, the disposition order must be tailored to the specific circumstances of the individual and must, to the extent possible, minimize the interference with that individual's liberty.

[102]   *Re Romas*, [2002] B.C.R.B.D. No. 66 (British Columbia Review Board), provides an example of the integration of the *Stone* approach to automatism and the *Winko* approach to Part XX.I of the *Criminal Code*. At trial (*R. v. Romas*), the accused was charged with an assault-related offence and claimed to have acted as a result of Confusional Sleep Arousal, a sleep disorder. Applying *Stone*, the accused was found NCR-MD. The trial judge referred the matter to the British Columbia Review Board for disposition. About six weeks later the Board, by a majority vote, ordered the accused absolutely discharged. In so ordering, the Board referred to several factors, all of which would seem applicable to the respondent assuming his current condition is consistent with that described at trial.

(ii) The Trial Judge's Application of the Principles in *R. v. Stone*

[103]   I am satisfied that the trial judge failed to appreciate the significance of the hereditary nature of the respondent's condition, failed to give effect to the respondent's well established history of sexsomnia, and failed to appreciate the significance of the strong likelihood of the recurrence of the events that triggered his sexsomnia. The trial judge also failed to appreciate that Dr. Shapiro's medical opinion that parasomnia did not constitute a mental disorder was largely irrelevant to the determination of whether, for policy reasons, the condition should be classified legally as a disease of the mind. These errors led to a failure to apply the proper legal standard when characterizing the respondent's automatism.

[104]   When addressing the cause of the respondent's condition, the trial judge acknowledged that causes internal to the accused, be they physical or mental, were generally treated as indicative of a disease of the mind, while causes external to the accused were generally indicative of a non-mental disorder automatism. The trial judge then said at para. 46:

The jurisprudence recognizes that somnambulism, as in the *Parks* case, is not suitable to this kind of analysis. Somnambulism is not a disease of the mind.

[105]   The trial judge was wrong to categorically indicate that somnambulism is not a disease of the mind. As *Parks* made clear, it may or may not be depending on the evidence. More significantly to the outcome of this case, I think the trial judge erred in dismissing the potential significance of the causes of the respondent's condition by referring to jurisprudence that had dismissed the internal/external cause distinction as being of no assistance in parasomnia cases. The trial judge should have considered whether, on the evidence, the causes of the parasomnia as explained by Dr. Shapiro offered any insight into the risk of recurrence and hence the potential danger to the public.

[106]   While the cause of parasomnia may not fit within the "external/internal" causal dichotomy described in the case law, Dr. Shapiro's evidence establishes that the predisposition for parasomnia, found in some three per cent of the adult population, is hereditary. A genetic predisposition is the epitome of an internal cause. Although that disposition does not cause the particular automatistic event, it does predispose the individual to that condition thereby increasing the risk of recurrence. The trial judge erred in discounting the significance of this internal cause of the respondent's condition. He did so based on a misapprehension of the "sleepwalking" case law and a failure to consider evidence relevant to the causal inquiry.

[107]   The trial judge's treatment of the "continuing danger" component of the meaning of "disease of the mind" reveals two errors. First, he found that prior sexsomnia incidents did not assist in assessing the danger to the public because those incidents did not involve criminal conduct. While technically the conduct did involve non-consensual sexual activity, I certainly accept that it was not conduct that should attract a criminal charge.

[108]   Even though the incidents involving former girlfriends did not lead to criminal charges, they were important in assessing the risk posed by the respondent's conduct. These events correspond to the psychiatric history of prior automatistic episodes stressed in *Stone*. The respondent's prior sexsomnia episodes demonstrate that his conduct toward L.O. was not an isolated, "one-off" incident. There were episodes both prior to and subsequent to the attack on L.O. during which the respondent engaged in sexual activity at a time when he was unaware of what he was doing and unable to control himself. In that condition the respondent could not distinguish between a consenting partner and a non-consenting victim. The identity of the subject of the sexual activity was a matter of chance, not a matter of choice.

[109]   I accept that it is perhaps more probable that the respondent would be asleep with or near someone with whom he had a relationship involving

consensual sexual relations. It cannot, however, be unexpected that the respondent will find himself asleep in the vicinity of persons with whom he has no relationship. One thinks of an airport or train station waiting room or the sleeping arrangements at a friend's cottage. There is also nothing in the evidence to suggest that the respondent could not move from room to room while in a parasomniac state and engage in non-consensual sexual activity with someone who happens to be in same building but in a different room.

[110]   With respect to the trial judge, his rejection of the prior sexsomnia incidents as having no value in considering whether the respondent posed a risk runs contrary to the fundamental nature of the defence advanced by the respondent. It was central to his position that he had no awareness of what he was doing and no control over his actions. It must follow that he was incapable of distinguishing between a consensual or non-consensual situation while in a parasomniac state. The trial judge should not have relied on a distinction that the accused was incapable of making to diminish the risk posed by the respondent.

[111]   The second error made by the trial judge in examining the "continuing danger" factor arises from his failure to consider the likelihood that the respondent would encounter the events or circumstances that triggered his parasomnia. *Stone*, at p. 440, explicitly directs trial judges to look to the likelihood of the recurrence of the triggering events and not just the likelihood of the recurrence of acts of violence while in an automatistic state.

[112]   The triggers in this case included alcohol, fatigue and stress. These are common place in most people's lives, particularly in the life of a busy, socially active, young man. Had the trial judge addressed the likelihood of the recurrence of the triggering events he would no doubt have found that it was virtually inevitable that some combination of these events would recur and recur with some frequency. On the analysis in *Stone*, the likelihood of recurrence of these triggering events offers significant support for a finding that the respondent's parasomnia should be characterized as a disease of the mind.

[113]   The trial judge also placed considerable emphasis on the firmness of Dr. Shapiro's evidence that the respondent's parasomnia did not constitute a disease of the mind. Dr. Shapiro's opinion that parasomnia did not constitute a disease of the mind, as opposed to his explanation of parasomnia and his opinion that the respondent was in a parasomniac state, had little or no evidentiary value. Nor was the force with which he held that opinion of any significance. As Martin J.A. observed in *Rabey*, at p. 474:

> Indeed, in strictness, a medical witness is not entitled to state that a particular condition is or is not a disease of the mind since that is a legal question. In practice, however, it is often convenient and permissible, in the discretion of the Judge, for a medical witness to testify in those terms.

[114]   The trial judge should not have been influenced by Dr. Shapiro's opinion as to the proper categorization of the respondent's medical condition when deciding whether as a matter of law and for policy reasons that condition should or should not be characterized as a disease of the mind.

[115]   Mr. Addario for the respondent ably, although ultimately unsuccessfully, defended the reasoning of the trial judge. Near the end of his oral submissions he opened a second front in support of his position that the appeal must be dismissed. Mr. Addario submitted that even if a strict application of the analysis set out in *Stone* might suggest an NCR-MD verdict, it would be grossly unfair and unjust to the respondent to label him NCR-MD. Mr. Addario submitted that as wrongheaded as it no doubt is, there is a very strong negative stereotype of persons found to be NCR-MD. Mr. Addario submits that the reality of the respondent's medical condition and his life in general could not be further from that stereotype. He contends that the respondent's parasomnia would not be regarded by any reasonable member of the community as the kind of mental disorder associated with a finding of NCR-MD. Mr. Addario forcefully argues that, just as the criminal justice system must be concerned with illegitimate automatism claims, it must be concerned that verdicts in automatism cases bear some resemblance to the community's concept of those who should or should not be found NCR-MD.

[116]   There is considerable force in Mr. Addario's submissions. Clearly no reasonable member of the community would, or should, regard the respondent as mentally ill. Indeed, the inappropriateness of labelling persons with parasomnia as mentally ill was acknowledged by Chief Justice Lane in *Burgess*, at p. 776.

[117]   I agree with Mr. Addario's contention that the result in criminal proceedings should, at least on a general level, reflect the community's perception of the appropriate result. Proper labelling is important to the maintaining of the integrity of the criminal justice process. It would be preferable if the *Criminal Code* allowed the court, where it was deemed necessary, to specifically identify in its verdict the condition that caused the involuntary actions, e.g. not criminally responsible on account of parasomnia: see *Ebrahim*, et al., at p. 612. Unfortunately the *Criminal Code* does not provide for that flexibility. Arguably, neither of the available verdicts, not guilty or NCR-MD, would be regarded by the community as particularly apt labels for the respondent.

[118]   The second part of Mr. Addario's submission would have the court accept the negative stereotyping of those found NCR-MD and decline to impose that verdict on the respondent because he does not fit that stereotype. No one should deny the existence of this negative stereotype and the harm it can do to those found NCR-MD. To give effect to Mr. Addario's submission would,

however, promote this negative stereotype. Were the court to decline to find the respondent NCR-MD because he does not fit the negative stereotype of persons so found, the court could be taken as accepting that those who are found NCR-MD do fit that stereotype.

[119]   The new mental disorder regime introduced into the *Criminal Code* in 1991 is intended to overcome the improper stereotyping of persons found NCR-MD and to provide for individualized assessment and treatment of those individuals: see *Winko*, at paras. 35-40. The courts can best play a role in the important task of overcoming the negative stereotypes associated with mental illness, not by shaping their verdicts to conform to those stereotypes, but by emphasizing both the basis for a finding of NCR-MD and by explaining what the verdict means. An NCR-MD verdict signals that an accused cannot be held responsible for what would otherwise be his or her criminal act. At the same time, it rejects any suggestion that the accused represents an automatic danger to the public. Instead, the NCR-MD verdict triggers an individualized, careful, current assessment of the accused's condition leading to a disposition tailored to the individual accused.

Doherty J.A. decided that, given *Criminal Code* limits on the powers of the court in the case of Crown appeals against an acquittal, the appropriate order was a new trial limited to the determination of whether the automatism constituted automatism resulting in an acquittal or mental disorder resulting in an NCRMD verdict. If the evidence remained the same Doherty J.A. indicated that the NCRMD verdict was the only reasonable verdict available on the current state of the law.

At his new trial, the Crown and defence agreed that the appropriate verdict was NCRMD. The Ontario Review Board held a disposition hearing and decided that Luedecke should be released absolutely as he no longer posed a significant threat to public safety. The Crown subsequently tried to have Luedecke comply with the provisions of the *Sex Offender Information Registration Act*. That application was dismissed because the Crown had failed to bring it in a timely fashion. See *R. v. Luedecke* (2010), 252 C.C.C. (3d) 542 (Ont. C.J.).

Justice Doherty is impeccably careful in his analysis and he clarifies the law of sane automatism in the light of *Stone*. On the issue of the so-called sexsomnia defence, in this case Luedecke got away lightly. See too Janine Benedet, Annotation to *Luedecke* (trial judgment) (2005), 35 C.R. (6th) 205 (Ont. C.J.) at 206-207. In contrast, Holly Phoenix, "Automatism : A Fading Defence" (2010) 56 Crim. L.Q. 328, is strongly critical. She argues that Luedecke was unnecessarily labelled and presented no significant threat as was found by the subsequent Review Board. This case shows again that in real life the evidence often presents in ways that engage more than one legal doctrine and that this may lead to difficulty and to an unsatisfactory result. Even accepting the evidence that the accused had problems with parasomnia on the night in question, it is hard to look beyond the fact that he was very drunk. The Court of Appeal does not detail the trial finding that at the party Luedecke consumed eight to twelve beers, a couple of drinks of rum and Coke, and a couple of vodkas. So if he was acting in an involuntary way this was to a large extent self-induced. The Court notes that although he had seen a sleep doctor he was not under treatment. So presumably the sleep disorder was not seen to be serious. Was the problem then more the alcohol?

R. v. BOUCHARD-LEBRUN

2011 CarswellQue 12785, 2011 SCC 58, [2011] 3 S.C.R. 575, 89 C.R. (6th) 1

Two young men, the accused and another, purchased pills of a type known as "*poire bleue*", which they took during the night of October 24. Hours later they decided to go and beat up L for the real or imagined reason that he wore an "upside-down cross" around his neck. Around 5:00 a.m., they illegally entered the building where L lived. They brutally attacked him by punching and kicking him many times. Another occupant of the building, D, went to L's aid but the accused threw D down steps and then stomped his head as he lay on the floor. The assault left D disabled and he will have to spend the rest of his life in hospital.

The trial judge accepted psychiatric evidence that at the material time the accused was suffering from toxic psychosis caused by the voluntary consumption of the pills. Two witnesses testified that he had been acting "weirdly" after taking the pills. There were signs of religious delirium during the attack with the accused making references to the Apocalypse, God and the devil. It was accepted that he was in a serious psychotic condition which disappeared days later. He had never experienced a psychotic episode before and was not an addict. The trial judge found that, because of that state of extreme intoxication, the accused had to be acquitted on the counts of breaking and entering with intent to commit a criminal offence, and attempting to break and enter. He then convicted the accused on the counts of aggravated assault on D and assault on L, on the basis that s. 33.1 of the *Criminal Code* provides that self-induced intoxication cannot be a defence to an offence against the bodily integrity of another person. The accused was sentenced to imprisonment for five years.

On appeal against his convictions, the accused argued that his psychosis should have led to a verdict of not criminally responsible on account of mental disorder under s. 16 of the *Criminal Code*. The Quebec Court of Appeal rejected the appeal as did the Supreme Court on the further appeal. We here consider the Court's determination that this was not a case for s. 16. We will revisit the judgment later on its ruling on the issue of intoxication.

LeBel J.: —

[61] For the purposes of the *Criminal Code*, "disease of the mind" is a legal concept with a medical dimension. Although medical expertise plays an essential part in the legal characterization exercise, it has long been established in positive law that whether a particular mental condition can be characterized as a "mental disorder" is a question of law to be decided by the trial judge. In a jury trial, the judge decides this question, not the jury. As Martin J.A. stated in an oft-quoted

passage from *Simpson*, "[i]t is the function of the psychiatrist to describe the accused's mental condition and how it is considered from the medical point of view. It is for the Judge to decide whether the condition described is comprehended by the term 'disease of the mind'" (p. 350). If the judge finds as a matter of law that the mental condition of the accused is a "mental disorder", it will ultimately be up to the jury to decide whether, on the facts, the accused was suffering from such a mental disorder at the time of the offence.

[62] Thus, the trial judge is not bound by the medical evidence, since medical experts generally take no account of the policy component of the analysis required by s. 16 *Cr. C.* (*Parks*, at pp. 899-900). Moreover, an expert's opinion on the legal issue of whether the mental condition of the accused constitutes a "mental disorder" within the meaning of the *Criminal Code* has "little or no evidentiary value" (*R. v. Luedecke*, 2008 ONCA 716, 269 O.A.C. 1, at para. 113).

[63] The respective roles of the expert, the judge and the jury were summarized in *R. v. Stone*, [1999] 2 S.C.R. 290. Writing for the majority, Bastarache J. stated the following:

> Taken alone, the question of what mental conditions are included in the term "disease of the mind" is a question of law. However, the trial judge must also determine whether the condition the accused claims to have suffered from satisfies the legal test for disease of the mind. This involves an assessment of the particular evidence in the case rather than a general principle of law and is thus a question of mixed law and fact. . . . The question of whether the accused actually suffered from a disease of the mind is a question of fact to be determined by the trier of fact. [Citation omitted; para. 197.]

[64] The central issue in this appeal is a question of law within the meaning of *Stone*. It is common ground that the appellant was in a psychotic condition that prevented him from distinguishing right from wrong. The main issue is whether a toxic psychosis caused exclusively by a single episode of intoxication constitutes a "mental disorder" within the meaning of s. 16 *Cr. C.*

[65] It can be seen at this point that the appellant's position poses a serious problem. To argue that toxic psychosis must always be considered a "mental disorder" is to say that the legal characterization exercise under s. 16 *Cr. C.* depends exclusively on a medical diagnosis. If the appellant's position were accepted, psychiatric experts would thus be responsible for determining the scope of the defence of not criminally responsible on account of mental disorder. This argument conflicts directly with this Court's consistent case law over the past three decades and cannot succeed. It would shift the responsibility for deciding whether the accused is guilty from the judge or jury to the expert.

E. *Specific Problem of a Toxic Psychosis that Results From the Voluntary Consumption of Alcohol or Drugs*

[69] When confronted with a difficult fact situation involving a state of toxic psychosis that emerged while the accused was intoxicated, a court should start from the general principle that temporary psychosis is covered by the exclusion from *Cooper*. This principle is not absolute, however: the accused can rebut the presumption provided for in s. 16(2) *Cr. C.* by showing that, at the material time, he or she was suffering from a disease of the mind that was unrelated to the intoxication-related symptoms. To determine whether an accused has discharged the burden of proof in this respect, the court should adopt the "more holistic approach" described by Bastarache J. in *Stone* (para. 203). As the Attorney General of Ontario ("AGO") suggested in this Court, it is ultimately this "more holistic approach" that will enable a court to determine whether the mental condition of an accused at the material time constitutes a "mental disorder" for the purposes of s. 16 *Cr. C.* (I.F., at paras. 22-23).

[70] In *Stone*, Bastarache J. proposed a flexible approach structured around two analytical tools and certain policy considerations. The purpose of the approach is to help the courts distinguish mental conditions that fall within the scope of s. 16 *Cr. C.* from those covered by *Cooper*'s exclusion of "self-induced states caused by alcohol or drugs" (p. 1159). In other words, a court should use this approach to determine whether a medically diagnosed disease of the mind constitutes a mental disorder in the legal sense.

[71] The *internal cause factor*, the first of the analytical tools described in *Stone*, involves comparing the accused with a normal person. In that case, Bastarache J. noted that "the trial judge must consider the nature of the trigger and determine whether a normal person in the same circumstances might have reacted to it by entering an automatistic state as the accused claims to have done" (para. 206). The comparison between the circumstances of the accused and those of a normal person will be objective and may be based on the psychiatric evidence. The more the psychiatric evidence suggests that a normal person, that is, a person suffering from no disease of the mind, is susceptible to such a state, the more justified the courts will be in finding that the trigger is external. Such a finding would exclude the condition of the accused from the scope of s. 16 *Cr. C.* The reverse also holds true.

[72] Although the trigger associated with the internal cause factor often involves a "psychological blow", there is no reason why it cannot consist of alcohol or drug use contemporaneous with the offence. What must therefore be determined is what state a normal person might have entered after consuming the same substances in the same quantities as the accused. Since certain factors such as fatigue and the pace of consumption may influence the effects of drugs, this comparison must take account of all the circumstances in which the accused

consumed the drugs that triggered the psychotic condition. If a normal person might also have reacted to similar drug use by developing toxic psychosis, it will be easier for the court to find that the mental disorder of the accused was purely external in origin (*Rabey*, at pp. 519 and 533; see also *Moroz*, at para. 46) and was not a disease of the mind within the meaning of the *Criminal Code*.

[73] The second analytical tool, the *continuing danger factor*, is directly related to the need to ensure public safety. The purpose of this factor is to assess the likelihood of recurring danger to others. Where a condition is likely to present a recurring danger, there is a greater chance that it will be regarded as a disease of the mind. To assess this danger, the court must consider, among other factors, "the psychiatric history of the accused and the likelihood that the trigger alleged to have caused the automatistic episode will recur" (*Stone*, at para. 214).

[74] Although Bastarache J.'s reasons were not explicit in this regard, it stands to reason that danger will be recurring only if it is likely to arise again independently of the exercise of the will of the accused. The recurrence of danger is not a factor linked to voluntary behaviour by the accused. This conclusion is consistent with the idea that the effect of the defence provided for in s. 16 *Cr. C.* is to exempt from criminal responsibility an accused whose actions are morally involuntary. The purpose of the defence of mental disorder is to ascertain whether the mental condition of the accused poses an *inherent* danger, that is, a danger that persists despite the will of the accused. As a corollary to this principle, a danger to public safety that might be voluntarily *created* by the accused in the future by consuming drugs would not be the result of a mental disorder for the purposes of s. 16 *Cr. C.*

[75] In *Stone*, Bastarache J. also stated that "a holistic approach to disease of the mind must also permit trial judges to consider other policy concerns which underlie this inquiry" (para. 218). The main policy consideration continues to be the need to protect society from the accused through the special procedure set out in Part XX.1 of the *Criminal Code*. Thus, if the circumstances of a case suggest that a pre-existing condition of the accused does not require any particular treatment and is not a threat to others, the court should more easily hold that the accused was not suffering from a disease of the mind at the time of the alleged events.

[76] The contextual approach required by *Stone* makes it possible to define the scope of this appeal. The purpose of the appeal is not to identify a rule to be applied to every case of toxic psychosis. And because every case has distinctive characteristics, it would be counterproductive to try to formulate an exhaustive definition of the mental conditions covered by *Cooper*'s exclusion of "self-induced states caused by alcohol or drugs". The instant case concerns just one type of toxic psychosis, namely one that resulted *exclusively* from a single episode of self-induced intoxication.

[77] Although the courts can seek assistance from the existing case law, it would be preferable for them to engage in an individualized analysis that takes account of the specific circumstances of each case. This means that the courts should determine on a case-by-case basis, applying the "more holistic approach" from *Stone*, whether the mental condition of each accused is included in or excluded from the definition of "disease of the mind" proposed by Dickson J. in *Cooper*. This approach is consistent with the line of authority based on *Rabey*, in which this Court endorsed Martin J.A.'s opinion that "[p]articular transient mental disturbances may not . . . be capable of being properly categorized in relation to whether they constitute 'disease of the mind' on the basis of a generalized statement and must be decided on a case-by-case basis" (pp. 519-20).

F. Application of the Principles to This Appeal

[78] In accordance with the approach set out above, I must now determine whether the appellant was suffering from a mental disorder within the meaning of s. 16 *Cr. C.* at the material time. To do this, it will be helpful to begin by referring to the trial judge's main findings of fact. Judge Decoste found that the appellant, who was highly intoxicated at the material time, was in a psychotic condition caused by the voluntary consumption of drugs. He wrote that [TRANSLATION] "the psychotic condition the accused was in when he committed these criminal acts originated in his drug use during the moments leading up to them" (para. 41). I would also note that the appellant's central argument is based on the contention that toxic psychosis is necessarily a "mental disorder" within the meaning of s. 16 *Cr. C.* because it is an "abnormal effect" of intoxication that affects only those who have a psychological predisposition or whose psyches are particularly fragile.

[79] The evidence in the record does not support the distinction drawn by the appellant between "normal effects" and "abnormal effects" of intoxication. Nor is it compatible with the argument that only persons who are predisposed to a mental disorder are likely to develop toxic psychosis as a result of drug use. For example, Dr. Faucher testified at trial that he saw cases of toxic psychosis [TRANSLATION] "every week" (A.R., at p. 967). As Thibault J.A. noted, the same witness also stated that half (50 percent) of subjects who take drugs containing PCP are likely to develop a psychotic condition when intoxicated. It thus appears that toxic psychosis is unfortunately a fairly frequent phenomenon that seems to result from the high toxicity of chemical drugs.

[80] The application of the first factor from *Stone* thus suggests that the taking of one "*poire bleue*" pill is a specific external factor that contradicts the appellant's argument, since it seems likely that the reaction of a normal person to such a pill would indeed be to develop toxic psychosis. This strongly suggests

that the appellant was not suffering from a mental disorder at the time he committed the impugned acts.

[81] The rapid appearance of psychotic symptoms generally indicates that the delusions of the accused can be attributed to a specific external factor. Dr. Faucher's expert assessment, which the trial judge preferred to that of Dr. Turmel, an expert called by the defence, revealed that the rapid reversal of symptoms is characteristic of a toxic psychosis caused by an episode of self-induced intoxication (A.R., at pp. 954-59). Moreover, Professor Parent has written on this topic that [TRANSLATION] "delusions that subside at the same rate as the drug are usually signs of *Substance Intoxication*" ("Les *Troubles psychotiques induits par une substance* en droit pénal canadien: analyse médicale et juridique d'un concept en pleine évolution", at p. 123). Such delusions therefore do not result from a disease of the mind within the meaning of the *Criminal Code*.

[82] In the instant case, the psychotic symptoms experienced by the appellant began to diminish shortly after he took the "*poire bleue*" pill and continued to do so until they disappeared completely on October 28, 2005. The Court of Appeal held that the disappearance of the symptoms showed that the symptoms of toxic psychosis coincided with the duration of the appellant's intoxication. Thibault J.A. could thus say that [TRANSLATION] "[t]he appellant suffered from no [disease of the mind] before committing the crimes, and once the effects of the drug consumption had passed, he was entirely sane" (para. 77). I see no valid reason to depart from this conclusion.

[83] As for the second factor from *Stone*, there is no evidence indicating that the mental condition of the accused is inherently dangerous in any way. Provided that the appellant abstains from such drugs in the future, which he is capable of doing voluntarily, it would seem that his mental condition poses no threat to public safety. Although I will not adopt a definitive position on this question, I might have concluded otherwise if the appellant had a dependency on drugs that affected his ability to stop using them voluntarily. The likelihood of recurring danger might then be greater.

[84] Finally, after considering all the circumstances of this case, I am satisfied that there is no valid reason to initiate the special procedure provided for in Part XX.1 of the *Criminal Code*. An accused whose mental condition at the material time can be attributed exclusively to a state of temporary self-induced intoxication and who poses no threat to others is not suffering from a mental disorder for the purposes of s. 16 *Cr. C*. The scheme of Part XX.1 applies only if the accused actually suffered from a disease of the mind at the material time. It is not intended to apply to accused persons whose temporary madness was induced artificially by a state of intoxication.

[85] In this context, I conclude that the appellant was not suffering from a "mental disorder" for the purposes of s. 16 *Cr. C.* at the time he committed the assault. He has failed to rebut the presumption that his toxic psychosis was a "self-induced stat[e] caused by alcohol or drugs" in accordance with the definition in *Cooper*. A malfunctioning of the mind that results *exclusively* from self-induced intoxication cannot be considered a disease of the mind in the legal sense, since it is not a product of the individual's inherent psychological makeup. This is true even though medical science may tend to consider such conditions to be diseases of the mind. In circumstances like those of the case at bar, toxic psychosis seems to be nothing more than a symptom, albeit an extreme one, of the accused person's state of self-induced intoxication. Such a state cannot justify exempting an accused from criminal responsibility under s. 16 *Cr. C.*

[88] In light of the case law, it is plausible to expect that the courts will have to perform this legal characterization exercise in circumstances much more difficult than the ones in the case at bar. One example would be a case in which the mental condition of the accused indicates an underlying mental disorder but the evidence also shows that the toxic psychosis was triggered by the consumption of drugs of a nature and in a quantity that could have produced the same condition in a normal person. In such circumstances, the courts should be especially meticulous in applying the "more holistic approach" from *Stone*.

R. v. FONTAINE

2017 SKCA 72, September 5, 2017

The accused F was charged with assault causing bodily harm against his common-law partner, L.

L testified that she and the accused had made plans to go out together on the evening of June 21, 2014. The accused left home early, without her, and failed to return. As a result, L arranged for her 16-year-old niece to look after their two children and went drinking. She later received a text message from the niece indicating that F had returned home and kicked in a door. L went home. She acknowledged being intoxicated at a level of eight on a scale of one to ten. She found F asleep in their bed. She was angry that he had kicked in the door. She testified that she struck him on the foot with her hand, pulled his leg and asked him to leave. She said the accused then got up off the bed "quite quickly", hit her in the face with his hand and threw her on the bed. Two cousins entered the bedroom and subdued F. L then struck him in the face several times with a closed fist. She sustained a bloody nose, a cut on her cheek and black swollen eyes. He had a bloodied mouth and swollen lips. The accused did not testify at trial.

The trial judge acquitted on the basis that the accused's act was an automatic and unthinking response to being startled from sleep in an aggressive fashion. There was no evidence that the defendant came to a state of alertness or consciousness, no words were spoken between them, and the exchange happened in mere moments. The accused's conduct had all the hallmarks of a reflexive action to a sudden and rather startling stimulus while in a state of sleep.

The Crown appealed the acquittal on the basis that, as per *R. v. Stone*, the accused bore the burden of proving he had struck his partner involuntarily and was required in that regard to have called expert psychiatric evidence.

Richards C.J.S. (Caldwell and Whitmore JJ.A. concurring):

[20] Voluntariness and intention are separate concepts. The former is an aspect of the *actus reas* of an offence. The latter involves the *mens rea* of the offence. . . .

[21] Unlike the Crown, Mr. Fontaine reads the trial judge's decision as turning on the straightforward notion that the Crown had failed to prove the *mens rea* of the alleged assault. This view is possible because the decision does make various references to "intent". Moreover, the trial judge invited counsel to make submissions during oral argument on the issue of intent and she concluded her reasons for decision by saying this:

> Plausible evidence regarding the defendant's actions raises a doubt in my mind based on reason and common sense as to the presence of the necessary intent. The Crown has failed to establish the requisite intent that is an essential ingredient of the offence charged. . . .

[22] However, read as a whole, the trial judge's decision is best and most fairly seen as being based on the concept of voluntariness, rather than intention. Notwithstanding that she sometimes used the word "intention" in her decision, the reality is that the authorities relied on by the trial judge deal with voluntariness and the heart of her analysis, reproduced below, was clearly directed at that question:

. . . .

B. *R v Stone* and its relevance to this case

[24] *R v Stone* is the leading Canadian authority on the law of automatism. In it, Bastarache J., writing for the majority of the Supreme Court, recalibrated the law in this area. More particularly, Bastarache J. held that, in cases involving automatism, the defence bears the burden of proving involuntariness on a balance of probabilities. In order to satisfy that burden, he said there must be both an assertion of involuntariness and confirming psychiatric evidence.

. . . .

[28] Claims of involuntariness can arise in or from a variety of situations and causes including ailments such as stroke or epilepsy; extreme intoxication; psychological shock; being stung by a swarm of bees; drugs; concussion; being propelled by the actions or grasp of another person; and somnambulism. See:

Don Stuart, *Canadian Criminal Law*, 6th ed (Scarborough: Carswell, 2011) at 115–116; *R v Hundal*, 1993 CanLII 120 (SCC), [1993] 1 SCR 867 at 875–876; *R v Jiang*, 2007 BCCA 270 (CanLII) at para 20, 220 CCC (3d) 55.

[29] Automatism has been defined in several ways, some of which are admittedly quite broad. Thus, for example, in *Bratty v Attorney-General for Northern Ireland*, [1963] AC 386 (HL) at 409, Lord Denning described automatism as:

> . . . an act which is done by the muscles without any control by the mind, such as a spasm, a reflex action or a convulsion; or an act done by a person who is not conscious of what he is doing, such as an act done whilst suffering from concussion or whilst sleep-walking. . . .

[30] However, in *R v Stone*, I do not understand Bastarache J. to have used "automatism" in a fully comprehensive sense, i.e., I do not understand him to have used automatism as a synonym for voluntariness. At paragraph 156, he defined automatism as "a state of impaired consciousness . . . in which an individual, though capable of action, has no voluntary control over that action". The notion of "a state of impaired consciousness" readily describes conditions such as those that underpinned *R v Stone* itself (psychological shock), *R v Parks* (somnambulism) and *R v Daviault* (extreme intoxication). It does not describe involuntary actions such as reflex responses. Accordingly, it is not insignificant that, at paragraph 170 of his decision, Bastarache J. referred with apparent approval to *R v Parks*, at page 896, where La Forest J. had classified automatism as "a sub-set of the voluntariness requirement".

. . . .

[32] Thus, automatism as addressed by *R v Stone* is best seen for present purposes as a particular sort of involuntary action. It is not, as the Crown suggests, an entirely general term that includes every possible kind of such action. In my view, circumstances involving reflex actions do not fall within the ambit of the approach prescribed by Bastarache J.

[33] There is something of an underlying policy rationale for treating dissociative states where the accused does not know what he or she is doing differently than involuntary actions that are the result of a reflex. As noted by Bastarache J. at paragraphs 175 and 176 of *R v Stone*, automatism raises special concerns because it is easily feigned and because knowledge of it rests with the accused. Moreover, the characteristics and nature of dissociative states resulting from such things as reactions to pharmaceuticals, psychological blows and somnambulism are well beyond the ordinary experience of a judge or jury. Accordingly, it is important that an accused who relies on the defence be required to call expert psychiatric evidence and to carry the burden of proving involuntariness in that instance. The same cannot be said, in my view, about reflex actions. They are a common part of human experience and, while

something that will legitimately arise only very rarely in criminal proceedings, they can ordinarily be meaningfully understood and evaluated by judges and juries without the assistance of expert testimony.

[34] As well, and relatedly, the less than comprehensive reach of *R v Stone* is underlined by the fact that the requirement for expert psychiatric evidence prescribed by Bastarache J. does not fit at all sensibly with the full range of involuntary actions. Take, for example, the situation where a person reacts after a swarm of bees enters the cabin of his vehicle and is charged with dangerous driving under s. 249(1)(a) of the Criminal Code. If that person argues his actions were involuntary, there would be little point in obliging him or her to call expert psychiatric evidence or, indeed, any expert evidence to prove that point. The same might be said, by way of further example, of the situation where A pushes B into C and B is then charged with assaulting C. B's contact with C will have been involuntary but nothing would be served by calling expert psychiatric evidence on the point. Indeed, it is difficult to see what a psychiatrist could possibly say about the situation.

[35] Finally, the reversal of the onus of proof described in *R v Stone* is, of course, an exceptional idea. Voluntariness is part of the *actus reus* and, as such, is something that the Crown would ordinarily be required to prove, albeit aided by the common sense notion that the acts of an apparently conscious person are usually voluntary. The law should not move easily away from this approach, particularly in light of the presumption of innocence reflected in ss. 7 and 11(d) of the *Charter*. Accordingly, I am not inclined to read *R v Stone* any more broadly than its terms suggest is required.

[36] Therefore, in conclusion, I do not understand *R v Stone* to be aimed at *all* involuntary acts, including reflexive ones. It follows that the Crown's argument on this point must fail.

Premenstrual Syndrome

On December 16, 1980, a 36-year-old English woman ended a love affair by deliberately running down her lover with her car and killing him. At trial she pled guilty to manslaughter because of diminished responsibility. She was discharged from custody and had her driver's licence revoked for one year. In a separate decision decided one day earlier, Sandie Smith, an East London barmaid, was placed on probation for carrying a knife and threatening to kill a policeman, though she was already on probation for having stabbed a fellow barmaid to death. In both of these cases the English courts found that the defendants were suffering from premenstrual syndrome (PMS), and as a result recognized PMS as a mitigating factor in sentencing these women. "Criminal Law: Premenstrual Syndrome in the courts?" (1984) 24 Washburn Law Journal 54-77.

PMS can be defined as "The recurrence of symptoms in the premenstruum with complete absence of symptoms in the postmenstruum". Symptoms of PMS occur in the same phase of the cycle each month: irritability, anxiety, tension, depression, hostility, decreased self-esteem, indecision, mood swings, impulsive behaviour, difficulty concentrating, social isolation, etc. The symptoms range from mild inconvenience to complete, although temporary, debilitation.

In most instances a woman with PMS understands her actions and the consequences but is simply powerless to control those actions.

Could PMS be a defence under existing Canadian law? Should it be a defence?

See, further, E. Meehan and K. MacRae, "Legal Implications of Premenstrual Syndrome: A Canadian Perspective" (1986) 135 C.M.A.J. 601 and a reply by Dr. Robinson in (1986) 135 C.M.A.J. 1340 ("the association between PMS and violent, impulsive or criminal acts is by no means firmly established").

In 1994 a more debilitating form of PMS called PMDD (Premenstrual Dysphoric Disorder) was added to the DSM-5. PMDD appears as a treatable depressive disorder in DSM-5.

PROBLEMS

1. The accused is charged with second degree murder. The victim, who was known to be gay, died from 79 knife wounds, including a cut throat. The accused stated to the police that he had had a few drinks with the victim, felt sick and laid down on a bed. He woke up suddenly and saw the victim naked, standing near him. He ran to the kitchen, grabbed the knife, killed the victim and simulated a theft. The accused's defence was that he was in a state of automatism caused by psychological shock. As a trial judge, rule as to the whether the defence of automatism should be left with the jury. Compare *Fournier v. R.* (1982), 30 C.R. (3d) 346, 70 C.C.C. (2d) 351 (Que. C.A.).

2. The accused is charged with the attempted murder of a police officer. He sat astride the officer who was lying on the sidewalk, and choked him with his hands. The police officer was rescued by a bystander, who struck the accused three times on the head before rendering him unconscious. The altercation between the accused and the officer had occurred when a car driven by the accused's brother, in which the accused was the passenger, had been stopped and the accused's brother arrested for impaired driving. The police evidence was that the accused had started the fight by karate-kicking the police officer in the chest. The defence was that, after some verbal abuse and physical resistance by the accused, the police officer had struck him in the face and the accused had no further recollection until he woke up in the hospital. An independent eyewitness testified that the police officer had struck the accused forcefully in the face. Should the defence of automatism succeed? Compare *R. v. Bartlett* (1983), 33 C.R. (3d) 247, 5 C.C.C. (3d) 321 (Ont. H.C.).

3. The accused was charged with aggravated assault upon her 7-year-old child. The defence introduced expert evidence to suggest that the accused may, as a result of depression, have suffered from intermittent explosive disorder, which may result in a dissociative state. The Crown expert testified to the contrary, citing the fact that the accused had some memory of the incident and the attack had purposive elements. Should the defence of sane automatism succeed? Compare *R. v. Bergamin* (1996), 3 C.R. (5th) 140, 111 C.C.C. (3d) 550 (Alta. C.A.).

4. The accused is charged with attempted murder of H contrary to s. 239 of the *Criminal Code* and assaulting H with a weapon contrary to s. 267(a). The accused visited H, a friend, one morning. He pulled a knife out of a drawer and stabbed H repeatedly. In the struggle he also stabbed H with a screwdriver. The testimony of the victim was that the accused was not intoxicated but was not himself, looked totally blank and was in a robotic state. After the stabbing the accused stole a vehicle and was involved in an accident. A defence forensic psychiatrist testified that the accused was in a dissociated state. The accused is a heroin addict. There was no apparent motive for the attack. He testified that he was suffering from depression and acute pain from heroin withdrawal. On the day in question the accused consumed approximately 52 Clonidine pills and 20 Imovane pills, mind-altering drugs which in sufficient quantity may produce disorders together with hallucinations. There was no evidence that the accused received any warnings about this medication, either via the containers or the doctor. The drugs had been prescribed for his addiction. As trial judge you are satisfied the accused did not consume any heroin that day. The defence was automatism. Give judgment. Compare *R. v. Vickberg* (1998), 16 C.R. (5th) 164 (B.C. S.C.).

5. The accused was charged with second degree murder for having caused the death of her husband. Her defence at trial was that she had acted in a state of non-mental disorder automatism. In this regard, two expert witnesses were called by the defence and one expert was called in reply by the Crown. All three experts agreed that the accused had no memory of the shooting. The defence experts concluded that she had acted in a state of automatism brought on shortly before the shooting by her traumatic relationship with her husband and the surrounding circumstances. The Crown's expert was of a different view. He agreed that the accused's amnesia was genuine but, in his opinion, it followed rather than preceded the shooting.

At the very outset of the trial, before any evidence had been called, defence counsel told the jury that he would be leading evidence to establish that the accused had been the victim of terrible abuse, mental and physical, for some 30 years. That assertion was not disputed. Defence counsel stated as well that, as a result of this abuse, the accused suffered at the time of the shooting from "battered wife syndrome". It was not disputed that she did.

The jury acquitted. Is there any ground of appeal for the Crown?

Compare *R. v. Graveline* (2006), 38 C.R. (6th) 42 (S.C.C.).

4. INTOXICATION

(a) Common Law

S.M. BECK AND G.E. PARKER, THE INTOXICATED OFFENDER —
A PROBLEM OF RESPONSIBILITY

(1966), 44 Can. Bar Rev. 563 at 570-573

What happens when an individual becomes intoxicated? The rather surprising answer, in view of the social and scientific interest in the problem, is that, in behavioural terms, we do not yet know with any degree of precision. An analysis of the experimental literature in 1940 evoked the following comment:

> In view of the psychiatric as well as lay interest in the effect of alcohol on these aspects [changes in volition, emotion and personality] of the individual, it is surprising how little attention they have received from experimental psychologists.

Another review in 1962 indicated little change:

> A review of the psychological literature since 1940 suggests that little progress has been made in developing a knowledge of how and in what way alcohol affects behaviour. It appears that a reformulation of the concepts that guide thinking about the action of alcohol in all areas is needed. Except in a few areas . , . , little creative effort appears to have been spent in research on the effect of alcohol on human behaviour. The exploratory experiment to find out what alcohol does, rather than to confirm some hypothesis, is rare.

It would be easy to conclude that because experimental psychology has so far told us little about the effects of alcohol on behaviour, the criminal law would not be justified in altering the criteria of responsibility. Medical science does know, in broad terms, what effects alcohol has on the individual, and this knowledge might well justify a change in the degree of responsibility attributed to the intoxicated offender.

It is certain that intoxication impairs perception, judgment and muscular coordination. Along with this impairment goes an increase in self-confidence, a lessening of inhibitions, and a release of sexual and aggressive impulses. The fact that an individual's repressed instincts may break through and manifest themselves in overt acts during intoxication has led some commentators to the incorrect conclusion that drunken offenders intend their acts in the same manner as do sober men. Their argument is as follows: all men have repressed desires — repressed intents — which they usally manage to control. The drunk is freed from his inhibitions and acts out these desires. His intent while drunk is thus his real intent and his acts are as purposive, or end-directed, as those of a sober man.

Psychoanalysts tell us, however, that people have repressed instincts, sexual and aggressive, not intents. Intents refer to cognitive functions. Alcohol brings about a diminution of the repressive mechanisms, allowing the instinctual to occur in behaviour. These repressive mechanisms are of emotional, not intellectual, origin. In simple terms, the emotional brakes which act as the restraint in all of us are released, and inhibited or self-controlled desires are converted into action. Striking confirmation of this effect of alcohol is provided by a recently published study of the sex offender by the Institute for Sex Research at Indiana University. The study, the most extensive of its kind ever undertaken, is a statistical analysis of interviews with 1,356 men convicted of rape, homosexuality, offences against children and a variety of other sexual crimes. The report shows that 67 percent of the men who threatened or used force on little girls were intoxicated at the time of their offences, as were 40 percent of the rapists whose victims were over 15. The report states that ". . . in very few cases does intoxication seem to do more than simply release pre-existing desires".

The same argument about "real" intent can be made in regard to the actions of a psychotic. Suppose the case of a person who, acting under the delusion that he has been commanded by God to make a sacrifice, kills his child. Certainly it could not be said that such a person's action was not purposive. In fact such a person might realize that ordinary people regard his act as wrong. Consequently he could be held responsible on a strict application of the M'Naghten rules. He would probably be declared insane, however, as most juries are not hindered by the rigidity of the rules when evidence of disease of the mind is so great. Few, if any, would object to that verdict as it would be clear that the offender had lost his power of self-control; that he was incapable of appreciating the moral quality of his act; and that he was incapable of exercising any, rational judgment in the matter.

But an acutely intoxicated person has also lost his power of self-control; his ability to make judgments is impaired, and he might be quite incapable of foreseeing the consequences of his acts.

> This effect of alcohol in depressing the inhibitory centres of the brain is of considerable medico-legal importance. It may lead to a failure to realize that a contemplated act is fraught with danger to oneself or others, or even if the possibility of danger be realized it may result in recklessness, that is, disregard of risk.

Indeed, the language of the report of the Royal Commission on the Law of Insanity in delineating the important differences between the wording of the M'Naghten rules and s. 16 of the *Canadian Criminal Code*, points up the similarity between the state of mind of a person who falls within the ambit of s. 16 and that of one who is acutely intoxicated.

Section 16 speaks of being "incapable of appreciating the nature and quality of an act". The M'Naghten rules say "as not to know the nature and quality of the act he was doing". The Commissioners concluded that:

> there is an important distinction to be drawn under Canadian law between a mental capacity, whether caused by drunkenness or disease of the mind, to "know" what is being done and a mental capacity to "foresee and measure the consequences of the act".
>
> The true test necessarily is, was the accused person at the very time of the offence . . . by reason of disease of the mind, unable fully to appreciate not only the nature of the act but the natural consequences that would flow from it? In other words, was the accused person, by reason of disease of the mind, deprived of the mental capacity to foresee and measure the consequences of the act?

Medical science clearly indicates that one who is acutely intoxicated might also fit within the above test, with the exception, of course, that his incapacity is not due to a disease of the mind (unless the individual is suffering from delirium tremens which is an alcoholic psychosis). The issue then comes back to voluntariness, for the truth is that the acutely intoxicated offender may have no more appreciation of the nature of an act and its consequences than the psychotic offender who may be excused from responsibility under s. 16(2) of the *Criminal Code*. Society, however, refuses to accept the plea of lack of responsibility from one who commits a crime in an intoxicated state. The act of becoming acutely intoxicated is itself judged as irresponsible and the consequences must be paid for. The result is a compromise between the requirement of the criminal law for a responsible or voluntary act, and the judgment of society that a wrongdoer not be exonerated simply because he was drunk. It is that compromise that we shall next examine.

Common law has long distinguished between voluntary and involuntary intoxication. In *R. v. Chaulk* (2007), 223 C.C.C. (3d) 174 (N.S. C.A.) the Court held that:

> Courts have consistently held that 'voluntary intoxication " means that the consuming of a substance where the person knew or had reasonable grounds for believing such might cause him to be impaired" (para. 45).

See too Trotter J. in *R. v. Goard* (2014), 310 C.C.C. (3d) 491 (Ont. S.C.J.).

Acquittals for involuntary intoxication have occurred on rare occasions (see Stuart, *Canadian Criminal Law: A Treatise* (7th ed., 2015 p. 140), in situations where the accused drank after being prescribed medicine by a doctor or dentist but only where the dangers of combining the medicine with alcohol were not properly explained or where a drink was spiked with alcohol. The test for involuntariness appears to be based in part on a negligence standard irrespective of whether the fault requirement for the offence charged is subjective or objective. No court has held that an alcoholic who falls off the wagon, takes a drink and can't stop drinking is to be considered to be in a state of involuntary intoxication.

Most of the complex jurisprudence that follows deals with voluntary intoxication.

R. v. BERNARD

[1988] 2 S.C.R. 833, 67 C.R. (3d) 113, 45 C.C.C. (3d) 1,
1988 CarswellOnt 93, 1988 CarswellOnt 971

The accused was charged with sexual assault causing bodily harm, contrary to s. 246.2(c) [now s. 272(c)] of the *Criminal Code*. The complainant testified that she had been forced to have sexual intercourse in her apartment without her consent and had then been subjected to serious bodily injury by the accused. There was evidence that the accused had punched the complainant twice with a closed fist, once above the eye, causing the eyelid to bleed profusely, and that he had threatened to kill her. The complainant testified that the accused had been drinking but was able to walk, to see everything, to talk clearly and to put albums on the record player. One of the accused's friends testified that he had been drinking on the night in question and, though he became rowdy, he was walking straight and talking. When the police arrived at the apartment he was awakened from a deep sleep and seemed to be suffering somewhat from his drinking. The accused stated that his drunkenness caused the attack on the complainant.

At trial before judge and jury, the accused did not testify. However, the Crown read evidence of a statement made to the police in which the accused admitted forcing the complainant to have sexual intercourse with him. He stated that he did know why he had done it, because he was drunk, and that "When I realized what I was doing, I got off". The trial judge directed the jury that there was no evidence of drunkenness except the accused's statement and, even if they found that he was drunk, drunkenness would be no defence to the charge alleged. The jury returned a verdict of guilty. The Ontario Court of Appeal dismissed an appeal from conviction, holding that the offence of sexual assault causing bodily harm was an offence of general intent, to which the defence of drunkenness did not apply. The accused appealed.

McINTYRE J. (BEETZ J. concurring): —

. . . .

There are two issues which arise in this appeal. The first is whether sexual assault causing bodily harm (*Criminal Code* s. 246.2(c)) is an offence requiring proof of specific or of general intent, and the second is whether evidence of self-induced drunkenness is relevant to the issue of guilt or innocence in an offence of general intent. Before dealing in detail with these questions, it will be helpful to make certain observations.

A distinction has long been recognized in the criminal law between offences which require the proof of a specific intent and those which require only the proof of a general intent. This distinction forms the basis of the defence of drunkenness and it must be understood and kept in mind in approaching this case. In *R. v. George*, [1960] S.C.R. 871, Fauteux J. said, at p. 877:

> In considering the question of *mens rea*, a distinction is to be made between (i) intention as applied to acts considered in relation to their purposes and (ii) intention as applied to acts considered apart from their purposes. A general intent attending the commission of an act is, in some cases, the only intent required to constitute the crime while, in others, there must be, in addition to that general intent, a specific intent attending the purpose for the commission of the act.

This statement makes the distinction clear. The general intent offence is one in which the only intent involved relates solely to the performance of the act in question with no further ulterior intent or purpose. The minimal intent to apply force in the offence of common assault affords an example. A specific intent offence is one which involves the performance of the *actus reus*, coupled with an intent or purpose going beyond the mere performance of the questioned act. Striking a blow or administering poison with the intent to kill, or assault with intent to maim or wound, are examples of such offences.

This distinction is not an artificial one nor does it rest upon any legal fiction. There is a world of difference between the man who in frustration or anger strikes out at his neighbour in a public house with no particular purpose or intent in mind, other than to perform the act of striking, and the man who strikes a similar blow with intent to cause death or injury. This difference is best illustrated by a consideration of the relationship between murder and manslaughter. He who kills intending to kill or cause bodily harm is guilty of murder, whereas he who has killed by the same act without such intent is convicted of manslaughter. The proof of the specific intent, that is, to kill or to cause bodily harm, is necessary in murder because the crime of murder is incomplete without it. No such intent is required, however, for the offence of manslaughter because it forms no part of the offence, manslaughter simply being an unlawful killing without the intent required for murder. The relevance of intoxication which could deprive an accused of the capacity to form the necesary specific intent in murder and its irrelevance in the crime of manslaughter can readily be seen.

The present law relating to the drunkenness defence has developed in this court from the application of principles set out in *Director of Public Prosecutions v. Beard*, [1920] A.C. 479 (H.L.), discussed and adapted in other United Kingdom cases, including *Attorney General for Northern Ireland v. Gallagher*, [1961] 3 All E.R. 299 (H.L.), *Bratty v. Attorney General for Northern Ireland*, [1961] 3 All E.R. 523 (H.L.), and *Director of Public Prosecutions v. Majewski*, [1977] A.C. 443 (H.L.). In this court, the matter has been dealt with in *R. v. George, supra*, and other cases, but particularly in *Leary v. The Queen* (1978), 1 S.C.R. 29. where Pigeon J., speaking for the majority of the court, said, at p. 57, that rape is a crime of general intention as distinguished from specific intention, a crime therefore "in which the defence of drunkenness can have no application". This may be said to have confirmed the law as it stands in Canada on this question and the appellant's principal attack in this court is upon that decision. It is not necessary for the purposes of this judgment to review in detail the authorities in this court on the question. It will be sufficient to summarize their effect in the following terms. Drunkenness in a general sense is not a true defence to a criminal act. Where, however, in a case which involves a crime of specific intent, the accused is so affected by intoxication that he lacks the capacity to form the specific intent required to commit the crime charged it may apply. The defence, however, has no application in offences of general intent.

The criticism of the law with respect to the defence of drunkenness is based on two propositions. It is said, firstly, that the distinction between the general intent and specific intent offences is artificial and is little more than a legal fiction. Secondly, it is said that it is illogical, because it envisages a defence of drunkenness in certain situations and not in others; it is merely a policy decision made by judges and not based on principle or logic. It will be evident from what I have said that I reject the first ground of criticism. As to the second criticism that it is based upon grounds of policy, I would say that there can be no doubt that considerations of policy are involved in this distinction. Indeed, in some cases, principally *Majewski, supra*, the distinction has been defended on the basis that it is sound social policy. The fact, however, that considerations of policy have influenced the development of the law in this field cannot, in my view, be condemned. In the final analysis all law should be based upon and consistent with sound social policy. No good law can be inconsistent with or depart from sound policy.

If the policy behind the present law is that society condemns those who, by the voluntary consumption of alcohol, render themselves incapable of self-control so that they will commit acts of violence causing injury to their neighbours, then in my view no apology for such policy is needed, and the resulting law affords no affront to the well established principles of the law or to the freedom of the individual. Furthermore, the existing law is not divorced from logical underpinnings as suggested in some academic writings. Not all the academic literature has been critical. A strong statement in support of the law on utilitarian or policy grounds made shortly after *Majewski* is by Sir Rupert Cross in *"Blackstone v. Bentham"* (1976), 92 L.Q.R. 516, where he said, at pp. 525-6:

> In reply to Bentham and the academics I would ask why it is "hard and unthinking" to refuse to allow people to exempt themselves from criminal responsibility for harm done by their bodies by incapacitating their minds from controlling them. Why should the requirement that intention or recklessness must be proved in order to establish liability for an assault not be subject to what appears to be the wholly reasonable retributive principle that it is unjust to those who remain sober to allow those who become drunk to allege that they were unaware of consequences of their bodily movements of which all sober people would have been aware? This is what Blackstone meant when he said that the law would not suffer any man "to privilege one crime by another." . . . Punishment is an evil and the less of it the better. But the evil of inflicting punishment is justified if the harm which is thus avoided is greater than that caused by the punishment. It may be asceticism to blame people for simply getting drunk,

but it is sound utilitarianism to seek to prevent people from doing certain kinds of harm while they are drunk. In so far as this object can be achieved by punishment, it is achieved most economically by singling out for punishment those who commit the kind of harm which the law seeks to prevent while they are drunk.

A.J. Ashworth ("Reason, Logic and Criminal Liability" (1975), 91 L.Q.R. 102) says, at p. 130:

> Moreover, it is hardly appropriate to regard a defence of acute intoxication as a simple denial of *mens rea*; it has been suggested that defences should not be classified solely according to the effect of the accused's condition, without reference to their cause. The criminal law permits reason to override the logical application of the traditional doctrines in cases of deliberately self-induced incapacities; to do otherwise would be tantamount to allowing a fraud on the law. It is submitted that, if the law provides no other means of imposing criminal liability in the cases of "voluntarily-induced" incapacities discussed in this article, then there are sufficient reasons for restricting the scope of the defences as the English Judges have done.

. . . .

In my view, the common law rules on the defence of drunkenness, though frequently the subject of criticism, have a rationality which not only accords with criminal law theory, but has also served society well. It is not questioned in this case that the defence of drunkenness, as it applies to specific intent offences, is supportable. It is submitted, however, that it should be extended to include all criminal charges. It is my view that this proposition is not sustainable.

Turning now to the issues raised, the first one is to consider whether the offence of sexual assault causing bodily harm is an offence requiring a general or specific intent. In *Swietlinski v. The Queen*, [1980] 2 S.C.R. 956, this court held that indecent assault, then an offence under the *Criminal Code*, was an offence of general intent. The indecent character of the assault was to be judged upon an objective view of the facts and not upon the mental state of the accused. It was said, at p. 968:

> What acts are indecent and what circumstances will have that character are questions of fact that will have to be decided in each case, but the determination of those questions will depend upon an objective view of the facts and circumstances in relation to the actual assault, and not upon the mental state of the accused.

and later at pp. 970-71:

> Because indecent assault is an offence of general or basic intent, the defence of drunkenness cannot apply where a person is charged with that offence.

This court dealt with the question of sexual assault *simpliciter* under s. 246(1)(*a*) in *R. v. Chase*, [1987] 2 S.C.R. 293.

. . . .

It would therefore be my view that the mental element of the offence in s.

246.2(*c*) is only the intention to commit the assault. The surrounding circumstances must be considered for evidence of its sexual nature and of the resulting bodily harm. The Crown need not show any further mental element (see J.D. Watt, *The New Offences Against the Person* (1984), at p. 113).

In my view, the comments in *Chase, supra*, are equally applicable to an offence under s. 246.2(*c*) which merely adds to the sexual assault *simpliciter* the requirement of bodily harm to the complainant. The resulting interference with the physical integrity of the complainant aggravates the seriousness of a sexual assault but the mental element remains the same. I would conclude that s. 246.2(*c*) creates an offence of general rather than specific intent.

The second issue, whether the defence of drunkenness applies to an offence of general intent includes the question of whether the court should overrule its earlier decision in *Leary*. The attack on *Leary* was based on its rejection of the defence for crimes of general intent. As already mentioned, nobody has suggested that it should not apply in cases of specific intent. The Chief Justice has expressed the view that evidence of self-induced intoxication should be a relevant consideration in determining whether the *mens rea* of any particular offence has been proved by the Crown. As I have indicated, I am unable to agree with this conclusion. The effect of such a conclusion would be that the more drunk a person becomes by his own voluntary consumption of alcohol or drugs, the more extended will be his opportunity for a successful defence against conviction for the offences caused by such drinking, regardless of the nature of the intent required for those offences.

The appellant made two principal arguments in seeking the reversal of the *Leary* rule. He contended that it relieves the Crown from the burden of proving *mens rea* in cases of general intent and, in effect, imposes strict liability upon proof of the *actus reus*. He also contended that the *Leary* rule violates s. 7 and s. 11(*d*) of the *Canadian Charter of Rights and Freedoms*.

In my opinion, both of these submissions must be rejected. I would say at the outset that in crimes of general intent the Crown is not relieved from proving any element of the offence. The effect of excluding the drunkenness defence from such offences is merely to prevent the accused from relying on his self-imposed drunkenness as a factor showing an absence of any necessary intent. While this court has consistently recognized the basic proposition that an accused person should not be subject to criminal sanction unless the Crown shows the existence of a blameworthy or criminal mental state associated with the *actus reus* of the crime, it does not follow that a person who so deprives himself by the voluntary consumption of alcohol or a drug of the normal power of self-restraint that a crime results, should be entitled to an acquittal. Compelling reasons grounded in logic, common sense, and sound social policy dictate otherwise.

As I indicated earlier, it is not necessary to review all of the authorities which have dealt with this issue. It is clear from a review of the cases, however, that until the early years of the nineteenth century drunkenness was considered "rather an aggravation than a defence": see Lord Birkenhead in *D.P.P. v. Beard, supra,* at p. 494. The early principle of the common law was that a voluntary destruction of will power would entitle a person to no more favourable treatment with regard to criminal conduct than a sober person. By the latter part of the 19th century this earlier rule was "mercifully relaxed" (see Lawton LJ. in *Majewski,* [1975] 2 All E.R. 296 (C.A.), at p. 305) in respect of crimes of specific intent where the capacity to form the required specific intent was not present because of intoxication: see the early cases such as *R. v. Doherty* (1887), 16 Cox. C.C. 306, per Stephen J., at p. 308. This new approach was given approval in *Beard's* case and the more modern authorities have been based upon it. This relaxation stems no doubt from a recognition of the severity of the penal consequence of most of the specific intent offences, as compared with the generally lesser penalties associated with the general intent offences. Therefore, the exclusion of the defence from general intent offences was not an exception to the general rule. The exception was the allowance of the defence in specific intent cases adopted to recognize the more complicated mental processes required for the crimes of special intent and the greater penalties involved. Some measure of relief for such cases was therefore provided. Otherwise, the common law preserved the general rule that a person may not by voluntary intoxication render himself immune from the consequences of his conduct.

. . . .

In *Leary,* this court followed the approach taken in the House of Lords in *Majewski,* where the House of Lords unanimously approved the distinction between general and specific intent on the basis that the rule had evolved to protect the community and that voluntary intoxication was a sufficient substitute for the fault element in crimes of general intent.

. . . .

This court in *Leary* approved the *Majewski* approach which has long been accepted in the law of Canada and, for the reasons which I have set out, it is my opinion that this court's judgment in *Leary* ought not to be overruled. I must re-emphasize that the *Leary* rule does not relieve the Crown from its obligation to prove the *mens rea* in a general intent offence. The fact that an accused may not rely on voluntary intoxication in such offences does not have that effect because of the nature of the offence and the mental elements which must be shown. The requisite state of mind may be proved in two ways. Firstly, there is the general proposition that triers of fact may infer *mens rea* from the *actus reus* itself: a person is presumed to have intended the natural and probable consequences of his actions. For example, in an offence involving the mere application of force, the minimal intent to apply that force will suffice to constitute the necessary *mens rea* and can be reasonably inferred from the act itself and the other evidence. Secondly, in cases where the accused was so intoxicated as to raise doubt as to the voluntary nature of his conduct, the Crown may meet its evidentiary obligation respecting the necessary blameworthy mental state of the accused by proving the fact of voluntary self-induced intoxication by drugs or alcohol. This was the approach suggested in *Majewski*. In most cases involving intoxication in general intent offences, the trier of fact will be able to apply the first proposition, namely, that the intent is inferable from the *actus reus* itself. As Fauteux J. observed in *George*, *supra*, at p. 879, it is almost metaphysically inconceivable for a person to be so drunk as to be incapable of forming the minimal intent to apply force. Hence, only in cases of the most extreme self-intoxication does the trier of fact need to use the second proposition, that is, that evidence of self-induced intoxication is evidence of the guilty mind, the blameworthy mental state.

The result of this two-fold approach is that for these crimes accused persons cannot hold up voluntary drunkenness as a defence. They cannot be heard to say: "I was so drunk that I did not know what I was doing". If they managed to get themselves so drunk that they did not know what they were doing, the reckless behaviour in attaining that level of intoxication affords the necessary evidence of the culpable mental condition. Hence, it is logically impossible for an accused person to throw up his voluntary drunkenness as a defence to a charge of general intent. Proof of his voluntary drunkenness can be proof of his guilty mind.

As I have endeavoured to show, the exclusion of the drunkenness defence in general intent cases is not without logical underpinnings but, whatever the logical weaknesses may be, an overwhelming justification for the exclusion may rest on policy, policy so compelling that it possesses its own logic. Intoxication, whether by alcohol or drugs, lies at the root of many if not most violent assaults: intoxication is clearly a major cause of violent crime. What then is preferable, a recognition of this fact and the adoption of a policy aimed at curbing the problem, or the application of what is said to be logic by providing in law that he who voluntarily partakes of that which is the cause of the crime should for that reason be excused from the consequences of his crime? If that is logic, I prefer policy.

It was argued by the appellant that the *Leary* rule converts the offence of sexual assault causing bodily harm into a crime of absolute liability in that the Crown need not prove the requisite intention for the completion of the offence. Therefore, it is said that *Leary* violates s. 7 and s. 11(*d*) of the *Charter*. In *Re Motor Vehicle Act Reference*, [1985] 2 S.C.R. 486 and in *R. v. Vaillancourt*, [1987] 2 S.C.R. 636, it was held that the requirement for a minimum mental state before the attachment of criminal liability is a principle of fundamental justice. Criminal offences, as a general rule, must have as one of their elements the requirement of a blameworthy mental state. The morally innocent ought not to be convicted. It is said that the *Leary* rule violates this fundamental premise. In my opinion, the *Leary* rule clearly does not offend this essential principle of criminal law but rather upholds it. The *Leary* rule recognizes that accused persons who have voluntarily consumed drugs or alcohol, thereby depriving themselves of self-control leading to the commission of a crime, are not morally innocent and are, indeed, criminally blameworthy. While the rule excludes consideration of voluntary intoxication in the approach to general intent offences, it nonetheless recognizes that it may be a relevant factor in those generally more serious offences where the *mens rea* must involve not only the intentional performance of the *actus reus* but, as well, the formation of further ulterior motives and purposes. It therefore intrudes upon the security of the person only in accordance with sound principle and within the established boundaries of the legal process. For these reasons, I would say that the *Charter* is not violated.

. . . .

I would therefore conclude that the courts below made no error and I would dismiss the appeal.

In any event, should it be considered that I am wrong in my approach to the *Leary* case, this is nonetheless a case in which the provisions of s. 613(1)(*b*)(iii) of the *Criminal Code* should be applied. . . . It is my view that there is no sufficient evidence of drunkeness to form any basis whatever for the defence of drunkenness.

WILSON J. (L'HEUREUX-DUBÉ J. concurring): — I have had the benefit of the reasons of the Chief Justice and of my colleagues McIntyre and La Forest JJ. I agree with McIntyre JJ. for the reasons given by him that sexual assault causing bodily harm is an offence of general intent requiring only the minimal intent to apply force. I agree with him also that in most cases involving general intent offences and intoxication the Crown will be able to establish the accused's blameworthy mental state by inference from his or her acts. I think that is the case here. The evidence of intoxication withheld from the trier of fact in this case could not possibly have raised a reasonable doubt as to the existence of the minimal intent to apply force. It is accordingly not necessary in this case to resort to self-induced intoxication as a substituted form of *mens rea*. And, indeed, I have some real concerns as to whether the imposition of criminal liability on that basis would survive a challenge under the *Canadian Charter of Rights and Freedoms*.

The facts are fully set out in the reasons of the Chief Justice and I refer to them only to underline why I agree with my colleague, McIntyre J., that the rule in *Leary v. The Queen*, [1978] 1 S.C.R. 29, should be preserved and applied in this case.

Sexual assault is a crime of violence. There is no requirement of an intent or purpose beyond the intentional application of force. It is first and foremost an assault. It is sexual in nature only because, objectively viewed, it is related to sex either on account of the area of the body to which the violence is applied or on account of words accompanying the violence. Indeed, the whole purpose, as I understand it, of the replacement of the offence of rape by the offence of sexual assault was to emphasize the aspect of violence and put paid to the benign concept that rape was simply the act of a man who was "carried away" by his emotions.

The appellant in his statement to the police admitted that he had forced the complainant to have sexual intercourse with him but claimed that because of his drunkenness he did not know why he had done this and that when he realized what he was doing he off" the complainant. There was evidence that the appellant had punched the complainant twice with his closed fist and had threatened to kill her. The doctor who examined the complainant testified that the complainant's right eye was swollen shut and that three stitches were required to close the wound. It is clear from this that there was intentional and voluntary, as opposed to accidental or involuntary, application of force.

The evidence of the appellant's intoxication consisted of his own statements to the police that he was drunk; the complainant's testimony that, while the appellant was acting out of character in making advances to her, he was able to walk, talk and put albums on the record player; a friend's testimony that prior to the incident the appellant had been drinking at a bar and had become "very rowdy" although still capable of talking and walking straight. By his own admission the appellant had sufficient wits about him after the violent assault to hide a bloodied towel and pillowcase from the police. There is no evidence that we are dealing here with extreme intoxication, verging on insanity or automatism, and as such capable of negating the inference that the minimal intent to apply force was present: see *R. v. Swietlinski*, (1978) 44 C.C.C. (2d) 267 (Ont. C.A.), at p. 294, aff'd [1980] 2 S.C.R. 956. The evidence of intoxication in this case was simply not capable of raising a reasonable doubt as to the existence of the minimal intent required. In this I agree with McIntyre J.

I am less confident about the proposition accepted by my colleague that self-induced intoxication may substitute for the mental element required to be present at the time the offence was committed although I realize that there are statements in judgments of this court to that effect. I do not believe, however, that the court has clearly adopted that proposition. The decision of the House of Lords in *Director of Public Prosecutions v. Majewski*, [1977] A.C. 443, may stand for the rather harsh proposition that even self-induced intoxication producing a state of automatism cannot constitute a defence to an offence of general intent such as assault but I doubt that our Canadian jurisprudence goes that far.

· · · ·

I believe that the *Leary* rule is perfectly consistent with an onus resting on the Crown to prove the minimal intent which should accompany the doing of the prohibited act in general intent offences. I view it as preferable to preserve the *Leary* rule in its more flexible form as Pigeon J. applied it, *i.e.*, so as to allow evidence of intoxication to go to the trier of fact in general intent offences only if it is evidence of extreme intoxication involving an absence of awareness akin to a state of insanity or automatism. Only in such a case is the evidence capable of raising a reasonable doubt as to the existence of the minimal intent required for the offence. I would not overrule *Leary*, as the Chief Justice would, and allow evidence of intoxication to go to the trier of fact in every case regardless of its possible relevance to the issue of the existence of the minimal intent required for the offence.

It was argued by the appellant and indeed accepted by the Chief Justice in his reasons that the *Leary* rule converts the offence of sexual assault causing bodily harm into a crime of absolute liability in that the Crown need not prove any mental element. This is said to offend s. 7 of the *Charter* as interpreted in *Re B.C. Motor Vehicle Act*, [1985] 2 S.C.R. 486 and in *R. v. Vaillancourt*, [1987] 2 S.C.R. 636. With all due respect to those who think differently I do not believe that the Crown is relieved from proving the existence of the required minimal intent by the operation of *Leary*. In *R. v. Sault Ste. Marie*, [1978] 2 S.C.R. 1299, Dickson J., as he then was, stated at p. 1310:

> In sharp contrast, "absolute liability" entails conviction on proof merely that the defendant committed the prohibited act constituting the *actus reus* of the offence. There is no relevant mental element. It is no defence that the accused was entirely without fault. He may be morally innocent in every sense, yet be branded as a malefactor and punished as such.

When the *Leary* rule is applied in this case the Crown must still prove beyond a reasonable doubt the existence of the required mental element of the intentional application of force. The offence cannot be said to be one of absolute liability in the sense that no mental element has to be proved in order to obtain a conviction. As Alan Mewett and Morris Manning write in *Criminal Law* (2nd ed. (1985)), at p. 210:

> The courts are not saying that crimes of general or basic intent do not require *mens rea*. Rather they are saying that those crimes have a *mens rea* of a type directed solely to the present and that drunkenness is not sufficient to negate that type of thought process.

Similarly, Glanville Williams argues in his *Textbook of Criminal Law* (2nd ed. (1983)), at pp. 475-76, that it is a misunderstanding to read even *Majewski, supra*, as transforming general intent offences into absolute liability offences because "even on a charge of a crime of basic intent the jury must have regard to all the evidence except the evidence of intoxication in determining the defendant's intention." In short, when evidence of intoxication is withheld from the jury the Crown still bears the burden of proving a blameworthy state of mind.

It was also argued by the appellant and accepted by the Chief Justice that the application of the *Leary* rule violates s. 11(*d*) of the *Charter* by allowing an accused to be convicted even although the trier of fact might well have a reasonable doubt as to the existence of the essential mental element of the offence or as to the availability of a defence which could raise a reasonable doubt as to the guilty of the accused: see *Vaillancourt, supra; R. v. Whyte*, [1988] 2 S.C.R. 3. Again I find myself in respectful disagreement with the Chief Justice and the appellant on this issue. To my mind, the operation of the *Leary* rule in this case does not have that result because the Crown still must prove that the accused applied force intentionally and the evidence of intoxication is withheld from the jury only because it is incapable of raising a reasonable doubt as to the accused's guilt. This is not a case in which self-induced intoxication is being resorted to as a substituted *mens rea* for the intentional application of force.

It is, my view, not strictly necessary in this case to address the constitutionality of substituting self-induced intoxication of general intent offences. The issue would, in my view, only arise in those rare cases in which the intoxication is extreme enough to raise doubts as to the existence of the minimal intent which characterizes conscious and volitional conduct. However, as both the Chief Justice and McIntyre J. have addressed the issue, I will express my own somewhat tentative views upon it.

This court has affirmed as fundamental the proposition that a person should not be exposed to a deprivation of liberty unless the Crown proves the existence of a blameworthy or culpable state of mind: see *Re B.C. Motor Vehicle Act, supra*, at pp. 513-20. It does not follow from this, however, that those who, through the voluntary consumption of alcohol or drugs incapacitate themselves from knowing what they are doing, fall within the category of the "morally innocent" deserving of such protection. This is not to say that such persons do not have a right under s. 7n or s. 12 of the *Charter* to be protected against punishment that is disproportionate to their crime and degree of culpability: see *Re B.C. Motor Vehicle Act, supra*, at pp. 532-34; *R. v. Smith*, [1987] 1 S.C.R. 1045. They do, especially if the consequences of their becoming intoxicated were not intended or foreseen.

The real concern over the substituted form of *mens rea* arises, it seems to me, under s. 11(*d*) of the *Charter*. While this court has recognized that in some cases proof of an essential element of a criminal offence can be replaced by proof of a different element, it has placed stringent limitations on when this can happen.

. . . .

In my tentative view, it is unlikely that in those cases in which it is necessary to resort to self-induced intoxication as the substituted element for the minimal intent, proof of the substituted element will "inexorably" lead to the conclusion that the essential element of the minimal intent existed at the time the criminal act was committed. But I prefer to leave this question open as it is unnecessary to decide it in order to dispose of this appeal.

I agree with my colleagues McIntyre and La Forest JJ. that, had there been error in the court below, no substantial wrong or miscarriage of justice resulted from it and that it would accordingly be appropriate to apply s. 613(1)(*b*)(iii) of the *Criminal Code*. I would dismiss the appeal.

DICKSON C.J. (LAMER J. concurring) (dissenting): —

. . . .

DRUNKENNESS AND *MENS REA*

In my view, the only issue the court needs to address may be put as follows: should evidence of self-induced intoxication be considered by the trier of fact, along with all other relevant evidence, in determining whether the prosecution has proved beyond a reasonable doubt the *mens rea* required to constitute the offence? I am of the opinion that the court should answer that question in the affirmative.

I wish to make clear at the outset, however, that nothing in these reasons is intended to apply with respect to the quite distinct issues raised by offences, such as driving while impaired, where intoxication or the consumption of alcohol is itself an ingredient of the offence. The *mens rea* of such offences can be left for consideration another day.

In *Leary v. The Queen*, [1978] 1 S.C.R. 29, Pigeon J. for the majority of the court, held that rape was an offence requiring proof of only "basic" or "general" intent rather than "specific" intent. Under that categorization, the court held, the jury should be instructed that evidence that drunkenness may have deprived the accused of the capacity to form the requisite intent should not be taken into account when considering whether the Crown had satisfied the burden of proving beyond a reasonable doubt that the accused had acted with the requisite intent. (See also *Swietlinski v. The Queen*, [1980] 2 S.C.R. 956, dealing with the offence of indecent assault). The offence of rape has now been removed from the *Criminal Code* and in its place are the sexual assault provisions. More recently, in *R. v. Chase*, [1987] 2 S.C.R. 293, the court held that sexual assault was a crime of "basic" or "general" intent. In *Chase*, however, drunkenness was not in issue and the propriety of maintaining the distinction between general and specific intent for purposes of evidence regarding intoxication was not considered. The present case raises that much more basis issue which, in my view, the court should reconsider.

In my dissent in *Leary*, I sought to advance the view that respect for basic criminal law principles required that the legal ficiton, the artificial "specific" intent threshold requirement, be abandoned. I do not intend in these reasons to repeat what I said in *Leary*. With due regard for *stare decisis*, as to which I will have more to say in a moment, and with the greatest of respect for those of a contrary view, I would only add that nothing I have heard or read since the judgment in *Leary* has caused me to abandon or modify in the slightest degree the views of dissent which I there expressed. Analysis of the *Leary* dissent may be summarized as follows.

First of all, one must recognize the fundamental nature of the *mens rea* requirement. To warrant the condemnation of a conviction and the infliction of punishment, one who has caused harm must have done so with a blameworthy state of mind. It is always for the Crown to prove the existence of a guilty mind beyond a reasonable doubt. Intoxication affects one's mental state, one's ability to perceive the circumstances in which one acts, and to appreciate possible consequences. In principle, therefore, intoxication is relevant to the mental element in crime, and should be considered, together with all other evidence, in determining whether the Crown has proved the requisite mental state beyond a reasonable doubt.

It is quite wrong, I think, to characterize the issue as whether the "defence of drunkeness" should apply to this or that offence. While this expression is commonly used, it is misleading and perhaps even unduly emotive. It suggests that those who would otherwise be liable for their criminal conduct will escape because they were drunk at the time the offence was committed. But, of course, no one suggests that special concessions should be made to drunken offenders. The issue is really whether the Crown should be relieved of the usual burden of proving the requisite mental element for the offence, because the accused was intoxicated. Should the jury be entitled to assess all of the evidence relevant to intent and be entitled to decide on the basis of all of the evidence whether the Crown has satisfied that burden?

The categories of "specific" intent on the one hand and "basic" or "general" intent on the other have evolved as an artificial device whereby evidence, otherwise relevant, is excluded from the jury's consideration. This court, in *Swietlinski*, has recognized that intoxication may as a matter of fact deprive an accused of "basic" or "general" intent. It is said, however, by those who support the classifiction that as a matter of policy, consideration of evidence of intoxication must be excluded. Indeed, a notable feature to be found in the analysis of many of those who support restricting the jury's use of evidence relating to drunkenness is the concession that while principle and logic lead in an opposite direction, the policy of protection of the public requires that principle and logic should yield: see, *e.g. Director of Public Prosecutions v. Majewski*, [1976] 2 All E.R. 142, at pp. 167-8 per Lord Edmund-Davies, quoted by Pigeon J. in *Leary, supra*, at pp. 52-3.

In my view, there are two fundamental problems with this approach. First, if the law is to be altered in the name of policy over principle, that is surely a task for Parliament rather than the courts. As Barwick C.J. of the High Court of Australia concluded in *O'Connor* (1980), 4 A. Crim. R. 348, at pp. 363-64:

> It seems to me to be completely inconsistent with the principles of the common law that a man should be conclusively presumed to have an intent which, in fact, he does not have, or to have done an act which, in truth, he did not do.

I can readily understand that a person who has taken alcohol or another drug to such an extent that he is intoxicated thereby to the point where he has no will to act or no capacity to form an intent to do an act is blameworthy and that his act of having ingested or administered the alcohol or other drug ought to be visited with severe consequences. The offence of being drunk and disorderly is not maintained these days in all systems of the common law. In any case it has not carried a sufficient penalty properly to express the public opprobrium which should attach to one who, by the taking of alcohol or the use of drugs, has become intoxicated to the point where he is the vehicle for unsocial or violent behaviour. But, though blameworthy for becoming intoxicated, I can see no ground for presuming his acts to be voluntary and relevantly intentional. For what is blameworthy there should be an appropriate criminal offence. But it is not for the Judges to create an offence appropriate in the circumstances: cf. *Knuller (Publishing, Printing & Promotions) Ltd. v. D.P.P.*, [1973] A.C. 435, at pp. 457-458, 464-465 and 490). It must be for the Parliament.

Secondly, even if it were appropriate for the courts to bend principle in the name of policy, so far as I am aware, there is no evidence that the artificiality of the specific intent requirement is actually required for social protection.

An unrestrained application of basic *mens rea* doctrine would not, in my opinion, open a gaping hole in the criminal law inimical to social protection. There are several reasons for this. To the extent that intoxication merely lowers inhibitions, removes self-restraint or induces unusal self-confidence or aggressiveness, it would be of no avail to an accused, as such effects do not relate to the *mens rea* requirement for volitional and intentional or reckless conduct. Similarly, intoxication would be of no avail to an accused who got drunk in order to gain the courage to commit a crime or to aid in his defence. Thirdly, one can trust in the good sense of the jury and that of our trial Judges to weigh all the evidence in a fair and responsbile manner, and they are unlikely to acquit too readily those who have committed offences while intoxicated.

The High Court of Australia held in *O'Connor, supra*, that the distinction between specific and general intent should not be followed and that in all cases, evidence of drunkenness should be left with the jury along with all other evidence relative to the issue of intent. The New Zealand Court of Appeal also rejected the artificial specific intent distinction: *R. v. Kamipeli*, [1975] 2 N.Z.L.R. 610.

. . . .

The experience in New Zealand and Australia, where the specific intent has been abandoned, suggests that the public will be adequately protected if the issue is left to the good sense of the jury. *O'Connor* was preceded in the State of Victoria by *R. v. Keogh*, [1964] V.R. 400. In *O'Connor*, Stephen J. explained as follows, at 358:

> A distrust of jurors and an anxiety that they may too readily be persuaded to an acquittal if evidence of the result of self-induced intoxication, particularly by drugs other than alcohol, were allowed, may have formed some part of the public policy on which the decision rests. I may say at once that I have, of course, no experience of English juries: but I have of juries in New South Wales. Starke J., a most experienced Judge in the hearing of criminal charges

in Victoria, having had as well a long and distinguished career as an advocate, expressed himself in the present case in relation to the impact of evidence of intoxication upon Victoria jurors. He said:

> "I, of course, have no knowledge of how English juries react. But over nearly 40 years' experience in this State I have found juries to be very slow to accept a defence based on intoxication. I do not share the fear held by many in England that if intoxication is accepted as a defence as far as general intent is concerned the floodgates will open and hordes of guilty men will descend on the community."

I share his views, as if they had been expressed about jurors in New South Wales. In my opinion, properly instructed jurors would be scrupulous and not indulgent in deciding an issue of voluntariness or of intention. Indeed, I am inclined to think that they may tend to think that an accused who had taken alchohol and particularly other drugs to the point of extreme intoxication had brought on himself what flowed from that state of intoxication.

The empirical evidence is to the same effect: see George Smith J., "Footnote to O'Connor's Case" (1981), 5 Crim. L.J. 270, reviewing the effects of the *O'Connor* decision in Australia, and concluding, after review of over 500 trials held in the District Court of New South Wales, that the actual impact on the acquittal rate was minimal (at p. 277):

> Certainly my inquiries would indicate that the decision in *O'Connor's* case, far from opening any floodgates has at most permitted an occasional drip to escape from the tap.

. . . .

III

STARE DECISIS

The real issue in this appeal, it seems to me, is whether the court should now overrule *Leary*. Let me say immediately that, even if a case were wrongly decided, certainty in the law remains an important consideration. There must be compelling circumstances to justify departure from a prior decision. On the other hand, it is clear that this court may overrule its own decisions and indeed, it has exercised that discretion on a number of occasions. . . .

There are at least four separate factors which find support in the jurisprudence of the court which in my submission lead to the conclusion that *Leary* should be overruled.

A. *Canadian Charter of Rights and Freedoms*

Since *Leary* was decided, the *Canadian Charter of Rights and Freedoms* has come into force. This court has held that legislation which imposes the sanction of imprisonment without proof of a blameworthy state of mind violates the guarantee of fundamental justice contained in s. 7 of the *Charter* and must be struck down unless it can meet the exacting test of s. 1 (see *Re B.C. Motor Vehicle Act*, [1985] 2 S.C.R. 486, *R. v. Vaillancourt*, [1987] 2 S.C.R. 636).

The appellant submits that *Leary* runs counter to s. 7 by providing that intoxication is no defence to a crime of general intent. In circumstances where the requisite mental intent is lacking due to an intoxicated condition, a general intent offence is converted into one of absolute liability in which proof of the commission of the actus reus by itself mandates conviction. It is also submitted that *Leary* runs counter to the presumption of innocence and the right to a fair hearing as guaranteed by s. 11(*d*) of the *Charter*, in so far as wrongful intent is irrebuttably presumed upon the showing of intoxication.

. . . .

In *Leary*, I expressed the opinion that the fundamental rationale for the *mens rea* presumption could be framed in the following terms, at p. 34:

> The notion that a court should not find a person guilty of an offence against the criminal law unless he has a blameworthy state of mind is common to all civilized penal systems. It is founded upon respect for the person and for the freedom of human will. A person is accountable for what he wills. When, in the exercise of the power of free choice, a member of society chooses to engage in harmful or otherwise undesirable conduct proscribed by the criminal law, he must accept the sanctions which that law has provided for the purpose of discouraging such conduct. Justice demands no less. But, to be criminal, the wrongdoing must have been consciously committed. To subject the offender to punishment, a mental element as well as a physical element is an essential concomitant of the crime. The mental state basic to criminal liability consists in most crimes in either (a) an intention to cause the *actus reus* of the crime, *i.e.* an intention to do the act which constitutes the crime in question, or (b) foresight or realization on the part of the person that his conduct will probably cause or may cause the *actus reus*, together with assumption of or indifference to a risk, which in all of the circumstances is substantial or unjustifiable. This latter mental element is sometimes characterized as recklessness.

In my view, that same principle is now given constitutional force in *Re B.C. Motor Vehicle Act, supra, Vaillancourt, supra.* In *Re B.C. Motor Vehicle Act, supra*, the court held, at p. 514, that "absolute liability in penal law offends the principles of fundamental justice." In *Vaillancourt*, Justice Lamer stated that the *B.C. Motor Vehicle Act Reference* "elevated *mens rea* from a presumed element in *Sault Ste. Marie, supra* to a constitutionally required element" (p. 652). While the court has not yet dealt directly with the extent to which objective foreseeability may suffice for the imposition of criminal liability (*Vaillancourt* at pp. 653-54), that issue is not raised in the present context.

The effect of the majority holding in *Leary* is to impose a form of absolute liability on intoxicated offenders, which is entirely inconsistent with the basic requirement for a blameworthy state of mind as a prerequisite to the imposition of the penalty of imprisonment mandated by the above-cited authorities. I agree with the observation of Professor Stuart in *Canadian Criminal Law* (2nd ed. 1987) that s. 7 of the *Charter* mandates the reversal of *Leary* and the assertion of "the fundamental principles of voluntariness and fault" in relation to intoxication and the criminal law (at p. 378). If the constitutional guarantee empowers the court to strike down legislation as in the two cases cited above, surely it provides a sufficient basis for overruling a prior decision of the court which fails to respect constitutionally entrenched values.

The majority holding in *Leary* also runs counter to the s. 11(*d*) right to be presumed innocent until proven guilty. With respect to crimes of general intent, guilty intent is in effect presumed upon proof of the fact of intoxication. Moreover, the presumption of guilt created by the *Leary* rule is irrebuttable.

The same argument made in the context of s. 7 can be made in relation to s. 11(*d*). By providing that intoxication is no defence to a crime of general intent, *Leary* renders the offence one of absolute liability and runs counter to the presumption of innocence by presuming an essential element required by s. 7 upon the proof of the fact of intoxication.

In my view, the *Leary* rule cannot be upheld by reference to s. 1, as it cannot survive the "proportionality" inquiry. While the protection of the public, said to underlie the *Leary* rule, could serve as an important objective, in my view the *Leary* rule does not achieve that objective in a manner consistent with the proportionality test of *Oakes, supra. Oakes* requires that "the measures adopted must be carefully designed to achieve the objective in question." As I have noted, there is no agreement in the case law as to how to distinguish between crimes of "general intent" and crimes of "specific intent". This distinction was plainly not in the minds of the *Code* drafters, and the mental elements of many crimes are not readily classified into one category or the other. There is no rational reason for protecting the public against some drunken offenders but not against others, particularly where the distinction is not based upon the gravity of the offence or the availability of included offences. If the public protection does require special measures, that should be accomplished through comprehensive legislation rather than ad hoc judicial recasting of some offences. For a recent review of possible legislative schemes, see Quigley, "Reform of the Intoxication Defence" (1987), 33 McGill L.J. 1.

The *Leary* rule in effect treats the deliberate act of becoming intoxicated as culpable in itself, but inflicts punishment measured by the unintended consequences of becoming intoxicated. Punishment acts as a deterrent where the conduct is intended or foreseen. There is no evidence to support the assertion that the *Leary* rule deters the commission of unintended crimes. Hence, there is no warrant for violating fundamental principles and convicting those who would otherwise escape criminal liability.

The *Leary* rule fails to satisfy the second branch of the proportionality test as well, namely, that the means chosen should impair as little as possible the right or freedom in question. In general intent offences, the jury is to be instructed to excise from their minds any evidence of drunkenness with the result that the Crown, because the accused is intoxicated, is relieved of proving *mens rea*, thereby placing the intoxicated person in a worse position than a sober person. Alternatively, the jury is required to examine the mental state of the accused, without reference to the alcohol ingested, and consequently find a fictional intent. In my view, imposition of this form of absolute liability goes well beyond what is required to protect the public from drunken offenders. As I have already indicated, striking down the artificial rule which precludes the trier of fact from considering evidence of intoxication in relation to *mens rea* has not produced an increase in the threat to public safety from drunken offenders in Australia, and there is no evidence to suggest that it would do so in Canada.

Finally, it is my view that there is a disproportionality between the effects of *Leary* on rights protected by the *Charter* and the objective of public safety. To paraphrase Lamer J. in *Re B.C. Motor Vehicle Act, supra*, at p. 521, it has not been demonstrated that risk of imprisonment of a few innocent persons is required to attain the goal of protecting the public from drunken offenders.

As stated in *R. v. Holmes*, [1988] 1 S.C.R. 914, at p. 940: "This effect, given the range of alternative legislative devices available to Parliament, is too deleterious to be justified as a reasonable limit under s. 1 of the *Charter*. Simply put, the provision exacts too high a price to be justified in a free and democratic society."

B. *Leary* Attenuated by Subsequent Cases

Since *Leary* there have been developments in the jurisprudence of the court which, in my submission, seriously undermine the view taken by the majority in *Leary*. The court has held that where the holding of a case has been "attenuated" by subsequent decisions, it may be appropriate to overrule that earlier decision: *Reference re the Agricultural Products Marketing Act*, [1978] 2 S.C.R. 1198.

In my view, *Leary* has also been undermined quite independently of the *Charter*. The court has consistently held that an honest but unreasonable mistaken belief in consent will negate the *mens rea* required for rape, indecent assault or sexual assaut: see *Pappajohn v. The Queen* [1980] 2 S.C.R. 120; *Sansregret v. The Queen*, [1985] 1 S.C.R. 570; *R. v. Bulmer*, [1987] 1 S.C.R. 782, and *R. v. Robertson*, [1987] 1 S.C.R. 918 at pp. 939-40. While the reasonableness of the accused's belief is a factor for the jury to consider in determining whether or not the belief was honestly held, a mistaken belief in consent need not be reasonable.

The *Leary* rule fits most awkwardly with that enunciated in *Pappajohn*. Lower courts have held that in the light of *Leary*, where intoxication is a factor in inducing a mistaken belief in consent, the jury must be instructed that while an honest but unreasonable belief will negate *mens rea* (*Pappajohn*) they are to disregard the effect that intoxication might have had in inducing that mistake

(*Leary*). In *R. v. Moreau* (1986), 26 C.C.C. (3d) 359 (Ont. C.A.), at pp. 386-7, Martin J.A. described the task of the jury as follows:

> It does not follow that the defence of honest belief in consent is unavailable on a charge of sexual assault to an accused who is voluntarily intoxicated. Where an issue arises on the evidence as to the accused's honest belief in consent, the defence of honest belief in consent must be put to the jury, notwithstanding the accused's self-induced intoxication. There may be a basis in the evidence for the accused's honest belief in consent apart altogether from his intoxication; there may even be reasonable grounds for that belief even though he was intoxicated. The intoxication may not be the cause of the mistaken belief. However, the accused cannot rely on his self-induced intoxication as the basis for his belief that the complainant consented. As Mayrand J.A. said in *R. v. Bresse, Vallieres and Theberge* (1978), 48 C.C.C. (2d) 78 at p. 87, 7 C.R. (3d) 50 (Que. C.A.):
>
> > One must distinguish the case in which, because of one's voluntary inebriation, a man takes no account of the refusal manifested by a woman from the case in which a man, because of the ambiguous conduct of the woman, believes sincerely that she consented to sexual relations. This *error of fact committed for reasons other than one's voluntary inebriation* is, in my opinion, a valid ground of defence. (Emphasis added.)
>
> In those circumstances the jury is required to engage in the difficult, and perhaps somewhat artificial task, of putting out of their minds the evidence of intoxcation on the issue whether the accused honestly believed that the complainant consented. The test is not whether a reasonable and sober person would have made the same mistake but whether the accused would have made the same mistake if he had been sober; see Glanville Williams, *Textbook on Criminal Law*, 2nd ed. (1983) at pp. 481-2. However, to hold that evidence of self-induced intoxication is relevant to the honesty of the accused's belief in consent where his belief is founded on his mistaken appreciation, due to intoxication, of the facts relating to the complainant's consent is, in my view, incompatible with the rule laid down in *Leary*, and would completely negate the policy rule that self-induced intoxication is not a defence in crimes of general intent.

In my view, the *Leary* qualification on the criminal law principle of general application with respect to mistake of fact unnecessarily and unduly complicates the jury's task. Indeed, I find it difficult to imagine how it is humanly possible to follow the jury instruction apparently mandated by the combination of *Leary* and *Pappajohn*. This confusing and anomalous result is entirely the product of the deviation from basic criminal-law principles which occurred in *Leary* and accordingly there is much to support the view that it should be overruled.

The inconsistency between *Leary* and *Pappajohn* has not gone unnoticed in the literature. In *Canadian Criminal Law* (2nd ed. 1987), at p. 378, Professor Stuart describes the collision between *Leary* and *Pappajohn* as a "glaring inconsistency". In "Regina v. O'Connor: *Mens Rea* Survives in Australia" (1981), 19 U.W.O. L. Rev. 281, at pp. 300-301, David H. Doherty observes:

> The two judgments are clearly inconsistent. *Pappajohn* confirms the essential requirement of a subjective mental culpability as a prerequisite to criminal liability. *Leary* creates a fundamental exception to that requirement. The facts of *Pappajohn* show that the judgments will inevitably come into conflict. The Supreme Court of Canada chose to avoid dealing with the confict in *Pappajohn* by ignoring the evidence of drinking by the accused.

It is to be hoped that in a later case the court will seek a more positive resolution to the problem. In seeking that resolution the majority position in *O'Connor* deserves emulation. After reading the opinions expressed in *O'Connor*, one concludes as did the minority in *Leary*, that the position taken in *Majewski* and adopted by the majority in *Leary* constitutes an illogical, unwarranted, and detrimental departure from the contemporary trend in criminal law which recognizes subjective mental blameworthiness at the time of the doing of the prohibited act as the sine qua non of criminal liability. The creation of exceptions to the principle compelled by considerations of public policy must be left to Parliament.

See also Peter J. Connelly, "Drunkenness and Mistake of Fact: Pappajohn v. The Queen; Swietlinski v. The Queen" (1981), 24 Crim. L.Q. 49; Christine Boyle, *Sexual Assault* (1984), at pp. 89-90.

C. *Leary* Creates Uncertainty

The third general consideration justifying the court in overruling *Leary* is the principle established in *Minister of Indian Affairs and Northern Development v. Ranville, supra,* where the court overruled its previous decision in *Commonwealth of Puerto Rico v. Hernandez*, [1975] 1 S.C.R. 228, on the ground that continued recognition of the *persona designata* category could only have the effect of creating doubt as to which procedure a party should follow. The prior decision itself was a cause of uncertainty, and therefore following the prior decision because of *stare decisis* would be contrary to the underlying value behind that doctrine, namely, clarity and certainty in the law. Similarly, in *Vetrovec, supra,* the court overruled previous decisions relating to corroboration and stated, "The law of corroboration is unduly and unnecessarily complex and technical".

I have already indicated the confusion created by the combination of *Leary* and *Pappajohn*. I suggest that the distinction between "general" and "specific" intent which *Leary* mandates and the notorious difficulty in articulating a clear and workable definition of specific intent falls squarely within the principle enunciated in *Ranville* and *Vetrovec*. Because that category is based on policy rather than principle, classification of offences as falling within or without the specific intent category is necessarily an ad hoc, unpredictable exercise.

The situation with respect to the offence of break and enter, raised by the companion case, *R. v. Quin* (reasons being delivered contemporaneously) provides an example. In *R. v. Campbell* (1974), 17 C.C.C. (2d) 320 (Ont. C.A.), the accused was charged with breaking and entering with intent pursuant to s. 306(1)(*a*). The Ontario Court of Appeal held that offence to be a crime of specific intent and hence drunkenness was relevant to the issue of intention. In *Quin*, the accused was charged with breaking and entering and committing an indictable offence pursuant to s. 306(1)(*b*). The same court held that under that subsection, the break and enter offence was one requiring only proof of general intent and hence evidence of intoxication could not be considered. A legal category which creates distinctions of this king, in my view, complicates and confuses the law to an unacceptable degree and, absent some compelling need for its retention, should be abandoned.

Another example of the complexity and uncertainty caused by the specific/general intent dichotomy is provided by *Swietlinski, supra*. In that case, the accused was charged with murder pursuant to s. 213(*d*) of the *Criminal Code*. The enumerated offence the accused was alleged to have committed was indecent assault. *Leary* had held that rape was an offence of general intent and in *Swietlinski*, the court applied *Leary* to the offence of indecent assault. However, because of the constructive murder provision, this would have led to a situation where the accused would be convicted of murder without any criminal intent. To avoid that result, the court held that where indecent assault formed the ingredient of constructive murder pursuant to s. 213, evidence of drunkenness could be taken into account in determining whether in fact the accused had the requisite intent for the offence of indecent assault. In other words, the court held quite explicitly that intoxication did logically bear upon the issue of intent to commit indecent assault, and that the only issue was whether, as a matter of policy, the jury should be told to put that evidence out of mind. In the light of *Vaillancourt*, *Swietlinski* is no longer significant for its result. Indeed, *Vaillancourt* and *Swietlinski* have this in common: both cases demonstrate the court's aversion to the imposition of liability without *mens rea*. In my view, to hold that evidence of intoxication can be taken into account with reference to an offence for certain purposes but not for other purposes is further reflection of the confusion, uncertainty, and lack of principle which motivates the specific/general intent dichotomy.

D. *Leary* Unfavourable to Accused

The fourth factor which bears directly upon whether or not the court should overrule *Leary* in my view, is that the *Leary* rule is one which operates against the accused by expanding the scope of criminal liability beyond normal limits. Respect for the principle of certainty and the institutional limits imposed upon the law-making function of the courts should constrain the court from overruling a prior decision where the effect would be to expand criminal liability. It is not for the courts to create new offences, or to broaden the net of liability, particularly as changes in the law through judicial decision operate retrospectively. The same argument does not apply, however, where the result of overruling a prior decision is to establish a rule favourable to the accused. In my submission, this principle underlies the decision of the court in *Paquette v. The Queen, supra*, at p. 197, where the court overruled its previous decision in *Dunbar v. The King, supra*, which had held that an accused who was a party to murder, but who had not himself committed the act, could not rely upon the defence of duresss. (See also *R. v. Santeramo* (1976), 32 C.C.C. (2d) 35 (Ont. C.A.), at p. 46 per Brooke J.A. "I do not feel bound by a judgment of this court where the liberty of the subject is in issue if I am convinced that that judgment is wrong.")

IV

DISPOSITION

The trial judge made no reference in his charge to the jury to the requirement that the Crown prove that the accused acted with the requisite intent. In my view, this is fatal to the conviction. Although the Crown presented a strong case against the accused at trial, no request was made by the respondent that this court apply the provision of s. 613(1)(b)(iii) of the *Criminal Code*, and in any event, it is not for this court to speculate as to the likely result had the jury been properly instructed.

It follows that the appeal should be allowed, the conviction set aside, and a new trial ordered.

LA FOREST J. (concurring in the result only): — I have had the advantage of reading the opinions prepared by the Chief Justice and Mr. Justice McIntyre. The requirement of *mens rea* in truly criminal offences is, as the Chief Justice had demonstrated, so fundamental that it cannot, since the *Charter*, be removed on the basis of judicially developed policy. It would be anomalous if the courts could infringe such a fundamental right on the basis of such policies when not demonstrated to be essential, while any attempt by Parliament to do so would be subjected to searching scrutiny under s. 1 as established by this court.

In my dissenting reasons in *R. v. Landry*, [1986] 1 S.C.R. 145, at p. 187, I set forth my views regarding the general issue posed here. I there observed that in the changed constitutional environment brought about by the *Charter*, if incursions are to be made upon fundamental legal values, it is for Parliament to do so, not the courts. It is the duty of Parliament to respond to the challenge of criminal activities. While the courts must sensitively consider actions taken by Parliament for the protection of the public generally, they must be forever diligent to prevent undue intrusions on our liberty. The courts are the protectors of our rights. It does not sit well for them to make rules intruding on fundamental rights even when this may appear to them to be desirable in a properly balanced system of criminal justice. That is Parliament's work. I added, at p. 189 of *Landry*:

> If Parliament in its wisdom finds it necessary to adjust the balance, it can do so. It is in a better position to provide for the precise balance and has a far better access to the knowledge required to achieve that balance than the courts. The courts can then perform their duty of scrutinizing Parliament's laws both in their general tenor and in their particular application to safeguard our traditional values.

Established common-law rules should not, it is true, lightly be assumed to violate the *Charter*. As a repository of our traditional values they may, in fact, assist in defining its norms. But when a common-law rule is found to infringe upon a right or freedom guaranteed by the *Charter*, it must be justified in the same way as legislative rules. No adequate justification was made here.

Accordingly, I am in general agreement with the law as stated by the Chief Justice. However, I agree with McIntyre J. that on the particular facts of this case no substantial wrong or miscarriage of justice has occurred and it is, therefore, a proper case to apply s. 613(1)(*b*)(iii) of the *Criminal Code*. For this reason, I would dispose of the case in the manner proposed by McIntyre J.

For comments on *Bernard*, see T. Quigley and A. Manson in 67 C.R. (3d) 168-182 and K. Campbell, "Intoxicated Mistakes" (1989) 32 Crim. L.Q. 110.

In *Daviault* a 6:3 majority of the Supreme Court adopted the Wilson compromise that extreme intoxication akin to automatism or insanity had, under the *Charter*, to be a defence to general intent crimes such as sexual assault. The majority, however, likening the defence to insanity, reversed the onus of proof.

(b) *Charter* Standards

R. v. DAVIAULT

[1994] 3 S.C.R. 63, 33 C.R. (4th) 165, 93 C.C.C. (3d) 21,
1994 CarswellQue 10, 1994 CarswellQue 118

The accused was charged with sexual assault. The complainant was a 65-year-old woman who was partially paralyzed and thus confined to a wheelchair. She knew the accused through his wife. At approximately 6 p.m. the accused, at her request, went to her home. He brought a 40-ounce bottle of brandy. The accused, aged 69, was a chronic alcoholic. He would later testify that he had already consumed seven or eight bottles of beer in a bar. The complainant drank part of a bottle of brandy and then fell asleep in her wheelchair. When she awoke during the night to go to the bathroom, the accused appeared, grabbed her chair, wheeled her into the bedroom, threw her on the bed and sexually assaulted her. The accused left the apartment at about 4 a.m. The trial judge found that he had drunk the rest of the bottle of brandy between 6 p.m. and 3 a.m. The accused testified he had no recollection of the events until he awoke nude in the complainant's bed. He denied sexually assaulting her. A pharmacologist called as an expert witness for the accused testified that the accused's alcoholic history made him less susceptible to the effects of alcohol. He estimated that if the accused had consumed seven or eight beers and 35 ounces of brandy his blood alcohol level would be between 400 and 600 milligrams per 100 millilitres of blood. That ratio would cause death or a coma in an ordinary person. According to the expert an individual with this level of alcohol in his blood might suffer an episode of "amnesia-automatism or 'blackout'". In such a state the individual loses contact with reality and the brain is temporarily dissociated from normal functioning. The individual has no awareness of his actions and likely no memory of them the next day. According to the witness it is difficult to distinguish between a person in a blackout and one simply acting while intoxicated. The latter state is more likely if the person has departed from his normal behaviour to act in a gratuitous or violent manner.

The trial judge found that the accused had committed the offence described by the complainant. However, he acquitted because he had a reasonable doubt about whether the accused, by virtue of extreme intoxication to the point of automatism within the meaning of the judgment of Wilson J. in *Bernard*, had possessed the minimal intent necessary to commit the offence. The Quebec Court of Appeal allowed the Crown appeal and substituted a conviction. The Quebec Court of Appeal decided the majority of the Supreme Court in *Bernard* had not held that self-induced intoxication resulting in a state akin to automatism or insanity was available as a defence to sexual assault. The accused appealed.

The majority of the Supreme Court allowed the appeal and ordered a new trial.

CORY J. (L'HEUREUX-DUBÉ, MCLACHLIN and IACOBUCCI JJ. concurring): —

Can a state of drunkenness which is so extreme that an accused is in a condition that closely resembles automatism or a disease of the mind as defined in s. 16 of the *Criminal Code*, R.S.C., 1985, c. C-46, constitute a basis for defending a crime which requires not a specific but only a general intent? That is the troubling question that is raised on this appeal.

. . . .

Categorization of Crimes as Requiring Either a Specific Intent or a General Intent

The distinction between crimes of specific and general intent has been acknowledged and approved by this court on numerous occasions.... On this issue, I am in general agreement with Sopinka J.'s presentation. The categorization of crimes as being either specific or general intent offences and the consequences that flow from that categorization are now well-established in this court. However, as he observes, we are not dealing here with ordinary cases of intoxication but with the limited situation of very extreme intoxication and the need, under the *Charter*, to create an exception in situations where intoxication is such that the mental element is negated. Sopinka J. sees no need for such an exception. This is where I must disagree with my colleague.

. . . .

The passage of the *Charter* makes it necessary to consider whether the decision in *Leary* contravenes s. 7 or 11(*d*) of the *Charter*. There have been some statements by this court which indicate that one aspect of the decision in *Leary* does infringe these provisions of the *Charter*. The first occurred in *R. v. Bernard*. . . . Wilson J. (L'Heureux-Dubé J. concurring), agreed with the conclusion reached by McIntyre and Beetz JJ. However, she advocated a modification of the rule set out in *Leary*. Her reasoning proceeds in this way. Sexual assault causing bodily harm is an offence of general intent which requires only a minimal intent to apply force. Ordinarily the Crown can establish the requisite mental state by means of the inferences to be drawn from the actions of the accused. Wilson J. found that the *Leary* rule was perfectly consistent with an onus resting upon the Crown to prove the minimal intent which should accompany the doing of the prohibited act in general intent offences, but she would have applied it in a more flexible form. In her view, evidence of intoxication could properly go before a jury in general intent offences if it demonstrated such extreme intoxication that there was an absence of awareness which was akin to a state of insanity or automatism. Only in such cases would she find that the evidence was capable of raising a reasonable doubt as to the existence of the minimal intent required for a general intent offence.

. . . .

The Alternative Options

What options are available with regard to the admissibility and significance of evidence of drunkenness as it may pertain to the mental element in general intent offences? One choice would be to continue to apply the *Leary* rule. Yet, as I will attempt to demonstrate in the next section, the rule violates the *Charter* and cannot be justified. Thus this choice is unacceptable.

Another route would be to follow *O'Connor* [(1980), 4 A. Crim. R. 348.] Evidence relating to drunkenness would then go to the jury along with all other relevant evidence in determining whether the mental element requirement had been met. It is this path that is enthusiastically recommended by the majority of writers in the field. Yet it cannot be followed. It is now well-established by this court that there are two categories of offences. Those requiring a specific intent and others which call for nothing more than a general intent. To follow *O'Connor* would mean that all evidence of intoxication of any degree would always go to the jury in general intent offences. This, in my view, is unnecessary. Further, in *Bernard, supra*, the majority of this court rejected this approach.

A third alternative, which I find compelling, is that proposed by Wilson J. in *Bernard*. I will examine the justifications for adopting this position in more detail shortly, but before doing that it may be helpful to review the nature of the *Charter* violations occasioned by a rigid application of the *Leary* rule.

How the Leary Rule Violates Sections 7 and 11(d) of the Charter

What then is the rule of law established by the decision in *Leary*? The conclusion of the majority in that case establishes that, even in a situation where the level of intoxication reached by the accused is sufficient to raise a reasonable doubt as to his capacity to form the minimal mental element required for a general intent offence for which he is being tried, he still cannot be acquitted. In such a situation, self-induced intoxication is substituted for the mental element of the crime. The result of the decision in *Leary*, applied to this case, is that the intentional act of the accused to voluntarily become intoxicated is substituted for the intention to commit the sexual assault or for the recklessness of the accused with regard to the assault. This is a true substitution of *mens rea*. First, it would be rare that the events transpiring from the consumption of alcohol through to the commission of the crime could be seen as one continuous series of events or as a single transaction. Secondly, the requisite mental element or *mens rea* cannot necessarily be inferred from the physical act or *actus reus* when the very voluntariness or consciousness of that act may be put in question by the extreme intoxication of the accused.

It has not been established that there is such a connection between the consumption of alcohol and the crime of assault that it can be said that drinking leads inevitably to the assault. Experience may suggest that alcohol makes it easier for violence to occur by diminishing the sense of what is acceptable behaviour. However, studies indicate that it is not in itself a cause of violence.

. . . .

In my view, the strict application of the *Leary* rule offends both ss. 7 and 11(*d*) of the *Charter* for a number of reasons. The mental aspect of an offence, or *mens rea*, has long been recognized as an integral part of crime. The concept is fundamental to our criminal law. That element may be minimal in general intent offences; nonetheless, it exists. In this case, the requisite mental element is simply an intention to commit the sexual assault or recklessness as to whether the actions will constitute an assault. The necessary mental element can ordinarily be inferred from the proof that the assault was committed by the accused. However, the substituted *mens rea* of an intention to become drunk cannot establish the *mens rea* to commit the assault.

R. v. Whyte, [1988] 2 S.C.R. 3, dealt with the substitution of proof of one element for proof of an essential element of an offence and emphasized the strict limitations that must be imposed on such substitutions. The position is put in this way at pp. 18-19:

> In the passage from *Vaillancourt* quoted earlier, Lamer J. recognized that in some cases substituting proof of one element for proof of an essential element will not infringe the presumption of innocence if, upon proof of the substituted element, it would be unreasonable for the trier of fact not to be satisfied beyond a reasonable doubt of the existence of the essential element. This is another way of saying that a statutory presumption infringes the presumption of innocence if it requires the trier of fact to convict in spite of a reasonable doubt. *Only if the existence of the substituted fact leads inexorably to the conclusion that the essential element exists, with no other reasonable possibilities, will the statutory presumption be constitutionally valid.* [Emphasis added.]

The substituted *mens rea* set out in *Leary* does not meet this test. The consumption of alcohol simply cannot lead inexorably to the conclusion that the accused possessed the requisite mental element to commit a sexual assault, or any other crime. Rather, the substituted *mens rea* rule has the effect of eliminating the minimal mental element required for sexual assault. Furthermore, *mens rea* for a crime is so well-recognized that to eliminate that mental element, an integral part of the crime, would be to deprive an accused of fundamental justice. See *R. v. Vaillancourt*, [1987] 2 S.C.R. 636.

. . . .

Sopinka J. refers to the common law rules of automatism in order to support his position that voluntariness is not a requirement of fundamental justice. With respect I cannot agree. The decision of this court in *Revelle v. The Queen*, [1981] 1 S.C.R. 576, predates the *Charter*. The rule that self-induced automatism cannot be a defence has never been subjected to a *Charter* analysis. In my view, automatism raises the same concerns as those presented in this case. Thus, to state that the rule in *Leary*, which precludes the accused from negating the mental element of voluntariness on the basis of an extreme state of intoxication, does not violate the *Charter* because the same principle has been developed in the context of the defence of automatism begs the very question which is now before this court. The presumption of innocence requires that the Crown bear the burden of establishing all elements of a crime. These elements include the mental element of voluntariness. That element cannot be eliminated without violating s. 11(*d*) and s. 7 of the *Charter*.

It was argued by the respondent that the "blameworthy" nature of voluntary intoxication is such that it should be determined that there can be no violation of the *Charter* if the *Leary* approach is adopted. I cannot accept that contention. Voluntary intoxication is not yet a crime. Further, it is difficult to conclude that such behaviour should always constitute a fault to which criminal sanctions should apply. However, assuming that voluntary intoxication is reprehensible, it does not follow that its consequences in any given situation are either voluntary or predictable. Studies demonstrate that the consumption of alcohol is not the cause of the crime. A person intending to drink cannot be said to be intending to commit a sexual assault.

Further, self-induced intoxication cannot supply the necessary link between the minimal mental element or *mens rea* required for the offence and the *actus reus*. This must follow from reasoning in *R. v. DeSousa*, [1992] 2 S.C.R. 944, and *R. v. Theroux, supra.* Here, the question is not whether there is some symmetry between the physical act and the mental element but whether the necessary link exists between the minimal mental element and the prohibited act; that is to say that the mental element is one of intention with respect to the *actus reus* of the crime charged. As well, as Sopinka J. observes, the minimum *mens rea* for an offence should reflect the particular nature of the crime. See *R. v. Creighton*, [1993] 3 S.C.R. 3. I doubt that self-induced intoxication can, in all circumstances, meet this requirement for all crimes of general intent.

In summary, I am of the view that to deny that even a very minimal mental element is required for sexual assault offends the *Charter* in a manner that is so drastic and so contrary to the principles of fundamental justice that it cannot be justified under s. 1 of the *Charter*. The experience of other jurisdictions which have completely abandoned the *Leary* rule, coupled with the fact that under the proposed approach, the defence would be available only in the rarest of cases, demonstrate that there is no urgent policy or pressing objective which need to be addressed. Studies on the relationship between intoxication and crime do not establish any rational link. Finally, as the *Leary* rule applies to all crimes of general intent, it cannot be said to be well-tailored to address a particular objective and it would not meet either the proportionality or the minimum impairment requirements.

. . . .

Far more writers have supported the approach advocated by Dickson J. in *Leary*, and adopted in *O'Connor*. In my view, the most vehement and cogent criticism of both *Majewski* and *Leary* is that they substitute proof of drunkenness for proof of the requisite mental element. The authors deplore the division of crimes into those requiring a specific intent and those which mandate no more than a general intent. They are also critical of the resulting presumption of recklessness, and of the loss of a requirement of a true *mens rea* for the offence. They would prefer an approach that would permit evidence of drunkenness to go to the jury together with all the other relevant evidence in determining whether the requisite *mens rea* had been established.

. . . .

I find further support for adopting the approach suggested by Wilson J. in studies pertaining to the effect of the *O'Connor* and *Kamipeli* decisions which have been undertaken in Australia and New Zealand. (Reference to these studies can be found in the English Law Commission's *Intoxication and Criminal*

Liability, supra, at pp. 60-63.) One of these studies was conducted in New South Wales, by means of a survey of approximately 510 trials (see Judge G. Smith, "Footnote to *O'Connor's* Case", *supra*. The author, Judge George Smith, concluded, at p. 277, that:

> Those figures disclose that a "defence" of intoxication which could not have been relied upon pre-*O'Connor* was raised in 11 cases or 2.16 percent of the total. Acquittals followed in three cases or 0.59 percent of the total, but only in one case or 0.2 percent of the total could it be said with any certainty that the issue of intoxication was the factor which brought about the acquittal.
>
> . . . .
>
> It seems to me that no one with any experience of the criminal courts should be greatly surprised at this result for the simple practical reason that any "defence" of drunkenness poses enormous difficulties in the conduct of a case. To name but one, if the accused has sufficient recollection to describe relevant events, juries will be reluctant to believe that he acted involuntarily or without intent whereas, if he claims to have no recollection, he will be unable to make any effective denial of facts alleged by the Crown.
>
> . . . .
>
> Certainly my inquiries would indicate that the decision in *O'Connor's* case, far from opening any floodgates has at most permitted an occasional drip to escape from the tap.

That study clearly indicates that the *O'Connor* decision has not had an effect of any significance on trials or on the numbers of acquittals arising from evidence of severe intoxication.

. . . .

It is obvious that it will only be on rare occasions that evidence of such an extreme state of intoxication can be advanced and perhaps only on still rarer occasions is it likely to be successful. Nonetheless, the adoption of this alternative would avoid infringement of the *Charter*.

I would add that it is always open to Parliament to fashion a remedy which would make it a crime to commit a prohibited act while drunk.

. . . .

It should not be forgotten that if the flexible "Wilson" approach is taken, the defence will only be put forward in those rare circumstances of extreme intoxication. Since that state must be shown to be akin to automatism or insanity, I would suggest that the accused should be called upon to establish it on the balance of probabilities. This court has recognized, in *R. v. Chaulk*, [1990] 3 S.C.R. 1303, that although it constituted a violation of the accused's rights under s. 11(*d*) of the *Charter*, such a burden could be justified under s. 1. In this case, I feel that the burden can be justified. Drunkenness of the extreme degree required in order for it to become relevant will only occur on rare occasions. It is only the accused who can give evidence as to the amount of alcohol consumed and its effect upon him. Expert evidence would be required to confirm that the accused was probably in a state akin to automatism or insanity as a result of his drinking.

. . . .

Should it be thought that the mental element involved relates to the *actus reus* rather than the *mens rea* then the result must be the same. The *actus reus* requires that the prohibited criminal act be performed voluntarily as a willed act. A person in a state of automatism cannot perform a voluntary willed act since the automatism has deprived the person of the ability to carry out such an act. It follows that someone in an extreme state of intoxication akin to automatism must also be deprived of that ability. Thus a fundamental aspect of the *actus reus* of the criminal act is absent. It would equally infringe s. 7 of the *Charter* if an accused who was not acting voluntarily could be convicted of a criminal offence. Here again the voluntary act of becoming intoxicated cannot be substituted for the voluntary action involved in sexual assault. To do so would violate the principle set out in *Vaillancourt, supra*. Once again to convict in the face of such a fundamental denial of natural justice could not be justified under s. 1 of the *Charter*.

Summary of Proposed Remedy

In my view, the *Charter* could be complied with, in crimes requiring only a general intent, if the accused were permitted to establish that, at the time of the offence, he was in a state of extreme intoxication akin to automatism or insanity. Just as in a situation where it is sought to establish a state of insanity, the accused must bear the burden of establishing, on the balance of probabilities, that he was in that extreme state of intoxication. This will undoubtedly require the testimony of an expert. Obviously, it will be a rare situation where an accused is able to establish such an extreme degree of intoxication. Yet, permitting such a procedure would mean that a defence would remain open that, due to the extreme degree of intoxication, the minimal mental element required by a general intent offence had not been established. To permit this rare and limited defence in general intent offences is required so that the common law principles of intoxication can comply with the *Charter*.

In light of the experience in Australia or New Zealand, it cannot be said that to permit such a defence would open the floodgates to allow every accused who had a drink before committing the prohibited act to raise the defence of drunkenness. As observed earlier, studies made in Australia and New Zealand indicate that there has not been any significant increase in the number of acquittals following the *O'Connor* and *Kamipelli* decisions.

Disposition

In the result, I would allow the appeal, set aside the order of the Court of Appeal and direct a new trial.

LAMER C.J.: — I have read the reasons of my colleagues, Justice Sopinka and Justice Cory. My views of the matter were enunciated through my concurrence in the reasons of Dickson C.J. in *R. v. Bernard*, [1988] 2 S.C.R. 833. While I now prefer characterizing the mental element involved as relating more to the *actus reus* than the *mens rea*, so that the defence clearly be available in strict liability offences, my views have not changed. I agree with my colleague Cory J.'s position on the law and, given my position in *Bernard*, which goes much further, I would of course support carving out, as he does, an exception to the rule laid down in *Leary v. The Queen*, [1978] 1 S.C.R. 29. I would accordingly allow the appeal and direct a new trial.

LA FOREST J.: — In *R. v. Bernard*, [1988] 2 S.C.R. 833, as well as in *R. v. Quin*, [1988] 2 S.C.R. 825, I, along with the Chief Justice, shared the view of then Chief Justice Dickson which strongly challenged the rule in *Leary v. The Queen*, [1978] 1 S.C.R. 29. While the majority of the court differed as to the specific interpretation of *Leary*, what is clear is that they rejected the view espoused by Dickson C.J. I am, therefore, left to choose between the approach set forth in McIntyre J.'s reasons in that case, developed here by Justice Sopinka, and those of Wilson J., developed here by Justice Cory. Of the two, I prefer the latter and accordingly (though I would be inclined to attribute the mental element he describes as going to the *actus reus*) I concur in the reasons of Cory J. and would dispose of this appeal in the manner proposed by him.

SOPINKA J. (GONTHIER and MAJOR JJ. concurring) (dissenting): —

. . . .

Central to [the *Charter*'s] values are the integrity and dignity of the human person. These serve to define the principles of fundamental justice. They encompass as an essential attribute and are predicated upon the moral responsibility of every person of sound mind for his or her acts. The requirement of *mens rea* is an application of this principle. To allow generally an accused who is not afflicted by a disease of the mind to plead absence of *mens rea* where he has voluntarily caused himself to be incapable of *mens rea* would be to undermine, indeed negate, that very principle of moral responsibility which the requirement of *mens rea* is intended to give effect to.

The second requirement of the principles of fundamental justice is that punishment must be proportionate to the moral blameworthiness of the offender. This was held to be a principle of fundamental justice in *R. v. Martineau*, [1990] 2 S.C.R. 633, and *R. v. Creighton*, *supra*. There are a few crimes in respect of which a special level of *mens rea* is constitutionally required by reason of the stigma attaching to a conviction and by reason of the severity of the penalty imposed by law. Accordingly, murder and attempted murder require a *mens rea* based on a subjective standard. No exception from the principle of fundamental justice should be made with respect to these offences and, as specific intent offences, drunkenness is a defence.

By contrast, sexual assault does not fall into the category of offences for which either the stigma or the available penalties demand as a constitutional requirement subjective intent to commit the *actus reus*. Sexual assault is a heinous crime of violence. Those found guilty of committing the offence are rightfully submitted to a significant degree of moral opprobrium. That opprobrium is not misplaced in the case of the intoxicated offender. Such individuals deserve to be stigmatized. Their moral blameworthiness is similar to that of anyone else who commits the offence of sexual assault and the effects of their conduct upon both their victims and society as a whole are the same as in any other case of sexual assault. Furthermore, the sentence for sexual assault is not fixed. To the extent that it bears upon his or her level of moral blameworthiness, an offender's degree of intoxication at the time of the offence may be considered during sentencing. Taking all of these factors into account, I cannot see how the stigma and punishment associated with the offence of sexual assault are disproportionate to the moral blameworthiness of a person like the appellant who commits the offence after voluntarily becoming so intoxicated as to be incapable of knowing what he was doing. The fact that the *Leary* rule permits an individual to be convicted despite the absence of symmetry between the *actus reus* and the mental element of blameworthiness does not violate a principle of fundamental justice.

It is further contended that the *Leary* rule violates the presumption of innocence because it permits an individual to be convicted despite the existence of a reasonable doubt as to whether or not that individual performed the *actus reus* of his or her own volition. This argument is premised upon the assumption that voluntariness is a constitutionally required element of the *actus reus* of an offence of universal application. Again, I do not think that this assumption is warranted.

. . . .

It is true that as a general rule, an act must be the voluntary act of an accused in order for the *actus reus* to exist. See *R. v. Parks*, [1992] 2 S.C.R. 871, at p. 896, per La Forest J., and *R. v. Theroux*, [1993] 2 S.C.R. 5, at p. 17, per McLachlin J. This, as in the case of *mens rea*, is a general rule of the criminal law, but when elevated to a principle of fundamental justice it too, exceptionally, is not absolute. One well-recognized exception is made relating to the defence of non-insane automatism. As I explain below, automatism does not apply to excuse an offence if the accused's state is brought on by his or her own fault.

The condition of automatism deprives the accused of volition to commit the offence but the general rule gives way to the policy that, in the circumstances, the perpetrator who by his or her own fault brings about the condition should not escape punishment. An accused person who voluntarily drinks alcohol or ingests a drug to the extent that he or she becomes an automaton is in the same position. The rules of fundamental justice are satisfied by a showing that the drunken state was attained through the accused's own blameworthy conduct.

Another criticism of the current rules governing the availability of the intoxication defence is that the distinction between offences of specific and general intent is illogical. Critics of the rule contend that there is no principled basis for distinguishing between offences of general and specific intent and thus there is no logical reason why intoxication should be a defence to offences of specific intent but not to offences of general intent.

The appellant does not, however, take issue with the proposition that in general the distinction between offences of specific and general intent is a valid one. His submission is that when drunkenness reaches the stage of automatism, the distinction should no longer apply. This essentially was the tentative view of Wilson J. as expressed in her *obiter* statement in *R. v. Bernard* to which I referred above.

Notwithstanding the position of the appellant, I propose to briefly address the criticism of the rule that it is illogical. In my view, the concept has strong policy underpinnings which, despite the fact that its definition and application may have produced some illogical results, have permitted it to survive for over 150 years in England and to be adopted in Canada and most states of the United States.

. . . .

The principles that emerge from the cases which serve as guidelines in classifying offences as specific or general intent offences are as follows. General intent offences as a rule are those which require the minimal intent to do the act which constitutes the *actus reus*. Proof of intent is usually inferred from the commission of the act on the basis of the principle that a person intends the natural consequences of his or her act. Without attempting to exhaust the policy reasons for excluding the defence of drunkenness from this category of offences, I would observe that it is seldom, even in cases of extreme drunkenness, that a person will lack this minimal degree of consciousness. Moreover, these are generally offences that persons who are drunk are apt to commit and it would defeat the policy behind them to make drunkenness a defence.

Specific intent offences are as a rule those that require a mental element beyond that of general intent offences and include "those generally more serious offences where the *mens rea* must involve not only the intentional performance of the *actus reus* but, as well, the formation of further ulterior motives and purposes" (per McIntyre J. in *R. v. Bernard, supra*, at p. 880). These are often referred to as "ulterior intent" offences. See *Majewski*, *supra*. Professor Colvin, in "A Theory of the Intoxication Defence" (1981), 59 Can. Bar Rev. 750, correctly points out that it is the further intent in addition to the basic intent that is the hallmark of ulterior intent offences. The policy behind this classification is in part the importance of the mental element over and above the minimal intent required for general intent offences. This distinction demands that the accused not be convicted if the added important mental state is negated by the drunken condition of the accused. Failure to prove the added element will often result in conviction of a lesser offence for which the added element is not required. One example is the offence of assault to resist or prevent arrest which is a specific intent offence. Absent the intent to resist arrest, the accused would be convicted of assault *simpliciter*, a general intent offence.

In addition to the ulterior intent offences there are certain offences which by reason of their serious nature and the importance of the mental element are classed as specific intent offences notwithstanding that they do not fit the criteria usually associated with ulterior intent offences. The outstanding example is murder. This is the most serious of criminal offences which carries a fixed penalty. By reason of the importance of the required mental element and the fixed penalty, this offence is classified as a specific intent offence. The defence of drunkenness is allowed so as to reduce the crime to manslaughter tempering the harshness of the law which precludes drunkenness as a consideration as to sentence. The classification of murder as a specific intent offence illustrates the proper application of policy in a case in which the application of the normal criteria might lead to a different result.

I accept that the application of the terms "specific" and "general" may lead to some illogical results. This is not surprising in light of the circumstances outlined above. Moreover, even the clearest unifying principle will in its application not produce perfect harmony. I am, however, convinced that the underlying policy of the *Leary* rule is sound. I am of the opinion that the criticism of the rule on the grounds of illogicality has been overdone. Applying criteria similar to the above, Professor Colvin has been able to explain "the broad pattern of the decisions emanating from the courts". See Colvin, *supra*, at p. 768.

. . . .

Conclusion

For all of these reasons, in my opinion the best course is for the court to reaffirm the traditional rule that voluntary intoxication does not constitute a defence to an offence of general intent, subject to the comments I have made with respect to improvements in the definition and application of the distinction between offences of specific and general intent. If a different approach is considered desirable because the *Leary* approach does not comport with social policy, Parliament is free to intervene. I note that this observation was made by

McIntyre J. in *R. v. Bernard* but Parliament has not intervened. It has been suggested that Parliament should create a new offence of dangerous intoxication. Such a recommendation was made by the Butler Committee in England and by the Law Reform Commission in Canada. (See Butler Committee Report on Mentally Abnormal Offenders (1975) (Cmnd. 6244, paras. 18.51-18.59) and Law Reform Commission of Canada, Recodifying Criminal Law, Report 30, vol. 1 (1986), at pp. 27-28.) Such legislation could be coupled with amendments to the *Criminal Code* to extend the defence of drunkenness to some or all offences to which it does not apply. Such changes, however, are for Parliament and not for this court to make.

In *Majewski*, Lord Elwyn-Jones L.C. summed up the situation in words with which I fully agree. He stated, at p. 475:

> It may well be that Parliament will at some future time consider, as I think it should, the recommendation in the Butler Committee Report on Mentally Abnormal Offenders (Cmnd. 6244, 1975) that a new offence of "dangerous intoxication" should be created. But in the meantime it would be irresponsible to abandon the common-law rule, as "mercifully relaxed," which the courts have followed for a century and a half.

Disposition

The trial judge stated that but for his opinion that the appellant's extreme state of drunkenness constituted a defence, he would have convicted the appellant. I agree with the Court of Appeal that the trial judge erred in law in this regard. The Court of Appeal was right, therefore, to substitute a conviction. I would dismiss the appeal.

The only description of the facts provided by the Supreme Court appears in the judgment of Sopinka J., who indicates that they were "not in dispute". The record appears incomplete. For further details gathered from the Crown factum and from communications with both counsel, see Patrick Healy, "Another Round on Intoxication", published in the Criminal Reports Forum issue on *Daviault*:

> He threw her from the chair onto the bed, began to fondle her under her dressing-gown, and then attempted to rape her. The victim struggled and demanded twice to go to the toilet. The accused insisted that they have sex. He said several times "We are going to make love". He spoke of going to Florida with the victim and more than once he called the victim by a name that was neither hers nor his wife's. He prevented her from going to the toilet and she urinated on him in the bed. When she attempted to call 911 for assistance, he struck her several times in the face with full force. He also struck the telephone from her hand. He pulled her up by her hair and demanded that she perform *fellatio*, at which point she squeezed and twisted his testicles. She testified that he showed no reaction to this. He then fell onto the bed. She dragged herself along the floor and pulled herself into the wheelchair. All this occurred over a period of about an hour. At about 4 a.m. he searched about to find the shirt that he had been wearing when he arrived. He found it, dressed himself and went home.

The victim testified that during the assault the accused did not appear to be drunk but she did state that the bottle of brandy and the glass from which she had been drinking were empty. The wife of the accused testified that Daviault came home at about 4:20 and did not appear to be drunk. He let himself into the house with his key, walked entirely straight, undressed and went to bed. She said that when he came home very drunk he was usually unable to open the door and slept fully dressed after passing out. On this occasion he also appeared quite calm and not "agitated or tormented" as he normally was after drinking strong liquor. She later noticed that his testicles had turned black.

On *Daviault*, see also, in the Criminal Reports, comments by Isabel Grant, Tim Quigley and Don Stuart. See also Martha Shaffer, "Criminal Responsibility and the *Charter:* The Case of *R. v. Daviault*" in Cameron (ed.), *The Charter's Impact on the Criminal Justice System* (1996) pp. 313-325.

The new trial ordered in *Daviault* resulted in a judicial stay of proceedings: (1995), 39 C.R. (4th) 269 (C.Q.). The complainant by then was deceased and disclosure of statements made originally to the police revealed inconsistencies such that the cross-examination would have been quite different. It was held that to proceed would be a denial of natural justice. See comment by Patrick Healy in (1995), 39 C.R. (4th) 272.

Public reaction to *Daviault* was swift. The Minister of Justice, Allan Rock, was reported to be "deeply troubled" by the ruling because of its "tremendous ramifications in sexual assault cases". It was widely condemned as giving the wrong message to those who drink and harm. Commentators used extravagant hypotheticals of rapists getting off on the basis of having had a few drinks. That such views were misreadings of the majority opinion is quite clear.

The number of acquittals that followed *Daviault* was wildly exaggerated.

Later, Martha Drassinower and Don Stuart, "Nine Months of Judicial Application of the *Daviault* Defence" (1995), 39 C.R. (4th) 280, surveyed reported and unreported judgments in the nine months following the Supreme Court's ruling. Eleven *Daviault* defences were considered at trial. Five were successful but two were subsequently reversed on appeal. Given what must have been thousands of criminal cases involving intoxicated accused over that period, the survey provides some validation of Justice Cory's prediction that the defence would be rarely used and would rarely succeed.

On February 24, 1995, the Minister of Justice, Allan Rock, tabled Bill C-72 in the House of Commons, purporting to provide that "extreme intoxication is not a defence to crimes of violence". **Is this amendment wise? Is it constitutional?**

Bill C-72

An Act to amend the *Criminal Code* (self-induced intoxication)

Preamble

WHEREAS the Parliament of Canada is gravely concerned about the incidence of violence in Canadian society;

WHEREAS the Parliament of Canada recognizes that violence has a particularly disadvantaging impact on the equal participation of women and children in society and on the rights of women and children to security of the person and to the equal protection and benefit of the law as guaranteed by sections 7, 15 and 28 of the *Canadian Charter of Rights and Freedoms*;

WHEREAS the Parliament of Canada recognizes that there is a close association between violence and intoxication and is concerned that self-induced intoxication may be used socially and legally to excuse violence, particularly violence against women and children;

WHEREAS the Parliament of Canada recognizes that the potential effects of alcohol and certain drugs on human behaviour are well-known to Canadians and is aware of scientific evidence that many intoxicants, including alcohol, may not cause a person to act involuntarily;

WHEREAS the Parliament of Canada shares with Canadians the moral view that people who, while in a state of self-induced intoxication, violate the physical integrity of others are blameworthy in relation to their harmful conduct and should be held criminally accountable for it;

WHEREAS the Parliament of Canada desires to promote and help to ensure the full protection of the rights guaranteed under sections 7, 11, 15 and 28 of the *Canadian Charter of Rights and Freedoms* for all Canadians, including those who are or may be victims of violence;

WHEREAS the Parliament of Canada considers it necessary to legislate a basis of criminal fault in relation to self-induced intoxication and general intent offences involving violence;

WHEREAS the Parliament of Canada recognizes the continuing existence of a common-law principle that intoxication to an extent that is less than that which would cause a person to lack the ability to form the basic intent or to have the voluntariness required to commit a criminal offence of general intent is never a defence at law;

AND WHEREAS the Parliament of Canada considers it necessary and desirable to legislate a standard of care, in order to make it clear that a person who, while in a state of incapacity by reason of self-induced intoxication, commits an offence involving violence against another person, departs markedly from the standard of reasonable care that Canadians owe to each other and is thereby criminally at fault;

NOW, THEREFORE, Her Majesty, by and with the advice and consent of the Senate and House of Commons of Canada, enacts as follows:

Self-induced Intoxication

When defence not available

33.1 (1) It is not a defence to an offence referred to in subsection (3) that the accused, by reason of self-induced intoxication, lacked the general intent or the voluntariness required to commit the offence, where the accused departed markedly from the standard of care as described in subsection (2).

Criminal fault by reason of intoxication

(2) For the purposes of this section, a person departs markedly from the standard of reasonable care generally recognized in Canadian society and is thereby criminally at fault where the person, while in a state of self-induced intoxication that renders the person unaware of, or incapable of consciously controlling, their behaviour, voluntarily or involuntarily interferes or threatens to interfere with the bodily integrity of another person.

Application

(3) This section applies in respect of an offence under this Act or any other Act of Parliament that includes as an element an assault or any other interference or threat of interference by a person with the bodily integrity of another person.

The effect of this most complex provision is to use a deemed fault provision to remove the *Daviault* defence to most general intent offences. Most such offences involve at least threats to bodily integrity so as to come within the ambit of subsection (3). However, s. 33.1 does not affect the common law defence of drunkenness available to specific intent crimes such as murder and robbery.

Whether s. 33.1 will survive *Charter* review remains to be seen. Lower courts have accepted that s. 33.1 flies in the face of the determination in *Daviault* that principles of fundamental justice require a defence of intoxication where this is akin to automatism. But they are divided on the further question of whether the s. 7 violation can be saved under s. 1 as a demonstrably justified reasonable limit. Rulings of constitutionality were reached in *Vickberg* (1998), 16 C.R. (5th) 164 (B.C. S.C.) and *Decaire* (September 11, 1998), (Ont. Gen. Div.). Section 33.1 was ruled unconstitutional in *Dunn* (1999), 28 C.R. (5th) 295 (Ont. Gen. Div.) and *Brenton* (1999), 28 C.R. (5th) 308 (N.W.T. S.C.). These rulings are fully discussed by Kelly Smith, "Section 33.1: Denial of *Daviault* Defence Should Be Held Constitutional" (2000), 28 C.R. (5th) 350. Lower courts in Ontario now accept that s. 33.1 is unconstitutional: see *R. v. Jensen*, [2000] O.J. No. 4870 (Ont. S.C.); *R. v. Cedeno* (2005), 27 C.R. (6th) 251 (Ont. C.J.); and *R. v. Fleming*, 2010 ONSC

8022. However, courts in some other provinces continue to find that the section can be saved under s. 1: see *R. v. Dow* (2010), 261 C.C.C. (3d) 399 (C.S. Que.) and *R. v. N. (S.)*, 2012 NUCJ. The Ontario Court of Appeal (see *R. v. Jensen* (2005), 27 C.R. (6th) 240 (Ont. C.A.)) and the Supreme Court of Canada have so far declined to rule on this question. The Supreme Court is not yet on record as justifying a s. 7 violation.

On the other hand, in *Mills* (1999), 28 C.R. (5th) 207 (S.C.C.), the Court spoke of a need for dialogue with Parliament which should allow for deference to legislative schemes. Furthermore, *Mills* also recognized that complainants in sexual assault cases have enforceable s. 15 rights which must be balanced not just as a matter of principles of fundamental justice. Isabel Grant, "Second Chances: Bill C-72 and the *Charter*" (1995) 33 Osgoode Hall L.J. 381, argues sex equality considerations should determine that s. 33.1 does not offend s. 7. The clear subtext to the negative reaction and Parliamentary response to *Daviault* was clearly grounded in that context. In *R. v. Dow* (2010), 261 C.C.C. (3d) 399 (Que. S.C.) Huot J. decided in a comprehensive ruling that s. 33.1 was demonstrably justified under s. 1. It was a reasonable alternative and protected vulnerable targets, in particular women and children. Another complication is that evidence was tendered at the Parliamentary committee hearings leading to Bill C-72 refuting the *Daviault* view that intoxication can lead to a state of automatism. See review by Smith, above, at 362-364. See, too, Joseph Wilkinson, "The Possibility of Alcoholic Automatism: Some Empirical Evidence" (1997) 2 Can. Crim. L. Rev. 217. Even if s. 33.1 survives *Charter* review in the Supreme Court, fundamental questions will remain as to the wisdom of the current legal regime for intoxication, rooted, as it still is, in the distinction between specific and general intent.

R. v. DALEY

52 C.R. (6th) 221, 2007 CarswellSask 707, 2007 CarswellSask 708, 226 C.C.C. (3d) 1, [2007] 3 S.C.R. 523

The Court makes it clear that where drunkenness is raised as a defence to a specific intent crime the issue is one of intent in fact rather than incapacity. In his lengthy judgment for the majority (four justices dissented on the basis the trial judge had in his direction to the jury not sufficiently related the law to the evidence) Justice Bastarache introduced new terminology for the different types of intoxication defences:

BASTARACHE J.:—

5.1.2.2 THE LEGALLY RELEVANT DEGREES OF INTOXICATION

41 Our case law suggests there are three legally relevant degrees of intoxication. First, there is what we might call "mild" intoxication. This is where there is alcohol-induced relaxation of both inhibitions and socially acceptable behaviour. This has never been accepted as a factor or excuse in determining whether the accused possessed the requisite *mens rea*. See *Daviault*, at p. 99. Second, there

is what we might call "advanced" intoxication. This occurs where there is intoxication to the point where the accused lacks specific intent, to the extent of an impairment of the accused's foresight of the consequences of his or her act sufficient to raise a reasonable doubt about the requisite *mens rea*. The court in *Robinson* noted that this will most often be the degree of intoxication the jury will grapple with in murder trials:

> In most murder cases, the focus for the trier of fact will be on the foreseeability prong of s. 229(a)(ii) of the *Criminal Code*, R.S.C. 1985, c. C 46, that is, on determining whether the accused foresaw that his or her actions were likely to cause the death of the victim. For example, consider the case where an accused and another individual engage in a fight outside a bar. During the fight, the accused pins the other individual to the ground and delivers a kick to the head, which kills that person. In that type of a case, the jury will likely struggle, assuming they reject any self defence or provocation claim, with the question of whether that accused foresaw that his or her actions would likely cause the death of the other individual. [para. 49]

A defence based on this level of intoxication applies only to specific intent offences.

42 It is important to recognize that the extent of intoxication required to advance a successful intoxication defence of this type may vary, depending on the type of offence involved. This was recognized by this court in *Robinson*, at para. 52, in regards to some types of homicides:

> [I]n cases where the only question is whether the accused intended to kill the victim (s. 229(a)(i) of the *Code*), while the accused is entitled to rely on any evidence of intoxication to argue that he or she lacked the requisite intent and is entitled to receive such an instruction from the trial judge (assuming of course that there is an "air of reality" to the defence), it is my opinion that intoxication short of incapacity will in most cases rarely raise a reasonable doubt in the minds of jurors. For example, in a case where an accused points a shotgun within a few inches of someone's head and pulls the trigger, it is difficult to conceive of a successful intoxication defence unless the jury is satisfied that the accused was so drunk that he or she was not capable of forming an intent to kill.

Although I would hesitate to use the language of capacity to form intent, for fear that this may detract from the ultimate issue (namely, actual intent), the point of this passage, it seems to me, is that, for certain types of homicides, where death is the obvious consequence of the accused's act, an accused might have to establish a particularly advanced degree of intoxication to successfully avail himself or herself of an intoxication defence of this type.

43 The third and final degree of legally relevant intoxication is extreme intoxication akin to automatism, which negates voluntariness and thus is a complete defence to criminal responsibility. As discussed above, such a defence would be extremely rare, and by operation of s. 33.1 of the *Criminal Code*, limited to non-violent types of offences.

The issue of the constitutionality of s. 33.1 was not before the Court in *Daley*.

R. v. BOUCHARD-LEBRUN

2011 CarswellQue 12785, 2011 SCC 58, [2011] 3 S.C.R. 575, 89 C.R. (6th) 1

We earlier considered the ruling that toxic psychosis exclusively resulting from the voluntary consumption of ecstasy pills could not result in a finding of not criminally responsible on account of mental disorder. The Court indicated that no *Charter* challenge had been made to s. 33.1, "which means that only the interpretation and application of that provision are in issue" (para. 28).

LeBel J.: —

[35] In a general sense, the appellant can reasonably argue that Parliament implicitly endorsed Sopinka J.'s dissent in *Daviault* by enacting s. 33.1 *Cr. C.* However, the enactment of that provision did not revive the *Leary* rule. It did not actually codify the position taken by the dissenting judges in *Daviault*; rather, it limited the scope of the rule stated by the majority. This means that the principles set out in *Daviault* still represent the state of the law in Canada, subject, of course, to the significant restriction set out in s. 33.1 *Cr. C. Daviault* would still apply today, for example, to enable an accused charged with a property offence to plead extreme intoxication. Indeed, the fact that the appellant was acquitted at trial on the charges against him under ss. 348(1)(*a*) and 463 *Cr. C.* affords an eloquent example of this.

G.   *Section 33.1 Cr. C. Applies in This Case*

[89] The foregoing conclusion leads to the question whether s. 33.1 *Cr. C.* is applicable. This provision applies where three conditions are met: (1) the accused was intoxicated at the material time; (2) the intoxication was self-induced; and (3) the accused departed from the standard of reasonable care generally recognized in Canadian society by interfering or threatening to interfere with the bodily integrity of another person (see generally *R. v. Vickberg* (1998), 16 C.R. (5th) 164 (B.C.S.C.); *R. v. Chaulk*, 2007 NSCA 84, 257 N.S.R. (2d) 99). Where these three things are proved, it is not a defence that the accused lacked the general intent or the voluntariness required to commit the offence.

[90] The self-induced intoxication to which s. 33.1 *Cr. C.* refers is limited in time. It corresponds to the period during which the substance consumed by the accused produced its effects. Section 33.1(2) *Cr. C.* leaves no doubt about this. It provides that a person "is . . . criminally at fault where the person, while in a state of self-induced intoxication that renders the person unaware of, or incapable

of consciously controlling, their behaviour, voluntarily or involuntarily interferes or threatens to interfere with the bodily integrity of another person". Section 33.1 *Cr. C.* is intended to prevent an accused from avoiding criminal liability on the ground that his or her state of intoxication at the material time *rendered the accused incapable* of forming the mental element or having the voluntariness required to commit the offence.

[91] Section 33.1 *Cr. C.* therefore applies to any mental condition that is a direct extension of a state of intoxication. It is also important to understand that no distinction based on the seriousness of the effects of self-induced intoxication is drawn in this provision. The appellant's suggestion that it applies only to the "normal effects" of intoxication is wrong. There is no threshold of intoxication beyond which s. 33.1 *Cr. C.* does not apply to an accused, which means that toxic psychosis can be one of the states of intoxication covered by this provision. It is so covered in the case at bar. The Court of Appeal therefore did not err in law in holding that s. 33.1 *Cr. C.* was applicable rather than s. 16 *Cr. C.*

It is startling that the Supreme Court proceeds to apply s. 33.1 which Parliament enacted to remove the *Daviault* defence of "extreme intoxication akin to insanity or automatism" from offences of general intent which affect bodily integrity. The Court simply noted the lack of a *Charter* challenge and proceeded to apply the section. Since the Court's majority decision in *Daviault* was squarely based on the view that this limited and rare defence was required by the *Charter* it seems too deferential and meek for the Court to have avoided the issue in this way. **Should the Court have ordered a new hearing with intervenors to consider this controversial issue and to decide whether the Court is still committed to the *Daviault* principles it declared previously?** See Dennis Baker and Rainer Knopff, "*Daviault* Dialogue: The Strange Journey of Canada's Intoxication Defence" (2014) 19.1 Rev. Const. Stud., arguing that the decision in *Bouchard-Lebrun* implicitly finds s. 33.1 constitutional, but that the Court chose not to do so explicitly for strategic purposes, in order to avoid criticism for being too deferential.

Our present law on voluntary intoxication as a defence is excessively complex. It is based on the following rules:

1. In most cases voluntary intoxication will be of no relevance at all because the accused, despite being intoxicated to some degree, will still have acted voluntarily and with the necessary *mens rea*, whatever that might be. This state of intoxication is described as "mild" in *R. v. Daley*, [2007] 3 S.C.R. 523, 226 C.C.C. (3d) 1, 52 C.R. (6th) 221.

2. If the offence is one of specific intent, then it is possible that the accused was intoxicated enough (even voluntarily) not to have formed that intent. In that case the onus is on the Crown to show that the *mens rea* element is proven (as it normally is with regard to all fault elements). This state of intoxication is referred to in *Daley* as "advanced".

3. If the offence is one of general intent then only self-induced intoxication, which is akin to automatism or insanity, will excuse. This will be very rare and will mean that neither the *actus reus* nor *mens rea* elements are made out. The onus of proof is on the accused to establish this claim on balance of probabilities (*Daviault*). This state of intoxication is referred to in *Daley* as "extreme".

4. If the general intent crime is related to bodily integrity s. 33.1 purports to abolish the *Daviault* defence for self-induced intoxication. The Supreme Court has yet to consider a *Charter* challenge to that provision. Lower court decisions conflict as to whether s. 33.1 is saved by s. 1.

See too the careful analysis of Justice Trotter (as he then was) in *R. v. Goard* (2014), 310 C.C.C. (3d) 491 (Ont. S.C.J.), in which several of these rules were in issue given multiple charges but convictions resulted. The bottom line is that you have to be very drunk indeed for the defence ever to be accepted.

In *R. v. Chaulk* (2007), 223 C.C.C. (3d) 174 (N.S. C.A.), Justice Bateman for the Court accepted *obiter* that "self-induced" for s. 33.1 purposes meant "voluntary". The accused "must intend to become intoxicated, either by voluntarily ingesting a substance knowing or having reasonable grounds to know it might be dangerous, or by recklessly ingesting such a substance."

Janine Benedet's C.R. comment is as follows:

> The Nova Scotia Court of Appeal here adopts a blended subjective/objective standard which requires intentional consumption of anything a reasonable person would know to be potentially intoxicating. Although the Court of Appeal declines to apply this test to the facts of this case, an attempt to do so raises some further questions. What if the accused is voluntarily consuming an intoxicant while trying to avoid becoming extremely intoxicated? Consider, for example, the party-goer who declines acid but accepts marijuana, relying on the fact that a small amount of marijuana has never caused him to do anything dangerous or criminal on prior occasions. If the marijuana is laced with acid, and the accused becomes out of control and violent, is this self-induced intoxication? One interpretation of the majority's reasons is that marijuana itself is a potential intoxicant and so the accused is guilty for voluntarily consuming it. Another is that for this accused only the acid is an intoxicant and it was not voluntarily ingested. On the facts of this case, if there was expert evidence that Chaulk's behaviour could not have been caused solely by alcohol, pot and caffeine, does he have a defence? The answer would seem to be "no" because a reasonable person would suspect that a drug offered by a stranger at a party might well be something intoxicating.

> Whether this is a good result depends in part on one's understanding of the reasons for the enactment of s. 33.1. The section is awkwardly drafted, but its underlying point seems to be that the person who voluntarily gets extremely drunk or high and then commits acts of violence has sufficient moral blameworthiness for conviction notwithstanding a lack of intent or volition at the moment of the violent act. Where the person who is trying to get only a little bit intoxicated, but in fact becomes extremely so, fits into this scheme is open to debate. Section 33.1 seems to invoke a standard of gross negligence or "marked departure", while the test articulated in this appeal for when intoxication is self-induced refers only to negligence *simpliciter*. The result seems to be that a person who negligently consumes any intoxicant that leads to violent acts committed in a state of automatism is deemed to be grossly negligent and therefore blameworthy. Note that the use of an objective standard could be avoided here by reliance on wilful blindness, namely that the accused suspected that the substance ingested might be intoxicating, or deliberately failed to inquire as to its contents. This is a concept that seems well suited to persons who point the finger at unnamed strangers bearing pills at parties.

PROBLEM

In the throes of an acrimonious separation, the accused, a cardiologist, stabbed to death his two young children while they were sleeping in their beds.

The evening of the murders the accused consumed windshield-wiper fluid and went on the Internet looking for ways to kill himself. The police found him hiding under his bed the next morning following a 911 call, after the accused spoke of suicide to his mother the previous evening. Had it not been for police, the accused would have likely died on account of the high degree of toxicity of the methanol (wiper fluid) and the substantial quantity he consumed.

From the outset of the trial the accused admitted having caused the deaths of the two children. However, the accused argued that he should be found not criminally responsible on account of his mental condition, which resulted from a combination of an adjustment disorder with anxiety and depressive mood, a suicidal crisis and the methanol intoxication. The only issue, then, was the accused's state of mind at the time of the events. At the same time, the accused knew of the effects of methanol intoxication, so that his intoxication could not be qualified as involuntary.

At the end of the trial, the jury found him not criminally responsible by reason of mental disorder.

The Crown appealed the verdict, arguing that the NCR defence should never have been submitted and the trial judge's jury instructions were deficient on the issue of the NCR defence. Rule.

Compare *R. c. Turcotte* (2013), 6 C.R. (7th) 43 (C.A. Que.), leave to appeal refused 2014 CarswellQue 1700, 2014 CarswellQue 1701 (S.C.C.).

R. v. TATTON

[2015] 2 S.C.R. 574, 323 C.C.C. (3d) 166, 20 C.R. (7th) 221

The accused was alone in his ex-girlfriend's home where he was living in a guest room. He was jealous and upset that she had terminated the relationship. He was drinking heavily and passed out. He woke up and decided to cook bacon. He put oil into a pan on the stove and set it to high. He left to go to Tim Hortons. He returned some 20 minutes later to find the house on fire. He called the fire department. The house and contents were destroyed. The accused was charged with the crime of arson under s. 434 of the *Criminal Code*, which requires proof that the person intentionally or recklessly caused damage by fire or explosion to the property of another.

The trial judge acquitted, holding that arson under s. 434 was a specific intent crime in the circumstances of the case. Given evidence of the accused's intoxication there was a reasonable doubt that he had the ability to connect the dots that fire would be the likely outcome of his actions. The Crown appealed. A majority of the Ontario Court of Appeal dismissed the appeal. According to the majority intentional or reckless arson under s. 434 required proof of specific intent such that the defence of intoxication was properly applied to acquit. The majority insisted on a subjective fault approach and considering the evidence of intoxication there was reasonable doubt as to whether the accused was reckless and actually foresaw the risk of fire in leaving the stove on high. In their view denying the defence of intoxication would require the jury to ignore the reality that the accused had been heavily drinking, and would be to apply an objective test. They pointed out that Parliament had enacted a separate crime of arson by negligence under s. 435. The dissenting judge was of the view that this ignored the established law that drunkenness was only a defence to specific intent crimes and that arson required intent or recklessness.

The Supreme Court of Canada allowed the Crown Appeal and ordered a new trial. They concluded that arson under s. 434 was a general intent crime for which voluntary intoxication was not a defence. The Court took the opportunity to explore afresh the distinction between general and specific intent.

Moldaver J, (McLachlin C.J. and Abella, Rothstein, Cromwell, Wagner and Gascon JJ. concurring);

(b) *The Appropriate Approach to Classifying Specific and General Intent Offences*

[30] The analysis of whether an offence is one of specific or general intent must start with a determination of the mental element of the offence in question. This is an exercise in statutory interpretation. Care should be taken not to turn it into a factual assessment based on the circumstances of the particular case.

[31] After the mental element of the provision has been determined, the next question is whether the crime is one of general or specific intent. The distinction between general and specific intent offences is not a precise science. Logic, intuition, and policy all play a part. The task has proved formidable to those who have been schooled in criminal law, and daunting to those who have not.

[32] Be that as it may, the place to begin in determining the appropriate classification of the offence is to look to existing jurisprudence. Where the jurisprudence has already determined the appropriate classification of the offence in a satisfactory manner, the task is straightforward. For example, this Court has established that sexual assault is a general intent offence, whereas robbery and murder are specific intent offences: see *Leary v. The Queen*, [1978] 1 S.C.R. 29, and *R. v. Chase*, [1987] 2 S.C.R. 293 (sexual assault); *R. v. George*, [1960] S.C.R. 871 (robbery); and *R. v. Cooper*, [1993] 1 S.C.R. 146 (murder). For these offences and for others that have been satisfactorily addressed by existing jurisprudence, there is no need to examine the question again. The framework that follows is meant to clarify, not change the law as set out in *Daviault*. However, if the jurisprudence is unclear, courts must examine the factors outlined in *Daviault*, as clarified below, to resolve the question.

[33] While *Daviault* made clear that there are two main considerations when determining if intoxication short of automatism can be considered — the "importance" of the mental element, and the social policy underlying the offence — it left certain questions unanswered. First, it provided no clear explanation of what is meant by the "importance" of the mental element. Second, it did not specify whether policy considerations should always play a role in the analysis or whether they should only come into play if an examination of the mental element left unclear how the offence should be characterized. I turn to these questions in the hope of bringing some added clarity to an area of the law that continues to perplex and confound.

(i) The "Importance" of the Mental Element

[34] *Daviault* specified that the nature of the mental element and its "relative importance" form the basis for the analysis. Although Sopinka J. did not explain what he meant by the "importance" of the mental element, it is clear that he was referring to the complexity of the thought and reasoning processes that make up the mental element of a particular offence. The thought and reasoning processes for general intent crimes are relatively straightforward. In contrast, specific intent crimes — those crimes with a more "important" mental element — require a more sophisticated reasoning process.

[35] For general intent crimes, the mental element simply relates to the performance of an illegal act. Such crimes do not require an intent to bring about certain consequences that are external to the *actus reus*: *Bernard*, at p. 863; *George*, at p. 877 (per Fauteux J.). Assault is a classic example. The accused must intentionally apply force; however, there is no requirement that he intend to cause injury. Likewise, crimes of general intent do not require actual knowledge of certain circumstances or consequences, to the extent that such knowledge is the product of complex thought and reasoning processes. In each instance, the mental element is straightforward and requires little mental acuity.

[36] To be clear, when I refer to a mental element that is "straightforward" and involving "little mental acuity", I am not creating a new legal standard for general intent offences. Rather, I am using these phrases synonymously with the descriptors used in *Daviault*: "minimal intent" and "minimal degree of consciousness": p. 123.

[37] In contrast, specific intent offences involve a heightened mental element. In *Daviault*, Sopinka J. limited his discussion of specific intent offences to crimes involving an ulterior purpose. For such crimes, the accused must not only intend to do the act that constitutes the *actus reus*, he must also act with an ulterior purpose in mind: Manning and Sankoff, at p. 386. For example, assault with intent to resist arrest is an offence containing an ulterior purpose. The accused must not only commit the assault, he must also act with the ulterior

purpose of resisting arrest. It is irrelevant whether he actually succeeds in resisting arrest; the offence simply requires that he act with that purpose in mind.

[38] Although Sopinka J. restricted his discussion of specific intent offences to crimes involving an ulterior purpose, it would be a mistake to assume that an ulterior purpose is always required. To the contrary, a heightened mental element could take the form of a requirement that the accused intend and bring about certain consequences, if the formation of that intent involves more complex thought and reasoning processes. Murder provides a classic example. Equally, a heightened mental element could take the form of a requirement that the accused have actual knowledge of certain circumstances or consequences, where the knowledge is the product of more complex thought and reasoning processes: see, e.g., M. T. Thornton, "Making Sense of *Majewski*" (1981), 23 *Crim. L.Q.* 464, at p. 482. Possession of stolen property is one such crime. The accused must actually know or be willfully blind to the fact that the goods he or she possesses are stolen. Although this offence contains no ulterior purpose, the knowledge component renders the mental element more acute. Intoxication is therefore available as a defence for such crimes.

[39] To summarize, specific intent offences contain a heightened mental element. That element may take the form of an ulterior purpose or it may entail actual knowledge of certain circumstances or consequences, where the knowledge is the product of more complex thought and reasoning processes. Alternatively, it may involve intent to bring about certain consequences, if the formation of that intent involves more complex thought and reasoning processes. General intent offences, on the other hand, require very little mental acuity.

(ii) The Role of Policy

[40] The second question that *Daviault* left unanswered is the stage at which policy ought to be considered. Confusion remains about whether policy should be considered in every case or whether it should only come into play if an examination of the mental element leaves it unclear how the offence should be characterized.

[41] In my view, the most logical approach is to first examine the nature of the mental element. Only when this analysis fails to yield a clear answer should one turn to policy considerations. As *Daviault* explains, policy considerations are closely tied to the nature of the mental element. General intent crimes involve such minimal mental acuity that it is difficult to see how intoxication short of automatism could deprive the accused of the low level of intent required. This provides a strong policy reason for precluding reliance on intoxication for these offences: *Daviault*, at p. 123. It also explains why it is constitutionally permissible to render the intoxication defence unavailable for general intent offences: *ibid.*, at pp. 99-100. In contrast, one can more readily understand how

the more complex thought and reasoning processes required for specific intent crimes may be negated by an accused's intoxication. For that reason, policy suggests that intoxication can be considered for specific intent crimes. The nature of the mental element is already intertwined with policy considerations. Thus, if an examination of the mental element clearly indicates how the offence should be characterized, there is little reason to resort to policy considerations.

[42] However, if an examination of the mental element does not provide a clear answer, policy considerations may help resolve the question. In the main, the policy assessment will focus on whether alcohol consumption is habitually associated with the crime in question. If it is, then allowing an accused to rely on intoxication as a defence would seem counterintuitive. For example, intoxication is often associated with the crime of sexual assault. Allowing self-induced intoxication to provide an accused with a defence would be to endorse, if not promote, the very behaviour that has historically proved to be a root cause of the problem. And while the law and common sense may not always coincide, we should not be looking for ways to send them scurrying in opposite directions. By the same token, where self-induced intoxication rarely, if ever, plays a role in the commission of a particular crime, preventing an accused from relying on it makes less sense from a policy perspective.

[43] As a general observation, and without setting out a general rule, alcohol habitually plays a role in crimes involving violent or unruly conduct: *Bernard*, at p. 880. It also tends to be prevalent in crimes involving damage to property. As such, it makes little sense from a policy perspective that it should provide a defence for crimes in which people or property are harmed or endangered: *Daviault*, at p. 123. Of course, there are well-established exceptions to this general proposition. Murder, for example, has long been considered a crime of specific intent for which the defence of intoxication is available. As *Daviault* explains, at p. 124, this is a function of the heightened thought and reasoning processes required, the gravity of the offence, the serious fixed punishment upon conviction, and the availability of the lesser included offence of manslaughter. It is therefore incorrect to state that intoxication may never be considered in crimes involving violence against people or damage to property. However, given the prevalence of alcohol in these crimes, there are likely to be strong policy reasons militating against an intoxication-based defence.

[44] Although the main focus of the policy inquiry will be on whether alcohol is habitually associated with the crime in question, there are other residual policy considerations that may also come into play. As noted in *Daviault*, the presence of a lesser included general intent offence in the main offence may be relevant. In such cases, an accused who successfully relies on intoxication to negate the heightened mental element of the main offence can still be convicted of the lesser included offence. Drunkenness will provide no defence to the lesser

offence. For example, an accused who successfully raises intoxication as a defence to a charge of assault with intent to resist arrest may still be convicted of the lesser included offence of assault. In these situations, the intoxicated offender will not escape punishment altogether. Consequently, there is less impetus to preclude the accused from advancing intoxication as a defence to the main offence.

[45] In addition, the presence of judicial sentencing discretion may be a factor to consider. If the crime is one for which the accused will receive a heavy minimum sentence upon conviction, it may be unduly harsh to preclude consideration of intoxication. However, if the judge has discretion to tailor the sentence to the facts of the case and to consider the accused's intoxication as part of that assessment, precluding the accused from advancing a defence of intoxication is less worrisome: *Daviault*, at p. 124.

(2) The Application of the Legal Framework to the Section 434 Offence

[46] The crime of arson has existed for many years, and the *Criminal Code* provisions have gone through many iterations. Over the years, courts have been divided on whether the offence of arson in s. 434 (and its predecessors) is a crime of general or specific intent: see, e.g., *R. v. Swanson* (1989), 48 C.C.C. (3d) 316 (Y.T.C.A.) (specific intent); *R. v. Hudson* (1993), 88 Man. R. (2d) 150 (C.A.) (specific intent); and *R. v. Muma* (1989), 51 C.C.C. (3d) 85 (Ont. C.A.) (general intent), relying on *R. v. Schmidtke* (1985), 19 C.C.C. (3d) 390 (Ont. C.A.).

[47] Applying the framework outlined above to the offence of arson in s. 434, I am satisfied that s. 434 is a general intent offence for which intoxication falling short of automatism is not available as a defence. For convenience, I repeat the provision:

> 434. Every person who intentionally or recklessly causes damage by fire or explosion to property that is not wholly owned by that person is guilty of an indictable offence and liable to imprisonment for a term not exceeding fourteen years.

[48] The *actus reus* is the damaging of property by fire. The mental element is the intentional or reckless performance of the illegal act — the causing of damage to property. No additional knowledge or purpose is needed. No complex thought or reasoning processes are required. On its face, the level of intent required for the offence would appear to be minimal.

[49] A majority of the Court of Appeal was concerned that if s. 434 were found to be a general intent offence, so as to preclude consideration of intoxication short of automatism, that would improperly transform the examination of recklessness into an objective inquiry. With respect, I cannot agree. Recklessness describes the act of one who sees the risk and acts without regard for the

consequences: *Sansregret v. The Queen*, [1985] 1 S.C.R. 570, at p. 582. It always involves a subjective inquiry — and this case is no exception. However, the offence of arson under s. 434 does not involve sophisticated reasoning. The risk of damage by fire is typically obvious, even when it involves a chain of events and not the simple application of a match to the property in question.

[50] I have difficulty seeing how intoxication short of automatism would prevent an accused from foreseeing the risk of causing damage to someone else's property by fire. Complex reasoning is not required to recognize the danger. Thus, preventing an accused from advancing the defence of intoxication does not transform recklessness into an objective inquiry. Rather, it recognizes the fact that intoxication short of automatism will not deprive an accused of the minimal intent required for this crime.

[51] In view of this conclusion, there is no need to resort to policy considerations to determine the availability of the defence of intoxication. However, had I found it necessary to do so, I would have reached the same conclusion.

[52] Section 434 involves damage to property. Damage to property is often associated with alcohol consumption. The present case is no exception. In my view, it would erode the policy underlying the offence of causing damage to property by fire if an accused could rely on self-induced intoxication as a defence.

[53] For these reasons, I am respectfully of the view that the trial judge and the majority of the Court of Appeal erred in characterizing s. 434 as a specific intent offence for which the defence of intoxication could be raised. Properly classified, s. 434 is a general intent offence, meaning that intoxication short of automatism may not be considered.

STEVE COUGHLAN, BRINGING CLARITY TO THE GENERAL/ SPECIFIC INTENT DISTINCTION: *R. v. TATTON*

(2015), 20 C.R. (7th) 240

Whether an offence should be regarded as a general or specific one has long been regarded as a particularly troublesome question in criminal law. The Supreme Court's decision in *Tatton* should go a long way towards clarifying the understanding of that distinction. Much of the previous discussion of specific and general intent has come in divided decisions of the Court, such as *R. v. George*,[17] *R. v. Leary*,[18] or *R. v. Daviault*[19] and indeed often in the decisions of

---

17 [1960] S.C.R. 871, 128 C.C.C. 289, 34 C.R. 1.
18 [1978] 1 S.C.R. 29, 33 C.C.C. (2d) 473.
19 [1994] 3 S.C.R. 63, 93 C.C.C. (3d) 21, 33 C.R. (4th) 165.

dissenting judges in those cases. If for no other reason than that *Tatton* represents an articulation of the rules by a unanimous Court, it is valuable.

The guidance offered by the Court with regard to classifying an offence as general or specific intent is also useful. Much of the confusion in the past, it is submitted, has come from focusing too much on the policy question, and has often reflected what might seem primarily to be goal-directed reasoning. That is, it could sometimes appear as though judges reasoned along lines more or less like this: "because this accused should not have the defence of intoxication, therefore this is a general intent offence" (or, of course, that the defence was specific intent because the defence should be available). *Tatton* makes unambiguous that the approach must look at the offence itself, not the impact on the particular accused: "This is an exercise in statutory interpretation. Care should be taken not to turn it into a factual assessment based on the circumstances of the particular case".[20] Further, although the Court acknowledges that policy factors are, along with the nature of the mental element, one of the two main considerations to be taken into account in deciding whether an offence is general or specific, they are decidedly secondary: "only when this analysis [the nature of the mental element] fails to yield a clear answer should one turn to policy considerations".[21]

The judgment in *Tatton* indicates that it is not intending to create a new standard for deciding whether offences are general or specific, but rather to clarify the existing test. One would hope, therefore, that for example the definitions offered by Justice Ritchie in *George* can still be relied upon: that a general intent relates to "acts done to achieve an immediate end" while specific intent relates to "acts done with the specific and ulterior motive and intention of furthering or achieving an illegal object". Put into question form, this amounts to asking for general intent "did you mean to do that" and for specific intent "why did you do that". Although many judges and commentators have suggested that the distinction is an illogical and troubled one (and there is no doubt that in its treatment in some past decisions that has been true), at the most basic level the difference between those two questions is relatively clear.

Part of the reason for the ructions over the distinction between general and specific intent is that, in and of itself, the distinction has virtually no consequence: it is a different rule, relating to intoxication, that matters. Drawing the general/specific distinction in the abstract is perhaps a useful guide to thinking for judges and lawyers. In considering whether the particular *mens rea* element of an offence has been made out it is necessary to think clearly about exactly what that element is, and terminology is generally useful in thinking clearly about issues. But beyond that it would be of no importance to distinguish the two types of intent, except for the rule relating to intoxication: intoxication is relevant to specific intent but irrelevant to general intent. Indeed, many judges

---

20 *Tatton*, para. 30.
21 *Tatton*, para. 41.

and commentators who argue against the "general/specific" distinction seem, in fact, to have objections to the intoxication rule, not to the distinction itself.[22]

This is a further reason that *Tatton* is a helpful decision. It does identify whether the intoxication defence should or should not be available as one of the – indeed the most important of the – policy considerations to be taken into account. However, policy considerations are firmly relegated to a secondary role, to be taken into account only if the distinction cannot clearly be drawn otherwise. That is as it should be. First, it makes the task simpler. "Should this person benefit from the defence of intoxication" is almost certainly a controversial question, but "am I asking <u>whether</u> the accused meant to do it, or <u>why</u> the accused meant to do it" is likely to be much more straightforward. Second, the proper way to reason in accordance with the rule of law is to ask first what type of offence is in question and then after that ask what the rules say about that type of offence: it is not to start by deciding whether the defence should be available and then inserting the rule which will achieve that result.

That general and specific intents can be readily distinguished in the abstract does not, of course, mean that it is always simple to tell which Parliament meant to set out in any particular offence. That is why, as the Court says, this "is an exercise in statutory interpretation" (para. 30). The Court was understandably reluctant to seem to lay down absolute rules, but one can argue that there are some pretty consistent patterns which assist in the statutory interpretation task. The fact that there are some hard cases does not mean there are no easy ones.

For example, many offences include a requirement that some action was committed to achieve a goal: "with intent to steal", "with intent to commit an indictable offence", "with intent to escape civil or criminal liability" or "for the purpose of compelling another person to abstain from doing anything that he or she has a lawful right to do" (ss. 343(c), 348(1)(a), 252 and 423(1) respectively). There do not seem to be any instances of offences which specify an intent in this way which have been found <u>not</u> to be specific intent offences. *R. v. Hibbert*[23] considered the meaning of "for the purpose of aiding any person to commit it" in a charge of aiding and found that desiring a goal was not an essential feature of having that goal as a purpose, but nothing in that decision suggests the offence is anything but specific intent. So if a statutory provision contains such a specified intent, it seems pretty likely that it will be a specific intent offence.[24]

Conversely, there are very few offences which have been found to be specific intent crimes which do <u>not</u> have such a clause in them, and in those cases there is generally some particular word in the offence which can be taken

---

22 See for example Don Stuart, "*R. v. Tatton:* Case Comment" (2014) 10 C.R. (6th) 108 or Tim Quigley, "Specific and General Nonsense?" (1987) 11 *Dal. L.J.* 75).

23 [1995] 2 S.C.R. 973, 99 C.C.C. (3d) 193, 40 C.R. (4th) 141.

24 Justice Bastarache in *R. v. Kerr*, 2004 SCC 44, [2004] 2 S.C.R. 371, 185 C.C.C. (3d) 1, 20 C.R. (6th) 199 at para. 33 refers to several offences which contain the phrases "with intent to" or "for the purpose of" and suggests: "Every other specific intent crime provision in the *Criminal Code* reads likewise." This is, it will be suggested, a slight overstatement, but only slight.

to implicitly include a goal. Counseling (whether "an offence" in s. 22 or "suicide" in s. 241(a)), for example, requires specific intent despite the fact that the offences in question do not contain any "with intent to" phrase. In that case, though, it is not simply because of some broad-based policy decision, but because of the interpretation of a particular word in the offence: that is, the word "counsel" in itself means not merely to say the words in question ("you should steal that") but to say the words with the intent that they be acted upon (see for example *R. v. Sharpe:*[25] "'[c]ounsel' can mean simply to advise; however in criminal law it has been given the stronger meaning of actively inducing.") So the specific intent in that offence can be tied to the interpretation of a particular term.

As a general proposition, then, the pattern primarily reflected in the case law is that an offence should be considered general intent unless there is something in its wording which seems to add specific intent. This is not to say, of course, that there is no possible scope for ambiguity. Some offences contain words which are notoriously difficult to deal with, such as "wilfully": see *R. v. Buzzanga [and Durocher]*[26] listing half a dozen meanings the word has been given in different offences, at least one of which was to render the offence in question a specific intent one. This means that it could be unclear, in a particular statutory provision, whether an offence containing the word "wilfully" is a general or specific one (see for example *R. v. Schmidtke*[27]). But that does not make the general/specific intent distinction more mysterious than any other piece of statutory interpretation: it is still a question of looking at the words of the statute and seeing whether one or more is meant to invoke a specific intent.

Similarly, sexual assault has been interpreted as a general intent offence in *R. v. Chase,*[28] clearly in very large part with the policy goal of not making intoxication a defence. However, almost uniquely among offences, the elements of sexual assault are nowhere set out in the *Code*, and so Parliament was in effect inviting the Court to interpret the offence in the way it thought most fit. No doubt one could disagree with the Court's conclusion that the offence should be seen as a general intent one, but not on the basis that that interpretation somehow ignores direction given in the statute!

The Court notes that the absence of a general part in the *Code* makes the task of interpreting provisions more difficult, as indeed does the inconsistency in drafting from section to section which is a result of that. But that does not have to mean that it is in principle any more difficult to look at wording to see whether it adds specific intent to an offence than it is to resolve any other matter of interpretation.

---

25 2001 SCC 2, [2001] 1 S.C.R. 45, 150 C.C.C. (3d) 321, 39 C.R. (5th) 72 at para. 56.
26 (1979), 25 O.R. (2d) 705, 49 C.C.C. (2d) 369 (Ont. C.A.).
27 (1985), 19 C.C.C. (3d) 390, 44 C.R. (3d) 392 (Ont. C.A.).
28 [1987] 2 S.C.R. 293, 37 C.C.C. (3d) 97, 59 C.R. (3d) 193.

As noted, the guidelines suggested above are not mentioned by the Court in *Tatton*. However, they are consistent with the result in that case. First, note that in the s. 430 offence of arson in issue there is no explicit "with intent to" clause, unlike arson in s. 435 which requires that the person act "with intent to deprive any other person". If we look for some *actus reus* word which might implicitly incorporate such a desire (as "counsel" does for s. 22), the only possibility is "cause", but that is clearly a non-starter: it is well-established that neither intention nor foreseeability are inherent parts of causing something.[29] Lacking any wording to add specific intent, s. 430 arson remains a general intent crime.

One proposal might be made, which admittedly does differ from what is said in *Tatton* but would be conceptually clearer. The Court notes (in accordance with established law) that some offences are called specific intent because they require "knowledge of certain circumstances" (para. 38) and therefore intoxication is available as a defence even though no ulterior purpose need be proven. Certainly that would be an exception to the guidelines offered above, but conceptually the matter could be regarded in a slightly different way. "Specific intent offences have the defence of intoxication" is not the same thing as "offences with the defence of intoxication are specific intent": that is, there is no obstacle to allowing intoxication to be relevant to whether an accused is guilty of a crime in ways not relating to whether they have specific intent. As noted earlier, the question of classification and the question of the intoxication rule are analytically distinct.

More to the point, "knowledge of circumstances" is not an intent at all, specific or general: it is knowledge. The Crown has to prove all elements of an offence, including knowledge elements, and a person might in fact fail to know some fact ("that person I assaulted was a peace officer" or "those goods I got cheap were stolen"), in which case that person is not guilty. Nothing in that reasoning about a knowledge element requires any classification of some putative "intent" which is nowhere in the wording of the statute. It is hard to see what of value is added to the analysis by incorporating such a step when the reason for the lack of knowledge is due to intoxication.

This is not merely a semantic point about the meaning of "know" compared to "intend". Part of the rationale for not allowing intoxication to be a defence to general intent crimes – indeed, the primary part of the rationale, applicable in all but the most extreme cases – is a factual one: "it is almost metaphysically inconceivable for a person to be so drunk as to be incapable of forming the minimal intent to apply force."[30] In contrast it is routine for ordinary states of intoxication to make people less aware of the facts around them. Treating the

---

29 See for example *R. v. Smithers* (1977), [1978] 1 S.C.R. 506, 34 C.C.C. (2d) 427 or *R. v. Maybin*, 2012 SCC 24, [2012] 2 S.C.R. 30, 283 C.C.C. (3d) 275, 92 C.R. (6th) 221.

30 McIntyre J. in *R. v. Bernard*, [1988] 2 S.C.R. 833, 45 C.C.C. (3d) 1, 67 C.R. (3d) 113 at para. 75, citing *George*.

two situations differently is therefore perfectly natural. Certainly the law has sometimes identified these "failure to prove knowledge" cases as examples of specific intent offences, but it would be both justified and conceptually clearer to recognize that as simply a different situation.

The Court observes that the task of distinguishing general and specific intent offences "has proved formidable to those who have been schooled in criminal law, and daunting to those who have not" (para. 31). The emphasis in *Tatton* on a two-step approach with policy considerations relegated to a secondary role which might potentially not arise at all shows great promise in remedying that state of confusion.

Can the revised approach to statutory interpretation of intent and policy considerations in *Tatton* justify the following current crime classification in Canadian criminal law (taken from Stuart, *Canadian Criminal Law* (7th ed. 2014) pp. 465-467)?

Specific intent	General intent
first or second degree murder	manslaughter
robbery	assaults
theft	sexual assaults
breaking and entry with intent	b & e and committing general intent crime
possess weapon for dangerous purpose	wilful damage to property
aiding or abetting any offence	pointing a firearm
attempting any offence	objective fault crimes

Don Stuart has long been one of the many commentators who view the conceptual distinction between general and specific intent as analytically invalid and not to be relied on to decide whether voluntary intoxication should be considered. S.H. Berner, in a 1971 U.B.C. L. Rev. article referenced by Moldaver J. in *Tatton*, criticizes the "analytical cul-de-sac" as well as anyone:

> Words like "intent" and "intention" are properly used to describe particular states of mind or attitudes which people may hold: which means that all that can be said in any case is that the particular state of mind or attitude in question did or did not exist. It makes no more sense to talk in term of "specific" and "general" intents, than to talk of "large" of "small" intents, or "red" or "white" intents" The adjectives are simply inappropriate. (at 334)

Stuart's law reform preference is for Parliament to enact a General Part declaring what fault element is required for each offence allowing for intoxication to be considered when subjective *mens rea* in any of its forms is required to be proved. For crimes based on objective fault where the test would be the *Charter* standard of a marked departure from the norm, drunkenness should not be considered, as is presently the case for manslaughter, dangerous driving and criminal negligence offences and arson by negligence under s. 436. The assumption on applying the normative objective fault standard is that the reasonable Canadian never drinks alcohol! See further Stuart, *Treatise*, pp. 490-

495 for other reform options such as a special verdict like that for insanity, an independent intoxication offence such as drunk and dangerous and a special verdict of guilty but intoxicated. Such reforms have proved too controversial to have been enacted in any jurisdiction. The anomaly is impaired driving prohibitions in every jurisdiction.

Chapter 7

JUSTIFICATIONS AND EXCUSES

1. WHY ALLOW COMMON LAW DEFENCES?

The reason for preserving common law defences in s. 8(3) in 1955 seems to lie in the acceptance of the pragmatic rationale of the English Royal Commission of 1880 which considered it "if not absolutely impossible, at least not practicable" to anticipate with acceptable precision every future defence. In the following extract Stephen raises another pragmatic consideration with considerable force.

J.F. STEPHEN, THE NINETEENTH CENTURY . . .

Quoted in G.L. Williams, "Necessity" (1978) Crim. L. Rev. 128 at 129-130

It appears to me that the two proposed enactments stand on entirely different principles. After the experience of centuries, and with a Parliament sitting every year, and keenly alive to all matters likely to endanger the public interests, we are surely in a position to say the power of declaring new offences shall henceforth be vested in Parliament only. The power which has at times been claimed for the judges of declaring new offences cannot be useful now, whatever may have been its value in earlier times.

On the other hand it is hardly possible to foresee all the circumstances which might possibly justify or excuse acts which might otherwise be crimes. A long series of authorities have settled certain rules which can be put into a distinct and convenient form, and it is of course desirable to take the opportunity of deciding by the way minor points which an examination of the authorities shows to be still open. In this manner rules can be laid down as to the effect of infancy, insanity, compulsion, and ignorance of law, and also as to the cases in which force may lawfully be employed against the person of another; but is it therefore wise or safe to go so far as to say that no other circumstances than those expressly enumerated shall operate by way of excuse or justification for what would otherwise be a crime? To do so would be to run a risk, the extent of which it is difficult to estimate, of producing a conflict between the *Code* and the moral feelings of the public. Such a conflict is upon all possible grounds to be avoided. It would, if it occurred, do more to discredit codification than anything which would possibly happen, and it might cause serious evils of another kind. Cases sometimes occur in which public opinion is at once violently excited and greatly divided, so that conduct is regarded as criminal or praiseworthy according to the sympathies of excited partisans. If the *Code* provided that nothing should amount to an excuse or justification which was not within the express words of the *Code*, it would, in such a case, be vain to allege that the conduct of the accused person was normally justifiable; that, but for the *Code*, it would have been legally justifiable; that every legal analogy was in its favour; and that the omission of an express provision about it was probably an oversight. I think such a result would be eminently unsatisfactory. I think the public would feel that the allegations referred to ought to have been carefully examined and duly decided upon.

To put the whole matter very shortly, the reason why the common-law definitions of offences should be taken away, whilst the common-law principles as to justification and excuse are kept alive, is like the reason why the benefit of a doubt should be given to a prisoner. The worst result that could arise from the abolition of the common-law offences would be the occasional escape of a person morally guilty. The only result which can follow from preserving the common law as to justification and excuse is, that a man morally innocent, not otherwise protected, may avoid punishment. In the one case you remove rusty spring-guns and man-traps from unfrequented plantations, in the other you decline to issue an order for the destruction of every old-fashioned drag or life-buoy which may be found on the banks of a dangerous river, but is not in the inventory of the Royal Humane Society.

This indeed does not put the matter strongly enough. The continued existence of the undefined common-law offences is not only dangerous to individuals, but may be dangerous to the administration of justice itself. By allowing them to remain, we run the risk of tempting the judges to express their disapproval of conduct which, upon political, moral, or social grounds, they consider deserving of punishment, by declaring upon slender authority that it constitutes an offence at common law; nothing, I think, could place the bench in a more invidious position, or go further to shake its authority.

. . . .

Besides the well-known matters dealt with by the *Code*, there are a variety of speculative questions which have been discussed by ingenious persons for centuries, but which could be raised only by such rare occurrences that it may be thought pedantic to legislate for them expressly beforehand, and rash to do so without materials which the course of events has not provided. Such cases are the case of necessity (two shipwrecked men on one plank), the case of a choice of evils (my horses are running away, and I can avoid running over A only by running over B), and some others which might be suggested.

. . . .

Any ingenious person may divert himself, as Hecato did, by playing with such questions. The Commission acted on the view that in practice the wisest answer to all of them is to say, "When the case actually happens it shall be decided;" and this is effected by the preservation of such parts of the common law as to justification and excuse as are not embodied in the *Code*. Fiction apart, there is at present no law at all upon the subject, but the judges will make one under the fiction of declaring it, if the occasion for doing so should ever arise.

Examples of common law defences recognized by Canadian courts are officially induced error of law, the voluntary intoxication defence to specific intent crimes and, as we shall see in this chapter, necessity, duress and entrapment.

2. AIR OF REALITY FOR DEFENCES

R. v. CINOUS

[2002] 2 S.C.R. 3, 49 C.R. (5th) 209, 162 C.C.C. (3d) 129,
2002 CarswellQue 261, 2002 CarswellQue 262 (S.C.C.)

Per McLachlin C.J.C. and Bastarache J. (L'Heureux-Dube, Gonthier, Binnie, LeBel JJ. concurring): —

Air of Reality

The key issue is whether there was an air of reality to the defence of self-defence in this case. It is our view that there is no air of reality to the defence: a properly instructed jury acting reasonably could not acquit the accused on the ground of self-defence, even if it accepted his testimonial evidence as true. Since the defence should never have been put to the jury, any errors made in the charge to the jury relating to that defence are irrelevant. The curative proviso of s. 686(1)(b)(iii) should be applied, and the conviction upheld.

This court has considered the air of reality test on numerous occasions. The core elements of the test, as well as its nature and purpose, have by now been clearly and authoritatively set out. See *R. v. Osolin*, [1993] 4 S.C.R. 595, 86 C.C.C. (3d) 481, 109 D.L.R. (4th) 478; *R. v. Park*, [1995] 2 S.C.R. 836, 99 C.C.C. (3d) 1; *R. v. Davis*, [1999] 3 S.C.R. 759, 139 C.C.C. (3d) 193, 179 D.L.R. (4th) 385. Nevertheless, a controversy has arisen in this case concerning the extent of a trial judge's discretion to keep from a jury defences that are fanciful or far-fetched. More narrowly, the contentious issue is the correct evidential standard to be applied in determining whether there is an air of reality to the defence of self-defence on the facts of this case.

In our view, the controversy can be resolved on the basis of existing authority, which we consider to be decisive. The correct approach to the air of reality test is well established. The test is whether there is evidence on the record upon which a properly instructed jury acting reasonably could acquit. See *Wu v. The King*, [1934] S.C.R. 609, 62 C.C.C. 90, [1934] 4 D.L.R. 459, *infra*; *R. v. Squire*, [1977] 2 S.C.R. 13, 29 C.C.C. (2d) 497, 69 D.L.R. (3d) 312; *Pappajohn v. The Queen*, [1980] 2 S.C.R. 120, 52 C.C.C. (2d) 481, 111 D.L.R. (3d) 1; *Osolin, supra; Park, supra; R. v. Finta*, [1994] 1 S.C.R. 701, 88 C.C.C. (3d) 417, 112 D.L.R. (4th) 513. This long-standing formulation of the threshold question for putting defences to the jury accords with the nature and purpose of the air of reality test. We consider that there is nothing to be gained by altering the current state of the law, in which a single clearly-stated test applies to all defences. See *Osolin, supra; Park, supra; Finta, supra*. There is no need to invent a new test, to modify the current test, or to apply different tests to different classes of cases.

(1) The Basic Features of the Air of Reality Test

The principle that a defence should be put to a jury if and only if there is an evidential foundation for it has long been recognized by the common law. This venerable rule reflects the practical concern that allowing a defence to go to the jury in the absence of an evidential foundation would invite verdicts not supported by the evidence, serving only to confuse the jury and get in the way of a fair trial and true verdict. Following *Pappajohn, supra*, the inquiry into whether there is an evidential foundation for a defence is referred to as the air of reality test. See *Park, supra,* at para. 11.

The basic requirement of an evidential foundation for defences gives rise to two well-established principles. First, a trial judge must put to the jury all defences that arise on the facts, whether or not they have been specifically raised by an accused. Where there is an air of reality to a defence, it should go to the jury. Second, a trial judge has a positive duty to keep from the jury defences lacking an evidential foundation. A defence that lacks an air of reality should be kept from the jury. *Wu, supra; Squire, supra; Pappajohn, supra; Osolin, supra; Davis, supra*. This is so even when the defence lacking an air of reality represents the accused's only chance for an acquittal, as illustrated by *R. v. Latimer*, [2001] 1 S.C.R. 3, 2001 SCC 1, 150 C.C.C. (3d) 129, 193 D.L.R. (4th) 577.

It is trite law that the air of reality test imposes a burden on the accused that is merely evidential, rather than persuasive. Dickson C.J. drew attention to the distinction between these two types of burden in *R. v. Schwartz*, [1988] 2 S.C.R. 443 at p. 466, 45 C.C.C. (3d) 97, 55 D.L.R. (4th) 1:

> Judges and academics have used a variety of terms to try to capture the distinction between the two types of burdens. The burden of establishing a case has been referred to as the "major burden," the "primary burden," the "legal burden" and the "persuasive burden". *The burden of putting an issue in play has been called the "minor burden," the "secondary burden," the "evidential burden," the "burden of going forward," and the "burden of adducing evidence."* [Emphasis added.]

The air of reality test is concerned only with whether or not a putative defence should be "put in play", that is, submitted to the jury for consideration. This idea was crucial to the finding in *Osolin* that the air of reality test is consistent with the presumption of innocence guaranteed by s. 11(d) of the *Canadian Charter of Rights and Freedoms*.

In applying the air of reality test, a trial judge considers the totality of the evidence, and assumes the evidence relied upon by the accused to be true. See *Osolin, supra; Park, supra*. The evidential foundation can be indicated by evidence emanating from the examination-in-chief or cross-examination of the accused, of defence witnesses, or of Crown witnesses. It can also rest upon the factual circumstances of the case or from any other evidential source on the record. There is no requirement that the evidence be adduced by the accused. See *Osolin, supra; Park, supra; Davis, supra*.

The threshold determination by the trial judge is not aimed at deciding the substantive merits of the defence. That question is reserved for the jury. See *Finta, supra; R. v. Ewanchuk*, [1999] 1 S.C.R. 330, 131 C.C.C. (3d) 481, 169 D.L.R. (4th) 193. The trial judge does not make determinations about the credibility of witnesses, weigh the evidence, make findings of fact, or draw determinate factual inferences. See *R. v. Bulmer*, [1987] 1 S.C.R. 782, 33 C.C.C. (3d) 385, 39 D.L.R. (4th) 641; *Park, supra*. Nor is the air of reality test intended to assess whether the defence is likely, unlikely, somewhat likely, or very likely to succeed at the end of the day. The question for the trial judge is whether the evidence discloses a real issue to be decided by the jury, and not how the jury should ultimately decide the issue.

Whether or not there is an air of reality to a defence is a question of law, subject to appellate review. It is an error of law to put to the jury a defence lacking an air of reality, just as it is an error of law to keep from the jury a defence that has an air of reality. See *Osolin, supra; Park, supra; Davis, supra*. The statements that "there is an air of reality" to a defence and that a defence "lacks an air of reality" express a legal conclusion about the presence or absence of an evidential foundation for a defence.

The considerations discussed above have led this court to reject unequivocally the argument that the air of reality test licenses an encroachment by trial judges on the jury's traditional function as arbiter of fact. As Cory J. stated in *Osolin, supra*, at p. 682:

> This is no more than an example of the basic division of tasks between judge and jury. It is the judge who must determine if evidence sought to be adduced is relevant and admissible. In the same way, it is the judge who determines if there is sufficient evidence adduced to give rise to the defence. If there has been sufficient evidence put forward, then the jury must be given the opportunity to consider that defence along with all the other evidence and other defences left with them in coming to their verdict.

Indeed, the air of reality inquiry has been found not only to be consistent with the traditional division of labour as between judge and jury, but actually to enhance the jury's ability to carry out its task. Again, Cory J.'s statement in *Osolin, supra*, at p. 683, is apposite:

> The jury system has in general functioned exceptionally well. Its importance has been recognized in s. 11(f) of the *Charter*. *One of the reasons it has functioned so very well is that trial judges have been able to direct the minds of jurors* to the essential elements of the offence and *to those defences which are applicable*. That process should be maintained. The charge to the jury must be directed to the essential elements of the crime with which the accused is charged and defences to it. *Speculative defences that are unfounded should not be presented to the jury. To do so would be wrong, confusing, and unnecessarily lengthen jury trials*. [Emphasis added.]

This court has held on many occasions that a single air of reality test applies to all defences. *Osolin, supra; Park, supra*, at para. 12. The test has been applied uniformly to a wide range of defences over the years. These include the defence of honest but mistaken belief in consent in sexual assault cases (*Pappajohn, supra; Bulmer, supra; Osolin, supra; Park, supra; R. v. Esau*, [1997] 2 S.C.R. 777, 116 C.C.C. (3d) 289, 148 D.L.R. (4th) 662; *Ewanchuk, supra; Davis, supra*), and other defences such as intoxication (*R. v. Robinson*, [1996] 1 S.C.R. 683, 105 C.C.C. (3d) 97, 133 D.L.R. (4th) 42; *R. v. Lemky*, [1996] 1 S.C.R. 757, 105 C.C.C. (3d) 137), necessity (*Latimer, supra*), duress (*R. v. Ruzic*, [2001] 1 S.C.R. 687, 2001 SCC 24, 153 C.C.C. (3d) 1, 197 D.L.R. (4th) 577), provocation (*R. v. Thibert*, [1996] 1 S.C.R. 37, 104 C.C.C. (3d) 1, 131 D.L.R. (4th) 675), and self-defence (*Brisson v. The Queen*, [1982] 2 S.C.R. 227, 69 C.C.C. (2d) 97, 139 D.L.R. (3d) 685; *R. v. Hebert*, [1996] 2 S.C.R. 272, 107 C.C.C. (3d) 42, 135 D.L.R. (4th) 577). Adopting different evidential standards for different classes of cases would constitute a sharp break with the authorities.

In dissent Arbour J. (Iacobucci and Major JJ. concurring) sought to revise the approach of the Supreme Court, mainly on her detailed analysis that the air of reality test developed in the context of the mistaken belief defence in sexual assault cases had departed from the common law "no evidence" test for withdrawal from the jury in favour of one of sufficiency of evidence which had usurped the fact-finding function of juries. The "no evidence" test should be adopted for defences such as self-defence especially where there were no special technical or policy considerations, no alternative defences and where it was the accused's only defence. See comment by Stuart, "*Cinous*: The Air of Reality Test Requires Weak Defences to be Withdrawn from Juries" (2002), 49 C.R. (5th) 392.

Whether the defence of self-defence should have been put to the jury in *Cinous* is canvassed later under self-defence.

The Court in *Cinous* only deals with defences without reverse onuses. The accused has a full persuasive burden of proof respecting defences of due diligence for regulatory offences (*Sault Ste. Marie*), officially induced error of law (*City of Lévis*), insanity (s. 16 and *Chaulk*), automatism (*Stone*) and extreme intoxication (*Daviault*). A number of other reverse onuses to establish lawful excuses would be abolished by Bill C-51.

3.   DEFENCE OF PERSON

Since 1892 the important law of self-defence in Canada has been notoriously complex. Former *Criminal Code* ss. 34(1), 34(2), 35 and 37 distinguished between situations of deadly and non-deadly self-defence, defence of those under protection and defence of strangers, and self-defence by an initial aggressor and simple self-defence. Unfortunately the sections were not drafted in parallel fashion to one another and often overlapped in unhelpful ways, so that in practice they were unwieldy. Successive Ministers of Justice ignored calls by the Law Reform Commission of Canada to clarify the law (Report No. 31: *Recodifying Criminal Law* (rev. ed., 1987, p. 36), Chief Justice Lamer in *R. v. McIntosh*, 36 C.R. (4th) 171, [1995] 1 S.C.R. 686 describing the provisions as "unbelievably confusing" and many writings of academics (e.g., Final Report: *Self-defence Review* (Ratushny Report) (1997)). Often appeals were granted and new trials ordered because the trial judge used the wrong section or misinterpreted it.

In practice, defence of person defences often turned on the application of ss. 34(1) and/or (2) which read as follows:

34. (1) Every one who is unlawfully assaulted without having provoked the assault is justified in repelling force by force if the force he uses is not intended to cause death or grievous bodily harm and is no more than is necessary to enable him to defend himself.

(2) Every one who is unlawfully assaulted and who causes death or grievous bodily harm in repelling the assault is justified if

(a) he causes it under reasonable apprehension of death or grievous bodily harm from the violence with which the assault was originally made or with which the assailant pursues his purposes, and

(b) he believes, on reasonable grounds, that he cannot otherwise preserve himself from death or grievous bodily harm.

In 2013 Parliament replaced all of the old self-defence provisions with what is now s. 34.

The old provisions, though badly drafted, had attempted to set out reasonably specific rules: if certain criteria were met then a person was entitled to act in self-defence; if additional criteria were met then that self-defence could involve deadly force; if still other criteria were met then the person could use deadly force despite having started the fight, and so on. The new provision, however, sets out a non-exhaustive list of relevant factors and directs the decision-maker to weigh some or all of them in the balance, with very little guidance.

A *Technical Guide for Practitioners,* published by the government when the new law came into force, notes that although the old law was badly worded it was generally felt that juries nonetheless performed well in sorting out legitimate self-defence claims from spurious ones. The goal of the new provision, therefore, was to make the law correspond to the approach actually taken by juries: "To achieve this objective, *the new defences extract from the old provisions the common core elements of each defence, and codify those core elements in a single simple framework that is capable of assessing a defence claim in any situation*" (emphasis in original). It also notes that:

> Replacing numerous circumstance-specific defences with a single generally-applicable defence means that some of the former threshold requirements are no longer part of the defence as threshold requirements. However, the new laws still allow for consideration of elements which previously served to distinguish the different versions of the defences under the old law. Specifically, *certain defence requirements under the old law (which could have been determinative of whether the defence succeeded or failed) are converted into factors that are not determinative in any case, but which may be taken into account in assessing the core defence elements, where relevant, on a case by case basis.* For instance, under the old self-defence laws, different versions of the defence applied, depending on whether the attack was provoked by the accused or not, whether the accused had a reasonable apprehension of death or not, and where the accused started the confrontation, whether he or she retreated before using deadly force. Under the new generally-applicable defence, these elements are no longer threshold requirements that must be met for the defence to succeed, but they may be relevant considerations to be taken into account depending on the facts of a given case. (emphasis in original)

There are considerations in the previous case law which are not explicitly included, or are ambiguously included, in s. 34. Given that the new section is apparently not intended to change the relevant considerations, but merely remove the rigid structure around the way in which they are to be considered, it seems likely that these factors will continue to be looked at. For example, under the old law the existence of several versions of the defence was in part an attempt to reflect proportionality, in the sense that deadly force could only be used in response to a similarly grave threat, and so on. However, the individual versions did not themselves make reference to proportionality: instead the general approach under s. 34(1) was that the accused could use "no more force than necessary". Courts frequently resorted to the principle that an accused cannot be "expected to weigh to a nicety, the exact measure of defensive action" (*R. v. Baxter* (1975), 27 C.C.C. (2d) 96 (Ont. C.A.)). Under the current law, s. 34(2)(g) simply directs triers of fact to consider the "nature and proportionality" of the response. Despite this wording the Ontario Court of Appeal in *R. v. Cunha*, 2016 ONCA 491, 337 C.C.C. (3d) 7, 29 C.R. (7th) 105 has continued to apply the generous *Baxter* formula to the new s. 34.

Similarly, previous case law gave much thought to whether a person was required to retreat rather than apply force in self-defence. The old provisions explicitly imposed an obligation to retreat on an initial aggressor but were silent about the issue in other circumstances. The courts, however, had long accepted that there was no duty to retreat from one's own home, and indeed in most instances no duty to retreat at all (see for example *R. v. Forde* (2011), 277 C.C.C. (3d) 1, 87 C.R. (6th) 409 (Ont. C.A.) and *R. v. Deegan* (1979), 49 C.C.C. (2d) 417 (Alta. C.A.). "Retreat" is not mentioned explicitly anywhere in s. 34, although s. 34(2)(b) invites consideration of "whether there were other means available to respond to the potential use of force". The relevance – or not – of retreating will need to be sorted out, but early indications suggest that courts are continuing to adopt the same approach as before (see *R. v. Cormier*, below).

An important consideration in the old provisions was whether the assault was provoked or not: in some circumstances a person would be disqualified from claiming self-defence if they had provoked the assault. Similarly, whether the accused was the initial aggressor was a factor which imposed additional obligations before that accused could claim self-defence. Neither of these factors is explicitly included in the new provision, though s. 34(2)(c) invites consideration of "the person's role in the incident".

Section 34 does more than create a new self-defence provision. It makes a person not guilty of "an offence" for performing an "act", not merely for applying force to repel force. Certainly striking a blow to defend against an assault would be included, but potentially so too could be theft (commandeering a car to escape an assault), destruction of property (breaking into a building to escape an assault) or other offences.

A major Supreme Court of Canada decision on self-defence, which was also the first case in Canada to consider the relevance of "battered women's syndrome", was *R. v. Lavallee*, [1990] 1 S.C.R. 852, 76 C.R. (3d) 329. Many of the considerations raised in *Lavallee* have been imported directly into the new s. 34, and it appears to have been quite significant in shaping the new defence. It is therefore likely that, to a very large degree, it will remain good law under the new provision.

R. v. LAVALLEE

[1990] 1 S.C.R. 852, 76 C.R. (3d) 329, 55 C.C.C. (3d) 97, 1990 CarswellMan 198, 1990 CarswellMan 377

The accused was a battered woman in a volatile common-law relationship who killed her partner late one night by shooting him in the back of the head as he left her room. A psychiatrist with extensive professional experience in the treatment of battered wives, Dr. Shane, prepared a psychiatric assessment of the accused which was used in support of her defence of self-defence. The accused was acquitted at trial but the Manitoba Court of Appeal ordered a new trial. On the accused's appeal the Supreme Court of Canada was faced with the decision of the Nova Scotia Court of Appeal in *R. v. Whynot*. That court followed what was then considered to be the law, that it was inherently unreasonable to apprehend death or grievous bodily harm unless and until the physical assault was actually in progress. The Supreme Court of Canada announced a change in the law. It was informed by the expert opinion led at the trial and by books and articles which it read for itself. Notice how the Court reasons; how it judicially notices legislative facts; how it decides the case; how it creates law.

WILSON J. (DICKSON C.J.C. and LAMER, L'HEUREUX-DUBÉ, SOPINKA, GONTHIER and MCLACHLIN JJ. concurring): —

The appellant did not testify but her statement made to police on the night of the shooting was put in evidence. Portions of it read as follows:

> Me and Wendy argued as usual and I ran in the house after Kevin pushed me. I was scared, I was really scared. I locked the door. Herb was downstairs with Joanne and I called for Herb but I was crying when I called him. I said, "Herb come up here please."Herb came up to the top of the stairs and I told him that Kevin was going to hit me actually beat on me again. Herb said he knew and that if I was his old lady things would be different, he gave me a hug. OK, we're friends, there's nothing between us. He said "Yeah, I know" and he went outside to talk to Kevin leaving the door unlocked. I went upstairs and hid in my closet from Kevin. I was so scared. . . My window was open and I could hear Kevin asking questions about what I was doing and what I was saying. Next thing I know he was coming up the stairs for me. He came into my bedroom and said "Wench, where are you?" And he turned on my light and he said "Your purse is on the floor" and he kicked it. OK then he turned and he saw me in the closet. He wanted me to come out but I didn't want to come out because I was scared. I was so scared. [The officer who took the statement then testified that the appellant started to cry at this point and stopped after a minute or two.] He grabbed me by the arm right there. There's a bruise on my face also where he slapped me. He didn't slap me right then, first he yelled at me then he pushed me and I pushed him back and he hit me twice on the right hand side of my head. I was scared. All I thought about was all the other times he used to beat me, I was scared, I was shaking as usual. The rest is a blank, all I remember is he gave me the gun and a shot was fired through my screen. This is all so fast. And then the guns were in another room and he loaded it the second shot and gave it to me. And I was going to shoot myself. I pointed it to myself, I was so upset. OK and then he went and I was sitting on the bed and he started going like this with his finger [the appellant made a shaking motion with an index finger] and said something like "You're my old lady and you do as you're told" or something like that. He said "wait till everybody leaves, you'll get it then" and he said something to the effect of "either you kill me or I'll get you" that was what it was. He kind of smiled and then he turned around. I shot him but I aimed out. I thought I aimed above him and a piece of his head went that way.

. . . .

Expert evidence on the psychological effect of battering on wives and common-law partners must, it seems to me, be both relevant and necessary in the context of the present case. How can the mental state of the appellant be appreciated without it? The average member of the public (or of the jury) can be forgiven for asking: Why would a woman put up with this kind of treatment? Why should she continue to live with such a man? How could she love a partner who beat her to the point of requiring hospitalization? We would expect the woman to pack her bags and go. Where is her self-respect? Why does she not cut loose and make a new life for herself? Such is the reaction of the average person confronted with the so-called "battered wife syndrome". We need help to understand it and help is available from trained professionals.

The gravity, indeed, the tragedy of domestic violence can hardly be overstated. Greater media attention to this phenomenon in recent years has revealed both its prevalence and its horrific impact on women from all walks of life. Far from protecting women from it, the law historically sanctioned the abuse of women within marriage as an aspect of the husband's ownership of his wife and his "right" to chastise her. One need only recall the centuries old law that a man is entitled to beat his wife with a stick "no thicker than his thumb".

Laws do not spring out of a social vacuum. The notion that a man has a right to "discipline" his wife is deeply rooted in the history of our society. The woman's duty was to serve her husband and to stay in the marriage at all costs "till death do us part" and to accept as her due any "punishment" that was meted out for failing to please her husband. One consequence of this attitude was that "wife battering" was rarely spoken of, rarely reported, rarely prosecuted, and even more rarely punished. Long after society abandoned its formal approval of spousal abuse, tolerance of it continued and continues in some circles to this day.

Fortunately, there has been a growing awareness in recent years that no man has a right to abuse any woman under any circumstances. Legislative initiatives designed to educate police, judicial officers and the public, as well as more aggressive investigation and charging policies, all signal a concerted effort by the criminal justice system to take spousal abuse seriously. However, a woman who comes before a judge or jury with the claim that she has been battered and suggests that this may be a relevant factor in evaluating her subsequent actions still faces the prospect of being condemned by popular mythology about domestic violence. Either she was not as badly beaten as she claims or she would have left the man long ago. Or, if she was battered that severely, she must have stayed out of some masochistic enjoyment of it.

. . . .

In my view, there are two elements of the defence under s. 34(2) of the *Code* which merit scrutiny for present purposes. The first is the temporal connection in s. 34(2)(*a*) between the apprehension of death or grievous bodily harm and the act allegedly taken in self-defence. Was the appellant "under reasonable apprehension of death or grievous bodily harm" from Rust as he was walking out of the room? The second is the assessment in s. 34(2)(*b*) of the magnitude of the force used by the accused. Was the accused's belief that she could not "otherwise preserve herself from death or grievous bodily harm" except by shooting the deceased based "on reasonable grounds"?

The feature common to both s. 34(2)(*a*) and s. 34(2)(*b*) is the imposition of an objective standard of reasonableness on the apprehension of death and the need to repel the assault with deadly force. . . .

If it strains credulity to imagine what the "ordinary man" would do in the position of a battered spouse, it is probably because men do not typically find themselves in that situation.

. . . .

It will be observed that subsection 34(2)(*a*) does not actually stipulate that the accused apprehend *imminent* danger when he or she acts. Case law has, however, read that requirement into the defence. . . . The sense in which "imminent" is used conjures up the image of "an uplifted knife" or a pointed gun. The rationale for the imminence rule seems obvious. The law of self-defence is designed to ensure that the use of defensive force is really necessary. It justifies the act because the defender reasonably believed that he or she had no alternative but to take the attacker's life. If there is a significant time interval between the original unlawful assault and the accused's response, one tends to suspect that the accused was motivated by revenge rather than self-defence. In the paradigmatic case of a one-time barroom brawl between two men of equal size and strength, this inference makes sense. How can one feel endangered to the point of firing a gun at an unarmed man who utters a death threat, then turns his back and walks out of the room? One cannot be certain of the gravity of the threat or his capacity to carry it out. Besides, one can always take the opportunity to flee or to call the police. If he comes back and raises his fist, one can respond in kind if need be. These are the tacit assumptions that underlie the imminence rule.

All of these assumptions were brought to bear on the respondent in *R. v. Whynot* (1983), 37 C.R. (3d) 198, 9 C.C.C. 449 (N.S.C.A.). The respondent, Jane Stafford, shot her sleeping common-law husband as he lay passed out in his truck. The evidence at trial indicated that the deceased "dominated the household and exerted his authority by striking and slapping the various members and from time to time administering beatings to Jane Stafford and the others" (at p. 452). The respondent testified that the deceased threatened to kill all of the members of her family, one by one, if she tried to leave him. On the night in question he threatened to kill her son. After he passed out, the respondent got one of the many shotguns kept by her husband and shot him. The Nova Scotia Court of Appeal held that the trial judge erred in leaving s. 37 (preventing assault against oneself or anyone under one's protection) with the jury. The court stated at p. 464:

> I do not believe that the trial Judge was justified in placing s. 37 of the *Code* before the jury any more than he would have been justified in giving them s. 34. Under s. 34 the assault must have been underway and unprovoked, and under s. 37 the assault must be such that it is necessary to defend the person assaulted by the use of force. No more force may be used than necessary to prevent the assault or the repetition of it. In my opinion, no person has the right in anticipation of an assault that may or may not happen, to apply force to prevent the imaginary assault.

The implication of the court's reasoning is that it is inherently unreasonable to apprehend death or grievous bodily harm unless and until the physical assault is actually in progress, at which point the victim can presumably gauge the requisite amount of force needed to repel the attack and act accordingly. In my view, expert testimony can cast doubt on these assumptions as they are applied in the context of a battered wife's efforts to repel an assault.

The situation of the appellant was not unlike that of Jane Stafford in the sense that she too was routinely beaten over the course of her relationship with the man she ultimately killed. According to the testimony of Dr. Shane these assaults were not entirely random in their occurrence.

. . . .

The cycle described by Dr. Shane conforms to the Walker Cycle Theory of Violence named for clinical psychologist, Dr. Lenore Walker, the pioneer researcher in the field of the battered wife syndrome. Dr. Shane acknowledged his debt to Dr. Walker in the course of establishing his credentials as an expert at trial. Dr. Walker first describes the cycle in the book *The Battered Woman* (1979). In her 1984 book, *The Battered Woman Syndrome*, Dr. Walker reports the results of a study involving 400 battered women. Her research was designed to test empirically the theories expounded in her earlier book. At pp. 95-96 of *The Battered Woman Syndrome* she summarizes the Cycle Theory as follows:

A second major theory that was tested in this project is the Walker Cycle Theory of Violence (Walker, 1979). This tension reduction theory states that there are three distinct phases associated in a recurring battering cycle: (1) tension building, (2) the acute battering incident, and (3) loving contrition. During the first phase, there is a gradual escalation of tension displayed by discrete acts causing increased friction such as name-calling, other mean intentional behaviours, and/or physical abuse. The batterer expresses dissatisfaction and hostility but not in an extreme or maximally explosive form. The woman attempts to placate the batterer, doing what she thinks might please him, calm him down, or at least, what will not further aggravate him. She tries not to respond to his hostile actions and uses general anger reduction techniques. Often she succeeds for a little while which reinforces her unrealistic belief that she can control this man . . .

The tension continues to escalate and eventually she is unable to continue controlling his angry response pattern. "Exhausted from the constant stress, she usually withdraws from the batterer, fearing she will inadvertently set off an explosion. He begins to move more oppressively toward her as he observes her withdrawal. . . . Tension between the two becomes unbearable" (Walker, 1979, p. 59). The second phase, the acute battering incident, becomes inevitable without intervention. Sometimes, she precipitates the inevitable explosion so as to control where and when it occurs, allowing her to take better precautions to minimize her injuries and pain.

"Phase two is characterized by the uncontrollable discharge of the tensions that have built up during phase one" (p. 59). The batterer typically unleashes a barrage of verbal and physical aggression that can leave the woman severely shaken and injured. In fact, when injuries do occur it usually happens during this second phase. It is also the time police become involved, if they are called at all. The acute battering phase is concluded when the batterer stops, usually bringing with its cessation a sharp physiological reduction in tension. This in itself is naturally reinforcing. Violence often succeeds because it does work.

In phase three which follows, the batterer may apologize profusely, try to assist his victim, show kindness and remorse, and shower her with gifts and/or promises. The batterer himself may believe at this point that he will never allow himself to be violent again. The woman wants to believe the batterer and, early in the relationship at least, may renew her hope in his ability to change. This third phase provides the positive reinforcement for remaining in the relationship, for the woman. In fact, our results showed that phase three could also be characterized by an absence of tension or violence, and no observable loving-contrition behaviour, and still be reinforcing for the woman.

Dr. Walker defines a battered woman as a woman who has gone through the battering cycle at least twice. As she explains in her introduction to The Battered Woman at p. xv, "Any woman may find herself in an abusive relationship with a man once. If it occurs a second time, and she remains in the situation, she is defined as a battered woman".

Given the relational context in which the violence occurs, the mental state of an accused at the critical moment she pulls the trigger cannot be understood except in terms of the cumulative effect of months or years of brutality.

. . . .

Another aspect of the cyclical nature of the abuse is that it begets a degree of predictability to the violence that is absent in an isolated violent encounter between two strangers. This also means that it may in fact be possible for a battered spouse to accurately predict the onset of violence before the first blow is struck, even if an outsider to the relationship cannot. Indeed, it has been suggested that a battered woman's knowledge of her partner's violence is so heightened that she is able to anticipate the nature and extent (though not the onset) of the violence by his conduct beforehand. In her article "Potential Uses for Expert Testimony: Ideas Toward the Representation of Battered Women Who Kill" (1986), 9 Women's Rights Law Reporter 227, psychologist Julie Blackman describes this characteristic at p. 229:

> Repeated instances of violence enable battered women to develop a continuum along which they can "rate" the tolerability or survivability of episodes of their partner's violence. Thus, signs of unusual violence are detected. For battered women, this response to the ongoing violence of their situations is a survival skill. Research shows that battered women who kill experience remarkably severe and frequent violence relative to battered women who do not kill. They know what sorts of danger are familiar and which are novel. They have had myriad opportunities to develop and hone their perceptions of their partner's violence. And, importantly, they can say what made the final episode of violence different from the others: they can name the features of the last battering that enabled them to know that this episode would result in life-threatening action by the abuser.

. . . .

Where evidence exists that an accused is in a battering relationship, expert testimony can assist the jury in determining whether the accused had a "reasonable" apprehension of death when she acted by explaining the heightened sensitivity of a battered woman to her partner's acts. Without such testimony I am skeptical that the average fact-finder would be capable of appreciating why her subjective fear may have been reasonable in the context of the relationship. After all, the hypothetical "reasonable man" observing only the final incident may have been unlikely to recognize the batterer's threat as potentially lethal. Using the case at bar as an example the "reasonable man" might have thought, as the majority of the Court of Appeal seemed to, that it was unlikely that Rust would make good on his threat to kill the appellant that night because they had guests staying overnight.

The issue is not, however, what an outsider would have reasonably perceived but what the accused reasonably perceived, given her situation and her experience.

Even accepting that a battered woman may be uniquely sensitized to danger from her batterer, it may yet be contended that the law ought to require her to wait until the knife is uplifted, the gun pointed or the fist clenched before her apprehension is deemed reasonable. This would allegedly reduce the risk that the woman is mistaken in her fear, although the law does not require her fear to be correct, only reasonable. In response to this contention, I need only point to the observation made by Huband J.A. that the evidence showed that when the appellant and Rust physically fought the appellant "invariably got the worst of it". I do not think it is an unwarranted generalization to say that due to their size, strength, socialization and lack of training, women are typically no match for men in hand-to-hand combat. The requirement imposed in *Whynot* that a battered woman wait until the physical assault is "underway" before her apprehensions can be validated in law would, in the words of an American Court, be tantamount to sentencing her to "murder by installment". . . . I share the view expressed by M.J. Willoughby in "Rendering Each Woman Her Due: Can a Battered Woman Claim Self-Defense When She Kills Her Sleeping Batterer" (1989), 38 Kan. L. Rev. 169, at p. 184, that "society gains nothing, except perhaps the additional risk that the battered woman will herself be killed, because she must wait until her abusive husband instigates another battering episode before she can justifiably act".

. . . .

Subsection 34(2) requires an accused who pleads self-defence to believe "on reasonable grounds" that it is not possible to otherwise preserve him or herself from death or grievous bodily harm. The obvious question is if the violence was so intolerable, why did the appellant not leave her abuser long ago? This question does not really go to whether she had an alternative to killing the deceased at the critical moment. Rather, it plays on the popular myth already referred to that a woman who says she was battered yet stayed with her batterer was either not as badly beaten as she claimed or else she liked it. Nevertheless, to the extent that her failure to leave the abusive relationship earlier may be used in support of the proposition that she was free to leave at the final moment, expert testimony can provide useful insights. Dr. Shane attempted to explain in his testimony how and why, in the case at bar, the appellant remained with Rust:

> She had stayed in this relationship, I think, because of the strange, almost unbelievable, but yet it happens, relationship that sometimes develops between people who develop this very disturbed, I think, very disturbed quality of a relationship. Trying to understand it, I think, isn't always easy and there's been a lot written about it recently, in the recent years, in psychiatric literature. But basically it involves two people who are involved in what appears to be an attachment which may have sexual or romantic or affectionate overtones.
>
> And the one individual, and it's usually the women in our society, but there have been occasions where it's been reversed, but what happens is the spouse who becomes battered, if you will, stays in the relationship probably because of a number of reasons.
>
> One is that the spouse gets beaten so badly — so badly — that he or she loses the motivation to react and becomes helpless and becomes powerless. And it's also been shown sometimes, you know, in — not that you can compare animals to human beings, but in laboratories, what you do if you shock an animal, after a while it can't respond to a threat of its life. It becomes just helpless and lies there in an amotivational state, if you will, where it feels there's no power and there's no energy to do anything.
>
> So in a sense it happens in human beings as well. It's almost like a concentration camp, if you will. You get paralyzed with fear.
>
> The other thing that happens often in these types of relationships with human beings is that the person who beats or assaults, who batters, often tries — he makes up and begs for forgiveness. And this individual, who basically has a very disturbed or damaged self-esteem, all of a sudden feels that he or she — we'll use women in this case because it's so much more common — the spouse feels that she again can do the spouse a favour and it can make her feel needed and boost her self-esteem for a while and make her feel worthwhile and the spouse says he'll forgive her and whatnot.

Apparently, another manifestation of this victimization is a reluctance to disclose to others the fact or extent of the beatings. For example, the hospital records indicate that on each occasion the appellant attended the emergency department to be treated for various injuries she explained the cause of those injuries as accidental. Both in its address to the jury and in its written submissions before this court the Crown insisted that the appellant's injuries were as consistent with her explanations as with being battered and, therefore, in the words of Crown counsel at trial, "the myth is, in this particular case, that Miss Lavallee was a battered spouse". In his testimony Dr. Shane testified that the appellant admitted to him that she lied to hospital staff and others about the cause of her injuries. In Dr. Shane's opinion this was consistent with her overall feeling of being trapped and helpless.

. . . .

The account given by Dr. Shane comports with that documented in the literature. Reference is often made to it as a condition of "learned helplessness", a phrase coined by Dr. Charles Seligman, the psychologist who first developed the theory by experimenting on animals in the manner described by Dr. Shane in his testimony. A related theory used to explain the failure of women to leave battering relationships is described by psychologist and lawyer Charles Patrick Ewing in his book, Battered Women Who Kill (1987). Ewing describes a phenomenon labelled "traumatic bonding" that has been observed between hostages and captors, battered children and their parents, concentration camp prisoners and guards, and batterers and their spouses.

. . . .

I emphasize at this juncture that it is not for the jury to pass judgment on the fact that an accused battered woman stayed in the relationship. Still less is it entitled to conclude that she forfeited her right to self-defence for having done so. I would also point out that traditional self-defence doctrine does not require a person to retreat from her home instead of defending herself: *R. v. Antley*, (1964), 42 C.R. 384, [1964] 2 C.C.C. 142 (C.A.). A man's home may be his castle but it is also the woman's home even if it seems to her more like a prison in the circumstances.

If, after hearing the evidence (including the expert testimony), the jury is satisfied that the accused had a reasonable apprehension of death or grievous bodily harm and felt incapable of escape, it must ask itself what the "reasonable person" would do in such a situation. The situation of the battered woman as described by Dr. Shane strikes me as somewhat analogous to that of a hostage. If the captor tells her that he will kill her in three days time, is it potentially reasonable for her to seize an opportunity presented on the first day to kill the captor or must she wait until he makes the attempt on the third day? I think the question the jury must ask itself is whether, given the history, circumstances and perceptions of the appellant, her belief that she could not preserve herself from being killed by Rust that night except by killing him first was reasonable. To the extent that expert evidence can assist the jury in making that determination, I would find such testimony to be both relevant and necessary.

. . . .

Obviously the fact that the appellant was a battered woman does not entitle her to an acquittal. Battered women may well kill their partners other than in self-defence. The focus is not on who the woman is, but on what she did. In "The Meaning of Equality for Battered Women Who Kill Men in Self-Defense"

(1985), 8 *Harv. Women's L. J.* 121, at 149, Phyllis Crocker makes the point succinctly:

> The issue in a self-defence trial is not whether the defendant is a battered woman, but whether she justifiably killed her husband. The defendant introduces testimony to offer the jury an explanation of reasonableness that is an alternative to the prosecution's stereotypic explanations. It is not intended to earn her the status of a battered woman, as if that would make her not guilty.

The trial judge, to his credit, articulated the same principle when introducing Dr. Shane's testimony in the course of his instructions to the jury. After referring to "the so-called battered spouse syndrome", he cautions:

> Let me say at the outset that I think it is better that we try not to attach labels to this. It doesn't matter what we call it. What is important is the evidence itself and how it impacts on the critical areas of the intent of the accused and the issue of self-defence.

. . . .

I would accordingly allow the appeal, set aside the order of the Court of Appeal, and restore the acquittal.

One of the key findings of *Lavallee* was that "imminence" of an assault was not a requirement of self-defence. Section 34(2)(b) now says that a court "shall consider. . .the extent to which the use of force was imminent". **Has the statute changed the law on this point?** (See the conclusion in *R. v. Ball*, 2013 BCSC 2371, reversed 2014 BCCA 120, para. 33 [B.C. S.C.] that "there must be evidence of a present use of force or a threat of force that is imminent".)

For comments by Donna Martinson, Marilyn MacCrimmon, Isabel Grant and Christine Boyle see "A Forum on Lavallee v. R.: Women and Self-Defence" (1991) 25 U.B.C. Law Rev. 23-68.

Although *Lavallee* has been widely heralded there have been some concerns expressed. Some question the reliability of the opinion of the expert given that it was based on so much hearsay evidence and that the trial Crown expected to have an opportunity to cross-examine the accused, but she was not called. The heavy reliance on the expert testimony as to the "cycle of learned helplessness" has produced the criticism that the particular research relied upon is suspect and unduly restrictive: see Neil Vidmar, "One or Many Words for a Camel? An Overview on Judicial Evaluation of Social Science Evidence", a paper presented to a Canadian Institute for the Administration of Justice conference, October 13-16, 1993. There is also the perspective that resting on expert medical opinion potentially medicalizes the problem and discounts the voice of the particular woman. This is very well-expressed by Professor Isabel Grant:

> A fundamental problem with developing a category like the "battered woman syndrome" is that we risk transforming the reality of this form of gender oppression into a psychiatric disorder. The victim of spousal violence becomes the abnormal actor, the one whose conduct must be explained by the expert. When a woman uses force to defend herself, it is evaluated with reference to a

male standard of reasonableness or to an exceptional standard for certain women, *i.e.*, those who are "battered women". The focus is on the irrationality of a woman's response and on the need for medical terminology to transform that irrational response into a reasonable one for a "battered woman". She must either be reasonable "like a man" or reasonable "like a battered woman". Trapped in this dichotomy, the "reasonable" woman may disappear.

The research of Dr. Lenore Walker, relied on by the Court in *Lavallee*, has been scathingly denounced:

> The battered woman syndrome illustrates all that is wrong with the law's use of science. The working hypothesis of the battered woman syndrome was first introduced in Lenore Walker's 1979 book, *The Battered Woman*. When it made its debut, this hypothesis had little more to support it beyond the clinical impressions of a single researcher. Five years later, Walker published a second book that promised a more thorough investigation of the hypothesis. However, this book contains little more than a patchwork of pseudo-scientific methods employed to confirm a hypothesis that its author and participating researchers never seriously doubted.

(Faigman and Wright, "The Battered Woman Syndrome in the Age of Science" (1997) 39 Arizona L. Rev. 67. See, further, Alan Gold's Netletter (ADGN/97-253 and ADGN/97-038). See, too, David Paciocco, *Getting Away with Murder; the Canadian Criminal Justice System* (Irwin Law, 1999), who dismisses the battered women's syndrome theory as "junk science" and little more than public interest advocacy dressed in the imposing garb of "study, experimentation and psychobabble" that imperils justice (p. 306).)

R. v. MALOTT

[1998] 1 S.C.R. 123, 121 C.C.C. (3d) 456,
1998 CarswellOnt 419, 1998 CarswellOnt 420

The accused was charged with murder. The accused and the deceased had lived as common-law spouses for almost 20 years. The deceased abused the accused physically, sexually, psychologically and emotionally. On the day of the shooting the accused was scheduled to go to a medical centre with the deceased to get prescription drugs for use in his illegal drug trade. She took a pistol from the deceased's gun cabinet. After driving to the medical centre she shot him to death. She then took a taxi to the deceased's girlfriend's home, shot her and stabbed her with a knife.

At trial, the accused testified to the extensive abuse which she had suffered and led expert evidence to show that she suffered from battered woman syndrome.

The jury found her guilty of second degree murder in the death of the deceased and of attempted murder of his girlfriend. The majority of the Court of Appeal affirmed the convictions. There was no air of reality to the defence of self-defence as it related to the charge of attempted murder. With respect to the deceased, the jury was clearly instructed that the perception of the accused, developed against the background of her abuse, was required to be assessed in determining if her actions were reasonable self-defence. The accused appealed, complaining about the adequacy of the trial judge's charge to the jury on the murder charge on the issue of battered woman syndrome as a defence.

The Supreme Court was unanimous in dismissing the appeal on the basis that the trial judge's charge on self-defence and the evidence of abuse while not perfect was adequate. There was a noteworthy *obiter* by the two female members of the Court.

L'HEUREUX-DUBÉ J. (MCLACHLIN J. concurring): —

... [G]iven that this court has not had the opportunity to discuss the value of evidence of "battered woman syndrome" since *R. v. Lavallee*, [1990] 1 S.C.R. 852 (S.C.C.), and given the evolving discourse on "battered woman syndrome" in the legal community, I will make a few comments on the importance of this kind of evidence to the just adjudication of charges involving battered women.

First, the significance of this court's decision in *Lavallee*, which first accepted the need for expert evidence on the effects of abusive relationships in order to properly understand the context in which an accused woman had killed her abusive spouse in self-defence, reaches beyond its particular impact on the law of self-defence. A crucial implication of the admissibility of expert evidence in *Lavallee* is the legal recognition that historically both the law and society may have treated women in general, and battered women in particular, unfairly. *Lavallee* accepted that the myths and stereotypes which are the products and the tools of this unfair treatment interfere with the capacity of judges and juries to justly determine a battered woman's claim of self-defence, and can only be dispelled by expert evidence designed to overcome the stereotypical thinking. The expert evidence is admissible, and necessary, in order to understand the reasonableness of a battered woman's perceptions, which in *Lavallee* were the accused's perceptions that she had to act with deadly force in order to preserve herself from death or grievous bodily harm. Accordingly, the utility of such evidence in criminal cases is not limited to instances where a battered woman is pleading self-defence, but is potentially relevant to other situations where the reasonableness of a battered woman's actions or perceptions is at issue (e.g. provocation, duress or necessity). See *R. v. Hibbert*, [1995] 2 S.C.R. 973 (S.C.C.), at p. 1021.

It is clear from the foregoing that "battered woman syndrome" is not a legal defence in itself such that an accused woman need only establish that she is suffering from the syndrome in order to gain an acquittal. As Wilson J. commented in *Lavallee*, at p. 890: "Obviously the fact that the appellant was a battered woman does not entitle her to an acquittal. Battered women may well kill their partners other than in self-defence." Rather, "battered woman syndrome" is a psychiatric explanation of the mental state of women who have been subjected to continuous battering by their male intimate partners, which can be relevant to the legal inquiry into a battered woman's state of mind. Second, the majority of the court in *Lavallee* also implicitly accepted that women's experiences and perspectives may be different from the experiences and perspectives of men. It accepted that a woman's perception of what is reasonable is influenced by her gender, as well as by her individual experience, and both are relevant to the legal inquiry. This legal development was significant, because it demonstrated a willingness to look at the whole context of a woman's experience in order to inform the analysis of the particular events. But it is wrong to think of this development of the law as merely an example where an objective test — the requirement that an accused claiming self-defence must *reasonably* apprehend death or grievous bodily harm — has been modified to admit evidence of the subjective perceptions of a battered woman. More important, a majority of the court accepted that the perspectives of women, which have historically been ignored, must now equally inform the "objective" standard of the reasonable person in relation to self-defence.

When interpreting and applying *Lavallee*, these broader principles should be kept in mind. In particular, they should be kept in mind in order to avoid a too rigid and restrictive approach to the admissibility and legal value of evidence of a battered woman's experiences. Concerns have been expressed that the treatment of expert evidence on battered women syndrome, which is itself admissible in order to combat the myths and stereotypes which society has about battered women, has led to a new stereotype of the "battered woman": see, e.g., Martha Shaffer, "The Battered Woman Syndrome Revisited: Some Complicating Thoughts Five Years After *R. v. Lavallee*" (1997), 47 U.T.L.J. 1, at p. 9; Sheila Noonan, "Strategies of Survival: Moving Beyond the Battered Woman Syndrome", in Ellen Adelberg and Claudia Currie, eds., *In Conflict with the Law: Women and the Canadian Justice System* (1993), 247, at p. 254; Isabel Grant, "The 'Syndromization' of Women's Experience", in Donna Martinson, et al., "A Forum on *Lavallee v. R.*: Women and Self-Defence" (1991), 25 U.B.C.L. Rev. 23, at pp. 53-54; and Martha R. Mahoney, "Legal Images of Battered Women: Redefining the Issue of Separation" (1991), 90 Mich. L. Rev. 1, at p. 42.

It is possible that those women who are unable to fit themselves within the stereotype of a victimized, passive, helpless, dependent, battered woman will not have their claims to self-defence fairly decided. For instance, women who have demonstrated too much strength or initiative, women of colour, women who are professionals, or women who might have fought back against their abusers on previous occasions, should not be penalized for failing to accord with the stereotypical image of the archetypal battered woman. See, e.g., Julie Stubbs and Julia Tolmie, "Race, Gender, and the Battered Woman Syndrome: An Australia Case Study" (1995), 8 C.J.W.L. 122. Needless to say, women with these characteristics are still entitled to have their claims of self-defence fairly adjudicated, and they are also still entitled to have their experiences as battered women inform the analysis. Professor Grant, *supra*, at p. 52, warns against allowing the law to develop such that a woman accused of killing her abuser must either have been "reasonable 'like a man' or reasonable 'like a battered woman'". I agree that this must be avoided. The "reasonable woman" must not be forgotten in the analysis, and deserves to be as much a part of the objective standard of the reasonable person as does the "reasonable man".

How should the courts combat the "syndromization", as Professor Grant refers to it, of battered women who act in self-defence? The legal inquiry into the moral culpability of a woman who is, for instance, claiming self-defence must focus on the *reasonableness* of her actions in the context of her personal experiences, and her experiences as a woman, not on her status as a battered woman and her entitlement to claim that she is suffering from "battered woman syndrome". This point has been made convincingly by many academics reviewing the relevant cases: see, e.g., Wendy Chan, "A Feminist Critique of Self-Defense and Provocation in Battered Women's Cases in England and Wales" (1994), 6 Women & Crim. Just. 39, at pp. 56-57; Elizabeth M. Schneider, "Describing and Changing: Women's Self-Defense Work and the Problem of Expert Testimony on Battering" (1992), 14 Women's Rts. L. Rep. 213, at pp. 216-17; and Marilyn MacCrimmon, "The Social Construction of Reality and the Rules of Evidence", in Donna Martinson et al., *supra*, at pp. 48-49. By emphasizing a woman's "learned helplessness", her dependence, her victimization, and her low self-esteem, in order to establish that she suffers from "battered woman syndrome", the legal debate shifts from the objective rationality of her actions to preserve her own life to those personal inadequacies which apparently explain her failure to flee from her abuser. Such an emphasis comports too well with society's stereotypes about women. Therefore, it should be scrupulously avoided because it only serves to undermine the important advancements achieved by the decision in *Lavallee*.

There are other elements of a woman's social context which help to explain her inability to leave her abuser, and which do not focus on those characteristics most consistent with traditional stereotypes. As Wilson J. herself recognized in *Lavallee*, at p. 887, "environmental factors may also impair the woman's ability to leave — lack of job skills, the presence of children to care for, fear of retaliation by the man, etc. may each have a role to play in some cases." To this list of factors I would add a woman's need to protect her children from abuse, a fear of losing custody of her children, pressures to keep the family together, weaknesses of social and financial support for battered women, and no guarantee that the violence would cease simply because she left. These considerations necessarily inform the reasonableness of a woman's beliefs or perceptions of, for instance, her lack of an alternative to the use of deadly force to preserve herself from death or grievous bodily harm.

How should these principles be given practical effect in the context of a jury trial of a woman accused of murdering her abuser? To fully accord with the spirit of *Lavallee*, where the reasonableness of a battered woman's belief is at issue in a criminal case, a judge and jury should be made to appreciate that a battered woman's experiences are both individualized, based on her own history and relationships, as well as shared with other women, within the context of a society and a legal system which has historically undervalued women's experiences. A judge and jury should be told that a battered woman's experiences are generally outside the common understanding of the average judge and juror, and that they should seek to understand the evidence being presented to them in order to overcome the myths and stereotypes which we all share. Finally, all of this should be presented in such a way as to focus on the reasonableness of the woman's actions, without relying on old or new stereotypes about battered women.

My focus on women as the victims of battering and as the subjects of "battered woman syndrome" is not intended to exclude from consideration those men who find themselves in abusive relationships. However, the reality of our society is that typically, it is women who are the victims of domestic violence, at the hands of their male intimate partners. To assume that men who are victims of spousal abuse are affected by the abuse in the same way, without benefit of the research and expert opinion evidence which has informed the courts of the existence and details of "battered woman syndrome", would be imprudent.

There has been relatively little consideration of the substance of the current self-defence provisions by Courts of Appeal, because courts have generally concluded that the old provisions continued to govern factual situations that arose before the new law took effect. Decisions interpreting the current provisions are beginning to appear.

R. v. CORMIER

(2017), 348 C.C.C. (3d) 97, 37 C.R. (7th) 63 (N.B. C.A.)

Cormier was charged with second degree murder after he stabbed and killed another man, Eldridge. There had been a series of text messages between the two, in the course of which Eldridge repeatedly verbally and possibly physically threatened Cormier, challenged him to a fight, and appeared at the home of Cormier's father, where Cormier had locked himself inside. After a hostile exchange through the ground-floor window in which Eldridge, accompanied by another person, tried to get Cormier to come out, Eldridge left the scene. However, Eldridge and his companion reappeared a few hours later, having threatened by text message to smash every window in the apartment unless Cormier paid an alleged debt. Cormier, accompanied by his father and by a friend, went outside: Cormier and the friend had knives, while Cormier's father had a metal pipe. There was conflicting evidence over the exact sequence of events, but there was evidence that Eldridge swung at Cormier with a pipe and that Cormier stabbed Eldridge, resulting in his death.

Cormier was convicted of murder at trial and appealed on the basis that the self-defence provision was not properly explained to the jury. In particular Cormier argued that the jury had been left with the understanding that, by leaving the apartment, he forfeited any self-defence claim. The New Brunswick Court of Appeal agreed that that was an incorrect view of the law and ordered a new trial.

Richard and Baird JJ.A. (Larlee J.A. concurring):

[40] Section 34(1) enumerates three criteria, all of which must be present for the defence to be available. In other words, self-defence is not applicable if the prosecution proves beyond a reasonable doubt that one of these criteria has not been met. They are:

1) Reasonable belief: the accused must reasonably believe that force or threat of force is being used against him or someone else (the subjective perception is objectively verified);

2) Defensive purpose: the subjective purpose for responding to the threat must be to protect oneself or others (this is a subjective state of mind); and

3) Reasonable response: the act committed must be reasonable in the circumstances (this is objectively assessed).

See *R. v. Bengy*, 2015 ONCA 397, [2015] O.J. No. 2958, at para. 28.

[41] The amendment codifies two elements of self-defence flowing from the Supreme Court's decision in *R. v. Lavallee*, [1990] 1 S.C.R. 852, [1990] S.C.J. No. 36; one being that imminence of the attack is not a rigid requirement in order for the defence to succeed, but is a factor to be considered when assessing the reasonableness of an accused's response; the other being the nature of the abusive relationship between the accused and the victim is also a factor when assessing the reasonableness of the accused's actions.

[42] The notion of "unlawful" assault as a requirement of the defence under the now repealed provisions is eliminated. Substituted is the concept of a reasonable perception of force or threat of force. In addition, the assessment of the reasonableness of the accused's response to a threat has changed. The Supreme Court in *R. v. Gunning*, 2005 SCC 27, [2005] 1 S.C.R. 627, had suggested that reasonableness could be substituted for the concept of "no more force than necessary" (para. 22). Whether an action is reasonable is now assessed through the lens of the nine non-exhaustive factors set out in s. 34(2).

[43] Professor Kent Roach, in an article titled A Preliminary Assessment of the New Self-Defence and Defence of Property Provisions 2012, 16 Canadian Criminal Law Review 275, comments on what he calls the "heart of the new

self-defence and defence of property" provisions; comments with which we agree. He states:

> The heart of the new self-defence and defence of property resides in section 34(1)(c) and section 35(1)(d) which respectively require that acts in defence of self and others and property be "reasonable in the circumstances." These requirements will be the critical and perhaps illusive issue in most cases. The new provisions, however, offer little guidance in determining this issue. In the case of self-defence, the new section 34(2) simply instructs the trier of fact to consider nine enumerated but non-exhaustive factors. In the case of defence of property, no legislative guidance is provided in determining what may be reasonable in the circumstances. One is tempted to suggest that the new section 34(2) offers too much in terms of factors that must be considered in determining whether the act was reasonable while section 35 fails to offer any guidance at all. The result in both cases, however, is the same. The reasonableness of any particular act will be seen as a prototypical question of judgment that is associated with jury determinations, whether or not the trial is one of those rare ones that is conducted with a jury. In other words, any assessment of the new provisions must of necessity be preliminary. The courts will have to flesh out the meaning of reasonableness and its relation to the previous self-defence and defence of property provisions in cases to come.

[44] Justice David Paciocco, in a paper titled The New Defence Against Force (2014), 18 Canadian Criminal Law Review 269, comments on the new self-defence provision as follows:

> Without question, this new defence against force is not only simpler than the pre-existing law of self-defence and defence of another, but it is also more generous. This is so even though the three fixed factual prerequisites now found in section 34 also existed for each of the now defunct self-defence provisions. What makes it possible for the new provision to operate more generously in cases of self-defence is the flexibility of its evaluative component. The old law variously imposed rigid fixed preconditions to self-defence including the absence of provocation, proportionality (commensurate force); necessity (required force); and even in some cases an attempt to quit or to flee. While decision-makers must consider similar factors under the new provisions, decision-makers now have discretion on the impact such factors will have, leaving them free to grant the defence in their absence, something not possible under the old law.

> Even though the prospect has been called more theoretical than real, there are also times when self-defence and defence of another could fail under the new provisions where they could have succeeded under the old. To take a simple example, some of the existing provisions permitted excessive force, even if it was not commensurate with the assault being defended against. The current law imposes no such limits, permitting the decision-maker to convict because the force used in self-defence exceeds the force that was threatened. Similarly, previous provisions used a narrow concept of provocation, permitted provocation to be considered in only some cases, and only then to determine what factors could be considered. Provocation was not an evaluative factor in its own right. Now the role of the accused in the incident, including but not limited to provocation, is an evaluative factor that the decision-maker is free to use in all cases. This makes it entirely possible for an accused to be denied the defence because he was the author of his own misfortune even when the previous provisions would not have allowed this to be considered.

[45] Early caselaw interpreting the amendment in question echoes the sentiment that the new self-defence provision appears to be easier to apply than its

predecessor. In *R. v. Levy*, 2016 NSCA 45, [2016] N.S.J. No. 211, Beveridge J.A. states:

> [...] On its face, the defence is far simpler. One section applies to all forms of self-defence. If there is an air of reality to self-defence, no offence is committed unless the Crown disproves at least one of the following: 1) that the accused believed on reasonable grounds that force or a threat of force was being used or made against them or another person; 2) the accused's acts were done for the purpose of defending or protecting themselves or another; 3) the act was reasonable in the circumstances. For the latter element, the trier of fact is directed to take into account the non-exclusive list of nine factors found in s. 34(2). [...] [para. 107]

[46] In a Technical Guide For Practitioners released by the Department of Justice titled Reforms to Self-Defence and Defence of Property: Technical Guide for Practitioners, Department of Justice, Canada, March 2013, the authors note that Parliament's intention was to simplify the legislative text; however, the amendment is not meant to substantially alter the principles of self-defence. In truth, however, the new provisions have substantially altered the principles of self-defence. In *R. v. Evans*, 2015 BCCA 46, [2015] B.C.J. No. 189, Frankel J.A. concludes the new provisions mark a substantive change in the law resulting in a more generous application which could lead to more acquittals than under the old regime. We agree.

. . . .

[54] In our respectful view, Crown's counsel's proposition that self-defence was not available because Mr. Cormier chose to open the door is one that is incorrect in law. At the very least, Mr. Cormier's decision to open the door would simply be one of the various factors to consider in determining the reasonableness of his response to the threats against his person. At no time, however, does the opening of the door to confront the aggressor, of itself, constitute a "barrier to self-defence". In our view, on a reasonable interpretation of the evidence in this particular case, Mr. Cormier's decision to open the door is irrelevant to the reasonableness of his response to the attack by Mr. Eldridge. We explain below.

[55] Crown counsel's argument at trial that Mr. Cormier should not have removed the barrier between himself and those who wanted to do him harm is analogous to those cases in which it has been argued that one has an obligation to retreat in the face of aggression. We therefore begin with a review of common law principles that govern those cases. Quite conveniently, Watt J.A. recently undertook the same review in *R. v. Sinclair*, 2017 ONCA 38. While he did so in the context of the self-defence provisions under the former s. 34(2) of the *Criminal Code*, some of the principles are nevertheless relevant to the present case. Recall that, under the former s. 34(2), self-defence was available in the face of an unlawful assault (by either the actual application of force or an attempt or threat, by act or gesture, to apply force), the reasonable apprehension of a risk of death or grievous bodily harm from the assault or its pursuit and a

reasonable belief that is not possible to preserve oneself from harm except by killing or seriously injuring the attacker. In *Sinclair*, prosecution counsel put to the jury that the accused had had ample opportunity to get away and the trial judge had, in his charge to the jury, addressed the question of retreat by telling the jury that "[w]hile there is no obligation on the defendant to retreat, the issue of retreat, whether a defendant could retreat, may be a relevant consideration in determining whether the defendant believed on reasonable grounds that he could not otherwise preserve himself from death or grievous bodily harm". Watt J.A. reviewed the governing principles in terms we readily adopt:

> A brief reminder about the obligation to retreat and the significance of evidence of a failure to do so when self-defence is put forward as a justification for killing another will assist in the resolution of this ground of appeal.

> First, former s. 34(2) does not, in express terms or by necessary implication, contain any reference to retreat. The subsection imposes no obligation on the self-defence claimant to retreat. In this respect, the former s. 34(2) differs from the former s. 35: *R. v. Cain*, 2011 ONCA 298, 278 C.C.C (3d) 228, at para. 9; *R. v. Abdalla*, 2006 BCCA 210, 209 C.C.C. (3d) 172, at para. 25; *Proulx*, at para. 44. Former s. 34(2) does not differ from the common law where retreat before using force is not an independent and imperative condition of a successful plea of self-defence: *R. v. Howe* (1958), 100 C.L.R. 448 (H.C.A.), at pp. 462-63.

> Second, the possibility of retreat is relevant to the second and third elements of the justification afforded by the former s. 34(2). In other words, the possibility of retreat is a relevant item of evidence for the jury to consider in deciding whether the accused:

> > i. had a reasonable apprehension of death or grievous bodily harm from the victim's assaultive conduct; and

> > ii. had a reasonable belief that it was not otherwise possible to save him or herself from death or grievous bodily harm except by killing or seriously harming the victim.

> See *Cain*, at para. 9; *Proulx*, at paras 47-49

> Third, the relevance of failure to retreat on these issues may disappear when an accused had no real opportunity to do so. The absence of any real opportunity to retreat may require an instruction that the accused's failure to do so is not relevant to the jury's assessment of the claim of self-defence: *Abdalla*, at para. 26.

> Fourth, where Crown counsel misstates the relevance of retreat, or failure to retreat, as for example by telling the jury that the accused is precluded from relying on self-defence because he had failed to retreat when the confrontation began, the trial judge would be required to give the jury a correcting instruction: *Cain*, at para. 11; *Proulx*, at para. 50; *Abdalla*, at para. 27.

> Finally, even where Crown counsel has not expressly misstated the relevance of retreat, a trial judge should consider whether a corrective instruction may be necessary to alleviate the risk that the jury may have understood the Crown to be making such an erroneous submission: *Cain*, at para. 11; *Proulx*, at para. 50. [paras. 84-89]

[56] *Sinclair* was a case in which the accused shot the victim to death in front of a bus shelter. Additional principles apply when an incident occurs in one's

home. In *R. v. Forde*, 2011 ONCA 592, [2011] O.J. No. 4049, LaForme J.A., for the Court, discusses retreat in this context. He notes it is well-established at common law that a person has "the right to defend him or herself in his or her own home without the duty to retreat from the home in face of an attack" (para. 38). He explains that retreat in anticipation of an attack is a factor for the jury to consider in assessing the reasonableness of self-defence but, in the case of an attack while in one's own home, not only is there no requirement to retreat, but "[r]ather, far from retreating, [an accused] would [also] have been entitled ... to use such force as was necessary to remove the complainant therefrom" (para. 42, quoting from *R. v. Antley* [1963] O.J. No. 853 (C.A.). LaForme J.A. also points to decisions of the British Columbia Court of Appeal, including *R. v. Proulx*, [1998] B.C.J. No. 1708 (C.A.), in which it was held that it is "a reversible error for the trial judge to fail to point out that the accused was not required to consider fleeing from his house" (para. 45).

[57] The case law generally speaks of one not having to retreat from one's own home. The rationale behind the principle that one does not have to retreat from one's own home is that one is legally entitled to use force to remove an intruder. The *Citizen's Arrest and Self-Defence Act* preserves this right for those in peaceable possession of property. Not only that, it extends the same right to one who is lawfully assisting a person whom they believe on reasonable grounds is in peaceable possession of property. Thus, under s. 35, not only could Mr. Cormier Sr. act to prevent Messrs. Eldridge and Beckingham from entering his property, but Mr. Cormier was legally entitled to assist him in doing so. As was stated in *Antley* and repeated in *Forde*, rather than requiring retreat in those circumstances, the law allows a person to use such force as necessary to remove the intruder. [Editors' note: *Cormier* is discussed again in the next section, dealing with s. 35 and Defence of Property.]

. . . .

[59] In our view, the principles governing "retreat" outlined above have analogous application to the present case. Here, prosecution counsel did not technically suggest Mr. Cormier had an obligation to retreat from his father's home. What counsel argued was that Mr. Cormier should have stayed inside the apartment and kept the door closed between himself and Mr. Eldridge. In some circumstances, that argument, if limited to addressing the factor to be considered under s. 34(2)(b), might be justified. However, the present circumstances do not justify that argument when one considers s. 35 of the *Criminal Code*. Mr. Cormier was lawfully entitled to assist his father in preventing an intrusion into the latter's apartment.

[60] Moreover, and of critical importance, Crown counsel at trial went further than simply arguing Mr. Cormier's failure to stay inside undermined his claim that his act vis-à-vis Mr. Eldridge was reasonable in the circumstances. Crown

counsel actually argued Mr. Cormicr's failure to remain inside negated self-defence. Such a claim clearly constitutes a misstatement of the law. As Watt J.A. points out in *Sinclair*, such a misstatement requires the trial judge to give a correcting instruction.

[61] Recall that Professor Roach alluded to cases in which there might be an overlap between defence of property and self-defence. In our view, this is one of those cases. The evidence revealed that Mr. Eldridge had repeatedly threatened Mr. Cormier over the course of the day. Twice Mr. Cormier retreated. After the last of these, Mr. Eldridge sent Mr. Cormier more threatening texts following which Messrs. Eldridge and Beckingham returned to the Cormier residence. Section 35 of the *Criminal Code* provides that one who believes they are in peaceable possession of property or who is assisting one who is in such possession and who believes on reasonable grounds that another person "is about to enter [...] the property without being entitled by law to do so" or is about to damage the property is justified to act to prevent this if the act is reasonable in the circumstances.

[62] Had the jurors been instructed on the application of s. 35, there is no question that, on a reasonable interpretation of the evidence, it would have been open for them to conclude that, when he armed himself with a knife and opened the door, Mr. Cormier did exactly what the law allows him to do under s. 35: use reasonable force to prevent Messrs. Eldridge and Beckingham from entering or damaging the property under the peaceful possession of Mr. Cormier Sr. Had the jury made this finding, it would have been holding that, when Mr. Cormier armed himself and opened the door to prevent an intrusion into his father's home, Mr. Cormier was properly acting in defence of property. Had the jury found that Mr. Cormier was justified in doing what he did up to that point, how can it be said that the door was a barrier to self-defence? The need for self-defence arguably only arose when Mr. Cormier reasonably apprehended the threat of imminent bodily harm when he saw Mr. Eldridge, armed with a pipe, coming at him. It is only at that point that Mr. Cormier used his knife to stab Mr. Eldridge.

[63] In our view, the jury should have been told that Mr. Cormier was lawfully entitled to repel Messrs. Eldridge and Beckingham from entering into or damaging Mr. Cormier Sr.'s home, provided what he did to that end was reasonable in the circumstances. There was no evidence the actual stabbing was done in defending Mr. Cormier Sr.'s property, which explains why defence counsel did not ask the judge to leave defence of property with the jury as a self-standing defence against the charge. The evidence, in its most favourable interpretation for Mr. Cormier, revealed that, when he struck out with the knife, it was to defend himself against Mr. Eldridge's imminent attack. This is quite possibly a case in which what began as the defence of property quickly morphed

into the defence of one's person. In these circumstances, the door was certainly not a barrier to self-defence and the factor set out in s. 34(2)(b) had no real application.

. . . .

[65] . . .Even if the jury held Mr. Cormier was, throughout the events, acting only to defend his person, his decision to open the door and to confront Mr. Eldridge would be but one factor to consider in assessing the reasonableness of Mr. Cormier's actions. The door would not constitute, of itself, a "barrier to self-defence".

The accused and his co-accused were inmates in a penitentiary. There had been considerable tension between the accused and a group of other inmates. The group had made threats that the accused took seriously. Fearing for his safety and anticipating an attack, the accused armed himself with knuckledusters and a stick. The co-accused got a knife. When one of the group members walked by, the accused hit him on the head repeatedly with the knuckledusters, while the co-accused stabbed him in the stomach. The injuries were fatal. The accused and co-accused were charged with first degree murder. In his charge to the jury the trial judge stated that the accused and the co-accused could not claim the defence of self-defence under s. 34(2) unless they believed that they were in imminent danger of death or serious bodily harm from the victim at the time they attacked him. The jury convicted the accused of manslaughter and the co-accused of second degree murder. On appeal the accused argued that the trial judge erred in his direction on s. 34(2). They argued they suffered from "prison environment syndrome" which was analogous to battered wife syndrome in that they lived in an environment in which inmates had to "kill or be killed". Should there be a new trial to consider such a defence? Should it succeed?

Compare *R. v. McConnell* (1996), 48 C.R. (4th) 199, [1996] 1 S.C.R. 1075 and see annotation by Christine Boyle (1996), 48 C.R. (4th) 200.

In *R. v. Cinous* (2002), 49 C.R. (5th) 209 (S.C.C.), the leading pronouncement on how the air of reality standard needs to be met before defences are put to juries (see earlier), the Court divided 6-3 (in a judgment over 100 printed pages(!)) over whether or not there was an air of reality to the defence of self-defence in the following circumstance.

The accused was charged with the first degree murder of a criminal accomplice, Mike. The accused testified that he and a friend had been involved in the theft and resale of computers along with Mike and another accomplice, Ice. About one month before the killing, he became convinced that Mike had stolen his gun. He told Mike and Ice that he wanted no more to do with them but they kept calling about doing thefts. He also testified that shortly after the gun went missing he began to hear rumours that Mike and Ice wanted to kill him, and that he was warned by a friend to watch out for them. One morning Mike and Ice called and asked the accused to participate in a computer theft. He agreed to meet with them that evening at his apartment. The accused testified that when they arrived, they kept their jackets on and whispered to one another as they sat in the living room. He saw Ice constantly placing his hand inside his coat. That made him suspect they were armed. The accused said he decided to participate in the theft to see if they really intended to kill him. They left the apartment and got into the accused's van to drive to the location of the theft. The accused said that he knew Mike and Ice wanted to kill him when he saw they had changed their gloves. Neither had changed to the black woollen gloves kept in the van compartment for computer thefts. Mike was wearing surgical latex gloves the accused associated with situations where bloodshed was expected. He had twice before seen them used on "burns" — attacks on criminals by other criminals. The accused drove. Ice sat next to him and Mike sat behind Ice. The accused testified Ice avoided making eye contact with him and kept touching his jacket as if he had a gun. He said he interpreted Ice's hand inside his jacket as a threat. The accused admitted that no other threats were made. The accused testified that he was sure that he was going to be killed and that the shot would more than likely come from behind — from Mike. Since he was driving, he could not get to his own gun quickly enough, were anything to happen. He felt trapped. He pulled into a populated and well-lit gas station to "release the pressure" and get himself out of this bad situation. He bought a bottle of windshield washer after returning to the van to get money from Ice. He poured the fluid in under the hood and brought the bottle back around to the back of the van. He opened the back door, "saw the opportunity", pulled out his gun and shot Mike in the back of the head. The accused testified that this was an instinctive reaction to a situation of danger. It did not occur to him to run away or to call the police.

Was there an air of reality to the defence?

4. DEFENCE OF PROPERTY

Defences of property were, since 1892, declared in extraordinarily complex *Code* provisions in ss. 38-42 which distinguished defences of movable property, dwelling houses and real property.

In 2013, at the same time that the self-defence provisions were amended, the old defence of property provisions were repealed and replaced by a single provision, s. 35.

R. v. CORMIER

(2017), 348 C.C.C. (3d) 97, 37 C.R. (7th) 63 (N.B. C.A.)

Cormier was previously discussed under the self-defence provisions: the accused had taken refuge inside his father's apartment against a person, Eldridge, who was threatening him. Eldridge and a friend had threatened by text to break all the windows, and Cormier (accompanied by others) went outside: in the resulting confrontation Cormier killed Eldridge. The primary issue in the case was self-defence, but the New Brunswick Court of Appeal also considered the new version of the Defence of Property provision in s. 35.

[47] As for the defence of property provisions, these appear to be very broad. Section 35 applies to a wide range of offences and to any type of property. The provision establishes the types of interference with "peaceable possession" of property that can trigger a defensive response. The defence is triggered upon a reasonably based belief of peaceable possession of property and of another person's specific actions regarding that property, i.e. either: (1) about to enter, entering or having entered to the property without lawful entitlement; (2) about to take, taking or having just taken the property; or (3) about to damage or destroy or in the process of damaging or destroying the property or making it inoperative. Upon the defence being triggered, an act committed to prevent the triggering event is justified provided it is "reasonable in the circumstances". The defensive purpose requirement is to be assessed subjectively. On the other hand, the reasonableness of the response is objectively assessed. However, unlike the enumeration of factors to aid assessing this in self-defence cases (s. 34(2)), s. 35 offers no legislative guidance.

[48] The extent of reasonableness under s. 35 remains to be jurisprudentially determined. Before the Citizen's Arrest and Self-Defence Act came into force, jurisprudence had clearly established that it was not reasonable to kill someone to prevent a crime directed only against property: *R. v. Gee*, [1982] 2 S.C.R. 286, per Dickson J. (as he then was) quoting Halsbury's Laws of England (4th ed.), vol. 11, at p. 630. This had long been the law, as noted in *Rossignol v. R.*, 2005 NBCA 11, dealing with the now repealed s. 41(1) of the *Criminal Code*, which allowed one in peaceable possession of real property to use as much force as necessary to prevent or stop a trespass:

> It is settled law that s. 41 of the Criminal Code does not apply when the force used by the person in possession of the real property to remove a trespasser causes the trespasser's death. Only the application of s. 34 could justify the use of such force: see *R. v. Price* (1835), 7 Car. & P. 178,173 E.R. 78, *R. v. Baxter* (1975), 27 C.C.C. (2d) 96 (Ont. C.A.), *R. v. Scopelliti* (1981), 34 O.R. (2d) 524 (C.A.), *R. v. Clark* (1983), 44 A.R. 141 (C.A.) and *R. v. Bacon*, [1999] Q.J. No. 19 (C.A.). [para. 12]

[49] Professor Kent Roach, in his article, laments the fact that Parliament was silent on the issue of proportionality in s. 35, although it made it a consideration

in self-defence cases by listing it as one of the factors to be considered under s. 34(2). Recall that "the nature and proportionality of the person's response to the use or threat of force" is listed as a factor in s. 34(2)(g). Professor Roach opines that "courts should read in such a proportionality requirement in the absence of clear legislation displacing the extensive proportionality jurisprudence". In the summary portion of his article, Professor Roach notes that absence of proportionality as a criterion in s. 35 opens up the "disturbing possibility that intentional killing in the defence of property could result in an acquittal".

[50] Frankly, it is difficult to conceive how the killing of an individual solely to defend one's property could ever be found to be a reasonable response in the circumstances. What usually occurs is that the force used to prevent interference with one's property is resisted and the aggression of the trespasser turns the situation into one of self-defence. Professor Roach makes this point:

> The old defence of property provisions provided that a trespasser who resisted an attempt to protect personal or real property would be deemed to have committed an assault. These complex provisions are not present in the new section 35. Nevertheless, this does not preclude frequent overlap between defence of property and self-defence provisions. For example, a person who is protecting property may also be able to claim self-defence if they have a reasonable belief that force or a threat of force is being used against them.

[51] For the reasons laid out below, we believe the present case is one in which there was in fact an overlap between defence of property and self-defence. In our view, it would have been open for the jury to conclude that what began as a defence of property situation quickly escalated into a defence of the person case.

5. NECESSITY

R. v. DUDLEY and STEPHENS

(1884), 14 Q.B.D. 273 (C.C.R.)

INDICTMENT for the murder of Richard Parker on the high seas within the jurisdiction of the Admiralty.

At the trial before Huddleston B., at the Devon and Cornwall Winter Assizes, November 7, 1884, the jury, at the suggestion of the learned judge, found the facts of the case in a special verdict which stated:

> that on July 5, 1884, the prisoners, Thomas Dudley and Edward Stephens, with one Brooks, all able-bodied English seamen, and the deceased also an English boy, between 17 and 18 years of age, the crew of an English yacht, a registered English vessel, were cast away in a storm on the high seas 1600 miles from the Cape of Good Hope, and were compelled to put into an open boat belonging to the said yacht. That in this boat they had no supply of water

and no supply of food, except two 1 lb. tins of turnips, and for three days they had nothing else to subsist upon. That on the fourth day they caught a small turtle, upon which they subsisted for a few days, and this was the only food they had up to the 20th day when the act now in question was committed. That on the 12th day the remains of the turtle were entirely consumed, and for the next eight days they had nothing to eat. That they had no fresh water, except such rain as they from time to time caught in their oilskin capes. That the boat was drifting on the ocean, and was probably more than 1000 miles away from land. That on the 18th day, when they had been seven days without food and five without water, the prisoners spoke to Brooks as to what should be done if no succour came, and suggested that some one should be sacrificed to save the rest, but Brooks dissented, and the boy, to whom they were understood to refer, was not consulted. That on the 24th of July, the day before the act now in question, the prisoner Dudley proposed to Stephens and Brooks that lots should be cast who should be put to death to save the rest, but Brooks refused to consent, and it was not put to the boy, and in point of fact there was no drawing of lots. That on that day the prisoners spoke of their having families, and suggested it would be better to kill the boy that their lives should be saved, and Dudley proposed that if there was no vessel in sight by the morrow morning the boy should be killed. The next day, the 25th of July, no vessel appearing, Dudley told Brooks that he had better go and have a sleep, and made signs to Stephens and Brooks that the boy had better be killed. The prisoner Stephens agreed to the act, but Brooks dissented from it. That the boy was then lying at the bottom of the boat quite helpless, and extremely weakened by famine and by drinking sea water, and unable to make any resistance, nor did he ever assent to his being killed. The prisoner Dudley offered a prayer asking forgiveness for them all if either of them should be tempted to commit a rash act, and that their souls might be saved. That Dudley, with the assent of Stephens, went to the boy, and telling him that his time was come, put a knife into his throat and killed him then and there; that the three men fed upon the body and blood of the boy for four days; that on the fourth day after the act had been committed the boat was picked up by a passing vessel, and the prisoners were rescued, still alive, but in the lowest state of prostration. That they were carried to the port of Falmouth, and committed for trial at Exeter. That if the men had not fed upon the body of the boy they would probably not have survived to be so picked up and rescued, but would within the four days have died of famine. That the boy, being in a much weaker condition, was likely to have died before them. That at the time of the act in question there was no sail in sight, nor any reasonable prospect of relief. That under these circumstances there appeared to the prisoners every probability that unless they then fed or very soon fed upon the boy or one of themselves they would die of starvation. That there was no appreciable chance of saving life except by killing some one for the others to eat. That assuming any necessity to kill anybody, there was no greater necessity for killing the boy than any of the other three men.

But whether upon the whole matter by the jurors found the killing of Richard Parker by Dudley and Stephens be felony and murder the jurors are ignorant, and pray the advice of the court thereupon, and if upon the whole matter the court shall be of opinion that the killing of Richard Parker be felony and murder, then the jurors say that Dudley and Stephens were each guilty of felony and murder as alleged in the indictment.

· · · ·

Dec. 9. The judgment of the court was delivered by LORD COLERIDGE C.J.: —

. . . .

There remains to be considered the real question in the case — whether killing under the circumstances set forth in the verdict be or be not murder. The contention that it could be anything else was, to the minds of us all, both new and strange, and we stopped the Attorney-General in his negative argument in order that we might hear what could be said in support of a proposition which appeared to us to be at once dangerous, immoral, and opposed to all legal principle and analogy. All, no doubt, that can be said has been urged before us, and we are now to consider and determine what it amounts to. First it is said that it follows from various definitions of murder in books of authority, which definitions imply, if they do not state, the doctrine, that in order to save your own life you may lawfully take away the life of another, when that other is neither attempting nor threatening yours, nor is guilty of any illegal act whatever towards you or any one else. But if these definitions be looked at they will not be found to sustain this contention. . . .

Is there, then, any authority for the proposition which has been presented to us? Decided cases there are none. . . .

The American case cited by my Brother Stephen in his Digest, from Wharton on Homicide, in which it was decided, correctly indeed, that sailors had no right to throw passengers overboard to save themselves, but on the somewhat strange ground that the proper mode of determining who was to be sacrificed was to vote upon the subject by ballot, can hardly, as my Brother Stephen says, be an authority satisfactory to a court in this country.

. . . .

Now, except for the purpose of testing how far the conservation of a man's own life is in all cases and under all circumstances, an absolute, unqualified, and paramount duty, we exclude from our consideration all the incidents of war. We are dealing with a case of private homicide, not one imposed upon men in the service of their Sovereign and in the defence of their country. Now it is admitted that the deliberate killing of this unoffending and unresisting boy was clearly murder, unless the killing can be justified by some well-recognized excuse admitted by the law. It is further admitted that there was in this case no such excuse, unless the killing was justified by what has been called "necessity." But the temptation to the act which existed here was not what the law has ever called necessity. Nor is this to be regretted. Though law and morality are not the same, and many things may be immoral which are not necessarily illegal, yet the absolute divorce of law from morality would be of fatal consequence; and such divorce would follow if the temptation to murder in this case were to be held by law an absolute defence of it. It is not so. To preserve one's life is generally speaking a duty, but it may be the plainest and the highest duty to sacrifice it. War is full of instances in which it is a man's duty not to live, but to die. The duty in case of shipwreck, of a captain to his crew, of the crew to the passengers, of soldiers to women and children, as in the noble case of the *Birkenhead*; these duties impose on men the moral necessity, not of the preservation, but of the sacrifice of their lives for others, from which in no country, least of all, it is to be hoped, in England, will men ever shrink, as indeed, they have not shrunk. It is not correct, therefore, to say that there is any absolute or unqualified necessity to preserve one's life. "Necesse est ut eam, non ut vivam," is a saying of a Roman officer quoted by Lord Bacon himself with high eulogy in the very chapter on necessity to which so much reference has been made. It would be a very easy and cheap display of commonplace learning to quote from Greek and Latin authors, from Horace, from Juvenal, from Cicero, from Euripides, passage after passage, in which the duty of dying for others has been laid down in glowing and emphatic language as resulting from the principles of heathen ethics; it is enough in a Christian country to remind ourselves of the Great Example whom we profess to follow. It is not needful to point out the awful danger of admitting the principle which has been contended for. Who is to be the judge of this sort of necessity? By what measure is the comparative value of lives to be measured? Is it to be strength, or intellect, or what? It is plain that the principle leaves to him who is to profit by it to determine the necessity which will justify him in deliberately taking another's life to save his own. In this case the weakest, the youngest, the most unresisting, was chosen. Was it more necessary to kill him than one of the grown men? The answer must be "No" —

> So spake the Fiend, and with necessity,
> The tyrant's plea, excused his devilish deeds.

It is not suggested that in this particular case the deeds were "devilish," but it is quite plain that such a principle once admitted might be made the legal cloak for unbridled passion and atrocious crime. There is no safe path for Judges to tread but to ascertain the law to the best of their ability and to declare it according to their judgment; and if in any case the law appears to be too severe on individuals, to leave it to the Sovereign to exercise that prerogative of mercy which the Constitution has intrusted to the hands fittest to dispense it.

It must not be supposed that in refusing to admit temptation to be an excuse for crime it is forgotten how terrible the temptation was; how awful the suffering; how hard in such trials to keep the judgment straight and the conduct pure. We are often compelled to set up standards we cannot reach ourselves, and to lay down rules which we could not ourselves satisfy. But a man has no right to declare temptation to be an excuse, though he might himself have yielded to it, nor allow compulsion for the criminal to change or weaken in any manner the legal definition of the crime. It is therefore our duty to declare that the prisoners' act in this case was wilful murder, that the facts as stated in the verdict are no legal justification of the homicide; and to say that in our unanimous opinion the prisoners are upon this special verdict guilty of murder.[1]

The court then proceeded to pass sentence of death upon the prisoners.[2]

PERKA v. R.

42 C.R. (3d) 113, [1984] 2 S.C.R. 233, 14 C.C.C. (3d) 385, 1984 CarswellBC 823

Dickson J. (Ritchie, Chouinard and Lamer JJ. concurring): — . . . .

I Facts

The appellants are drug smugglers. At trial, they led evidence that in early 1979 three of the appellants were employed, with 16 crew members, to deliver, by ship (the Samarkanda), a load of cannabis (marijuana) worth $6,000,000 or $7,000,000 from a point in international waters off the coast of Colombia, South America, to a drop point in international waters 200 miles off the coast of Alaska. The ship left Tumaco, Colombia, empty with a port clearance document stating the destination to be Juneau, Alaska. For three weeks the ship remained in international waters off the coast of Colombia. While there, a DC-6 aircraft made four trips, dropping into the water shrimp nets with a total of 634 bales of cannabis which were retrieved by the ship's longboats.

A "communications" package was also dropped from a light aircraft, giving instructions for a rendezvous with another vessel, the Julia B., which was to pick up the cargo of cannabis from the Samarkanda in international waters off the coast of Alaska. En route, according to the defence evidence, the vessel began to encounter a series of problems; engine break-downs, overheating generators and malfunctioning navigation devices, aggravated by deteriorating weather. In the meantime the fourth appellant, Nelson, part-owner of the illicit cargo, and three other persons left Seattle in a small boat, the Whitecap, intending to rendezvous with the Samarkanda at the drop point in Alaska. The problems of the Samarkanda intensified as fuel was consumed. The vessel became lighter, the intakes in the hull for sea water, used as a coolant, lost suction and took in air instead, causing the generators to overheat. At this point the vessel was 180 miles from the Canadian coastline. The weather worsened. There

---

1 My brother Grove has furnished me with the following suggestion, too late to be embodied in the judgment but well worth preserving: "If the two accused men were justified in killing Parker, then if not rescued in time, two of the three survivors would be justified in killing the third, and of the two who remained the stronger would be justified in killing the weaker, so that three men might be justifiably killed to give the fourth a chance of surviving."— C.

2 This sentence was afterwards commuted by the Crown to six months' imprisonment.

were 8-to-10-foot swells and a rising wind. It was finally decided for the safety of ship and crew to seek refuge on the Canadian shoreline for the purpose of making temporary repairs. The Whitecap found a sheltered cove on the west coast of Vancouver Island, No Name Bay. The Samarkanda followed the Whitecap into the bay but later grounded amidships on a rock because the depth sounder was not working. The tide ran out. The vessel listed severely to starboard, to the extent that the Captain, fearing the vessel was going to capsize, ordered the men to offload the cargo. That is a brief summary of the defence evidence.

Early on the morning of 22nd May 1979 police officers entered No Name Bay in a marked police boat with siren sounding. The Samarkanda and the Whitecap were arrested, as were all the appellants except Perka and Nelson, the same morning. The vessels and 33.49 tons of cannabis marijuana were seized by the police officers.

Charged with importing cannabis into Canada and with possession for the purpose of trafficking, the appellants claimed that they did not plan to import into Canada or to leave their cargo of cannabis in Canada. They had planned to make repairs and leave. Expert witnesses on marine matters called by the defence testified that the decision to come ashore was, in the opinion of one witness, expedient and prudent and, in the opinion of another, essential. At trial, counsel for the Crown alleged that the evidence of the ship's distress was a recent fabrication. Crown counsel relied on the circumstances under which the appellants were arrested to belie the "necessity" defence; when the police arrived on the scene most of the marijuana was already onshore, along with plastic ground sheets, battery-operated lights, liquor, food, clothing, camp stoves, and sleeping bags. Nevertheless, the jury believed the appellants and acquitted them.

. . . .

II THE NECESSITY DEFENCE

(a) *History and Background*

From earliest times it has been maintained that in some situations the force of circumstances makes it unrealistic and unjust to attach criminal liability to actions which, on their face, violate the law. Aristotle, *Nicomachean Ethics*, translated by Sir David Ross, Book III, p. 49, 1110a, discusses the jettisoning of cargo from a ship in distress and remarks that "any sensible man does so" to secure the safety of himself and his crew. Pollard, arguing for the defendant in the case of *Renniger v. Fogossa* (1551), 1 Plowden 1 at 18, 75 E.R. 1, maintained:

> . . . in every law there are some things which when they happen a man may break the words of the law, and yet not break the law itself; and such things are exempted out of the penalty of the law, and the law privileges them although they are done against the letter of it, for

breaking the words of the law is not breaking the law, so as the intent of the law is not broken. And therefore the words of the law of nature, of the law of this realm, and of other realms, and of the law of God also will yield and give way to some acts and things done against the words of the same laws, and that is, where the words of them are broken to avoid greater inconveniences, or through necessity, or by compulsion.

In *Leviathan*, Pelican ed. (1968), c. 27, at p. 157, Hobbes writes:

> If a man by the terrour of present death, be compelled to doe a fact against the law, he is totally excused; because no law can oblige a man to abandon his own preservation. And supposing such a law were obligatory: yet a man would reason thus, If I doe it not, I die presently; if I doe it I die afterwards; therefore by doing it there is time of life gained; Nature therefore compels him to the fact.

To much the same purpose Kant, in *Metaphysical Elements of Justice*, translated by Ladd (1965), discussing the actions of a person who, to save his own life, sacrifices that of another, says at p. 41:

> A penal law applying to such a situation could never have the effect intended, for the threat of an evil that is still uncertain (being condemned to death by a Judge) cannot outweigh the fear of an evil that is certain (being drowned). Hence, we must judge that, although an act of self-preservation through violence is not inculpable, it still is unpunishable.

In those jurisdictions in which such a general principle has been recognized or codified it is most often referred to by the term "necessity". Classic and harrowing instances which have been cited to illustrate the arguments both for and against this principle include the mother who steals food for her starving child, the shipwrecked mariners who resort to cannibalism (*R. v. Dudley*, (1884), 14 Q.B.D. 273 (C.C.R.)) or throw passengers overboard to lighten a sinking lifeboat (*U.S. v. Holmes*, 26 F. Cas. 360 (1842)), and the more mundane case of the motorist who exceeds the speed limit taking an injured person to the hospital.

. . . .

In Canada the existence and the extent of a general defence of necessity was discussed by this court in *Morgentaler v. R.*, [1976] 1 S.C.R. 616, 30 C.R.N.S. 209, 20 C.C.C. (2d) 449. As to whether or not the defence exists at all I had occasion to say at p. 678:

> On the authorities it is manifestly difficult to be categorical and state that there is a law of necessity, paramount over other laws, relieving obedience from the letter of the law. If [such a principle exists] it can go no further than to justify non-compliance in urgent situations of clear and imminent peril when compliance with the law is demonstrably impossible.

. . . .

In the present appeal the Crown does not challenge the appellants' claim that necessity is a common law defence preserved by the *Criminal Code*, R.S.C. 1970, c. C-34, s. 7(3). Rather, the Crown claims, the trial judge erred in: (1)

instructing the jury on the defence in light of the facts; and (2) imposing the burden of disproof of the defence upon the Crown, rather than imposing the burden of proof on the appellants.

(b) *The Conceptual Foundation of the Defence*

In *Morgentaler v. R.*, *supra*. I characterized necessity as an "ill-defined and elusive concept". Despite the apparently growing consensus as to the existence of a defence of necessity, that statement is equally true today.

This is no doubt in part because, though apparently laying down a single rule as to criminal liability, the "defence" of necessity in fact is capable of embracing two different and distinct notions. As Macdonald J.A. observed succinctly but accurately in the *Salvador* case [*R. v. Salvador* (1981), 21 C.R. (3d) 1, 59 C.C.C. (2d) 521 (N.S.C.A.)], at p. 542:

> Generally speaking, the defence of necessity covers all cases where non-compliance with law is excused by an emergency or justified by the pursuit of some greater good.

Working Paper 29, Criminal Law — The General Part: Liability and Defences (1982), of the Law Reform Commission of Canada at p. 93 makes this same point in somewhat more detail:

> The rationale of necessity, however, is clear. Essentially it involves two factors. One is the avoidance of greater harm or the pursuit of some greater good, the other is the difficulty of compliance with law in emergencies. From these two factors emerge two different but related principles. The first is a utilitarian principle to the effect that, within certain limits, it is justifiable in an emergency to break the letter of the law if breaking the law will avoid a greater harm than obeying it. The second is a humanitarian principle to the effect that, again within limits, it is excusable in an emergency to break the law if compliance would impose an intolerable burden on the accused.

Despite any superficial similarities, these two principles are in fact quite distinct and many of the confusions and difficulties in the cases (and, with respect, in academic discussions) arise from a failure to distinguish between them.

Criminal theory recognizes a distinction between "justifications" and "excuses". A "justification" challenges the wrongfulness of an action which technically constitutes a crime. The police officer who shoots the hostage-taker, the innocent object of an assault who uses force to defend himself against his assailant, the Good Samaritan who commandeers a car and breaks the speed laws to rush an accident victim to the hospital, these are all actors whose actions we consider *rightful*, not wrongful. For such actions people are often praised, as motivated by some great or noble object. The concept of punishment often seems incompatible with the social approval bestowed on the doer.

In contrast, an "excuse" concedes the wrongfulness of the action but asserts that the circumstances under which it was done are such that it ought not to be attributed to the actor. The perpetrator who is incapable, owing to a disease of the mind, of appreciating the nature and consequences of his acts, the person who labours under a mistake of fact, the drunkard, the sleepwalker: these are all actors of whose "criminal" actions we disapprove intensely, but whom, in appropriate circumstances, our law will not punish.

Packer, *The Limits of the Criminal Sanction*, expresses the distinction thus at p. 113:

> Conduct that we choose not to treat as criminal is "justifiable" if our reason for treating it as noncriminal is predominantly that it is conduct that we applaud, or at least do not actively seek to discourage: conduct is "excusable" if we deplore it but for some extrinsic reason conclude that it is not politic to punish it.

It will be seen that the two different approaches to the "defence" of necessity from Blackstone forward correspond, the one to a justification, the other to an excuse. As the examples cited above illustrate, the criminal law recognizes and our *Criminal Code* codifies a number of specific categories of justification and of excuse. The remainder, those instances that conform to the general principle but do not fall within any specific category such as self-defence on the one hand or insanity on the other, purportedly fall within the "residual defence" of necessity.

As a "justification" this residual defence can be related to Blackstone's concept of a "choice of evils". It would exculpate actors whose conduct could reasonably have been viewed as "necessary" in order to prevent a greater evil than that resulting from the violation of the law. As articulated, especially in some of the American cases, it involves a utilitarian balancing of the benefits of obeying the law as opposed to disobeying it, and, when the balance is clearly in favour of disobeying, exculpates an actor who contravenes a criminal statute. This is the "greater good" formulation of the necessity defence: in some circumstances, it is alleged, the values of society, indeed of the criminal law itself, are better promoted by disobeying a given statute than by observing it.

With regard to this conceptualization of a residual defence of necessity, I retain the scepticism I expressed in *Morgentaler v. R.*, *supra*, at p. 678. It is still my opinion that "No system of positive law can recognize any principle which would entitle a person to violate the law because on his view the law conflicted with some higher social value." The *Criminal Code* has specified a number of identifiable situations in which an actor is justified in committing what would otherwise be a criminal offence. To go beyond that and hold that ostensibly illegal acts can be validated on the basis of their expediency would import an undue subjectivity into the criminal law. It would invite the courts to second-guess the Legislature and to assess the relative merits of social policies underlying criminal prohibitions. Neither is a role which fits well with the judicial function. Such a doctrine could well become the last resort of scoundrels and, in the words of Edmund Davies L.J. in *Southwark London Borough Council v. Williams*, [1971] Ch. 734 at 746 (C.A.), it could "very easily become simply a mask for anarchy".

Conceptualized as an "excuse", however, the residual defence of necessity is, in my view, much less open to criticism. It rests on a realistic assessment of human weakness, recognizing that a liberal and humane criminal law cannot hold people to the strict obedience of law in emergency situations where normal human instincts, whether of self-preservation or of altruism, overwhelmingly impel disobedience. The objectivity of the criminal law is preserved; such acts are still wrongful, but in the circumstances they are excusable. Praise is indeed not bestowed, but pardon is, when one does a wrongful act under pressure which, in the words of Aristotle in the *Nicomachean Ethics* p. 49, ll10a10, "overstrains human nature and which no one could withstand".

George Fletcher, *Rethinking Criminal Law* (1978), describes this view of necessity as "compulsion of circumstance", which description points to the conceptual link between necessity as an excuse and the familiar criminal law requirement that in order to engage criminal liability the actions constituting the *actus reus* of an offence must be voluntary. Literally this voluntariness requirement simply refers to the need that the prohibited physical acts must have been under the conscious control of the actor. Without such control, there is, for purposes of the criminal law, no act. The excuse of necessity does not go to voluntariness in this sense. The lost alpinist who on the point of freezing to death breaks open an isolated mountain cabin is not literally behaving in an involuntary fashion. He has control over his actions to the extent of being physically capable of abstaining from the act. Realistically, however, his act is not a "voluntary" one. His "choice" to break the law is no true choice at all; it is remorselessly compelled by normal human instincts. This sort of involuntariness is often described as "moral or normative involuntariness". Its place in criminal theory is described by Fletcher at pp. 804-805 as follows:

> The notion of voluntariness adds a valuable dimension to the theory of excuses. That conduct is involuntary — even in the normative sense — explains why it cannot fairly be punished. Indeed, H.L.A. Hart builds his theory of excuses on the principle that the distribution of punishment should be reserved for those who voluntarily break the law. Of the arguments he advances for this principle of justice, the most explicit is that it is preferable to live in a society where we have the maximum opportunity to choose whether we shall become the subject of criminal liability. In addition, Hart intimates that it is ideologically dcsirable for the government to treat its citizens as self-actuating, choosing agents. This principle of respect for individual autonomy is implicitly confirmed whenever those who lack an adequate choice are excused for their offences.

I agree with this formulation of the rationale for excuses in the criminal law. In my view this rationale extends beyond specific codified excuses and embraces the residual excuse known as the defence of necessity. At the heart of this defence is the perceived injustice of punishing violations of the law in circumstances in which the person had no other viable or reasonable choice available; the act was wrong but it is excused because it was realistically unavoidable.

Punishment of such acts, as Fletcher notes at p. 813, can be seen as purposeless as well as unjust:

> ... involuntary conduct cannot be deterred and therefore it is pointless and wasteful to punish involuntary actors. This theory ... of pointless punishment, carries considerable weight in current Anglo-American legal thought.

Relating necessity to the principle that the law ought not to punish involuntary acts leads to a conceptualization of the defence that integrates it into the normal rules for criminal liability rather than constituting it as a *sui generis* exception and threatening to engulf large portions of the criminal law. Such a conceptualization accords with our traditional legal, moral and philosophic views as to what sorts of acts and what sorts of actors ought to be punished. In this formulation it is a defence which I do not hesitate to acknowledge and would not hesitate to apply to relevant facts capable of satisfying its necessary prerequisites.

(c) *Limitations on the Defence*

If the defence of necessity is to form a valid and consistent part of our criminal law it must, as has been universally recognized, be strictly controlled and scrupulously limited to situations that correspond to its underlying rationale. That rationale, as I have indicated, is the recognition that it is inappropriate to punish actions which are normatively "involuntary". The appropriate controls and limitations on the defence of necessity are therefore addressed to ensuring that the acts for which the benefit of the excuse of necessity is sought are truly "involuntary" in the requisite sense.

In *Morgentaler v. R.*, *supra*, I was of the view that any defence of necessity was restricted to instances of non-compliance "in urgent situations of clear and imminent peril when compliance with the law is demonstrably impossible". In my opinion this restriction focuses directly on the "involuntariness" of the purportedly necessitous behaviour by providing a number of tests for determining whether the wrongful act was truly the only realistic reaction open to the actor or whether he was in fact making what in fairness could be called a choice. If he was making a choice, then the wrongful act cannot have been involuntary in the relevant sense.

The requirement that the situation be urgent and the peril be imminent tests whether it was indeed unavoidable for the actor to act at all. In Lafave and Scott, *Criminal Law*, at p. 388, one reads:

> It is sometimes said that the defence of necessity does not apply except in an emergency — when the threatened harm is immediate, the threatened disaster imminent. Perhaps this is but a way of saying that, until the time comes when the threatened harm is immediate, there are generally options open to the defendant to avoid the harm, other than the option of disobeying the literal terms of the law — the rescue ship may appear, the storm may pass; and so the defendant must wait until that hope of survival disappears.

At a minimum the situation must be so emergent and the peril must be so pressing that normal human instincts cry out for action and make a counsel of patience unreasonable.

The requirement that compliance with the law be "demonstrably impossible" takes this assessment one step further. Given that the accused had to act, could he nevertheless realistically have acted to avoid the peril or prevent the harm, without breaking the law? *Was there a legal way out?* I think this is what Bracton means when he lists "necessity" as a defence, providing the wrongful act was not "avoidable". The question to be asked is whether the agent had any real choice: could he have done otherwise? If there is a reasonable legal alternative to disobeying the law, then the decision to disobey becomes a voluntary one, impelled by some consideration beyond the dictates of "necessity" and human instincts.

The importance of this requirement that there be no reasonable legal alternative cannot be overstressed.

Even if the requirements for urgency and "no legal way out" are met, there is clearly a further consideration. There must be some way of assuring proportionality. No rational criminal justice system, no matter how humane or liberal, could excuse the infliction of a greater harm to allow the actor to avert a lesser evil. In such circumstances we expect the individual to bear the harm and refrain from acting illegally. If he cannot control himself we will not excuse him. According to Fletcher, this requirement is also related to the notion of voluntariness:

> . . . if the gap between the harm done and the benefit accrued becomes too great, the act is more likely to appear voluntary and therefore inexcusable. For example, if the actor has to blow up a whole city in order to avoid the breaking of his finger, we might appropriately expect him to endure the harm to himself. His surrendering to the threat in this case violates our expectations of appropriate and normal resistance and pressure. Yet as we lower the degree of harm to others and increase the threatened harm to the person under duress we will reach a threshold at which, in the language of the Model Penal Code, "a person of reasonable firmness" would be "unable to resist". Determining this threshold is patently a matter of moral judgment about what we expect people to be able to resist in trying situations. A valuable aid in making that judgment is comparing the competing interests at stake and assessing the degree to which the actor inflicts harm beyond the benefit that accrues from his action.

I would therefore add to the preceding requirements a stipulation of proportionality expressable, as it was in *Morgentaler v. R.*, *supra*, by the proviso that the harm inflicted must be less than the harm sought to be avoided.

(d) *Illegality or Contributory Fault*

The Crown submits that there is an additional limitation on the availability of the defence of necessity. Citing *R. v. Salvador*, *supra*, it argues that because the appellants were committing a crime when their necessitous circumstances arose they should be denied the defence of necessity as a matter of law.

. . . .

In any event, I have considerable doubt as to the cogency of such a limitation. If the conduct in which an accused was engaging at the time the peril arose was illegal, then it should clearly be punished, but I fail to see the relevance of its illegal character to the question of whether the accused's subsequent conduct in dealing with this emergent peril ought to be excused on the basis of necessity. At most the illegality — or, if one adopts Jones J.A.'s approach, the immorality — of the preceding conduct will colour the subsequent conduct in response to the emergency as also wrongful. But that wrongfulness is never in any doubt. Necessity goes to *excuse* conduct, not to *justify* it. Where it is found to apply it carries with it no implicit vindication of the deed to which it attaches. That cannot be over-emphasized. Were the defence of necessity to succeed in the present case, it would not in any way amount to a vindication of importing controlled substances or to a critique of the law prohibiting such importation. It would also have nothing to say about the comparative social utility of breaking the law against importing as compared to obeying the law. The question, as I have said, is never whether what the accused has done is wrongful. It is always and by definition wrongful. The question is whether what he has done is voluntary. Except in the limited sense I intend to discuss below, I do not see the relevance of the legality or even the morality of what the accused was doing at the time the emergency arose to this question of the voluntariness of the subsequent conduct.

. . . .

In my view the better approach to the relationship of fault to the availability of necessity as a defence is based once again on the question of whether the actions sought to be excused were truly "involuntary". If the necessitous situation was clearly foreseeable to a reasonable observer, if the actor contemplated or ought to have contemplated that his actions would likely give rise to an emergency requiring the breaking of the law, then I doubt whether what confronted the accused was in the relevant sense an emergency. His response was in that sense not "involuntary". "Contributory fault" of this nature, but only of this nature, is a relevant consideration to the availability of the defence.

. . . .

(e) *Onus of Proof*

Although necessity is spoken of as a defence, in the sense that it is raised by the accused, the Crown always bears the burden of proving a voluntary act. The prosecution must prove every element of the crime charged. One such element is the voluntariness of the act. Normally, voluntariness can be presumed, but if the accused places before the court, through his own witnesses or through cross-examination of Crown witnesses, evidence sufficient to raise an issue that the situation created by external forces was so emergent that failure to act could endanger life or health and upon any reasonable view of the facts, compliance with the law was impossible, then the Crown must be prepared to meet that issue. There is no onus of proof on the accused.

. . . .

(f) *Preliminary Conclusions as to the Defence of Necessity*

It is now possible to summarize a number of conclusions as to the defence of necessity in terms of its nature, basis and limitations: (1) the defence of necessity could be conceptualized as either a justification or an excuse; (2) it should be recognized in Canada as an excuse, operating by virtue of s. 7(3) of the *Criminal Code*; (3) necessity as an excuse implies no vindication of the deeds of the actor; (4) the criterion is the moral involuntariness of the wrongful action; (5) this involuntariness is measured on the basis of society's expectation of appropriate and normal resistance to pressure; (6) negligence or involvement in criminal or immoral activity does not disentitle the actor to the excuse of necessity; (7) actions or circumstances which indicate that the wrongful deed was not truly involuntary do disentitle, (8) the existence of a reasonable legal alternative similarly disentitles; to be involuntary the act must be inevitable, unavoidable and afford no reasonable opportunity for an alternative course of action that does not involve a breach of the law; (9) the defence applies only in circumstances of imminent risk where the action was taken to avoid a direct and immediate peril; and (10) where the accused places before the court sufficient evidence to raise the issue, the onus is on the Crown to meet it beyond a reasonable doubt.

(g) *The Judge's Charge*

The trial judge concluded that there was before him an adequate body of evidence to raise the issue of necessity and proceeded to direct the jury with respect to the defence. As I have earlier indicated, the Crown disputes whether the defence was open to the accused in the circumstances of the case and submits further that if it was in fact available the trial judge erred in his direction.

In my view the trial judge was correct in concluding that on the evidence before him he should instruct the jury with regard to necessity. There was evidence before him from which a jury might conclude that the accused's actions in coming ashore with their cargo of cannabis were aimed at self-preservation in response to an overwhelming emergency. I have already indicated that in my view they were not engaged in conduct that was illegal under Canadian criminal law at the time the emergency arose, and that, even if they were, that fact alone would not disentitle them to raise the defence. The question then becomes whether the trial judge erred in charging the jury in the terms that he did.

The summary of conclusions with regard to necessity in the forgoing section indicates that for the defence to succeed an accused's actions must be, in the relevant sense, an "involuntary" response to an imminent and overwhelming peril. The defence cannot succeed if the response was disproportionate to the peril or if it was not "involuntary" in the sense that the emergency was not "real" or not imminent or that there was a reasonable alternative response that was not illegal.

In the course of his charge on the issue of necessity the trial judge instructed the jury, using the specific words that appear in *Morgentaler*, to the effect that they must find facts which amount to "an urgent situation of clear and imminent peril when compliance with the law is demonstrably impossible" in order for the appellants' non-compliance with the law against importation and possession of cannabis to be excused. That is the correct test. It is, with respect, however, my view that in explaining the meaning and application of this test the trial Judge fell into error.

The trial Judge was obliged, in my opinion, to direct the jury's attention to a number of issues pertinent to the test for necessity. Was the emergency a real one? Did it constitute an immediate threat of the harm purportedly feared? Was the response proportionate? In comparing this response to the danger that motivated it, was the danger one that society would reasonably expect the average person to withstand? Was there any reasonable legal alternative to the illegal response open to the accused? Although the trial judge did not explicitly pose each and every one of these questions, in my view his charge was adequate to bring the considerations underlying them to the jury's attention on every issue except the last one, the question of a reasonable alternative.

This issue was the determining obstacle to the success of the defence of necessity in a number of the cases referred to earlier, including *Gilkes, Doud, Byng* and, for the present case most notably, because of the similarity of its factual basis, *Salvador*. Indeed, in most cases where the defence is raised, this consideration will almost certainly be the most important one.

In his charge, the trial judge did not advert to this requirement. He did tell the jury that they must find facts capable of showing that "compliance with the law was demonstrably impossible" but on his recharge he put before the jury a significantly different test. The test, he said, is:

> . . . can you find facts from this evidence, and that means all the evidence, of course, that the situation of the Samarkanda at sea was so appallingly dire and dangerous to life that a reasonable doubt arises as to whether or not their decision was justified?

And again, at the conclusion of the recharge:

> There is no need for the evidence to show you that a certainty of death would result unless the action complained of by the Crown was taken. It doesn't go so far as that. You

have to look at it as reasonable people and decide on any reasonable view of the matter, would these people have been justified in doing what they did? That is all that necessity means.

Both of these passages imply that the crucial consideration was whether the accused acted reasonably in coming into shore with their load of cannabis rather than facing death at sea. That is not sufficient as a test. Even if it does deal with the reality of the peril, its imminence and the proportionality of putting into shore, it does not deal at all with the question of whether there existed any other reasonable responses to the peril that were not illegal. Indeed, aside from the initial repetition of the *Morgentaler* formula, the trial judge did not advert to this consideration at all, nor did he direct the jury's attention to the relevance of evidence indicating the possibility of such alternative courses of action. In these respects I believe he erred in law. He did not properly put the question of a "legal way out" before the jury.

In my view, this was a serious error and omission going to the heart of the defence of necessity. The error justifies a new trial.

. . . .

V CONCLUSION

On the basis of all the above, it is my conclusion that the Court of Appeal was correct in the result in ordering a new trial and was correct in sustaining the trial judge's decision to withhold the botanical defence from the jury.

I would dismiss the appeals.

Appeals dismissed.

[Wilson J. delivered a lengthy dissent. She accepted the distinction between justification and excuse but was of the view that necessity could sometimes be pleaded as a justification, not only as an excuse.]

Is it necessary to distinguish justification from excuse? What legal consequences flow from the distinction? How does one determine whether the situation should be labelled a justification or an excuse? Should consequences flow from labels?

R. v. LATIMER

[2001] 1 S.C.R. 3, 39 C.R. (5th) 1, 150 C.C.C. (3d) 129,
2001 CarwellSask 4, 2001 CarswellSask 5

The defence of necessity received another high-profile test in this heartwrenching case. A father was on trial for the first degree murder of Tracy, his 12-year-old daughter, who had a severe form of cerebral palsy. Tracy was quadriplegic and her physical condition rendered her immobile. Her condition was permanent, caused by neurological damage at the time of her birth. She was said to have the mental capacity of a four-month-old baby, and could communicate only by means of facial expressions, laughter and crying. She was completely dependent on others for her care. She suffered five to six seizures daily. It was thought that she experienced a great deal of pain. This could not be reduced by medication since this would conflict with her anti-epileptic medication and her difficulty in swallowing. She had to be spoon-fed, and her lack of nutrients caused weight loss. There was evidence that Tracy could have been fed with a feeding tube into her stomach, an option that would have improved her nutrition and health, and that might also have allowed for more effective pain medication to be administered. The accused and his wife rejected this option as intrusive and the first step to artificially preserving her life. Tracy had a serious disability but was not terminally ill. She had undergone numerous surgeries including the implanting of metal rods to support her spine. The Latimers learned that the doctors wished to perform additional surgery on a dislocated hip which involved removing her upper thigh bone. According to the accused's wife they perceived this as mutilation.[3]

The accused decided to take his daughter's life. While his wife and Tracy's siblings were at church, he carried Tracy to his pickup truck, seated her in the cab, and inserted a hose from the truck's exhaust pipe into the cab. She died from the carbon monoxide. The accused at first maintained that she had simply passed away in her sleep, but later confessed to having taken her life. Charged with first degree murder, the jury found him guilty of second degree murder. The

---

3 The above facts are taken from the Supreme Court's review of the record. The tragic context has been further described by Professor Barney Sneiderman, "The Latimer Mercy-Killing Case: A Rumination on Crime and Punishment" (1997) 5 Health L.J. 1 at 1-2 as follows:

> Gravely affected since birth by cerebral palsy, Tracy Latimer was a "totally body-involved spastic quadriplegic", whose constant muscle spasms and seizures had wrenched her body into a twisted frozen position. She had the mental age of a two- or three-month-old baby, weighed 38 pounds, wore diapers, often needed suppositories to unplug her bowels, had impaired vision, and could not sit up, talk, or feed herself. Her parents kept a bucket at hand when feeding her as she had difficulty in swallowing and would constantly vomit. She spent her days either in bed or propped in a wheelchair, tightly fitted to prevent her thrashing about during her daily seizure episodes.
>
> Tracy had undergone a number of surgical procedures to relieve the painful muscular tension afflicting her grossly contorted body; muscles had been cut at the top of her legs, her toes, her heel cords, and knees. There was also surgery on her spine; stainless steel rods were inserted on each side to relieve the cramping of her stomach and lungs. Because Tracy was on anticonvulsant medication to control her seizures, her parents were fearful that using narcotics to control her pain could prove fatal by depressing her respiration (a concern shared by Tracy's orthopaedic surgeon). She was in constant pain from a dislocated hip, and Latimer was appalled at the prospect of impending surgery that would involve the removal of part of her hip and thigh bone. And there would be more surgery to come.

Sneiderman's sources are the reported decision in (1995), 41 C.R. (4th) 1 (Sask. C.A.), the trial transcript and newspaper accounts. The notion Tracy was in constant pain has been disputed: see Ruth Enns, A Voice Unheard. The Latimer Case and People with Disabilities (1999). An appendix at pp.166-170 shows that Tracy's mother's communication books had multiple entries as to her happiness and smiles.

trial judge had withdrawn the defence of necessity from the jury by the following instruction:

> [W]hile the doctrine of necessity can sometimes operate to excuse criminal misconduct, I must tell you as a matter of law that the doctrine does not apply in this case. The defence of necessity exists only where the perpetrator's decision to break the law is inescapable and unavoidable and necessary to avert some imminent risk of peril. It arises only in cases where there is no option, no other choice. That was not the situation here. There was an option, albeit not a particularly happy one. The option was to persevere in the attempts to make Tracy comfortable in her life, however, disagreeable and heartwrenching those attempts may have been. (41 C.R. (4th) at 38)

The sentence was life imprisonment with no parole eligibility for ten years.

In dismissing Latimer's appeal the Saskatchewan Court of Appeal held that the trial judge had properly withdrawn the defence of necessity from the jury given the *Perka* criteria. A majority, over the dissent of Chief Justice Bayda, rejected the argument for a constitutional exemption from the mandatory sentence.

At the second trial, ordered by the Supreme Court for other reasons, the charge was second degree murder. The trial proceeded on the basis the accused had been motivated by concern for his daughter's present and future pain. For very similar reasons to those offered in the first trial, the trial judge, Noble J., withdrew the defence of necessity but only after the addresses by counsel. The jury again convicted but were visibly upset when asked to make a recommendation whether parole eligibility should be set at more than ten years. They recommended one year! This reality was a factor Noble J. took into account in opting for a constitutional exemption and imposing a sentence of one year followed by probation for one year less one day. During the second trial, defence counsel asked the trial judge for a ruling, in advance of his closing submissions, on whether the jury could consider the defence of necessity. The trial judge told counsel that he would rule on necessity after the closing submissions. Some of the defence counsel's address referred to the defence of necessity. The judge later ruled that the defence was not available.

The Saskatchewan Court of Appeal affirmed the conviction but reversed the sentence. It imposed the mandatory minimum sentence of life imprisonment without parole eligibility for ten years. The Supreme Court in a short unanimous judgment dismissed the accused's further appeals against conviction and sentence.

Per curiam: —

. . . .

(1) The Availability of the Defence of Necessity
(a) The Three Requirements for the Defence of Necessity

We propose to set out the requirements for the defence of necessity first, before applying them to the facts of this appeal. The leading case on the defence of necessity is *Perka v. The Queen* . . . .

. . . .

Dickson J. insisted that the defence of necessity be restricted to those rare cases in which true "involuntariness" is present. The defence, he held, must be "strictly controlled and scrupulously limited" (p. 250). It is well-established that the defence of necessity must be of limited application. Were the criteria for the defence loosened or approached purely subjectively, some fear, as did Edmund Davies L.J., that necessity would "very easily become simply a mask for anarchy": *Southwark London Borough Council v. Williams*, [1971] Ch. 734 (C.A.), at p. 746.

Perka outlined three elements that must be present for the defence of necessity. First, there is the requirement of imminent peril or danger. Second, the accused must have had no reasonable legal alternative to the course of action he or she undertook. Third, there must be proportionality between the harm inflicted and the harm avoided.

To begin, there must be an urgent situation of "clear and imminent peril": *Morgentaler v. The Queen*, [1976] 1 S.C.R. 616, at p. 678. In short, disaster must be imminent, or harm unavoidable and near. It is not enough that the peril is foreseeable or likely; it must be on the verge of transpiring and virtually certain to occur. In *Perka*, Dickson J. expressed the requirement of imminent peril at p. 251: "At a minimum the situation must be so emergent and the peril must be so pressing that normal human instincts cry out for action and make a counsel of patience unreasonable". The *Perka* case, at p. 251, also offers the rationale for this requirement of immediate peril: "The requirement . . . tests whether it was indeed unavoidable for the actor to act at all". Where the situation of peril clearly should have been foreseen and avoided, an accused person cannot reasonably claim any immediate peril.

The second requirement for necessity is that there must be no reasonable legal alternative to disobeying the law. *Perka* proposed these questions, at pp. 251-52: "Given that the accused had to act, could he nevertheless realistically have acted to avoid the peril or prevent the harm, without breaking the law? *Was there a legal way out?*" (emphasis in original). If there was a reasonable legal alternative to breaking the law, there is no necessity. It may be noted that the requirement involves a realistic appreciation of the alternatives open to a person; the accused need not be placed in the last resort imaginable, but he must have no reasonable legal alternative. If an alternative to breaking the law exists, the defence of necessity on this aspect fails.

The third requirement is that there be proportionality between the harm inflicted and the harm avoided. The harm inflicted must not be disproportionate to the harm the accused sought to avoid.

. . . .

Evaluating proportionality can be difficult. It may be easy to conclude that there is no proportionality in some cases, like the example given in *Perka* of the person who blows up a city to avoid breaking a finger. Where proportionality can quickly be dismissed, it makes sense for a trial judge to do so and rule out the defence of necessity before considering the other requirements for necessity. But most situations fall into a grey area that requires a difficult balancing of harms. In this regard, it should be noted that the requirement is not that one harm (the harm avoided) must always clearly outweigh the other (the harm inflicted). Rather, the two harms must, at a minimum, be of a comparable gravity. That is, the harm avoided must be either comparable to, or clearly greater than, the harm inflicted. As the Supreme Court of Victoria in Australia has put it, the harm inflicted "must not be out of proportion to the peril to be avoided": *R. v. Loughnan*, [1981] V.R. 443, at p. 448.

Before applying the three requirements of the necessity defence to the facts of this case, we need to determine what test governs necessity. Is the standard objective or subjective? A subjective test would be met if the person believed he or she was in imminent peril with no reasonable legal alternative to committing the offence. Conversely, an objective test would not assess what the accused believed; it would consider whether in fact the person *was* in peril with no reasonable legal alternative. A modified objective test falls somewhere between the two. It involves an objective evaluation, but one that takes into account the situation and characteristics of the particular accused person. We conclude that, for two of the three requirements for the necessity defence, the test should be the modified objective test.

The first and second requirements — imminent peril and no reasonable legal alternative — must be evaluated on the modified objective standard described above. As expressed in *Perka*, necessity is rooted in an objective standard: "involuntariness is measured on the basis of society's expectation of appropriate and normal resistance to pressure" (p. 259). We would add that it is appropriate, in evaluating the accused's conduct, to take into account personal characteristics that legitimately affect what may be expected of that person. The approach taken in *R. v. Hibbert*, [1995] 2 S.C.R. 973, is instructive. Speaking for the court, Lamer C.J. held, at para. 59, that:

> it is appropriate to employ an objective standard that takes into account the particular circumstances of the accused, including his or her ability to perceive the existence of alternative courses of action.

While an accused's perceptions of the surrounding facts may be highly relevant in determining whether his conduct should be excused, those perceptions remain relevant only so long as they are reasonable. The accused person must, at the time of the act, honestly believe, on reasonable grounds, that he faces a situation of imminent peril that leaves no reasonable legal alternative open. There must be a reasonable basis for the accused's beliefs and actions, but it would be proper to take into account circumstances that legitimately affect the accused person's ability to evaluate his situation. The test cannot be a subjective one, and the accused who argues that *he* perceived imminent peril without an alternative would only succeed with the defence of necessity if his belief was reasonable given his circumstances and attributes. We leave aside for a case in which it arises the possibility that an honestly held but mistaken belief could ground a "mistake of fact" argument on the separate inquiry into *mens rea*.

The third requirement for the defence of necessity, proportionality, must be measured on an objective standard, as it would violate fundamental principles of the criminal law to do otherwise. Evaluating the nature of an act is fundamentally a determination reflecting society's values as to what is appropriate and what represents a transgression. Some insight into this requirement is provided by George Fletcher, in a passage from *Rethinking Criminal Law* (1978), at p. 804. Fletcher spoke of the comparison between the harm inflicted and the harm avoided, and suggested that there was a threshold at which a person must be expected to suffer the harm rather than break the law. He continued:

> Determining this threshold is patently a matter of moral judgment about what we expect people to be able to resist in trying situations. A valuable aid in making that judgment is comparing the competing interests at stake and assessing the degree to which the actor inflicts harm beyond the benefit that accrues from his action.

The evaluation of the seriousness of the harms must be objective. A subjective evaluation of the competing harms would, by definition, look at the matter from the perspective of the accused person who seeks to avoid harm, usually to himself. The proper perspective, however, is an objective one, since evaluating the gravity of the act is a matter of community standards infused with constitutional considerations (such as, in this case, the s. 15(1) equality rights of the disabled). We conclude that the proportionality requirement must be determined on a purely objective standard.

(b) The Application of the Requirements for Necessity in This Case

The inquiry here is not whether the defence of necessity should in fact *excuse* Mr. Latimer's actions, but whether the jury should have been left to consider this defence. The correct test on that point is whether there is an air of reality to the defence.

. . . .

The question is whether there is sufficient evidence that, if believed, would allow a reasonable jury — properly charged and acting judicially — to conclude that the defence applied and acquit the accused.

For the necessity defence, the trial judge must be satisfied that there is evidence sufficient to give an air of reality to each of the three requirements. If the trial judge concludes that there is no air of reality to any one of the three requirements, the defence of necessity should not be left to the jury.

In this case, there was no air of reality to the three requirements of necessity.

The first requirement is imminent peril. It is not met in this case. The appellant does not suggest he himself faced any peril; instead he identifies a peril to his daughter, stemming from her upcoming surgery which he perceived as a form of mutilation. Acute suffering can constitute imminent peril, but in this case there was nothing to her medical condition that placed Tracy in a dangerous situation where death was an alternative. Tracy was thought to be in pain before the surgery, and that pain was expected to continue, or increase, following the surgery. But that ongoing pain did not constitute an emergency in this case. To borrow the language of Edmund Davies L.J. in *Southwark London Borough Council*, *supra*, at p. 746, we are dealing not with an emergency but with "an obstinate and long-standing state of affairs". Tracy's proposed surgery did not pose an imminent threat to her life, nor did her medical condition. In fact, Tracy's health might have improved had the Latimers not rejected the option of relying on a feeding tube. Tracy's situation was not an emergency. The appellant can be reasonably expected to have understood that reality. There was no evidence of a legitimate psychological condition that rendered him unable to perceive that there was no imminent peril. The appellant argued that, for him, further surgery *did* amount to imminent peril. It was not reasonable for the appellant to form this belief, particularly when better pain management was available.

The second requirement for the necessity defence is that the accused had no reasonable legal alternative to breaking the law. In this case, there is no air of reality to the proposition that the appellant had no reasonable legal alternative to killing his daughter. He had at least one reasonable legal alternative: he could have struggled on, with what was unquestionably a difficult situation, by helping Tracy to live and by minimizing her pain as much as possible. The appellant might have done so by using a feeding tube to improve her health and allow her to take more effective pain medication, or he might have relied on the group home that Tracy stayed at just before her death. The appellant may well have thought the prospect of struggling on unbearably sad and demanding. It was a human response that this alternative was unappealing. But it was a reasonable legal alternative that the law requires a person to pursue before he can claim the defence of necessity. The appellant was aware of this alternative but rejected it.

The third requirement for the necessity defence is proportionality; it requires the trial judge to consider, as a question of law rather than fact, whether the harm avoided was proportionate to the harm inflicted. It is difficult, at the conceptual level, to imagine a circumstance in which the proportionality requirement could be met for a homicide. We leave open, if and until it arises, the question of whether the proportionality requirement could be met in a homicide situation. In England, the defence of necessity is probably not available for homicide: *R. v. Howe*, [1987] 1 A.C. 417 (H.L.), at pp. 453 and 429; Smith and Hogan, *Criminal Law* (9th ed. 1999), at pp. 249-51. The famous case of *R. v. Dudley and Stephens* (1884), 14 Q.B.D. 273, involving cannibalism on the high seas, is often cited as establishing the unavailability of the defence of necessity for homicide, although the case is not conclusive: see Card, Cross and Jones, *Criminal Law* (12th ed. 1992), at p. 352; Smith and Hogan, *supra*, at pp. 249 and 251. The Law Reform Commission of Canada has suggested the defence should not be available for a person who intentionally kills or seriously harms another person: *Report on Recodifying Criminal Law* (1987), at p. 36. American jurisdictions are divided on this question, with a number of them denying the necessity defence for murder: P.H. Robinson, *Criminal Law Defenses* (1984), vol. 2, at pp. 63-65; see also *United States v. Holmes*, 26 F. Cas. 360 (C.C.E.D. Pa. 1842) (No. 15,383). The American *Model Penal Code* proposes that the defence of necessity *would* be available for homicide: American Law Institute, *Model Penal Code and Commentaries* (1985), at para. 3.02, pp. 14-15; see also W.R. LaFave and A.W. Scott, *Substantive Criminal Law* (1986), vol. 1, at p. 634.

Assuming for the sake of analysis only that necessity could provide a defence to homicide, there would have to be a harm that was seriously comparable in gravity to death (the harm inflicted). In this case, there was no risk of such harm. The "harm avoided" in the appellant's situation was, compared to death, completely disproportionate. The harm inflicted in this case was ending a life; that harm was immeasurably more serious than the pain resulting from Tracy's operation which Mr. Latimer sought to avoid. Killing a person — in order to relieve the suffering produced by a medically manageable physical or mental condition — is not a proportionate response to the harm represented by the non-life-threatening suffering resulting from that condition.

We conclude that there was no air of reality to *any* of the three requirements for necessity. As noted earlier, if the trial judge concludes that even one of the requirements had no air of reality, the defence should not be left to the jury. Here, the trial judge was correct to remove the defence from the jury. In considering the defence of necessity, we must remain aware of the need to respect the life, dignity and equality of all the individuals affected by the act in question. The fact that the victim in this case was disabled rather than able-bodied does not affect our conclusion that the three requirements for the defence of necessity had no air of reality here.

In *R. v. Morgentaler, Smoling and Scott* (1985), 48 C.R. (3d) 1 (Ont. C.A.) the Court considered whether Dr. Henry Morgentaler could rely on the defence of necessity for having provided therapeutic abortions without complying with the law in force at the time concerning such abortions. The Court held:

> ... the defence of necessity is not premised on dissatisfaction with the law. The defence of necessity recognizes that the law must be followed, but there are certain factual situations which arise which may excuse a person for failure to comply with the law. It is not the law which can create an emergency giving rise to a defence of necessity, but it is the facts of a given situation which may do so.

This was not a case where two or more doctors agreed to procure the miscarriage of a female person who was in immediate need of medical services in order to avoid danger to her life or health, and in which case the defence of necessity would be a live issue. The defence of necessity cannot be resorted to as an excuse for medical practitioners in Canada to agree in the circumstances of this case to procure abortions on their own opinion of the danger to life or health and at a place of their own choosing in complete disregard of the provisions of s. 251 of the *Criminal Code*.

The decision in *Latimer* that there was no evidentiary foundation for the defence of necessity to be put to the jury is in stark contrast to the three *Morgentaler* trials in Quebec where the necessity defence was weak but nevertheless left with the jury. **Should the defence of necessity have been put in *Latimer*?**

Latimer is clearly a hard case. It engages the emotions of disabled persons who understandably feel vulnerable if the accused was not to be punished for deliberately taking an innocent life without consent. There is also understandable fear that a lenient sentence would encourage other similar actions and moves to decriminalize assisted suicide and euthanasia. See further David Lepofsky, "The *Latimer* Case: Murder is Still Murder When the Victim is a Child With a Disability" (2001) Queen's L.J. 319.

In June 1995, the Special Senate Committee on Euthanasia and Assisted Suicide handed down its report, recommending that counselling suicide, assisting suicide, and non-voluntary euthanasia should all remain criminal offences. They also recommended, however, that "the *Criminal Code* be amended to provide for a less severe penalty in cases where there is the essential element of compassion or mercy".

Chief Justice Bayda carefully considered public outrage expressed against the sentence and four other mercy killing cases, two involving consent, where the charges were reduced from murder and the sentences were probation. This is a powerful judgment: see, too, Tim Quigley, "*R. v. Latimer*: Hard Cases Make Interesting Law" (1995), 41 C.R. (4th) 89 at 96-98. At its heart the concern is for equal justice. Unfortunately, it was not even referred to by the Supreme Court. See, too, Barney Sneiderman, "The *Latimer* Mercy-Killing Case: A Rumination of Crime and Punishment" (1997) 5 Health L.J. 1 and "The Case of Robert Latimer. A Commentary on Crime and Punishment" (1999) 37 Alta. L. Rev. 1017. The latter article was relied on by defence counsel in the Supreme Court but is not even acknowledged by the Court. For a wide range of views on the Supreme Court's decision see comments by Barney Sneiderman, Archibald Kaiser, Allan Manson and Stuart in the C.R.'s. In *R. v. Ferguson*, 54 C.R. (6th) 197, 228 C.C.C. (3d) 385, [2008] 1 S.C.R. 96 the Supreme Court firmly decided that constitutional exemptions were not available in the case of minimum sentences. See comments by Steve Coughlan and Paul Calarco.

In the U.K. the absolute authority of *Dudley and Stephens* that necessity can never be a defence to a deliberate killing may have been weakened by a ruling of the Court of Appeal: *Re. A (Children) (Conjoined Twins: Surgical Separation)*, [2000] 4 All E.R. 961 (C.A.). The Court ruled that necessity would legalize an operation to separate conjoined twins against the wishes of their Catholic parents. The operation would result in the instant death of one of the twins but would likely save the other from death for a normal life. The defence of necessity is fully reviewed by Brooke L.J. and also relied on by Ward L.J. and Walker L.J. It somehow rests on the view that death was not intended. Brooke L.J. refers to a real life example:

> At the coroner's inquest conducted in October 1987 into the Zeebrugge [ferry] disaster, an army corporal gave evidence that he and dozens of other people were near the foot of a rope ladder. They were all in the water and in danger of drowning. Their route to safety, however, was blocked for at least ten minutes by a young man who was petrified by cold or fear (or both) and was unable to move up or down. Eventually the corporal gave instructions that the man should be pushed off the ladder, and he was never seen again (at para. 311).

For a full review of *Latimer* and the *Conjoined Twins* case see Gary Trotter, "Necessity and Death: Lessons from *Latimer* and the Case of the Conjoined Twins" (2003) 40 Alberta L. Rev. 817. Professor Trotter argues that necessity should be rejected as a defence to intentional killings and that the *Conjoined Twins* case must be confined to its "idiosyncratic context".

For an argument that mandatory minimum sentences for murder are not appropriate in the context of euthanasia see Nadia E. Thomas, "Sentencing Murder: Did Robert Latimer Deserve the Mandatory Minimum?" (2002), 7 Can. Crim. L. Rev. 93.

---

1. The accused is charged with speeding and dangerous driving. He was clocked on radar at 120 k.p.h. in a 50 k.p.h. zone. He was operating his vehicle in a heavily built-up residential area and was observed maintaining this speed over a distance of several city blocks. During this time he was being closely followed by another automobile. The automobile alternately slowed and accelerated with the second vehicle always maintaining a distance of seven to eight feet from the lead vehicle. The accused testified that each time he speeded up he did so to ensure maintenance of interval between himself and the car behind him to avoid the hazard presented by the other driver's tailgating. The driver of the other vehicle admitted that he was crowding the accused intentionally as he was "out for thrills". The accused relies on necessity. What do you, as Crown counsel, argue?
Compare *R. v. Fry* (1977), 36 C.C.C. (2d) 396 (Sask. Prov. Ct.), *R. v. Kennedy* (1972), 18 C.R.N.S. 80, 7 C.C.C. (2d) 42 (N.S. Co. Ct.) and *R. v. Morris* (1994), 32 C.R. (4th) 191 (B.C. S.C.).

2. The accused is charged with fishing in a place where, at that time, fishing was prohibited by law. The waters had been closed to fishing from 1400 hours that day. The basis of his defence is that, owing to the very inclement weather the day before, his punts, used for collecting the herring from the gillnets, were beached. The accused was therefore unable to retrieve all his nets before 1400 hours although he worked all morning and did manage to retrieve some. Give judgment.
Compare *R. v. Pootlass* (1978), 1 C.R. (3d) 378 (B.C. Prov. Ct.).

3. The accused is a police constable and at the material time was driving a police cruiser. He received a radio call that a bank alarm had gone

off at the Bank of Montreal a few blocks away. He was advised that the robbers were armed and still on the premises. He turned on the siren and roof lights and headed for the bank. As he approached the bank he was aware of a stop sign which required him to stop at the intersection. Because of the emergency and his concern for the safety of the people in the bank, he decided not to stop. He slowed to 20 k.p.h., looked both ways, and entered the intersection without stopping. He collided with a car coming from his right. He was aware of his exemption under the circumstances from the speed provisions of the *Highway Traffic Act*, but realized there was no other exemption. The accused is charged with failing to stop and advances the defence of necessity. Result?

Compare *R. v. Walker* (1979), 48 C.C.C. (2d) 126 (Ont. Co. Ct.).

4. The accused is charged with having committed an assault on his wife. The assault allegedly occurred in the accused's truck as they were returning from an evening at the tavern. The accused was driving. He was sober but his wife was drunk. His wife became agitated about an occurrence earlier that evening and demanded that they return to town. The accused refused to turn around and his wife threatened to jump. She reached for the door handle and he grabbed her and pulled her back. She grabbed at the steering wheel and the truck nearly went into the ditch. The accused grabbed her around the neck and held her in that fashion all the way home. Grounds of necessity?

Compare *R. v. Morris* (1981), 23 C.R. (3d) 175, 61 C.C.C. (2d) 163 (Alta. Q.B.).

5. The accused was charged with trespassing contrary to a provincial statute. The trespass occurred on the grounds of Litton Industries. The accused testified that she believed Litton Industries to manufacture component systems for the Cruise missile and that the Cruise missile was aimed at targets in other countries which could trigger a nuclear conflict. She believed Litton Industries was committing a serious offence and she was prepared to commit the offence of trespass to avert this evil. She testified she was involved in the protest because "I have to!" The defence relied on necessity.

Compare *R. v. Young* (1984), 39 C.R. (3d) 290 (Ont. Prov. Ct.).

6. The accused, a 33-year-old mother of five young children, was charged with defrauding the Ministry of Community and Social Services of more than $1,000. It was alleged that during a common-law relationship over a ten-year period she had misrepresented that her partner and the father of four of the children had not been living with her. It was further alleged that as a result she had obtained family benefits to which she was not entitled. Over the ten years until final separation she had received benefits of some $130,000. On the final separation the accused went to a women's shelter.

The trial judge found that the accused had failed to disclose that the parties were from time to time living together and that as a result she had received family benefits to which she was not entitled. However, there was evidence that he was abusive and spent any money he had on alcohol. She testified she was afraid to tell General Welfare that he was living with her in case the welfare cheque was made out to him. She feared he would drink away the money and they would be without food or shelter or both. Should the defence of necessity succeed?

Compare *R. v. LaLonde* (1995), 37 C.R. (4th) 97 (Ont. Gen. Div.) and see comment by Shella Noonan, "*LaLonde:* Evaluating The Relevance of BWS Evidence" (1995), 37 C.R. (4th) 110.

7. The accused is charged with impaired driving and driving over the legal limit. He was found driving erratically on the streets of a small town at midday. He was trying to drive himself to hospital after an unsuccessful suicide attempt. He had been drinking heavily and he tried to poison himself with carbon monoxide from his truck inside his garage. He woke up, confused, to discover the truck had run out of gas. He decided to go for help in another vehicle. In his confused, highly emotional and drunk state it did not occur to him to go to a neighbour for help or to call 911. Should his defence of necessity succeed?

Compare *R. v. Desrosiers* (2007), 48 C.R. (6th) 85 (Ont. C.J.). See too *R. v. McCain* (2003), 15 C.R. (6th) 360 (Ont. C.J.).

8. The accused had a history of depression and moved into the forests and engaged in periods of fasting for spiritual cleansing. After a 60-day fast he walked for several hours in the cold to look for food. He believed he was in a desperate situation due to lack of food and hypothermia. He broke into a house where he ate some food and wrapped himself in blankets. The owner of the house found him unconscious. He is charged with breaking and entering a dwelling house and committing mischief. Should his defence of necessity result in acquittal?

Compare *R. v. John Doe* (2007), (sub nom. *R. v. Nelson*) 228 C.C.C. (3d) 302, 54 C.R. (6th) 393 (B.C. C.A.).

9. The accused was driving with excessive alcohol in his blood. His cousin had fallen and suffered a significant cut to his head. The accused unsuccessfully phoned emergency services. It was snowing and after midnight so he decided to drive rather than approach neighbours he did not know.

Compare *R. v. Costoff* (2010), 74 C.R. (6th) 369 (Ont. C.J.) and *R. v. Primus* (2010), 261 C.C.C. (3d) 159 (C.A. Que.).

6. DURESS

(a) Section 17 and Common Law

See ss. 17 and 18 of the *Criminal Code*.

R. v. CARKER (NO. 2)

[1967] S.C.R. 114, 2 C.R.N.S. 16, [1967] 2 C.C.C. 190, 1966 CarswellBC 169

RITCHIE J.: — This is an appeal by the Attorney-General of British Columbia from a judgment of the Court of Appeal of that Province, from which Mr. Justice MacLean dissented, and by which it was ordered that the respondent's conviction for unlawfully and wilfully damaging public property and thereby committing mischief, should be set aside and that a new trial should be had.

At the trial the respondent admitted having damaged the plumbing fixtures in the cell where he was incarcerated at Oakalla Prison Farm in British Columbia but, through his counsel, he sought to introduce evidence to show that he had committed this offence under the compulsion of threats and was therefore entitled to be excused for committing it by virtue of the provisions of s. 17 of the *Criminal Code* and that he was also entitled to avail himself of the common-law defence of "duress" having regard to the provision of s. 7 of the *Criminal Code*.

. . . .

I agree with the learned trial judge and with MacLean J.A. that in respect of proceedings for an offence under the *Criminal Code* the common-law rules and principles respecting "duress" as an excuse or defence have been codified and exhaustively defined in s. 17.

. . . .

At the outset of the proceedings at the trial in the present case and in the absence of the jury, Mr. Greenfield, who acted on behalf of the accused, informed the court that he intended to call evidence of compulsion and duress and he elected to outline the nature of this evidence which was that the offence had been committed during a disturbance, apparently organized by way of protest, to damage property at the Prison Farm in the course of which a substantial body of prisoners, shouting in unison from their separate cells, threatened the respondent, who was not joining in the disturbance, that if he did not break the plumbing fixtures in his cell he would be kicked in the head, his arm would be broken and he would get a knife in the back at the first opportunity.

. . . .

There can be little doubt that the evidence outlined by Mr. Greenfield, which was subsequently confirmed by the evidence given by the ringleaders of the disturbance in mitigation of sentence, disclosed that the respondent committed the offence under the compulsion of threats of death and grievous bodily harm, but although these threats were "immediate" in the sense that they were continuous until the time that the offence was committed, they were not threats of "immediate death" or "immediate grievous bodily harm" and none of the persons who delivered them was present in the cell with the respondent when the offence was committed. I am accordingly of opinion that the learned trial judge was right in deciding that the proposed evidence did not afford an excuse within the meaning of s. 17 of the *Criminal Code*.

. . . .

In support of the suggestion that the threat in the present case was "immediate and continuous" Mr. Justice Norris relied on the case of *Subramaniam v. Public Prosecutor*, in which the Privy Council decided that the trial Judge was wrong in excluding evidence of threats to which the appellant was subjected by Chinese terrorists in Malaya. In that case it was found that the threats were a continuous menace up to the moment when the appellant was captured because the terrorists might have come back at any time and carried them into effect. Section 94 of the Penal Code of the Federated Malay States, which the appellant sought to invoke in that case provided:

> 94. Except murder and offences included in Chapter VI punishable with death, nothing is an offence which is done by a person who is compelled to do it by threats, which, at the time of doing it, reasonably cause the apprehension that instant death to that person will otherwise be the consequence.

The distinctions between the *Subramaniam* case and the present one lie in the fact that Subramaniam might well have had reasonable cause for apprehension that instant death would result from his disobeying the terrorists who might have come back at any moment, whereas it is virtually inconceivable that "immediate death" or "grievous bodily harm" could have come to Carker from those who were uttering the threats against him as they were locked up in separate cells, and it is also to be noted that the provisions of s. 17 of the *Criminal Code* are by no means the same as those of s. 94 of the Penal Code of the Federated Malay States; amongst other distinctions the latter section contains no provision that the person who utters the threats must be present when the offence is committed in order to afford an excuse for committing it.

. . . .

The evidence outlined to the learned trial judge discloses that the criminal act was committed to preserve the respondent from future harm coming to him, but there is no suggestion in the evidence tendered for the defence that the accused did not know that what he was doing would "probably cause" damage. Accepting the outline made by defence counsel as being an accurate account of the evidence which was available, there was in my view nothing in it to support the defence that the act was not done "wilfully" within the meaning of s. 371(1) and 372(1) of the *Criminal Code* and there was accordingly no ground to justify the learned trial judge in permitting the proposed evidence to be called in support of such a defence.

In view of all the above, I would allow this appeal, set aside the judgment of the Court of Appeal and restore the conviction.

Appeal allowed and conviction restored.

R. v. PAQUETTE

[1977] 2 S.C.R. 189, 39 C.R.N.S. 257, 30 C.C.C. (2d) 417,
1976 CarswellOnt 415F, 1976 CarswellOnt 28

MARTLAND J.: — The facts which give rise to this appeal are as follows:

During the course of a robbery at the Pop Shoppe, in the City of Ottawa, on March 18, 1973, an innocent bystander was killed by a bullet from a rifle fired by one Simard. The robbery was committed by Simard and one Clermont, both of whom, together with the appellant, were jointly charged with non-capital murder. Simard and Clermont pleaded guilty to this charge.

The appellant was not present when the robbery was committed or when the shooting occurred. The charge against him was founded upon s. 21(2) of the *Criminal Code*. Section 21 provides as follows:

21(1) Every one is a party to an offence who
  (*a*) actually commits it,
  (*b*) does or omits to do anything for the purpose of aiding any person to commit it, or
  (*c*) abets any person in commiting it.
  (2) Where two or more persons form an intention in common to carry out an unlawful purpose and to assist each other therein and any one of them, in carrying out the common purpose, commits an offence, each of them who knew or ought to have known that the commission of the offence would be a probable consequence of carrying out the common purpose is a party to that offence.

The appellant made a statement to the police, which was admitted in evidence at the trial and which described his involvement in the matter as follows: On the day of the robbery Clermont telephoned the appellant for a ride as his own car was broken. Clermont asked the appellant where he used to work and was told at the Pop Shoppe. Clermont told him to drive to the Pop Shoppe because Clermont wanted to rob it, and, when the appellant refused, Clermont pulled his gun and threatened to kill him. Simard was picked up later and also a rifle. The appellant drove them to the Pop Shoppe. The appellant had been threatened with revenge if he did not wait for Clermont and Simard. The appellant, in his statement, stated he was afraid and drove around the block. After the robbery and homicide Clermont and Simard attempted twice, unsuccessfully, to get into the appellant's car. Three of the Crown's witnesses supported this latter statement.

The appellant did not testify at trial but relied on the above statement and two other statements also introduced at the trial by the Crown to support his argument that he had no intention in common with Simard and Clermont to carry out the robbery; *i.e.*:

(1) an oral statement to a police officer on his arrest that he had been threatened with death "if he squealed";

(2) the written statement to the police outlined above in which he stated that he had only participated in the robbery by driving because he was threatened with death;

(3) a statement to his girlfriend the day after the robbery that he was forced to do it. The trial Judge charged the jury as follows:

> Now, the defence are asserting that Paquette participated in this robbery because he was compelled to do so, and in that connection I charge you that if Paquette joined in the common plot to rob the Pop Shoppe under threats of death or grievous bodily harm, that would negative his having a common intention with Simard to rob the Pop Shoppe, and you must find Paquette not guilty.

The appellant was acquitted. The Crown appealed to the Court of Appeal for Ontario [19 C.C.C. (2d) 154, 5 O.R. (2d) 1]. The reasons delivered by that court make it clear that the appeal would have been dismissed had it not been for the decision of this court in *Dunbar v. The King*, 67 C.C.C. 20, [1936] 4 D.L.R. 737.

The relevant portions of the majority judgment in that case are as follows [at pp. 27-8 C.C.C., pp. 743-4 D.L.R.]:

> On January 15, 1936, three men entered and robbed a branch of the Canadian Bank of Commerce in Vancouver and in the course of the robbery the teller was fatally shot. The appellant Dunbar was not among those who entered the bank but he had brought the robbers to the bank in an automobile and after the robery was over drove back for them and took them away to the house where they had all been living together. He subsequently shared with them in the proceeds of the robbery. He had a criminal record, had met one or other of the robbers in the penitentiary and had been living with them in the same house for some days prior to the robbery. He knew when driving the car to the bank that his associates were going there with the purpose of robbing the bank, that these men were armed and that in the course of such robbery it was not improbable that someone might be killed. His sole excuse for his conduct was that he had acted under compulsion as one of his associates had threatened his life unless he accompanied them and had further threatened that if he did anything to betray them that he would be killed. The point of alleged misdirection most stressed by counsel for the prisoner before us was a statement as follows: —
>
> "If you accept Dunbar's evidence that he was so bereft of reason that his reasoning faculties were suspended and that he was really in the position of having his hand held by somebody, that he had two men standing over him — you had this story of the thing put to

you in the way that he would have you believe — well, then it seems to me there should be some evidence to show his mental condition."

Section 20 of the *Criminal Code*, dealing with compulsion, excludes murder and robbery, and therefore is inapplicable to this case, but it was argued that if compulsion were shown it might be sufficient to negative any common intention under the provision of s. 69(2) of the *Code*. It seems to me that this argument fails to recognize the distinction between intention and the motive giving rise to intention.

If Dunbar's story of the threat to him was true then he was faced with a choice between endangering his own life or assisting those about to commit a robbery which might, as he knew, be accompanied by murder of an innocent person. The motive giving rise to his choice between these two courses is irrelevant. This being so, in my opinion the issue was not unfairly put before the jury in the learned trial judge's charge. I would, therefore, dismiss the appeal.

Counsel for the Crown submits that the principles of law applicable to the excuse or defence of duress or compulsion are exhaustively codified in s . 17 [am. 1974-75-76, c. 105, s. 29] of the *Criminal Code*, and that the appellant is precluded from relying upon this provision because of the exception contained at the end of it. Section 17 provides:

> 17. A person who commits an offence under compulsion by threats of immediate death or grievous bodily harm from a person who is present when the offence is committed is excused for committing the offence if he believes that the threats will be carried out and if he is not a party to a conspiracy or association whereby he is subject to compulsion, but this section does not apply where the offence that is committed is treason, murder, piracy, attempted murder, assisting in rape, forcible abduction, robbery, causing bodily harm or arson.

In my opinion, the application of s. 17 is limited to cases in which the person seeking to rely upon it has himself committed an offence. If a person who actually commits the offence does so in the presence of another party who has compelled him to do the act by threats of immediate death or grievous bodily harm, then, if he believes the threats would be carried out, and is not a party to a conspiracy whereby he is subject to such compulsion, he is excused for committing the offence. The protection afforded by this section is not given in respect of the offences listed at the end of the section, which include murder and robbery.

The section uses the specific words "a person who commits an offence". It does not use the words "a person who is a party to an offence". This is significant in the light of the wording of s. 21(1) which, in para. (*a*), makes a person a party to an offence who "actually commits it". Paragraphs (*b*) and (*c*) deal with a person who aids or abets a person committing the offence. In my opinion, s. 17 codifies the law as to duress as an excuse for the actual commission of a crime, but it does not, by its terms, go beyond that. *R. v. Carker (No. 2)*, [1967] 2 C.C.C. 190, [1967] S.C.R. 114, 2 C.R.N.S. 16, in which reference was made to s. 17 having codified the defence or excuse of duress, dealt with a situation in which the accused had actually committed the offence.

The appellant, in the present case, did not himself commit the offence of robbery or of murder. He was not present when the murder occurred, as was the case in *R. v. Farduto* (1912), 21 C.C.C. 144, and *R. v. Warren* (1973), 14 C.C.C. (2d) 188, 24 C.R.N.S. 349, to which counsel for the Crown referred. In the former case the accused provided the razor with which the murderer cut the throat of the victim in his presence. The court was of the view that the trial judge could conclude that there was no case of such compulsion as would constitute an excuse. In the latter case the accused, the brother of the actual murderer was present with him over a period of time after the robbery occurred and before the deceased was killed in his presence. The report does not indicate the nature of the compulsion alleged. The emphasis appears to have been on the subnormal intelligence of the accused making him willing to go along with what was suggested to him.

The appellant could only be considered to be a party to the murder on the basis of the application of s. 21(2). Section 21(1) is not applicable because the offence to which he is alleged to be a party is murder, and it is clear that he did not commit murder, nor did he aid or abet in its commission.

Subsection (2) is only applicable if it is established that the appellant, in common with Simard and Clermont, formed an intention to commit robbery. The question in issue is as to whether the trial judge erred in law in telling the jury that if the appellant joined in the plot to rob under threats of death or of grievous bodily harm, this would negative such common intention.

I have already stated my reasons for considering s. 17 to be inapplicable. That being so, the appellant is entitled, by virtue of s. 7(3) of the *Code* to rely upon any excuse or defence available to him at common law. The defence of duress to a charge of murder against a person who did not commit the murder, but who was alleged to have aided and abetted, was recently considered by the House of Lords in *Director of Public Prosecutions for Northern Ireland v. Lynch*, [1975] A.C. 653, in which the decided cases were fully reviewed. The facts in that case were as follows [headnote]:

> The defendant drove a motor car containing a group of the I.R.A. in Northern Ireland on an expedition in which they shot and killed a police officer. On his trial for aiding and abetting the murder there was evidence that he was not a member of the I.R.A. and that he acted unwillingly under the orders of the leader of the group, being convinced that, if he disobeyed, he would himself be shot. The trial judge held that the defence of duress was not available to him and the jury found him guilty. The Court of Criminal Appeal in Northern Ireland upheld the conviction.

The House of Lords, by a three to two majority, held that on a charge of murder the defence of duress was open to a person accused as a principal in the second degree (aider and abettor) and ordered a new trial.

The conclusion of Lord Morris of Borth-y-Gest is stated at p. 677, as follows:

> Having regard to the authorities to which I have referred it seems to me to have been firmly held by our courts in this country that duress can afford a defence in criminal cases. A recent pronouncement was that in the Court of Appeal in 1971 in the case above referred

to (*Reg. v. Hudson*, [1971] 2 Q.B. 202). The court stated that they had been referred to a large number of authorities and to the views of writers of textbooks. In the judgment of the court delivered by Lord Parker C.J. and prepared by Widgery L.J. the conclusion was expressed, at p. 206, that "it is clearly established that duress provides a defence in all offences including perjury (except possibly treason or murder as a principal)."

We are only concerned in this case to say whether duress could be a possible defence open to Lynch who was charged with being an aider and abettor. Relying on the help given in the authorities we must decide this as a matter of principle. I consider that duress in such a case can be open as a possible defence. Both general reasoning and the requirements of justice lead me to this conclusion.

Lord Wilberforce, at pp. 682-3, cited with approval a passage from the dissenting reasons of Bray C.J., in *R. v. Brown and Morley*, [1968] S.A.S.R. 467 at 494:

"The reasoning generally used to support the proposition that duress is no defence to a charge of murder is, to use the words of Blackstone cited above, that 'he ought rather to die himself, than escape by the murder of an innocent.' Generally speaking I am prepared to accept this proposition. Its force is obviously, considerably less where the act of the threatened man is not the direct act of killing but only the rendering of some minor form of assistance, particularly when it is by no means certain that if he refuses the death of the victim will be averted, or conversely when it is by no means certain that if he complies the death will be a necessary consequence. It would seem hard, for example, if an innocent passer-by seized in the street by a gang of criminals visibly engaged in robbery and murder in a shop and compelled at the point of a gun to issue misleading comments to the public, or *an innocent driver compelled at the point of a gun to convey the murderer to the victim*, were to have no defence. Are there any authorities which compel us to hold that he would not?"

I am in agreement with the conclusion reached by the majority that it was open to Lynch, in the circumstances of that case, to rely on the defence of duress, which had not been put to the jury. If the defence of duress can be available to a person who has aided and abetted in the commission of murder, then clearly it should be available to a person who is sought to be made a party to the offence by virtue of s. 21(2). A person whose actions have been dictated by fear of death or of grievous bodily injury cannot be said to have formed a genuine common intention to carry out an unlawful purpose with the person who has threatened him with those consequences if he fails to co-operate.

Paquette created two bases upon which the accused could be found not guilty: that he did not have a common intention with Clermont and Simard (and therefore that the elements of s. 21(2) were not proven in the first place); and that as a party rather than a principal he was entitled to rely on the common law defence of duress, rather than the stricter statutory version.

Both of those points were addressed in the next case to deal with duress, *R. v. Hibbert*. We have looked at *Hibbert* before, in considering the meaning of the word "purpose". Hibbert was convicted of aggravated assault as a party under s. 21(1)(b), on the basis that he had done something "for the purpose" of aiding another person to carry out a shooting: he had gone with B to C's apartment building and arranged for C to come to the lobby, at which point B had shot C four times. Hibbert argued that he had only performed the actions in order not to be shot himself and therefore did not truly have the "purpose" of aiding in the shooting. The Supreme Court of Canada, as we saw earlier, rejected that argument and found that the elements of s. 21(1)(b) were made out. The Court also noted that this approach to s. 21(1)(b) was inconsistent with the approach in *Paquette* to s. 21(2); as a result, they overturned that aspect of the decision in *Paquette*, holding that the presence of duress would not prevent a "common intention" from being formed. However, they continued to find that the duress might itself constitute a defence and elaborated upon one of the requirements of the common law version of that defence.

R. v. HIBBERT

[1995] 2 S.C.R. 973, 40 C.R. (4th) 141, 99 C.C.C. (3d) 193,
1995 CarswellOnt 117, 1995 CarswellOnt 530

LAMER C.J. (LA FOREST, L'HEUREUX-DUBÉ, SOPINKA, GONTHIER, CORY, MCLACHLIN, IACOBUCCI and MAJOR JJ. concurring): —

. . . .

The "Safe Avenue of Escape" Requirement in the Common Law of Duress

The second and third issues raised by the appellant have to do with the so-called "safe avenue of escape" rule. The court must decide whether such a rule in fact exists, and, if it does, whether the availability of a "safe avenue" is to be determined on an objective or subjective basis. In my opinion, it is best to start the analysis by examining the juristic nature of the defence of duress and its relationship to other common law defences, since I am of the view that by so doing the answers to the questions posed in the present appeal will become clear.

(1) The Relation Between Duress and Other Excuses

As I have explained, the common law defence of duress, properly understood, is not based on the idea that coercion negates *mens rea*. Rather, it is one of a number of defences that operate by justifying or excusing what would otherwise be criminal conduct. Once duress is recognized as providing a defence of this type, it becomes apparent that much can be learned about its juristic nature by examining other existing legal excuses or justifications, such as the defences of necessity, self-defence and provocation, and by considering the extent to which analogies between these defences and the defence of duress can be drawn and sustained.

. . . .

The similarities between defences of duress and necessity have been noted on previous occasions by other commentators. . . . . In *Perka* the status of the defence of necessity in the common law of Canada was firmly established. In his majority reasons, Dickson J. summarized the considerable debate in the academic literature over the question of whether the defence of necessity should be conceptualized as a "justification" or an "excuse". Dickson J. described the justification-based approach to the defence of necessity . . . . He went on to reject this basis for the defence. Instead, he adopted an understanding of the defence of necessity based on the alternative concept of an "excuse" . . . . The common law defences of necessity and duress apply to essentially similar factual situations. Indeed, to repeat Lord Simon of Glaisdale's observation, "[d]uress is . . . merely a particular application of the doctrine of 'necessity'". In my view, the similarities between the two defences are so great that consistency and logic requires that they be understood as based on the same juristic principles. Indeed, to do otherwise would be to promote incoherence and anomaly in the criminal law. In the case of necessity, the court has already considered the various alternative theoretical positions available, in *Perka*, *supra*, and has expounded a conceptualization of the defence of necessity as an excuse, based on the idea of normative involuntariness. In my opinion, the need for consistency and coherence in the law dictates that the common law defence of duress also be based on this juridical foundation. If the defence is viewed in this light, the answers to the questions posed in the present appeal can be seen to follow readily from the reasons of Dickson J. in *Perka*.

(a) The Safe Avenue of Escape Requirement

The so-called "safe avenue of escape" requirement in the law of duress is, in my view, simply a specific example of a more general requirement, analogous to that in the defence of necessity identified by Dickson J. — the requirement that compliance with the law be "demonstrably impossible". As Dickson J. explained, this requirement can be derived directly from the underlying concept of normative involuntariness upon which the defence of necessity is based. As I am of the view that the defence of duress must be seen as being based upon this same theoretical foundation, it follows that the defence of duress includes a similar requirement — namely, a requirement that it can only be invoked if, to adopt Dickson J.'s phrase, there is "no legal way out" of the situation of duress the accused faces. The rule that the defence of duress is unavailable if a "safe avenue of escape" was open to the accused is simply a specific instance of this general requirement — if the accused could have escaped without undue danger, the decision to commit an offence becomes, as Dickson J. observed in the context of necessity, "a voluntary one, impelled by some consideration beyond the dictates of 'necessity' and human instincts".

(b) Is the Existence of a Safe Avenue of Escape to Be Determined Subjectively or Objectively?

How this question is answered depends, in my view, on how one conceives of the notion of "normative involuntariness" upon which the defence of duress is based. That is, is an action "normatively involuntary" when the actor believes that he has no real choice, or is this the case only when there is in fact no reasonable alternative course of action available?

Cogent arguments can be made in support of each of these positions. The issue can be framed in slightly different terms. The question of when a person "could not help doing what he did", and thus performs a normatively involuntary act can, however, be understood in two different ways. On the one hand, it can be argued that actors who perform acts that appear reasonable in relation to their knowledge of their surrounding circumstances "cannot help" what they did, even if their understanding of their situation is objectively unreasonable. Put another way, it can be argued that a person's acts are normatively involuntary if he or she honestly believes there are no reasonable alternatives, even if he or she has overlooked an alternative that a reasonable person would have been aware of. On the other hand, it can also be argued that an actor's failure to take steps to inform himself or herself of the true state of affairs is itself a choice, and that a decision based on the resulting erroneous view of the circumstances is thus not normatively involuntary, since it could have been avoided. In my opinion, the latter argument accords most closely with the view of normative involuntariness adopted by the court in *Perka*, which, as I have explained, should be seen as the theoretical foundation of both the defences of duress and necessity. As Dickson J.'s reasons in *Perka* suggest, a degree of objectivity is inherent to excuses that are based on the notion of normative involuntariness, to the extent that this concept turns on the objective availability, or lack of availability, of true choice. Indeed, Dickson J. clearly indicates that the operative standard for the defence of necessity is to be an objective one, based on whether "there is a reasonable legal alternative to disobeying the law".

However, simply adopting the second of the two arguments set out above does not fully resolve the issue of the standard to be applied in assessing whether a safe avenue of escape existed. Even if it is accepted that an actor's failure to take steps to acquire reasonable knowledge of his or her full range of options can, in itself, constitute a form of choice, it can still be argued that this only holds true when the actor is able to acquire and process additional information. That is, a person does not "choose" inaction when he or she is incapable in the first place of acting, or of knowing when to act. Thus, an argument can be made for framing the objective standard used in determining the availability of alternative options, such as "safe avenues of escape", in terms of the particular actor's capacities and abilities. This argument reflects a more general concern about the application of the negligence standard in criminal law, which Hart, *supra*, has summarized in the following terms:

> If our conditions of liability are invariant and not flexible, i.e. if they are not adjusted to the capacities of the accused, then some individuals will be held liable for negligence though they could not have helped their failure to comply with the standard.

This court has previously indicated that when assessing the reasonableness of an accused's conduct for the purposes of determining whether he or she should be excused from criminal responsibility, it is appropriate to employ an objective standard that takes into account the particular circumstances of the accused, including his or her ability to perceive the existence of alternative courses of action. For instance, in *R. v. Lavallee*, [1990] 1 S.C.R. 852, a self-defence case, Wilson J., writing for a majority of the court, declared (at p. 889):

> I think the question the jury must ask itself [in a case of self-defence] is whether, given the history, circumstances and perceptions of the appellant, her belief that she could not preserve herself from being killed by [her "common-law" spouse] that night except by killing him first was reasonable.

The defences of self-defence, duress and necessity are essentially similar, so much so that consistency demands that each defence's "reasonableness" requirement be assessed on the same basis. Accordingly, I am of the view that while the question of whether a "safe avenue of escape" was open to an accused who pleads duress should be assessed on an objective basis, the appropriate objective standard to be employed is one that takes into account the particular circumstances and human frailties of the accused.

It should be noted that the question of what sort of objective standard is to be used when assessing the "reasonableness" of the conduct of persons raising an excuse-based defence is different in several key respects from the issue that was before the court in *R. v. Creighton*, [1993] 3 S.C.R. 3. In that case, in the course of considering the *mens rea* for "unlawful act manslaughter" under s. 222(5)(*a*) of the *Criminal Code*, a majority of the court was of the view that (at p. 61, per McLachlin J.):

> [C]onsiderations of principle and policy dictate the maintenance of a single, uniform legal standard of care for [offences with a mens rea of negligence], subject to one exception: incapacity to appreciate the nature of the risk which the activity in question entails.

Although I dissented on this point in *Creighton* (while concurring in the result), I now consider myself bound by the majority judgment. However, I do not believe that *Creighton* is applicable when what is at issue is the standard of reasonableness to be used in establishing the availability of an excuse-based defence, as opposed to the determination of liability under an offence that is defined in terms of a mental state of negligence. In my view, the relevant "considerations of policy and principle" in such cases are quite different from those identifiable in the context of negligence-based offences. Offences defined in terms of negligence typically impose criminal liability on an accused person for the consequences that flowed from his or her inherently hazardous activities — activities that he or she voluntarily and willingly chose to engage in. In *Creighton, supra*, the majority was of the view that people "may properly be held to [a strict objective standard] as a condition of choosing to engage in activities which may maim or kill other innocent people" (p. 66). Even if a person fails to foresee the probable consequences of their freely chosen actions, these actions remain the product of genuine choice. In contrast, excuse-based defences, such as duress, are predicated precisely on the view that the conduct of the accused is involuntary, in a normative sense — that is, that he or she had no realistic alternative course of action available. In my view, in determining whether an accused person was operating under such constrained options, his or her perceptions of the surrounding facts can be highly relevant to the determination of whether his or her conduct was reasonable under the circumstances, and thus whether his or her conduct is properly excusable.

. . . .

D. Assessing the Charge to the Jury

. . . .

It is quite possible that the jury determined that the appellant aided the assault "intentionally", in the sense that he performed acts that he knew would probably assist Bailey to commit the assault because he believed that if he did not Bailey would kill him. The jurors might have thus concluded that the appellant's *mens rea* was not "negated" by duress, under circumstances in which they might well have concluded that his conduct could be excused if they had been aware of the existence of the common law defence of duress, properly conceptualized.

Appeal allowed; new trial ordered.

(b) *Charter* Standard of Moral Involuntariness

R. v. RUZIC

[2001] 1 S.C.R. 687, 41 C.R. (5th) 1, 153 C.C.C. (3d) 1,
2001 CarswellOnt 1239, 2001 CarswellOnt 1238 (S.C.C.)

The accused was charged with importing two kilograms of heroin into Canada. The accused admitted having imported the narcotics but claimed that she was then acting under duress. She conceded that her claim of duress did not meet the immediacy and presence requirements of s. 17 of the *Criminal Code* but challenged the constitutionality of s. 17 under s. 7 of the *Charter* and raised the common law defence of duress. She was acquitted at trial and the Crown's appeal was dismissed. The Crown appealed further. The Supreme Court was unanimous in dismissing the appeal and holding that s. 17 was in part unconstitutional.

LeBel J.: —

. . . .

An expert witness testified at trial that, in 1994, large paramilitary groups roamed Belgrade and engaged in criminal and mafia-like activities. The same expert maintained that people living in Belgrade during that period did not feel safe. They believed the police could not be trusted. There was a real sense that the rule of law had broken down. There was a series of encounters between Mirkovic and the respondent while she was walking her dog. Each time he approached her, he knew more about her, although she had shared no details of her life with him. He phoned her at home. He told her he knew her every move. Ms. Ruzic alleged that his behaviour became more and more intimidating, escalating to threats and acts of physical violence. On one occasion, he burned her arm with a lighter. On another, he stuck a syringe into her arm and injected her with a substance that smelled like heroin and made her nauseous. She indicated that these physical assaults were coupled with sexual harassment and finally threats against her mother.

On April 25, 1994, Mirkovic phoned the respondent and instructed her to pack a bag and meet him at a hotel in central Belgrade. Once there, he allegedly strapped three packages of heroin to her body and indicated that she was to take them to a restaurant in Toronto. He gave her a false passport, a bus ticket from Belgrade to Budapest and some money. He told her to fly from Budapest to Athens, and then from Athens to Toronto. When she protested, he warned her that, if she failed to comply, he would harm her mother.

. . . .

A. Are Statutory Defences Owed Special Deference by Reviewing Courts?

. . . .

The appellant now appeared to concede that the scope of s. 17 is susceptible to *Charter* review, but maintained that the courts should assume a posture of deference when undertaking such an assessment. The prosecution contends it belongs to Parliament to decide when otherwise criminal conduct should be excused, because determining who can rely on the statutory defence of duress and in what circumstances is an inherently policy-driven exercise. The appellant asserts that the legislature is best placed to determine what constitutes "morally involuntary" conduct for the purpose of invoking s. 17, given the difficult value judgments involved in defining duress. The appellant submits that the appropriate standard of review would restrict courts to consider simply whether the restrictions on the defence are irrational or arbitrary. As a corollary of its approach, the Crown did not seek to justify s. 17 under s. 1 of the *Charter*. Before the court, it argued rather that, if properly construed, s. 17 would not even infringe the *Charter*.

. . . .

Soon after the *Charter* came into force, Lamer J. pointed out in *Re B.C. Motor Vehicle Act*, that courts have not only the power but the duty to evaluate the substantive content of legislation for *Charter* compliance. In the realm of criminal law, the courts routinely review the definition of criminal offences to ensure conformity with *Charter* rights. This has included the *mens rea* element of an offence: *e.g.*, *R. v. Vaillancourt* and *R. v. Wholesale Travel Group*. These powers and responsibilities extend equally to statutory defences. courts would be abdicating their constitutional duty by abstaining from such a review. Defences and excuses belong to the legislative corpus that the *Charter* submits to constitutional review by the courts.

. . . .

[S]tatutory defences do not warrant more deference simply because they are the product of difficult moral judgments. The entire body of criminal law expresses a myriad of policy choices. Statutory offences are every bit as concerned with social values as statutory defences.

. . . .

B. Is it a Principle of Fundamental Justice That Only Morally Voluntary Conduct Can Attract Criminal Liability?

. . . .

The notion of moral voluntariness was first introduced in *Perka v. The Queen*, for the purpose of explaining the defence of necessity and classifying it as an excuse. It was borrowed from the American legal theorist George Fletcher's discussion of excuses in *Rethinking Criminal Law* (1978). A person acts in a morally involuntary fashion when, faced with perilous circumstances, she is deprived of a realistic choice whether to break the law. By way of illustration in *Perka*, Dickson J. evoked the situation of a lost alpinist who, on the point of freezing to death, breaks into a remote mountain cabin. The alpinist confronts a painful dilemma: freeze to death or commit a criminal offence. Yet as Dickson J. pointed out, the alpinist's choice to break the law "is no true choice at all; it is remorselessly compelled by normal human instincts", here of self-preservation. The court in *Perka* thus conceptualized the defence of necessity as an excuse. An excuse, Dickson J. maintained, concedes that the act was wrongful, but withholds criminal attribution to the actor because of the dire circumstances surrounding its commission.

Extending its reasoning in *Perka* to the defence of duress, the court found in *R. v. Hibbert* that it too rests on the notion of moral voluntariness. In the case of the defences of necessity and duress, the accused contends that he should avoid conviction because he acted in response to a threat of impending harm. The court also confirmed in *Hibbert* that duress does not ordinarily negate the *mens rea* element of an offence. Like the defence of necessity, the court classified the defence of duress as an excuse, like that of necessity. As such, duress operates to relieve a person of criminal liability only after he has been found to have committed the prohibited act with the relevant *mens rea*. Thus duress, like necessity, involves the concern that morally involuntary conduct not be subject to criminal liability. Can this notion of "moral voluntariness" be recognized as a principle of fundamental justice under s. 7 of the *Charter*? Let us examine possible avenues which have been put forward by the respondent towards such recognition.

1. Moral Voluntariness and Moral Blameworthiness

As we will see below, this court has recognized on a number of occasions that "moral blameworthiness" is an essential component of criminal liability which is protected under s. 7 as a "principle of fundamental justice". The respondent in the case at bar attempts to link the principles of "moral blameworthiness" and "moral voluntariness" as a means of securing the constitutional status of the defence of duress. Laskin J.A. in the court below has followed this line of reasoning. However, the appellant argues that "moral blamelessness" only arises in the absence of either the *actus reus* or the *mens rea* of an offence. One who acts under duress, he contends, remains a morally responsible agent whose behaviour is not blame-free. Further, the appellant submits that moral involuntariness is too vague and amorphous a concept to constitute a principle of fundamental justice. This controversy about the concepts of moral blamelessness and moral involuntariness brings us back to the foundations of criminal responsibility. In the analysis of duress and of its relationship with the tenets of the criminal justice system, is it appropriate to equate moral blamelessness with moral involuntariness?

· · · ·

It should be emphasized that this court, in cases like *Sault Ste. Marie* and *Re B.C. Motor Vehicle Act*, has referred to moral innocence in the context of the discussion of the mental element of an offence. *Hibbert*, on the other hand, held that the defence of duress does not normally negate *mens rea*. Rather, it operates to excuse a wrongful act once the *actus reus* and *mens rea* components of the offence have been made out. Laskin J.A. conceded this point, but countered that moral blameworthiness is a broader concept, extending beyond the traditional elements of an offence. Both Laskin J.A. and the respondent rely heavily, in this respect, on Professor Martha Shaffer's article "Scrutinizing Duress: The Constitutional Validity of Section 17 of the *Criminal Code*" (1998), 40 C.L.Q. 444, in making this argument.

Professor Shaffer acknowledges in her article that moral blameworthiness is an ambiguous concept, the meaning of which this court has not had occasion to discuss in any significant way. I am reluctant to do so here, particularly since, in my opinion, conduct that is morally involuntary is not always intrinsically free of blame. Moral involuntariness is also related to the notion that the defence of duress is an excuse. Dickson J. maintained in *Perka* that an excuse acknowledges the wrongfulness of the accused's conduct. Nevertheless, the law refuses to attach penal consequences to it because an "excuse" has been made out. In using the expression "moral involuntariness", we mean that the accused had no "real" choice but to commit the offence. This recognizes that there was indeed an alternative to breaking the law, although in the case of duress that choice may be even more unpalatable — to be killed or physically harmed.

Let us consider again the situation of the lost alpinist: can we really say he is blameless for breaking into somebody else's cabin? The State refrains from punishing him not because his actions were innocent, but because the circumstances did not leave him with any other realistic choice than to commit the offence. As Fletcher puts it, excuses absolve the accused of personal accountability by focussing, not on the wrongful act, but on the circumstances of the act and the accused's personal capacity to avoid it. Necessity and duress are characterized as concessions to human frailty in this sense. The law is designed for the common man, not for a community of saints or heroes.

To equate moral involuntariness with moral innocence would amount to a significant departure from the reasoning in *Perka* and *Hibbert*. It would be contrary to the court's conceptualization of duress as an excuse. Morally involuntary conduct is not always inherently blameless. Once the elements of the offence have been established, the accused can no longer be considered blameless. This court has never taken the concept of blamelessness any further than this initial finding of guilt, nor should it in this case. The undefinable and potentially far-reaching nature of the concept of moral blamelessness prevents us from recognizing its relevance beyond an initial finding of guilt in the context of s. 7 of the *Charter*. Holding otherwise would inject an unacceptable degree of uncertainty into the law. It would not be consistent with our duty to consider as "principles of fundamental justice" only those concepts which are constrained and capable of being defined with reasonable precision. I would therefore reject this basis for finding that it is a principle of fundamental justice that morally involuntary acts should not be punished.

2. Moral Voluntariness and Voluntariness in the Physical Sense

The respondent's second approach, which relates moral voluntariness back to voluntariness in the physical sense, rests on firmer ground. It draws upon the fundamental principle of criminal law that, in order to attract criminal liability, an act must be voluntary. Voluntariness in this sense has ordinarily referred to the *actus reus* element of an offence. It queries whether the actor had control over the movement of her body or whether the wrongful act was the product of a conscious will. Although duress does not negate ordinarily *actus reus per se* (just as it does not ordinarily negate *mens rea* as we have just seen), the principle of voluntariness, unlike that of "moral blamelessness", can remain relevant in the context of s. 7 even after the basic elements of the offence have been established. Unlike the concept of "moral blamelessness", duress in its "voluntariness" perspective can more easily be constrained and can therefore more justifiably fall within the "principles of fundamental justice", even after the basic elements of the offence have been established.

Let us examine the notion of "voluntariness" and its interplay with duress more closely. As Dickson J. stated in *Rabey v. The Queen*, "it is a basic principle that absence of volition in respect of the act involved is always a defence to a crime. A defence that the act is involuntary entitles the accused to a complete and unqualified acquittal." Dickson J.'s pronouncement was endorsed by the court in *R. v. Parks*. The principle of voluntariness was given constitutional status in *Daviault*, where Cory J. held for the majority that it would infringe s. 7 of the *Charter* to convict an accused who was not acting voluntarily, as a fundamental aspect of the *actus reus* would be absent. More recently, in *R. v. Stone*, [1999] 2 S.C.R. 290, the crucial role of voluntariness as a condition of the attribution of criminal liability was again confirmed in an appeal concerning the defence of automatism.

In introducing the concept of moral voluntariness in *Perka*, the court specifically linked it to the more familiar notion of physical voluntariness discussed above. Dickson J. acknowledged that the two concepts are not identical. The lost alpinist, for instance, does not act in a literally involuntary fashion; he is physically capable of avoiding the criminal act. Fletcher puts forth another example, more pertinent to the defence of duress. Suppose someone puts a knife in the accused's hand and forces it into the victim's chest. The accused's body is literally overpowered, as is her will. Consider next the situation of someone who gives the accused a knife and orders her to stab the victim or else be killed herself. Unlike the first scenario, moral voluntariness is not a matter of physical dimension. The accused here retains conscious control over her bodily movements. Yet, like the first actor, her will is overborne, this time by the threats of another. Her conduct is not, in a realistic way, freely chosen.

What underpins both of these conceptions of voluntariness is the critical importance of autonomy in the attribution of criminal liability. The treatment of criminal offenders as rational, autonomous and choosing agents is a fundamental organizing principle of our criminal law. Its importance is reflected not only in the requirement that an act must be voluntary, but also in the condition that a wrongful act must be intentional to ground a conviction. *Sault Ste. Marie, Re B.C. Motor Vehicle Act*, and *Vaillancourt* all stand for the proposition that a guilty verdict requires intentional conduct or conduct equated to it like recklessness or gross negligence. Like voluntariness, the requirement of a guilty mind is rooted in respect for individual autonomy and free will and acknowledges the importance of those values to a free and democratic society: *Martineau.* Criminal liability also depends on the capacity to choose — the ability to reason right from wrong. As McLachlin J. observed in *Chaulk* in the context of the insanity provisions of the *Criminal Code,* this assumption of the rationality and autonomy of human beings forms part of the essential premises of Canadian criminal law.

Punishing a person whose actions are involuntary in the physical sense is unjust because it conflicts with the assumption in criminal law that individuals are autonomous and freely choosing agents: see Shaffer, *supra*, at pp. 449-50. It is similarly unjust to penalize an individual who acted in a morally involuntary fashion. This is so because his acts cannot realistically be attributed to him, as his will was constrained by some external force. . . .

Although moral involuntariness does not negate the *actus reus* or *mens rea* of an offence, it is a principle which, similarly to physical involuntariness, deserves protection under s. 7 of the *Charter*. It is a principle of fundamental justice that only voluntary conduct — behaviour that is the product of a free will and controlled body, unhindered by external constraints — should attract the penalty and stigma of criminal liability. Depriving a person of liberty and branding her with the stigma of criminal liability would infringe the principles of fundamental justice if the accused did not have any realistic choice. The ensuing deprivation of liberty and stigma would have been imposed in violation of the tenets of fundamental justice and would thus infringe s. 7 of the *Charter*.

B. Do the Immediacy and Presence Requirements in Section 17 Infringe the Principle of Involuntariness in the Attribution of Criminal Responsibility?

. . . .

The appellant argues that the immediacy and presence requirements do not dictate that the threatener be physically present at the scene of the crime. Rather, they require a temporal connection between the commission of the offence and the threatener's presence, in the sense that the threatener must be able to execute the threat immediately should the accused fail to comply. The respondent replies that the appellant's proposed interpretation would stretch the language of s. 17 beyond recognition. As counsel for one of the interveners put it during the hearing of this appeal, it would amount to construing presence as absence and immediate as sometime later.

The plain meaning of s. 17 is quite restrictive in scope. Indeed, the section seems tailor-made for the situation in which a person is compelled to commit an offence at gun point. The phrase "present when the offence is committed", coupled with the immediacy criterion, indicates that the person issuing the threat must be either at the scene of the crime or at whatever other location is necessary to make good on the threat without delay should the accused resist. Practically speaking, a threat of harm will seldom qualify as immediate if the threatener is not physically present at the scene of the crime.

The court has in the past construed s. 17 in a narrow fashion. *R. v. Carker* and *Paquette v. The Queen*, are the two leading cases on the interpretation of s. 17. . . .

. . . .

I agree with the respondent that a threat will seldom meet the immediacy criterion if the threatener is not physically present at or near the scene of the offence. The immediacy and presence requirements, taken together, clearly preclude threats of future harm.

Neither the words of s. 17 nor the court's reasons in *Carker* and *Paquette* dictate that the target of the threatened harm must be the accused. They simply require that the threat must be made to the accused. Section 17 may thus include threats against third parties. However, the language of s. 17 does not appear capable of supporting a more flexible interpretation of the immediacy and presence requirements. Even if the threatened person, for example, is a family member, and not the accused person, the threatener or his accomplice must be at or near the scene of the crime in order to effect the harm immediately if the accused resists. Thus, while s. 17 may capture threats against third parties, the immediacy and presence criteria continue to impose considerable obstacles to relying on the defence in hostage or other third party situations.

Thus, by the strictness of its conditions, s. 17 breaches s. 7 of the *Charter* because it allows individuals who acted involuntarily to be declared criminally liable. Having said that, it will be interesting to see how the common law addresses the problem of duress, especially with respect to the immediacy component. In that regard, we will have the opportunity to see how the common law on duress in Canada, Great Britain, Australia, and even in some U.S. jurisdictions is often more liberal than what s. 17 provides and takes better account of the principle of voluntariness. This will confirm the view that s. 17 is overly restrictive and therefore breaches s. 7 of the *Charter*. We recall that the principles of fundamental justice may be distilled from the "legal principles which have historically been reflected in the law of this and other similar states" (*Seaboyer*). Examining the common law of other states like Great Britain and Australia to confirm our interpretation of s. 7 will therefore be relevant. The analysis of duress in common law will also be useful as it will shed some light on the appropriate rules which had to be applied to the defence of the accused in the case at bar and which will now be applied in all other cases, once s. 17 of the *Criminal Code* is partially struck down.

D. The Common Law of Duress

. . . .

[The Court then examined the Canadian common law of duress as illustrated in *Paquette*, *Hibbert* and *Langlois*.[4] It then reviewed the English common law of duress which was seen as generally similar to its Canadian counterpart. The Court found that in the Australian common law of duress there were some differences from state to state but that overall, the state courts appear to have followed quite closely the English courts' approach. Examining the American common law of duress, LeBel J. concluded that while in some states the defence is subject to quite strict constraints, several American cases have displayed a flexible view of the temporal criterion in the context of duress. While the common law was not unanimous in the United States, a substantial consensus had thus grown in Canada, England and Australia to the effect that the criterion of immediacy is no longer a generally accepted component of the defence. Rather, the common law only required a "strict temporal connection" which was somewhat more relaxed than "immediate" harm.]

E. The Breach of Section 7 of the *Charter*: Conclusion in the Case at Bar

At the heart of Laskin J.A.'s decision is a concern that the immediacy and presence requirements are poor substitutes for the safe avenue of escape test at common law. In his view, their focus on an instantaneous connection between the threat and the commission of the offence misses the point in a number of special cases. He highlights two situations in particular. The first is the battered woman who is coerced by her abusive partner to break the law. Even though her partner is not present when she commits the offence and is therefore unable to execute it immediately, a battered woman may believe nonetheless that she has no safe avenue of escape. Her behaviour is morally involuntary, yet the immediacy and presence criteria, strictly construed, would preclude her from

---

4   Editors' note: In *R. v. Langlois* (1993), 19 C.R. (4th) 87, 80 C.C.C. (3d) 28 (Que. C.A.) the trial judge, in opening the common law defence in this case, directed the jury that duress involved three essential requirements.
    First, there had to be either explicit or implicit threats of death or serious injury.
    Second, the threats had to be "immediate": respondent had no right to yield to threats if he had an obvious safe avenue of escape. He had a duty to try by all possible means to avoid committing the crime, to escape.

. . . .

As to the third element, the judge directed the jury that a person subjected to threats was expected to show reasonable courage:

> . . . la Loi ne protège pas une personne qui commet des infractions criminelles sous l'effet de menaces si cette personne n'est pas normalement et raisonnablement courageuse dans les circonstances particulières de sa situation.

The jury was then told that society expects a higher standard or additional degree of courage from someone who has chosen a calling that normally requires courage, such as a police officer. Penitentiary employees were also expected to show "the kind of courage one does not demand of an accountant or schoolteacher".

resorting to s. 17. There may also be other situations in which a person is so psychologically traumatized by the threatener that he complies with the threat, even though it was not immediate and to the objective observer, there was a legal way out. The second scenario described by Laskin J.A. is the case of a person like Ms. Ruzic, for whom effective police protection was unavailable. Do the immediacy and presence requirements demand that a person go to the authorities if he has the opportunity to do so, even when he believes it would be useless or even dangerous to do so? It should be noted that in this second scenario, a court might face a delicate task in assessing the validity of a claim that, in a foreign land, no police protection was available. It illustrates some of the difficulties in the practical implementation of a defence of duress which involves a risk of abuse through unverifiable assertions of danger and harm.

Nevertheless, s. 17's reliance on proximity as opposed to reasonable options as the measure of moral choice is problematic. It would be contrary to the principles of fundamental justice to punish an accused who is psychologically tortured to the point of seeing no reasonable alternative, or who cannot rely on the authorities for assistance. That individual is not behaving as an autonomous agent acting out of his own free will when he commits an offence under duress.

The appellant's attempts at reading down s. 17, in order to save it, would amount to amending it to bring it in line with the common law rules. This interpretation badly strains the text of the provision and may become one more argument against upholding its validity. The underinclusiveness of s. 17 infringes s. 7 of the *Charter*, because the immediacy and presence requirements exclude threats of future harm to the accused or to third parties. It risks jeopardizing the liberty and security interests protected by the *Charter*, in violation of the basic principles of fundamental justice. It has the potential of convicting persons who have not acted voluntarily.

F. Can the Infringement Be Justified Under Section 1?

Having found that the immediacy and presence requirements infringe s. 7 of the *Charter*, I turn now to consider whether the violation is a demonstrably justifiable limit under s. 1. The government, of course, bears the burden of justifying a *Charter* infringement. Consistent with its strategy in the courts below, the appellant made no attempt before this court to justify the immediacy and presence criteria according to the s. 1 analysis. I therefore conclude at the outset that the appellant has failed to satisfy its onus under s. 1.

Moreover, it is well established that violations of s. 7 are not easily saved by s. 1. Indeed, the court has indicated that exceptional circumstances, such as the outbreak of war or a national emergency, are necessary before such an infringement may be justified: *R. v. Heywood, Re B.C. Motor Vehicle Act*. No such extraordinary conditions exist in this case. Furthermore, I am inclined to agree with Laskin J.A. that the immediacy and presence criteria would not meet the proportionality branch of the s. 1 analysis. In particular, it seems to me these requirements do not minimally impair the respondent's s. 7 rights. Given the appellant's failure to make any submissions on the issue, the higher standard of justification for a violation of s. 7, and my doubts concerning proportionality, I conclude that the immediacy and presence conditions cannot be saved by s. 1.

. . . .

H. The Jury Charge

. . . .

Viewed in its entirety, the trial judge's charge explained adequately the elements of the defence of duress at common law to the members of the jury.

The charge contained all the elements required by the common law rules on duress. The criterion of the safe avenue of escape was well explained as was the objective component of this test. Notwithstanding the argument of the appellant, the law does not require an accused to seek the official protection of police in all cases. The requirement of objectivity must itself take into consideration the special circumstances where the accused found herself as well as her perception of them. Herold J. drew the attention of the jury both to that objective component and to the subjective elements of the defence. This argument must thus fail.

As to the immediacy of the threat, as Laskin J.A.'s reasons point out, Herold J. brought home to the jury the fact that the threat had to be a real threat affecting the accused at the time of the offence. This instruction at least implied that the jury had to consider the temporal connection between the threat and the harm threatened, although it would have been preferable to say so in so many express words.

There was no misdirection either on the burden of proof. The accused must certainly raise the defence and introduce some evidence about it. Once this is done, the burden of proof shifts to the Crown under the general rule of criminal evidence. It must be shown, beyond a reasonable doubt, that the accused did not act under duress. . . .

Disposition

The appellant's submissions cannot be accepted. The immediacy and presence requirements of s. 17 of the *Criminal Code* infringe s. 7 of the *Charter*. As the infringement has not been justified under s. 1, the requirements of immediacy and presence must be struck down as unconstitutional. The Court of Appeal and the trial judge were right in allowing the common law defence of duress go to the jury, and the trial judge adequately instructed the jury on the defence.

Is *Ruzic* consistent with *Stone*? Is *Ruzic* consistent with *Latimer*?

Does turning "moral involuntariness" into a principle of fundamental justice itself provide a broader defence than the Court really intends? The defence of provocation, for example, (discussed below) requires that a reasonable person would have lost self-control in the circumstances. Would that amount to morally involuntary behaviour on the definition in *Ruzic*? If so, *Ruzic* seems to mean that provocation should be a complete defence, and applicable to any crime, rather than (as it is now) a partial defence applicable only to murder. See Steve Coughlan, "Duress, Necessity, Self-Defence and Provocation: Implications of Radical Change?" (2002) 7 Can. Crim. L. Rev. 147.

For critical comments on *Ruzic,* see Stanley Yeo, "Defining Duress" (2002) 45 Crim. L.Q. 293 and Ben Berger "Emotions and the Veil of Voluntarism: The Loss of Judgment in Canadian Criminal Defences" (2006) 51 McGill L.J. 99. In the years that have passed since *Ruzic* the new *Charter* standard of moral involuntariness has surprisingly yet to be applied in contexts other than duress. For an argument that *Ruzic* should inform the development of a substantive defence of entrapment see Paul M. Hughes, "Temptation and Culpability in the Law of Duress and Entrapment" (2006) 51 Crim. L.Q. 342.

The Court's decision in *Ruzic* further complicated an already confused area of the law. After *Paquette,* the statutory version of duress applied to principals but the less strict common law version was available to parties: *Ruzic* made part but not all of that common law version available to principals. The next major decision on duress came in *R. v. Ryan*, and the Court took the opportunity to try to eliminate much of this confusion and to make the statutory and common law versions of the defence as close to identical as possible.

The actual issue in *Ryan* was a novel one. In all previous uses of the defence, a person had been told to commit a crime by some third party who threatened harm to the accused for failing to do so. The accused in *Ryan* was never threatened in that way: rather, in response to a history of abuse at the hands of her husband, she attempted to hire someone to kill him. At trial and at the Nova Scotia Court of Appeal, it was found that she could not plead self-defence but that she could rely on the defence of duress. The central issue before the Supreme Court was whether duress was available at all in these circumstances: they held that it was not.

R. v. RYAN

290 C.C.C. (3d) 477, 98 C.R. (6th) 223, [2013] 1 S.C.R. 14

LeBel and Cromwell JJ.:

[1] This appeal raises a novel question: may a wife, whose life is threatened by her abusive husband, rely on the defence of duress when she tries to have him murdered? The Nova Scotia courts concluded that she may and acquitted the respondent, Nicole Ryan, of counselling the commission of her husband's murder. The Crown appeals.

[2]   As we see it, the defence of duress is available when a person commits an offence while under compulsion of a threat made *for the purpose of compelling* him or her to commit it. That was not Ms. Ryan's situation. She wanted her husband dead because he was threatening to kill her and her daughter, not because she was being threatened for the purpose of compelling her to have him killed. That being the case, the defence of duress was not available to her, no matter how compelling her situation was viewed in a broader perspective. It is also our view, however, that the uncertainty surrounding the law of duress coupled with the Crown's change of position between trial and appeal created unfairness to Ms. Ryan's defence in this case. As a result, we would allow the appeal and enter a stay of proceedings.

. . . .

[34]   The next issue is what order should be made, given our conclusion that the Court of Appeal erred in law and the appeal of the Crown should be allowed. In our view, the interests of justice require that a stay of proceedings be entered as the Court is authorized to do in the clearest of cases by s. 695 of the *Code*. . . .

[35]   It is apparent that the law of duress was unclear, which made resort to it as a defence unusually difficult. Coupled with that consideration is the problem in this case that the Crown changed its position about the applicable law between the trial and the appeal process. The trial proceeded on the basis that duress was available as a matter of law to Ms. Ryan if the facts supported it. She therefore went to trial on the basis that the issues were mainly the factual ones relating to whether she had pointed to evidence capable of raising a reasonable doubt about the various components of duress. Presumably, decisions about the conduct of the defence were made on this basis and might have been made differently had the legal position later adopted by the Crown on appeal, that duress was not open to her in law, been known at the time of trial. There is therefore a serious risk that some of the consequences of those decisions could not be undone in the context of a new trial and this raises concern about the fairness of ordering a new trial. In addition, the abuse which she suffered at the hands of Mr. Ryan took an enormous toll on her, as, no doubt, have these protracted proceedings, extending over nearly five years, in which she was acquitted at trial and successfully resisted a Crown appeal in the Court of Appeal. There is also the disquieting fact that, on the record before us, it seems that the authorities were much quicker to intervene to protect Mr. Ryan than they had been to respond to her request for help in dealing with his reign of terror over her. A stay of proceedings is warranted only in the clearest of cases (see *R. v. Power*, [1994] 1 S.C.R. 601, at p. 615). In our opinion, Ms. Ryan's case falls into the residual category of cases requiring a stay: it is an exceptional situation that warrants an exceptional remedy. In all of the circumstances, it would not be fair to subject

Ms. Ryan to another trial. In the interests of justice, a stay of proceedings is required to protect against this oppressive result. . . .

(2) The Statutory Defence of Duress Post-*Ruzic*

[43]   What, therefore, remains of s. 17 after *Ruzic*? The Court did not strike down s. 17 in its entirety; it was found unconstitutional only "in part" (para. 1). As a result, the following four requirements of the statutory defence remain intact after the Court's ruling in *Ruzic*:

> 1. there must be a threat of death or bodily harm directed against the accused or a third party;
>
> 2. the accused must believe that the threat will be carried out;
>
> 3. the offence must not be on the list of excluded offences; and
>
> 4. the accused cannot be a party to a conspiracy or criminal association such that the person is subject to compulsion.

[44]   However, the Court in *Ruzic* did not leave the statutory defence in place simply stripped of its unconstitutional portions. The Court supplemented the interpretation and application of s. 17 with elements from the common law defence of duress, which it found to be "more consonant with the values of the Charter" (para. 56). In other words, the Court in *Ruzic* used the common law standard to interpret the affirmative requirements of the statute (see D. M. Paciocco, "No-one Wants to Be Eaten: The Logic and Experience of the Law of Necessity and Duress" (2010), 56 Crim. L.Q. 240, at p. 273).

[45]   Where ambiguities or gaps exist in the partially struck-down s. 17, the common law defence of duress operates to clarify and flesh out the statutory defence:

> The analysis of duress in common law will also be useful as it will shed some light on the appropriate rules which had to be applied to the defence of the accused in the case at bar *and which will now be applied in all other cases*, once s. 17 of the *Criminal Code* is partially struck down. [Emphasis added; *Ruzic*, at para. 55.]

[46]   In *Ruzic*, the Court articulated and analyzed the following three key elements of the common law defence of duress, which now operate in s. 17 cases alongside the four requirements remaining in the statutory defence: (1) no safe avenue of escape; (2) a close temporal connection; and (3) proportionality (see *Parent*, at pp. 549-50).

(a) No Safe Avenue of Escape

[47]   The defence of duress "focuses on the search for a safe avenue of escape" (*Ruzic*, at para. 61). Following the decision in *Hibbert*, the Court in *Ruzic* concluded that the defence does not apply to persons who could have

legally and safely extricated themselves from the situation of duress. In order to rely on the defence, the accused must have had no safe avenue of escape, as measured on the modified objective standard of the reasonable person similarly situated.

(b) A Close Temporal Connection

[48]   There must be "a close temporal connection between the threat and the harm threatened" (*Ruzic*, at para. 96). The close connection between the threat and its execution must be such that the accused loses the ability to act voluntarily. The requirement of a close temporal connection between the threat and the harm threatened is linked with the requirement that the accused have no safe avenue of escape. As the Court in *Ruzic* indicated, a threat that is "too far removed in time . . . would cast doubt on the seriousness of the threat and, more particularly, on claims of an absence of a safe avenue of escape" (para. 65).

[49]   As long as the immediacy and presence requirements in s. 17 remained intact, the safe avenue of escape and close temporal connection factors had little relevance. A threat of immediate death or bodily harm which the recipient believes will be carried out by a person present ensured a close temporal connection and would most likely leave no safe avenue of escape. However, once the immediacy and presence requirements were struck from s. 17, the common law requirements of no safe avenue of escape and the close temporal connection became a critical means of assessing whether the accused's actions were morally involuntary.

[50]   In addition, once the immediacy and presence requirements were struck, it followed that the accused's belief that the threat would be carried out must be evaluated on a modified objective standard of the reasonable person similarly situated. Section 17 provides that a person will be excused "if the person believes that the threats will be carried out". On its face, therefore, the section requires a purely subjective belief, a lower standard that made sense when the threat was clearly immediate and the threatener physically present on the scene. Once the immediacy and presence requirements are removed, however, measuring the accused's belief that the threat will be carried out necessarily demands a higher standard of evaluation. In other words, the accused's actual belief must also be reasonable.

[51]   By reading in the requirements of safe avenue of escape and close temporal connection, the purely subjective standard becomes an evaluation based on a modified objective standard. These two elements, in conjunction with the belief that the threat will be carried out, must be analyzed as a whole: the accused cannot reasonably believe that the threat would be carried out if there was a safe avenue of escape and no close temporal connection between the threat and the harm threatened.

[52]   The addition of the common law requirements to replace the now defunct immediacy and presence elements of s. 17 thus act to temper the once purely subjective belief as to the threat. Furthermore, they bring the statutory provision in line with the principle of moral involuntariness. Considering that society's opinion of the accused's actions is an important aspect of the principle, it would be contrary to the very idea of moral involuntariness to simply accept the accused's subjective belief without requiring that certain external factors be present. . .

(c) Proportionality

[53]   The defence of duress requires proportionality between the threat and the criminal act to be executed. In other words, the harm caused must not be greater than the harm avoided. Proportionality is measured on the modified objective standard of the reasonable person similarly situated, and it includes the requirement that the accused will adjust his or her conduct according to the nature of the threat: "The accused should be expected to demonstrate some fortitude and to put up a normal resistance to the threat" (*Ruzic*, at para. 62).

[54]   Proportionality is a crucial component of the defence of duress because, like the previous two elements, it derives directly from the principle of moral involuntariness: only an action based on a proportionally grave threat, resisted with normal fortitude, can be considered morally involuntary. Furthermore, since the principle of moral involuntariness was judged to be a principle of fundamental justice in *Ruzic*, it must be read into s. 17 in order to comply with the statutory interpretation rule that courts must prefer the constitutional interpretation of a statute.

(3) The Common Law Defence of Duress Post-*Ruzic*

[55]   Following this Court's analysis in *Ruzic*, we can conclude that the common law of duress comprises the following elements:

- an explicit or implicit threat of death or bodily harm proffered against the accused or a third person. The threat may be of future harm. Although, traditionally, the degree of bodily harm was characterized as "grievous", the issue of severity is better dealt with at the proportionality stage, which acts as the threshold for the appropriate degree of bodily harm;

- the accused reasonably believed that the threat would be carried out;

- the non-existence of a safe avenue of escape, evaluated on a modified objective standard;

- a close temporal connection between the threat and the harm threatened;

- proportionality between the harm threatened and the harm inflicted by the accused. This is also evaluated on a modified objective standard;

• the accused is not a party to a conspiracy or association whereby the accused is subject to compulsion and actually knew that threats and coercion to commit an offence were a possible result of this criminal activity, conspiracy or association.

[56]   We will discuss these elements in turn.

(a) Threat of Death or Bodily Harm

[57]   For an accused to be able to rely on the common law defence of duress, there must have been a threat of death or bodily harm. This threat does not necessarily need to be directed at the accused: *Ruzic*, at para. 54. It can be either explicit or implied: *R. v. Mena* (1987), 34 C.C.C. (3d) 304 (Ont. C.A.), at p. 320; see also *R. v. McRae* (2005), 77 O.R. (3d) 1 (C.A.).

[58]   The strict immediacy or imminence requirement found in the defence of necessity was not imported into the common law defence of duress. Rather, this immediacy requirement is "interpreted as a requirement of a close connection in time, between the threat and its execution in such a manner that the accused loses the ability to act freely": *Ruzic*, at para. 65. This position was also held in *Langlois*, where Fish J.A. (as he then was) held that the issue is not the immediacy or imminence of the threat, but whether "the accused failed to avail himself or herself of some opportunity to escape or to render the threat ineffective": *R. v. Langlois* (1993), 80 C.C.C. (3d) 28 (Que. C.A.), at p. 50. The lack of a strict immediacy requirement not only strengthens the assertion that threats can be made to third parties, but also supports the conclusion in *Ruzic*, at para. 86, that the threats made can be of future harm.

[59]   The harm threatened must be death or bodily harm. Traditionally, courts have qualified this bodily harm as needing to be "grievous" or "serious" (see, for example, *Hibbert*, at paras. 21 and 23). However, this higher threshold is not necessary in light of the existence of the proportionality requirement — inherent in the principle of moral involuntariness — which acts as the ultimate barrier for those who seek to rely on the defence.

[60]   At s. 2, the *Criminal Code* defines the term "bodily harm" as "any hurt or injury to a person that interferes with the health or comfort of the person and that is more than merely transient or trifling in nature". Removing the "grievous" or "serious" element of the bodily harm requirement and dealing with the requisite degree of harm at the proportionality stage will not unduly broaden the common law defence of duress. The two-pronged nature of the proportionality requirement, a concept which we will more fully develop below, will prevent such an outcome. First, the harm caused must be measured against the harm threatened. Second, the accused must meet society's standards for the reasonable person similarly situated, which includes a capacity to resist the threat to some degree.

[61]   Theoretically, it could be possible to have caused less harm than threatened, yet still not be afforded the defence of duress because the behaviour and reaction of the accused as a whole is judged unacceptable for that individual in that particular circumstance. For example, inflicting quite minor harm in reaction to the threat of quite minor harm might fulfill the "equal or lesser harm" requirement, but would certainly not constitute a situation where society would be ready to excuse the act as morally involuntary.

[62]   If the threat is of insufficient seriousness, the offence committed in reaction to that threat cannot be proportional. The voluntariness of an act depends on its proportionality: an individual cannot claim to have lost the ability to act freely when the harm threatened does not meet society's threshold. For these reasons, the degree of bodily harm that will make the defence available is best dealt with at the proportionality stage.

[63]   Therefore, in order to fulfill this first requirement of the common law defence of duress, there must have been an explicit or implicit, present or future threat of death or bodily harm, directed at the accused or a third person.

   (b) Reasonable Belief that Threat Will Be Carried Out

[64]   In addition, the accused must have reasonably believed that the threat would be carried out. This element is analyzed on a modified objective basis, that is, according to the test of the reasonable person similarly situated.

   (c) No Safe Avenue of Escape

[65]   This element of the common law defence was specifically addressed in *Ruzic*, at para. 61. Once again, the test, evaluated on a modified objective basis, is that of a reasonable person similarly situated:

> The courts will take into consideration the particular circumstances where the accused found himself and his ability to perceive a reasonable alternative to committing a crime, with an awareness of his background and essential characteristics. The process involves a pragmatic assessment of the position of the accused, tempered by the need to avoid negating criminal liability on the basis of a purely subjective and unverifiable excuse.

In other words, a reasonable person in the same situation as the accused and with the same personal characteristics and experience would conclude that there was no safe avenue of escape or legal alternative to committing the offence. If a reasonable person similarly situated would think that there was a safe avenue of escape, the requirement is not met and the acts of the accused cannot be excused using the defence of duress because they cannot be considered as morally involuntary.

(d) Close Temporal Connection

[66]   The element of close temporal connection between the threat and the harm threatened, mentioned above, serves to restrict the availability of the common law defence to situations where there is a sufficient temporal link between the threat and the offence committed.

[67]   This requirement in no way precludes the availability of the defence for cases where the threat is of future harm. For example, the accused in *Ruzic* was able to rely on the defence even though the threat was to harm her mother in the event that she did not smuggle the drugs from Belgrade to Toronto as ordered, a task that would take several days to accomplish.

[68]   The first purpose of the close temporal connection element is to ensure that there truly was no safe avenue of escape for the accused. If the threat is too far removed from the accused's illegal acts, it will be difficult to conclude that a reasonable person similarly situated had no option but to commit the offence. The temporal link between the threat and the harm threatened is necessary to demonstrate the degree of pressure placed on the accused.

[69]   The second purpose of the close temporal connection requirement is to ensure that it is reasonable to believe that the threat put so much pressure on the accused that between this threat and the commission of the offence, "the accused los[t] the ability to act freely": *Ruzic* at para. 65. It thus serves to determine if the accused truly acted in an involuntary manner.

(e) Proportionality

[70]   Proportionality is inherent in the principle of moral involuntariness. "[T]his involuntariness is measured on the basis of society's expectation of appropriate and normal resistance to pressure": *Perka*, at p. 259. Part of the analysis involves making a determination of whether the harm threatened is equal to or greater than the harm caused.

[71]   The test for determining whether an act was proportional is therefore two-pronged, and was set out by Dickson J. in *Perka*, at p. 252:

> There must be some way of assuring proportionality. No rational criminal justice system, no matter how humane or liberal, could excuse the infliction of a greater harm to allow the actor to avert a lesser evil. . . . According to Fletcher, this requirement is also related to the notion of voluntariness ([G. P. Fletcher, *Rethinking Criminal Law* (1978)], at p. 804):
>
> > . . . if the gap between the harm done and the benefit accrued becomes too great, the act is more likely to appear voluntary and therefore inexcusable. . . . Determining this threshold is patently a matter of *moral judgment about what we expect people to be able to resist in trying situations*. A valuable aid in making that judgment is comparing the competing interests at stake and assessing the degree to which the actor inflicts harm beyond the benefit that accrues from his action. [Emphasis added.]

[72] In other words, the "moral voluntariness" of an act must depend on whether it is proportional to the threatened harm. To determine if the proportionality requirement is met, two elements must be considered: the difference between the nature and magnitude of the harm threatened and the offence committed, as well as a general moral judgment regarding the accused's behaviour in the circumstances. These elements are to be evaluated in conjunction on a modified objective basis.

[73] The first element of proportionality requires that the harm threatened was equal to or greater than the harm inflicted by the accused: *Ruzic*, at para. 62; also see *R. v. Latimer*, 2001 SCC 1, [2001] 1 S.C.R. 3, at para. 31. The second element of proportionality requires a more in-depth analysis of the acts of the accused and a determination as to whether they accord with what society expects from a reasonable person similarly situated in that particular circumstance. It is at this stage that we examine if the accused demonstrated "normal" resistance to the threat. Given that the defence of duress "evolved from attempts at striking a proper balance between those conflicting interests of the accused, of the victims and of society" (*Ruzic*, at para. 60), proportionality measured on a modified objective standard is key.

[74] The evaluation of the proportionality requirement on a modified objective standard differs from the standard used in the defence of necessity, which is purely objective. While the defences of duress and necessity share the same juristic principles, according to Lamer C.J. in *Hibbert*, this does not entail that they must employ the same standard when evaluating proportionality. The Court in *Ruzic* noted that the two defences, although both categorized as excuses rooted in the notion of moral or normative involuntariness, target different types of situations. Furthermore, the temporality requirement for necessity is one of imminence, whereas the threat in a case of duress can be carried out in the future. It is therefore not so anomalous that the courts have attributed differing tests for proportionality, especially when we consider that the defences may apply under noticeably different factual circumstances.

(f) Participation in a Conspiracy or Criminal Association

[75] This statutory element has been recognized as also relevant to the common law. Recent jurisprudence has concluded that those who seek to rely on the common law defence of duress cannot do so if they knew that their participation in a conspiracy or criminal association came with a risk of coercion and/or threats to compel them to commit an offence: see *R. v. Li* (2002), 162 C.C.C. (3d) 360 (Ont. C.A.), at paras. 20-33; *R. v. Poon*, 2006 BCSC 1158 (CanLII), at para. 7; *R. v. M.P.D.*, 2003 BCPC 97, [2003] B.C.J. No. 771 (QL), at para. 61.

[76]   In *Li*, the Ontario Court of Appeal stated that voluntarily joining a conspiracy or criminal organization also has an impact on whether there was a safe avenue of escape. In that case, the accused persons had approached a criminal organization of their own volition and had later been threatened by this same group. In its analysis on the presence of an air of reality, the court stated the following:

> As can be seen, the Supreme Court [in *Ruzic*] recognized the *juxtaposition between a safe avenue of escape and the voluntary assumption of the risk in the first place*. Both are front and centre in the case in appeal. In considering the appellants' claim that calling the local police would have been ineffective because they not only feared for themselves but also for their families in China and elsewhere, the court should be reminded of their initiative in approaching the Snakeheads in the first place, and the fact that the threats of retaliation against them and their families was sweetened by the inducement of retiring their debts to this organization [Emphasis added; para. 32.]

[77]   The Court of Appeal's conclusion stands for the proposition that courts must take into account the accused's voluntary assumption of risk, a natural corollary of the unavailability of the defence of duress to those who wilfully engage in criminal conspiracies or organizations. This is consistent with the principle of moral involuntariness. An accused that, because of his or her criminal involvement, knew coercion or threats were a possibility cannot claim that there was no safe avenue of escape, nor can he or she truly be found to have committed the resulting offence in a morally involuntary manner.

[78]   Therefore, to rely on the common law defence of duress, the accused must not be a party to a conspiracy or association whereby he or she is subject to compulsion and actually knew that threats and coercion to commit an offence were a possible result of this criminal activity, conspiracy or association. In *Ruzic*, at para. 70, LeBel J. states: "Like s. 17 of the *Criminal Code*, the English jurisprudence has precluded resort to the defence where the threats are made by a criminal organization which the accused voluntarily joined and knew might pressure him to engage in criminal activity (*R. v. Lewis* (1992), 96 Cr. App. R. 412; *R. v. Heath*, [1999] E.W.J. No. 5092 (QL))" (emphasis added).

[79]   There is division of opinion as to whether the accused's knowledge of potential threats or coercion is evaluated on a subjective or objective standard. According to Yeo, the above-cited conclusion in *Ruzic* is consistent with Australian law, which only denies the defence of duress to those who were actually aware of the risk of being coerced by the criminal association: S. Yeo, "Defining Duress" (2002), 46 Crim. L.Q. 293, at p. 315. A subjective standard is also applied in the United States: *United States v. Burnes*, 666 F.Supp.2d 968 (D. Minn. 2009); United States v. Gamboa, 439 F.3d 796 (8th Cir. 2006); *United States v. Montes*, 602 F.3d 381 (5th Cir. 2010). Baker, however, seems to reject a purely subjective standard. According to him, the test should be whether the

accused "recklessly or negligently placed himself in a situation in which it was probable that he would be forced to commit a criminal act" (at para. 25-044).

[80]   We think that the subjective standard is more in line with the principle of moral involuntariness. If the accused voluntarily puts him or herself in a position where he or she could be coerced, then we cannot conclude that there was no safe avenue of escape and that the ensuing actions were morally involuntary.

IV. Summary

[81]   The defence of duress, in its statutory and common law forms, is largely the same. The two forms share the following common elements:

- There must be an explicit or implicit threat of present or future death or bodily harm. This threat can be directed at the accused or a third party.

- The accused must reasonably believe that the threat will be carried out.

- There is no safe avenue of escape. This element is evaluated on a modified objective standard.

- A close temporal connection between the threat and the harm threatened.

- Proportionality between the harm threatened and the harm inflicted by the accused. The harm caused by the accused must be equal to or no greater than the harm threatened. This is also evaluated on a modified objective standard.

- The accused is not a party to a conspiracy or association whereby the accused is subject to compulsion and actually knew that threats and coercion to commit an offence were a possible result of this criminal activity, conspiracy or association.

[82]   Certain differences remain.

[83]   The first is that, as was established in *Paquette* and confirmed in *Ruzic*, the statutory defence applies to principals, while the common law defence is available to parties to an offence. The second is that the statutory version of the defence has a lengthy list of exclusions, whereas it is unclear in the Canadian common law of duress whether any offences are excluded. This results in the rather incoherent situation that principals who commit one of the enumerated offences cannot rely on the defence of duress while parties to those same offences, however, can.

[84]   This is an unsatisfactory state of the law, but one which we think we are not able to confront in this case. Although we had the benefit of extensive argument about the parameters of the common law and statutory defences of duress, understandably no argument was presented about the statutory

exclusions. In addition, some courts have found some of these exclusions to be constitutionally infirm. We accordingly leave to another day the questions of the status of the statutory exclusions and what, if any, exclusions apply at common law.

Until *Ryan*, it had seemed as though the proportionality requirement was limited to a comparison of the harm avoided and the harm caused, which seemed to make it a criterion which existed independently of the moral involuntariness requirement. *Ryan* makes clearer that proportionality is not simply such a comparison, but also involves a "general moral judgment regarding the accused's behaviour in the circumstances" (para. 72). On this basis proportionality is a *part of* the analysis to determine whether behaviour was morally involuntary, not an additional consideration. This approach reduces the danger arising out of *Ruzic* (and referred to above) that the moral involuntariness principle of fundamental justice could have unintended effects such as making provocation a complete defence.

In both *Ruzic* and *Ryan* the Supreme Court expressly left open the constitutionality of excluding the defence of duress in the case of the listed offences. **Do you think that a s. 7 *Charter* challenge could succeed on the basis of the moral involuntariness standard or that of arbitrariness?**

In *R. v. Fraser* (2002), 3 C.R. (6th) 308 (N.S. Prov. Ct.), the Court held that the exclusion of robbery from the s. 17 duress defence might result in the conviction of the morally involuntary. The exclusion of robbery was struck down. At trial both accused relied on the common law defence of duress. The Court found the defence made out in the case of one of the accused who was therefore acquitted. See too *R. v. Allen* (2014), 318 C.C.C. (3d) 335, 16 C.R. (7th) 272 (Sask. Q.B.) (striking down exclusion of robbery and assault with a weapon).

The 92-page judgment of Justice Mainella for the Manitoba Court of Appeal in *R. v. Willis* (2016), 344 C.C.C. (3d) 443, 33 C.R. (7th) 239 (Man. C.A.), leave to appeal refused 2017 CarswellMan 192, 2017 CarswellMan 193 (S.C.C.) provides an extraordinarily detailed and rich analysis of the history of and philosophy behind the Hale view, dating back to the seventeenth century and reflected in Canada's *Criminal Code* since 1892, that duress can never be a defence to murder.

The Court describes differing approaches to this controversial issue in common law jurisdictions, noting that most jurisdictions still rely on Hale and a careful review of reform efforts in Canada. The Manitoba justices advance a staunch and detailed defence of the moralistic view that, apart from self-defence, murdering an innocent person can never meet the proportionality requirement of moral involuntariness.

Justice Mainella strongly criticizes the contrary view, advanced in *obiter*, by the Ontario Court of Appeal in *R. v. Aravena*, 2015 ONCA 250, 323 C.C.C. (3d) 54, 20 C.R. (7th) 131, leave to appeal refused 2016 CarswellOnt 5400, 2016 CarswellOnt 5401 (S.C.C.), leave to appeal refused 2016 CarswellOnt 5404, 2016 CarswellOnt 5405 (S.C.C.), leave to appeal refused 2016 CarswellOnt 5410, 2016 CarswellOnt 5411 (S.C.C.) that the statutory exclusion of the defence of duress to the offence of murder in s. 17 of the *Code* potentially infringes s. 7 of the *Charter*. Justice Mainella reasons as follows:

- The Ontario Court of Appeal was wrong in suggesting that modern English case authorities were based on a "deterrence-based policy argument" and the view that duress is a justification, not an excuse. It was a misunderstanding of history to rationalize the bar to the defence of duress from the offence of murder on a utilitarian basis.
- The judges in *Howe* returned the law to its traditional deontological foundation that protection of the sanctity of life requires a bright-line rule for the defence of duress, as exists for the defence of necessity based on *R. v. Dudley and Stephens*.
- *Aravena* may cast uncertainty on the defence of necessity. The Supreme Court of Canada has always attempted to keep the defences of duress and necessity as consistent as possible on a juristic basis. In *R. v. Latimer* the Supreme Court of Canada stated that it was "difficult, at the conceptual level, to imagine a circumstance in which the proportionality requirement [of necessity] could be met for a homicide" (para. 40). A reasoned argument could be made on the basis of *Aravena* that *Dudley and Stephens* is no longer the law, at least in Ontario, with respect to the defence of necessity and the offence of murder.
- *Aravena* had placed an undue emphasis on the unfairness of a threatened individual being expected to sacrifice himself or herself rather than commit murder.

Do you agree with the Manitoba or the Ontario Court of Appeal? See comments on *Willis* by Stuart, "High Time for the Supreme Court or Parliament to Reform our Complex Duress Defence" (2016), 33 C.R. (7th) 313 and Coughlan, "Doing the Right Thing: Duress as a Defence to Murder" (2016), 33 C.R. (7th) 317.

Professor Payan Akhavan "Should Duress Apply to All Crimes? A Comparative Appraisal of Moral Involuntariness and the Twenty Crimes Exception Under Section 17 of the Criminal Code" (2009) 13 Can. Crim. L. Rev. 271, however, argues that all of Canada's 20 crime exceptions are out of step with modern trends in other countries and should be struck down under *Ruzic* and the common law changed. See too Terry Skolnik, "Three Problems with Duress and Moral Involuntariness" (2016) 63 Crim. L.Q. 124.

Professor Martha Shaffer has persuasively argued that a revised law of duress must be broad to deal fairly with the experiences of battered women coerced into crime: see "Coerced into Crime: Battered Women and the Defence of Duress" (1999) 4 Can. Crim. L. Rev. 272 and "Scrutinizing Duress: The Constitutional Validity of Section 17 of the *Criminal Code*" (1998) 34 Crim. L.Q. 444.

For comments on *Ryan* see Steve Coughlan, "Welcome Clarity Around Duress" (2013), 98 C.R. (6th) 252, Carissima Mathen and Michael Plaxton, "*R. v.*

Ryan: Leaving Battered Women to the 'Justification' of Self-defence" (2013), 98 C.R. (6th) 258, and Archie Kaiser, "*Ryan*: A Troubling and Doctrinally Meandering Case Sets the Stage for the Law Reform Process and an Independent Inquiry" (2013), 98 C.R. (6th) 261. The Court expressed no opinion on whether the courts below had properly dismissed the defence of self-defence or whether the defence of necessity was available (see further Coughlan's C.R. comment). For an argument that the *Charter* analysis of duress in *Ryan* leads to the conclusion that equivalent changes should be made to the defence of necessity, see Steve Coughlan, "The Rise and Fall of Duress (or How Duress Changed Necessity Before Being Excluded by Self-defence)" (2013) 39 Queen's L.J. 83.

1. **The accused is charged with impaired driving. She admits that she was very drunk when she drove, but her defence is that she was compelled to do so to escape a sure beating at the hands of her enraged husband. She had been celebrating with fellow workers and her husband had discovered her with another male when he had gone to look for her four hours after he had expected her to return. In a state of rage he had smashed the window of the car in which she was seated and had also rammed the car when she drove off.**
Compare *R. v. Smith* (1977), 40 C.R.N.S. 390 (B.C. Prov. Ct.).

2. **The accused is charged with kidnapping contrary to s. 247(I)(c) of the *Criminal Code*. At the instigation of her husband she had lured a 20-year-old woman, whom she had previously known, into her husband's automobile on the pretext that she was going to a fashion show. The husband then grabbed the victim and tied her up while the accused drove her to a place where they were going to hold her. A ransom demand was made of the victim's father but the ransom was not paid and eventually the victim was released. Two weeks after the kidnapping and the failed extortion attempt, the accused confessed her participation to the police. Her defence was that she had acted entirely out of fear of her husband, who had previously assaulted her and had warned her that, if she did not do what he said, she would never see her daughter again, as the daughter would be kidnapped and taken to the United States.**
Compare *R. v. Robins* (1982), 66 C.C.C. (2d) 550 (Que. C.A.).

3. **The accused, Drazen Erdemovic, was indicted on May 29, 1996 before the Trial Chamber of the International Tribunal for the Prosecution of Persons Responsible for Serious Violations of International Humanitarian Law committed in the Territory of the former Yugoslavia since 1991. The case against Erdemovic was based on his own evidence. He had come forward to unburden himself and accept punishment. Erdemovic had been a member of a Sabotage Unit of the Serbian Army. On July 16, 1995, the Unit was ordered to a farm where they were told they would act as a firing squad to kill Muslims. Busloads of over 1000 Bosnian Muslim men and boys arrived and were executed that day. Erdemovic personally shot**

about 70 people. The accused pleaded guilty to a count of a crime against humanity but offered an explanation:

> Your Honour, I had to do this, they told me; "If you are sorry for them, stand up, line up with them and we will kill you too". I am not sorry for myself but for my family, my wife and son. . . and I could not refuse because they would have killed me. That is all I wish to add.

The Trial Chamber accepted his plea of guilt and sentenced him to ten years: see *The Prosecutor v. Drazen Erdemovic,* Case No. IT-96-22-T, T.Ch.I, 29 Nov. 1996. Later the issue before the Appeals Chamber at The Hague, Netherlands (majority judgment issued on October 7, 1997) was whether duress was a defence to such a charge. If there is to be such a defence is it material that the Muslim civilians would in any case have been killed by other soldiers?

7. PARTIAL DEFENCES TO MURDER

(a) Provocation

Under s. 232 of the *Criminal Code*, provocation as there defined is a partial defence to a murder charge in that it reduces it to a conviction of manslaughter.

R. v. HILL

(1985), [1986] 1 S.C.R. 313, 51 C.R. (3d) 97, 25 C.C.C. (3d) 322, 1986 CarswellOnt 1005, 1985 CarswellOnt 132

DICKSON C.J.C. (BEETZ, ESTEY, CHOUINARD and LA FOREST JJ. concurring): —

Gordon James Elmer Hill was charged with committing first degree murder at the city of Belleville, county of Hastings, on the person of Verne Pegg, contrary to s. 218(1) [now s. 235] of the *Criminal Code*, R.S.C. 1970, c. C-34. He was found by the jury not guilty of first degree murder but guilty of second degree murder. He was sentenced to imprisonment for life without eligiblity for parole until ten years of his sentence had been served.

I. THE FACTS

At trial both parties agreed that it was the acts of Hill which caused the death of Pegg, but disagreed otherwise. The position of the Crown at trial was that Hill and Pegg were homosexual lovers and that Hill had decided to murder Pegg after a falling out between them. The Crown argued that Hill deliberately struck Pegg in the head while Pegg lay in bed. This did not kill Pegg, who immediately ran from the bedroom into the bathroom to try and stop the flow of blood from his head. Realizing that he had been unsuccessful, Hill took two knives from the kitchen and stabbed Pegg to death.

Hill's version of the events was very different. He admitted to causing the death of Pegg, but put forward two defences: self-defence and provocation. Hill testified that he had known Pegg for about a year through the latter's involvement with the "Big Brother" organization. Hill stated that on the night in question he had been the subject of unexpected and unwelcome homosexual advances by Pegg while asleep on the couch in Pegg's apartment. Pegg pursued Hill to the bathroom and grabbed him, at which time Hill picked up a nearby hatchet and swung it at Pegg in an attempt to scare him. The hatchet struck Pegg in the head. Hill then ran from the apartment but returned shortly afterward. Upon re-entering the apartment, he was confronted by Pegg, who threatened to kill him. At this point. Hill obtained two knives from the kitchen and stabbed Pegg to death.

Hill was arrested, after a car chase with the police, at the wheel of a Pontiac automobile owned by Pegg. At the scene of arrest Hill denied knowing Pegg, but later he made a statement to the police which was substantially similar to his oral testimony at trial.

V. THE DEFENCE OF PROVOCATION

The defence of provocation appears to have first developed in the early 1800s. Tindal C.J. in *R. v. Hayward* (1833), 6 C. & P. 157 at 159, told the jury that the defence of provocation was derived from the law's "compassion to human infirmity". It acknowledged that all human beings are subject to uncontrollable outbursts of passion and anger which may lead them to do violent acts. In such instances, the law would lessen the severity of criminal liability.

Nevertheless, not all acts done in the heat of passion were to be subject to the doctrine of provocation. By the middle of the 19th Century, it became clear that the provoking act had to be sufficient to excite an ordinary or reasonable person under the circumstances. As Keating J. stated in *R. v. Welsh* (1869), 11 Cox C.C. 336 at 338:

> The law is, that there must exist such an amount of provocation as would be excited by the circumstances in the mind of a reasonable man, and so as to lead the jury to ascribe the act to the influence of that passion.

The *Criminal Code* codified this approach to provocation by including under s. 215 three general requirements for the defence of provocation. First, the provoking wrongful act or insult must be of such a nature that it would deprive an ordinary person of the power of self-control. That is the initial threshold which must be surmounted. Secondly, the accused must actually have been provoked. As I have earlier indicated, these two elements are often referred to as the objective and subjective test of provocation respectively. Thirdly, the accused must have acted on the provocation on the sudden and before there was time for his or her passion to cool.

(a) *The Objective Test of Provocation and the Ordinary Person Standard*

In considering the precise meaning and application of the ordinary person standard or objective test, it is important to identify its underlying rationale. Lord Simon of Glaisdale has perhaps stated it most succinctly when he suggested in *Camplin, supra*, at p. 726, that:

> ... the reason for importing into this branch of the law the concept of the reasonable man [was] ... to avoid the injustice of a man being entitled to rely on his exceptional excitablity or pugnacity or ill-temper or on his drunkenness.

If there were no objective test to the defence of provocation, anomalous results could occur. A well-tempered, reasonable person would not be entitled to benefit from the provocation defence and would be guilty of culpable homicide amounting to murder, while an ill-tempered or exceptionally excitable person would find his or her culpability mitigated by provocation and would be guilty only of manslaughter. It is society's concern that reasonable and non-violent behaviour be encouraged that prompts the law to endorse the objective standard. The criminal law is concerned, among other things, with fixing standards for human behaviour. We seek to encourage conduct that complies with certain societal standards of reasonableness and responsibility. In doing this, the law quite logically employs the objective standard of the reasonable person.

With this general purpose in mind, we must ascertain the meaning of the ordinary person standard. What are the characteristics of the "ordinary person"? To what extent should the attributes and circumstances of the accused be ascribed to the ordinary person? To answer these question, it is helpful to review the English developments, I shall begin with the English cases.

(i) English Law of Provocation and the Ordinary Person Standard

In *R. v. Lesbini*, [1914] 3 K.B. 1116, the English Court of Criminal Appeal refused to take into account the mental deficiency of the accused in assessing the availability of the provocation defence. It confirmed the threshold objective test for provocation, whereby there must be sufficient provocation to excite a reasonable person. A reasonable or ordinary person was not one with mental deficiencies. In *Mancini v. Pub. Prosecutions Dir.*, [1942] A.C. 1, the House of Lords endorsed the *Lesbini* case and further elaborated the objective test of provocation. Viscount Simon L.C. stated, at p. 9:

The test to be applied is that of the effect of the provocation on a reasonable man, as was laid down by the Court of Criminal Appeal in *Rex v. Lesbini*, so that an unusually excitable or pugnacious individual is not entitled to rely on provocation which would not have led an ordinary person to act as he did.

The ordinary or reasonable person, therefore, was one of normal temperament and average mental capacity.

In 1954, the House of Lords was faced with the question of whether, in applying the objective test of provocation, it should take into account certain physical characteristics of the accused. In *Bedder v. D.P.P.*, [1954] 1 W.L.R. 1119, a sexually impotent man killed a prostitute after she taunted him about his physical condition. The House of Lords had to determine whether, in applying the objective test of provocation, the sexual impotence of the accused should be taken into account. The test would then have been whether an ordinary person who was sexually impotent would have been provoked. The court rejected this approach and held that the peculiar physical characteristics of the accused were not to be ascribed to the ordinary person for the purposes of the objective test.

Despite the House of Lords' conclusion that the physical characteristics of the accused were irrelevant to the determination of whether a reasonable person would have been provoked, it appears that the court was primarily concerned with the difficulty of distinguishing "temperament" from "physical defects". As Lord Simonds L.C. stated, at p. 1121:

It appears to that court, as it appears to me, that "no distinction is to be made in the case of a person who, though it may not be a matter of temperament, is physically impotent, is conscious of that impotence, and therefore mentally liable to be more excited unduly if he is 'twitted' or attacked on the subject of that particular infirmity". The court thereupon approved and reiterated the proposition that the question for the jury was whether on the facts . . . from the evidence the provocation was in fact enough to lead a reasonable person to do what the accused did.

The *Bedder* approach to the ordinary person standard is no longer the law in England. In *Camplin*, *supra*, the House of Lords expressly rejected the narrow objective test articulated in *Bedder*. The *Camplin* case involved a youth of 15 years of age who maintained that he had been provoked by a homosexual assault. The House of Lords unanimously concluded that the ordinary person, for the purposes of the objective test of provocation, was to be an ordinary person of the same age and sex as the accused. It should be noted that in *Camplin* the trial judge had specifically directed the jury to take age and sex into account and the appeal sought to establish that this was wrong. In the present case, there was no such instruction.

In justifying its shift away from the *Bedder* approach, the House of Lords relied in part on legislative changes in the law of provocation introduced after the *Bedder* opinion. Specifically, in 1957, s. 3 of the *Homicide Act, 1957* (5 & 6 Eliz. 2, c. 11), was passed; it provides:

> 3. Where on a charge of murder there is evidence on which the jury can find that the person charged was provoked (whether by things done or by things said or by both together) to lose his self-control, the question whether the provocation was enough to make a reasonable man do as he did shall be left to be determined by the jury: and in determining that question the jury shall take into account everything both done and said according to the effect which, in their opinion, it would have on a reasonable man.

The phrase "the jury shall take into account everything" was interpreted to allow a consideration of relevant characteristics in connection with the objective test.

Lord Diplock clarified the underlying rationale for expanding the notion of the ordinary person when he wrote, at p. 717:

> To taunt a person because of his race, his physical infirmities or some shameful incident in his past may well be considered by the jury to be more offensive to the person addressed, however equable his temperament, if the facts on which the taunt is founded are true than it would be if they were not.

On a similar note, Lord Morris of Borth-y-Gest held, at p. 721:

> If the accused is of particular colour or particular ethnic origin and things are said which to him are grossly insulting it would be utterly unreal if the jury had to consider whether the words would have provoked a man of a different colour or ethnic origin — or to consider how such a man would have acted or reacted.

Taking these considerations into account, Lord Simon of Glaisdale formulated the objective test as follows, at p. 727:

> I think that the standard of self-control which the law requires before provocation is held to reduce murder to manslaughter is still that of the reasonable person ... but that, in determining whether a person of reasonable self-control would lose it in the circumstances, the entire factual situation, which includes the characteristics of the accused, must be considered.

One conceptual difficulty was acknowledged by Lord Diplock. He recognized at p. 717 that:

> ... in strict logic there is a transition between treating age as a characteristic that may be taken into account in assessing the gravity of the provocation addressed to the accused and treating it as a characteristic to be taken into account in determining what is the degree of self-control to be expected of the ordinary person.

In most cases, it is appropriate to assume that the level of self-control or degree of reasonableness is the same regardless of certain physical differences. Age, however, in Lord Diplock's view posed a more difficult problem. He resolved this problem with respect to age by appealing to the acknowledged importance of the law's compassion to human infirmity. On a more general level, he rejected the solution of separating out the inquiry into two phases as overly complicated for the jury.

(ii) Canadian Case Law

The Supreme Court of Canada has also had occasion to provide guidance on the ordinary person standard for provocation. In *Taylor v. R.*, [1947] S.C.R. 462, 3 C.R. 475, 89 C.C.C. 209 [Ont.], a case in which the accused was drunk at the time of his alleged provocation, Kerwin J. at p. 471 made clear that for the purposes of the objective test of provocation the "criterion is the effect on the ordinary person . . . the jury is not entitled to take into consideration any alleged drunkenness on the part of the accused".

This court again rejected a consideration of the drunkenness of the accused in connection with the objective test in *Salamon v. R.*, [1959] S.C.R. 404, 30 C.R. 1, 123 C.C.C. 1 [Ont.]. Fauteux endorsed the trial judge's instruction to the jury [quoted at p. 410] not to consider "the character, background, temperament, or condition of the accused" in relation to the objective test of provocation. Similarly, Cartwright J. (dissenting on another issue) wrote, at p. 415, that the trial judge correctly "made it plain that on this [objective] branch of the inquiry no account should be taken of the idiosyncrasies of the appellant and that the standard was that of an ordinary person".

Finally, in *Wright v. R.*, [1969] S.C.R. 335, [1969] 3 C.C.C. 258 [Sask.], a son was charged with the shooting death of his father. The evidence suggested that there had been some difficulties in their relationship. The father was said to have been a bad-tempered and violent man who had mistreated his son on a number of occasions. The accused had not seen his father for a period of about five years until a few days prior to the fatal incident. On the evening of the shooting, the accused had spent most of the day drinking with his friends. In considering the objective test of provocation, the court rejected the relevance of the quality of the accused's relationship with his father, the mentality of the accused or his possible drunkenness. Fauteux J. quoted, at p. 340, the words of Lord Simmonds L.C. in *Bedder*, *supra*, that the purpose of the objective test is:

> . . . to invite the jury to consider the act of the accused by reference to a certain standard or norm of conduct and with this object the "reasonable" or the "average" or the "normal" man is invoked.

The court went on to state, at p. 340:

> While the character, background, temperament, idiosyncrasies, or the drunkenness of the accused are matters to be considered in the second branch of the enquiry, they are excluded from consideration in the first branch. A contrary view would denude of any sense the objective test.

Appellate Courts at the provincial level have also considered the nature of the ordinary person standard of provocation. In *R. v. Clark* (1975), 22 C.C.C.

(2d) 1 (Alta. C.A.), the "morbid jealousy" and "slight mental degeneration" [p. 15] suffered by the accused was held not to be relevant to the objective test. According to Clement J.A., at p. 16:

> In the first branch of the inquiry, the objective test, which in essence has to be determined as a standard of comparison is the reaction that might be expected from ordinary human nature to the wrongful act, or to the alleged insult in the present case.

In *R. v. Parnerkar* (1972), 16 C.R.N.S. 347, 5 C.C.C. (2d) 11, affirmed [1974] S.C.R. 449, 21 C.R.N.S. 129, 10 C.C.C. (2d) 253, the Saskatchewan Court of Appeal held that the cultural and religious background of the accused was not relevant to the determination of the objective test. The accused, born in India, was alleged to have been provoked by, *inter alia*, the deceased's statement: "I am not going to marry you because you are a black man." The court's ruling seems to narrow unduly the conception of the ordinary person and rigidly prohibit a consideration of the physical characteristics of the accused along the lines of the *Bedder* case. I should note that *Parnerkar* was affirmed by this court on appeal; however, this particular question was not addressed.

In more recent decisions, appellate courts at the provincial level appear to be moving towards the *Camplin, supra*, approach. The Ontario Court of Appeal's decision in the present appeal, and *Daniels v. R.* (1983), 7 C.C.C. (3d) 542 (C.A.), reflect this trend. In *Daniels* case, Laycraft J.A. held that in instructing the jury on the objective test of provocation the trial judge should tell the jury to take into account all of the external events putting pressure on the accused. He stated at p. 554:

> The purpose of the objective test prescribed by s. 215 is to consider the actions of the accused in a specific case against the standard of the ordinary person. Hypothetically, the ordinary person is subjected to the same external pressures of insult by acts or words as was the accused. Only if those pressures would cause an ordinary person to lose self-control does the next question arise whether the accused did, in fact, lose self-control. In my view, the objective test lacks validity if the reaction of the hypothetical ordinary person is not tested against all of the events which put pressure on the accused.

(iii) The Appropriate Content of the Ordinary Person Standard

What lessons are to be drawn from this review of the case law? I think it is clear that there is widespread agreement that the ordinary or reasonable person has a normal temperament and level of self-control. It follows that the ordinary person is not exceptionally excitable, pugnacious or in a state of drunkenness.

In terms of other characteristics of the ordinary person, it seems to me that the "collective good sense" of the jury will naturally lead it to ascribe to the ordinary person any general characteristics relevant to the provocation in question. For example, if the provocation is a racial slur, the jury will think of an ordinary person with the racial background that forms the substance of the insult. To this extent, particular characteristics will be ascribed to the ordinary person. Indeed, it would be impossible to conceptualize a sexless or ageless ordinary person. Features such as sex, age, or race do not detract for a person's characterization as ordinary. Thus particular characteristics that are not peculiar or idiosyncratic can be ascribed to an ordinary person without subverting the logic of the objective test of provocation. As Lord Diplock wrote in *Camplin*, *supra*, at pp. 716-17:

> ... the "reasonable man" man has never been confined to the adult male. It means an ordinary person of either sex, not exceptionally excitable or pugnacious, but possessed of such powers of self-control as everyone is entitled to expect that his fellow citizens will exercise in society as it is today.

It is important to note that in some instances certain characteristics will be irrelevant. For example, the race of a person will be irrelevant if the provocation involves an insult regarding a physical disability. Similarly, the sex of an accused will be irrelevant if the provocation relates to a racial insult. Thus the central criterion is the relevance of the particular feature to the provocation in question. With this in mind, I think it is fair to conclude that age will be a relevant consideration when we are dealing with a young accused person. For a jury to assess what an ordinary person would have done if subjected to the same circumstances as the accused, the young age of an accused will be an important contextual consideration.

I should also add that my conclusion that certain attributes can be ascribed to the ordinary person is not meant to suggest that a trial judge must in each case tell the jury what specific attributes it is to ascribe to the ordinary person. The point I wish to emphasize is simply that, in applying their common sense to the factual determination of the objective test, jury members will quite naturally and properly ascribe certain characteristics to the "ordinary person".

(b) *The Subjective Test and Actual Provocation*

Once a jury has established that the provocation in question was sufficient to deprive an ordinary person of the power of self-control, it must still determine whether the accused was so deprived. It may well be that an ordinary person would have been provoked but in fact the accused was not. This second test of provocation is called "subjective" because it involves an assessment of what actually occurred in the mind of the accused. At this stage, the jury must also consider whether the accused reacted to the provocation on the sudden and before there was time for his passion to cool.

In instructing the jury with the respect to the subjective test of provocation, the trial judge must make clear to the jury that its task at this point is to ascertain whether the accused was *in fact* acting as a result of provocation. In this regard, a trial judge may wish to remind the jury members that, in determining whether an accused was actually provoked, they are entitled to take into account his or her mental state and psychological temperament.

VI. The Validity of the Judge's Charge

To apply this statement of the law to the present appeal, we must return to the actual words of the trial judge. When instructing the jury on the objective test of provocation, he began by stating [quoted at p. 90]:

> First, the actual words must be such as would deprive an ordinary person of self-control. In considering this part of the defence you are not to consider the particular mental make-up of the accused: rather the standard is that of the ordinary person. You will ask yourselves: Would the words or acts in this case have caused an ordinary person to lose his self-control?

He later added:

> You will consider that evidence and you will decide whether the words and acts were sufficient to cause an ordinary person to lose his self-control.

In my view, this part of the charge was well-stated and correct in law. The trial judge did not err in failing to specify that the ordinary person, for the purpose of the objective test of provocation, is to be deemed to be of the same age and sex as the accused. Although this type of instruction may be helpful in clarifying the application of the ordinary person standard. I do not think it wise or necessary to make this a mandatory component of all jury charges or provocation. Whenever possible, we should retain simplicity in charges to the jury and have confidence that the words of the *Criminal Code* will provide sufficient guidance to the jury. Indeed, in this area of the law I take heed of the words of Lord Goddard C.J. in *R. v. McCarthy*, [1954] 2 Q.B. 105 at 112:

> No court has ever given, nor do we think ever can give, a definition of what constitutes a reasonable or average man. That must be left to the collective good sense of the jury . . . .

It has been suggested that the instruction of the trial judge on the subjective prong of the provocation defence had the effect of misleading the jury on the appropriate content of the ordinary person standard. The charge stated [quoted in part at p. 90]:

> . . . you will then secondly consider whether the accused acted on the provocation on the sudden before there was time for his passion to cool. In deciding this question you are not restricted to the standard of the ordinary person. You will take into account the mental, the emotional, the physical characteristics and the age of this accused . . . .

In my opinion, these words would not have misled the average juror with respect to the objective test, particularly when viewed in the context of the charge as a whole.

I have the greatest of confidence in the level of intelligence and plain common sense of the average Canadian jury sitting on a criminal case. Juries are perfectly capable of sizing the matter up. In my experience as a trial judge I cannot recall a single instance in which a jury returned to the courtroom to ask for further instructions on the provocation portion of a murder charge. A jury frequently seeks further guidance on the distinction between first degree murder, second degree murder and manslaughter, but rarely, if ever, on provocation. It sems to be common ground that the trial judge would not have been in error if he had simply read s. 215 of the *Code* and left it at that, without embellishment. I am loath to complicate the task of the trial judge, in cases such as the case at bar, by requiring him or her as a matter of law to point out to the members of the jury that in applying the objective test they must conceptualize an "ordinary person" who is male and young. The accused is before them. He is male and young. I cannot conceive of a Canadian jury conjuring up the concept of an "ordinary person" who would be either female or elderly, or banishing from their minds the possibility that an "ordinary person" might be both young and male. I do not think anything said by the judge in the case at bar would have lead the jury to such an absurdity.

VII. CONCLUSION

I find that the trial judge's charge to the jury on the ordinary person standard in the defence of provocation was consistent with the requirements of the *Criminal Code* and correct in law. It was not necessary to direct the jury that the ordinary person means an ordinary person of the same age and sex as the accused. I would therefore allow the appeal and restore the conviction.

McIntyre J. gave a concurring judgment. Three separate dissenting judgments were delivered by Lamer, Wilson and LeDain JJ. None of the dissenters unequivocally favoured a mandatory direction to the jury as had the House of Lords in *Camplin*. In general, the dissenting justices were of the view that this trial judge's direction had excluded age from consideration under the "ordinary person" test and that this had in the circumstances been unfairly prejudicial to the accused.

Should the Supreme Court have adopted the full *Camplin* approach?

In *R. v. Jackson* (1991), 68 C.C.C. (3d) 385 at 410, the Ontario Court of Appeal applied the "modified objective test" of *Hill* to consider "whether a reasonable young adult would have been deprived of self-control by an assault committed by a long-time friend, lover, provider and protector in the course of an argument which signalled the end of this long-standing relationship". This issue was not addressed when the Supreme Court dismissed the further appeal: [1993] 4 S.C.R. 573, 26 C.R. (4th) 178, 86 C.C.C. (3d) 385.

For a view that the provocation defence contributes to homophobia and violence against gay men and lesbians see N. Kathleen (Sam) Banks, "The 'Homosexual Panic' Defence in Canadian Criminal Law" (1997), 1 C.R. (5th) 371.

R. v. PARENT

[2001] 1 S.C.R. 761, 41 C.R. (5th) 199, 154 C.C.C. (3d) 1,
2001 CarswellQue 851, 2001 CarswellQue 852

The accused and his estranged wife were involved in divorce litigation over the division of their assets, some of which were held in a corporation. Their financial situation had deteriorated to the point the accused's shares were seized and put up for sale. The wife attended the sale, allegedly intending to buy the shares. The accused was also present. He carried a loaded gun with a locked security catch in his pocket. His wife suggested that they speak and they went into a nearby room. He testified that she said in effect "I told you that I would wipe you out completely". He then felt a hot flush rising and he shot. He said he did not know what he was doing any more and did not intend to kill her. She died from six wounds.

At trial on a charge of first degree murder he argued that the verdict should be reduced to manslaughter on the basis of lack of criminal intent or provocation. The jury found him guilty of manslaughter. The Court of Appeal upheld the verdict.

The Supreme Court allowed the appeal and ordered a new trial on second degree murder.

McLACHLIN C.J.C. for a unanimous court: —

The jury had three possible offences before it: first degree murder, second degree murder and manslaughter. All three offences require proof of an act of killing (*actus reus*) and the corresponding criminal intention (*mens rea*). In relation to murder, the defence of provocation does not eliminate the need for proof of intention to kill, but operates as an excuse that has the effect of reducing murder to manslaughter.

The Crown argues that the trial judge erred in suggesting that anger is capable of negating the intention to kill and that the jury could reduce the offence to manslaughter on this basis. More particularly, the Crown suggests that the judge's directions wrongly treated anger as a matter that could negate the criminal intent or *mens rea* of the offence; wrongly suggested that negation of intent can reduce the offence to manslaughter; and wrongly left open the suggestion that anger alone can establish provocation, when in fact other requirements must be met pursuant to s. 232 of the *Criminal Code*, R.S.C. 1985, c. C-46. The gravamen of the Crown's submission is that the trial judge's direction on intention was confusing and wrong and left it open to the jury to convict the accused of manslaughter, not on the basis of provocation (which the trial judge correctly defined), but on the erroneous basis that a high degree of anger short of provocation, as defined in law, could negate the criminal intent or *mens rea* of the offence.

Anger can play a role in reducing murder to manslaughter in connection with the defence of provocation. Anger is not a stand-alone defence. It may form part of the defence of provocation when all the requirements of that defence are met: (1) a wrongful act or insult that would have caused an ordinary person to be deprived of his or her self-control; (2) which is sudden and unexpected; (3) which in fact caused the accused to act in anger; (4) before having recovered his or her normal control: *R. v. Thibert*, [1996] 1 S.C.R. 37, 104 C.C.C. (3d) 1, 131 D.L.R. (4th) 675. Again, anger conceivably could, in extreme circumstances, cause someone to enter a state of automatism in which that person does not know what he or she is doing, thus negating the voluntary component of the *actus reus*: *R. v. Stone*, [1999] 2 S.C.R. 290, 134 C.C.C. (3d) 353, 173 D.L.R. (4th) 66. However, the accused did not assert this defence. In any event, the defence if successful would result in acquittal, not reduction to manslaughter.

So it seems clear that the trial judge misdirected the jury on the effect of anger in relation to manslaughter. His directions left it open to the jury to find the accused guilty of manslaughter, on the basis of the anger felt by the accused, even if they concluded that the conditions required for the defence of provocation were not met. The directions raise the possibility that the jury's verdict of manslaughter may have been based on erroneous legal principles, unless they were corrected in the recharge to the jury.

. . . .

I would allow the appeal and direct a new trial on second degree murder.

For a full analysis of *Parent* see Gary Trotter, "Anger, Provocation, and the Intent for Murder: A Comment on *R. v. Parent*" (2002) 47 McGill L.J. 669. See too Wayne Gorman, "*R. v. Parent*" (2002) 45 Crim. L.Q. 412.

R. v. TRAN

[2010] 3 S.C.R. 350, 2010 CarswellAlta 2281, 2010 CarswellAlta 2282, 261 C.C.C. (3d) 435, 80 C.R. (6th) 1

The accused suspected that his estranged wife was having a relationship with another man and had made attempts at surveillance. He entered his estranged wife's home unexpected and uninvited, using keys he had purported to return. He found his wife in bed with her boyfriend, and attacked the two of them. He then ran from the bedroom to the kitchen, returned with two butcher knives, and renewed his attack, stabbing the boyfriend several times. The accused then confronted his estranged wife and slashed her with the knife, during which time the boyfriend managed to crawl into the living room. The accused followed him to that room, renewing his attack. He eventually stabbed the boyfriend 17 times, killing him, and also injured his estranged wife.

At trial, the only defence raised was that murder should be reduced to manslaughter based on provocation. The trial judge held that the Crown had failed to disprove the elements of provocation, acquitted the accused of second degree murder, and convicted him of manslaughter. The Court of Appeal held that there was no air of reality to the defence of provocation and substituted a conviction for second degree murder.

CHARRON J. (for seven justices): —

[6] The preceding overview of the facts reflects the trial judge's findings and uncontested items of evidence. I agree with the Court of Appeal that, on those facts, there was no air of reality to the defence of provocation. In my respectful view, the trial judge proceeded on wrong legal principles concerning the requirements for the defence of provocation and, as a result, erred in law in finding that there was an evidential basis in this record for that defence.

[7] Specifically, there was no "insult" within the meaning of s. 232 of the *Criminal Code*, R.S.C. 1985, c. C-46. As rightly concluded by the Court of Appeal, the appellant's view of his estranged wife's sexual involvement with another man after the couple had separated — found at trial to be the "insult" — cannot in law be sufficient to excuse "a loss of control in the form of a homicidal rage" and constitute "an excuse for the ordinary person of whatever personal circumstances or background" (Watson J.A., at para. 64). In addition, the uncontradicted evidence about the appellant's knowledge that his wife was involved with another man and his own conduct in entering her home and bedroom, unexpected and uninvited, belied any notion that this supposed "insult" would have struck "upon a mind unprepared for it" as required by law (Hunt J.A., at para. 18). Finally, there was no air of reality to the appellant "acting on the sudden at the time of the killing" (Watson J.A., at para. 77).

[8] As a conviction for murder was inevitable, both on the law and on the trial judge's essential findings of fact, the Court of Appeal properly substituted a verdict of second degree murder and remitted the matter for sentencing. I would dismiss the appeal.

2. Analysis

[10] As the opening words of the provision make plain, the defence will only apply where the accused had the necessary intent for murder and acted upon this intent. Parliament thus carefully limited the application of the defence. The requirements of the defence contained in s. 232 have been described variously by the Court as comprising either two, three or four elements. For example, in *R. v. Hill*, [1986] 1 S.C.R. 313, Dickson C.J. identified three general requirements for the defence of provocation:

> First, the provoking wrongful act or insult must be of such a nature that it would deprive an ordinary person of the power of self-control. That is the initial threshold which must be surmounted. Secondly, the accused must actually have been provoked. As I have earlier indicated, these two elements are often referred to as the objective and subjective tests of

provocation respectively. Thirdly, the accused must have acted on the provocation on the sudden and before there was time for his or her passion to cool. [p. 324]

In *R. v. Thibert*, [1996] 1 S.C.R. 37, Cory J. for the majority of the Court collapsed these three requirements into two elements, one objective and the other subjective, describing them as follows:

First, there must be a wrongful act or insult of such a nature that it is sufficient to deprive an ordinary person of the power of self-control as the objective element. Second, the subjective element requires that the accused act upon that insult on the sudden and before there was time for his passion to cool. [Emphasis in original deleted; para. 4.]

Subsequently, in *R. v. Parent*, 2001 SCC 30, [2001] 1 S.C.R. 761, the Court reiterated the test in *Thibert* but framed it in terms of four required elements:

... (1) a wrongful act or insult that would have caused an ordinary person to be deprived of his or her self-control; (2) which is sudden and unexpected; (3) which in fact caused the accused to act in anger; (4) before having recovered his or her normal control . . . . [para. 10]

[11] These various formulations do not differ in substance. While it may be conceptually convenient in any given case to formulate the requirements of the defence in terms of distinct elements and to treat each of these elements separately, it is important to recognize that the various components of the defence may overlap and that s. 232 must be considered in its entirety.

[12] Before discussing the requirements contained in s. 232, it is useful to briefly review the historical development of the defence. As we shall see, prevailing social mores and judicial attitudes have played an important role in defining what amounts to provocation at law.

2.1 Historical Development of the Defence

[13] The defence of provocation, presently codified in s. 232 of the *Criminal Code*, has its origins in the English common law. More specifically, its precursor lies in the sixteenth century concept of "chance-medley" killings. As the English jurist Sir Edward Coke described it, "[h]omicide is called chancemedley . . . for that it is done by chance (without premeditation) upon a sudden brawle, shuffling, or contention" (*The Third Part of the Institutes of the Laws of England: Concerning High Treason, and Other Pleas of the Crown and Criminal Causes* (1817), at p. 56). During these killings, persons were considered to act "in the Time of their Rage, Drunkenness, hidden Displeasure, or other Passion of Mind" (*Statute of Stabbing (1604)*, 2 Jas I, c. 8). Such killings were considered less morally reprehensible than deliberate "cold-blooded" killings and, informed by the value of honour that formed an important aspect of that period's social context, were viewed as partially excused.

[14] During the seventeenth century, another trend in the law of homicide emerged. It provided that anyone charged with murder was presumed to have acted with "malice aforethought", for which the punishment at the time was death. In response to the severity of the law, the courts resorted to the separate crime of manslaughter to take into account certain human frailties that would operate to rebut the presumption. One such concession to human frailty was that the accused had been provoked into committing the act (Department of Justice, *Reforming Criminal Code Defences: Provocation, Self-Defence and Defence of Property: A Consultation Paper* (1998), at p. 2). However, not any provocation would suffice; it had to be significant: see G. R. Sullivan, "Anger and Excuse: Reassessing Provocation" (1993), 13 *Oxford J. Leg. Stud.* 421, at p. 422.

[15] By the eighteenth century, the doctrine of provocation had become entrenched in the common law. Initially, the accused's state of mind, and in particular whether he was sufficiently deprived of self-control to have acted without malice in responding to the provocation, was the focus of the defence. Eventually, however, the courts set out to create greater certainty by establishing specific categories of "provocative events" that were considered "significant" enough to result in a loss of self-control. In the seminal case, *R. v. Mawgridge* (1707), Kel J. 119, 84 E.R. 1107, Lord Holt C.J. set out four categories of provocation. One category envisaged a husband catching a man in the act of adultery with his wife. The basis of the provocation, he wrote, was that "jealousy is the rage of a man, and adultery is the highest invasion of property" (p. 1115). Interestingly, while the killing of a sexual rival caught in the act of committing adultery with one's wife was seen as a proper basis for the defence, the killing of one's wife for infidelity was not: F. Stewart and A. Freiberg, *Provocation in Sentencing Research Report* (2nd ed. 2009), at para. 2.1.2. Another category included an "affron[t]" of "pulling . . . the nose, or filliping upon the forehead" (*Mawgridge*, at p. 1114). These categories carried the vestiges of a social view that privileged notions of preserving a man's honour. As Sullivan has described it:

> A violent response in such circumstances was not so much a matter to be condoned but to be required of a man of honour. The core perception of mitigating anger at this time was not of an emotion rendering the agent out of control but as a hot-blooded response informed and controlled by a rational understanding of the nature and degree of the provocation offered. It was a case of hot-blooded yet controlled vindication of one's honour rather than spontaneous, uncontrolled fury. [p. 422]

[16] By the middle of the nineteenth century, attempts to identify further categories were abandoned and the defence became more generalized. In *R. v. Hayward* (1833), 6 Car. & P. 157, 172 E.R. 1188, at p. 1189, Tindal C.J. told the jury that the defence was derived from the law's "compassion to human infirmity". The Law Commissioners' Digest of 1839 provided that the provocative conduct must be "a wrongful act or insult", which required that the

conduct be inherently offensive (Law Commission of Great Britain, *Partial Defences to Murder*, Consultation Paper No. 173 (2003), at para. 1.27, citing "Fourth Report of Her Majesty's Commissioners on Criminal Law", in *Reports from Commissioners* (1839), 235). These developments occurred at the same time as another critical one. While an objective standard was always implicit in the defence, a more formal standard of self-control expected to be exercised by the "reasonable man" in the circumstances was eventually proposed: *R. v. Welsh* (1869), 11 Cox C.C. 336. Ultimately, the objective element came to play a heightened role in the operation of the defence as the recognized grounds of provocation were abandoned (see T. Macklem, "Provocation and the Ordinary Person" (1987-1988), 11 *Dal. L.J.* 126, at p. 130).

[17] As this brief historical review demonstrates, the social context has always played an important role in defining what amounts to provocation at law. In 1949, Lord Goddard C.J. summarized the relationship between the defence and social context in the following manner:

> At a time when society was less secure and less settled in its habits, when the carrying of swords was as common as the use of a walking stick at the present day, and when duelling was regarded as involving no moral stigma if fairly conducted, it is not surprising that the courts took a view more lenient towards provocation than is taken to-day when life and property are guarded by an efficient police force and social habits have changed.

> (*R. v. Semini*, [1949] 1 K.B. 405, at p. 409)

[18] The common law defence of provocation was adopted and codified in the Canadian *Criminal Code* from its inception in 1892. The wording of s. 232 remains substantially unaltered. The same cannot be said of the social context in which it is embedded. The continued appropriateness of the defence has been a source of controversy, both in Canada and abroad. Some commentators and reviewing bodies have recommended that the defence be abandoned altogether, leaving provocation, when relevant, as a factor to be considered in sentencing. For a discussion of such reform proposals in Canada and elsewhere, see D. E. Ives, "Provocation, Excessive Force in Self-Defence and Diminished Responsibility", in Law Commission of Great Britain, *Partial Defences to Murder: Overseas Studies*, Consultation Paper 173 (App. B) (2003), 73, at pp. 78-81; Australia, Victorian Law Reform Commission, *Defences to Homicide: Final Report* (2004); New Zealand Law Commission, *The Partial Defence of Provocation*, Report 98 (2007).

[19] Parliament has not chosen this course and the defence continues to exist in Canada. This does not mean, however, that the defence in its present articulation should not continue to evolve to reflect contemporary social norms, and in particular, *Charter* values. Just as at common law the notion of an "insult . . . sufficient to deprive an ordinary person of the power of self-control", now

codified under s. 232, is not frozen in time. By incorporating this objective element, the defence of provocation is necessarily informed by contemporary social norms and values. These include society's changed views regarding the nature of marital relationships and the present reality that a high percentage of them end in separation.

[20] It is with these considerations in mind that I turn to an examination of the defence as contained in s. 232 of the *Criminal Code*.

2.2 *Provocation Under Section 232 of the Criminal Code*

[21] Viewing the provision as a whole, I offer some preliminary comments about the juridical nature of the defence. A criminal law defence is usually characterized as providing either an excuse or a justification for the impugned conduct. As Professor K. Roach rightly observes: "As a partial defence that reduces murder to manslaughter, provocation does not fit easily into the excuse/ justification framework" (*Criminal Law* (4th ed. 2009), at p. 358). In *R. v. Manchuk*, [1938] S.C.R. 18, at pp. 19-20, this Court explained that "provocation . . . neither justifies nor excuses the act of homicide. But the law accounts the act and the violent feelings which prompted it less blameable because of the passion aroused by the provocation, . . . though still sufficiently blameable to merit punishment — and it may be punishment of high severity — but not the extreme punishment of death."

[22] Thus, the accused's conduct is partially *excused* out of a compassion to human frailty. While the call for compassion was particularly compelling in times when the alternative was the death penalty, the rationale subsists today, given the serious consequences to the offender flowing from a conviction for murder. It is not sufficient, however, that an accused's sudden reaction to a wrongful act or insult may be explained from a purely subjective standpoint. The provision incorporates an objective standard against which the accused's reaction must be measured — that which may be expected of the "ordinary person" in like circumstances. Not all instances of loss of self-control will be excused. Rather, the requisite elements of the defence, taken together, make clear that the accused must have a *justifiable* sense of being wronged. This does not mean, and in no way should be taken as suggesting, that the victim is to be blamed for the accused's act, nor that he or she deserved the consequences of the provocation. Nor does it mean that the law sanctions the accused's conduct. Instead, the law recognizes that, as a result of human frailties, the accused reacted inappropriately and disproportionately, but understandably to a sufficiently serious wrongful act or insult.

[23] In my view, the requirements of s. 232 are most usefully described as comprising two elements, one objective and the other subjective. As Cory J. for the majority of the Court put it in *Thibert*:

> First, there must be a wrongful act or insult of such a nature that it is sufficient to deprive an ordinary person of the power of self-control as the objective element. Second, the subjective element requires that the accused act upon that insult on the sudden and before there was time for his passion to cool. [Emphasis in original deleted; para. 4.]

[24] I will review each element in turn.

2.2.1 The Objective Element: A Wrongful Act or Insult Sufficient to Deprive an Ordinary Person of the Power of Self-Control

[25] For the purpose of discussion, the objective element may be viewed as two-fold: (1) there must be a wrongful act or insult; and (2) the wrongful act or insult must be sufficient to deprive an ordinary person of the power of self-control.

[26] While the concepts "wrongful act" and "insult" are not defined, the following limitation is set out in s. 232(3):

> 232. . . .
>
> (3) For the purposes of this section, the questions
>
>> (a) whether a particular wrongful act or insult amounted to provocation, and
>>
>> (b) whether the accused was deprived of the power of self-control by the provocation that he alleges he received,
>
> are questions of fact, but no one shall be deemed to have given provocation to another by doing anything that he had a legal right to do, or by doing anything that the accused incited him to do in order to provide the accused with an excuse for causing death or bodily harm to any human being.

The second branch of s. 232(3) is not at issue in this case and I do not propose to discuss the limitation on the defence in circumstances where the accused himself incites the act of provocation with a view to providing himself with an excuse for committing the offence. The "legal right" limitation on the defence, however, merits further discussion in the context of this case.

[27] It is well established that the phrase "legal right" does not include all conduct not specifically prohibited by law. For example, the fact that a person may not be subject to legal liability for an insult directed at the accused does not mean that he or she has the "legal right" to make the insult within the meaning of s. 232(3) and that provocation is not open to the accused. To require that an insult be specifically prohibited by law would effectively render the word

"insult" under s. 232(2) redundant, as any such "insult" would necessarily be a "wrongful act". The phrase "legal right" has been defined, rather, as meaning a right which is sanctioned by law, such as a sheriff proceeding to execute a legal warrant, or a person acting in justified self-defence (*Thibert*, at para. 29, citing *R. v. Haight* (1976), 30 C.C.C. (2d) 168 (Ont. C.A.), at p. 175, and *R. v. Galgay*, [1972] 2 O.R. 630 (C.A.), at p. 649). Interpreted in this manner, the notion of legal right serves to carve out from the ambit of s. 232 legally sanctioned conduct which otherwise could amount, in fact, to an "insult".

[28] There has been academic criticism of this approach. Professor Roach argues, for example, that the concept of legal right could be rethought in the context of domestic violence. He writes: "It could be argued that people have a legal right to leave relationships and even to make disparaging comments about ex-partners. The Court's continued refusal to recognize this broader interpretation of a legal right could deny women the equal protection and benefit of the law" (p. 359).

[29] In my view, these concerns, while legitimate, are better addressed at the stage when the gravity of the "insult" is objectively measured as against the ordinary person standard. In other words, while one spouse undoubtedly has a legal right to leave his or her partner, in some circumstances the means by which that spouse communicates this decision may amount *in fact* to an "insult", within the ordinary meaning of the word. However, to be recognized *at law*, the insult must be of sufficient gravity to cause a loss of self-control, as objectively determined. The fact that the victim has the "legal right", in the broad sense of the term, to leave the relationship is an important consideration in the assessment of this objective standard.

[30] The "ordinary person", as a legal concept, has generally been assimilated in the case law to the well-known "reasonable person" and the two terms are often used interchangeably: e.g., *Hill*, at p. 331. While I believe that the two fictional entities share the same attributes, at first blush some may question this as a logical inconsistency, given that a "reasonable" person would not commit culpable homicide in the first place. Indeed, "reasonableness" often defines the standard of conduct which is expected at law, and conduct which meets this standard, as a general rule, does not attract legal liability. The inconsistency is resolved when it is recalled that the defence is only a partial one, and that the defendant, even if successful, will still be guilty of manslaughter. The use of the term "ordinary person" therefore reflects the normative dimensions of the defence; that is, behaviour which comports with contemporary society's norms and values will attract the law's compassion. Meeting the standard, however, will only provide a *partial* defence. In this context, it seems to me that the label "ordinary person" is more suitable and this may explain Parliament's choice of

words. Cory J. for the majority of the Court in *Thibert* explained how the ordinary person standard should be interpreted:

> Yet, I think the objective element should be taken as an attempt to weigh in the balance those very human frailties which sometimes lead people to act irrationally and impulsively against the need to protect society by discouraging acts of homicidal violence. [para. 4]

[31] Applying this objective standard has not been without difficulty. A central concern has been the extent to which the accused's personal characteristics and circumstances should be considered when applying the "ordinary person" test. Traditionally, Canadian courts, endorsing the approach of their English counterparts, adopted a restrictive approach, prohibiting any reference to the accused's characteristics or circumstances (*Bedder v. Director of Public Prosecutions*, [1954] 1 W.L.R. 1119 (H.L.); *Salamon v. The Queen*, [1959] S.C.R. 404; *Wright v. The Queen*, [1969] S.C.R. 335). However, this approach required the court to completely ignore relevant contextual circumstances in making its determinations.

[32] Recognizing this deficiency, a broader approach was eventually adopted in conceptualizing the "ordinary person" so as to account for some, but not all, of the individual characteristics of the accused. As Dickson C.J. explained in *Hill*, this more flexible approach is essentially a matter of common sense:

> ... the "collective good sense" of the jury will naturally lead it to ascribe to the ordinary person any general characteristics relevant to the provocation in question. For example, if the provocation is a racial slur, the jury will think of an ordinary person with the racial background that forms the substance of the insult. To this extent, particular characteristics will be ascribed to the ordinary person. Indeed, it would be impossible to conceptualize a sexless or ageless ordinary person. Features such as sex, age, or race, do not detract from a person's characterization as ordinary. Thus particular characteristics that are not peculiar or idiosyncratic can be ascribed to an ordinary person without subverting the logic of the objective test of provocation. [Emphasis added; p. 331.]

[33] I emphasize the words of caution that, in adopting this more flexible approach, care must be taken not to subvert the logic of the objective test. Indeed, if all of the accused's characteristics are taken into account, the ordinary person *becomes* the accused. As Dickson C.J. noted, this approach would lead to the anomalous result that "[a] well-tempered, reasonable person would not be entitled to benefit from the provocation defence . . . while an ill-tempered or exceptionally excitable person would find his or her culpability mitigated by provocation and would be guilty only of manslaughter" (p. 324).

[34] Further, an individualized approach ignores the cardinal principle that criminal law is concerned with setting standards of human behaviour. As Dickson C.J. put it: "It is society's concern that reasonable and non-violent behaviour be encouraged that prompts the law to endorse the objective standard"

(p. 324). Similarly, McIntyre J. in concurring reasons expanded upon this purpose, stating:

> The law fixes a standard for all which must be met before reliance may be placed on the provocation defence. Everyone, whatever his or her idiosyncracies, is expected to observe that standard. It is not every insult or injury that will be sufficient to relieve a person from what would otherwise be murder. The "ordinary person" standard is adopted to fix the degree of self-control and restraint expected of all in society. [p. 336]

It follows that the ordinary person standard must be informed by contemporary norms of behaviour, including fundamental values such as the commitment to equality provided for in the *Canadian Charter of Rights and Freedoms*. For example, it would be appropriate to ascribe to the ordinary person relevant racial characteristics if the accused were the recipient of a racial slur, but it would not be appropriate to ascribe to the ordinary person the characteristic of being homophobic if the accused were the recipient of a homosexual advance. Similarly, there can be no place in this objective standard for antiquated beliefs such as "adultery is the highest invasion of property" (*Mawgridge*, at p. 1115), nor indeed for any form of killing based on such inappropriate conceptualizations of "honour".*

[35] Finally, the particular circumstances in which the accused finds himself will also be relevant in determining the appropriate standard against which to measure the accused's conduct. This is also a matter of common sense, as it would be impossible to conceptualize how the ordinary person might be expected to react without considering the relevant context. Again here, however, care must be taken not to "subver[t] the logic of the objective [inquiry]" and assimilate circumstances that are peculiar to the individual accused into the objective standard (*Hill*, at p. 331). For example, in determining the appropriate objective standard, it will be relevant for the trier of fact to know that the alleged provocation occurred in circumstances where the deceased was wrongfully firing the accused from his long-term employment. This context is necessary to set the appropriate standard. But the standard does not vary depending on the accused's peculiar relationship or particular feelings about his employer or his employment. Personal circumstances may be relevant to determining whether the accused was in fact provoked — the subjective element of the defence — but they do not shift the ordinary person standard to suit the individual accused. In other words, there is an important distinction between contextualizing the objective standard, which is necessary and proper, and individualizing it, which only serves to defeat its purpose.

---

* Editors' note. This *obiter* reference to honour killing was relied in the *Shafia* trial in Kingston in 2012 to dismiss any such defence. A father, wife and son were convicted of first degree murder in the drowning deaths of three daughters and a former wife of the father. This horrific trial prompted the publication of a special issue by various authors on so-called honour crimes: (2012) 16 Can. Crim. L. Rev. 103-246.

2.2.2 The Subjective Element: The Provocation Must Have Caused the Accused to Lose Self-Control and Act While Out of Control

[36] Once it is established that the wrongful act or insult was sufficient to deprive an ordinary person of the power of self-control, the inquiry turns to a consideration of the subjective element of the defence. The subjective element can also be usefully described as two-fold: (1) the accused must have acted in response to the provocation; and (2) on the sudden before there was time for his or her passion to cool.

[37] The inquiry into whether the accused was in fact acting in response to the provocation focuses on the accused's subjective perceptions of the circumstances, including what the accused believed, intended or knew. In other words, the accused must have killed because he was provoked and not because the provocation existed (*R. v. Faid*, [1983] 1 S.C.R. 265, at p. 277, citing Professor G. L. Williams in his *Textbook of Criminal Law* (1978), at p. 480).

[38] The requirement of suddenness was introduced into the defence as a way of distinguishing a response taken in vengeance from one that was provoked. Therefore, suddenness applies to both the act of provocation and the accused's reaction to it. The wrongful act or insult must itself be sudden, in the sense that it "must strike upon a mind unprepared for it, that it must make an unexpected impact that takes the understanding by surprise and sets the passions aflame" (*R. v. Tripodi*, [1955] S.C.R. 438, at p. 443). Further, the intentional killing must have been committed by the accused "before there was time for his passion to cool": s. 232(2) of the *Criminal Code*.

2.3 *The Role of the Judge and Jury*

[39] As noted earlier, s. 232(3) provides that determining whether a particular wrongful act or insult amounted to provocation and whether the accused was deprived of the power of self-control by the provocation are questions of fact. Consistent with the wording of this provision, it remains with the jury, and not the trial judge, to weigh the evidence in order to determine whether the Crown has discharged its burden of disproving that the killing was caused by provocation (*R. v. Fontaine*, 2004 SCC 27, [2004] 1 S.C.R. 702, at para. 56, citing *R. v. Schwartz*, [1988] 2 S.C.R. 443).

[40] However, the interpretation of a legal standard (the elements of the defence) and the determination of whether there is an air of reality to a defence constitute questions of law, reviewable on a standard of correctness. The term "air of reality" refers to the inquiry into whether there is an evidential foundation for a defence. Statements that there is or is not an air of reality express a legal conclusion about the presence or absence of an evidential foundation for a defence: *R. v. Cinous*, 2002 SCC 29, [2002] 2 S.C.R. 3, at paras. 50 and 55; *R.*

v. Osolin, [1993] 4 S.C.R. 595, at p. 682; *Parnerkar v. The Queen*, [1974] S.C.R. 449, at p. 461. Thus, this inquiry is not a review of the trial judge's assessment of the evidence but of the judge's legal conclusions in relation to the defence of provocation: *R. v. Ewanchuk*, [1999] 1 S.C.R. 330, at para. 21.

[41] In a jury trial, the judge is the gatekeeper and judge of the law and must therefore put the defence to the jury only where there is evidence upon which a "reasonable jury acting judicially" could find that the defence succeeds (*Faid*, at p. 278). For the defence to succeed, the jury must have a reasonable doubt about whether each of the elements of provocation was present. This necessarily requires that there be a sufficient evidential basis in respect of each component of the defence before it is left to the jury: the evidence must be reasonably capable of supporting the inferences necessary to make out the defence before there is an air of reality to the defence (*Fontaine*, at para. 56; *R. v. Reddick*, [1991] 1 S.C.R. 1086, at p. 1088, citing *Pappajohn v. The Queen*, [1980] 2 S.C.R. 120, at p. 133). In a trial by judge alone, the trial judge must instruct himself or herself accordingly. Therefore, the trial judge errs in law if he or she gives effect to the defence of provocation in circumstances where the defence should not have been left to a jury, had the accused been tried by a jury.

3. Application to the Case

[42] As stated at the outset, I agree with the Court of Appeal that there was no air of reality to the defence of provocation in this case. The conduct in question does not amount to an "insult"; nor does it meet the requirement of suddenness.

[43] As for the objective element of the defence, the appellant does not suggest that he was provoked by a "wrongful act". Rather, his contention is that, in the context of his relationship with Ms. Duong, his discovery of her sexual involvement with Mr. An Tran amounted to an insult at law. The facts do not support this contention.

[44] First, it is difficult to see how the conduct of Ms. Duong and Mr. An Tran could constitute an insult on any ordinary meaning of the word. The general meaning of the noun "insult" as defined in the *Shorter Oxford English Dictionary on Historical Principles* (6th ed. 2007), vol. 1, at p. 1400, is "[a]n act or the action of attacking; (an) attack, (an) assault." Likewise, the action of insulting means to "[s]how arrogance or scorn; boast, exult, esp. insolently or contemptuously. . . . Treat with scornful abuse; subject to indignity; . . . offend the modesty or self-respect of." Here, Ms. Duong and Mr. An Tran were alone in the privacy of her bedroom, neither wanting nor expecting the appellant to show up. In these circumstances, I agree with Hunt J.A. that "[n]othing done by the complainant or the victim comes close to meeting the definition of insult. Their behaviour was not only lawful, it was discreet and private and entirely passive vis-à-vis the [appellant]. They took pains to keep their relationship

hidden. . . . Their behaviour came to his attention only because he gained access to the building by falsely saying he was there to pick up his mail" (para. 17).

[45] Further, there was nothing sudden about the discovery. The appellant is the one whose appearance came as a total surprise to Ms. Duong and Mr. An Tran, not the other way around. On the factual findings made by the trial judge, the appellant had not only suspected his wife's relationship with another man, but he made deliberate attempts to surveillance her activity, including by eavesdropping on her conversations. The night before the tragic events, the appellant told his godmother that he now knew who the man was whom his wife was seeing (trial judge's reasons, at p. 26). Therefore, it cannot be said that his discovery, upon entering Ms. Duong's bedroom unannounced and uninvited, "str[uck] upon a mind unprepared for it".

[46] Finally, I also agree with Watson J.A. that on "the subjective side of the question", the trial judge's findings of "[o]utward excitement and anger" could not be decisive (para. 76). The appellant did not testify about his state of mind. The evidence shows, as Watson J.A. notes, that he

> was measuring his actions on what he was saying and doing. The trial judge should have addressed whether he could have regained his self control by the time he went into the living room and finished off the victim — not merely whether he was still angry and excited. The trial judge found his anger continued but she failed to direct herself to consider whether the continuation of his anger amounted to a continuing lack of the power of self control without an opportunity to recover it. [para. 76]

As Watson J.A. rightly concluded, "there was on the trial judge's fact findings no air of reality to his acting on the sudden at the time of the killing" (para. 77).

4. Disposition

[47] The Court of Appeal properly substituted a conviction for second degree murder and returned the matter to the trial court for sentencing. As Watson J.A. stated: "In light of the law, and of the trial judge's findings of fact, and of the overwhelming evidence, a conviction for murder was unavoidable" (para. 81). I would dismiss the appeal.

Appeal dismissed; conviction for second degree murder upheld.

The Court says in *Tran*:

"it would be appropriate to ascribe to the ordinary person relevant racial characteristics if the accused were the recipient of a racial slur, but it would not be appropriate to ascribe to the ordinary person the characteristic of being homophobic if the accused were the recipient of a homosexual advance". **Does this mean that *Hill* is wrongly decided?**

This case is an important and helpful review of the long-controversial partial defence to murder and is now the starting place for judicial analysis.

This defence has little to do with theories of justification or excuse but is all about a long-established doctrine to sometimes avoid the rigours of the fixed penalty for murder — in Canada, formerly death and now life imprisonment. Without the fixed penalty we would not need the partial defence of provocation. This legislative change seems unlikely so the courts must soldier on.

On the facts the Supreme Court unanimously finds that there was no air of reality to the provocation defence, as there was no insult given that the new couple was discrete and the accused did not act on the sudden because he had suspicions in advance of his discovery. It is arguable that the Court has become too restrictive. **What if a wife has suspicions that her husband is abusing a daughter? She investigates and opens a door to find him touching his daughter inappropriately. If she loses control and kills him can she not have the benefit of the partial defence to reduce her criminal culpability?** The child abuse will constitute a wrongful act for these purposes but, applying *Tran*, she did not act on the sudden. This result may seem severe. **Is *Tran* authority that the suddenness requirement can never be met if there is any prior suspicion?**

It will be important not to generalize *Tran* to other defences such as self-defence and duress where the individualized approach to tests of objective reasonableness is now well-established and not subject to the special limits characterizing the uneven law of provocation.

There were signs in 2013 that lower courts favoured more flexibility respecting the air of reality test for putting the partial defence of provocation to the jury. In *R. v. Rothgordt* (2013), 296 C.C.C. (3d) 233, 99 C.R. (6th) 304 (B.C. C.A.) the Crown version was that the attack was based on concerns as to sexual identity (which seems to be homophobia). However, Chief Justice Finch for the B.C. Court of Appeal indicated that the defence version of an attack by the victim was different and the issue was a matter for the jury. In *R. v. Angelis* (2013), 296 C.C.C. (3d) 143, 99 C.R. (6th) 315 (Ont. C.A.), even though the relationship had become dysfunctional for two months since the accused learned that his wife had been having an affair, Justice Laskin accepted for the Ontario Court of Appeal that there was an air of reality for provocation given the victim's clawing attack on the accused's penis, which was both wrongful and sudden.

There were even signs of a loosening attitude in the Supreme Court. In *R. v. Buzizi*, 2 C.R. (7th) 225, [2013] 2 S.C.R. 248, 297 C.C.C. (3d) 287, Justice Fish led an admittedly brittle 3-2 majority to hold that the trial judge had erred in holding that there was no air of reality for provocation where the main defence was self-defence. In *R. v. Gauthier*, 2013 SCC 32, 2 C.R. (7th) 269, [2013] 2 S.C.R. 403, 298 C.C.C. (3d) 277, which did not concern provocation, Wagner J. for the Court held that there was no rule preventing incompatible defences being put to the jury provided there was an evidentiary foundation for each.

However, majority decisions of the Supreme Court have now sent an unmistakable messages that the partial defence of provocation to murder is to be a narrow defence which should rarely pass the air of reality test.

In *R. v. Cairney*, [2013] 3 S.C.R. 420, 302 C.C.C. (3d) 1, 5 C.R. (7th) 223, the accused was residing in an apartment where the victim lived with his spouse;

the victim had a history of abusing his spouse, and Cairney knew that. On the date in question Cairney had a shotgun and confronted the victim about his abusive behaviour; the victim said: "What are you going to do, shoot me? You don't have the guts to shoot me." The victim then got up and started to leave the apartment. C testified that he told F "Get back here, I want to talk to you" to which the victim responded "Fuck you, you goof. This is none of your business, I'll do with Fran whatever I want". Cairney testified that he was upset because he thought the victim was "laughing me off"; he testified that he "saw red", followed the victim out of the apartment and into a stairwell and fatally shot him. A 5-2 majority found no air of reality to the requirement that an ordinary person would have lost self-control.

In *R. v. Pappas*, [2013] 3 S.C.R. 452, 302 C.C.C. (3d) 295, 5 C.R. (7th) 271, the accused had been the victim of extortion over a period of time by the victim, which was based on the victim threatening to reveal details about Pappas' offshore investments to the Canada Revenue Agency, and threatening to harm his mother if he chose to stop paying or went to the police. Pappas went to the victim's home to end the extortion and threats, taking a loaded handgun with him, but not immediately revealing it. The victim refused to discontinue his extortion, saying "You're the best cash out I have and I got great fucking insurance". Pappas took this as an implied threat against his mother. At this point, Pappas said he "snapped" and "everything was just automatic" as he pulled out his gun and shot the victim. In this case a 6-2 majority found no air of reality to the provocation claim.

Academic commentators welcomed the flexibility offered in *Buzizi* (see Micah Rankin, *R. v. Buzizi*: A More Generous Air of reality Test for the Subjective Dimension of the Provocation Defence" (2013), 2 C.R. (7th) 261) but the return to a narrow view of air of reality has been strongly criticized: see Peter Sankoff, "*R. v. Cairney*: Predictable Responses and the Shrinking Defence of Provocation" (2013), 5 C.R. (7th) 254, Gerry Ferguson "Provocation: Air of Reality and the Ordinary Person Test" (2012), 94 C.R. (6th) 32, and Don Stuart, "The Supreme Court Strangles the Defence of Provocation" (2013), 5 C.R. (7th) 249.

In *R. v. Hill* (2015), 330 C.C.C. (3d) 1, 23 C.R. (7th) 224 (Ont. C.A.) the accused strangled G on January 22, 2008. He hid her body and buried it in a bush near his home the next day. He was charged with second degree murder. He pled guilty to the included offence of manslaughter. The Crown rejected the plea and the accused was convicted on the charge of second degree murder. For the Ontario Court of Appeal Justice Doherty (Gillese and Brown JJ.A. concurring) ordered a new trial. The Court held that there was here an air of reality for the partial defence of provocation. The jury could have had a reasonable doubt that the accused strangled the victim on the sudden in response to unanticipated verbal and physical abuse. He also identified errors in the charge. Since this was a case of anger not fear comparing the accused's size and athleticism to that of the victim had no relevance and might have raised issues of reasonableness, justifiability and proportionality that are not part of the defence. Nor should the trial judge have directed the jury to consider whether the provocative act was sufficient to cause an ordinary person to do the very things the accused did.

This nuanced judgment continues a very long tradition in the Ontario Court of Appeal to be relatively generous on the issue of the partial defence to murder.

However in 2015 Parliament moved to restrict the defence. On June 18, 2015 on the eve of the federal election royal consent was given to the *Zero Tolerance for Barbaric Cultural Practices Act*, S.C. 2015, c. 29. The government background to this bill when it was introduced in the Senate indicated that:

> The Bill would complement existing Canadian initiatives, both at home and abroad, to put an end to barbaric cultural practices that go against Canadian values because they cause harm to women and girls and prevent their full participation in society. These practices, which include early and forced marriage, 'honour'-based violence and female genital mutilation/cutting, have no place in Canada's free and democratic society.

The Act is focused mainly on preventing the entry into Canada of those intent on practicing polygamy and a number of provisions respecting forced marriages. However it also amended the key provocation provision under s. 232(2) to read as follows:

> Conduct of the victim that would constitute an indictable offence under this Act that is punishable by five years or more imprisonment and that is of such a nature as to be sufficient to deprive an ordinary person of the power of self-control is provocation for the purposes of this section, if the accused acted on it on the sudden and before there was time for their passion to cool. [emphasis added].

The *Criminal Code* amendments in part 3 of this Act, including the provocation amendment, were to come into force "on a day to be fixed by order of the Governor General in Council". This turned out to be July 16, 2015: SI/2015-67. At that date the Explanatory Note indicated that

> The amendments limit the application of the defence of provocation so that it will no longer be available in honour killings and many spousal homicides.

This replacing of the traditional triggering test of "a wrongful act or insult" by an "indictable offence punishable by five years or more" is clearly much more limiting than the drafters intended and will also add complexity. An extremely offensive racial taunt would, for example, not suffice. In terms of so-called honour killings the change was unnecessary as the Supreme Court in *R. v. Tran*, [2010] 3 S.C.R. 350, 261 C.C.C. (3d) 435, 80 C.R. (6th) 1 had already indicated that honour killings will not ground the provocation defence (see para. 34). *Tran* was relied on in the horrific *R. v. Shafia* trial in Kingston in 2012 to dismiss any such defence. A father, wife and son were convicted of first degree murder in the drowning deaths of three daughters and a former wife of the father.

For further strong criticism of the amendment see Professor Kent Roach, "Vandalizing the Criminal Code with Irrational and Arbitrary Restrictions on Provocation" (2015) 62 Crim. L.Q. 403.

If this drastic narrowing of the defence of provocation is not reconsidered by the new federal government there will be a strong case for resorting to ss. 7 or 12 of the *Charter* to strike down the mandatory minimum of life imprisonment for murder to achieve a flexible penalty. All murderers should be punished and likely sent to jail for a long time but judges who have presided over murder trials know well that culpability is not always equal or necessarily deserving of life imprisonment.

The partial defence of provocation is presently extremely controversial and has been under review by the Department of Justice for years: see *Reforming Criminal Code Defences: Provocation, Self-defence and Defence of Property* (Department of Justice, 1998) pp.1-20. A study by a Federal-Provincial-Territorial working group, reported in the Justice study at pp. 5-6, of 115 reported cases in which the defence of provocation was raised, warns against generalizations or special interest solutions. Sixty-two cases involved domestic homicides. In 55 cases men killed women and in 7 women killed men. The remaining 53 cases involving men killing men. Sixteen of these cases involved alleged homosexual advances. In all types of cases the study revealed that the defence of provocation was more often than not unsuccessful.

Some see the solution as being the abolition of the mandatory life sentence for murder. See Peter MacKinnon, "Two Views of Murder" (1985) 53 Can. Bar Rev. 130; "Annotation to Latimer" (1996), 41 C.R. (4th) 6; and Tim Quigley, "*R. v. Latimer.* Hard Cases Make Interesting Law" (1995), 41 C.R. (4th) 89 at 98. See too Steve Coughlan, "Reforming Homicide Law to Separate Guilt from Sentence: An International Gloss" (2008) 13 Can. Crim. L. Rev. 1. There have been no indications of any federal government seeming amenable to this solution.

The Supreme Court has spoken to the issue of sentencing in provoked murder cases. In *Stone* (1999), 24 C.R. (5th) 1 (S.C.C.), the accused stabbed his wife 47 times after she verbally insulted him and a "whoosh" came over him. The defence of provocation was left with the jury and they returned a verdict of manslaughter. The trial judge imposed a sentence of four years, taking into account 18 months' pre-trial custody as equivalent to three years. On the sentence appeal, Justice Bastarache for a court unanimous on this point rejected the Crown's position that an accused should not gain a "double benefit" of considering provocation in reducing a verdict from murder to manslaughter under s. 232 of the *Code* and then again on sentencing. Rather, s. 232 provided an accused with a single benefit of a reduction of a verdict of murder to one of manslaughter to allow for consideration of the provoked nature of the killing in the determination of the appropriate penalty. A spousal connection between offender and victim was recognized as an aggravating factor in sentencing under s. 718.2(a)(ii) and previously under the common law, which applied to this case (the sentencing had been before the new section came into effect). However, the Crown had failed to establish that the sentencing judge did not properly consider the domestic nature of this offence in reaching his decision on sentence.

In 2009 the U.K. Parliament abolished the defence of provocation but replaced it by a narrower partial defence of lack of control, which has been criticized as "incoherent". See Andrew Ashworth's case comment in (2012) 7 Crim. L. Rev. 539 and Simester and Sullivan's *Criminal Law* (5th ed., 2013) pp. 395-406. The main statutory elements are: no considered desire for revenge, a justifiable sense of being wronged and a person of D's age and sex might have reacted in a similar way. There is no requirement of suddenness.

(b) Voluntary Intoxication

At common law there are two partial defences to murder. We earlier saw that voluntary intoxication may reduce a murder charge to manslaughter since murder is considered to be a specific intent crime.

(c) Cumulative Effect on Intent (rolled up charge)

There is also the possibility, especially under Ontario case law, of what has become known as the "rolled up" charge which asks the jury to consider the cumulative effect of all the factors on whether the Crown has proved the intent required for murder.

R. v. NEALY

(1986), 54 C.R. (3d) 158, 30 C.C.C. (3d) 460,
1986 CarswellOnt 136 (Ont. C.A.)

CORY J.A.: —

. . . .

A brief history of the facts will suffice for the purposes of this appeal.

During the early morning hours of 20th August 1982 the appellant, Patrick Nealy, stabbed and killed Larry Casimiri. At the time, Nealy was 23 years old and Casimiri was 33 years old, married, with three children.

Earlier, during the afternoon of 19th August, Nealy injected into his arm a drug known as "stovetop". He thought that the plateau from that injection occurred late in the afternoon. In the evening, he and his girlfriend, Alison McKinley, drank together at the St. Charles Tavern. This is a bar which was frequented by members of the gay community and was well known to Nealy. While at this tavern, Nealy and his girlfriend met the deceased and two friends of the deceased. Some time around 11:00 p.m., Nealy and his girlfriend, together with the deceased and his two friends, proceeded to the Albany Tavern. This tavern as well was often frequented by members of the gay community.

Both the appellant and the deceased continued to drink at the Albany Tavern. The deceased danced with Nealy's girlfriend. According to Nealy, after dancing with her, Casimiri repeatedly said that Nealy's girlfriend "had nice tits and that he was going to fuck her". Nealy told Casimiri to keep quiet. Eventually, the two men began pushing and then punching each other. Nealy suggested to Casimiri that they continue their fight outside. Casimir left the Albany Tavern and Nealy followed him.

Before Nealy left the tavern, he removed a knife from his girlfriend's purse and placed it in his belt with the handle exposed. Once out on the street, the men continued to fight. To many of the witnesses, it appeared that Nealy was the aggressor and better-co-ordinated. Casimiri, although heavier-set, appeared drunk and unco-ordinated. It was Nealy's evidence that he was upset by what Casimiri had said about his girlfriend and that he was afraid of Casimiri, who came at him, as he said, "like a grizzly bear".

Nealy stated that he had the knife only to frighten Casimiri and he warned Casimiri to "back off". In any event, he stabbed Casimiri several times — on his evidence, three times. With the last stroke of the knife, Casimiri collapsed in front of a van parked on King Street and Nealy fled. Nealy testified that he had not intended to kill Casimiri and that he was angry with himself for what had happened and sorry for what he had done.

At the opening of the trial, Nealy entered a plea of not guilty to the charge of murder but guilty of manslaughter. This plea was not accepted by the Crown and the trial proceeded. Despite the plea, Nealy raised the issue of self-defence at trial.

At the conclusion of the evidence it was clear that the jury would have to consider: first, the issue of drunkenness and the effect upon the accused of the alcohol consumed; second, the question of self-defence; third, the question of provocation; and fourth, the effect that the alcohol he had consumed, coupled with the fear and anger experienced by the accused, would have upon the issue of whether he ever formed the requisite intent to murder Casimiri.

. . . .

The trial judge, early in his charge, read to the jury s. 212(*a*)(iii) and advised them of the intent that was required in order to find the accused guilty of murder.

Later he told the jury that he was going to deal specifically with self-defence, provocation and drunkenness. He dealt first, in an exemplary manner, with self-defence. He then said that the second defence was drunkenness, and gave instructions with regard to it, and lastly dealt with what he termed the "third defence" of provocation. Each of these aspects of the charge was, to a certain extent, "compartmentalized". It is conceded that he did not at any time instruct the jury as to the cumulative effect that the consumption of alcohol and the fear and anger that were experienced by Nealy as a result of his dispute with the deceased might have had upon Nealy's ability to form the requisite intent to commit murder.

It would, I think, have been better if the trial judge, at the conclusion of his reference to these three specific elements, had advised the jury as to the possible cumulative effect of the evidence.

In this case, it would have been preferable if the jury had been instructed along these lines: first, that, in considering whether the accused formed the requisite intent, they were to take into account the alcohol that had been consumed by Nealy; further, that they were to consider the evidence which Nealy had given as to his fear and anger as a result of the words uttered by Casimiri in the Albany Tavern and the punching and shoving which followed both inside the tavern and on the street. The jury should have been told that, even if the words spoken by Casimiri, coupled with his actions, did not raise in their minds a reasonable doubt as to whether or not Nealy had been "provoked" as that term is defined in s. 215 of the *Code*, or that Nealy was incapable of forming the required intent by reason of the consumption of alcohol, the jury was still to consider all these surrounding circumstances in coming to a conclusion as to whether Nealy possessed the requisite intent needed to commit murder pursuant to s. 212 (*a*) of the *Code*.

That, I believe, is the position that has been adopted by this court. In *R. v. Clow* (1985), 44 C.R. (3d) 228 at 231 (Ont. C.A.), there appears a statement of this court which is applicable to the facts of this case:

> It is respectfully submitted that the learned trial Judge erred in failing to instruct the jury as to the cumulative effects of consumption of alcohol or drugs, provocation and excessive force in self-defence as it might relate to the requisite specific intent 'to mean to cause death or to mean to cause bodily harm which she knew was likely to cause death and was reckless as to whether death ensued'.

We agree.

In *R. v. Trecroce* (1980), 55 C.C.C. (2d) 202 (Ont. C.A.), Martin J.A. stated at p. 211:

> That is not to say, of course, that a jury, if they consider that the accused was honestly defending himself, may not entertain a reasonable doubt whether acting instinctively in the excitement of the moment he really contemplated the consequences of his actions and actually had the requisite intent for murder even though that inference might normally be drawn from his acts apart from the circumstances that he was defending himself.

And in *R. v. Campbell* (1977), 17 O.R. (2d) 673, 1 C.R. (3d) 309, S-49, 38 C.C.C. (2d) 6 (C.A.), Martin J.A. again stated at p. 683:

> Provocation may, of course, inspire the intent required to constitute murder. There may, however, be cases where the conduct of the victim amounting to provocation produces in the accused a state of excitement, anger or disturbance, as a result of which he might not contemplate the consequences of his acts and might not, in fact, intend to bring about those consequences. The accused's intent must usually be inferred from his conduct and the surrounding circumstances, and in some cases the provocation afforded by the victim, when considered in relation to the totality of the evidence, might create a reasonable doubt in the mind of the jury whether the accused had the requisite intent. Thus, in some cases, the provocative conduct of the victim might be a relevant item of evidence of the issue of intent whether the charge be murder or attempted murder. This, I take it, was the view of Eveleigh, J., in *R. v. Bruzas, supra*, at p. 369. Provocation in that aspect, however, does not operate as a 'defence' but rather as a relevant item of evidence on the issue of intent.

The case referred to, *R. v. Campbell, supra*, was one of attempted murder. The argument there advanced on behalf of the accused was that provocation within the meaning of the *Code* would reduce the offence to attempted manslaughter. That argument was rejected because provocation is applicable only to reduce an act which would otherwise be murder to manslaughter. Nevertheless it was held in that case that acts of provocation, whether in murder or attempted murder, and by implication whether or not sufficient to satisfy the *Code* definition, might be relevant to the issue of intent.

R. v. *Clow*, *supra*, was relied upon and followed by this court in R. v. *Desveaux* (1986), 51 C.R. (3d) 173, 26 C.C.C. (3d) 88. In that case as well the statement of principle contained in R. v. *Clow* was a fundamental element in the decision of the court.

Although the question has not been specifically considered by the Supreme Court of Canada, there are some statements in various reasons of that court that lend support to the position set forth in R. v. *Clow* and R. v. *Desveaux*. In R. v. *Faid*, [1983] 1 S.C.R. 265, 33 C.R. (3d) 1, 2 C.C.C. (3d) 513 at 517-18, Dickson J. was considering the question as to whether or not excessive force in self-defence could result in a conviction of manslaughter. He stated:

> . . . though the facts on which the defence of self-defence was unsuccessfully sought to be based may in some cases go to show that the defendant acted under provocation or that, although acting unlawfully, he lacked the intent to kill or cause grievous bodily harm. In such cases a verdict of manslaughter would be proper.

In *Brisson v. R.*, [1982] 2 S.C.R. 227, 29 C.R. (3d) 289, 69 C.C.C. (2d) 97 [Que.], the court was once again considering whether excessive force in self-defence could reduce a charge of murder to manslaughter. Dickson J., speaking on behalf of the court, stated at p. 258-59:

> To summarize, I would reject the notion that excessive force in self-defence, *unless related to intent under s. 212 of the Code* or to provocation, reduces what would otherwise be murder to manslaughter. [The italics are mine.]

In R. v. *Gee*, [1982] 2 S.C.R. 286, 29 C.R. (3d) 347, 68 C.C.C. (2d) 516, 43 N.R. 128 at 137, Dickson J., speaking for the majority, stated:

> In my view, it cannot be said that force can be partially justified. Success under s. 27 leads to acquittal. If the defence under s. 27 does not succeed, the jury should render the verdict which would have been rendered, absent s. 27. This may be a verdict of manslaughter, not because of partial justification under s. 27 but because the special mental element required for guilt of murder has not been proven. In other words, the half-way house is not to be found in s. 27 but, if at all, in s. 212.

These authorities emphasize the importance of the issue of intent. Further, they indicate that all the circumstances surrounding the act of killing must be taken into account in determining whether or not the accused had the intent required for the commission of murder. It may well be that the evidence does not give rise to a reasonable doubt as to whether there was provocation or whether the accused lacked the ability to form that intent as a result of consuming alcohol or drugs. Nevertheless, the evidence adduced on these issues, viewed cumulatively, may be of great importance in determining the crucial issue of intent.

Not every case where the consumption of alcohol and some form of provocation is involved will require a specific direction as to the cumulative effect of these factors. Still, it will be preferable in most cases and essential in some that such a direction be given. In the circumstances of this case, fairness required no less than the addition to the charge of two or three sentences which would be sufficient to bring to the jury's mind the necessity of considering all the pertinent facts in resolving the issue of intent.

The omission of the trial judge to give such a direction coupled with the improper aspects of the cross-examination of the accused, are sufficient to require a direction for a new trial. In the result, I would, with some regret, allow the appeal and direct a new trial.

In *R. v. Kent* (2005), 29 C.R. (6th) 33 (B.C. C.A.) Justice Low, writing for the B.C. Court of Appeal, could find no clear advice from the Supreme Court as to the use of a rolled up charge. The Court found that in the circumstances of this case a rolled up charge was unnecessary and might have confused the jury into thinking provocation was not available where there was a murderous intent. The accused's wife became angry when the accused returned home with drugs he had bought with money she had given him for groceries. According to the accused she said many mean things, including that her ex-husband would not have slept with his sister, as the accused had. This made him mad and he strangled her. The Court found that there was an air of reality for provocation and ordered a new trial.

In *R. v. Mohamed*, 2011 ONCA 260 (Ont. C.A.) the Ontario Court of Appeal noted that the concern that the jury will compartmentalize the evidence in a murder case is the greatest where a discrete defence has been left to the jury. The danger is that the jury, having rejected a defence such as provocation, will not consider the provocation evidence when dealing with intent. In *Mohamed* the trial judge had rightly found no air of reality to the defence of provocation and there was no concern that the jury would not consider all the circumstances in the face of explicit and repeated instructions to do so. See too *R. v. Flores* (2011), 83 C.R. (6th) 93 (Ont. C.A.).

8. GENERAL REVIEW QUESTIONS

1. Jack and Jill have had a tempestuous love affair for over a year. Jack had always been highly strung. He had also endured periods of acute depression for which he had received several weeks of psychiatric counselling. He always seemed to fear the worst. Actually his often-expressed suspicions that Jill was dating another man were well-grounded. Her other boyfriend, Bill, with whom she was much more emotionally involved, demanded that she "ditch" Jack. She decided on the strategy of

first calming him with alcohol and then playing him a pre-recorded message on a cassette, during which she would leave his apartment. She carried her unloaded pistol in her purse for "protection". They had about five whiskys each at a local pub in less than two hours. As Jack was driving Jill to his apartment, Jill for some unknown reason — probably as a result of her intoxication — departed from her plan and started to play her cassette tape in the car. The message began brutally: "Jack, I've had enough. You are physically repulsive and a mental wreck. I love Bill and have done so passionately for two months . . .". It is not clear what happened next. All that is known is that Jack's car suddenly veered off the road, somersaulted and struck a fence. Miraculously Jack and Jill were unhurt. According to Jack, he was devastated by the message and he might well have lunged at Jill while he was still driving. In any event his mind was blank until he realized he had been in an accident, that Jill was pointing a gun at him and that he then stabbed her repeatedly with a screwdriver, which had been on the dashboard. A third party on the scene says Jack had a dull glazed look about him, he was shouting "You bitch! You bitch!" hysterically and it was extremely difficult to stop Jack's convulsive-like assault. Jill later died of the multiple wounds. Her pistol was found on the front seat of the car.

Jack stands charged with second degree murder. His defence counsel asks you for a brief as to his viable total or partial defences. Discuss relevant authorities and comment on the strength or weakness of each defence.

2. Jamie has had a tortured adolescence struggling with his sexual identity. At the age of 16 he recently came to terms with the fact that he was gay. Until his arrest he was living with his lover, Fred, a chartered accountant, aged 28. One of Jamie's former girlfriends, Bettie, realized Jamie's preference had changed. She became partly jealous and partly plain vicious. Whenever she saw Jamie she taunted him with anti-gay remarks. One night Jamie and Fred had been at a bar for several hours. Each had consumed about ten beers. Bettie came up to them. Just the sight of her made his blood boil. She again taunted him with several anti-gay remarks before moving off. Jamie told Fred he'd had enough. "The next time", said Jamie, "I'll thrash her to teach her a lesson she'll never forget." Fred said, "She deserves it." Jamie found a stick used to prop up a window and put it on the bar table. An hour and two beers later — during which time Jamie was morose — Bettie again arrived. She went up to Jamie and said: "You all deserve AIDS. It's God's way of disapproving." Jamie would testify, "This was the last straw. I saw red again, picked up the stick and hit, hit, hit." In fact Bettie was knocked unconscious with about six very heavy blows. She died in hospital several days later. The fatal assault took less than a minute. Fred just watched, only intervening after the sixth blow, saying "That's enough".

You are an articled clerk to the prosecutor. She has charged both Jamie and Fred with first degree murder on the basis that they committed murder contrary to s. 229(a) that was planned and deliberate under s. 231(2). She is incensed by the wanton violence and will press hard for a conviction of

first degree murder. She asks you for a legal memorandum assessing the strengths and weaknesses of all possible full and partial defences and the likely verdict. She notes there is no possibility of the defence of insanity.

9. ENTRAPMENT

R. v. MACK

[1988] 2 S.C.R. 903, 67 C.R. (3d) 1, 44 C.C.C. (3d) 513,
1988 CarswellBC 701, 1988 CarswellBC 767

LAMER J.: —

INTRODUCTION

The central issue in this appeal concerns the doctrine of entrapment. The parties, in essence, ask this court to outline its position on the conceptual basis for the application of the doctrine and the manner in which an entrapment claim should be dealt with by the courts. Given the length of these reasons due to the complexity of the subject, I have summarized my findings on pages 964 to 966 of these reasons.

The Facts

The appellant was charged with unlawful possession of a narcotic for the purpose of trafficking. He testified at trial and, at the close of the case for the defence, brought an application for a stay of proceedings on the basis of entrapment. The application was refused and a conviction entered by Wetmore Co. Ct. J., sitting without a jury, in written reasons reported in (1983), 34 C.R. (3d) 228. A notice of appeal from that decision was filed with the British Columbia Court of Appeal but the appeal books were not filed within the time prescribed. Counsel for the appellant sought and obtained, with the consent of Crown Counsel, an order dispensing with the requirement that transcripts of evidence be filed and permitting counsel to base their arguments solely on the reasons for judgment of Wetmore Co. Ct. J. The Chief Justice of British Columbia directed that a panel of five judges hear the appeal. For the reasons given by Craig J.A., on behalf of the court, the appeal was dismissed. This decision is now reported at (1985), 49 C.R. (3d) 169. Leave to appeal was granted by this court.

It is necessary to describe in some detail the relevant facts. In view of the particular procedural history of this appeal, I think it is appropriate to reproduce in its entirety the summary of the evidence provided for in the reasons for judgment of Wetmore Co. Ct. J. (at pp. 234-37):

> Through information obtained from an officer of the Ontario Provincial Police, one Momotiuk was brought to British Columbia. This man had apparently been dealing in narcotics in Kenora, Ontario. He was placed under police "handlers" in Vancouver, he visited the accused on a number of occasions, and eventually a transaction was set up whereby the accused would deliver cocaine to Momotiuk.
>
> The accused testified. He first met Momotiuk in 1979 in Montreal where the accused was visiting one Franks. The accused understood Franks and Momotiuk to be associated in some clothing franchise.
>
> The accused at this time was attempting to develop some property for sale near De Roche, British Columbia, and told Franks and Momotiuk of this and both expressed some interest in buying. Both arrived in British Columbia in October 1979. In the course of this visit the accused says that Momotiuk told him he was a drug trafficker in Kenora and wanted some "Thai pot". The accused says he had no interest.
>
> Momotiuk, according to the accused, called later still wanting to make drug deals, and the accused told him he was interested only in real estate deals.
>
> The accused again went to a yoga retreat near Montreal in December 1979. Franks and Momotiuk visited him there. Momotiuk produced some cocaine, which he and Franks used, and again asked the accused to become a supplier. A few days later they met again. At this time conversation was directed to show Momotiuk as an importer of drugs on a large scale, and again the accused was invited to join in and refused.
>
> In January and February there were approximately seven telephone calls from Momotiuk to the accused soliciting his involvement. The accused says he refused.
>
> In mid-February 1980 Momotiuk visited the accused again, asking him to supply drugs. The accused says he told Momotiuk he was not interested and asked to be left alone. Momotiuk continued to visit two or three times and also telephoned.
>
> In March the accused says Momotiuk arrived again. They went for a walk in the woods. Momotiuk produced a pistol and was going to show the accused his marksmanship. He was dissuaded because of the probability of startling the horses nearby. The accused says that at this remote area Momotiuk said, "A person could get lost." This the accused says was a threat. He says the matter of drugs was again raised and the accused says he was adamant that he had no knowledge of drugs sources.
>
> The accused was asked to phone him twice and did not. One Matheson attended at the accused's residence on 13th March with a message that Momotiuk was very excited and wanted to see him at the Biltmore Hotel. The accused says he wanted nothing to do with Momotiuk but was terrified of him and agreed to go into town to the Biltmore. He also says that Matheson told him Momotiuk had some friends with him. This the accused took to be other members of this illegal syndicate.
>
> While en route to the city he twice noted a car which seemed to be following him. This was probably so, because undercover police officers were doing a surveillance at the time. On arrival at the hotel he met Momotiuk. Again he was informed of the syndicate. He was asked then if he wished to see the buying power. The accused agreed. He was directed to a car outside the hotel. In this car was an open briefcase with $50,000 exposed. The custodian, unknown to the accused, was an undercover policeman.
>
> The accused returned to the hotel, Momotiuk asked him to get a sample and gave him $50 for this purpose.
>
> The accused left and went to a supplier he had known of from years back. This supplier, one Goldsmith, now dead, heard the accused's story and agreed to supply "in order to get Doug (Momotiuk) off me". He obtained the sample and delivered it to Momotiuk, who tested

it and said to get as much as he could. He returned to the supplier and offered $35,000 to $40,000 for a pound.

At the meeting the following day the accused had still not acquired the drugs and he says that at this point he was told to get his act together, in a threatening way.

I need not detail the accused's evidence of the following two days. He obtained 12 ounces of cocaine, and was to pay $27,000 for it. This credit, he says, was extended to him by Goldsmith on the basis of payment when delivered to Momotiuk. It was in the course of this delivery that he was arrested.

It is on the basis of this testimony that the accused says he was entrapped. Momotiuk, Matheson and Franks did not testify. Neither did "Bonnie", the accused's former wife, who was apparently present at one of the Montreal meetings, where cocaine was produced and some discussion took place.

The accused has drug convictions in 1972 and 1976, two in 1978 and one in 1979. Those in 1976, one in 1978 and one in 1979 involved cocaine. He says his former use of drugs arose to relieve back pain, but in 1978 he discovered relief from yoga and gave up the use of narcotics. The offence in 1979 was a fall from grace when he met up with old friends.

Decisions of the Courts Below

Wetmore Co. Ct. J. held that the judgment of Estey J. in *Amato v. The Queen*, [1982] 2 S.C.R. 418, and of the British Columbia Court of Appeal in *R. v. Jewitt* (1983), 34 C.R. (3d) 193 (rev'd on other grounds, [1985] 2 S.C.R. 128), established that entrapment is recognized as part of the abuse of process doctrine and a stay of proceedings arising from a finding of entrapment is not a "defence" in the traditional sense of that word. This distinction between a "stay" and a "defence" was important in terms of the burden and standard of proof. Wetmore Co. Ct. J. decided the evidential burden rested on the party seeking the stay to satisfy a court on a balance of probabilities that there had been entrapment which would constitute an abuse of the courts' processes. He stated at p. 232:

> To ask the court to preclude either side — the state, represented by the prosecution, or the defence — from the adjudication of their differences must involve satisfying the court that its processes cannot result in the attainment of justice through the traditional avenue of a full and open trial. To make that finding, it seems fundamental to a system of justice in a free and democratic society that the court must be satisfied that its processes have been so abused that those very processes are precluded from attaining justice. Satisfaction in such a state of affairs existing must be more than a reasonable suspicion.

In Wetmore Co. Ct. J.'s view, the presumption of innocence until proven guilty beyond a reasonable doubt was not violated. He stated that this presumption applied at trial while a motion for a stay was to really determine whether the appellant would have a trial. It was not significant that in this case the motion came at the end of the proceeding: "What counsel is asking is that I stop the proceedings before a verdict. This amounts to aborting the trial" (p. 234). Wetmore Co. Ct. J.'s view of the nature of the entrapment claim may be discerned in the following passage, at p. 234:

> This evidentiary burden is of great importance in the matter of entrapment because fundamental to any such finding is the conclusion that the accused had no disposition to

commit the crime but succumbed to improper enticement by authorities of the state. As in all matters of the mental element in criminal matters, the state of mind usually comes from inferences from established facts. I must test those facts to say then which is more probable as to the accused's predisposition, not merely if something is rationally possible.

After reviewing the evidence, Wetmore Co. Ct. J. noted, at p. 237, that the appellant's evidence found support in the testimony of the police officers to some extent: "They agree that Momotiuk was difficult to 'handle'". The stay was refused, however, because the appellant had not met the burden of proof. Wetmore Co. Ct. J. concluded, at p. 237:

> In fairness to the accused, I should say that, if I were to decide this issue on the basis of the Crown having to negate entrapment beyond a reasonable doubt, I would have such a doubt.
>
> I find, however, that it is far more probable that the accused became involved in this transaction for profit, rather than through persistent inducement and fear. Given his record and the alacrity with which he produced on seeing the $50,000 in March 1980, I find it much more probable that he then saw a situation of profit and acted upon it. There is no doubt in my mind that the opportunity was made available through the tactics of the police and their agent, but that falls short of entrapping a person into the commission of an act that he had no intention of doing.

The British Columbia Court of Appeal held that having regard to this court's decision in *Jewitt, supra*, and the opinion of several of the Justices in *Amato, supra*, entrapment is available in response to a criminal charge as an aspect of abuse of process but not as a substantive defence. It was further held that the determination of the existence of entrapment is a question of law to be decided by the trial judge. The appellant bore the onus of proof on a balance of probabilities, since an accused claiming entrapment is seeking to have the case disposed of on the basis of police misconduct as opposed to the merits.

Having decided the applicable legal issues, the Court of Appeal referred to the trial judge's conclusion that the appellant acted out of a desire for profit. Craig J.A. then stated at p. 183: "I think that the judge was right in concluding that there was no entrapment in this case." The appeal was therefore dismissed.

[Justice Lamer then thoroughly reviewed the American and Canadian jurisprudence and summarized his conclusions.]

. . . .

Summary

In conclusion, and to summarize, the proper approach to the doctrine of entrapment is that which was articulated by Estey J. in *Amato, supra*, and elaborated upon in these reasons. As mentioned and explained earlier there is entrapment when,

(a) the authorities provide a person with an opportunity to commit an offence without acting on a reasonable suspicion that this person is already engaged in criminal activity or pursuant to a *bona fide* inquiry;

(b) although having such a reasonable suspicion or acting in the course of a *bona fide* inquiry, they go beyond providing an opportunity and induce the commission of an offence.

It is neither useful nor wise to state in the abstract what elements are necessary to prove an entrapment allegation. It is, however, essential that the factors relied on by a court relate to the underlying reasons for the recognition of the doctrine in the first place.

Since I am of the view that the doctrine of entrapment is not dependent upon culpability, the focus should not be on the effect of the police conduct on the accused's state of mind. Instead, it is my opinion that as far as possible an objective assessment of the conduct of the police and their agents is required. The predisposition, or the past, present or suspected criminal activity of the accused, is relevant only as a part of the determination of whether the provision of an opportunity by the authorities to the accused to commit the offence was justifiable. Further, there must be sufficient connection between the past conduct of the accused and the provision of an opportunity, since otherwise the police suspicion will not be reasonable. While predisposition of the accused is, though not conclusive, of some relevance in assessing the initial approach by the police of a person with the offer of an opportunity to commit an offence it is never relevant as regards whether they went beyond an offer, since that is to be assessed with regard to what the average non-predisposed person would have done.

The absence of a reasonable suspicion or a *bona fide* inquiry is significant in assessing the police conduct because of the risk that the police will attract people who would not otherwise have any involvement in a crime and because it is not a proper use of the police power to simply go out and test the virtue of people on a random basis. The presence of reasonable suspicion or the mere existence of a *bona fide* inquiry will, however, never justify entrapment techniques: the police may not go beyond providing an opportunity regardless of their perception of the accused's character and regardless of the existence of an honest inquiry. To determine whether the police have employed means which go further than providing an opportunity, it is useful to consider any or all of the following factors:

— the type of crime being investigated and the availability of other techniques for the police detection of its commission;

— whether an average person, with both strengths and weaknesses, in the position of the accused would be induced into the commission of a crime;

— the persistence and number of attempts made by the police before the accused agreed to committing the offence;
— the type of inducement used by the police including: deceit, fraud, trickery or reward;
— the timing of the police conduct, in particular whether the police have instigated the offence or became involved in ongoing criminal activity;
— whether the police conduct involves an exploitation of human characteristics such as the emotions of compassion, sympathy and friendship;
— whether the police appear to have exploited a particular vulnerability of a person such as a mental handicap or a substance addiction;
— the proportionality between the police involvement, as compared to the accused, including an assessment of the degree of harm caused or risked by the police, as compared to the accused, and the commission of any illegal acts by the police themselves;
— the existence of any threats, implied or express, made to the accused by the police or their agents;
— whether the police conduct is directed at undermining other constitutional values.

This list is not exhaustive, but I hope it contributes to the elaboration of a structure for the application of the entrapment doctrine. Thus far, I have not referred to the requirement in *Amato, supra*, per Estey J., that the conduct must, in all the circumstances, be shocking or outrageous. I am of the view that this is a factor which is best considered under the procedural issues to which I will now turn.

Procedural Issues

The resolution of the issues surrounding the manner in which an entrapment claim should be considered at trial is, in my view, entirely dependant upon the conceptual basis for the defence, outlined earlier. If I were of the opinion that there was a substantive or culpability-based defence of entrapment, I would readily come to the conclusion that the defence raised a question of fact, which should be decided by a jury when there is a sufficient evidentiary basis on which to raise the defence, and I would hold that the onus would rest on the Crown to disprove the existence of entrapment beyond a reasonable doubt. Having come to the opposite viewpoint on the rationale for recognizing the doctrine of entrapment, I am not persuaded that the adoption of rules which historically, and by virtue of the *Charter*, conform to most substantive defences is either necessary or correct. It seems to me, however, that this court must be clear on how an entrapment claim is to be handled, as a brief review of some lower court decisions suggests that there is, at present, and understandably so, a great deal of confusion on the matter.

A. Who Decides: Judge or Jury?

Both the appellant and respondent agree that objective entrapment, involving police misconduct and not the accused's state of mind, is a question to be decided by the trial judge, and that the proper remedy is a stay of proceedings. I too am of this view. The question of unlawful involvement by the state in the instigation of criminal conduct is one of law, or mixed law and fact.

. . . .

Supporting the view that a judge should decide is the decision of the Court of Appeal in the present case, referred to earlier. Further, Tallis J.A. (Cameron J.A. concurring) in *R. v. Mistra* (1986), 32 C.C.C. (3d) 97 (Sask. C.A.), at p. 122, appears to have approved the decision of the British Columbia Court of Appeal in the present case and in *R. v Showman*, (unreported). In *Jewitt, supra*, at the level of the Court of Appeal, Anderson J.A. gave four reasons for his conclusion that the issue of entrapment is one to be decided by a trial judge (*supra*, at pp. 219-20). I am in complete agreement with the first and the fourth of these reasons. Anderson J.A. began by observing, at p. 219:

> ... the courts have always been the masters of their own process and it is for the courts alone to determine whether there has been an abuse of process. All issues relating to abuse of process require a factual determination but it does not follow that such a determination should be made by a jury.

And he concluded at p. 220:

> ... as a matter of policy, the issue of entrapment should be left to the courts so that standards and guidelines may be established by case law. Such a development will be impossible if issues of entrapment are left to juries.

Anderson J.A. made reference to potential prejudice arising should the issue go to the jury, for the jury may find the accused guilty because of the accused's criminal record or bad reputation (citing Frankfurter J. in *Sherman, supra*, at p. 382). I am not concerned by this for two reasons: firstly, as I noted earlier, in most cases the accused will have committed the offence and his or her guilt is not in issue; secondly, in my view the past criminal conduct of the accused is not relevant to the analysis, except where it relates to the reasonable suspicions of the police. The last point made by Anderson J.A. was that an accused could ask for evidence to be excluded by a trial judge under s. 24(2) of the *Charter* because of entrapment, and be denied that request and yet, in the same case, a jury may find that the police conduct brought the administration of justice into disrepute. He felt that such a result should be avoided. I prefer to express no opinion in this case on the propriety of a s. 24(2) application to exclude evidence because of entrapment. I am, however, of the view that the reasons which support a judicial determination of applications under s. 24(2) for the exclusion of evidence are equally relevant to the present discussion.

This court has held that the determination of whether the admission of evidence obtained in violation of a *Charter* right would bring the administration of justice into disrepute is one which should be made by a trial judge (*R. v. Therens*, [1985] 1 S.C.R. 613, per Le Dain J., at p. 653). In articulating how a trial judge should engage him or herself in that analysis, I stated in *Collins, supra*, that a judge should consider the question from the perspective of a reasonable person, "dispassionate and fully apprised of all the circumstances", and I commented that "The reasonable person is usually the average person in the community but only when that community's current mood is reasonable" (*supra*, at p. 282). The issue there, as here, is maintaining respect for the values which, over the long term, hold the community together. One of those very fundamental values is the preservation of the purity of the administration of justice. In my opinion a judge is particularly well suited to make this determination and this finding should be guided by the above quoted comments from *Collins, supra*. Further, as noted by Anderson J.A. in *Jewitt, supra*, and commented on by Vallerand J.A. in *Baxter, supra*, if one of the advantages of allowing claims of entrapment is the development of standards of conduct on the part of the state, it is essential that decisions on entrapment, and those allowing the claim especially, be carefully explained so as to provide future guidance; this is not something the jury process lends itself to. Accordingly, I am of the firm opinion that the issue of entrapment should be resolved by the trial judge for policy reasons.

Finally, I am of the view that before a judge considers whether a stay of proceedings lies because of entrapment, it must be absolutely clear that the Crown had discharged its burden of proving beyond a reasonable doubt that the accused had committed all the essential elements of the offence. If this is not clear and there is a jury, the guilt or innocence of the accused must be determined apart from evidence which is relevant only to the issue of entrapment. This protects the right of an accused to an acquittal where the circumstances so warrant. If the jury decides the accused has committed all of the elements of the crime, it is then open to the judge to stay the proceedings because of entrapment by refusing to register a conviction. It is not necessary nor advisable in this case to expand on the details of procedure. Because the guilt or innocence of the accused is not in issue at the time an entrapment claim is to be decided, the right of an accused to the benefit of a jury trial in s. 11(*f*) of the *Charter* is in no way infringed.

B. Who Bears the Burden of Proof and on What Standard?

. . . .

I have come to the conclusion that it is not inconsistent with the requirement that the Crown prove the guilt of the accused beyond a reasonable doubt to place the onus on the accused to prove on a balance of probabilities that the conduct of the state is an abuse of process because of entrapment. I repeat: the guilt or innocence of the accused is not in issue. The accused has done nothing that entitles him or her to an acquittal; the Crown has engaged in conduct, however, that disentitles it to a conviction. This point was made by Dickson C.J. in *Jewitt, supra*, in a passage cited earlier. This court in *Jewitt*, and more recently in *R. v. Keyowski*, [1988] 1 S.C.R. 657, affirmed that a court may only enter a stay for an abuse of process in the "clearest of cases" (*Jewitt, supra*, at p. 137; *Keyowski, supra*, at p. 659). It is obvious to me that requiring an accused to raise only a reasonable doubt is entirely inconsistent with a rule which permits a stay in only the "clearest of cases". More fundamentally, the claim of entrapment is a very serious allegation against the state. The state must be given substantial room to develop techniques which assist it in its fight against crime in society. It is only when the police and their agents engage in a conduct which offends basic values of the community that the doctrine of entrapment can apply. To place a lighter onus on the accused would have the result of unnecessarily hampering state action against crime. In my opinion the best way to achieve a balance between the interests of the court as guardian of the administration of justice, and the interests of society in the prevention and detection of crime, is to require an accused to demonstrate by a preponderance of evidence that the prosecution is an abuse of process because of entrapment. I would also note that this is consistent with the rules governing s. 24(2) applications (*Collins, supra*, at p. 277), where the general issue is similar to that raised in entrapment cases: would the administration of justice be brought into disrepute?

Before turning to the particular case at bar I would like to comment on the requirement in *Amato, supra*, that "In the result, the scheme so perpetrated must in all the circumstances be so shocking and outrageous *as to bring the administration of justice into disrepute*" (at p. 446, emphasis in original). I would, upon reconsideration, prefer to use the language adopted by Dickson C.J. in *Jewitt, supra*, and hold that the defence of entrapment be recognized in only the "clearest of cases". The approach set out in these reasons should provide a court with the necessary standard by which to judge the particular scheme. Once the accused has demonstrated that the strategy used by the police goes beyond the limits described earlier, a judicial condonation of the prosecution would by definition offend the community. It is not necessary to go further and ask whether the demonstrated entrapment would "shock" the community, since the accused has already shown that the administration of justice has been brought into disrepute.

In conclusion, the onus lies on the accused to demonstrate that the police conduct has gone beyond permissible limits to the extent that allowing the prosecution or the entry of a conviction would amount to an abuse of the judicial process by the state. The question is one of mixed law and fact and should be resolved by the trial judge. A stay should be entered in the "clearest of cases" only.

Disposition

In determining whether the doctrine of entrapment applies to the present appeal, this court is restricted to the summary of evidence provided by Wetmore Co. Ct. J. in his reasons. I am of the view that a stay of proceedings should be entered in this case. While the trial judge had the advantage of hearing the testimony of the appellant, and normally findings on entrapment cases should not be disturbed because of this, I am concerned that in this case too much emphasis was placed on the appellant's state of mind. Earlier in my summary of the decisions below I cited a passage from the trial judge's reasons wherein he stated that the fundamental issue was the appellant's state of mind and his predisposition to crime. This, perhaps, explains why in his conclusion the trial judge stated the appellant was not entrapped because he acted out of a desire to profit from the transaction. If the trial judge had been permitted only to evaluate the conduct of the police objectively, I think he might well have, and in any event, ought to have come to the conclusion the police conduct amounted to entrapment.

From the facts it appears that the police had reasonable suspicion that the appellant was involved in criminal conduct. The issue is whether the police went too far in their efforts to attract the appellant into the commission of the offence.

Returning to the list of factors I outlined earlier, this crime is obviously one for which the state must be given substantial leeway. The drug-trafficking business is not one which lends itself to the traditional devices of police investigation. It is absolutely essential, therefore, for police or their agents to get involved and gain the trust and confidence of the people who do the trafficking or who supply the drugs. It is also a crime of enormous social consequence which causes a great deal of harm in society generally. This factor alone is very critical and makes this case somewhat difficult.

The police do not appear, however, to have been interrupting an ongoing criminal enterprise, and the offence was clearly brought about by their conduct and would not have occurred absent their involvement. The police do not appear to have exploited a narcotics addiction of the appellant since he testified that he had already given up his use of narcotics. Therefore, he was not, at the time, trying to recover from an addiction. Nonetheless, he also testified that he was no longer involved in drugs and, if this is true, it suggests that the police were indeed trying to make the appellant take up his former lifestyle. The persistence of the police requests, as a result of the equally persistent refusals by the appellant, supports the appellant's version of events on this point. The length of time, approximately six months, and the repetition of requests it took before the appellant agreed to commit the offence also demonstrate that the police had to go further than merely providing the appellant with the opportunity once it became evident that he was unwilling to join the alleged drug syndicate.

Perhaps the most important and determinative factor in my opinion is the appellant's testimony that the informer acted in a threatening manner when they went for a walk in the woods, and the further testimony that he was told to get his act together after he did not provide the supply of drugs he was asked for. I believe this conduct was unacceptable. If the police must go this far, they have gone beyond providing the appellant with an opportunity. I do not, therefore, place much significance on the fact that the appellant eventually committed the offence when shown the money. Obviously the appellant knew much earlier that he could make a profit by getting involved in the drug enterprise and he still refused. I have come to the conclusion that the average person in the position of the appellant might also have committed the offence, if only to finally satisfy this threatening informer and end all further contact. As a result I would, on the evidence, have to find that the police conduct in this case was unacceptable. Thus, the doctrine of entrapment applies to preclude the prosecution of the appellant. In my opinion, the appellant has met the burden of proof and the trial judge should have entered a stay of proceedings for abuse of process.

I would accordingly allow the appeal, set aside the conviction of the appellant and enter a stay of proceedings.

Appeal allowed.

R. v. BARNES

[1991] 1 S.C.R. 449, 3 C.R. (4th) 1, 63 C.C.C. (3d) 1,
1991 CarswellBC 915, 1991 CarswellBC 11 (S.C.C.)

1   LAMER C.J. (WILSON, LA FOREST, SOPINKA, GONTHIER, CORY and STEVENSON JJ. concurring): — This case involves a consideration of the defence of entrapment as set out by this court in *R. v. Mack*, [1988] 2 S.C.R. 903. In particular, this court is asked whether the accused was subjected to random virtue-testing by an undercover police officer in the city of Vancouver. . . . .

Facts

2   On January 12, 1989, the appellant sold one gram of hashish to an undercover police officer near the Granville Mall area of Vancouver. The parties do not dispute the facts surrounding the sale, which are as follows.

3   The undercover officer was involved in a "buy-and-bust" operation conducted by the Vancouver Police Department. In a buy-and-bust operation, undercover police officers attempt to buy illicit drugs from individuals who appear, in the opinion of the officers, to be inclined to sell such drugs. If an officer is successful, the individual is immediately arrested for trafficking.

4   This particular operation was undertaken by the Department with respect to the Granville Mall area in the city of Vancouver, which covers a six-block section of Granville Street. On the day of the arrest, the undercover officer approached the accused, Philip Barnes, and his friend, as they were walking towards Granville Street. The officer testified at trial that she approached the accused and his friend because she had "a hunch, a feeling that they'd — possibly might be in possession". She believed that he and his friend fit the description of persons who possibly had drugs in their possession and who would be willing to sell to her: "I had a feeling. They fit my general criteria. I look for males hanging around, dressed scruffy and in jeans, wearing a jean jacket or leather jacket, runners or black boots, that tend to look at people a lot." The officer indicated that there was nothing else that aroused her suspicions.

5   The officer approached the accused and asked him if he had any "weed". He said "no", but his friend repeated to him: "She wants some weed." The accused again responded negatively. The officer persisted and the accused then agreed to sell a small amount of cannabis resin to the officer for $15. Shortly afterwards, the accused was arrested by another officer and small amounts of cannabis resin and marijuana were seized from his person.

6   The accused was tried in the County Court of Vancouver before Leggatt Co. Ct. J., and was found guilty of trafficking in cannabis resin, of the included offence of possession of cannabis resin for the purpose of trafficking, and of possession of marijuana. The accused conceded that he sold illicit drugs to the officer, but argued that a judicial stay for entrapment should be directed. He claimed that he had no intention of selling drugs on the day in question, but felt sorry for the undercover officer; he agreed to sell only because he believed that his friend wanted to meet a woman and that this was a way of gaining an introduction. The trial judge held that the police officer had engaged in "random virtue testing", which was unacceptable according to the judgment of this court in *Mack, supra*, and therefore ordered a judicial stay of the proceedings.

7   The British Columbia Court of Appeal allowed the Crown's appeal and ordered a new trial.

. . . .

Analysis

Did the police officer engage in random virtue-testing?

14   To resolve this appeal, this court must consider whether the conduct of the undercover police officer was acceptable in light of the guidelines set out in *Mack, supra*. In *Mack*, I attempted to define the circumstances in which police conduct in the course of investigating and uncovering criminal activity ceases to be acceptable and, instead, amounts to the unacceptable entrapment of individuals. The defence of entrapment is based on the notion that limits should be imposed on the ability of the police to participate in the commission of an offence. As a general rule, it is expected in our society that the police will direct their attention towards uncovering criminal activity that occurs without their involvement.

. . . .

16   It is apparent that the police officer involved in this case did not have a "reasonable suspicion" that the accused was already engaged in unlawful drug-related activity. The factors that drew the officer's attention to this particular accused — his manner of dress, the length of his hair — were not sufficient to give rise to a reasonable suspicion that criminal acts were being committed. Furthermore, the subjectiveness of the officer's decision to approach the accused, based on a "hunch" or "feeling" rather than extrinsic evidence, also indicates that the accused did not, as an individual, arouse a reasonable suspicion.

17   Consequently, the police conduct in this case will amount to entrapment unless the officer presented the accused with the opportunity to sell drugs in the course of a *bona fide* inquiry. In my opinion, the police officer involved in this case was engaged in such a *bona fide* investigation. First, there is no question that the officer's conduct was motivated by the genuine purpose of investigating and repressing criminal activity. The police department had reasonable grounds for believing that drug-related crimes were occurring throughout the Granville Mall area. The accused was not, therefore, approached for questionable motives unrelated to the investigation and repression of crime.

18   Secondly, the police department directed its investigation at a suitable area within the city of Vancouver. As I noted in *Mack, supra*, the police may present the opportunity to commit a particular crime to persons who are associated with a location where it is reasonably suspected that criminal activity is taking place. I stated, at p. 956:

> Of course, in certain situations the police may not know the identity of specific individuals, but they do know certain other facts, such as a particular location or area where it is reasonably suspected that certain criminal activity is occurring. In those cases it is clearly permissible to provide opportunities to people associated with the location under suspicion, even if these people are not themselves under suspicion.

The police department in this case focused its investigation on an area of Vancouver, a section of Granville Street covering approximately six city blocks, where it was reasonably suspected that drug-related crimes were occurring. In my opinion, they would not have been able to deal with the problem effectively had they restricted the investigation to a smaller area. Although there were particular areas within the Granville Mall where drug trafficking was especially serious, it is true that trafficking occurred at locations scattered generally throughout the Mall. It is also true that traffickers did not operate in a single place. It would be unrealistic for the police to focus their investigation on one specific part of the Mall given the tendency of traffickers to modify their techniques in response to police investigations. The trial judge admitted that the Mall was "known as an area of considerable drug activity". Similarly, the Court of Appeal found support in the evidence given at trial by Staff Sergeant Davies of the Vancouver City Police. In discussing the police department's activities in 1988, Staff Sergeant Davies indicated, at p. 370, that:

> (a) Of the 2,294 persons charged with drug offences, approximately 22% were from incidents in the Granville Mall area;
>
> (b) 506 arrests were made on the mall resulting in 659 charges — 289 for trafficking, 199 for possession for the purpose of trafficking;
>
> (c) 315 arrests were made in "buy and bust" operations resulting in 475 charges.

The Court of Appeal concluded, at p. 372:

> The evidence at trial disclosed that sales of narcotics took place up and down the mall and it was for that reason that the undercover officer walked up and down the mall approaching persons and providing an opportunity to sell illicit drugs to her.

19   It is, therefore, my opinion that the police department was engaged, in these circumstances, in a *bona fide* inquiry.

20   I note that in many cases, the size of the area itself may indicate that the investigation is not *bona fide*. This will be so particularly when there are grounds for believing that the criminal activity being investigated is concentrated in part of a larger area targeted by the police. In this case, however, for the reasons discussed above, it was reasonable for the Vancouver Police Department to focus its investigation on the Granville Mall.

21   The accused argues that although the undercover officer was involved in a *bona fide* inquiry, she nevertheless engaged in random virtue-testing since she approached the accused without a reasonable suspicion that he was likely to commit a drug-related offence. She approached the accused simply because he was walking near Granville Street.

22   In my respectful opinion, this argument is based on a misinterpretation of *Mack*. I recognize that some of my language in *Mack* might be responsible for this misinterpretation. In particular, I stated, at p. 956:

> In those cases [where there is a particular location where it is reasonably suspected that certain crimes are taking place] it is clearly permissible to provide opportunities to people associated with the location under suspicion, even if these people are not themselves under suspicion. This latter situation, however, is only justified if the police acted in the course of a bona fide investigation and are not engaged in random virtue-testing.

23   This statement should not be taken to mean that the police may not approach people on a random basis, in order to present the opportunity to commit an offence, in the course of a *bona fide* investigation. The basic rule articulated in *Mack* is that the police may only present the opportunity to commit a particular crime to an individual who arouses a suspicion that he or she is already engaged in the particular criminal activity. An exception to this rule arises when the police undertake a *bona fide* investigation directed at an area where it is reasonably suspected that criminal activity is occurring. When such a location is defined with sufficient precision, the police may present any person associated with the area with the opportunity to commit the particular offence. Such randomness is permissible within the scope of a *bona fide* inquiry.

24   Random virtue-testing, conversely, only arises when a police officer presents a person with the opportunity to commit an offence without a reasonable suspicion that:

(a) the person is already engaged in the particular criminal activity, or

(b) the physical location with which the person is associated is a place where the particular criminal activity is likely occurring.

25   In this case, the accused was approached by the officer when he was walking near the Granville Mall. The notion of being "associated" with a particular area for these purposes does not require more than being present in the area. As a result, the accused was associated with a location where it was reasonably believed that drug-related crimes were occurring. The officer's conduct was therefore justified under the first branch of the test for entrapment set out in *Mack*.

26   For these reasons, it is my opinion that the officer did not engage in random virtue-testing in this case. I would, therefore, dismiss the appeal and uphold the decision of the Court of Appeal ordering a new trial.

. . . .

65   MCLACHLIN J. (dissenting): — This appeal raises the question of when undercover police should be allowed to interfere with members of the public

who are not under suspicion. This court laid out the basic principles governing undercover intrusion into private activity in *R. v. Mack*, [1988] 2 S.C.R. 903. The present case raises issues as to the ambit of the *Mack* test and its application. With the greatest respect, I cannot agree with the application of the *Mack* test adopted in this case by the Court of Appeal and endorsed by my colleague, Chief Justice Lamer. To accept this application would, in my considered opinion, represent endorsing a measure of state intrusion into the private affairs of citizens greater than any heretofore sanctioned by this court under the *Canadian Charter of Rights and Freedoms* and out of step with the philosophy and principles which guided the decisions of this court in *R. v. Dyment*, [1988] 2 S.C.R. 417; *R. v. Duarte*, [1990] 1 S.C.R. 30; *R. v. Kokesch*, [1990] 3 S.C.R. 3; and *R. v. Wong*, [1990] 3 S.C.R. 36.

. . . . I . . . take the view that determining whether the police were acting pursuant to a *bona fide* inquiry requires consideration of more than the two factors referred to by Lamer C.J. More particularly, it involves consideration of whether the state's interest in repressing criminal activity in the particular case outweighs the interest which individuals have in being able to go about their daily lives without courting the risk that they will be subjected to the clandestine investigatory techniques of agents of the state. . . .

70   *Mack* therefore stands for the proposition that determination of entrapment must involve a balancing between the individual interest in being left alone and the state's interest in the repression of crime. Only where considerations such as fairness, justice and the need for protection from crime tip the balance in favour of the state will police conduct which offends the individual interests at stake be acceptable.

72   To paraphrase La Forest J. in *Wong, supra*, the notion is that individuals should be free to go about their daily business — to go shopping, to visit the theatre, to travel to and from work, to name but three examples — without courting the risk that they will be subjected to the clandestine investigatory techniques of agents of the state. A further risk inherent in overbroad undercover operations is that of discriminatory police work, where people are interfered with not because of reasonable suspicion but because of the colour of their skin or, as in this case, the quality of their clothing and their age.

73   It follows, from the fact that the concept of unlawful entrapment represents a balancing of conflicting interests, that the test for entrapment must likewise permit the measuring of relative harms. A test which does not permit weighing of the infringement on individual freedom and privacy in determining whether entrapment has occurred is to that extent deficient. As Lamer J. put it in the passage cited in *Mack*, what must be determined "in any given case" is where the proper balance lies.

74   While comments of Lamer J. in *Mack* on what constitutes a *bona fide* inquiry leave room for consideration of the individual interest in being left alone and not being induced into crime, the application of *Mack* proposed by him in this case permits little or no recognition of the interest of the individual in being left alone. All that is required is that the police act from a proper motive and that there be a suspicion of criminal activity within a general geographic area targeted by the police. That established, there is no room for consideration of factors vital to the balancing process, for example, the size of the area, the number of innocent people going about legitimate activities who might be interfered with by the operation, and the seriousness of the crime in question.

75   In advocating a more refined test for *bona fide* inquiry than does Lamer C.J., I am motivated by concern for the implications of the test he proposes. That test would permit the police to extend their Granville Mall operation to all of Vancouver if statistics could be found to suggest that drug offences were occurring throughout Vancouver generally. The example is extreme. Yet it indicates the deficiency I see in the test proposed by Lamer C.J. In my view, a more sensitive test than that proposed by Lamer C.J. — one which permits appreciation of all relevant factors — is required.

76   I conclude that determination that the police were operating in the course of a bona fide inquiry within the meaning of *Mack* requires the court to consider not only the motive of the police and whether there is crime in the general area, but also other factors relevant to the balancing process, such as the likelihood of crime at the particular location targeted, the seriousness of the crime in question, the number of legitimate activities and persons who might be affected, and the availability of other less intrusive investigative techniques. In the final analysis, the question is whether the interception at the particular location where it took place was reasonable having regard to the conflicting interests of private citizens in being left alone from state interference and of the state in suppressing crime. If the answer to this question is yes, then the inquiry is *bona fide*.

77   In proposing a test that involves the balancing of conflicting interests, I am not insensitive to the criticism sometimes made that balancing formulas may lack certainty and predictability and accord too much discretion to reviewing judges. Notwithstanding such criticisms, a balancing approach remains the only rational way to address problems such as that presented in this case. Balancing formulas provide a way of channelling diverse information into an analytic framework, a framework which, while perhaps less than precise, is far superior to voting by "gut reaction". A balancing process, where conflicting interests are articulated and weighed against each other, forces us to face squarely the real policy issues involved in the case, to make explicit what otherwise, rightly or wrongly, may be assumed. Our constitutional law is embedded in the notion of

defining and balancing strongly felt interests in society. The rules which elaborate that law must address the same concerns.

78   In point of fact, the test which I propose offers sufficient guidance to the police, in my view. It may reasonably be predicted, for example, that where there is no evidence of the likelihood of offences being committed at the place where the undercover operative is stationed, the interception is unlikely to be *bona fide* in the absence of a countervailing state interest of compelling proportions.

79   Having set out the considerations which should be addressed in determining whether an inquiry is *bona fide*, I turn to the facts of this case. In my view, the factors to which I have referred negate Lamer C.J.'s conclusion that the entire Granville Mall represents a suitable area within the city of Vancouver for the carrying out of a *bona fide* police inquiry. Granville Mall, located in downtown Vancouver, occupies a six-block stretch of Granville Street, a major north-south thoroughfare running through the entire city. The diversity of the Granville Mall area — which features theatres and restaurants, major department stores, large office towers, and within the radius of one block, the Vancouver Art Gallery, convention facilities and the Law Courts — means that on a daily basis literally thousands of individuals will frequent the Mall and thus fall subject to the clandestine investigatory techniques of the police on the policy proposed in this case.

80   Lamer C.J. bases his conclusion that targeting the entirety of Granville Mall as a site for undercover operations constituted a *bona fide* police inquiry, on the absence of improper motive and the fact that it was reasonably suspected that drug-related crimes were occurring on the mall. He refers to the trial judge's observation that Granville Mall is "known as an area of considerable drug activity". With the greatest respect, I cannot agree with Lamer C.J.'s conclusion at p. 461 that "[it] would be unrealistic for the police to focus their investigation on one specific part of the Mall". There is no evidence whatsoever that trafficking took place at the location of the undercover interception. Nor is there any evidence that traffickers systematically rotated locations to avoid detection. Indeed, the trial judge, in ordering a stay of proceedings, noted the legitimate character of much of the mall and held that the accused "was not at the immediate centre of drug trafficking". What evidence there is, established that the Granville Mall Skytrain station is known to the police as the "hub" of drug activity on the mall. That information suggests that it would be perfectly realistic for the police to focus their investigation on one specific part of the mall — namely, the very hub of drug activity, the Skytrain station.

81   As indicated above, I cannot agree that the fact that crime may be said to occur generally within a given area suffices to establish a *bona fide* inquiry, given proper police motives. Other factors must be considered. The first is the

likelihood of crime in the particular area targeted. There was no evidence that trafficking was likely to occur in the intersection where the accused was intercepted — the intersection between a major hotel, an office tower and two department stores. On the contrary, as the finding of the trial judge reflects, drug trafficking was centred elsewhere on the mall. The fact that trafficking occurred at different locations in the six-block area of the mall does not establish that trafficking was likely to occur at the intersection where the accused was intercepted.

82   What evidence there is of drug activity on Granville Mall came from Staff Sergeant Kenneth Michael Davies, who, significantly, was called as "an expert in the areas of police enforcements [sic] practice and techniques regarding drug enforcement in the Granville Mall area and the downtown Vancouver area and, in particular, the operation of undercover operations". Staff Sergeant Davies noted that the hub of drug activity on Granville Mall had migrated northward from the McDonald's restaurant to the Skytrain station. He also stated that recently a greater proportion of the drug trafficking has been occurring indoors, in bars and restaurants along the mall. He offered no evidence whatsoever that the particular intersection in question here — Granville and Georgia — had ever been a known site of drug activity. Moreover, in cross-examination, he appeared to disapprove expressly of the conduct engaged in by the undercover policewoman:

> Q [The suspects] are noticed walking across the street in a crosswalk; that's it. They're not standing — not seen standing where a bunch of people were standing. They haven't come from a place where there is any suspicion of drug trafficking. They're just walking across the street?
>
> A If that's all there was, I personally wouldn't direct my operator to approach these people, given the very limited information you're giving me.

83   The statistics produced by Staff Sergeant Davies all relate to the entirety of the mall, with no attempt to discriminate between different locations where or times when the offences in question were committed. To rely on these numbers in support of the view that the police were justified in extending their operation to the entire six-block area of the mall is fraught with peril. Statistics are only as good as the questions upon which they are based. We have absolutely no idea what questions were asked in order to produce the numbers relied on by the Crown. It is entirely possible that the vast majority of the drug offences which occurred on Granville Mall took place close to the Skytrain station on Granville Street, the acknowledged hub of drug activity on Granville Mall. It is equally possible that none of the offences occurred at the intersection where the accused was intercepted. Again, it is possible that the vast majority of the drug offences which occurred on Granville Mall occurred on certain days or at specific times of day — weekends or late evenings, for example — and not at 6:00 p.m. on a weekday, which is when the transaction in question here occurred.

I conclude that the statistics relied on in this case fall far short of justifying granting to the police unfettered licence to carry out their operation anywhere within a six-block stretch of downtown Vancouver without restriction as to the area and the times of day to be covered. In short, it is not established that the police could reasonably have suspected trafficking at the place and time where the accused was intercepted.

84   A second factor relevant to determining the appropriateness of the investigation is the impact that the investigation may have on law-abiding citizens pursuing legitimate activities. Here the possibility of this undercover operation's interfering with legitimate activities was high. As already noted, the intersection in question is bounded by department stores, an office tower and a major hotel. Theatres, the Art Gallery and the Law Courts are nearby. This factor, while not in itself conclusive, weighs against the right of undercover police to intercede at will.

85   On the other side of the balance must be weighed the seriousness of the criminal activity which the police have targeted. It is apparent that the state interest in repressing crime may receive greater weight when the police target serious criminal offences. The offence here in question, while not to be condoned, cannot be considered as serious. In *Kokesch, supra*, Sopinka J. for the majority took judicial notice of the fact that narcotics offences involving marijuana are generally regarded as less serious than those involving "hard" drugs such as cocaine and heroin. The same might be said of offences involving hashish, the substance involved in this case. The amount, moreover, was small. In short, this was not the sort of serious drug offence which would more readily tip the balance in favour of the state.

86   I turn finally to the availability of alternative investigatory techniques for detecting the sort of criminal activity at issue. There were alternative ways of apprehending drug pedlars such as the appellant. Simple observation by undercover operatives (as opposed to interception) is one. I am left with some doubt as to whether the apprehension of drug pedlars on Granville Mall requires giving the police carte-blanche to intercept large numbers of law-abiding citizens as these citizens visit the theatre or leave major office towers or department stores.

87   I arrive then at the conclusion that in the case at bar the individual interest in being left alone and free to pursue one's daily business without being confronted by undercover police operatives vastly outweighs the state interest in the repression of crime. It follows that the police officer in this case cannot be said to have been acting pursuant to a *bona fide* inquiry. Any other conclusion would be, in my respectful opinion, unfitting in a society which heralds the constitutional protection of individual liberties and places a premium on "being left alone".

88   I would allow the appeal and restore the stay of proceedings.

L'Heureux-Dubé J. agreed with the majority on the merits but dissented on the issue of jurisdiction. She would have substituted convictions.

It is often believed that the *Mack* and *Barnes* regime makes it difficult to obtain entrapment stays to control abusive police sting operations. However, a computer survey of 152 cases between 1989 and 2009 found a success rate of entrapment arguments of 18%, particularly in drug cases: David Tanovich, "Rethinking the *Bona Fides* on Entrapment" (2011) 43 U.B.C. L. Rev. 417. Tanovich calls for greater use of the *Mack* approach as an important remedy against discriminatory law enforcement. He notes that the reasonable suspicion test has now been given greater scrutiny in other contexts. It seems likely, however, that stays for entrapment will not markedly increase unless the Supreme Court returns to *Barnes* to limit the meaning of a *bona fide* inquiry. That appeared to occur in the B.C. Court of Appeal ruling in *R. v. Swan* (2009), 65 C.R. (6th) 240 (B.C. C.A.), that a police drug investigation should be stayed where the police phoned a list of cell phone numbers compiled through anonymous sources and other tips. Justice Prowse for the Court found that there was no reasonable suspicion or *bona fide* investigation. See similarly *R. v. Gladue* (2012), 92 C.R. (6th) 434 (Alta. C.A.), leave to appeal refused (2012), 443 N.R. 394 (note) (S.C.C.) and *R. v. Le* (2016), 28 C.R. (7th) 187 (B.C. C.A.), leave to appeal refused 2016 CarswellBC 3004, 2016 CarswellBC 3005 (S.C.C.) but see *R. v. Olazo* (2012), 287 C.C.C. (3d) 379 (B.C. C.A.) and *R. v. Seymour* (2016), 343 C.C.C. (3d) 412, 35 C.R. (7th) 365 (Man. C.A.).

On the other hand, the Supreme Court in *R. v. Imoro*, 80 C.R. (6th) 27, [2010] 3 S.C.R. 62 had no difficulty in agreeing with the Ontario Court of Appeal that a trial judge had wrongly found entrapment in a case where an undercover officer had followed up a tip that a black man was selling drugs from his apartment. A brief conversation outside the apartment could not constitute entrapment. Furthermore, the accused had invited the officer into his apartment and the officer had actually witnessed a drug transaction. Justice LeBel described this as not an inducement to commit a crime but as an engagement in criminal activities. The trial judge had not stayed the proceedings but had excluded the evidence under s. 24(2). The Ontario Court of Appeal determined that a stay would have been the only proper remedy. The Supreme Court left this issue open.

Entrapment failed in *R. v. Chiang* (2012), 92 C.R. (6th) 420 (B.C. C.A.) (police placing advert for sexy young girls in classified ad for underage prostitution) and in *R. v. Faqi* (2011), 89 C.R. (6th) 409 (Alta. C.A.) (drug investigation in every downtown bar being *bona fide* investigation and trial judge wrongly finding racial profiling where black man approached because of manner of dress). See too Brent Kettles "The Entrapment Defence in Internet Child Luring Cases (2011) 16 Crim. L. Rev. 89, who suggests that the defence will rarely succeed because of the way courts conceptualize "opportunity to offend" and "*bona fide* inquiry". See too in this context *R. v. Bayat* (2011), 91 C.R. (6th) 190 (Ont. C.A.) (no entrapment where officer initiating online contact with accused and pretending to be a 13-year-old girl).

In *R. v. Clothier* (2011), 266 C.C.C. (3d) 19 (Ont. C.A.) the Court rejected the defence of entrapment in the case of the provincial offence of selling tobacco to a person under 19. The use of random test shoppers was held to be an appropriate police technique for this regulatory offence.

Chapter 8

PARTIES TO A CRIME

1. CO-PRINCIPALS

R. v. BALL

(2011), 82 C.R. (6th) 72, 267 C.C.C. (3d) 532 (B.C. C.A.), leave to appeal
refused (2011), 430 N.R. 390 (note) (S.C.C.)

The two accused were among a larger group of people who got into an altercation at a bar with two brothers; eventually the group of four or five pursued the brothers from the bar and assaulted them in an alleyway. One of the brothers died from the injuries suffered, but the evidence against the accused only established that they had struck the surviving brother. The accused were convicted of manslaughter, and one issue on appeal was whether they could be convicted of that offence not merely as aiders or abettors, but as principals.

RYAN J.A.: —

21   Section 21(1) of the *Criminal Code* provides:

> Every one is a party to an offence who
> (a) actually commits it;
>
> (b) does or omits to do anything for the purpose of aiding any person to commit it; or
>
> (c) abets any person in committing it.

22   Section 21(2) is not directly engaged by this appeal, but as there is some reference to it in the case law I reproduce it here for ease of reference:

> 21(2) Where two or more persons form an intention in common to carry out an unlawful purpose and to assist each other therein and any one of them, in carrying out the common purpose, commits an offence, each of them who knew or ought to have known that the commission of the offence would be a probable consequence of carrying out the common purpose is a party to that offence.

23   Two persons may both be actual committers for the purposes of s. 21(1)(a) (referred to in the case law variously as "co-principals", "joint-principals", "co-

perpetrators" or "joint-perpetrators") even though each has not performed every act which makes up the *actus reus* of the offence. As Martin J.A. explained in *R. v. Mena* (1987), 34 C.C.C. (3d) 304: 57 C.R. (3d) 172 (O.C.A.) at page 309:

> Unquestionably, more than one person may actually commit an offence. Perhaps the simplest example of joint perpetrators is where two accused attack the victim intending to kill him or her and the combined effect of the blows struck by the two accused is to kill the victim. In those circumstances, both the accused have murdered the deceased: see Smith and Hogan, *Criminal Law*, 5th ed. (1983), at p. 120.
>
> > At common law, a principal in the first degree is one who has committed the fact with his own hands, or through an innocent agent: see Russell on Crime, 12th ed. Vol. I (1964), at p. 131. It was well established that, if several persons combined to commit a crime and each person committed a different part of the crime, every such person was a principal in the first degree. In Russell on Crime, supra, the author states at p. 131:
> >
> > > All the facts of the case must be taken into account, so that where it appears that there is a joint enterprise afoot between two (or more) persons in which each has an active part to perform in order to effect the criminal purpose then each participant is equally a principal in the first degree. Thus in burglary if A hoists B through a half-open window and B then goes to the closed door of the house and opens it from the inside thus admitting A, both are principals in the first degree to burglary. So also there may be joint action in cases of stealing and other crimes. In certain circumstances each of the participants may do his part in the absence of the others and even may not know by whom the other parts were executed. [Footnotes omitted.] [Emphasis added.]

Glanville Williams in *Criminal Law: The General Part*, 2d ed. (1961) states at p. 349:

> Two persons may be guilty as joint perpetrators. Hence where a body of men beat a constable (some with sticks, some by throwing stones, some with their fists), and the constable died of the aggregate violence, the judge directed the jury that "If several persons act together in pursuance of a common intent, every act done in furtherance of such intent by each of them is, in law, done by all" (*R. v. Macklin* (1838), 2 Lewin 225).
>
> Part of a crime may be committed by one principal, another by another. Thus, in burglary, one may break and the other enter. Other illustrations are in forgery, where different persons execute different parts of the document (though in the absence of one another), and in libel, where D composes, E prints, and F publishes. In these cases, it is not necessary for the various perpetrators to be present at the same time. It is even possible for two persons to manipulate the controls of a car at the same time so that both are driving. [Footnotes omitted.]

In *Textbook of Criminal Law*, 2d ed. (1983), Glanville Williams says at p. 330:

> Two persons may be guilty as joint perpetrators; and part of a crime may be committed by one perpetrator, another by another. Thus, in robbery, which involves the two elements of theft and threat, one person may steal while his companion makes the threat of force, and the two are co-perpetrators.
>
> It is, I think, clear that in the above passage the author is referring to the case where two people have acted in concert to commit a robbery as a joint enterprise.

24   This conclusion is logical. Where two people rob a bank with a gun, only one person can carry and point the weapon, and it may be more convenient for a second, not occupied with a weapon, to scoop up the cash. The robbers have not, individually performed all elements of the offence, yet they both have committed the crime in the sense that they are co-perpetrators. There is no need in such a case to turn to accessorial principles to determine guilt. So also with an attack by two or more on two (or more) victims - an attacker may strike only one victim while others strike the second, or they may all strike both. The attackers are all actual committers. Again, there is no need to resort to accessorial principles to find a basis for conviction.

25   Where two persons commit a crime as co-perpetrators it may be the case that they have agreed to do so before embarking on the endeavour. For purposes of liability under s. 21(1)(a) of the *Code*, however, agreement to carry out a common purpose is not necessary. The question is whether there is an indication of common participation, not a common purpose.

. . . .

28   It follows that where co-perpetrators engage in a deadly assault, the Crown need not prove which of the attackers struck the fatal blow or blows...

29   In the case at bar the trial judge found that the Clarke, Ball and Rosborough, members of the Woolnough party, jointly participated in an attack on the Johnston brothers as they left the Rec Room after they were advised by staff to leave. If this conclusion is not wrong, all of the attackers are responsible for the injuries received by both men.

30   In my view the trial judge was entitled to reach the conclusion that he did on the evidence. The Woolnough party was together in the Rec Room when Mark Woolnough and Ian Johnston almost came to blows. Bradley Johnston was nearby when this confrontation occurred and left with his brother when advised to do so. Both men were attacked at the same time by a group of individuals after they left the pub. The trial judge found that the group that attacked the Johnston brothers consisted of members of the Woolnough party. It matters little that each attacker did not lay a hand on each person assaulted. What matters is that all played a part in the attack, whether it was striking one brother or the both of them. In such a case the blow of one is the blow of them all.

31   I would not accede to this ground of appeal.

     The Court of Appeal concluded that the accused could be found guilty as principals. They also found that the accused could be found guilty as either aiders or abettors under ss. 21(1)(b) and 21(1)(c).

In the mass first degree murder case of *R. v. Pickton* (2010), 77 C.R. (6th) 12 (S.C.C.) a 6-3 majority found that a direction to find guilt if "he was otherwise an active participant" in killings adequately conveyed the law on potential routes to criminal liability.

2. AIDING AND ABETTING

See ss. 21-23 of the *Criminal Code*.

DUNLOP and SYLVESTER v. R.

[1979] 2 S.C.R. 881, 8 C.R. (3d) 349, 47 C.C.C. (2d) 93,
1979 CarswellMan 91, 1979 CarswellMan 158

DICKSON J. (LASKIN C.J.C., ESTEY and SPENCE JJ. concurring): — The appellants were twice tried and convicted on a charge of rape. The indictment alleges that on June 26, 1975, they did unlawfully have sexual intercourse with B.R. without her consent. They were sentenced to serve six years in penitentiary. In an appeal taken following the second trial, the Manitoba Court of Appeal found error on the part of the trial judge, but by a three to two majority sustained the conviction by applying s. 613(1)(*b*)(iii) of the *Code* [37 C.C.C. (2d) 90]. It is from that judgment that the present appeal is taken.

[The complainant in the case had been raped by a group of about 18 members of a motorcycle gang. She identified Dunlop and Sylvester as two of the people who had raped her. They both denied the assault, and testified that although they had delivered beer to the location where the rapes occurred and had observed a woman having intercourse, they stayed for only three minutes, did not have intercourse with the complainant, and did not in any way assist anyone else to do so.

There was no dispute that if the Crown had proven beyond a reasonable doubt that the complainant's version of events was true, then the accused were guilty as principals to the offence. However, the trial judge also instructed the jury that an alternative way in which the accused could be found guilty was as parties to the offence under s. 21(1) or 21(2) of the *Criminal Code*. If that were correct, it could only be relevant if the jury did not accept the complainant's identification evidence, but nonetheless could find the accused guilty based on their testimony as to their behaviour.]

Section 21(1) of the Criminal Code

On s. 21(1) of the *Code*, the jury was instructed as follows:

Secondly, I should also instruct you on the law relating to parties to an offence. Section 21(1) of the *Criminal Code*, reads as follows:

"Every one is a party to an offence who:
(a) actually commits it,
(b) does or omits to do anything for the purpose of aiding any person to commit it, or
(c) abets any person in committing it."

Abets, that word abets means encourages, supports, upholds. It is another way of expressing a person giving assistance to someone committing the offence. Everyone who aids and encourages the person in the commission of the offence is as guilty as the person who commits the actual criminal act.

To find that the accused is guilty of aiding or abetting the commission of an offence by another person, it is only necessary to show that he understood what was being done and by some act on his part assisted or encouraged the attainment of that act.

Mere presence at the scene of a crime is not sufficient to ground culpability. Something more is needed: encouragement of the principal offender; an act which facilitates the commission of the offence, such as keeping watch or enticing the victim away, or an act which tends to prevent or hinder interference with accomplishment of the criminal act, such as preventing the intended victim from escaping or being ready to assist the prime culprit. Thus, in an early work, *Foster's Crown Law*, p. 350, we read:

in order to render a person an accomplice and a principal in felony, he must be aiding and abetting at the fact, or ready to afford assistance if necessary, and therefore if A. happeneth to be present at a murder, for instance, and taketh no part in it, nor endeavoureth to prevent it, nor apprehendeth the murderer, nor levyeth hue and cry after him, this strange behaviour of his, though highly criminal, will not of itself render him either principal or accessory.

The leading case of *R. v. Coney* (1882), 8 Q.B.D. 534, decided that non-accidental presence at the scene of the crime was not conclusive of aiding and abetting. The accused were present at a prize fight, then illegal, though taking no part in the management of the fight. It did not appear that the accused said or did anything. The Chairman of the Quarter Sessions directed the jury that, prize fights being illegal, all persons who went to a fight to see the combatants strike each other, and being present when they did so, were guilty of assault unless they were casually passing by. If they stayed at the place, they encouraged it by their presence although they did not say or do anything. Eight of the 11 judges hearing the case reserved were of the opinion that the direction was not correct. Two passages from the judgment of Cave J. at p. 539 bear repeating:

Now it is a general rule in the case of principals in the second degree that there must be participation in the act, and that, although a man is present whilst a felony is being committed, if he takes no part in it, and does not act in concert with those who commit it, he will not be a principal in the second degree merely because he does not endeavour to prevent the felony, or apprehend the felon.

and [at p. 540]:

Where presence may be entirely accidental, it is not even evidence of aiding and abetting. Where presence is *prima facie* not accidental it is evidence, but no more than evidence, for the jury.

Hawkins J., in a well-known passage had this to say, pp. 557-8:

> In my opinion, to constitute an aider and abettor some active steps must be taken by word, or action, with the intent to instigate the principal, or principals. Encouragement does not of necessity amount to aiding and abetting, it may be intentional or unintentional, a man may unwittingly encourage another in fact by his presence, by misinterpreted words, or gestures, or by his silence, on non-interference, or he may, encourage intentionally by expressions, gestures, or actions intended to signify approval. In the latter case he aids and abets, in the former he does not. It is no criminal offence to stand by, a mere passive spectator of a crime, even of a murder. Non-interference to prevent a crime is not itself a crime. But the fact that a person was voluntarily and purposely present witnessing the commission of a crime, and offered no opposition to it, though he might reasonably be expected to prevent and had the power to do so, or at least to express his dissent, might under some circumstances, afford cogent evidence upon which a jury would be justified in finding that he wilfully encouraged and so aided and abetted. But it would be purely a question for the jury whether he did so or not. So if any number of persons arrange that a criminal offence shall take place, and it takes place accordingly, the mere presence of any of those who so arranged it would afford abundant evidence for the consideration of a jury of an aiding and abetting.

In this court the question of aiding and abetting was canvassed in *Preston v. The King*, 93 C.C.C. 81, [1949] S.C.R. 156, 7 C.R. 72. The appellant and another were accused of having set fire to a school. Mr. Justice Estey delivered the majority judgment in this court, in the course of which he stated (p. 159) that in order to find the appellant guilty of aiding, abetting, counselling or procuring, it was only necessary to show that he understood what was taking place and by some act on his part encouraged or assisted in the attainment thereof. Later he said (p. 160) that mere presence does not constitute aiding and abetting, but presence under certain circumstances may itself be evidence thereof. He proceeded to review the evidence and concluded, p. 85 C.C.C., p. 161 S.C.R.:

> If appellant's explanation was not believed by the jury there was *evidence in addition to his mere presence* upon which they might well conclude that he was guilty of aiding, abetting, counselling or procuring. (Emphasis added.)

Two Canadian cases make the distinction between presence with prior knowledge, and accidental presence. In *R. v. Dick* (1947), 87 C.C.C. 101, 2 C.R. 417 (Ont. C.A.), the accused was charged with the murder of her husband. According to her own statement, she met her husband and Bohozuk, a friend, and they went with her in a borrowed car, her husband in the front seat and Bohozuk in the back. The two men began to quarrel, both were drinking; Bohozuk pulled a gun and shot Mr. Dick. It was not a happy marriage, nor were Mr. Dick and Bohozuk on best of terms. There was some surrounding evidence casting doubt upon the non-involvement of the accused. As Chief Justice Robertson noted, she did not admit that there was any design, nor that she knew Bohozuk intended to shoot Dick, nor even that she knew Bohozuk had a weapon with him. Yet the trial judge gave only general directions on aiding and abetting to the jury. Robertson C.J.O. concluded at p. 116 C.C.C., pp. 432-3 C.R.:

Now, while it may be that a jury might infer from the evidence a good deal that is not expressly admitted, it is not at all certain that this jury did infer that the appellant knew more than she admits knowing of Bohozuk's then present purpose. This jury should have been instructed that if they found that the appellant was no more than passively acquiescent at the time of the shooting, and that she had no reason to expect that there would be any shooting until it actually occurred, then s. 69 did not apply:

In the result, a new trial was ordered.

In *R. v. Hoggan*, [1966] 3 C.C.C. 1, 47 C.R. 256 (Alta. C.A.), the charge was that the accused aided and abetted in wilfully attempting to defeat the course of justice by attempting to dissuade a witness from giving evidence. Johnson J.A. concluded at p. 5 C.C.C., p. 260 C.R.:

> There are two things that must be proved before an accused can be convicted of being a party by aiding and abetting. It must first be proved that he had knowledge that the principal intended to commit the offence and that the accused aided and abetted him. Where there is no knowledge that an offence is to be committed, the presence of an accused at the scene of the crime cannot be a circumstance which would be evidence of aiding and abetting.

The basis for Johnson J.A.'s approach to aiding and abetting is found in *Preston* and *Coney*, both of which he cites.

The case of *R. v. Salajko*, [1970] 1 C.C.C. 352, 9 C.R.N.S. 145 (Ont. C.A.), is like the instant case in many respects. A girl was raped by 15 young men in a lonely field. Three were charged. Two of these were identified as having had intercourse with the girl. She admitted, however, that the third accused, Salajko, though seen to be near the girl with his pants down while she was being raped by others, did not have intercourse with her. The Crown placed its case against him on s. 21 (1)(*b*) and (*c*) of the *Criminal Code*. One might be forgiven for thinking that it was open to the jury to infer encouragement by conduct, but the Ontario Court of Appeal thought otherwise. Chief Justice Gale, delivering the judgment of the court, stated that in the absence of evidence to suggest something in the way of aiding, or counselling, or encouraging on the part of the accused with respect to that which was being done by the others, there was simply no evidence upon which a jury could properly arrive at a verdict of guilty against the particular accused. The learned Chief Justice also found error in the trial judge's charge which seemed to indicate that a person could abet another in the commission of an offence if, knowingly, he stood by while the offence was being committed.

Finally, there are the cases of *R. v. Black*, [1970] 4 C.C.C. 251, 10 C.R.N.S. 17, and *R. v. Clarkson*, [1971] 3 All E.R. 344. The victim in *Black's* case was conveyed to a clubhouse where he was subjected to various sordid indignities. Many of the accused took an active part in torturing the victim while others stood around laughing and yelling. The British Columbia Court of Appeal confirmed the convictions, being of the view that the spectators furnished encouragement to the perpetrators of the outrages and their mere presence in the circumstances of the case ensured against the escape of the victim. There was thus something more than "mere presence", as in *R. v. Coney, supra*. Most important, the trial judge directed the jury in language drawn from the judgment of Hawkins J. in *Coney* and reviewed the evidence relating to the presence of the accused in clear terms.

In contrast to *R. v. Black* is the case of *R. v. Clarkson*, a decision of the Court Martial Appeal Court. A girl was raped in a room in a barracks in Germany by a number of soldiers. Another group of soldiers clustered outside the door and later "piled in" to the room. They remained there for a considerable time while the girl was raped. There was no evidence that the appellants had done any physical act, or uttered any word, which involved direct physical participation or verbal encouragement. There was no evidence that they touched the girl, or did anything to prevent others from assisting her or to prevent her from escaping. The Appeal Court held that it was not enough that the presence of the accused, in fact, gave encouragement, "It must be proved that the accused intended to give encouragement; that he *wilfully* encouraged" (p. 347). There must be, the court held, an intention to encourage and encouragement in fact. The convictions were quashed.

The case at bar

In the case at bar I have great difficulty in finding any evidence of anything more than mere presence and passive acquiescence. Presence at the commission of an offence can be evidence of aiding and abetting if accompanied by other factors, such as prior knowledge of the principal offender's intention to commit the offence or attendance for the purpose of encouragment. There was no evidence that while the crime was being committed either of the accused rendered aid, assistance or encouragement to the rape of B.R. There was no evidence of any positive act or omission to facilitate the unlawful purpose. One can infer that the two accused knew that a party was to be held, and that their presence at the dump was not accidental or in the nature of casual passers-by, but that is not sufficient. A person cannot properly be convicted of aiding or abetting in the commission of acts which he does not know may be or are intended: *per* Viscount Dilhorne in *Director of Public Prosecutions for Northern Ireland v. Maxwell*, [1978] 3 All E.R. 1140 at p. 1144 (H.L.). One must be able to infer that the accused had prior knowledge that an offence of the type committed was planned, *i.e.*, that their presence was with knowledge of the intended rape. On this issue, the Crown elicited no evidence.

In concluding that there was evidence of a nature which would permit the jury to draw an inference that the accused were more than merely present at a crime and had done nothing to prevent it, Mr. Justice Matas referred to the earlier meeting of the Spartans at the dump (with Sylvester and Dunlop present) when Douglas was introduced as a prospect, the presence of members of the group at the Waldorf beverage room where the complainant and her friend were spending some time, the bringing of the complainant by Douglas to the dump, the reappearance of a group of Spartans at the same location (where the gang rape took place), the arrival of the accused with a substantial quantity of beer, and the observation by both accused of intercourse taking place by the complainant and one male, but with other men nearby.

The activities of Douglas are twice mentioned by Mr. Justice Matas, but it must be recalled that Douglas was not one of the accused. Dunlop and Sylvester bear no responsibility for what he may or may not have done. Apart from presence earlier in the evening at the dump and at the Waldorf beverage room, the evidence Mr. Justice Matas marshalls against Dunlop and Sylvester is (i) their arrival at the dump with a substantial quantity of beer, and (ii) their observation of intercourse. In my view, for the reasons I have earlier sought to express, neither of these facts is capable in law of affording evidence that the appellants aided and the commission of the crime of rape. They go only to mere presence and not to complicity.

With great respect, I am unable to find in the evidence to which Mr. Justice Matas alludes, or elsewhere, any facts as distinguished from surmise or suspicion, upon which any jury could conclude beyond reasonable doubt that the accused had assumed a role which would qualify them as aiders and abettors under s. 21(1) of the *Code*.

In these circumstances, in my view, the trial judge erred in charging the jury on the alternative bases of (i) principal offender, and (ii) aider and abettor.

Conclusion

If the trial judge was in error in charging upon s. 21(2), which is admitted and, as I believe, in error in his recharge on s. 21(1), what disposition is to be made of the case? The majority view in the Manitoba Court of Appeal was that the trial judge had not erred in his answer to the jury's question. As to the admitted error in charging as to common intention under s. 21(2), Mr. Justice Matas said [at p. 101]:

> But it is apparent from the juror's question that the members were not troubled by the concept of common intention. In any event, in light of all the evidence and the whole charge, I am satisfied that no substantial wrong or miscarriage of justice occurred.

The difficulty one faces is that we do not know, and will never know, whether the jury found the appellants guilty because they had had intercourse with the complainant, or by reason of the operation of s-ss. (1) or (2) of s. 21 of the *Code*. We do know from the question of the jury, and its timing, that after two hours and 25 minutes of deliberation the jury had not accepted the evidence of the complainant as to direct participation by the appellants. Fifteen minutes after resuming deliberation, following the recharge, the guilty verdict was returned.

I do not think this is an appropriate case for the application of s. 613(1)(b)(iii). I am unable to say that the verdict would have been the same in the absence of error. For the following reasons given by Mr. Justice Hall, I would direct a verdict of acquittal, rather than have the applicants undergo a third trial [at p. 98]:

> The accused have been subjected to two trials and a like number of appeals. They have been in custody over a year. The doubt raised on their innocence or guilt should be resolved now. The substance of the case is their denial against the testimony of B.R., without much more. In the circumstances, the needs of justice would be met by directing a verdict of acquittal, rather than having the accused submit to a trial for the third time.

I would allow the appeals, set aside the judgment of the Manitoba Court of Appeal, and direct a verdict of acquittal in respect of each appellant.

MARTLAND J. (dissenting) (RITCHIE and PIGEON JJ. concurring): — The appellants were convicted by a jury on a charge of rape. The facts giving rise to this charge are stated in the reasons of my brother Dickson.

It is not disputed that mere presence at the scene of a crime is not, in itself, sufficient to establish aiding or abetting the commission of an offence, but the trial Judge did not instruct the jury that it was. He charged the jury that "it is only necessary to show that he understood what was being done and by some act on his part assisted or encouraged the attainment of that act".

. . . .

In my opinion, there was evidence on which the jury could conclude that the appellants had aided and abetted the commission of the offence. The jury had been properly instructed as to what was necessary in order to establish aiding and abetting. The sufficiency of that evidence was solely a matter for the determination of the jury and was not a matter to be decided by the Court of Appeal.

Martland J. regarded the response of the trial judge to the jury in question as not offensive when read in the context of the evidence of that evening's events. The minority accordingly would have dismissed the appeal. Pratte J. (Beetz J. concurring) agreed that the appeal should be disposed of in the manner proposed by Dickson J. but on the narrower ground relating to the response of the trial judge to the jury's question.

Appeals allowed; acquittals entered.

Kulbacki, a 20-year-old man, owned a motor vehicle and was sitting in the front passenger seat while a 16-year-old female drove the car at speeds over 90 m.p.h. on an unimproved municipal highway. He did and said nothing to stop, prevent, or attempt to stop or prevent the driver from driving in that manner. **Is**

he guilty of dangerous driving? See *R. v. Kulbacki*, 47 C.R. 233, [1966] 1 C.C.C. 167, 1965 CarswellMan 41 (Man. C.A.).

R. v. LAURENCELLE

(1999), 28 C.R. (5th) 157, 1999 CarswellBC 2109 (B.C.C.A.)

1   ESSON J.A. (orally):— The appeal by Ms. Laurencelle is against her conviction by a Provincial Court judge on a charge of unlawful confinement.

2   The facts of the case are these. At about 10:30 on a Saturday evening in July, Robert McCarron was kidnapped by four men from the parking lot of a grocery store. They used knives to force him to go with them to a nearby house. Two of the men were never identified; one of them was identified as Bradley McCandless ("McCandless") and another as Jeromy Biron ("Biron"). McCandless subsequently pleaded guilty to charges of kidnapping and unlawful confinement and, I believe, two other charges that arose out of the overall incident.

3   The victim was kept in the house from Saturday evening until the following Tuesday when he escaped. He was the only witness at the trial of the appellant. He surmised from what he observed that the house was the home of the appellant and Biron and, as well, the appellant's daughter was there at times. In the course of the original kidnapping, the complainant was threatened by two of the men and assaulted by McCandless. All of this took place without the appellant knowing anything about it at that stage. At about 11:00 p.m. McCandless forced the victim to turn over various items, including his bank card and keys, and also forced him to reveal his personal identification number so that his bank card could be used. With the bank card and that information, McCandless was able to liberate some $2,400 from the bank account apparently in several stages over the period of time the victim was held.

4   During the time of his confinement, the victim was kept bound by tape around his legs and his hands were also bound with tape. McCandless was the prime player in taking those steps. The victim was allowed to use the washroom on a number of occasions by McCandless, who would cut the tape from him and escort him to the washroom, then re-apply the tape after he came out of the washroom.

5   The appellant first had knowledge of anything to do with this at about 11:30 p.m. on the Saturday evening when she arrived home with her daughter. She was heard by the victim to say "What's going on?", and it appeared to him that they then went to another room and had a conversation of which he did not know the contents. The appellant's contact with the complainant consisted of her providing him with water on more than one occasion, and on one occasion

removing the tape from his hands so that he could smoke a cigarette. She attempted to comfort him. The victim said that, after her first conversation with McCandless on the Saturday evening, she appeared to be afraid of McCandless, and she told the victim that she was afraid of McCandless and Biron. The evidence of that statement by her, I note, was led by the Crown in his direct evidence. She was asked by the victim when he would be let go, she assured him that he would be let go and that he would be okay.

6   From time to time between the Saturday evening and the Tuesday when the escape took place, McCandless left the residence to re-appear with new clothing and other personal items which the victim assumed were purchased with his bank card. There is no evidence that the appellant shared in any way from the fruits of these crimes. The victim could not say definitely whether he and the appellant were ever alone in the house, although as far as he knew, they were not. She took no part in tying him up, assaulting or threatening him, other than the one incident of untying him so that he could smoke a cigarette. The victim said he was not afraid of the appellant and that he did not believe that the appellant was involved in the kidnapping or the confinement. In his evidence, he said this:

> *Q* And, in fact, her involvement with you to the limited extent that it was, appeared to you to make—an attempt to make you more comfortable, is that right?
>
> *A* That's right.
>
> *Q* And she expressed concern to you for your wellbeing, your health, your safety, etcetera?
>
> *A* Yeah, she did.
>
> . . . .
>
> *Q* And you didn't see Ms. Laurencelle with any new belongings?
>
> *A* No I didn't.
>
> . . . .
>
> *Q* So if I understand you correctly, Ms. Laurencelle took no active part in anything relating to you, isn't that right?
>
> *A* Yeah, I don't think so.

7   The appellant alleges these errors on the part of the trial judge:

> 1. The learned Trial Judge erred in finding that the Appellant's act of caring for the Complainant made her a party to the offence.

2. The learned Trial Judge erred in finding that the Appellant's omission of failing to leave the Residence made her a party to the offence.

3. The verdict was unreasonable and unsupported by the evidence.

8   It is common ground that the applicable law is as stated by the Supreme Court of Canada in *Dunlop and Sylvester v. The Queen* (1979), 47 C.C.C. (2d) 93 (S.C.C.). Dickson J. (later C.J.C.) said at p. 106:

> In order for an accused person to be convicted as a party to an offence, the Crown must prove that accused actually committed the offence, or that she aided or abetted another to commit it within the meaning of s. 21 of the *Criminal Code*. The Crown must therefore prove that an accused who was present during the commission of an offence was more than passively acquiescent to the commission of the offence.

The principal submission of the appellant is that there was nothing that went beyond passive acquiescence on her part.

9   The trial judge in convicting the appellant on this count said this:

> There was no indication that the accused was aware that the kidnapping and confinement was going to take place, but upon entering her own home some short time after the offence she saw the complainant or the victim bound. She knew what had occurred and unfortunately for her made a wrong decision.

> At that point in time she could have left and there would have been no burden on her to do anything else and she could not have become involved in this matter. She did not leave immediately. In fact, she did not leave at all. She stayed. She stayed in the home. She allowed the victim and Bradley McCandless and Biron to remain, which is more than passive acquiescence. She helped in the care of the victim and as I said she allowed her home to be used as a place of confinement, thereby encouraging the other co-accused in their venture.

> It was reported by the victim that she said she was afraid of Brad and Jeromy. It is left open to the court to wonder why she said that. Was she afraid or equally plausible, was this said to instill fear in the victim? She was free to come and go at any time. There was a safe avenue of escape available at all times. There was no evidence before me to indicate any reason why she could not walk out the door. She chose not to do that.

> She may have been doing it in a kindly manner, but nonetheless, she was unlawfully confining the victim under all the circumstances that I heard this morning and I find her guilty of count two.

10   I should mention that the Crown laid the same charges against the appellant as they did against McCandless, which included kidnapping and robbery and I believe a fourth count, thus the reference to count two. The trial judge did dismiss the other counts so we are dealing only with unlawful confinement.

11   It is my view, with respect, that the passage which I have quoted from the judge's reasons indicates that she lost sight of the principle that the burden

of proving participation was on the Crown. She appears to have imposed a duty on the appellant to leave the house, and perhaps more importantly, she found that the appellant "allowed" McCandless and Biron to remain. In my view, the evidence provides no reasonable basis for finding a duty to leave or for finding that the appellant allowed McCandless and Biron to remain and continue the confinement. The evidence, since it all comes from the victim, is very hazy as to what the appellant's relationship was to the house but, from what little evidence there is, it can be taken that she and Biron were both living there and both, to that extent, had some control over the premises. There is no basis for asserting that the appellant had sole control, and certainly no basis as a matter of common sense for suggesting that she had any effective way of requiring McCandless and Biron to leave. This case is quite different from the various cases which have found that control can lead to a person being found a party by allowing premises or automobiles to be used in an unlawful manner.

12   The judge's observation that she was left to wonder whether the appellant said to the victim that she was afraid in order to instill fear in him is mere speculation. It would almost seem to imply an assumption that the accused should have given evidence, since it was only the accused who could have "left it open to the court to wonder" why she said that. However that may be, it was not an appropriate basis upon which to reject the otherwise contradicted evidence that she had expressed fear. I will observe finally on that point that the suggestion that she was being devious in saying she was afraid is inconsistent with her other behaviour towards the victim.

13   The Crown submits that the acts of kindness amounted to aiding and abetting the offence of confinement. With respect, I can find no adequate basis for making that connection. For those reasons, I would allow the appeal, set aside the conviction, and direct that an acquittal be entered.

In *R. v. Arias-Jackson*, 52 C.R. (6th) 1 (*sub nom.* R. v. Jackson), [2007] 3 S.C.R. 514, a 5-2 majority confirmed the conviction of aiding marijuana production where the accused had been found in a wilderness camp tent near a drier on a marijuana production site. To the dissenters this was a conviction wrongly based on mere presence contrary to *Dunlop*. However, in *R. c. Rochon*, 299 C.C.C. (3d) 202, [2012] 2 S.C.R. 673, a 6-1 majority confirmed the acquittal of a mother of aiding and abetting marijuana production. She became aware her son was growing marijuana on her property. He refused her request to stop but she did not report him to the police.

In *R. v. Dooley* (2009), 249 C.C.C. (3d) 449 (Ont. C.A.), leave to appeal refused [2010] 2 S.C.R. vi, the Ontario Court of Appeal confirmed the conviction of both parents of the second degree murder of a son, one as perpetrator and one as aiding or abetting. The jury had been properly directed that failure by a parent to perform his or her parental duty to protect could be viewed as a form of aid to the other parent to continue the abuse. However, in a similar parental abuse case in *R. v. Palombi* (2007), 222 C.C.C. (3d) 528 (Ont. C.A.), the Court ordered a new trial where the trial judge had not charged the jury that aiding required an intent to assist rather than mere awareness of abuse.

R. v. BRISCOE

[2010] 1 S.C.R 411, 2010 CarswellAlta 589, 2010 CarswellAlta 588,
73 C.R. (6th) 224, 253 C.C.C. (3d) 140

The accused was charged with kidnapping, aggravated assault and first degree murder. He had been one of a group of five people who had lured a 13-year-old girl to a secluded area. Two of the other male members of the group raped her and she was killed by the application of various types of force by several members of the group. Briscoe did not apply any force which contributed to her death, though he stood by and watched the rape and murder. The Crown's theory was that another member of the group, Laboucan, was the mastermind who had formulated the plan, selected the victim and communicated the plan to the others. Briscoe's actions constituted aiding the offences. He had driven the group to and from the crime scene, chosen a secluded location, provided and transported weapons (a wrench and a mallet), at an early point held the victim and told her to shut up, and had threatened a friend of the victim who was also present. The Crown also submitted that, even apart from Briscoe's acts of assistance, his presence coupled with his knowledge of the plan made him an abettor. His presence could lend courage to the attackers, discourage rescue, and give the victim further reason to feel helpless and lost and futile. The trial judge agreed that the external elements were proven but held that the Crown had not proven the *mens rea* for party liability beyond a reasonable doubt. The Supreme Court of Canada ordered a new trial.

CHARRON J. (for the Court): —

[13] Canadian criminal law does not distinguish between the principal offender and parties to an offence in determining criminal liability. Section 21(1) of the *Criminal Code* makes perpetrators, aiders, and abettors equally liable:

21. (1) Every one is a party to an offence who

(*a*) actually commits it;

(*b*) does or omits to do anything for the purpose of aiding any person to commit it; or

(*c*) abets any person in committing it.

The person who provides the gun, therefore, may be found guilty of the same offence as the one who pulls the trigger. The *actus reus* and *mens rea* for aiding or abetting, however, are distinct from those of the principal offence.

[14] The *actus reus* of aiding or abetting is doing (or, in some circumstances, omitting to do) something that assists or encourages the perpetrator to commit

the offence. While it is common to speak of aiding and abetting together, the two concepts are distinct, and liability can flow from either one. Broadly speaking, "[t]o aid under s. 21(1)(*b*) means to assist or help the actor. . . . To abet within the meaning of s. 21(1)(*c*) includes encouraging, instigating, promoting or procuring the crime to be committed": *R. v. Greyeyes*, [1997] 2 S.C.R. 825, at para. 26. The *actus reus* is not at issue in this appeal. As noted earlier, the Crown argued at trial that Mr. Briscoe was both an aider and an abettor. The trial judge's finding that Mr. Briscoe performed the four acts of assistance described above is not disputed.

[15] Of course, doing or omitting to do something that resulted in assisting another in committing a crime is not sufficient to attract criminal liability. As the Court of Appeal for Ontario wrote in *R. v. F. W. Woolworth Co.* (1974), 3 O.R. (2d) 629, "one does not render himself liable by renting or loaning a car for some legitimate business or recreational activity merely because the person to whom it is loaned or rented chooses in the course of his use to transport some stolen goods, or by renting a house for residential purposes to a tenant who surreptitiously uses it to store drugs" (p. 640). The aider or abettor must also have the requisite mental state or *mens rea*. Specifically, in the words of s. 21(1)(*b*), the person must have rendered the assistance *for the purpose* of aiding the principal offender to commit the crime.

[16] The *mens rea* requirement reflected in the word "purpose" under s. 21(1)(*b*) has two components: intent and knowledge. For the intent component, it was settled in *R. v. Hibbert*, [1995] 2 S.C.R. 973, that "purpose" in s. 21(1)(*b*) should be understood as essentially synonymous with "intention". The Crown must prove that the accused intended to assist the principal in the commission of the offence. The Court emphasized that "purpose" should not be interpreted as incorporating the notion of "desire" into the fault requirement for party liability. It is therefore not required that the accused desired that the offence be successfully committed (*Hibbert*, at para. 35). The Court held, at para. 32, that the perverse consequences that would flow from a "purpose equals desire" interpretation of s. 21(1)(*b*) were clearly illustrated by the following hypothetical situation described by Mewett and Manning:

> If a man is approached by a friend who tells him that he is going to rob a bank and would like to use his car as the getaway vehicle for which he will pay him $100, when that person is . . . charged under s. 21 for doing something for the purpose of aiding his friend to commit the offence, can he say "My purpose was not to aid the robbery but to make $100"? His argument would be that while he knew that he was helping the robbery, his desire was to obtain $100 and he did not care one way or the other whether the robbery was successful or not.

(A. W. Mewett and M. Manning, *Criminal Law* (2nd ed. 1985), at p. 112)

The same rationale applies regardless of the principal offence in question. Even in respect of murder, there is no "additional requirement that an aider or abettor subjectively approve of or desire the victim's death" (*Hibbert*, at para. 37 (emphasis deleted)).

[17] As for knowledge, in order to have the intention to assist in the commission of an offence, the aider must know that the perpetrator intends to commit the crime, although he or she need not know precisely how it will be committed. That sufficient knowledge is a prerequisite for intention is simply a matter of common sense. Doherty J.A. in *R. v. Maciel*, 2007 ONCA 196, 219 C.C.C. (3d) 516, provides the following useful explanation of the knowledge requirement which is entirely apposite to this case (at paras. 88-89):

> ... a person who is alleged to have aided in a murder must be shown to have known that the perpetrator had the intent required for murder under s. 229(a): *R. v. Kirkness* (1990), 60 C.C.C. (3d) 97 (S.C.C.) at 127.

The same analysis applies where it is alleged that the accused aided a perpetrator in the commission of a first degree murder that was planned and deliberate. The accused is liable as an aider only if the accused did something to assist the perpetrator in the planned and deliberate murder and if, when the aider rendered the assistance, he did so for the purpose of aiding the perpetrator in the commission of a planned and deliberate murder. Before the aider could be said to have the requisite purpose, the Crown must prove that the aider knew the murder was planned and deliberate. Whether the aider acquired that knowledge through actual involvement in the planning and deliberation or through some other means, is irrelevant to his or her culpability under s. 21(1).

[18] It is important to note that Doherty J.A., in referring to this Court's decision in *R. v. Kirkness*, [1990] 3 S.C.R. 74, rightly states that the aider to a murder must "have known that the perpetrator had the intent required for murder". While some of the language in *Kirkness* may be read as requiring that the aider share the murderer's intention to kill the victim, the case must now be read in the light of the above-noted analysis in *Hibbert*. The perpetrator's intention to kill the victim must be known to the aider or abettor; it need not be shared. *Kirkness* should not be interpreted as requiring that the aider and abettor of a murder have the same *mens rea* as the actual killer. It is sufficient that he or she, armed with *knowledge* of the perpetrator's intention to commit the crime, acts with the intention of assisting the perpetrator in its commission. It is only in this sense that it can be said that the aider and abettor must intend that the principal offence be committed.

. . . .

[25] In this case, I agree with Martin J.A. that the trial judge erred in law by failing to consider wilful blindness. As he noted, even Mr. Briscoe's own

statements to the police suggest that he had a "strong, well-founded suspicion that someone would be killed at the golf course" (para. 30) and that he may have been wilfully blind to the kidnapping and prospect of sexual assault. His statements also show that he deliberately chose not to inquire about what the members of the group intended to do because he did not want to know. As he put it, "whatever you guys wanna do just do it. Don't do it around me I don't want to see nothing I don't know what the fuck you're gonna do." The trial judge relied heavily upon the statements in his reasons but did not refer to the doctrine of wilful blindness. Of course, whether Mr. Briscoe had the requisite *mens rea* for the three offences was a question for the trier of fact, and Mr. Briscoe is entitled to the benefit of any reasonable doubt on this issue. However, from a legal standpoint, it is my respectful view that the evidence cried out for an analysis on wilful blindness. In these circumstances, the Court of Appeal rightly concluded that the trial judge's failure to consider Mr. Briscoe's knowledge from that perspective constitutes a legal error which necessitates a new trial on all charges.

In *R. v. Simpson* (1988), 62 C.R. (3d) 137 (S.C.C.), the Supreme Court unanimously held that the unlawful purpose in s. 21(2) must be different from the offence actually charged. The "unlawful purpose" and the "offence" committed in the course of the pursuit of the unlawful purpose were different. This settled a long-standing conflict of opinion in lower courts.

R. v. LOGAN

[1990] 2 S.C.R. 731, 79 C.R. (3d) 169, 58 C.C.C. (3d) 391,
1990 CarswellOnt 1002, 1990 CarswellOnt 110

The accused were convicted of attempted murder. During a robbery a person was shot and severely injured. Neither accused did the shooting. Johnson admitted to being one of the robbers but stated that he had no intention to shoot and that there had been no discussion concerning the use of guns. Logan had boasted of being involved in planning the robberies. The trial judge instructed the jury that there could be convictions, under s. 21(2), if the Crown established beyond a reasonable doubt that the accused knew or ought to have known that someone would probably shoot with the intention of killing. The Court of Appeal allowed appeals with respect to the convictions for attempted murder and substituted convictions for robbery. The Crown appealed.

LAMER C.J.C. (DICKSON C.J.C., WILSON, GONTHIER and CORY JJ. concurring): —

The appellant is challenging the constitutionality of s. 21(2) in general and, in particular, of the objective component of the section ("ought to have known").

However, the Court of Appeal, quite correctly, did not declare the objective component of s. 21(2) inoperative for all offences. They dealt specifically with the operation of the provision in relation to the offence of attempted murder and the possibility that a party to an attempted murder could be convicted upon proof of objective intent, whereas a conviction of the principal would require proof of subjective intent. More generally, as a basis for their decision, the court determined that it is a principle of fundamental justice that a party to *any* offence cannot be found guilty of the offence based on a lower standard of requisite *mens rea* than that required for convicting the principal.

For this proposition, the court relied on our judgment in *Vaillancourt*. In that case, this court held that for a few offences the principles of fundamental justice require that a conviction cannot stand unless there is proof beyond a reasonable doubt of a minimum degree of *mens rea*, and that legislation providing for any lesser degree violates the *Charter* and is inoperative. Murder was one of those offences.

With respect, I cannot construe *Vaillancourt* as saying that, as a general proposition, Parliament cannot ever enact provisions requiring different levels of guilt for principal offenders and parties. Although I readily admit that, as a matter of policy, the proposition seems more equitable than not, I am not ready to characterize it as a principle of fundamental justice. It must be remembered that within many offences there are varying degrees of guilt, and it remains the function of the sentencing process to adjust the punishment for each individual offender accordingly. The argument that the principles of fundamental justice prohibit the conviction of a party to an offence on the basis of a lesser degree of *mens rea* than that required to convict the principal could be supported only, if at all, in a situation where the sentence for a particular offence is fixed. However, currently in Canada the sentencing scheme is flexible enough to accommodate the varying degrees of culpability resulting from the operation of ss. 21 and 22.

That said, however, there are a few offences with respect to which the operation of the objective component of s. 21(2) will restrict the rights of an accused under s. 7. If an offence is one of the few for which s. 7 requires a minimum degree of *mens rea*, *Vaillancourt* does preclude Parliament from providing for the conviction of a party to that offence on the basis of a degree of *mens rea* below the constitutionally-required minimum.

Requisite mens rea for conviction pursuant to s. 21(2)

Therefore, the question whether a party to an offence had the requisite *mens rea* to found a conviction pursuant to s. 21(2) must be answered in two steps. Firstly, is there a minimum degree of *mens rea* which is required as a principle of fundamental justice before one can be convicted as a principal for this particular offence? This is an important initial step because if there is no such constitutional requirement for the offence, the objective component of s. 21(2) can operate without restricting the constitutional rights of the party to the offence. Secondly, if the principles of fundamental justice do require a certain minimum degree of *mens rea* in order to convict for this offence, then that minimum degree of *mens rea* is constitutionally required to convict a party to that offence as well.

Step 1: Section 7 and Attempted Murder

With respect to the case at bar, then, the first question which must be answered is whether the principles of fundamental justice require a minimum degree of *mens rea* in order to convict an accused of attempted murder. *Ancio* established that a specific intent to kill is the *mens rea* required for a principal on the charge of attempted murder. However, as the constitutional question was not raised or argued in that case, it did not decide whether that requisite *mens rea* was a *constitutional* requirement. The case simply interpreted the offence as currently legislated.

In *R. v. Martineau*, a judgment handed down this day, this court has decided, as a constitutional requirement, that no one can be convicted of murder unless the Crown proves beyond a reasonable doubt that the person had *subjective* foresight of the fact that the death of the victim was likely to ensue. Because of both the stigma and the severe penal consequences which result from a conviction for murder, the Constitution requires at least that degree of intent.

As defined in *Ancio*, the elements of *mens rea* for attempted murder are identical to those for the most severe form of murder, murder under s. 212(*a*)(i) [now s. 229 (*a*)(i)]. For each, the accused must have had the specific intent to kill. All that differs is the "consequences" component of the *actus reus*. Quite simply, an attempted murderer is, if caught and convicted, a "lucky murderer". Therefore, it would seem logical that the requisite *mens rea* for a murder conviction, as described in *Martineau*, must be the same for a conviction of attempted murder. However, logic is not sufficient reason to label something a "constitutional requirement". As I have stated in *Vaillancourt*, the principles of fundamental justice require a minimum degree of *mens rea* for only a very few offences. The criteria by which these offences can be identified are, primarily, the stigma associated with a conviction and, as a secondary consideration, the penalties available.

The stigma associated with a conviction for attempted murder is the same as it is for murder. Such a conviction reveals that, although no death ensued from the actions of the accused, the intent to kill was still present in his or her mind. The attempted murderer is no less a killer than a murderer: he may be lucky — the ambulance arrived early, or some other fortuitous circumstance — but he still has the same killer instinct. Secondly, while a conviction for attempted murder does not automatically result in a life sentence, the offence is punishable by life and the usual penalty is very severe.

It should be noted that, as a basis for a constitutionally-required minimum degree of *mens rea*, the social stigma associated with a conviction is the most important consideration, not the sentence. Few offences have a high minimum sentence such as that for murder. For some offences there is a high maximum and a low minimum penalty available; for other offences the maximum penalty is much reduced and there is no minimum imposed whatsoever. In either situation, the fact that a lesser sentence is available or imposed, by statute or through the exercise of judicial discretion, in no way ends the inquiry. The sentencing range available to the Judge is not conclusive of the level of *mens rea* constitutionally required. Instead, the crucial consideration is whether there is a continuing serious social stigma which will be imposed on the accused upon conviction.

For example, the offence of theft in the most serious circumstances is punishable by a maximum of ten years or, in less serious circumstances, a maximum of two years if the Crown proceeds by indictment; if the Crown proceeds summarily, the maximum is six months. The constitutional *mens rea* requirement would not, under s. 7, be triggered by any punishment within these ranges which the sentencing Judge decided to impose. Whether the actual or available punishment is severe or not, the social stigma associated with being labelled dishonest will be automatically and unavoidably imposed upon conviction. It is because of this stigma that the principles of fundamental justice will require a minimum degree of *mens rea*, that is, as I said in *Vaillancourt*, at p. 653, "proof of some dishonesty".

For these reasons, the *mens rea* for attempted murder cannot, without restricting s. 7 of the *Charter*, require of the accused less of a mental element than that required of a murderer under s. 212(*a*)(i), that is, subjective foresight of the consequences. While Parliament, as I have already implied, could well extend our definition of attempted murder in *Ancio* to include the unsuccessful murderers of s. 212(*a*)(ii), it cannot go further and include objective foresight as being sufficient for a conviction without restricting s. 7 of the *Charter*.

Step 2: *Mens Rea* for Attempted Murder Pursuant to S. 21(2)

Having completed the initial step of the inquiry, one can proceed to the second step in determining the requisite *mens rea* for the conviction of a party pursuant to s. 21(2) on a charge of attempted murder. When the principles of fundamental justice require *subjective* foresight in order to convict a principal of attempted murder, that same minimum degree of *mens rea* is constitutionally required to convict a party to the offence of attempted murder. Any conviction for attempted murder, whether of the principal directly or of a party pursuant to s. 21(2), will carry enough stigma to trigger the constitutional requirement. To the extent that s. 21(2) would allow for the conviction of a party to the offence of attempted murder on the basis of objective foresight, its operation restricts s. 7 of the *Charter*.

Section 1 Analysis

Given the finding that s. 7 is restricted in the present case, can that restriction be found to be a reasonable limit demonstrably justified in a free and democratic society? The s. 1 analysis to be followed in answering this question has been set out in the decision of this court in *R. v. Oakes*, [1986] 1 S.C.R. 103, 50 C.R. (3d) 1, 24 C.C.C. (3d) 321.

. . . .

However, even though Parliament has sought to achieve an important legislative objective by enacting the restriction in issue in this appeal and even though such restriction is rationally connected to that objective, I am of the view that it does not satisfy the proportionality test because it unduly impairs an accused's rights under s. 7 of the *Charter*: see *Vaillancourt, supra*, at p. 651.

The objective component of s. 21(2) unduly impairs rights under s. 7 of the *Charter* when it operates with respect to an offence for which a conviction carries severe stigma and for which, therefore, there is a constitutionally-required minimum degree of *mens rea*. The words "ought to know" allow for the possibility that while a party may not have considered and accepted the risk that an accomplice may do something with the intent to kill in furtherance of the common purpose, the party, through this negligence, could still be found guilty of attempted murder. In other words, parties could be held to be criminally negligent with respect to the behaviour of someone else. For most offences under the *Criminal Code*, a person is convicted for criminal negligence only if consequences have ensued from their actions. While a person may be convicted, absent consequences, for criminal negligence (*e.g.*, dangerous operation of a motor vehicle), none of these forms of criminal negligence carry with them the stigma of being labelled a "killer". In a situation where s. 21(2) is operating in relation to the offence of attempted murder, no consequences have resulted from the actions of the party, and yet the party could be convicted of this offence and suffer severe accompanying stigma and penalty.

Because of the importance of the legislative purpose, the objective component of s. 21(2) can be justified with respect to most offences. However, with respect to the few offences for which the Constitution requires subjective intent, the stigma renders the infringement too serious and outweighs the legislative objective, which therefore cannot be justified under s. 1.

Conclusion

I would, therefore, as did the Court of Appeal, declare inoperative the words "or ought to have known" when considering under s. 21(2) whether a person is a party to any offence where it is a constitutional requirement for a conviction that foresight of the consequences be subjective, which is the case for attempted murder. Once these words are deleted, the remaining section requires, in the context of attempted murder, that the party to the common venture know that it is probable that his accomplice would do something with the intent to kill in carrying out the common purpose.

I would dismiss the appeal. I would restrict my answers to the constitutional questions as follows:

> 1. Does s. 21(2) of the *Criminal Code* contravene the rights and freedoms guaranteed by section 7 and/or section 11(*d*) of the *Canadian Charter of Rights and Freedoms*?

> Yes, on charges where subjective foresight is a constitutional requirement, to the extent that a party may be convicted if that person objectively "ought to have known" that the commission of the offence would be a probable consequence of carrying out the common purpose.

> 2. If the answer to question 1 is in the affirmative, is section 21(2) of the *Criminal Code* justified under section 1 of the *Canadian Charter of Rights and Freedoms*, and therefore not inconsistent with the *Constitution Act, 1982*?

> No.

L'Heureux-Dubé and Sopinka JJ. delivered separate concurring opinions.

A question which sometimes arises is whether the fact that a person changes his or her mind about committing an offence constitutes a defence. For principals the answer will generally be "no": either the person will have already committed the offence, will have done enough to be guilty of an attempt or will not be guilty in the first place. For parties, however, there will sometimes be the defence of "abandonment", as the Supreme Court explains in the next case.

R. v. GAUTHIER

2013 SCC 32, [2013] 2 S.C.R. 403, 298 C.C.C. (3d) 277, 2 C.R. (7th) 269

WAGNER J:

[38] . . . a defence of abandonment [for s. 21(2)] has three essential elements: (1) there must be an intention to abandon or withdraw from the unlawful purpose, (2) there must be timely communication of this abandonment or withdrawal from the person in question to those who wish to continue, and (3) the notice so communicated to those who continue to participate in the common purpose must be unequivocal.

[39] This appeal raises the issue of the application of the defence of abandonment in the context of the form of participation in a crime provided for in s. 21(1) of the *Criminal Code*.

. . . .

[The Court held that there were additional considerations when party liability was based on aiding or abetting rather than on common intention to carry out an unlawful purpose. In the latter context, they held, "[c]ommunicating the intention to abandon the common purpose reduces the resources available to carry out the unlawful purpose and in so doing cancels out the effects of the participation of the withdrawing or abandoning person" (para. 45). The same is not true, they held, for aiders and abettors.]

[46] . . . Aiders and abettors generally do much more than promise their support in carrying out an unlawful purpose in the future. They perform concrete acts to aid the principal offender to commit the offence or to abet him or her in committing it. Their criminal liability and their moral culpability are proportional to these acts and stem from the fact that they have performed them. Thus, merely communicating in unequivocal terms their intention to cease participating in the commission of the offence will not be enough "to break the chain of causation and responsibility", to repeat the words of Sloan J. from Whitehouse.

[47] Where a person's participation in a crime is more than a simple promise to carry out a common unlawful purpose — where, for example, the person is a party to the offence within the meaning of s. 21(1) of the *Criminal Code* — requiring an unequivocal communication of the intention to cease participating in the commission of the offence (the *Whitehouse* test) means that the accused must show that he or she took reasonable steps to neutralize the effects of his or her participation. As one author explains, using a colourful image to make his point, the intention to withdraw must be accompanied by acts that are likely to cancel out the effects of the acts that have already been performed to aid or abet the offender:

> Once the arrow is in the air, it is no use wishing to have never let it go — "Please God, let it miss!" The archer is guilty of homicide when the arrow gets the victim through the heart. The withdrawer, it is true, does not merely change his mind: he withdraws — but is that relevant if the withdrawal has no more effect on subsequent events than the archer's repentance? [Emphasis added.]

(J. C. Smith, Commentary on *R. v. Mitchell*, [1999] Crim. L.R. 497)

. . . .

[50] One who is a party to an offence on the basis that he or she did or omitted to do anything for the purpose of aiding any person to commit the offence, or abetted any person in committing it (s. 21(1) of the *Criminal Code*), or on the basis that he or she had formed with other persons an intention to carry out an unlawful purpose and to assist each other therein and that an offence was committed in carrying out the common purpose (s. 21(2) of the *Criminal Code*), may raise the defence of abandonment if the evidence shows

(1) that there was an intention to abandon or withdraw from the unlawful purpose;

(2) that there was timely communication of this abandonment or withdrawal from the person in question to those who wished to continue;

(3) that the communication served unequivocal notice upon those who wished to continue; and

(4) that the accused took, in a manner proportional to his or her participation in the commission of the planned offence, reasonable steps in the circumstances either to neutralize or otherwise cancel out the effects of his or her participation or to prevent the commission of the offence.

Fish J. was the sole dissenter on the basis that the fourth requirement had not been adopted before and was too restrictive.

3. COUNSELLING

Section 22 of the *Criminal Code* provides that:

(1) Where a person counsels another person to be a party to an offence and that other person is afterwards a party to that offence, the person who counselled is a party to that offence, notwithstanding that the offence was committed in a way different from that which was counselled.

(2) Every one who counsels another person to be a party to an offence is a party to every offence that the other commits in consequence of the counselling that the person who counselled knew or ought to have known was likely to be committed in consequence of the counselling.

(3) For the purposes of this Act, "counsel" includes procure, solicit or incite.

The court has noted that although "counsel" could have the ordinary meaning simply of advising, for criminal law purposes it must be limited to cases of actively inducing (*R. v. Sharpe*, 2001 SCC 2, [2001] 1 S.C.R. 45, 150 C.C.C. (3d) 321, 39 C.R. (5th) 72, para. 56).

The court has also described, in *R. v. Hamilton*, 2005 SCC 47, 198 C.C.C. (3d) 1, 30 C.R. (6th) 243, [2005] 2 S.C.R. 432, the external and fault elements of the offence:

29 In short, the *actus reus* for counselling is the deliberate encouragement or active inducement of the commission of a criminal offence. And the *mens rea* consists in nothing less than an accompanying intent or conscious disregard of the substantial and unjustified risk inherent in the counselling: that is, it must be shown that the accused either intended that the offence counselled be committed, or knowingly counselled the commission of the offence while aware of the unjustified risk that the offence counselled was in fact likely to be committed as a result of the accused's conduct. (emphasis in original).

Hamilton is discussed at greater length in Chapter 9 under "Liability for Offence not Committed".

4.   ACCESSORY AFTER FACT

R. v. DUONG

(1998), 15 C.R. (5th) 209, 124 C.C.C. (3d) 392,
1998 CarswellOnt 1784 (Ont. C.A.)

The accused was charged with being an accessory after the fact to a murder committed by one L. Two people were killed in December 1993. There were reports in the newspapers and on television connecting L to the homicides. The accused and L had been friends for five or six years. L called the accused and asked if he could stay at the accused's apartment. L indicated he was "in trouble for murder" and had no place to go. The accused had seen the media reports of the homicides and knew that L was in trouble. The accused allowed L to hide in his apartment for about two weeks. The police raided the apartment and found L hiding in the bedroom. The accused was specifically asked by the police what L told him about the homicides and he replied that he had told him he was in trouble but that the accused said he didn't want to know anything more because he knew he would be in trouble for helping him hide.

L was charged with two counts of first degree murder and three counts of attempted murder. After a lengthy trial he was convicted of two counts of second degree murder and two counts of attempted murder. The accused was convicted and appealed.

Section 23(1) of the *Criminal Code* provides:

An "accessory after the fact" to an offence is one who, knowing that a person has been a party to the offence, receives, comforts or assists that person for the purpose of enabling that person to escape.

DOHERTY J.A. (CATZMAN and AUSTIN JJ.A. concurring): —

There is little Canadian case law dealing with the knowledge requirement in s. 23(1), perhaps because the language of s. 23(1) is unambiguous. In *R. v. Vinette* (1974), [1975] 2 S.C.R. 222, 19 C.C.C. (2d) 1 (S.C.C.), the accused was charged with being an accessory after the fact to manslaughter. Both the majority (per Pigeon J. at p. 231 S.C.R., p. 7 C.C.C.) and the dissent (per Laskin C.J.C. at pp. 225-26 S.C.R., pp. 2-3 C.C.C.) accepted that the Crown had to prove that an accused charged with being an accessory after the fact to a homicide had knowledge of "the unlawful killing." Similarly, in *R. v. A. (M.)*, released March 22, 1996, this court proceeded on the basis that knowledge of the offence committed by the person aided was an essential element of the charge of being an accessory after the fact. See, also, D. Watt, "Accesssoryship After the Fact: Substantive Procedural and Evidentiary Considerations" (1981), 21 C.R. (3d) 307 at pp. 308, 318-19; V. Rose, *Parties to an Offence* (1982) at pp. 164-66, 194.

In other jurisdictions where provisions like s. 23(1) were in effect, or the common law prevailed, courts required that the Crown prove that the accessory after the fact knew of the specific offence committed by the person assisted: *R. v. Levy*, [1912] 1 K.B. 158 (Eng. Ct. of Crim. App.) at p. 160; *R. v. Tevendale*, [1955] V.L.R. 95 (Australia Vict. Sup. Ct.); *R. v. Carter* (1990), 47 A. Crim. R. 55 (Queensland C.A.) at p. 63; P. Gillies, *Criminal Law* (1990) at pp. 765-66. For example, in *R. v. Carter, supra*, Carter J. said at p. 63:

> It follows that in this case it was incumbent upon the Crown to establish the fact that the principal offender had done the acts said to constitute the offence of murder, that the accused knew that and, with that knowledge, received or assisted Carter in order to enable him to escape punishment.

The authorities referred to by Crown counsel rely on statutory language which is very different from that found in s. 23(1). These statutes create a more generic offence involving the hindering of an investigation, or interference with the apprehension or conviction of a person. For example, in *R. v. Morgan*, [1972] 1 Q.B. 436 (Eng. C.A.), the relevant statutory provision provided:

> Where a person has committed an arrestable offence, any other person who, *knowing or believing him to be guilty of the offence or of some other arrestable offence,* does without lawful authority or reasonable excuse any act with intent to impede his apprehension or prosecution shall be guilty of an offence. [Emphasis added.]

Parliament could have enacted similar legislation. It has not, however, done so and it is beyond the authority of the courts to enact such legislation by judicial fiat. I am not moved by the Crown's further contention that the requirement that the Crown prove that the accessory had knowledge of the offence committed by the person aided will allow individuals to escape justice when they aid someone believing that person has committed crime "x" when in fact the person has committed crime "y". If that is the effect of the present legislation, it is for Parliament to decide whether the statutory prohibition should be expanded. Moreover, it seems to me that the circumstances posited by the Crown would give rise to a charge of obstructing justice under s. 139(2) of the *Criminal Code*.

A charge laid under s. 23(1) must allege the commission of a specific offence (or offences) and the Crown must prove that the alleged accessory knew that the person assisted was a party to that offence. The Crown will meet its burden if it proves that the accused had actual knowledge of the offence committed. Whether wilful blindness will suffice is addressed below. The further question of whether recklessness as to the offence committed by the principal would be sufficient need not be decided in this case.

The appellant argues that wilful blindness can only be relied on by the Crown if the Crown proves that an accused whose suspicions were aroused had the means available to verify the accuracy of those suspicions. The appellant goes on to contend that he could have turned only to Lam to verify his suspicions and that the record does not suggest that Lam would have admitted his culpability in the murders. It follows, says the appellant, that he did not have the means available to him to verify his suspicions and should not, therefore, be held culpable on the basis of wilful blindness. The appellant cites no authority for this proposition.

Wilful blindness is explained in *Sansregret v. R.*, [1985] 1 S.C.R. 570 at p. 584, 18 C.C.C. (3d) 223 at p. 235:

> ... wilful blindness arises where a person who has become aware of the need for some inquiry declines to make the inquiry because he does not wish to know the truth. He would prefer to remain ignorant. The culpability in recklessness is justified by consciousness of the risk and by proceeding in the face of it, *while in wilful blindness it is justified by the accused's fault in deliberately failing to inquire when he knows there is reason for inquiry.* [Emphasis added.]

More recently, in *R. v. Hawkins*, [1995] 4 S.C.R. 55 at pp. 110-11, (*sub. nom. R. v. Jorgensen*) 102 C.C.C. (3d) 97 at p. 135, Sopinka J. described wilful blindness in these terms in reference to a charge of selling obscene material:

> ... *It is well established in criminal law that wilful blindness will also fulfil a mens rea requirement.* If the retailer becomes aware of the need to make further inquiries about the nature of the videos he was selling yet deliberately chooses to ignore these indications and does not make any further inquiries, then the retailer can be nonetheless charged under s. 163(2)(a) for "knowingly" selling obscene materials. *Deliberately choosing not to know something when given reason to believe further inquiry is necessary can satisfy the mental element of the offence. . . .*
>
> A finding of wilful blindness involves an affirmative answer to the question: Did the accused shut his eyes because he knew or strongly suspected that looking would fix him with knowledge? [Emphasis added.]

These authorities make it clear that where the Crown proves the existence of a fact in issue and knowledge of that fact is a component of the fault requirement of the crime charged, wilful blindness as to the existence of that fact is sufficient to establish a culpable state of mind. Liability based on wilful blindness is subjective. Wilful blindness refers to a state of mind which is aptly described as "deliberate ignorance" (Don Stuart, Canadian Criminal Law, 3rd ed. (1995), at p. 209). Actual suspicion, combined with a conscious decision not to make inquiries which could confirm that suspicion, is equated in the eyes of the criminal law with actual knowledge. Both are subjective and both are sufficiently blameworthy to justify the imposition of criminal liability.

The appellant's submission misunderstands the basis upon which liability is imposed where wilful blindness exists. Liability turns on the decision not to inquire once real suspicions arise and not on the hypothetical result of inquiries which were never made. Where an accused chooses to make no inquiries, preferring to remain "deliberately ignorant", speculation as to what the accused would have learned had he chosen to make the necessary inquiries is irrelevant to the determination of the blameworthiness of that accused's state of mind.

The appellant also submits that even if wilful blindness has application in the circumstances of this case, the trial judge erred in finding that the appellant was wilfully blind to the fact that Lam was a party to murder. This is in essence an argument that the trial judge's finding is unreasonable. It was urged that the appellant's statements to the police suggested only that he suspected that Lam had some connection, perhaps as a witness, to the homicides. The appellant submits that a finding of knowledge that Lam was a party to murder based on those statements was more speculation than reasonable inference.

It was certainly open to trial counsel to advance the argument now urged upon this court. I cannot say, however, that the trial judge's rejection of that argument and his conclusion that the appellant's suspicions extended to a suspicion that Lam had been a party to murder was unreasonable. It was open to him to infer that the appellant's statements revealed a state of mind which encompassed the suspicion that Lam was in trouble because he had been a party to murder. The fact that the appellant may have contemplated other possible connections between Lam and the murders afforded no bar to a finding that he was wilfully blind to the fact that Lam was a party to murder.

See also *R. v. Shalaan*, [1998] 1 S.C.R. 88, 121 C.C.C. (3d) 223, where the Supreme Court of Canada affirmed the decision of the Nova Scotia Court of Appeal in a murder case. The accused's husband had been killed in his home, while only the accused and a young person were present, and only one of those two people could have committed the killing. The trial judge ((1996), 153 N.S.R. (2d) 35, 108 C.C.C. (3d) 220 (N.S.S.C.)) had held that he was not persuaded beyond a reasonable doubt that the accused had performed the killing, and in fact was convinced that it was the young person who had committed the offence. He also held that the Crown had not proven that the accused had aided or abetted the crime, or had known in advance it would be committed. If she was guilty, then, it was only as an accessory after the fact, which he held required the Crown to prove:

> (i)   The identity of Fayezah Jassim Shalaan as the offender;
> (ii) The time and place of the offence as set out in the Indictment;
> (iii) That T.A. committed murder;
> (iv) That Fayezah Jassim Shalaan knew that T.A. had committed murder;
> (v)   That Fayezah Jassim Shalaan helped T.A. to escape from justice by receiving, comforting, or assisting him;
> (vi) That the purpose of Fayezah Jassim Shalaan in receiving, comforting, or assisting T.A. was to help him escape from justice. (para. 18)

The trial judge held that the Crown had proven all the elements but (iii). With regard to that element, he noted that the young person had already been tried for the offence in a different court and had been found not guilty. In those circumstances, he held, a conviction of the accused as an accessory after the fact was not possible:

> ¶ 22...Section 23.1 refers to where the principal "cannot be convicted of the offence." Although the section does not describe or limit the basis upon which a conviction of a principal cannot be convicted, various legal texts and cases have referred to specifics such as the ability to locate or compel the attendance of such a person, an incapacity based on infancy under Section 13 of the *Code*, and even the death of a principal before indictment or trial...In my opinion Section 23.1 refers to these types of specifics and not a situation where the principal has been previously acquitted.

> ¶ 23 In my opinion we are all still left with the common law, and the obiter in *Vinette*, as interpreted by Moir J.A. in *Anderson*, and that is, if the principal was acquitted, the accessory must be acquitted.

> ¶ 24 Under these circumstances for me to find the accused guilty on this charge would, in my opinion, be perverse and result in inconsistent verdicts. It might well be inclined, I submit, to bring the administration of justice into disrepute.

The Nova Scotia Court of Appeal ((1997), 159 N.S.R. (2d) 285, 115 C.C.C. (3d) 450)) overturned this verdict. After an extensive review of the history of the provision and case law from Canada, the United States and Great Britain, the Court of Appeal concluded:

> ¶ 29...It is clear from [s. 23.1] and s. 592 of the *Code* it is not necessary to convict a principal in order to convict an accessory. While the language does not refer to the acquittal of the principal, in my view the words "whether or not the principal" is convicted, are broad enough to encompass the acquittal of the principal. Those provisions have changed the common law.

The Supreme Court of Canada affirmed this result.

5. GENERAL REVIEW QUESTION

1. **A group of five youths, aged 17 to 19 and including A and B, are in a Kingston bar watching the televising of a National Hockey League play-off game between the Montreal Canadiens and Quebec Nordiques, won by Quebec 4-1. During this game each consumes only about three beers. During the second period a Quebec supporter, Pierre, is discovered in the bar. He is sitting alone. His actions are limited to smiling a lot and applauding Quebec goals. After the game the group of five corner Pierre outside the bar and begin deriding him and elbowing him. B shouts "Let's beat up the Frog". A leaves the group momentarily, goes to the back of the bar premises, picks up a four-foot-long loose fence picket, returns and proceeds to savagely beat Pierre, who has fallen to the ground. B removes his leather belt from his jeans and is about to join the attack when Pierre lapses into unconsciousness. The group runs off. C, a passing pedestrian who is a doctor, turns Pierre over, starts to examine him but then departs. Later C explains "Ontario doctors were on work-stoppage". An ambulance is summoned by another passer-by. It only arrives 35 minutes later as the ambulance service is involved in a rash of hospital transfers due to the**

doctors' work-stoppage. Pierre dies in transit. The autopsy assigns the death to a combination of the beating, the delay and Pierre's previously undiagnosed heart aneurism.

The responsible Crown Attorney is appalled by the incident. He asks you for a memorandum of law and advice as to the maximum viable charges (discussing possible defences) against A (the attacker), B (the bystander) and C (the doctor).

Chapter 9

INCOMPLETE CRIMES

1. ATTEMPTS

See ss. 24 and 463 of the *Criminal Code*.

R. v. ANCIO

[1984] 1 S.C.R. 225, 39 C.R. (3d) 1, 10 C.C.C. (3d) 385,
1984 CarswellOnt 41, 1984 CarswellOnt 799

MCINTYRE J. (DICKSON, BEETZ, ESTEY, CHOUINARD, LAMER and WILSON JJ. concurring): — This appeal [from 63 C.C.C. (2d) 309] involves consideration of the mental element required for proof of the crime of attempted murder, the subject of this court's earlier judgment in *Lajoie v. R.*, [1974] S.C.R. 399, 20 C.R.N.S. 360, [1974] 10 C.C.C. (2d) 313, affirming 16 C.R.N.S. 180, 4 C.C.C. (2d) 402.

At the date of the events which give rise to this appeal the respondent had been married some 25 years. His wife had left the matrimonial home and was living with one Kurely. The respondent was depressed and had been drinking to excess on the date in question. He telephoned his wife at Kurely's residence and told her he was afraid that their 23-year-old son was about to commit suicide and asked her to meet him. She refused to co-operate. Later the same evening the respondent broke into a friend's home while its owners were absent and took away three shotguns. He sawed off the barrel of one, loaded it and, taking some extra ammunition with him, went to Kurely's apartment building and gained entry by breaking the glass in the front door. On hearing the noise caused by the breaking glass, Kurely came from his bedroom to investigate, carrying a chair with a jacket hanging on it. He saw the respondent, carrying the shotgun, ascending the stairs to the second floor. He threw the chair and jacket, hitting the respondent. The gun went off. The blast missed Kurely by some three feet but put a hole in the jacket, which had been on the chair. A struggle followed, in which Kurely appears to have wrestled the gun from the respondent. When the police arrived, having been called during the course of the fight between the two men, Kurely was on the floor with his head partly under a bed and with the respondent upon him striking him weakly.

Shortly after his arrest the respondent stated to the police:

> I just went over to see my wife. I had phoned her earlier. I broke the window and went in. Then I heard what sounded like a gun go off. You are lucky you got there when you did. I had him by the throat and I would have killed him.

According to the respondent's account of events, the gun was discharged accidentally, although under tests conducted by the police the weapon was not found to be prone to accidental discharge.

The respondent was charged with a number of offences arising out of this affair but only one, that of attempted murder, is involved in this appeal. It was contained in the first count of the information and was in these terms:

> . . . did attempt to murder Michael Kurely by discharging a sawed off shotgun at him contrary to s. 222 of the *Criminal Code* of Canada [R.S.C. 1970, c. C-34].

He elected trial by judge alone and was convicted. The conviction was quashed in the Court of Appeal and a new trial directed. This appeal is taken by leave of this court.

. . . .

The Crown contended in this court that the Court of Appeal was in error in holding that the *mens rea* in attempted murder was limited to an intention to cause death (s. 212(a)(i)), or an intention to cause bodily harm knowing it to be likely to cause death and being reckless whether death ensues (s. 212(a)(ii)). The Crown's position was stated in its factum in these words:

> . . . the intention for attempted murder is not restricted to an actual intention to kill or an intention to cause grievous bodily harm that one knows is likely to cause death and is reckless whether death ensues or not, but *extends to an intention to do that which constitutes the commission of the offence of murder as defined in ss. 212 and 213 am. 1974-75-76, c. 93, s. 13; c. 105, s. 29; since am. 1980-81-82-83, c. 125 s. 15 of the Criminal Code. It is the Crown's position that s. 24 and s. 213(d) in combination can form the basis for a conviction of attempted murder.* (The italics are mine)

The respondent supported the judgment of the Court of Appeal, which followed the judgment of this court in *Lajoie v. R.*, *supra*. In that case it was held that a conviction for attempted murder could be sustained where the Crown had shown on the part of the accused either an intent to kill the potential victim or an intent to cause bodily harm which he knows is likely to cause death and is reckless whether death ensues or not. Although reference was made in *Lajoie* to the possibility of committing attempted murder as defined in s. 213 (see the concluding sentence on p. 408), the respondent and the Court of Appeal in the case at bar adopted the view that this was merely obiter. . . . . .

. . . .

The respondent submitted that the Crown's position, that s. 213(*d*) coupled with s. 24(1) described a further intent sufficient to warrant a conviction for attempted murder, should not be accepted because there was no authority to extend the concept of a constructive intent further than *Lajoie* had taken it. While contending on the facts of this case that he was not obliged to go further, he argued that in reason and logic a specific intent to kill should be the only intent sufficient to ground a conviction for attempted murder. It was said that the effect of the Crown's argument in extending the concept of an attempt to s. 213(*d*) of the *Criminal Code* would be to justify a conviction for attempted murder in the absence of any mental element with respect to the causing of death which would be to ignore the words of s. 24(1) specifically requiring an intent to commit the offence in question.

Lying at the heart of the controversy which arises in this case is the judgment of this court in *Lajoie, supra.*

. . . .

A great deal of the confusion surrounding the nature of the intent required to found a conviction for attempted murder may well stem from an assumption that murder and attempted murder are related offences which must share the same mental elements. A brief review of the historical development of the law relating to the two offences demonstrates that the crime of attempt developed as a separate and distinct offence from the offence of murder.

In very early times murder was simply the killing of a human being. The law was concerned with the injury done to the family of the deceased and the compensation which should follow. The consequence of the killing was the important feature and the intent or *mens rea* was of little if any significance. Special mental elements were recognized in statutes as early as the 13th Century, and by the 14th Century the concept of malice aforethought had developed: see *Act of the King's Charters of Pardon, 1389* (13 Ric. 2, star. 2), c. 1. Thus two elements came to be recognized in murder: the killing, and the malice aforethought, which in modern times has come to mean the necessary intent or intents.

As the common law developed, the mental element required for the commission of murder expanded to include both constructive intent and knowledge of the likelihood of death as a result of a person's acts, with recklessness as to whether death ensued or not.

. . . .

The offence of attempts developed much later than the offence of murder. In early times an attempt to commit an offence was not itself a crime. It was considered that in the absence of a guilty act intention alone was not punishable.

The modern offence of attempting the commission of a crime is said to have its origins in the Court of Star Chamber. An early venture into this field is found in the *Case of Duels* (1615), 2 State Tr. 1033, which involved proceedings against one William Priest for sending a written challenge to duel and one Richard Wright for carrying it and a stick that was to be the measure of the length of the weapons to be employed. It was asserted by Sir Francis Bacon, then Attorney General, at p. 1041, that:

> For the Capacity of this court, I take this to be a ground infallible: that wheresoever an offence is capital, or matter of felony, though it be not acted, there the combination or practice tending to that offence is punishable in this court as a high misdemeanor. So practice to impoison, though it took no effect; waylaying to murder, though it took no effect; and the like; have been adjudged heinous misdemeanors punishable in this court. Nay, inceptions and preparations in inferior crimes, that are not capital, as suborning and preparing of witnesses that were never deposed, or deposed nothing material, have likewise been censured in this court, as appeareth by the decree in *Garnon's Case*.

The court in its decree gave effect to the Attorney General's submission saying, in part, at p. 1046:

> And the court with one consent did declare their opinions: That by the ancient law of the land, all inceptions, preparations, and combinations to execute unlawful acts, though they never be performed, as they be not to be punished capitally, except it be in case of treason, and some other particular cases of statute law, so yet they are punishable as misdemeanors and contempts: and that this court was proper for offences of such nature.

The practice of the Court of Star Chamber in this respect became firmly established in that court (see Hall, *General Principles of Criminal Law*, 2nd ed. (1960), p. 565 *et seq.*) and was in time adopted in the Court of King's Bench. It has been said that the origin of the doctrine of criminal attempt as it is known in the common-law was Lord Mansfield's judgment in *R. v. Scofield* (1784), Cald. Mag. Rep. 397. Scofield was charged in an indictment with "wickedly, unlawfully and maliciously intending devising and contriving to feloniously set fire to, burn and consume a certain house".

. . . .

Whether *Scofield* was the starting point for the common-law doctrine is doubted by Hall (pp. 569-70) but the question seems to have been settled in *R. v. Higgins* (1801), 102 E.R. 269 (K.B.), where it was said, at p. 274, by Grose J.:

> First, as to the offence itself, it must be admitted that an attempt to commit a felony is in many cases at least a misdemeanor . . .

Any doubt remaining regarding the existence of the offence of attempted murder in England was set to rest by the enactment of the *Offences Against the Person Act, 1861* (24 & 25 Vict.), c. 100, ss. 11 to 15. These sections made it a felony to attempt the commission of murder in the various ways described.

In Canada the common-law offence of attempt was codified in the *1892 Criminal Code* as s. 64.

. . . .

A minor change in the 1953-54 *Code* changed the section to its present form in s. 24.

. . . .

The section has therefore covered the law of attempt in general since the codification of the law in 1892. In addition, particular provision has been made in the *Criminal Code* for the offence of attempted murder . . . .

. . . .

It is clear from the foregoing that in common law and under the criminal law of Canada criminal attempt is itself an offence separate and distict from the crime alleged to be attempted. As with any other crime, the Crown must prove a *mens rea*, that is, the intent to commit the offence in question, and the *actus reus*, that is, some step towards the commission of the offence attempted going beyond mere acts of preparation. Of the two elements the more significant is the *mens rea*. In *R. v. Cline* [(1956), 115 C.C.C. 18], Laidlaw J.A., speaking for the Ontario Court of Appeal, said, at p. 27:

> Criminal intention alone is insufficient to establish a criminal attempt. There must be *mens rea* and also an *actus reus*. But it is to be observed that whereas in most crimes it is the *actus reus* which the law endeavours to prevent, and the *mens rea* is only a necessary element of the offence, in a criminal attempt the *mens rea* is of primary importance and the *actus reus* is the necessary element.

And in *Russell on Crime*, 12th ed. (1964), vol. 1, p. 175, it is said:

> Since the mischief contained in an attempt depends upon the nature of the crime intended, the criminality lies much more in the intention than in the acts done.

This proposition was accepted by Goddard L.C.J. in *Whybrow* [(1951), 35 Cr. App. R. 51], at p. 147, where he stated that "the intent becomes the principal ingredient of the crime".

The common-law recognition of the fundamental importance of intent in the crime of attempt is carried forward into the *Criminal Code*. A reading of s. 24 of the *Code* and all its predecessors since the enactment of the first *Code* in 1892 confirms that the intent to commit the desired offence is a basic element of the offence of attempt. Indeed, because the crime of attempt may be complete without the actual commission of any other offence and even without the performance of any act unlawful in itself, it is abundantly clear that the criminal element of the offence of attempt may lie solely in the intent. As noted by

Glanville Williams, *Criminal Law: The General Part*, 2nd ed. (1961), p. 642, para. 207, in discussing attempts:

> An *actus reus* . . . need not be a crime apart from the state of mind. It need not even be a tort or a moral wrong or a social mischief.

The question now arises: What is the intent required for an attempt to commit murder? As has been indicated earlier, the Crown's position is that the intent required for a conviction on a charge of attempt to murder is the intent to do that which will, if death is caused, constitute the commission of murder as defined in ss. 212 and 213 of the *Code*, so that a combination of ss. 24 and 213(*d*) can form the basis for a conviction of attempted murder. The respondent, on the other hand, argues that, although the authorities presently limit the intent to that which would constitute murder as defined in s. 212 of the *Code*, logic and principle dictate that the intent should be limited to the specific intent to kill described in s. 212(*a*)(i).

While it is clear from ss. 212 and 213 of the *Criminal Code* that an unintentional killing can be murder, it is equally clear that, whatever mental elements may be involved and whatever means may be employed, there cannot be a murder without a killing. Section 24 of the *Code* defines, in part, the offence of attempt as "having an intent to commit an offence". As Estey J. observed in *R. v. Quinton*, [1947] S.C.R. 234 at 235-36, 3 C.R. 6, 88 C.C.C. 231, in referring to the then s. 72 (now s. 24):

> This section requires that one to be guilty of an attempt must intend to commit the completed offence and to have done some act toward the accomplishment of that objective.

The completed offence of murder involves a killing. The intention to commit the complete offence of murder must therefore include an intention to kill. I find it impossible to conclude that a person may intend to commit the unintentional killings described in ss. 212 and 213 of the *Code*. I am then of the view that the *mens rea* for an attempted murder cannot be less than the specific intent to kill.

As I have said earlier, there is a division of opinion upon this point and strong arguments have been raised in favour of the Crown's position that a "lesser intent", such as that provided in s. 212(*a*)(ii), or even no intent at all relating to the causing of death, as provided in s. 213(*d*), may suffice to found a conviction for attempted murder. This view is supported in *Lajoie, supra*. In my view, with the utmost respect for those who differ, the sections of the *Criminal Code* relied on in that case do not support that position.

As noted above, Martland J.'s analysis of the intent required to found a conviction for attempted murder is based primarily on the change in wording of s. 222. In my opinion, emphasis on the amendment of this section is unwarranted, for two reasons. Firstly, s. 222 does not define or create the offence of attempted murder. The scheme of the *Criminal Code* in relation to attempts has been the same from its inception. One section defines the offence of attempts generally

(s. 72 of the 1927 *Code*, now s. 24). Another sets out the penalties of attempts (s. 57 of the 1927 Code, now s. 421), and a third creates a separate penalty for attempted murder (s. 264 of the 1927 *Code*, s. 210 in *Lajoie*, now s. 222). Rather than defining or creating an offence, s. 222 merely fixes a penalty for a specific attempt. Despite the categorization of the various means of committing murder set out in the old s. 264, there is no essential difference between the old and the new sections in this respect.

Secondly, the elimination of the words "with intent to commit murder" from s. 264 is not significant. Section 24 defines an attempt as "having an intent to commit an offence". Because s. 24 is a general section it is necessary to "read in" the offence in question. The offence of attempted murder then is defined as "having an intent to commit murder". This does not differ from the old s. 264 reference to "with intent to commit murder", which Martland J. acknowledged was interpreted, in *R. v. Flannery* [[1923] 3 W.W.R. 97], to require the specific intent to kill.

Martland J. placed further emphasis on s. 222 of the *Criminal Code* by relying on the words "attempts by any means" to support his conclusion that murder may be attempted in any of the "ways" set out in ss. 212 and 213. In my view, the reference to "any means" in s. 222 refers to ways in which a murder could be accomplished, such as by poisoning, shooting, or stabbing. The earlier version of s. 222 (s. 232 in 1892, s. 264 in 1906) listed the various methods by which a killing could be effected, but the illustrations were replaced in the 1953-54 revision with a general reference to murder "by any means". In any event, ss. 212 and 213 have nothing to do with the means of killing. They are concerned solely with describing the mental elements which will suffice to make a completed killing murder. The fact that certain mental elements, other than an intent to kill, may lead to a conviction for murder where there has been a killing does not mean that anything less than an intent to kill will suffice for an attempt at murder.

It was argued, and it has been suggested in some of the cases and academic writings on the question, that it is illogical to insist upon a higher degree of *mens rea* for attempted murder, while accepting a lower degree amounting to recklessness for murder. I see no merit in this argument. The intent to kill is the highest intent in murder and there is no reason in logic why an attempt to murder, aimed at the completion of the full crime of murder, should have any lesser intent. If there is any illogic in this matter, it is in the statutory characterization of unintentional killing as murder. The *mens rea* for attempted murder is, in my view, the specific intent to kill. A mental state falling short of that level may well lead to conviction for other offences, for example, one or other of the various aggravated assaults, but not to a conviction for an attempt at murder. For these reasons, it is my view that *Lajoie*, *supra*, should no longer be followed.

I would accordingly dismiss the Crown's appeal and confirm the Court of Appeal's order for a new trial.

RITCHIE J.: — 1 am unable to distinguish this case from that of *Lajoie v. R.*, [*supra*], which is a unanimous judgment of this court and by which I feel bound. I would therefore allow this appeal.

Appeal dismissed.

R. v. SORRELL and BONDETT

(1978), 41 C.C.C. (2d) 9, 1978 CarswellOnt 1205 (Ont. C.A.)

Ontario Court of Appeal, DUBIN, MARTIN and BLAIR JJ.A. April 27, 1978.

BY THE COURT: — The Attorney-General of Ontario appeals against the acquittal of the respondents on a charge of attempted robbery.

The respondents were tried at Kingston before His Honour Judge Campbell, sitting without a jury, on an indictment containing three counts.

Count 1 charged the respondents jointly with, on or about March 3, 1977, attempting to rob Peter Mason of Aunt Lucy's Fried Chicken store at 240 Montreal St. in Kingston. Count 2 charged the respondent Sorrell with carrying, at the time and place aforesaid, a concealed weapon, to wit: a Smith and Wesson revolver. Count 3 charged the respondent Sorrell with having in his possession, at the time and place aforesaid, a Smith and Wesson revolver, knowing the same was obtained by an offence committed in Canada punishable on indictment. The respondent Sorrell, on arraignment, pleaded guilty to the charge of carrying a concealed weapon contained in count 2; his plea of guilty was accepted by the trial judge after the evidence was completed, and he was sentenced to imprisonment for 18 months. The trial judge acquitted the respondent Sorrell on count 3, on the ground that the Crown had failed to prove the necessary element of guilty knowledge. The Crown does not appeal the acquittal of Sorrell on count 3, and we are not further concerned with it.

On the evening of Thursday, March 3, 1977, Miss Dawn Arbuckle was the cashier at Aunt Lucy's Fried Chicken store at 240 Montreal St. in Kingston. The store is located at the corner of Montreal and Markland Sts., the customer entrances being on Montreal St. Mr. Peter Mason was the manager of the store. The regular closing time for the store was 11:00 p.m., but, on the evening in question, since almost all the chicken had been sold, the manager decided to close the store earlier, and locked the customer entrances at approximately 10:45 p.m. Around 10 minutes to 11:00 Miss Arbuckle noticed two men, wearing balaclavas, on the Markland St. side of the store; they then came to one of the customer entrances in Montreal St. The area outside the store was illuminated, and the lights normally on in the store, when open, were still on.

One of the men was wearing a blue ski jacket and the other was wearing a brown coat. The balaclavas worn by the two men were pulled down completely over their heads, and one man was also wearing sunglasses. Miss Arbuckle said that the balaclava worn by one man was blue and white in colour, and that worn by the other man was brown and white.

One of the men rapped on the door and on the window. The manager, who had been mopping the floor, turned around and said, "Sorry we are closed", and returned to his mopping. The two men turned toward each other, and made a gesture of surprise. At this time Miss Arbuckle noticed that one of the men had a silver-coloured gun in his hand. The two men then walked away on Montreal Street in the direction of Princess St.; whereupon Mr. Mason, the manager, telephoned the police. Two officers in a cruiser responded to the call, drove to the area and saw two men, whose clothing corresponded to the description that the officers had been given, walking on Montreal St. The officers drove past the two men, then made a U-turn and drove back towards them.

As the officers passed the two men, before making the U-turn, they saw one of the men throw "an article of material" towards a snow bank on the side of the street. The two men, who proved to be the respondents, were then arrested. The respondent Sorrell had a loaded .357 Magnum revolver concealed in his waistband. The gun was loaded with six Dominion .38 shells, and another five Dominion .38 shells were removed from the respondent Sorrell's pants' pocket.

An officer conducted a search of the immediate area where the respondents had been arrested, and found a brown balaclava on a snowbank on the side of Montreal St. The point on Montreal St. where the respondents were arrested was some 411 yards from the Aunt Lucy's store, where the attempted robbery is alleged to have occurred. The officer proceeded along Montreal St. in the direction of the Aunt Lucy's store, and found a blue balaclava in the middle of the sidewalk on Montreal St. at the intersection of Raglan St.

Neither of the respondents testified in his defence.

The Crown appeals against the acquittal of the respondents on the charge of attempted robbery on the ground that the trial judge erred in law in holding that the acts of the respondents did not go beyond mere preparation, and hence did not constitute an attempt.

Section 24 of the *Code* defines an attempt as follows:

> 24(1) Every one who, having an intent to commit an offence, does or omits to do anything for the purpose of carrying out his intention is guilty of an attempt to commit the offence whether or not it was possible under the circumstances to commit the offence.
>
> (2) The question whether an act or omission by a person *who has an intent to commit an offence* is or is not mere preparation to commit the offence, and too remote to constitute an attempt to commit the offence, is a question of law. (Emphasis supplied.)

In order to establish the commission of the offence of attempted robbery charged, it was necessary for the Crown to prove that the respondents:

(i)   intended to do that which would in law amount to the robbery specified in the indictment (*mens rea*), and

> (ii) took steps in carrying out that intent which amounted to more than
> mere preparation (*actus reus*).

By virtue of s. 24(2) of the *Code*, the existence of element (i) is a question of fact, but whether the steps taken are sufficient to satisfy element (ii) is a question of law.

In *R. v. Cline*, 115 C.C.C. 18 at p. 29, Laidlaw J.A., in his much-quoted judgment, said:

> (1) There must be *mens rea* and also an *actus reus* to constitute a criminal attempt, but the criminality of misconduct lies mainly in the intention of the accused. . . . (5) The *actus reus* must be more than mere preparation to commit a crime. But (6) when the preparation to commit a crime is in fact fully complete and ended, the next step done by the accused for the purpose and with the intention of committing a specific crime constitutes an *actus reus* sufficient in law to establish a criminal attempt to commit that crime.

Thus, proof of the respondents' intention to commit the robbery particularized in the indictment, which is a question of fact, was the central issue in the case. Mr. Doherty for the Crown contended before us that on the facts found by the trial judge, he erred in law in failing to draw the legal conclusion of guilt required by the facts accepted by him as proved, and, in particular, erred in law in holding that the acts of the respondents, found by him to have been proved, had not gone beyond mere preparation. Counsel for the respondents, on the other hand, contended that the trial judge's reasons for judgment, considered in their entirety, show that he acquitted the respondents because he entertained a reasonable doubt whether they had the intent to rob the Aunt Lucy's store, the existence of which intent was essential to constitute the attempt charged.

A detailed examination of the trial judge's reasons for judgment is necessary in order to endeavour to ascertain the basis upon which he acquitted the respondents. The trial judge said:

> Turning to count 1, that is the count that affects both Sorrel and Bondett, namely, this attempted robbery count. There are many conclusions that I have drawn from the credible evidence, beyond a reasonable doubt, and I say that those conclusions complete substantially the Crown's case subject only — and I say only — to the thorny question as to whether or not the events in question constitute an attempt within the meaning of the *Criminal Code*.

After referring to certain discrepancies in the evidence of the Crown witnesses, which he did not consider material, the trial judge continued:

> The Crown's case on count 1 has been proved beyond a reasonable doubt in my finding on the matters of identity of the accused, the date, the place and, subject only to what I am going to be saying on the matter of attempt, as to the allegation that the attempted robbery, if there was an attempted robbery, was committed in respect of Peter Mason of Aunt Lucy's Kentucky Fried Chicken.

He then held that Mr. Mason, as the manager of the store, had the custody of the money in the store, and said:

It brings me down then to the sole remaining question, did what took place at the time and at the place, as referred to by the witnesses Arbuckle and Mason, constitute an attempt at robbery? I may say that I found the evidence of both of those witnesses to be satisfactory, credible, and my findings are based on that evidence. I as well look to the evidence at the trial as to the manner of departure from the premises — from in front of the premises — by the two accused and the actions that they were performing when seen and practically immediately apprehended by the police. I am finding that between them they rid themselves of the balaclavas which could raise the inference of guilty mind; but that, of course, raises the question: a mind having a sense of guilt of what? They may have thought that what they did at the front of the store was criminal in some way and that they should take some steps to cover up — whether they were right in that belief or not. Was what they had actually done illegal as being an attempt to rob, whether they believed it or not, that still leaves to me the question: was what they did within the ambit of an attempt to rob? The inference is pretty plain, and I think I would be naive to conclude otherwise, that they were up to no good on that occasion, that they may well have had robbery of the store in mind. But, again, I am driven back to the provisions of the *Code* that differentiate between mere preparation and the actual commencement of steps to commit the robbery

I am obliged to counsel for their references to cases on the point, one of which endeavours to lay down tests for the assistance of the court, and subsequent cases, but all of which have their own set of facts and circumstances with which the court then in those cases had to deal. It is an extremely thin line, but whether thin or otherwise, if my finding is that that line had been crossed beyond mere preparation, the finding — if it were to be made — that the line had been crossed would be sufficient to bring me to a conclusion beyond a reasonable doubt. Nevertheless, the fineness of the line is a bother to me. I am conscious of the fact that the accused timed their arrival at the store such that they could expect a fund of money to be in the till, such they could expect there would likely be few if any persons there other than the store personnel, and that they had costumed themselves for the purpose of disguising their features to render subsequent identification difficult, but I am also of the view that it is important for me to consider the fact that apart from rattling the door and perhaps rattling on the window — that would be consistent with an innocent person's endeavour to get in the food store — there was no gesture or threat of violence or threat of force. The case before me is attempted robbery and not attempted break, enter and theft, or break and enter with intent, or conspiracy, or whatever. So that the endeavour to open the door would — were one of those other charges to have been before me, and I am not saying in any way that it should have been before me — what was done by way of attempt to open the door could relate more to a charge of attempted breaking rather than the charge of robbery. In brief, in my finding, the accused by virtue of I suppose good luck of not having been able to progress further in doing whatever they were going to do had not yet crossed the line between preparation and attempt. Accordingly, I am finding that count 1 as regards both accused has not been proved on that narrow ground, and I have endorsed the indictment on count 1: both accused not guilty.

It will be observed that while the trial judge made an express finding that he was satisfied beyond a reasonable doubt that the respondents were the two men who had approached the store, and that one of them had a gun, he made no similar finding with respect to the existence of the necessary intent to rob. Mr. O'Hara, on behalf of the respondent Sorrell particularly emphasized the following passages in the trial judge's reasons, relative to intent, which Mr. O'Hara characterized as "powerful expressions of doubt", namely: ". . . they may well have had robbery of the store in mind", and ". . . what was done by way of attempt to open the door could relate more to a charge of attempted breaking rather than the charge of robbery". In our view, the trial judge's reasons are more consistent with a finding that the necessary intent to commit robbery was not proved beyond a reasonable doubt, than with a finding that such intent was established by the evidence. In any event, the Crown has not satisfied us that the trial judge found the existence of an intent to rob.

The Crown's right of appeal under s. 605(1)(*a*) of the *Code* is confined to a ground of appeal that involves a question of law alone. The failure of the trial judge to draw the appropriate inference of intent from the facts found by him, is an error of fact, and does not raise a question of law.

. . . .

If the trial judge had found that the respondents intended to rob the store, the acts done by them clearly had advanced beyond mere preparation, and were sufficiently proximate to constitute an attempt: see *Henderson v. The King*, 91 C.C.C. 97, [1948] S.C.R. 226, *per* Kerwin J., at p. 98 C.C.C., p. 228 S.C.R., *per* Estey J., at pp. 114-16 C.C.C., pp. 243-6 S.C.R., *per* Locke J., at pp. 116-17 C.C.C., p. 246 S.C.R.; *R. v. Carey*, 118 C.C.C. 241, [1957] S.C.R. 266, 25 C.R. 177, *per* Kerwin C.J.C., at pp, 246-7, *per* Rand J., at p. 251. If the trial judge had found that the respondents had the necessary intent his finding that the acts done by the respondents did not go beyond mere preparation and did not constitute attempted robbery, would constitute an error of law that would not only warrant, but require our intervention.

Because of the doubt that he entertained that the respondents had the necessary intent to commit robbery, however, his error in law in holding that the respondents' acts did not go beyond mere preparation, could not have affected the verdict of acquittal, unless, of course, his self-misdirection with respect to what constituted mere preparation, led him into error in entertaining a reasonable doubt whether the requisite intent had been proved. This question is one of considerable difficulty. The following passage (included in those previously quoted), would tend to support the conclusion that the trial judge was led into error with respect to the existence of the necessary intent by self-misdirection that the respondents' acts had not gone beyond mere preparation:

> It is an extremely thin line, but whether thin or otherwise, if my finding is that that line had been crossed beyond mere preparation, the finding — if it were to be made — that the line had been crossed would be sufficient to bring me to a conclusion beyond a reasonable doubt. Nevertheless, the fineness of the line is a bother to me.

The trial judge then proceeded, however, to refer to the matters in the passages previously quoted, relating to the issue of intent, which gave him difficulty in finding that the required mental element was present. The issue of intent was basic and, the trial judge, in our view, could not logically or appropriately make a determination whether the acts of the respondents went beyond mere preparation until he had first found the intent with which those acts were done.

The issue whether the acts of the respondents went beyond mere preparation could not be decided in the abstract apart from the existence of the requisite intent.

In the present case, there was no evidence of the intent to rob other than that furnished by the acts relied on as constituting the *actus reus*. There was no extrinsic evidence in the form of statements of intention, or admissions by the respondents showing what their intention was.

The prosecution in this case was forced to rely exclusively upon the acts of the accused, not only to constitute the *actus reus*, but to supply the evidence of the necessary *mens rea*. This court in *R. v. Cline, supra*, rejected the so-called "unequivocal act" test for determining when the stage of attempt has been reached. That test excludes resort to evidence *aliunde*, such as admissions, and holds that the state of attempt has been reached only when the acts of the accused show unequivocally on their face the criminal intent with which the acts were performed. We are of the view that where the accused's intention is otherwise proved, acts which on their face are equivocal may, none the less, be sufficiently proximate to constitute an attempt. Where, however, there is no extrinsic evidence of the intent with which accused's acts were done, acts of the accused, which on their face are equivocal, may be insufficient to show that the acts were done with the intent to commit the crime that the accused is alleged to have attempted to commit, and hence insufficient to establish the offence of attempt.

Counsel for the respondents while conceding that the trial judge's reasons are not free of ambiguity, submitted that they are reasonably open to the interpretation that he was searching for evidence that satisfied him beyond a reasonable doubt that the accused intended to rob the store in question, and at the end of his quest was not satisfied beyond a reasonable doubt, that the acts done by the accused supplied the necessary proof of intent.

We think that this submission accurately states the basis upon which the trial judge acquitted the respondents, and the Crown has not satisfied us that, but for the self-misdirection with respect to which complaint is made, the verdict of the trial judge would not necessarily have been the same. It is not to the point that, on the evidence, we would have reached a different conclusion with respect to the respondent's intentions.

. . . .

Appeal dismissed.

R. v. DEUTSCH

[1986] 2 S.C.R. 2, 52 C.R. (3d) 305, 27 C.C.C. (3d) 385,
1986 CarswellOnt 120, 1986 CarswellOnt 1009

LE DAIN J.: — This appeal, which involves a charge of attempting to procure a person to have illicit sexual intercourse with another person contrary to s. 195(1)(a) of the *Criminal Code*, raises two issues: the distinction between attempt and mere preparation, and the meaning of "illicit sexual intercourse".

The appeal is from the judgment of the Ontario Court of Appeal on March 17, 1983 setting aside the acquittal of the appellant by Graburn Co. Ct. J. on August 13, 1982 of the charge of attempting to procure a person to have illicit sexual intercourse with another person and ordering a new trial of the appellant on that charge.

During the period covered by the indictment, which is the three months ending on or about September 3, 1981, the appellant was carrying on a business known as Global Franchises Marketing, which was engaged in selling franchises of various kinds. During this period the appellant placed an advertisement in newspapers in Ottawa, Hamilton and Toronto inviting applications for the position of secretary/sales assistant and conducted interviews with three women who responded to the advertisement and with a police officer who posed as an applicant for the position and recorded the interview on a tape recorder. The advertisement read as follows:

ENJOY TRAVEL

SECRETARY — Sales Assistant to Sales Executive. $600-$800 per month to start plus commission, bonuses, company benefits and expenses. Must be free to travel extensively. Call 746-2440 ask for Mel.

In the interviews the appellant indicated that a secretary/sales assistant would be expected to have sexual intercourse with clients or potential clients of the company where that appeared to be necessary to conclude a contract. The appellant also indicated that a successful secretary/sales assistant could earn as much as $100,000 per year through commission or bonus on the sale of franchises. The appellant did not make an offer of employment to the three applicants who testified at his trial. After hearing what the position required they said they were not interested and the interviews terminated. Nor did he make an offer of employment to the police officer who posed as an applicant, but when she told him she was interested in the position, despite its requirements, he told her to think it over and let him know.

The appellant was tried upon an indictment containing two counts: attempting to procure female persons to become common prostitutes, and attempting to procure female persons to have illicit intercourse with another person. Graburn Co. Ct. J. acquitted the appellant on both counts. He found that the appellant intended that a person hired for the position should have sexual relations with clients or potential clients, but he held, as a matter of law, that the acts or statements of the appellant did not, in the absence of an offer of employment, constitute the *actus reus* of an attempt to procure. In his opinion they were mere preparation. He accordingly did not find it necessary to decide whether the sexual intercourse contemplated by the appellant would be illicit sexual intercourse within s. 195(1)(*a*) or make those who engaged in it common prostitutes within s. 195(1)(*d*), as it then read.

The Ontario Court of Appeal (Martin, Houlden and Robins JJ.A.) (1983), 5 C.C.C. (3d) 41, dismissed the appeal from the acquittal on the charge of attempting to procure female persons to become common prostitutes, but allowed the appeal from the acquittal on the charge of attempting to procure female persons to have illicit sexual intercourse with another person and directed a new trial of the appellant on that count of the indictment. The court held that the trial judge erred in concluding that the acts or statements of the appellant could not, in the absence of an offer of employment, constitute an attempt to procure rather than mere preparation. It held that there was evidence from which the trial judge could have concluded that there was both the *mens rea* and the *actus reus* required for an attempt to procure. The court also held that the sexual intercourse contemplated by the appellant would be illicit sexual intercourse within s. 195(1)(*a*). The appellant appeals from the judgment of the Court of Appeal with respect to the second count of the indictment.

The appellant, who appeared in person on the appeal, expressed his grounds of appeal in several different ways, but in my opinion there are only two issues that require consideration by the court:

1. Whether the Court of Appeal erred in holding that the acts or statements of the appellant could, as a matter of law, constitute an attempt to procure rather than mere preparation; and
2. Whether the Court of Appeal erred in holding that the sexual intercourse contemplated by the appellant would be illicit sexual intercourse within s. 195(1)(*a*) of the *Code*.

. . . .

[The Court first considered the second issue and concluded that the Court of Appeal did not err in holding that the sexual intercourse contemplated by the appellant would be "illicit sexual intercourse" within s. 195(1)(a) of the *Code*.]

. . . .

I turn now to the question whether the acts or statements of the appellant could, as a matter of law, constitute the *actus reus* of an attempt to procure a person to have illicit sexual intercourse with another person, contrary to s. 195(1)(*a*) of the *Code*. The general provision of the *Code* defining the constituent elements of an attempt to commit an offence is s. 24, which provides:

24. (1) Every one who, having an intent to commit an offence, does or omits to do anything for the purpose of carrying out his intention is guilty of an attempt to commit the offence whether or not it was possible under the circumstances to commit the offence.

(2) The question whether an act or omission by a person who has an intent to commit an offence is or is not mere preparation to commit the offence, and too remote to constitute an attempt to commit the offence, is a question of law.

The issue is whether, if there was the necessary intent, the acts of the appellant were mere preparation to commit the offence of procuring a person to have illicit sexual intercourse with another person or whether any of them was a step in the commission of the offence, and the extent to which that distinction is to turn on the relative remoteness of the act in question from what would have been the completion of the offence. This issue, as s. 24 indicates, is a question of law. The appellant contends that the Court of Appeal erred in holding that one of the acts of the appellant could, if there was the necessary intent, constitute the *actus reus* of an attempt to procure.

The trial judge found that the appellant "intended that the women in question should have sexual relations with prospective customers and clients", but that the acts of the appellant consisting of the advertisements, the interviews and what was said during the interviews concerning the requirements of the position and the money to be earned, were mere preparation and too remote from the complete offence of procuring to constitute the *actus reus* of an attempt to procure. He said:

. . . .

I consider that the interview and its content was an act remotely leading to the commission of the offence, and was not an act immediately connected with it, nor sufficiently proximate to it so as to constitute an attempt; the latter language being used by the Ontario Court of Appeal in the case of *Sorrell and Bondett* which was decided in 1978 and is reported in 41 C.C.C. (2d) at p. 9.

. . . .

Several different tests for determining whether there is the *actus reus* of attempt, as distinct from mere preparation to commit an offence, have been identified as reflected at one time or another in judicial decisions and legislation. All of them have been pronounced by academic commentators to be unsatisfactory in some degree. For a thorough analysis of the various tests, with suggestions for an improved test, see Meehan, *The Law of Criminal Attempt — A Treatise*, 1984, chapter 5, and Stuart, *Canadian Criminal Law*, 1982, pp. 529ff. There is a succinct appraisal of the various tests in the English Law Commission's Report No. 102 of 1980 entitled, Criminal Law: Attempt, and Impossibility in Relation to Attempt, Conspiracy and Incitement. It has been frequently observed that no satisfactory general criterion has been, or can be, formulated for drawing the line between preparation and attempt, and that the application of this distinction to the facts of a particular case must be left to common sense judgment.

. . . .

In my opinion the distinction between preparation and attempt is essentially a qualitative one, involving the relationship between the nature and quality of the act in question and the nature of the complete offence, although consideration must necessarily be given, in making that qualitative distinction, to the relative proximity of the act in question to what would have been the completed offence, in terms of time, location and acts under the control of the accused remaining to be accomplished. I find that view to be compatible with what has been said about the *actus reus* of attempt in this court and in other Canadian decisions that should be treated as authoritative on this question.

The most recent expression of opinion in this court on what constitutes an attempt to commit an offence is the judgment in *R. v. Ancio*, [1984] 1 S.C.R. 225, where the issue was the intent required for attempted murder. McIntyre J., in the course of a review of the development of the law of attempt, said with reference to the *mens rea* and the *actus reus* of attempt at p. 247:

> As with any other crime, the Crown must prove a *mens rea*, that is, the intent to commit the offence in question and the *actus reus*, that is, some step towards the commission of the offence attempted going beyond mere acts of preparation. Of the two elements the more significant is the *mens rea*.

McIntyre J. referred with approval to the judgment of Laidlaw J.A. in *R. v. Cline, supra*, particularly for what it said concerning the relative importance of *mens rea* in attempt, but that judgment has also been treated as helpful for what it said concerning the application of the distinction between preparation and attempt. With reference to this question Laidlaw J.A. said at p. 28:

> The consummation of a crime usually comprises a series of acts which have their genesis in an idea to do a criminal act; the idea develops to a decision to do that act; a plan may be made for putting that decision into effect; the next step may be preparation only for carrying out the intention and plan; but when that preparation is in fact fully completed, the next step in the series of acts done by the accused for the purpose and with the intention of committing the crime as planned cannot, in my opinion, be regarded as remote in its connection with that crime. The connection is in fact proximate.

Laidlaw J.A. offered six propositions by way of guidance for determination of the requisite *mens rea* and *actus reus* of attempt, the last two of which, with reference to the *actus reus*, are as follows:

> (5) The *actus reus* must be more than mere preparation to commit a crime. But (6) when the preparation to commit a crime is in fact fully complete and ended, the next step done by the accused for the purpose and with the intention of committing a specific crime constitutes an *actus reus* sufficient in law to establish a criminal attempt to commit that crime.

The extent to which some version of the proximity test, which was formulated in *R. v. Eagleton* (1854), Dears. C.C. 376 (C.C.R.), and applied in the much-criticized case of *R. v. Robinson*, [1915] 2 K.B. 342 (C.C.A.), as a "last step" or "last stage" test (*cf.* English Law Commission, op cit., pp. 335-36), is to be applied in drawing the distinction between preparation and attempt has also been the subject of commentary in this court. In *Henderson v. The King*, [1948] S.C.R. 226, where one of the issues was whether there had been an attempt to rob a bank, Estey J., who was one of the majority holding that there had been an attempt, said at p. 244:

> Counsel for the accused referred to a number of cases in which the attempted crime was either against the person or that of obtaining by false pretences. He contended that any act not "immediately connected with" the completed crime would be too remote to constitute an attempt. Even under the cases which he cited the accused may still have one or more acts to do, and these may be separated by an intervening period of time, in order to complete the offence and yet may be guilty of an attempt.

Among the cases referred to by Estey J. in support of this statement were *R. v. Cheeseman* (1862), 169 E.R. 1337, where Blackburn J. said at p. 1339, "But, if the actual transaction has commenced which would have ended in the crime if not interrupted, there is clearly an attempt to commit the crime", and *R. v. White*, [1910] 2 K.B. 124, where Bray J. said at p. 130: " . . . the completion or attempted completion of one of a series of acts intended by a man to result in killing is an attempt to murder even although this completed act would not, unless followed by other acts, result in killing. It might be the beginning of the attempt, but would none the less be an attempt." Taschereau J., dissenting, in *Henderson*, although he differed in the result, would not appear to have applied a different concept of proximity. He said, after referring to the authorities, including *Eagleton* and *Robinson*, at pp. 234-35:

> Although it may be said that no one could doubt the express purpose of the bandits, I do not believe that it can be held that the mere fact of going to the place where the contemplated crime is to be committed, constitutes an attempt. There must be a closer relation between the victim and the author of the crime; there must be an act done which displays not only a preparation for an attempt, but a commencement of execution, a step in the commission of the actual crime itself.

In *Detering v. The Queen*, [1982] 2 S.C.R. 583, which involved a conviction for attempted fraud, Laskin C.J. raised a question, as I read his reasons, as to the weight to be given to the proximity test in the essential task under s. 24 of the *Code* of distinguishing between preparation and attempt. With reference to the contention of counsel that "proximity was an essential requirement in the sense, to put it generally, that the actions of the accused must go beyond mere preparation and close (a question of degree) to the realization of his purpose", Laskin C.J. said at p. 586:

This leaves for consideration the so-called proximity principle. It may well be that this is envisaged by the reference to remoteness in s. 24(2), but I do not see that it advances the essential issue in attempt which requires going beyond mere preparation. Nor do I find cogency in the appellant's submission that if there is impossibility this does not bring any act of the accused closer to realization so as to establish proximity. I read s. 24(1) as making a different distinction, one merely requiring proof of intent and of accused going beyond mere preparation by making, as in this case, a false representation even though not resulting in full realization of his objective.

In my opinion, relative proximity may give an act which might otherwise appear to be mere preparation the quality of attempt. That is reflected, I think, in the conclusion of the majority in *Henderson* and in the conclusion of the Ontario Court of Appeal with respect to *actus reus* in *R. v. Sorrell and Bondett* (1978), 41 C.C.C. (2d) 9. But an act which on its face is an act of commission does not lose its quality as the *actus reus* of attempt because further acts were required or because a significant period of time may have elapsed before the completion of the offence.

In the case at bar the Court of Appeal agreed with the trial judge on the applicable meaning of "procure". The meaning selected by the trial judge and approved by the Court of Appeal was "to cause, or to induce, or to have a persuasive effect upon the conduct that is alleged." Martin J.A. expressed his agreement at p. 49 with the following statement of the issue by the trial judge: "The question for decision is did Mr. Deutsch attempt to cause or attempt to induce or attempt to have a persuasive effect upon the woman in question to have illicit sexual intercourse with another person. . . ." I agree that the sources referred to by the trial judge and Martin J.A. support the meaning given by them to the word "procure".

The Court of Appeal differed with the trial judge as to what would have constituted the completed offence of procuring a person to have illicit sexual intercourse with another person. The trial judge held that the offence of procuring would have been completed, in the particular context of this case, by the acceptance of an offer of employment. The Court of Appeal held, citing *R. v. Johnson* (1963), 48 Cr. App. R. 25, and *R. v. Gruba*, [1969] 2 C.C.C. 365, that the offence of procuring a person to have illicit sexual intercourse with another person is not committed unless sexual intercourse actually takes place. In the appeal to this court the respondent accepted this statement of the law as to what is required for the complete offence of procuring a person to have illicit sexual intercourse with another person. It was not challenged, and I accept it for purposes of deciding whether the acts of the appellant could, as a matter of law, constitute the *actus reus* of an attempt to procure.

I agree with the Court of Appeal that if the appellant had the necessary intent to induce or persuade the women to seek employment that would require them to have sexual intercourse with prospective clients then the holding out of the large financial rewards in the course of the interviews, in which the necessity of having sexual intercourse with prospective clients was disclosed, could constitute the *actus reus* of an attempt to procure. It would clearly be a step, and an important step, in the commission of the offence. Before an offer of employment could be made in such circumstances an applicant would have to seek the position, despite its special requirement. Thus such inducement or persuasion would be the decisive act in the procuring. There would be little else that the appellant would be required to do towards the completion of the offence other than to make the formal offer of employment. I am further of the opinion that the holding out ot the large financial rewards in the course of the interviews would not lose its quality as a step in the commission of the offence, and thus as an *actus reus* of attempt, because a considerable period of time might elapse before a person engaged for the position had sexual intercourse with prospective clients or because of the otherwise contingent nature of such sexual intercourse.

For these reasons I would dismiss the appeal. I agree with the Court of Appeal that because the trial judge did not make a finding as to whether or not there was the necessary intent to procure there must be a new trial.

One of the most heated debates in Anglo-American criminal law has been as to whether courts should acquit in some cases of attempting the impossible. The embers were fanned by a complex decision of the House of Lords in *Haughton v. Smith*, [1974] 3 W.L.R. 1 (H.L.), to the effect that there were distinctions to be made. It is generally accepted by writers that a court should be able to convict of an attempt to commit a crime which, in the circumstances, was physically impossible to commit. One example is a would-be assassin throwing a bomb that will never explode. The major difference of opinion is between those who favour criminal responsibility and those who do not for cases of attempts which would only be criminal if the facts were as the accused wrongly supposed them to be. The classic examples are stealing an umbrella that turns out to be your own or stabbing a corpse thinking it was a live person. Glanville Williams urged Canadian courts:

> to lend no ear to the arguments of those who would persuade them, notwithstanding the clear and wise words of the *Code*, to introduce questions of impossibility into the law of attempt and its associated crimes: "Attempting the Impossible — A Reply" (1979), 22 Crim. L.Q. 49 at 57.

The Supreme Court agreed with Glanville Williams' position with its decision in *Dynar*.

UNITED STATES v. DYNAR

[1997] 2 S.C.R. 462, 8 C.R. (5th) 79, 115 C.C.C. (3d) 481,
1997 CarswellOnt 1981, 1997 CarswellOnt 1982

The U.S. government requested the extradition of D, a Canadian citizen who had been the subject of a failed "sting" operation by the FBI. D had agreed to launder money which he had been told were the proceeds of crime. Since it was a sting, the money was not in fact the proceeds of crime: under Canadian (but not American) law at the time, this meant that had D actually received the funds and laundered them, he would not have committed any offence. In fact the money was never delivered to him. The issue for the Supreme Court was whether D's conduct would have amounted to a criminal attempt under Canadian law.

CORY and IACOBUCCI JJ. (LAMER C.J.C., LA FOREST, L'HEUREUX-DUBÉ, and GONTHIER JJ. concurring): —

. . . .

(2) The Law of Attempt

The *Criminal Code* creates the crime of attempt to commit an offence:

24. (1) Every one who, having an intent to commit an offence, does or omits to do anything for the purpose of carrying out the intention is guilty of an attempt to commit the offence *whether or not it was possible under the circumstances to commit the offence.* [Emphasis added.]

On its face, the statute is indifferent about whether or not the attempt might possibly have succeeded. Therefore it would seem, at first blush, not to matter that Mr. Dynar could not possibly have succeeded in laundering money known to be the proceeds of crime. So long as he attempted to do so, he is guilty of a crime.

In our view, s. 24(1) is clear: the crime of attempt consists of an intent to commit the completed offence together with some act more than merely preparatory taken in furtherance of the attempt. This proposition finds support in a long line of authority. [Citations omitted.] In this case, sufficient evidence was produced to show that Mr. Dynar intended to commit the money-laundering offences, and that he took steps more than merely preparatory in order to realize his intention. That is enough to establish that he attempted to launder money contrary to s. 24(1) of the *Criminal Code*.

However, the respondent argues that Parliament did not intend by s. 24(1) to criminalize all attempts to do the impossible, but only those attempts that the common law has classified as "factually impossible". An attempt to do the factually impossible, according to the respondent, is an attempt that runs up against some intervening obstacle and for that reason cannot be completed. The classic example involves a pickpocket who puts his hand into a man's pocket intending to remove the wallet, only to find that there is no wallet to remove.

Traditionally, this sort of impossibility has been contrasted with "legal impossibility". An attempt to do the legally impossible is, according to those who draw the distinction, an attempt that must fail because, even if it were completed, no crime would have been committed. See Eric Colvin, *Principles of Criminal Law* (2nd ed. 1991), at pp. 355-56.

According to the respondent, the *Criminal Code* criminalizes only attempts to do the factually impossible. An attempt to do the legally impossible, in the absence of an express legislative reference to that variety of impossibility, is not a crime.

As support for this interpretation, the respondent offers two arguments. The first is that Parliament based s. 24(1) on an English provision whose purpose was to overrule a decision of the House of Lords that had made factual impossibility a defence. See Barry Brown, "'Th'attempt, and not the deed, Confounds us': Section 24 and Impossible Attempts" (1981), 19 *U.W.O. L. Rev.* 225 at pp. 228-29. On the strength of this argument, the New Zealand Court of Appeal accepted that New Zealand's equivalent to s. 24(1) criminalizes attempts whose completion is factually impossible but not those whose completion is legally impossible. See *R. v. Donnelly*, [1970] N.Z.L.R. 980 (C.A.) at pp. 984 and 988.

The respondent's second argument is that Parliament, had it intended to criminalize attempts to do the legally impossible, would have used the words "whether or not it was factually or legally impossible" in s. 24(1). As examples of statutes that were intended to criminalize attempts to do the legally impossible, the respondent cites provisions of statutes from the United Kingdom and from the United States . . . .

. . . .

A third argument, which the respondent does not advance, is that the words "under the circumstances" restrict the scope of s. 24(1) to attempts to do the factually impossible. An attempt that is not possible "under the circumstances", according to this argument, is by implication possible under some other set of circumstances. Otherwise, there would be no need to mention circumstances — the mere mention of impossibility would suffice.

. . . .

In addition there is another way of turning the same language to the respondent's advantage. "Circumstances", in ordinary parlance, are facts. Laws, by contrast, are not circumstances. Accordingly, applying the rule that *expressio unius est exclusio alterius*, the mention in s. 24(1) of attempts that are circumstantially or factually impossible may be taken to exclude attempts that are legally impossible. The question, as one Canadian writer has framed it, is whether "'the circumstances' referred to in [s. 24(1)] include the legal status of the actor's conduct". Brown, *supra*, at p. 229.

Still another argument in favour of the respondent's position, though one that reflects judicial policy rather than the strict ascertainment of legislative intent, is that penal statutes, if ambiguous, should be construed narrowly, in favour of the rights of the accused. "[T]he overriding principle governing the interpretation of penal provisions is that ambiguity should be resolved in a manner most favourable to accused persons". *R. v. McIntosh*, [1995] 1 S.C.R. 686, at para. 38.

Although some of these arguments have a certain force, what force they have is greatly attenuated when it is realized that the conventional distinction between factual and legal impossibility is not tenable. The only relevant distinction for purposes of s. 24(1) of the *Criminal Code* is between imaginary crimes and attempts to do the factually impossible. The criminal law of Canada recognizes no middle category called "legal impossibility". Because Mr. Dynar attempted to do the impossible but did not attempt to commit an imaginary crime, he can only have attempted to do the "factually impossible". For this reason, Mr. Dynar's proposal that s. 24(1) criminalizes only attempts to do the factually impossible does not help him.

As we have already indicated, an attempt to do the factually impossible is considered to be one whose completion is thwarted by mere happenstance. In theory at least, an accused who attempts to do the factually impossible could succeed but for the intervention of some fortuity. A legally impossible attempt, by contrast, is considered to be one which, even if it were completed, still would not be a crime. One scholar has described impossible attempts in these terms:

> Three main forms of impossibility have set the framework for contemporary debate. First, there is impossibility due to inadequate means (Type I). For example, A tries to kill B by shooting at him from too great a distance or by administering too small a dose of poison; C tries to break into a house without the equipment which would be necessary to force the windows or doors. . . .
>
> The second form of impossibility arises where an actor is prevented from completing the offence because some element of its *actus reus* cannot be brought within the criminal design (Type II). For example, A tries to kill B by shooting him when he is asleep in bed, but in fact B has already died of natural causes; C tries to steal money from a safe which is empty. . .
>
> The third form of impossibility arises where the actor's design is completed but the offence is still not committed because some element of the *actus reus* is missing (Type III). For example, A may take possession of property believing it to have been stolen when it has not been; B may smuggle a substance for reward believing it to be a narcotic when it is sugar. (Colvin, *supra*, at pp. 355-56.)

According to Professor Colvin, factually impossible attempts are those that fall into either of the first two categories. Legally impossible attempts are those that fall into the third category.

Colvin's schema appears attractive. But in fact it draws distinctions that do not stand up on closer inspection. There is no legally relevant difference between the pickpocket who reaches into the empty pocket and the man who takes his own umbrella from a stand believing it to be some other person's umbrella. Both have the *mens rea* of a thief. The first intends to take a wallet that he believes is not his own. The second intends to take an umbrella that he believes is not his own. Each takes some steps in the direction of consummating his design.

And each is thwarted by a defect in the attendant circumstances, by an objective reality over which he has no control: the first by the absence of a wallet, the second by the accident of owning the thing that he seeks to steal. It is true that the latter seems to consummate his design and still not to complete an offence; but the semblance is misleading. The truth is that the second man does not consummate his design, because his intention is not simply to take the particular umbrella that he takes, but to take an umbrella that is not his own. That this man's design is premised on a mistaken understanding of the facts does not make it any less his design. A mistaken belief cannot be eliminated from the description of a person's mental state simply because it is mistaken.

If it were otherwise, the effect would be to eliminate from our criminal law the defence of mistaken belief. If mistaken beliefs did not form part of an actor's intent — if an actor's intent were merely to do what he in fact does — then a man who honestly but mistakenly believed that a woman had consented to have sexual relations with him and who on that basis actually had sexual relations with that woman, would have no defence to the crime of sexual assault. His intention, on this limited understanding of intention, would have been to sleep with the particular woman with whom he slept; and that particular woman, by hypothesis, is one who did not consent to sleep with him. Substituting the one description ("a woman who did not consent to sleep with him") for the other ("the particular woman with whom he slept"), it would follow that his intention was to sleep with a woman who had not consented to sleep with him. But of course, and as we have already strenuously urged, intention is one thing and the truth is another. Intention has to do with how one sees the world and not necessarily with the reality of the world.

Accordingly, there is no difference between an act thwarted by a "physical impossibility" and one thwarted "following completion". Both are thwarted by an attendant circumstance, by a fact: for example, by the fact of there being no wallet to steal or by the fact of there being no umbrella to steal. The distinction between them is a distinction without a difference. Professor Colvin himself agrees that "[t]he better view is that impossibility of execution is never a defence to inchoate liability in Canada" (p. 358).

There is, however, a relevant difference between a failed attempt to do something that is a crime and an imaginary crime. [Citation omitted.] It is one thing to attempt to steal a wallet, believing such thievery to be a crime, and quite another thing to bring sugar into Canada, believing the importation of sugar to be a crime. In the former case, the would-be thief has the *mens rea* associated with thievery. In the latter case, the would-be smuggler has no *mens rea* known to law. Because s. 24(1) clearly provides that it is an element of the offence of attempt to have "an intent to commit an offence", the latter sort of attempt is not a crime.

Nor should it be. A major purpose of the law of attempt is to discourage the commission of subsequent offences. See Williams' *Textbook of Criminal Law, supra*, at pp. 404-5. [Citations omitted.] But one who attempts to do something that is not a crime or even one who actually does something that is not a crime, believing that what he has done or has attempted to do is a crime, has not displayed any propensity to commit crimes in the future, unless perhaps he has betrayed a vague willingness to break the law. Probably all he has shown is that he might be inclined to do the same sort of thing in the future; and from a societal point of view, that is not a very worrisome prospect, because by hypothesis what he attempted to do is perfectly legal.

Therefore, we conclude that s. 24(1) draws no distinction between attempts to do the possible but by inadequate means, attempts to do the physically impossible, and attempts to do something that turns out to be impossible "following completion". All are varieties of attempts to do the "factually impossible" and all are crimes. Only attempts to commit imaginary crimes fall outside the scope of the provision. Because what Mr. Dynar attempted to do falls squarely into the category of the factually impossible — he attempted to commit crimes known to law and was thwarted only by chance — it was a criminal attempt within the meaning of s. 24(1). The evidence suggests that Mr. Dynar is a criminal within the contemplation of the Canadian law and so the double criminality rule should be no bar to his extradition to the United States.

In *R. v. Alicandro* (2009), 63 C.R. (6th) 330 (Ont. C.A.), leave to appeal refused (2010), 410 N.R. 383 (note) (S.C.C.) it was held that internet luring is an inchoate offence akin to attempt and impossibility is not a defence. A belief that the victim was underage was sufficient to prove the offence even though the person was an adult police officer.

2. CONSPIRACY

See s. 465 of the *Criminal Code*.

R. v. CELEBRITY ENTERPRISES LTD. (NO. 2)

(1977), 42 C.C.C. (2d) 478, 1977 CarswellBC 607 (B.C. C.A.)

APPEAL by the Crown from the accused's acquittal by Trainor Co. Ct. J., [1977] 4 W.W.R. 144, on a charge of conspiracy to produce a public mischief. The indictment contained two counts: count 1, conspiracy to live on the avails of prostitution; and count 2, conspiracy to produce a public mischief. The accused were convicted on count 1 and acquitted on count 2. The accused appealed from their conviction on count 1 and the Crown appealed the acquittal on count 2. The court dealt with the accused's appeal first, and the judgment in that appeal is reported at 41 C.C.C. (2d) 540. Following are the reasons for *judgment on the Crown* appeal.

ROBERTSON J.A. (orally): — The learned trial judge held that count 2 disclosed no offence known to the law and he accordingly entered an acquittal upon it. Against that acquittal the Crown has cross-appealed. Count 2 reads in part:

> they did conspire together and with Eleanor Harrigan and Tony Pizani and other persons unknown, to effect an unlawful purpose, to wit, produce a public mischief at or in the premises located at 1019 Seymour Street, and known as the New Penthouse Cabaret, with intent thereby to corrupt public morals, contrary to the form of the Statute.

I am unable to see how one can eliminate from the count the words "produce a public mischief". If then the offence charged is conspiracy to produce a public mischief at common law, it is bad in view of the holding by the House of Lords in *Director of Public Prosecutions v. Withers*, [1975] A.C. 842, that there is no such offence. If the offence charged is conspiracy to produce a public mischief under the *Criminal Code*, it is bad because, while the *Code* makes certain defined kinds of public mischief offences, it does not provide that public mischief with intent to corrupt public morals is an offence.

As an alternative argument Mr. Jaques submits that one may treat the count as a charge of conspiracy to corrupt public morals. Assuming — contrary to my view — that one can so read the charge, the question arises whether a conspiracy to corrupt public morals is a conspiracy to effect an unlawful purpose within the meaning of s. 423(2)(*a*) of the *Criminal Code*. An unlawful purpose must be a purpose which is unlawful by the law of Canada, and it is of no significance that counsel for the accused has conceded that a conspiracy to corrupt public morals is by the common law of England an indictable offence, because s. 8 of the *Criminal Code* provides that

> 8. Notwithstanding anything in this Act or any other Act no person shall be convicted (*a*) of an offence at common law . . .

If something that someone does is not something of which he can be convicted, that something cannot, in my opinion, be "unlawful" in the sense in which the word is used in s. 423(2)(*a*).

It is consistent with this that, since s. 8 came into force in 1955, there is no reported case in Canada where there has been conviction of conspiracy to effect an unlawful purpose where there has not been a breach of either a Dominion statute or a provincial statute.

I would, therefore, dismiss the cross-appeal.

McFarlane and Taggart JJ.A. concurred.

R. v. GRALEWICZ

[1980] 2 S.C.R. 493, 54 C.C.C. (2d) 289,
1980 CarswellOnt 661F, 1980 CarswellOnt 661

CHOUINARD J. (RITCHIE, DICKSON, BEETZ and ESTEY JJ. concurring): —
Upon motion of the appellants the following information was quashed by order
of Judge Brown of the Provincial Court (Criminal Division) of the District of
York:

> That Roman Adolfe Gralewicz, John Royce, Roy Norris Willis, Roger Desjardins,
> Richard Thomasson, Edwin Aldon Williams, Hedley Harnum, Andre Bansept, William
> Lisenchuk, Walter Mercer, and George Baldo between the 1st day of January, 1971 and the
> 21st day of January, 1977, in the Province of Ontario and elsewhere in the Dominion of
> Canada, unlawfully did conspire and agree together, the one with the other and with John
> Robert Lazarus, John Pearson, Glen Patrick Milley, Ian Joseph Vickers, Lawrence Carey,
> George Keagan, Donald Roy Swait, Arthur Hunt, Michael Dabour, John Richard Wood,
> Kenneth Henry McGuire, and with another person or persons unknown to effect an unlawful
> purpose, to wit: to prevent members of the Seafarers' International Union of Canada from
> participating in the lawful activities of their Union, in accordance with Section 110(1) of the
> *Canada Labour Code,* R.S.C. 1970, Chapter L-1 as amended, by committing the following
> acts, to wit:
>
> (1) Threats and assaults upon members of the said Union;
> (2) Possession and use of offensive weapons;
> (3) Defrauding members of the said Union through falsifying expenses;
> (4) Violations of the articles of the said Union's Constitution as they relate to elections, trials
>   and individual rights,
> (5) Unlawfully preventing the said Union members from obtaining employment,
>
> Thereby committing an offence contrary to Section 423(2)(a) of the *Criminal Code,* R.S.C.
> 1970, Chapter C-34.

. . . .

In the appellants' submission an agreement to prevent anyone from
exercising his freedom under s. 110 of the *Canada Labour Code,* R.S.C. 1970,
c. L-1, to participate in the lawful activities of his union does not amount to a
conspiracy to effect an unlawful purpose within the meaning of s. 423(2) of the
Criminal Code.

Section 110(1) [rep. & sub. 1972, c. 18, s. 1] of the *Canada Labour Code*
reads as follows:

> 110(1) Every employee is free to join the trade union of his choice and to participate in
> its lawful activities.

The first submission advanced on behalf of the appellants is that:

> The *Canada Labour Code* is a complete and exhaustive code provided by the Parliament of
> Canada for the conduct of those industrial relations which come under federal jurisdiction. It

was not the intention of Parliament that its provisions should be enforced by resort to the *Criminal Code* or to any other statute since it provides its own mechanisms for enforcement.

In the appellants' submission, s. 110 is merely declaratory and contains no requirement and no prohibition. It does not create an offence. Various offences are created by ss. 184 and 185 [rep. & sub. *idem*] relating to interference with the freedoms of employees and employers recognized by s. 110 but none in the nature of that alleged in the information. Section 186 [rep. & sub. *idem*] enacts a general prohibition to the effect that "no person shall seek by intimidation or coercion to compel a person to become or refrain from becoming or to cease to be a member of a trade union." This deals with membership, not with participation in the lawful activities of a union.

The only section of the Act under which a prosecution could be contemplated for preventing members of a union from participating in the lawful activities of their union would be s. 191(1) [rep. & sub. *idem*]:

> 191(1) Subject to section 190, every person other than an employer or a trade union who violates or fails to comply with any provision of this Part other than section 148, 184 or 185 is guilty of an offence and liable on summary conviction to a fine not exceeding one thousand dollars.

Counsel for the respondent conceded however, and rightly so in my opinion, that this section could not apply because the words "violates or fails to comply" imply a prohibition or a requirement and there are none in section 110.

I see little merit in the appellants' first submission and I can but conclude as suggested by the respondent that "the fact that within a code of labour relations there is no specific sanction to enforce the rights of employees to participate in the lawful activities of their union does not sanctify otherwise criminal conduct".

The appellants further submit that their conduct as charged in the information does not constitute an offence under the *Criminal Code*. In their submission:

> If a statute does not expressly provide a penalty then, the only possible offence one can commit with respect to it, is the one set out in s. 115(1) of the *Criminal Code*.
> 115(1) Every one who, without lawful excuse, contravenes an Act of the Parliament of Canada by wilfully doing anything that it forbids or by wilfully omitting to do anything that it requires to be done, is, unless some penalty or punishment is expressly provided by law, guilty of an indictable offence and is liable to imprisonment for two years.

Section 115(1) has no application here since s. 110(1) of the *Canada Labour Code* contains no prohibition and no requirement.

The only specific offences in the *Criminal Code* related to interference with union membership are those by employers under s. 382.

As regards interference with the right of a person to do something or to abstain from doing something s. 381 enacts:

381(1) Every one who, wrongfully and without lawful authority, for the purpose of compelling another person to abstain from doing anything that he has a lawful right to do, or to do anything that he has a lawful right to abstain from doing,

(a) uses violence or threats of violence to that person or to his wife or children, or injures his property,
(b) intimidates or attempts to intimidate that person or a relative of that person by threats that, in Canada or elsewhere, violence or other injury will be done to or punishment inflicted upon him or a relative of his, or that the property of any of them will be damaged,
(c) persistently follows that person about from place to place,
(d) hides any tools, clothes or other property owned or used by that person, or deprives him of them or hinders him in the use of them,
(e) with one or more other persons follows that person, in a disorderly manner, on a highway,
(f) besets or watches the dwelling-house or place where that person resides, works, carries on business or happens to be, or
(g) blocks or obstructs a highway,

is guillty of an offence punishable on summary conviction.

(2) A person who attends at or near or approaches a dwelling-house or place, for the purpose only of obtaining or communicating information, does not watch or beset within the meaning of this section.

The appellants have not been charged under section 381. We were told by counsel that the respondent never relied on this section and that any similarity between allegations in the information and s. 381 is purely coincidental.

On the other hand, as recognized by counsel for the appellants, "it is evident that there may be interference with the rights of a person to do what he has the right to do other than by the means set out in section 381. However, those other means of interference do not attract criminal law sanctions unless, of course, they constitute crimes in themselves."

In this case what the appellants have been charged with is conspiracy "to effect an unlawful purpose, to wit: to prevent members of the Seafarers' International Union of Canada from participating in the lawful activities of their Union, in accordance with s. 110(1) of the *Canada Labour Code*".

It is, therefore, necessary to determine whether preventing members of a union from participating in the lawful activities of their union is an unlawful purpose within the meaning of s. 423(2) of the *Criminal Code*, or what is the meaning of unlawful purpose.

According to the appellants' counsel an unlawful purpose can only be one prohibited by statute either federal or provincial:

In our respectful submission, the law does not create offences consisting of conspiracies to do acts not themselves prohibited by law under the guise of a conspiracy to effect an unlawful purpose. If the act which is the subject of the conspiracy is not prohibited by statute, it cannot form an unlawful act or purpose as the subject of a conspiracy.

They rely principally on *R. v. Celebrity Enterprises Ltd. et al., supra* [at p. 146], where Judge Trainor acquitted the accused of a count of conspiracy "to effect an unlawful purpose, to wit, produce a public mischief . . . with intent thereby to corrupt public morals, contrary to the form of the statute".

Analyzing the sections of the *Criminal Code* dealing with public mischief (s. 128 [rep. & sub. 1972, c. 13, s. 8]), mischief (s. 387) and offences tending to corrupt morals (ss. 159 and following) as well as other sections, Judge Trainor determined that none applied to the case and that consequently the unlawful purpose charged did not relate to an offence under the *Criminal Code*.

It would relate, however, to an offence at common law. While no such generalized offence as conspiracy to effect a public mischief was known to the law (*R. v. Withers*, [1975] A.C. 842), a conspiracy to corrupt morals was indictable (*Shaw v. Director of Public Prosecutions*, [1962] A.C. 220; *Knuller (Publishing, Printing and Promotions) v. Director of Public Prosecutions*, [1973] A.C. 435).

Judge Trainor was of the opinion that unlawful purpose does not extend to common law offences and he stated at p. 176:

> I cannot accept the Crown's invitation to follow *Shaw* and *Knuller* and either extend the meaning of "unlawful purpose" to include a purpose not authorized by law or to hold that a common law offence can be an unlawful purpose. In my view our law has developed clearly and surely to the point that the "unlawful purpose" in s. 423(2) must be one contrary to law. Although the point is not before me I would think this reasoning applies equally to "unlawful means" in s. 423(2)(*b*).
>
> By contrary to law I mean prohibited by federal or provincial legislation. Thus would be included all summary conviction offences under the *Criminal Code* and other federal legislation and offences created by provincial legislation.

That decision was upheld by the British Columbia Court of Appeal (1979), 42 C.C.C. (2d) 478, where speaking for the court Robertson J.A. states at p. 480:

> If something that someone does is not something of which he can be convicted, that something cannot, in my opinion, be "unlawful" in the sense in which the word is used in s. 243(2)(*a*).

Leave to appeal to this court was refused, [1978] 1 S.C.R. xi.

All the Canadian cases in which conduct was held capable of being the subject of a criminal conspiracy to effect an unlawful purpose were based on conduct prohibited by legislation: see *Wright, McDermott and Feely v. The Queen*, [1964] 2 C.C.C. 201, [1964] S.C.R. 192, *R. v. Layton, Ex p. Thodas et al.*, [1970] 5 C.C.C. 260, 10 C.R.N.S. 290; *R. v. Chapman and Grange* (1973), 11 C.C.C. (2d) 84; *R. v. Jean Talon Fashion Centre Inc.* (1975), 22 C.C.C. (2d) 223. Counsel for the respondent recognized that there are no Canadian cases where a charge of conspiracy was upheld based on conduct not prohibited by legislation.

The respondent relies, however, on the following passage by Fauteux J., as he then was, in *Wright, McDermott & Feeley, supra*, at p. 202 C.C.C., pp. 193-4 S.C.R.:

While marginal notes in the body of an Act form no part of the Act, the marginal note appended to s. 408(2) accurately designates as "Common law conspiracy" the offence described in this section which, as defined by Lord Denman C.J. in *R. v. Jones* (1832), 4 B. & Ad. 345 at p. 349, consists in a combination "to do an unlawful act, or a lawful act by unlawful means". Common-law conspiracy is one of the few common-law offences which, upon the 1954 revision of the *Cr. Code*, Parliament thought advisable to perpetuate by codification: *Martin's Criminal Code*, 1955, p. 35. Hence the law pertaining to this offence, its elements and the wide embracing import of the term "unlawful purpose", remains unchanged.

But all that was decided in that case was that unlawful purpose extends to a breach of a provincial statute, in that case the Ontario provincial *Police Act*. After the above passage, Fauteux J. continues:

While the term, as shown in *Harrisons Law of Conspiracy*, 1924, encompasses more than criminal offences, sufficient it is to say, for the purpose of this case, that the purpose alleged in the charge, to wit, the obtention from a constable of information which it is his duty not to divulge, is an unlawful purpose. In the language of Lord Mansfield, in *R. v. Bembridge* (1783), 3 Doug. 327 at p. 332, ". . . a man accepting an office of trust concerning the public, especially if attended with profit, is answerable criminally to the King for misbehaviour in his office." The fact that the purpose or the breach of trust contemplated by the conspirators, whether as their ultimate aim or only as a means to it, be, it carried into effect, punishable either under s. 103 of the *Cr. Code* (*vide, R. v. McMorran* (1948), 91 C.C.C. 19 at pp. 26 *et seq.*, 5 C.R. 338 at pp. 345 *et seq.*) or under s. 60 of the *Ontario Provincial Police Act*, adequately manifests the unlawfulness of the purpose within the meaning of the law attending common-law conspiracies.

When the *Criminal Code* was revised in 1954, s. 8 was introduced:

8. Notwithstanding anything in this Act or any other Act no person shall be convicted
    (*a*) of an offence at common law
    (*b*) of an offence under an Act of the Parliament of England, or of Great Britain, or of the United Kingdom of Great Britain and Ireland, or
    (*c*) of an offence under an Act or ordinance in force in any province, territory or place before that province, territory or place became a province of Canada,
but nothing in this section affects the power, jurisdiction or authority that a court, Judge, Justice or Magistrate had, immediately before the 1st day of April 1955, to impose punishment for contempt of court.

It follows that common-law conspiracy would have ceased to be part of Canadian criminal law had it not been retained as a statutory offence. But to make it a statutory offence does not necessarily mean that it was embodied with all its implications and uncertainties recognized by the decisions of the English Courts when no decisions in Canada had ever gone as far as those of the English Courts. And Fauteux J. in the above cited passage clearly does not say that.

The *Withers* case, *supra*, is authority to the effect "that it is not open to the courts nowadays either to create new offences or so to widen existing offences as to make punishable conduct of a type hitherto not subject to punishment". The more so in Canada and Cartwright J., as he then was, speaking for himself and five other members of this court, stated in *Frey v. Fedoruk et al.* 97 C.C.C. 1 at p. 14, [1950] S.C.R. 517 at p. 530:

> To so hold would, it seems to me, be to assert the existence of what is referred to in Stephen's *History of the Criminal Law of England*, vol. 2, p. 190, as *"the power which has in some instances been claimed for the Judges of declaring anything to be an offence which is injurious to the public although it may not have been previously regarded as such"*.
> The writer continues: *"The power, if it exists at all, exists at common law."*
> In my opinion, this power has not been held and should not be held to exist in Canada. I think it safer to hold that no one shall be convicted of a crime unless the offence with which he is charged is recognized as such in the provisions of the *Criminal Code*, or can be established by the authority of some reported case as an offence known to the law. I think that if any course of conduct is now to be declared criminal, which has not up to the present time been so regarded, such declaration should be made by Parliament and not by the courts. [Emphasis added.]

It is difficult for me to see how the mere enactment of conspiracy as a statutory offence would have the effect of extending its scope beyond what it had been held to extend to at common law by the Canadian courts prior to its becoming a statutory offence while at the same time Parliament enacted s. 8 to exclude common-law offences from the ambit of the criminal law of Canada. I am, therefore, of the opinion, that in s. 423(2)(*a*) unlawful purpose means contrary to law, that is prohibited by federal or provincial legislation.

But even assuming that the meaning of unlawful purpose could be extended as far as it was at English common law prior to the 1977 amendments I do not believe that it would comprise a purpose to prevent members of a union from participating in the lawful activities of their union. (The law concerning conspiracy has been modified in England by the *Criminal Law Act*, 1977 (U.K.), c. 45, and in brief it now relates to the commission of an *offence*, meaning an offence triable in England and Wales.)

In Kenny's *Outlines of Criminal Law*, 19th ed. (1966), to which reference is made in the *Withers* case, *supra*, unlawful purpose as it then stood is described as follows at pp. 428-30:

> 451. The term "unlawful" is here used in a sense which, unhappily, has never yet been defined with precision. The purposes which it comprises appear to be of the following species.
>
> (i) Agreements to commit a substantive crime; *e.g.* a conspiracy to steal, or even merely to incite someone else to steal. This extends to all cases where it would be criminal for any of the conspirators to commit the act agreed upon, even though there be in the gang other persons in whom it would be no offence to commit it; and to all "crimes", even non-indictable ones, *e.g.* non-payment of poor rates. A conspiracy to obstruct the *course of justice* can exist without there being any obstruction of the *police* (*e.g.* to fabricate evidence, or to keep witnesses away from the court). It therefore differs from a conspiracy to *obstruct the police* in the execution of their duty, for this may not be concerned in any way with the course of public justice, but have as its object, for example, to prevent the police from maintaining public order or keeping the highway clear.
>
> (ii) Agreements to commit any tort that is malicious or fraudulent. Some say that agreements to commit any tort, of whatever kind, are indictable as conspiracies. But the weight of authority

seems to be in favour of limiting the rule to torts of fraud or malice thus excluding, for instance, a trespass committed *bona fide* by persons eager to assert their supposed right of way.

(iii) Agreements to commit a breach of contract under circumstances that are peculiarly injurious to the public.

(iv) Agreements to do certain other acts, which (unlike all those hitherto mentioned) are not breaches of law at all, but which nevertheless are outrageously immoral or else are, in some way, extremely, injurious to the public. We may quote, as instances, agreements to facilitate the seduction of a woman; or to run slackly in a race so as to enable a confederate to win his bets: or to hiss a play unfairly; or to defraud a shipowner by secretly putting stowaways on board. Similar criminality would arise in agreements to raise by false reports the price of the Funds or of any other vendible commodity; or so to carry on trade as to diminish the revenue; or to persuade a prosecutor not to appear at the trial; or to give false information to the police; or to indemnify a prisoner's bail. On the other hand, it is doubtful whether an agreement to make loud noises for the purpose of disturbing an invalid neighbour would be indictable as a conspiracy. And a thrifty combination of poor-law authorities to marry a female pauper to a pauper of another parish, in order to relieve the ratepayers of the woman's parish, is not a conspiracy. Yet some combinations for procurement of marriage will amount to conspiracy; *e.g* taking a young woman of property from the custody of her relations in order to marry her to one of the conspirators. And although some combinations "in restraint of trade" may be so far illegal as to be unenforceable, it is now settled that they do not necessarily constitute a criminal offence. As to the question whether a conspiracy formed in England to effect some unlawful purpose abroad would be indictable here, the House of Lords has laid it down that a conspiracy to commit a crime abroad is not indictable in this country unless the contemplated crime is one for which an indictment would lie here, and that a conspiracy to attain a lawful object by unlawful means, rather than to commit a crime, is not triable here when the unlawful means and the ultimate object are both outside the jurisdiction. (I have omitted the footnotes and the references thereto.)

Reviewing this extensive list I do not see one head under which would come the conduct described in the information.

This is understandable because as it appears to me, to prevent members of a union from participating in the lawful activities of their union is not necessarily unlawful nor "outrageously immoral", nor "extremely injurious to the public". It is possible to conceive of many situations where to do that would not be so. This seems to be recognized by the Court of Appeal when speaking for the Court, Brooke J.A. says [at p. 191]:

The *Canada Labour Code* is silent as to acts by others outside of the employer-employee relationship which may interfere with the exercise by the employee of the right or freedom to participate in lawful activities of the union. This is no doubt in recognition of the right or freedom of others to perhaps peacefully persuade such employee as to his participation in the lawful activities of the trade union.

But then Brooke J.A. goes on to say:

But that is quite a different matter than acts or an agreement which has the purpose of preventing or depriving an employee from exercising his right or freedom to participate in the lawful activities of his union.

The distinction that is drawn here appears to me to relate to the means rather than to the purpose. The purpose in either case is the same, namely, that there be no participation by an employee in the lawful activities of his union. Only the means differ: persuasion in the first case, intimidation or other unlawful means in the other.

But we are not here concerned with the means. This information is not laid under s. 423(2)(*b*), nor under s. 381, nor under any other section charging a specific crime. It is laid under s. 423(2)(*a*) and, in my opinion, as laid it does not set out an offence known to the law of Canada.

I would allow the appeal, set aside the judgment of the Court of Appeal and that of the Supreme Court of Ontario, and restore the order of the Provincial Court quashing the information.

McINTYRE J. (dissenting) (MARTLAND J. concurring): —

.   .   .   .

The principal question raised in this appeal is whether the information discloses an offence known to the law. The fact that Crown counsel considered that a particular section of the *Criminal Code* was not relied upon in drafting the information does not preclude this court from considering the effect of the section and finding that the unlawful purpose, alleged in the information, falls within the terms of s. 381 of the *Criminal Code*. While the information, to disclose an offence, must allege a conspiracy to effect an unlawful purpose, specific reference to a numbered section of the *Criminal Code* is not necessary.

Section 110 [rep. & sub. 1972, c. 18, s. 1] of the *Canadian Labour Code*, R.S.C. 1970, c. L-1, confers rights upon employees to join trade unions and participate in their lawful activities. While it may be doubtful if any effective sanction for the enforcement or protection of such rights appears in the *Canada Labour Code*, s. 381 of the *Criminal Code* makes it an offence and, therefore, an unlawful purpose to use the means therein described to compel a person to abstain from doing anything he has a lawful right to do. The information alleges a conspiracy to prevent members of the Seafarers' International Union of Canada from participating in the lawful activities of their union by committing the acts described in the infomation, thereby making the use of the described means a part of the unlawful purpose alleged. Such a conspiracy would, therefore, be a conspiracy to effect an unlawful purpose, and would be an offence within s. 423(2)(*a*) of the *Criminal Code*. I am, of course, far from saying that the Crown would be able to prove its case at trial, but I am of the view that an offence has been alleged in the information and the trial should proceed.

To the argument, which could be raised by counsel for the appellants, that reliance on s. 381 of the *Criminal Code* could take the appellants by surprise and prejudice them in their defence, there is a short answer. This argument might well have force where a previously unmentioned issue is raised after the completion of the evidence at a trial and before judgment, or even where it is produced during a trial when the defence has already adopted a position without consideration of the effect or influence such a change in the Crown position might have. However, that does not apply here where no trial has been commenced, and the appellants would have, from the outset, abundant notice of the problems they face.

· · · ·

Appeal dismissed.

R. v. INNOCENTE

(2004), 187 C.C.C. (3d) 533, 2004 CarswellNS 260 (N.S.C.A.)

In May 1995 Innocente hired a person named Craig Henneberry to do work at his house. Eventually Innocente and Henneberry became involved in an enterprise transporting illegal narcotics from Montreal to Halifax. Henneberry flew with Innocente to Montreal and met Francois Germain: Henneberry subsequently made about a dozen trips in which he picked up drugs at Germain's apartment and drove them back to Innocente's home in Nova Scotia. In early July of 1995 Innocente and Henneberry had a falling out and Henneberry stopped his involvement in transporting the drugs. Innocente was charged with and convicted of having conspired with Craig Henneberry to traffic in cannabis resin between June 1, 1995 and July 30, 1995.

In this later case, Innocente was charged with having conspired with five people (including Francois Germain but not including Craig Henneberry) to traffic in cannabis resin and cocaine between March 25, 1996 and May 17, 1996. At this later trial, he sought to plead "autrefois convict": that is, that he had already been in jeopardy for this behaviour at the earlier trial and had been convicted of it, and so could not be placed on trial a second time for the offence. The decision is heavily fact-dependant, but the basic issue is straightforward. The Crown argued that there were two separate and independent conspiracies: the earlier one of which Innocente had already been convicted, and this second, later one. Innocente argued that there was only one conspiracy, which stretched through the entire period from June 1, 1995 to May 17, 1996, and included, at various times, all of the co-conspirators named in the two indictments, and different drugs at different times.

BY THE COURT: —

1   Daniel Joseph Innocente pleads the special plea of *autrefois convict* to a charge of conspiracy to traffic in a narcotic. He relies upon a previous conviction and sentence on a charge of conspiracy to traffic in a narcotic as the basis for the plea. Pursuant to S. 607(3) of the *Criminal Code*, I am deciding whether he has established the special plea, without a jury, before calling upon him to plead further.

. . . .

72   I am satisfied that the two conspiracies alleged - that for which the accused was convicted on the first count of the Henneberry indictment and the conspiracy alleged in the Poirier indictment - are, in fact, one and the same conspiracy. It seems clear, based on the information that was available to the Crown at the time of the Henneberry trial, that the indictment could have been amended at that time to reflect (at the very least) a time period extending into 1996 and the involvement of Mr. Germain as a co-conspirator with Mr. Innocente.

73   Another basis for the Crown's submissions that there were two conspiracies rather than one is that the indictments referred to different narcotics. The Henneberry indictment referred only to cannabis resin, while the Poirier indictment referred to cannabis resin and cocaine. The Crown submits, essentially, that the addition of cocaine to the later indictment creates a new conspiracy. However, the conspiracies alleged involved the supply of drugs to enable Mr. Innocente to traffic in drugs. There was no limit to the types of drugs that would be involved in these transactions. Mr. Henneberry did not specifically recall all of the drugs that might have been involved, but he did testify that he had transported cannabis resin in the Thunderbird on the first trip.

74   I conclude that the likely introduction of cocaine in the period after March 26, 1996, did not trigger a new conspiracy or the end of the previous one. The enterprise commenced in May 1995 with the purchase of the Thunderbird and its registration in the name of Hélène Guitard, with Mr. Innocente retaining control and ownership of the vehicle, and with Mr. Innocente's discussions with Mr. Germain and Mr. Henneberry. Mr. Innocente engaged Mr. Henneberry to drive the vehicle, but only as driver. As Mr. Henneberry said, he was not a partner of Mr. Innocente, but was working for him. The conspiracy of which Mr. Henneberry was a part was one involving Mr. Innocente and Mr. Germain, for the sale and purchase of drugs, as opposed to the mere movement of drugs. Even if the introduction of cocaine represented the introduction of another object of the conspiracy, this does not necessarily end the existing conspiracy. A conspiracy can have more than one object.

75   The decision in *R. v. Saunders* (1990), 56 C.C.C. (3d) 220 (S.C.C.) (*sub nom. R. v. Rooke and De Vries*) does not assist the Crown. In that case the accused were charged with conspiracy to import heroin, but the evidence at trial was that one accused had been involved in the importation of cocaine rather than heroin. The trial judge instructed the jury that it could convict as long as the accused had conspired to traffic a narcotic, regardless of which narcotic. The Court of Appeal, [1987] B.C.J. No. 1351, ordered a new trial, and the Supreme Court of Canada dismissed the further appeal. McLachlin J. (as she then was) wrote (at p. 223):

It is a fundamental principle of criminal law that the offence, as particularized in the charge, must be proved.... [O]nce the Crown has particularized the narcotic in a charge, the accused cannot be convicted if a narcotic other than the one specified is proved. The Crown chose to particularize the offence in this case as a conspiracy to import heroin. Having done so, it was obliged to prove the offence thus particularized. To permit the Crown to prove some other offence characterized by different particulars would be to undermine the purpose of providing particulars, which is to permit "the accused to be reasonably informed of the transaction alleged against him, thus giving him the possibility of a full defence and a fair trial": *R. v. Côté* (1977), 33 C.C.C. (2d) 353 at p. 357....

Crown counsel suggests that the import of the decision of the Court of Appeal is that the Crown will necessarily fail in every case if it cannot prove that the conspiracy related to a particular narcotic, as opposed to and prohibited narcotic. I cannot accept that suggestion. I agree with Crown counsel that the gravamen of the offence is conspiracy to import a narcotic, rather than a particular kind of narcotic. The purpose of specifying the narcotic in a case such as this is to identify the transaction which is the basis of the alleged conspiracy. The fundamental requirement that the charge must provide sufficient particulars to reasonably permit the accused to identify the specific transaction may be met in a variety of ways. Where the Crown has evidence of the particular drug involved, this may properly be required to be provided as a particular identifying the transaction. But where the Crown is uncertain as to the particular drug which was the subject of the conspiracy, it may properly decline to give particulars of the drug. The charge may nevertheless stand, provided that it sufficiently clearly identifies the alleged conspiracy in some other way. There must be a new trial in this case, not because a conviction for conspiracy to import a narcotic cannot be supported without proof of the type of narcotic involved, but rather because the Crown chose in this case to particularize the drug involved and failed to prove the conspiracy thus particularized.

76   Relying on *Saunders*, the Crown claims that because it did not specify cocaine in the Henneberry indictment, such an allegation would substantially alter the charges against Mr. Innocente and increase his jeopardy without any evidence to support a request for an amendment. However, it does not appear to me that the court said it was impossible to find a conspiracy as alleged on the indictment providing the indictment was properly amended during the trial. In *Saunders*, the court pointed out that no amendment had been sought at trial or at the Court of Appeal, and that it would be unfair and prejudicial to the accused to permit an amendment that fundamentally and retroactively changed the nature of what the Crown was required to prove (pp. 223-224).

77   *Saunders* stands for the proposition that if the Crown specifies a particular narcotic, it must prove that narcotic, and that the Crown can seek to amend the particulars in the indictment pursuant to section 601. The basis for the position the court took in *Saunders* was the necessity for the accused to be aware of the transaction upon which the Crown relies to found the charge. The Crown is bound by its own particularization of the offence. This does not mean that the Crown can rely on that particularization in order to defeat a plea of *autrefois convict*.

78   Once again, I find the reasoning in *A.A.B.* helpful on this point. As in that case, the transaction that forms the basis of the *autrefois* plea was a continuing

transaction which could have captured both indictments had the necessary amendments been sought.

79   Another instructive case is the Ontario Court of Appeal's decision in *R. v. Paterson, Ackworth and Kovach* (1985), 18 C.C.C. (3d) 137 (affirmed at 39 C.C.C. (3d) 575 (S.C.C.)). In that case, the three accused were charged with conspiracy to traffic in cannabis resin. One accused was also charged with conspiracy to traffic in methamphetamine. The trial judge concluded that there had been a single conspiracy to traffic in both methamphetamine and cannabis resin, rather than the two conspiracies charged in the indictment. Martin J.A. quoted the following comment of the trial judge (at pp. 141-142):

> ... I am forced to reject the central arch-stone of the Crown's case, namely, that there were two conspiracies and not just one. To me, the Crown has totally failed to show that there were separate conspiracies in methamphetamine and cannabis resin. Indeed, it is my view ... that the Crown has proved one conspiracy to traffic, with two objects - the selling of a mix of so-called hard and soft drugs.
>
> The Crown, in attempting to breathe life into the two-conspiracy theory, has artfully attempted to segregate the evidence - especially the wire-tap evidence - into two separate segments or compartments, but, as I review that evidence, it simply cannot be jammed into the allegedly water-tight compartments raised in the Crown theory....
>
> The result I am driven to on this aspect of the case is that the Crown has totally failed to establish a "two conspiracy" case, as charged in the indictment. As it seems to me, the Crown has tried to package and compartmentalize the totality of the evidence to suit a preconceived theory, but the evidence does not, in my view of it, fit the artificial structure invented by the Crown. Rather, the Crown has proved a single conspiracy with two objects and multiple participants....

80   Martin J.A. went on to state the following propositions, among others (at p. 143):

> A single conspiracy may have more than one illegal object and it is proper to allege in one count a conspiracy to commit several crimes. If the prosecution proves a conspiracy to do any one of the prohibited acts alleged in the indictment as the objects of the conspiracy, that is sufficient to support a conviction....
>
> Where there is but one agreement, and not separate agreements as to the different unlawful objects, there can only be one conviction....

81   The Court of Appeal took no issue with the trial judge's finding that there was actually a single conspiracy where the Crown had charged two separate conspiracies (nor, indeed, did the Supreme Court of Canada). In this case, as in *Paterson*, I am forced to the conclusion that the Crown has forced an "artificial structure" of two conspiracies onto what is, in fact, an allegation of a single conspiracy to traffic in narcotics. The two indictments - the Henneberry and Poirier indictments - as formulated by the Crown in fact allege a single conspiracy. The details include the participation of Mr. Innocente and Mr.

Germain in a scheme to transport narcotics from Montreal to Halifax by way of couriers (such as Mr. Henneberry) driving a Thunderbird automobile modified to conceal drugs in a secret compartment, and by other drivers and other means until the arrest of Mr. Germain and Mr. Poirier on May 15, 1996.

CONCLUSION

82   I conclude that Mr. Innocente's plea of *autrefois convict* in relation to the Poirier indictment must succeed. Accordingly, Mr. Innocente is discharged in respect of the charge before the court. The charge is dismissed.

3. LIABILITY FOR OFFENCE NOT COMMITTED

R. c. DÉRY

2006 SCC 53, 2006 CarswellQue 9479, 2006 CarswellQue 9480, 213 C.C.C. (3d) 289, [2006] 2 S.C.R. 669, 43 C.R. (6th) 94

The judgment of the court was delivered by Fish J.: —

5   December brings with it, in Canada and elsewhere, a holiday season widely and joyously celebrated by "raising a glass". Liquor merchants must frequently replenish their shelves to keep the glasses filled. In the Quebec City region, the Société des alcools du Québec ("SAQ") is forced by the increased demand to stock more of its products than its secure warehouses can contain. The inevitable overflow is stored temporarily in trailers parked outdoors at an SAQ compound.

6   An unrelated investigation resulted in the interception of discussions between Mr. Déry, Daniel Savard and others, concerning the possibility of stealing this liquor stored outdoors. On the strength of the intercepted conversations, Messrs. Déry and Savard were both charged with conspiracy to commit theft and conspiracy to possess stolen goods.

7   There was no evidence that either accused had taken any steps to carry out the proposed theft, and the trial judge was not persuaded that they had at any point agreed to steal or possess the liquor that was the object of their covetous musings: (2002), 7 C.R. (6th) 325. In the absence of a proven agreement, the judge quite properly felt bound to acquit the accused of the conspiracies charged. On each count, however, he convicted both co-accused of attempting to conspire, which he believed to be an included offence.

8   A majority of the Court of Appeal of Quebec affirmed their convictions at trial: [2005] Q.J. No. 5350 (QL), 2005 QCCA 483; [2005] Q.J. No. 5351 (QL),

2005 QCCA 484. Forget J.A., dissenting, would have allowed their appeals on the ground that attempted conspiracy is an offence unknown to Canadian law.

9   This further appeal, by Mr. Déry alone, comes to this court as of right. The decisive issue is whether there is any legal basis for concluding that attempt to conspire to commit an indictable offence is a crime in Canada. In the absence of a statutory basis for concluding that the crime exists, there is of course no need to find authority that it does not: s. 9(a) of the *Criminal Code*, R.S.C. 1985, c. C-46, makes clear that no one in Canada may be convicted of "an offence at common law". To affirm Mr. Déry's convictions, we must therefore find that attempt to conspire has until now lain dormant within the statutory confines of the *Criminal Code*, ready to be roused by a proper sounding of its governing provisions.

10   Like Forget J.A., I would let sleeping laws lie.

. . . .

40   The argument in favour of attempted conspiracy is that the provisions governing inchoate liability can be stacked one upon the other, like building blocks. Pursuant to s. 463(d), attempting to commit any "offence for which the offender may be prosecuted by indictment" is an indictable offence punishable by half the maximum penalty for the attempted offence. Conspiracy to commit an indictable offence is itself an indictable offence, punishable by the maximum penalty provided for the underlying substantive offence: s. 465(1)(c). Likewise, it is argued, attempt to conspire is an offence punishable by half the penalty provided for the completed conspiracy.

41   I agree with Forget J.A. that this argument is seductive in appearance but unsound in principle (para. 79). It assumes, but does not establish, that attempt to conspire is an offence under the *Criminal Code*, and it leaves unresolved the question whether the definition of attempt in s. 24 captures, as a matter of law, an attempt to conspire.

42   In virtue of s. 24, a test of proximity separates "mere preparation" from attempt:

> 24. (1) Every one who, having an intent to commit an offence, does or omits to do anything for the purpose of carrying out the intention is guilty of an attempt to commit the offence whether or not it was possible under the circumstances to commit the offence.

> (2) *The question whether an act or omission by a person who has an intent to commit an offence is or is not mere preparation to commit the offence, and too remote to constitute an attempt to commit the offence*, is a question of law.

43   The intent of the legislator in s. 24(2) is to fix the threshold of criminal responsibility. Applying the test provided, courts must situate on a continuum

from antisocial contemplation to prohibited conduct — or bad thought to substantive crime — the point where the criminal law intervenes. This continuum was aptly described a half-century ago by Laidlaw J.A. in *R. v. Cline* (1956), 115 C.C.C. 18 (Ont. C.A.):

> The consummation of a crime usually comprises a series of acts which have their genesis in an idea to do a criminal act; the idea develops to a decision to do that act; a plan may be made for putting that decision into effect; the next step may be preparation only for carrying out the intention and plan; but when that preparation is in fact fully completed, the next step in the series of acts done by the accused for the purpose and with the intention of committing the crime as planned cannot, in my opinion, be regarded as remote in its connection with that crime. The connection is in fact proximate. [p. 28]

44   In *Dynar*, Cory and Iacobucci JJ. observed that conspiracy is an act that precedes the next step after preparing to carrying out a plan:

> *Conspiracy is in fact a more "preliminary" crime than attempt*, since the offence is considered to be complete before any acts are taken that go beyond mere preparation to put the common design into effect. The Crown is simply required to prove a meeting of the minds with regard to a common design to do something unlawful . . . [Emphasis added; para. 87.]

And they explained that "the reason for punishing conspiracy before any steps are taken towards attaining the object of the agreement is *to prevent the unlawful object from being attained, and therefore to prevent this serious harm from occurring*" (para. 90 (emphasis added)). The serious harm referred to is not the conspiracy but the substantive offence. By criminalizing conspiracy, the legislature has intervened earlier along the continuum because of the increased danger represented by a cohort of wrongdoers acting in concert. See G. Côté-Harper, P. Rainville and J. Turgeon, *Traité de droit penal canadien* (4th ed. 1998), at pp. 661-63.

45   The question this court must now answer is whether acts that precede a conspiracy are sufficiently proximate to a substantive offence to warrant criminal sanction. In *Dungey*, Dubin J.A. answered this question in the negative:

> Notwithstanding that the charge was one of conspiracy, the conduct of the respondent should be viewed as a step preparatory to committing the substantive offence of fraud and, in that sense, what he did would be too remote to constitute an attempt. [p. 98]

In *R. v. Chan* (2003), 178 C.C.C. (3d) 269 (Ont. C.A.), Simmons J.A. was of a similar view:

> Strictly inchoate crimes are a unique class of criminal offences in the sense that they criminalize acts that precede harmful conduct but do not necessarily inflict harmful consequences in and of themselves. It can thus be appreciated that it could extend the criminal law too far to reach behind those acts and criminalize behaviour that precedes those acts. [para. 69]

46   I agree with these observations. In *Dungey*, Dubin J.A. left the door open to a possible exception for substantive conspiracy precisely because, in that context, "the question of remoteness would not arise" (p. 99) since substantive conspiracies are themselves the legislative focus of the perceived harm, and not simply the risk of its possible commission.

47   Given that conspiracy is essentially a crime of intention, and "[c]riminal law should not patrol people's thoughts" (*Dynar*, at para. 169, per Major J.), it is difficult to reach further than the law of conspiracy already allows. Even if it were possible, it has never been the goal of the criminal law to catch all crime [Translation] "in the egg", as the Attorney General for Canada has put it in this case (factum, at para. 58). In this sense, conspiracies are criminalized when hatched. And they can only be hatched by agreement.

48   This basic element of conspiracy — agreement — exposes the otherwise hidden criminal intentions of the parties to it. This demonstrates their commitment to a prohibited act. By contrast, the criminal law intervenes later in the progression from thought to deed where someone acts alone. Overt steps are then thought necessary to disclose and establish with sufficient certainty the criminal intention that is an essential element of the attempt to commit an offence.

49   By its very nature, moreover, an agreement to commit a crime in concert with others enhances the risk of its commission. Early intervention through the criminalization of conspiracy is therefore both principled and practical.

50   Likewise, the criminalization of attempt is warranted because its purpose is to prevent harm by punishing behaviour that demonstrates a substantial risk of harm. When applied to conspiracy, the justification for criminalizing attempt is lost, since an attempt to conspire amounts, at best, to a risk that a risk will materialize.

51   Finally, though Mr. Déry discussed a crime hoping eventually to commit it with others, neither he nor they committed, or even agreed to commit, the crimes they had discussed. The criminal law does not punish bad thoughts of this sort that were abandoned before an agreement was reached, or an attempt made, to act upon them.

52   For these reasons, I would allow the appeal, set aside Mr. Déry's convictions and order that acquittals be entered instead.

In *R. v. F. (J.)* (2013), 99 C.R. (6th) 1, [2013] 1 S.C.R. 565 Moldaver J. for the Court distinguished *Déry* to allow for the possibility of a person being a party to a conspiracy. However, liability on that basis would depend on the person specifically aiding in the formation of the conspiracy, not merely aiding in the commission of the offence at which the conspiracy was aimed. Steve Coughlan in a C.R. annotation argues that this is a sensible balance at a policy level which will neither over- nor under-criminalize. Compare criticism by Micah Rankin, "Party Liability for Conspiracy After *R. v. F. (J.)*" (2013), 99 C.R. (6th) 24.

R. v. HAMILTON

[2005] 2 S.C.R. 432, 30 C.R. (6th) 243, 198 C.C.C. (3d) 1,
2005 CarswellAlta 1037, 2005 CarswellAlta 1038 (S.C.C.)

FISH J. (MCLACHLIN C.J., BASTARACHE, BINNIE, LEBEL and DESCHAMPS JJ. concurring): —

1   The respondent, René Luther Hamilton, offered for sale through the Internet access to a "credit card number generator" — in terms that extolled its use for fraudulent purposes. As part of the same package of "Top Secret Files", he also offered for sale bomb "recipes" and information on how to commit burglaries.

2   Mr. Hamilton was charged under s. 464(a) of the *Criminal Code*, R.S.C. 1985, c. C-46, in four separate counts, with counselling the commission of indictable offences that were not in fact committed.

3   The trial judge was not satisfied that Mr. Hamilton had acted with the requisite *mens rea*, or culpable intent, and she therefore acquitted him on all four counts: (2002), 3 Alta. L.R. (4th) 147, 2002 ABQB 15. The Court of Appeal for Alberta dismissed the Crown's appeal: (2003), 25 Alta. L.R. (4th) 1, 2003 ABCA 255.

4   The Crown now appeals to this court on the ground that the trial judge erred as to the *mens rea* of counselling. In the Crown's view, it is unnecessary to prove that the person who counselled the offence intended that it be committed; recklessness is sufficient.

5   The Crown contends that even if recklessness is insufficient, the trial judge erred in confounding "motive" and "intent." With respect, I agree that the trial judge erred in this regard and that her verdict, but for this error, might very well have been different, at least on the count for counselling fraud. She acquitted Mr. Hamilton of that offence because, in her own words, "[h]is *motivation* was monetary" (para. 53; emphasis added).

6   I would therefore allow the Crown's appeal, order a new trial on the count for counselling fraud and dismiss the appeal with respect to the three remaining counts.

7   Mr. Hamilton was charged under s. 464 of the *Criminal Code* with counselling four indictable offences that were not committed: making explosive

substances with intent; doing anything with intent to cause an explosion; break and enter with intent; and fraud.

8   The charges resulted from an advertisement, or "teaser", sent by Mr. Hamilton through the Internet to more than 300 people whose addresses he had acquired from published lists. His advertisement read, in part:

HAVE YOU EVER HEARD OF A SOFTWARE PROGRAM THAT CAN PRODUCE AND DISPLAY VALID WORKING CREDIT CARD NUMBERS AT THE TOUCH OF A KEY!!!!

WELL IT'S ARRIVED ..... THE TIME IS NOW!!

THE AUTOMATIC CREDIT CARD NUMBER GENERATOR!!!!!!!!!

...

ALL VALID AND FULLY FUNCTIONAL!!

...

*YOU CAN ALSO Extrapolate NEW CREDIT CARD NUMBERS OFF OF YOUR EXISTING ALREADY VALID REAL CREDIT CARDS!!!! 100% valid numbers!

SIMPLE TO USE??? - ABSOLUTELY!!

...

IMAGINE THE THINGS THAT YOU COULD DO WITH THIS PROGRAM, AND THE VALID CREDIT CARD NUMBERS IT GENERATES!!

THE POSSIBILITIES ARE ENDLESS!!!

...

ALSO AVAILABLE IS THE OVERSEA'S AT&T CALLING CARD NUMBER GENERATOR!!!!!

FREE LONG DISTANCE??? YUPPERS! YES INDEED, ABSOLUTELY!!!!!

*THIS SIMPLE EASY TO USE PROGRAM PRODUCES VALID OVERSEA'S AT&T CALLING CARD NUMBERS.. WITH ONE STROKE OF THE KEY!!! ....

...

*GET ANY CREDIT CARD YOU WANT

...

ALL OF THESE METHODS *HAVE BEEN PROVEN TO WORK OVER AND OVER, TIME AND TIME AGAIN!!* THESE ARE THE SECRETS THAT MILLIONAIRES AND GOVERNMENT INSIDERS ONLY TELL THEIR FRIENDS ABOUT!!

Don't delay ... This Extraordinary and Valuable Information including the Card Generator Programs can be yours Today for ONLY $50 (US FUNDS).

...

IF YOU DOWNLOAD THE PROGRAMS AND USE THEM ... WE ACCEPT NO LIABILITY FOR YOUR ACTIONS!

...

DON'T MISS OUT ON THIS CHANCE TO GET YOUR HANDS ON THESE TWO AMAZING PROGRAMS, THAT WILL FOREVER CHANGE YOUR LIFE .. ! IF YOU MISS THE CHANCE NOW, IT MIGHT NOT COME AROUND AGAIN ..... AS THESE SOFTWARE PROGRAMS ARE NOT SOLD IN RETAIL STORES, FOR OBVIOUS REASONS!!

...

Looking forward to seeing you well on your way to a wealthy lifestyle!! [Emphasis added.]

9   Mr. Hamilton also created a web site advertising the Top Secret files, and was shown to have made at least 20 sales.

10   The trial judge found that Mr. Hamilton had seen a computer-generated list of the contents of the Top Secret files. They contained document descriptions such as "bombs.txt", "bombs2.txt", "bombs3.txt", "How to Break into a House.txt", and "visa hacking.txt". Mr. Hamilton testified that he had not read these files, and the trial judge, without making an express finding, appears to have accepted his evidence in this regard. The Top Secret files were organized into two zip files, which consisted of roughly 2000 pages of text. Only 13 pages related to the counselling charges that concern us here.

11   A document describing a credit card number generator that was not part of the Top Secret files was also discovered on Mr. Hamilton's computer. As well, a handwritten list of Visa numbers was seized in his possession. Of the listed numbers, all but one were found by the judge to be "valid" (para. 15), in the sense of "usable". But no complaints were received by the bank regarding their improper use. The trial judge accepted Mr. Hamilton's evidence that he did not use the credit card numbers he had generated.

12   The trial judge acquitted Mr. Hamilton on all counts and the Court of Appeal affirmed the acquittals.

III

13   The Crown contends that recklessness satisfies the fault requirement of counselling and that, even if intent (as opposed to recklessness) must be proved, the trial judge erred in grafting onto the required element of intention an additional requirement of motive.

14   At common law, counselling or procuring a felony was a substantive offence, whether or not the felony was subsequently committed: *R. v. Brousseau* (1917), 56 S.C.R. 22. The charges that concern us here are now codified in s. 464(a) of the *Criminal Code*, which provides:

> 464. . . .(a) every one who counsels another person to commit an indictable offence is, if the offence is not committed, guilty of an indictable offence and liable to the same punishment to which a person who attempts to commit that offence is liable;

15   The *actus reus* for counselling will be established where the materials or statements made or transmitted by the accused actively induce or advocate — and do not merely describe — the commission of an offence: *R. v. Sharpe*, [2001] 1 S.C.R. 45, 2001 SCC 2, McLachlin C.J., at para. 57.

16   The *mens rea*, or fault element, for counselling was recently considered in *R. v. Janeteas* (2003), 172 C.C.C. (3d) 97, which involved an appeal by the accused against his conviction on one count of counselling murder and two counts of counselling unlawful bodily harm. The trial judge had instructed the jury that they could convict the accused of these offences only if they were satisfied beyond a reasonable doubt that he had counselled their commission "with the intent that his advice or counselling ... *be accepted*" (para. 14; emphasis added).

17   The Ontario Court of Appeal found this instruction to be inadequate. In the court's view, it was not enough for the jury to conclude that the accused intended that his counselling of the offences "be accepted" or "be taken seriously" (para. 43) by the persons counselled to commit then; the accused must have intended as well that the offence counselled be in fact committed (para. 46).

18   In the present case, the trial judge described counselling as a "dual *mens rea* offence" (para. 37) and the Court of Appeal in *Janeteas* cited this characterization of the requisite mental element in its reasons (at para. 19).

19   *Janeteas* was decided on an unusual set of facts and in light of concessions by Crown counsel as to the inadequacy of the trial judge's instructions to the jury. Moreover, authorities cited by the Court of Appeal – none of them binding on this court – do support the proposition that counselling is a "dual intent" offence. But the court in *Janeteas* did take care to say that it would have reached the same result even if it were found sufficient for conviction that the accused, in counselling the commission of the offences, was reckless as to the consequences.

20   In my respectful view, a judicial determination of the fault element for counselling should not be made to depend on whether the required *mens rea* is characterized as "dual". I find it preferable to begin instead by considering why

the counselling of crime is prohibited and then to examine the ordinary meaning of the words used by Parliament to achieve its purpose.

21   Our concern here is with the imposition of criminal liability on those who counsel others to commit crimes. In this context, "counsel" includes "procure, solicit or incite": see s. 22(3) of the *Criminal Code*.

22   In their relevant senses, the *Canadian Oxford Dictionary* (2nd ed. 2004) defines "counsel" as "advise" or "recommend (a course of action)"; "procure", as "bring about"; "solicit", as "ask repeatedly or earnestly for or seek or invite", or "make a request or petition to (a person)"; and "incite", as "urge". "Procure" has been held judicially to include "instigate" and "persuade": *R. v. Gonzague* (1983), 4 C.C.C. (3d) 505 (Ont. C.A.).

23   Those who encourage the commission of crimes in any of these ways are criminally responsible for their conduct by way of "secondary liability".

24   The rationale underlying secondary liability was described by the Law Reform Commission of Canada as "straightforward, obvious and justifiable" – in principle, though not always in practice: Working Paper 45, *Secondary Liability: Participation in Crime and Inchoate Offences* (1985), at p. 5.

25   According to the Commission (at pp. 5-6):

> . . . the rationale for secondary liability is the same as that for primary liability. Primary liability attaches to the commission of acts which are outlawed as being harmful, as infringing important human interests and as violating basic social values. Secondary liability attaches on the same ground to their attempted commission, to counselling their commission and to assisting their commission.
>
> This is clear with participation. If the primary act (for example, killing) is harmful, then doing it becomes objectionable. But if doing it is objectionable, it is also objectionable to get another person to do it, or help him do it. For while killing is objectionable because it causes actual harm (namely, death), so too inducing and assisting killing are objectionable because of the potential harm: *they increase the likelihood of death occurring.*
>
> The same arguments hold for inchoate crimes. Again, if the primary act (for example, killing), is harmful, society will want people not to do it. Equally, it will not want them even to try to do it, or to counsel or incite others to do it. *For while the act itself causes actual harm, attempting to do it, or counselling, inciting or procuring someone else to do it, are sources of potential harm – they increase the likelihood of that particular harm's occurrence.* Accordingly, society is justified in taking certain measures in respect of them: outlawing them with sanctions, and authorizing intervention to prevent the harm from materializing. [Emphasis added.]

26   These passages, in my view, aptly explain why Parliament has imposed criminal responsibility on those who counsel, procure, solicit or incite others to commit crimes, whether or not the crimes are in fact committed.

27   And it seems to me that the plain meaning of the terms used by Parliament to achieve this purpose point to a fault element that combines advertent conduct with a "conscious disregard of unjustified (and substantial) risk" that it entails: L. Alexander and K. D. Kessler, "*Mens rea* and Inchoate Crimes" (1997), 87 J. Crim. L. & Criminology 1138, at p. 1175 (emphasis in original).

28   The "substantial and unjustified risk" standard of recklessness has venerable roots in Canada and in other common law jurisdictions as well: see, for example, *Leary v. The Queen*, [1978] 1 S.C.R. 29 at p. 35 (Dickson J., as he then was, dissenting on other grounds); and, generally, M.L. Friedland and K. Roach, *Criminal Law and Procedure: Cases and Materials* (8th ed. 1997), at pp. 508 ff, where Herbert Wechsler explains, at p. 510-11, why the American Law Institute required in its Model Penal Code that the risk consciously disregarded be both "substantial" and "unjustifiable".

29   In short, the *actus reus* for counselling is the deliberate encouragement or active inducement of the commission of a criminal offence. And the *mens rea* consists in nothing less than an accompanying intent or conscious disregard of the substantial and unjustified risk inherent in the counselling: that is, it must be shown that the accused either intended that the offence counselled be committed, or knowingly counselled the commission of the offence while aware of the unjustified risk that the offence counselled was in fact likely to be committed as a result of the accused's conduct.

30   I would resist any temptation to depart in this case from that relatively demanding standard. The Internet provides fertile ground for sowing the seeds of unlawful conduct on a borderless scale. And, at the hearing of the appeal, Crown counsel expressed with eloquence and conviction the urgent need for an appropriate prophylactic response.

31   In my view, however, this task must be left to Parliament. Even if they were minded to do so, courts cannot contain the inherent dangers of cyberspace crime by expanding or transforming offences, such as counselling, that were conceived to meet a different and unrelated need. Any attempt to do so may well do more harm than good, inadvertently catching morally innocent conduct and unduly limiting harmless access to information.

. . . .

IV

34   In determining that the *actus reus* of counselling was made out, the trial judge stated:

> In my view the teaser, viewed objectively, actively promotes the use of the credit card generator. The legal disclaimers do not discourage use. Rather they serve as a message that

the use of the numbers generated is illegal, and attempt to limit liability, which furthers rather than limits the message which is to use the numbers in a cautious fashion.

The Top Secret files sent out by Mr. Hamilton which relate to the charges amount to "How To" guides. The bomb documents contain recipes for bombs together with instructions for assembly and then instructions on how to detonate the bomb. "How to Break into a House" gives instructions in a step by step fashion for a style of break in and theft. The [Visa] hacker, or credit card number generator, is similar. [paras. 20-21]

35   The trial judge appears to have accepted Mr. Hamilton's evidence that he did not read the files relating to bombs and to burglaries and found as a fact that he had no intention to induce the recipients of his "teaser" to either build bombs or commit burglaries. This finding of fact was not reviewable in the Court of Appeal and is not subject to review in this court, since the Crown's right of appeal is limited in both instances to questions of law alone.

36   Mr. Hamilton's acquittal on the count for counselling fraud does not stand on the same footing.

37   At least as regards the credit card number generator, the trial judge concluded that the documents offered for sale — and sold — by Mr. Hamilton "actively promote or encourage the actions described in them" (para. 22). Applying the test set out in *R. v. Dionne* (1987), 79 N.B.R. (2d) 297 (C.A.), she found that the documents "are likely to incite and are 'with a view to' inciting the offence" (para. 22).

38   Nothing in the evidence suggests that Mr. Hamilton intended these documents to be read in a different manner or that they be used for a different purpose. Moreover, the trial judge expressly found that Mr. Hamilton had "subjective knowledge that the use of false credit card numbers is illegal" (para. 53).

39   The trial judge nonetheless acquitted Mr. Hamilton on the charge of counselling fraud because she had "a doubt that Mr. Hamilton had subjective intent to counsel fraud" (para. 53). And she explained her conclusion this way:

. . . His *motivation* was monetary, and he sought to pique the curiosity of readers who might acquire the information in the same way that he was initially attracted to the information. Further, he struck me as utterly unsophisticated and naïve to the point that he cannot be said to have been wilfully blind or reckless. [Emphasis added; para. 53.]

40   Essentially, on my reading of this passage, the trial judge acquitted Mr. Hamilton on this count because his motivation was mercenary as opposed to malevolent.

41   In my respectful view, this was an error of law requiring our intervention.

42   The distinction between motive and intent has been well understood by Canadian courts since at least 1979, when Dickson J. stated:

> In ordinary parlance, the words "intent" and "motive" are frequently used interchangeably, but in the criminal law they are distinct. In most criminal trials, the mental element, the *mens rea* with which the court is concerned, relates to "intent", i.e. the exercise of a free will to use particular means to produce a particular result, rather than with "motive", i.e. that which precedes and induces the exercise of the will. The mental element of a crime ordinarily involves no reference to motive: ...(*Lewis v. The Queen*, [1979] 2 S.C.R. 821, at p. 831)

43   Cory and Iacobucci JJ. also underlined this distinction in *Dynar v. United States*, [1997] 2 S.C.R. 462, emphasizing the importance, as a matter of legal policy, of maintaining it with vigilance: "It does not matter to society, in its efforts to secure social peace and order, what an accused's motive was, but only what the accused intended to do. It is no consolation to one whose car has been stolen that the thief stole the car intending to sell it to purchase food for a food bank" (para. 81). See also *R. v. Hibbert*, [1995] 2 S.C.R. 973.

44   In this case, of course, the motive attributed to the accused was far less laudable. He sought to make "a quick buck" by encouraging the intended recipients of his Internet solicitation to purchase a device that generated credit card numbers easily put to fraudulent use.

45   The trial judge's conclusion that Mr. Hamilton did not intend to induce the recipients to use those numbers is incompatible with the plain meaning of the "teaser" e-mail and with her other findings of fact, including her finding that Mr. Hamilton well understood that use of the generated numbers was illegal. Her assertion that "[h]is motivation was monetary" immediately after her reference to these facts demonstrates an error of law as to the *mens rea* for counselling the commission of a crime, and warrants a new trial.

V

46   I would for these reasons allow the appeal on the count for counselling fraud and order a new trial on that count, but dismiss the appeal in relation to the three remaining counts.

CHARRON J. (MAJOR and ABELLA JJ. concurring) (dissenting):

[The dissenting judges disagreed that recklessness could be a sufficient basis for convicting an accused of counselling an offence, arguing that only actual intention should be sufficient.]

. . . .

C. The *Actus reus* for Counselling an Offence not Committed

67   As stated earlier, only *mens rea* is at issue on this appeal. However, in order to properly determine the fault requirement for any offence, it is necessary to consider the *actus reus* of the offence so as to identify the circumstances and consequences to which the offence is directed. The *actus reus* under s. 464 consists of "counsel[ling] another person to commit an indictable offence" (or an offence punishable on summary conviction). Hence, there must be:

(a) an act of counselling;
(b) communicated to another person;
(c) in respect of the commission of an offence.

It is readily apparent from the language of the provision that the interpretation of the word "counsel", in large part, will determine the scope of criminal liability.

68   In its ordinary sense, counselling means simply to advise. If given that meaning, the scope of targeted activity would potentially be very wide. The simple communication of information on "how to" commit an offence would suffice to make out the *actus reus* of the offence. The criminalization of all such communications could easily be justified on the basis that society seeks to protect itself against the potential harm occasioned by acts of counselling — the increased likelihood that the counselled offence be committed. After all, it is at least arguable that the communication of this kind of information may plant a seed in the recipient's mind and increase the likelihood of the crime materializing. Should then all such communications be banned? More significantly, should they be subject to society's severest sanction, the criminal law?

69   We must ask ourselves if the resulting encroachment on freedom of speech would exact too high a cost. If "counsel" meant simply to advise, a lawyer's advice to a client on the law with respect to the various means of committing an offence could potentially be caught. Movies, video games, textbooks, and other literary works that describe or depict the commission of an offence may be subject to state scrutiny. I would think it obvious that such a prohibition on expression would be too wide. It is for this reason, as we shall see, that such an interpretation of the word "counsel" has been rejected in the criminal context.

70   The requisite *actus reus* of the offence of counselling was considered in *R. v. Dionne* (1987), 79 N.B.R. (2d) 297 (C.A.). Mr. Dionne was charged with counselling indictable offences that were not committed. He was alleged to have counselled an undercover officer to commit the offences of threatening and

assault causing bodily harm. The trial judge instructed the jury on the requisite elements of the offences as follows, at para. 20:

> [Translation] Taking each count individually, the offence is complete if, first of all, the accused had the intention of having injury caused, or of having threats made by telephone, as the case may be, and secondly, if the accused conveyed his intention to someone else with a view to having that person cause the injuries, or make the threats by telephone.

71   On appeal, the New Brunswick Court of Appeal held that these instructions were erroneous. The *actus reus* of the offence of counselling could not be made out on the basis of a mere passive communication by an accused of his desire that an offence be committed — more was required. Ayles J.A. stated as follows, at para. 21:

> [Translation] In my opinion, those instructions are incorrect since the offence of incitement implies actions which are more serious than those of conveying one's intention to have injuries inflicted upon someone, with a view to having those injuries inflicted. *The actions or words must be capable of inducing a person to commit the intended offences, and passive communication of one's intention does not constitute an offence even if the object is to have injuries inflicted upon someone.* [Emphasis added.]

72   This court considered *Dionne* and expressly adopted this "stronger meaning of actively inducing" in *R. v. Sharpe*, [2001] 1 S.C.R. 45, 2001 SCC 2, at para. 56. In order for the *actus reus* to be proven, the words communicated by the accused, viewed objectively, must be seen as actively inducing, procuring or encouraging the commission of an offence. This restricted interpretation of the meaning of counselling is not only consonant with the definition of "counsel" under s. 22(3), it ensures that the scope of the offence remains within the justifiable limits of the criminal law. It is this concern of potential overbreadth that informed this court's adoption in *Sharpe* of a more restricted meaning of counselling.

73   The need to carefully circumscribe the scope of an offence prohibiting a form of communication was discussed at length in *R. v. Keegstra*, [1990] 3 S.C.R. 697. In that case, the constitutional validity of s. 319(2), which prohibits communications that wilfully promote hatred against an identifiable group, was challenged on the basis that it unduly restricted the freedom of expression under s. 2(b) of the *Canadian Charter of Rights and Freedoms*. This court, by majority decision, upheld the constitutional validity of the provision. It did so on the basis that s. 319(2) possessed sufficient definitional safeguards to ensure that it captured only the harm to which the prohibition is targeted and, as such, did not unduly restrict the s. 2(b) guarantee.

74   Hence, as held in *Sharpe*, nothing short of active inducement or encouragement will suffice to make out the *actus reus* of the offence of counselling. In other words, when viewed objectively, the communication must be one that actively seeks to persuade the person counselled to commit the crime.

In this way, the scope of targeted activity is not extended to the mere possibility of planting a seed in the recipient's mind; it is limited to those communications that are likely to cause that seed to sprout, creating a resolve to commit the crime. It is only then that the potential risk justifies the criminal prohibition. However, it is well established that it is not necessary that the person counselled be in fact persuaded: *R. v. Walia* (1975), 9 C.R. (3d) 293 (B.C.C.A.), at pp. 293-95; *R. v. Glubisz* (1979), 47 C.C.C. (2d) 232 (B.C.C.A.), at pp. 235 and 241-42; *R. v. Gonzague* (1983), 4 C.C.C. (3d) 505 (Ont. C.A.), at pp. 508-9. The focus on a prosecution for counselling is on the counsellor's conduct and state of mind, not that of the person counselled.

D. The *Mens Rea* for Counselling an Offence Not Committed

75   No constitutional challenge is raised in this case. Nonetheless, the court must be mindful of the potential overbreadth of a criminal sanction whose sole target is speech. As reiterated in *Sharpe*, Parliament is presumed to have intended to enact legislation in conformity with the *Charter* (para. 33). This concern over the potential sweep of the provision does not end with the analysis of the requisite *actus reus* and the level of risk targeted by Parliament. The persons who could potentially fall within the reach of the criminal law must be considered. Because of the stigma attached to a criminal prosecution and to a conviction, it is important that the offence not catch the morally innocent.

76   The requisite *mens rea* is not expressly set out in s. 464. However, this is not unusual. The mental element of an offence is not always described in the enactment. Often it must be inferred from the nature of the prohibited activity and the harm it is meant to guard against. In this case, because of the nature of the offence, our earlier discussion on the requisite *actus reus* can largely inform the determination of the necessary *mens rea*. As we have seen, it is not sufficient that the communication simply raise the possibility of affecting its recipient; it must actively seek to persuade that person to commit the crime. It follows that the counsellor must, at the very least, intend to persuade the person counselled to commit the offence. In this respect, it is my view that mere recklessness as to the counselled person's reaction to the communication is insufficient. In other words, it is not enough that the counsellor, knowing that the communication is objectively capable of persuading a person to commit an offence, goes ahead and does the act anyway. If mere recklessness as to the communication's potential power of persuasion were to suffice, some may argue that the publication of Shakespeare's *Henry VI*, with its famous phrase "let's kill all the lawyers", should be subject to state scrutiny!

[The dissenting judges also disagreed that the trial judge had erred by confusing "motive" and "intention".]

84   The trial judge concluded that Mr. Hamilton did not have the necessary *mens rea* on any standard. The Court of Appeal saw no reason to interfere with her conclusion. Nor do I. My colleague Fish J. is of the view that the trial judge erred by confounding "motive" and "intent". He rests this conclusion on the trial judge's finding that Mr. Hamilton's motivation was monetary. With respect, I disagree. The trial judge's consideration of Mr. Hamilton's motivation must be examined in the context of the evidence before her, and her reasons must be read as a whole.

85   Mr. Hamilton testified that he had not intended to induce the commission of any criminal offence. He had not written any of the files; he had himself purchased them off the Internet and did not even know what much of the information was about. The files consisted of roughly 2,000 pages of text, only 13 of which related to the charges before the court. In particular, he had not read any of the files about bombs or break and enters. The teaser made no reference to these files. As for the material on the credit card generator, he thought readers would simply be interested, as he had been, in discovering how easy it was to generate valid credit card numbers. He did not think anyone could use the credit card numbers without a valid name, expiry date or security number. Notably, at the relevant time Mr. Hamilton had never owned a credit card. The trial judge, as she was entitled to do, accepted Mr. Hamilton's testimony. She concluded as follows, at paras. 53-54:

> On all the evidence I find that Mr. Hamilton ought to have known he was counselling fraud. The teaser and his subjective knowledge that the use of false credit card numbers is illegal make this conclusion irresistible. However, I have a doubt that Mr. Hamilton had subjective intent to counsel fraud. His motivation was monetary, and he sought to pique the curiosity of readers who might acquire the information in the same way that he was initially attracted to the information. Further, he struck me as utterly unsophisticated and naïve to the point that he cannot be said to have been wilfully blind or reckless.
>
> I also find that Mr. Hamilton did not intend the fraud be carried out nor was he wilfully blind or reckless as to the risk of deprivation which would result (to use the *Theroux* test). In my view the evidence points to a conclusion that Mr. Hamilton was inviting others to do as he had done: to satisfy their curiosity by seeing how easy it is to generate the numbers and to expect that they cannot use them without the expiry date. In other words, he did not specifically intend that the fraud would be carried out. Nor, in all of the circumstances, ought he to have known that the fraud would be carried out. It follows that there could not be a conclusion that he was wilfully blind or reckless as to the consequences of the fraud. Rather, Mr. Hamilton was trying to make money by selling information on the Internet. In my view, on all of the evidence, it cannot be found he counselled fraud.

86   The trial judge was entitled to consider motive. It is a piece of circumstantial evidence that may assist in determining an accused's state of

mind. In reading her reasons as a whole, I see no reason to interfere with the conclusion reached by the Court of Appeal on this issue, at para. 44:

> The trial judge did not err as alleged by the Crown. As she was entitled to do, the trial judge considered motive as part of her fact findings. But her decision was based on other facts relating to the respondent's knowledge. She found, for example, that the respondent had not read most of the "Top Secret" files. She also found that he was not interested in their contents and that he was, overall, "naive, lazy or ignorant". Dealing with the credit card number generator, the trial judge accepted the respondent's testimony that he did not think any generated numbers could be used because they lacked an expiry date. On the basis of these facts, she found the respondent lacked sufficient knowledge of the consequences of his actions to satisfy the *mens rea* requirement. It is clear that she understood the nature of the test she was bound to apply and did not err in law.

IV. Disposition

87   For these reasons, I would dismiss the appeal.

Chapter 10

GROUP RESPONSIBILITY:

CORPORATIONS, CRIMINAL ORGANIZATIONS AND TERRORIST GROUPS

1. CORPORATIONS

(a) Common Law

CANADIAN DREDGE AND DOCK CO. v. R.

[1985] 1 S.C.R. 662, 45 C.R. (4th) 289, 19 C.C.C. (3d) 1, 59 N.R. 241,
1985 CarswellOnt 939, 1985 CarswellOnt 96

This is the leading decision on the difficult issue of the "identification doctrine" under which Canadian courts for many years imputed fault, including *mens rea*, to corporations. The case concerned appeals of several corporate accused against their *Criminal Code* convictions for conspiracy to defraud. The charges stemmed from bids for dredging contracts found to have been collusive. The Supreme Court rejected arguments that the companies were not guilty as the bids had been conducted by managers acting in fraud of the companies or contrary to corporate instructions.

The Supreme Court confirmed the convictions and took the opportunity to assert and justify the identification doctrine for holding corporations responsible for *mens rea* offences.

ESTEY J.: —

The position of the corporation in criminal law must first be examined. Inasmuch as all criminal and quasi-criminal offences are creatures of statute the amenability of the corporation to prosecution necessarily depends in part upon the terminology employed in the statute. In recent years there has developed a system of classification which segregates the offences according to the degree of intent, if any, required to create culpability.

(a) *Absolute Liability Offences*

Where the Legislature by the clearest intendment establishes an offence where liability arises instantly upon the breach of the statutory prohibition, no particular state of mind is a prerequisite to guilt. Corporations and individual persons stand on the same footing in the face of such a statutory offence. It is a case of automatic primary responsibility. Accordingly, there is no need to establish a rule for corporate liability nor a rationale therefore. The corporation is treated as a natural person.

(b) *Offences of Strict Liability*

Where the terminology employed by the Legislature is such as to reveal an intent that guilt shall not be predicated upon the automatic breach of the statute — but rather upon the establishment of the *actus reus*, subject to the defence of due diligence, an offence of strict liability arises. See *R. v. City of Sault Ste. Marie*, [1978] 2 S.C.R. 1299. As in the case of an absolute liability offence, it matters not whether the accused is corporate or unincorporate, because the liability is primary and arises in the accused according to the terms of the statute in the same way as in the case of absolute offences. It is not dependent upon the attribution to the accused of the misconduct of others. This is so when the statute, properly construed, shows a clear contemplation by the Legislature that a breach of the statute itself leads to guilt, subject to the limited defence above noted. In this category, the corporation and the natural defendant are in the same position. In both cases liability is not vicarious but primary.

(c) *Offences Requiring Mens Rea*

These are the traditional criminal offences for which an accused may be convicted only if the requisite *mens rea* is demonstrated by the prosecution. At common law a corporate entity could not generally be convicted of a criminal offence. Corporate criminal immunity stemmed from the abhorrence of the common law for vicarious liability in criminal law, and from the doctrine of *ultra vires*, which regarded criminal activities by corporate agents as beyond their authority and beyond corporate capacity. At the other extreme in the spectrum of criminal offences there are certain crimes which cannot in any real sense be committed by a corporation as a principal, such as perjury and bigamy, whatever the doctrine of corporate criminal liability may be. As a corporation may only act through agents, there are basically only three approaches whereby criminal intent could be said to reside or not reside in the corporate entity:

> (i)   a total vicarious liability for the conduct of any of its agents whatever their level of employment or responsibility so long as they are acting within the scope of their employment;

(ii) no criminal liability unless the criminal acts in question have been committed on the direction or at the request, express or clearly implied of the corporation as expressed through its board of directors;

(iii) a median rule whereby the criminal conduct, including the state of mind, of employees and agents of the corporation is attributed to the corporation so as to render the corporation criminally liable so long as the employee or agent in question is of such a position in the organization and activity of the corporation that he or she represents its *de facto* directing mind, will, centre, brain area or ego so that the corporation is identified with the act of that individual. There is said to be on this theory no responsibility through vicarious liability or any other form of agency, but rather a liability arising in criminal law by reason of the single identity wherein is combined the legal entity and the natural person; in short, a primary liability. This rule stands in the middle of the range or spectrum. It is but a legal fiction invented for pragmatic reasons.

. . . .

This [median] rule of law was seen as a result of the removal of the officer or managerial level employee from the general class of "inferior servants or agents" for whose acts the corporate employer continued (as in the case of the human employer) to be immune from vicarious liability in criminal law. This result is generally referred to as the "identification" theory. It produces the element of *mens rea* in the corporate entity, otherwise absent from the legal entity but present in the natural person, the directing mind. This establishes the "identity" between the directing mind and the corporation which results in the corporation being found guilty for the act of the natural person, the employee. . . . The essence of the test is that the identity of the directing mind and the company coincide so long as the actions of the former are performed by the manager within the sector of corporation operation assigned to him by the corporation. The sector may be functional, or geographic, or may embrace the entire undertaking of the corporation. The requirement is better stated when it is said that the act in question must be done by the directing force of the company when carrying out his assigned function in the corporation. It is no defence to the application of this doctrine that a criminal act by a corporate employee cannot be within the scope of his authority unless expressly ordered to do the act in question. Such a condition would reduce the rule to virtually nothing. Acts of the ego of a corporation taken within the assigned managerial area may give rise to corporate criminal responsibility, whether or not there be formal delegation; whether or not there be awareness of the activity in the board of directors or the officers of the company; and, as discussed below, whether or not there be express prohibition.

. . . .

Generally the directing mind is also guilty of the criminal offence in question. Glanville Williams, in *Textbook of Criminal Law* (1978), states, at p. 947:

> . . . the director or other controlling officer will almost always be a co-perpetrator of or accessory in the offence . . . .

. . . .

The corporation is but a creature of statute, general or special, and none of the provincial corporation statutes and business corporations statutes, or the federal equivalents, contain any discussion of criminal liability or liability in the common law generally by reason of the doctrine of identification. It is a court-adopted principle put in place for the purpose of including the corporation in the pattern of criminal law in a rational relationship to that of the natural person. The identity doctrine merges the board of directors, the managing director, the superintendent, the manager or anyone else delegated by the board of directors to whom is delegated the governing executive authority of the corporation, and the conduct of any of the merged entities is thereby attributed to the corporation. . . . A corporation may, by this means, have more than one directing mind. This must be particularly so in a country such as Canada where corporate operations are frequently geographically widespread. The transportation companies, for example, must of necessity operate by the delegation and subdelegation of authority from the corporate centre; by the division and subdivision of the corporate brain; and by decentralizing by delegation the guiding forces in the corporate undertaking.

The Court in *Dredge and Dock* decided that there could be corporate responsibility on the identification doctrine whether or not there had been formal delegation, awareness of the activity in the board of directors or offices of the company, or express authorization or prohibition. However, the Court also noted that the identification doctrine could not be used where the criminal act of the directing mind had been totally in fraud of the corporation or where the act was intended to, or did result in, benefit exclusively to the directing mind.

The Australian scholar, Professor Brent Fisse (see, for example, "Corporate Criminal Responsibility" (1991) 15 Crim. L.J. 166 and "Criminal Law: The Attribution of Criminal Liability to Corporations: A Statutory Model" (1991) 13 Sydney L. Rev. 277) and others have called for a new approach for holding corporations responsible for intentional crimes. The argument is that under the identification doctrine the imputing of intent of employees to the corporate entity misses the point. Corporate behaviour is not just the sum of individual employee behaviour but must be considered in the context of the organizational structure and culture.

Professor Pamela Bucy, "Corporate Ethos: A Standard for Imposing Corporate Criminal Liability" (1991) 75 Minnesota L. Rev. 1095, has recently proposed a standard of corporate criminal liability which turns on whether there was a corporate ethos which encouraged the commission of crime. The inquiry is not only into whether the actors were sufficiently high in the hierarchy but also looks at such aspects as company goals and practices, the reaction to past offences and the existence and sufficiency of compliance programs.

(b) *Criminal Code* Provisions for Organizations (2003)

Twenty-six miners died in the Westray mine explosion in Nova Scotia. Manslaughter charges were laid against two mine managers based on breaches of health and safety regulations. After protracted proceedings they were dropped. In 2003 the federal government, with all party consent, responded by enacting[1] a new and severe regime to hold corporations and other organizations criminally responsible.

There are now two avenues to criminal responsibility:

Offences of negligence — organizations

22.1 In respect of an offence that requires the prosecution to prove negligence, an organization is a party to the offence if

(a) acting within the scope of their authority

(i) one of its representatives is a party to the offence, or

(ii) two or more of its representatives engage in conduct, whether by act or omission, such that, if it had been the conduct of only one representative, that representative would have been a party to the offence; and

(b) the senior officer who is responsible for the aspect of the organization's activities that is relevant to the offence departs — or the senior officers, collectively, depart — markedly from the standard of care that, in the circumstances, could reasonably be expected to prevent a representative of the organization from being a party to the offence.

Other offences — organizations

22.2 In respect of an offence that requires the prosecution to prove fault — other than negligence — an organization is a party to the offence if, with the intent at least in part to benefit the organization, one of its senior officers

(a) acting within the scope of their authority, is a party to the offence;

(b) having the mental state required to be a party to the offence and acting within the scope of their authority, directs the work of other representatives of the organization so that they do the act or make the omission specified in the offence; or

(c) knowing that a representative of the organization is or is about to be a party to the offence, does not take all reasonable measures to stop them from being a party to the offence.

---

1 S.C. 2003, c. 21, s. 2.

The massive width of these new provisions becomes clearer when one reads the definitions in s. 2 of the *Criminal Code* of the terms "organization" and "senior officer":

"organization" means

(a) a public body, body corporate, society, company, firm, partnership, trade union or municipality, or

(b) an association of persons that

(i) is created for a common purpose,

(ii) has an operational structure, and

(iii) holds itself out to the public as an association of persons;

"senior officer" means a representative who plays an important role in the establishment of an organization's policies or is responsible for managing an important aspect of the organization's activities and, in the case of a body corporate, includes a director, its chief executive officer and its chief financial officer;

The responsibility of the organization is no longer dependant on establishing fault in the "directing mind" but extends to a much lower level.

For a full analysis of the new law, see Todd Archibald, Kenneth Jull and Kent Roach, "The Changed Face of Corporate Liability" (2004) 48 Crim. L.Q. 306 and Paul Dusome, "Criminal Liability under Bill C-45: Paradigms, Prosecutors, Predicaments" (2007) 53 Crim. L.Q. 98. The authors suggest that the expansion of corporate liability is overdue. However, they criticize the new regime as being too broad, for a counter-intuitive extension of corporate liability for subjective intent offences to senior officers, and for blurring the distinction between regulatory and criminal liability.

For analysis of the few cases that have discussed the key term "senior officer" see Todd Archibald, Ken Jull and Kent Roach, "Critical Developments in Corporate Criminal Liability: Senior Officers, Wilful Blindness, and Agents in Foreign Jurisdictions" (2013) 60 Crim. L.Q. 92 and "Corporate Criminal Liability: Myriad Complexity in the Scope of Senior Officer" (2014) 60 Crim. L.Q. 386.

2.   CRIMINAL ORGANIZATIONS[2]

In 1997 the *Criminal Code* was amended[3] to include a wide variety of measures against "criminal organizations". Before considering the new

---

2 Many of the notes in this section first appeared in Stuart, "Politically Expedient but Potentially Unjust Criminal Legislation against Gangs" (1998) 69 Int. Rev. Penal Law 245. This was a much-expanded version of a paper of like name first published in (1997) 2 Can. Crim. L. Rev. 207. See too Michael Moon, "Outlawing the Outlaws: Importing R.I.C.O.'s Notion of Criminal Enterprise into Canada to Combat Organized Crime" (1999) 24 Queen's L.J. 451.

3 S.C. 1997, c. 23.

substantive provisions we need first to assess their political origins in gang violence in Quebec.

(a) Biker Violence

The immediate context was the eve of a 1997 federal election and the perceived need to respond to a plea by the Quebec Attorney General and Quebec mayors for measures to address a violent and protracted fight between two biker gangs: the Hells Angels and the Rock Machine. That strife, focused in Quebec, had led to bombings and some 30 deaths. One bomb blast killed an innocent passer-by, a young boy. Members of the public were understandably outraged and frightened.

The federal Minister of Justice and the Solicitor General of Canada described[4] the new Bill C-95 as "tough new measures to target criminal gang activity" which had been developed through "extensive consultations with police across Canada" and a two-day national forum. That forum, held in Ottawa on September 27-28, 1996, had brought together "police, representatives from provincial and federal governments, the legal community, private industry and academics". The purpose of the forum had been to "examine the increasingly complex problem of organized crime in Canada, and to recommend integrated, effective measures to address it".

Consideration of whether any measures were necessary was thus a question not on the agenda.

The centrepiece, explained the Ministers, was a new offence of "participation in a criminal organization". This did not criminalize mere membership in a criminal organization and laid the groundwork for the targeted use of new investigative tools to be directed against criminal organizations. These included special peace bonds, new powers to seize proceeds of crime, including access to income tax information, a new possession of explosive offence, tougher and consecutive sentencing provisions, greater powers to resort to electronic surveillance and a new reverse onus bail provision for those charged with the new offences. Bill C-95 was extremely complex, consisting of over 50 pages of detailed *Criminal Code* amendments. It passed with all party consent through Parliament in a day with no meaningful committee review, for example, of the extensive police powers which read like a police wish list.

(b) Participation in Criminal Organization (Gangsterism) (1997)

The new crime in s. 467.1(1) of participation in a criminal organization, often dubbed gangsterism in the media, extended criminal responsibility beyond the already wide net for accessories or conspirators. Under s. 467.1(2) there must be a mandatory consecutive sentence and double criminality for a participant in

---

4 Department of Justice News Release, "Federal Government Introduces National Anti-gang Measures", April 17, 1997.

a criminal organization who is a party to an offence committed in association with the organization.

The lynchpin is the definition of "criminal organization" inserted in 1997 into the *Criminal Code* definition s. 2 as follows:

> "Criminal organization" means any group, association or other body consisting of five or more persons, whether formally or informally organized,
>
> (a) having as one of its primary activities the commission of an indictable offence under this or any other Act of Parliament for which the maximum punishment is imprisonment for five years or more, and
>
> (b) any or all of the members of which engage in or have, within the preceding five years, engaged in the commission of a series of such offences.

This extended far beyond a cohesive gang committed to violence. This legislation does not just reach such broadly-structured gangs as the Mafia, the Hells Angels[5] or the Triads. It could certainly be applied to low-level members of a highly organized gang, to those only very loosely associated in crime and to those who have never been violent. Only one of the group has to have committed a series of offences within five years. There is no requirement of gang continuity.

Consider the following hypothetical example of drugs distribution in a predominantly black area of Toronto. A buys a quantity of drugs from a high-level drug dealer. Rather than attempt to sell the drugs himself he approaches fellow black friends, B and C, and acquaintances, D and E, with an offer of easy money. A is the only one with a criminal record of three offences within the last three years — selling marijuana and two breaking and entry. A arranges for the five to meet in a park to split up the cache. The meeting takes place but B and D do not attend. A subsequently meets with them separately. Under Bill C-95 this is a criminal organization. It does not matter that there was no meeting of the minds required for the crime of conspiracy or that this was not an ongoing or structured group. The possible application of Bill C-95's array of strong new measures to such a group came at a time of a major Commission Report documenting systemic racism against black youths in Toronto,[6] particularly in the enforcement of drug laws.

At its widest the complex new crime of participation in organized crime was committed by proof of

1. an association with an informal group of five or more;

2. knowledge that at least one of the group has been committing serious crimes within the last five years; and

3. being a party to an indictable offence in association with the group.

---

5 In *Brown v. Durham Regional Police Department* (1996), 106 C.C.C. (3d) 302 (Ont. Gen. Div.), a civil action against the police, the Court heard detailed evidence about motorcycle gangs in Canada. Ferguson J. noted that "the evidence showed that even organized clubs like the Hells Angels chapters appear to operate more as a brokerage of criminals than as a cohesive vertical hierarchy of criminal activity" (at 317).

6 *Report of the Commission on Systemic Racism in the Ontario Criminal Justice System* (1995).

Section 467.1 has breathtaking scope and could surely be applied to most engaged in criminal conduct. It could certainly be applied to the above-described temporary group of drug traffickers.[7] It is expressly a form of guilt by association long shunned by common law jurisdictions which normally require proof by the state of an individual act with personal fault relating to that act or a shared purpose. The requirement of being a party to an offence does require proof of some individual act and personal fault. However, this could merely be that required for liability as an accessory rather than perpetrator and could include anyone assisting another to commit a crime such as driving the getaway vehicle, or even merely providing it.

The new Canadian anti-gang provision is unlike the Italian *associazione di tipo Mafioso*,[8] which criminalizes membership in certain criminal associations. It is also distinguishable from the French *association de malfaiteurs*,[9] which penalizes group preparation equally to the completed offence.

The Canadian scheme appears to be a much wider version of the United States RICO model. Passed in 1970 as a weapon against organized crime, the *Racketeer Influenced and Corrupt Organizations Act*[10] requires proof of an "enterprise"[11] and a connected "pattern of racketeering activity".[12] Although the RICO net is itself notoriously wide, there is, in contrast to the Canadian model, a requirement of an ongoing structure of persons associated in time and purpose and organized for consensual decision-making.[13]

It has been suggested[14] that a proper definition of organized crime should embrace the elements of corruption, violence, sophistication, continuity, structure, discipline, ideology, multiple enterprises, involvement in legitimate enterprises and a "bonding" ritual.

Professor Christopher Blakesley reviewed[15] several national studies presented at an international conference in Alexandria, Egypt from November

---

7 Robert Gordon, "Criminal Business Organizations, Street Gangs and "Wanna-be Groups": A Vancouver Perspective" (2000) 42 Can. J. of Crim. 39 distinguishes the highly organized for-profit crime business, organized street gangs and the "wanna-be" unorganized groups which are typically young offenders.

8 In the 1987 show trial of alleged Sicilian Mafia members in Palermo, 344 were convicted and sentenced to a total of 2665 years in prison. By 1989 only 60 persons remained in prison: see Jean-Paul Brodeur, "Organized Crime: Trends in the Literature", a report to the Departments of Justice and the Solicitor General (May 1966) at 28-29.

9 There are so few prosecutions that the crime is not listed in the French Department of Justice statistics: Brodeur, *ibid.* at 28.

10 18 U.S.C. ss. 1961-1964.

11 Under s. 1961(4) an "enterprise" may be "any individual, partnership, corporation, association, or other legal entity, or any union or group of individuals associated in fact although not a legal entity".

12 A wide list of federal and state offences are enumerated as predicate offences ranging from murder to mail fraud: s. 1961.

13 See Christopher Blakesley, "The Criminal Justice System Facing The Challenge of Organized Crime: Section II. The Special Part", at p. 14 of an unpublished explanatory note written in preparation for the XVIth International Congress of Penal Law held in Budapest, Hungary, September 5-11, 1999.

14 Michael Maltz, "Defining Organized Crime", in Handbook of Organized Crime in the United States (1994) at 26

15 "General Report. The Criminal Justice System Facing the Challenge of Organised Crime" (1998) 69 Int. Rev. Penal Law 69.

8-12, 1997, as to the dangers of adopting ill-considered criminal legislation on organized crime and concluded as follows:

> It is easy to fall into the trap: politicians gain popularity and votes by looking "tough on crime", especially organised crime. They become even more popular when they are able to say bad things about courts that try to rectify the constitutional problems created by bad laws. Sadly, often the news media exacerbate the problem by pandering to public fear and appetite for salacious material. Outcries from interest groups are shrill, raising the cost to anyone who wishes to promote reasoned and constitutional laws. This all creates an atmosphere that tends to ignore the larger picture and which may actually hurt the battle against crime, while damaging human rights and democracy.[16]

(c) Fiasco of Manitoba Warriors Trial[17]

That the new anti-gang measures were not narrowly targeted became clear in the case of gangsterism charges laid in the trial of the Manitoba Warriors in Winnipeg.

In October 1998, police and prosecutors threw the new book at 35 accused. Most were charged with drugs and weapons charges and the new participation in a criminal organization offence involving the Manitoba Warriors. This was alleged to be a predominantly Aboriginal street gang. The Crown proceeded by direct indictment. Of those charged, all but two were Aboriginal. The hype and complexity escalated to such an extent that the Manitoba government constructed a custom-built high security court in an old mustard-seed cleaning plant. Many applied for bail. None succeeded. Review applications also failed. The new reverse onus bail provision for organized crime may have contributed to this extraordinary detention. The remand centre conditions were severe with contact visits severely limited. At appearances in the special courthouse accused were chained to the floor in special separate cubicles.

The public gallery was limited to 35 seats with an obstructed view which would not have permitted them to see the jury. After 20 months of pre-trial motions and guilty pleas only 15 accused remained. Finally outside counsel were employed to reach a plea bargain. As part of the deal the participation in a criminal organization charges were withdrawn. In all 32 guilty pleas were entered on drug charges including trafficking of cocaine in Winnipeg hotels. Only two guilty pleas were entered at an early stage to the participation in a criminal organization charges and these only involved lesser participants. The cost of building the courthouse was $3.3 million and the total cost of this trial has been estimated at $7 million.

The final outcome of this show trial is a monument to State folly. Roland Penner, a former Attorney General for Manitoba, has described it as "politically

---

16 *Ibid.* at 4.

17 This account was first published in Stuart, "Time to Recodify Criminal Law and Rise Above Law and Order Expediency: Lessons from the Manitoba Warrior Prosecution", (2001) 28 Manitoba L.J. 89. The major sources for this account are the judgment of Krindle J. in *R. v. Pangman* (2000), 32 C.R. (5th) 272 (Man. Q.B.) dismissing the application for a change of venue, a CBC Magazine program "The Indian Courthouse" of November 15, 1999 and "Gang-related Charges Dropped Against Alleged Warriors", *The Globe and Mail*, July 8, 2000.

motivated, expensive and constitutionally invalid".[18] Professor David Deutscher suggests it was "too complex, with too many accused and too many charges to have a chance of success".[19]

Only the most avid and self-congratulatory prosecutor could pronounce this trial as a success and a vindication of the anti-gang measures.[20] In terms of organized crime this street gang was, as even the Crown counsel put it, "in the junior leagues". Having endured this extraordinary use of State power, the Manitoba Warriors has been given notoriety and experienced an extraordinary use of State power which may lead, in a counterproductive way, to a more cohesive group in the future. As suggested by defence counsel Richard Peck:

> This has given them identity, empowerment and a sense of belonging which has been denied to them by society at large.[21]

Shouldn't this matter have been treated as a routine drugs conspiracy trial with discretion exercised to target only the major participants? At worst this was State action based on false stereotypes of Aboriginal people.

(d) Widening Gangsterism Laws (2001)[22]

The political cycle started again on the eve of another federal election in 2001. On September 12, 2000, a Montreal crime reporter was shot several times the day after he had published an expose of organized crime. By September 14, 2000, a Quebec Minister, Serge Menard, was calling for new and clearer organized laws to prohibit mere membership in criminal gangs like the Hells Angels and the Rock Machine and the use of the notwithstanding clause to trump any *Charter* claim of freedom of association. It is stunning that this initiative came from a province in which the invocation of the *War Measures Act* in 1970 and the banning of the F.L.Q. terrorist group led to the arrests of hundreds of innocent Quebecois. Canada does not need laws of guilt by association or any overriding of *Charter* rights.[23]

On the eve of the election a Parliamentary sub-committee on organized crime[24] held *in camera* hearings. Some MPs seemed troubled by the experience of the Manitoba Warriors trial. But no MP subsequently saw this test case as pointing to the dangers of Parliament's overbroad anti-gang quick fix. The

---

18 *Globe and Mail, ibid.*

19 *Ibid.*

20 "Fontaine made fool of himself", *Winnipeg Free Press*, July 12, 2000. The remarks are attributed to Crown Attorney Bob Morrison at the final sentence hearing and were directed against remarks of Phil Fontaine, then National Chief of the Assembly of First Nations, who had been critical of the process.

21 *Winnipeg Free Press*, July 13, 2000.

22 For further analysis of our complex gangsterism laws see David Freedman, "The New Law of Criminal Organizations in Canada" (2006) 85 Can. Bar Rev. 171 and Karen Katz, "Law Gone to Politics, Politics Gone to Law: The Evolution of Canada's Organized Crime Legislation" (2011) 57 Crim. L.Q. 58.

23 See too Kent Roach, "Panicking over Criminal Organizations: We Don't Need Another Offence" (2000), 44 Crim. L.Q. 1.

24 Sub-committee on Organised Crime of the Standing Committee on Justice and Human Rights, *Combatting Organised Crime* (October, 2000).

Committee released a hastily drafted report with numerous recommendations to toughen the anti-gang laws. During the election campaign all politicians agreed that something more needed to be done about gangs. No politician dared to raise questions.

After the election Bill C-24 proceeded rapidly through a committee hearing. It contained 70 printed pages of complicated amendments to the *Criminal Code* and other federal statutes. The *Proceeds of Crime (Money Laundering) Act* was substantially widened to embrace the seizure, freezing and confiscation of proceeds of most indictable offences rather than the 40 previously listed as "enterprise crimes". There are new offences to single out intimidation against people in the justice system including witnesses, jurors, prosecutors, guards, judges and politicians.

It also snuck in a Ministerial power to designate in ss. 25.1 and 25.2 police officers to break the law whether the target was organized crime or not. This power to designate can even be delegated to other police officers and is general rather than case-specific. It is the antithesis of the rule of law. Despite the opposition of the CBA and others it also became law. Critics were fobbed off on a promise of Parliamentary review.

We concentrate here on the bill's widening of the criminal organization definition and the anti-gang offences. Since Bill C-24 the new definition of a criminal organization is found in s. 467.1 as follows:

> "criminal organization" means a group, however organized, that is composed of three or more persons and that has as one of its main purposes or main activities the facilitation or commission of one or more serious offences that, if committed, would likely result in the direct or indirect receipt of a material benefit, including a financial benefit, by the group or by any of the persons who constitute the group. It does not include a group of persons that forms randomly for the immediate commission of a single offence.

Under the same section

> "serious offence" means an indictable offence under this or any other Act of Parliament for which the maximum punishment is imprisonment for five years or more, or another offence that is prescribed by regulation.

The Department of Justice Backgrounder "Highlights of the Organized Crime Bill" released on its website on April 5, 2001 explains that a new definition of criminal organization was drafted to respond to concerns expressed by police and prosecutors that the current definition was "too complex and too narrow in scope". Ironically by this time convictions had been registered in Quebec under the new gangsterism laws against members of the Hells Angels and Rock Machine.[25] The Department of Justice nevertheless pressed on with the broadening of the existing definition in three ways by:

1. reducing the number of people required to constitute a criminal organization from five to three;

---

25 Two mega-trials of bikers in Quebec produced huge problems of cost, drain on legal aid, severance motions, disclosure, delay and complexity: see Anne-Marie Boisvert, "Mega Trials: The Disturbing Situation in Quebec" (2004), 15 C.R. (6th) 181.

2. removing the requirement that at least one of the members be involved in committing crimes for the organization within the past five years; and

3. extending the scope of offences which define criminal organizations, previously limited to indictable offences punishable by five years or more, to all serious crimes.

The bill removes the feeble limits on the definition of organized crime previously in place. To speak of a criminal organization of three seems laughable until we remember the huge scope of State power this definition will authorize. The Backgrounder explains that the inclusion of serious offences is to include "signature" crimes such as prostitution or gambling. This glosses over the reality that prostitution *per se* is not a crime. The power to add a list of crimes by regulation unreviewable by Parliament is the antithesis of democracy or the rule of law. The new definition does add one limit exclusion of a group formed "randomly for the immediate commission of a single offence". This is a welcome recognition of the need for continuity but it is very weak protection and is unlikely to exclude loose collectivities to distribute drugs to others and thereby involving multiple offences.

The Backgrounder also stresses that what is made criminal, subject to consecutive penalties as before, is *knowing participation* in activities that further the organization's objectives. Here the Backgrounder is shockingly misleading. When three new offence definitions the bill creates are examined,[26] it is clear that these elements of knowledge and participation are so comprised as to be a sham:

Participation in activities of criminal organization

467.11 (1) Every person who, for the purpose of enhancing the ability of a criminal organization to facilitate or commit an indictable offence under this or any other Act of Parliament, knowingly, by act or omission, participates in or contributes to any activity of the criminal organization is guilty of an indictable offence and liable to imprisonment for a term not exceeding five years.

Prosecution

(2) In a prosecution for an offence under subsection (1), it is not necessary for the prosecutor to prove that

    (a) the criminal organization actually facilitated or committed an indictable offence;

    (b) the participation or contribution of the accused actually enhanced the ability of the criminal organization to facilitate or commit an indictable offence;

    (c) the accused knew the specific nature of any indictable offence that may have been facilitated or committed by the criminal organization; or

    (d) the accused knew the identity of any of the persons who constitute the criminal organization.

---

26 See too the further definition of criminal organization. Under s. (2) facilitation of an offence does not require knowledge of a particular offence the commission of which is facilitated, or that an offence actually be committed. Under s. (3) committing an offence means being a party to it or counselling any person to be a party to it.

Factors

(3) In determining whether an accused participates in or contributes to any activity of a criminal organization, the court may consider, among other factors, whether the accused

    (a) uses a name, word, symbol or other representation that identifies, or is associated with, the criminal organization;

    (b) frequently associates with any of the persons who constitute the criminal organization;

    (c) receives any benefit from the criminal organization; or

    (d) repeatedly engages in activities at the instruction of any of the persons who constitute the criminal organization.

Commission of offence for criminal organization

467.12 (1) Every person who commits an indictable offence under this or any other Act of Parliament for the benefit of, at the direction of, or in association with, a criminal organization is guilty of an indictable offence and liable to imprisonment for a term not exceeding fourteen years.

Prosecution

(2) In a prosecution for an offence under subsection (1), it is not necessary for the prosecutor to prove that the accused knew the identity of any of the persons who constitute the criminal organization.

Instructing commission of offence for criminal organization

467.13 (1) Every person who is one of the persons who constitute a criminal organization and who knowingly instructs, directly or indirectly, any person to commit an offence under this or any other Act of Parliament for the benefit of, at the direction of, or in association with, the criminal organization is guilty of an indictable offence and liable to imprisonment for life.

Prosecution

(2) In a prosecution for an offence under subsection (1), it is not necessary for the prosecutor to prove that

    (a) an offence other than the offence under subsection (1) was actually committed;

    (b) the accused instructed a particular person to commit an offence; or

    (c) the accused knew the identity of all of the persons who constitute the criminal organization.

It can be seen that knowledge is expressly not required to be proved of the crime to be facilitated or committed or of the identity of the members of the criminal organization. That is a knowledge requirement that has no real meaning and points to absolute responsibility which is unconstitutional where the liberty interest is at stake.[27] So too it is express that no crime need to have been facilitated or committed by the criminal organization or even made more likely. Even the Backgrounder acknowledges the "provisions could target anyone (not just members)". Contrast the focus in conspiracy jurisprudence on a meeting of the

---

27 *Motor Vehicle Reference* (1985), 48 C.R. (3d) 289 (S.C.C.); *Pontes* (1995), 41 C.R. (4th) 201 (S.C.C.).

minds on a common purpose. As Justice Dickson put it in *Cotroni, Papalia* (1979):[28]

> The word "conspire" derives from two Latin words, "con" and "spirare", meaning "to breathe together". To conspire is to agree....There must be evidence beyond a reasonable doubt that the alleged conspirators acted in concert in pursuit of a common goal".[29]

Charter challenges to the new scheme based on vagueness, overbreadth and lack of fault were rejected by Fuerst J. in *R. v. Lindsay* (2004), 20 C.R. (6th) 376 (Ont. S.C.). The Court, however, read into the knowledge requirement a requirement of proof of knowledge of the composition of the criminal organization although not of the identity of those in the group. In contrast in *R. v. Accused No. 1*, 2005 CarswellBC 2982, 134 C.R.R. (2d) 274 (B.C. S.C.), Holmes J. struck down the new definition of criminal organization as too vague and too broad. However, her decision was soon reversed by the B.C.C.A. in *R. v. Terezakis* (2007), 51 C.R. (6th) 165, 223 C.C.C. (3d) 344 (B.C. C.A.), leave to appeal refused (2008), 226 C.C.C. (3d) vi (note) (S.C.C.). In 2009 the Ontario Court of Appeal had little difficulty rejecting the appeal in *Lindsay* (2009), 245 C.C.C. (3d) 301 (Ont. C.A.).[30] In *R. v. Venneri*,[31] Fish J., speaking for the Court, did not find vagueness. He held that "criminal organization" requires a finding of a degree of organization or structure, knowledge of the organization, and that "in association with" requires the commission of a criminal offence "in connection" with the organization.

The new three-category approach to participation in organized crime is anything but simple and will itself add to the complexity of trials. Quite apart from the Manitoba Warriors prosecution, gangsterism trials in Alberta and Quebec have followed the pattern of excessive length, complexity and cost. Even before this legislation it was never desirable to have mass trials.

3.   TERRORIST GROUPS[32]

(a)   9/11 Attacks

Seeing those planes explode into the World Trade Center buildings, the towers falling and the horrifying destruction of life are memories we will always have. We all feel more vulnerable. Most expected our government to be proactive

---

28 45 C.C.C. (2d) 1 (S.C.C.).

29 *Ibid.* at 17-18.

30 See the comprehensive and highly critical review by Miles Hastie, "The Separate Offence of Committing a Crime 'In Association with' a Criminal Organization: Gangs Symbols and Signs of Constitutional Problems" (2009) 14 Can. Crim. L. Rev. 79.

31 2012 SCC 33, [2012] 2 S.C.R. 211, 93 C.R. (6th) 223.

32 Most of the notes in this section first appeared in Stuart, "The Anti-Terrorism Bill C-36: An Unnecessary Law and Order Quick Fix that Permanently Stains the Canadian Criminal Justice System" (2002) 14.1 Nat. J. of Const. L. 153. Compare however Stanley Cohen, "Safeguards and Justification for Canada's New Terrorism Act" (2002) 14.1 Nat. J. of Const. L. 99. See too 24 conference essays from a U. of T. conference in Daniels, Macklem & Roach (ed.), *The Security of Freedom. Essays on Canada's Anti-Terrorism Bill* (2001, U. of T. Press).

on our behalf. It is easy to support the allocation of significant sums of government money for preventive measures such as better airport security, medicine to counteract anthrax, more anti-terrorist police and CSIS personnel, and even for our military assistance to the United State's uncomfortable war in Afghanistan. Those planning or committing acts of violent terrorism should be arrested, prosecuted and severely punished.

However, the complex new criminal laws which Bill C-36 added to our permanent laws led to opposition in some quarters at the time they were rushed through Parliament, opposition which still continues. Some argue that when the State turns to its power to investigate, detain, punish and imprison, the standard of justification should be high, even in extraordinary times. Basic principles of a criminal justice system that deserves the name require the State to prove both that the individual acted and was at fault, that responsibility be fairly labelled and that any punishment be proportionate to the accused's actions.

(b)   Definition of Terrorism

To many critics the fatal flaw in Bill C-36 is its very wide definition of "terrorist activity" in s. 83.01. It decides who can be charged as a terrorist and against whom extensive new investigative powers can be exercised. In one respect the definition may be unduly narrow. There is no wisdom in requiring proof of a motive under s. 83.01(1)(b)(i)(A) of "a political, religious or ideological purpose, objective or cause". For years criminal law has sought to avoid proof of a bad motive as a requirement for criminal responsibility. It is too hard to prove and may, as here, lead to curious results. Why should a violent terrorist with unfathomable motives not be included? On this point the government was stubbornly adamant. Perhaps the political problem may be that if the government had conceded that point, its case for special new laws would have been even weaker. The unfortunate reality of retaining the motive clause is that there will be religious and political targeting.

A most contentious aspect of the new definition remains the wide extension in s. 83.01(1)(b)(ii)(E) to those who intend to cause "serious interference with or serious disruption of an essential service, facility or system, whether public or private, other than as a result of advocacy, protest, dissent or stoppage of work that is not intended to result in the conduct or harm referred to in any of clauses (A) to (C)" [which include intending to cause a serious risk to the safety of the public].

At first reading the bill purported to exempt "lawful protest". That exemption was not worth the paper it was written on as most protesters in Canada have, when charged, been convicted of at least obstruction offences. The government finally removed the word "lawful" from "protest". This may afford some protection to protesters. However, it refused to remove clause (E) altogether as so many, including then Liberal backbencher Irwin Cotler,[33] had urged. The overbreadth dangers have been reduced but remain a serious concern.

---

33 See Cotler, "Thinking Outside the Box: Foundational Principles for a Counter-Terrorism Law and Policy", in *The Security of Freedom, ibid.* at 111-129.

Do you think that the following activities could still be investigated, charged and punished as terrorism?

1. Aboriginal groups' blockading of logger roads to assert Aboriginal title.

2. Anti-globalization protests, such as those which occurred in Quebec City.

3. Disruptive passive resistance inspired by Mahatma Gandhi.

4. Labour union stoppages of many types.

5. Sending aid to an Afghanistan refugee group later determined to be involved in terrorist activity.

6. Community groups sponsoring Muslim immigration into Canada where an immigrant is allegedly involved in terrorist activities in the country of origin, even if this was some time in the past.

7. A person claiming refugee status in Canada has to establish fear of political persecution from his or her country of origin. It would not be difficult for opponents in that country to provide intelligence to Canada that the refugee had participated in terrorism.

8. Gangs of bikers or even a couple of youths out to disrupt the town.

Equally, if not even more contentious, is the alternative way the legislation permits persons to be branded as terrorists. The Governor-in-Council, on the recommendation of the Solicitor General, is now empowered to name by regulation a list of terrorist entities (s. 83.05). This designation is based on a determination by the Government, in private and without public debate and based merely on reasonable grounds rather than proof in a court of law. There is strong argument that this power violates the presumption of innocence in s. 11(d), which requires proof beyond reasonable doubt of essential elements before a fair and independent tribunal.[34] The Government amendments did include a provision (s. 83.05(5)) for after-the-event review by a judge but there is a power for a judge to prevent disclosure of information for reasons of national security. In this definition of terrorism, there is a great difference between what the Government told Canadians it intended and what the bill says. In its original Backgrounder entitled "Highlights of Anti-Terrorism Act" the claim was that:

> This definition and designation framework will provide clear guidance to police, prosecutors, the courts and the public on what constitutes a terrorist group or activity while protecting the lawful activities of legitimate political or lobby organizations.

> Recently UN Secretary General Kofi Annan has urged UN members to agree on a definition of terrorism as any action:

---

34 See further Kent Roach, "Listing and the Law" (2009) 55 Crim. L.Q. 1.

> intended to cause death or serious bodily harm to civilians or non-combatants with the purpose of intimidating a population or compelling a government or an international organization to do or abstain from doing any act.[35]

Similarly in *Suresh v. Canada*,[36] in the context of a review of the controversial power to detain on security certificates without any charge, the Supreme Court adopted as a definition of terrorism for the *Immigration Act* that from the International Convention for the Suppression of Terrorism of any:

> act intended to cause death or serious bodily injury to a civilian, or to any other person not taking part in the hostilities in a situation of armed conflict, when the purpose of such act, by its nature or context, is to intimidate a population, or to compel a government or an organization to do or abstain from doing any act.[37]

These definitions are considerably narrower than those to be found in the very complex definition in ATA.

(c)   Broad New Offences

Being branded as a terrorist in one of these ways is not an offence. The bill creates new offences of Participating, Facilitating, Instructing and Harbouring.[38] We will focus critical attention here on the new offence of knowingly participating or contributing to terrorist activities. Similar criticism could be advanced against the other three offences. So what on earth, some might say, is wrong with creating a crime of knowingly participating in terrorist activity? The Backgrounder gives as an example the act of knowingly recruiting into the group new individuals for the purpose of enhancing the ability of the terrorist group to aid, abet or commit indictable offences.

The problem is that Parliament, just as it did earlier in the case of the creation of a crime of knowingly participating in a criminal organization, has cynically legislated out of existence any meaningful test of knowledge or meaningful test of participating or contributing. Here again the devil is in the detail.

The definition section is s. 83.18(1):

> Every one who knowingly participates in or contributes to, directly or indirectly, any activity of a terrorist group for the purpose of enhancing the ability of any terrorist group to facilitate or carry out a terrorist activity is guilty of an indictable offence and liable to imprisonment for a term not exceeding ten years.

So there is here a fault requirement of actual knowledge plus a purpose of enhancing the terrorist group's ability to facilitate or carry out a terrorist activity.

---

35   Report of March 21, 2005.
36   [2002] 1 S.C.R. 3.
37   *Ibid.* at para. 98.
38   For a full analysis see Kent Roach, "The New Terrorism Offences and the Criminal Law", *The Security of Freedom* at 151-172. See too Martha Shaffer, "Effectiveness of Anti-Terrorism Legislation. Does Bill C-36 Give Us What We Need?" *The Security of Freedom* at 195-204. She also called for withdrawal of the bill.

Yet consider the next subsection, which had a strange and revealing heading "Prosecution" in the original bill:

> (2) An offence may be committed under subsection (1) whether or not
>
>> (a) a terrorist group actually facilitates or carries out a terrorist activity;
>>
>> (b) the participation or contribution of the accused actually enhances the ability of a terrorist group to facilitate or carry out a terrorist activity; or
>>
>> (c) the accused knows the specific nature of any terrorist activity that may be facilitated or carried out by a terrorist group.

Then we find a definition of participating or contributing which includes acts as vague as

> (b) providing or offering to provide a skill or an expertise for the benefit of, at the direction of or in association with a terrorist group
>
> (d)...remaining in any country for the benefit of, at the direction of or in association with a terrorist group.

Bar Association representatives pointed out to the Parliamentary committee that clause (b) is inconsistent with the proper legal representation of those affected by these new terrorist laws. The Government did not bother to respond. Clause (d) is particularly stunning. It establishes guilt by association wherever you are in the world and whatever you are doing! The maximum sentence on conviction for such knowing participation in terrorism is 10 years (s. 83.18). This must be served consecutive to a sentence for any other offence (s. 83.26).

When such criminalization is read in conjunction with the wide ways you can be branded as a terrorist, there would be good arguments that such provisions violate s. 7 *Charter* protections requiring meaningful act and fault requirements. The Supreme Court has held that you cannot substitute elements to avoid fault standards[39] and that minimum fault standards established by the Court cannot be watered down.[40] Excluding a mistaken belief defence respecting an essential element of a crime has been held to be unconstitutional.[41] The Court has re-asserted as a fundamental principle that the State prove a voluntary physical act.[42] In Bill C-36 there is often no real act requirement and there is no clear requirement that the accused knew that the group is involved in the acts which constitute terrorism. Other *Charter* arguments would be vagueness and overbreadth and disproportionate punishment contrary to the cruel and unusual punishment protection of s. 12.

---

39 *Vaillancourt*, [1987] 2 S.C.R. 636.
40 *Supra* note 36.
41 *Hess and Nguyen*, [1990] 2 S.C.R. 906.
42 *Ruzic* (2001), 41 C.R. (5th) 1 (S.C.C.). The Court also speaks of no criminal responsibility where there is "moral involuntariness".

Charter challenges were rejected by the Ontario Court of Appeal in the 2010 appeals of *Khawaja* and *U.S. v. Nadarajah*.[43] The Court seemed little interested in taking the *Charter* arguments seriously and much more concerned to impose long prison sentences. It contented itself with a detailed analysis of the complex ATA provisions and found that the *mens rea* provisions required a specific and high degree of moral culpability, and that the scheme was not too vague or overbroad. When *Khawaja* reached the Supreme Court,[44] the Court decided that the terrorism provisions in the *Criminal Code* were not overbroad or grossly disproportional under s. 7. To reach this result McLachlin C.J.C. for the Court resorted to reading down. She adopted a purposive interpretation of *actus reus* and *mens rea* requirements of s. 83.18 excluding convictions: (i) for innocent or socially useful conduct undertaken absent any specific intent to enhance the abilities of a terrorist group to facilitate or carry out a terrorist activity; and (ii) for conduct that a reasonable person would not view as capable of materially enhancing the abilities of a terrorist group to facilitate or carry out a terrorist activity. For a critical comment see Peter Sankoff, "*Khawaja*: Mixed Messages on the Meaning of Intention, Purpose and Desire" (2013), 97 C.R. (6th) 280.

Even if these new provisions are *Charter*-proof the larger issue is whether the new offences risk injustice in the form of unfair labelling and huge and dangerous overreaching of State power.

(d)   Three-Year Review

In 2006, the three-year review proceeded through Parliament. Some argued that the government of the day should withdraw the whole ATA as thorough overkill and unnecessary given existing *Criminal Code* offences and State powers. This did not occur. Canadian governments of any stripe have clearly fallen for the worldwide lure of special anti-terrorist laws. It is interesting to note proposals made by then backbencher Irwin Cotler that were not accepted by the Liberal government at the time of passage:[45]

1. Removal of the motive requirement of a religious or an ideological purpose as this provides an unnecessary defence and could be relied on for discriminatory law enforcement;

2. Delete clause E, which ensnares those intending to disrupt essential services, as this could be stretched to characterize as terrorist acts of protestors never intended to be caught;

3. Prior notice before being listed as a terrorist group;

---

43   (2011), 82 C.R. (6th) 122 (Ont. C.A.), leave to appeal allowed (2011), 425 N.R. 399 (note) (S.C.C.), affirmed [2012] 3 S.C.R. 555, 97 C.R. (6th) 223 and (2011), 81 C.R. (6th) 285 (Ont. C.A.), leave to appeal allowed (2011), 425 N.R. 398 (note) (S.C.C.), affirmed [2012] 3 S.C.R. 609, 97 C.R. (6th) 267.

44   97 C.R. (6th) 223, [2012] 3 S.C.R. 555.

45   *Wholesale Travel Group Inc.,* [1991] 3 S.C.R. 154.

4. Crime of facilitation should require that the facilitator know the group is engaged in terrorism;

5. Meaningful oversight by a Parliamentary officer or the Security Intelligence Review Commission;

6. Judicial rather than ministerial authority to authorize foreign intercepts originating or ending in Canada;

7. No suppression of information depriving an accused of the right to know and contest State evidence; and

8. The inclusion of an anti-discrimination clause

The government did not respond to such concerns or to the amendments urged in such detail and with such persuasive force by Professor Kent Roach before the Senate ATA Review Committee.[46]

A major problem with a broad definition of terrorism and broad offences is that this can be used for racial profiling. Professor Ed Morgan[47] has suggested that the approach to this complex issue being developed by our courts should not be applied in other contexts such as immigration and border crossing, given ubiquitous threat of mass violence since the 9/11 attacks. This view is surprisingly insensitive to the experience of Muslim and Arab Canadians who have presented significant anecdotal and survey evidence to Parliamentary committees that they have been, and continue to be, racially targeted under ATA and immigration powers. Principles being developed in the context of criminal trials seem equally applicable.[48]

For a comprehensive comparative review of anti-terrorism laws in the United States, the U.K., Australia and Canada, see Kent Roach, "The 9/11 Effect: Comparative Counter-terrorism" (Cambridge University Press, 2011).

In 2015 the Conservative government of the time brought in further anti-terrorism provisions in Bill C-51, *An Act to enact the Security of Canada Information Sharing Act and the Secure Air Travel Act, to amend the Criminal Code, the Canadian Security Intelligence Service Act and the Immigration and Refugee Protection Act and to make related and consequential amendments to other Acts*. Many of the provisions in that Act dealt with the sharing of information between government agencies or dealt with the powers of CSIS. However, the

---

46 Kent Roach, "The Three Year Review of Canada's Anti-terrorism Act: The Need for Greater Restraint and Fairness, Non-Discrimination and Special Advocates" (2005). See too Kent Roach, "The Parliamentary Review of the Anti-Terrorist Act" (2007) 52 Crim. L.Q. 281. See also Kent Roach, "Ten Ways to Improve Canadian Anti-Terrorism Law" (2005) 51 Crim. L.Q. 102, Stuart, "Avoiding Myths and Challenging Minister of Justice Cotler to Undo the Injustices of Our Anti-Terrorism Act" (2005) 51 Crim. L.Q. 53 and Maureen Webb, "Essential Liberty or a Little Temporary Safety? The Review of the Canadian Anti-Terrorist Act" (2005) 51 Crim. L.Q. 53.

47 "Racial Profiling as an Investigative Tool", *Law Times*, October 15, 2002,

48 See too Sujit Choudhry & Kent Roach, "Racial and Ethnic Profiling: Statutory Definition, Constitutional Remedies and Democratic Accountability" (2003) 41 Osgoode Hall L.J. 1 and Teem Bahdi, "No Exit : Racial Profiling and Canada's War Against Terrorism" (2003) 41 Osgoode Hall L.J. 293. See especially David Tanovich, *The Colour of Justice* (Irwin Law, 2006) at 105-118.

Act also added new provisions to the *Criminal Code*, relating to new offences, investigative powers and other procedures.

Among these new provisions was the offence of advocating or promoting commission of terrorism offences (s. 83.221), which was in addition to the existing offence of instructing to carry out terrorist activity (s. 83.22). Critics suggested that changes like this went too far: for example, Canadians who spoke in support of Crimean citizens who used violence to resist the Russian invasion of their territory would seem to be committing the offence.

Similarly, the new provisions make it easier for police to arrest a person on suspicion of terrorist activity: rather than requiring a belief that such an act "will" be carried out it is sufficient to believe such an act "may" be carried out (s. 83.3(2)). For criticism of the new provisions and the approach to terrorism, see Craig Forcese and Kent Roach, *False Security: The Radicalization of Canadian Anti-terrorism* (Toronto: Irwin Law, 2015).

The Liberal government subsequently in power has indicated that amending these anti-terrorism provisions is on its legislative agenda, but at the time of this writing no legislation has been introduced.

Chapter 11

SENTENCING

1. PRINCIPLES OF SENTENCING

See, generally, Allan Manson, *The Law of Sentencing* (Irwin Law, 2001), and Manson, Trotter, Healy, Roberts and Ives, eds., *Sentencing and Penal Policy in Canada*, 3rd ed. (Emond Montgomery, 2016).

R. v. C.A.M.

[1996] 1 S.C.R. 500, 46 C.R. (4th) 269, 105 C.C.C. (3d) 327,
1996 CarswellBC 1000, 1996 CarswellBC 1000F

The accused pleaded guilty to a number of counts of sexual assault, incest and assault with a weapon, arising from a largely uncontested pattern of sexual, physical and emotional abuse inflicted upon his children over a number of years. The trial judge, remarking that the offences were as egregious as any he had ever had occasion to deal with, sentenced the accused to a cumulative sentence of 25 years' imprisonment, with individual sentences running both consecutively and concurrently. The Court of Appeal reduced the sentence to 18 years and 8 months.

The appeal was allowed and a sentence of 25 years' imprisonment restored. In the course of his reasons Chief Justice Lamer wrote, for the Court:

Did the Court of Appeal err in holding that retribution is not a legitimate principle of sentencing?

As a second and independent ground of appeal, the Crown argues that the Court of Appeal erred in law by relying on the proposition that "retribution is not a legitimate goal of sentencing" in reducing the sentence imposed by Filmer Prov. Ct. J. to 18 years and 8 months. In my reading of the judgment of the Court of Appeal below, I find little evidence that the passing remarks of Wood J.A. in relation to the legitimacy of retribution played a significant role in his conclusion that the respondent's sentence ought to be reduced to 18 years and 8 months' imprisonment. It should be noted that Rowles J.A., in her concurring reasons, did not even discuss retribution as a principle of sentencing. Similarly, there is no evidence that Filmer Prov. Ct. J. placed any explicit reliance on the objective of "retribution" in initially rendering his stern sentence. Accordingly, whether or not Wood J.A. erred as a strict matter of law in his discussion of the philosophical merits of retribution as a principle of sentencing, I conclude that Wood J.A.'s discussion of retribution was not a decisive element in the majority of the Court of Appeal's conclusion that the sentence of the respondent ought to be reduced to below 19 years. Therefore, I am persuaded that the remarks of Wood J.A. in relation to retribution did not constitute a reversible error.

However, given the continued judicial debate over this issue, particularly in recent judgments of the British Columbia Court of Appeal (see, e.g., *R. v. Hicks* (1995), 56 B.C.A.C. 259, at para. 14 (rejecting retribution), *R. v. Eneas*, [1994] B.C.J. No. 262, at paras. 45 and 46 (endorsing retribution); *R. v. M. (D.E.S.)* (1993), 80 C.C.C. (3d) 371, at p. 376 (rejecting retribution); *R. v. Hoyt*, [1992] B.C.J. No. 2315, at paras. 21 and 22 (rejecting retribution); *R. v. Pettigrew* (1990), 56 C.C.C. (3d) 390, at pp. 394-95 (endorsing retribution)), it would be prudent for this court to clarify briefly the existing state of Canadian law in this important area.

It has been recognized by this court that retribution is an accepted, and indeed important, principle of sentencing in our criminal law. As La Forest J. acknowledged in discussing the constitutionality of the dangerous offender provisions of the *Criminal Code* in *R. v. Lyons*, [1987] 2 S.C.R. 309, at p. 329:

> In a rational system of sentencing, the respective importance of prevention, deterrence, retribution and rehabilitation will vary according to the nature of the crime and the circumstances of the offender. No one would suggest that any of these functional considerations should be excluded from the legitimate purview of legislative or judicial decisions regarding sentencing.

This court has since re-endorsed this passage on a number of occasions as a proper articulation of some of the guiding principles of sentencing in a number of subsequent cases. See *Luxton*, *supra*, at p. 721; *Goltz*, *supra*, at p. 503; and *Shropshire*, *supra*, at para. 23.

The Canadian Sentencing Commission in its 1987 Report on Sentencing Reform also endorsed retribution as a legitimate and relevant consideration in the sentencing process. While the Commission noted that strict retributivist theory on its own fails to provide a general justification for the imposition of criminal sanctions, the Commission argued that retribution, in conjunction with other utilitarian justifications of punishment (*i.e.*, deterrence and rehabilitation), contributes to a more coherent theory of punishment (*supra*, at pp. 141-42, 143-45). More specifically, the Commission argued that a theory of retribution centred on "just deserts" or "just sanctions" provides a helpful organizing principle for the imposition of criminal sanctions (at p. 143). Indeed, as the Commission noted, retribution frequently operates as a principle of restraint, as utilitarian principles alone may direct individualized punishments which unfairly exceed the culpability of the offender. As the Report stated at pp. 133-34:

The ethical foundation of retributivism lies in the following principle: it is immoral to treat one person as a resource for others. From this principle it follows that the only legitimate ground for punishing a person is the blameworthiness of his or her conduct. It also follows that sanctions must be strictly proportionate to the culpability of a person and to the seriousness of the offence for which that person has been convicted.... According to these principles, all exemplary sentences (i.e. the imposition of a harsher sanction on an individual offender so that he or she may be made an example to the community) are unjustified, because they imply that an offender's plight may be used as a means or as a resource to deter potential offenders.

See, similarly, B. P. Archibald, *Crime and Punishment: The Constitutional Requirements for Sentencing Reform in Canada* (1988) 22 R.I.T. 307, at p. 18. With these considerations in mind, the Commission explicitly defined the fundamental purpose of sentencing with reference to the normative goal of imposing "just sanctions". As the Commission cast the guiding purpose of criminal sentencing, at p. 153:

In furtherance of the overall purpose of the criminal law of maintaining a just, peaceful and safe society, the fundamental purpose of sentencing is to preserve the authority of and promote respect for the law through the imposition of just sanctions.

A majority of this court has since expressed approval of this passage as an accurate statement of the essential goals of sentencing. See *R. v. Jones*, [1994] 2 S.C.R. 229, at p. 291 (although I dissented on the merits of the case). Retribution, as an objective of sentencing, represents nothing less than the hallowed principle that criminal punishment, in addition to advancing utilitarian considerations related to deterrence and rehabilitation, should also be imposed to sanction the moral culpability of the offender. In my view, retribution is integrally woven into the existing principles of sentencing in Canadian law through the fundamental requirement that a sentence imposed be "just and appropriate" under the circumstances. Indeed, it is my profound belief that retribution represents an important unifying principle of our penal law by offering an essential conceptual link between the attribution of criminal liability and the imposition of criminal sanctions. With regard to the attribution of criminal liability, I have repeatedly held that it is a principle of "fundamental justice" under s. 7 of the *Charter* that criminal liability may only be imposed if an accused possesses a minimum "culpable mental state" in respect of the ingredients of the alleged offence. See *Martineau, supra*, at p. 645. See, similarly, *Re B.C. Motor Vehicle Act, supra*; *R. v. Vaillancourt*, [1987] 2 S.C.R. 636. It is this mental state which gives rise to the "moral blameworthiness" which justifies the state in imposing the stigma and punishment associated with a criminal sentence. See *Martineau*, at p. 646. I submit that it is this same element of "moral blameworthiness" which animates the determination of the appropriate quantum of punishment for a convicted offender as a "just sanction". As I noted in *Martineau* in discussing the sentencing scheme for manslaughter under the *Code*, it is a recognized principle of our justice system that "punishment be meted out with regard to the level of moral blameworthiness of the offender"

(p. 647). See the similar observations of W.E.B. Code in "Proportionate Blameworthiness and the Rule Against Constructive Sentencing" (1992), 11 C.R. (4th) 40, at pp. 41-42.

However, the meaning of retribution is deserving of some clarification. The legitimacy of retribution as a principle of sentencing has often been questioned as a result of its unfortunate association with "vengeance" in common parlance. See, *e.g.*, *R. v. Hinch and Salanski*, *supra*, at pp. 43-44; *R. v. Calder* (1956), 114 C.C.C. 155 (Man. C.A.), at p. 161. But it should be clear from my foregoing discussion that retribution bears little relation to vengeance, and I attribute much of the criticism of retribution as a principle to this confusion. As both academic and judicial commentators have noted, vengeance has no role to play in a civilized system of sentencing. See Ruby, *Sentencing*, *supra*, at p. 13. Vengeance, as I understand it, represents an uncalibrated act of harm upon another, frequently motivated by emotion and anger, as a reprisal for harm inflicted upon oneself by that person. Retribution in a criminal context, by contrast, represents an objective, reasoned and measured determination of an appropriate punishment which properly reflects the moral culpability of the offender, having regard to the intentional risk-taking of the offender, the consequential harm caused by the offender, and the normative character of the offender's conduct. Furthermore, unlike vengeance, retribution incorporates a principle of restraint; retribution requires the imposition of a just and appropriate punishment, and nothing more. As R. Cross has noted in *The English Sentencing System* (2nd ed. 1975), at p. 121: "The retributivist insists that the punishment must not be disproportionate to the offender's deserts."

Retribution, as well, should be conceptually distinguished from its legitimate sibling, denunciation. Retribution requires that a judicial sentence properly reflect the moral blameworthiness of that particular offender. The objective of denunciation mandates that a sentence should also communicate society's condemnation of that particular offender's conduct. In short, a sentence with a denunciatory element represents a symbolic, collective statement that the offender's conduct should be punished for encroaching on our society's basic code of values as enshrined within our substantive criminal law. As Lord Justice Lawton stated in *R. v. Sargeant* (1974), 60 Cr. App. R. 74, at p. 77:

> society, through the courts, must show its abhorrence of particular types of crime, and the only way in which the courts can show this is by the sentences they pass.

The relevance of both retribution and denunciation as goals of sentencing underscores that our criminal justice system is not simply a vast system of negative penalties designed to prevent objectively harmful conduct by increasing the cost the offender must bear in committing an enumerated offence. Our criminal law is also a system of values. A sentence which expresses denunciation is simply the means by which these values are communicated. In short, in addition to attaching negative consequences to undesirable behaviour, judicial sentences should also be imposed in a manner which positively instills the basic set of communal values shared by all Canadians as expressed by the *Criminal Code*.

As a closing note to this discussion, it is important to stress that neither retribution nor denunciation alone provides an exhaustive justification for the imposition of criminal sanctions. Rather, in our system of justice, normative and utilitarian considerations operate in conjunction with one another to provide a coherent justification for criminal punishment. As Gonthier J. emphasized in *Goltz, supra*, at p. 502, the goals of the penal sanction are both "broad and varied". Accordingly, the meaning of retribution must be considered in conjunction with the other legitimate objectives of sentencing, which include (but are not limited to) deterrence, denunciation, rehabilitation and the protection of society. Indeed, it is difficult to perfectly separate these interrelated principles. And as La Forest J. emphasized in *Lyons*, the relative weight and importance of these multiple factors will frequently vary depending on the nature of the crime and the circumstances of the offender. In the final analysis, the overarching duty of a sentencing judge is to draw upon all the legitimate principles of sentencing to determine a "just and appropriate" sentence which reflects the gravity of the offence committed and the moral blameworthiness of the offender.

2. SENTENCING REFORM: REDUCED USE OF INCARCERATION

Major amendments to the *Criminal Code* came into force on September 3, 1996 when Bill C-41 was proclaimed in force. Mr. Justice Vancise of the Saskatchewan Court of Appeal hails the amendments as providing a framework under which there should be less custodial sentencing: "To Change or Not to Change — That is the Issue" (1996), 1 Can. Crim. L. Rev. 263. In addition to a number of specific amendments to sentencing powers, Bill C-41 declared the Purpose and Principles of Sentencing in ss. 718, 718.1 and 718.2. These were first considered by the Ontario Court of Appeal in *Priest*.

R. v. PRIEST

(1996), 1 C.R. (5th) 275, 110 C.C.C. (3d) 289,
1996 CarswellOnt 3588 (Ont. C.A.)

The accused was a 19-year-old first offender. He had no prior record. He pleaded guilty to breaking and entering a convenience store and stealing computer games and accessories worth approximately $2,700. He confessed when confronted by the store owner. All of the stolen property was recovered and there were no aggravating features involved in the offence. There was no violence or vandalism. There was no breach of trust involved. All of the stolen property was recovered. At the sentencing hearing, which lasted for less than five minutes, the accused was unrepresented by counsel. There was no presentence report or other information about the accused's background, family, roots in the community, education or work history. Crown counsel suggested a sentence of 30 to 60 days. Taking judicial notice of the prevalence of the crime of breaking and entering in the community and stating that general deterrence was for that reason the primary sentencing consideration, the trial judge imposed a sentence of one year's imprisonment. The accused appealed. The sentencing of the appellant took place on July 15, 1996. On August 22, Carthy J.A. ordered the appellant released on bail pending appeal and ordered that the appeal be expedited. Thus, when the appeal came before the Court of Appeal on August 30, the accused had already served five weeks in jail. Crown counsel conceded that the sentence could not stand and suggested that it be reduced to time served and probation for one year, with conditions that the accused report to a probation officer and seek and maintain employment.

ROSENBERG J.A: —

It is obvious that the original sentence of one year imprisonment cannot stand. In imposing the sentence that he did, the trial judge ignored principles and procedural guidelines that have been laid down by this court on many occasions.

Prevalence of the Crime

In imposing the sentence, the trial judge found that general deterrence was the paramount consideration. In stressing general deterrence to the exclusion of all other objectives, he relied upon the apparent prevalence of the offence of break and enter in Hearst. It is not necessary to decide in this case whether the trial judge had sufficient information before him from which he could safely conclude that there was a serious problem of break and enter in Hearst. I note, however, that unlike some cases that have come before this court, there were no statistics placed before the trial judge and he based his opinion on the court dockets of persons accused of the crime of break and enter.

The principles to be applied where there appears to be an unusually high incidence of a particular crime in the community have been set down by this court. In 1978, Arnup J.A. in *R. v. Sears* (1978), 39 C.C.C. (2d) 199 at p. 200, (Ont. C.A.), pointed out that prevalence of a particular crime in the community can never be more than one factor to be taken into account .... This court has specifically spoken on this principle in relation to break and enter in *R. v. Rohr* (1978), 44 C.C.C. (2d) 353 (Ont. C.A.). In that case the youthful appellant had broken into an aquatic centre, done considerable damage, and stolen some $600 worth of goods from the snack bar. The 16-year-old appellant had no prior record but was sentenced to six months imprisonment pursuant to the trial judge's policy of imposing lengthy jail terms even on first offenders for break and enter because of the increase in the number of break-ins in the community. Martin J.A. made it clear that even where break and enter is prevalent in a particular community, it is a circumstance to be taken into consideration, but not the exclusive consideration.

The trial judge was entirely wrong to state that due to the apparent prevalence of the crime of break and enter in Hearst, general deterrence was the paramount objective in sentencing this accused. This was a serious error in principle and wholly distorted the decision as to the appropriate disposition.

This court has stressed that before imposing a sentence of imprisonment upon a first offender, the trial judge should have either a presentence report or some very clear statement with respect to the accused's background and circumstances. That principle has particular application in the case of a youthful offender like this appellant. This requirement of a presentence report or statement about the offender is not a mere formality. As discussed below, the trial judge has a duty to consider whether any disposition other than imprisonment would be appropriate. Without some understanding of the accused's background, the trial judge cannot possibly make that determination. Based on the scanty information before him, the trial judge would have no means of determining that imprisonment was the appropriate sanction for this appellant.

Youthful First Offender

The primary objectives in sentencing a first offender are individual deterrence and rehabilitation. Except for very serious offences and offences involving violence, this court has held that these objectives are not only paramount but best achieved by either a suspended sentence and probation or a very short term of imprisonment followed by a term of probation .... It has been an important principle of sentencing in this province that the sentence should constitute the minimum necessary intervention that is adequate in the particular circumstances. This principle implies that trial judges consider community-based dispositions first and impose more serious forms of punishment only when necessary. These principles have now been codified in the recently proclaimed ss. 718 and 718.2 of the *Criminal Code*, R.S.C. 1985, c. C-46. Section 718(*c*) instructs that separation of offenders from society is an appropriate objective of sentencing "where necessary". Section 718.2(*d*) directs that an offender should not be deprived of liberty "if less restrictive sanctions may be appropriate in the circumstances". The principle embodied in now s. 718.2(*e*) was of particular significance in this case. It provides that "all available sanctions other than imprisonment that are reasonable in the circumstances should be considered for all offenders, with particular attention to the circumstances of aboriginal offenders". Although these sections had not been proclaimed when the appellant appeared before Judge Cloutier, the provisions to a large extent codify existing practice and principles in this province, especially in relation to first offenders.

. . . .

Proportionality

In the recently proclaimed s. 718.1, Parliament sets out the fundamental principle of sentencing:

> 718.1 A sentence must be proportionate to the gravity of the offence and the degree of responsibility of the offender.

Although only now codified, this principle is well established in this country. Chief Justice Lamer in *R. v. M. (C.A.)*, [1996] 1 S.C.R. 500 at p. 530, 105 C.C.C. (3d) 327 at p. 349, noted that this principle now has a constitutional dimension:

> Within broader parameters, the principle of proportionality expresses itself as a constitutional obligation. As this court has recognized on numerous occasions, a legislative or judicial sentence that is grossly disproportionate, in the sense that it is so excessive as to outrage standards of decency, will violate the constitutional prohibition against cruel and unusual punishment under s. 12 of the *Charter*.

The principle of proportionality is rooted in notions of fairness and justice. For the sentencing court to do justice to the particular offender, the sentence imposed must reflect the seriousness of the offence, the degree of culpability of the offender, and the harm occasioned by the offence. The court must have regard to the aggravating and mitigating factors in the particular case. Careful adherence to the proportionality principle ensures that this offender is not unjustly dealt with for the sake of the common good.

The sentence imposed by the trial judge in this case was wholly disproportionate to what occurred. This was a break-in of non-residential premises. There were a number of mitigating factors that were completely ignored by the trial judge. The appellant had no prior record; he confessed to the offence; he returned all of the stolen goods; and he pled guilty at an early opportunity. The trial judge was required to give effect to these mitigating factors in imposing sentence on this appellant.

While I hesitate to label the sentence grossly disproportionate, it approaches that standard. It was well above the threshold of the "clearly unreasonable" or "demonstrably unfit" sentence requiring intervention by this court.

The Role of the Courts

In his reasons for sentence, the trial judge stated that the citizens of Hearst must know that the court is doing its job. He was rightly concerned with the need to protect society and that the courts be seen to be doing their part. The courts of this country must accept the fundamental purpose of sentencing that imposition of appropriate sanctions can contribute to the maintenance of a safe and peaceful society. As Parliament has stated in the recently proclaimed s. 718 of the *Criminal Code*, the purpose of sentencing is also to contribute to respect for the law and maintenance of a just society. Respect for the law is not enhanced when overly harsh sanctions are imposed and a trial court ignores well established sentencing principles. The trial court does not fulfil its duty to fashion a sanction that will contribute to the maintenance of a more just society when it imposes a sentence on the offender that is far beyond the usual penalty imposed for this offence in other parts of the province and the country. The offender and the offender's family would harbour a well-justified sense of grievance over the offender's treatment by the judicial system. Chief Justice Lamer made this crucial point in *R. v. M. (C.A.)*, *supra*, at pp. 558-59 S.C.R., p. 369 C.C.C. He was there discussing the rationale for the objectives of denunciation and retribution in a just system of punishment. His statements, however, have a broader application. He said:

> The relevance of both retribution and denunciation as goals of sentencing underscores that our criminal justice system is not simply a vast system of negative penalties designed to prevent objectively harmful conduct by increasing the cost the offender must bear in committing an enumerated offence. Our criminal law is also a system of values. A sentence which expresses denunciation is simply the means by which these values are communicated. In short, in addition to attaching negative consequences to undesirable behaviour, judicial sentences should also be imposed in a manner which positively instills the basic set of communal values shared by all Canadians as expressed in the *Criminal Code*.

This positive aspect of sentencing, reinforcing the basic values of the society, can only be achieved if the court exercises its broad discretion in sentencing in a just manner having regard to established principles. Section 717(1) (now s. 718.3) of the *Criminal Code* emphasizes that the sentence to be imposed is in the discretion of the trial judge. That discretion is, however, not unfettered. The various principles and objectives of sentencing set out by this court and in the *Criminal Code* are designed to guide the exercise of the discretion. The substantial deference that appeal courts are required to pay to the exercise of the trial judge's discretion is not unlimited. In *R. v. M. (C.A.)*, *supra*, at p. 374, Chief Justice Lamer described the imposition of sentence by the trial judge as a "delicate art" where the judge attempts to balance carefully the societal goals of sentencing against the moral blameworthiness of the offender and the circumstances of the offence, "while at all times taking into account the needs and current conditions of and in the community". Regrettably, the sentencing judge failed to exercise his discretion in this careful and measured way.

For the foregoing reasons, we allowed the appeal and reduced the sentence to time served (approximately five weeks) and one year probation on the statutory terms and on the special terms that the appellant report forthwith to a probation officer and thereafter once per month if required and that he make reasonable efforts to seek and maintain employment or education.

The sentencing reforms in Bill C-41 contained s. 718.2(e), aimed at reducing the use of incarceration. That section provides:

718.2 A court that imposes a sentence shall also take into consideration the following principles:

...(e) all available sanctions other than imprisonment that are reasonable in the circumstances should be considered for all offenders, with particular attention to the circumstances of aboriginal offenders.

The correct approach to applying s. 718.2, and in particular the issue of sentencing Aboriginal offenders, was discussed in the following case:

R. v. GLADUE

[1999] 1 S.C.R. 688, 133 C.C.C. (3d) 385, 23 C.R. (5th) 197, 1999 CarswellBC 778, 1999 CarswellBC 779 (S.C.C.)

The judgment of the court was delivered by CORY and IACOBUCCI JJ.:—

. . . .

52   Canada is a world leader in many fields, particularly in the areas of progressive social policy and human rights. Unfortunately, our country is also distinguished as being a world leader in putting people in prison. Although the United States has by far the highest rate of incarceration among industrialized democracies, at over 600 inmates per 100,000 population, Canada's rate of approximately 130 inmates per 100,000 population places it second or third highest: see Federal/Provincial/Territorial Ministers Responsible for Justice, *Corrections Population Growth: First Report on Progress* (1997), Annex B, at p. 1; Bulletin of U.S. Bureau of Justice Statistics, *Prison and Jail Inmates at Midyear 1998* (March 1999); The Sentencing Project, *Americans Behind Bars: U.S. and International Use of Incarceration, 1995* (June 1997), at p. 1. Moreover, the rate at which Canadian courts have been imprisoning offenders has risen sharply in recent years, although there has been a slight decline of late: see Statistics Canada, "Prison population and costs" in *Infomat: A Weekly Review* (February 27, 1998), at p. 5. This record of incarceration rates obviously cannot instil a sense of pride.

[In particular, the Court held that the section's specific reference to the circumstances of Aboriginal offenders was meant to respond to the overrepresentation of Aboriginal persons in Canadian prisons.]

58   If overreliance upon incarceration is a problem with the general population, it is of much greater concern in the sentencing of aboriginal Canadians. In the mid-1980s, aboriginal people were about 2 percent of the population of Canada, yet they made up 10 percent of the penitentiary population. In Manitoba and Saskatchewan, aboriginal people constituted

something between 6 and 7 percent of the population, yet in Manitoba they represented 46 percent of the provincial admissions and in Saskatchewan 60 percent: see M. Jackson, "Locking Up Natives in Canada" (1988-89), 23 *U.B.C. L. Rev.* 215 (article originally prepared as a report of the Canadian Bar Association Committee on Imprisonment and Release in June 1988), at pp. 215-16. The situation has not improved in recent years. By 1997, aboriginal peoples constituted closer to 3 percent of the population of Canada and amounted to 12 percent of all federal inmates: Solicitor General of Canada, Consolidated Report, *Towards a Just, Peaceful and Safe Society: The Corrections and Conditional Release Act—Five Years Later* (1998), at pp. 142-55. The situation continues to be particularly worrisome in Manitoba, where in 1995-96 they made up 55 percent of admissions to provincial correctional facilities, and in Saskatchewan, where they made up 72 percent of admissions. A similar, albeit less drastic situation prevails in Alberta and British Columbia: Canadian Centre for Justice Statistics, *Adult Correctional Services in Canada, 1995-96* (1997), at p. 30.

[The Court also held that the traditional approach of many Aboriginal peoples to societal problems corresponded well with the amendments to the *Criminal Code* aimed at incorporating more restorative principles. Ultimately they laid down a series of guidelines to assist judges in applying s. 718.2(e).]

93   Let us see if a general summary can be made of what has been discussed in these reasons.

1 Part XXIII of the *Criminal Code* codifies the fundamental purpose and principles of sentencing and the factors that should be considered by a judge in striving to determine a sentence that is fit for the offender and the offence.

2 Section 718.2(e) mandatorily requires sentencing judges to consider all available sanctions other than imprisonment and to pay particular attention to the circumstances of aboriginal offenders.

3 Section 718.2(e) is not simply a codification of existing jurisprudence. It is remedial in nature. Its purpose is to ameliorate the serious problem of overrepresentation of aboriginal people in prisons, and to encourage sentencing judges to have recourse to a restorative approach to sentencing. There is a judicial duty to give the provision's remedial purpose real force.

4 Section 718.2(e) must be read and considered in the context of the rest of the factors referred to in that section and in light of all of Part XXIII. All principles and factors set out in Part XXIII must be taken into consideration in determining the fit sentence. Attention should be paid to the fact that Part XXIII, through ss. 718, 718.2(e), and 742.1, among other provisions, has placed a new emphasis upon decreasing the use of incarceration.

5 Sentencing is an individual process and in each case the consideration must continue to be what is a fit sentence for this accused for this offence in this community. However, the effect of s. 718.2(e) is to alter the method of analysis which sentencing judges must use in determining a fit sentence for aboriginal offenders.

6   Section 718.2(e) directs sentencing judges to undertake the sentencing of aboriginal offenders individually, but also differently, because the circumstances of aboriginal people are unique. In sentencing an aboriginal offender, the judge must consider:

(A) The unique systemic or background factors which may have played a part in bringing the particular aboriginal offender before the courts; and

(B) The types of sentencing procedures and sanctions which may be appropriate in the circumstances for the offender because of his or her particular aboriginal heritage or connection.

7   In order to undertake these considerations the trial judge will require information pertaining to the accused. Judges may take judicial notice of the broad systemic and background factors affecting aboriginal people, and of the priority given in aboriginal cultures to a restorative approach to sentencing. In the usual course of events, additional case-specific information will come from counsel and from a pre-sentence report which takes into account the factors set out in #6, which in turn may come from representations of the relevant aboriginal community which will usually be that of the offender. The offender may waive the gathering of that information.

8   If there is no alternative to incarceration the length of the term must be carefully considered.

9   Section 718.2(e) is not to be taken as a means of automatically reducing the prison sentence of aboriginal offenders; nor should it be assumed that an offender is receiving a more lenient sentence simply because incarceration is not imposed.

10   The absence of alternative sentencing programs specific to an aboriginal community does not eliminate the ability of a sentencing judge to impose a sanction that takes into account principles of restorative justice and the needs of the parties involved.

11   Section 718.2(e) applies to all aboriginal persons wherever they reside, whether on- or off-reserve, in a large city or a rural area. In defining the relevant aboriginal community for the purpose of achieving an effective sentence, the term "community" must be defined broadly so as to include any network of support and interaction that might be available, including in an urban centre. At

the same time, the residence of the aboriginal offender in an urban centre that lacks any network of support does not relieve the sentencing judge of the obligation to try to find an alternative to imprisonment.

12   Based on the foregoing, the jail term for an aboriginal offender may in some circumstances be less than the term imposed on a non-aboriginal offender for the same offence.

13   It is unreasonable to assume that aboriginal peoples do not believe in the importance of traditional sentencing goals such as deterrence, denunciation, and separation, where warranted. In this context, generally, the more serious and violent the crime, the more likely it will be as a practical matter that the terms of imprisonment will be the same for similar offences and offenders, whether the offender is aboriginal or non-aboriginal.

Parliament's goal in enacting s. 718(2)(e) and the Court's goal in *Gladue* was to respond to the problem of Aboriginal over-representation in prisons by seeing to it that special care was taken at the sentencing stage in the case of Aboriginal offenders. In practice it is far from clear that even that limited goal has been achieved.

HONOURING THE TRUTH, RECONCILING FOR THE FUTURE

Summary of the Final Report of the Truth and Reconciliation Commission of Canada (2015)

R. v. Gladue was a landmark decision by the Supreme Court of Canada involving section 718.2(e) of the *Criminal Code*, in the case of an Aboriginal woman from British Columbia. On September 16, 1995, Jamie Tanis Gladue was celebrating her nineteenth birthday when she got into a violent disagreement with her boyfriend and stabbed him. She was eventually convicted of manslaughter. At her sentencing hearing, the judge took into account her youth, her status as a mother, and the absence of any serious criminal history. She was sentenced to three years imprisonment. When the Supreme Court dismissed her appeal of the sentence in 1999, the Court approvingly quoted a study to the effect that "the prison has become for many young native people the contemporary equivalent of what the Indian residential school represented for their parents."

The Court noted that Aboriginal people constituted 12% of federal prisoners, and included the following statement in its ruling:

> The figures are stark and reflect what may fairly be termed a crisis in the Canadian criminal justice system. The drastic overrepresentation of aboriginal peoples within both the Canadian prison population and the criminal justice system reveals a sad and pressing social problem. It is reasonable to assume that Parliament, in singling out aboriginal offenders for distinct sentencing treatment in s. 718.2(e), intended to attempt to redress this social problem to some degree. The provision may properly be seen as Parliament's direction to members of the

judiciary to inquire into the causes of the problem and to endeavour to remedy it, to the extent that a remedy is possible through the sentencing process.

The judgment continues: "The fact that the reference to aboriginal offenders is contained in section 718.2(e), in particular, dealing with restraint in the use of imprisonment, suggests that there is something different about aboriginal offenders which may specifically make imprisonment a less appropriate or less useful sanction."

R. v. Gladue is a much-cited judgment and it has in some jurisdictions resulted in the introduction of more extensive pre-sentence or Gladue reports that provide the sentencing judge with contextual information on the background of Aboriginal offenders. Producing these reports has not been without difficulty and controversy. In 2012, the Globe and Mail reported,

> Saskatchewan, Alberta and Manitoba have barely begun to produce [Gladue] reports. While the number in Alberta has shot up from 14 in 2011 to 100 that are now in production, most of them are being prepared by probation officers—who are trained to assess risk factors but have no particular understanding of aboriginal culture and history. In Quebec, *Gladue* reports are almost unheard of.

Many jurisdictions work with Aboriginal community groups to prepare *Gladue* reports. This is a good practice because probation officers who prepare pre-sentence reports generally do not have cultural training to work with Aboriginal offenders, families, and communities to prepare adequate Gladue reports prior to sentencing.

There are some concerns that defence lawyers may not always request a Gladue report or use it to their clients' advantage. One defence lawyer noted, "The lawyer is not compensated for the report and yet we are expected to do multiple hours of work that we are not paid for. Sometimes we are asked to review the report. That can take 3 hours. More time is spent on the *Gladue* report than other PSRs [Pre-Sentence Reports] because of the structure of the program."

Gladue reports can often be difficult for offenders and their families. One *Gladue* report writer stated, "The interviews are very hard. They are very emotional. Especially if a person is in custody. I've had guys say, 'I can't talk about that because I can't cry in here.' Sometimes I wonder if we are re-traumatizing them."

However, some judges see that they have a greater responsibility. In *R. v. Jesse Armitage*, which was heard in the first official Canadian court established to adhere to the principles expressed in *R. v. Gladue* and accordingly called a "*Gladue* court," Justice Nakatsuru wrote his entire judgment in unusually simple prose:

> In the *Gladue* court at Old City Hall, accused persons who share a proud history of the first people who lived in this nation, not only have a right to be heard, but they also have a right to fully understand. Their voices are heard by the judges. And they must also know that we have heard them ... I know that all accused, whether they have any Aboriginal blood or not, should have this right. Judges struggle to make sure they do. However, when judges write

their decisions, they are writing for different readers, different audiences. Judges write not only for the parties before them. Judges write to other readers of the law. Lawyers. Other judges. The community. In this case, I am writing for Jesse Armitage.

In his ruling, Justice Nakatsuru noted that Jesse Armitage's grandmother was a residential school Survivor, and that her own children have struggled with alcoholism; and that Armitage came from a broken home. The judge went on to say,

> If I could describe Mr. Armitage as a tree, his roots remain hidden beneath the ground. I can see what he is now. I can see the trunk. I can see the leaves. But much of what he is and what has brought him before me, I cannot see. They are still buried. But I am sure that some of those roots involve his Aboriginal heritage and ancestry. They help define who he is. They have been a factor in his offending. They must be taken into account in his sentencing.

Times have changed. The former Harper Conservative Government constantly repeated a mantra of "serious time for serious crime" and has introduced a number of new mandatory minima prison sentences for various offences, particularly for firearms and drug offences. Kent Roach, "Rates of Imprisonment and Criminal Justice Policy" (2008) 53 Crim. L.Q. 273, raises concerns that this will substantially increase Canada's imprisonment rates. He notes that Canada's current rate of imprisonment is 110 per 100,000 whereas that in the United States is a staggering 738 per 100,000. See too Adelina Iftene and Allan Manson, "Recent Criminal Legislation and the Challenge for Prison Health Care" (2012) Canadian Medical Association Journal 1, pointing to increased overcrowding, double bunking and a shortage of prison health care resources.

In *R. v. Ferguson* (2008), 54 C.R. (6th)197 (S.C.C.) the Supreme Court added further rigidity in deciding that constitutional exemptions were not available in the case of minimum sentences. See C.R. comments by Steve Coughlan and Paul Calarco. Coughlan sees the decision as consistent with the rule of law. Calarco suggests that the rigidity may make claims of cruel and unusual punishment under s. 12 of the *Charter* more likely to succeed.

The message of the 3-2 majority Court of Appeal in *R. v. Arcand* (2010), 83 C.R. (6th) 199 (Alta. C.A.) delivered at the start of a lengthy analysis of Canadian sentencing policies and realities, is that courts of appeal need to be far more aggressive in intervening to control rampant sentencing disparity through a scheme of starting-point prison sentences for particular crimes:

FRASER C.J., COTE and WATSON J.J.A.—

> We must face up to five sentencing truths. First, it is notorious amongst judges, of whom there are now approximately 2,100 in this country at three court levels, that one of the most controversial subjects, both in theory and practical application, is sentencing. That takes us to the second truth. The proposition that if judges knew the facts of a given case, they would all agree, or substantially agree on the result, is simply not so. The third truth. Judges are not the only ones who know truths one and two, and thus judge shopping is alive and well in Canada - and fighting hard to stay that way. All lead inescapably to the fourth truth. Without reasonable uniformity of approach to

sentencing amongst trial and appellate judges in Canada, many of the sentencing objectives and principles prescribed in the Code are not attainable. This makes the search for just sanctions at best a lottery, and at worst a myth. Pretending otherwise obscures the need for Canadian courts to do what Parliament asked: minimize unjustified disparity in sentencing while maintaining flexibility. The final truth. If the courts do not act to vindicate the promises of the law, and public confidence diminishes, then Parliament will. [para. 8]

This is a concern not evident in sentencing judgments of other courts of appeal. See, for example, *R. v. Tuglavina* (2011), 83 C.R. (6th) 356 (N.L. C.A.) and *R. v. Kummer* (2011), 83 C.R. (6th) 379 (Ont. C.A.), which assert an approach of setting flexible guidelines, and accept and justify the Supreme Court's approach that appeal courts should show deference to sentencing decisions of trial judges. The message of the majority of the Alberta Court of Appeal can be read as encouraging the current Parliamentary trend to fixed minimum sentences. Although this would make sentencing easier it is likely that many judges at all levels, and including Alberta judges, would not favour such rigidity or lack of trust in the judiciary. Not all crimes are the same and minimum sentences allow for no individual factors to be taken into account.

There used to be only a few minimum penalties in the *Criminal Code*. Now as a legacy of the Harper Conservative Government there are over 100. These law and order amendments came at a time when United States courts and policy experts on both sides of the border have become acutely aware of the danger, injustice and costs of such sentencing rigidity. The current Liberal Government has promised a review of such penalties but nothing has materialized in the first two years. We shall see that fortunately courts are now applying constitutional barriers mostly by reinterpreting the *Charter* standard against cruel and unusual punishment and broadening the reasonable hypothetical approach.

The authoritative breakthrough came with the decision of the Supreme Court in *R. v. Nur*, [2015] 1 S.C.R. 773, 322 C.C.C. (3d) 149, 18 C.R. (7th) 227. Chief Justice McLachlin for a 6-3 majority held that a three- and five-year mandatory minimum for firearms offences violated s. 12 on the basis of reasonable foresight of gross disproportionality for some offenders.

According to the Chief Justice, with LeBel, Abella, Cromwell, Karakatsanis and Gascon JJ. concurring, a challenge to a mandatory sentencing provision under s. 12 of the *Charter* raises two questions: first, whether the provision amounts to cruel and unusual punishment in the sense of gross disproportionality for that accused; and, if not, second, whether the provision would result in cruel and unusual punishment for other offenders whose circumstances are reasonably foreseeable. The jurisprudence in respect of this approach is, held the majority, long and settled, workable, and provides sufficient certainty. The term "reasonable hypothetical" might be helpful but the focus remains squarely on whether the sentence would be grossly disproportionate in reasonably foreseeable cases. Fanciful or remote situations may be excluded because the exercise must be grounded in experience and common sense. However, it is not necessary that the projected application be common or likely. Where a challenge is advanced under s. 12, a court must determine what is a proportionate sentence and then determine whether the mandatory minimum sentence requires the imposition of a sentence that is grossly disproportionate to the fit and proportionate sentence.

Here the majority held that the three-year minimum sentence for a first offence would result in grossly disproportionate sentences in reasonably foreseeable cases because the offence covers a wide range of potential conduct. Although most cases within that range may well merit the mandatory minimum sentence, conduct at the far end of the range may not. The provision foreseeably catches licensing offences that involve little or no moral fault and little or no danger to the public. Although firearms are inherently dangerous, a three-year term of imprisonment for essentially a licensing infraction is out of sync with the norms of sentencing and legitimate expectations in a free and democratic society. Therefore, the three-year minimum sentence for first offenders violated s. 12. The five-year minimum sentence for second or subsequent offenders would also be grossly disproportionate for less serious offenders. The five-year term goes far beyond what is necessary in order to protect the public, to express moral condemnation, and to discourage others from engaging in such conduct. Neither violation could be saved under s. 1. The sentences imposed on the two appellants were appropriate and therefore the appeals were dismissed.

Moldaver J. concurred in the result but dissented on the constitutional issue, with Rothstein and Wagner JJ. concurring. The reasonable hypothetical approach did not justify striking down the provisions because the licensing-type cases relied upon by the majority were not grounded in experience or common sense. There had not been a single licensing-type case where the mandatory minimum could be regarded as grossly disproportionate. There also had not been any cases in which a licensing-type offence had been prosecuted by indictment. The reasonable hypothetical approach assumed that the Crown would elect to proceed by indictment when the fair, just, and appropriate election would be to elect to proceed summarily. This does not accord with common sense because the Crown election has been purposely integrated into the legislative scheme and is a clear expression of Parliamentary intention to provide prosecutors with the discretion to divert less serious cases into summary proceedings.

The majority judgment rejected the dissenters' notion that a different analysis must be adopted for hybrid offences and that the proper approach is to consider whether proceeding on indictment is an abuse of process. The *Nur* Court did not find it necessary to consider the s. 7 or s. 15 challenges. See strong criticisms advanced by Rosemary Cairns Way, "A Disappointing Silence: Mandatory Minimums and Substantive Equality" (2015) 18 C.R. (7th) 297, shared by Tim Quigley (2015), 18 C.R. (7th) 227. She argues that the majority ruling is disappointing in its focus on the abstract concept of a reasonable foreseeability, rather than the empirical question of the utility of mandatory minimum sentences, which have a discriminatory and disparate impact on vulnerable groups

In *R. v. Lloyd*, [2016] 1 S.C.R. 130, 334 C.C.C. (3d) 20, 27 C.R. (7th) 205 a 6 3 majority decided that a one-year mandatory minimum for repeat drug trafficking offences violated s. 12 given reasonable hypotheticals and that the violation could not be saved under s. 1. The nine justices unanimously and firmly rejected the notion that a *Charter* challenge on mandatory minimum sentences can be based on proportionality as a principle of fundamental justice under s. 7. Instead the Court decides that the issue must be addressed under the tougher gross disproportionality standard for cruel and unusual punishment under s. 12.

The joint dissenting opinion of Justices Wagner, Gascon and Brown attacked the reasonable hypotheticals used by the majority and relied on early Supreme Court s. 12 jurisprudence to suggest that the *Charter* argument should only succeed in "very rare" cases. The dissenters, all recent appointees, did not address any of the Chief Justice's policy arguments advanced so eloquently and comprehensively in *Nur* against the proliferation of mandatory minimums. It is to the credit of Justice Moldaver that he joined in *Lloyd* with the majority even though he had argued so strongly against the Chief Justice's approach in his dissenting opinion in *Nur*.

The approach in *Nur* and *Lloyd* must now be taken to have settled the framework for s. 12 challenges. Under that approach many of the 100 or so current mandatory minimums should fall.

Curiously *R. v. Safarzadeh-Markhali*, [2016] 1 S.C.R. 180, 334 C.C.C. (3d) 1, 27 C.R. (7th) 265 finds the same nine justices of the Supreme Court agreeing that a pre-trial custody limit in the *Truth in Sentencing Act* can be struck down under s. 7 on the fundamental principle of justice recognized in cases such as *Bedford* that a law cannot be overbroad. The calculation of pre-trial credit for sentencing purposes is clearly a matter of sentencing. Some lower courts have also relied on s. 7 to strike down mandatory sentences as overbroad. The Supreme Court has not made it clear whether this avenue of challenge is now also closed.

In *R. v. Lloyd* the Court reasoned that mere proportionality in sentencing is *not* a principle of fundamental justice under s. 7:

> Recognition of the principle of proportionality in sentencing as a principle of fundamental justice under s. 7 would also have implications for the respective roles of Parliament and the courts. The principle of proportionality is an admirable guide for judges seeking to impose fit sentences within the legal parameters established by Parliament. But it is not an overarching constitutional principle that allows judges to subvert the norms of punishment enacted by Parliament. Those norms are judged only by the standard of s. 12.

> It has been said that "proportionality in sentencing could aptly be described as a principle of fundamental justice": *R. v. Ipeelee*, 2012 SCC 13, [2012] 1 S.C.R. 433, at para. 36. However, this does not mean that proportionality constitutes a new principle of fundamental justice distinct from the well-established principle of gross disproportionality under s. 7 of the *Charter*.

> Parliament has the power to make policy choices with respect to the imposition of punishment for criminal activities and the crafting of sentences that it deems appropriate to balance the objectives of deterrence, denunciation, rehabilitation and protection of society. Courts owe Parliament deference in a s. 12 analysis [pars. 43-45].

The Supreme Court in *Lloyd* chooses to distance itself from the words of Justice LeBel in *R. v. Ipeelee*, 2012 SCC 13, [2012] 1 S.C.R. 433, 280 C.C.C. (3d) 265, 91 C.R. (6th) 1 at para. 36 that "proportionality in sentencing could aptly be described as a principle of fundamental justice".

The view that gross disproportionality under s. 12 rather than proportionality under s. 7 is the approach to be adopted for mandatory minimums appears to be pragmatic rather than principled. The Court reached that position without even acknowledging the weight of Canadian academic opinion that a higher standard of proportionality should be recognized. See, for example, Palma Paciocco, "Proportionality, Discretion and the Roles of Judges and Prosecutors at

Sentencing" (2014) 18 Can. Crim. L. Rev. 241, Justice David Paciocco, "The Law of Minimum Sentences: Judicial Responses and Responsibility" (2015) 19 Can. Crim. L. Rev. 173 and T. Quigley, "Pre-trial Sentencing Credit Rule Contrary to Section 7 Charter Proportionality Standard for Sentencing" (2014), 13 C.R. (7th) 63.

The fundamental principle of sentencing declared in s. 718.1 of the *Criminal Code* has been applied by our courts on a daily basis for almost 20 years following Parliament's acceptance of the work of the Sentencing Commission. Surely that principle as time passed had a strong claim to be recognized as a principle of fundamental justice in s. 7

> as a legal principle, about which there is a significant societal consensus that is fundamental to the way in which the legal system ought fairly to operate and. . .identified with sufficient precision to yield a manageable standard (*Malmo Levine*, 2003 SCC 74, para. 113).

The Court in *Lloyd* was clearly intent on giving the current Parliament room to maneuver by suggesting it could narrow minima or give judges power to depart from minima in exceptional circumstances. The Court noted that a statutory exemption was the solution in many countries and had been recommended by the Canadian Bar Association. In 2011 the C.B.A. struck a committee of Crown and defence lawyers as well as policymakers to study the issue and report to the Uniform Law Conference of Canada. The majority of the Court in *Lloyd* implicitly retreats from the strong policy arguments advanced by Chief Justice McLachlin in *Ferguson* against a constitutional exemption solution to minimum sentences. Chief Justice McLachlin suggested in that decision that it would be hard to judge claims of exceptional circumstances and that an exemption would be contrary to the rule of law on the ground of uncertainty. The unruly ball is now tossed into the government's court.

In the meantime s. 12 challenges to mandatory minimums continue. An obvious candidate for challenge has been the simplistic mandatory grid for sentencing for possession of marijuana for trafficking: 6 months for 6-200 plants, 1 year for 201-500 plants and 2 years for 501 or more plants found at the time of the police raid. Most challenges have succeeded.

3. TOOLS OF SENTENCING

Discharges

See s. 730 of the *Criminal Code*.

In *R. v. Derksen* (1972), 20 C.R.N.S. 129, 9 C.C.C. (2d) 97 (B.C. P.C.), on a charge of possession of cannabis resin, the prosecutor asked that the Court grant an absolute or conditional discharge since it was a first offence. Ostler J. expressed concern that it could not be in the best interests of an accused and not contrary to the public interest to approach all unremarkable cases of this sort with a uniform policy of a discharge; to do so would be seen by many as condoning the offence and inviting a further breach. He concluded:

> In fine, it is my opinion that the discharge — the finding of guilt without the usual concomitant of conviction — should never be applied routinely to any criminal offence, in effect labelling the enactment violable. It should be used frugally, selectively and judiciously, as Parliament obviously intended. If it is considered that an absolute or conditional discharge is the appropriate penalty for a first offence under this section, then Parliament should so declare. The courts should not compromise or circumvent the law.

In *R. v. Fallofield* (1973), 22 C.R.N.S. 342, 13 C.C.C. (2d) 450 (B.C. C.A.), the defendant had been convicted of possession of stolen goods of a value of less than $200; while delivering refrigerators to a new apartment building, he took some left-over pieces of carpet of a value of $33.07. Evidence at the trial showed the defendant to be a corporal in the Armed Services, married, no previous record, and that a conviction could very possibly affect his future career in the Navy. The Court of Appeal reviewed the discharge cases to that date and, with the caveat that the discretion to grant a discharge should not be fettered, offered the following conclusions respecting what is now s. 730:

(1) The section may be used in respect of *any* offence other than an offence for which a minimum punishment is prescribed by law or the offence is punishable by imprisonment for 14 years or for life or by death.

(2) The section contemplates the commission of an offence. There is nothing in the language that limits it to a technical or trivial violation.

(3) Of the two conditions precedent to the exercise of the jurisdiction, the first is that the court must consider that it is in the best interests of the accused that he should be discharged either absolutely or upon condition. If it is not in the best interests of the accused, that, of course, is the end of the matter. If it is decided that it is in the best interests of the accused, then that brings the next consideration into operation.

(4) The second condition precedent is that the court must consider that a grant of discharge is not contrary to the public interest.

(5) Generally, the first condition would presuppose that the accused is a person of good character, without previous conviction, that it is not necessary to enter a conviction against him in order to deter him from future offences or to rehabilitate him, and that the entry of a conviction against him may have significant adverse repercussions.

(6) In the context of the second condition the public interest in the deterrence of others, while it must be given due weight, does not preclude the judicious use of the discharge provisions.

(7) The powers given by s. 662.1 [now s. 730] should not be exercised as an alternative to probation or suspended sentence.

(8) Section 662.1 should not be applied routinely to any particular offence. This may result in an apparent lack of uniformity in the application of the discharge provisions. This lack will be more apparent than real and will stem from the differences in the circumstances of cases.

The relationship between being granted a discharge and having a criminal record is complex. Under s. 730(3) of the *Criminal Code* a discharged accused "shall be deemed not to have been convicted of the offence". A 1972 amendment to the *Criminal Records Act* prescribed that one subject to a discharge could apply to the Parole Board, subject to a shorter waiting period, for a pardon. A pardon "vacated" a record. This amendment thwarted the aim of the discharge provisions and risked misinformation and confusion. It was only amended in 1992.

Subsequently, in *the Safe Streets and Communities Act*, S.C. 2012, c. 1, the entire concept of a "pardon" was removed from Canadian law and replaced with a "record suspension". A record suspension only "requires that the judicial record of the conviction be kept separate and apart from other criminal records" and with some exceptions "removes any disqualification or obligation to which the applicant is, by reason of the conviction, subject under any Act of Parliament" (*Criminal Records Act*, s. 2.3(b)). A person convicted of an offence can apply, after a certain period of time, for a record suspension. If it is granted then under s. 6(2) of the *Criminal Records Act* "[n]o such record shall be disclosed to any person, nor shall the existence of the record or the fact of the conviction be disclosed to any person, without the prior approval of the Minister".

Note that only "a person who has been convicted of an offence" can apply for a record suspension: a person who received a discharge has *not* been convicted of an offence. However, under s. 6.1 of the *Criminal Records Act* "the existence of the record or the fact of the discharge" cannot be disclosed to anyone without the prior approval of the Minister. This occurs automatically after a certain period of time: one year in the case of an absolute discharge and three years in the case of a conditional discharge. That is the same consequence that would flow from successful application for a record suspension. The effect of this is two-fold: a discharged accused will without application receive the same benefit as if he or she had applied for a record suspension, but that will not occur immediately. As a result, for a discharged accused, the answer to the question "have you been convicted of an offence" is from the start "no", but the answer to the question "do you have a criminal record" is "yes" until the appropriate time has passed, at which point it becomes "no".

Fines

See s. 734 of the *Criminal Code*, and compare the counterpart provisions with respect to summary conviction offences in s. 787.

Probation

See s. 731 of the *Criminal Code*.

In *R. v. Sangster* (1973), 21 C.R.N.S. 339 (Que. C.A.), the trial judge had given a suspended sentence of five years' imprisonment and placed the accused on probation for three years. Kaufman J.A. dismissed the Crown's appeal but noted:

> I do, however, wish to point out that the true intent of s. 663 (1)(a) of the *Code* is to suspend "the passing of sentence", and not the sentence itself. With respect, I therefore consider it unwise to indicate to an accused the precise sentence which might be imposed on him should he fail to observe the conditions set by the court. To do so may well put the judge in a predicament: keep his word and sentence an accused to a term of imprisonment which might be considerably longer than the circumstances would warrant or, in the alternative, give a proper sentence, but lose credibility. Neither situation is good — the first an injustice to the accused, the second an unnecessary embarrassment to the court.
>
> This should not be taken to mean that an accused cannot be told that failure to abide by the conditions might entail serious consequences, indeed even imprisonment for a lengthy period. But I do think that no court should bind itself in so absolute a fashion that all room for discretion will have vanished.

The court may suspend the passing of sentence and place the accused on probation when there is no minimum punishment provided (*cf. R. v. Bradshaw*, [1976] 1 S.C.R. 162, 29 C.R.N.S. 221, 21 C.C.C. (2d) 69). The court may fine the accused and place him or her on probation or the court may imprison the accused and place him or her on probation. (The imprisonment in such a case cannot be for a period longer than two years: *R. v. Nutter, Collishaw and Dulong* (1972), 7 C.C.C. (2d) 224 (B.C. C.A.)). The court cannot fine the accused and place him on probation and imprison him or her: *R. v. Smith* (1972), 7 C.C.C. (2d) 468 (N.W.T.) and *R. v. Blacquiere* (1975), 24 C.C.C. (2d) 168 (Ont. C.A.).

Section 732.1 provides that the court may prescribe, besides the statutory conditions listed, "such other *reasonable* conditions as the court considers desirable for securing the good conduct of the accused and for preventing a repetition by him of the same offence or the commission of other offences". The condition imposed then cannot be as additional punishment. In *R. v. Ziatas* (1973), 13 C.C.C. (2d) 287 (Ont. C.A.), the trial judge, on an assault charge, fined the accused and placed him on probation for one year with the condition that he not operate a motor vehicle during that period. The condition was struck out on appeal because:

> we are all of the view that he proceeded upon a wrong principle, inasmuch as he imposed this term of the probation order as an additional punishment to be imposed upon the accused, whereas his only power, if he had any jurisdiction to impose the condition under s. 663(2) of the *Criminal Code*, was to impose such reasonable conditions as he considered desirable for securing the good conduct of the accused and for preventing the repetition by him of the same offence or the commission of other offences.

In *R. v. Gladstone* (1978), 2 C.R. (3d) S-9, 40 C.C.C. (2d) 42 (B.C. Co. Ct.), the accused was convicted of breach of a regulation made under the *Fisheries Act* and the Court made it a condition of probation that he surrender his permit to fish for a period of one month. The appeal court allowed the accused's appeal and noted:

> A condition of probation based upon s. 663(2)(*h*) [now s. 732.1] should be reasonable and it should be designed to secure the good conduct of the accused and to prevent a repetition by the accused of the same offence or the commission of other offences. The primary purpose of a condition of probation attached under 663(2)(*a*) to (*h*) inclusive, should be for the rehabilitation of the accused, not the imposition of punishment. That is particularly relevant when a condition of probation has been prescribed following the suspension of sentence, as distinct from a condition of probation being imposed following the passing of sentence, be it the imposition of a term in jail, or of a fine.
>
> In this case the comments expressed by the learned Provincial Court Judge in sentencing the accused indicate that his primary purpose in directing the accused to surrender his permit to fish was to punish the accused, because he had violated his privilege to fish under the permit, and also to deter the accused and other native people from a repetition of the offence.
>
> In my respectful view, the condition attached by the learned Provincial Court Judge to the probation order was inappropriate for several reasons. First, having suspended sentence, he in effect punished the accused by depriving him of his permit to fish for a period of 30 days. Secondly, in view of the particular circumstances of the accused — that he was a native Indian, no longer employable, in receipt of Social Assistance, and who represented that he was catching fish to smoke for winter food for himself and his family — I am not persuaded that it was a "reasonable condition" within the general purview of s. 663(2)(*h*). Thirdly, the primary purpose of the condition was not directed to the rehabilitation of tlhe accused. Fourthly, the effect of the condition was to

prohibit the accused from fishing under his permit for one month, as distinct from restricting the accused from fishing under the permit for specified periods of time within the period of one month.

In view of the accused's alleged lack of understanding of the precise terms of his permit to fish, including the requirement that fish be "marked" (which may have been caused by his difficulty in hearing), a condition of probation under s. 663(2)(a), that the accused be required to report to and be under the supervision of a fisheries officer for a fixed period of time would have been more appropriate. It would have had the primary purpose of encouraging the rehabilitation of the accused. It would have enabled a fisheries officer to ensure that the accused clearly understood the terms of his permit. Alternatively, a condition of probation under s. 663(2)(h) that the accused report for several weeks to a fisheries officer on the completion of each weekly period of fishing under the permit, to demonstrate to such fisheries officer that any fish caught had been "marked" properly, would have complied with the scope and purpose of s. 663(2)(h).

In *R. v. Pawlowski* (1971), 5 C.C.C. (2d) 87 (Man. C.A.), the accused's probation order which provided for restitution also contained a condition that he pay costs of $1000. The magistrate said he was assessing heavy costs to indicate to the accused disapproval of his actions and because of his lack of remorse. Dickson J.A., struck out the condition as illegal and said that s. 737(2)(h) did not authorize the imposition of punishment by means of a fine nor a requirement to pay costs.

In *R. v. DeKleric*, [1969] 2 C.C.C. 367 (B.C.C.A.), the magistrate suspended the passing of sentence and imposed a condition of probation that the accused pay the sum of $500 in favour of the Vancouver Superannuated Police Officer's Association. Davey C.J.B.C. noted:

> However, I cannot part with this case without some remarks about condition (3), which required the respondent to pay the sum of $500 to the Vancouver Superannuated Police Officers' Association at the rate of $100 per month. It seems to me, with the greatest respect to this experienced Magistrate, that that is quite wrong. If the circumstances required a fine, it should have been imposed as a fine. If the circumstances required as a condition of suspended sentence, restitution or reparation to the injured parties within the meaning of the provisions of the *Code* which allow such a condition to be imposed as a term of the suspended sentence, then It should have been done that way. This innovation is a most dangerous one. It can lead to the greatest abuses, and for myself I hope it is the last time we see such a condition imposed as a term of any suspended sentence.
>
> I have considered whether we should impose a fine or not. If we impose a fine, then this is no longer a suspended sentence. The only consequence of breach of the recognizance will be an action to recover the amount of the recognizance. Under a suspended sentence, if the respondent is in breach of the conditions of the recognizance, he may be brought before the court to have an appropriate sentence imposed in the light of the conditions which then exist. That is what I think should be done.

Restitution

Sections 738-741.2 authorize orders of restitution. In *R. v. Dashner* (1974), 25 C.R.N.S. 340, 15 C.C.C. (2d) 139 (B.C. C.A.), the accused, convicted on two counts of assault causing bodily harm, was fined and placed on probation. One condition of the probation order required the accused to pay each victim $500 within two months. This condition was struck out on appeal and McFarlane J.A. noted:

> I think, however, that great care should be taken to ensure that restitution or reparation will not be made a condition of a probation order unless the court is satisfied that the convicted person

is able to pay and that the circumstances come clearly within the paragraph, particularly that the amount ordered represents "actual loss or damage sustained". My reason for this view is that breach of a probation order is itself an offence under the *Criminial Code* which may involve very serious consequences.

I think assistance in the task of interpretation and application of s. 737(2)(*e*) may be found in para. (*h*) which authorizes:

> (*h*) . . . such other reasonable conditions as the court considers desirable for securing the good conduct of the accused and for preventing a repetition by him of the same offence or the commission of other offences.

It appears that the general purpose of probation orders is to secure the good conduct of the convicted person as opposed to compensating victims of crime. The remedies available to them by ordinary civil suit and under the *Criminal Injuries Compensation Act*, 1972 (B.C.), c. 17, should not be overlooked: nor the difference between compensation on the one hand and restitution or reparation on the other.

So, too, in *R. v. Groves* (1977), 39 C.R.N.S. 366, 37 C.C.C. (2d) 429 (Ont. H.C.), where McEwan P.C.J. had made it a condition that the accused pay to his victim, a police officer, $500 for his pain and suffering which resulted from the accused twisting and bending the officer's little finger. The officer had received workmen's compensation for his injury during his absence from duty. He was still experiencing discomfort at the date of the trial. On appeal, O'Driscoll J. noted the lack of discovery mechanisms in the criminal process for accurately determining extent of loss and concluded:

> In my view, had Parliament intended to confer upon the criminal courts a remedial power to order an offender to compensate a victim for pain and suffering, it would have set out its intent in clear language. Indeed, it seems to me, that the word "actual" as used in the section suggests that Parliament intended to restrict its scope to those damages that are relatively concrete and easily ascertainable and as such exclude such vague, amorphous and difficult matters as "pain and suffering". Consequently, I am of the opinion that an order under s. 663(2)(*e*) should be restricted to those damages in the nature of special damages.

The amount of restitution is to be fixed by the sentencing judge. In *R. v. Shorten* (1976), 29 C.C.C. (2d) 528 (B.C. C.A.), the accused were convicted of welfare fraud. The trial judge fined the accused and placed them on probation with a condition requiring restitiution in such amounts and at such times as the probation officer should order. In striking out this condition McIntyre J.A. stated:

> It seems to me that the condition in question can be attacked from either of two angles: (1) Because the judge has delegated to the probation officer the duty to form a judicial opinion of the convicted person's ability from time to time to pay. (2) Because the judge has delegated to the probation officer the power to make an order or orders. It is apparent that the trial judge, in what may well have been a commendable effort to make a realistic order which would offer some hope of compliance did attempt to delegate his functions in dealing with sentence. This part of his order cannot stand.
>
> In reaching this conclusion I am not overlooking the provisions of s. 738(3) of the *Criminal Code* which provide for the modification of a probation order after its making. The operation of this section, however, depends upon an application by prosecutor or accused. No such application has been made and the possible operation of that section in these circumstances is therefore not before us.

In addition to the restitution that can be made as part of a probation order, a number of recent changes to the *Code* provide for victim surcharges and other restitution orders: see ss. 737-741.2.

Community Service

See s. 732.1(3)(f): provides for conditions of community service not exceeding 240 hours over 18 months.

In *R. v. Stennes* (1975), 35 C.R.N.S. 123 (B.C. C.A.), the accused was sentenced to a six-month term to be followed by probation for two years with a number of conditions including the condition that he do 40 hours of community work per month. The Court of Appeal noted:

> Counsel for the appellant took the initial objection that the probation order was a nullity under the provisions of the *Criminal Code*, R.S.C. 1970, c. C-34, s. 663(l)(*b*) [am. 1972, c. 13, s. 58], for the reason that the condition which I have mentioned as being that numbered 7, that the appellant do 40 hours of community work per month, was the equivalent of a fine, and that a probation order could be given only in addition to fining or imposing a term of imprisonment, and that as imprisonment had already been imposed in this case no fine could be also imposed.
>
> I find no substance to that argument. In my view a condition in a probation order to do certain work, if appropriate, is not a fine, and I so hold. Accordingly, that submission must fall to the ground. I will have something to say later about the terms of the condition itself.

Later in the judgment, however, the condition was struck out as "inappropriate" with no discussion as to why.

By contrast, in *R. v. Shaw* (1977), 36 C.R.N.S. 358 (Ont. C.A.), the Ontario Court of Appeal approved of conditions of community service projects in respect of two youths convicted of trafficking in marijuana and L.S.D. The Court added:

> Not only do I think that the provisions in the probation orders relating to this matter are valid, but in appropriate cases should be more extensively used.

Intermittent Sentence

See s. 732, available for sentences not exceeding 90 days. Note that if an intermittent sentence is imposed, then the court must order probation. It might be advisable to consider as a term of the probation that the offender attend at the detention centre on time and in a sober condition.

Recognizance to Keep the Peace

See ss. 810, 810.1 and 811 of the *Criminal Code*. Along with the authority specified in these sections the magistrate has a common law jurisdiction to bind over a person to keep the peace: see *R. v. White; Ex parte Chonan* (1969), 5 C.R.N.S. 30, [1969] 1 C.C.C. 19 (B.C. S.C.).

Imprisonment

Maximum sentences for indictable offences range from life (e.g., manslaughter: s. 236), 14 years (e.g., incest: s. 155(2)), ten years (e.g., obstructing justice in a judicial proceeding: s. 139(2)), five years (e.g., for an offence for which no punishment is specially provided: s. 743), and two years (e.g., wilful obstruction of a peace officer: s. 129). The maximum is generally six months in the case of offences punishable by summary conviction (e.g., assault: s. 266(b) and s. 787). In 1994 Parliament increased the maximum penalty for several hybrid offences when proceeded against by way of summary conviction to 18 months: see, e.g., assault causing bodily harm (s. 267) and sexual assault (s. 271).

For a long time Canada had just a few minimum imprisonment sentences (e.g., life for first or second degree murder and 14 days for a second conviction for impaired driving). In recent years Parliament has, however, added a number notably for firearms and drug offences.

Where the accused is convicted of more than one offence and receives more than one prison sentence the judge has a discretion to declare that the sentences be served concurrently or consecutively (s. 718.3(4)). In addition, under s. 745.51 a judge can order, where an accused is found guilty of multiple murders, that the periods of ineligibility for parole can be consecutive.

Conditional Sentences

See ss. 742-742.7. If a court has decided to impose a sentence of imprisonment of less than two years, these sections, which came into force in September, 1996, permit a court to order that the offender serve the sentence in the community where the court is satisfied that such an order would not endanger the safety of the community. The court is obliged to impose certain conditions and also may impose others. The pattern for granting conditional discharges is controversial and inconsistent: see, for example, Tim Quigley, "Uneven Deference on Conditional Sentencing" (2003), 12 C.R. (6th) 117.

R. v. PROULX

2000 SCC 5, [2000] 1 S.C.R. 61, 140 C.C.C. (3d) 449, 30 C.R. (5th) 1,
2000 CarswellMan 32, 2000 CarswellMan 33

The judgment of the court was delivered by LAMER C.J. — ...

127   At this point, a short summary of what has been said in these reasons might be useful:

1. Bill C-41 in general and the conditional sentence in particular were enacted both to reduce reliance on incarceration as a sanction and to increase the use of principles of restorative justice in sentencing.

2. A conditional sentence should be distinguished from probationary measures. Probation is primarily a rehabilitative sentencing tool. By contrast, Parliament intended conditional sentences to include both punitive and rehabilitative aspects. Therefore, conditional sentences should generally include punitive conditions that are restrictive of the offender's liberty. Conditions such as house arrest should be the norm, not the exception.

3. No offences are excluded from the conditional sentencing regime except those with a minimum term of imprisonment, nor should there be presumptions in favour of or against a conditional sentence for specific offences.

4. The requirement in s. 742.1(a) that the judge impose a sentence of imprisonment of less than two years does not require the judge to first impose a sentence of imprisonment of a fixed duration before considering whether that sentence can be served in the community. Although this approach is suggested by the text of s. 742.1(a), it is unrealistic and could lead to unfit sentences in some cases. Instead, a purposive interpretation of s. 742.1(a) should be adopted. In a preliminary determination, the sentencing judge should reject a penitentiary term and probationary measures as inappropriate. Having determined that the appropriate range of sentence is a term of imprisonment of less than two years, the judge should then consider whether it is appropriate for the offender to serve his or her sentence in the community.

5. As a corollary of the purposive interpretation of s. 742.1(a), a conditional sentence need not be of equivalent duration to the sentence of incarceration that would otherwise have been imposed. The sole requirement is that the duration and conditions of a conditional sentence make for a just and appropriate sentence.

6. The requirement in s. 742.1(b) that the judge be satisfied that the safety of the community would not be endangered by the offender serving his or her sentence in the community is a condition precedent to the imposition of a conditional sentence, and not the primary consideration in determining whether a conditional sentence is appropriate. In making this determination, the judge should consider the risk posed by the specific offender, not the broader risk of whether the imposition of a conditional sentence would endanger the safety of the community by providing insufficient general deterrence or undermining general respect for the law. Two factors should be taken into account: (1) the risk of the offender re-offending; and (2) the gravity of the damage that could ensue in the event of re-offence. A consideration of the risk posed by the offender should include the risk of any criminal activity, and not be limited solely to the risk of physical or psychological harm to individuals.

7. Once the prerequisites of s. 742.1 are satisfied, the judge should give serious consideration to the possibility of a conditional sentence in all cases by examining whether a conditional sentence is consistent with the fundamental purpose and principles of sentencing set out in ss. 718 to 718.2. This follows from Parliament's clear message to the judiciary to reduce the use of incarceration as a sanction.

8. A conditional sentence can provide significant denunciation and deterrence. As a general matter, the more serious the offence, the longer and more onerous the conditional sentence should be. There may be some circumstances, however, where the need for denunciation or deterrence is so pressing that incarceration will be the only suitable way in which to express society's condemnation of the offender's conduct or to deter similar conduct in the future.

9. Generally, a conditional sentence will be better than incarceration at achieving the restorative objectives of rehabilitation, reparations to the victim and the community, and promotion of a sense of responsibility in the offender and acknowledgment of the harm done to the victim and the community.

10. Where a combination of both punitive and restorative objectives may be achieved, a conditional sentence will likely be more appropriate than incarceration. Where objectives such as denunciation and deterrence are particularly pressing, incarceration will generally be the preferable sanction. This may be so notwithstanding the fact that restorative goals might be achieved. However, a conditional sentence may provide sufficient denunciation and deterrence, even in cases in which restorative objectives are of lesser importance, depending on the nature of the conditions imposed, the duration of the sentence, and the circumstances of both the offender and the community in which the conditional sentence is to be served.

11. A conditional sentence may be imposed even where there are aggravating circumstances, although the need for denunciation and deterrence will increase in these circumstances.

12. No party is under a burden of proof to establish that a conditional sentence is either appropriate or inappropriate in the circumstances. The judge should consider all relevant evidence, no matter by whom it is adduced. However, it would be in the offender's best interests to establish elements militating in favour of a conditional sentence.

13. Sentencing judges have a wide discretion in the choice of the appropriate sentence. They are entitled to considerable deference from appellate courts. As explained in *M. (C.A.)*, *supra*, at para. 90: "Put simply,

absent an error in principle, failure to consider a relevant factor, or an overemphasis of the appropriate factors, a court of appeal should only intervene to vary a sentence imposed at trial if the sentence is demonstrably unfit".

The *Safe Streets and Communities Act*, S.C. 2012, c. 1, s. 34, limited conditional sentences by enacting the following *Criminal Code* provision:

742.1 If a person is convicted of an offence and the court imposes a sentence of imprisonment of less than two years, the court may, for the purpose of supervising the offender's behaviour in the community, order that the offender serve the sentence in the community, subject to the conditions imposed under section 742.3, if

(a) the court is satisfied that the service of the sentence in the community would not endanger the safety of the community and would be consistent with the fundamental purpose and principles of sentencing set out in sections 718 to 718.2;

(b) the offence is not an offence punishable by a minimum term of imprisonment;

(c) the offence is not an offence, prosecuted by way of indictment, for which the maximum term of imprisonment is 14 years or life;

(d) the offence is not a terrorism offence, or a criminal organization offence, prosecuted by way of indictment, for which the maximum term of imprisonment is 10 years or more;

(e) the offence is not an offence, prosecuted by way of indictment, for which the maximum term of imprisonment is 10 years, that

    (i) resulted in bodily harm,

    (ii) involved the import, export, trafficking or production of drugs, or

    (iii) involved the use of a weapon; and

(f) the offence is not an offence, prosecuted by way of indictment, under any of the following provisions:

    (i) section 144 (prison breach),

    (ii) section 264 (criminal harassment),

    (iii) section 271 (sexual assault),

    (iv) section 279 (kidnapping),

    (v) section 279.02 (trafficking in persons — material benefit),

    (vi) section 281 (abduction of person under fourteen),

    (vii) section 333.1 (motor vehicle theft),

    (viii) paragraph 334(*a*) (theft over $5000),

    (ix) paragraph 348(1)(e) (breaking and entering a place other than a dwelling-house),

    (x) section 349 (being unlawfully in a dwelling-house), and

    (xi) section 435 (arson for fraudulent purpose).

TABLE OF CASES

The bold entries reflect those cases where the text of the judgment is given.

A (Children) (Conjoined Twins: Surgical Separation), Re 982

Adgey v. R. 763

Application under s. 83.28 of the Criminal Code, Re 10

B.C. Electric Ry. v. Loach 316

Beaver v. R. 367, 472, 473, 738, 739

Bedford v. Canada (Attorney General) 59, 70, 71, **79**, 108, 229, 417, 1206

Brown v. Durham Regional Police Department 1174

Buch v. Amory Mortgage Co. 258

Canada (Attorney General) v. Bedford *See* Bedford v. Canada (Attorney General)

Canada (Attorney General) v. Charles 773

Canada v. Pharmaceutical Society (Nova Scotia) 49

Canadian Dredge and Dock Co. v. R. 1167, 1170

Canadian Foundation for Children v. Canada (A.G.) *See* Canadian Foundation for Children, Youth & the Law v. Canada (Attorney General)

Canadian Foundation for Children, Youth & the Law v. Canada (Attorney General) 49, 71, 253, 777

Canadian National Transportation Ltd. v. Canada (Attorney General) 390

Carter v. Canada (Attorney General) 229

Centre for Addiction and Mental Health v. R. 788

City of Lévis *See* Lévis (City) v. Tétreault; Lévis (City) v. 2629-4470 Québec Inc.

Clements (Litigation Guardian of) v. Clements 357

Cooper v. R. 789

Corporation of the City of London v. Polewsky 405

Davis v. State 594

D.P.P. v. Morgan 686

Dunlop and Sylvester v. R. 1082, 1092

Edington v. Fitzmaurice 362

Fagan v. Commissioner of Metropolitan Police 262

Fournier v. R. 865

Frey v. Fedoruk 2, 5

Haughton v. Smith 1130

Hill v. Hamilton-Wentworth (Regional Municipality) Police Services Board 552

Hunter v. Southam Inc. 47, 48

Johnson v. R. 755

Jones v. National Coal Board 134

Kilbride v. Lake 309

Kjeldsen v. R. 798

Law v. Canada (Minister of Human Resources Development) 719

Lévis (City) v. Tétreault; Lévis (City) v. 2629-4470 Québec Inc. 404, 405, **769**

Lévis (Ville) c. Tétrault *See* Lévis (City) v. Tétreault; Lévis (City) v. 2629-4470 Québec Inc.

Marshall v. R. 192

Molis v. R. 774

Moore v. R. 268

O'Grady v. Sparling 510, 511

Pappajohn v. R. 473, **597**, 627, 632, 725, 738

People v. Beardsley 296

Perka v. R. 963, 976

Phillips v. Ford Motor Co. 134

PHS Community Services Society v. Canada (Attorney General) 58, 59, 70, 71

Pichette v. Quebec (Deputy Minister of Revenue) 418

Prostitution Reference 49

Quebec (Attorney General) v. A. 720

Québec (Autorité des marchés financiers) c. Souveraine, cie d'assurance générale 773

R. v. A. (J.) 689, 703
R. v. A. (No. 2) 664
R. v. Abbey 799
R. v. Accused No. 1 1181
R. v. Adams 551
R. v. Ali 315
R. v. Alicandro 736, 1135
R. v. Allen 1019
R. v. Ancio 493, **1111**
R. v. Anderson 524
R. v. Angelis 1046
R. v. Aravena 1019, 1020
R. v. Arcand 1203
R. v. Archer 774
R. v. Arias-Jackson 1094
R. v. Arkell 470
R. v. Armstrong 493
R. v. B. (D.) 777
R. v. B. (T.B.) 229
R. v. Ball (2011) 1079
R. v. Ball (2013) 944
R. v. Banwait 465
R. v. Barnes 1066, 1076
R. v. Barron 577
R. v. Bartlett 865
R. v. Barton 705, 710
R. v. Bauman 775
R. v. Baxter 934
R. v. Beatty 541, 551, 552, 554, 555, 716
R. v. Beauchamp 422, 424
R. v. Beaver *See* Beaver v. R.
R. v. Bedford *See* Bedford v. Canada
    (Attorney General)
R. c. Bélanger 551
R. v. Bergamin 866
R. v. Bernard 870, 892, 893, 923
R. v. Berryman 315
R. v. Blacquiere 1210
R. v. Blaue 342
R. v. Blondin 506, 738
R. v. Bolduc and Bird 230
R. v. Bouchard-Lebrun 855, **910**, 911
R. v. Boulanger 473, **497**
R. v. Bradshaw 1210
R. v. Brar 431
R. v. Brenton 907
R. v. Briscoe 504, **1093**
R. v. Brocklebank 540

R. v. Brooks 472
R. v. Brown 418
R. v. Browne 280
R. v. Budget Car Rentals (Toronto) Ltd.
    192
R. v. Bulmer 628, 632
R. v. Burger 551
R. v. Burt 187, 191, 192
R. v. Butler 49, 133
R. v. Buzizi 1046, 1047
R. v. Buzzanga and Durocher 484, **485**,
    493
R. v. C.A.M. 1189
R. v. Cairney 1046
R. v. Campbell and Mlynarchuk 750
R. v. Campione 803
R. v. Cancoil Thermal Corp. 405
R. v. Canhoto 540
R. v. Carker (No. 2) 986
R. v. Carriere 577
R. v. Carson 257
R. v. Cedeno 907
R. v. Celebrity Enterprises Ltd. (No. 2)
    1135
R. v. Chalk 210
R. v. Chapin 391
R. v. Chapman 737
R. v. Charters 763
R. v. Chartrand 493
R. v. Chase 622
R. v. Chaulk (1990) 77, 78, 786, **802**, 933
R. v. Chaulk (2007) 869, 912
R. v. Chiang 1076
R. v. Cinous 929, 933, 956
R. v. City of Sault Ste. Marie 367, **374**,
    383, 397, 404, 405, 417, 933
R. v. Clark 11, 16, 23
R. v. Clarke 737
R. v. Clay 70
R. v. Clemente 473
R. v. Clothier 1077
R. v. Collins (1987) 17
R. v. Collins (1989) 468, 739
R. v. Cormier 935, **949**, **958**
R. v. Cornejo 681
R. v. Costoff 985
R. v. Cotroni 1181
R. v. Crangle 684

R. v. Creaghan 762
R. v. Creighton 320, 361, 458, 472, 473, 477, **532**, 540, 547, 551, 552, 555, **564**, 577, 578, 715, 716
R. v. Cribbin 335
R. v. Cuerrier 230, **231**, 247, 248, 251, 252
R. v. Cunha 934
R. v. Czibulka 431
R. v. Daley 908, 910, 911, 912
R. v. Darrach (S.C.C.) 658, 664, 680
R. v. Darrach (Ont. C.A.) 685, **717**
R. v. Dashner 1211
R. v. Daviault 716, 719, **892**, 886, 904, 905, 907, 908, 911, 912, 933
R. v. Davis (1978) 576
R. v. Davis (1999) 632, **633**
R. v. De Ciantis 551
R. v. Deans 787
R. v. Decaire 907
R. v. Deegan 935
R. v. DeKleric 1211
R. v. Delorey 551
R. v. Derksen 1207
R. c. Déry 1149
R. v. DeSousa 320, 472, 555, **556**, 564, 577, 578
R. v. Desbiens 551
R. v. Desrosiers 985
R. v. Deutsch 1124
R. v. Devgan 315
R. v. Dooley 1092
R. v. Dorosh 763
R. v. Dow 908
R. v. Downey 108
R. v. Dragos 736
R. v. Drainville 767, 768
R. v. Dubeau 775
R. v. Dudley and Stephens 959, 982, 1020
R. v. Dunn (1977) 774
R. v. Dunn (1999) 907
R. v. Duong 1104
R. v. Edelenbos 427
R. v. Edwards 421
R. v. Ellis-Don Ltd. 412
R. v. Ereddia 424
R. v. Esau 635

R. v. Esop 750
R. v. Ewanchuk 666, 679, 680, 686, 689, 703, 704, 717
R. v. F. (D.L.) 335
R. v. F. (J.) 527, **553**, 554, 556, 1152
R. v. Fallofield 1208
R. v. Faqi 1076
R. v. Fatima 325, 334
R. v. Ferguson 982, 1203, 1207
R. v. Ferrari 326
R. v. Finlay 472
R. v. Finta 472
R. v. Fleming 907
R. v. Flores 1054
R. v. Fontaine 861
R. v. Forde 935
R. v. Fraser 1019
R. v. Fry 983
R. v. Gale 257
R. v. Gauthier 1046, **1101**
R. v. Gentles 358
R. v. Ghomeshi 711, 715
R. v. Gingrich 472
R. v. Gladstone 1210
R. v. Gladue (1999), 1198, 1201
R. v. Gladue (2012) 1076
R. v. Goard 869, 912
R. v. Godin 555, 577, 578
R. v. Gosset 472, 555
R. v. Gould 551
R. v. Goulis 18
R. v. Gralewicz 1137
R. v. Graveline 867
R. v. Grottoli 419
R. v. Groves 1212
R. v. H. (A.D.) 472, **474**
R. v. Hamilton 493, 502, 1103, **1153**
R. v. Harbottle 323, 325, 333, 339
R. v. Harding 493
R. v. Harshbarger 576
R. v. Henry 6, 9
R. v. Hess; R. v. Nguyen 726, 736, 1185
R. v. Hibbert 480, 992, **993**, 1005
R. v. Hill (1985) 1022, 1045
R. v. Hill (2015) 1047
R. v. Hoffart 736
R. v. Holliday 82
R. v. Howe 684

R. v. Hundal 361, **362**, 472, **528**
R. v. Hutchinson 248, 252, 705
R. v. Imoro 1076
R. v. Innocente 1145
R. v. Ipeelee 1206
R. v. J. (K.R.) 74
R. v. Jackson 1031
R. v. Jacobsen 424
R. v. Jensen 907, 908
R. v. Jiang 551
R. v. Jobidon 214, 226, 229, 248, 579, 665
R. v. Jones 775
R. v. Jorgensen 502
R. v. K. (M.M.) 465
R. v. Kahnapace 431
R. v. Keegstra 492
R. v. Kennedy 983
R. v. Kent 1054
R. v. Khawaja 59, 478, 479, 1186
R. v. King 297
R. v. Kingsbury 762
R. v. Knoblauch 787
R. v. Kouri 125
R. v. Krushel 573
R. v. Kubassek 253
R. v. Kulbacki 1089
R. v. Kummer 1204
R. v. Kundeus 738, **741**, 747
R. v. L. (J.) 541, 552
R. v. Laba 77, 843
R. v. Labaye 125, 133
R. v. Ladue 739
R. v. Lagace 505
R. v. LaLonde 985
R. v. Latimer 493, **974**, 982, 983, 1008, 1020
R. v. Laurencelle 1089
R. v. Lavallee 935, 944, 945
R. v. Le 1076
R. v. Lebenfish 6
R. v. Leclerc 577, 578
R. v. Legare 494, 736
R. v. Levigne 736
R. v. Levkovic 473
R. v. Lewis 478, 479
R. v. Lifchus 92, 94
R. v. Lilgert 555

R. v. Lillyman 593
R. v. Lindsay 1181
R. v. Livermore 635
R. v. Lloyd 1205, 1206, 1207
R. v. Logan 472, **1096**
R. v. Lohnes 180
R. v. Lucki 303
R. v. Luedecke 843, 854
R. v. Mabior 230, **237**, 247, 248, 251, 252
R. v. Mac 22
R. v. MacDonald (2008) 431
R. v. MacDonald (2014) 760
R. v. MacFadden 315
R. v. MacIntyre 774
R. v. Mack 1056, 1076
R. v. MacMillan Bloedel Ltd. 420
R. v. Maidment 419
R. c. Mailhot 788
R. v. Malcolm 680
R. v. Malmo-Levine 49, 70, **118**, 133, 401
R. v. Malott 945
R. v. Mara 133
R. v. Martineau 25, **441**, 452, 454, 457, 458, 472, 554, 747
R. v. Mastel 736, 737
R. v. Maybin 347, 357
R. v. McCain 985
R. v. McCaughan 551
R. v. McConnell 956
R. v. McCraw 723
R. v. McDonald 226
R. v. McIlwane 229
R. v. McIntosh 933
R. v. McLeod 739
R. v. Meiler 453, 458
R. v. Menezes 358
R. v. Michael 313
R. v. Michaud 80, 417
R. v. Miller 265
R. v. Mills 114, 719, 720, 908
R. v. Mohamed 1054
R. v. Moo 431
R. v. Moquin 227
R. v. Morelli 199, 736
R. v. Morgentaler 25

R. v. Morgentaler, Smoling and Scott 981, 982
R. v. Morris (1981) 984
R. v. Morris (1994) 983
R. v. Motor Vehicle Reference 1180
R. v. Mulligan 364
R. v. Mullins-Johnson 100
R. v. Murphy 257
R. v. Murray 493
R. v. N. (S.) 908
R. v. Naglik 472, 509
R. v. Nealy 1050
R. v. Nelson 472
R. v. Nette 326, 333, 334, 335, 339
R. v. Nur 1204
R. v. Nurse 578
R. v. Nutter, Collishaw and Dulong 1210
R. v. Nygaard and Schimmens 465, 468
R. v. O. (J.M.) 736
R. v. O. (M.) 687
R. v. O.D. 736
R. v. O'Connor 114, 595, 719
R. v. O'Leary 358
R. v. Oakes 72, 74, 77, 78, **103**, 408, 417, 806
R. v. Olazo 1076
R. v. Oommen 802
R. v. Ortt 365
R. v. Osolin 632
R. v. Osvath 688
R. v. P. 252
R. v. P. (L.T.) 736
R. v. Page 622
R. v. Paice 226
R. c. Palin 552
R. v. Palombi 1092
R. v. Pangman 1176
R. v. Pappajohn *See* Pappajohn v. R.
R. v. Pappas 1047
R. v. Paquette 480, **988**, 992, 993, 1005, 1008
R. v. Paré 19
R. v. Parent 1032, 1033
R. v. Parish 577
R. v. Parks 298, **822**
R. v. Patterson 431
R. v. Pawlowski 1211
R. v. Peckham 786

R. v. Pengelley 736
R. v. Peters 472
R. v. Peterson 283
R. v. Pham 203, 210
R. v. Phan 358
R. v. Pickton 1082
R. v. Pierce Fisheries Ltd. 418
R. v. Pontes 404, 405, 1180
R. v. Pootlass 983
R. v. Priest 1193
R. v. Priestap 480
R. v. Primus 985
R. v. Pritchard 471
R. v. Proulx 788, **1214**
R. v. Prue; R. v. Baril 756
R. v. R.D.S. 155, 162
R. v. Rabey (Ont. C.A.) 806
R. v. Raham 421
R. v. Reddick 632
R. v. Reeves 806
R. v. Reid 358
R. v. Relkie 551
R. v. Reyat 578
R. v. Robins 1021
R. c. Rochon 1092
R. v. Roks 459
R. v. Ronish 503
R. v. Rothgordt 1046
R. v. Roy 551
R. v. Ruzic 997, 1008, 1019, 1020, 1185
R. v. Ryan (1967) 307
R. v. Ryan (2013) 1008, 1019, 1020
R. v. S. (J.) 457
R. v. S. (J.H.) 96
R. v. Safarzadeh-Markhall 69, 1206
R. v. Sangster 1209
R. v. Sansregret *See* Sansregret v. R.
R. v. Sault Ste. Marie *See* R. v. City of Sault Ste. Marie
R. v. Scharf 577
R. v. Schwartz 102
R. v. Scott 23
R. v. Seaboyer; R. v. Gayme 638, 654, 655, 656, 657, 658, 689, 704, 720
R. v. Sedley 1
R. v. Settle 551
R. v. Seymour 1076
R. v. Shalaan 1107

R. v. Shand 453, 457, 458, 459
R. v. Shanks 323
R. v. Sharpe 1103
R. v. Shaw 1213
R. v. Shearing 114, 715, 720
R. v. Shiner 773
R. v. Shorten 1212
R. v. Simpson (1977) 799
R. v. Simpson (1988) 1096
R. v. Simpson (2015) 753
R. v. Sinclair 357
R. v. Sit 453
R. v. Slater 736
R. v. Smale 257, 627
R. v. Smith (App. Ct.) 339
R. v. Smith (B.C. Prov. Ct.) 1021
R. v. Smith (N.W.T. Terr. Ct.) 1210
R. v. Smith (Sask. C.A.) 460
R. v. Sorrell and Bondett 1118
R. v. Starr 94
R. v. Steer 18
R. v. Stennes 1213
R. v. Stone 298, 833, 854, 862, 933,
    1008, 1049
R. v. Strickland 664
R. v. Strong 471
R. v. Stucky 390
R. v. Swaby 305
R. v. Swain 78, 786, 806
R. v. Swan 57, 58, 1076
R. v. Szostak 789
R. v. T. (K.) 577
R. v. T. (W.A.) 689
R. v. T.S. 680
R. v. Talbot 334, 335
R. v. Tatton 24, 913, 924
R. v. Tayfel 552
R. v. Terezakis 1181
R. v. Termertzoglou 664
R. v. Terrence 196
R. v. Thain 736
R. v. Théroux 363, 473, **494**, 497
R. v. Thompson 246
R. v. Thornton (Ont. C.A.) 276
R. v. Tolson 738, 739
R. v. Toma 315
R. v. Townsend 458
R. v. Tran 1033, 1045, 1046, 1048

R. v. Transport Robert, R. v. William
    Cameron Trucking (*sub nom.* **R. v.**
    1260448 Ontario Inc.) 413, 417
R. v. Travers 465
R. v. Trecroce 787
R. v. Tremblay 133
R. c. Truchon 551
R. v. Tuglavina 1204
R. c. Turcotte 913
R. v. Tutton and Tutton 511, 523, 527,
    528, 552, 553
R. v. Ubhi 540
R. v. V. (K.B.) 627
R. v. Vaillancourt *See* Vaillancourt v. R.
R. v. Vantroba 555
R. c. Venneri 472, 1181
R. v. Vickberg 866, 907
R. v. W. (D.J.) 554
R. v. W. (G.) 229
R. v. Walker 984
R. v. Walle 366
R. v. Weaver 632
R. v. Welch 229
R. v. Whelan 774
R. v. White; ex parte Chonan 1213
R. v. Wholesale Travel Group Inc. 383,
    390, **406**, 412, 737, 1186
R. v. Williams (1992.) 405
R. v. Williams (2003) 252
R. v. Willis 1019
R. v. Wilson 420
R. v. Windle 801
R. v. Wolfe 304
R. v. Wudrich 554
R. v. Young 984
R. v. Zhao 579
R. v. Ziatas 1210
Rabey v. R. 297, 812
Ranieri, Re 788
Reference Re Firearms Act (Canada)
    35, 390
Reference Re Section 94(2) of the Motor
    Vehicle Act (B.C.) 78, **398**, 1180
Rodriguez v. B.C. (A.G.) 229
Sansregret v. R. 473, **500**, 597, **611**
Schreiber v. Canada (Attorney General)
    17
Schwartz v. R. 801, 802

Simpson v. R. 424
Smithers v. R. 316, 326, 335, 339
Stapleton v. R. 801
State v. Anderson 594
Suresh v. Canada (Minister of Citizenship
   & Immigration) 1184
The Queen v. Bingapore 345
Thornton v. R. (S.C.C.) 280
U.S. v. Freeman 784

U.S. v. Nadarajah 1186
United States v. Dynar 493, **1130**
Vaillancourt v. R. 431, 441, 453, 471,
   472, 1185
Waite v. R. 523
Winko v. Forensic Psychiatric Institute
   787, 788
Woolmington v. D.P.P. 85, 366
Yuill v. Yuill 135